INVINCIBLE

TRUEMAN'S *Specific* Series®

NTA UGC-NET/SET

For JRF and Eligibility Test for Assistant Professor

(and Ph.D Entrance Exams)

Subject Code: 08

COMMERCE

NEW SYLLABUS with

Previous Years' Papers

By
M. Shivani
M.Com, MBA

Authentic & Dependable

Produced and Published by
Danika Publishing Company
(Publishers of Trueman's *Specific* Series)
4352/4C, Ansari Road,
Daryaganj, New Delhi - 110002
Ph.: 011-23242482, 41501988
e-mail: danikabooks@yahoo.com

Can be had from
Invincible Publishers
2nd Floor, SAS Tower, Medicity, Sector 38,
Gurugram (Haryana)

ISBN : 9788189301989

New Edition : 2026

Price : Rs. 850/-

Data Processing :
Inhouse

Printed at :
Dhruv Printers
New Delhi.

Subject to New Delhi Jurisdiction only

PUBLISHERS' NOTE

The present work is a humble attempt to satisfy the needs of students appearing for UGC NET/SET Examinations. Syllabus and Guidelines for Paper II have been given in the book. After theory and MCQs, model papers are provided for practice. We have also incorporated questions asked in previous NET examinations. The book in the present form shall serve as a reliable evocative book for those preparing for NET/SET examinations.

Any suggestions for the improvement shall be thankfully acknowledged.

— With Best Wishes

CONTENTS

UGC-NET NEW SYLLABUS

The Test will consist of two papers as given below:

Paper	Marks	Number of Questions	MCQs	Duration
I	100	50	The questions will be generic in nature, intending to assess the teaching/research aptitude of the candidate. It will primarily be designed to test reasoning ability, comprehension, divergent thinking and general awareness of the candidate.	03 hours All the questions will be compulsory.
II	200	100	This will be based on the subject selected by the candidate.	

The Test will be conducted in Computer Based Test (CBT) mode only, and will be held on different dates at various centres in India.

Syllabus for all NET Subjects can be downloaded from the UGC website:**https://www.ugcnetonline.in/syllabus-new.php.**

SYLLABUS

UNIT-1 BUSINESS ENVIRONMENT AND INTERNATIONAL BUSINESS

- Concepts and elements of business environment: Economic environment- Economic systems, Economic policies(Monetary and fiscal policies); Political environment- Role of government in business; Legal environment- Consumer Protection Act, FEMA; Socio-cultural factors and their influence on business; Corporate Social Responsibility (CSR)
- Scope and importance of international business; Globalization and its drivers; Modes of entry into international business
- Theories of international trade; Government intervention in international trade; Tariff and non-tariff barriers; India's foreign trade policy
- Foreign direct investment (FDI) and Foreign portfolio investment (FPI); Types of FDI, Costs and benefits of FDI to home and host countries; Trends in FDI; India's FDI policy
- Balance of payments (BOP): Importance and components of BOP
- Regional Economic Integration: Levels of Regional Economic Integration; Trade creation and diversion effects; Regional Trade Agreements: European Union (EU), ASEAN, SAARC, NAFTA
- International Economic institutions: IMF, World Bank, UNCTAD
- World Trade Organisation (WTO): Functions and objectives of WTO; Agriculture Agreement; GATS; TRIPS; TRIMS

UNIT-2 ACCOUNTING AND AUDITING

- Basic accounting principles; concepts and postulates
- Partnership Accounts: Admission, Retirement, Death, Dissolution and Insolvency of partnership firms
- Corporate Accounting: Issue, forfeiture and reissue of shares; Liquidation of companies; Acquisition, merger, amalgamation and reconstruction of companies
- Holding company accounts
- Cost and Management Accounting: Marginal costing and Break-even analysis; Standard costing; Budgetary control; Process costing; Activity Based Costing (ABC); Costing for decision-making; Life cycle costing, Target costing, Kaizen costing and JIT
- Financial Statements Analysis: Ratio analysis; Funds flow Analysis; Cash flow analysis

- Human Resources Accounting; Inflation Accounting; Environmental Accounting
- Indian Accounting Standards and IFRS
- Auditing: Independent financial audit; Vouching; Verification ad valuation of assets and liabilities; Audit of financial statements and audit report; Cost audit
- Recent Trends in Auditing: Management audit; Energy audit; Environment audit; Systems audit; Safety audit

UNIT-3 BUSINESS ECONOMICS

- Meaning and scope of business economics
- Objectives of business firms
- Demand analysis: Law of demand; Elasticity of demand and its measurement; Relationship between AR and MR
- Consumer behavior: Utility analysis; Indifference curve analysis
- Law of Variable Proportions: Law of Returns to Scale
- Theory of cost: Short-run and long-run cost curves
- Price determination under different market forms: Perfect competition; Monopolistic competition; Oligopoly- Price leadership model; Monopoly; Price discrimination
- Pricing strategies: Price skimming; Price penetration; Peak load pricing

UNIT-4 BUSINESS FINANCE

- Scope and sources of finance; Lease financing
- Cost of capital and time value of money
- Capital structure
- Capital budgeting decisions: Conventional and scientific techniques of capital budgeting analysis
- Working capital management; Dividend decision: Theories and policies
- Risk and return analysis; Asset securitization
- International monetary system
- Foreign exchange market; Exchange rate risk and hedging techniques
- International financial markets and instruments: Euro currency; GDRs; ADRs
- International arbitrage; Multinational capital budgeting

UNIT-5 BUSINESS STATISTICS AND RESEARCH METHODS

- Measures of central tendency
- Measures of dispersion
- Measures of skewness
- Correlation and regression of two variables
- Probability: Approaches to probability; Bayes' theorem
- Probability distributions: Binomial, poisson and normal distributions
- Research: Concept and types; Research designs
- Data: Collection and classification of data
- Sampling and estimation: Concepts; Methods of sampling - probability and non-probability methods; Sampling distribution; Central limit theorem; Standard error; Statistical estimation
- Hypothesis testing: z-test; t-test; ANOVA; Chi-Vsquare test; Mann-Whitney test (U-test); Kruskal-Wallis test (H-test); Rank correlation test
- Report writing

UNIT-6 BUSINESS MANAGEMENT AND HUMAN RESOURCE MANAGEMENT

- Principles and functions of management
- Organization structure: Formal and informal organizations; Span of control
- Responsibility and authority: Delegation of authority and decentralization
- Motivation and leadership: Concept and theories
- Corporate governance and business ethics
- Human resource management: Concept, role and functions of HRM; Human resource planning; Recruitment and selection; Training and development; Succession planning
- Compensation management: Job evaluation; Incentives and fringe benefits
- Performance appraisal including 360 degree performance appraisal
- Collective bargaining and workers' participation in management
- Personality: Perception; Attitudes; Emotions; Group dynamics; Power and politics; Conflict and negotiation; Stress management
- Organizational Culture: Organizational development and organizational change

UNIT-7 BANKING AND FINANCIAL INSTITUTIONS

- Overview of Indian financial system
- Types of banks: Commercial banks; Regional Rural Banks (RRBs); Foreign banks; Cooperative banks
- Reserve Bank of India: Functions; Role and monetary policy management
- Banking sector reforms in India: Basel norms; Risk management; NPA management
- Financial markets: Money market; Capital market; Government securities market
- Financial Institutions: Development Finance Institutions (DFIs); Non-Banking Financial Companies (NBFCs); Mutual Funds; Pension Funds
- Financial Regulators in India
- Financial sector reforms including financial inclusion
- Digitisation of banking and other financial services: Internet banking; mobile banking; Digital payments systems
- Insurance: Types of insurance- Life and Non-life insurance; Risk classification and management; Factors limiting the insurability of risk; Re-insurance; Regulatory framework of insurance- IRDA and its role

UNIT-8 MARKETING MANAGEMENT

- Marketing: Concept and approaches; Marketing channels; Marketing mix; Strategic marketing planning; Market segmentation, targeting and positioning
- Product decisions: Concept; Product line; Product mix decisions; Product life cycle; New product development
- Pricing decisions: Factors affecting price determination; Pricing policies and strategies
- Promotion decisions: Role of promotion in marketing; Promotion methods - Advertising; Personal selling; Publicity; Sales promotion tools and techniques; Promotion mix
- Distribution decisions: Channels of distribution; Channel management
- Consumer Behaviour; Consumer buying process; factors influencing consumer buying decisions
- Service marketing
- Trends in marketing: Social marketing; Online marketing; Green marketing; Direct marketing; Rural marketing; CRM
- Logistics management

UNIT-9 LEGAL ASPECTS OF BUSINESS

- Indian Contract Act, 1872. Elements of a valid contract; Capacity of parties; Free consent; Discharge of a contract; Breach of contract and remedies against breach; Quasi contracts;
- Special contracts: Contracts of indemnity and guarantee; contracts of bailment and pledge; Contracts of agency
- Sale of Goods Act, 1930: Sale and agreement to sell; Doctrine of Caveat Emptor; Rights of unpaid seller and rights of buyer
- Negotiable Instruments Act, 1881: Types of negotiable instruments; Negotiation and assignment; Dishonour and discharge of negotiable instruments
- The Companies Act, 2013: Nature and kinds of companies; Company formation; Management, meetings and winding up of a joint stock company
- Limited Liability Partnership: Structure and procedure of formation of LLP in India
- The Competition Act, 2002: Objectives and main provisions
- The Information Technology Act, 2000: Objectives and main provisions; Cyber crimes and penalties
- The RTI Act, 2005: Objectives and main provisions
- Intellectual Property Rights (IPRs) : Patents, trademarks and copyrights; Emerging issues in intellectual property
- Goods and Services Tax (GST): Objectives and main provisions; Benefits of GST; Implementation mechanism; Working of dual GST

UNIT-10 INCOME-TAX AND CORPORATE TAX PLANNING

- Income-tax: Basic concepts; Residential status and tax incidence; Exempted incomes; Agricultural income; Computation of taxable income under various heads; Deductions from Gross total income; Assessment of Individuals; Clubbing of incomes
- International Taxation: Double taxation and its avoidance mechanism; Transfer pricing
- Corporate Tax Planning: Concepts and significance of corporate tax planning; Tax avoidance versus tax evasion; Techniques of corporate tax planning; Tax considerations in specific business situations: Make or buy decisions; Own or lease an asset; Retain; Renewal or replacement of asset; Shut down or continue operations
- Deduction and collection of tax at source; Advance payment of tax; E-filing of income-tax returns

❖❖

UNIT 1

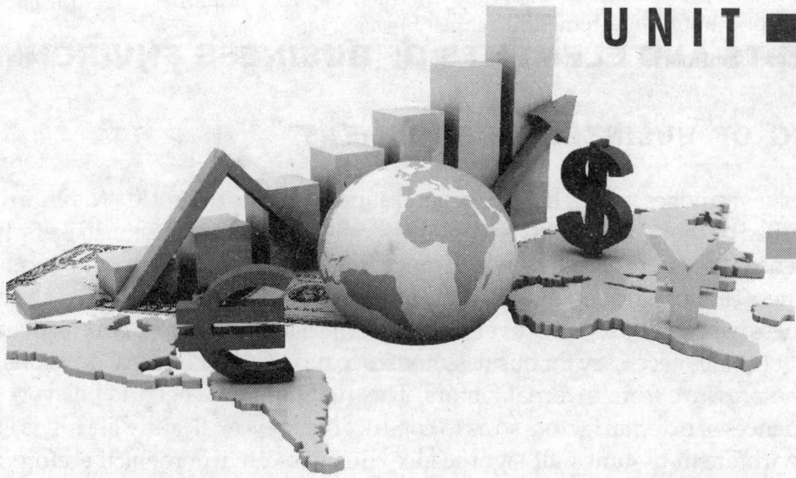

BUSINESS ENVIRONMENT AND INTERNATIONAL BUSINESS

SYLLABUS

- Concepts and elements of business environment: Economic environment- Economic systems, Economic policies(Monetary and fiscal policies); Political environment- Role of government in business; Legal environment- Consumer Protection Act, FEMA; Socio-cultural factors and their influence on business; Corporate Social Responsibility (CSR)
- Scope and importance of international business; Globalization and its drivers; Modes of entry into international business
- Theories of international trade; Government intervention in international trade; Tariff and non-tariff barriers; India's foreign trade policy
- Foreign direct investment (FDI) and Foreign portfolio investment (FPI); Types of FDI, Costs and benefits of FDI to home and host countries; Trends in FDI; India's FDI policy
- Balance of payments (BOP): Importance and components of BOP
- Regional Economic Integration: Levels of Regional Economic Integration; Trade creation and diversion effects; Regional Trade Agreements: European Union (EU), ASEAN, SAARC, NAFTA
- International Economic institutions: IMF, World Bank, UNCTAD
- World Trade Organisation (WTO): Functions and objectives of WTO; Agriculture Agreement; GATS; TRIPS; TRIMS

CONCEPTS AND ELEMENTS OF BUSINESS ENVIRONMENT

MEANING OF BUSINESS ENVIRONMENT

Business involves activities, which links an organization with outside world. Within an organization, a business is governed by the behaviour of its employees, management or decision makers. But externally a business is influenced by a score of factors, which range from customers to competitors and government. Therefore, a business cannot be independent of the influence of these external factors. It should also be noted that a business has absolute control over all the internal factors, it has no control over the external factors. So often it becomes necessary for business houses to modify their internal decisions and policies, on the basis of the pressure from external factors. This highlights the need to be ever- cognizant of changes and influences of external factors so as to conduct business on healthy lines. It is in this context that business environment assumes all significance. Business environment therefore refers to the influences and pressures exerted by external factors on the business.

In other words. The combination of internal and external factors that influence a company's operating situation. The business environment can include factors such as : clients & suppliers; its competitors and owners; improvement in technology; laws and government activities; and market, social and economic trends.

The term Business Environment refers to the aggregate of all forces, factors and institutions which are external to and beyond the control of individual business enterprises and their management; but which influence their functioning. In other words, business environment may be defined as all those conditions and forces external to a business unit under which it operates.

Importance of Business Environment. There is a mutual interdependence between business and its environment. A business enterprise is an open system. It continuously interacts with its environment. Business takes inputs (raw materials, capital, labour, energy etc.) from its environment and transform them into goods and services and then send them back to the environment.

Business and its external environment interact in the following ways :

- Exchange of information
- Exchange of resources
- Exchange of influence and power.

Managerial Response to Changes in Business Environment. The management of business enterprise respond to environmental forces in different ways depending upon their goals, values, beliefs and competence. Various ways that managers may show the responses to changes in business environment are :

- Wait and Watch
- Anticipation and Adoption
- Innovative Approach
- Autonomous commanding thrusts.

EMERGING TRENDS

Like in any other environment, business environments to witness various changes in the fashion of it's working over the time. These changes are referred to as business trends.

- Network Marketing
- Franchising
- Business Process Outsourcing
- Aggregator
- Knowledge Process Outsourcing
- Digital Economy
- E-Commerce
- M-Commerce

The following Figure would help to understand the various factors which constitute the business environment.

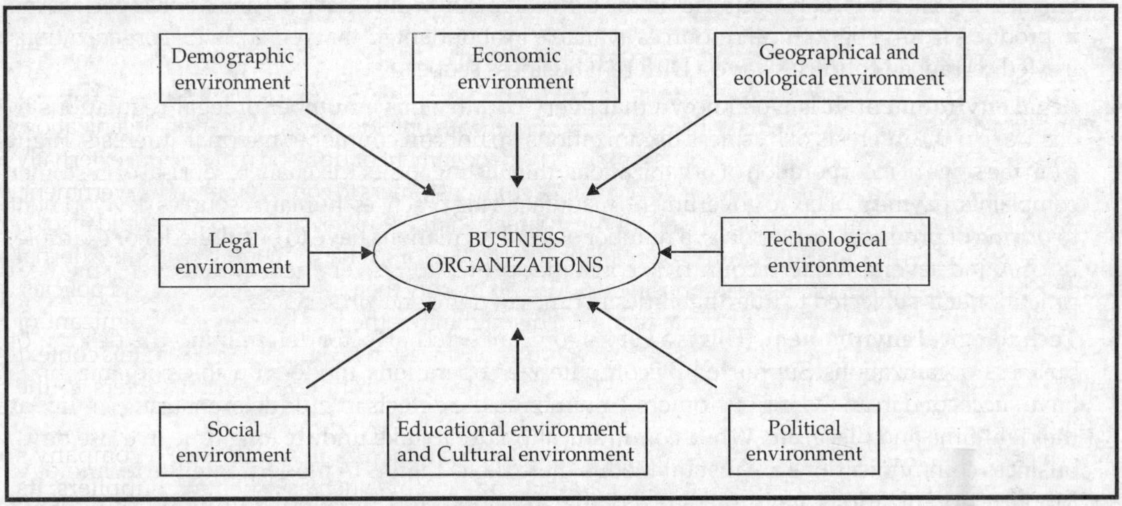

Constituents of Business Environment

From the above Figure, it would be clear that business organizations function in an environment subject to the influence of various constituents. Each one of the constituents have in turn a number of factors influencing them. For example, economic environment has micro and macro environmental factors affecting it. To develop a right perspective about business environment, let us discuss briefly about each one of the external environment constituents.

1. **Demographic environment.** This refers to the size and behaviour of population in a country. Suppose a country has a huge size of population, then, the country would provide extensive business or marketing opportunities for all types of business organizations. On the other hand, a country with low size of population would force the business organizations to seek external market for their products or services. Similarly, if the population in a country is well - tuned to 'use and throw concept' [like most of the Western countries] then there would be limited scope for repair shops and employment scope in that segment would be almost nil. But alternatively this would give wide marketing opportunities for manufacturing organizations.
2. **Economic environment.** Economic environment refers to the overall economic factors like economic philosophy of the country, economic structure, planning, economic policies, controls and regulations, etc. All these have a serious impact on the functioning of business organizations in a country. For example, in a Capitalistic economic system, business organizations would be subjected to limited government regulations and controls. They would be more governed by market forces [demand and supply] rather than by other factors. On the other hand, in a Socialist system, the government would determine everything on behalf of the country. In a communist set up, the government has absolute control over every aspect of production but in case of private enterprise this may not exist at all. In a Mixed economic system, government would be selective in allowing the presence of private enterprises in certain activities, reserving some spheres completely for governmental operations. Hence, the economic philosophy of the country directly determines the scope and functions of business organizations in that country.
3. **Geographical and ecological environment.** Geographical environment refers to climatic conditions and natural resources, which determines the manufacturing scope and the nature of the products

that could be marketed. For example, a country like Kenya has to manufacture more products based on forest resources, while the Gulf countries can produce only crude, Japan can have business in fish, fruits, etc., Countries in the tropical region would have organizations specializing in products from geographical resources available in abundant in that region, while organizations in Mediterranean countries have a Different business scope.

4. **Legal environment.** It is well known that every country has a number of legal regulations to ensure that the interests of business organizations do not run counter to national interests. Right from the stage of incorporation of organizations, their listing in stock exchange, reprisal of customer complaints, payment of tax to government, manufacturing practices, human resources development to pricing of products and services, a number of legal regulations have to be fulfilled. For example, in USA and several western countries, consumer protection is very active, that even *a* medical practitioner is subjected to huge liabilities in times of deficiency in services.
5. **Technological environment.** This is a very significant external factor determining the destiny of business organizations. Supported by computerized operations, modern business organizations have succeeded in analyzing customers, minimizing the defects in products, ensuring service at the right time and place, etc. While communication use to take unduly long time in those days, business communications are instantaneous these days, thanks to modern satellite technology. Modern organizations have recognized that research and development alone can ensure organizational growth and stability. They have become more and more proactive and remain as change agents of the economy. Governments has also become more technology conscious that right from police controls to registration of title deeds, computerizations has been adopted. Customer service through call centers is the latest necessity of organizations. Manufacturing activities have become more and more technically sophisticated. Therefore business environment has become highly dynamic.
6. **Social environment.** Social environment today has brought compulsions on business organizations to adhere to certain business ethics and morals. Social responsibility of business is an important force that modern business organizations cannot wriggle out of their duties and responsibilities towards the society. For example, every leather manufacturing or process unit is made to install pollution prevention system. Similarly, the expectations of various interests in the society have undergone a sea of change. The shareholders, promoters and owners expect a reasonable return on their investments. The workers expect security of service, terminal benefits, accident relief and various other compensations from the organizations. Government expects the business units to *pay* tax regularly and participate in social improvement. The distributors and agents expect the organizations to ensure smooth delivery process and demand more commission and compensation. Suppliers expect the organizations to give them continuous business and prompt payment of bills. Therefore each social group has a specific interest, the combination of all these, exerts enormous pressure on the business unit. A business unit which succeeds in meeting the interests of all these groups remains successful and grows.
7. **Educational and cultural environment.** Educational environment in a country determines the quality of population. A country with very high illiterate population would always experience political and economic instability. Similarly, lack of education may also give scope for the existence of superstitious beliefs, fatalistic attitude, etc. People's choice of goods and services would be more governed, by their religious faiths and beliefs. For instance, in the colonial days, the Indian population was a victim of the Britisher's divide and rule tactics. The economic development of a country completely depends on the literacy level which alone can pave the way for improvement in science and technology, modernization, industrialization, etc. In such a country, the business opportunities are plenty.

Cultural environment refers to the values, norms, customs, ethics, goals and other accepted behavioural pattern of people in a country. In olden days, religion was the basis of all activities in a society. The religious leaders and institutions determined what business people should do and what people must consume. In India, the existence of caste system has done more damage than any good. Caste based politics has become the order of the day. Under the pretext of working for backward and downtrodden people, several persons have amassed fortune. This is worsened by political support and policies.

8. **Political environment.** Political stability is one important factor which determines the business growth or downfall. A country with relative political stability would witness inflow of foreign capital and collaboration. By political stability we mean that the policies of government remaining consistent. As the business decisions are based on government policies, frequent changes in these policies would force business organizations to change their policies too, which makes functioning very difficult.

   Sometimes, when the policies determined by a party in power are reversed by the succeeding party forming the government, there would be far reaching changes in business environment. For example, India was following a policy of protectionism till late 1908's. Hence, the industrial development and economic development could not take place at a rapid rate. In the absence of competition, the business organizations, made people to accept inferior quality goods and services. Once, the liberalization policy is adopted, the scene has completely changed. Today, no business can survive unless it provides quality goods or services on par with the multinational corporations. Until the disintegration of USSR, India was simply following USSR's lines, but after the disintegration, India has to literally fend for itself. With the pressures mounted by the Western countries, India had to accept various trade and monetary policies. This has brought about a complete change in business environment.

OBJECTIVE OF BUSINESS ENVIRONMENT

Following are main objectives of business environment:

1. **Knowledge of Information.** By studying the business environment, we can know the changes of business. This information is very useful for our business. Every businessman should be aware of the current environment of business. With this, he can think about the future of his business in such environment.
2. **Basis of Decisions.** One of the main objective of the study of business environment is that it can provide all the information which is needed for taking good decisions. Suppose, you completed your internal business environment study. With this study, you can take decision relating to purchase, sale, salary and price because you know your competitor, you know your suppliers and you know your customers.
3. **Helpful in making of Policies.** For making good business policies, we need to know and scan business through business environment.
4. **Technological Planning.** Today, technology is changing very fastly 3 years ago, I have to search software for downloading business software but today I can use all business software online free of cost. This has become possible due to changes of web technology. So, you have to study technological environment. With this, you can make better technological planning for your business.
5. **Survive in the Business.** Sometime industry may face recession. Production may be unlimited but sales will be limited. Only those business enterprises will be able to survive which will estimate all these situations in advance through business environment study.

IMPORTANCE OF BUSINESS ENVIRONMENT

There is a close and continuous interaction between the business and its environment. This interaction helps in strengthening the business firm and using its resources more efficiently. As stated above, the business environment is multifaceted, complex, and dynamic in nature and has a far-reaching impact on the survival and growth of the business. To be more specific, proper understanding of the social, political, legal and economic environment helps the business in the following ways:

(1) **Determining Opportunities and Threats.** The interaction between the business and its environment would identify opportunities for and threats to the business. It helps the business enterprises for meeting the challenges successfully.

(2) **Giving Direction for Growth.** The interaction with the environment leads to opening up new frontiers of growth for the business firms. It enables the business to identify the areas for growth and expansion of their activities.

(3) **Continuous Learning.** Environmental analysis makes the task of managers easier in dealing with business challenges. The managers are motivated to continuously update their knowledge, understanding and skills to meet the predicted changes in realm of business.

(4) **Image Building.** Environmental understanding helps the business organisations in improving their image by showing their sensitivity to the environment within which they are working. For example, in view of the shortage of power, many companies have set up Captive Power Plants (CPP) in their factories to meet their own requirement of power.

(5) **Meeting Competition.** It helps the firms to analyse the competitors' strategies and formulate their own strategies accordingly.

(6) **Identifying Firm's Strength and Weakness.** Business environment helps to identify the individual strengths and weaknesses in view of the technological and global developments.

COMPONENTS OF GENERAL ENVIRONMENT OF A BUSINESS

The following are the key components of general environment of a business.

1. **Economic environment.** Economic environment consists of economic factors that influence the business in a country. These factors include gross national product, corporate profits, inflation rate, employment, balance of payments, interest rates, consumer income etc.
2. **Social environment.** It describes the characteristics of the society in which the organization exists. Literacy rate, customs, values, beliefs, life-style, demographic features and mobility of population are part of the social environment. It is important for managers to notice the direction in which the society is moving and formulate progressive policies according to the changing social scenario.
3. **Political environment.** It comprises of political stability and the policies of the government. Ideological inclination of political parties, personal interest on politicians, influence of party forums etc. create political environment. For example, Bangalore established itself as the most important IT centre of India mainly because of political support.
4. **Legal environment.** This consists of legislation that is passed by the parliament and state legislatures. Examples of such legislation specifically aimed at business operations include the Trade mark Act 1969, Essential Commodities Act 1955, Standards of Weights and Measures Act 1969 and Consumer Protection Act 1986.
5. **Technological environment.** It includes the level of technology available in a country. It also indicates the pace of research and development and progress made in introducing modern technology in production. Technology provides capital intensive but cost effective alternative to

traditional labor intensive methods. In a competitive business environment technology is the key to development.

ELEMENTS OF THE BUSINESS ENVIRONMENT

Main elements or factors of Business Environment are :

1. Micro business Environment

This is also known as internal business environment because business has power to control it. In this environment, factors can be divided in the following way.

1st Supplier. A supplier provides raw material to business. This is also main factor of business environment because it affects business very closely. If supplier delay to supply raw materials or stop to supply then production of business will be stopped due to lack of raw material supply. So, for controlling this factor, it is the duty of businessman to make good relation with more than one supplier so that, if one stop or delay at this time, goods can be purchased from other supplier.

2nd Customers. Customers are those people or companies which buy goods from our business. Business sells them its finished product. But from time to time tastes of customers also change. So, according to the taste of business customers, new products must be supplied by business. This is the formula for business perpetuity..

3rd Market Intermediaries. For promoting sale, it is required to advertise by different way, so market intermediaries include sales man and middle man. This environment is under control of business because, if business starts selling with more ads, his selling will surely increase.

4th Competitors. Competitors of business also create internal business environment. According to competitors policies, business changes its policies for winning in competition.

5th Financial Intermediaries. As business grows, it needs more money for its growth; either this money can be obtained by issuing new shares or by borrowing money from financial intermediaries. So, financial intermediaries plays a vital role in business environment. If they provides loan at very low rate, at that time business can get and grow fastly but, if they increase the interest rate, at that time business will not get loan at this rate and its growth may decrease due to lack of fund.

2. Macro Business Environment or External Factors of Business Environment

(i) **Economical Environment.** Economic environment is main element of business environment. Economy is factor which affects business in the following way:

(a) ***Economic policies.*** Economic policies related to budget, industrial policy, fiscal policy, export and import policy and business should see what changes are done in these and business has to change their business policies according to these changes.

(b) ***Economic regulation.*** Different laws and regulations are at international level and national level. These are all called economic regulation and business has to respect all of these while it is operating business.

(ii) **Natural Environment.** Natural environment is also external factor of business. Because, business can not fully control natural environment. Many points like season, raining, floods, earth quake are natural and happens according to fluctuation in it. These are also main element of business because business has to face all these factors. But some of loss from these factors can be transferred with effective schemes of insurance.

(iii) **Demographic Factors.** Size of population and their growth rate includes demographic element and factor of business environment. Increasing trend of population will increase demand of products and support business to produce more products. But if death rate is increasing or demographic factor like religion are preventing to use the products of business then. At that time business enterprise has to change its plan according to situation.

(iv) **Technological Environment.** This is fully concerned with changing technology and its effect on product. Many technical products are fastly changed by coming new technology. At that time business also have to cover new products according to changes in technology.

(v) **Political Environment.** Political environment is composition of three factors which are following :

(a) legislature (b) executive (c) judiciary

All above factor affects business and business has to make rules and regulation according to Govt. and political rules and regulation.

(vi) **International Environment.** International environment includes WTO, IMF, WB, SAARC and G20 meetings and their rules and regulations can effect on any type of business. Business has to exist in world market, and then it should understand their effect and take action according to these rules and regulation.

Types of Business Environment

Confining business environment to uncontrollable external factors, it may be classified as

(a) Economic environment

(b) Non-economic environment

The economic environment includes economic conditions, economic policies and economic system of the country. Non-economic environment comprises social, political, legal, technological, demographic and natural environment. All these have a bearing on the strategies adopted by the firms and any change in these areas is likely to have a far-reaching impact on their operations.

ECONOMIC ENVIRONMENT

The economic environment is composed of various set of economic policies, economic system, strategy for economic growth and development, resource endowment, size of market and status of infrastructural facilities in a country. All these affect the business environment in one way or the other. To understand the impact of these on business environment, let us discuss each one of these components in detail.

1. Economic System

Economic system refers to the organizations and institutions created for the purpose of satisfying the wants of human beings. In a country, available resources have to be utilized to manufacture and distribute goods and services, which would meet the needs of the people so that they are satisfied. These institutions and organizations function with their own rules and regulations. The economic system has certain broad characteristics.

(i) The economic system always functions with scarcity of resources. How the system effectively and efficiently uses the resources will determine the extent to which the needs of the people are met.

(ii) An economic system comprises of people. That is, a society of human beings alone can constitute economic system.

(iii) A set of institutions are created and used for the purpose of smooth functioning of an economic system. For example, banks, technology, government, price mechanism, planning etc., are all institutions through which the system operate.

(iv) The basic objective with which an economic system functions is to satisfy the wants of the people. Unless there is want for a commodity or service, nothing can be produced. Hence, the economic system allocates the resources in such a way that the wants of the people are satisfied.

On the basis of the above characteristics of an economic system, it should be clear that the economic system is very dynamic in nature. That is, the economic system undergoes changes with every change in the institutions, though the rate of change would differ from institution to institution.

The economic system functions to answer three vital questions:

(a) what to produce

(b) how to produce and

(c) for whom to produce.

Answering these questions assumes enormous significance as that would determine every activity within a country.

The first question **'What to produce'** depends on what is wanted. The economic system would throw signals through which the requirements of the people could be understood. But not all wants could be satisfied. This is because; a country may not be gifted with all the necessary resources to produce all the goods. Hence, depending upon the resource endowment a country would decide what it could produce. Then there is a problem of prioritizing the available resources among the goods to be produced. Resources should not be used for the production of unwarranted goods. The production of goods, which are harmful to human beings, like narcotic drugs, should be prevented. Hence, considering the availability of resources, the economic system should opt to produce only goods that would satisfy the wants of human beings. In this context it is also necessary to weigh the individual requirements and the national requirements for goods. The latter should be given preference over the former.

The second question **'How to produce'** addresses basically, issues relating to selection of right strategy, technology and investment. For example, a country like India, with very huge population should not prefer capital -intensive technology, as that would lead to more unemployment of human resources. Similarly, while selecting the technology, a country should weigh a number of considerations like relevance of technology, cost of technology, support in case of failures, consequences of the technology used, etc. Another vital aspect is the investment that a country has to make while selecting the strategy and the technology. A very important question is whether the available funds should be invested in sophisticated research and development or meeting the basic needs of the people. Hence, the second question would ultimately determine the efficiency with which the last question the available resources are utilized.

'For whom to produce' implies that based on the resource utilization, the country as a whole should benefit and not few segments. Hence, having produced the goods and services, how they could be equitably distributed is an important aspect. The distribution of national product would differ from country to country depending upon the economic system in vogue.

It has been already pointed out that the way in which the above three questions are answered depends on the economic system which functions in a country. To understand how these answers differ among the economic systems, we should understand the different types of economic systems. In the next section the details of different types of economic systems are discussed.

Types of Economic System

Economic system can be broadly classified into three categories: Capitalism, Socialism and Mixed economy. A number of other types also emerged but all of them came close to any one of the above three type of systems. Such systems include: communism and Marxism. Let us now discuss the features, strengths and weaknesses of each one of these systems.

(I) Capitalism

Capitalism is an economic system based on the principle of free enterprise. Individual ownership of resources is an important feature. With control and command over resources, individuals can conduct any type of business. The object in such a system is to maximize private gains. Any type of enterprise or production of any commodity or service is permitted, so long it is wanted by the society. In such a system the market forces determine the resource allocation and price. That is, the demand and supply forces together determine what to produce, how to produce and for whom to produce. Price mechanism is the nucleus of the capitalistic society. The price mechanism clearly reflects the wants of the people. Once this is known, the producers will allocate the resources to manufacture and sell the products in great demand. While doing so, there is no control or regulation over production. In other words, oligopoly environment prevails. But each producer differentiates his product that he would be able to survive in the market.

But capitalism has a number of weaknesses. The important ones are discussed below :

(i) Economic inequality is invariably found in capitalistic societies. Individuals and organizations with ownership of resources hold over the market for their product or service, will be able to maximize their gains. Those who have no such property would remain poor and become poorer. So it is said that under capitalism, rich becomes richer and poor becomes poorer. The inequality in wealth and income widens over a period under capitalism.

(ii) The scope for the emergence of monopolies in capitalistic societies is very high. Organizations by virtue of their economic power would be able to easily eliminate rivals and competitors in the market. There is also possibility of such monopolies influencing the government in policy making and intervention.

(iii) Though it is said that capitalism would always lead to ideal allocation of resources and fuller utilization of resources, in reality the experience is that resources are held by individuals and organizations and under utilization is the result. Sometimes, products which are not really of national priority are produced and forced on the public, through advertisements and sales promotion techniques.

(iv) Though it is expected that in capitalistic societies the output would increase to optimal level, in practice this is never found. Producers always restrict output to maintain a high price and also maximize profit. So excess capacity would exist in many industries.

(v) In a capitalistic society the divide between the haves and have-nots widen over the period. Existence of poverty among the sophisticated sections of people is also seen. This results in built up of frustration in the society. Over a period this might lead to revolution and social upheaval.

(II) Socialism

Socialism refers to an economic system in which the following features are predominant:

(a) The resources are owned by the State or state owned institutions.

(b) Production takes place in the interest of the society and not for maximizing profits of individuals or organizations. Government decides the type of productive efforts to be permitted. In other words, in a socialist country, government can adopt licensing system and other types of regulations to prevent the emergence of monopolist and exploitative tendencies.

(c) Maximization of Community welfare is the objective than profit maximization.

(d) Another very important feature is that government ensures equitable distribution of national product. Public distribution system assumes enormous significance in such an economic system.

On the whole, the socialistic society differs from capitalist society in every sense. In the broad spectrum of economic systems, socialism and capitalism occupy two extremes. In the world today, pure capitalistic society is not seen in any country. Even in USA, government interference in various economic activities is found. For example, in the field of national defence, atomic energy, space technology, social security, etc., the presence of government is almost complete. Government also retains the right to interfere in the market system, whenever there is deliberate and intentional attempt to monopolize the resource ownership or the market. Similarly, in the erstwhile Soviet Union, socialistic principles were followed. But even here, there were instances of private ownership of property, enterprises, etc., were reported. That is why it is very difficult to come across pure capitalistic or socialistic societies.

MERITS

1. Collective ownership eliminate emergence and existence of monopolies. 2. Resources utilization is planned and achieved in the interest of the society. 3. Government with its control over the resources is able to ensure full utilization of resources and avoid wastage and production of unnecessary goods. 4. As equality in distribution is the fundamental feature of socialism, there is no scope for widening inequalities and the government takes steps to narrow the gap between the rich and the poor through various measures.

LIMITATIONS

1. Excessive dependence on government decisions often result in delay in offering any public service. 2. Bureaucratic control becomes an integral part of the socialistic principles. As a result the benefits and its direction of flow is determined by the bureaucrats. 3. Government by undertaking excessive responsibility on its shoulders, abets inefficiency and corruption in the society. 4. No incentive and motivation for individual excellence or achievements is possible in such a society and so innovations and inventions do not really take place in large scale in such a society. 5. With governmental presence in every walk of life, efficiency and productivity suffer. 6. Lack of support for individual liberty kills initiative.

(III) Mixed Economy

Evolution of the concept of Mixed economy

There was no reference to the mixed economic system in Economic literature in the past. Economists were mainly familiar and advocated the Laissez faire or free enterprise system, as several countries could develop fast following the free enterprise system, in which there was no or little government intervention. The entire economic system operated with the price mechanism at its center point. The producers produced what the consumers wanted and this provided very little scope for the government to intervene in the system. The Classical economists and their ardent supporters believed that the invisible hand will direct the economy and with private initiative and enterprise, every country should be able to record a faster growth as proved in the case of UK, USA, Europe, Australia, and other countries.

But over a period under the leadership of Karl Marx, a new economic system was developed called socialism, in which there was no scope for any private enterprise as everything was owned and controlled by the government. The government decided the type of developmental activities and the requirements of the society and used the available resources in the provision of these requirements. Several countries like USSR, Communist China, Vietnam, Cuba and others preferred this socialist system in which government is made the custodian of the society.

The main reason for the emergence of this new economic system was the failure of capitalism during the 1929 depression to revive every economy from depression. Keynes himself thought that capitalism without some of its evils could certainly help economic recovery. Hence, a time came when economists felt that cent per cent free enterprise or cent per cent government governed economic development cannot work satisfactorily. A compromise between these extremes was thought of as an ideal economic system. The new system called 'mixed economic system' which contained the merits of both the capitalism and socialism and appeared to be fully promising. This mixed economic system is adopted by India as indicated by the First Industrial Policy Resolution 1948.

Characteristics of Mixed Economy

(i) **Co-existence of public and private sectors.** In a mixed economy, one will find the existence of both the private and public sectors. In such a system, the government will undertake the responsibility to build and develop certain sector activities and leave the other activities for the private initiative. In India, the government announced the adoption of the mixed economy system through its 1948 Industrial Policy Resolution. The government clearly earmarked the industries to be completely under the state control, the industries which are to owned and controlled by the state as well as the private sector and industries which are completely left for the private sector. In this way the Resolution provided for the simultaneous existence of both private and public sectors.

(ii) **State participation in economic development.** This is the second feature of mixed economy, according to which the state reserves its right to design and decide the type of development to be achieved. In such a set up, the government strives to promote the welfare of the country by ensuring social order, social justice and establishing all the necessary institutions which are required to achieve the desired pattern of growth and development.

(iii) **Distribution of ownership and control of resources.** This is the next feature of mixed economy. In this system, the government itself enters the field of production so that the available resources are fully utilized. This will also help to avoid concentration of wealth in the hands of few and enable distribution of ownership and control of productive activities. As a result there is no scope for exploitation of any group, say labor, by any other group. In this way the weaker section of the community is well protected and taken care of. Only the mixed economy will enable the government to attain the objectives of the Directive Principles of the Indian Constitution.

(iv) **Directing the investment in socially desirable projects and channels.** Mixed economy facilitates the flow of investment into channels which confers the society with several benefits. For example, the Indian government has invested huge amount in several projects to develop the infrastructural facilities. This forms the basis for the development of other sectors. The investment in these infrastructural areas will not come forth from the private sector as the return is nil. Hence, the government in a mixed economic set up provides the thrust by developing the necessary background and strength which will encourage the private sector to invest in profitable opportunities. In this way the government plays a key role in a mixed economic system.

(v) **Scope for achieving balanced economic development.** Left to itself, the private sector would establish its enterprises only in urban or sub-urban areas and that too in already well developed states. This will mean other areas will have no scope for development. But in a mixed economy, the government will itself undertake the initiative to set up industries in backward areas and encourage the private initiative to set up industries in such areas by offering several concessions and exemptions. In the absence of mixed economy, several states in India would have remained industrially backward.

(vi) Ultimate control and regulation in the hands of government. This feature of mixed economy clearly spells out that in every activity affecting the economy, the government will be the ultimate authority. Though the private sector is assigned its role to perform, the government will still monitor and control the way in which the private initiative is performing its role. Infact, according to the 1948 Industrial Policy Resolution, the government made it clear that the industries already established by the private sector belonging to that category in which new industries will be established by the government alone, the government would undertake the review of the working of these industries in private sector after a period of ten years and if found unsatisfactory, they would be taken over by the government. Though this was criticized as a threat of nationalization, yet through such a provision the government underlines its authority. Similarly in the banking and insurance sectors, the government nationalized banks emphasizing its powers to control and regulate any sector.

(vii) Co-operation in the field of economic development. According to this feature of mixed economy, the government formulates the design for development and invites the private sector to participate in the development. It clearly spells out the guidelines which would govern such cooperative efforts and the limits of freedom granted to the private sector. In case of India, the government prepares the plans for development and spells out the areas left for the private initiative and the areas that will be under state control. Hence, there is scope for the development of private sector, though only according to the design developed by the government.

(IV) Marxism

Marxism is essentially socialism in different garb. The pure socialism is proved to be impractical and it made role of government the center point. Most of the government could not fit in this role effectively. Further capitalism with its explicit goals threatened the success of socialism. It was at this juncture that Karl Marx came up with his ideology, which led to the evolution of Marxian socialism. Marx succeeded through his logical reasoning that economics dominates every activity of a society. This leads to class struggle. When one struggle is tackled another one crop up. The continued onslaught of the capitalist on the society would result in the creation of haves and have-nots. This division of the society would widen with the continuance of capitalism, which ultimately will result in class struggle. Marx explained through his theory of value that every product should be valued in accordance with the value of labor contained in it. But the laborers are rewarded at a very much lesser rate than what they create. That is,, every laborer contribute more by way of his work to produce the product but he is paid a very low wages. The difference is the gain realized by the capitalists. The capitalists would accumulate profits this way at the cost of worsening labor condition. Over a period the divide between the proprietary class and the labor class would widen that much, that there would be social upheaval. Karl Marx predicted class war and argued that unless the capitalist class realizes this, there would be severe impact on production and economic condition of a country. His argument came true in the case of France that the French revolution broke out in 1789.

(V) Communism

Communism is Marx's prediction at the fall of capitalism. Marx argued that the widening inequalities in a society coupled with class struggle should ultimately sound the death knell of capitalism. He is of the view that when capitalism falls, the communism will emerge in which, the laborers will lead the country. The government will own all the resources and determine the needs of the society. It will also decide various other issues of macro and micro importance. Government will turn out to be the custodian of the society and in a pure communistic society; people will lead a life where basic necessities are provided by the government. Unemployment will be very low as every one is occupied in some avocation or other.

But the way in which communism was practiced in China created an impression that the government would be oppressive in its approach that will force the people to lead a life of slavery. One has to work to earn his bread. Military type of regimentation was enforced that common people were subjected to absolute control and regulation by government. The economy remained closed without any international relations, both economic and social. There is no two party systems and the nominated representatives of the Communist party attend to all the governmental responsibilities. Market mechanism is completely absent in such a system, as government determined everything on behalf of the country.

As has been already pointed out depending upon the economic system, the business environment will change. In a capitalist system, the environment provides opportunities for every one who wants to maximize gains. In a socialist system, the government undertakes the responsibility of providing everything to the citizens. In a Marxist economy, it is ultimately the laborers who will hold the reins. In a Communist economy, it is the group of administrators who run the economy in the interest of the society.

2. Economic Policies

Economic policies include fiscal policy, monetary policy, foreign trade policy, licensing policy, technology policy, price policy, etc. These policies lay the framework within which every organization has to function.

(I) Fiscal Policy

By Fiscal policy we mean, the government's tax rates, public expenditure and public borrowing. Through these the government can effectively encourage consumption, investment and saving habits and also restrict them. For example, suppose there is inflation in a country. Inflation implies that the people have high purchasing power and so there is increase in demand for goods. To curb this, the government may raise the personal tax and also the corporate tax. Consequently, individuals will be left with lesser disposable income and to minimize tax, they may start saving through various tax - saving schemes. As far as the corporates are concerned, they have to part with more by way of tax to the government and this would bring down the rate of profit and dividend declared. As a result the corporates would resort to upward price revision, which might lead to further fall in demand for their products and services. During deflationary period, the government would reduce the tax so as to encourage more spending and investment. Even in tax policy, the government can be selective in taxing more of rich and exempting the poor completely. This would facilitate income re-distribution and improve the conditions of poor.

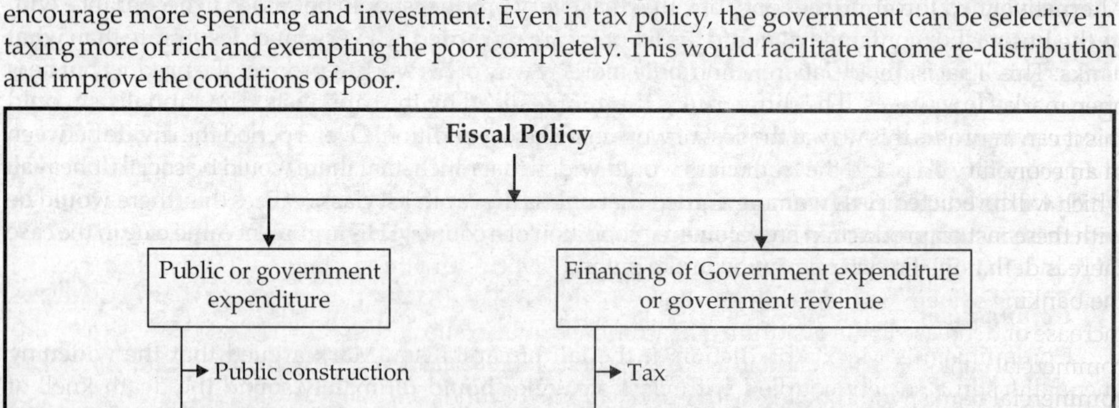

Similarly, by altering its expenditure on various public projects, the government would be able to influence the prevailing economic condition. Government expenditures are incurred on infrastructural development, public utility services like hospitals, new industrial units of very huge size, etc. For instance, suppose there is inflation in a country. The government would reduce its level of expenditure, thereby reducing the income of the people. With lesser income, the demand would go down and so the price. At the time of deflation, the government would expand its public expenditure by investing in a number of public projects, so that there will be income generation for demand generation which will revive the economy.

Public borrowing is one more instrument in the hands of the government to influence the economic condition in a country. This involves government issuing bonds and encouraging common public and other institutions to buy them. By this, the government would be able to bring down the level of purchasing power in the economy and control the inflation. During deflation, the government would redeem the bonds so that with more purchasing power, the economy would be able to revive.

(II) Monetary Policy

Monetary policy refers to the set of policies determined and implemented by the central bank of a country to control the economic condition. The central bank of a country has the basic responsibility to maintain the price level and money supply in a country. This is possible only when the central bank has certain instruments. These instruments available with the central bank to control the money supply and price level are called monetary policy instruments. They can also be termed as Credit control policy. Credit controls can be of two types: Quantitative credit controls and Qualitative credit controls. The former aims at limiting the money supply, while the latter is used to channelize the available credit in the country.

Quantitative credit control policy includes three tools: bank rate, open market operations and variable reserve ratio. Bank rate refers to the rate at which the central bank would re-discount the eligible bills already discounted by the commercial- banks. In simple words, bank rate of interest which a central bank charges on the loans and advances to a commercial bank. These loans and advances are for a period of more than 90 days. By revising the bank rate upwards, the central bank would be able to make the discounting by business organizations with commercial banks costly. This would discourage discounting and thereby money supply in the economy, would come down. Alternatively, by lowering the bank rate, the central bank makes credit available at a cheaper rate, and so the business organizations would go for a larger discounting of eligible bills with commercial banks. This liberal credit policy would have expansionary effects on the economy. Similarly, using open market operations, the central bank can buy or sell the securities in the open market and through this it can increase or contract money supply in the economy. For example, suppose there is inflation in an economy. To bring down the money supply, the central bank would sell the securities it has, which will be bought by the commercial banks and other institutions. In this process the excess money with these institutions would be siphoned off, there by they have to restrict credit. Alternatively when there is deflation, the central bank would buy the securities and the money equivalent transferred to the banking system would facilitate adoption of liberal credit. Variable reserve ratio refers to the increase or decrease in the quantum of Statutory liquidity ratio and the Cash reserve ratio which the commercial banks have to maintain as a proportion of their total deposits. By increasing the ratios, the commercial banks would be left with lesser volume of funds and so this will reduce their lending capacity. By reducing the ratio, the commercial banks would be left with more funds with which they can make lending liberal. All these policies would have a direct impact on the business organizations and their operations.

Instruments or Methods of Monetary Policy

- Quantitative
  - Bank rate
  - Open market operations
  - Change in minimum reserve ratio or Cash Reserve ratio
  - Change in Liquidity Reserve ratio or Statutory Liquidity ratio
- Qualitative
  - Change in margin Requirements of Loans
  - Rationing of Credit
  - Direct Action
  - Moral Suasion

(III) Foreign Trade Policy

The foreign trade policy determines the scope for trade between countries. It would directly affect the business prospects of the business organizations. A liberal policy would extend the scope for exports and imports, while a restrictive policy would narrow the scope. Similarly, if protectionism is favored, then the business organizations will have lesser market threats from multinational corporations. Alternatively if liberalization is the policy, then every domestic business organization has to tune itself to every type of challenge posed by the business giants from abroad. Foreign trade policy also includes the exchange rate policy and exchange controls and customs duties. All these are fundamental to the growth of a business organization. For example, suppose there is full convertibility, then the business organizations would be able to export and import and make payments with lesser restrictions. On the other hand, if there is only partial convertibility, the scope for trade is correspondingly less and the business organizations have to go through a sickening process of getting licenses for export or import and route all their payments through proper channel. Customs duties also play a vital role in determining the volume of external trade. A rise in customs duties would discourage domestic demand because the price of imported goods and services would go up and remain at a high level compared to the domestically produced goods and services. A reduction in custom duty would encourage imports and be favourable to the domestic manufacturers.

Government frequently changes the foreign trade policy, keeping in view the requirements of the country and the economic condition. To tide over the Glance of payments difficulties, government may resort to various policy measures like devaluation, exchange clearing agreements, tariffs and duties, exchange control regulations, etc. These tools would be suitably modified to achieve the desired goals. For example, to encourage exports and discourage imports, the government may devalue the currency, by which the imports of Indian goods abroad become cheaper and the imports of foreign goods in India become costlier. Hence the business organizations have to continuously monitor the changes in the trade policies so as to position themselves accordingly.

(IV) Licensing Policy

In the pre-liberalization days, India adopted licensing policy to regulate the growth of industries in India. Since the days of independence, India adopted licensing policy, which in effect made the government control the growth of industries in accordance with the national priorities. For example, in India, till 1985, the industries in India were classified into four categories: industries completely owned by public sector, industries where both public and private sector participation was permitted, small scale industries and cottage industries. Except the first category in all the other categories, private sector presence was permitted through licensing. This resulted in several adverse effects, which were all explained in detail by the Dutt committee report. But till 1985, liberalization was never accepted as a part of growth strategy. But after 1985, the situation slowly changed and by 1991 India adopted a policy of liberalization. Consequently, the business scope and prospects of the Indian business organization changed since 1991. As has been already pointed out they were exposed to market competition and threats after liberalization. Performance has become a necessity for survival. By about the end of 20th century, the government also proceeded to disinvest several public sector units thereby opening up the challenges all the more for Indian industries. Therefore, the licensing policy and its direction have a lot of impact on the business organizations.

(V) Technology Policy

One of the most important economic policies is the technology policy. Improvement in technology is a condition for growth and survival of any organization. From a stage of man-dependent environment, the business organizations are all fast becoming machine-dependent [computer dependent]. Right from the stage of enquiries down up to planning the logistics, computers are widely used. Only from the mid-90's the government started adopting a favourable technology policy. Apart from permitting free imports of computers and components as well as telecommunication equipments, the government has devised a number of schemes like Software Technology Park, to give a Philip to the technology in India. Computerization has come to stay in telecommunication, railways, roadways, postal services, educational services, medical services, engineering, financial services, etc. This liberal technology policy has resulted in the growth of new industrial segment, viz., information technology.

(VI) Price Policy

This refers to the controls that government has on the price in a country. This is necessary, because, unless price is controlled, there is bound to be inflation and then economic instability. Further in Indian context, nearly 35% of the population is living below the poverty line. They do not have any permanent employment. Especially the rural poverty is very serious. To overcome this situation, the government resorts to price control policy. All the essential and basic necessity goods are subjected to price control. While the poor and downtrodden are provided the essential goods at a controlled and subsidized rate through public distribution, the others are expected to meet their requirements through open market. Through demand and supply management, the government makes all the efforts to keep the prices under control. For instance, by building up buffer stocks, the government overcomes the shortage of food commodities during adverse period. Similarly, specific concessions are given to industrial units located in backward regions and rural areas. This helps them to run on sound basis. As regards the manufactured products, the government adopts the administered price mechanism to control the prices. For example, the cooking gas is supplied to the public at one price, to the commercial establishments at a different price. This helps to minimize the strain of the population using LPG as cooking media. Similarly till April 2002, petrol and diesel were subjected to administered price controls. Sugar, cement, etc., are also subjected to administered price. Hence, through price policy the government protects the interests of the people and this policy has a direct impact on the functioning of the business organization in our country.

3. Economic Planning

Economic planning is made for reducing economic risks. Under this planning, we can select best alternative for increasing the economic strength of company. Economic planning's other name is central planning and central economic planning.

In economic planning, we have to make plan regarding optimum use of our resources in producing goods. We also have to make plan to produce optimum quantity of output. We can use economic planning at small level and at large level like investment decisions of Govt.

MNCs uses economic planning for effective division of their resources in their different departments and branches. They also uses statistical techniques for calculating correlation of company's sale and other sale and on this basis, they make plan to increase sale.

POLITICAL ENVIRONMENT

The Role Government in Business Environment

Government is a very powerful institution which can create a favourable business environment. We can study its role under the following heads:

Role

1. **Government: Regulator of Business.** The entire regulatory legislations and policies stand covered under this segment. On the one hand, there is a very large indirect area of government control over the functioning of private sector business through budgetary and monetary policies.

   But against this there is also a fast expanding area of direct administrative or physical controls through which the government seeks to ensure that private investment and production in industry and the use of scarce resources conform to government's basic socio-economic objectives.

   They have become necessary tools in a system which seeks to avoid total nationalisation of resources.

   Government's regulatory functions with regard to trade, business and industry aim at laying down the limits for the private enterprise. The regulatory functions of the Government include (i) restraints on private activities, (ii) control of monopoly and big business, (iii) development of public enterprises as an alternative to private enterprises to ensure competitive dualism, (iv) maintenance of a proper socio-economic infrastructure.

2. **Government: Promoter of Business.** The promotional role of the government in relation to industries can be seen as providing finance to industry, in granting various incentives and in creating infrastructure facilities for industrial growth and investment.

   For example, our government has identified certain backward areas as 'No Industry Districts'. To promote development of such areas, Government provides subsidies and tax holiday to attract investment in backward areas.

   In this way the government will help the process of balanced development and thereby remove regional disparities. The government is assisting the development of small scale industries. The District Industrial Centers are assisting the development of small industries. The government is actively helping the industrial development of the country by providing finance to them through the development banks.

3. **Government as an Entrepreneur.** The impressive growth of the public sector in India from a small beginning bears testimony to the role of the government as an entrepreneur.

   Private investors are solely guided by private profit motive and hence they are not interested in developing products of common public use and social services which yield relatively lower returns. But as a "social entrepreneur" the government does not hesitate to take them up.

4. **Government as the Planner.** In its role as a planner, the government indicates various priorities in the Five Year Plans and also the sectoral allocation of resources. Mixed economies are democratically planned economies.
   - The government tries to manage the economy and its business activities through the exercise of planning. Planning is the most important activity in a modern mixed economy. The idea of economic planning can be traced to three different sources: Rationalism, Socialism and Nationalism.
   - Economists advocate a planned economy on the ground that it can be a rational economy which can utilise the available resources in an optimal manner.
   - In other words, the planned economy is a rational economy which attempts to secure the maximum return with minimum wastage of productive resources.
   - The socialists advocate a planned economy because it helps to achieve some desirable social ends like economic equality. An unplanned economy, left to it, is incapable of attaining the social ends.
   - The nationalists advocate a planned economy because a planned economy is a powerful economy.
   - The nationalists want to use planning as a weapon to strengthen the military power of the country. Hitler in Germany and Mussolini in Italy resorted to planning to achieve political motive.
   - Planning operation involves a number of steps. The first stage in planning is the formulation of socio-economic objectives of the plan and their definition in quantitative terms.
   - Such objectives include growth, justice, eradication of poverty, price stability etc. In the second stage, the plan lays down the physical and financial targets.
   - The third stage is concerned with execution. The Planning Commission is only an advisory body and it has no power to execute the plan.
   - The various government departments take necessary measures to execute the plan. Executing a plan is more difficult than making it.

LEGAL ENVIRONMENT OF BUSINESS IN INDIA

To understand the legal environment of business in India we are taking account of long history of company law in India. The Companies Act, 1956, is the successor to the Indian Companies Act of 1913 and is a consolidation of many successive Amendment Acts, statutory rules and principles laid down in decisions of the Courts in India and in England. Several Acts were passed from 1850 onwards. The first Act, passed in 1850, was known as the Joint Stock Companies Act. This was followed by two Acts of 1857 and 1860; but the Act of 1866, which followed soon after, repealed all the previous enactments; and this Act itself was repealed in turn by the Act of 1882. This last-mentioned Act remained on the statute book up to 1913, though in the meantime, it was amended several times to meet the demands of the commercial world. The Indian Companies Act of 1913 was passed with the object of consolidating and amending the law relating to trading companies and was mainly based upon the English Companies Act of 1908, with certain additional provisions to meet the peculiar business conditions prevailing in this country. Since the Indian Act closely followed the English Company Law, the decisions of the English Courts under the latter were also generally followed by the Courts in India. This Act of 1913, however, did not provide for certain peculiarities of the Indian commercial world, such as the managing agency, and was, therefore, found to be highly unsatisfactory in several respects in the course of its working. Eventually, extensive amendments were introduced in the Act by the

Indian Companies (Amendment) Act of 1935, which came into operation on 15th January 1937. The vast number of amendments introduced by this Act of 1937, however, involved a few omissions; but they were sought to be removed by frequent amendments in the subsequent years.

The Act of 1913 was, however, repealed by the present Companies Act (1 of 1956) which was brought into force from 1st April 1956. This followed the acceptance by the Government of the recommendations of what is known as the Bhabha Committee which consisted of some Members of Parliament. This Committee submitted a detailed report in 1952, and a Bill incorporating the amendments suggested by it was introduced in the Lok Sabha in 1953 and became subsequently Act 1 of 1956. This Act, while adopting the scheme and most of the provisions of the UK Companies Act of 1948, marked a distinct improvement on the Act of 1913 in several respects and sought to ensure an efficient and honest management of companies governed by the Act.

The Companies Act, 1956, for the first time also provided for a greater measure of Governmental control over the formation and management of joint stock companies. This was considered desirable in the public interest and in order to prevent the diversion of company's funds for purpose which thwarted national economic policies or approved economic objectives.

The basic objectives underlying the law were to provide:

(i) a minimum standard of good behaviour and business honesty in company promotion and management;

(ii) due recognition of the legitimate interest of shareholders and creditors and of the duty of managements not to prejudice to jeopardise those interests;

(iii) provision for greater and effective control over and voice in the management for shareholders;

(iv) a fair and true disclosure of the affairs of companies in their annual published balance sheet and profit and loss accounts;

(v) a higher standard of accounting and auditing;

(vi) recognition of the rights of shareholders to receive reasonable information and facilities for exercising an intelligent judgement with reference to the management;

(vii) a ceiling on the share of profits payable to managements as remuneration for services rendered;

(viii) a check on their transactions where there was a possibility of conflict of duty and interest;

(ix) a provision for investigation into the affairs of any company managed in a manner oppressive to a minority of the shareholders or prejudicial to the interest of the company as a whole; and

(x) enforcement of the performance of their duties by those engaged in the management of public companies or of private companies which were subsidiaries of public companies by providing sanctions in the case of breach and subjecting the later also to the more restrictive provisions of law applicable to public companies.

CONSUMER PROTECTION ACT

Plight of the Indian Consumer

An examination of the important problems facing the Indian consumer would make clear the need for more effective Government intervention and consumer movement to safeguard consumer rights. The following factors make his plight miserable:

(i) Short supply of many goods and services, especially of essential items, is a very serious problem afflicting the Indian consumer. This demand-supply imbalance has produced all the associated evils of profiteering, hoarding and black marketing, corruption, irresponsiveness and arrogance towards consumers.

(ii) The Indian consumer is also the victim of lack of effective or workable competition.

(iii) Many products with which consumers in advanced countries are quite familiar are still new to a very large segment of the Indian consumers. The unfamiliarity of the consumers with product features makes the sale of substandard, inferior or even defective products easier in India than in advanced countries.

(iv) Due to low literacy levels and unsatisfactory information flows, the Indian consumers, by and large, are not conscious of all their rights. This encourages irresponsible and unscrupulous business attitudes and tactics.

(v) It has been said that the legal process in India is comparatively time-consuming and cumbersome. This discourages the consumers from seeking the redressal of their grievance by means of the judicial process.

(vi) Consumerism in India is not well organised and developed.

(vii) Though the public sector has been developed and expanded to serve the public interest by providing effective competition to the private sector, increasing production, improving distribution, *etc.* it has yet to produce benefits that are commensurate with the investment. It is an irony that though consumer welfare is an avowed objective of the public sector, in certain areas the poor performance of the public sector monopolistic has made the plight of the consumer more miserable.

(viii) Though there are a number of laws to safeguard the interests of consumers, they are not effectively implemented and enforced to achieve the objectives.

The above factors call for effective State intervention and consumerism to ensure the rights of consumers.

Government Measures

In India, the Government has taken a number of measures to protect consumer interests. The various Government measures may be classified into:

(i) **Statutory Regulation.** Government of India has armed itself with a number of statutory weapons to control the production, supply, distribution, price and quality of a large number of goods and services. It is empowered to regulate the terms and conditions of sale, the nature of trade and commerce, etc.

Important legislations in this respect includes the MRTP Act, Industries Development and Regulation Act, Essential Commodities Act, Prevention of Food Adulteration Act, Prevention of Black marketing and Maintenance of Supplies of Essential Commodities Act, Trade Marks and Merchandise Marks Act, Sale of Goods Act, Indian Patents and Designs Act, Agricultural Products Grading and Marketing Act, Drugs Act and Drugs Control Act; Indian Standard Institute's Certification Act, Standard Weight and Measures Act, Imports and Exports Control Act, Packaged Commodities Order, Price and Stock Display Order, Consumer Protection Act, etc.

There are, thus, a good number of laws to protect consumer interests. But a common complaint is that these laws are not effectively implemented.

The Monopolies and Restrictive Trade Practices Act, 1969, contains provisions to deal with monopolistic and restrictive trade practices that are prejudicial to public interest. One of the significant aspects of the MRTP (Amendment) Act of 1984 is the incorporation of provisions to control unfair trade practices.

(ii) **Growth and Expansion of Public Sector.** There have been a significant growth and expansion of the public sector in India. One of the most important objectives of the public sector is the enhancement of consumer welfare by increasing production, improving efficiency in production and supply, making available goods and services at fair prices, curbing private monopolies and reducing market imperfections, improving the distribution system and so on. The public sector, in fact, is expected to implement the societal marketing concept.

The Government has developed the public distribution system to reduce the hardships of consumers, especially of the vulnerable sections, by making essential consumer goods available more equitably and at fair prices. There is, however, a common complaint that some of the items, especially the foodgrains supplied by the system, are of inferior quality.

A well developed consumerism is essential for the protection of consumer rights. Consumerism has the following important roles to play:

(a) ***Consumer Education.*** The consumer is given information about various consumer goods and services. This relates to prices, what the consumer can expect, standard trade practices, *etc.*

(b) ***Product Rating.*** In order to guide the consumer in his choice of products, some of the agencies carry out tests and submit reports on them

(c) ***Liaison with Government and with Producers.*** Another important role of consumer organisations is to maintain liaison with producers on the one hand and Government authorities on the other. As Government is the key factor in meeting most consumer needs in India, these organisations have to realise that they have a larger role in that direction, especially in India.

Consumer Protection Act, 2019

The new Consumer Protection Act was passed by Parliament in 2019. It came into force in July 2020 and replaced the Consumer Protection Act, 1986.

Need for the New Act

- The Digital Age has ushered in a new era of commerce and digital branding, as well as a new set of customer expectations. Digitisation has provided easy access, a large variety of choices, convenient payment mechanisms, improved services and shopping as per convenience. However, there are also associated challenges related to consumer protection.
- To help address the new set of challenges faced by consumers in the digital age, the Indian Parliament passed the landmark Consumer Protection Bill, 2019 which aims to provide timely and effective administration and settlement of consumer disputes.

Consumer Protection Act 2019 Details

- Consumer Protection Act, 2019 is a law to protect the interests of the consumers. This Act provides safety to consumers regarding defective products, dissatisfactory services, and unfair trade practices.
- The basic aim of the Consumer Protection Act, 2019 is to save the rights of the consumers by establishing authorities for timely and effective administration and settlement of consumers' disputes.

Rights of the Consumers

- Consumers have the right to information on various aspects of goods and services. This could be information about the quantity, quality, purity, potency, price, and standard of goods or services.

- To be protected from hazardous goods and services. Right to protection against goods and services that can be dangerous to life and property.
- To be protected from unfair or restrictive trade practices.
- Consumers have the right to access a variety of goods and services at competitive prices.
- Consumers should have the right to redressal.

Salient Provisions of the Consumer Protection Act, 2019

New Definition of Consumer

- The new Act has widened the definition of 'consumer'.

Definition of Consumer

- As per the Act, a person is called a consumer who avails the services and buys any good for self-use. Worth to mention that if a person buys any good or avails any service for resale or commercial purposes, he/she is not considered a consumer. This definition covers all types of transactions i.e. offline and online through teleshopping, direct selling or multi-level marketing.

Central Consumer Protection Authority

- The Act proposes the establishment of the Central Consumer Protection Authority (CCPA) as a regulatory authority.
- The CCPA will protect, promote and enforce the rights of consumers and regulate cases related to unfair trade practices, misleading advertisements, and violation of consumer rights.
- CCPA would be given wide-ranging powers.
  - The CCPA will have the right to take suo-moto actions, recall products, order reimbursement of the price of goods/services, cancel licenses, impose penalties and file class-action suits.
  - The CCPA will have an investigation wing to conduct independent inquiry or investigation into consumer law violations.

Consumer Disputes Redressal Commission

- The Act has the provision of the establishment of Consumer Disputes Redressal Commissions (CDRCs) at the national, state and district levels to entertain consumer complaints.
- As per the notified rules, the State Commissions will furnish information to the Central Government on a quarterly basis on vacancies, disposal, the pendency of cases and other matters.
- The CDRCs will entertain complaints related to:
  - Overcharging or deceptive charging
  - Unfair or restrictive trade practices
  - Sale of hazardous goods and services which may be hazardous to life.
  - Sale of defective goods or services
- As per the Consumer Disputes Redressal Commission Rules, there will be no fee for filing cases up to Rs. 5 lakh.

E-Filing of Complaints

- The new Act provides flexibility to the consumer to file complaints with the jurisdictional consumer forum located at the place of residence or work of the consumer. This is unlike the earlier condition where the consumer had to file a complaint at the place of purchase or where the seller has its registered office address.

- The new Act also contains enabling provisions for consumers to file complaints electronically and for hearing and/or examining parties through video-conferencing.
- Consumers will also not need to hire a lawyer to represent their cases.

Product Liability & Penal Consequences

- The Act has introduced the concept of product liability.
  - A manufacturer or product service provider or product seller will now be responsible for compensating for injury or damage caused by defective products or deficiency in services.
- This provision brings within its scope, the product manufacturer, product service provider and product seller, for any claim for compensation. The term 'product seller' would also include e-commerce platforms.

Penalties for Misleading Advertisement

- The CCPA may impose a penalty on a manufacturer or an endorser, for a false or misleading advertisement. The CCPA may also sentence them to imprisonment.

Provision for Alternate Dispute Resolution

- The new Act provides for mediation as an Alternate Dispute Resolution mechanism. For mediation, there will be a strict timeline fixed in the rules.
- As per the recently notified rules, a complaint will be referred by a Consumer Commission for mediation, wherever scope for early settlement exists and parties agree to it. The mediation will be held in the Mediation Cells to be established under the aegis of the Consumer Commissions. There will be no appeal against settlement through mediation.

Unfair Trade Practices

- The new Act has armed the authorities to take action against unfair trade practices too.
- The Act introduces a broad definition of Unfair Trade Practices, which also includes the sharing of personal information given by the consumer in confidence unless such disclosure is made in accordance with the provisions of any other law.

The Central Consumer Protection Council

- The Consumer Protection Act empowers the Central Government to establish a Central Consumer Protection Council. It will act as an advisory body on consumer issues.
  - As per the notified Central Consumer Protection Council Rules, the Central Consumer Protection Council would be headed by the Union Minister of Consumer Affairs, Food and Public Distribution with the Minister of State as Vice Chairperson and 34 other members from different fields.
  - The Council, which has a three-year tenure, will have a Minister-in-charge of consumer affairs from two States from each region – North, South, East, West, and NER. There is also a provision for having working groups from amongst the members for specific tasks.

Applicability

- This Act is applicable to all the products and services, until or unless any product or service is especially debarred out of the scope of this Act by the Central Government.

Consumer Protection Act, 2019 Significance

Empowering Consumers

- The new Act will empower consumers and help them in protecting their rights through its various rules and provisions. The new Act will help in safeguarding consumer interests and rights.
  - Consumer-driven businesses such as retail, e-commerce would need to have robust policies dealing with consumer redressal in place.
  - The new Act will also push consumer-driven businesses to take extra precautions against unfair trade practices and unethical business practices.

Inclusion of the E-commerce Sector

- The earlier Act did not specifically include e-commerce transactions, and this lacuna has been addressed by the new Act.
  - E-commerce has been witnessing tremendous growth in recent times. The Indian e-commerce market is expected to grow to US$ 200 billion by 2026.
- The Act also enables regulations to be notified on e-commerce and direct selling with a focus on the protection of interests of consumers. This would involve rules for the prevention of unfair trade practices by e-commerce platforms.
  - As per the notified rules, every e-commerce entity is required to provide information relating to return, refund, exchange, warranty and guarantee, delivery and shipment, modes of payment, grievance redressal mechanism, payment methods, the security of payment methods, charge-back options, etc. including country of origin which are necessary for enabling the consumer to make an informed decision at the pre-purchase stage on its platform.
  - The e-commerce platforms will have to acknowledge the receipt of any consumer complaint within forty-eight hours and redress the complaint within one month from the date of receipt under this Act. This will bring e-commerce companies under the ambit of a structured consumer redressal mechanism.
  - E-commerce entities that do not comply will face penal action.

Time-bound Redressal

- A large number of pending consumer complaints in consumer courts have been common across the country. The new Act by simplifying the resolution process can help solve consumer grievances speedily.
- A main feature of the Act is that under this, the cases are decided in a limited time period.

Responsible Endorsement

- The new Act fixes liability on endorsers considering that there have been numerous instances in the recent past where consumers have fallen prey to unfair trade practices under the influence of celebrities acting as brand ambassadors.
- This will make all stakeholders – brands, agencies, celebrities, influencers and e-commerce players – a lot more responsible. The new Act would force the endorser to take the onus and exercise due diligence to verify the veracity of the claims made in the advertisement to refute liability claims.

Upholding Consumer Interests

- For the first time, there will be an exclusive law dealing with Product Liability.
- Product liability provisions will deter manufacturers and service providers from delivering defective products or deficient services.
- The new legislation empowers the National Consumers Dispute Redressal Committee as well as the State Commission to declare null and void any terms of a contract while purchasing a product. This will go a long way in protecting consumers, who are often subject to contract conditions that favour a seller or manufacturer.

Alternate Dispute Redressal Mechanism

- The provision of Mediation will make the process of dispute adjudication simpler and quicker.
- This will provide a better mechanism to dispose of consumer complaints in a speedy manner and will help in the disposal of a large number of pending cases in consumer courts across the nation.

Simplified Process for Grievance Redressal

- The new Act would ease the overall process of consumer grievance redressal and dispute resolution process. This will help reduce inconvenience and harassment for the consumers.
- The enhanced pecuniary jurisdiction and provisions providing statutory recognition to mediation processes, enabling filing of complaints from any jurisdiction and for hearing parties through video-conferencing will increase accessibility to judicial forums and afford crucial protection in times when international e-commerce giants are expanding their base.

Consumer Protection Act, 2019 Concerns

State Regulation

- As part of the Consumer Protection Act, 2019, the Ministry of Consumer Affairs will compile a code of conduct for advertisers and agencies, a move designed to curb unfair practices and misleading claims. The planned code will detail penalties for advertisers and their agencies and publishers if misleading advertising and false claims are found.
- There have been concerns that this approach would mark a move from self-regulation to a more federated oversight.

Implementational Challenges

- The existing vacancies at the district commission level would undermine the effective implementation of the new Act.

Lack of Differentiated Approach

- As per the proposed rules for the e-commerce businesses, companies are not allowed to "manipulate the price" of goods and services offered on their platforms to gain unreasonable profit or discriminate between consumers of the same class or make any arbitrary classification of consumers affecting their rights under the Act.
- The clause on the manipulation of price by e-commerce companies appears irrelevant as sometimes, the e-commerce companies would want to reduce the price to enhance sales volume. For a country with market size of around $25 billion, the guidelines should have taken a deeper view of the e-commerce ecosystem, covering all prevailing business models between consumers, marketplaces and sellers.

FOREIGN EXCHANGE MANAGEMENT ACT, 1999 (FEMA)

For a long time, India has had an adverse balance of payment position in international trade, i.e., imports were more than exports; due to which there was shortage of foreign exchange in India. Foreign Exchange Regulation Act was introduced in 1947. This was later replaced with 'the Foreign Exchange Regulation Act, 1973' (FERA), which came into effect on 1st Jan., 1974.

Government initiated the process of liberalisation of Indian economy in 1991. Foreign Investment in various sectors was permitted. This increased flow of foreign exchange to India and foreign exchange reserves have increased substantially. In view of this, FERA has been repealed and FEMA has been passed. The act has been made effective from 1st June, 2000.

PROVISIONS UNDER FEMA

- Free transactions on current account subject to reasonable restrictions that may be imposed.

  m RBI control over capital account transactions.
- Control over realisation of export proceeds.
- Dealing in foreign exchange through 'Authorised Persons' like Authorised Dealer/Money Changer/Off-shore banking unit.
- Adjudication of Offences.
- Appeal provisions including Special Director (Appeals) and Appellate Tribunal.
- Directorate of Enforcement.

As per Statement of Objects to the FEMA Bill, the object of FEMA is to consolidate and amend the law relating to foreign exchange with the object of facilitating external trade and payments and for promoting the orderly development and maintenance of foreign exchange markets in India.

Reserve Bank of India is the overall controlling authority in respect of FEMA.

ENFORCEMENT OF FEMA

Though RBI exercises overall control over foreign exchange transactions, enforcement of FEMA has been entrusted to a separate 'Directorate of Enforcement' formed for this purpose.

FEMA makes provisions in respect of dealings in foreign exchange. Broadly, all current account transactions are free. However, Central Government can impose reasonable instructions by issuing rules. [Section 3 of FEMA]

Capital Account Transactions are permitted to the extent specified by RBI by issuing regulations. [Section 6 of FEMA].

FEMA envisages that RBI will have a controlling role in management of foreign exchange. Since RBI cannot directly handle foreign exchange transactions, it authorises 'Authorised Persons' to deal in foreign exchange as per directions issued by RBL. [Section 10 of FEMA].

RBI is empowered to issue directions to such 'Authorised Persons' under section 11 of FEMA. These directions are issued through AP (DIR) circulars.

FEMA also makes provisions for enforcement, penalties, adjudication and appeals.

NON-RESIDENT INDIAN AND PIO UNDER FEMA

There are many Indians staying abroad. Many of them have taken the citizenship of that country, but they have their roots in India. Such 'non-residents of Indian nationality' or 'persons of Indian origin residing abroad' are often called 'NRI'. They are given several facilities in India without losing their status as 'foreign citizen'.

Definition of NRI

'Non-Resident Indian' (NRI) means an individual resident outside India who is citizen of India or is an 'Overseas Citizen of India' cardholder within the meaning of section 7(A) of the Citizenship Act, 1955.

'Overseas Citizen of India' –

Cardholders registered as such under Notification No. 26011/4/98 F.I. dated 19.8.2002 issued by Central Government are deemed to be 'Overseas Citizen of India' cardholders'.

Thus, a person resident outside India will be 'NRI', if:

(a) He is citizen of India

(b) He is an Overseas Cardholder.

For the purpose of Foreign exchange Management Regulations, 2000, NRI means a person resident outside India who is a citizen of India.

Person of Indian Origin

'Person of Indian Origin' (PIO) means a citizen of any country other than Bangladesh or Pakistan, if:

(i) He at any time held Indian passport.

(ii) He or either his parents or any of his grandparents was a citizen of India by virtue of the Constitution of India or the Citizenship Act, 1955.

(iii) The person is a spouse of an Indian citizen or a person.

The definition has been modified for various purposes in various regulations.

For the purpose of Foreign Exchange Management Regulations, 2000, citizen of 'Sri Lanka' is also excluded in addition to citizen of Bangladesh and Pakistan.

INCOME TAX DEFINITION

Income tax classifies persons as 'Resident', 'Resident but not ordinarily resident' and 'Non-resident'. The definition under FEMA and definitions under Income Tax are not same, and there are variations, though sometimes they match.

Investment Facilities available to NRI and PIOs at a Glance

NRIs and PIOs have been given some special facilities for investment in India. These are, of course, in addition to facilities available to other foreign investors. They also have some facilities after return to India. These are discussed at appropriate places, but summarised below to know facilities at a glance.

(a) **Bank Accounts and Deposits:**
- NRE Account
- FCNR (B) account
- NRO Account

(b) **Repatriation: Upto USD 1 million per year from NRO account, subject to income tax deduction (TDS)**

(c) **Investments on repatriation basis:**
- FDI
- Government dated securities/treasury bills
- Units of domestic mutual funds
- Bonds issued by PSU in India

- Shares in PSU dis-invested by Government of India
- Shares and convertible debentures under FDI scheme
- Shares and debentures of Indian companies through PIS
- Deposits with Indian companies, NBFC, Housing Finance companies and other Financial Institutions
- National Pension Scheme
- Investment Vehicle

(d) **Investment on non-repatriation basis:**

- Units of money market mutual funds of India
- Capital of firm or proprietary concern in India, not engaged in agricultural or plantation activity or real estate business
- Chit funds
- Postal savings

(e) **Immovable property:**

- Immovable property other than agricultural/plantation property or a farm house
- Sale proceeds to the extent of repatriable funds used in acquiring immovable property can be repatriated without any lock-in period upto two residential properties
- Refund of application/earnest money together with interest subject to TDS, if original payment was made out of NRE/FCNR (B) account or inward remittance

(f) **Transmission of inheritance:**

No permission required

(g) **Housing Loans:**

NRI/PIO can obtain housing loans for purchase of property in India.

(h) **Facilities to returning NRI/PIO:**

- May continue to hold, own transfer or invest in foreign currency, foreign security or any immovable property situated outside India, if such currency, security or property was held or owned when resident outside India
- RFC account. Proceeds of sale of assets held outside India can be credited to RFC account.

(i) **Rupee Loan to NRI employees of Indian companies for acquiring ESOP:**

Banks can give rupee loans to NRI employees of Indian companies for acquiring shares of companies, within limits.

Indian Resident under FEMA

Person resident in India means the following [section 2(v) of FEMA

- A person residing in India for more than 182 days during the course of preceding financial year. However, it does not include a person who has gone out of India or who stays outside India for employment outside India or carrying on business or vocation outside India or for any other purpose, in such circumstances as would indicate his intention to stay outside India for an uncertain period.
- A person residing in India for more than 182 days during the course of preceding financial year. However, it does not include a person who has come to or stays in India, in either case, otherwise than

  (a) He has come for or taking employment in India

  (b) For carrying on business or vocation in India

(c) For any other purpose, in such circumstances as would indicate his intention to stay in India for an uncertain period.

In other words, even in this case, residing in India in previous year for 182 days is essential.

- Any person or body corporate registered or incorporated in India.
- An office, branch or agency outside India owned or controlled by a person resident outside India
- An office, branch or agency outside India owned or controlled by a person resident in India.

Broadly, 'person resident of India' includes persons of India (except those staying abroad for work or business or other purpose) and foreign persons who come to India or stay in India for employment, carrying out business or other purpose. Even office, branch or agency can be 'person'.

Person residing for less or more than 182 days in previous year

If a person stayed in India during 2001-2002 for less than 182 days, he will not be a 'resident' during 2002-03 even if he resides in India for more than 182 days in that year, as what is relevant is 'preceding year'. However, if he resides in India for over 182 days in 2002-03, he will be 'resident' in 2003-04. But if he leaves India for the purpose of taking up employment outside India during 2003-04, or for any other purpose as business/vocation outside India, or for any other purpose as would indicate his intention to stay outside India for an uncertain period, he would cease to be person resident in India from the date of his departure.

Even if a person is a foreign citizen, if he has not left India for any of aforesaid purposes during 2003-04, he would be considered, 'person resident in India' during the financial year 2003-04.

Difference between stay and reside

There is distinction between 'stay' and 'reside'. 'Stay' means physical presence in India while 'reside' indicates permanency. Thus, even if an airplane pilot 'stays' in India for more than 182 days during his transit travel, it cannot be said that he 'resides' in India.

Difference between income tax and FEMA provisions:

One major distinction between Income Tax and FEMA provisions is that for purpose of Income Tax, purpose of stay (in India or abroad) is not relevant, only duration of stay is relevant.

Person going out for certain/uncertain period

If a person stays in India for over 182 days during financial year 2001-02 but goes out next year on 10-08-2002 for employment, business, or any other purpose with intention to stay outside India for uncertain period, he will not be considered 'resident' during 2002-03 from the day he leaves India. However, if he goes abroad for a certain period and stays abroad, he will be treated as 'resident' in 2002-03, even if his stays in India was less than 182 days in 2002-03. The reason is that he has gone out for a specific period and his stay in previous year was more than 182 days. However, in 2003-04, he will not be 'resident' as he did not stay in India for more than 182 days during 2002-03. If a person leaves India on 1-03-2003 to take up the employment abroad, he will be considered as a person resident outside India w.e.f. 1-3-2003 for the financial year April 2002 – March 2003, even though his stay in India was for more than 182 days.

Functions of RBI under FEMA

Foreign Exchange Management Act ("FEMA") envisages that Reserve Bank of India ("RBI") will have a key role in management of foreign exchange. The main functions of RBI under FEMA are as follows:

(a) Controlling dealings in foreign exchange by giving general or special permission for dealing in foreign exchange, excluding those cases where specific provisions have been made in Act, Rules or Regulations – Section 3.
(b) RBI cannot impose any restrictions on current account transactions. These can be imposed only by Central Government in consultation with RBI – Section 5. However, in certain cases, prior approval of RBI is required for current account transactions as provided in Foreign Exchange Management (Current Account Transactions) Rules, 2000.
(c) Specifying conditions for payment in respect of capital account transaction – Section 6(2).
(d) Regulate / prohibit / restrict the following, by issuing Regulations:
- Transfer or issue of foreign security to resident and Indian security to non-resident;
- Borrowing and lending in foreign exchange or to a foreign person;
- Export / import of currency or currency notes;
- Transfer of immovable property outside India;
- Giving guarantee or surety where foreign exchange transaction is involved – Section 6(3)

(e) Specify (by regulation) period and manner in which foreign exchange due from export of goods and services should be received – Section 8.
(f) To grant exemption from realisation and repatriation in cases specified under Section 9.
(g) Granting authorisation to 'Authorised Person' to deal in foreign exchange, to give directions to them and to inspect the authorised person – Sections 10, 11 & 12.

Key Updates in FEMA Amendments (2024-2025)

1. **Cross-Border Share Swaps & Foreign Investment**
   - The amendments simplify share swaps for Indian companies expanding abroad through mergers and acquisitions.
   - Investments from countries sharing land borders with India now require government approval, irrespective of the sector.
   - Overseas Citizen of India (OCI) investors will now be treated similarly to Non-Resident Indians (NRIs) in certain non-repatriation investments.
2. **Promotion of INR Trade Settlement**
   - The Reserve Bank of India (RBI) revised FEMA regulations to encourage trade settlements in INR.
   - Authorized Dealer bank branches overseas can now open INR accounts for non-residents to facilitate transactions with Indian residents.
   - Non-residents can also use repatriable INR accounts (such as Special Rupee Vostro Accounts) for investments and transactions with other non-residents.
3. **Foreign Currency Accounts for Exporters**
   - Indian exporters can now open foreign currency accounts abroad to manage trade proceeds efficiently.
   - Cross-border transactions are permitted in all foreign currencies, including local currencies of trade partners.
4. **Alignment with Startup Regulations**
   - The turnover threshold for startups to qualify for FDI benefits has increased from Rs. 25 crore to Rs. 100 crore.
   - Startups will now retain their status for up to 10 years after incorporation.

5. **Regulatory Clarity on Control & Investor Groups**
   - The definition of "control" has been standardized across various financial laws.
   - Foreign Portfolio Investors (FPIs) with more than 50% common control will be classified as a single investor group.

SOCIO-CULTURAL FACTORS AND THEIR INFLUENCE ON BUSINESS

Social and cultural factors affecting business include belief systems and practices, customs, traditions and behaviours of all people in given country, fashion trends and market activities influencing actions and decisions. Socio-cultural perspective is one of the most important factor influencing decision of marketing managers and strategic goals of companies entering new foreign markets. It should be noted that legal factors affecting business is also considered as one of the major socio-cultural factors that can influence companies. Proper identification of this factor during strategic analysis (PEST analysis, STEEP analysis, SWOT analysis, TOWS analysis) could lead to better strategic alignment of company to society (during international development).

Social factors affecting Businesses

- social classes and their influence on the society,
- average disposable income level,
- wealth of people,
- economic inequalities,
- level of education,
- access to education (free, paid),
- level and access to health-care,
- health consciousness in society (smoking, drinking, drug use, safe driving, etc.),
- buying habits and consumer preferences,
- average retirement age (for men and women),
- personality of average consumer,
- reputation of company in society,
- conflicts within society,
- susceptibility to influence,
- social organization (communities, social groups, gangs, ad-hoc gatherings, etc.),
- uncertainty avoidance dominating in society (or other G. Hofstede socio-cultural factors).

Cultural factors affecting Business

- fashion trends,
- lifestyle,
- social media influence (blogging, etc.) vs traditional media (press, TV, radio),
- dominant communication technology in social groups,
- participation in cultural events,
- willingness to pay for tickets,
- popular actors, music styles, design forms, etc.
- creativity of people,
- relative population of local (folk) artists vs. global imported culture,
- various other determinants of culture.

Socio-cultural factors and Demography

- population growth rate,
- birth control regulations and incentives,
- age distribution (ageing of societies can change demand),
- life expectancy rate,
- sex distribution (differences between number of men and women in society),
- average family size and family structure,
- relative influence of minorities in society,
- immigration rate,
- emigration rate,
- social diversity (of income, education, race, gender, etc.).

Beliefs and Value Systems within Society

- majority and minority religions,
- influence of religious leaders on social behaviours,
- role of religion as a binding/dividing factor in society,
- dominant beliefs in society,
- eating habits connected with religion,
- belief in superstitions (Friday 13th, 13th floor in buildings, etc.) and myths,
- role of science in relation to religion,
- customs, traditions during holidays (worship days).

Common attitudes in Society

- attitudes toward banking, saving money and investing,
- attitudes toward ecological products, recycling, global warming, etc.,
- attitudes toward renewable energy sources, green products,
- attitudes toward imported products and services, foreign investments, etc.,
- attitudes toward work and career, possibility of development,
- attitudes toward leisure and retirement,
- attitudes toward learning and self-development,
- attitudes toward others (diverse people, counties, companies, etc.),
- attitudes toward safety (police, military, etc.) and privacy,
- attitudes toward ethical/unethical behaviours and Corporate Social Responsibility,
- attitudes toward management practices (negotiation, business activities, etc.).

CORPORATE SOCIAL RESPONSIBILITY (C.S.R.)

Corporate social responsibility (CSR) is a self-regulating business model that helps a company be socially accountable – to itself, its stakeholders, and the public. By practicing corporate social responsibility, also called corporate citizenship, companies can be conscious of the kind of impact they are having on all aspects of society including economic, social, and environmental. To engage in CSR means that, in the normal course of business, a company is operating in ways that enhance society and the environment, instead of contributing negatively to it.

Corporate social responsibility is a broad concept that can take many forms depending on the company and industry. Through CSR programs, philanthropy, and volunteer efforts, businesses can benefit society while boosting their own brands. As important as CSR is for the community, it is equally valuable for a company. CSR activities can help forge a stronger bond between employee and corporation; they can boost morale and can help both employees and employers feel more connected with the world around them.

In order for a company to be socially responsible, it first needs to be responsible to itself and its shareholders. Often, companies that adopt CSR programs have grown their business to the point where they can give back to society. Thus, CSR is primarily a strategy of large corporations. Also, the more visible and successful a corporation is, the more responsibility it has to set standards of ethical behavior for its peers, competition, and industry.

SCOPE AND IMPORTANCE OF INTERNATIONAL BUSINESS

International business is much broader than international trade. It includes not only international trade (i.e., export and import of goods and services) but also a wide variety of other ways in which the firms operate internationally. International Management professionals are familiar with the language, culture, economic and political environment, and business practices of countries in which multinational firms actively trade and invest.

Major forms of business operations that constitute international business are as follows.

- **Merchandise exports and imports.** Merchandise means goods that are tangible, i.e., those that can be seen and touched. When viewed from this perceptive, it is clear that while merchandise exports mean sending tangible goods abroad, merchandise imports means bringing tangible goods from a foreign country to one's own country.
- **Service exports and imports.** Service exports and imports involve trade in intangibles. It is because of the intangible aspect of services that trade in services is also known as invisible trade.
- **Licensing and franchising.** Permitting another party in a foreign country to produce and sell goods under your trademarks, patents or copyrights in lieu of some fee is another way of entering into international business. It is under the licensing system that Pepsi and CocaCola are produced and sold all over the world by local bottlers in foreign countries.
- **Foreign investments.** Foreign investment is another important form of international business. Foreign investment involves investments of funds abroad in exchange for financial return. Foreign investment can be of two types: direct and portfolio investments.
- **Monopoly Power.** It might arrive from patent rights, technological advantages, product segregation etc. Another reason for internationalization is limited market information.
- **Benefiting from currency exchange.** Those who add an international business to their assortment may also advantage from currency fluctuations. For example, when the U.S. dollar is down, you might be able to export more as foreign customers benefit from the favorable currency exchange rate.
- **Limitations of Domestic Market.** Some demographic trends such as a contraction in birth rate decline in domestic demand, fully tapped market potential have adverse effects on some businesses. When the domestic market is small, international business is the option for growth. Depression in the home market drives companies to explore foreign markets.
- **Increased revenues.** One of the top advantages of international business is that you may be capable to enlarge your number of probable clients. Each country you add to your list can open up a new path to business growth and increased revenues.

- **Growth opportunities.** Foreign markets both developed country and developing country provide considerable expansion opportunities for the firms from a developing country. MNCs are interested in no. of developing countries due to initially increasing in their income and population of the predictable 1 billion increases in world population during 2000 to 2015; only about 3% will be in the high-income countries, foreign markets, both developed and developing countries after ample opportunities for developing country firms also.
- **Expand and diversify.** International business can enlarge and expand its activities. This is because it earns very high profits. It also gets financial help from the government.
- **Opportunity to specialize.** International markets can open up avenues for a new line of service or products. It can also give you an opportunity to specialize in a different area to serve that market.

GLOBALIZATION AND ITS DRIVERS

Globalization means several things to several people. For some it is a new paradigm – a set of fresh beliefs, working methods and economic, political and socio-cultural realities in which the previous assumptions are no longer valid. For developing countries, it means integration with the world economy. In simple economic terms, globalisation refers to the process of integration of the world into one huge market. Such unification calls for the removal of all trade barriers among countries. Even political and geographical barriers become irrelevant.

At the company level, globalisation means two things:

(a) the company commits itself heavily with several manufacturing locations around the world and offers products in several diversified industries and

(b) it also means the ability to compete in domestic markets with foreign competitors. In the popular sense, globalisation refers mainly to multi-plant operations.

A company which has gone global is called in Multinational (MNC) or a Transitional (TNC). An MNC is, therefore, one that by operating in more than one country, gains through Research and Development (R&D), leading to substantial production, marketing and financial advantages in its costs and reputation that are not available to purely domestic competitors. The global company views the world as one market, minimises the importance of national boundaries, raises capital and markets wherever it can do the job best.

To be specific, a global company has three characteristics:

(i) It is a conglomerate of multiple units (located in different parts of the globe) but all linked by common ownership.

(ii) Multiple units draw on a common pool of resources such as money, credit, information, patents, trade names and control systems.

(iii) The units respond to some common strategy.

Nestle International is an example of an enterprise that has become multinational. It sells its products in most countries and manufactures in many. Besides, its managers and shareholders are from many nations. The other MNCs whose names can be mentioned here are IBM, GE, McDonald, Ford, Shell, Philips, Sony, and Uniliver.

Why do Companies Go Global?

There are several reasons why companies go global. The primary motive for going global is that there is money in the overseas markets.

The MNCs from the laid - the US, Europe and Japan - have huge assets and more than quarter of these assets are found in foreign markets.

The other reasons for seeking international markets are:

1. One reason could be the rapid shrinking of time and distance across the globe thanks to faster communication, speedier transportation, growing financial flows and rapid technological changes.
2. It is being realised that the domestic markets are no longer adequate and rich. Japanese have flooded the US market with automobiles and electronics because the home market was not large enough to absorb whatever was produced. Some European companies have gone global for similar reasons.
3. Raymond Vernon has propounded a theory explaining why companies go international. Though propounded in the late 1960s, Vernon's theory is relevant even today.

ADVANTAGES OF GLOBALISATION

- Free flow of capital and increase in the total capital employed.
- Free flow of technology.
- Increase in Industrialization.
- Spread of production facilities throughout the globe.
- Balanced development of world economies.
- Increase in production and consumption.
- Commodities at lower price with high quality.
- Increase in jobs and income.
- Higher standard of living.
- Balanced human development.

DISADVANTAGES OF GLOBALISATION

- Loss of domestic industries.
- Exploits human resource.
- Decline in income.
- Unemployment.
- Transfer of Natural resources.
- Widening gap between rich and poor.
- Dominance of foreign institutions.

Called product-cycle theory, Vernon's hypothesis proceeds on the following lines:

Companies that develop attractive new products sell them first in their home markets. Sooner or later, foreigners may learn about these products. At this stage, most companies would export the product or service rather than produce it abroad. But as foreign demand grows, the economics of foreign production changes. Eventually, the foreign market becomes large enough to justify foreign investment.

MODES OF ENTRY INTO INTERNATIONAL BUSINESS

There are seven major modes of entering an international market.

Exporting

An item produced in a domestic market can be sold abroad. Storing and processing is mainly done in the supplying firm's home country. Export can increase the sales volume. When a firm receives canvassed items and exports them, it is called Passive Export.

Alternately, if a strategic decision is taken to establish proper processes for organizing the export functions and for obtaining foreign sales, it is known as Active Export.

- **Advantages.** Low investment; Less risks.
- **Disadvantages.** Unknown market; No control over foreign market; Lack of information about external environment.

Licensing

In this mode of entry, the manufacturer of the home country leases the right of intellectual properties, i.e., technology, copyrights, brand name, etc., to a manufacturer of a foreign country for a predetermined fee. The manufacturer that leases is known as the licensor and the manufacturer of the country that gets the license id known as the licensee.

- **Advantages.** Low investment of licensor; Low financial risk of licensor; Licensor can investigate the foreign market; Licensee's investment in R&D is low; Licensee does not bear the risk of product failure; Any international location can be chosen to enjoy the advantages; No obligations of ownership, managerial decisions, investment etc.
- **Disadvantages.** Limited opportunities for both parties involved; Both parties have to manage product quality and promotion; One party's dishonesty can affect the other; Chances of misunderstanding; Chances of trade secrets leakage of the licensor.

Franchising

In this mode, an independent firm called the franchisee does the business using the name of another company called the franchisor. In franchising, the franchisee has to pay a fee or a fraction of profit to the franchisor. The franchisor provides the trademarks, operating process, product reputation and marketing, HR and operational support to the franchisee.

- **Advantages.** Low investment; Low risk; Franchisor understands market culture, customs and environment of the host country; Franchisor learns more from the experience of the franchisees; Franchisee gets the R&D and brand name with low cost; Franchisee has no risk of product failure.
- **Disadvantages.** Franchising can be complicated at times; Difficult to control; Reduced market opportunities for both franchisee and franchisor; Responsibilities of managing product quality and product promotion for both; Leakage of trade secrets.

Turnkey Project

It is a special mode of carrying out international business. It is a contract under which a firm agrees - for a remuneration - to fully carry out the design, create, and equip the production facility and shift the project over to the purchaser when the facility is operational.

Mergers & Acquisitions

In Mergers & Acquisitions, a home company may merge itself with a foreign company to enter an international business. Alternatively, the home company may buy a foreign company and acquire the foreign company's ownership and control. M&A offers quick access to international manufacturing facilities and marketing networks.

- **Advantages.** Immediate ownership and control over the acquired firm's assets; Probability of earning more revenues; The host country may benefit by escaping optimum capacity level or overcapacity level.

JOINT VENTURE

When two or more firms join together to create a new business entity, it is called a joint venture. The uniqueness in a joint venture is its shared ownership. Environmental factors like social, technological, economic and political environments may encourage joint ventures.

- **Advantages.** Joint ventures provide significant funds for major projects; Sharing of risks between or among partners; Provides skills, technology, expertise, marketing to both parties.
- **Disadvantages.** Conflicts may develop; Delay in decision-making of one affects the other party and it may be costly; The venture may collapse due to the entry of competitors and the changes in the partner's strength; Slow decision-making due to the involvement of two or more decision-makers.

- **Disadvantages.** Complex process and requires experts from both countries; No addition of capacity to the industry; Government restrictions on acquisition of local companies may disrupt business; Transfer of problems of the host country's to the acquired company.

Wholly Owned Subsidiary

Wholly Owned Subsidiary is a company whose common stock is fully owned by another company, known as the parent company. A wholly owned subsidiary may arise through acquisition or by a spin-off from the parent company.

THEORIES OF INTERNATIONAL TRADE

The exchange of goods across national borders is termed as international trade. Countries differ widely in terms of the products and services traded. Countries rarely follow the trade structure of other nations; rather they evolve their own product portfolios and trade patterns for exports and imports. Besides, nations have marked differences in their vulnerabilities to the upheavals in exogenous factors.

Trade is crucial for the very survival of countries that have limited resources, such as Singapore or Hong Kong (presently a province of China), or countries that have skewed resources, such as those located in the Caribbean and West Asian regions. However, for countries with diversified resources, such as India, the US, China, and the UK, engagement in trade necessitates a logical basis.

Trade theories also offer an insight, both descriptive and prescriptive, into the potential product portfolio and trade patterns. They also facilitate in understanding the basic reasons behind the evolution of a country as a supply base or market for specific products.

The principles of the regulatory frameworks of national governments and international organizations are also influenced to a varying extent by these basic economic theories.

The theory of mercantilism attributes and measures the wealth of a nation by the size of its accumulated treasures. Accumulated wealth is traditionally measured in terms of gold, as earlier gold and silver were considered the currency of international trade. Nations should accumulate financial wealth in the form of gold by encouraging exports and discouraging imports.

The theory of mercantilism aims at creating trade surplus, which in turn contributes to the accumulation of a nation's wealth. Between the sixteenth and nineteenth centuries, European colonial powers actively pursued international trade to increase their treasury of goods, which were in turn invested to build a powerful army and infrastructure.

The colonial powers primarily engaged in international trade for the benefit of their respective mother countries, which treated their colonies as exploitable resources. The first ship of the East India Company arrived at the port of Surat in 1608 to carry out trade with India and take advantage of its rich resources of spices, cotton, finest muslin cloth, etc.

Other European nations—such as Germany, France, Portugal, Spain, Italy—and the East Asian nation of Japan also actively set up colonies to exploit the natural and human resources.

Mercantilism was implemented by active government interventions, which focused on maintaining trade surplus and expansion of colonization. National governments imposed restrictions on imports through tariffs and quotas and promoted exports by subsidizing production.

The colonies served as cheap sources for primary commodities, such as raw cotton, grains, spices, herbs and medicinal plants, tea, coffee, and fruits, both for consumption and also as raw material for industries. Thus, the policy of mercantilism greatly assisted and benefited the colonial powers in accumulating wealth.

Advantages of International Business

- **A Country may Import.** Things which it cannot Produce International trade enables a country to consume things, which either cannot be produced within its borders or production may cost very high. Therefore, it becomes cost cheaper to import from other countries through foreign trade.
- **Maximum Utilisation of Resources.** International trade helps a country to utilise its resources to the maximum limit. If the country does not take up imports and exports, then its resources remain unexploited. Thus, it helps to eliminate the wastage of resources.
- **Benefit to Consumer.** Imports and exports of different countries provide opportunities to the consumer to buy and consume those goods, which cannot be produced in their own country. They therefore get a diversity in choices.
- **Reduces Trade Fluctuations.** By making the size of the market large with large supplies and extensive demand, international trade reduces trade fluctuations. The prices of goods tend to remain more stable.
- **Utilisation of Surplus Produce** International trade enables different countries to sell their surplus produce to other countries and earn foreign exchange.
- **Fosters International Trade.** International' trade fosters peace, goodwill and mutual understanding among nations. Economic inter-dependence of countries often leads to close cultural relationship and thus, avoid war between them.

Disadvantages of International Business

- **Import of Harmful Goods.** Foreign trade may lead to import harmful goods like cigarettes, drugs etc. which may ruin the health of the residents of the country. E.g. The people of China suffered greatly through optimum imports.
- **It may Exhaust Resources.** International trade leads to intensive cultivation of land. Thus, it has the operations of law of diminishing returns in agricultural countries. It also makes a poor nation by giving too much burden over the resources.
- **Over Specialisation** Over specialisation may be disastrous for a country. A substitute may appear and ruin the economic lives of millions.
- **Danger of Starvation.** A country might depend for her food mainly on foreign countries. In times of war, there is a serious danger of starvation for such countries.
- **One Country may Gain at the Expense of Another.** One of the serious drawbacks of foreign trade is that one country may gain at the expense of other due to certain accidental advantages. The industrial revolution in Great Britain ruined Indian handicrafts during the 19th century.
- **It may Lead to War.** Foreign trade may lead to war in different countries competing with each other in finding out new markets and sources of raw material for their industries and frequently come into clash. This was one of the causes of first and second world war.

INTERNATIONAL BUSINESS THEORIES

Adam Smith's Model

Adam Smith describes trade taking place as a result of countries having absolute advantage in production of particular goods, relative to each other. Within Adam Smith's framework, absolute advantage refers to the instance where one country can produce a unit of a good with less labor than another country.

In Book IV of his major work the Wealth of Nations, Adam Smith, discussing gains from trade, provides a literary model for absolute advantage based upon the example of growing grapes from Scotland. He makes the argument that while it is possible to grow grapes and produce wine in Scotland, the investment in the factors of production would cost thirty times than more than the cost of purchasing an equal quantity from a foreign country. The minimization of aggregate real costs and efficient resource allocation through trade without strong consideration for comparative costs form the basis of Adam Smith's model of absolute advantage in international trade.

Ricardian Model

The law of comparative advantage was first proposed by David Ricardo.

The Ricardian theory of comparative advantage became a basic constituent of neoclassical trade theory. Any undergraduate course in trade theory includes a presentation of Ricardo's example of a two-commodity, two-country model. For the modern development, see Ricardian trade theory extensions

The Ricardian model focuses on comparative advantage, which arises due to differences in technology or natural resources. The Ricardian model does not directly consider factor endowments, such as the relative amounts of labor and capital within a country.

Specific Factors Model

The specific factors model is an extension of the Ricardian model. It was due to Jacob Viner's interest in explaining the migration of workers from the rural to urban areas after the Industrial revolution.

In this model labor mobility among industries is possible while capital is assumed to be immobile in the short run. Thus, this model can be interpreted as a short-run version of the Heckscher-Ohlin model. The "specific factors" name refers to the assumption that in the short run, specific factors of production such as physical capital are not easily transferable between industries. The theory suggests that if there is an increase in the price of a good, the owners of the factor of production specific to that good will profit in real terms

Heckscher-Ohlin Model

In the early 1900s, a theory of international trade was developed by two Swedish economists, Eli Heckscher and Bertil Ohlin. This theory has subsequently become known as the Heckscher-Ohlin model (H-O model). The results of the H-O model are that the pattern of international trade is determined by differences in factor endowments. It predicts that countries will export those goods that make intensive use of locally abundant factors and will import goods that make intensive use of factors that are locally scarce.

The H-O model makes the following core assumptions:

- Labor and capital flow freely between sectors equalising factor prices across sectors within a country.
- The amount of labor and capital in two countries differ (difference in endowments)
- Technology is the same among countries (a long-term assumption)
- Tastes are the same upon countries

Stolper-Samuelson Theory

According to the Stolper-Samuelson theorem, the export of a product which is relatively cheap, abundant resource makes this resource more scarce in the domestic market. Thus, the increased demand for the abundant resource leads to an increase in its price and an increase in its income.

Simultaneously, the income of the resource used intensively in the import-competing product decreases as its demand falls.

Simply put, this theorem indicates that an increase in the price of a product rises the income earned by resources that are used intensively in its production. Conversely, a decrease in the price of a product reduces the income of the resources that it uses intensively. The abundant resource that have comparative advantage realizes an increase in income, and the scare resource realizes a decrease in its income regardless of industry. This trade theory concludes that some people will suffer losses from free trade even in the long-term.

Empirical Evidences of the Heckscher-Ohlin Model

In 1953, Wassily Leontief published a study in which he tested the validity of the Heckscher-Ohlin theory. The study showed that the United States was more abundant in capital compared to other countries, therefore the United States would export capital-intensive goods and import labor-intensive goods. Leontief found out that the United States' exports were less capital intensive than its imports. The result became known as Leontief's paradox.

New trade Theory

New trade theory tries to explain empirical elements of trade that comparative advantage-based models above have difficulty with. These include the fact that most trade is between countries with similar factor endowment and productivity levels, and the large amount of multinational production (i.e., foreign direct investment) that exists. New trade theories are often based on assumptions such as monopolistic competition and increasing returns to scale. One result of these theories is the home-market effect, which asserts that, if an industry tends to cluster in one location because of returns to scale and if that industry faces high transportation costs, the industry will be located in the country with most of its demand, in order to minimize cost.

New New Trade Theory

New new trade theory is a theory of international trade inaugurated by Marc Melitz in 2003. It discovered that efficiency of firms in a country changes much and those firms engaged in international trade have higher productivity than firms which produce only for domestic market. As it is fitted to big data age, the research produced many follows and the trend is now called New new trade theory in comparison to Paul Krugman's new trade theory.

Gravity Model

The Gravity model of trade presents a more empirical analysis of trading patterns. The gravity model, in its basic form, predicts trade based on the distance between countries and the interaction of the countries' economic sizes. The model mimics the Newtonian law of gravity which also considers distance and physical size between two objects. The model has been shown to have significant empirical validity.

Ricardian Trade Theory Extensions

According to Eaton and Kortum, in the 21 century, "the Ricardian framework has experienced a revival. Much work in international trade during the last decade has returned to the assumption that countries gain from trade because they have access to different technologies. ... This line of thought has brought Ricardo's theory of comparative advantage back to center stage." The Ricardian trade theory was expanded and generalized multiple times: notably to treat many-country many-product situation and to include intermediate input trade, and choice of production techniques. In Ricardian framework, capital goods (comprising fixed capital) are treated as goods which are produced and consumed in the production.

New Trade Theory of International Trade

Countries do not necessarily trade only to benefit from their differences but they also trade so as to increase their returns, which in turn enable them to benefit from specialization. International trade enables a firm to increase its output due to its specialization by providing a much larger market those results in enhancing its efficiency.

The theory helps explain the trade patterns when markets are not perfectly competitive or when the economies of scale are achieved by the production of specific products. Decrease in the unit cost of a product resulting from large scale production is termed as economies of scale.

Since fixed costs are shared over an increased output, the economies of scale enable a firm to reduce it's per unit average cost of production and enhance its price competitiveness.

(i) **Internal Economies of Scale.** Companies benefit by the economies of scale when the cost per unit of output depends upon their size. The larger the size, the higher are the economies of scale. Firms that enhance their internal economies of scale can decrease their price and monopolize the industry, creating imperfect market competition. This in turn results in the lowering of market prices due to the imperfect market competition.

Internal economies of scale may lead a firm to specialize in a narrow product line to produce the volume necessary to achieve cost benefits from scale economies.

Industries requiring massive investment in R&D and creating manufacturing facilities, such as branded software by Microsoft, microprocessors by Intel or AMD, and aircrafts by Boeing or Airbus, need to have a global market base so as to achieve internal economies of scale and compete effectively.

(ii) **External Economies of Scale.** If the cost per unit of output depends upon the size of the industry, not upon the size of an individual firm, it is referred to as external economies of scale. This enables the industry in a country to produce at a lower rate when the industry size is large compared to the same industry in another country with a relatively smaller industry size.

The dominance of a particular country in the world market in a specific products sector with higher external economies of scale is attributed to the large size of a country's industry that has several small firms, which interact to create a large, competitive critical mass rather than a large-sized individual firm.

However, external economies of scale do not necessarily lead to imperfect markets but may enable the country's industry to achieve global competitiveness. Although no single firm needs to be large, a number of small firms in a country may create a competitive industry that other countries may find difficult to compete with.

The automotive component industry o India and the semiconductor industry in Malaysia are illustrations of external economies of scale. The development of sector-specific industrial clusters, such as brassware in Moradabad, hosiery in Tirupur, carpets in Bhadoi, semi-precious stones in jaipur, and diamond polishing in Surat, may also be attributed to external economies

The new trade theory brings in the concept of economies of scale to explicate the Leontief paradox. Such economies of scale may not be necessarily linked to the differences in factor endowment between the trading partners. The higher economies of scale lead to increase in returns, enabling countries to specialize in the production of such goods and trade with countries with similar consumption patterns.

Besides intra-industry trade, the theory also explains intra-firm trade between the MNEs and their subsidiaries, with a motive to take advantage of the scale economies and increase their returns.

GOVERNMENT INTERVENTION IN INTERNATIONAL TRADE

A government's political objectives often contradict economic proposals so that its market efficiency and international competitiveness become better. First of all the chapter discusses the different ways in which governments intervene in the international trade process, why do they do so and the economic and non-economic effects their actions have on the participants in the process. After that, it studies the role of the General Agreement on Tariffs and Trade and the World Trade Organization in the international trade arena. Finally, it discusses the different ways in which firms can deal with adverse trading conditions.

Objectives

- Conflicting Results of Trade Policies
- Economic Rationales for Governmental Intervention
- Noneconomic Rationales for Government Intervention
- Instruments of Trade Control
- Dealing with Governmental Trade Influences

Conflicting Results of Trade Policies

The governments not just intervene in trade to attain economic, social and/or political objectives, at also pursue political rationality along with it. However, it's almost impossible to help the struggling constituencies without penalizing the prosperous. The conflicting goals are not the only threat; retaliation against protectionist actions is another persisting threat.

Conomis Rationales for Governmental Intervention

Another reason why governments impose policies on their agricultural sector is that they believe because of their intervention the rate of income growth would increase. Few examples of such interventions that lead to increased economic activity are investment policies-the provision of public goods, such as the research and development of new technologies and infrastructural development (roads, schools, health facilities).

Sometimes, the private sector won't be able to make these investments as private investors would not be likely to get the full benefit from investment in public goods because it is not possible or too expensive to exclude the non service payers created. It also happens that the consumption by one consumer fails to reduce the availability of the good or service for others. Consumers therefore don't go in to paying for the good or service hence there is no market formation. Finally, due to the excessive capital requirements of the investment the private sector won't be able to mobilize necessary financial resources. The public sector regarding most of these investments is capable of recovering the costs of intervention through user fees or through taxation of the commodities or the regional populations benefitting from the investment.

The second rationale for government intervention in the agricultural sector is the correction of market failures. In case of market imperfections, the prices of goods or services will not reflect their true scarcity values because the private sector cannot develop the institutions required for efficient market functioning. In rural credit markets there may be a lack of information on alternative lending and borrowing opportunities in other regions, or there may be no formal lending institutions to mobilize savings all of which may result in market failure. Another such example is market power; private sector suppliers (or consumers) can influence prices because they are not abundant and also because there is a lack of other market outlets for the buyers or sellers. These conditions are mostly found in factor markets (those for labour, credit, and land) and also sometimes in remote rural commodity markets.

Unemployment

Among the most effective types of political pressure there are the organized labor's efforts to preserve domestic jobs. When imports are limited, local jobs are retained as firms and consumers have only one choice, to purchase domestically produced goods and services. For the effectiveness of such measures in limiting unemployment however the protectionist country has to be relatively small. These measures may also lead to retaliation. Thus the governments have to maintain balance between the costs of higher prices and the costs of unemployment and displaced production resulting from free trade.

Infant-Industry Argument

According to the infant industry argument, first presented by Alexander Hamilton in 1792, a government should protect emerging industries so that the country gets a comparative advantage from international competition till the time its firms are ready to compete in world markets effectively. Eventual competitiveness happens due to the movement along the learning curve along with the efficiency gains from achieving the economies of large-scale production. Nonetheless, for infant-industry protection a particular segment of the economy (typically local consumers) needs to incur the initial higher cost of inefficient local production.

TARIFF BARRIERS

In simplest terms, a tariff is a tax. It adds to the cost of imported goods and is one of several trade policies that a country can enact.

Who Collects a Tariff?

Tariffs are paid to the customs authority of the country imposing the tariff. Tariffs on imports coming into the United States, for example, are collected by Customs and Border Protection, acting on behalf of the Commerce Department. In the U.K., it's HM Revenue & Customs (HMRC) that collects the money.

Tariffs are often created to protect infant industries and developing economies but are also used by more advanced economies with developed industries. Here are five of the top reasons tariffs are used:

Protecting Domestic Employment

The levying of tariffs is often highly politicized. The possibility of increased competition from imported goods can threaten domestic industries. These domestic companies may fire workers or shift production abroad to cut costs, which means higher unemployment and a less happy electorate. The unemployment argument often shifts to domestic industries complaining about cheap foreign labor, and how poor working conditions and lack of regulation allow foreign companies to produce goods more cheaply. In economics, however, countries will continue to produce goods until they no longer have a comparative advantage (not to be confused with an absolute advantage).

Protecting Consumers

A government may levy a tariff on products that it feels could endanger its population. For example, South Korea may place a tariff on imported beef from the United States if it thinks that the goods could be tainted with a disease.

Infant Industries

The use of tariffs to protect infant industries can be seen by the Import Substitution Industrialization (ISI) strategy employed by many developing nations. The government of a developing economy will levy tariffs on imported goods in industries in which it wants to foster growth. This increases the prices of imported goods and creates a domestic market for domestically produced goods while protecting those industries from being forced out by more competitive pricing. It decreases unemployment and allows developing countries to shift from agricultural products to finished goods.

Criticisms of this sort of protectionist strategy revolve around the cost of subsidizing the development of infant industries. If an industry develops without competition, it could wind up producing lower quality goods, and the subsidies required to keep the state-backed industry afloat could sap economic growth.

National Security

Barriers are also employed by developed countries to protect certain industries that are deemed strategically important, such as those supporting national security. Defense industries are often viewed as vital to state interests, and often enjoy significant levels of protection. For example, while both Western Europe and the United States are industrialized, both are very protective of defense-oriented companies.

Retaliation

Countries may also set tariffs as a retaliation technique, if they think that a trading partner has not played by the rules. For example, if France believes that the United States has allowed its wine producers to call its domestically produced sparkling wines "Champagne" (a name specific to the Champagne region of France) for too long, it may levy a tariff on imported meat from the United States. If the U.S. agrees to crack down on the improper labeling, France is likely to stop its retaliation. Retaliation can also be employed if a trading partner goes against the government's foreign policy objectives.

Types of Tariffs and Trade Barriers

There are several types of tariffs and barriers that a government can employ:

Specific Tariffs

A fixed fee levied on one unit of an imported good is referred to as a specific tariff. This tariff can vary according to the type of good imported. For example, a country could levy a $15 tariff on each pair of shoes imported, but levy a $300 tariff on each computer imported.

Ad Valorem Tariffs

The phrase ad valorem is Latin for "according to value," and this type of tariff is levied on a good based on a percentage of that good's value. An example of an ad valorem tariff would be a 15% tariff levied by Japan on U.S. automobiles. The 15% is a price increase on the value of the automobile, so a $10,000 vehicle now costs $11,500 to Japanese consumers. This price increase protects domestic producers from being undercut but also keeps prices artificially high for Japanese car shoppers.

Licenses

A license is granted to a business by the government and allows the business to import a certain type of good into the country. For example, there could be a restriction on imported cheese, and licenses would be granted to certain companies allowing them to act as importers. This creates a restriction on competition and increases prices faced by consumers.

Import Quotas

An import quota is a restriction placed on the amount of a particular good that can be imported. This sort of barrier is often associated with the issuance of licenses. For example, a country may place a quota on the volume of imported citrus fruit that is allowed.

Voluntary Export Restraints (VER)

This type of trade barrier is "voluntary" in that it is created by the exporting country rather than the importing one. A voluntary export restraint is usually levied at the behest of the importing country and could be accompanied by a reciprocal VER. For example, Brazil could place a VER on the exportation of sugar to Canada, based on a request by Canada. Canada could then place a VER on the exportation of coal to Brazil. This increases the price of both coal and sugar but protects the domestic industries.

How Do Tariffs Affect Prices?

Tariffs increase the prices of imported goods. Because of this, domestic producers are not forced to reduce their prices from increased competition, and domestic consumers are left paying higher prices as a result. Tariffs also reduce efficiencies by allowing companies that would not exist in a more competitive market to remain open.

The figure illustrates the effects of world trade without the presence of a tariff. In the graph, DS means domestic supply and DD means domestic demand. The price of goods at home is found at price P, while the world price is found at P*. At a lower price, domestic consumers will consume Qw worth of goods, but because the home country can only produce up to Qd, it must import Qw-Qd worth of goods.

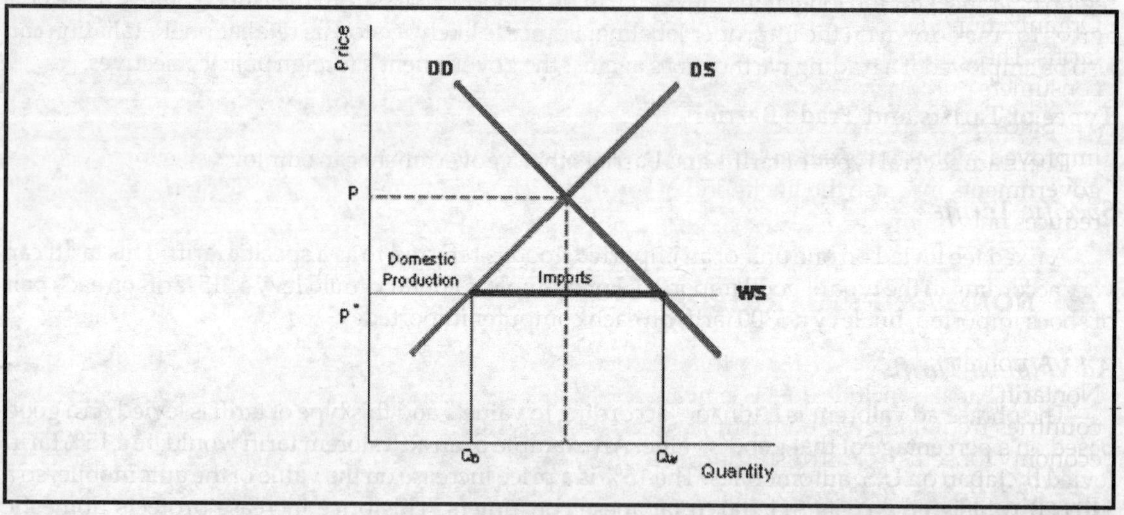

Price without the influence of a tariff

When a tariff or other price-increasing policy is put in place, the effect is to increase prices and limit the volume of imports. In Figure, price increases from the non-tariff P* to P′. Because the price has increased, more domestic companies are willing to produce the good, so Qd moves right. This also shifts Qw left. The overall effect is a reduction in imports, increased domestic production, and higher consumer prices. (To learn more about the movement of equilibrium due to changes in supply and demand, read Understanding Supply-Side Economics.)

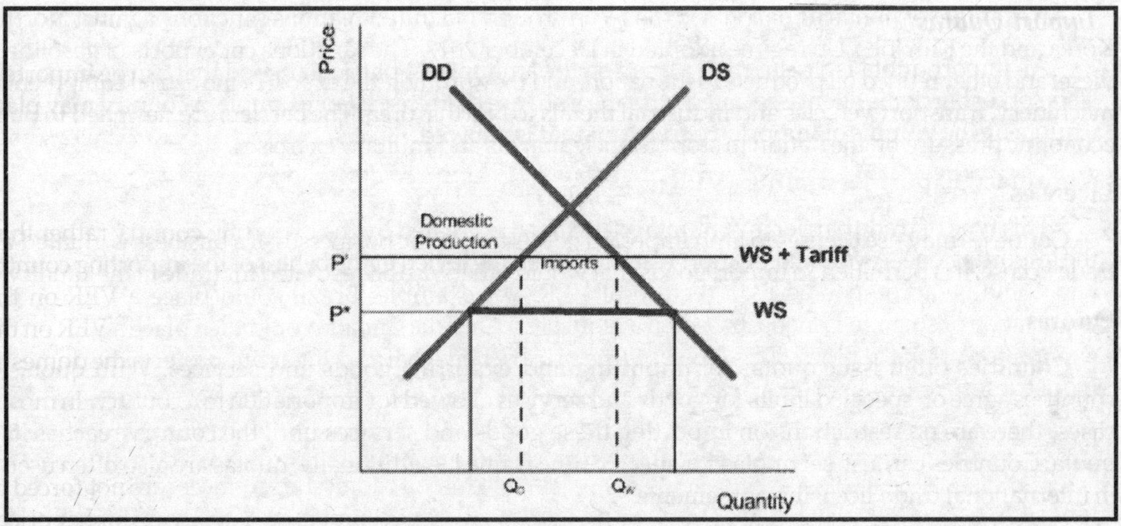

Price under the effects of a tariff

Tariffs and Modern Trade

The role tariffs play in international trade has declined in modern times. One of the primary reasons for the decline is the introduction of international organizations designed to improve free trade, such as the World Trade Organization (WTO). Such organizations make it more difficult for a country to levy tariffs and taxes on imported goods, and can reduce the likelihood of retaliatory taxes. Because of this, countries have shifted to non-tariff barriers, such as quotas and export restraints. Organizations like the WTO attempt to reduce production and consumption distortions created by tariffs. These distortions are the result of domestic producers making goods due to inflated prices, and consumers purchasing fewer goods because prices have increased.

Since the 1930s, many developed countries have reduced tariffs and trade barriers, which has improved global integration and brought about globalization. Multilateral agreements between governments increase the likelihood of tariff reduction, while enforcement of binding agreements reduces uncertainty.

NON-TARIFF BARRIERS

A nontariff barrier is a way to restrict trade using trade barriers in a form other than a tariff. Nontariff barriers include quotas, embargoes, sanctions, levies and other restrictions. Large, developed countries frequently use nontariff barriers to control the amount of trade it conducts with another economy for selfish or altruistic purposes.

Breaking Down Non-tariff Barrier

Countries commonly use nontariff barriers in international trade, and they typically base these barriers on the availability of goods and services, and political alliances with trading countries. Overall, any barrier to international trade will influence the economy because it limits the functions of standard market trading. The lost revenue resulting from the barrier to trade is called an economic loss.

Countries can set various types of alternative barriers in place of standard tariffs. Such barriers often release countries from paying added tax on imported goods and create other barriers that have a meaningful yet different monetary impact.

An example of nontariff barriers is the recent round of United Nations sanctions against North Korea and the Kim Jong Un regime adopted in December 2017. The sanctions cut exports of gasoline, diesel and other refined oil products to the nation, and they prohibit the export of industrial equipment, machinery, transport vehicles and industrial metals to North Korea. The barriers are designed to put economic pressure on the nation to stop its nuclear arms and military exercises.

Licenses

Countries may use licenses to limit imported goods to specific businesses. If a business is granted a trade license, it is permitted to import goods that would otherwise be restricted for trade in the country.

Quotas

Countries often issue quotas for importing and exporting goods and services. With quotas, countries agree on specified limits for goods and services allowed for importation to a country. In most cases, there are no restrictions on importing these goods and services until the country reaches its quota. Countries can also set quotas for specific time frames. Additionally, quotas are also often used in international trade licensing agreements.

Embargoes

Embargoes restrict the trade of specified goods and services. An embargo is a measure a government will use for specific political or economic circumstances.

Sanctions

Countries impose sanctions on other countries to limit their trade activity. Sanctions can include increased administrative actions or additional customs and trade procedures that slow or limit a country's ability to trade.

Voluntary Export Restraints

Exporting countries sometimes use voluntary export restraints. Voluntary export restraints set limits on the number of goods and services a country will export to specified countries. These restraints are typically based on availability and political alliances.

Standard Tariffs

Countries can use nontariff barriers in place of or in conjunction with standard tariff barriers, which are taxes that an exporting country pays to an importing country for goods or services. Tariffs are the most common type of trade barrier, and they increase the cost of goods and services in an importing country.

INDIA'S FOREIGN TRADE POLICY

The integration of the domestic economy through the twin channels of trade and capital flows has accelerated in the past two decades which in turn led to the India's GDP reaching Rs 167.73 trillion (US$ 2.30 trillion) in 2017-18*. Simultaneously, the per capita income also nearly trebled during these years. India's trade and external sector had a significant impact on the GDP growth as well as expansion in per capita income. India's GDP during the first half of 2018-19 stood at Rs 89.88 trillion (US$ 1.29 trillion).

Total exports from India (Merchandise and Services) increased 15.48 per cent year-on-year during April-November 2018 to US$ 351.99 billion, while total imports increased by 16.86 per cent year-on-year to US$ 428.18 billion according to data from the Ministry of Commerce & Industry. Exports from the country recorded their highest growth in 2017-18.

According to Mr Suresh Prabhu, Minister for Commerce and Industry, the Government of India is keen to grow exports and provide more jobs for the young, talented, well-educated and even semi-skilled and unskilled workforce of India.

Capital Inflows

India's foreign exchange reserves were US$ 393.29 billion in the week up to December 21, 2018, according to data from the RBI.

External Sector

- In November 2018, India and Iran had signed a bilateral agreement to settle oil trades in Indian currency through public sector bank United Commercial Bank (UCO) Bank.
- In June 2018, a Memorandum of Understanding (MoU) was signed between the Governments of India and China to export non-basmati rice to China. As of October 2018, total 24 mills got clearance to export the same.
- Bilateral trade between India and China reached US$ 84.44 billion in 2017 with 40 per cent increase in Indian exports to China.
- In August 2018, US upgraded India's status as a trading partner on par with its North Atlantic Treaty Organization (Nato) allies.
- India's external sector has a bright future as global trade is expected to grow at 4 per cent in 2018 from 2.4 per cent in 2016.
- Bilateral trade between India and Ghana is rising exponentially and is expected to grow from US$ 3 billion to US$ 5 billion over the coming three years, stated Mr Aaron Mike Oquaye Junior, Ghana's Ambassador to India.
- India has revised its proposal on trade facilitation for services (TFS) at the World Trade Organisation (WTO) and has issued a new draft, with the contents being more meaningful and acceptable to other member countries.
- The Union Cabinet, Government of India, has approved the proposed Memorandum of Understanding (MoU) between Export-Import Bank of India (EXIM Bank) and Export-Import Bank of Korea (KEXIM).
- The Goods and Services Network (GSTN) has signed a memorandum of understanding (MoU) with Mr Ajay K Bhalla, Director General of Foreign Trade (DGFT), to share realised foreign exchange and import-export code data, process export transactions of taxpayers under goods and services tax (GST) more efficiently, increase transparency and reduce human interface.
- In March 2017, the Union Cabinet approved the signing of the customs convention on the international transport of goods, Transports Internationaux Routiers (TIR) making India the 71st signatory to the treaty, which will enable the movement of goods throughout these countries in Asia and Europe and will allow the country to take full benefit of the International North South Transportation Corridor (INSTC).
- Mr Richard Verma, the United States Ambassador to India, has verified that India-US relations across trade, defence and social ties will be among the top priorities of the newly elected US President Mr Donald Trump's administration.

Foreign Trade Policy

- In the Mid-Term Review of the Foreign Trade Policy (FTP) 2015-20 the Ministry of Commerce and Industry has enhanced the scope of Merchandise Exports from India Scheme (MEIS) and

Service Exports from India Scheme (SEIS), increased MEIS incentive raised for ready-made garments and made- ups by 2 per cent, raised SEIS incentive by 2 per cent and increased the validity of Duty Credit Scrips from 18 months to 24 months.

- As of December 2018, Government of India is planning to set up trade promotion bodies in 15 countries to boost exports from Small and Medium Enterprises (SME) in India.
- In September 2018, Government of India increased the duty incentives for 28 milk items under the Merchandise Export from India Scheme (MEIS).
- All export and import-related activities are governed by the Foreign Trade Policy (FTP), which is aimed at enhancing the country's exports and use trade expansion as an effective instrument of economic growth and employment generation.
- The Department of Commerce has announced increased support for export of various products and included some additional items under the Merchandise Exports from India Scheme (MEIS) in order to help exporters to overcome the challenges faced by them.
- The Central Board of Excise and Customs (CBEC) has developed an 'integrated declaration' process leading to the creation of a single window which will provide the importers and exporters a single point interface for customs clearance of import and export goods.
- As part of the FTP strategy of market expansion, India has signed a Comprehensive Economic Partnership Agreement with South Korea which will provide enhanced market access to Indian exports. These trade agreements are in line with India's Look East Policy. To upgrade export sector infrastructure, 'Towns of Export Excellence' and units located therein will be granted additional focused support and incentives.
- RBI has simplified the rules for credit to exporters, through which they can now get long-term advance from banks for up to 10 years to service their contracts. This measure will help exporters get into long-term contracts while aiding the overall export performance.
- The Government of India is expected to announce an interest subsidy scheme for exporters in order to boost exports and explore new markets.

FOREIGN DIRECT INVESTMENT (FDI)

Foreign direct investment (FDI) is an investment made by a firm or individual in one country into business interests located in another country. Generally, FDI takes place when an investor establishes foreign business operations or acquires foreign business assets, including establishing ownership or controlling interest in a foreign company. Foreign direct investments are distinguished from portfolio investments in which an investor merely purchases equities of foreign-based companies. Foreign direct investments are commonly made in open economies that offer a skilled workforce and above-average growth prospects for the investor, as opposed to tightly regulated economies. Foreign direct investment frequently involves more than just a capital investment. It may include provisions of management or technology as well. The key feature of foreign direct investment is that it establishes either effective control of, or at least substantial influence over, the decision-making of a foreign business.

The Bureau of Economic Analysis (BEA), which tracks expenditures by foreign direct investors into U.S. businesses, reported total FDI into U.S. businesses of $259.7 billion in 2017, marking a 32% decrease from the prior year. As per usual, acquisitions made up the overwhelming majority of new foreign direct investments into the U.S., totalling $253.2 billion. Meanwhile, greenfield investments, a type of FDI defined by the BEA as investments to either establish a new business or to expand an existing foreign-owned business, comprised a much lighter $6.5 billion.

METHODS OF FOREIGN DIRECT INVESTMENT

Foreign direct investments can be made in a variety of ways, including the opening of a subsidiary or associate company in a foreign country, acquiring a controlling interest in an existing foreign company, or by means of a merger or joint venture with a foreign company.

The threshold for a foreign direct investment that establishes a controlling interest, per guidelines established by the Organisation of Economic Co-operation and Development (OECD), is a minimum 10% ownership stake in a foreign-based company. However, that definition is flexible, as there are instances where effective controlling interest in a firm can be established with less than 10% of the company's voting shares.

Types of Foreign Direct Investment

Foreign direct investments are commonly categorized as being horizontal, vertical or conglomerate. A horizontal direct investment refers to the investor establishing the same type of business operation in a foreign country as it operates in its home country, for example, a cell phone provider based in the United States opening up stores in China. A vertical investment is one in which different but related business activities from the investor's main business are established or acquired in a foreign country, such as when a manufacturing company acquires an interest in a foreign company that supplies parts or raw materials required for the manufacturing company to make its products.

A conglomerate type of foreign direct investment is one where a company or individual makes a foreign investment in a business that is unrelated to its existing business in its home country. Since this type of investment involves entering an industry the investor has no previous experience in, it often takes the form of a joint venture with a foreign company already operating in the industry.

FOREIGN PORTFOLIO INVESTMENT (FPI)

Foreign portfolio investment (FPI) consists of securities and other financial assets passively held by foreign investors. It does not provide the investor with direct ownership of financial assets and is relatively liquid depending on the volatility of the market. Foreign portfolio investment differs from foreign direct investment (FDI), in which a domestic company runs a foreign firm, because although FDI allows a company to maintain better control over the firm held abroad, it may face more difficulty selling the firm at a premium price in the future.

Foreign portfolio investment is part of a country's capital account and shown on its balance of payments (BOP). The BOP measures the amount of money flowing from one country to other countries over one monetary year. It includes the country's capital investments, monetary transfers, and the number of exports and imports of goods and services.

Differences Between FPI and FDI

FPI lets an investor purchase stocks, bonds or other financial assets in a foreign country. Because the investor does not actively manage the investments or the companies that issue the investments, he does not have control over the securities or the business. However, since the investor's goal is to create a quick return on his money, FPI is more liquid and less risky than FDI.

In contrast, FDI lets an investor purchase a direct business interest in a foreign country. For example, an investor living in New York purchases a warehouse in Berlin so a German company can expand its operations. The investor's goal is to create a long-term income stream while helping the company increase its profits.

The investor controls his monetary investments and actively manages the company into which he puts money. He helps build the business and waits to see his return on investment (ROI). However, because the investor's money is tied up in a company, he faces less liquidity and more risk when trying to sell his interest.

The investor also faces currency exchange risk, which may decrease the value of his investment when converted from the country's currency to U.S. dollars, and political risk, which may make the foreign economy and his investment amount volatile.

Example of Foreign Portfolio Investment

In 2016, the United States received approximately 84% of total remittances, which was the majority of outflows for FPI. The United Kingdom, Singapore, Hong Kong and Luxembourg rounded out the top five countries receiving FPI, with approximately 81% of the combined share. Net inflows from all countries were $451 million. Outflows were approximately $1.3 billion. Approximately 84% of investments were in Philippine Stock Exchange-listed securities pertaining to property companies, holding firms, banks, telecommunication companies, food, beverage and tobacco companies.

Types of FDIs

Foreign Direct Investment can be broadly classified into two types : Outward FDIs and Inward FDIs. This classification is based on the types of restrictions imposed and various prerequisites required for these investments. An outward bound FDI is backed by the government against all types of associated risks. This form of FDI is subject to tax incentives as well as disincentives of various forms. Risk coverage provided to the domestic industries and subsidies granted to the local firms stand in the way of outward FDIs, which are also known as direct investment abroad.

Different economic factors encourages inward FDIs. These include interest loan, tax breaks, grants, subsidies and the removal of restrictions and limitations. Factors detrimental to the growth of FDIs include necessities of differential performance and limitations related with ownership patterns.

Other categorisations of FDI exist as well.

Vertical Foreign Direct Investment takes place when a multinational corporations owns some shares of a foreign enterprise, which supplies input for it or used the output produced by the MNC.

Horizontal Foreign Direct Investment happens when a multinational company carries out a similar business operation in different nations.

Foreign Direct Investment is guided by different motives. FDIs that are undertaken to strengthen the existing market structure or explore the opportunities of new market can be called market seeking FDIs. Resource seeking FDIs are aimed at factors of production which have more operational efficiency than those available in the home country of the investors.

Some Foreign Direct Investment involves the transfer of strategic asset. FDI activities may also be carried out to ensure optimisation of available opportunities and economies of scale. In this case, the foreign direct investment is termed as 'efficiency seeking'.

There are two strategic kinds of FDI

(1) **Horizontal foreign direct investment.** If FDI is made in way which in same sector as a company have activity in at home. To give an example for Horizontal Foreign Direct Investment, we can say that If Ariston makes investment on Caribbean and Scandinavian nation it can be counted as horizontal foreign direct investment. Authorities suggest that studying on horizontal foreign direct investment may be very helpful to understand the vertical foreign investment.

(2) **Vertical foreign direct investment.** If a company or multi national establishment (MNE) supplies production resources for a company's local transactions, or this kind of foreign

direct investment can take place with selling the final product of a local company in their company's country.

After briefly defining the foreign direct investment, now on next part, we will be studying on benefits and costs of the foreign direct investment for a country.

FDI: Benefits for Economy of Host Country

In order to get more positives from FDI freely, improving countries have started to dilate and make more suitable laws and FDI policies and attempted to reach most suitable arrangement to get interest the FDI makers. Professors of economy who supports the liberal market perspective suggest that the gain of FDI to a landlord country so preponderate the costs that practical nationalism is an ideology which has been unable to imply.

Four determined benefits will be studied on this part for the landlord country: effects on resource – transfer , the effect on employment, effect on balance of payments, and the aspect of competition.

Effects on Resource – Transfer

Foreign direct investment can add great amount of value to a landlord economy with providing cash and capital, innovative technology, and governance sources that might the directly invested country does not have and with the help of three important resource the country's economy's expanding rate can be increased. That type of source transport can contribute to the stimulating the fiscal expanding of the landlord economy. There are three elements in Resource – Transfer Effect, which are Capital, Technology and Management.

Capital

When we get to talk about the capital, multinational enterprises (MNEs) spend money and make investment for long term basis, get into jeopardy and use their corporate identities only when the projects makes money well. After the free capital transfer across nations regulations, capital-holders are very likely to seek highest rate of return. It causes that the countries which are in need of capital, try to attract MNEs to invest. A lot of MNEs , with the help of their big size and financial strength, get accessibility to fiscal instruments and opportunities which may not be ready to use to company's of landlord nation. These funds are likely to be ready to use for MNEs. That situation is caused by the multi national enterprises' popularity, huge MNEs more easily access to money from capital markets than host country firms would. That situation helps MNEs to invest their money to host country and get higher return rate with the help of the MNEs, the host country gets the investment.

For example, after the seeing that definition we may think, as an example to capital transfer, the efforts of Turkish government to find a partner for their tele-communication company of Turk Telekom. That partnership was thought as an opportunity to grow for that company mentioned.

One professor suggests three general advantages of FDI on capital, these are ; (1) company presidents have less risk with the help of free flow of capital around the world. With the different financial instruments, president can distribute the risk. (2) If the money and capital markets become worldwide, that situation increase the quality of capital and money governance and management, gathers more modern regulations. (3) With the integration to international system of capital flowing, country's governments must have some limit to make bad policies.

Technology

If a company wants to grow, must be able to use and follow technology very well. That sentence is generally approved by the authorities. Technology can create a movement and mobility in the economy which may be able to facilitate economic improvement and industrialization. There are two different ways of effect of technology to take place in landlord country. Both of the are very valuable and can not be ignored. Technology may take place in a process of production or it can take place in final product (for example., smart phones we use). Although, there are too many nations which do not have enough technology and innovation, they also have to have their own research and improvement for their economic growth. Last sentences is also specifically accurate for less improved nations.

It is evident that the having appropriate technology has a great amount of correlation with being improved country or not. If a country has enough technology, they can directly evacuate their technology to different country and make great money. Because technology is an expensive resource.

Technologies which are taken from improved countries are more willing to bring modernism and liberalism to the landlord country.

Management

Foreign expertise for management which are gained by FDI is very helpful for the landlord country. The mentioned benefits take place with different ways. First, the investing MNE can train the host country's citizen to expertise on their respectively occupation. This way is thought to be cheaper. Secondly, the investing MNE can bring their own employees from their company's nation and with making this, the invested company's brunch may has already trained employees to manage the business in landlord company. These benefits sometimes get less if the mentioned benefits are unique for the investing MNE's company. That problem cause infectivity in management and governance of the landlord's branch of the company. With creating suitable management team is accepted to increase the efficiency of the company and also the landlord country's nation's management traditions.

For this concept, one of experienced professor offers three benefits in managerial way. Such as more accurate training and high level of regulations can help to increase effectiveness of management, being skillful on investment possibilities can be increased by entrepreneurial soul, the employees who get training, takes arising externalities.

Employment Effects

Employment is effected by foreign direct investment (FDI) directly and also indirectly. Facilitating of employment is most important effect of FDI in the countries with high working power but having less capital to invest. This kind of impact takes place when the MNE hires a lot of host country's citizen. This is the direct effect of employment. The indirect effect of employment is creating jobs in domestic resource provider as a outcome of FDI of the MNE and increased local spending.

Some argue that not all the "newly created employments" established by FDI shows net additions in employment. For example; If we think about FDI by German chemical company in the Greece., some argue that the employment established by this FDI have been less than break even with creating employment lost in chemical companies from Greece, which have started to lose market share to foreigner chemical investor. As a result of this kind of substation effects the real number of the employment which is created by FDI of the German chemical company may be less than it is expected.

That employment effect helps and creates leverage for the investing MNEs when the MNE and the landlord country's government negotiate about a conflict. Create employment is always important task for a government.

Balance of Payments Effects

Balance of Payment is a country's balance-of-payment is the difference between the payments to and receipts from other countries. FDI can have beneficial and negative effects on a country's balance of payment. FDIs effect on a country's balance of payment accounts is an significant regulation topic for most landlord policy makers. There are three possible balance of payments outcome of FDI.

- **Initial Capital Inflow.** If a MNE invest directly on a country, that multi national enterprise gathers their own money to spend and invest.
- **Substitute for Imports.** If a MNE produce goods in a country and If these goods were imported earlier, this kind of situation will look good on balance of payments.
- **Inflow of payments from export of goods and services.** If a MNE produce goods in a country and If these goods are exported, this kind of situation creates good values on balance of payments.

Costs of the Foreign Direct Investment

Three costs of FDI concern host countries. They arise from possible adverse effects on competition within the host nation, adverse effects on the balance of payments, and the perceived loss of national sovereignty and autonomy.

Adverse Effect on Competition

This aspect basically be summarized with saying the MNEs which directly invests to another country may have "too much" power and kill off competition. Even though the landlord country's government seems to be satisfied with the positive effects of the FDI, sometimes they start to have some concerns with the gaining or being too much strength of foreign investor can cause deadly effect on the competition. Eventually, the foreigner investor or the MNE can become the monopoly in sectors of landlord country's economy. This kind of concerns take place in countries which have small amount of big companies operate locally.

Adverse Effect on Balance of Payments

This aspect can be summarized with saying; when a foreign subsidiary imports a substantial number of its inputs from abroad, there is a debit on the current account of the host country's balance of payments.

The landlord country's company's balance of payment possibly effected adversely with two concepts showed below.

- The money and capital generated by the FDI will not be staying in the landlord country's account forever. Eventually the MNE which invested on landlord country, will take their money and takes their home nation.
- If a foreign group member country imports great amount of production from abroad, the figures will take place on landlord country's debit account in balance of payments accounts.

FDI & GOVT. INITIATIVES

Trends in Foreign Direct Investment (FDI) in India (2024-2025)

Current Status of FDI in India

India has continued to attract significant Foreign Direct Investment (FDI), despite global economic challenges. As of September 2024, India's cumulative FDI inflows since April 2000 crossed the **$1 trillion milestone**. However, net FDI inflows declined in FY24 to **$26.5 billion**, down from **$42 billion in FY23**, largely due to **geopolitical tensions, high borrowing costs, and global economic uncertainties**0430.

Key Trends and Insights

1. **Sectoral Shifts in FDI**
   - **Manufacturing sector** FDI has surged by 69% over the past decade, increasing from **$98 billion (2004-2014) to $165 billion (2014-2024)**0400.
   - FDI in **digital services** (e.g., IT, telecommunications, e-commerce) has been rising, while **physical FDI** (e.g., infrastructure, construction) has relatively declined0430.
   - The **services, computer software & hardware, telecommunications, and automobiles** sectors continue to be the most attractive for foreign investors0400.
2. **Geopolitical and Economic Challenges**
   - The **Russia-Ukraine conflict, high interest rates, and global trade slowdowns** have led to **subdued FDI growth** in India and worldwide0430.
   - Investor caution has resulted in higher **repatriation/disinvestment**, contributing to the decline in net FDI inflows0430.
3. **Top Investing Countries**
   - **Mauritius (25%) and Singapore (24%)** remain the largest sources of FDI in India, followed by **the US (10%), the Netherlands (7%), Japan (6%), and the UK (5%)**0400.
4. **Government Reforms to Attract FDI**
   - The Indian government has introduced **liberalized FDI policies**, such as increasing sectoral caps and reducing regulatory barriers in **insurance, pharmaceuticals, and private security**0400.
   - Faster approvals through the **Foreign Investment Facilitation Portal (FIFP)** and measures to ease business regulations are expected to boost FDI0410.
5. **China Plus One Strategy & India's Position**
   - India has been attempting to capitalize on the **China Plus One** strategy, where companies are shifting manufacturing out of China. However, **Vietnam, Thailand, and Malaysia** have benefited more from this trend0400.
   - India needs **faster dispute resolution, better logistics infrastructure, and a streamlined regulatory process** to improve its attractiveness0400.

Trends in Foreign Direct Investment (FDI) in India's Service Sector

India's service sector continues to be a major recipient of Foreign Direct Investment (FDI), contributing significantly to the country's economic growth. Below are the latest trends in FDI inflows into the service sector:

1. **Consistent Growth in FDI Inflows:** The service sector remains a dominant segment for FDI inflows, with areas such as financial services, IT, telecom, education, and healthcare attracting substantial investments. In recent years, this sector has accounted for nearly 50% of total FDI inflows in India.
2. **Key Sub-Sectors Driving Growth**
   - **IT and Business Process Management (BPM):** India's IT sector remains a strong attraction for investors, with leading global tech companies expanding their presence.
   - **Telecommunications:** Increased digital adoption and the rollout of 5G have made this sector a focal point for foreign investments.
   - **FinTech and Financial Services:** A surge in digital banking and payment solutions has driven investments in this sector.

- **Healthcare and Pharmaceuticals:** The post-pandemic demand for healthcare infrastructure and biotech innovations has led to higher FDI inflows.

3. **Geographical Focus:** Metropolitan cities such as Bengaluru, Hyderabad, and Mumbai continue to attract the most FDI due to their established ecosystems in IT, finance, and services.
4. **Government Policies Supporting FDI:** The Indian government has liberalized FDI regulations in several service sub-sectors, allowing up to 100% FDI in areas like telecom and insurance under the automatic route. Reforms in data protection laws and taxation policies have also improved investor confidence.
5. **Challenges and Risks**
   - Regulatory changes and compliance requirements remain a concern for foreign investors.
   - Global economic uncertainties and geopolitical factors could impact FDI flows into India.
   - Infrastructure and bureaucratic hurdles continue to pose operational challenges.
6. **Future Outlook:** With India's digital transformation and the increasing global focus on the services industry, the service sector is expected to maintain a strong FDI inflow trajectory. Strategic initiatives like 'Digital India' and 'Startup India' are further enhancing the investment climate.

Foreign Direct Investment (FDI) in India's Information Technology (IT) Sector

Foreign Direct Investment (FDI) in India's Information Technology (IT) sector has been witnessing significant growth, driven by the country's digital transformation, robust startup ecosystem, and government incentives. Here are the latest trends:

1. **Increased FDI in IT & Software Sector**
   - The IT and software sector continues to be one of the largest recipients of FDI in India. Between **April 2000 and September 2024**, the sector attracted substantial investment, reinforcing India's status as a global tech hub.
   - The sector benefited from **FDI inflows exceeding $85 billion** during this period, making it a major contributor to India's overall FDI inflows.
2. **Rise of Emerging Technologies**
   - Foreign investors are increasingly focusing on **artificial intelligence (AI), machine learning (ML), cloud computing, and cybersecurity**.
   - Companies from the **US, Japan, and Europe** have been actively investing in Indian firms specializing in these technologies.
3. **Government Policies Boosting FDI**
   - The Indian government allows **100% FDI under the automatic route** in IT and software development.
   - The **PLI (Production-Linked Incentive) scheme** has further attracted foreign investors by providing financial incentives to companies investing in the **semiconductor and IT hardware sectors**.
   - The **Startup India** initiative and **Digital India** campaign have also facilitated higher investments in the IT sector.
4. **Increased Focus on IT Services & SaaS**
   - The **Software-as-a-Service (SaaS) sector** is becoming a major FDI attraction, with firms like Zoho, Freshworks, and Chargebee leading the charge.
   - Indian IT service giants like **TCS, Infosys, and Wipro** are securing more foreign contracts, leading to increased FDI in the outsourcing sector.

5. **FDI in IT-Enabled Services (ITeS)**
   - Global tech companies, including **Amazon, Google, and Microsoft**, are expanding their data centers in India, contributing to FDI growth in IT-enabled services.
   - **Bangalore, Hyderabad, and Pune** remain top destinations for foreign tech investment.
6. **Challenges & Future Prospects**
   - While the sector continues to attract FDI, challenges include **data privacy concerns, cybersecurity threats, and regulatory uncertainties.**
   - India's push for **semiconductor manufacturing and AI-driven innovation** is expected to attract further FDI in 2025 and beyond.

Key Trends in FDI in the Construction Industry (2024-2025)

1. **Surge in FDI Inflows**
   - FDI in the construction sector more than doubled in the financial year 2023-24, contributing significantly to India's total FDI inflows of $70.9 billion during this period.
   - The construction industry has attracted over $32 billion in FDI since 2000, ranking as the sixth-largest recipient of foreign investment globally.
2. **Government Initiatives Driving Investment**
   - Major government programs such as the **Smart Cities Mission** and **Pradhan Mantri Awas Yojana (PMAY)** continue to boost foreign investments, focusing on urban infrastructure, affordable housing, and transportation.
   - In the 2024-25 budget, the Indian government allocated **Rs. 11.11 lakh crore ($134 billion)** for infrastructure development, reinforcing the sector's attractiveness to foreign investors
3. **India's Position in the Global Market**
   - By 2025, India is expected to be the **third-largest construction market in the world**, after China and the U.S.
   - The industry is projected to reach **$1.4 trillion** by 2025, fueled by rising incomes, housing shortages, and population growth.
4. **Technological Advancements and Sustainable Construction**
   - The sector is increasingly adopting **AI, digital tools, and green building technologies** to enhance efficiency and sustainability.
   - The growing demand for **smart cities and eco-friendly buildings** is attracting foreign firms specializing in sustainable urban development.
5. **Real Estate and Cement Industry Growth**
   - The real estate sector is projected to reach **$1 trillion by 2030** and **$5.8 trillion by 2047**, supporting the demand for construction activities.
   - Cement production is expected to grow by 12% annually to meet the demand for rural housing and large-scale government infrastructure projects.

Major Contributors to FDI in Construction

- **Top investor countries:** Singapore (24%), Mauritius (25%), USA (10%), Netherlands (7%), Japan (6%).
- **Top recipient states:** Maharashtra (30%), Karnataka (22%), Gujarat (17%), Delhi (14%), Tamil Nadu (5%).

Trends of Foreign Direct Investment in the Service Sector

The service sector has been able to draw the highest amount of foreign direct investment equity in the country, totalling up to $240.57 billion during 2000-2015. In 2015 the total amount of foreign direct investment in this sector amounted to $27.63 billion (DIPP, 2015). From 1991-2000, the share of service sector in the foreign direct investment in India was 15.2% as compared to the share in 2000-2011 is 19.9%.

The notable increase in the foreign investments in the service sector from the year 2014 was due to the current government coming in power and introducing a more investor-friendly climate. The major reason for such a rise in foreign direct investment in this respective sector includes the various initiatives taken by the government. The investment cap has risen in various sectors including the insurance sector from 26% to 49% and others including defence and railways. Changes in the timelines of the approval of foreign direct investment projects have also contributed to such growth of investment in this sector (IBEF, 2016).

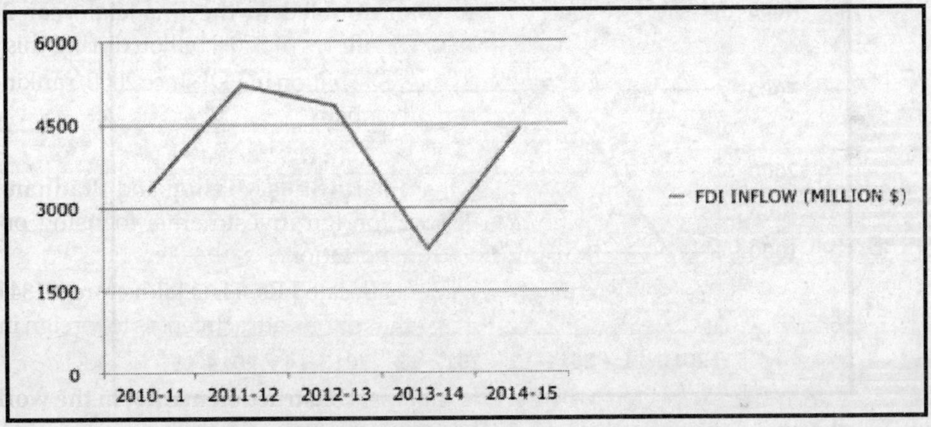

The inflow of foreign direct investment in the service sector

Trends of Foreign Direct Investment in the Information Technology Sector

The information technology sector is the second most attractive industry for foreign investments in India. The total inflows in this sector have reached the mark of $108.13 billion in 2015 since 2000 and in the year 2015, it amounted to $34.3 billion (DIPP, 2015). Some notable motivation in this regard is that the IT industry in the country is rapidly growing and the availability of cheap labour that is highly attracting the companies from the overseas market. Again the turning year in this regard is the year 2014.

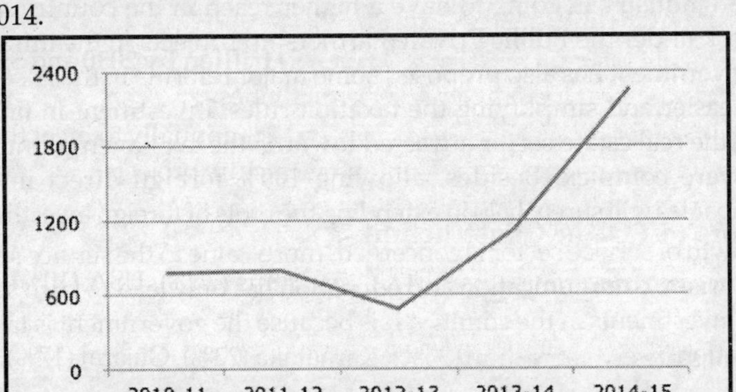

The inflow of foreign direct investment (in million $) in hardware and software industry

Trends of Foreign Direct Investment in the Construction Industry

The construction business is again a major sector attracting foreign direct investment in the country from the past 15 years. The industries draw $113.8 billion foreign direct investment starting from the year 2000 till 2015. Various initiatives introduced by the Indian government such as Make in India helps to attract a large amount of foreign direct investment in this sector. However, the influx of foreign direct investment in the year 2015 dipped to $0.67 billion (DIPP, 2015). It is observed that even though the amount of investment is decreasing from the year 2011 itself, but its cumulative inflows from the year 2000 have been the second highest, only after service sector. The rise of foreign direct investment in such sector owes it to the rising opportunities in the power sector including power generation, distribution, transmission and equipment. Besides, the infrastructure sector has also gained momentum on an average from the year 2000. Foreign direct investment in the construction sector contributes 9% to the total foreign direct investment inflows in the country (IBEF, 2016b).

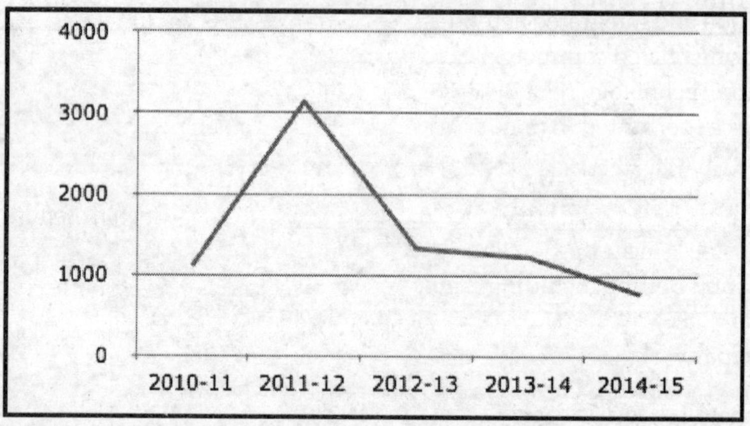

The inflow of foreign direct investment (in million $) in the construction sector

Roots of Foreign Direct Investment

Foreign Direct Investment has been able to expand its roots in the country and is still the prospects of investment is higher. The business environment in India has become investor friendly because of the various policies formed by the government that are promising in this regard. Some notable policies have been made in the sectors mentioned above that can prove to be advantageous in the coming period of time for the economy of the country.

The construction industry is going to have a higher reach in the country as the Government has proposed to work under the Public Private Partnership projects in the infrastructure projects. Along with it, the government has also proposed some major reforms in the IT sector by making the fundraising norms easier and simplifying the taxation rules. Investment in financing, insurance, business sector and the real estate sector attracted towards the tax haven countries as the rules for foreign investors were complex. Besides, allowing 100% foreign direct investment in Asset Reconstruction Companies will surely help in extending the roots of foreign investments in the country.

As far as the growth of service sector is concerned, more value to the service sectors including the health, transport, tourism, communication and education has only lead to such sector becoming the topmost sectors for investments in the country. It is because the government is taking steps towards digitization of the nation.

FDI Policy of India

Government of India has taken various effective steps to simplify the Foreign Direct investment policy. The Foreign Direct Investment Policy (FDI Policy) of the Government of India prescribes the foreign investment cap in specified industrial sectors. But in the recent times many activities have been transferred to unrestricted sectors in which 100% Foreign Direct investment is permitted. Broadly, the industrial sectors are categorized as:

1. Restricted
2. Prohibited
3. Unrestricted Sectors (Up to 100% foreign ownership)

All the sectors other than those mentioned below subject to terms and conditions in the FDI policy come under unrestricted sectors for example:

- Mining (except Mining and mineral separation of titanium bearing minerals and ores, its value addition and integrated activities).
- Manufacturing related commercial activities.
- Information Technology related activities.
- E-commerce (permitted in marketplace model and not the inventory based model. Also, it applies only to Business to Business e-commerce and not business to consumer e-commerce).

Prohibited Sectors

- Lottery Business including Government/private lottery, online lotteries etc.
- Gambling and Betting including casinos etc.
- Chit funds
- Nidhi company
- Trading in Transferable Development Rights (TDRs)
- Real Estate Business or Construction of Farm Houses.
- Manufacturing of cigars, cheroots, cigarillos and cigarettes, of tobacco or of tobacco substitutes
- Activities/sectors not open to private sector investment are Atomic Energy and Railway Operations.

Sector	Entry Route
Upto 20% foreign ownership	
Banking- Public Sector (Subject to Banking Companies (Acquisition & Transfer of Undertakings) Acts 1970/80)	Government permission necessary
Upto 26% foreign ownership	
Broadcasting Content Service (Terrestrial Broadcasting FM (FM Radio) and Up-linking of 'News & Current Affairs' TV	Government permission necessary
Channels (Other conditions specified by Ministry of Information and Broadcasting, Government of India))	Government permission necessary
Print Media (Publishing of newspaper and periodicals dealing with news and current affairs and Publication of Indian editions of foreign magazines dealing with news and current affairs)	Government permission necessary
Up to 49% foreign ownership	
Defense Industry (subject to Industrial License under the Industries (Development & Regulation) Act, 1951) and other regulations	Automatic up to 49% and above 49% under Government route with approval of Cabinet Committee on Security for state of the art technology

Sector	Entry Route
Cable Networks (Other Multi System Operators not undertaking upgradation of networks towards digitalization and addressability and Local Cable Operators)	Automatic
Petroleum and Natural Gas (Petroleum refining by the Public Cabinet Committee Sector Undertakings (PSU), without any disinvestment or dilution of domestic equity in the existing PSUs.)	Automatic route
Scheduled Air Transport Service/ Domestic Scheduled Passenger Airline	Automatic route
Insurance	Automatic route
Private Security Agencies	Automatic route
Telecom & related Services (including Telecom Infrastructure Providers Category-I) All telecom services including Telecom Infrastructure Providers Category-I, viz. Basic, Cellular, United Access Services, Unified License (Access Services), Unified License, National/International Long Distance, Commercial V-Sat, Public Mobile Radio Trunked Services	Automatic up to 49% and Government route beyond 49% and up to 100%.
Commodity Exchange	Automatic route
Single Brand product retail trading	Automatic up to 49% and Government route beyond 49%
Asset Reconstruction Company	Automatic up to 49% and Government route beyond 49%
Pension Sector	Automatic route
Power Exchanges (Power Exchanges registered under the Central Electricity Regulatory Commission (Power Market) Regulations, 2010.)	Automatic route
Infrastructure Company in the Securities Market (namely, stock exchanges, depositories and clearing corporations, in compliance with SEBI Regulations)	Automatic route
Upto 51% foreign ownership	
Multi Brand Retail Trading	Government
Upto 74% foreign ownership	
Credit Information Companies	Automatic route
Civil Aviation (Ground Handling Services subject to sectoral regulations and security clearance)	Automatic up to 49% and Government route beyond 49% and up to 74%
Airports (Existing projects)	Automatic up to 74% and Government route beyond 74%
Satellites (Establishment and operation, subject to the sectoral guidelines of Department of Space/ISRO)	Government
Banking & Finance - Private Sector	Automatic up to 49% and Government route beyond 49% and up to 74%.

BALANCE OF PAYMENTS (BOP)

The balance of payments is rarely a way of listing receipts and payments in international transactions for a country. Balance of payment is an application of double-entry book keeping and if entry is done in a proper way, debits and credits will always balance; hence in a way, the balance of payment will always be in equilibrium. It is important to understand in what way the balance of payments can be in disequilibrium and in what sense it will always be in equilibrium.

Account of a Country's Balance of Payments

I. Credits		
1.	Exports of goods	1100
2.	Exports of services	300
3.	Unrequired receipts (Gifts, indemnities, *etc.*) from foreigners	200
4.	Capital receipts (borrowing from capital, repayment by or sale of assets to, foreigners)	400
	Total Receipts	**2000**
II. Debits		
5.	Imports of goods	1600
6.	Imports of services	100
7.	Unrequired payments (gifts, indemnities, *etc.* to foreigners)	160
8.	Capital payments (lending to, capital repayments to or purchase of assets from foreigners)	140
	Total Payments	**2000**

Credit entries show all the ways in which a country can acquire foreign currency. Debit entries show all the ways in which a country can spend the foreign exchange.

Items (1), (2), (3), (5), (6), and (7) enumerate all the payments and receipts made for the current period of time; they all have a flow dimension and refer to a certain value of exports per time period. The balance of payments of a country always refer to a certain time period, usually a calendar year.

Items (4) and (8) express changes in stock and refer to capital receipts and payments. Government, corporation and individuals borrow money from abroad, which leads to inflow of foreign currencies, and these transactions will be entered as items in (4). Similarly, Government, corporation and individuals lend money abroad, leading to outflow of foreign currencies and these transactions will be entered as items in (8).

Total of Credit side of Balance of payment should always equal debit side.

Various Balances

(i) **Balance of Trade.** It is difference between item (1) and (5) of above Table. In case exports of goods is Rs. 1100 crore and imports of goods is Rs 1600 crore, balance of trade will be 1100–600=–500. Balance of trade is the difference in the revenue through exports and foreign currency spent on imports. Balance of trade need not always balance. If the country exports more goods than it imports, it is said to have a favourable balance or surplus in its balance of trade. If it imports more goods than it exports, it has a deficit or unfavourable balance of trade. Even though the country had a deficit in its balance of trade, this might be offset by items on other accounts.

(ii) **Balance of services.** It is the difference between export of services and import of services. From above Table, balance of services is calculated from differences between item (2) and item (6). In case export of services is Rs. 300 crore and import of services is Rs. 100 crore, balance of trade will be Rs. 300 crore – Rs. 100 crore = Rs. 200 crore.

(iii) **Balance of unrequited transfers.** It is the difference between unrequired receipts and unrequited payments. From Table, balance of unrequited transfer is calculated from differences between item (3) and item (7). In case of unrequited receipts of Rs. 200 crore and unrequited payment of Rs. 160 crore, balance of unrequited transfers will be: Rs. 200 crore minus Rs. 160 crore is equal to Rs. 40 crore.

(iv) **Balance on current account.** It shows the flow aspect of a country's international transactions. Balance on current account can be calculated by adding up the balance of trade, services and unrequited transfers. All the goods and services produced within the country and exported during the time period in question, are entered on the credit side of the balance of current account, and all the goods and services imported and consumed within the country during the same period are entered on the debit side of the balance of current account. All the international transactions entering a country's system of national accounting should be listed on the country's balance of current account.

Balance on current A/C = -500 + 200 + 40 = –360

(v) **Balance on capital account.** All items of a flow nature should be included in the balance of current account and that all items expressing changes in stock should enter the balance of capital account. If a country has a deficit on the balance of current account, the country has spent more abroad during the period than it has earned. A way to settle this is by a transaction on the capital account. The country can deplete part of its stock to an amount equal to the deficit on the balance of current account. This can be done by borrowing from abroad, selling assets or by depleting its reserves of foreign currency. Balance on current account can be calculated by deriving the difference between item (4) and item (6). If capital receipts is Rs 400 crore and capital payment is Rs 140, then balance on capital account is: Rs 400 crore minus Rs 140 crore is equal to Rs 260 crore. Balance of capital account should be equal to balance on current account, but of opposite sign. Adding up of balances of capital account and current account leads to balance of payments which should always be zero.

(vi) **Various balances calculated from Table.**

1. Balance of Trade — 1100 – 1600 = –500
   items (1) minus (5)
2. Balance of services
   items (2) minus (6) — 300 – 100 = +200
3. Balance of unrequited transfers — 200 – 160 = + 40
   items (3) minus (7)
4. Balance of current account
   items (1) + (2) + (3) – [(5)+(6)+(7)] — = 1600 – 1860 = –260
5. Balance of capital account
   item (4) minus (8) — = +260
6. Balance of payments + 260+(–260) — = 0
   balance of current account
   plus balance of capital account

Components of BoP

The BoP consists of three main components-current account, capital account, and financial account. As mentioned earlier, the BoP should be zero. The current account must balance with the combined capital and financial accounts.

Current Account

The current account monitors the flow of funds from goods and services trade (import and export) between countries. Now this includes money received or spent on manufactured goods and raw materials. It also includes revenue from tourism, transportation receipts, revenue from specialized services (medicine, law, engineering), and royalties from patents and copyrights. In addition, the current account includes revenue from stocks.

Capital Account

The capital account monitors the flow of international capital transactions. These transactions include the purchase or disposal of non-financial assets (for example, land) and non-produced assets. The capital account also includes money received from debt-forgiveness and gift taxes. In addition, the capital account records the flow of the financial assets by migrants leaving or entering a country and the transfer, sale, or purchase of fixed assets.

Financial Account

The financial account monitors the flow of funds pertaining to investments in businesses, real estate, and stocks. It also includes government-owned assets such as gold and Special Drawing Rights (SDRs) held with the International Monetary Fund (IMF). In addition, it includes foreign investments and assets held abroad by nationals. Similarly, the financial account includes a record of the assets owned by foreign nationals.

Why is BoP important?

The BoP statement provides a clear picture of the economic relations between different countries. It is an integral aspect of international financial management.

To begin with, the BoP statement provides information pertaining to the demand and supply of the country's currency. The trade data shows a clear picture of whether the country's currency is appreciating or depreciating in comparison with other countries. Next, the country's BoP determines its potential as a constructive economic partner. In addition, a country's BoP indicates its position in international economic growth.

By studying its BoP statement and its components closely, a country would be able to identify trends that may be beneficial or harmful to the economy and take appropriate measures.

REGIONAL ECONOMIC INTEGRATION

There are several stages in the process of economic integration, from a very loose association of countries in a preferential trade area, to complete economic integration, where the economies of member countries are completely integrated.

A regional trading bloc is a group of countries within a geographical region that protect themselves from imports from non-members in other geographical regions, and who look to trade more with each other. Regional trading blocs increasingly shape the pattern of world trade - a phenomenon often referred to as regionalism.

Levels of Regional Economic Integration:

Political Union
Fiscal Union
Monetary Union
Common Market
Customs Union
Free Trade Area
Preferential Trade Area
Independent Economy

Increasing Intergation ↑

Preferential Trade Area

Preferential Trade Areas (PTAs) exist when countries within a geographical region agree to reduce or eliminate tariff barriers on selected goods imported from other members of the area. This is often the first small step towards the creation of a trading bloc. Agreements may be made between two countries (bi-lateral), or several countries (multi-lateral).

Free Trade Area

Free Trade Areas (FTAs) are created when two or more countries in a region agree to reduce or eliminate barriers to trade on all goods coming from other members. The North Atlantic Free Trade Agreement (NAFTA) is an example of such a free trade area, and includes the USA, Canada, and Mexico.

Customs Union

A customs union involves the removal of tariff barriers between members, together with the acceptance of a common (unified) external tariff against non-members.

Countries that export to the customs union only need to make a single payment (duty), once the goods have passed through the border. Once inside the union goods can move freely without additional tariffs. Tariff revenue is then shared between members, with the country that collects the duty retaining a small share.

The advantages of a customs union

Without a unified external tariff, trade flows would become distorted. If, for example, Germany imposes a 10% tariff on Japanese cars, while France imposes a 2% tariff, Japan would export its cars to French car dealers, and then sell them on to Germany, thereby avoiding 80% of the tariff. This is avoided if a common tariff is shared between Germany and France (and other members of the customs union.)

A common external tariff effectively removes the possibility of arbitrage and, some would argue, is one of the fundamental building blocks of economic integration.

The disadvantages of a customs union

Union members must negotiate collectively with non-members or organisations like the WTO as a single group of countries. While this is essential to maintain the customs union, it means that members are not free to negotiate individual trade deals.

For example, if a member wishes to protect a declining or infant industry it cannot do so through imposing its own tariffs. Equally, if it wishes to open up to complete free trade, it cannot do so if a common tariff exists.

Also, it makes little sense for a particular member to impose a tariff on the import of a good that is not produced at all within a that country.

There is also a potential disadvantage to a single member in how the tariff revenue is allocated. Members that trade relatively more with countries outside the union, such as the UK, may not get their 'fair share' of tariff revenue.

The UK's status as a customs union member is one of the dilemmas facing the UK as a result of Brexit. If it wishes to create individual trade deals with, say the USA and China, it cannot retain its current status as a full member of the customs union.

Common Market

A common (or single) market is the most significant step towards full economic integration. In the case of Europe, the single market is officially referred to a the 'internal market'.

The key feature of a common market is the extension of free trade from just tangible goods, to include all economic resources. This means that all barriers are eliminated to allow the free movement of goods, services, capital, and labour.

In addition, as well as removing tariffs, non-tariff barriers are also reduced and eliminated.

For a common market to be successful there must also be a significant level of harmonisation of micro-economic policies, and common rules regarding product standards, monopoly power and other anti-competitive practices. There may also be common policies affecting key industries, such as the Common Agricultural Policy (CAP) and Common Fisheries Policy (CFP).

Full Economic Union

Economic union is a term applied to a trading bloc that has both a common market between members, and a common trade policy towards non-members, although members are free to pursue independent macro-economic policies.

The European Union (EU) is the best known Economic union, and came into force on November 1st 1993, following the signing of the Maastricht Treaty (formally called the Treaty on European Union.)

Monetary Union

Monetary union is the first major step towards macro-economic integration, and enables economies to converge even more closely. Monetary union involves scrapping individual currencies, and adopting a single, shared currency, such as the Euro for the Euro-17 countries, and the East Caribbean Dollar for 11 islands in the East Caribbean. This means that there is a common exchange rate, a common monetary policy, including interest rates and the regulation of the quantity of money, and a single central bank, such as the European Central Bank or the East Caribbean Central Bank.

Fiscal Union

A fiscal union is an agreement to harmonise tax rates, to establish common levels of public sector spending and borrowing, and jointly agree national budget deficits or surpluses. The majority of EU states agreed a fiscal compact in early 2012, which is a less binding version of a full fiscal union.

Economic and Monetary Union

Economic and Monetary Union (EMU) is a key stage towards compete integration, and involves a single economic market, a common trade policy, a single currency and a common monetary policy.

Complete Economic Integration

Complete economic integration involves a single economic market, a common trade policy, a single currency, a common monetary policy, together with a single fiscal policy, including common tax and benefit rates - in short, complete harmonisation of all policies, rates, and economic trade rules.

TRADE CREATION AND DIVERSION

When customs unions are established the flow of trade between countries involved in the new union and those outside will be affected. Customs unions eliminate barriers to trade between members, which is assumed to provide a considerable incentive to increase trade between members and to reduce trade between members and non-members. It is often easiest to appreciate the effect of a customs union by considering what happens when one country joins an existing union.

Outside a union, and operating independently, a single nation will look to exploit its comparative advantage. In a free trade environment, countries will trade with who they like, attempting to exploit their own comparative cost advantage through specialisation. They will export goods they produce most efficiently, and import goods from low-cost countries who have exploited their own comparative cost advantage to produce cheap exports. In a situation where countries do not trade freely, by imposing tariffs, or by favouring one country over another in terms of tariff levels, trade will be distorted and the pattern of trade will change. Inefficient producers may be protected and encouraged, at the expense of more efficient imports.

The creation of a customs union, with common external tariffs, will further alter the existing pattern of trade flows. The assumption is that before the union, members imposed differential tariffs on different countries to protect their own industries. Taking a hypothetical example from an actual historical period, we shall assume that, prior to joining the European 'common market' in 1973, the UK could produce butter at 130p per kilograms (kg), on average. At the same time, New Zealand could produce the same quantity for 100p, and Denmark could produce it for 120p. Hence, prior to the formation of a customs union, New Zealand has a comparative advantage in butter, and is the most efficient. Denmark is the second most efficient producer, and the UK is the least efficient.

Let us assume that, in order to protect its inefficient farmers equally, the UK imposes differential tariffs on New Zealand and Denmark in order to raise the imported price above its own (high cost) butter. For example, imposing a high 32% tariff on 'very' low priced New Zealand butter would raise its price to 132p per kg (100p to 132p), as would imposing only a 10% tariff on low priced Danish butter (120p to 132p). We will also assume that, with these tariffs in place, a total demand of 30m kg of butter exists in the UK each year, with UK farmers supplying 20m kg (the maximum it can produce), and New Zealand and Danish farmers supply 5m kg each.

Once a union is created, members agree to eliminate tariffs between themselves. The effect of this is that, facing lower priced, zero-tariff, imports from members, consumers increase their demand for these goods, and new trade will be created - a process called trade creation. The terms trade creation and trade diversion are closely associated with Chicago School economist Jacob Viner (The Customs Union Issue, 1950).

For example, if Denmark and the UK form a customs union, tariffs on Danish butter must now be reduced, and once they are completely removed, the free market price of 120p will be highly attractive to UK consumers. UK consumers will now consume more butter in total because average butter prices will have fallen with the removal of tariffs on Danish butter, and total demand for butter rises. For example, total output and consumption might increase to 32m kgs (up by 2m), with UK farmers down from 20m to 15m, New Zealand exports collapsing to just 2m, and Denmark increasing its output and sales of butter to the UK to 10m (from 5m to 10m). Total consumption has gone up from 30m (20 + 5 + 5), to 32m (15 + 2 + 15). The additional 2m kgs of butter produced and consumed is the new trade created as a result of the removal of barriers by union members.

Furthermore, this will enable a dynamic reaction within Denmark and the UK. Over time, as countries (Denmark and the UK) become more integrated, increased trade will generate further efficiency gains, such as through the application of economies of scale. Prices may fall even further, relative to those of non-member countries, and the process of trade creation continues. For example, with increased sales, Denmark can specialise further in butter production, and produce on large scale, bringing prices down even further (perhaps nearer to the New Zealand level). Also, the UK can now free up its resources, and move them out of butter production and into goods and services for which the UK has a comparative advantages over Denmark. Hence, over time, trade creation will continue as a positive long-term effect of a customs union.

The major loser in this is the previous trading partner left outside the bloc - less trade now exists between new members and their old trading partners. The process of efficient producers losing out to inefficient ones is generally referred to as trade diversion. For example, after Denmark and the UK form a customs union, New Zealand, which was the most efficient butter producer, suffers a loss of sales to the UK, from 5m to 2m, with trade diverted from New Zealand to Denmark. However, there is some debate about the use of the term trade diversion. In its simplest form it means any trade diverted away from efficient global producers as a result of the creation of a customs union. Other economists regard trade diversion as relating to the long-term loss of trade resulting from inefficient producers (such as Denmark, in our hypothetical example) becoming more efficient following membership of the union. For example, if the price of Danish butter falls from 120p to 95p as a result of trade expansion within the union, it is now 5p cheaper than New Zealand in the open market, and more trade may now be diverted away from the formerly highly efficient New Zealand. Whichever definition is accepted, it is clear that in this case the union has distorted trade.

Finally, we also need to consider the loss of tariff revenue that might follow the diversion of trade from non-member countries. Given that, in our simple example, imports from New Zealand have fallen causing a loss of tariff revenue, and tariff revenue from Danish butter has been eliminated, it is necessary to weigh up the welfare gains and losses from the formation of the customs union. There is no simple answer to this, and it is quite possible that a union could result in either a net loss, or a net gain.

REGIONAL TRADE AGREEMENTS

The EU manages trade relations with third countries in the form of trade agreements. They are designed to create better trading opportunities and overcome related barriers.

EU's trade policy is also used as a vehicle for the promotion of European principles and values, from democracy and human rights to environment and social rights.

Classification

Trade agreements differ depending on their content:

- Economic Partnership Agreements (EPAs) - support development of trade partners from African, Caribbean and Pacific countries
- Free Trade Agreements (FTAs) - enable reciprocal market opening with developed countries and emerging economies by granting preferential access to markets
- Association Agreements (AAs) - bolster broader political agreements

The EU also enters into non-preferential trade agreements, as part of broader deals such as Partnership and Cooperation Agreements (PCAs).

Negotiations of trade agreements are conducted in accordance with the rules set out in Article 218 of the Treaty of the Functioning of the European Union.

European Union (EU)

Ongoing trade negotiation processes between EU and third countries include:

- Japan - a Free Trade Agreement (FTA) to enter into force on 1 February 2019; negotiating directives were adopted in 2012 and deal was ratified end of 2018.
- Singapore - split FTA pending adoption in the Council; negotiating directives were adopted under ASEAN, the Association of South East Asian Nations, in 2007.
- Vietnam - split FTA in pre-signature phase, with entry into force expected in 2019; negotiating directives were adopted under ASEAN in 2007.
- Mexico - text for the modernisation of the EU-Mexico Global Agreement to be finalised by end of 2018; negotiating directives were adopted in 1999.
- MERCOSUR - negotiations are ongoing on a trade agreement, part of the Association Agreement, with the South American trade bloc of Argentina, Brazil, Paraguay and Uruguay; negotiating directives were adopted in 1999.
- Chile - negotiations to modernise the existing FTA are ongoing; negotiating directives were adopted in 2017.
- Australia and New Zealand - FTA negotiations are ongoing; negotiating directives were adopted in 2018.

New Architecture of Trade Agreements

On 22 May 2018, the Council adopted conclusions addressing the way in which trade agreements are negotiated and concluded.

This set out the key principles which will underpin the Council's approach towards trade negotiations from now on.

Concretely, the Council focused in particular on two issues:

- the European Commission's intention to recommend splitting between separate agreements related to investment and other trade provisions
- on the Council's role in trade negotiations.

Role of the Council

The Council plays a crucial role in shaping a new trade agreement.

In the opening stages, the Council authorises the European Commission to negotiate a new trade agreement on behalf of the EU. This is done through a "negotiating mandate". With the related authorisation, the Council providers negotiating directives which include the objectives, scope and possible time limits of the negotiations.

The Commission then negotiates with the partner country on behalf of the EU, in close cooperation with the Council and the European Parliament.

After agreement on the text of the deal is reached with partners, the Commission submits formal proposals for adoption to the Council.

Following discussions, the Council adopts a decision for the signature of the agreement on behalf of the EU. It then transmits the signed agreement to the European Parliament for consent.

In the final stages, after the European Parliament gives its consent, the Council adopts the decision to conclude the agreement.

TRADING PRINCIPLES

The EU abides by the principles of the World Trade Organisation (WTO).

In June 2018, in the context of growing trade tensions across the world, the European Council stressed the need to preserve and deepen the rules-based multilateral system.

The EU also expressed its openness to improve, together with like-minded partners, the functioning of the WTO.

Trade agreements are generally very complex because they are legal texts covering a wide range of activities, from agriculture to intellectual property. But they share a number of fundamental principles.

ASEAN Trade Agreements (ATAs)

ASEAN (Association of Southeast Asian Nations) is a regional organization formed in 1967 with ten member countries in Southeast Asia. One of its major goals is to promote **economic integration** and **free trade** among member states and with global partners through **trade agreements.**

1. **ASEAN Trade in Goods Agreement (ATIGA)**
   - **Signed**: 2009 (in effect since 2010)
   - **Objective**: To establish a single market and production base through **free flow of goods**.
   - **Key Features**:
     - Elimination of **import duties** on **99% of goods** traded among ASEAN members.
     - Simplified **Rules of Origin (ROO)**.
     - Streamlined **customs procedures** and **trade facilitation**.
     - Promotes **non-tariff measures (NTMs)** transparency.
2. **ASEAN Framework Agreement on Services (AFAS)**
   - **Objective**: Liberalize the **services sector** (banking, insurance, telecommunications, etc.).
   - **Key Features**:
     - Allows **cross-border movement** of services and professionals.
     - Encourages cooperation and mutual recognition agreements (MRAs) for **qualifications**.
3. **ASEAN Comprehensive Investment Agreement (ACIA)**
   - **Signed**: 2009
   - **Objective**: Create a **liberal, facilitative, transparent**, and **competitive** investment environment.
   - **Key Features**:
     - Protects and promotes **intra-ASEAN investment**.
     - Ensures **national treatment** and **most-favored-nation (MFN)** status.
     - Includes provisions for **investor protection** and **dispute settlement**.
4. **ASEAN Free Trade Agreements (ASEAN+1 FTAs)**

   ASEAN has signed **free trade agreements with key partners**, known as **ASEAN+1 FTAs**. These include:

- **ASEAN-China Free Trade Area (ACFTA)**
  - In effect since **2010**
  - One of the **world's largest free trade areas**
  - Covers trade in goods, services, investment, and economic cooperation
- **ASEAN-Korea FTA (AKFTA)**
  - Effective since **2007**
  - Tariff elimination on over 90% of products
- **ASEAN-Japan Comprehensive Economic Partnership (AJCEP)**
  - In effect since **2008**
  - Covers trade in goods, services, investment, and technical cooperation
- **ASEAN-India FTA (AIFTA)**
  - In effect since **2010**
  - Aims at eliminating tariffs on a large number of goods
- **ASEAN-Australia-New Zealand FTA (AANZFTA)**
  - In effect since **2010**
  - Covers goods, services, investment, intellectual property, and competition policy

5. **Regional Comprehensive Economic Partnership (RCEP)**
   - **Signed**: 2020 | **In force**: 2022
   - Includes **ASEAN + 5** major partners: China, Japan, South Korea, Australia, New Zealand
   - **World's largest trade bloc**
     - Covers **30% of global GDP and population**
     - Simplifies trade rules, **harmonizes ROO**, and promotes investment, services, and e-commerce.

Benefits of ASEAN Trade Agreements

- **Lower tariffs** and better **market access**
- Enhanced **regional supply chains**
- Promotes **foreign direct investment (FDI)**
- Greater **economic integration and cooperation**
- Boosts **competitiveness** of ASEAN firms in global markets

Challenges

- Uneven development levels among member states
- Implementation and compliance issues
- Complex ROO and non-tariff barriers (NTBs)
- Balancing national interests with regional goals

SAARC TRADE AGREEMENT

The objective of the SAPTA is to promote and sustain mutual trade and the economic co-operation among the member states through exchange of trade concessions. SAPTA therefore is the first step towards higher levels of trade and economic co-operation in the region.

The basic principles:

- Overall reciprocity and mutuality of advantages
- Step by step negotiations and periodic reviews so as to improve and extend the preferential trade arrangement, in stages
- Inclusion of all products, manufactures and commodities in their raw semi- processes and processed forms
- Special and favourable treatment to Least Developed Contacting States

Main Components

- Tariff
- Para Tariff
- Non Tariff

Direct Trade Measures

SAPTA specified four negotiating approaches namely, product by product basis, across the board tariff reduction, sectoral basis and direct trade measures. However it was agreed that tariff concessions would initially be negotiated on a product - by- product basis. The agreement also provides for negotiation of tariff concessions to be an ongoing process. The SAPTA envisages that concessions on tariff para-tariff and non tariff measures will be negotiated step -buy step improved and extended in successive stages.

National Schedules of Concessions

The process of negotiation on the schedule of concession, which forms an integral part of the Agreement, commenced in 1993. For this purpose, the Inter Governmental Group on Trade Liberalization (IGG) was set up. The IGG met on six occasions in various capitals. At the sixth meeting held in Kathmandu on 20th and 21st April 1995, the delegations held intensive rounds of bilateral and multilateral negotiations and agreed on the National Schedule of concessions to be granted by individual member states to other member states under the SAPTA Agreement.

Four rounds of trade negotiations were concluded under SAPTA covering over 5000 commodities. Each Round contributed to an incremental trend in the product coverage and the deepening of tariff concessions over previous Rounds.

During the first and the second rounds, trade negotiations were conducted on a product by product basis. In the third and the fourth rounds, negotiations were conducted on chapter wise.

Maintenance of SAPTA Concession

The Agreement on the South Asian Free Trade Area (SAFTA) which was implemented with effect from 1st January 2006 will supercede the SAARC Preferential Trading Arrangement (SAPTA). On the issue of maintaining SAPTA concessions for LDCs, the Committee agreed that once the Non-LDCs member states complete the Trade Liberalization Programme (TLP) for LDC member states, SAPTA concessions would cease for LDC member states. However, if any item on which SAPTA concessions are available to LDC, appear in the sensitive lists of non-LDC, they shall maintain the same level of concession through derogation. The Committee has further agreed that if the items under TLP enjoy tariff preferences under SAPTA, the Non-LDCs shall reduce their tariff on those items to a rate not higher than the rate applicable for LDCs under SAPTA on the date agreed for base rate for TLP. It was also agreed at the first SAFTA Ministerial Council Meeting held in April that LDCs should also maintain concessions under SAPTA for Non LDCs until the completion of TLP irrespective of whether the products are in the sensitive lists or not (Please contact the Department of Commerce for further clarifications).

NAFTA TRADE AGREEMENT

The North American Free Trade Agreement, which eliminated most tariffs on trade between Mexico, Canada and the United States, went into effect on January 1, 1994. NAFTA's purpose is to encourage economic activity between North America's three major economic powers. Numerous tariffs, particularly those related to agriculture, textiles and automobiles, were gradually phased out between Jan. 1, 1994 and January 1, 2008.

President Trump campaigned on a promise to repeal NAFTA and other trade agreements he deemed unfair to the United States, and on August 27, 2018, he announced a new trade deal with Mexico to replace it. The U.S. - Mexico Trade Agreement, as it is called, will maintain duty-free access for agricultural goods on both sides of the border and eliminate non-tariff barriers while encouraging more agricultural trade between Mexico and the United States and will effectively replace NAFTA. On September 30, the United States and Canada agreed to a deal to replace NAFTA, which will now be called the USMCA - The United States Mexico Canada Agreement. In a joint press release from the U.S. and Canada Trade Offices, representatives said the following:

"USMCA will give our workers, farmers, ranchers and businesses a high-standard trade agreement that will result in freer markets, fairer trade and robust economic growth in our region. It will strengthen the middle class, and create good, well-paying jobs and new opportunities for the nearly half billion people who call North America home."

The three countries signed the agreement on November 30, 2018.

Why NAFTA was Formed

About one-fourth of all U.S. imports, such as crude oil, machinery, gold, vehicles, fresh produce, livestock and processed foods, originate from Canada and Mexico, which are the United States' second- and third-largest suppliers of imported goods. In addition, approximately one-third of U.S. exports, particularly machinery, vehicle parts, mineral fuel/oil and plastics, are destined for Canada and Mexico.

The legislation was developed during George H. W. Bush's presidency as the first phase of his Enterprise for the Americas Initiative. The Clinton administration, which signed NAFTA into law in 1993, believed it would create 200,000 U.S. jobs within two years and 1 million within five years because exports play a major role in U.S. economic growth. The administration anticipated a dramatic increase in U.S. imports from Mexico under the lower tariffs.

Additions to NAFTA

NAFTA was supplemented by two other regulations: the North American Agreement on Environmental Cooperation (NAAEC) and the North American Agreement on Labor Cooperation (NAALC). These side agreements were intended to prevent businesses from relocating to other countries to exploit lower wages, more lenient worker health and safety regulations, and looser environmental regulations.

NAFTA did not eliminate regulatory requirements on companies wishing to trade internationally, such as rule of origin regulations and documentation requirements that determine whether certain goods can be traded under NAFTA. The free-trade agreement also contains administrative, civil and criminal penalties for businesses that violate any of the three countries' laws or customs procedures.

North American Industry Classification System

The three signatory countries developed a new collaborative business-classification system that allows for the comparison of business activity statistics across North America. The North American Industry Classification Systemorganizes and separates industries according to their production processes.

The NAICS replaced the U.S. Standard Industrial Classification system, allowing businesses to be classified systematically in an ever-changing economy. The new system enables easier comparability between all countries in North America. To ensure that the NAICS remains relevant, the intention is to review the system every five years.

The three parties responsible for the formation and continued maintenance of the NAICS are the Instituto Nacional de Estadistica y Geografia in Mexico, Statistics Canada and the United States Office of Management and Budget through its Economic Classification Policy Committee, which also includes the Bureau of Economic Analysis, Bureau of Labor Statistics and the Bureau of Census. The first version of the classification system was released in 1997. A revision in 2002 reflected the substantial changes occurring in the information sector. The most recent revision, in 2017, created 21 new industries by reclassifying, splitting or combining 29 existing industries.

This classification system allows for more flexibility than the SIC's four-digit structure by implementing a hierarchical six-digit coding system and classifying all economic activity into 20 industry sectors. Five of these sectors are primarily those that produce goods, with the remaining 15 sectors being strictly those that provide some type of service. Every company receives a primary NAICS code that indicates its main line of business. A company receives its primary code based on the code definition that generates the largest portion of the company's revenue at a specified location in the past year.

The first two digits of an NAICS code indicate the company's economic sector. The third digit designates the company's subsector. The fourth digit indicates the company's industry group. The fifth digit reflects the company's NAICS industry. The sixth designates the company's specific national industry.

NAFTA's Impact

Debate continues surrounding NAFTA's impact on its signatory countries. While the United States, Canada and Mexico have all experienced economic growth, higher wages and increased trade since NAFTA's implementation, experts disagree on how much the agreement actually contributed to these gains, if at all (for more details, see NAFTA's Winners and Losers). The results are hard to isolate, and other significant developments have occurred on the continent and globally in the past quarter-century.

From the beginning, NAFTA critics were concerned that the agreement would result in U.S. jobs relocating to Mexico, despite the supplementary NAALC. NAFTA affected thousands of U.S. auto workers in this way, for example. Many companies moved their manufacturing to Mexico and other countries with lower labor costs, although NAFTA may not have been the reason for those moves. Under the USMCA, those concerns, like NAFTA, may be history.

INTERNATIONAL ECONOMIC INSTITUTION

At the Bretton Woods Conference in 1944 it was decided to establish a new monetary order that would expand international trade, promote international capital flows and contribute to monetary stability. The IMF and the World Bank were borne out of this Conference of the end of World War

II. The World Bank was established to help the restoration of economies disrupted by War by facilitating the investment of capital for productive purposes and to promote the long-range balanced growth of international trade. On the other hand, the IMF is primarily a supervisory institution for coordinating the efforts of member countries to achieve greater cooperation in the formulation of economic policies. It helps to promote exchange stability and orderly exchange relations among its member countries. It is in this context that the present chapter reviews the purpose and working of some of the international financial institutions and the contributions made by them in promoting economic and social progress in developing countries by helping raise standards of living and productivity to the point of which development becomes self-sustaining.

International Sources of Finance

One major source of financing is international non-profit agencies. There are several regional development banks such as the Asian Development Bank, the African Development Bank and Fund and the Caribbean Development Bank. The primary purpose of these agencies is to finance productive development projects or to promote economic development in a particular region. The Inter-American Development Bank, for example, has the principal purpose of accelerating the economic development of its Latin American member countries. In general, both public and private entities are eligible to borrow money from such agencies as long as private funds are not available at reasonable rates and terms. Although the interest rate can vary from agency to agency, these loan rates are very attractive and very much in demand.

Of all the international financial organisations, the most familiar is the World Bank, formally known as the International Bank for Reconstruction and Development (IBRD). The World Bank has two affiliates that are legally and financially distinct entities, the International Development Association (IDA) and the International Finance Corporation (IFC). Exhibit 1 provides a comparison among IBRD, IDA and IFC in terms of their objectives, member countries, lending terms, lending qualifications as well as other details. All three organisations have the same central goals: to promote economic and social progress in poor or developing countries by helping raise standards of living and productivity to the point at which development becomes self-sustaining.

Toward this common objective, the World Bank, IDA and IFC have three interrelated functions and these are to lend funds, to provide advice and to serve as a catalyst in order to stimulate investments by others. In the process, financial resources are channelled from developed countries to the developing world with the hope that developing countries, through this assistance, will progress to a level that will permit them, in turn, to contribute to the development process of other less fortunate countries. Japan is a prime example of a country that has come full circle. From being a borrower, Japan is now a major lender to these three organisations. South Korea is moving in a direction similar to that of Japan nearly a quarter of a century ago.

INTERNATIONAL MONETARY FUND (IMF)

The International Monetary Fund (IMF) came into official existence on December 27, 1945, when 29 countries signed its Articles of Agreement (its Charter) agreed at a conference held in Bretton Woods, New Hampshire, USA, from July 1-22, 1944. The IMF commenced financial operations on March 1, 1947. Its current membership is 188 countries. Its Total Quotas are SDR 476 billion (about US$ 755.7 billion at the exchange rate), following a 45 per cent quota increase effective from January 22,1999.

- **Staff.** Approximately 2,700 from 110 countries.

- **Accounting Unit.** Special Drawing Right (SDR). As of August 23, 1999, SDR I equalled US $1.370280.

IMF is a cooperative institution that 182 countries have voluntarily joined because they see the advantage of consulting with one another on this forum to maintain a stable system of buying and selling their currencies so that payments in foreign currency can take place between countries smoothly and without delay. Its policies and activities are guided by its Charter known as the Articles of Agreement.

IMF lends money to members having trouble meeting financial obligations to other members, but only on the condition that they undertake economic reforms to eliminate these difficulties for their own good and that of the entire membership. Contrary to widespread perception, the IMF has no effective authority over the domestic economic policies of its members. What authority the IMF does possess is confined to requiring the member to disclose information on its monetary and fiscal policies and to avoid, as far as possible, putting restrictions on exchange of domestic for foreign currency and on making payments to other members.

There are several major accomplishments to the credit of the International Monetary System. For example, it

- sustained a rapidly increasing volume of trade and investment;
- displayed flexibility in adapting to changes in international commerce;
- proved to be efficient (even when there were decreasing percentages of reserves to trade);
- proved to be hardy (it survived a number of pre-1971 crises, speculative and otherwise, and the down-and-up swings of several business cycles);
- allowed for a growing degree or international cooperation;
- established a capacity to accommodate reforms and improvements.

To an extent, the fund served as an international central bank to help countries during periods of temporary balance of payments difficulties by protecting their rates of exchange. Because of that, countries did not need to resort to exchange controls and other barriers to restrict world trade.

Origins of IMF

The need for an organisation like the IMF became evident during the great depression that ravaged the world economy in the 1930s. A widespread lack of confidence in paper money led to a spurt in the demand for gold and severe devaluation in the national currencies. The relation between money and the value of goods became confused as did the relation between the value of one national currency and another.

In the 1940s, Harry Dexter (US) and John Maynard Keynes (UK) put forward proposals for a system that would encourage the unrestricted conversion of one currency into another, establish a clear and unequivocal value for each currency and eliminate restrictions and practices such as competitive devaluations. The system required cooperation on a previously unattempted scale by all nations in establishing an innovative monetary system and an international institution to monitor it. After much negotiations in the difficult war time conditions, the international community accepted the system and an organisation was formed to supervise it.

The IMF began operations in Washington DC in May 1946. It then had 39 members. The IMF's membership now is 188.

Members and Administration

On joining the IMF, each member country contributes a certain sum of money called a 'quota subscription', as a sort of credit union deposit. Quotas serve various purposes.

- They form a pool of money that the IMF can draw from to lend to members in times of financial difficulty.
- They form the basis of determining the Special Drawing Rights (SDR).
- They determine the voting power of the member.

Statutory Purposes

The purposes of the International Monetary Fund are:

- To promote international monetary cooperation through a permanent institution that provides the machinery for consultation and collaboration on international monetary problems.
- To facilitate the expansion and balanced growth of international trade and to contribute, thereby, to the promotion and maintenance of high levels of employment and real income and to the development of the productive resources of all members as primary objectives of economic policy.
- To promote exchange stability, to maintain orderly exchange arrangements among members and to avoid competitive exchange depreciation.
- To assist in the establishment of a multilateral system of payments in respect of current transactions between members and in the elimination of foreign exchange restrictions which hamper the growth of world trade.
- To give confidence to members by making the general resources of the Fund temporarily available to them under adequate safeguards, thus providing them with opportunity to correct maladjustment in their balance of payments without resorting to measures destructive to national or international prosperity.
- In accordance with the above, to shorten the duration and lessen the degree of disequilibrium in the international balances of payments of members.

Financial Assistance

The IMF lends money only to member countries with balance of payments problems. A member country with a payments problem can immediately withdraw from the IMF the 25 per cent of its quota. A member in greater difficulty may request for more money from the IMP and can borrow up to three times its quota provided the member country undertakes to initiate a series of reforms and uses the borrowed money effectively. The frequently used mechanisms by the IMF to lend money are:

1. Standby Arrangements
2. Extended Arrangements
3. Structural Adjustment Mechanism (With low interest rates)

Regular IMF Facilities

- Standby Arrangements (SBA) are designed to provide short-term balance of payments assistance for deficits of a temporary or cyclical nature, such arrangements are typically for 12 to 18 months. Drawings are phased on a quarterly basis, with their release made conditional on meeting performance criteria and the completion of periodic programme reviews. Repurchases are made 31/4 to 5 years after each purchase.
- Extended Fund Facility (EFF) is designed to support medium-term programmes that generally run for three years. The EFF aims at overcoming balance of payments difficulties stemming from macroeconomic and structural problems. Performance criteria are applied, similar to those in standby arrangements and repurchases are made in 4½ to 10 years.

Concessional IMF Facility

- Enhanced Structural Adjustment Facility (ESAF) was established in 1987 and enlarged and extended in 1994. Designed for low-income member countries with protracted balance of payments problems, ESAF drawings are loans and not purchases of other members' currencies. They are made in support of three year programmes and carry an annual interest rate of 0.5 per cent, with a 5th year grace period and a 10 year maturity. Quarterly benchmarks and semiannual performance criteria apply; 80 low income countries are currently eligible to use the ESAF.

SDRs

As time passed, it became evident that the Fund's resources for providing short-term accommodation to countries in monetary difficulties were not sufficient. To resolve the situation, the Fund, after much debate and long deliberations, created new drawing rights in 1969. Special Drawing Rights (SDRs), sometimes called paper gold, are special account entries on the IMF books designed to provide additional liquidity to support growing world commerce. Although SDRs are a form of money not convertible to gold, their gold value is guaranteed, which helps to ensure their acceptability. Initially, SDRs worth $9.5 billion were created.

Participant nations may use SDRs as a source of currency in a spot transaction, as a loan for clearing a financial obligation, as a security for a loan, as a Swap against currency, or in a forward exchange operation. A nation with a balance of payments need may use its SDRs to obtain usable currency from another nation designated by the fund. A participant also may use SDRs to make payments to the Fund, such as repurchases. The Fund itself may transfer SDRs to a participant for various purposes including the transfer of SDRs instead of currency to a member using the Fund's resources.

THE WORLD BANK

The World Bank group is a multinational financial institution established at the end of World War II (1944) to help provide long-term capital for the reconstruction and development of member countries. The group is important to multinational corporations because it provides much of the planning and financing for economic development projects involving billions of dollars for which private businesses can act as contractors and suppliers of goods and engineering related services.

The purpose for the setting up of the Bank are :

- To assist in the reconstruction and development of territories of members by facilitating the investment of capital for productive purposes, including the restoration of economies destroyed or disrupted by war, the reconversion of productive facilities to peacetime needs and encouragement of the development or productive facilities and resources in less developed countries.
- To promote private foreign investment by means of guarantees or participation in loans and other investments made by private investors; and when private capital is not available on reasonable terms, to supplement private investment by providing, on suitable conditions, finance for productive purposes out of its own capital, funds raised by it and its other resources.
- To promote the long-range balanced growth of international trade and the maintenance of equilibrium in balance of payments by encouraging international investment for the development of the productive resources of members, thereby assisting in raising productivity, the standard of living and condition of labour in their territories.

- To arrange the loans made or guaranteed by it in relation to international loans through other channels so that the more useful and urgent projects, large and small alike, can be dealt with first.
- To conduct its operations with due regard to the effect of international investment on business conditions in the territories of members and, in the immediate post-war years, to assist in bringing about a smooth transition from a wartime to a peacetime economy.

The World Bank is the International Bank for Reconstruction and Development (IBRD) and the International Development Association (IDA). The IBRD has two affiliates, the International Finance Corporation (IFC) and the Multilateral Investment Guarantee Agency (MIGA). The Bank, the IFC and the MIGA are sometimes referred to as the "World Bank Group".

UNCTAD

United Nations Conference on Trade and Development (UNCTAD), permanent organ of the United Nations (UN) General Assembly, established in 1964 to promote trade, investment, and development in developing countries. Headquartered in Geneva, Switzerland, UNCTAD has approximately 190 members.

Negotiations at UNCTAD's meetings resulted in the Global System of Trade Preferences (1988), an agreement that reduced tariffs and removed or reduced nontariff trade barriers among participating developing countries; the Common Fund for Commodities (1989), an intergovernmental financial institution that provides assistance to developing countries that are heavily dependent on commodity exports; and various agreements for debt relief. In the 1990s UNCTAD's efforts were directed toward the challenges globalization poses to developing countries, and special attention was focused on measures to help the poorest and least developed countries become integrated into the world economy.

The highest policy-making body of UNCTAD is the Conference, which meets once every four years to set policy guidelines and to formulate a program of work. The UNCTAD Secretariat, whose members form part of the UN Secretariat, performs policy analysis, monitors and implements the decisions of UNCTAD's intergovernmental bodies, and provides for technical cooperation and exchanges of information. It comprises four divisions-on globalization and development strategies; international trade; investment, technology, and enterprise development; and services infrastructure-as well as the Office of the Special Co-ordinator for Least Developed, Land-locked, and Island Developing Countries (OSC-LDC). The Trade and Development Board, UNCTAD's executive body, is responsible for the operations of the organization when the Conference is not in session.

WORLD TRADE ORGANIZATION (W.T.O.)

GATT was an international body having its headquarters at Geneva and was founded in 1947 by 23 member countries including India. The body now comprises of 162 member countries of which around two-thirds are developing nations.

According to the approved GAIT accord, a Preparatory Committee would be set up, which in turn would set up the World Trade Organization (WTO), to become operational in early 1995. The WTO will act as a permanent watchdog on the International Trade and will enjoy the status similar to that of UNIDO wherein each member nation will have single voting right.

GATT was converted from a provisional agreement into a formal international organisation called World Trade Organization (WTO) with effect from January 1, 1995. WTO will serve as a single institutional framework encompassing GATT and all the result of the Uruguay Round.

It will be directed by a Ministerial Conference that will meet at least once every two years and its regular business will be overseen by a General Council. The WTO is a more powerful body with enlarged functions than the GATT and is envisaged to play a major role in the world economic affairs.

Role of WTO in International Trade

(i) WTO's aim is to liberalise international trade.
(ii) WTO establishes rules regarding international trade and sees that these rules are obeyed.
(iii) 153 countries of the world are currently members of the WTO.
(iv) It is seen that the developed countries have unfairly retained trade barriers. On the other hand, WTO rules have forced developing countries to remove trade barriers.

Functions of WTO

The former GATT was not really an organisation; it was merely a legal arrangement. On the other hand, the WTO is a new international organisation set up as a permanent body. It is designed to play the role of a watchdog in the spheres of trade in goods, trade in services, foreign investment, intellectual property rights, etc. Article III has set out the following five functions of WTO;

(i) The WTO shall facilitate the implementation, administration and operation and further the objectives of this Agreement and of the Multilateral Trade Agreements, and shall also provide the frame work for the implementation, administration and operation of the Plurilateral Trade Agreements.
(ii) The WTO shall provide the forum for negotiations among its members concerning their multilateral trade relations in matters dealt with under the Agreement in the Annexes to this Agreement.
(iii) The WTO shall administer the Understanding on Rules and Procedures Governing the Settlement of Disputes.
(iv) The WTO shall administer Trade Policy Review Mechanism.
(v) With a view to achieving greater coherence in global economic policy making, the WTO shall cooperate, as appropriate, with the international Monetary Fund (IMF) and with the International Bank for Reconstruction and Development (IBRD) and its affiliated agencies.

Objectives of WTO

Important objectives of WTO are mentioned below:

(i) to implement the new world trade system as visualised in the Agreement;
(ii) to promote World Trade in a manner that benefits every country;
(iii) to ensure that developing countries secure a better balance in the sharing of the advantages resulting from the expansion of international trade corresponding to their developmental needs;
(iv) to demolish all hurdles to an open world trading system and usher in international economic renaissance because the world trade is an effective instrument to foster economic growth;
(v) to enhance competitiveness among all trading partners so as to benefit consumers and help in global integration;
(vi) to increase the level of production and productivity with a view to ensuring level of employment in the world;
(vii) to expand and utilize world resources to the best;
(viii) to improve the level of living for the global population and speed up economic development of the member nations.

India and WTO

India is one of the founding members of the World Trade Organisation (WTO) and participation in the WTO rule based system implies greater stability, transparency and predictability in the governance of international trade.

The importance of WTO in promoting multilateral trade is being increasingly acknowledged. The WTO rules envisage non-discrimination in the form of national treatment and most favoured nation (MFN) treatment to our exports in the markets of other WTO members.

National treatment ensures that our exports to other member countries would not be discriminated vis-a-vis their domestic products. MFN treatment likewise ensures non-discrimination among various members in their tariff regimes and also other rules and regulations.

Emerging from continued discussions in various multilateral for a , developmental issues along with trade related issues are being increasingly focused at the international level. Poverty concerns of developing countries along with development and trade policies are also being given cognisance.

Need has been felt for integration of trade policies with development strategies, increasing support to areas of finance and debt relief, recognising the importance of technology for development, improvement in market access for developing countries in sectors like textiles, clothing and agriculture, and providing better access to the dispute settlement mechanisms for these countries.

The issue of abuse of the anti-dumping procedure*, the problems of rules of origin criteria, technical barriers to trade, regional trading blocs, etc., are also being considered at various levels in the WTO.

The Government of India has taken several steps to implement the policy commitments made under some of the agreements, particularly under the Agreement on Tariffs and Quantitative Restrictions Agreement on Agriculture (AoA), Trade Related Intellectual Property Rights (TRIPs), Trade Related Investment Measures (TRIMs), General Agreement on Trade in Services (GATS), apart from others. A strategy for tariff negotiations is, however, required.

The additional 'non-trade' issues relating to transparency in government procurement practices trade and competition policy, trade and environment, and trade and labour standards proposed in the Singapore and the Geneva Ministerial need to be addressed for negotiations.

The commitments regarding the technical barriers to trade, social agenda covering labour standards and environmental and phyto-sanitary issues also require establishment of certain national standards and technical regulations in a standardised and transparent system.

At the same time, there are some issues on which India has expressed certain reservations. These are:

- During the implementation of WTO agreements in the last six years, India has experienced certain imbalances and inequities in the WTO agreements. It is found that some developed countries have not fulfilled their obligations in letter and spirit of the WTO agreements, and many of the Special and Differential Treatment clauses, in favour of developing countries, added in various WTO agreements have remained in operational.
- Taking advantage of the exception clauses provided in the WTO, most industrialised countries are still enforcing various regulations on foreign producers and suppliers.
- Extending the scope of the investment regime in WTO beyond Trade Related Investment Measures and General Agreements on Trade in Services, is not appropriate.
- A multilateral framework cannot guarantee an increase in FDI inflows although it threatens to adversely affect the quality of the inflows.
- There are also other asymmetries present, as the WTO does not address the responsibilities of corporations which often impose trade restrictive clauses on their subsidiaries.

- WTO has not been able to ensure abolition of non-trade barriers being imposed on labour and environmental considerations, including the linkage in certain Generalised System of Preferences (GSP) schemes to these issues.

The present negotiations strategy is based on the decisions taken at the Doha Ministerial in November 2001. The Doha Declaration focused mainly on TRIPs agreement, public health, trade and environment and the implementation related issues and concerns. Elaborate timetables on work programme for current negotiations in agriculture and services and other issues have been worked out.

The Doha Conference presented mixed results for India. India's main concern was to speed up implementation of various agreements and to undo the imbalances and inequities present in some WTO agreements. From India's point of view, faster removal of the textile quotas maintained by developed countries like the USA was the most important implementation issue, which was, however, met with limited success. As far as environmental issues are concerned, the Doha declaration has mandated negotiations to clarify WTO rules in the light of multilateral environmental agreements. These negotiations could lead to developed countries raising barriers against goods from developing countries on the pretext of environmental protection.

India had also reservations on starting negotiations on four new 'non-trade' areas, namely, multilateral investment, global rules on competition, transparency in government procurement and trade facilitation, i.e., framing of uniform custom's procedures for clearance of goods. India could secure only a two-year respite and the study process would continue for two more years, i.e., up to the Fifth Ministerial Conference, when a decision about negotiations will be taken on the basis of an explicit consensus.

Apart from mandated negotiations in agriculture and services where the process has already started, negotiations on market access for non- agricultural products is quite important for India, as reduction or elimination of tariffs, tariff peaks and tariff escalation as well as removal of non-tariff barriers will be quite helpful in exports. India would, of course, have to make offers even though the negotiations will be carried out under less than full reciprocity as far as developing countries are concerned.

WTO AGRICULTURE AGREEMENT

After over 7 years of negotiations the Uruguay Round multilateral trade negotiations were concluded on December 15, 1993 and were formally ratified in April 1994 at Marrakesh, Morrocco. The WTO Agreement on Agriculture was one of the many agreements which were negotiated during the Uruguay Round.

The implementation of the Agreement on Agriculture started with effect from 1.1.1995. As per the provisions of the Agreement, the developed countries would complete their reduction commitments within 6 years, i.e., by the year 2000, whereas the commitments of the developing countries would be completed within 10 years, i.e., by the year 2004. The least developed countries are not required to make any reductions.

The products which are included within the purview of this agreement are what are normally considered as part of agriculture except that it excludes fishery and forestry products as well as rubber, jute, sisal, abaca and coir.

The WTO Agreement on Agriculture contains provisions in 3 broad areas of agriculture and trade policy : market access, domestic support and export subsidies.

Market Access

This includes tariffication, tariff reduction and access opportunities. Tariffication means that all non-tariff barriers such as quotas, variable levies, minimum import prices, discretionary licensing, state trading measures, voluntary restraint agreements etc. need to be abolished and converted into an equivalent tariff. Ordinary tariffs including those resulting from their tariffication are to be reduced by an average of 36% with minimum rate of reduction of 15% for each tariff item over a 6 year period. Developing countries are required to reduce tariffs by 24% in 10 years. Developing countries as were maintaining Quantitative Restrictions due to balance of payment problems, were allowed to offer ceiling bindings instead of tariffication.

Special safeguard provision allows the imposition of additional duties when there are either import surges above a particular level or particularly low import prices as compared to 1986-88 levels.

It has also been stipulated that minimum access equal to 3% of domestic consumption in 1986-88 will have to be established for the year 1995 rising to 5% at the end of the implementation period.

Domestic Support

For domestic support policies, subject to reduction commitments, the total support given in 1986-88, measured by the Total Aggregate Measure of Support (total AMS), should be reduced by 20% in developed countries (13.3% in developing countries). Reduction commitments refer to total levels of support and not to individual commodities. Policies which amount to domestic support both under the product specific and non product specific categories at less than 5% of the value of production for developed countries and less than 10% for developing countries are also excluded from any reduction commitments. Policies which have no or at most minimal, trade distorting effects on production are excluded from any reduction commitments ('Green Box'-Annex 2 of the Agreement on Agriculture www.wto.org. The list of exempted green box policies includes such policies which provide services or benefits to agriculture or the rural community, public stock-holding for food security purposes, domestic food aid and certain de-coupled payments to producers including direct payments to production limiting programmes, provided certain conditions are met.

INDIA'S COMMITMENTS

Market Access

As India was maintaining Quantitative Restrictions due to balance of payments reasons (which is a GATT consistent measure), it did not have to undertake any commitments in regard to market access. The only commitment India has undertaken is to bind its primary agricultural products at 100%; processed foods at 150% and edible oils at 300%. Of course, for some agricultural products like skimmed milk powder, maize, rice, spelt wheat, millets etc. which had been bound at zero or at low bound rates, negotiations under Article XXVIII of GATT were successfully completed in December, 1999, and the bound rates have been raised substantially.

Domestic Support

India does not provide any product specific support other than market price support. During the reference period (1986-88), India had market price support programmes for 22 products, out of which 19 are included in our list of commitments filed under GATT. The products are - rice, wheat, bajra, jawar, maize, barley, gram, groundnut, rapeseed, toria, cotton, Soyabean (yellow), Soyabean (black), urad, moong, tur, tobacco, jute, and sugarcane. The total product specific AMS was (-) Rs. 24,442 crores during the base period. The negative figure arises from the fact that during the base period, except for tobacco and sugarcane, international prices of all products was higher than domestic prices, and the product specific AMS is to be calculated by subtracting the domestic price from the international price and then multiplying the resultant figure by the quantity of production.

Non-product specific subsidy is calculated by taking into account subsidies given for fertilizers, water, seeds, credit and electricity. During the reference period, the total non-product specific AMS was Rs. 4581 crores. Taking both product specific and non-product specific AMS into account, the total AMS was (-) Rs. 19,869 crores i.e. about (-) 18% of the value of total agricultural output.

Since our total AMS is negative and that too by a huge magnitude, the question of our undertaking reduction commitments did not arise. As such, we have not undertaken any commitment in our schedule filed under GATT. The calculations for the marketing year 1995-96 show the product specific AMS figure as (-) 38.47% and non-product specific AMS as 7.52% of the total value of production. We can further deduct from these calculations the domestic support extended to low income and resource poor farmers provided under Article 6 of the Agreement on Agriculture. This still keeps our aggregate AMS below the *de minimis* level of 10%.

In India, exporters of agricultural commodities do not get any direct subsidy. The only subsidies available to them are in the form of:

(a) exemption of export profit from income tax under section 80-HHC of the Income Tax Act and this is also not one of the listed subsidies as the entire income from Agriculture is exempt from Income Tax per se.

(b) subsidies on cost of freight on export shipments of certain products like fruits, vegetables and floricultural products. We have in fact indicated in our schedule of commitments that India reserves the right to take recourse to subsidies (such as, cash compensatory support) during the implementation period.

Mandated Negotiations

Article 20 of the Agreement on Agriculture (AoA) (www.wto.orgmandates that negotiations for continuing the reform process in agriculture will be initiated one year before the end of the implementation period. As the implementation period for developed countries culminated at the end of the year 2000, the negotiations on the Agreement on Agriculture have begun in January 2000.

These negotiations are being conducted in special sessions of the WTO Committee on Agriculture (COA) at Geneva. The following are the broad parameters for carrying out negotiations:

- Experience of member countries in implementation of reduction commitments till date;
- The effects of reduction commitments on World Trade in Agriculture;
- Non trade concerns, special and differential treatment to developing country members and the objective of establishing a fair and market oriented agricultural trading system; and
- Identifying further commitments necessary to achieve the long-term objectives of the Agreement.

During extensive deliberations in the WTO Committee on Agriculture and in the General Council, member countries had agreed to broadly adhere to the mandate of Article 20 of the Agreement. In pursuance of the same, in the first phase of the negotiations, members have submitted 47 negotiating proposals, which were discussed in Seven Special Sessions of the CoA. With the approval of the Cabinet Committee on WTO Matters, India also submitted its negotiating proposals to the WTO on 15th January 2001, in the areas of market access, domestic support, export competition and food security. These proposals were drawn up and drafted based on inputs received from wide ranging consultations with various stakeholders and keeping in view India's objectives in the negotiations, which are to protect its food and livelihood security concerns and to protect all domestic policy measures taken for poverty alleviation, rural development and rural employment as also to create opportunities for expansion of agricultural exports by securing meaningful market access in developed countries. India also co-sponsored two papers, one on "Market Access" along with 11 other developing countries and another on "Export Credits for Agricultural Products" along with 9 other countries/ group of countries.

GATS

The creation of the GATS was one of the landmark achievements of the Uruguay Round, whose results entered into force in January 1995. The GATS was inspired by essentially the same objectives as its counterpart in merchandise trade, the General Agreement on Tariffs and Trade (GATT): creating a credible and reliable system of international trade rules; ensuring fair and equitable treatment of all participants (principle of non-discrimination); stimulating economic activity through guaranteed policy bindings; and promoting trade and development through progressive liberalization.

While services currently account for over 60 percent of global production and employment, they represent no more than 20 per cent of total trade (BOP basis). This — seemingly modest — share should not be underestimated, however. Many services, which have long been considered genuine domestic activities, have increasingly become internationally mobile. This trend is likely to continue, owing to the introduction of new transmission technologies (e.g. electronic banking, tele-health or tele-education services), the opening up in many countries of long-entrenched monopolies (e.g. voice telephony and postal services), and regulatory reforms in hitherto tightly regulated sectors such as transport. Combined with changing consumer preferences, such technical and regulatory innovations have enhanced the "tradability" of services and, thus, created a need for multilateral disciplines.

- All WTO Members, some 140 economies at present, are at the same time Members of the GATS and, to varying degrees, have assumed commitments in individual service sectors.
- The GATS applies in principle to all service sectors, with two exceptions.

  Article I(3) of the GATS excludes "services supplied in the exercise of governmental authority". These are services that are supplied neither on a commercial basis nor in competition with other suppliers. Cases in point are social security schemes and any other public service, such as health or education, that is provided at non-market conditions.

  Further, the Annex on Air Transport Services exempts from coverage measures affecting air traffic rights and services directly related to the exercise of such rights.
- The GATS distinguishes between four modes of supplying services: cross-border trade, consumption abroad, commercial presence, and presence of natural persons.

  Cross-border supply is defined to cover services flows from the territory of one Member into the territory of another Member (e.g. banking or architectural services transmitted via telecommunications or mail);

  Consumption abroad refers to situations where a service consumer (e.g. tourist or patient) moves into another Member's territory to obtain a service;

  Commercial presence implies that a service supplier of one Member establishes a territorial presence, including through ownership or lease of premises, in another Member's territory to provide a service (e.g. domestic subsidiaries of foreign insurance companies or hotel chains);

  Presence of natural persons consists of persons of one Member entering the territory of another Member to supply a service (e.g. accountants, doctors or teachers). The Annex on Movement of Natural Persons specifies, however, that Members remain free to operate measures regarding citizenship, residence or access to the employment market on a permanent basis.

- The supply of many services is possible only through the simultaneous physical presence of both producer and consumer. There are thus many instances in which, in order to be commercially meaningful, trade commitments must extend to cross-border movements of the consumer, the establishment of a commercial presence within a market, or the temporary movement of the service provider himself.
- The GATS expressly recognizes the right of Members to regulate the supply of services in pursuit of their own policy objectives, and does not seek to influence these objectives. Rather, the Agreement establishes a framework of rules to ensure that services regulations are administered in a reasonable, objective and impartial manner and do not constitute unnecessary barriers to trade.
- Obligations contained in the GATS may be categorized into two broad groups: General obligations, which apply directly and automatically to all Members and services sectors, as well as commitments concerning market access and national treatment in specifically designated sectors. Such commitments are laid down in individual country schedules whose scope may vary widely between Members. The relevant terms and concepts are similar, but not necessarily identical to those used in the GATT; for example, national treatment is a general obligation in goods trade and not negotiable as under the GATS.

  (a) **General obligations.** MFN Treatment: Under Article II of the GATS, Members are held to extend immediately and unconditionally to services or services suppliers of all other Members "treatment no less favourable than that accorded to like services and services suppliers of any other country". This amounts to a prohibition, in principle, of preferential arrangements among groups of Members in individual sectors or of reciprocity provisions which confine access benefits to trading partners granting similar treatment.

  Derogations are possible in the form of so-called Article II-Exemptions. Members were allowed to seek such exemptions before the Agreement entered into force. New exemptions can only be granted to new Members at the time of accession or, in the case of current Members, by way of a waiver under Article IX:3 of the WTO Agreement. All exemptions are subject to review; they should in principle not last longer than 10 years. Further, the GATS allows groups of Members to enter into economic integration agreements or to mutually recognize regulatory standards, certificates and the like if certain conditions are met.

  Transparency: GATS Members are required, inter alia, to publish all measures of general application and establish national enquiry points mandated to respond to other Member's information requests.

  Other generally applicable obligations include the establishment of administrative review and appeals procedures and disciplines on the operation of monopolies and exclusive suppliers.

  (b) **Specific Commitments.** Market Access: Market access is a negotiated commitment in specified sectors. It may be made subject to various types of limitations that are enumerated in Article XVI(2). For example, limitations may be imposed on the number of services suppliers, service operations or employees in the sector; the value of transactions; the legal form of the service supplier; or the participation of foreign capital.

  National Treatment: A commitment to national treatment implies that the Member concerned does not operate discriminatory measures benefiting domestic services or service suppliers. The key requirement is not to modify, in law or in fact, the conditions of competition in favour of the Member's own service industry. Again, the extension of national treatment in any particular sector may be made subject to conditions and qualifications.

Members are free to tailor the sector coverage and substantive content of such commitments as they see fit. The commitments thus tend to reflect national policy objectives and constraints, overall and in individual sectors. While some Members have scheduled less than a handful of services, others have assumed market access and national treatment disciplines in over 120 out of a total of 160-odd services.

The existence of specific commitments triggers further obligations concerning, inter alia, the notification of new measures that have a significant impact on trade and the avoidance of restrictions on international payments and transfers.

- Each WTO Member is required to have a Schedule of Specific Commitments which identifies the services for which the Member guarantees market access and national treatment and any limitations that may be attached. The Schedule may also be used to assume additional commitments regarding, for example, the implementation of specified standards or regulatory principles. Commitments are undertaken with respect to each of the four different modes of service supply.

  Most schedules consist of both sectoral and horizontal sections. The "Horizontal Section" contains entries that apply across all sectors subsequently listed in the schedule. Horizontal limitations often refer to a particular mode of supply, notably commercial presence and the presence of natural persons. The "Sector-Specific Sections" contain entries that apply only to the particular service.
- The majority of current commitments entered into force on 1 January 1995, i.e. the date of entry into force of the WTO. New commitments have since been scheduled by participants in extended negotiations (see below) and by new Members that have joined the WTO.
- Yes, any Member is free to expand or upgrade its existing commitments at any time.
- Pursuant to Article XXI, specific commitments may be modified subject to certain procedures. Countries which may be affected by such modifications can request the modifying Member to negotiate compensatory adjustments; these are to be granted on an MFN basis.
- The GATS permits Members in specified circumstances to introduce or maintain measures in contravention of their obligations under the Agreement, including the MFN requirement or specific commitments. The relevant Article provides cover, inter alia, for measures necessary to:
  - protect public morals or maintain public order;
  - protect human, animal or plant life or health; or
  - secure compliance with laws or regulations not inconsistent with the -Agreement including, among others, measures necessary to prevent deceptive or fraudulent practices.

  Moreover, the Annex on Financial Services entitles Members, regardless of other provisions of the GATS, to take measures for prudential reasons, including for the protection of investors, depositors, policy holders or persons to whom a fiduciary duty is owed by a financial service supplier, or to ensure the integrity and stability of the financial system.

  Finally, in the event of serious balance-of-payments difficulties Members are allowed to temporarily restrict trade, on a non-discriminatory basis, despite the existence of specific commitments.
- Developing country interests have inspired both the general structure of the Agreement as well as individual Articles. In particular, the objective of facilitating the increasing participation of developing countries in services trade has been enshrined in the Preamble to the Agreement

and underlies the provisions of Article IV. This Article requires Members, inter alia, to negotiate specific commitments relating to the strengthening of developing countries' domestic services capacity; the improvement of developing countries' access to distribution channels and information networks; and the liberalization of market access in areas of export interest to these countries.

While the notion of progressive liberalization is one of the basic tenets of the GATS, Article XIX provides that liberalization takes place with due respect for national policy objectives and Members' development levels, both overall and in individual sectors. Developing countries are thus given flexibility for opening fewer sectors, liberalizing fewer types of transactions, and progressively extending market access in line with their development situation. Other provisions ensure that developing countries have more flexibility in pursuing economic integration policies, maintaining restrictions on balance of payments grounds, and determining access to and use of their telecommunications transport networks and services. In addition, developing countries are entitled to receive technical assistance from the WTO Secretariat.

- The GATS, including its Annexes and Related Instruments, sets out a work programme which is normally referred to as the "built-in" agenda. The programme reflects both the fact that not all services-related negotiations could be concluded within the time frame of the Uruguay Round, and that Members have already committed themselves, in Article XIX, to successive rounds aimed at achieving a progressively higher level of liberalization (see below). In addition, various GATS Articles provide for issue-specific negotiations intended to define rules and disciplines for domestic regulation (Article VI), emergency safeguards (Article X), government procurement (Article XIII), and subsidies (Article XV). These negotiations are currently under way.

  At the sectoral level, negotiations on basic telecommunications were successfully concluded in February 1997 and negotiations in the area of financial services in mid-December 1997. In these negotiations, Members achieved significantly improved commitments with a broader level of participation.
- No. The results of sectoral negotiations are new specific commitments and/or MFN exemptions related to the sector concerned. Thus, they are neither legally independent from other sector-specific commitments nor constitute agreements different from the GATS. The new commitments and MFN exemptions have been incorporated into the existing Schedules and Exemption Lists by way of separate Protocols to the GATS.
- In services, the Uruguay Round was only a first step in a longer-term process of multilateral rule-making and trade liberalization. Observers tend to agree that, while the negotiations succeeded in setting up the principle structure of the Agreement, the liberalizing effects have been relatively modest. Barring exceptions in financial and telecommunication services, most schedules have remained confined to confirming status quo market conditions in a relatively limited number of sectors. This may be explained in part by the novelty of the Agreement and the perceived need of Members to gather experience before considering wider and deeper commitments. Moreover, many administrations needed time to develop the necessary regulation — including quality standards, licensing and qualification requirements — that ensures that external liberalization is compatible with, and conducive to, core policy objectives (quality, equity, etc.) in socially or infrastructurally important services.

  More than ten years have passed since the Agreement's inception, and the economic importance of services — in terms of production, income, employment and trade — has continued to rise. There thus appears ample scope for new and/or improved commitments in new negotiations.

- Under Article XIX, Members are (self-) committed to launch successive rounds of services negotiations with a view to achieving a progressively higher level of liberalization. The first such round was to begin no later than five years from the date of entry into force of the Agreement and, accordingly, started in January 2000.

TRIPS

The areas of intellectual property that it covers are: copyright and related rights (i.e. the rights of performers, producers of sound recordings and broadcasting organizations); trademarks including service marks; geographical indications including appellations of origin; industrial designs; patents including the protection of new varieties of plants; the layout-designs of integrated circuits; and undisclosed information including trade secrets and test data.

The three main features of the Agreement are:

- **Standards.** In respect of each of the main areas of intellectual property covered by the TRIPS Agreement, the Agreement sets out the minimum standards of protection to be provided by each Member. Each of the main elements of protection is defined, namely the subject-matter to be protected, the rights to be conferred and permissible exceptions to those rights, and the minimum duration of protection. The Agreement sets these standards by requiring, first, that the substantive obligations of the main conventions of the WIPO, the Paris Convention for the Protection of Industrial Property (Paris Convention) and the Berne Convention for the Protection of Literary and Artistic Works (Berne Convention) in their most recent versions, must be complied with. With the exception of the provisions of the Berne Convention on moral rights, all the main substantive provisions of these conventions are incorporated by reference and thus become obligations under the TRIPS Agreement between TRIPS Member countries. The relevant provisions are to be found in Articles 2.1 and 9.1 of the TRIPS Agreement, which relate, respectively, to the Paris Convention and to the Berne Convention. Secondly, the TRIPS Agreement adds a substantial number of additional obligations on matters where the pre-existing conventions are silent or were seen as being inadequate. The TRIPS Agreement is thus sometimes referred to as a Berne and Paris-plus agreement.
- **Enforcement.** The second main set of provisions deals with domestic procedures and remedies for the enforcement of intellectual property rights. The Agreement lays down certain general principles applicable to all IPR enforcement procedures. In addition, it contains provisions on civil and administrative procedures and remedies, provisional measures, special requirements related to border measures and criminal procedures, which specify, in a certain amount of detail, the procedures and remedies that must be available so that right holders can effectively enforce their rights.
- **Dispute settlement.** The Agreement makes disputes between WTO Members about the respect of the TRIPS obligations subject to the WTO's dispute settlement procedures.

In addition the Agreement provides for certain basic principles, such as national and most-favoured-nation treatment, and some general rules to ensure that procedural difficulties in acquiring or maintaining IPRs do not nullify the substantive benefits that should flow from the Agreement. The obligations under the Agreement will apply equally to all Member countries, but developing countries will have a longer period to phase them in. Special transition arrangements operate in the situation where a developing country does not presently provide product patent protection in the area of pharmaceuticals.

The TRIPS Agreement is a minimum standards agreement, which allows Members to provide more extensive protection of intellectual property if they so wish. Members are left free to determine the appropriate method of implementing the provisions of the Agreement within their own legal system and practice.

Substantive Standards of Protection

Copyright

During the Uruguay Round negotiations, it was recognized that the Berne Convention already, for the most part, provided adequate basic standards of copyright protection. Thus it was agreed that the point of departure should be the existing level of protection under the latest Act, the Paris Act of 1971, of that Convention. The point of departure is expressed in Article 9.1 under which Members are obliged to comply with the substantive provisions of the Paris Act of 1971 of the Berne Convention, i.e. Articles 1 through 21 of the Berne Convention (1971) and the Appendix thereto. However, Members do not have rights or obligations under the TRIPS Agreement in respect of the rights conferred under Article 6b is of that Convention, i.e. the moral rights (the right to claim authorship and to object to any derogatory action in relation to a work, which would be prejudicial to the author's honour or reputation), or of the rights derived therefrom. The provisions of the Berne Convention referred to deal with questions such as subject-matter to be protected, minimum term of protection, and rights to be conferred and permissible limitations to those rights. The Appendix allows developing countries, under certain conditions, to make some limitations to the right of translation and the right of reproduction.

In addition to requiring compliance with the basic standards of the Berne Convention, the TRIPS Agreement clarifies and adds certain specific points.

Article 9.2 confirms that copyright protection shall extend to expressions and not to ideas, procedures, methods of operation or mathematical concepts as such.

Article 10.1 provides that computer programs, whether in source or object code, shall be protected as literary works under the Berne Convention (1971). This provision confirms that computer programs must be protected under copyright and that those provisions of the Berne Convention that apply to literary works shall be applied also to them. It confirms further, that the form in which a program is, whether in source or object code, does not affect the protection. The obligation to protect computer programs as literary works means e.g. that only those limitations that are applicable to literary works may be applied to computer programs. It also confirms that the general term of protection of 50 years applies to computer programs. Possible shorter terms applicable to photographic works and works of applied art may not be applied.

Article 10.2 clarifies that databases and other compilations of data or other material shall be protected as such under copyright even where the databases include data that as such are not protected under copyright. Databases are eligible for copyright protection provided that they by reason of the selection or arrangement of their contents constitute intellectual creations. The provision also confirms that databases have to be protected regardless of which form they are in, whether machine readable or other form. Furthermore, the provision clarifies that such protection shall not extend to the data or material itself, and that it shall be without prejudice to any copyright subsisting in the data or material itself.

Article 11 provides that authors shall have in respect of at least computer programs and, in certain circumstances, of cinematographic works the right to authorize or to prohibit the commercial rental to the public of originals or copies of their copyright works. With respect to cinematographic works, the exclusive rental right is subject to the so-called impairment test: a Member is excepted from the obligation unless such rental has led to widespread copying of such works which is materially impairing the exclusive right of reproduction conferred in that Member on authors and their successors in title. In respect of computer programs, the obligation does not apply to rentals where the program itself is not the essential object of the rental.

According to the general rule contained in Article 7(1) of the Berne Convention as incorporated into the TRIPS Agreement, the term of protection shall be the life of the author and 50 years after his death. Paragraphs 2 through 4 of that Article specifically allow shorter terms in certain cases. These provisions are supplemented by Article 12 of the TRIPS Agreement, which provides that whenever the term of protection of a work, other than a photographic work or a work of applied art, is calculated on a basis other than the life of a natural person, such term shall be no less than 50 years from the end of the calendar year of authorized publication, or, failing such authorized publication within 50 years from the making of the work, 50 years from the end of the calendar year of making.

Article 13 requires Members to confine limitations or exceptions to exclusive rights to certain special cases which do not conflict with a normal exploitation of the work and do not unreasonably prejudice the legitimate interests of the right holder. This is a horizontal provision that applies to all limitations and exceptions permitted under the provisions of the Berne Convention and the Appendix thereto as incorporated into the TRIPS Agreement. The application of these limitations is permitted also under the TRIPS Agreement, but the provision makes it clear that they must be applied in a manner that does not prejudice the legitimate interests of the right holder.

Related Rights

The provisions on protection of performers, producers of phonograms and broadcasting organizations are included in Article 14. According to Article 14.1, performers shall have the possibility of preventing the unauthorized fixation of their performance on a phonogram (e.g. the recording of a live musical performance). The fixation right covers only aural, not audiovisual fixations. Performers must also be in position to prevent the reproduction of such fixations. They shall also have the possibility of preventing the unauthorized broadcasting by wireless means and the communication to the public of their live performance.

In accordance with Article 14.2, Members have to grant producers of phonograms an exclusive reproduction right. In addition to this, they have to grant, in accordance with Article 14.4, an exclusive rental right at least to producers of phonograms. The provisions on rental rights apply also to any other right holders in phonograms as determined in national law. This right has the same scope as the rental right in respect of computer programs. Therefore it is not subject to the impairment test as in respect of cinematographic works. However, it is limited by a so-called grand-fathering clause, according to which a Member, which on 15 April 1994, i.e. the date of the signature of the Marrakesh Agreement, had in force a system of equitable remuneration of right holders in respect of the rental of phonograms, may maintain such system provided that the commercial rental of phonograms is not giving rise to the material impairment of the exclusive rights of reproduction of right holders.

Broadcasting organizations shall have, in accordance with Article 14.3, the right to prohibit the unauthorized fixation, the reproduction of fixations, and the rebroadcasting by wireless means of broadcasts, as well as the communication to the public of their television broadcasts. However, it is not necessary to grant such rights to broadcasting organizations, if owners of copyright in the subject-matter of broadcasts are provided with the possibility of preventing these acts, subject to the provisions of the Berne Convention.

The term of protection is at least 50 years for performers and producers of phonograms, and 20 years for broadcasting organizations (Article 14.5).

Article 14.6 provides that any Member may, in relation to the protection of performers, producers of phonograms and broadcasting organizations, provide for conditions, limitations, exceptions and reservations to the extent permitted by the Rome Convention.

Trademarks

The basic rule contained in Article 15 is that any sign, or any combination of signs, capable of distinguishing the goods and services of one undertaking from those of other undertakings, must be eligible for registration as a trademark, provided that it is visually perceptible. Such signs, in particular words including personal names, letters, numerals, figurative elements and combinations of colours as well as any combination of such signs, must be eligible for registration as trademarks.

Where signs are not inherently capable of distinguishing the relevant goods or services, Member countries are allowed to require, as an additional condition for eligibility for registration as a trademark, that distinctiveness has been acquired through use. Members are free to determine whether to allow the registration of signs that are not visually perceptible (e.g. sound or smell marks).

Members may make registrability depend on use. However, actual use of a trademark shall not be permitted as a condition for filing an application for registration, and at least three years must have passed after that filing date before failure to realize an intent to use is allowed as the ground for refusing the application (Article 14.3).

The Agreement requires service marks to be protected in the same way as marks distinguishing goods.

The owner of a registered trademark must be granted the exclusive right to prevent all third parties not having the owner's consent from using in the course of trade identical or similar signs for goods or services which are identical or similar to those in respect of which the trademark is registered where such use would result in a likelihood of confusion. In case of the use of an identical sign for identical goods or services, a likelihood of confusion must be presumed (Article 16.1). The TRIPS Agreement contains certain provisions on well-known marks, which supplement the protection required by Article 6b is of the Paris Convention, as incorporated by reference into the TRIPS Agreement, which obliges Members to refuse or to cancel the registration, and to prohibit the use of a mark conflicting with a mark which is well known. First, the provisions of that Article must be applied also to services. Second, it is required that knowledge in the relevant sector of the public acquired not only as a result of the use of the mark but also by other means, including as a result of its promotion, be taken into account. Furthermore, the protection of registered well-known marks must extend to goods or services which are not similar to those in respect of which the trademark has been registered, provided that its use would indicate a connection between those goods or services and the owner of the registered trademark, and the interests of the owner are likely to be damaged by such use (Articles 16.2 and 3).

Members may provide limited exceptions to the rights conferred by a trademark, such as fair use of descriptive terms, provided that such exceptions take account of the legitimate interests of the owner of the trademark and of third parties (Article 17).

Initial registration, and each renewal of registration, of a trademark shall be for a term of no less than seven years. The registration of a trademark shall be renewable indefinitely (Article 18).

Cancellation of a mark on the grounds of non-use cannot take place before three years of uninterrupted non-use has elapsed unless valid reasons based on the existence of obstacles to such use are shown by the trademark owner. Circumstances arising independently of the will of the owner of the trademark, such as import restrictions or other government restrictions, shall be recognized as valid reasons of non-use. Use of a trademark by another person, when subject to the control of its owner, must be recognized as use of the trademark for the purpose of maintaining the registration (Article 19).

It is further required that use of the trademark in the course of trade shall not be unjustifiably encumbered by special requirements, such as use with another trademark, use in a special form, or use in a manner detrimental to its capability to distinguish the goods or services (Article 20).

Geographical Indications

Geographical indications are defined, for the purposes of the Agreement, as indications which identify a good as originating in the territory of a Member, or a region or locality in that territory, where a given quality, reputation or other characteristic of the good is essentially attributable to its geographical origin (Article 22.1). Thus, this definition specifies that the quality, reputation or other characteristics of a good can each be a sufficient basis for eligibility as a geographical indication, where they are essentially attributable to the geographical origin of the good.

In respect of all geographical indications, interested parties must have legal means to prevent use of indications which mislead the public as to the geographical origin of the good, and use which constitutes an act of unfair competition within the meaning of Article 10b is of the Paris Convention (Article 22.2).

The registration of a trademark which uses a geographical indication in a way that misleads the public as to the true place of origin must be refused or invalidated ex officio if the legislation so permits or at the request of an interested party (Article 22.3).

Article 23 provides that interested parties must have the legal means to prevent the use of a geographical indication identifying wines for wines not originating in the place indicated by the geographical indication. This applies even where the public is not being misled, there is no unfair competition and the true origin of the good is indicated or the geographical indication is accompanied be expressions such as "kind", "type", "style", "imitation" or the like. Similar protection must be given to geographical indications identifying spirits when used on spirits. Protection against registration of a trademark must be provided accordingly.

Article 24 contains a number of exceptions to the protection of geographical indications. These exceptions are of particular relevance in respect of the additional protection for geographical indications for wines and spirits. For example, Members are not obliged to bring a geographical indication under protection, where it has become a generic term for describing the product in question (paragraph 6). Measures to implement these provisions shall not prejudice prior trademark rights that have been acquired in good faith (paragraph 5). Under certain circumstances, continued use of a geographical indication for wines or spirits may be allowed on a scale and nature as before (paragraph 4). Members availing themselves of the use of these exceptions must be willing to enter into negotiations about their continued application to individual geographical indications (paragraph 1). The exceptions cannot be used to diminish the protection of geographical indications that existed prior to the entry into force of the TRIPS Agreement (paragraph 3). The TRIPS Council shall keep under review the application of the provisions on the protection of geographical indications (paragraph 2).

Industrial Designs

Article 25.1 of the TRIPS Agreement obliges Members to provide for the protection of independently created industrial designs that are new or original. Members may provide that designs are not new or original if they do not significantly differ from known designs or combinations of known design features. Members may provide that such protection shall not extend to designs dictated essentially by technical or functional considerations.

Article 25.2 contains a special provision aimed at taking into account the short life cycle and sheer number of new designs in the textile sector: requirements for securing protection of such designs, in particular in regard to any cost, examination or publication, must not unreasonably impair the opportunity to seek and obtain such protection. Members are free to meet this obligation through industrial design law or through copyright law.

Article 26.1 requires Members to grant the owner of a protected industrial design the right to prevent third parties not having the owner's consent from making, selling or importing articles bearing or embodying a design which is a copy, or substantially a copy, of the protected design, when such acts are undertaken for commercial purposes.

Article 26.2 allows Members to provide limited exceptions to the protection of industrial designs, provided that such exceptions do not unreasonably conflict with the normal exploitation of protected industrial designs and do not unreasonably prejudice the legitimate interests of the owner of the protected design, taking account of the legitimate interests of third parties.

The duration of protection available shall amount to at least 10 years (Article 26.3). The wording "amount to" allows the term to be divided into, for example, two periods of five years.

Patents

The TRIPS Agreement requires Member countries to make patents available for any inventions, whether products or processes, in all fields of technology without discrimination, subject to the normal tests of novelty, inventiveness and industrial applicability. It is also required that patents be available and patent rights enjoyable without discrimination as to the place of invention and whether products are imported or locally produced (Article 27.1).

There are three permissible exceptions to the basic rule on patentability. One is for inventions contrary to order public or morality; this explicitly includes inventions dangerous to human, animal or plant life or health or seriously prejudicial to the environment. The use of this exception is subject to the condition that the commercial exploitation of the invention must also be prevented and this prevention must be necessary for the protection of order public or morality (Article 27.2).

The second exception is that Members may exclude from patentability diagnostic, therapeutic and surgical methods for the treatment of humans or animals (Article 27.3(a)).

The third is that Members may exclude plants and animals other than micro-organisms and essentially biological processes for the production of plants or animals other than non-biological and microbiological processes. However, any country excluding plant varieties from patent protection must provide an effective sui generis system of protection. Moreover, the whole provision is subject to review four years after entry into force of the Agreement (Article 27.3(b)).

The exclusive rights that must be conferred by a product patent are the ones of making, using, offering for sale, selling, and importing for these purposes. Process patent protection must give rights not only over use of the process but also over products obtained directly by the process. Patent owners shall also have the right to assign, or transfer by succession, the patent and to conclude licensing contracts (Article 28).

Members may provide limited exceptions to the exclusive rights conferred by a patent, provided that such exceptions do not unreasonably conflict with a normal exploitation of the patent and do not unreasonably prejudice the legitimate interests of the patent owner, taking account of the legitimate interests of third parties (Article 30).

The term of protection available shall not end before the expiration of a period of 20 years counted from the filing date (Article 33).

Members shall require that an applicant for a patent shall disclose the invention in a manner sufficiently clear and complete for the invention to be carried out by a person skilled in the art and may require the applicant to indicate the best mode for carrying out the invention known to the inventor at the filing date or, where priority is claimed, at the priority date of the application (Article 29.1). If the subject-matter of a patent is a process for obtaining a product, the judicial authorities shall have the authority to order the defendant to prove that the process to obtain an identical product is different from the patented process, where certain conditions indicating a likelihood that the protected process was used are met (Article 34).

Layout-designs of Integrated Circuits

Article 35 of the TRIPS Agreement requires Member countries to protect the layout-designs of integrated circuits in accordance with the provisions of the IPIC Treaty (the Treaty on Intellectual Property in Respect of Integrated Circuits), negotiated under the auspices of WIPO in 1989.

These provisions deal with, inter alia, the definitions of "integrated circuit" and "layout-design (topography)", requirements for protection, exclusive rights, and limitations, as well as exploitation, registration and disclosure. An "integrated circuit" means a product, in its final form or an intermediate form, in which the elements, at least one of which is an active element, and some or all of the interconnections are integrally formed in and/or on a piece of material and which is intended to perform an electronic function.

A "layout-design (topography)" is defined as the three-dimensional disposition, however expressed, of the elements, at least one of which is an active element, and of some or all of the interconnections of an integrated circuit, or such a three-dimensional disposition prepared for an integrated circuit intended for manufacture.

The obligation to protect layout-designs applies to such layout-designs that are original in the sense that they are the result of their creators' own intellectual effort and are not commonplace among creators of layout-designs and manufacturers of integrated circuits at the time of their creation. The exclusive rights include the right of reproduction and the right of importation, sale and other distribution for commercial purposes. Certain limitations to these rights are provided for.

In addition to requiring Member countries to protect the layout-designs of integrated circuits in accordance with the provisions of the IPIC Treaty, the TRIPS Agreement clarifies and/or builds on four points. These points relate to the term of protection (ten years instead of eight, Article 38), the applicability of the protection to articles containing infringing integrated circuits (last sub clause of Article 36) and the treatment of innocent infringers (Article 37.1).

The conditions in Article 31 of the TRIPS Agreement apply mutatis mutandis to compulsory or non-voluntary licensing of a layout-design or to its use by or for the government without the authorization of the right holder, instead of the provisions of the IPIC Treaty on compulsory licensing (Article 37.2).

Protection of Undisclosed Information

The TRIPS Agreement requires undisclosed information — trade secrets or know-how — to benefit from protection. According to Article 39.2, the protection must apply to information that is secret, that has commercial value because it is secret and that has been subject to reasonable steps to keep it secret. The Agreement does not require undisclosed information to be treated as a form of property, but it does require that a person lawfully in control of such information must have the possibility of preventing it from being disclosed to, acquired by, or used by others without his or her consent in a manner contrary to honest commercial practices. "Manner contrary to honest commercial practices" includes breach of contract, breach of confidence and inducement to breach, as well as the acquisition of undisclosed information by third parties who knew, or were grossly negligent in failing to know, that such practices were involved in the acquisition.

The Agreement also contains provisions on undisclosed test data and other data whose submission is required by governments as a condition of approving the marketing of pharmaceutical or agricultural chemical products which use new chemical entities. In such a situation the Member government concerned must protect the data against unfair commercial use. In addition, Members must protect such data against disclosure, except where necessary to protect the public, or unless steps are taken to ensure that the data are protected against unfair commercial use.

Control of Anti-competitive Practices in Contractual Licences

Article 40 of the TRIPS Agreement recognizes that some licensing practices or conditions pertaining to intellectual property rights which restrain competition may have adverse effects on trade and may impede the transfer and dissemination of technology (paragraph 1).

Member countries may adopt, consistently with the other provisions of the Agreement, appropriate measures to prevent or control practices in the licensing of intellectual property rights which are abusive and anti-competitive (paragraph 2).

The Agreement provides for a mechanism whereby a country seeking to take action against such practices involving the companies of another Member country can enter into consultations with that other Member and exchange publicly available non-confidential information of relevance to the matter in question and of other information available to that Member, subject to domestic law and to the conclusion of mutually satisfactory agreements concerning the safeguarding of its confidentiality by the requesting Member (paragraph 3).

Similarly, a country whose companies are subject to such action in another Member can enter into consultations with that Member (paragraph 4).

TRIMS

The Agreement on TRIMs of the WTO is based on the belief that there is strong connection between trade and investment. Restrictive measures on investment are trade distorting. Several restrictive measures on investment are prohibiting trade and hence are not allowable. According to the TRIMs provision, countries should not adopt the *investment measures* which restrict and distort trade.

Investment measures are those steps used traditionally against foreign investment by host countries. Here, the TRIMs instruct that WTO members may not apply any measure that discriminates against foreign investment that violates basic WTO principles (like the MFN). WTO gives a list of prohibited investment measures or TRIMs like local content requirement, export obligation, technology transfer requirement etc. that violates trade. Few exemptions to developing countries are also provided under TRIMs. The Committee on TRIMs monitors the operation and implementation of the TRIMs Agreement and offers consultation for member countries.

The objective of TRIMs is to ensure fair treatment of investment in all member countries.

As per the TRIMs Agreement, members are required to notify the WTO Council for Trade in Goods of their existing TRIMs that are inconsistent with the agreement.

TRIMs and Foreign Investment Policy Changes in India

India has made several foreign investment liberalisation measures since the launch of the New Industrial Policy in 1991. Regulations for both FDI and FPI were simplified and now foreign investment is allowed in almost all sectors.

- WTO prohibit investment restricting measures that discriminates foreign investment.
- The argument of WTO is that such investment restricting steps are violating trade itself (WTO is an institution formed to promote trade).
- Historically countries impose measures that restrict foreign investment (called as investment measures and WTO term this as Trade Related Investment Measures).
- Under TRIMs, the WTO names the list of investment measures that discriminates foreign investment and hence violates the basic WTO principle of National Treatment.
- These measures include – local content requirement, domestic employment, technology transfer requirement etc.

Recent TRIMS and Foreign Investment Policy Changes in India (2024-2025)

India has made several regulatory updates to its foreign investment policies, particularly in compliance with the **Trade-Related Investment Measures (TRIMS) Agreement** and **Foreign Direct Investment (FDI) regulations.** Below are key developments:

1. **TRIMS Compliance and Policy Shifts**
   - India has gradually eased certain **local content requirements** and **export obligations** in sectors such as electronics, automobiles, and telecom to align with the TRIMS agreement under the **World Trade Organization (WTO).**
   - The government continues to **phase out protectionist policies** that conflict with TRIMS, such as mandatory sourcing requirements in specific industries. However, some strategic sectors (e.g., defense and infrastructure) still maintain certain investment restrictions for national security reasons.
2. **RBI's Updated Master Directions on Foreign Investment (2025)**
   The **Reserve Bank of India (RBI)** updated its **Master Directions on Foreign Investment** in January 2025 to enhance clarity and flexibility for foreign investors:
   - **Downstream Investments by Foreign-Owned or Controlled Companies (FOCCs):** These investments are now on par with direct FDI, allowing for greater **equity swaps, deferred consideration,** and **post-closing price adjustments** without prior RBI approval.
   - **Reporting Requirements:** Entities transitioning from a resident to FOCC status must now report the change within **30 days** via Form-DI.
   - **Foreign Investment for Financial Sector:** Companies in the **financial services sector** can now receive foreign investment to meet **Net-Owned Fund (NOF) requirements** without prior government approval, simplifying regulatory compliance.
3. **FDI Policy Changes and Trends (2024-2025):** The government has introduced several **FDI liberalization measures**, particularly in high-growth industries:
   - **Technology & IT Sector:** Continues to attract the highest FDI, with relaxed norms for **data centers, cloud computing, and AI-driven investments.**
   - **Manufacturing & Infrastructure:** Boosted by the **"Make in India"** initiative, with **100% FDI allowed under the automatic route** in several subsectors.
   - **Retail & E-commerce:** Stricter **compliance and consumer protection laws,** but increasing FDI flows due to rising online shopping demand.
   - **Digital Infrastructure & Fintech:** Emerging as **FDI hotspots**, particularly for blockchain, digital payments, and cybersecurity firms.
   - **Investment from Neighboring Countries:** Increased scrutiny, particularly for investments from China and Pakistan, requiring prior government approval.
4. **Changes in FEMA Regulations (2024-2025):** The **Foreign Exchange Management Act (FEMA)** has been updated to boost FDI and international trade transactions:
   - **Special Non-Resident Rupee Accounts:** Non-residents can now use **repatriable INR accounts** for FDI in non-debt instruments.
   - **Encouragement of INR for Trade:** India has signed agreements with **UAE, Indonesia, and Maldives** to facilitate trade in INR, reducing reliance on USD.
   - **Eased Restrictions for Indian Exporters:** Exporters can now **hold foreign currency accounts overseas**, simplifying trade settlements.

MULTIPLE CHOICE QUESTIONS

1. What is the primary goal of an economic system?
   (1) Social equality
   (2) Profit maximisation
   (3) Resource allocation
   (4) Environmental conservation
2. Which economic system is characterised by private ownership of resources and minimal government intervention?
   (1) Capitalism (2) Socialism
   (3) Communism (4) Mixed economy
3. In a market economy, prices are determined by
   (1) Government authorities
   (2) Supply and demand
   (3) Central planners (4) Labour unions
4. Fiscal policies are primarily concerned with:
   (1) Money supply
   (2) Taxation and government spending
   (3) Interest rates (4) Exchange rates
5. Monetary policy is controlled by
   (1) The President
   (2) The Central Bank
   (3) The Parliament
   (4) International organisations
6. Expansionary fiscal policy is typically used to
   (1) Control inflation
   (2) Reduce government spending
   (3) Stimulate economic growth
   (4) Increase interest rates
7. Which of the following is a tool of monetary policy?
   (1) Government expenditure
   (2) Discount rate
   (3) Progressive taxation
   (4) Fiscal deficit
8. The main goal of contractionary fiscal policy is to
   (1) Increase unemployment
   (2) Control inflation
   (3) Boost consumer spending
   (4) Expand government expenditure
9. What is the purpose of the legal environment in business?
   (1) Setting ethical standards
   (2) Resolving disputes
   (3) Promoting social responsibility
   (4) Regulating competition
10. Which economic policy tool is used to regulate the overall money supply in an economy?
    (1) Fiscal policy
    (2) Exchange rate policy
    (3) Monetary policy
    (4) Trade policy
11. The Keynesian economic theory is associated with
    (1) Laissez-faire economics
    (2) Supply-side economics
    (3) Demand-side economics
    (4) Monetarism
12. What is the main focus of supply-side economics?
    (1) Reducing government spending
    (2) Cutting taxes to stimulate production
    (3) Controlling inflation through interest rates
    (4) Increasing social welfare programs
13. Which economic system emphasizes collective or state ownership of resources?
    (1) Capitalism (2) Socialism
    (3) Mixed economy (4) Market economy
14. The Gross Domestic Product (GDP) measures:
    (1) The total population of a country
    (2) The total output of goods and services
    (3) The level of unemployment
    (4) The inflation rate
15. What does the term "inflation" refer to in an economic context?
    (1) Decrease in the money supply
    (2) Increase in the overall price level of goods and services
    (3) Expansion of government expenditure
    (4) Reduction in consumer spending

16. Which economic policy aims to influence the money supply by buying or selling government securities?
(1) Fiscal policy (2) Monetary policy
(3) Exchange rate policy
(4) Trade policy

17. A budget deficit occurs when
(1) Government expenditures exceed revenues
(2) Revenues exceed government expenditures
(3) There is a balanced budget
(4) Interest rates rise sharply

18. What is the primary function of the Federal Reserve in the United States?
(1) Fiscal policy implementation
(2) Monetary policy regulation
(3) Taxation decisions
(4) Social welfare program administration

19. Which economic policy tool is more likely to be implemented during a recession?
(1) Expansionary fiscal policy
(2) Contractionary fiscal policy
(3) Neutral fiscal policy
(4) Monetarist policy

20. What is the purpose of a trade policy in the business environment?
(1) Regulating competition
(2) Promoting international trade
(3) Setting ethical standards
(4) Resolving legal disputes

Directions: Each of the following items consists of two statements, one labelled as Assertion (A) and other labelled as Reason (R). You are to examine these two statements carefully and decide if the (A) and the (R) are individually true and if so, whether (R) is the correct explanation of (A). Select your answers to these items using the codes given below:
(1) Both (A) and (R) are true, and the (R) is the correct explanation of the (A).
(2) Both (A) and (R) are true, but the (R) is not the correct explanation of the (A).
(3) (A) is true, but the (R) is false.
(4) Both (A) and (R) are false.

21. **Assertion (A):** Fiscal policy is primarily concerned with controlling interest rates.
Reason (R): Interest rates are a tool of monetary policy, not fiscal policy.

22. **Assertion (A):** In a socialist economic system, the means of production are privately owned.
Reason: Socialism emphasizes collective or state ownership of resources.

23. **Assertion (A):** The legal environment in business only focuses on resolving disputes.
Reason (R): The legal environment also plays a role in setting ethical standards and promoting social responsibility.

24. **Assertion (A):** The goal of contractionary fiscal policy is to boost consumer spending.
Reason (R): Contractionary fiscal policy aims to control inflation.

25. **Assertion (A):** The Keynesian economic theory is associated with demand-side economics.
Reason (R): Keynesian economics suggests that government intervention can help stabilise the economy during downturns.

26. What is the primary role of government in a business environment?
(1) Profit maximisation
(2) Resource allocation
(3) Regulatory oversight
(4) International trade promotion

27. Which government agency is responsible for overseeing and regulating monetary policy in the United States?
(1) Securities and Exchange Commission (SEC)
(2) Federal Reserve
(3) Department of Justice
(4) Federal Trade Commission (FTC)

28. In the context of business, what is the purpose of lobbying?
(1) Direct marketing
(2) Influencing government decisions
(3) Stock trading
(4) Employee training

29. Consumer Protection Act primarily focuses on:
(1) Ensuring fair competition
(2) Safeguarding consumers against unfair trade practices
(3) Regulating international trade
(4) Promoting employee rights

30. FEMA stands for
(1) Federal Emergency Management Agency
(2) Foreign Exchange Management Act
(3) Federal Employment and Management Association
(4) Financial and Economic Management Act

31. What is the role of FEMA in the business environment?

(1) Regulating consumer protection
(2) Managing emergencies and disasters
(3) Overseeing monetary policy
(4) Controlling international trade

32. Which government body is responsible for enforcing antitrust laws in the United States?
(1) Department of Commerce
(2) Federal Trade Commission (FTC)
(3) Securities and Exchange Commission (SEC)
(4) Environmental Protection Agency (EPA)

33. What is the main purpose of antitrust laws?
(1) Protecting consumers from fraud
(2) Promoting fair competition and preventing monopolies
(3) Ensuring workplace safety
(4) Regulating international trade

34. The concept of corporate social responsibility (CSR) suggests that businesses should:
(1) Maximise profits at any cost
(2) Only focus on shareholder interests
(3) Consider the impact on society and the environment
(4) Ignore legal regulations

35. Which legal environment factor is concerned with the rights and responsibilities of individuals and organisations in their relationships with each other?
(1) Regulatory oversight
(2) Civil liberties
(3) Contract law
(4) Antitrust laws

36. What is the purpose of a cease and desist order issued by a government agency?
(1) Encouraging business expansion
(2) Prohibiting specific business activities
(3) Facilitating international trade
(4) Promoting ethical behaviour

37. The Sherman Antitrust Act is aimed at
(1) Ensuring workplace safety
(2) Regulating international trade
(3) Preventing unfair competition and monopolies
(4) Protecting consumers from fraud

38. Which government agency is responsible for enforcing environmental regulations in the United States?
(1) Department of Labour
(2) Environmental Protection Agency (EPA)
(3) Federal Communications Commission (FCC)
(4) Food and Drug Administration (FDA)

39. What is the primary purpose of environmental regulations?
(1) Encouraging pollution
(2) Ensuring workplace safety
(3) Promoting ethical behaviour
(4) Protecting the environment

40. Which legal concept involves unauthorised use or reproduction of someone else's intellectual property?
(1) Trademark infringement
(2) Patent violation
(3) Copyright infringement
(4) Contract breach

41. What does the acronym GDPR stand for in the context of legal regulations?
(1) General Data Protection Regulation
(2) Government Development and Policy Regulation
(3) Global Digital Privacy Rule
(4) General Disclosure and Privacy Rights

42. The purpose of the Dodd-Frank Wall Street Reform and Consumer Protection Act is to:
(1) Promote insider trading
(2) Regulate the financial industry and protect consumers
(3) Encourage fraudulent activities
(4) Deregulate the banking sector

43. What is the main objective of the Whistleblower Protection Act?
(1) Punishing whistleblowers
(2) Protecting individuals who report wrongdoing
(3) Promoting corruption
(4) Encouraging unethical behaviour

44. Which government body oversees and enforces labour laws in the United States?
(1) Department of Commerce
(2) Department of Labour
(3) Federal Reserve
(4) Securities and Exchange Commission (SEC)

45. The Sarbanes-Oxley Act is primarily focused on:
(1) Protecting the environment
(2) Regulating international trade
(3) Ensuring workplace safety

(4) Enhancing corporate governance and financial reporting

Directions: Each of the following items consists of two statements, one labelled as Assertion (A) and other labelled as Reason (R). You are to examine these two statements carefully and decide if the (A) and the (R) are individually true and if so, whether (R) is the correct explanation of (A). Select your answers to these items using the codes given below:

(1) Both (A) and (R) are true, and the (R) is the correct explanation of the (A).
(2) Both (A) and (R) are true, but the (R) is not the correct explanation of the (A).
(3) (A) is true, but the (R) is false.
(4) Both (A) and (R) are false.

46. **Assertion (A):** The Consumer Protection Act primarily focuses on promoting fair competition.

Reason (R): Fair competition is essential for ensuring consumer rights and preventing fraudulent practices.

47. **Assertion (A):** FEMA controls international trade.

Reason (R): FEMA stands for the Federal Emergency

48. What does the term "socio-cultural factors" refer to in a business context?
(1) Economic conditions
(2) Social and cultural influences
(3) Government regulations
(4) Technological advancements

49. Which of the following is an example of a socio-cultural factor influencing business decisions?
(1) Interest rates
(2) Demographic trends
(3) Fiscal policies
(4) Currency exchange rates

50. How can changing demographics affect businesses?
(1) By impacting interest rates
(2) By influencing consumer preferences and demands
(3) By regulating competition
(4) By controlling government spending

51. Corporate Social Responsibility (CSR) involves
(1) Maximising profits at any cost
(2) Ignoring environmental concerns
(3) Balancing financial goals with social and environmental responsibilities
(4) Minimising employee benefits

52. Which of the following is a potential benefit of practicing CSR for businesses?
(1) Increased environmental degradation
(2) Enhanced brand reputation
(3) Reduced employee satisfaction
(4) Higher profit margins

53. How do socio-cultural factors impact marketing strategies?
(1) They have no influence on marketing
(2) They shape consumer behaviour and preferences
(3) They only affect government policies
(4) They determine interest rates

54. Which statement best describes the influence of cultural diversity on the workplace?
(1) It hinders creativity and innovation
(2) It has no impact on organisational performance
(3) It enhances creativity and innovation
(4) It leads to increased employee turnover

55. The "buy local" movement is an example of
(1) Economic factors
(2) Socio-cultural factors
(3) Political factors
(4) Technological factors

56. What is the primary goal of a diverse and inclusive workplace?
(1) Reducing employee turnover
(2) Maximising profits
(3) Enhancing employee well-being and productivity
(4) Controlling interest rates

57. Which of the following is a potential challenge of cultural diversity in the workplace?
(1) Increased creativity
(2) Enhanced problem-solving skills
(3) Communication barriers
(4) Improved teamwork

58. How does consumer awareness of environmental issues influence business practices?
(1) It has no impact on business practices
(2) It encourages businesses to ignore environmental concerns
(3) It promotes sustainable and eco-friendly practices

(4) It increases interest rates

59. Which term refers to the shared values, attitudes, and beliefs of a group of people?
(1) Demographics (2) Culture
(3) Economics (4) Technology

60. What is the significance of understanding cultural nuances in international business?
(1) It is irrelevant to international business practices
(2) It helps in ignoring local customs and traditions
(3) It facilitates effective communication and relationship-building
(4) It leads to cultural homogenisation

61. Which of the following is a key aspect of CSR in relation to employees?
(1) Minimising employee benefits
(2) Maximising working hours
(3) Ensuring a safe and healthy work environment
(4) Ignoring employee rights

62. How can businesses contribute to social sustainability?
(1) Ignoring labour rights
(2) Fostering diversity and inclusion
(3) Maximising environmental degradation
(4) Reducing community engagement

63. The concept of "fair trade" is related to
(1) Political factors (2) Economic factors
(3) Socio-cultural factors
(4) Technological factors

64. What is the primary purpose of a code of ethics in business?
(1) Encouraging unethical behaviour
(2) Promoting corruption
(3) Providing guidance on ethical conduct
(4) Ignoring consumer rights

65. Which statement best describes the impact of socio-cultural factors on product design?
(1) Socio-cultural factors have no influence on product design
(2) They shape consumer preferences and needs, influencing product design
(3) Product design is solely determined by economic factors
(4) Technological advancements override socio-cultural considerations

66. How does CSR contribute to stakeholder engagement?
(1) By prioritising profits over stakeholder interests
(2) By ignoring environmental concerns
(3) By demonstrating a commitment to ethical practices and social responsibility
(4) By minimising employee benefits

67. The concept of "cultural intelligence" refers to:
(1) Ignoring cultural diversity in the workplace
(2) The ability to understand and adapt to different cultures
(3) Discriminating against employees from diverse backgrounds
(4) Avoiding international business opportunities

Directions: Each of the following items consists of two statements, one labelled as Assertion (A) and other labelled as Reason (R). You are to examine these two statements carefully and decide if the (A) and the (R) are individually true and if so, whether (R) is the correct explanation of (A). Select your answers to these items using the codes given below:
(1) Both (A) and (R) are true, and the (R) is the correct explanation of the (A).
(2) Both (A) and (R) are true, but the (R) is not the correct explanation of the (A).
(3) (A) is true, but the (R) is false.
(4) Both (A) and (R) are false.

68. **Assertion (A):** Socio-cultural factors have no impact on marketing strategies.
Reason (R): Marketing strategies are solely based on economic considerations.

69. **Assertion (A):** The primary goal of a diverse and inclusive workplace is to maximise profits.
Reason (R): A diverse and inclusive workplace has no impact on organisational performance.

70. **Assertion (A):** Communication barriers are not a potential challenge of cultural diversity in the workplace.
Reason (R): Cultural diversity enhances communication skills among employees.

71. **Assertion (A):** Understanding cultural nuances is irrelevant to international business practices.
Reason (R): International business is solely driven by economic factors.

72. **Assertion (A):** The concept of "fair trade" is primarily related to economic factors.
Reason (R): Economic considerations override socio-cultural factors in fair trade practices.

73. What does international business involve?
(1) Local trade only
(2) Domestic trade only
(3) Business activities across national borders
(4) Regional trade only

74. Which of the following is an example of an intangible aspect of international business?
(1) Goods (2) Services
(3) Technology (4) Currency

75. What is the primary objective of international business?
(1) Maximising domestic sales
(2) Minimising global competition
(3) Expanding operations beyond national borders
(4) Reducing technological advancements

76. Which factor is a driver of globalisation?
(1) Protectionism
(2) Economic self-sufficiency
(3) Cultural diversity
(4) Technological advancements

77. What is a key advantage of globalisation for businesses?
(1) Increased competition
(2) Limited market access
(3) Reduced market potential
(4) Expanded market opportunities

78. What is a mode of entry into international business that involves minimal risk and allows companies to test the market?
(1) Exporting (2) Licensing
(3) Franchising (4) Joint ventures

79. Which entry mode allows a company to grant another firm the right to use its intellectual property in exchange for fees or royalties?
(1) Exporting (2) Licensing
(3) Franchising (4) Joint ventures

80. In which entry mode do two or more firms join together to create a new business entity with shared ownership and control?
(1) Exporting (2) Licensing
(3) Franchising (4) Joint ventures

81. What is a limitation of exporting as a mode of entry into international business?
(1) High risk
(2) Limited market access
(3) Complex regulations
(4) Limited control over marketing activities

82. Which mode of entry allows a company to maintain control over its products, services, and brand image in a foreign market?
(1) Exporting (2) Licensing
(3) Franchising
(4) Wholly owned subsidiaries

83. What is the term for the practice of a company producing goods or services in different countries to take advantage of local resources and cost differences?
(1) Offshoring (2) Outsourcing
(3) Insourcing (4) Onshoring

84. What is a challenge associated with cultural diversity in international business?
(1) Increased innovation
(2) Improved communication
(3) Potential misunderstandings and conflicts
(4) Simplified negotiation processes

85. Which statement is true regarding the importance of international business for economic growth?
(1) International business hinders economic growth
(2) International business has no impact on economic growth
(3) International business promotes economic growth through increased trade and investment
(4) Economic growth is unrelated to international business activities

86. How does technological advancement contribute to the scope of international business?
(1) By limiting communication and connectivity
(2) By reducing the speed of information exchange
(3) By facilitating global communication and trade
(4) By restricting access to information

87. What is a primary driver of globalisation?
(1) Economic self-sufficiency
(2) Technological stagnation
(3) Protectionism
(4) Technological advancements

88. Which mode of entry is suitable for companies seeking to enter a foreign market with minimal financial investment?
(1) Exporting (2) Licensing
(3) Franchising (4) Joint ventures

89. How do cultural differences impact international business negotiations?
(1) They simplify negotiations
(2) They have no impact on negotiations
(3) They may lead to misunderstandings and misinterpretations
(4) They limit innovation

90. What is a potential disadvantage of joint ventures as a mode of entry?
(1) Limited market access
(2) Reduced financial risk
(3) Shared control and decision-making
(4) Enhanced local market knowledge

91. What role does globalisation play in creating interconnected markets?
(1) It limits market access
(2) It reduces competition
(3) It increases market segmentation
(4) It promotes interconnectedness and integration of markets

92. What is a characteristic of a wholly owned subsidiary as a mode of entry?
(1) Shared ownership and control
(2) Limited financial commitment
(3) High level of control over operations
(4) Minimal market knowledge

Directions: Each of the following items consists of two statements, one labelled as Assertion (A) and other labelled as Reason (R). You are to examine these two statements carefully and decide if the (A) and the (R) are individually true and if so, whether (R) is the correct explanation of (A). Select your answers to these items using the codes given below:
(1) Both (A) and (R) are true, and the (R) is the correct explanation of the (A).
(2) Both (A) and (R) are true, but the (R) is not the correct explanation of the (A).
(3) (A) is true, but the (R) is false.
(4) Both (A) and (R) are false.

93. **Assertion (A):** International business only involves local trade.
Reason (R): Domestic trade is the primary focus of international business.

94. **Assertion (A):** Exporting is a mode of entry that allows companies to maintain control over their products in a foreign market.
Reason (R): In exporting, companies have limited control over their products once they enter a foreign market.

95. **Assertion (A):** Cultural diversity in international business negotiations simplifies the process.
Reason (R): Cultural differences have no impact on negotiation dynamics.

96. **Assertion (A):** Offshoring involves the practice of producing goods or services in different countries to take advantage of local resources and cost differences.
Reason (R): Offshoring is not related to cost considerations.

97. **Assertion (A):** Globalisation promotes interconnectedness and integration of markets.
Reason (R): Globalisation hinders international trade and economic integration.

98. According to the theory of comparative advantage, what is the basis for international trade?
(1) Absolute advantage
(2) Equal resource endowment
(3) Differences in opportunity costs
(4) Fixed exchange rates

99. Which theory suggests that countries should specialise in the production of goods for which they have the lowest opportunity cost?
(1) Mercantilism
(2) Absolute advantage
(3) Comparative advantage
(4) Factor proportions theory

100. What is the main idea behind the theory of absolute advantage?
(1) Countries should focus on producing goods with the highest opportunity cost.
(2) Countries should specialise in the production of goods they can produce most efficiently.
(3) Countries should not engage in international trade.
(4) Fixed exchange rates benefit all countries.

101. Which theory emphasises the role of factor endowments in determining trade patterns?
(1) Mercantilism
(2) Absolute advantage
(3) Comparative advantage
(4) Factor proportions theory

102. What is a reason for government intervention in international trade?
(1) To encourage free trade
(2) To promote fair competition
(3) To reduce tariffs
(4) To discourage exports

103. Which of the following is an example of a tariff barrier?
(1) Quotas (2) Import restrictions
(3) Subsidies (4) Excise duties

104. What is the purpose of imposing quotas as a non-tariff barrier?
(1) To encourage imports
(2) To restrict the quantity of imports
(3) To lower tariffs
(4) To promote free trade

105. Which non-tariff barrier involves setting a limit on the quantity of a specific good that can be imported?
(1) Quotas (2) Embargoes
(3) Subsidies (4) Dumping

106. How do subsidies act as a non-tariff barrier?
(1) They encourage imports
(2) They reduce the cost of exports
(3) They discourage domestic production
(4) They promote fair competition

107. What is the primary objective of anti-dumping measures?
(1) To promote free trade
(2) To encourage fair competition
(3) To discourage the export of goods at below-market prices
(4) To lower import restrictions

108. What is the primary focus of India's Foreign Trade Policy?
(1) Encouraging imports
(2) Discouraging exports
(3) Promoting free trade
(4) Boosting exports and enhancing competitiveness

109. Which organisation formulates and implements India's Foreign Trade Policy?
(1) Reserve Bank of India (RBI)
(2) Ministry of Finance
(3) Ministry of Commerce and Industry
(4) Securities and Exchange Board of India (SEBI)

110. What is the significance of the Most Favored Nation (MFN) status in international trade?
(1) It grants preferential treatment to specific countries
(2) It imposes higher tariffs on specific countries
(3) It discourages free trade
(4) It ensures equal treatment for all trading partners

111. What is the role of the World Trade Organisation (WTO) in international trade?
(1) Imposing tariffs on member countries
(2) Facilitating negotiations and resolving trade disputes
(3) Restricting trade barriers
(4) Discouraging member countries from engaging in trade

112. Which agreement aims to promote international trade by reducing trade barriers?
(1) Kyoto Protocol
(2) Paris Agreement
(3) General Agreement on Tariffs and Trade (GATT)
(4) North American Free Trade Agreement (NAFTA)

113. What is the objective of the Make in India initiative?
(1) To promote imports
(2) To discourage exports
(3) To boost domestic manufacturing and attract foreign investment
(4) To limit industrial growth

114. Which trade policy tool involves selling goods in a foreign market at a price lower than the cost of production?
(1) Quotas (2) Embargoes
(3) Subsidies (4) Dumping

115. How does India's Foreign Trade Policy aim to support small and medium-sized enterprises (SMEs)?
(1) By imposing high tariffs on their products
(2) By discouraging their participation in international trade
(3) By providing incentives and support to enhance their competitiveness
(4) By restricting their access to global markets

116. Which type of tariff is imposed as a fixed charge for each unit of a good imported?
(1) Ad valorem tariff (2) Specific tariff
(3) Compound tariff (4) Prohibitive tariff

117. How does the government of a country benefit from imposing tariffs on imports?
(1) By encouraging free trade
(2) By promoting fair competition

(3) By generating revenue through tariff collections

(4) By lowering trade barriers

Directions: Each of the following items consists of two statements, one labelled as Assertion (A) and other labelled as Reason (R). You are to examine these two statements carefully and decide if the (A) and the (R) are individually true and if so, whether (R) is the correct explanation of (A). Select your answers to these items using the codes given below:

(1) Both (A) and (R) are true, and the (R) is the correct explanation of the (A).

(2) Both (A) and (R) are true, but the (R) is not the correct explanation of the (A).

(3) (A) is true, but the (R) is false.

(4) Both (A) and (R) are false.

118. Assertion (A): The theory of comparative advantage suggests that countries should produce goods for which they have the highest opportunity cost.

Reason (R): Comparative advantage is based on the principle of producing goods more efficiently.

119. Assertion (A): Government intervention in international trade is solely aimed at promoting imports.

Reason (R): Protectionist measures are designed to protect domestic industries from foreign competition.

120. Assertion (A): Quotas and subsidies both act as non-tariff barriers in international trade.

Reason (R): Quotas limit the quantity of imports, while subsidies reduce the cost of exports.

121. Assertion (A): Anti-dumping measures aim to encourage the export of goods at below-market prices.

Reason (R): Anti-dumping measures are implemented to prevent unfair trade practices.

122. Assertion (A): India's Foreign Trade Policy focuses solely on restricting exports.

Reason (R): The primary objective of India's Foreign Trade Policy is to boost exports and enhance competitiveness.

123. What does FDI stand for in the context of international business?

(1) Foreign Domestic Investment

(2) Foreign Developmental Investment

(3) Foreign Direct Investment

(4) Foreign Domestic Income

124. Which of the following is a characteristic of Foreign Portfolio Investment (FPI)?

(1) Involves a significant degree of control and management

(2) Represents a long-term investment in foreign assets

(3) Investors actively participate in the decision-making of the company

(4) Involves the purchase of financial assets such as stocks and bonds

125. What is the primary purpose of FDI?

(1) To purchase foreign financial assets

(2) To gain access to foreign markets and resources

(3) To engage in short-term trading activities

(4) To minimise control over foreign businesses

126. Which type of FDI involves a foreign investor acquiring a substantial ownership stake in a foreign company?

(1) Horizontal FDI (2) Vertical FDI

(3) Greenfield FDI (4) Brownfield FDI

127. In which type of FDI does a company invest in a similar business abroad as it operates domestically?

(1) Horizontal FDI (2) Vertical FDI

(3) Greenfield FDI (4) Brownfield FDI

128. What is the significance of the "market-seeking" motive for FDI?

(1) To access resources and raw materials

(2) To take advantage of cost differences in production

(3) To tap into a large consumer base in the foreign market

(4) To minimise political risks

129. What is a potential benefit of FDI for the host country?

(1) Loss of control over key industries

(2) Increased competition in the domestic market

(3) Technology transfer and job creation

(4) Dependence on foreign investment

130. How can FDI contribute to the home country's economy?

(1) By reducing unemployment

(2) By increasing dependence on foreign markets

(3) By limiting technological advancements

(4) By discouraging domestic entrepreneurship

131. What is a potential cost of FDI to the home country?
(1) Technology transfer
(2) Job creation
(3) Loss of control over key industries
(4) Enhanced economic growth

132. Which trend is commonly associated with the globalisation of FDI?
(1) Increased protectionism
(2) Reduced cross-border investments
(3) Decline in international business activities
(4) Growing interconnectedness of global economies

133. What is a potential benefit of FDI for the host country's balance of payments?
(1) Increased imports
(2) Trade deficits
(3) Inflows of foreign exchange
(4) Currency devaluation

134. How does FDI differ from FPI in terms of control over the invested entity?
(1) FDI involves minimal control, while FPI involves significant control
(2) FDI involves significant control, while FPI involves minimal control
(3) Both FDI and FPI involve equal levels of control
(4) FDI and FPI have no control over the invested entities

135. What is a common motive for FDI known as the "efficiency-seeking" motive?
(1) Access to a large consumer base
(2) Cost differences in production
(3) Political stability
(4) Technology transfer

136. How does FDI contribute to technological advancements in the host country?
(1) By limiting access to advanced technologies
(2) By discouraging innovation
(3) By transferring advanced technologies from the foreign investor
(4) By promoting technological stagnation

137. What is a potential benefit of FDI for the host country's infrastructure development?
(1) Deterioration of existing infrastructure
(2) Dependency on foreign infrastructure
(3) Enhanced infrastructure development
(4) Stagnation in infrastructure projects

138. How can FDI contribute to the host country's human capital development?
(1) By limiting access to education and training opportunities
(2) By discouraging skill development initiatives
(3) By promoting knowledge transfer and skill enhancement
(4) By stagnating the growth of the workforce

139. What is a potential disadvantage of FDI for the host country's local businesses?
(1) Increased competition and market opportunities
(2) Improved access to resources
(3) Loss of market share and potential bankruptcy
(4) Enhanced innovation and entrepreneurship

140. What is the role of India's FDI policy in regulating foreign investment in the country?
(1) To discourage FDI and promote protectionism
(2) To limit access to key industries for foreign investors
(3) To provide a framework for attracting and regulating FDI
(4) To promote FDI without any regulations

141. Which sector in India generally requires government approval for FDI beyond a certain threshold?
(1) Information Technology (IT)
(2) Agriculture
(3) Defense (4) Retail

142. How does India's FDI policy aim to attract foreign investors?
(1) By imposing strict restrictions and barriers
(2) By limiting incentives and benefits for foreign investors
(3) By providing a conducive and transparent environment for investment
(4) By discouraging technological advancements

Directions: Each of the following items consists of two statements, one labelled as Assertion (A) and other labelled as Reason (R). You are to examine these two statements carefully and decide if the (A) and the (R) are individually true and if so, whether (R) is the correct explanation of (A). Select your answers to these items using the codes given below:
(1) Both (A) and (R) are true, and the (R) is the correct explanation of the (A).

(2) Both (A) and (R) are true, but the (R) is not the correct explanation of the (A).

(3) (A) is true, but the (R) is false.

(4) Both (A) and (R) are false.

143. Assertion (A): FDI and FPI both involve significant control over the invested entities.

Reason (R): FDI and FPI are interchangeable terms with no distinction in terms of control.

144. Assertion (A): The "market-seeking" motive for FDI aims to minimise dependence on foreign markets.

Reason (R): The "market-seeking" motive focuses on tapping into a large consumer base in the foreign market.

145. Assertion (A): FDI always leads to a loss of control over key industries in the home country.

Reason (R): FDI may or may not result in a loss of control depending on the level of investment and ownership.

146. Assertion (A): FDI contributes to the host country's balance of payments through increased imports.

Reason (R): FDI leads to trade deficits and outflows of foreign exchange in the host country.

147. Assertion (A): India's FDI policy primarily focuses on discouraging foreign investors.

Reason (R): India's FDI policy aims to provide a conducive and transparent environment to attract foreign investors.

148. What does BOP stand for in the context of economics?

(1) Balance of Power

(2) Balance of Payments

(3) Business Operating Profit

(4) Budgetary Oversight Policy

149. What is the main purpose of the Balance of Payments (BOP) system?

(1) To regulate fiscal policy

(2) To monitor international trade and financial transactions

(3) To control inflation rates

(4) To assess domestic production levels

150. Which component of the BOP records the value of all goods and services exported and imported by a country?

(1) Current Account (2) Capital Account

(3) Financial Account (4) Reserve Account

151. What is the primary focus of the Capital Account in the BOP?

(1) Recording international trade in goods and services

(2) Measuring financial investments and capital transfers

(3) Monitoring government expenditures

(4) Assessing domestic production levels

152. Which component of the BOP includes foreign aid, grants, and remittances?

(1) Current Account (2) Capital Account

(3) Financial Account (4) Reserve Account

153. How does a trade surplus impact a country's BOP?

(1) It increases the Current Account balance

(2) It decreases the Capital Account balance

(3) It has no impact on the BOP

(4) It reduces the Financial Account balance

154. What is the significance of the Financial Account in the BOP?

(1) It records international trade in goods and services

(2) It measures financial investments and capital transfers

(3) It monitors government expenditures

(4) It assesses domestic production levels

155. Which transaction would contribute to a debit entry in the BOP?

(1) Export of goods

(2) Receipt of foreign aid

(3) Import of services

(4) Repayment of a loan to a foreign entity

156. What is the purpose of the Reserve Account in the BOP?

(1) To record international trade in goods and services

(2) To measure financial investments and capital transfers

(3) To hold official reserves such as gold and foreign currencies

(4) To assess domestic production levels

157. How does a country achieve a trade surplus in the Current Account?

(1) By exporting more goods and services than it imports

(2) By importing more goods and services than it exports

(3) By increasing government expenditures

(4) By reducing foreign aid and grants

158. What does the term "capital transfers" refer to in the BOP context?

(1) Financial investments between countries
(2) Movements of financial capital within a country
(3) One-time transfers of ownership of assets and liabilities
(4) Trade in goods and services

159. How does a country achieve a trade deficit in the Current Account?
(1) By exporting more goods and services than it imports
(2) By importing more goods and services than it exports
(3) By increasing government expenditures
(4) By reducing foreign aid and grants

160. What is the primary impact of a trade deficit on a country's BOP?
(1) It increases the Current Account balance
(2) It decreases the Capital Account balance
(3) It reduces the Financial Account balance
(4) It decreases the Reserve Account balance

161. Which of the following is an example of a capital transfer in the BOP?
(1) Payment for imported goods
(2) Payment for services provided by a foreign entity
(3) Debt repayment to a foreign lender
(4) Inheritance received from a foreign relative

162. What is the role of the Financial Account in the BOP?
(1) To record international trade in goods and services
(2) To measure financial investments and capital transfers
(3) To monitor government expenditures
(4) To assess domestic production levels

163. How does foreign aid impact the Current Account in the BOP?
(1) It increases the Current Account balance
(2) It decreases the Capital Account balance
(3) It has no impact on the BOP
(4) It reduces the Financial Account balance

164. What is the significance of the Current Account balance in the BOP?
(1) It represents the overall financial position of a country
(2) It measures financial investments and capital transfers
(3) It assesses the flow of goods and services in and out of a country
(4) It monitors government expenditures

165. How does a country achieve a surplus in the Capital Account of the BOP?
(1) By reducing financial investments and capital transfers
(2) By increasing financial investments and capital transfers
(3) By decreasing the flow of goods and services
(4) By reducing government expenditures

166. What is the impact of a surplus in the Capital Account on a country's overall BOP?
(1) It improves the overall BOP position
(2) It worsens the overall BOP position
(3) It has no impact on the overall BOP position
(4) It decreases the Current Account balance

167. Which of the following transactions would contribute to a credit entry in the BOP?
(1) Export of goods
(2) Import of services
(3) Repayment of a loan to a foreign entity
(4) Receipt of foreign aid

Directions: Each of the following items consists of two statements, one labelled as Assertion (A) and other labelled as Reason (R). You are to examine these two statements carefully and decide if the (A) and the (R) are individually true and if so, whether (R) is the correct explanation of (A). Select your answers to these items using the codes given below:
(1) Both (A) and (R) are true, and the (R) is the correct explanation of the (A).
(2) Both (A) and (R) are true, but the (R) is not the correct explanation of the (A).
(3) (A) is true, but the (R) is false.
(4) Both (A) and (R) are false.

168. Assertion (A): The Balance of Payments (BOP) is primarily concerned with monitoring domestic production levels.
Reason (R): BOP focuses on assessing the flow of goods and services in and out of a country.

169. Assertion (A): A trade surplus in the Current Account leads to an increase in the Financial Account balance.
Reason (R): A trade surplus indicates higher exports than imports, leading to increased financial inflows.

170. **Assertion (A):** Capital transfers in the BOP involve continuous flows of financial capital between countries.
Reason (R): Capital transfers in the BOP refer to one-time transfers of ownership of assets and liabilities.

171. **Assertion (A):** A trade deficit in the Current Account has no impact on the Financial Account balance.
Reason (R): A trade deficit indicates higher imports than exports, leading to decreased financial inflows.

172. **Assertion (A):** The Capital Account in the BOP represents the overall financial position of a country.
Reason (R): The Capital Account measures financial investments and capital transfers.

173. What is the highest level of regional economic integration?
(1) Free Trade Area (2) Customs Union
(3) Common Market (4) Economic Union

174. Which level of regional economic integration involves a common external trade policy?
(1) Free Trade Area (2) Customs Union
(3) Common Market (4) Economic Union

175. What is the primary goal of regional economic integration?
(1) To create trade barriers between member countries
(2) To promote economic cooperation and integration
(3) To discourage international trade
(4) To limit the movement of goods and services

176. Which effect occurs when a regional trade agreement leads to the diversion of trade from more efficient external suppliers to less efficient internal suppliers?
(1) Trade Creation Effect
(2) Trade Diversion Effect
(3) Trade Neutral Effect
(4) Trade Expansion Effect

177. Which level of regional economic integration allows for the free movement of goods, services, and factors of production among member countries?
(1) Free Trade Area (2) Customs Union
(3) Common Market (4) Economic Union

178. What is the primary characteristic of a Free Trade Area (FTA)?
(1) Common external trade policy
(2) Elimination of tariffs and quotas within the region
(3) Free movement of factors of production
(4) Coordination of monetary policies

179. Which regional economic integration level involves a common currency and a common monetary policy?
(1) Free Trade Area (2) Customs Union
(3) Common Market (4) Economic Union

180. What is the primary difference between a Customs Union and a Common Market?
(1) Customs Union involves the free movement of factors of production, while a Common Market does not.
(2) Common Market involves a common external trade policy, while a Customs Union does not.
(3) Customs Union involves the elimination of tariffs and quotas, while a Common Market does not.
(4) Common Market involves the free movement of factors of production, while a Customs Union does not.

181. Which regional trade agreement is also known as the European Common Market?
(1) NAFTA (2) ASEAN
(3) EU (4) SAARC

182. Which regional economic integration level involves a common external tariff and a common trade policy toward non-member countries?
(1) Free Trade Area (2) Customs Union
(3) Common Market (4) Economic Union

183. Which organisation is the Association of Southeast Asian Nations?
(1) EU (2) NAFTA
(3) ASEAN (4) SAARC

184. What is the main objective of SAARC (South Asian Association for Regional Cooperation)?
(1) To promote economic cooperation among South American countries
(2) To facilitate regional economic integration in Southeast Asia
(3) To enhance economic collaboration among South Asian countries
(4) To establish a common market in North America

185. Which regional trade agreement aims to eliminate barriers to trade and promote economic cooperation among North American countries?

(1) EU (2) NAFTA
(3) ASEAN (4) SAARC

186. What is the main characteristic of a Free Trade Area (FTA)?
(1) Common external trade policy
(2) Elimination of tariffs and quotas within the region
(3) Free movement of factors of production
(4) Coordination of monetary policies

187. Which effect occurs when a regional trade agreement leads to an increase in overall economic welfare due to the creation of new trade opportunities?
(1) Trade Creation Effect
(2) Trade Diversion Effect
(3) Trade Neutral Effect
(4) Trade Expansion Effect

188. What is the primary goal of the European Union (EU)?
(1) To promote economic cooperation in North America
(2) To establish a common market in Southeast Asia
(3) To achieve political and economic integration among European countries
(4) To enhance economic collaboration in South America

189. Which regional trade agreement involves the United States, Canada, and Mexico?
(1) EU (2) NAFTA
(3) ASEAN (4) SAARC

190. Which regional economic integration level allows for the coordination of fiscal and monetary policies among member countries?
(1) Free Trade Area (2) Customs Union
(3) Common Market (4) Economic Union

191. Which of the following is an example of a Customs Union?
(1) NAFTA (2) EU
(3) ASEAN (4) SAARC

192. What is the main objective of NAFTA (North American Free Trade Agreement)?
(1) To promote economic cooperation in Southeast Asia
(2) To achieve political and economic integration among European countries
(3) To eliminate barriers to trade and enhance economic collaboration in North America
(4) To establish a common market in South America

Directions: Each of the following items consists of two statements, one labelled as Assertion (A) and other labelled as Reason (R). You are to examine these two statements carefully and decide if the (A) and the (R) are individually true and if so, whether (R) is the correct explanation of (A). Select your answers to these items using the codes given below:
(1) Both (A) and (R) are true, and the (R) is the correct explanation of the (A).
(2) Both (A) and (R) are true, but the (R) is not the correct explanation of the (A).
(3) (A) is true, but the (R) is false.
(4) Both (A) and (R) are false.

193. Assertion (A): A Common Market involves the free movement of goods, services, and factors of production.
Reason (R): A Common Market is a higher level of economic integration than a Customs Union.

194. Assertion (A): ASEAN aims to achieve political and economic integration among Southeast Asian countries.
Reason (R): ASEAN primarily focuses on promoting economic cooperation in South America.

195. Assertion (A): NAFTA involves a common external tariff and a common trade policy toward non-member countries.
Reason (R): NAFTA is a Free Trade Area with no common external trade policy.

196. Assertion (A): The European Union (EU) has the goal of promoting economic cooperation in Asia.
Reason (R): The EU aims to achieve political and economic integration among European countries.

197. Assertion (A): The Trade Diversion Effect occurs when a regional trade agreement leads to increased overall economic welfare.
Reason (R): The Trade Diversion Effect results from the creation of new trade opportunities.

198. What is the primary purpose of the IMF?
(1) To promote international trade
(2) To provide financial assistance and stability to member countries
(3) To regulate global commodity prices
(4) To facilitate regional economic integration

199. Which institution focuses on poverty reduction and development projects in middle-income and creditworthy low-income countries?
(1) World Bank (2) IMF
(3) UNCTAD (4) WTO

200. What is the main function of the World Bank?
(1) To regulate global financial markets
(2) To provide short-term financial assistance to countries facing balance of payments problems
(3) To promote long-term economic development and poverty reduction
(4) To establish international trade agreements

201. Which organisation aims to promote international trade and development and address the special needs of developing countries?
(1) IMF (2) World Bank
(3) UNCTAD (4) WTO

202. In what year was the IMF established?
(1) 1944 (2) 1951
(3) 1960 (4) 1971

203. What is the IMF's primary tool for providing financial assistance to member countries facing balance of payments problems?
(1) Structural Adjustment Programs
(2) Special Drawing Rights (SDRs)
(3) International Reserves
(4) Poverty Reduction Strategy Papers

204. Which institution is often referred to as the "lender of last resort"?
(1) World Bank (2) IMF
(3) UNCTAD (4) WTO

205. What is the main source of funding for the World Bank?
(1) Member contributions
(2) Bond issues
(3) Special Drawing Rights (SDRs)
(4) Corporate donations

206. Which UN agency focuses on trade and development issues, including promoting the interests of developing countries in the global economic system?
(1) UNICEF (2) UNDP
(3) UNCTAD (4) UNESCO

207. What is the primary purpose of the World Bank's International Finance Corporation (IFC)?
(1) To provide financial assistance to middle-income countries
(2) To promote private sector investment in developing countries
(3) To regulate global financial markets
(4) To address global environmental issues

208. What is a key function of the IMF's Structural Adjustment Programs (SAPs)?
(1) Promoting short-term economic stability
(2) Facilitating regional economic integration
(3) Encouraging government spending
(4) Implementing long-term development projects

209. Which organisation provides trade-related technical assistance and capacity-building support to developing countries?
(1) IMF (2) World Bank
(3) UNCTAD (4) WTO

210. How does the IMF aim to achieve exchange rate stability among member countries?
(1) By fixing exchange rates for all member currencies
(2) By allowing member countries to freely float their currencies
(3) By establishing a common global currency
(4) By coordinating exchange rate policies

211. What is the primary role of the IMF's Poverty Reduction and Growth Trust (PRGT)?
(1) To provide short-term financial assistance to member countries
(2) To promote long-term economic development and poverty reduction
(3) To regulate global commodity prices
(4) To facilitate regional economic integration

212. In which year was the World Bank established?
(1) 1944 (2) 1951
(3) 1960 (4) 1945

213. What is the primary function of the UNCTAD's Division on Investment and Enterprise?
(1) To promote international trade agreements
(2) To provide financial assistance to developing countries
(3) To regulate global financial markets
(4) To enhance the contribution of investment to development

214. Which organisation aims to ensure the stability of the international monetary and financial system?
(1) World Bank (2) IMF
(3) UNCTAD (4) WTO

215. What is the primary focus of the World Bank's International Development Association (IDA)?
(1) Providing short-term financial assistance to middle-income countries
(2) Promoting private sector investment in developing countries

(3) Addressing global environmental issues
(4) Offering concessional loans and grants to the world's poorest countries

216. Which UN agency is responsible for coordinating global efforts to achieve sustainable development goals?
(1) UNDP (2) UNICEF
(3) UNCTAD (4) UNEP

Directions: Each of the following items consists of two statements, one labelled as Assertion (A) and other labelled as Reason (R). You are to examine these two statements carefully and decide if the (A) and the (R) are individually true and if so, whether (R) is the correct explanation of (A). Select your answers to these items using the codes given below:
(1) Both (A) and (R) are true, and the (R) is the correct explanation of the (A).
(2) Both (A) and (R) are true, but the (R) is not the correct explanation of the (A).
(3) (A) is true, but the (R) is false.
(4) Both (A) and (R) are false.

217. Assertion (A): The IMF primarily focuses on promoting long-term economic development and poverty reduction.
Reason (R): The IMF provides financial assistance and stability to member countries facing balance of payments problems.

218. Assertion (A): The World Bank's International Finance Corporation (IFC) promotes private sector investment in developing countries.
Reason (R): The IFC is the World Bank's primary tool for providing financial assistance to middle-income countries.

219. Assertion (A): UNCTAD focuses on promoting the interests of developed countries in the global economic system.
Reason (R): UNCTAD provides concessional loans and grants to the world's poorest countries.

220. Assertion (A): The IMF's Structural Adjustment Programs (SAPs) primarily aim to implement long-term development projects.
Reason (R): SAPs are designed to promote short-term economic stability.

221. Assertion (A): The World Bank's International Development Association (IDA) provides concessional loans and grants to the world's poorest countries.
Reason (R): IDA's focus is on promoting private sector investment in developing countries.

222. When was the World Trade Organisation (WTO) established?
(1) 1944 (2) 1951
(3) 1995 (4) 2000

223. What is the primary objective of the WTO?
(1) To regulate global financial markets
(2) To promote long-term economic development
(3) To facilitate regional economic integration
(4) To ensure the smooth flow of international trade

224. Which round of multilateral trade negotiations led to the establishment of the WTO?
(1) Kennedy Round (2) Tokyo Round
(3) Uruguay Round (4) Doha Round

225. What is the primary function of the WTO's Dispute Settlement Body (DSB)?
(1) To negotiate trade agreements
(2) To provide financial assistance to developing countries
(3) To settle disputes among member countries
(4) To monitor global commodity prices

226. Which agreement aims to regulate the trade of agricultural products and address issues such as subsidies and market access?
(1) GATS (2) TRIPS
(3) Agriculture Agreement
(4) TRIMS

227. What does GATS stand for in the context of the WTO?
(1) General Agreement on Tariffs and Subsidies
(2) General Agreement on Trade in Services
(3) General Agreement on Textiles and Standards
(4) General Agreement on Technology and Science

228. Which agreement focuses on the protection of intellectual property rights, including patents and copyrights?
(1) GATS (2) TRIPS
(3) Agriculture Agreement
(4) TRIMS

229. What does TRIMS stand for in the context of the WTO?
(1) Trade-Related Investment Measures
(2) Trade-Related Intellectual Property Standards

(3) Trade-Related Investment Standards
(4) Trade-Related Intellectual Property Measures

230. Which round of WTO negotiations aims to address issues related to trade barriers, agriculture, and services?
(1) Kennedy Round (2) Doha Round
(3) Tokyo Round (4) Uruguay Round

231. What is the primary goal of the WTO's Trade-Related Aspects of Intellectual Property Rights (TRIPS) Agreement?
(1) To eliminate subsidies in the agricultural sector
(2) To regulate trade in services
(3) To protect intellectual property rights globally
(4) To address trade-related investment measures

232. Which agreement aims to prevent discriminatory and trade-distorting measures that affect international investment?
(1) GATS (2) TRIPS
(3) Agriculture Agreement
(4) TRIMS

233. What is the primary focus of the WTO's General Agreement on Tariffs and Trade (GATT)?
(1) Regulation of trade in services
(2) Protection of intellectual property rights
(3) Elimination of tariffs and trade barriers
(4) Promotion of long-term economic development

234. Which agreement addresses the issue of trade-distorting subsidies in the agricultural sector?
(1) GATS (2) TRIPS
(3) Agriculture Agreement
(4) TRIMS

235. What is the primary purpose of the WTO's General Council?
(1) To negotiate trade agreements
(2) To provide financial assistance to developing countries
(3) To settle disputes among member countries
(4) To oversee the implementation of trade agreements

236. Which agreement focuses on measures that affect the trade of goods and services through their impact on foreign investment?
(1) GATS (2) TRIPS
(3) Agriculture Agreement
(4) TRIMS

237. In which city is the headquarters of the World Trade Organisation (WTO) located?
(1) Geneva (2) New York
(3) Paris (4) Brussels

238. What is the primary function of the WTO's Trade Policy Review Body (TPRB)?
(1) To negotiate trade agreements
(2) To provide financial assistance to developing countries
(3) To settle disputes among member countries
(4) To conduct regular reviews of member countries' trade policies

239. Which agreement aims to regulate the trade of services, including sectors such as finance, telecommunications, and education?
(1) GATS (2) TRIPS
(3) Agriculture Agreement
(4) TRIMS

240. What is the primary purpose of the WTO's Committee on Trade and Development?
(1) To negotiate trade agreements
(2) To provide financial assistance to developing countries
(3) To settle disputes among member countries
(4) To address the trade concerns of developing countries

241. Which agreement aims to promote fair competition and prevent anti-competitive practices in international trade?
(1) GATS (2) TRIPS
(3) Agriculture Agreement
(4) TRIMS

242. **Assertion (A):** The WTO's Dispute Settlement Body (DSB) primarily negotiates trade agreements.

Reason (R): The DSB is responsible for settling disputes among member countries.
(1) Both (A) and (R) are true, and the (R) is the correct explanation of the (A).
(2) Both (A) and (R) are true, but the (R) is not the correct explanation of the (A).
(3) (A) is true, but the (R) is false.
(4) Both (A) and (R) are false.

ANSWERS

1. (3)	**2.** (1)	**3.** (2)	**4.** (2)	**5.** (2)	**6.** (3)	**7.** (2)	**8.** (2)	**9.** (2)	**10.** (3)
11. (3)	**12.** (2)	**13.** (2)	**14.** (2)	**15.** (2)	**16.** (2)	**17.** (1)	**18.** (2)	**19.** (1)	**20.** (2)
21. (3)	**22.** (3)	**23.** (3)	**24.** (3)	**25.** (1)	**26.** (3)	**27.** (2)	**28.** (2)	**29.** (2)	**30.** (2)
31. (4)	**32.** (2)	**33.** (2)	**34.** (3)	**35.** (3)	**36.** (2)	**37.** (3)	**38.** (2)	**39.** (4)	**40.** (3)
41. (1)	**42.** (2)	**43.** (2)	**44.** (2)	**45.** (4)	**46.** (3)	**47.** (3)	**48.** (2)	**49.** (2)	**50.** (2)
51. (3)	**52.** (2)	**53.** (2)	**54.** (3)	**55.** (2)	**56.** (3)	**57.** (3)	**58.** (3)	**59.** (2)	**60.** (3)
61. (3)	**62.** (2)	**63.** (3)	**64.** (3)	**65.** (2)	**66.** (3)	**67.** (2)	**68.** (4)	**69.** (4)	**70.** (3)
71. (4)	**72.** (3)	**73.** (3)	**74.** (2)	**75.** (3)	**76.** (4)	**77.** (4)	**78.** (1)	**79.** (2)	**80.** (4)
81. (4)	**82.** (4)	**83.** (1)	**84.** (3)	**85.** (3)	**86.** (3)	**87.** (4)	**88.** (1)	**89.** (3)	**90.** (3)
91. (4)	**92.** (3)	**93.** (4)	**94.** (3)	**95.** (4)	**96.** (3)	**97.** (3)	**98.** (3)	**99.** (3)	**100.** (2)
101. (4)	**102.** (2)	**103.** (4)	**104.** (2)	**105.** (1)	**106.** (2)	**107.** (3)	**108.** (4)	**109.** (3)	**110.** (4)
111. (2)	**112.** (3)	**113.** (3)	**114.** (4)	**115.** (3)	**116.** (2)	**117.** (3)	**118.** (3)	**119.** (3)	**120.** (1)
121. (3)	**122.** (3)	**123.** (3)	**124.** (4)	**125.** (2)	**126.** (4)	**127.** (1)	**128.** (3)	**129.** (3)	**130.** (1)
131. (3)	**132.** (4)	**133.** (3)	**134.** (2)	**135.** (2)	**136.** (3)	**137.** (3)	**138.** (3)	**139.** (3)	**140.** (3)
141. (3)	**142.** (3)	**143.** (4)	**144.** (3)	**145.** (3)	**146.** (4)	**147.** (3)	**148.** (2)	**149.** (2)	**150.** (1)
151. (2)	**152.** (1)	**153.** (1)	**154.** (2)	**155.** (3)	**156.** (3)	**157.** (1)	**158.** (3)	**159.** (2)	**160.** (4)
161. (4)	**162.** (2)	**163.** (1)	**164.** (3)	**165.** (2)	**166.** (1)	**167.** (1)	**168.** (3)	**169.** (2)	**170.** (3)
171. (4)	**172.** (3)	**173.** (4)	**174.** (2)	**175.** (2)	**176.** (2)	**177.** (3)	**178.** (2)	**179.** (4)	**180.** (4)
181. (3)	**182.** (2)	**183.** (3)	**184.** (3)	**185.** (2)	**186.** (2)	**187.** (1)	**188.** (3)	**189.** (2)	**190.** (4)
191. (2)	**192.** (3)	**193.** (1)	**194.** (3)	**195.** (4)	**196.** (3)	**197.** (4)	**198.** (2)	**199.** (1)	**200.** (3)
201. (3)	**202.** (1)	**203.** (2)	**204.** (2)	**205.** (2)	**206.** (3)	**207.** (2)	**208.** (1)	**209.** (4)	**210.** (4)
211. (2)	**212.** (1)	**213.** (4)	**214.** (2)	**215.** (4)	**216.** (1)	**217.** (3)	**218.** (2)	**219.** (4)	**220.** (3)
221. (3)	**222.** (3)	**223.** (4)	**224.** (3)	**225.** (3)	**226.** (3)	**227.** (2)	**228.** (2)	**229.** (1)	**230.** (2)
231. (3)	**232.** (4)	**233.** (3)	**234.** (3)	**235.** (4)	**236.** (4)	**237.** (1)	**238.** (4)	**239.** (1)	**240.** (4)
241. (4)	**242.** (3)								

UNIT

2

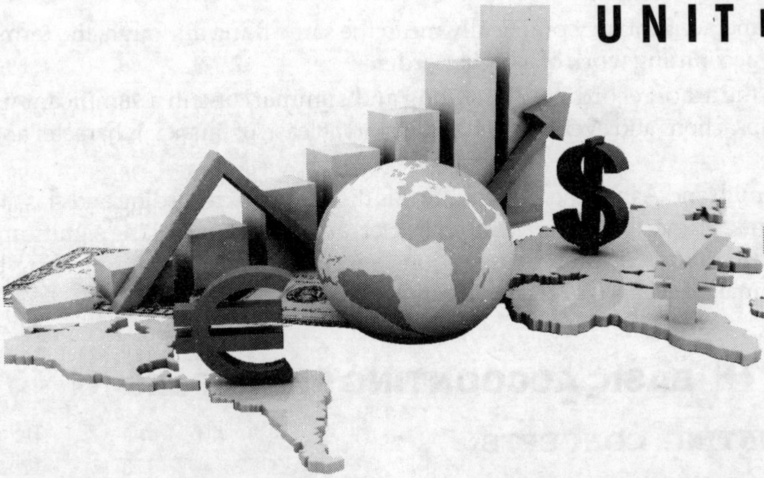

ACCOUNTING AND AUDITING

SYLLABUS

- Basic accounting principles; concepts and postulates
- Partnership Accounts: Admission, Retirement, Death, Dissolution and Insolvency of partnership firms
- Corporate Accounting: Issue, forfeiture and reissue of shares; Liquidation of companies; Acquisition, merger, amalgamation and reconstruction of companies
- Holding company accounts
- Cost and Management Accounting: Marginal costing and Break-even analysis; Standard costing; Budgetary control; Process costing; Activity Based Costing (ABC); Costing for decision-making; Life cycle costing, Target costing, Kaizen costing and JIT
- Financial Statements Analysis: Ratio analysis; Funds flow Analysis; Cash flow analysis
- Human Resources Accounting; Inflation Accounting; Environmental Accounting
- Indian Accounting Standards and IFRS
- Auditing: Independent financial audit; Vouching; Verification ad valuation of assets and liabilities; Audit of financial statements and audit report; Cost audit
- Recent Trends in Auditing: Management audit; Energy audit; Environment audit; Systems audit; Safety audit

ACCOUNTING

Book keeping is the art of keeping accounts in a regular and systematic manner. This means that a firm has to record the events affecting it in such a way that a correct picture can emerge whenever needed. 'Events' in a firm need not be very big; usually they are small but, sometimes, they are big. Purchase of machinery worth Rs. 5 lakhs and stationary worth Rs. 5 are both events. A systematic record of all events, big and small, is essential.

Book keeping and accountancy practically mean the same thing although, the term accountancy is usually used for accounting work of a higher order.

Accounting is the art of recording, classifying and summarising in a significant manner and in terms of money, transactions and events which are, in part at least, of financial character and interpreting the results thereof.

According to Smith and Ashburne, "Accounting is the science of recording and classifying business transactions & events, primarily of a financial character, and the act of making significant summaries, analyses and interpretations of those transactions and events and communicating the results to persons who must make decisions or form judgement."

BASIC ACCOUNTING PRINCIPLES

BASIC ACCOUNTING CONCEPTS

Business Entity Concept. Accountants treat a business as distinct from the persons who own it; it then becomes possible to record transactions of the business with the proprietor, also without such a distribution, the affairs of the firm will be all mixed up with the private affairs of the proprietor and the true picture of the firm will not be available.

This concept has now been extended to accounting separately for various divisions for a firm in order to ascertain the result for each division separately. It has been of immense value in determining results by each responsibility center - Responsibility Accounting.

Money Measurement Concept. This assumption implies that only those transactions and events are recorded in accounting which can be expressed in monetary terms. An event, even though important like a quarrel between the production manager and the sales manager, will not be recorded unless its monetary effect can be measured with a fair degree of accuracy. It should be remembered that money enables various things of diverse nature to be added up together and dealt with. The use of a building and the use of clerical services can be aggregated only through money values and not otherwise.

Cost concept. Transactions are entered in books of account at the moments actually involved. Suppose a firm purchases a piece of land for Rs. 150000 but considers it as worth Rs. 300000. The purchase of land will be recorded at Rs. 150000 and not any more. This is one of the most important concepts, it prevents arbitrary values being put on transactions chiefly those resulting in acquisition of assets. Of course, sometimes accountants have necessarily to be satisfied with an estimate only. If we take an example of machinery: The amount of depreciation has to be charged to accounts each year in respect of machinery . The amount has to be an estimate since the future life of the machinery cannot be known precisely.

Going Concern Concept. It is assumed that the business will exist for the foreseeable future and transactions are recorded from this point of view. It is this that necessitates distinction between expenditure that will render benefit over a long period and that whose benefit will be exhausted quickly, say within the year. Of course, if it is certain that the business will exist only for a limited time, the accounting record will keep the expected life in the view.

A firm is said to be a going concern when there is neither the intention nor the necessity to wind up its affairs or curtail substantially the scale of its operations. In other words, it should continue to operate at its present scale.

Dual - Aspect Concept. Each transaction has two aspects; if a business has acquired an asset, it must have resulted in one of the following:

(i) some other asset has been given up;

(ii) the obligation to pay for it has arisen

(iii) There has been a profit, leading to an increase in the amount that the business owes to the proprietor or

(iv) the proprietor has contributed money for the acquisition of the asset.

The reverse is also true. If, for instance, there is an increase in the money owed to others, there must have been an increase in assets or a loss. At any time

Assets = Liabilities + Capital or

Capital = Assets - liabilities

In other words, capital, *i.e.* the owner's share of the assets of the firm is always what is left out of asset after paying off outsiders.

A transaction must affect one of the things mentioned above.

Income or profits arises only when there has been an increase in the owners share of the assets of the firm (called owner's equity) but not if the increase has resulted from money contributed by the owners himself. Any increase in the owner's equity is called revenue and anything that reduces the owner's equity is expense (or loss); profit results only where the total of revenues exceeds the total of expenses or losses.

Realisation Concept. Accounting is a historical record of transaction; it records what has happened. It does not anticipate events, though anticipated adverse effect of events that have already occurred are usually recorded. This is of great importance in stopping business firms from inflating their profits by recording sales and incomes that are only likely to accrue unless money has been realised either cash has been received or a legal obligation to pay has been assumed by the customer no sale can be said to have taken place and no profits or income can be said to have arisen.

Accrual Concept. When an event takes place or a transaction is entered into, its consequences are bounded to follow. For example, if one borrows Rs. 100000 @ 15% P.A. at the end of the year Rs. 15000 will become due as interest. If the amount is paid, the record will certainly show it. If, however, the amount is not yet paid, there is the liability to pay the amount and there being no corresponding increase in the total assets, the capital will stand reduced. This must be brought into the record. The accrual concept demands that all transactions or events, not yet settled in cash, must be taken into account.

Periodicity Postulate. Truly speaking the measurement of income of a business entity can be accurately made only when it is liquidated. But the going concern postulate assumes the continuity of business for many years. The owners, investors, Government *etc.* are impatient and unwilling to wait till the business is terminated. They are interested in regular reports and accounts at proper intervals to know "how things are going?" This means that the financial statements must be prepared on a periodic basis rather than waiting until the business is liquidated.

To facilitate the preparation of financial statements on a periodic basis, accountants follow periodic postulate. According to this postulate, the life of the business is divided into appropriate segments for understanding the result shown by the business. Such a segment or time interval is called 'accounting period', which is usually of one year. Accounting period is the interval of time at the end of which income or revenue statement and balance sheets are prepared in order to show the result of operations and change in resources.

Matching Concept. It is based on periodic postulate. The primary objective of a business is to earn profit. It is for this reason that major share of attention of the accountant is absorbed involving technique for measuring profit. In order to measure the profits for the period, revenues should be matched with the costs (expenses) of that period. Thus matching concept implies the matching expenses against related revenues.

Basically matching concept involves two questions (a) what criteria should be used as a basis for associating costs with present and future periods and (b) how shall the expiration of products and service factors be measured.

The various bases used for determining the period in which the revenue is realised are sales basis, cash basis and the production basis. The second step is to find out the costs and expenses to be matched with revenues. Accountant must estimate the life span of the asset and allocate a part of the expired cost occur during that accounting period until its useful life is ended. Matching concept also requires the application of personal judgement in making the estimates for doubtful debts, discounts etc.

CAPITAL AND REVENUE TRANSACTIONS

The transactions in accounting may be classified into:

1. **Capital transactions.** The transactions which provide benefits or supply services to a business unit for more than one year or one operating cycle of business are known as capital transactions.
2. **Revenue transactions.** The transactions which provide benefit or supply services to a business unit for one accounting period only are known as revenue transactions.

These transactions are further divided into expenditures and receipts as shown below:

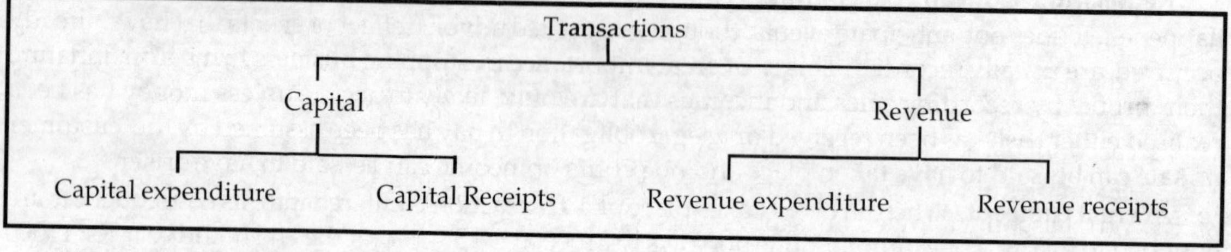

(a) **Capital Expenditure.** The capital expenditure is that expenditure the benefits of which is enjoyed or consumed not in one year only but over many years. It is the expenditure incurred which results in the purchase or acquisition of asset and properties which may be used for many years. Such an expenditure is of a non-recurring nature. The following expenditures are usually treated as capital expenditure.

(i) Any expenditures which results in the acquisition of fixed assets such as land, buildings, plant and machinery, furniture, plants etc.

(ii) Any expenditure incurred in connection with the acquisition of any asset, its transportation, its erection *etc.* such as brokerage paid in buying land, the freight or cartage paid to workers for installing the machine.

(iii) Any expenditure incurred in connection for the extension or improvement of any assets.

(iv) Expenditure which increases the revenue earning capacity of business, such as cost of making additions on the building or the amount spent on renovation of the old machinery.

(v) Expenditure incurred to acquire the right to carry on business, such as preliminary expenses, cost of patent.

(vi) Legal charges incurred in connection with acquiring or defending suits for protecting fixed assets, right *etc.*

All items of a capital nature are shown in the Balance Sheet. The main purpose of incurring such expenditure is to earn income over a period of years or increase the earning capacity of the business concern with the aid of such expenditure.

(b) **Revenue Expenditure.**

When the benefits of an expenditure is limited to the year in which it is incurred, it is treated as revenue expenditure. So all expenses which are incurred during the regular course of business are regarded as revenue expenditure. In other words, any expenditure which is not a capital expenditure and which is incurred for carrying the day to day business activities is called revenue expenditure. The following types of expenses are treated as revenue expenditure:

(i) Expenses that are incurred in day to day running of business such as wages, salaries, rent, postage, insurance etc.

(ii) Expenditure incurred for buying goods for resale.

(iii) Expenditure incurred for maintaining the assets such as repairs.

(iv) Depreciation on fixed assets.

(v) Interest on loan taken for running the business.

All items of revenue nature are shown in profit and loss account. The purpose of incurring such expenditure is to maintain the business. The amount spend is relatively small, but not always the benefit of such an expenditure is exhausted in a short period, in any case not more than a year.

There is one important aspect of revenue expenditure. It is as follows:

Deferred Revenue Expenditure. It is as follows:

Sometimes, it is perceived that the benefit of a revenue expenditure may be available beyond the current period. In such cases, the expenditure is classified as deferred revenue expenditure and is written off over a period of 3 to 4 years instead of charging it to the profit and loss account of the period in which it is incurred.

Examples of Deferred revenue expenditure are as follows :

(i) Discount allowed on issue of debentures.

(ii) Development expenditure of mines and minerals.

(iii) Expenditures on an advertisement campaign or a scientific expenditure.

(c) **Capital receipts.** Receipts of any amount is a capital receipt, if :

(i) It is realized from the sale of fixed assets such as plant and machinery, furniture, land, *etc.*

(ii) It is received by way of loan, capital (including premium in issue of shares) or contribution to capital fund of non-profit organizations, such as specific donation of life membership fees paid by members to the club.

(iii) It accrues in view to some sources of income.

(d) **Revenue Receipts.** A receipt would be revenue receipt, if:

(i) It accrues on account of sale of goods and services.

(ii) It is of commercial nature and yields some income to the business on a regular basis, such as royalty, consultancy fee *etc.*

(iii) It is of recurring nature such as interest on investments, dividend, rent of property, commission earned *etc.*

Distinction between Capital expenditure and Revenue expenditure

Capital expenditure	Revenue expenditure
1. It is incurred for acquisition of fixed assets.	1. It is incurred for running the business.
2. These are incurred in increasing the value of fixed assets.	2. They do not increase the value of fixed assets.
3. They increase the earning capacity of the business.	3. They are incurred to maintain the earning capacity of the business.
4. The benefit of such expenditure extends to more than one year.	4. The benefits is limited to one year only.
5. These expenses are of a non-recurring nature.	5. These expenses are of a recurring nature.
6. They are shown in the Balance Sheet.	6. They are shown in trading and P& L A/C.

The expenditure is capital or revenue expenditure can be explained with the following example:

Example.

Which of the following expenditures are capital, revenue and deferred revenue expenditure?

(a) Cost of air-conditioning in the office of the General Manager.
(b) Cost of overhauling and painting a second hand truck newly purchased.
(c) Cost of the annual taxes paid and the annual insurance premium paid on the truck mentioned above.
(d) Wages paid to workers for installation of machinery.
(e) Cost of making more exits in a cinema hall under orders of the Government.
(f) Cost of re-decorating a cinema hall.
(g) Cost of putting up a gallery in a theatre hall.
(h) Cost of acquiring the goodwill of an old firm.
(i) Cost of heavy advertisements for a new product and removal of works to a new and better site.
(j) Temporary rooms constructed for storing raw materials for the construction of a big building.
(k) A machinery costing Rs. 5000 has to be sold. It realises Rs. 3000. A new machine is purchased for Rs. 9000.

Solution.

(a) This is capital expenditure because the benefit of this expenditure will be available for a number of years. In any case, the machine which has been installed will be there and can be disposed of whenever desired.
(b) When a second hand machine is purchased, all expenditure incurred in the beginning to make it fit for working is treated as capital expenditure. The value of the machine is increased by the amount spent. Therefore, the cost of overhauling and painting the truck will be capital expenditure.
(c) Annual taxes and annual premium paid on the truck are revenue expenditures because they do not add to the value of the truck and their benefit will be exhausted within the year.
(d) This is capital expenditure because it is, necessary to put the machine in working condition.
(e) Making more exits in a cinema hall does not increase the capacity of the hall and therefore, it should be treated as revenue expenditure.
(f) Cost of re-decorating a cinema hall is also not capital expenditure because it does not add to the capacity of the hall. But the cost is fairly heavy and the benefit will be there for a number of years. Therefore, the cost of re-decoration should be treated as deferred revenue expenditure.

(g) When a new gallery is put up, it will increase the number of seats in the hall. Therefore, this cost should be treated as capital expenditure.

(h) This is capital expenditure because the use of that firm's name will benefit the purchaser for a long time.

(i) This expenditure is heavy but not of capital nature because no new asset is acquired. But since the benefit of the expenditure will be available for a number of years, it should be treated as deferred revenue expenditure.

(j) The cost of construction of temporary rooms should be treated as capital expenditure because it is necessary for the construction of the main building. The cost of the rooms will be added to the cost of the building.

(k) There is a loss of Rs. 2000 on sale of the old machinery. This is revenue loss. Rs. 9000 has been spent on acquiring a new machinery. It is capital expenditure.

PARTNERSHIP ACCOUNTS

The Indian Partnership Act defines partnership as 'the relation between persons who have agreed to share the profits of a business carried on by all or any of them acting for all.' The essential features of partnership, therefore, are:

1. An association of two or more persons;
2. An agreement entered into by all persons concerned;
3. Existence of a business;
4. The carrying on of business by all or any of them acting for all;
5. Sharing of profit of the business (including losses).

From the accounts point of view, the main thing to remember is that the relations among the partners will be governed by natural agreement. The agreement is known as Partnership Deed. It should be comprehensive to avoid disputes later on. It is usual, therefore, to find the following clauses in a Partnership Deed :

1. The name of the firm and the nature of the partnership business.
2. The commencement and duration of the business.
3. The amount of capital to be contributed by each partner.
4. The rate of interest to be allowed to each partner on his capital and on his loan to the firm and to be charged on his drawings.
5. The disposal of profits, particularly the ratio in which profits are to be shared.
6. The amount to be allowed to each partner as drawings and the timings of such drawings.
7. Whether a partner will be allowed a salary.
8. Any variations in the usual rights and duties of partners.
9. The method by which goodwill is to be calculated on the retirement or death of a partner.
10. The procedure by which a partner may retire and the method of payment of his dues to him.
11. The basis of determination of the sum due to the executors of a deceased partner and the method of payment.
12. The treatment of losses arising out of the insolvency of a partner.
13. The procedure to be followed for settlement of disputes among partners.
14. Preparation of accounts and their audit.

The Deed has to be properly stamped.

Duties of Partners

(a) Every partner is bound to diligently carry on the business of the firm to the greatest common advantage. Unless the agreement provides, there is no salary.

(b) Every partner must be just and faithful to the other partners.

(c) A partner is bound to keep and render true, proper, and correct accounts of the partnership and must permit other partners to inspect and copy such accounts.

(d) Every partner is bound to indemnify the firm for any loss caused by his wilful neglect or fraud in the conduct of the business.

(e) A partner must not carry on a competing business, nor use the property of the firm for his private purposes. In both cases he must hand over to the firm any profit or gains made by him but he must himself suffer any loss that might have occurred.

(f) Every partner is bound to share the losses equally with the others.

(g) A partner is bound to act within the scope of his authority.

(h) No partner can assign or transfer his partnership interest to any other person so as to make him a partner in the business.

Powers of Partners. The above relates to relations among the partners themselves. When it comes to dealing with outsiders or third parties, the partners are supposed to have the power to act in certain matters and not to have such power in others. In other words, unless a public notice has been given to the contrary, certain contracts entered into by a partner on behalf of the partnership, even without consulting other partners, will be binding on the firm. In case of a trading firm, the implied powers of partners are the following:

(a) Buying and selling goods.

(b) Receiving payments on behalf of the firm and giving valid receipts.

(c) Drawing cheques, accepting and endorsing bills of exchange and promissory notes in the name of the firm.

(d) Borrowing money on behalf of the firm with or without pledging the stock in trade.

(e) Engaging servants for the business of the firm.

In certain cases a partner has no powers. This is to say that third parties cannot bind the firm unless the partners have agreed. These cases are:

(a) Submitting a dispute relating to the fine to arbitration.

(b) Opening a bank account on behalf of the firm in the name of a partner.

(c) Compromise or relinquishment of any claim or portion of claim by the firm.

(d) Withdrawal of a suit or proceedings filed on behalf of the firm.

(e) Admission of any liability in a suit of proceedings against the firm.

(f) Acquisition of immovable property belonging to the firm.

(g) Entering into partnership on behalf of the firm.

The rights, duties and powers of partners can be changed by mutual consent.

Kinds of Partners. Besides the usual partners who contribute to the capital of the firm and take part in its business, the following special types of partners may be noted.

(i) **Sleeping or Dormant Partner** is one who is in reality a partner but whose name does not appear in any way as partner and who is not known to outsiders as partner. He is liable to those third parties who subsequently discover that he was or is a partner. He has no duties to perform but he has the right of access to books of account and of examining and copying them.

(ii) **Nominal Partner** is a person whose name is used as if he were member of the firm, but who, really, is not a partner. He is liable to third parties for all acts of the firm as if he were a real partner.

(iii) **Partner in Profit Only** is one who gets a share of the profits and does not share losses. He is liable to outsiders. He does not take part in the management of the business.

(iv) **Partner by Estoppel or holding Out** is one who without really being a partner, so behaves as to lead others to believe him to be a partner. Similarly, if one is declared to be a partner and does not disclaim the partnership, one will be treated as partner by holding out. Such persons are liable to those third parties who extend credit to the firm on the belief that such persons are partners.

(v) **Sub-Partner** is one who gets a share of profits of the firm from one of the partners. A sub-partner has no rights against the firm and he is not liable for its debts.

(vi) **An Incoming Partner** is one who is newly admitted to the firm, is not liable for the debts and obligations of the firm incurred before his joining the firm unless he so agrees.

(vii) **A Retiring or Outgoing Partner** continues to be liable for obligations incurred before his retirement, and will continue to be liable even for future obligations if he does not give public notice of his retirement.

(viii) **Minor Partner.** A minor can be admitted to the benefits of an existing partnership with the consent of all the partners. The minor is not personally liable for the debts of the firm but his share in the partnership property and profits of the firm will be liable for the firm's debts and obligations. He can bring a suit for accounts and for his distributive share when he wants to sever his connections with the firm, but not otherwise. But he has the right of access to the accounts of the firm including the right to examine and copy. Within six months of his attaining majority or on his coming to know that he enjoys the benefits of partnership (whichever date is later), he has to elect whether or not he wants to continue as partner. He must give public notice of his decision not to continue as partner, otherwise he will be deemed to have elected to be a Full-fledged partner. On his election as a partner, he will become liable for the debts of the firm since he was admitted to the benefits of the firm. If he repudiates his partnership, all his liabilities will cease from the date of the public notice to this effect.

ADMISSION OF A PARTNER

When a new partner is admitted into a partnership, certain adjustments in accounts become necessary. Chiefly, this is because the new partner will acquire a share in the profits of the firm and because of this, the old partner will stand to lose. Suppose, A and B are partners sharing profits in the ratio 3 : 2. If their profits are Rs. 20,000, A will get Rs. 12,000 and B will get Rs. 8,000. If C is admitted and is given, one-fourth 'share in profits, then out of the Rs. 20,000 he will get Rs. 5,000. The remaining Rs. 15,000 will be divided between A and B; A will get Rs. 9,000 and B will get Rs. 6,000. Thus on C's admission A loses Rs. 3,000 per year and B loses Rs. 2,000 per year. C will have to compensate A and B for this loss. It is no argument to say that on C's admission the profits will not remain at Rs. 20,000; extra profits will arise and therefore, A and B will both get more than what they previously got. But it should be noted that the additional profits will be earned by the combined efforts of all the partners, A, B and C. Therefore, if A & B get a share of the extra profits they are not particularly obliged to C. Out of the present profits of Rs. 20,000 they have to give up a share in favour of C and, therefore, they are entitled to a compensation. The problem of the compensation is the chief problem while dealing with admission of a partner. This is tackled through goodwill.

(A) **Goodwill.** Goodwill is the value of the reputation of a firm in respect of profits expected in future over and above the normal rate of profits. The implication of the above is that there is always a certain normal rate of profit earned by various firms. A firm will be said to possess goodwill only if the future profits of the firm are expected to be more than this normal rate of profit. Suppose, a firm employs a capital of Rs. 1 lakh. The rate of profit earned by firms in general is 10%. If this firm earns Rs. 10,000 or less per year, there will be no goodwill for this firm. But if the profit earned is more than Rs. 10,000 say, Rs. 18,000, then the goodwill will attach to the extra Rs. 8,000. Usually this figure of extra profits (or super profits as it is known) will be multiplied by 3 or 4 or 5 representing the number of years' purchase of super profits. In examination problems, very often goodwill is not valued in this manner but may be valued as so many years' purchase of the average profits of a number of years. If, for instance, it is said that goodwill is to be valued at three years' purchase of five years' average profits, it means that, first of all, average for 5 years profits will be ascertained and then that average will be multiplied by three. The product will be the amount of goodwill. If the profits for 5 years total Rs. 50,000, the average comes to Rs. 10,000; three years' purchase of goodwill will be Rs. 30,000.

One can see that there can be no goodwill if the firm has not been working properly and that goodwill will exist only if the firm has worked hard and well. If a new partner joins the firm how will be enjoy the fruits of the past labours on the part of the previous partners. This is another reason why a new partner has to compensate the existing partners. Usually, therefore, when a new partner joins the firm, he has to bring in the required sum of capital as well as another sum of money representing the compensation for old partners. This sum will be based upon goodwill. If, in the above example, where goodwill has been valued at Rs. 30.000, the incoming partner is to have one-fifth share in future profits, he will be required to pay Rs. 6,000 in addition to whatever he has to bring in as his capital. This Rs. 6,000 belongs to old partners and will be credited to their Capital Accounts. However, it is not always necessary that the new partner should pay his share of goodwill in cash. There are various ways in which goodwill can be dealt with on the admission of a partner.

Following are the ways:

(i) ***Goodwill raised or when the new partner cannot pay his share of goodwill in cash.*** This means that goodwill is simply brought into books at its proper value. This is what is meant by raising goodwill. This is done by debiting goodwill and crediting the old partners in the old profit sharing ratio. Suppose, A and B carry on business sharing profits and loss in the ratio of 5 : 3. C is admitted and is given of profits. He pays Rs. 25,000 as his capital. But is unable to pay anything for goodwill which is valued at Rs. 40,000. In this case the entries will be

1.	Cash Account	Dr.	25,000	
	To C's Capital Account			25,000
	Amount brought in by C as his capital on his admission.			
2.	Goodwill Account	Dr.	40,000	
	To A's Capital Account			25,000
	To B's Capital Account			15,000
	Goodwill raised at its proper value in books and credited to A and B in their profit sharing ratio.			

The effect will be that the capitals of A and B will increase and there will be a new account, namely, Goodwill Account. This will appear in the Balance Sheet on the asset side.

A point to note is that if goodwill is already appearing in books, the entry is to be made for the difference only. Suppose, in the above case when goodwill has been valued at Rs. 40,000, goodwill already appears in books at Rs. 16,000. This means that Goodwill Account stands debited with this figure and that on C's admission this figure is to be raised to Rs. 40,000. This can be done by debiting goodwill account by another Rs. 24,000. Therefore, the entry will be

Goodwill Account	Dr.	24,000	
To A's Capital Account		15,000	
B's Capital Account			9,000

If the amount of goodwill already appearing in books is more than the present value, then it means that there is a loss to be suffered by the old partners. Suppose, goodwill is now valued at Rs. 40,000, but appears in books already at Rs. 48,000. This means that the Goodwill Account has to be credited by Rs. 8,000 in order to reduce it to Rs. 40,000. Both A and B will be debited in their profit sharing ratio. The entry is:

A's Capital Account	Dr.	5,000	
B's Capital Account	Dr.	3,000	
To Goodwill Account			8,000

In all the cases discussed above, Goodwill will appear at Rs. 40,000 after C's admission and will be shown in the Balance Sheet at this figure.

(ii) **Goodwill raised and written off immediately.** It may not be considered proper by a firm to continue to show goodwill in the Balance Sheet. This is because goodwill is an asset which can be realised or converted into cash only if the firm is dissolved. Therefore, if goodwill is raised on the admission of a partner, it is often written off immediately. This is done by debiting all partners, including the new partner, in the new profit sharing ratio and by crediting goodwill. Suppose, in the above case when goodwill is raised at Rs. 40,000, it has to be written off. The entry for writing off will be

A's Capital Account	Dr.	20,000	
B's Capital Account	Dr.	12,000	
C's Capital Account	Dr.	8,000	
The Goodwill Account			40,000

With this entry the Goodwill Account will cease to exist. Capital Accounts of all partners are reduced. Goodwill, naturally, will not appear in the Balance Sheet.

(iii) **Goodwill brought in cash.** In this case, Cash Account is debited and Goodwill Account is credited. Then, immediately, the Goodwill Account is transferred to the Capital Accounts of 'the old partners in the old profit sharing ratio'. Suppose, A and B carry on business sharing profits and losses in the ratio of 3 : 1. C is admitted and is given one-fifth share of profits. He is required to bring in Rs. 20,000 as capital and his share of goodwill 'which is– valued at Rs. 25,000'. In this case C will have to pay Rs. 5,000 for goodwill, i.e., one-fifth of Rs. 25,000. The entries will be as follow:

1. Cash Account	Dr.	25,000	
To C's Capital Account			20,000
To Goodwill Account			5,000
Amount brought in by C as his capital and goodwill.			

2. Goodwill Account Dr. 5,000
   To A's Capital Account 3,750
   To B's Capital Account 1,250
   Goodwill brought in by C credited to A and B in their profit sharing ratio.

The net effect of these two entries is that there is an increase of Rs. 25,000 in cash and an increase of Rs. 3,750 in the Capital Account of A, Rs. 1,250 in the Capital Account of B and a credit to the Capital Account of C of Rs. 20,000. Goodwill Account has been closed and, therefore, will not appear in the Balance Sheet.

One point, however, is to be noted. It has been made clear above that goodwill is a compensation to old partners. Therefore, the amount brought in as goodwill by the incoming partner should be credited to the old partners in the ratio of their sacrifice and not in the old profit sharing ratio. Suppose, in the above case, on C's admission the new profit sharing ratio is one-half, one-fourth and one-fourth. This means that on C's admission B does not stand to lose at all. He previously received one-fourth of profit and now also he receives one-fourth of profit. It is A who is suffering the entire loss on C's admission because his share of profit has come down from three-fourths to one-half. Therefore, the entire amount of goodwill brought in by C should be given to A. This is why the cash brought in as goodwill by the incoming partner should be credited to old partners in the ratio of sacrifice made by them. This ratio of sacrifice can be calculated by finding out how much the previous partners lose. Suppose, A and B were sharing profits in the ratio of 5 : 3. C is admitted and the new profit sharing ratio is 2 :1:1. This means that A will now get one half, B will get one-fourth and C one-fourth. A loses 5/8–1/2, *i.e.*, 1/8. B also loses 1/8, *i.e.*, 3/8–1/4. Therefore, on C's admission, both A and B lose equally. The amount brought in by C should he credited to the Capital Accounts of A and B equally.

There is a way in which goodwill can be credited to partners in the ratio of their sacrifices automatically. This requires the three following steps :

(a) Credit the whole of the cash brought in by the new partner (for goodwill as well as for his capital) to his Capital Account. Suppose C is required to pay Rs. 40,000 as capital and Rs. 10,000 as goodwill for one-fifth share of profits. The entry under this step will be

Cash Account	Dr.	50,000	
To C's Capital Account			50,000

(b) Raise goodwill at full value and credit old partners in the old profit sharing ratio. Suppose, A and B were sharing profits and losses in the ratio of 3 : 2. Then taking the above example of C's admission, and therefore, valuing goodwill at Rs. 50,000, i.e., 10,000., the following entry will be made

Goodwill Account	Dr.	50,000	
To A's Capital Account			30,000
To B's Capital Account			20,000

(c) Write off goodwill to all partners, including the new one, in the new profit sharing ratio. Suppose the new profit sharing ratio is 5 : 3 : 2. In that case the entry will be

A's Capital Account	Dr.	25,000	
B's Capital Account	Dr.	15,000	
C's Capital Account	Dr.	10,000	
To Goodwill Account			50,000

The effect of these three entries is that A has been credited with Rs. 5,000, i.e., Rs. 30,000 minus Rs. 25,000. B has been credited with Rs. 5,000 i.e., Rs. 20,000 minus Rs. 15,000. C's Capital Account which was previously credited at Rs. 50,000 has been debited with Rs. 10,000 and, therefore, has been reduced to Rs. 40,000. We can pass the entries in the straightforward manner also but we will have to calculate the ratio of sacrifice made by A and B on C's admission. The sacrifice is

A $3/5 - 5/10 = 1/10$

B $2/5 - 3/10 = 1/10$

The sacrifice made by both partners is equal. Therefore, we can, alternatively, pass the following entries

		Dr.	Cr.
(1)	Cash Account Dr.	50,000	
	To C's Capital Account		40,000
	To Goodwill Account		10,000
(2)	Goodwill Account Dr.	10,000	
	To A's Capital Account		5,000
	To B's Capital Account		5,000

The student must note that this treatment of goodwill is necessary only when goodwill is brought in cash.

If goodwill is to be withdrawn by partners, then the only additional entry required is to debit the Capital Accounts of the partners concerned and to credit cash.

(iv) **Goodwill paid privately.** When the amount of goodwill is paid to the old partners outside the books privately, no entry is required. In this case the amount to be paid to each partner will be calculated as shown in number (iii) above but, there will be no entry in the books.

(B) ***Revaluation of assets and liabilities.*** When a new partner joins firm, it is desirable to bring all appreciation or reduction in the value of assets into account as on the date of admission. Similarly, if the books contain any liability which has not to be paid or if the books do not contain a liability which has to be paid, suitable entries should be passed. The purpose of such entries is to make a proper Balance Sheet on the date of admission. Also, all profits which have accrued but not yet brought into books and similarly, all losses which have occurred, but not yet recorded, should now be brought into books so that the capital accounts of the old partners reflect the proper figure. One result of passing of such entries will be that any subsequent profits or losses will be automatically shared by the incoming partner along with others. To record such profits or losses, an account, named Profit and Loss Adjustment Account or Revaluation Account, is opened. This account is debited with all reductions in the value of assets and increase in liabilities. The account is credited with increase in that value of assets and decrease in liabilities. The difference in the two sides of the account will show profit or loss. This is transferred to the capital accounts of old partners in the old profit sharing ratio. The entries to be passed are

1. Revaluation Account Dr.

To the Assets (individually) which show a decrease	with the reduction in the value of the assets.
To Liabilities (individually) which have to be increased	with the increase in the liabilities.

2.	Assets Account (individually)	Dr.	with the increase in the value of assets.
	Liabilities Account (individually)	Dr.	with the reduction in the amount of liabilities.
	To Revaluation Account		
3.	Revaluation Account	Dr.	with the profit in the profit sharing ratio.
	To Capital Accounts of old partners		
Or	Capital Account of old partners	Dr.	with the loss in old profit sharing ratio.
	To Revaluation Account		

As a result of the above entries the capital accounts of the old partners will change and the assets and liabilities will have to be adjusted to their proper values. It is at these figures that they will appear in the Balance Sheet.

(C) ***Reserves etc. in the Balance Sheet.*** Whenever a new partner is admitted, any reserves, etc. which may be lying in the Balance Sheet should be transferred to the Capital Accounts of the old partners in the old profit sharing ratio. In examination problems it should be done even if there are no instructions on this point.

(D) ***Finding out the new profit sharing ratio.*** When a new partner is admitted, in absence of any other agreement, it is assumed that the old partners, as between themselves, will continue to share profits in the old profit sharing ratio. 'This means that after giving the share to the new partner as per agreement with him, the remaining share of profits should be divided among the old partners in the old ratio'. For doing this the new partner's share should be deducted from 1 and then the remainder should be divided up in the old ratio. Suppose A and B share profits in the ratio of three-fourths and one-fourth. C is admitted and is given one-fifth share of profits. Deducting one-fifth from 1, we have four-fifths. If four-fifths are divided between A and B in the ratio of 3 : 1 the share of A comes to three-fifths, *i.e.*, $\frac{4}{5}\times\frac{3}{4}$ Similarly, the share of B comes to one-fifth, *i.e.*, $\frac{4}{5}\times\frac{1}{4}$. Thus the new profit sharing ratio of the three partners comes to three-fifth, one-fifth and one-fifth or 3 : 1 : 1. Sometimes, a partner purchases a certain share of profits from one partner and another share of profit from another partner. Suppose A and B share profits in the ratio of 3 :1. C is admitted and he purchases one-fourth share of profit from A. In that case, the share of profit of A will be three-fourths minus one-fourth, *i.e.*, one-half. There is no change in B is share of profits and, therefore, the new ratio will be one-half, one-fourth and one-fourth. Suppose A and B share in the ratio of 3: 2 and C is admitted taking one-tenth of profits from each of the partners. In that case A's profit will be 3/5–1/10, viz., 5/10 and B's share of profit will be 2/5 –1/10 *viz.*, 3/10, and C's profit will be1/10+1/10, *i.e.*, 2/10. The new ratio, therefore, is 5 : 3 : 2.

(E) **Capitals in the profit sharing ratio.** It is sometimes agreed that on the admission of a partner the capitals of the partners should also be made in the profit sharing ratio. This question should be taken up after making all adjustments in respect of goodwill transfer or profit or loss on revaluation of assets and reserves, etc. Suppose as a result of these adjustments A's capital stands at Rs. 45,000 and B's capital stands at Rs. 34,000. C is admitted who pays Rs. 20,000 as his share of capital. The new profit sharing ratio is

5 : 3 : 2. The capitals of A and B are also to be in the same ratio as that of profits. This means that C's capital is Rs. 20,000 for one-fifth share of profits. Accordingly, the total capital of the firm should be Rs. 1 lakh. Therefore, according to the profit sharing ratio A's capital should be Rs. 50,000 and B's capital should be Rs. 30,000. A, therefore, should bring in Rs. 5,000 and B should be paid Rs. 4,000. We can get at these figures in another way also. If for one-fifth share of 'profits', the capital is Rs. 20,000, for three-tenths share of profits the capital should be 20,000 × 5 x 3/10 or Rs. 30,000. This is what B's capital should be. Similarly, for five-tenth share of profits the capital should be 20,000 × 5 × 5/10 or Rs. 50,000.

Sometimes, the new partner is asked to bring in capital according to his profit sharing ratio. Suppose A's capital is Rs. 45,000 and B's capital is Rs. 35,000, making a total of Rs. 80,000. C is admitted for one-fifth share of profits and is to pay a proportionate amount as capital. It is clear that A and B together get four-fifths share of profits for which the capital is Rs. 80,000. For a full share the capital comes to Rs. 1 lakh, *i.e.*, 80,000 × 5/4. If C is to get one-fifth share of profits and has to pay a proportionate amount as capital, he must pay Rs. 20,000 *i.e.*, one fifth of Rs. 1 lakh. This figure can also be obtained in another way. A and B's share of profit is 4/5. C's share of profit is 1/5. C's share, therefore, is 1/4 of the combined share of A and B, *i.e.*, 1/5 ÷ 4/5. Therefore, C's capital should be 1/4 of the total of A's and B's capital. Therefore, he must pay 1/4 of Rs. 80,000 or Rs. 20,000 as his capital.

(F) **Amounts of assets and liabilities not to be changed.** Sometimes on the admission of a partner, it is desired that the effect of changes in the amounts of assets and liabilities should be brought into books without having to show the assets and liabilities at their new figures. This means that the partners concerned will pass entries in their capital accounts to record the changes but will leave the assets and liabilities to be shown in the balance sheet at their old figures. The method to do this is to find out the loss or profit or revaluation by a Memorandum Revaluation Account. This will be debited with losses and credited with gains, but double entry will not be completed in the accounts of the assets and liabilities concerned. The net result of this account, Memorandum Revaluation Account, is transferred to the capital accounts of old partners in the old ratio. Then, immediately this entry is reversed by transferring the amount to the capital account of all partners in the new ratio. If revaluation shows a profit, first the profit will be transferred to the credit side of old partners in old ratio, and then the amount will be debited to the capital accounts of all partners, including the new partners, in the new ratio. If it is a loss, first the capital accounts of old partners will be debited in the old profit sharing ratio and then the capital accounts of all partners will be credited in the new profit sharing ratio. In this manner the double entry is completed by crediting and debiting the capital accounts only. The assets and liabilities will continue to appear at their old figures. It should be noted that, in a question like this, it is understood that Goodwill Account will have to be written off if it is to be raised first.

RETIREMENT OF A PARTNER

Retirement means discontinuation of partnership. The reason for a partner discontinuing may be illness, old age or misunderstanding between the partners. Once a partner retires, his all relations with the firm and other partners terminate. On retirement of a partner the partnership dissolves. It becomes necessary for the firm to find out the amount payable to him. Hence, it becomes necessary to make certain adjustments in the accounts.

(A) **Calculation of new profit sharing ratio of the remaining partners.** The remaining partners well have to agree amongst themselves on this point. For instance, if A, B & C were sharing profits and losses in the ratio of 5 : 3: 2 and B retires, it is up to A and C to agree that in future the profits and losses will be shared in the ratio of say, 3/5 to A and 2/5 to C, or A and C may agree that B's share of profits will be taken equally by the other two partners. B was getting 3/10; half of their is 3/20. Therefore, 3/20 will be added to A's share and 3/20 will be added to c's share. A's share will be 5/10 + 3/20 or 13/20 and C's share will be 2/10 + 3/20 or 7/20. The new ratio, therefore is 13 : 7.

If there is no fresh agreement among the remaining partners, it is presumed that they will take the share of the retiring partner in the same ratio as they were having previously. To continue the above example, A and C will take B's share in the ratio of 5 : 2 in absence of agreement. That means 5/7 of 3/10 or $\frac{15}{70}$ will be taken by A and $\frac{2}{7}$ of $\frac{3}{10}$ will be taken by C. The new share for A will be 5/10 + $\frac{15}{70}$ or $\frac{5}{7}$. Similarly C's share will be 2/10 + 6/70 or 20/70 or 2/7. He can arrive at these ratios in a more convenient manner. The previous ratio 5 : 3 : 2. The partner with '3' goes, so let us remove this figure. The ratio remains as 5 : 2. Therefore A will get 5/7 and C well get 2/7.

(B) **Treatment of Goodwill on the retirement of a partner.** In case of retirement of a partner, there is no question of goodwill being dealt with in the form of cash. Goodwill is only raised in the books or rather, goodwill is recorded in the books at its proper figure. If, for instance, there is no goodwill account already appearing in books, goodwill account will be raised at its full figure. But if in books there is already a goodwill account, then goodwill account should be raised only for the difference. On the other hand, if the present value of goodwill is less than the book figure, the goodwill account will have to be credited to bring it down to its proper value. Of course, goodwill is valued according to the method given in partnership deed. If the Deed is silent, the retiring partner and the other partners will have to come to an agreement on question of the value of goodwill.

Goodwill may be recorded in any of the following ways :

(a) When Goodwill is raised at its full value in the books of the firm:

Debit Goodwill account

Credit all partners (including the retiring one) in the old profit sharing ratio.

This entry should be passed only for the difference if already a goodwill account appears in the books. If the present value of goodwill is less then the book figure, the above noted entry will be reversed. In this case goodwill account will appear in balance sheet of the company at its present figure.

(b) When goodwill is raised at its full value and then written off or when goodwill account is not allowed to remain in the books.

(i) Debit Goodwill Account

Credit all partners (including the retiring one) in the old profit sharing ratio.

Goodwill Account	Dr.	20000	
To A's Capital A/C			12000
To B's Capital A/C			4000
To C's Capital A/C			4000

(ii) Debit-the remaining partners, in the new profit sharing ratio and credit goodwill. Suppose A, B and C were partners sharing in the ratio of 3 : 1 : 1. B retires and goodwill on that occasion is valued at Rs. 20000.

The two entries will be :

Goodwill raised at Rs. 20000 and credited to all the partners.

A's Capital account	Dr.	15000
C's Capital account	Dr.	5000
To Goodwill account		20000

Goodwill account written off to the capital accounts of A and C in the new profit sharing ratio which is $\frac{3}{4}$ th and $\frac{1}{4}$ th.

(c) When only retiring partner's share of goodwill is raised. The method is debit the remaining partners and credit the retiring partner with his share of goodwill. Instead of one entry, two entries can be passed, viz.

(i) Debit Goodwill account Credit retiring partner's capital account	with his share of goodwill only.
(ii) Debit remaining partners capital account Credit Goodwill account	in the ratio of the gain of the remaining partners.

(d) When goodwill is raised with the share of retiring partner and then written off–In that case existing partner's capital account as per gaining ratio will be debited and retiring partners capital account will be credited by the amount of retiring partner's share of goodwill. For example,

Suppose A, B and C are partners sharing profits and losses in the ratio of 1/2, 1/3, 1/6. B retires and goodwill for that purpose is valued at Rs. 30000. The new profit sharing ratio will be 3/5 and 2/5, this means that A's gain is 1/10 or (3/30) i.e. 3/5 – 1/2, C's gain is 7/30 i.e. 2/5–1/6. The ratio of gain, therefore, is 3 : 7 as between A and C. Therefore the amount is Rs. 10000 which will have to be credited to B as goodwill should be debited to A and C in the ratio of 3 : 7. The entry will be:

A's capital account	Dr.	3000	
C's capital account	Dr.	7000	
To B's Capital account			10000

The following two entries can be passed:

Goodwill account	Dr.	10000	
To B's capital account			10000

Goodwill account raised at B's share which is 1/3

A's Capital account	Dr.	3000	
C's Capital Account	Dr.	7000	
To Goodwill account			10000

Goodwill account written off

The truth of the above can be tested by raising goodwill at full value and then writing off in the new ratio. The two entries are given below:

Goodwill account	Dr.	30000	
To A's Capital account			15000
To B's Capital account			10000
To C's Capital account			5000
C's Capital account	Dr.	18000	
A's Capital account	Dr.	12000	
To goodwill account			30000

The net effect of these two entries is that A has been debited with Rs. 3000 and C has been debited with Rs. 7000. These figures are the same as worked out previously.

(C) **Revaluation of assets and liabilities.** Revaluation of assets and liabilities is a must on the retirement of a partner unless the deed specifically says that they are not to be revalued. Even those assets which do not appear in the books but which belong to the firm have to be revalued. The method of recording the revaluation is the same as given in the case of admission of partners. Revaluation account will be debited with reduction in the values of assets and increase in the amount of liabilities. This account will be credited with increase in the value of assets and reduction in the amount of liabilities. The profit of loss or revaluation must be transferred to the capital accounts of all partners (including the retiring partners) in the old profit sharing ratio.

(D) **Accounting treatment of undistributed profits/losses at the time of retirement of a partner.** Where a partner retires, the reserve accumulated profit or losses appearing in the Balance sheet are shared by all partners, including the retiring partners in their profit-sharing ratio. For this purpose the following entries are passed :

(a) For distribution of reserve and profits :

General Reserve A/C Dr.
Profit & Loss A/C Dr.
To Partners Capital A/C
(Individually)

(b) For distribution of past losses between all partners in their profit sharing ratio:

All partner's capital A/C Dr.
To Profit & Losses A/C.

(E) **How the account of a retiring partner settled.** For the settlement of retiring partners account first of all the amount due to retiring party will be calculated by crediting his capital account with beginning balance of his capital, interest on Capital, share of profit on revaluation of assets and liabilities, his share of goodwill and reserve fund and debiting the capital with drawings, interest on drawings and his share of loss in revaluation of assets and liabilities.

Settlement of Total Amount due to the Retiring Partner

The amount due to the retiring/outgoing partners may be paid by anyone of the following manner:

(i) The amount may be paid off immediately from business in cash. The entry for this purposes will be:

Retiring Partner's Capital A/C Dr.
To Cash/Bank A/C

(ii) The amount due to him may be transferred to a loan Account which is to be paid gradually with interest.

(a) For transferring to Loan account :

Retiring partner's capital A/C Dr.

To Retiring Partner's Loan A/C

(b) For the amount of interest :

Interest A/C Dr

To Retiring partner's loan A/C

(c) For the payment of instalment:

Retiring partner's capital A/C

To Cash/Bank A/C.

DEATH OF A PARTNER

The problems which arise in case of death of a partner are similar to those of a retiring partner except that the death of a partner may occur at any time whereas the retirement of a partner is planned *i.e.* he is allowed to retire on the last date of an accounting period.

The accounting treatment of the death of a partner is almost the same as in case of retirement. The legal representative of deceased partner will be entitled to receive from the firm, the amount due on account of the following:

(i) Capital standing to the credit of his Capital Account.
(ii) Interest on Capital, if any, to the date of death of the partner.
(iii) Share in the goodwill of the firm.
(iv) Share in the revaluation of assets and liabilities.
(v) Share in the accumulated reserves.
(vi) Share in the undistributed profits.
(vii) Share in the profit of the firm from the last Balance-sheet to the date of his death.
(viii) Share in the Joint Life Policy.
(ix) Salary, if any, due to him till the date of his death.

Further the amount due to deceased partner is reduced by:

(a) Drawings, (b) Interest on Drawing and (c) Undistributed losses, if any, should be transferred to his Executor's Account. Then the amount may be paid immediately or by installments. If payment is made by installments, it will carry interest – 6% p.a.

Deceased Partner's Capital Amount

Dr. Cr.

Particulars	Rs.	Particulars	Rs.
To Drawings	–	By Balance b/d	–
To Interest on Drawings	–	By Reserve Fund	–
To Loss on Revaluation	–	(Share in Reserve Fund)	–
To Profit and Loss A/C	–	By Int. on Capital A/C	–
(upto date of death)	–	(upto date of death)	–
To Deceased Partner's	–	By Joint Life Policy A/C	–
Executor's A/C	–	(Balancing Figures)	–
By Goodwill A/C	–	By Profit and Loss A/C	–
		(up to date of death)	–

At the time of death of a Partner, deceased Partner's executors are entitled to share the profits earned by the firm from the beginning of the year till his death.

The deceased Partner's share of profit is to be determined on the basis of time or turnover:

(a) **Time Basis.** If the time basis is used, the profit will be assumed to have arisen uniformly over the year. Suppose the total profit for a year is Rs. 48,000 and a partner dies after three months of the close of previous year, the profits for the three months will be Rs. 12,000 i.e. 48,000 x 3/12. If the deceased partner took 3/10 of profits his share of profits till the date of death will be Rs. 3600.

(b) **Turnover or Sales Basis.** If profit till the date of death is to be ascertained on the basis of sales or turnover, we should know
   (i) the sales for the whole year, and
   (ii) sales upto the date of death. Suppose a partner dies on 1st March, 1998, accounts being closed on 31 December. The profit till the date of death is to be ascertained on the basis of sales, assuming profits for 1998 will be the same as for 1997.

The following information is available for 1997.

Sales for 1997	Rs.	1,20,000
Sales for Jan. & Feb. 1998	Rs.	30,000
Profit for 1997	Rs.	24,000

Then profit on the basis of sales will be

If the deceased partner was entitled to 1/4th share in profits, his estate has to be credited by Rs. 1,500 for profits till the date of death.

Joint Life Policy

A joint life policy is an assurance policy taken on the joint lives of all the partners. If any partner dies then amount of the policy is paid by the Life Insurance Corporation. This amount can be very well used to settle the account of the executor of the deceased partner without disturbing the position of the business.

There are three methods of dealing with the Joint Life Policy:

Ist Method. When the premium is treated as business expense. Under this method, the premium paid on the joint life policy is debited to the profit and loss account and whatever amount is received from the corporation on the date of death of a partner is divided among the partners in their profit sharing ratio.

The following journal entries will be passed:

1st and subsequent years:

(i) On payment of premium:
   Insurance Premium A/C
   To Bank Dr.

(ii) When premium paid transferred to Profit and Loss Account:
   Profit and Loss A/C Dr.
   To Insurance premium A/C
   Last year: Repeat the first two years entries

(iii) When the amount of policy realised on surrender or maturity or death of a partner:
   Bank A/C Dr.
   To Joint Life Policy A/C

(iv) When the amount realised on policy transferred to all partners in their profit-sharing ratio:

Joint life policy A/C Dr.

To all partner's Capital A/Cs

IInd Method. When premium paid is treated as an asset. Under this method, the premium paid is treated as an asset and joint life policy is also treated as an asset because after two years premium have been paid, a policy has surrender value; surrender value of a policy is the amount which the insurance company is prepared to pay to the firm when the policy is surrendered.

The following journal entries are made in this method :

(i) When premium is paid on policy :

Joint life policy A/C Dr.

To Bank

(ii) When joint life policy is brought down to its surrender value:

Profit and Loss A/C Dr.

To Joint Life Policy A/C

Note. The above mentioned entries will be repeated until any partner dies or till maturity of policy.

(iii) When the amount of policy realised on its surrender, maturity or death of a partner :

Bank A/C Dr.

To Joint Life Policy A/C

(iv) When the balance of policy transferred to partner's accounts:

Joint life policy A/C Dr.

To all partners Capital A/C

IIIrd Method. When premium paid is treated as an asset and reserve is maintained. Under this method, Joint life policy Account and Joint Life Policy Reserve Account, both are maintained at Surrender value:

(i) When premium is paid:

Joint Life Policy A/C Dr.

To Bank

(ii) When a reserve equal to premium paid is created out of P&L A/C

Profit & Loss A/C Dr.

To Joint Life Policy Reserve A/C

(iii) When excess of Joint Life Policy over surrender value is written off to Joint Life Reserve Account:

Joint life policy reserve A/C Dr.

To Joint life policy

On the death of a partner:

(iv) When the amount of Joint life policy is received:

Bank A/C Dr.

To Joint life policy A/C

(v) When the balance of Joint policy reserve account is transferred to Joint life policy account:

Joint life policy reserve A/C Dr.

To Joint life policy A/C

(vi) When balance of Joint life policy is distributed amongst the partners:

Joint life policy A/C Dr.

To Partner's Capital A/Cs

DISSOLUTION OF A PARTNERSHIP FIRM

Concept of Dissolution of Partnership and Dissolution of a Firm. The term 'Dissolution' stands for discontinuation. Under the Indian Partnership Act, 1932, the dissolution may be either of partnership or of a firm.

Dissolution of partnership refers to the change in the existing relations of the partners. The firm continues its business. It may take place on admission/retirement/death/insolvency of a partner or on change in the profit sharing ratio.

Dissolution of a firm means the dissolution of partnership between all the partners of the firm alongwith the termination of firm's business.

It is clear from the above discussion that dissolution of a partnership may or may not include dissolution of firm, but dissolution of firm necessarily means dissolution of partnership.

Circumstances under which a Firm is dissolved. A Partnership firm may be dissolved with or without the intervention of the court.

(1) ***Dissolution without the Intervention of the court.***

A Partnership firm may be dissolved without the intervention of the court in any of the following ways:

(a) ***Dissolution by agreement.*** A partnership firm comes into existence by mutual agreement and therefore it can also be dissolved by the mutual consent of all the partners.

(b) ***Compulsory dissolution.*** In the following cases partnership firm will have to be compulsorily dissolved.

(i) by the adjudication of all the partners or of all the partners but one as insolvent, or

(ii) by the business of firm becoming unlawful due to the happening of any such event.

(c) ***Dissolution on the happening of certain contingencies.*** In the absence of any contract to the contrary, a firm will be dissolved on the happening of the following contingencies:

(i) On the expiry of the fixed period for which the firm was constituted.

(ii) On the completion of the adventure or undertaking for carrying out which the firm was constituted.

(iii) On the death of a partner and

(iv) On the adjudication of a partner as insolvent.

(d) ***Dissolution by notice.*** When a Partnership is at will, the firm may be dissolved by any partner giving a notice in writing to all the other partners of his intention to dissolve the firm.

(2) ***Dissolution by the court.***

The court may dissolve a firm in the following cases :

(a) When a partner becomes of unsound mind or as permanently incapacitated for doing partnership work.

(b) When a partner is found guilty of misconduct.

(c) When the business of the firm cannot be carried on except at a loss.

(d) When a partner disregards the provisions of the partnership consistently.

(e) Any other ground which in the opinion of the court is just and equitable.

Accounting Procedure that should be adopted for dissolution of a Partnership Firm.

Accounting on Dissolution. Following procedure must be adopted for accounting purpose.

A. Open three accounts in the following consecutive order viz.
   (a) Realisation A/C
   (b) Partner's Capital A/C
   (c) Cash or Bank A/C

B. Close and transfer all ledger accounts existing on the date of dissolution to one of the above three accounts. List of ledger accounts are provided in the form of Balance Sheet. The process of transferring should be adopted as follows:
   (a) All liabilities from liability side of Balance Sheet are transferred as follows.
      (i) Capital A/C balance, General Reserve, Reserve Fund, Compensation Fund etc. to the credit side of partner's capital A/C. Note that reserves to be divided amongst partners in their profit sharing ratio.
      (ii) Partner's loan amount to the credit side of Partner's Loan A/C.
      (iii) All other liabilities to the credit side of Realisation A/C at book (Balance Sheet) values.
   (b) Different assets appearing on Asset side of Balance Sheet are transferred as follows:
      (i) Cash and Bank Balance on Debit side of Bank A/C.
      (ii) Profit and Loss A/C (Dr) Balance to the Debit side of partner's capital A/C, distributed between partner's in their profit sharing ratio.
      (iii) All other assets to Debit side of Realisation A/C at book value.

   By doing this, all assets and liabilities accounts are closed. Realisation A/C shall now act as representative account for assets and liabilities.

C. The assets of the firm may be disposed of in one of the following ways:
   (a) Sale of asset for cash in open market : Cash is received so cash/Bank A/C is debited, whereas asset is going out for the business, hence Realisation A/C will be credited.
   (b) Asset taken over by a partner. Partner is receiver of asset, hence partner's capital A/C is debited. Realisation A/C is credited for asset is moving out from the business.
   (c) Asset given away in discharge of a liability. Sometimes a particular liability is discharged by giving it away one of the asset of the firm. Here debit and credit effect is given to Realisation A/C because it represent both the asset and the liability. Here Realisation A/C is already debited as well credited for similar amounts hence no entry.

   Note: Once assets and liabilities are transferred to Realisation A/C, they get closed. Realisation A/C will represent them instead of individual asset or liability being given any effect.

D. Liability of the firm may be discharged or settled in one of the following ways:
   (i) Payment in cash or cheque – In this case following entry will be passed.
      Realisation A/C Dr.
      To Cash A/C
   (ii) Liability taken over by a partner
      When a partner takes over a liability his capital A/C will be credited and Realisation A/c debited for liability being settled by a partner.

Note:

(a) If nothing is mentioned about discharge of a particular liability than it is assumed that the same is paid in cash at book value.

(b) If nothing is mentioned about the disposal of asset, then it is assumed that same is sold in cash at book value.

E. Balance Realisation A/C and distribute the Profit/Loss amongst the partners in profit sharing ratio. Thus, Realisation A/C will be closed.

(i) If there is Profit on realisation.

Realisation A/C Dr.

To All Partner's Capital A/Cs

(In the profit- sharing ratio)

(ii) If there is loss on realisation.

All Partner's Capital A/Cs Dr.

To Realisation A/C

F. **Capital A/C Balance of Partners.**

The difference will be paid or received through Cash/Bank A/C.

(i) In case of Payment by a partner having a debit balance in his capital Account.

Cash/Bank A/C Dr.

To concerned partner's capital A/C

(ii) In case of payment to a partner having a credit balance in his Capital Account

Concerned partner's capital A/C Dr.

To Cash/Bank A/C

G. The Cash/Bank A/C must automatically tally.

SPECIMEN OF LEDGER ACCOUNTS REALISATION ACCOUNT

Dr. Particular	Amount (Rs.)	Particular	Cr. Amount (Rs.)
To sundry Assets Stock Furniture Debtors Machinery etc. (at book value)		By Sundry Assets Creditors Bills Payable etc. By Cash/Bank A/C (Assets Realised)	
To Cash/Bank A/C (Crs. Paid)		By partner's capital A/C (assets taken over at agreed value)	
To partner's capital A/C (for taking liability)		By partners capital A/C (loss) (Bal. Fig.)	
To Cash/Bank A/C (Realisation Exp paid)			
To partner's capital A/C (for realisation expenses)			
To partner's capital A/C (profit) (Bal. Figure)			

PARTNERS CAPITAL ACCOUNT

To Profit & loss A/C (loss)		By opening Balance	
		By General Reserve (P & L (A/C)	
To Realisation A/C (Assets taken over)		By Realisation A/C (Credit for Realisation Expenses)	
To Realisation A/C (Loan on Realisation)		By Realisation A/C (Liability taken over)	
To Cash/Bank A/C (Settlement)		By Realisation A/C (Profit on Realisation)	

CASH BANK ACCOUNT

To opening Balance		By Realisation A/C (Liabilities Paid)	
To Realisation A/C (Assets Realisation)		By Realisation A/C (Expenses paid)	
To Partners Capital A/C (Cash brought in)		By partners capital A/C (final settlement)	

Deal with realisation expenses when the firm is dissolved.

1. When the realisation expenses are paid by the firm.

   Realisation Account Dr.

   To Cash/Bank Account

2. When the realisation expenses are paid by the partner on behalf of the firm.

   Realisation Account Dr.

   To partner's Capital A/C

3. (i) When the firm is agreed to pay the partner a fixed amount towards realisation expenses irrespective of the actual expenses.

   Realisation Account Dr.

   To partner's Capital A/C

   (ii) For the payment of actual expenses by the firm on behalf of partner

   Partner's Capital A/C Dr.

   To cash A/C

   However, if a partner himself pays realisation expenses and agreeing not to get reimbursed, no entry is required.

H. (i) Accounting treatment of Unrecorded assets and unrecorded liabilities at the time of dissolution of firm.

For Unrecorded Asset

Cash A/C Dr.

or

Bank A/C Dr.
or
Partner's Capital A/C Dr.
To Realisation Account

Such assets are either realised in cash or by cheque or are taken over by a partner.

For Unrecorded Liabilities

Realisation Account Dr.
To Cash/Bank/Partners Capital

Such Liabilities should be paid off, or a partner might undertake to pay.

(ii) **Treatment of Goodwill.** The accounting treatment of goodwill in case of dissolution of a firm may be summarised as under.

	If Goodwill is already appearing in the books.		If Goodwill is not appearing in the books.	
(a) On transfer to Realisation A/C	Realisation A/C To Goodwill A/C	Dr.	The question of transfer does not arise at all.	
(b) On sale for cash	Cash/Bank A/C To Realisation A/C	Dr.	Cash/Bank A/C To Realisation A/C	Dr.
(c) On being taken over by any of the partners	Concerned Partner's Capital A/C To Realisation A/C	Dr.	Concerned Parter's Capital A/C To Realisation A/C	Dr.

(iii) **Realisation Account.** At the time of dissolution all assets are to be disposed off and all liabilities are to be paid off in order to close the books of accounts. These assets are realised and liabilities are paid off through a common account which is called realisation Account.

The main object of such an account is to show the profit or loss on realisation of assets and payment of liabilities.

Distinguish between Revaluation A/C and Realisation A/C

	Revaluation Account	Realisation Account
1.	Revaluation Account is prepared at the time of admission, retirement or death of a Partner.	Realisation Account is prepared at the time of dissolution of a partnership firm.
2.	It is prepared for determining the profit or loss on revaluation of assets and liabilities.	It is prepared for determining the profit or loss on realisation of assets and settlement of liabilities.
3.	Profit or loss on revaluation of assets and liabilities is distributed among old partners in their profit-sharing ratio.	Profit or loss on realisation Account is distributed among all partners in their profit-sharing ratio.
4.	It contains only those assets and liabilities which are revalued.	It contains all assets and liabilities.

INSOLVENCY OF PARTNERSHIP FIRMS

If there are two partners and one of them is insolvent, then the solvent partner will have to bear all the loss that there might be because of the insolvency of the other partner. Suppose the position after realisation of assets is :

	Rs		Rs
A's Capital	15000	Loss on Realisation	10000
B's Capital	2000	Cash	7000
	17000		17000

A and B share in the ratio of 3:2. In that case the loss on realisation will be debited to A, Rs. 6000 and to B, Rs. 4000 converting B's credit balance into a debit balance of Rs. 2000. If B is solvent he will pay Rs. 2000 and thus A will get Rs. 9000. But if B is insolvent, the Rs. 2000 payable by B will be a loss and will have to be transferred to the debit of A's capital account. This will reduce his credit balance to Rs. 7000 and thus he will get Rs. 7000 only.

The position is more complicated when there are two or more solvent partners and the others are insolvent. If the capital accounts of the insolvent partners show a debit balance (and thus loss to the firm) the question arises as to whether this loss is like the other losses to be borne in the profit sharing ratio or whether it is a special loss to be dealt with differently. Before the decision in Garner Vs Murray, it was thought that the loss due to insolvency of a partner was an ordinary loss and was to be borne by the other partners in the profit sharing ratio. Suppose the position of a firm after realisation is

A's capital	10000	C's Capital	3000
B's Capital	5000	Cash	12000
	15000		15000

All partners share equally. If C is unable to contribute anything, the amount of Rs. 3000 owing from him will be a loss and this loss (before Garner Vs Murray) will be shared by A and B equally. Thus A will get Rs. 8500 *i.e.* Rs. 10000 minus Rs. 1500 and B will get Rs. 3500 *i.e.* Rs. 5000 minus Rs. 1500.

Garner Vs Murray

The decision in Garner Vs Murray changed the position outlined above. The judgement laid down the following rules :

(a) Solvent partners should bring cash equal to their share of the loss or realisation.

(b) The loss on account of the insolvent partner should be borne in the ratio of capitals after (a).

The net result is that the loss due to the insolvency of a partner is not to be shared by the solvent partners in the ratio in which they share profits or losses but in the ratio of capitals just before dissolution. In the above example, the loss on account of C's insolvency will be debited to A and B in the ratio of 10 : 5. Thus A will be debited with Rs. 2000 and B with Rs. 1000. A will get Rs. 8000 and B will get Rs. 4000.

It follows from the above that should a solvent partner's capital account show a debit balance he will not be responsible for loss due to an insolvent partner. This is so even if he is richer than the other solvent partners.

Fixed and Fluctuating Capitals

The loss on account of an insolvent partner has to be borne in the ratio of capitals just before dissolution. This raises another point. Often adjustments are to be made in the Capital Accounts, for example, of undistributed profits. On dissolution, such profits must be distributed. This will change the capitals. If the capitals are fixed, the adjustments will be made in the current accounts really and hence the capitals will not be changed. Therefore, the ratio for distributing loss due to an insolvent partner will not change because of undistributed profits or reserves. If the capitals are fluctuating the undistributed profits or reserves (or other adjustments prior to dissolution) will change capitals and also the ratio for sharing the insolvent partner's loss. Suppose after realisation, the position is:

A's capital	10,000	C's Capital	5,000
B's Capital	5,000	Cash	16,000
	15,000		15000

Reserve has to be credited to all partners (who are presumably equal). A's capital account becomes Rs. 12,000 ; B's capital account will be Rs. 7,000 and C's capital account will show a debit balance of Rs. 3,000. If the capitals are fixed, C's loss (Rs. 3,000) will be borne by A and B in the ratio of 10 : 5. But if the capitals are fluctuating, the ratio will be 12 : 7.

All Partners Insolvent

Should all partners be insolvent the resultant loss will have to be borne by creditors. In such a case it is better not to transfer the creditors to the Realisation Account; otherwise, the Realisation Account should be prepared in the usual way. All the available cash should be paid to the creditors ; the amount remaining unpaid should be transferred to the Profit and Loss Account. The capital accounts of partners will be closed by transfer to the Deficiency Account.

Piece Meal Distribution

When a firm is dissolved, assets are gradually sold so as to realise the best price. The amounts thus realised are used, naturally, to first pay outsiders and then the available amounts are distributed among the partners-again first to pay off their loans, if any, to the firm and then their capitals. After paying the creditors, the amounts are paid proportionately to discharge the loans. When it comes to the turn of capitals, the monies should be so distributed that the ultimate loss, i.e. amounts left unpaid, should be in the profit sharing ratio. Obviously, the loss has to be shared by the partners in their profit sharing ratio.

For this, two methods are followed – either the proportionate capitals method or the maximum loss method. Suppose all creditors and partners 'loans have been paid off and the partners capitals' are A Rs.30,000, B 25,000 and C Rs.20,000. The partners share profits and losses in the ratio of 5:3:2. If Rs.30,000 is available for distribution among the partners we can proceed in one of the following two ways:

1. **Proportionate Capitals.** The total of capitals is Rs. 75,000; had the capitals been in proportion to the profit sharing ratio, these would have been Rs. 37, 500, Rs. 22,500 and Rs.15,000. A's capital is lower than that "required"; hence taking A's capital as the base, the capitals of B and C should have been

B:	30,000 × 3/5	Rs.	18,000
C:	30,000 × 2/5	Rs.	12,000

It means that first of all the monies available should be so distributed as to bring down the capitals of B and C to Rs.18,000 and Rs.12,000 respectively.

As between B and C, taking B's capital as the base, C's capital should have been Rs. 16,667 i.e. 25,000 x 2/3. Hence, first the capital of C should be reduced to Rs.16,667 by paying Rs.3,333. Once the capitals are in the profit sharing ratio, the available amounts can be distributed in the profit sharing ratio. The payment will, therefore, be as shown below:

	Capitals		
	A	B	C
	Rs.	Rs.	Rs.
Amount due	30,000	25,000	20,000
Amount paid to C			3,333
(to bring the capital to Rs. 16,667		25,000	16,667
Amounts paid to B and C (to bring their capitals – to Rs. 18,000 and Rs. 12,000 respectively)		7,000	4,667
	30,000	18,000	12000
Balance in proportion to the profit sharing ratio	7,500	4,500	3,000
Balance still due (or Loss if there are no further assets to realise)	22,500	13,500	9,000

2. **Cash Distribution.** The main question is how to distribute cash among partners for return of capital. One must note that the profit and loss on realisation of assets will not be known for sometime and must be distributed in such a way that the amount finally left unpaid are in the ratio in which profit and losses are shared. The available cash cannot be distributed in the profit sharing ratio because that will leave the balance unpaid out of proportion. The cash available cannot be distributed in the ratio of capital because, then the partner will be forced to bear the final loss which may be different from the profit sharing ratio.
3. **Maximum Loss.** Comparing the total of amounts due to the partners as capital with the amount available, the loss can be ascertained on the assumption that no further amounts will be received. This is the maximum loss. It should be distributed among the partners in the profit sharing ratio-if a minus figure results, that should be dealt with according to Garner vs. Murray. The total of the balances in the capitals will be equal to the amount in hand and partners will be paid accordingly. In the example given above, the total of capitals is Rs. 75,000 and the available amount is Rs. 30,000. Hence the maximum loss is Rs. 45,000.

The following shows how Rs. 30,000 should be distributed.

	Capitals		
	A	B	C
	Rs.	Rs.	Rs.
Capital	30,000	25,000	20,000
Less: Maximum Loss (in the profit sharing ratio)	22,500	13,500	9,000
Balance, and amount paid	7,500	11,500	11,000

CORPORATE ACCOUNTING

Accounting is one of the key functions for almost any business. It may be handled by a bookkeeper or an accountant at a small firm, or by sizable finance departments with dozens of employees at larger companies. The reports generated by various streams of accounting, such as cost accounting and management accounting, are invaluable in helping management make informed business decisions. While basic accounting functions can be handled by a bookkeeper, advanced accounting is typically handled by qualified accountants who possess designations such as Certified Public Accountant (CPA) in the United States, or Chartered Accountant (CA), Certified General Accountant (CGA) or Certified Management Accountant (CMA) in Canada.

ACCOUNTING: CREATING FINANCIAL STATEMENTS

The financial statements that summarize a large company's operations, financial position and cash flows over a particular period are concise statements based on thousands of financial transactions. As a result, all accounting designations are the culmination of years of study and rigorous examinations combined with a minimum number of years of practical accounting experience.

ACCOUNTING: GENERALLY ACCEPTED ACCOUNTING PRINCIPLES

In most cases, accountants use generally accepted accounting principles (GAAP) when preparing financial statements. GAAP is a set of standards related to balance sheet identification, outstanding share measurements and other accounting issues, and its standards are based on double-entry accounting, a method which enters each expense or incoming revenue in two places on a company's balance sheet.

ACCOUNTING: EXAMPLE OF DOUBLE ENTRY ACCOUNTING

To illustrate double-entry accounting, imagine a business issues an invoice to one of its clients. An accountant using the double-entry method enters a debit under the accounts receivables column on the balance sheet and a credit under the income statement's revenue column. When the client pays the invoice, the accountant credits accounts receivables and debits cash. Double-entry accounting is also called balancing the books, as all of the accounting entries are balanced against each other. If the entries aren't balanced, the accountant knows there must be a mistake somewhere in the ledger.

ACCOUNTING: FINANCIAL ACCOUNTING VS. MANAGEMENT ACCOUNTING

Financial accounting refers to the processes accountants use to generate the annual accounting statements of a firm. Management accounting uses much of the same processes but utilizes information in different ways. Namely, in management accounting, an accountant generates monthly or quarterly reports that a business's management team can use to make decisions about how the business operates.

ACCOUNTING: FINANCIAL ACCOUNTING VS. COST ACCOUNTING

Just as management accounting helps businesses make decisions about management, cost accounting helps businesses make decisions about costing. Essentially, cost accounting considers all of the costs related to producing a product. Analysts, managers, business owners and accountants use this information to determine what their products should cost. In cost accounting, money is cast as an economic factor in production, whereas in financial accounting, money is considered to be a measure of a company's economic performance.

CORPORATE ACCOUNTING ISSUES

Private equity funds have become more vigilant in tracking precisely why some of their portfolio companies are not doing well. At least two cases of alleged fraud by the companies invested in doctoring of books or fudging the minutes of meetings are well known.

In 2011, PE firms Bain Capital and TPG Capital dragged Lilliput Kidswear to court over alleged accounting fraud. This year, private equity firm SAIF Partners alleged that home-grown kids' wear retailer Catmoss was cooking its books.

However, not all investigations PE firms engage in are to detect or pinpoint fraud. Often it is because of lack of quality information on the performance of their portfolio companies. The poor corporate governance environment combined with intense competition for investment encourages promoters to manipulate their financial performance. It is not often detected with the level of due diligence that is currently being seen. The numerous recent cases of fraud in the private equity industry suggest that while a forensic review of the internal financial data of an investment target can identify red flags, it cannot be relied upon to uncover fraud. It is equally challenging for private equity investors to understand the performance of their portfolio companies once the investment is complete. The majority of investors hold minority positions and promoters treat private equity funding not as a strategic partnership but as another source of capital that they can control. This leaves investors with very limited tools to monitor the performance of portfolio companies post investment. With corporate governance standards still evolving and auditing standards that have not fully matured, private equity investors in India face serious challenges when applying due diligence and risk mitigation practices from developed markets to India. Simply put, these practices do not work when investing in India.

India is not unique in this regard but the problem is more severe here because corporate governance culture is still evolving and accounting and regulatory standards are not fully matured. At Kroll, we have seen similar frauds in the Middle East and Latin America because those PE markets are also characterized by minority stakes where fund managers have limited say in the management of the company and there is a general lack of information post-investment.

For example, we have seen a portfolio company in a Latin American country where executives had created bonus and pension plans more or less concealed in the numbers and not discovered until an executive retired and was being paid a fairly rich pension. That is very different from a typical Kroll investigation in more developed markets where frauds relate to theft of intellectual property or employees creating fictitious vendors. In emerging markets, it tends to be more subtle and more embedded in the corporate governance culture of the company. The areas where Kroll has seen the biggest increase in fraud-related investigations in the private equity industry are export-oriented industries where the customers of the portfolio companies are based abroad and it is difficult for PE funds to identify conflicts of interest. Businesses that rely on government approvals and are dependent on cash transactions such as real estate and infrastructure as well as businesses that are not generating sufficient cash despite growing top and bottom lines are more vulnerable to fraud.

FORFEITURE

When shares are allotted to an applicant, he and the company enter into a contract automatically. Then such an applicant is bound to pay the allotment money and all the various call monies till the shares are fully paid up. But if the shareholder fails to pay any of the calls (one or more) on the authorization of the board of Directors, the said shares can be forfeited. Forfeiture essentially means cancellation.

Before such forfeiture is done a notice must be given to the shareholder. The notice must provide the shareholder with a minimum of 14 days to make the payment due, or his shares will be forfeited. Even after such notice if the shareholder does not pay, then the shares will be canceled.

When the said shares are forfeited the shareholder ceases to be a member of the company. He loses all his rights and interests that a shareholder might enjoy. And once his name is removed from the register of shareholders he also losses all the money he has already paid towards the share capital. Such money will not be refunded.

When the shares have forfeited all entries regarding the issue of such shares have to be reversed. So the following adjustments are made for forfeiture of shares:

i. Share Capital – debited with total amounts called up.
ii. Unpaid Call A/c (Allotment, First Call etc.) – credited with the portion of the amount called up but unpaid.
iii. Share Forfeiture A/c – credited with the amount already paid by the defaulter.

Points to be noted:

- If the company maintains a Calls in Arrears account, then that account will be credited with the unpaid portion of the amount instead of Share Allotment A/c or Share Call A/c.
- The balance in the Share Forfeiture A/c is shown under the Share Capital on the liabilities side of the balance sheet. This account will remain till the said shares forfeited are reissued by the company.

If the shares were initially issued at a premium then the forfeiture treatment changes a little. If at the time of the forfeiture the entire amount of premium has already been received by the company, then the entries remain the same, i.e., as if the shares were issued at par. Please note that the Share Premium Account will not be debited in this case.

However, at the time when the shares are forfeited if the entire, or part of the share premium is unpaid, certain adjustments must be made to Share Premium A/c. In such a case the Share Premium A/c will be debited by the amount of premium not received. So if none of the premium is received, the entry will be reversed completely. So both Share Capital account and Share Premium A/c (for the amount not received) will be debited.

When the shares were initially issued at a discount and then forfeited, such a discount must be written off. So an adjustment entry will be passed to give this effect. So the discount applicable on the shares forfeited is written back by crediting the Discount on Issue A/c.

At times the directors of the company may decide to reissue the shares forfeited. The reissue can be done at par, premium or discount. Generally, the shares will be reissued at a discount. The maximum discount, however, will be restricted to the amount received on forfeiture of such shares plus their original discount if any. This discount given will be written off from the Share Forfeiture A/c.

LIQUIDATION OF COMPANIES

Liquidation is a process through which a company which is running is shut down and its existence comes to an end. This often happens when the companies are unable to pay its creditors and hence need to sell off its assets to pay of them. Though in another version this could be a voluntary act as well where law ensures that all the debts of a company into existence is paid before it is closed or shut down.

Indian Banking Industry is in the throes of a crisis. NPA (non performing assets) have been piling up. The total amount of stressed assets in trillions of INR. Freeing up this money is crucial for the banking sector. In order for a market to function and economy to thrive, there needs to be a proper flow of money. If the input and output of cash is not balanced in a system, it will have greater chances of collapsing. Based upon this simple principle, debts owed by Companies need to be recovered so as to save the financial institutions and also to maintain the equilibrium in the market. Till 29th November 2016 the procedure for recovery of debts was governed by many statues in India like Sick Industrial Companies Act, Recovery of Debt Due to Banks and Financial Institutions, Securitization and Reconstruction of Financial Assets and Enforcement of Security Interest Act (SARFAESI).

And because of having so many statues, it was rather cumbersome to understand and proceed for the recovery of money in case of default from a debtor. This lead to the need of having a comprehensive statue that would deal with such issue in a time bound manner. Consequently, Central Government on 30th November 2016 enacted the Insolvency and Bankruptcy Code, 2016.

This Code has radically changed and simplified the entire procedure for the liquidation of corporate persons. This code also provides for the insolvency and bankruptcy of individuals and the partnerships firms. A new option o fresh start is also provided for those small partnership firms and businessmen who would want to pay their debts and start afresh.

The Insolvency and Bankruptcy Code, 2016 has shifted the entire load from the shoulder of creditors to a new entity called Resolution Professional. It is his duty, under the statue, to conduct the entire process of insolvency and liquidation of corporate person. Since the entire procedure has changed and the code has made significant changes in Companies Act, 2013 it is required that we look into the code and understand the technicalities.

Initiating Proceedings for insolvency resolution and liquidation under Bankruptcy Code

The Code empowers both financial and operational creditors with the right to initiate the proceedings by filing application before the adjudicating authority. In case of Corporate Persons, the adjudicating authority is National Company Law Tribunal. A financial Creditor is one to who financial debt is owed or to who such debt is legally assigned. An operational creditor is one to who operational debt is owed. Operational Debt includes any debt in respect of provisions of goods and services.

This means that Operational Creditors generally arise form import-export dealings. Any person, other than financial creditor or operational creditor can initiate the proceedings provided he submits the required documents like book of accounts etc. Such person is called Corporate Applicant.

The resolution will start only after the admission of this application. The entire process of resolution and liquidation needs to be finished with a period of 180 days. However, the Adjudicating Authority, if it thinks fit, can extend this period with a maximum period of 90 days. Hence the maximum time that can be taken in 180+90 days.

Admission of Application for Resolution and Liquidation

Once the application is accepted, a notice will be issued in public regarding such application. Along with this notice, an interim resolution professional will be appointed whose primary task will be to collect all the relevant information and constitute a committee of creditors.

From the date of admission of application or also called the date of commencement, a moratorium period will begin during which the assets of the debtor cannot be interfered with in any way. Even the execution of any judgments, decrees or orders will not take place against such assets during moratorium period.

Resolution Professional: What is his role?

Once the interim resolution professional creates the committee of creditors his part of job is done. However, the committee may continue with the interim resolution professional or may appoint new resolution professional. The newly appointed resolution professional has a larger responsibility.

He will have to conduct, manage and supervise the entire resolution process till the debtor is discharged. The Resolution Professional shall make information memorandum which will contain all the relevant information required to make resolution plan.

Based upon this memorandum he shall submit a resolution plan to the committee. This resolution can be submitted to resolution professional by anyone. The committee of creditors than decide whether to admit or reject the resolution plan.

Liquidation of a Company or Other Incorporated Body: The Process

After the admission of resolution plan by the committee, Official Liquidator is appointed and the process of liquidation commences. Official Liquidator creates Liquidation estate which includes all the attachable assets of the corporate person. Official Liquidator shall consolidate, verify, admit, determine and evaluate the claims of the creditors.

In the meantime, certain transactions that are detrimental to the creditors or which were entered into for the purpose of deceiving creditors are avoided. These transactions are preferred transactions, undervalued transaction, defrauding transactions and Extortionate Credit Transaction.

These kinds of transactions are avoided mainly because such transactions were entered into in order to deceive the creditor and deny them their share.

After the Official Liquidator is thorough with the claims of the creditors, he distributes the assets according to the list of priority of creditors. The Insolvency and Bankruptcy Code, 2016 has entire changed the priority list of creditors.

The priority of creditor list is as follows:

1. The insolvency resolution process costs and the liquidation costs to be paid in full.
2. Workmen's Dues and Secured Creditor.
3. Wages and dues to employees (other than workmen)
4. Financial debts to unsecured creditors.
5. Central and state governments and debts owed to a secured creditors for any amount unpaid following the enforcement of security interests
6. Any remaining debts and dues.
7. Preference Shareholders
8. Equity Shareholders or partners

After the distribution of assets to the satisfaction of the amount of debts, dissolution of Corporate Person takes place. This order can be appealed to National Company Law Appellant Tribunal. The final adjudicating authority is Supreme Court.

Appeals

An appeal can be made against the order of the adjudicating authority to National Company Law Appellate Tribunal (NCLAT). The application needs to be filed within 30 days of the order.

However, the tribunal may allow to file after the expiry of this term provided it believes that there was sufficient cause for the delay. Appeal can be made on the following grounds:

- The approved resolution plan is in contravention of the provisions of any law for the time being in force.
- there has been material irregularity in exercise of the powers by the resolution professional during the corporate insolvency resolution period.
- The debts owed to Operational Creditors of the corporate debtor have not been provided for in the resolution plan in the manner specified by the Board.
- The Insolvency resolution process costs have not been provided for repayment in priority to all other debts.
- The resolution plan does not comply with any other criteria specified by the Board.
- An appeal against a liquidation order passed may be filed on grounds of material irregularity or fraud committed in relation to such a liquidation order.

The highest adjudicating authority up to which appeals will lie is Supreme Court. The code also talks about fast track resolution which will get completed within a period of 90 days. However, the same has not been notified and central government is yet to form rules for the same.

ACQUISITION

An acquisition is a situation whereby one company purchases most or all of another company's shares in order to take control. An acquisition occurs when a buying company obtains more than 50% ownership in a target company. As part of the exchange, the acquiring company often purchases the target company's stock and other assets, which allows the acquiring company to make decisions regarding the newly acquired assets without the approval of the target company's shareholders. Companies perform acquisitions for various reasons. They may seek to achieve economies of scale, greater market share, increased synergy, cost reductions, or new niche offerings. If they wish to expand their operations to another country, buying an existing company may be the only viable way to enter a foreign market, or at least the easiest way: The purchased business will already have its own personnel (both labor and management), a brand name, and other intangible assets, which helps to ensure that the acquiring company will start off with a solid customer base. Acquisitions often become a part of a company's growth strategy when it is more beneficial to acquire an existing firm's operations than it is to expand its own. Sometimes expanding compromises efficiency. Whether because the company is becoming too bureaucratic or it runs into physical or logistical resource constraints, eventually its marginal productivity peaks. To find higher growth and new profits, the large firm may look for promising young companies to acquire and incorporate into its revenue stream. When an industry attracts too many competitor firms or when the supply from existing firms ramps up too much, companies may look to acquisitions to reduce excess capacity, eliminate the competition, or focus on the most productive providers. If a new technology emerges that could increase productivity, a company may decide that it is more cost-efficient to purchase a company that has successfully implemented the technology rather than spending on internal research and development, which can often be too costly and time-consuming.

Acquisition and a Takeover

Although there is no technical difference between an acquisition and a take over and both words are often used interchangeably, they carry slightly different connotations. Typically, "takeover" suggests that the target company resists or opposes the purchase. In contrast, "acquisition" describes a more amicable transaction and is often used in conjunction with "merger", which occurs when the purchasing company and target company combine to form a new company.

Friendly and Hostile Acquisitions

Acquisitions can be either friendly or hostile. Friendly acquisitions occur when the target firm expresses its agreement to be acquired. Hostile acquisitions don't have the same agreement from the target firm, and the acquiring firm must actively purchase large stakes of the target company to gain a majority.

Friendly acquisitions often work towards a mutual benefit for both the acquiring and target companies. The companies develop strategies to ensure that the acquiring company purchases the appropriate assets, including the review of financial statements and other valuations, and that the purchase accounts for any obligations that may come with the assets. Once both parties agree to the terms and meet any legal stipulations, the purchase proceeds.

Unfriendly acquisitions, commonly referred to as hostile takeovers, occur when the target company does not consent to the acquisition. In this case, the acquiring company must gather a majority stake to force the acquisition. To acquire the necessary stake, the acquiring company can produce a tender offer designed to encourage current shareholders to sell their holdings in exchange for an above-market-value price. A 30-day acquisition notice must be filed with the Securities and Exchange Commission (SEC) with a copy directed to the target company's board of directors.

Share Prices and Acquisitions

In either case, the acquiring company often offers a premium on the market price of the target company's shares to entice shareholders to sell. For example, News Corp.'s bid to acquire Dow Jones back in 2007 was equal to a 65% premium over the stock's market price.

When a firm acquires another entity, there usually is a predictable short-term effect on the stock price of both companies. In general, the acquiring company's stock will fall while the target company's stock will rise.

The target company's stock usually goes up because of the premium that the acquiring company pays.

The acquiring company's stock usually goes down for several reasons. First, as we mentioned above, the acquiring company must pay more than the target company currently is worth. Beyond that, there are often several uncertainties involved with acquisitions. Here are some of the problems the takeover company could face during an acquisition:

- A turbulent integration process: problems associated with integrating different workplace cultures
- Lost productivity because of management power struggles
- Additional debt or expenses that must be incurred to make the purchase
- Accounting issues that weaken the takeover company's financial position, including restructuring charges and goodwill

Ways of Financing an Acquisition

A purchasing company can finance an acquisition by raising private equity, receiving a bank loan, or striking a mezzanine financing deal that involves elements of both debt and equity financing. It's also common for sellers to finance part of an acquisition; seller financing is more common in conjunction with a bank loan.

Since the financial crisis of 2007-2008, raising money to acquire a target company has become more difficult. Lenders have modified their criteria for providing credit by raising down payment requirements and carefully scrutinizing potential cash flow.

Private equity financing often takes the form of venture capital – a professionally managed pool of funds that invest in high-growth opportunities – or private equity firms. This isn't always the case, but it has proven to be an effective means of raising funds from dispersed sources and channeling them toward entrepreneurial opportunities.

Equity financing involves the buyer company selling securities in order to raise money, then using that money for both the acquisition transaction and to provide additional cash for the new company.

Bank financing takes a variety of forms. The most common is to receive a cash flow-based loan, in which the bank scrutinizes the cash flow, debt load, and profit margins of the target company.

The target company's financials are more important than the acquiring firm's; the target company is the asset that eventually generates the returns that are used to pay back the loan. If there is seller financing involved, the target company may take over the actual note after the acquiring company makes the down payment.

Asset-based financing is another option. In an asset-based loan, the lender looks at the collateral (the inventory, receivables, and fixed assets of the target firm) rather than the cash flow and debt loan.

Evaluating an Acquisition Candidate

Before acquiring, it is imperative for a company to evaluate whether its target is a good candidate. In fact, officers of companies have a fiduciary duty to perform thorough due diligence before making any acquisition.

The first step in evaluating an acquisition candidate is determining whether the asking price is reasonable. The metrics investors use to place a value on an acquisition target vary per industry; one of the primary reasons acquisitions fail is that the asking price for the target company exceeds these metrics.

Potential buyers should also examine the target company's debt load. A company with reasonable debt at a high-interest rate is a prime acquisition candidate as a larger company could refinance for much less. Unusually high liabilities, however, should alert potential investors to potential dangers. What's been called the worst deal in the history of U.S. finance, Bank of America's 2008 acquisition of Countrywide Financial, occurred through a failure to recognize such liabilities.

Most businesses have been party to or are aware of the potential of lawsuits; however, huge companies, such as Walmart, get sued several times daily. A good acquisition candidate is one that is not dealing with a level of litigation that exceeds what is reasonable and normal for its industry and size.

A good acquisition target has clean and organized financial statements. This makes it easier for the investor to exercise due diligence and execute the takeover with confidence; it also helps prevent unwanted surprises from being unveiled after the acquisition is complete.

Three of Finance History's Largest Acquisitions

The late 1990s experienced a series of multi-billion-dollar acquisitions not previously witnessed. From Yahoo!'s 1999 $6 billion purchase of Broadcast.com to @Home's almost $7 billion purchase of Excite, companies were interested in the growth now, profitability later (if ever) phenomenon. In the first few weeks of 2000, such acquisitions reached their zenith.

AOL and Time Warner

AOL, the most publicized online service of its time, built a then-remarkable subscriber base of 30 million people by offering a software suite (available on compact discs!) that entitled users to hundreds of free hours. Yes, internet usage was once measured in hours!

Meanwhile, Time Warner was decried as an "old media" company, despite having tangible businesses (publishing, television, et al.) and an enviable income statement. In a masterful display of overweening confidence, the young upstart purchased the venerable giant for $164 billion, dwarfing all records. The relative importance of the two companies was revealed in the new entity's name, AOL Time Warner.

Two years later, AOL Time Warner lost $99 billion. The new company's market value fell by $200 billion, significantly more than the size of the original acquisition. A few years later, the companies cited irreconcilable differences and ended their union. Today, Time Warner is a $60.0 billion company; its erstwhile purchaser was acquired by Verizon in 2015 for $4.4 billion.

Vodafone and Mannesmann

Yet AOL's ephemeral takeover of Time Warner is merely the Western Hemisphere's record holder. A few months earlier, British telecommunications company, Vodafone, completed a rancorous, if not completely, hostile takeover of German wireless provider Mannesmann. The Vodafone/Mannesmann deal cost $183 billion, in 1999 dollars—or more precisely, $183 billion in 1999 Vodafone stock. Vodafone offered, and Mannesmann ultimately accepted. The deal would have been historic even without the superlative currency figure, as it represented the first foreign takeover in modern German history. Today, Mannesmann survives under the name Vodafone D2, operating exclusively in Germany as the wholly owned subsidiary of its U.K. parent.

Express Scripts and Medco

Worldwide acquisitions tailed off considerably in the ensuing decade. The value of all corporate acquisitions in 2011 was lower than the corresponding number from 14 years earlier. In fact, the largest proposed acquisition of the period never even got off the ground. Like the Vodafone/Mannesmann deal, it would have involved America's second-largest mobile provider, AT&T, buying America's fourth-largest mobile provider, T-Mobile, for $39 billion. (Continuing the parallel, T-Mobile is a subsidiary of Germany's Deutsche Telekom.) Even though the deal was endorsed by many diverse parties, most state attorney generals, multiple labor unions, and the U.S. Department of Justice cited antitrust violations and sued. The principals pulled out, leaving a far less publicized deal as the biggest buy out of the year.

In 2012, St. Louis-based Express Scripts purchased Medco for $29 billion. Both companies administer prescription drug programs, process and pay claims, and indirectly act as bulk purchasers for their large customer bases. Since the acquisition, it's estimated that one in three Americans now falls under the Express Scripts aegis.

After the Acquisition

Most of the attention during an acquisition goes towards valuation, market shares, and legalities. Little notice is given to what happens in the aftermath, even though the success of an acquisition usually hinges on how the new company handles its many responsibilities. A new, logical corporate structure needs to be established. Resources need to be re-allocated towards their most valuable ends. Accounting processes and information must be combined in a legal, tax-efficient way. Pre-existing business relationships should be re-assessed, including relationships with staff.

Except in rare cases, the acquiring company must learn and become acquainted with new operations, customers, and suppliers. The new owners should meet the new employees, who are likely to be anxious about their job status and a changing culture. It's the responsibility of new leadership to communicate effectively, make honest and fair decisions, and try to minimize the risks and costs involved in this transition.

There are new logistics for the delivery of goods and services and for the integration of technology. When mergers involve large numbers of new employees, a new business command structure needs to be designed, articulated, and executed.

Some companies hire third-parties help to smooth this transition. Some consultants specialize in merger and acquisition (M&A) transitions and accounting integration. This can be especially helpful for management that has never been involved in an acquisition before.

Ultimately, the success or failure of an M&A deal hinges on the reaction of shareholders and customers. One mark of a successful acquisition: the acquiring firm (or the new, combined entity) displays higher earnings per share (EPS) than it previously had. This is considered an accretive acquisition. If EPS is lower following an acquisition, it is considered dilutive.

Merger

A merger is an agreement that unites two existing companies into one new company. There are several types of mergers and also several reasons why companies complete mergers. Mergers and acquisitions are commonly done to expand a company's reach, expand into new segments, or gain market share. All of these are done to please shareholders and create value.

A merger is the voluntary fusion of two companies on broadly equal terms into one new legal entity. The firms that agree to merge are roughly equal in terms of size, customers, scale of operations, etc. For this reason, the term "merger of equals" is sometimes used.

Mergers are most commonly done to gain market share, reduce costs of operations, expand to new territories, unite common products, grow revenues and increase profits, all of which should benefit the firms' shareholders. After a merger, shares of the new company are distributed to existing shareholders of both original businesses.

In 2015, there was a record $4.30 trillion worth of mergers and acquisitions announced. Deal making continues to be a popular way to grow revenue and earnings for companies of varying size.

Types of Mergers

There are five main types of company mergers:

- **Conglomerate.** This is a merger between two or more companies engaged in unrelated business activities. The firms may operate in different industries or different geographical regions. A pure conglomerate involves two firms that have nothing in common. A mixed conglomerate, on the other hand, takes place between organizations that, while operating in unrelated business activities, are actually trying to gain product or market extensions through the merger. Companies with no overlapping factors will only merge if it makes sense from a shareholder wealth perspective, that is, if the companies can create synergy. A conglomerate merger was formed when The Walt Disney Company merged with the American Broadcasting Company (ABC) in 1995.
- **Congeneric.** A congeneric merger is also known as a Product Extension merger. It occurs when two or more companies operate in the same market or sector with overlapping factors, such as technology, marketing, production processes, research and development (R&D), join to form a new business entity. A product extension merger is achieved when a new product line from one company is added to an existing product line of the other company. When two companies become one under a product extension, they are able to gain access to a larger group of consumers and, thus, bigger market share. An example of a congeneric merger is

Citigroup's 1998 union with Travelers Insurance, two companies with complementing products.

- **Market Extension.** This type of merger occurs between companies that sell the same products but compete in different markets. Companies that engage in a market extension merger seek to gain access to a bigger market and, thus, a bigger client base. To extend their markets, Eagle Bancshares and RBC Centura merged in 2002.
- **Horizontal.** A horizontal merger occurs between companies operating in the same industry. The merger is typically part of consolidation between two or more competitors offering the same products or services. Such mergers are common in industries with fewer firms, and the goal is to create a larger business with greater market share and economies of scale since competition among fewer companies tends to be higher. The 1998 merger of Daimler-Benz and Chrysler is considered a horizontal merger.
- **Vertical.** When two companies that produce parts or services for a specific finished product merge, the union is referred to as a vertical merger. Vertical merger occurs when two companies operating at different levels within the same industry's supply chain combine their operations. Such mergers are done to increase synergies achieved through the cost reduction which results from merging with one or more supply companies. One of the most well-known examples of a vertical merger took place in 2000 when internet provider America Online (AOL) combined with media conglomerate Time Warner.

Examples of Mergers

Anheuser-Busch InBev is an example of how mergers work and unite companies together. The company is the result of multiple mergers, consolidation, and market extensions in the beer market. The newly named company, Anheuser-Busch InBev, is the result of the mergers of three large international beverage companies - Interbrew (Belgium), Ambev (Brazil), and Anheuser-Busch (United States). Ambev merged with Interbrew uniting the number three and five largest brewers in the world. When Ambev and Anheuser-Busch merged, it united the number one and two largest brewers in the world. This example represents both horizontal merger and market extension as it was industry consolidation but also extended the international reach of all the combined company's brands.

The largest mergers in history have totaled over $100 billion each. In 2000, Vodafone acquired Mannesmann for $181 billion to create the world's largest mobile telecommunications company. In 2000, AOL and Time Warner vertically merged in a $164 million deal considered one of the biggest flops ever. In 2014, Verizon Communications bought out Vodafone's 45% stake in Vodafone Wireless for $130 billion.

Due to the large number of mergers, a mutual fund emerged, giving investors a chance to profit from merged deals. The fund captures the spread, or amount left between the offer price and trading price. The Merger Fund from Westchester Capital Funds has been around since 1989. The fund invests in companies that have publicly announced a merger or takeover. To invest in the fund, a minimum amount of $2,000 is required, and the fund does charge a higher 2.12% expense ratio. Since its inception in 1989, the fund has returned an average of 6.1% annually.

Amalgamation

In corporate finance, an amalgamation is the combination of two or more companies into a larger single company.

In accounting an amalgamation, or consolidation, refers to the combination of financial statements. For example, a group of companies reports their financials on a consolidated basis which includes the individual statements of several smaller businesses.

An amalgamation is, in fact, a specific subset within a broader group of "business combinations". There are three main types of business combinations, which are outlined below in more detail. It's important to understand the subtle differences when talking about mergers, acquisitions, and amalgamations.

1. **Acquisition (two survivors).** The purchasing company acquires more than 50% of the shares of the acquired company and both companies survive.
2. **Merger (one survivor).** The purchasing company buys the selling company's assets. The sale of the acquired company's assets leads to the survival of only the purchasing company.
3. **Amalgamation (no survivors).** This third option creates a new company in which none of the pre-existing companies survive.

As you can see with the above examples, the difference comes down to the surviving companies. In an amalgamation, a new company is created and none of the old companies survive.

Amalgamations are often done when competing companies engaged in similar business would achieve some synergy or cost savings by combining their operations, which can be quantified in a financial model. By contrast, it can also occur when companies want to enter new markets or get into new business and mergers and acquisitions as a way to achieve that. Here is a list of reasons why companies perform consolidations:

- Access to new markets
- Access to new technologies
- Access to new clients / geographies
- Cheaper financing for a bigger company
- Cost savings (synergies) achieved through bargaining power with suppliers and clients
- Eliminating competition

An amalgamation typically requires investment bankers, lawyers, accountants, and the executives at each of the combining companies. The bankers will typically perform extensive financial modeling and valuation to evaluate the potential transaction and advise the individual corporations. In parallel to this process, the lawyers will work with the bankers and their corporate clients to determine which of the above legal structures is optimal: acquisition, merger, or amalgamation.

Reconstruction of Companies

Reconstruction is a process of the company's reorganization, concerning legal, operational, ownership and other structures, by revaluing assets and reassessing the liabilities. There are two methods of reconstruction which are internal reconstruction and external reconstruction. The former is the method in which the reconstruction is undertaken without winding up the company and forming a new one, while the latter, is one whereby the existing company loses its existence, and a new company is set up to take over the business of the existing company.

Reconstruction is required when the company is incurring losses for many years, and the statement of account does not reflect the true and fair position of the business, as a higher net worth is depicted, than that of the real one. Here, in the given article, we are going to talk about all the important differences between internal and external reconstruction.

Comparison Chart

Basis for comparison	Internal reconstruction	External reconstruction
Meaning	Internal reconstruction refers to the method of corporate restructuring wherein existing company is not liquidated to form a new one.	External reconstruction is one in which the company undergoing reconstruction is liquidated to take over the business of existing company.

Basis for comparison	Internal reconstruction	External reconstruction
New company	No new company is formed.	New company is formed.
Use of specific terms in Balance Sheet	Balance Sheet of the company contains "And Reduced".	No specific terms are used in the Balance sheet.
Capital reduction	Capital is reduced and the external liability holders waive their claims.	No reduction in the capital
Approval of court	Approval of court is must.	No approval of court is required.
Transfer of Assets and Liabilities	No such transfer takes place.	Assets and liabilities of existing company are transferred to the new company.

Definition of Internal Reconstruction

A recourse undertook by the enterprise, in which substantial changes are made in the company's capital structure, without resorting to the liquidation of the existing company, is called internal reconstruction. In finer terms, it is the inner rearrangement of the company's financial structure, in which the company undergoing reconstruction continues to exist.

Internal Reconstruction focuses on relieving the company from debts and losses by negotiating with the creditors and reducing the outstanding amount towards them, so as to reach a favorable position. The methods given below are generally employed to effect the internal reconstruction process:

- Alteration of Share Capital
- Sub-division and Consolidation of Shares
- Conversion of shares into stock or stock into shares.
- Variation of Shareholder's rights
- Reduction of Share Capital
- Compromise/Arrangement
- Surrender of Shares.

In this process, the assets are restated, to represent fair values, and liabilities are restated to show the settable amount, and thus the balance sheet shows a true picture. In this scheme, trading losses and fictitious assets are written off, against the claim sacrificed by the debenture holders, creditors, etc.

Definition of External Reconstruction

External Reconstruction is a process in which the company's financial affairs are wound up, and a new company is formed to take over the assets and liabilities of the existing company, after the reorganization of the financial position. It requires the approval of shareholders, creditors and National Company Law Tribunal (NCLT).

In external reconstruction, the undertaking is being continued by the company but is in substance transferred to a company which is not an external one, but another entity that comprises of almost same shareholders, to be carried on by the transferee company. The accounting treatment of external reconstruction is same as the amalgamation in the nature of the purchase.

Key Differences Between Internal and External Reconstruction

The following points are relevant on account of the differences between internal and external reconstruction:

1. Internal reconstruction can be defined as the reorganization of the company, without liquidating the existing company and forming a new one. On the other hand, an external reconstruction is a form of corporate restructuring wherein the existing company is liquidated to give birth to a new company, for continuing the business of the existing one.

2. No new company is formed in internal reconstruction. Conversely, the new company is formed in the external reconstruction, to take over the business of the existing company.
3. In internal reconstruction, the capital of the company is reduced, and external liabilities such as debenture holders and creditors waive their claims by giving a discount. On the other hand, in external reconstruction, there is no reduction in the capital of the company.
4. In internal reconstruction, court's approval is mandatory, because the reduction in capital may affect the rights of the shareholders, which requires confirmation from the court. As against, in external reconstruction, there is no such approval required.
5. When the company undergoes internal reconstruction process, the Balance sheet prepared after the process contains the terms, "And Reduced." On the contrary, there are no specific terms used in the Balance Sheet in the case of external reconstruction.
6. In internal reconstruction, since there is no new company is formed, there is no transfer of assets and liabilities. Unlike, external reconstruction, assets, and liabilities of the old company are transferred to the new company.

HOLDING COMPANY ACCOUNTS

A holding company is a company which acquires all or majority of equity shares of any other company (called subsidiary company) in order to have control over subsidiary company. The subsidiary company continues to operate as before. The only noticeable change is as regards shareholders. After the acquisition of shares, the holding company is a major shareholder.

The Companies Act 1956 defines a subsidiary company and section 4 of the companies Act lays down that a company shall be deemed to be a subsidiary company of another if, but only if

(a) That other controls the composition of its board of directors, or

(b) The other company:

  (i) holds more than half in nominal value of its equity share capital, or

  (ii) if it is a company formed before 1st April 1956 with both equity and preference shareholders having the same voting rights, the other company exercises or controls more than half of its total voting power, or

  (iii) it is a subsidiary of any company which is that other company's subsidiary. For example, company B is a subsidiary of company A and company C is the subsidiary of company B. By virtue of above provision, company C will be taken as subsidiary of company A also.

Types of Holding Companies

Depending upon the purpose for which holding companies are created, they are of following types:

I. **Pure-holding Company.** A company which holds majority shares of other company is called Pure-holding Company.

II. **Parent Holding Company.** An existing company which consolidates other competing Limits is called parent holding company.

III. **Off Spring Holding Company.** It is a new company formed to take over the shares of many existing companies.

IV. **Intermediate Holding Company.** A holding company which is itself a subsidiary is called intermediate holding company.

V. **Mixed or Operating Holding or Investment holding Company.** When a company controls another company only for financial gains, it is called an investment holding company.

Financial year of the Holding Company and its Subsidiaries

The individual Companies which are subsidiaries of a holding enjoy separate legal status and as such can close their financial year on any date. However it seems to be the intention of the companies Act 1956 that the financial year of the subsidiary may end with that of the holding company. Section 213(1) of the companies Act, therefore provides that the central government may, if finds desirable, issue the necessary direction to subsidiary of a holding company to extend its financial year.

The maximum time gap between the close of the financial year of the holding company and its subsidiary can be of 6 months. If at any time it is more than six months, the Central Government on application of the board of directors of either of the company, can give orders to reduce the time gap to six months.

Presentation of Final Accounts

The final accounts of the holding company and its subsidiaries can be presented before shareholders in two ways, *i.e.,*

I. Presenting separately the final accounts of all the subsidiaries giving details of the manner in which these accounts are dealt with in the accounts of the holding company.

II. Preparing and Presenting the annual accounts i.e., profit/loss accounts and balance sheets of the holding company and its subsidiary in the consolidated form.

In India law does not require a holding company to present a consolidated balance sheet and a consolidated profit/loss account incorporating the operations of its subsidiaries in its own final accounts.

Calculation of Cost of Control or Gain on Acquisition *i.e.,* Calculation of Goodwill or Capital Reserve on Consolidation:

If the holding company pays more than the net worth of the subsidiary company because of its reputation, this difference between the net worth and the price paid for them is debited to "Goodwill or cost of control" account, if the purchase price paid by the holding company is less than the net assets of the subsidiary company this gain is of capital nature and is transferred to Capital Reserve Account.

Goodwill = Cost of investment is more than the net assets acquired

Or

Cost of investment is more than the net worth of shares acquired

Capital Reserve = Cost of investment is less than the net assets acquired

Calculation of Minority Interest (Partly Owned Subsidiary)

In certain cases holding company does not acquire all the shares of the subsidiary company or when the holding company acquires more than half but less than all the shares of the subsidiary that means some of the shares in the subsidiary are held by outsiders. In such a situation outsiders will also have a claim against the net assets of the company alongwith holding company. The proportion of net assets/shareholders holding small number of shares, is known as Minority Interest. The usual practice is to show all assets and liabilities of the subsidiary company in the consolidated balance sheet. The proportion of net assets belonging to minority shareholders, is shown on the liability side under the heading 'Minority Interest."

Minority Interest is not a liability in reality but it is that part of capital of the group which belongs to outsiders. While calculating minority interest all accumulated profits or losses of the subsidiary must be adjusted in its share capital.

Minority shareholders are not concerned with whether the profits are capital profits or revenue profits. In other words, no distinction is made between pre-acquisition and post-acquisition profits for calculating minority interest. The share of total profits for which minority shareholders have a claim will be adjusted in their share of capital to find out value of minority interest.

Distinction Between Capital Profits and Revenue Profits

If the holding company acquires shares in the subsidiary company on its balance sheet date, all the reserves and profits of the subsidiary are treated as capital profits and are adjusted for calculating gain or loss on acquisition. Profits earned and reserve built up after the date of acquisition are treated as revenue profits and revenue reserves and are shown in the consolidated balance sheet.

Capital profits are adjusted for ascertaining Cost of Control/Goodwill or Capital Reserve. Date of acquisition of shares in the subsidiary company is important for dividing the profits/reserves into capital and revenue.

Capital Losses and Revenue Losses

Debit balance of profit and loss account of subsidiary company at the time of acquisition of shares by the holding company is to be treated as capital losses and are adjusted while calculating cost of control and debited to Goodwill Account. Pre-acquisition losses are capital losses.

Revenue losses or post-acquisition losses of subsidiary company are treated as:

(a) Share of holding company are deducted from the revenue profits of the holding company or added to its (holding Co.) accumulated losses and shown on the asset side of the consolidated balance sheet.

(b) Share of minority shareholders are deducted from their share of capital.

Unrealised Profit

When some goods are sold above the cost price by holding company to subsidiary company or vice versa remains unsold at the date of consolidation, the profits of the supplier cannot be considered as realised from the view point of the group. Such unrealised profit of the group must be eliminated and the value of closing stock must be adjusted so that it could be shown at cost in the Consolidated Balance Sheet. There are three opinions to deal with this problem. These are

(i) Eliminate the profit attributable to the group. This opinion presumes that transaction is complete so far as minority shareholders are concerned. This opinion is followed in the problems of this book.

(ii) The entire profit is eliminated from the stock. The profit of the majority and minority shareholders are reduced in proportion to their interest.

(iii) The third opinion is advanced by AICPA (American Institute of Certified Public Accountants). According to this thought the whole such profit is eliminated from stock and from the profits of majority shareholders.

Unclaimed Dividend

Unclaimed dividend is that part of total dividend which has been declared but not claimed by some shareholders so far.

If unclaimed dividend appears in the balance sheet of the subsidiary company then it should be divided into two parts:

(i) Dividend unclaimed by outside shareholders.

(ii) Dividend unclaimed by holding company or any other group company.

The first part of unclaimed dividend shall appear as liability in the consolidated balance sheet and the second part shall be eliminated being inter-group transaction.

Proposed Dividend

If dividend is proposed by the subsidiary company then the proposed dividend should be deducted from P& L A/C of the subsidiary Company. The proposed dividend is deducted from profits because it is appropriation to profits.

It must be noted here that if proposed dividend is appearing in the balance sheet of the subsidiary then it should not be deducted from profits as it is already debited to P/L appropriation accounts.

In case proposed dividend appears in the balance sheet of the subsidiary company then it need not appear as such in the consolidated balance sheet. Holding company share of such proposed dividend is added to Profit/Loss account of holding company, minority's share of proposed dividend can be added to minority interest or the share of minority can be shown as current liability in the consolidated balance sheet.

Share Premium

The treatment of share premium depends upon the fact that to whom it relates. Share premium of holding company generally remain unchanged in the consolidated balance sheet. But if control was acquired by holding company by issue of its own shares at premium, such premium should be adjusted against goodwill in consolidated balance sheet.

Share Premium of Subsidiary Company which exists at the time of acquisition of share is taken as pre-acquisition profit (capital profit). If share premium arises by issue of shares to outsiders after acquisition of control, the proportionate share of minority shareholders is added to 'Minority Interest' and the proportionate amount of share premium of Holding Company shall be added to share premium of holding company.

Preliminary Expenses

Preliminary expenses may be treated as Capital Loss and adjusted in calculation of cost of control at the time of consolidation of accounts.

Provision for Taxation

If any provision for tax is created by the subsidiary, it should be treated as current liability. So it should be shown on the liability side of consolidated balance sheet.

Contingent Liabilities

A liability which may or may not materialise is known as contingent liability. For the purpose of consolidation contingent liabilities are categorised as:

I. Internal Contingent Liabilities or Intra-Group Contingent Liabilities.

II. External Contingent Liabilities

In Individual balance sheets contingent Liabilities are generally shown in foot-note.

While preparing consolidated balance sheet, contingent liability in respect of a transaction between holding company and subsidiary company (internal contingent liabilities) will disappear from the footnote as they are actual liability.

Consolidation of Profit/Loss Account

Consolidated Profit/Loss account is prepared in order to ascertain the result (Profit/Loss) of the current year of the group. While consolidating the Profit/Loss account, the items appearing in the Profit/Loss account of the holding company and its subsidiaries have to be aggregated. During the process of aggregation the following adjustments have to made.

I. **Inter-Company Transfer of Goods.** If goods were transferred by holding company to subsidiary company or vice-versa then inter company transfers must be eliminated from both purchases and sales appearing in the consolidated Profit/Loss account.

II. **Unrealised Profit.** Intra-group unrealised profit on sales should be reduced from (i) the trading profits of the selling company (ii) the stock of the purchasing company. The reduction should be confined to the holding company's share of such profits. The unrealised profits is treated by passing the following entry:

P/L (Consolidated) A/C. Dr.

To Stock Reserve A/C

III. **Pre-acquisition Profits or Losses of Subsidiary.** The proportionate share of pre-acquisition share of profits of subsidiary that belong to the holding company is credited to capital reserve (or goodwill as the case may be) by debiting consolidated Profit/Loss account. In other words the following entry is passed.

Consolidated P/L A/C Dr.

To Capital Reserve

To Goodwill

Note: In case of Pre-acquisition losses the reverse entry shall be passed.

IV. **Inter-company Dividends and Interest.** Dividends received by the holding company from the subsidiary company should be eliminated from both the sides of the consolidated profit/loss account. Similarly debenture interest due or received from each other should be eliminated. It should be noted here that no adjustment is required for interest on debentures and dividends, as the tax is payable to outsiders and Government authorities.

V. **Proposed Dividend of Subsidiary**

(a) If the subsidiary company has recorded the proposed dividend in its books and the holding company has also recorded it for its share of dividends, the holding company's share should be eliminated from both the sides of the consolidated Profit/Loss Account.

(b) If the holding company has not passed entries for proposed dividends of the subsidiary company, the debit in respect of proposed dividend should be reduced by the holding company's share in such proposed dividends.

VI. **Capitalisation of Post-acquisition Profit.** If some of the post-acquisition profits has been utilised by the subsidiary in payment of bonus shares, the same should be transferred to Capital Reserve.

VII. **Arrears of Preference Dividend.** Arrears of dividends on cumulative preference shares are payable if there are profits. If there are enough profits and consolidated Profit/Loss account is to be prepared then the arrears of dividend on preference shares held by the minority shareholders should be debited to the consolidated Profit/Loss account and credited to minority interest account.

In Brief, the following entry can be passed:

Consolidated P/L A/C Dr.

To Minority Interest A/C

VIII. **Revaluation of Assets.** If the fixed assets of the subsidiary company were revalued at the time of acquisition of shares and the revaluation was not recorded by subsidiary in its books then the excess or short depreciation should be adjusted by debiting or crediting consolidated Profit/Loss account and debiting or crediting the respective asset account.

IX. **Subsidiary is Transfer to Reserves.** If the subsidiary company has transferred its profits then such reserve is categorised into two parts *i.e.*, holding company's share in reserve and minority shareholders share in reserve. The reserve appropriated from the subsidiary's Profit/Loss appropriation account appear in group accounts as a 'Minority Interest' in the consolidated Profit/Loss account.

X. **Minority Shareholders Share.** The share of outside shareholders in Currents years net profit (*i.e.*, profit after depreciation, taxation but before adjustment of unrealised profit on stock) is debited to consolidated Profit/Loss account and credited to minority interest.

COST AND MANAGEMENT ACCOUNTING

MARGINAL COSTING

Marginal Costing is a costing technique wherein the marginal cost, i.e. variable cost is charged to units of cost, while the fixed cost for the period is completely written off against the contribution.

The term marginal cost implies the additional cost involved in producing an extra unit of output, which can be reckoned by total variable cost assigned to one unit. It can be calculated as:

Marginal Cost = Direct Material + Direct Labor + Direct Expenses + Variable Overheads

Characteristics of Marginal Costing

- **Classification into Fixed and Variable Cost:** Costs are bifurcated, on the basis of variability into fixed cost and variable costs. In the same way, semi variable cost is separated.
- **Valuation of Stock:** While valuing the finished goods and work in progress, only variable cost are taken into account. However, the variable selling and distribution overheads are not included in the valuation of inventory.
- **Determination of Price:** The prices are determined on the basis of marginal cost and marginal contribution.
- **Profitability:** The ascertainment of departmental and product's profitability is based on the contribution margin.

In addition to the above characteristics, marginal costing system brings together the techniques of cost recording and reporting.

Marginal Costing Approach

The difference between product costs and period costs forms a basis for marginal costing technique, wherein only variable cost is considered as the product cost while the fixed cost is deemed as a period cost, which incurs during the period, irrespective of the level of activity.

Facts Concerning Marginal Costing

- **Cost Ascertainment.** The basis for ascertaining cost in marginal costing is the nature of cost, which gives an idea of the cost behavior, that has a great impact on the profitability of the firm.
- **Special technique.** It is not a unique method of costing, like contract costing, process costing, batch costing. But, marginal costing is a different type of technique, used by the managers for the purpose of decision making. It provides a basis for understanding cost data so as to gauge the profitability of various products, processes and cost centers.
- **Decision Making.** It has a great role to play, in the field of decision making, as the changes in the level of activity pose a serious problem to the management of the undertaking.

Marginal Costing assists the managers in taking end number of business decisions, such as replacement of machines, discontinuing a product or service, etc. It also helps the management in ascertaining the appropriate level of activity, through break even analysis, that reflect the impact of increasing or decreasing production level, on the company's overall profit.

Break-even Analysis

A break-even analysis is a financial tool which helps you to determine at what stage your company, or a new service or a product, will be profitable. In other words, it's a financial calculation for determining the number of products or services a company should sell to cover its costs (particularly fixed costs). Break-even is a situation where you are neither making money nor losing money, but all your costs have been covered.

Break-even analysis is useful in studying the relation between the variable cost, fixed cost and revenue. Generally, a company with low fixed costs will have a low break-even point of sale. For an example, a company has a fixed cost of Rs.0 (zero) will automatically have broken even upon the first sale of its product.

Components of Break Even Analysis

Fixed Costs

Fixed costs are also called as the overhead cost. These overhead costs occur after the decision to start an economic activity is taken and these costs are directly related to the level of production, but not the quantity of production. Fixed costs include (but are not limited to) interest, taxes, salaries, rent, depreciation costs, labour costs, energy costs etc. These costs are fixed no matter how much you sell.

Variable Costs

Variable costs are costs that will increase or decrease in direct relation to the production volume. These cost include cost of raw material, packaging cost, fuel and other costs that are directly related to the production.

Contribution Margin

Break-even analysis also deals with the contribution margin of a product. The excess between the selling price and total variable costs is known as contribution margin. For an example, if the price of a product is Rs.100, total variable costs are Rs. 60 per product and fixed cost is Rs. 25 per product, the contribution margin of the product is Rs. 40 (Rs. 100 – Rs. 60). This Rs. 40 represents the revenue collected to cover the fixed costs. In the calculation of the contribution margin, fixed costs are not considered.

When is Break even analysis used?

Starting a new business. If you wish to start a new business, a break-even analysis is a must. Not only it helps you in deciding, whether the idea of starting a new is viable, but it will force you to be realistic about the costs, as well as guide you about the pricing strategy.

Creating a new product. In the case of an existing business, you should still do a break-even analysis before launching a new product—particularly if such a product is going to add a significant expenditure.

Changing the business model. If you are about to the change your business model, like, switching from wholesale business to retail business, you should do a break-even analysis. The costs could change considerably and this will help you to figure out the selling prices need to change too.

Breakeven analysis is useful for the following reasons:

- It helps to determine remaining/unused capacity of the concern once the breakeven is reached. This will help to show the maximum profit on a particular product/service that can be generated.
- It helps to determine the impact on profit on changing to automation from manual (a fixed cost replaces a variable cost).
- It helps to determine the change in profits if the price of a product is altered.
- It helps to determine the amount of losses that could be sustained if there is a sales downturn.

Additionally, break-even analysis is very useful for knowing the overall ability of a business to generate a profit. In the case of a company whose breakeven point is near to the maximum sales level, this signifies that it is nearly impractical for the business to earn a profit even under the best of circumstances.

Therefore, it's the management responsibility to monitor the breakeven point constantly. This monitoring certainly reduces the breakeven point whenever possible.

Ways to monitor Break even point

- **Pricing analysis.** Minimize or eliminate the use of coupons or other price reductions offers, since such promotional strategies increase the breakeven point.
- **Technology analysis.** Implementing any technology that can enhance the business efficiency, thus increasing capacity with no extra cost.
- **Cost analysis.** Reviewing all fixed costs constantly to verify if any can be eliminated can surely help. Also, review the total variable costs to see if they can be eliminated. This analysis will increase the margin and reduce the breakeven point.
- **Margin analysis.** Push sales of the highest-margin (high contribution earning) items and pay close attention to product margins, thus reducing the breakeven point.
- **Outsourcing.** If an activity consists of a fixed cost, try to outsource such activity (whenever possible), which reduces the breakeven point.

Benefits of Break-even analysis

Catch missing expenses. When you're thinking about a new business, it's very much possible that you may forget about few expenses. Therefore, if you do a break-even analysis you have to review all your financial commitments to figure out your break-even point. This analysis certainly restricts the number of surprises down the road.

Set revenue targets. Once the break-even analysis is complete, you will get to know how much you need to sell to be profitable. This will help you and your sales team to set more concrete sales goals.

Make smarter decisions. Entrepreneurs often take decisions in relation to their business based on emotion. Emotion is important i.e. how you feel, though it's not enough. In order to be a successful entrepreneur, your decisions should be based on facts.

Fund your business. This analysis is a key component in any business plan. It's generally a requirement if you want outsiders to fund your business. In order to fund your business, you have to prove that your plan is viable. Furthermore, if the analysis looks good, you will be comfortable enough to take the burden of various ways of financing.

Better Pricing. Finding the break-even point will help in pricing the products better. This tool is highly used for providing the best price of a product that can fetch maximum profit without increasing the existing price.

Cover fixed costs. Doing a break-even analysis helps in covering all fixed cost.

STANDARD COSTING

Standard costing is the practice of substituting an expected cost for an actual cost in the accounting records. Subsequently, variances are recorded to show the difference between the expected and actual costs. This approach represents a simplified alternative to cost layering systems, such as the FIFO and LIFO methods, where large amounts of historical cost information must be maintained for inventory items held in stock.

Standard costing involves the creation of estimated (i.e., standard) costs for some or all activities within a company. The core reason for using standard costs is that there are a number of applications where it is too time-consuming to collect actual costs, so standard costs are used as a close approximation to actual costs.

Since standard costs are usually slightly different from actual costs, the cost accountant periodically calculates variances that break out differences caused by such factors as labor rate changes and the cost of materials. The cost accountant may periodically change the standard costs to bring them into closer alignment with actual costs.

Advantages of Standard Costing

Though most companies do not use standard costing in its original application of calculating the cost of ending inventory, it is still useful for a number of other applications. In most cases, users are probably not even aware that they are using standard costing, only that they are using an approximation of actual costs. Here are some potential uses:

- **Budgeting.** A budget is always composed of standard costs, since it would be impossible to include in it the exact actual cost of an item on the day the budget is finalized. Also, since a key application of the budget is to compare it to actual results in subsequent periods, the standards used within it continue to appear in financial reports through the budget period.
- **Inventory costing.** It is extremely easy to print a report showing the period-end inventory balances (if you are using a perpetual inventory system), multiply it by the standard cost of each item, and instantly generate an ending inventory valuation. The result does not exactly match the actual cost of inventory, but it is close. However, it may be necessary to update standard costs frequently, if actual costs are continually changing. It is easiest to update costs

for the highest-dollar components of inventory on a frequent basis, and leave lower-value items for occasional cost reviews.

- **Overhead application.** If it takes too long to aggregate actual costs into cost pools for allocation to inventory, then you may use a standard overhead application rate instead, and adjust this rate every few months to keep it close to actual costs.
- **Price formulation.** If a company deals with custom products, then it uses standard costs to compile the projected cost of a customer's requirements, after which it adds a margin. This may be quite a complex system, where the sales department uses a database of component costs that change depending upon the unit quantity that the customer wants to order. This system may also account for changes in the company's production costs at different volume levels, since this may call for the use of longer production runs that are less expensive.

Nearly all companies have budgets and many use standard cost calculations to derive product prices, so it is apparent that standard costing will find some uses for the foreseeable future. In particular, standard costing provides a benchmark against which management can compare actual performance.

Problems with Standard Costing

Despite the advantages just noted for some applications of standard costing, there are substantially more situations where it is not a viable costing system. Here are some problem areas:

- **Cost-plus contracts.** If you have a contract with a customer under which the customer pays you for your costs incurred, plus a profit (known as a cost-plus contract), then you must use actual costs, as per the terms of the contract. Standard costing is not allowed.
- **Drives inappropriate activities.** A number of the variances reported under a standard costing system will drive management to take incorrect actions to create favorable variances. For example, they may buy raw materials in larger quantities in order to improve the purchase price variance, even though this increases the investment in inventory. Similarly, management may schedule longer production runs in order to improve the labor efficiency variance, even though it is better to produce in smaller quantities and accept less labor efficiency in exchange.
- **Fast-paced environment.** A standard costing system assumes that costs do not change much in the near term, so that you can rely on standards for a number of months or even a year, before updating the costs. However, in an environment where product lives are short or continuous improvement is driving down costs, a standard cost may become out-of-date within a month or two.
- **Slow feedback.** A complex system of variance calculations is an integral part of a standard costing system, which the accounting staff completes at the end of each reporting period. If the production department is focused on immediate feedback of problems for instant correction, the reporting of these variances is much too late to be useful.
- **Unit-level information.** The variance calculations that typically accompany a standard costing report are accumulated in aggregate for a company's entire production department, and so are unable to provide information about discrepancies at a lower level, such as the individual work cell, batch, or unit.

The preceding list shows that there are many situations where standard costing is not useful, and may even result in incorrect management actions. Nonetheless, as long as you are aware of these issues, it is usually possible to profitably adapt standard costing into some aspects of a company's operations.

Standard Cost Variances

A variance is the difference between the actual cost incurred and the standard cost against which it is measured. A variance can also be used to measure the difference between actual and expected sales. Thus, variance analysis can be used to review the performance of both revenue and expenses.

There are two basic types of variances from a standard that can arise, which are the rate variance and the volume variance. Here is more information about both types of variances:

- **Rate variance.** A rate variance (which is also known as a price variance) is the difference between the actual price paid for something and the expected price, multiplied by the actual quantity purchased. The "rate" variance designation is most commonly applied to the labor rate variance, which involves the actual cost of direct labor in comparison to the standard cost of direct labor. The rate variance uses a different designation when applied to the purchase of materials, and may be called the purchase price variance or the material price variance.
- **Volume variance.** A volume variance is the difference between the actual quantity sold or consumed and the budgeted amount, multiplied by the standard price or cost per unit. If the variance relates to the sale of goods, it is called the sales volume variance. If it relates to the use of direct materials, it is called the material yield variance. If the variance relates to the use of direct labor, it is called the labor efficiency variance. Finally, if the variance relates to the application of overhead, it is called the overhead efficiency variance.

Thus, variances are based on either changes in cost from the expected amount, or changes in the quantity from the expected amount. The most common variances that a cost accountant elects to report on are subdivided within the rate and volume variance categories for direct materials, direct labor, and overhead. It is also possible to report these variances for revenue.

It is not always considered practical or even necessary to calculate and report on variances, unless the resulting information can be used by management to improve the operations or lower the costs of a business. When a variance is considered to have a practical application, the cost accountant should research the reason for the variance in detail and present the results to the responsible manager, perhaps also with a suggested course of action.

Standard Cost Creation

At the most basic level, you can create a standard cost simply by calculating the average of the most recent actual cost for the past few months. In many smaller companies, this is the extent of the analysis used. However, there are some additional factors to consider, which can significantly alter the standard cost that is used. They are:

- **Equipment age.** If a machine is nearing the end of its productive life, it may produce a higher proportion of scrap than was previously the case.
- **Equipment setup speeds.** If it takes a long time to setup equipment for a production run, the cost of the setup, as spread over the units in the production run, is expensive. If a setup reduction plan is contemplated, this can yield significantly lower overhead costs.
- **Labor efficiency changes.** If there are production process changes, such as the installation of new, automated equipment, then this impacts the amount of labor required to manufacture a product.
- **Labor rate changes.** If you know that employees are about to receive pay raises, either through a scheduled raise or as mandated by a labor union contract, then incorporate it into the new standard. This may mean setting an effective date for the new standard that matches the date when the cost increase is supposed to go into effect.

- **Learning curve.** As the production staff creates an increasing volume of a product, it becomes more efficient at doing so. Thus, the standard labor cost should decrease (though at a declining rate) as production volumes increase.
- **Purchasing terms.** The purchasing department may be able to significantly alter the price of a purchased component by switching suppliers, altering contract terms, or by buying in different quantities.

Any one of the additional factors noted here can have a major impact on a standard cost, which is why it may be necessary in a larger production environment to spend a significant amount of time formulating a standard cost.

BUDGETARY CONTROL

Budgetary control is the process of determining various actual results with budgeted figures for the enterprise for the future period and standards set then comparing the budgeted figures with the actual performance for calculating variances, if any. First of all, budgets are prepared and then actual results are recorded.

The comparison of budgeted and actual figures will enable the management to find out discrepancies and take remedial measures at a proper time. The budgetary control is a continuous process which helps in planning and co-ordination. It provides a method of control too. A budget is a means and budgetary control is the end-result.

Budgetary control involves the follows:

(a) The objects are set by preparing budgets.:

(b) The business is divided into various responsibility centres for preparing various budgets.

(c) The actual figures are recorded.

(d) The budgeted and actual figures are compared for studying the performance of different cost centres.

(e) If actual performance is less than the budgeted norms, a remedial action is taken immediately.

Objectives of Budgetary Control

Budgetary control is essential for policy planning and control. It also acts an instrument of co-ordination.

The main objectives of budgetary control are the follows:

1. To ensure planning for future by setting up various budgets, the requirements and expected performance of the enterprise are anticipated.
3. To operate various cost centres and departments with efficiency and economy.
4. Elimination of wastes and increase in profitability.
5. To anticipate capital expenditure for future.
6. To centralise the control system.
7. Correction of deviations from the established standards.
8. Fixation of responsibility of various individuals in the organization.

Essentials of Budgetary Control

There are certain steps which are necessary for the successful implementation budgetary control system.

1. **Organization for Budgetary Control.** The proper organization is essential for the successful preparation, maintenance and administration of budgets. A Budgetary Committee is formed, which comprises the departmental heads of various departments. All the functional heads are entrusted with the responsibility of ensuring proper implementation of their respective departmental budgets.

   The Chief Executive is the overall in-charge of budgetary system. He constitutes a budget committee for preparing realistic budgets A budget officer is the convener of the budget committee who co-ordinates the budgets of different departments. The managers of different departments are made responsible for their departmental budgets.

2. **Budget Centres.** A budget centre is that part of the organization for which the budget is prepared. A budget centre may be a department, section of a department or any other part of the department. The establishment of budget centres is essential for covering all parts of the organization. The budget centres are also necessary for cost control purposes. The appraisal performance of different parts of the organization becomes easy when different centres are established.

3. **Budget Manual.** A budget manual is a document which spells out the duties and also the responsibilities of various executives concerned with the budgets. It specifies the relations amongst various functionaries.

4. **Budget Officer.** The Chief Executive, who is at the top of the organization, appoints some person as Budget Officer. The budget officer is empowered to scrutinize the budgets prepared by different functional heads and to make changes in them, if the situations so demand. The actual performance of different departments is communicated to the Budget Officer. He determines the deviations in the budgets and the actual performance and takes necessary steps to rectify the deficiencies, if any.

   He works as a coordinator among different departments and monitors the relevant information. He also informs the top management about the performance of different departments. The budget officer will be able to carry out his work fully well only if he is conversant with the working of all the departments.

5. **Budget Committee.** In small-scale concerns the accountant is made responsible for preparation and implementation of budgets. In large-scale concerns a committee known as Budget Committee is formed. The heads of all the important departments are made members of this committee. The Committee is responsible for preparation and execution of budgets. The members of this committee put up the case of their respective departments and help the committee to take collective decisions if necessary. The Budget Officer acts as convener of this committee.

6. **Budget Period.** A budget period is the length of time for which a budget is prepared and employed. The budget period depends upon a number of factors. It may be different for different industries or even it may be different in the same industry or business.

   The budget period depends upon the following considerations:

   (a) The type of budget i.e., sales budget, production budget, raw materials purchase budget, capital expenditure budget. A capital expenditure budget may be for a longer period i.e. 3 to 5 years purchase, sale budgets may be for one year.

   (b) The nature of demand for the products.

   (c) The timings for the availability of the finances.

   (d) The economic situation of the country.

   (e) The length of trade cycles.

   All the above-mentioned factors are taken into account while fixing period of budgets.

7. **Determination of Key Factor.** The budgets are prepared for all functional areas. These budgets are interdependent and inter-related. A proper co-ordination among different budgets is necessary for making the budgetary control a success. The constraints on some budgets may have an effect on other budgets too. A factor which influences all other budgets is known as Key Factor or Principal Factor.

   There may be a limitation on the quantity of goods a concern may sell. In this case, sales will be a key factor and all other budgets will be prepared by keeping in view the amount of goods the concern will be able to sell. The raw material supply may be limited, so production, sales and cash budgets will be decided according to raw materials budget. Similarly, plant capacity may be a key factor if the supply of other factors is easily available.

   The key factor may not necessarily remain the same. The raw materials supply may be limited at one time but it may be easily available at another time. The sales may be increased by adding more sales staff, etc. Similarly, other factors may also improve at different times. The key factor also highlights the limitations of the enterprise. This will enable the management to improve the working of those departments where scope for improvement exists.

Advantages of Budgetary Control

The budgetary control system help in fixing the goals for the organization as whole and concerted efforts are made for its achievements. It enables 'economies in the enterprise.

Some of the advantages of budgetary control are:

1. **Maximization of Profits.** The budgetary control aims at the maximization of profits of the enterprise. To achieve this aim, a proper planning and co-ordination of different functions is undertaken. There is a proper control over various capital and revenue expenditures. The resources are put to the best possible use.
2. **Co-ordination.** The working of different departments and sectors is properly coordinated. The budgets of different departments have a bearing on one another. The co-ordination of various executives and subordinates is necessary for achieving budgeted targets.
3. **Specific Aims.** The plans, policies and goals are decided by the top management. All efforts are put together to reach the common goal, of the organization. Every department is given a target to be achieved. The efforts are directed towards achieving some specific aims. If there is no definite aim then the efforts will be wasted in pursuing different aims.
4. **Tool for Measuring Performance.** By providing targets to various departments, budgetary control provides a tool for measuring managerial performance. The budgeted targets are compared to actual results and deviations are determined. The performance of each department is reported to the top management. This system enables the introduction of management by exception.
5. **Economy.** The planning of expenditure will be systematic and there will be economy in spending. The finances will be put to optimum use. The benefits derived for the concern will ultimately extend to industry and then to national economy. The national resources will be used economically and wastage will be eliminated.
6. **Determining Weaknesses.** The deviations in budgeted and actual performance will enable the determination of weak spots. Efforts are concentrated on those aspects where performance is less than the stipulated.
7. **Corrective Action.** The management will be able to take corrective measures whenever there is a discrepancy in performance. The deviations will be regularly reported so that necessary action is taken at the earliest. In the absence of a budgetary control system the deviations can be determined only at the end of the financial period.

8. **Consciousness.** It creates budget consciousness among the employees. By fixing targets for the employees, they are made conscious of their responsibility. Everybody knows what he is expected to do and he continues with his work uninterrupted.
9. **Reduces Costs.** In the present day competitive world budgetary control has a significant role to play. Every businessman tries to reduce the cost of production for increasing sales. He tries to have those combinations of products where profitability is more.
10. **Introduction of Incentive Schemes.** Budgetary control system also enables the introduction of incentive schemes of remuneration. The comparison of budgeted and actual performance will enable the use of such schemes.

Limitations of Budgetary Control

Despite of many good points of budgetary control there are some limitations of this system. Some of the limitations are discussed as follows:

1. **Uncertain Future.** The budgets are prepared for the future period. Despite best estimates made for the future, the predictions may not always come true. The future is always uncertain and the situation which is presumed to prevail in future may change. The change in future conditions upsets the budgets which have to be prepared on the basis of certain assumptions. The future uncertainties reduce the utility of budgetary control system.
2. **Budgetary Revision Required.** Budgets arc prepared on the assumptions that certain conditions will prevail. Because of future uncertainties, assumed conditions may not prevail necessitating the revision of budgetary targets. The frequent revision of targets will reduce the value of budgets and revisions involve huge expenditures too.
3. **Discourage Efficient Persons.** Under budgetary control system the targets are given to every person in the organization. The common tendency of people is to achieve the targets only. There may be some efficient persons who can exceed the targets but they will also feel contented by reaching the targets. So budgets may serve as constraints on managerial initiatives.
4. **Problem of Co-ordination.** The success of budgetary control depends upon the co-ordination among different departments. The performance of one department affects the results of other departments. To overcome the problem of co-ordination a Budgetary Officer is needed. Every concern cannot afford to appoint a Budgetary Officer. The lack of co-ordination among different departments results in poor performance.
5. **Conflict Among Different Departments.** Budgetary control may lead to conflicts among functional departments. Every departmental head worries for his department goals without thinking of business goal. Every department tries to get maximum allocation of funds and this raises a conflict among different departments.
6. **Depends Upon Support of Top Management.** Budgetary control system depends upon the support of top management. The management should be enthusiastic for the success of this system and should give full support for it. If at any time there is a lack of support from top management then this system will collapse.

PROCESS COSTING

A manufacturing unit that can differentiate its processes and produces a standard product will use process costing method to determine cost of production. This is done by allocating all process cost to the total units produced.

In simple words, if an unit passes through different processes and the processes are easily distinguishable then the cost of the unit will be cost of process that it goes through.

In process costing a separate account is opened for every process and on completion of the process the cost is transferred to the next process.

Illustration

A paper manufacturing unit has the following processes

❍ Making pulp ❍ Beating ❍ Pulp to paper ❍ Finishing

Let us assume the costs incurred for producing 1000 units is

Making pulp	Rs. 10000
Beating	Rs. 20000
Pulp to paper	Rs. 15000
Finishing	Rs. 30000
Total Costs	Rs. 75000
Total units	1000
Cost per unit	Rs. 75

The above illustration is a simple presentation of process costing. However in an actual unit there will be Work in Progress at any given period end. So the steps for process costing will be

- To determine the total production that is: Opening stock at beginning of period + Production during the period – Rejections if any + Equivalent units of Work in process
  (To convert the number of WIP units to finished product equivalent lets understand this example : Say 500 units are in WIP and they are 50% complete then the finished product equivalent will be 500 + 50% = 250)
- To determine the total costs, both direct and indirect costs incurred for the opening stock and current production are to be considered.
- Allocation of the costs incurred for the entire inventory is done by dividing the total costs by equivalent units of production.

As we know, there will be Work in progress during the opening and closing of a period and thus an organization needs to decide on the cost flow assumptions. For computing costs under process costing the organization can use either the FIFO or weighted average cost flow assumption.

Under the FIFO method it is assumed that the material that comes in first is transferred out first and hence the two methods (FIFO and weighted average) vary while treating opening inventory. The treatment of Work in progress in both the methods is as follows :

Steps	**Weighted Average**	**First in first out**
Total production	Units transferred out + Ending inventory WIP	Beginning WIP+Units transferred out + ending inventory WIP
Total Costs	Beginning WIP costs + costs incurred during the period	Total costs incurred during the period
Cost allocation	Total costs / total units	Total costs / total units

The above is a simple chart differentiating the two methods. In case of WIP there will be percentage of completion that will have to be looked into and equivalent units will have to be computed. Let us understand the same with an example, the assumption is that the percentage of completion is the same for both material and labour.

Opening inventory	5000, 40% complete
Units started during the period	12000
Closing inventory	4000, 60% complete

Under the FIFO method, the computation of total production will be as follows :

Opening inventory – 5000 × 60% (since 40% has been completed) = Rs. 3000

Completed units (Units started – closing inventory) – 12000-4000= Rs. 8000Closing inventory – 4000 × 60% = Rs. 2400

Total production is 3000+8000+2400= Rs. 13400

Taking the same example let us calculate total production under the weighted average method

Completed units 12000-4000= Rs. 8000

Closing WIP 4000*60%= Rs. 2400

Total production= Rs. 10400

Similarly the costs will have to be determined and assigned to the Equivalent units of production.

In our day to day lives too there are many activities that can be segregated into defined processes. And the time involved can be assigned to each process. The cumulative time for all the processes will be the time of the entire activity.

Process costing includes the following methods of costing :

Unit Costing

This method applies to businesses that produce a single product. In this method the total cost is divided by number of units to derive per unit cost.

This is mostly used in industries dealing in- Cement manufacturing, paper manufacturing, textiles.

Operating costing

This applies to service industry wherein the services are defined and distinguished.

This is mostly used by Hospitals, Railways.

Operation Costing

This is similar to process costing. The only difference being that instead of process the cost for various operations is considered.

This is mostly used in industries dealing in Toy manufacturing

Therefore process costing is widely used method of costing. It can be easily applied to manufacturing as well as service industries.

Activity Based Costing (ABC)

Activity-based costing (ABC) is an accounting method that identifies and assigns costs to overhead activities and then assigns those costs to products. An activity-based costing (ABC) system recognizes the relationship between costs, overhead activities, and manufactured products, and through this relationship, it assigns indirect costs to products less arbitrarily than traditional methods.

Some costs are difficult to assign through this method of cost accounting. Indirect costs, such as management and office staff salaries, are sometimes difficult to assign to a product. For this reason, this method has found its niche in the manufacturing sector.

Activity-based costing (ABC) is mostly used in the manufacturing industry since it enhances the reliability of cost data, hence producing nearly true costs and better classifying the costs incurred by the company during its production process.

This costing system is used in target costing, product costing, product line profitability analysis, customer profitability analysis, and service pricing. It is also hugely popular since organizations can develop a much better corporate focus and strategy if costs are better grasped.

Definition of Activities in ABC System

The ABC system of cost accounting is based on activities, which is any event, unit of work, or task with a specific goal, such as setting up machines for production, designing products, distributing finished goods, or operating machines. Activities consume overhead resources and are considered cost objects.

Under the ABC system, an activity can also be considered as any transaction or event that is a cost driver. A cost driver, also known as an activity driver, is used to refer to an allocation base. Examples of cost drivers include machine setups, maintenance requests, power consumed, purchase orders, quality inspections, or production orders.

There are two categories of activity measures: transaction drivers, which involves counting how many times an activity occurs, and duration drivers, which measure how long an activity takes to complete. Unlike traditional cost measurement systems that depend on volume count such as machine hours and/or direct labor hours to allocate indirect or overhead costs to products, the ABC system classifies five broad levels of activity that are, to a certain extent, unrelated to how many units are produced. These levels include batch-level activity, unit-level activity, customer-level activity, organization-sustaining activity, and product-level activity.

How ABC System Improves Costing Process

Activity-based costing enhances the costing process in three ways. First, it expands the number of cost pools that can be used to assemble overhead costs. Instead of accumulating all costs in one company-wide pool, it pools costs by activity. It also creates new bases for assigning overhead costs to items such that costs are allocated based on the activities that generate costs instead of on volume measures, such as machine hours or direct labor costs. Finally, ABC alters the nature of several indirect costs, making costs previously considered indirect- such as depreciation, inspection, or power- traceable to certain activities. Alternatively, ABC transfers overhead costs from high-volume products to low-volume products, raising the unit cost of low-volume products.

Costing for Decision Making

Many business decisions require a firm knowledge of several cost concepts. Different types of costs have differing characteristics. Consequently, when reviewing a business case to determine which path to take, it is useful to understand the following cost concepts:

- **Fixed, variable, and mixed costs.** A fixed cost, such as rent, does not change in lock step with the level of activity. Conversely, a variable cost, such as direct materials, will change as the level of activity changes. Those few costs that change somewhat with activity are considered mixed costs. It is important to understand the distinction, since a decision to alter an activity may or may not alter costs. For example, shuttering a facility may not terminate the associated building lease payments, which are fixed for the duration of the lease.
- **By-product costs.** A product may be an incidental by-product of a production process (such as sawdust at a lumber mill). If so, it does not really have any cost, since its cost would have been incurred anyways as a result of the production of the main product. Thus, selling a by-product at any price is profitable; no price is too low.
- **Allocated costs.** Overhead costs are allocated to manufactured goods only because it is required by the accounting standards (for the production of financial statements). There is no cause-and-effect between the creation of one additional unit of production and the incurrence of additional overhead. Thus, there is no reason to include allocated overhead in the decision to set a price for one additional unit.

- **Discretionary costs.** Only a few costs can actually be dropped without causing any short-term harm to an organization. Examples are employee training and maintenance. Over the long-term, delaying these expenditures will eventually have a negative effect. Thus, managers need to understand the impact of their decisions over a period of time when determining which costs to cut back.
- **Step costs.** Though some costs are essentially fixed, it may be necessary to make a large investment in them when the activity level increases past a certain point. Adding a production shift is an example of a step cost. Management should understand the activity volumes at which step costs can be incurred, so that it can manage around them - perhaps delaying sales or outsourcing work, rather than incurring step costs.

All of the cost concepts noted here are critical elements of many types of management decisions.

Life Cycle Costing

Life cycle costing, or whole-life costing, is the process of estimating how much money you will spend on an asset over the course of its useful life. Whole-life costing covers an asset's costs from the time you purchase it to the time you get rid of it.

Buying an asset is a cost commitment that extends beyond its price tag. For example, think of a car. The car's price tag is only part of the car's overall life cycle cost. You also need to consider expenses for car insurance, interest, gas, oil changes, and any other necessary maintenance to keep the car running. Not planning for these additional costs can set you back.

The cost to buy, use, and maintain a business asset adds up. Whether you're purchasing a car, a copier, a computer, or inventory, you should consider and budget for the asset's future costs.

Life Cycle Costing Process

Conducting a life cycle cost assessment helps you better predict how much your business will pay when you acquire a new asset.

To calculate an asset's life cycle cost, estimate the following expenses:

- Purchase
- Installation
- Operating
- Maintenance
- Financing (e.g., interest)
- Depreciation
- Disposal

Add up the expenses for each stage of the life cycle to find your total.

You might use past data to help you create a more accurate cost prediction. To simplify the process, start with your fixed costs. Fixed costs for businesses are the expenses that stay the same from month to month. Then, estimate variable costs, which are expenses that change.

Life Cycle Costing Process for Intangible Assets

You can also use life cycle costing to determine how much your intangible assets will cost. Intangible assets are non-physical property, such as patents, your business's brand, and your reputation.

Although it is more difficult to add up the whole-life cost of an intangible asset than a tangible asset (physical property), it's still possible. Consider the total cost of acquiring and maintaining an intangible asset.

For example, patents cost thousands of dollars. You might also need to hire a lawyer to help you obtain one. And, you will need to pay fees to maintain your patent.

Or, consider your business's brand. You might spend money on all the things that go into creating your brand, such as developing a logo, registering your name, and setting up a small business website. Further, you will spend money on marketing and maintaining your brand.

Life Cycle Costing Assessment Example

Let's say you want to buy a new copier for your business.

Purchase. The purchase price is $2,500.

Installation. You spend an additional $75 for setup and delivery.

Operating. You need to buy ink cartridges and paper for it, so you estimate you will spend $1,000 on these supplies over the course of its useful life. And, you expect the total electricity the copier will use to be $300.

Maintenance. If the copier breaks, you estimate repairs will total $450.

Financing. You purchase the copier with your store credit card, which has an interest rate of 3.5% per month. You pay off the printer the next month, meaning you owe $87.50 in interest ($2,500 X 3.5%).

Depreciation. You predict the copier will lose value by $150 each year.

Disposal. You estimate it will cost $100 to hire an independent contractor to remove the copier from your business.

Although the purchase price of the copier is $2,500, the life cycle cost of the copier could end up costing your business over $4,500.

Purpose of the Life Cycle Cost Analysis

As mentioned, conducting a life cycle cost analysis helps you estimate how much an asset will cost you over the course of its life.

Take a look at some of the reasons why knowing an asset's total cost can guide your business decisions.

1. **Choose between two or more assets.** Using life cycle costing helps you make purchasing decisions. If you only factor in the initial cost of an asset, you could end up spending more in the long run. For example, buying a used asset might have a lower price tag, but it could cost you more in repairs and utility bills than a newer model.

   Life cycle cost management depends on your ability to make a smart investment. When you are deciding between two or more assets, consider their overall costs, not just the price tag in front of you.

2. **Determine the asset's benefits.** How do you know if you should buy an asset? Generally, you weigh the pros and cons of your purchase. But if you only consider the initial, short-term cost, you won't know if the asset will benefit your business financially in the long run.

   By using life cycle costing, you can more accurately predict if the asset's return on investment (ROI) is worth the expense. If you only look at the asset's current purchase cost and don't factor in future costs, you will overestimate the ROI.

3. **Create accurate budgets.** When you know how much an asset's total price is, you can create budgets that represent your business's actual expenses. That way, you won't underestimate your business's costs.

   A budget is made up of expenses, revenue, and profits. If you underestimate an asset's cost on your budget, you are overestimating your profits. Failing to account for expenses can result in overspending and negative cash flow.

Target Costing

Target costing is not just a method of costing, but rather a management technique wherein prices are determined by market conditions brought about by several factors, such as homogeneous products, level of competition, no/low switching costs for the end customer, etc. When these factors come into the picture, management wants to control the costs, as they have little or no control over the selling price.

CIMA defines target cost as "a product cost estimate derived from a competitive market price."

In industries such as FMCG, construction, healthcare, and energy, competition is so intense that prices are determined by supply and demand in the market, and hence producers can't effectively control selling prices. They can only control, to some extent, their costs, so management's focus is on influencing every component of product, service, or operational costs.

The key objective of target costing is to enable management to use proactive cost planning, cost management, and cost reduction practices where costs are planned and calculated early in the design and development cycle, rather than during the later stages of product development and production.

Key Features of Target Costing

- The price of the product is determined by market conditions. The company is a price taker rather than a price maker.
- The minimum required profit margin is already included in the target selling price.
- It is part of management strategy to focus on cost reduction and effective cost management.
- Product design, specifications, and customer expectations are already built in while formulating the total selling price.
- The difference between the current cost and the target cost is the "cost reduction," which management wants to achieve.
- A team is formed to integrate activities such as designing, purchasing, manufacturing, marketing, etc. to find and achieve the target cost.

Advantages of Target Costing:

- It shows management's commitment to process improvements and product innovation to gain competitive advantages.
- The product is created from the expectation of the customer and hence cost is also based on similar lines. Thus, the customer feels more value is delivered.
- With the passage of time, the company's operations improve drastically, creating economies of scale.
- The company's approach to designing and manufacturing products becomes market-driven.
- New market opportunities can be converted into real savings to achieve the best value for money rather than to simply realize the lowest cost.

KAIZEN COSTING

Kaizen costing is a method of reducing managing costs. It's also referred to as continuous improvement costing. The method is aimed at cost reduction below standard level, but without negative effects on quality, staff, safety, etc.

The idea is similar to target costing, where managers try to achieve the result with lower resources. However, target costing is used on design stage, while kaizen costing - during the manufacturing stage. What's more important, kaizen costing requires high involvement of employees, while target costing - only some designers.

There are two approaches to kaizen costing:

- Asset specific - all improvement activities are related to reduction of use of chosen asset or resource.

- Product specific - improvement activities are related to different resources related to one product.

The main types of cost that should be reduced are:

- Working with suppliers to reduce costs in supply chain
- Costs of product redesign
- Waste
- Legal costs
- Recruitment and training costs (more effective methods of training)
- Manufacturing costs (using learning curve effect)
- Marketing, sales, distribution
- Disposal

The standard costing is approach to control costs looking at variances in comparison to actual costs. That becomes cause of the main criticism of standard costing. Managing by exceptions (only in case of variance) is not efficient enough. Kaizen costing goes further and improves costs continuously.

Kaizen costing	Standard costing
Cost reduction targets are set and applied monthly	Standards are set annually or semi-annually
Variance analysis involves target Kaizen costs versus actual cost reduction amounts	Variance analysis involves comparing actual to standard costs
Investigation occurs when target reductions are not attained	Investigation occurs when standards are not met

Targets for kaizen costs are set monthly based on following procedure:

1. Per product actual cost in the previous year = total actual cost of last year / actual production in last year.
2. Estimated amount of total current year actual cost = Per product actual cost in the previous year × Estimated production for the current year.
3. Kaizen cost target for the current year = Estimated amount of total current year actual cost × Ratio of cost reduction target.
4. Assignment cost to each plant = Cost directly controlled in single plant / cost directly controlled in all plants
5. Kaizen cost target for each plant = Kaizen cost target for the current year / Assignment ratio

The Kaizen costing can use Hoshin Kanri approach of bottom-up path, where lower managers propose reduction levels. This however requires highly engaged staff.

Kaizen Costing Principles

- It lays no emphasis on the present existing situation, by disregarding all ideas implemented in the production process;
- The system does not strive for perfection, rather seeking gradual improvements in the existing situation, at an acceptable cost;
- It allows managers to exercise discretion in the application of their knowledge and personal skills;
- It encourages collective decision—making, i.e. the ideas of many are better than that of one single person;

- There are no limits to the level of improvements that can be implemented.
- Kaizen involves setting standards and then continually improving these standards to achieve long-term sustainable improvements.
- The focus is on eliminating waste, improving processes and systems and improving productivity.
- Involves all employees and all areas of the business.

The main advantages are:

- Encouraging and empowering employees lead to better results
- Employee suggestion system helps to find ways of cost reduction
- Lean thinking helps reducing resources absorption

The potential **disadvantages** are:

- Kaizen is a permanent change system
- Kaizen can increase the burden on lower level of management
- Kaizen costs can lead to diminishing returns if not implemented wisely

JUST IN TIME (JIT)

The just-in-time inventory system is a management strategy that aligns raw-material orders from suppliers directly with production schedules. Companies use this inventory strategy to increase efficiency and decrease waste by receiving goods only as they need them for the production process, which reduces inventory costs. This method requires producers to forecast demand accurately.

The JIT inventory supply system is a shift away from other just-in-case strategies, in which producers hold large inventories to have enough product to absorb maximum market demand.

One example of a JIT system would be a car manufacturer that operates with low inventory levels relying on its supply chain to deliver the parts it needs to build cars. The parts needed to manufacture the cars do not arrive before or after the manufacturer needs them; instead, they arrive just as the manufacturer needs them.

Just-in-Time Inventory System Advantages

JIT inventory controls have several advantages over traditional models. Production runs remain short, which means manufacturers can move from one product to another easily. This method reduces costs by minimizing warehouse needs. Companies also spend less money on raw materials because they buy just enough resources to make just the ordered products and no more.

System Disadvantages

The disadvantages of JIT inventories involve disruptions in the supply chain. If a raw materials supplier has a breakdown and cannot deliver the goods on time, one supplier can shut down the entire production process. A sudden order for goods that surpasses expectations may delay delivery of finished products to clients.

Case Study

Toyota uses JIT inventory controls as part of its business model. Toyota sends off orders for parts only when it receives new orders from customers. The company started this method in the 1970s, and it took over 15 years to perfect. Several elements of JIT manufacturing need to occur for Toyota to succeed. The company must have steady production, high-quality workmanship, no machine breakdowns at the plant, reliable suppliers and quick ways to assemble machines that put together vehicles.

Toyota's JIT concept almost came to a crashing halt in February 1997. A fire at an Aisin-owned brake parts plant decimated its capacity to produce a P-valve for Toyota vehicles. The company was the sole supplier of the part, and the fact that the plant remained closed for weeks could have devastated Toyota's supply line. The auto manufacturer ran out of P-valve parts after just one day. Production lines shut down for two days until a supplier of Aisin could manufacture the valves. Other suppliers for Toyota also had to shut down because the auto manufacturer didn't need other parts to complete any cars on the assembly line. The fire cost Toyota nearly $15 billion in revenue and 70,000 cars due to its two-day shutdown, but it could have been much worse.

FINANCIAL STATEMENTS

A financial statement is a collection of data organised according to logical and consistent accounting procedures. Its purpose is to convey an understanding of some financial aspects of a business firm. It may show a position at a moment in time, as in the case of a balance sheet, or may reveal a series of activities over a given period of time, as in the case of an income statement. Thus the term *financial statements* refers to the two statements:

(i) The position statement or the balance sheet;

(ii) The income statement or the profit and loss account.

These statements are used to convey to management and other interested outsiders the profitability and financial position of a firm. According to John N. Myer, 'The financial statements are composed of data which are the result of a combination of:

(a) recorded facts concerning the business transaction,

(b) conventions adopted to facilitate the accounting technique,

(c) postulates or assumptions made to and

(d) personal judgements used in the application of the conventions and postulates.

The following points explain the nature of financial statements:

1. **Recorded Facts.** The term 'recorded facts' refers to the data taken out from the accounting records. The records are maintained on the basis of actual cost data. The original cost or historical cost is the basis of recording various transactions.

   The figures of various accounts such as cash in hand, cash at bank, bills receivables, sundry debtors, fixed assets *etc.* are taken as per the figures recorded in the accounting books. The assets purchased at different times and at different prices are put together and shown at cost prices. As recorded facts are not based on replacement costs, the financial statements do not show current financial condition of the concern.

2. **Accounting conventions.** Certain accounting conventions are followed while preparing financial statements. The convention of valuing inventory at cost or market price, whichever is lower, is followed. The valuing of assets at cost less depreciation principle for balance sheet purposes is followed. The convention of materiality is followed in dealing with small things like pencils, pens, postage stamps, *etc.* These items are treated as expenditure in the year in which they are purchased even though they are assets in nature. The stationary is valued at cost and not on the principle of cost or market price whichever is less. The use of accounting conventions makes financial statements comparable, simple and realistic.

3. **Postulate.** The accountant makes certain assumptions while making accounting records. One of these assumptions is that the enterprise is treated as a going concern. The other alternative to this postulate is that the concern is to be liquidated, this is untenable if management shows an intention to liquidate the concern. So the assets are shown on a going

concern basis. Another important assumption is to present that the value of money will remain the same in different periods. Though there is a drastic change in purchasing power of money the assets purchased at different times will be shown at the amount paid for them. While preparing profit and loss account, the revenue is treated in the year in which the sale was undertaken even though the sale price may be received in a number of years. The assumption is known as realisation postulate.

4. **Personal judgement.** Even though certain standard accounting conventions are followed in preparing financial statements but still personal judgement of the accountant plays an important part. For example, in applying the cost or market value whichever is less to inventory valuation the accountant will have to use his judgement in computing the cost in a particular case. There are a number of methods for valuing stock *viz.* last in first out, first in first out, average cost method, standard cost, base stock method, *etc.* The accountant will use one of these methods for valuing materials. The selection of depreciation method, to use one of the several methods for estimating uncollectable debts, to determine the period for writing off intangible assets are some of the examples where judgement of the accountant will play an important role in choosing the most appropriate course of action.

Objectives of Financial Statements

(i) To provide reliable financial information about economic resources and obligations of a business firm.

(ii) To provide other needed information about changes in such economic sources and obligations.

(iii) To provide reliable information about charges in net resources (resources less obligations) arising out of business activities.

(iv) To provide financial information that assists in estimating the earning potential of business.

(v) To disclose, to the extent possible, other information related to the financial statements that is relevant to the needs of the users of these statements.

Types of Financial Statements

Generally Accepted Accounting Principles (GAAP) specify that a complete set of financial statements must include;

(i) A balance sheet.

(ii) An income statement.

(iii) A statement of changes in owner's accounts.

(iv) A statement of changes in financial position.

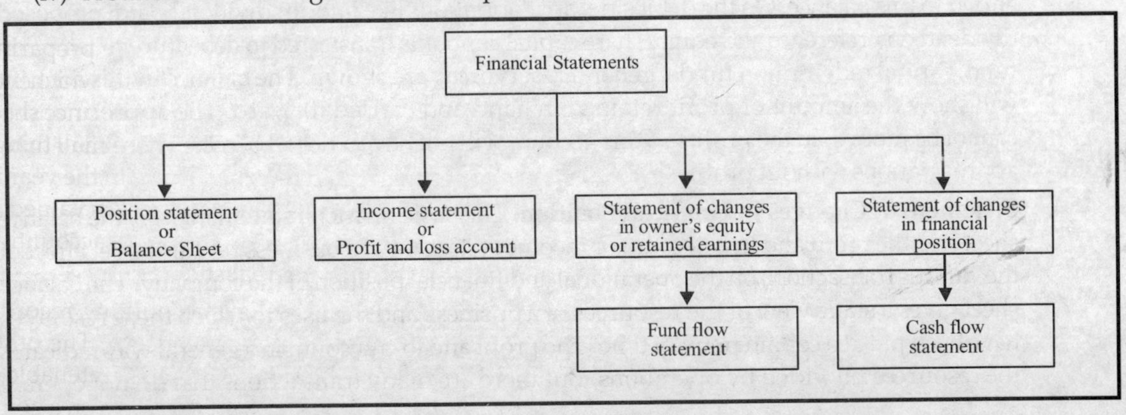

1. **Balance Sheet.** The balance sheet is one of the important statements depicting the financial strength of the concern. It shows on the one hand the properties that it utilises and on other hand the sources of those properties. The balance sheet shows all the assets owned by the concern and all the liabilities and claims it owes to owners and outsiders. The balance sheet is prepared on a particular date. The right hand side shows properties and assets and the liabilities are shown on the left hand side. Normally there is no particular sequence for showing various assets and liabilities. The companies Act, 1956 has prescribed a particular form for showing assets and liabilities in the balance sheet for companies registered under this act. These companies are also required to give figures for the previous year alongwith the current year's figures.
2. **Income statement (or Profit and Loss Account).** Income statement is prepared to determine the operational position of the concern. It is a statement of revenues earned and the expenses incurred for earning that revenue. If there is excess of revenues over expenditures it will show a profit and if the expenditures are more than the income then there will be a loss. The income statement is prepared for a particular period, generally a year. When income statement is prepared for the year ending on 31st December 1996 then all revenues and expenditures falling due in that year will be taken into account irrespective of their receipt or payment.

   The income statement may be prepared in the form of a Manufacturing Account to find out the cost of production, in the form of trading account to determine gross profit or gross loss, in the form of a profit and loss account to determine net profit or net loss. A statement of Retained Earnings may also be prepared to show the distribution of profits.
3. **Statement of Changes in Owner's Equity (or Retained Earnings).** The term owners equity refers to the claims of the owners of the business (shareholders) against the assets of the firm. It consists of two elements;

   (i) paid-up share capital, *i.e.* the initial amount of funds invested by the shareholders and

   (ii) retained earnings/reserves and surplus representing undistributed profits.

   The statement of changes in owners equity simply shows the beginning balance of each owner's equity account, the reason for increase and decrease in each and its ending balance. However, in most-cases, the only owner's equity account that changes significantly is Retained Earnings and hence the statement of changes in owner's equity becomes a statement of retained earnings.

   A statement of retained earnings is also known as Profit and Loss Appropriation Account or income disposal statement. As the name suggests it shows appropriations of earnings. The previous year's balance is first brought forward. The net profit during the current year is added to this balance. On the debit side, appropriations like interim dividend paid, proposed dividend on preference and equity share capital, amounts transferred to debenture redemption fund, capital redemption funds, general reserve, *etc.* are shown. The balance in this account will show the amount of profit retained in hand and carried forward. The appropriations cannot be more than the profits so this account will not have a debit balance. There can not be appropriations without profits.
4. **Statement of Changes in Financial Position.** The basic financial statements, *i.e.* the balance sheet and the profit and loss account or income statement of a business reveal the set effect of the various transactions on the operational and financial position of the company. The balance sheet gives a static view of the resources of a business and the uses to which these resources have been put at a certain point of time. The profit and loss account in a general way indicates the resources provided by operations. But there are many transactions that do not operate

through profit and loss account. Thus, for a better understanding another statement called statement of changes in financial position has to be prepared to show the changes in assets and liabilities from the end of one period to the end of another part of time. The objective of this statement is to show the movement of funds (working capital or cash) during particular period. The statement of changes in financial position may take any of the following two forms:

(a) ***Funds flow statement.*** The funds flow statement is designed to analyse the changes in the financial condition of a business enterprise between two periods. The word fund is used to denote working capital.

This statement will show the sources from which the funds are received and the uses to which these have been put. This statement enables the management to have an idea about the sources of funds and their use for various purposes. This statement help the management in policy formulation and performance appraisal.

(b) ***Cash flow statement.*** A statement of changes in the financial position of a firm on cash basis is called cash flow statement. It summarises the causes of changes in cash position of a business enterprise between dates of two balance sheets. This statement is very much similar to the statement of changes in working capital *i.e.* funds flow statement. A cash flow statement focuses attention on cash changes only. It describes the sources of cash and its uses.

Final Account

Preparation of final accounts is the last step in the accounting cycle. Final accounts are prepared to achieve the objectives of accountancy. In order to know the profit or loss earned by a firm 'trading and profit and loss account' *i.e.* income statement is prepared. Balance sheet or financial position statement will show the financial condition of the firm on a particular date. These two statements are prepared to give the final results of the business. That is why, both these are collectively called as 'final Accounts'.

Thus, final accounts include :

(i) Trading and profit and loss account or income statement and

(ii) Balance sheet or position statement.

Final accounts are the means of conveying to management, owners and interested outsiders a picture of profitability and financial position of the business. The preparation of final accounts is the end product of the accounting process which gives a concise accounting information of the accounting period after the accounting period is over. These accounts summarise all accounting information recorded in the subsidiary books and the ledger running into thousands of pages.

Procedure. Once the trial Balance is prepared traders prepares final accounts *i.e.* trading account, profit and loss account and balance sheet. Trading and profit and loss account are prepared by transferring from the trial balance, all revenues accounts and expenses accounts and accounts concerning goods by passing closing entries. All remaining account *i.e.* assets accounts, liabilities accounts and capital accounts are shown in Balance Sheet.

Trading Account

Income statement is made up of two accounts *i.e.* trading account and profit and loss account. Trading concerns *i.e.* those concern which purchase goods from one market and sell it in another market, prepare trading account. This account is prepared to know the trading results of the business *i.e.* how much profit the business has earned from buying and selling during a particular period. Trading account shows 'Gross profit' or 'Gross Loss' *i.e.* difference between net proceeds of sale and cost of goods sold.

Format of Trading Account

Trading Account for the year ending

Dr. **Cr.**

Particulars	Amount Rs.	Particulars	Amount Rs.
To opening stock To purchase A/C Less–Purchases returns Less–Discount on purchases To direct expenses To wages To carriage and Cartage To Manufacturing expenses To Coal, water & freight To factory lighting To fuel & Power To Motive Power To carriage & freight To wages & salaries To Octroi To factory, rent & taxes To duty on imported goods To Gross profit/loss		By sale Less sales return By closing stock	

Closing Entries in Respect of Trading Account

The accounts written in the trading account are closed with the help of passing closing entries in journal. Accounts having debit balance are closed by crediting them and accounts having credit balance are closed by debiting them. Following are the closing entries in respect of Trading Account.

(i) For transferring the accounts on the debit side of trading account.

Trading Account Dr.
To stock (Opening) A/C.
To Purchases A/C
To sales return A/C
To factory fuel and power A/C
To Freight and carriage A/C
To Manufacturing expenses A/C.

(ii) For transferring the account on the credit side of trading account.

Sales Account Dr.

Purchases return account Dr.

Stock (closing) Account Dr.

To trading Account

(iii) At this stage the trading account will reveal the gross profit or loss. For transferring the gross profit-

Stock (closing) Account Dr.

To profit and loss A/C

For transferring gross loss

Profit and loss Account Dr.

To trading Account

Profit and Loss Account

Profit and Loss account is prepared to calculate the net profit of the business. Net Profit is the surplus remaining after charging against gross profit all the expenses, including depreciation and other provisions, properly attributable to the normal activities of the particular business. The objectives of preparing profit and loss account can be summed up as under;

(i) Provides information about net profit.

(ii) Comparison of Current years income with that of the previous years can be made.

(iii) Concrete steps may be taken to increase the net profit in future through analysis of expenses.

(iv) Proper allocation of net profit can be made among partners and provisions for various types of Reserves as also for research and development programmes can be made.

Format of Profit and Loss Accounts for the year ending

Particular	Rs.	Particular	Rs.
To Gross loss b/d **To selling & distribution expenses.** Advertisement Travelling, salaries Expenses & commission Bad debts Godown rent Export expenses Carriage outward Bank charges Agents commission		By Gross Profit b/d By interest Received By discount By commission By rent from tenants By income from invest-ment By apprenticeship-premium By interest on debenture	
B/f			

C/f			
Unkeep of Motor lorries		By income from any other sources	
To Management Expenses			
Rent, Rate and taxes		By Miscellaneous revenue	
Heating and lighting			
Office salaries		By Receipts	
Printing & Telegrams		By Net Loss transferred to capital A/C.	
Telephone charges			
Legal charges			
Audit fees			
Insurance			
General expenses			
To Depreciation and Maintenance			
Depreciation			
Repairs & Maintenance			
To financial expenses			
Discount allowed			
Interest on Capital			
Interest on loans			
Discount on Bills			
To Extra ordinary expenses			
Loss by fire (not covered by insurance)			
Cash defecations			
To net profit transferred to capital A/C			

Closing Entries in Respect of profit and Loss Account

1. The gross profit or loss is transferred to profit and loss account and thus profit and loss account is opened by gross profit or gross loss.

   Where there is gross profit:

   Trading Account Dr.
   To profit and Loss Account

   When there is gross loss:

   Profit and loss Account Dr.
   To trading Account.

2. Profit and loss account is debited with all indirect expenses and losses. For transfer of various expenses and losses following entry is passed :

   Profit and loss Account Dr.
   To various expenses A/C
   To various losses A/C

3. Profit and loss account is credited with miscellaneous incomes accounts. For transfer of various Incomes, following entry is passed :

   Various Incomes Accounts Dr.

   To Profit and Loss accounts

4. The results of the account is either net profit or net loss. The profit and loss account is closed by transferring the net profit or net loss to capital A/C.

   When these is net profit:

   Profit and Loss A/C Dr.

   To capital A/C

   When there is net loss:

   Capital account Dr.

   To Profit and Loss A/C

Balance Sheet

Balance sheet is basically a simple statement about a business enterprise. It is a 'sheet' of all those ledger 'Balances' pertaining to the assets owned and liabilities owned by the business on a particular day. Balance sheet is prepared with a view to measure the correct financial position of a business in a systematic standard form.

The Committee on Technology of American Institute of Certified Public Accountant (AICPA) defines the balance sheet as 'list of balances in the assets and liability accounts. This list depicts the position of assets and liabilities of a specific business at a specific point of time.'

Balance sheet and trial balance both are statements and are prepared by almost all enterprises. Inspite of differences, they resemble in following :

(1) Both contain the cash balance.

(2) Both are prepared from the ledger.

(3) Both are not accounts but statements.

(4) Accounts having no balance do not appear in either of the two.

Important Adjustments

(i) **Closing Stock.** Closing stock means unsold or unused stock of goods remaining at the end of the accounting period. Closing stock needs adjustments at the time of preparing final account. The adjustment entry for closing stock is as under :

   Closing stock account Dr.

   To trading account.

   The impact of this entry will be that closing stock becomes an asset and appears in the balance sheet and the trading A/C is credited with closing stock.

(ii) **Outstanding Expenses.** 'Those expenses which have been incurred and are due for payment *i.e.* not paid as yet, are called outstanding expenses'. For example, Rs. 1000 p.m. is paid as a salary to an employee but during the year 1988, only Rs. 10000 are paid as salary. Two months salary *i.e.* Rs. 2000 which is due but not paid is outstanding salary. All such expenses must be accounted for in that accounting year in which they are accrued irrespective of the fact whether they are paid or not. In order to bring this fact into books of account, following adjusting entry will be passed at the end of the year.

Salary A/C Dr.

To outstanding salary A/C

The two fold effect of the above adjustment entry will be :

(a) Outstanding expenses will be shown on the debit side of the trading or profit & loss account by way of addition to the expenses.

(b) Outstanding expenses account represents liability and it will be shown on the liabilities side of the balance sheet.

(iii) **Prepaid or unexpired expenses.** There are certain expenses which are paid in advance or paid for the future period which is not set over or not yet expired since such expenses are already paid, they are also recorded in books of accounts of that period for which they do not relate. Therefore such prepaid expenses must be adjusted in the books of accounts to arrive at the true results. Generally insurance, taxes, telephone rent *etc.* are paid in advance. For *e.g.*, if a fire insurance policy is taken for a year paying Rs. 1000 as insurance premium on 1st April 1988, the policy will expire on 31st March 1989. If accounts are closed on 31st Dec. 1988, premium from Ist Jan, 1989 to 31st March 1989, will be prepaid expenses i.e. Rs. 250 will be prepaid expenses. The following adjustment entry will be passed :

Prepaid insurance A/C Dr.

To insurance A/C

The two fold effect of this entry will be :

(a) Prepaid expenses will be shown in the trading A/C or profit and loss account by way of deduction from the expenses.

(b) Prepaid expenses represents benefit receivable i.e. an asset and therefore it will be shown on the assets side of the balance sheet.

(iv) **Accrued Incomes.** That income which has been carried but not received during the accounting year is called accrued income. Income like interest on investments, rent of property, sublet *etc.* are many a time earned by the business during a particular accounting period but actually not received during that period. For example, if the business has invested Rs. 10000 in 5% securities on 1st Jan. 1988 but during the year Rs. 350 has been received as interest on securities, then Rs. 150 interest on securities will be accrued interest for the year 1988. The following adjustment entry will be passed :

Accrued interest A/C Dr.

To interest A/C

The two fold effect of above entry will be

(a) accrued income will be shown on the credit side of profit and loss account by way of addition to the income.

(b) It will be a benefit receivable *i.e.* an asset to the business and therefore, it will be shown on the assets side of the balance sheet.

(v) **Unearned incomes or income received in advance:** Income received but not earned during the accounting year is called as income received in advance. It is the income received in advance for which business in responsible, for example building has been given to a tenant on Rs. 200 p.m. but during the year Rs. 3000 has been received. Then Rs. 600 will be unearned income, for unearned income following adjustment entry will be passed :

Rent A/C Dr.

To unearned rent A/C

The effect of this entry will be:

(a) It is shown on the credit side of profit and loss account by way of deduction from the income.

(b) Unearned income will be shown on the liabilities side of the Balance sheet.

(vi) **Depreciation:** Depreciation is permanent decrease or reduction in the value of the assets. When an asset is employed for earning purpose, it is necessary that depreciation must be charged to the profit of the year in order to show correct profit or loss and to show the asset at its correct value in the balance sheet.

Generally, depreciation is charged at some percentage on the value of an asset, for example, if a machine is purchased for Rs. 10000 on Ist Jan. 1988 and depreciates at 10% p.a.. Following entries will be passed to adjust depreciation.

Depreciation A/C Dr.
To Machinery A/C

The two fold effect of this entry will be :

(a) Depreciation is shown on the debit side of the profit & loss account.

(b) Depreciation is shown on the asset side by way of deduction from the value of asset.

(vii) **Interest on capital and Drawings.** Charging interest on capital is based on the argument that the same amount of capital were invested else where the proprietor would have received interest thereon. In order to ascertain the efficiency it is a common practice to charge interest on capital employed by the proprietors. The adjusting entry will be :

Interest an capital A/C Dr.
To capital A/C

(a) Interest on capital like an expense, will be shown on the debit side of the profit & loss account.

(b) Interest on capital will be shown on the liability side of the Balance sheet by way of addition to the capital.

The proprietors may also realise that when he draws money for private use, the firm losses interest therefore the proprietor may be debited with the interest on the money drawn by him. Interest will depend on the amount and the data of drawings. The adjusting entry will be :

Capital A/C Dr.
To Interest or drawing A/C

The two fold effect of this entry will be:

(a) Interest on drawings like a revenue will be shown on the credit side of the profit and loss A/C.

(b) Interest on Capital will be shown on the liabilities side of the Balance sheet by way of reduction in the capital.

(viii) **Reserves for Bad and Doubtful Debts.** It is very difficult to carry on a business only by making cash sales. Sometimes it becomes necessary to sell goods on credit also. When goods are sold on credit the amounts receivable from all debtors may not be recovered fully. Some debts may become irrecoverable due to many reasons like death, insolvency, insanity or dishonesty of the debtor. Such debts are called as 'Bad debts'. It is loss for the business. Therefore, it is one shown on the debit side of profit and loss A/C and secondly, shown as a deduction from the amount of sundry debtors in balance sheet. The following entry is passed for its adjustment.

Bad debts A/C To concerned debtor A/C (Being adjustment entry passed for irrecoverable debts).	Dr.	xxx

The bad debt A/C is closed by transferring its balance to profit and loss A/C by a closing entry. The concerned debtor A/C gets reduced to the extent of the bad debts.

Doubtful Debts

Debts created by selling goods on credit in an accounting year may not become bad in the same year. They may become bad in the subsequent year. In such cases the bad debts arising on account of selling goods on credit in one year fall upon the next year or subsequent year. So it is advised to ascertain the amount of debts which may become bad out of the debts of a year before preparing final accounts of the year. Such debts are called as 'Doubtful debts'. These are calculated or estimated by a trader on the basis of past experience. It is generally calculated at a fixed percentage on the total debtors of a trader at the end of an accounting period. The amount of doubtful debts is once placed on the debt side of profit and loss A/C and secondly it is shown as a deduction from the amount of sundry debtors in Balance sheet. The following entry is passed for adjustment.

Profit and Loss A/C Dr.	xxx
To provision for doubtful debts	xxx
(Being a provision is made towards doubtful debts)	

The debt to the profit and loss account will reduce the year's profit suitably for the possible loss and the amount will be carried forward to the next year. Next year when bad debts actually occur and are written off, the bad debts accounts will be debited to the provision for bad debts account, the amount of bad debts will be debited to the profit and loss account since debit was already given to it last year. It should be noted that the customer account on sundry debtors account is not affected by creation of the provision for bad debts. The provision for bad and doubtful debts account are deducted from the amount of book debts in the balance sheet but the two accounts are separate.

Sometimes, the balance in the provision for bad and doubtful debts account is more than sufficient to meet the bad debts and the new provision required. The remaining amount then is credited to the profit and loss account.

(ix) **Reserve for Discount on debtors and creditors.** Debtors are sometimes allowed a discount to induce them for a prompt payment. The traders maintains a reserve for them which is called reserve for discount on sundry debtors. It is shown on the debit side of profit and loss A/C and deducted from the sundry debtors in the balance sheet. It should be kept in mind that while calculating the reserve for discount the reserve for bad debts should be deducted from the sundry debtors in the balance sheet. For *e.g.*, debtors own Rs. 10000, reserve for discount is Rs. 500. A reserve for bad debts @ 5% will not be calculated on Rs. 10000 but on Rs. 9500 (Rs. 10000- Rs. 500).

When discount is allowed, following journal entry is passed :

Discount A/C Dr.

To debtor's personal A/C

Following entry is passed to create a provision for discount on debtors.

Profit & Loss A/C Dr.

To Provision for discount on debtors A/C.

The discount allowed will be transferred to the provision for discount on debtors account by passing following entry:

Provision for discount on debtors A/C Dr

To discount A/C

Such provision will be shown on the debt side of profit and loss A/C. The provision will be shown by way of deduction from sundry debtors (after deduction of further bad debts and provision for doubtful debts) on the assets side of the balance sheet.

FINANCIAL STATEMENTS ANALYSIS

RATIO ANALYSIS

Ratio, broadly speaking is the numerical relationship between two numbers. And hence ratio analysis of statement stands for the process of determining and presenting the relationship of items and groups of items in the statements. When relations among various accounting data supplied by financial statements are worked out, they are termed as accounting ratios. Ratio may be expressed in the following three ways:

(a) **Ratio.** Specially the simple division of one number by another *e.g.*, current asset to current liability ratio is 2:1.

(b) **Rate.** The ratio between two numerical facts, usually over a period of time *e.g.*, stock turnover is three times a year.

(c) **Percentage.** A special type of rate which expresses the relation in hundredth *e.g.*, gross profit is 25% on sale. While determining a ratio it is well to understand. It is desirable to divide the "more favourable" one by the "less favourable".

Nature of Ratio Analysis

An accounting ratio shows the mathematical relationship between two figures that have a meaningful relation with each other e.g., net sales and profit, and current assets and current liabilities. No meaning can be attached to the ratio between two figures that are unrelated to each other. Ratio analysis uses financial ratios indicating a quantitative relationship to make qualitative judgements on various aspects of the business.

Interpretation of Ratios

The technique of interpretation of ratios involves the comparisons of existing ratios against defined standards. The standards of comparison may consist of the following:

(i) Ratios calculated from the past financial statements of the same company.

(ii) Ratio evolved using the projected financial expectations from the company in the future. These would help corrective action to be initiated in the present.

(iii) Ratios of a few carefully identified competitors, who have similar operations as a reflection on the company's relative performance.

(iv) Ratio of the industry of which the firm is a member.

Classification of Ratios

Classification of ratios depends upon the objective for which they are calculated. It may also depend upon the availability of data. Analysis of financial statement is made with a view to ascertain the efficiency and financial soundness of the company as such ratios can be classified on the basis of profitability, turnover and financial capability. On the basis of purpose, ratios may be classified as under:

A. **Profitability Ratios**
   - (a) Gross profit ratio
   - (b) Net profit ratio and operating net profit ratios
   - (c) Expenses ratios
   - (d) Operating ratio
   - (e) Net profit to net worth ratio
   - (f) Net profit to fixed assets ratio
   - (g) Return on investment or capital employed
   - (h) Return on equity capital
   - (i) Earning per share

B. **Activity or Performance or Turnover Ratio**
   - (a) Stock or inventory turnover ratio
   - (b) Total capital turnover ratio
   - (c) Fixed assets turnover ratio
   - (d) Working capital turnover ratio
   - (e) Debtors turnover ratio

C. **Financial Ratios**
   - (a) Liquid ratios or short term financial or solvency ratios
     - (i) Current ratio
     - (ii) Liquid ratio
   - (b) Solvency ratios or long term financial ratios
     - (i) Debt equity ratio
     - (ii) Total debt ratio
     - (iii) Interest coverage or debt service ratio
     - (iv) Fixed assets ratio
     - (v) Proprietary ratio
     - (vi) Solvency ratio or debt to total funds ratio
     - (vii) Capital gearing ratio.

Significance of Return on Investment - (ROI)

Return on investment ratio measures, the operational efficiency and borrowing policy of the enterprise. It also shows how effectively the capital employed in the business is used. It shows the earning capacity of the net assets of the business. The ratio judges the performance of the business. It can be used for comparing the performance of even dissimilar business or different departments of the same business.

Uses of Return on Investment - (ROI)

1. It measures overall profitability of the business
2. Return on investment is a very significant ratio for measuring operational efficiency of the management.
3. It is used for comparing the performance of the different departments and sections of the enterprise.
4. Return on investment helps in making investment decisions.
5. Return on investment helps in determining the price of the product.

Use and Significance of Ratio Analysis

The ratio analysis is one of the most powerful tools of financial analysis. It is used as a device to analyse and interpret the financial health of enterprise. Just like a doctor examines his patient by recording his body temperature, blood pressure *etc.*, before making his conclusion regarding the illness and before giving his treatment. A financial analyst analyses the financial statements with various tools of analysis before commenting upon the financial health or weaknesses of enterprise. 'A ratio known as a symptom like blood pressure, the pulse rate or the temperature of an individual.' It is with help of ratios that the financial statements can be analysed more clearly and decisions made from such analysis.

The use of ratios is not confined to financial managers only. As discussed earlier, there are different parties interested in the ratio analysis for knowing the financial position of a firm for different purposes. The supplier of goods on credit, banks, financial institutions, investors, shareholders and management all make use of ratio analysis as a tool in evaluating the financial position and performance of a firm for granting credit, providing loans or making investments in the firm. With the use of ratio analysis one can measure the financial condition of a firm and can point out whether the condition is strong, good, questionable or poor. The conclusions can also be drawn as to whether the performance of the firm is improving or deteriorating. Thus, ratios have wide applications and are of immense use today.

(a) **Managerial Uses of Ratio Analysis**

(i) ***Helps in decision-making.*** Financial statements are prepared primarily for decision making. But the information provided in financial statements is not an end in itself and no meaningful conclusion can be drawn from these statements alone. Ratio analysis helps in making decisions from the information provided in these financial statements.

(ii) ***Helps in financial forecasting and planning.*** Ratio Analysis is of much help in financial forecasting and planning. Planning is looking ahead and the ratios calculated for a number of years work as a guide for the future. Meaningful conclusions can be drawn for future from these ratios. Thus, ratio analysis helps in forecasting and planning.

(iii) ***Helps in communicating.*** The financial strength and weakness of a firm are communicated in a more easy and understandable manner by the use of ratios. The information contained in the financial statements is conveyed in a meaningful manner to the one for whom it is meant. Thus, ratios help in communication and enhance the value of the financial statements.

(iv) ***Helps in co-ordination.*** Ratios even help in co-ordination which is of utmost importance in effective business management. Better communication of efficiency and weakness of an enterprise results in better co-ordination in the enterprise.

(v) ***Helps in Control.*** Ratio analysis even helps in making effective control of the business. Standard ratios can be based upon proforma financial statements and variances or deviations, if any, can be found by comparing the actual with the standards so as to take a corrective action at the right time. The weaknesses or otherwise, if any, come to the knowledge of the management which helps in effective control of the business.

(vi) ***Other Uses.*** These are so many other uses of the ratio analysis. It is essential part of the budgetary control and standard costing. Ratios are of immense importance in the analysis and interpretation of financial statements as they bring the strength or weakness of a firm.

(b) **Utility to Shareholders/Investors.** An investor in the company will like to assess the financial position of the concern where he is going to invest. His first interest will be the security of his investment and then a return in the form of dividend or interest. For the first purpose he will try to assess the value of fixed assets and the loans raised against them. The investor will feel satisfied only if the concern has sufficient amount of assets. Long-term solvency ratios will help him in assessing financial concern. Profitability ratios, on the other hand, will be useful to determine profitability position. Ratio analysis will be useful to the investor in making up his mind whether the present financial position of the concern warrants further investment or not.

(c) **Utility to Creditors.** The creditors or suppliers extend short-term credit to the concern. They are interested to know whether financial position of the concern warrants their payments at a specified time or not. The concern pays short-term creditors out of its current assets. If the current assets are quite sufficient to meet current liabilities then the creditor will not hesitate in extending credit facilities. Current and acid-test ratios will give an idea about the current financial position of the concern.

(d) **Utility to Employees.** The employees are also interested in the financial position of the concern especially profitability. Their wage increases and amount of fringe benefits are related to the volume of profits earned by the concern. The employees make use of information available in financial statements. Various profitability ratios relating to gross profit, operating profit, net profit *etc.* enable employees to put forward their viewpoint for the increase in wages and other benefits.

(e) **Utility to Government.** Government is interested to know the overall strength of the industry. Various financial statements published by industrial units are used to calculate ratios for determining short-term, long-term and overall financial position of the concerns. Profitability indexes can also be prepared with the help of ratios. Government may base its future policies on the basis of industrial information available from various units. The ratios may be used as indicators of overall financial strength of public as well as private sector. In the absence of the reliable economic information, governmental plans and policies may not prove successful.

SUMMARY OF RATIOS

Objective of Analysis (1)	Ratios to be computed (2)	Basic Components (3)
(a) Short-term Financial Position or Test of Liquidity	1. Current Ratio	$\frac{\text{Current Assets}}{\text{Current Liabilities}}$
	2. Quick or Acid Test or Liquid Ratio (for immediate solvency)	$\frac{\text{Liquid/Quick Assets}}{\text{Current Liabilities}}$
	3. Absolute Liquid Ratio	$\frac{\text{Absolute Liquid Assets}}{\text{Current Liabilities}}$
(b) Current assets Movement or Efficiency or Activity Ratios	1. Inventory/Stock Turnover Ratio	$\frac{\text{Cost of Goods sold}}{\text{Average Inventory at Cost}}$
	2. Debtors or Receivables Turnover Ratio/Velocity	$\frac{\text{Net Credit Annual Sales}}{\text{Average Trade Debtors}}$
	3. Average Collection Period	$\frac{\text{Total Trade Debtors}}{\text{Sales per day}}$

	4. Creditors/payables Turnover Ratio/velocity	$\frac{\text{Net Credit Annual Purchase}}{\text{Average Trade Creditors}}$
	5. Average Payment Period	$\frac{\text{Total Trade Creditors}}{\text{Average Daily Purchases}}$
	6. Working Capital Turnover Ratio	$\frac{\text{Cost of Sales}}{\text{Net Working Capital}}$
(c) Analysis of Long-term Financial Position or Test of Solvency	1. Debt-Equity Ratio	$\frac{\text{Outsider's Funds}}{\text{Shareholders' Funds}}$ OR $\frac{\text{External Equities}}{\text{Internal Equities}}$
	2. Funded Debt to Total Capitalisation Ratio	$\frac{\text{Funded Debt}}{\text{Total Capitalisation}} \times 100$
	3. Ratio of Long-term Debt to Shareholders, Funds (Debt-Equity)	$\frac{\text{Long-term Debt}}{\text{Shareholders' Funds}}$
	4. Proprietary or Equity Ratio	$\frac{\text{Shareholder's Funds}}{\text{Total Assets}}$
	5. Solvency Ratio	$\frac{\text{Total Liabilities to Outsiders}}{\text{Total Assets}}$
	6. Fixed Assets Net Worth Ratio	$\frac{\text{Fixed Assets (after depreciation)}}{\text{Shareholders' funds}}$
	7. Fixed Assets Ratio or Fixed Assets to Long-term Funds	$\frac{\text{Fixed Assets (after depreciation)}}{\text{Total Long-term Funds}}$
	8. Ratio of Current Assets to Proprietors' Funds	$\frac{\text{Current Assets}}{\text{Shareholders' Funds}}$
	9. Debt-Service, or Interest Coverage Ratio	$\frac{\text{Net Profit (before interest \& taxes)}}{\text{Fixed Interest Charges}}$
	10. Total Coverage, or Fixed-Charge Coverage	$\frac{\text{EBIT}}{\text{Total Fixed Charges}}$

	11. Preference Dividend	$\dfrac{\text{Net Profit (before interest \& Income tax)}}{\text{Preference Dividend}}$
		Annual Cash flow (before interest & Income tax)
	Coverage Ratio	
	12. Cash to Debt-Service	$\dfrac{CF}{1+\dfrac{\text{Interest on debt}}{1-\text{Tax rate}}}$
	Ratio or Debt Cash Flow	$=\dfrac{CF}{1+\dfrac{SFD}{1-T}}$
	Coverage	
(d) Analysis of Profitability	1. Gross Profit Ratio	$\dfrac{\text{Gross Profit}}{\text{Net Sales}}\times 100$
(i) General Profitability	2. Operating Ratio	$\dfrac{\text{Operating Cost}}{\text{Net Sales}}\times 100$
	3. Expense Ratio	$\dfrac{\text{Particular Expenses}}{\text{Net Sales}}\times 100$
	4. Net Profit Ratio	$\dfrac{\text{Net Profit after tax}}{\text{Net Sales}}\times 100$
	5. Operating Profit Ratio	$\dfrac{\text{Operating Profit}}{\text{Net Sales}}\times 100$
(ii) Overall Profitability	1. Return on Shareholders' Investments or Net Worth (ROI.)	$\dfrac{\text{Net Profit (after interest \& tax)}}{\text{Shareholders' Funds}}\times 100$
	2. Return on Equity Capital	$\dfrac{\text{NetProfit after tax - Preference Div.}}{\text{Paid-up Equity Capital}}\times 100$
	3. Earnings Per Share (E.P.S.)	$\dfrac{\text{NetProfit after tax - Preference Div.}}{\text{Number of Equity Share}}$
	4. Return on Gross Capital Employed	$\dfrac{\text{Adjusted Net Profit}}{\text{Gross Capital Employed}}\times 100$
	5. Return on Net Capital Employed	$\dfrac{\text{Adjusted Net Profit}}{\text{Net Capital Employed}}\times 100$
	6. Capital Turnover Ratio	$\dfrac{\text{Sales or Cost of Sales}}{\text{Capital Employed}}$

	7. Dividend Yield Ratio	$\frac{\text{Dividend Per Share}}{\text{Market value per share}}$
	8. Dividend Pay-out Ratio or Pay-out Ratio	$\frac{\text{Dividend Per Equity Share}}{\text{Earnings per share}}$
	9. Price-Earning Ratio (P/E Ratio)	$\frac{\text{Market Price per Equity Share}}{\text{Earnings per share}}$
(e) Analysis of Capital Structure or Leverage	1. Capital Gearing Ratio	$\frac{\text{Eq. Share Capital + Reserves \& Surplus}}{\text{Pref. Capital + Long-term debt bearing fixed interest}}$
	2. Total Investment to Long-term Liabilities	$\frac{\text{Shareholders' funds + Long-term Liabilities}}{\text{Long-term Liabilities}}$
	3. Debt Equity Ratio	$\frac{\text{Outsiders' Funds}}{\text{Shareholders'Funds}}$
	4. Ratio of Fixed Assets to Funded Debt	$\frac{\text{Fixed Assets}}{\text{Funded Debt}}$
	5. Ratio of Current Liabilities to Proprietors Funds	$\frac{\text{Current Liabilities}}{\text{Shareholders' Funds}}$
	6. Ratio of Reserves to Equity Capital	$\frac{\text{Reserves}}{\text{Equity Share Capital}} \times 100$
	7. Financial Leverage	$\frac{\text{Int. \& Tax (EBIT)}}{\text{EBIT – Inter \& Pref. Divd.}}$
	8. Operating Leverage	$\frac{\text{Contribution}}{\text{EBIT}}$

FUND FLOW ANALYSIS

The Funds Flow Statement is a statement which shows the movement of funds and is a report of the financial operations of the business undertaking. It indicates various means by which funds were obtained during a particular period and the ways in which these funds were employed. In simple words, it is a statement of sources and applications of funds.

In a **narrow sense**, it means cash only and a funds flow statement prepared on this basis is called a cash flow statement. Such a statement enumerates net effects of the various business transactions on cash and takes into account receipts and disbursements of cash.

In a **broader sense**, the term 'funds' refers to money values in whatever form it may exist. Here 'funds' means all financial resources, used in business whether in the form of men, material, money, machinery and others.

In a **popular sense**, the term 'funds' means working capital *i.e.*, the excess of current assets over current liabilities. The working capital concept of funds has emerged due to the fact that total resources of a business are invested partly in fixed assets in the form of fixed capital and partly kept in the form of liquid or near liquid form as working capital.

The term 'flow' means movement and includes both 'inflow' and 'outflow'. The term 'flow of funds' means transfer of economic values from one asset of equity to another. Flow of funds is said to have taken place when any transaction makes changes in the amount of funds available before happening of the transaction. If the effect transactions results in the increase of funds, it is called as a source of funds and if it results in the decrease of funds, it is known as an application of funds. Further, in case the transactions does not change funds, it is said to have not resulted in the flow of funds. According to the working capital concept of funds, the term 'flow of funds' refers to the movement of funds in the working capital. If any transactions results in the increase in working capital, it is said to be a source or inflow of funds and if it results in the decrease of working capital, it is said to be an application or out-flow of funds.

According to I.C.W.A., 'Fund flow Statement is a statement either prospective or retrospective setting out the sources and applications of the funds of an enterprises. The purpose of the statement is to indicate clearly the requirement of funds and how they are proposed to be raised and the efficient, utilisation and application of the same'.

Uses, Significance and Importance of Funds Flow Statement

A funds flow statement is an essential tool for the financial analysis and is of primary importance to the financial management. Now-a-days, it is being widely used by the financial analysts, credit granting institutions and financial managers. The basic purpose of a funds flow statement is to reveal the changes in the working capital on the two balance sheet dates. It also describes the sources from which additional working capital has been financed and the uses to which working capital has been applied. Such a statement is particularly useful in assessing the growth of the firm, its resulting financial needs and in determining the best way of financing these needs. By making use of projected funds flow statements, the management can come to know the adequacy or inadequacy of working capital even in advance. One can plan the intermediate and long-term financing of the firm, repayment of long-term debts, expansion of the business, allocation of resources *etc.* The significance or importance of funds flow statement can be well followed from its various uses given below:

(i) **It helps in the analysis of financial operations.** The financial statements reveal the net effect of various transactions on the operational and financial position of a concern. The balance sheet gives a static view of the resources of a business and the uses to which these resources have been put at a certain point of time. But it does not disclose the causes for changes in the assets and liabilities between two different points of time. The funds flow statement explains causes for such changes and also the effect of these changes on the liquidity position of the company. Sometimes a concern may operate profitably and yet its cash position may become more and more worse. The funds flow statement gives a clear answer to such a situation explaining what has happened to the profits of the firm.

(ii) **It throws light on many perplexing questions of general interest** which otherwise may be difficult to be answered, such as

(a) Why were the net current assets lesser in spite of higher profits and vice versa?

(b) Why more dividends could not be declared in spite of available profits?

(c) How was it possible to distribute more dividends than the present earnings ?
(d) What happened to the net profit? Where did they go?
(e) What happened to the proceeds of sale of fixed assets or issue of shares, debentures, etc.?
(f) What are the sources of the repayment of debt?
(g) How was the increase in working capital financed and how it will be financed in future?

(iii) **It helps in the formation of a realistic dividend policy.** Sometimes a firm has sufficient profits available for distribution as dividend but yet it may not be advisable to distribute dividend for lack of liquid or cash resources. In such cases, a funds flow statement helps in the formation of a realistic dividend policy.

(iv) **It helps in the proper allocation of resources.** The resources of a concern are always limited and it wants to make the best use of these resources. A projected funds flow statement constructed for the future helps in making managerial decisions. The firm can plan the deployment of its resources and allocate them among various applications.

(v) **It acts as a future guide.** A projected funds flow statement also acts as a guide for future to the management. The management can come to know the various problems it is going to face in near future for want of funds. The firm's future needs of funds can be projected well in advance and also the timing of these needs. The firm can arrange to finance these needs more effectively and avoid future problems.

(vi) **It helps in appraising the use of working capital.** A funds flow statement helps in explaining how efficiently the management has used its working capital and also suggests ways to improve working capital position of the firm.

(vii) **It helps in knowing the overall credit worthiness of a firm.** The financial institutions and banks such as State Financial Institutions, Industrial Development Corporation, Industrial Finance Corporation of India, Industrial Development Bank of India, *etc.*, all ask for funds flow statements constructed for a number of years before granting loans to know the credit worthiness and paying capacity of the firm. Hence, a firm seeking financial assistance from these institutions has no alternative but to prepare funds flow statements.

Procedure for Preparing a Funds Flow Statement

Funds Flow statement is a method by which we study changes in the financial position of a business enterprise between beginning and ending financial statements dates. Hence, the funds flow statement is prepared by comparing two balance sheets and with the help of such other information derived from the accounts as may be needed. Broadly speaking, the preparation of a funds flow statement consists of two parts :

A. Statement or Schedule of Changes in Working Capital

Working Capital means the excess of current assets over current liabilities. Statement of changes in working capital is prepared to show the changes in the working capital between the two balance sheet dates. This statement is prepared with the help of current assets and current liabilities derived from the two balance sheets.

As, Working Capital = Current Assets – Current Liabilities.

So,

(i) An increase in current assets increases working capital.
(ii) A decrease in current assets decreases, working capital.
(iii) An increase in current liabilities decreases working capital and
(iv) A decrease in current liabilities increases working capital.

The change in the amount of any current asset or current liability in the current balance sheet as 621 compared to that of the previous balance sheet either results in increase or decrease in working capital. The difference is recorded for each individual current asset and current liability. In case a current asset in the current period is more than in the previous period, the effect is an increase in working capital and it is recorded in the increase column . But if a current liability in the current period is more than in the previous period, the effect is decrease in working capital and it is recorded in the decrease column or vice versa. The total increase and the total decrease are compared and the difference shows the net increase or net decrease in working capital. It is worth noting that schedule of changes in working capital is prepared only from current assets and current liabilities and the other information is not of any use for preparing this statement. A typical form of statement or schedule of changes in working capital is as follows:

STATEMENT OR SCHEDULE OF CHANGES IN WORKING CAPITAL

Particulars	Previous Year	Current Year	Effect on Working Capital	
			Increase	Decrease
Current Assets:				
Cash in hand				
Cash at bank				
Bills Receivable				
Sundry Debtors				
Temporary Investments				
Stocks/Inventories				
Prepaid Expenses				
Accrued Incomes				
Total Current Assets				
Current Liabilities:				
Bills Payable				
Sundry Creditors				
Outstanding Expenses				
Bank Overdraft				
Short-term advances				
Dividends Payable				
Proposed dividends				
Provision for taxation				
Total Current Liabilities				
Working Capital (CA-CL)				
Net Increase or Decrease in Working Capital				

B. Statement of Sources and Application of Funds

Funds flow statement is a statement which indicates various sources from which funds (working capital) have been obtained during a certain period and the uses or applications to which these funds have been put during that period. Generally, this statement is prepared in two formats:

(a) Report Form

(b) T-Form or An Account Form or Self Balancing Type.

SPECIMEN OF REPORT FORM OF FUNDS FLOW STATEMENT

	Rs.
Sources of Funds:	
Funds from Operations	
Issue of Share Capital	
Raising of long-term loans	
Receipts from partly paid shares, called up	
Sales of non current (fixed) assets	
Non-trading receipts, such as dividends received	
Sale of Investments (long-term)	
Decrease in Working Capital (as per schedule of changes in Working Capital)	
Total	
Applications or Uses of Funds:	
Funds Lost in Operations	
Redemption of Preference Share Capital	
Redemption of Debentures	
Repayment of long-term loans	
Purchase of non-current (fixed) assets	
Purchase of long-term Investments	
Non-trading payments	
Payments of dividends	
Payment of tax	
Increase in Working Capital (as per schedule of changes in Working Capital)	
Total	

T Form or An Account Form or Self Balancing Type
FUNDS FLOW STATEMENT
(For the year ended..........)

Sources	*Rs.*	*Applications*	*Rs.*
Funds from Operations		Funds lost in Operations	
Issue of Share Capital		Redemption of Preference Share Capital	
Issue of Debentures		Redemption of Debentures	
Raising of long-term loans		Repayment of long-term loans	
Receipts from partly paid shares, called up		Purchase of non-current (fixed) assets	
Sale of non-current (fixed) assets		Purchase of long-term Investments	
Non-trading receipts such as dividends		Non-trading payments	
Sale of long-term Investments		Payment of Dividends	
Net Decrease in Working Capital		Payment of tax	
		Net Increase in Working Capital	

Sources of Funds

The following are the sources from which funds generally flow (come), into the business :

(a) Funds from Operations or Trading Profits

Trading profits or the profits from operations of the business are the most important and major source of funds. Sales are the main source of inflow of funds into the business as they increase current assets (cash, debtors or bills receivable) but at the same time funds flow out of business for expenses and cost of goods sold. Thus, the net effect of operations will be a source of funds if inflow from sales exceeds the outflow for expenses and cost of goods sold and vice-versa. But it must be remembered that funds from operations do not necessarily mean the profit as shown by the profit and loss account of a firm, because there are many non-fund or non-operating items which may have been either debited or credited to profit and loss account. The examples of such items on the debit side of a profit and loss account are the following:

Amortization of fictitious and intangible assets such as goodwill, Preliminary expenses and Discount on issue of shares and debentures written off; Appropriation of Retained Earnings, such as Transfers to Reserves, *etc.*, Depreciation and depletion Loss on sale of fixed assets ; Payment of dividend, *etc.* The non-fund items are those which may be operational expenses but they do not affect funds of the business, *e.g.*, for depreciation charged to profit and loss account, funds really do not move out of business. Non-operating items are those which although may result in the outflow of funds but are not related to the trading operations of the business, such as loss on sale of machinery or payment of dividends. The methods of calculating funds from operations have been discussed in the following pages.

Basically, there are two methods of calculating funds from operations:

(1) **The first method** is to prepare the profit and loss account afresh by taking into consideration only fund and operational items which involve funds and are related to the normal operations of the business. The balancing figure in this case will be either funds generated from operations or funds lost in operations depending upon whether the income or credit side of profit and loss account exceeds the expense or debit side of profit and loss account or vice-versa.

(2) **The second method** (which is generally used) is to proceed from the figure of net profit or net loss as arrived at from the profit and loss account already prepared. Funds from operations by this method can be calculated as under:

CALCULATION OF FUNDS FROM OPERATION	
Closing Balance of P & L A/C or Retained Earnings (as given in the balance sheet)	Rs.
Add: Non-fund and Non-operating items which have been already debited to P & L A/C:	
(i) Depreciation and Depletion	
(ii) Amortization of fictitious and Intangible Assets such as:	
(a) Goodwill	
(b) Patents	
(c) Trade marks	
(d) Preliminary Expenses	
(e) Discount on Issue of Shares, etc.	
(iii) Appropriation of Retained Earnings, such as:	
(a) Transfer to General Reserve	
(b) Dividend Equalisation Fund	
(c) Transfer to Sinking Fund	
(d) Contingency Reserve, etc.	
(iv) Loss on Sale of any non-current (fixed) assets such as :	
(a) Loss on sale of land and building	
(b) Loss on sale of machinery	
(c) Loss on sale of furniture	
(d) Loss on sale of long-term investments, etc.	
(v) Dividends including:	
(a) Interim Dividend	
(b) Proposed Dividend (if it is an appropriation of profits and not taken as current liability)	
(vi) Provision for Taxation (if it is not taken as Current Liability)	
(vii) Any other non-fund/non-operating items which have been debited to P/L	
Total (A)	

Less Non-fund or Non-operating items which have already been credited to P & L A/C	
(i) Profit or Gain from the sale of non-current (fixed) assets such as:	
(a) Profit on sale of land and building	
(b) Profit on sale of plant & machinery	
(c) Profit on sale of long-term investments, etc.	
(ii) Appreciation in the value of fixed assets, such as increase in the value of land if it has been credited to P & L A/C	
(iii) Dividends Received	
(iv) Excess Provision re-transferred to P&L A/C or written off	
(v) Any other non-operating item which has been credited to P&L A/C	
(vi) Opening balance of P& L A/C or Retained Earnings (as given in the balance sheet)	
Total (B)	
Total (A) – Total (B) = Funds generated by operations	

Funds from operations can also be calculated by preparing Adjusted Profit and Loss Account as follows:

ADJUSTED PROFIT AND LOSS ACCOUNT

	Rs.			Rs.
To Depreciation & Depletion or amortization of fictitious and intangible assets, such as: Goodwill, Patents, Trade Marks, Preliminary Expenses *etc.*			By Opening Balance (of P & L A/C)	
To Appropriation of Retained Earnings, such as: Transfers to General Reserve, Dividend Equalisation Fund, Sinking Fund, *etc.*			By Transfers from excess provisions	
To Loss on Sales of any non current or fixed asset			By Appreciation in the value of fixed assets	
To Dividends (including interim dividend)			By Dividends received	
			By Profit on sale of fixed or non-current assets	
			By Funds from Operations (balancing figure in case debit side exceeds credit side)	

To Proposed Dividend (if not taken as a current liability)		
To Provision for taxation (if not taken as a current liability)		
To Closing balance (of P & L A/C)		
To Funds lost in Operations (balancing figure, in case credit side exceeds the debit side)		

(b) Issue of Share Capital

If during the year there is any increase in the share capital, whether preference or equity, it means capital has been raised during the year. Issue of shares is a source of funds as it constitutes inflow of funds. Even the calls received from partly paid shares constitutes an inflow of funds. It should also be remembered that it is the net proceeds from the issue of share capital which amounts to a source of funds and hence in case shares are issued at premium, even the amount of premium collected shall become a source of funds. The same is true when shares are issued at discount ; it will not be the nominal value of shares but the actual realisation after deducting discount that shall amount to inflow of funds. But sometimes shares are issued otherwise than in cash, the following rules must be followed:

(i) Issue of shares for making of partly paid shares as fully paid out of accumulated profits in the form of bonus shares is not a source of funds.

(ii) Issues of shares for consideration other than current assets such as against purchase of land, machines, *etc.* does not amount to inflow of funds.

(iii) Conversion of debentures or loans into shares also does not amount to inflow of funds.

In all the three cases mentioned above, both the amounts involved are non-current and do not involve any current assets or funds.

(c) Issue of Debentures and Raising of Loans, etc.

Issue of debentures or raising of loans (long-term), whether secured or unsecured results in the flow of funds into the business. The inflow of funds is the actual proceeds from the issue of such debentures or raising of loans, *i.e.*, including the amount of premium or excluding discount, if any. However, loans raised for consideration other than a current asset, such as for purchase of building, will not constitute inflow of funds because in that case the accounts involved are only fixed or non-current.

(d) Sale of Fixed (non-current assets) and Long-term or Trade Investments

When any fixed or non-current asset like land, building, plant and machinery, furniture, long-term investments, *etc.* are sold it generates funds and becomes a source of funds. However, it must be remembered that if one fixed asset is exchanged for another fixed asset, it does not constitute an inflow of funds because no current assets are involved.

(e) Non-Trading Receipts

Any non-trading receipt like dividend received, refund of tax, rent received, *etc.* also increases funds and is treated as a sources of funds because such an income is not included in the funds from operations.

(f) Decrease in Working Capital

If the working capital decreases during the current period as compared to the previous period, it means that there has been a release of funds from working capital and it constitutes a source of funds.

Application or Uses of Funds

(a) **Funds lost in operations.** Sometimes the result of trading in a certain year is a loss and some funds are lost during that period in trading operations. Such loss of funds in trading amounts to an outflow of funds and is treated as an application of funds.

(b) **Redemption of preference share capital.** If during the year any preference shares are redeemed, it will result in the outflow of funds and is taken as an application of funds. When the shares are redeemed at premium or discount, it is the net amount paid (including premium or excluding discount, as the case may be). However, if shares are redeemed in exchanges of some other type of shares or debentures, it does not constitute an outflow of funds as no current account is involved in that case.

(c) **Repayment of loans or redemption of debentures, etc..** In the same way as redemption of preference share capital, redemption of debentures or repayment of loans also constitute an application of funds.

(d) **Purchase of any non-current or fixed asset.** When any fixed or non-current asset like land, building, plant and machinery, furniture, long-term investments, etc. are purchased, funds outflow from the business. However, if fixed assets are purchased for a consideration of issue of shares or debentures or if some fixed asset is exchanged for another, it does not involve any funds and hence not an application of funds.

(e) **Payments of Dividends and Tax.** Payments of dividends and tax are also applications of funds. It is the actual payment of dividend (may be interim dividend) and tax which should be taken as an outflow of funds and not the mere declaration of dividend or creating of a provision for taxation.

(f) **Any other non-trading payment.** Any payment or expense not related to the trading operations of the business amounts to outflow of funds and is taken as an application of funds. The examples could be drawings in case of sole trader or partnership firms, loss of cash, *etc.*

CASH FLOW ANALYSIS

Cash plays a very important role in the entire economic life of a business. A firm needs cash to make payments to its suppliers, to incur day-to-day expenses and to pay salaries, wages, interest and dividends, *etc.* In fact, what blood is to a human body, cash is to a business enterprise. It is very essential for a business to maintain an adequate balance of cash. But many a times, a concern operates profitably and yet it becomes very difficult to pay taxes and dividends. This may be because:

(i) although huge profits have been earned, yet cash may not have been received or

(ii) even if cash has been received, it may have drained out (used) for some other purposes. This movement of cash is of vital importance to the management.

A statement of changes in the financial position affirm on cash basis is called a cash flow statement. Such a statement enumerates net effects of the various business transactions on cash and takes into account receipts and disbursements of cash. A cash flow statement summarises the causes of changes in cash position of a business enterprise between dates of two balance sheets. This statement is very much similar to the statement of changes in financial position prepared on working capital basis, *i.e.*, a funds flow statement, except that a cash flow statement focuses attention on cash instead of working capital. It is called a cash flow statement because it describes the inflow (sources) and outflow (uses) of cash.

DIFFERENCE BETWEEN FUNDS FLOW STATEMENT AND CASH FLOW STATEMENT

	Basis of Difference	Funds Flow Statement	Cash Flow Statement
(i)	Basis of Concept	It is based on a wider concept of funds, *i.e.*, Working capital.	It is based on a narrower concept of funds *i.e.*, cash.
(ii)	Basis of Accounting	It is based on accrual basis of accounting.	It is based on cash basis of accounting.
(iii)	Schedule of change in working Capital	Schedule of changes in working capital is prepared to show the changes in current assets and current liabilities.	No such schedule of changes in working capital is prepared.
(iv)	Method of Preparing	Fund Flow Statement reveals the sources and applications of funds. The net difference between sources and applications of funds represents net increase or decrease in working capital.	It is prepared by taking the opening balance of cash, adding to this all the inflows of cash and deducting the out flows of cash from the the difference represents the closing balance of cash.
(v)	Basis of Usefulness	It is useful in planning intermediate and long term financing.	It is more useful for short-term analysis and cash planning of the business.

Uses and Significance of Cash Flow Statement

Cash flow statement is of vital importance to the financial management. It is an essential tool of financial analysis for short-term planning. The chief advantages of cash flow statement are as follows:

(i) Since a cash flow statement is based on the cash basis of accounting, it is very useful in the evaluation of cash position of a firm.

(ii) A projected cash flow statement can be prepared in order to know the future cash position of a concern so as to enable a firm to plan and coordinate its financial operations properly. By preparing this statement, a firm can come to know as to how much cash will be generated into the firm and how much cash will be needed to make various payments and hence the firm can well plan to arrange for the future requirements of cash.

(iii) A comparison of the historical and projected cash flow statements can be made so as to find the variations and deficiency or otherwise in the performance so as to enable the firm to take immediate and effective action.

(iv) A series of intra-firm and inter-firm cash flow statements reveals whether the firm's liquidity (short-term paying capacity) is improving or deteriorating over a period of time and in comparison to other firms over a given period of time.

(v) Cash flow statement helps in planning the repayment of loans, replacement of fixed assets and other similar long-term planning of cash. It is also significant for capital budgeting decisions.

(vi) It better explains the causes for poor cash position inspite of substantial profits of a firm by throwing light on various applications of cash made by the firm. It further helps in answering some intricate questions like – what happened to the net profits ? Where did the profits go? Why more dividends could not be paid in spite of sufficient available profit ?

(vii) Cash flow analysis is more useful and appropriate than funds flow analysis for short-term financial analysis as for a very short period it is cash which is more relevant then the working capital for forecasting the ability of the firm to meet its immediate obligations.

Procedure for Preparing a Cash Flow Statement

Cash flow statement shows the impact of various transactions on cash position of a firm. It is prepared with the help of financial statements, *i.e.*, balance sheet and profit and loss account and some additional information. A cash flow statement starts with the opening balance of cash and balance at bank, all the inflows of cash are added to the opening balance and the out flows of cash are deducted from the total. The balance, *i.e.* opening balance of cash and bank balance plus in flows of cash minus outflows of cash is reconciled with the closing balance of cash. The preparation of cash flow statement involves the determining of:

(a) **Sources of Cash Inflows.**

The main sources of cash inflows are

(i) Cash flow from operations;
(ii) Increase in existing liabilities or creation of new liabilities and
(iii) Reduction in or Sale of Assets;
(iv) Non-trading Receipts.

(b) **Application of Cash or Cash Outflows.**

(i) Cash lost in operations;
(ii) Decrease in or discharge of liabilities;
(iii) Increase in or purchase of assets and
(iv) Non-trading payments.

Generally, cash flow statement is prepared in two forms:

(a) Report form
(b) T-Form or an Account Form or Self Balancing Type

SPECIMEN OF REPORT FORM OF CASH FLOW STATEMENT

	Rs.
Cash balance in the beginning	
Add: Cash inflows:	
Cash flow from operations	
Sale of assets	
Issue of shares	
Issue of debentures	
Raising of loans	
Collection from debtors	
Non trading receipts such as:	
Dividend received	
Income tax refund	
Less: Applications or Outflows of cash:	
Redemption of Preference shares	
Redemption of debentures	
Repayment of loans	
Purchase of assets	
Payment of dividend	
Payment of taxes	
Cash lost in operations	
Cash Balance at the end	

T–FORM OR AN ACCOUNT FORM OF CASH FLOW STATEMENT

	Rs.		Rs.
Cash balance in the beginning		Outflow of Cash:	
Add. Cash inflows:		Redemption of Preference Shares	
Cash flow from operation		Redemption of Debentures	
Sale of Assets		Repayment of Loans	
Issue of Shares		Purchase of Assets	
Issue of Debentures		Payment of Dividends	
Raising of Loans		Payment of Tax	
Collection from Debtors		Cash lost in Operations	
Dividends Received		Cash Balance at the end	
Refund of tax			

Sources of Cash Inflows

A. Cash from Operations or Cash from Operating Profit.

Cash from trading operations during the year is a very important source of cash inflows. The net effect of various transactions in a business during a particular period is either net profit or net loss. Usually, net profit results in inflow of cash and net loss in outflow of cash. But it does not mean that cash generated from trading operations in a year shall be equal to the net profit or that cash lost in operations shall be identical with net loss. It may either be more or less. Even, there may be a net loss in a business but yet there may be a cash inflow from operations. It is so because of certain non-operating (expenses or incomes) charged to the income statement, *i.e.*, Profit and Loss Account.

How to Calculate Cash from Operations or Cash from Operating Profit?

There are three methods of determining cash from operations:

(a) **From Cash Sales.** Cash from operations can be calculated by deducting cash purchases and cash operating expenses from cash sales, *i.e.*

Cash from Operations = (Cash Sales) – (Cash Purchases + Cash Operating Expenses)

Cash sales are calculated by deducting credit sales or increase in receivables from the total sales. From the cash sales, the cash purchases and cash operating expenses are to be deducted. In the absence of any information, all expenses may be assumed to be cash expenses. In case outstanding and prepaid expenses are known/given, any decrease in outstanding expenses or increase in prepaid expenses should be deducted from the corresponding figure. Thus, cash from operations under this method can be tabulated as follows:

(a) CALCULATION OF CASH FROM OPERATIONS

	Amount
Sales	
Less. Credit Sales or Increase in accounts receivables.	
Cash Sales	
Less. Cash Purchases (Purchases–Credit Purchases or increase in payables)	
Less. Cash from Operating expenses (after adjusting prepaid and Outstanding expenses)	
Cash from Trading Operations.	

(b) **From Net Profit/ Net Loss.** Cash from operations can also be calculated with the help of net profit or net loss. Under this method, net profit or net loss is adjusted for non-cash and non-operating expenses and incomes as follows:

(b) CALCULATION OF CASH FROM TRADING OPERATIONS

	Amount
Net Profit (as given)	
Add: Non cash and non-operating items which have already been debited to P & L A/C:	
Depreciation	
Transfer to Reserves	
Transfer to provisions	
Goodwill written off	
Preliminary expenses written off	
Other intangible assets written off	
Loss on sale or disposal of fixed assets	
Increase in Accounts Payable	
Increase in outstanding expenses	
Decrease in prepaid expenses	
Less: Non-cash and non-operating items which have already been credited to P & L A/C:	
Increase in Accounts Receivables	
Decrease in Outstanding Expenses	
Increase in Prepaid Expenses	
Cash from Operations	

(c) **Cash from Operating Profit.** Cash from operating profit is also calculated with the help of net profit or net loss. The difference in this method as compared to the above discussed method is that increase or decrease in accounts payable and accounts receivable is not adjusted while finding cash from operations and it is directly shown in the cash flow statement as an inflow or outflow of cash as the cash may be. The cash from operations so calculated is generally called operating profit.

CALCULATION OF CASH FROM OPERATING PROFIT

	Amount
Net Profit (as given) or Closing Balance of Profit and Loss A/C	
Add: Non-cash and non-operating items which have already been debited to P & L A/C:	
Depreciation	
Transfers to Reserves and Provisions	
Writing off intangible assets	
Outstanding Expenses (current year)	
Prepaid Expenses (previous year)	
Loss on Sale of fixed Assets	
Dividend Paid, etc.	

Less: Non-cash and non-operating items which have already been credited to P & L A/C:
Profit on Sale or disposal of fixed assets
Non-trading receipts such as dividend received, rent received, *etc.*
Re-transfers from provisions
(excess provisions charged back)
Outstanding income (current year)
Pre-received income (in previous year)
Opening balance of P & L A/C
Cash from Operating Profit

(i) **Outstanding/Accrued Expenses.** The outstanding/accrued expenses represent those expenses which are although charged to profit and loss account but no cash is paid during the year. For this reason, outstanding/accrued expenses of the current year are added back while calculating cash from operating profit. However, if some outstanding expenses of the previous year are also given, these may be assumed to have been paid during the year and hence shown as an outflow of cash in the cash flow statement.

(ii) **Prepaid Expenses.** Prepaid expenses are those expenses which are paid in advance and hence result in the outflow of cash but are not charged to profit and loss account because they do not relate to the current period of profit and loss account. For this reason, prepaid expenses of the current year should be taken as an outflow of cash in the cash flow statement. But the expenses, if any, paid in the previous year do not involve outflow of cash in the current year but are charged to profit and loss account. Therefore, prepaid expenses of the previous year (related to the current year) should be added back while calculating cash from operating profit.

B. Increase in Existing Liabilities or Creation of New Liabilities

If there is an increase in existing liabilities or a new liability is created during the year, it results in the flow of cash into the business. The liability may be either a fixed long-term liability such as Equity Share Capital, Preference Share Capital, Debentures, long-term loans, *etc.* or a current liability such as sundry creditors, bills payable, *etc.*

The inflow of cash may be either Actual or Notional

There is an actual inflow of cash when cash is actually received and generally long-term liabilities result into actual inflow of cash, *e.g.*

For Issue of Shares, during the year, the journal entry shall be

Cash A/C ...Dr.
To Share Capital A/C

So, actual cash flows into the business. In the same manner, issue of debentures, raising of loans for cash, *etc.* result into actual inflows of cash. But when the fixed liabilities are created in consideration of purchase of assets, *i.e.*, other than cash, there is no inflow of actual cash. The journal entry for the issue of debentures in lieu of purchase of machinery is:

Plant and Machinery A/C ...Dr.
To Debentures A/C
(It does not involve actual flow of cash)

Usually, current liabilities result into inflow of notional cash. For example, increase in Sundry Creditors implies purchase of goods on credit. In this case, although no cash is actually received but we may say that creditors have given us loans which have been utilised in purchasing goods from them. Hence, increase in the current liabilities may be taken as a source of inflow of cash and decrease in current liabilities as an outflow of cash.

C. Reduction in or Sale of Assets

Whenever a reduction in or sale of any asset-fixed or current-takes place (otherwise than depreciation) it results into inflow of actual or notional cash. There is an actual inflow of cash when assets are sold for cash and notional cash flows in when assets are sold or disposed off on credit. Thus, sale of building, machinery or even reduction in current assets like stocks, debtors, *etc.* result in inflow of actual or notional cash.

D. Non-Trading Receipts

Sometimes, there may be non-trading receipts like dividend received, rent received, refund of tax, etc. such receipts or incomes are although non-trading in nature but they result into inflow of cash and hence taken in the cash flow statement.

Applications of Cash or Cash Outflows

A. **Cash lost in Operations.** Sometimes the net result of trading in a particular period is a loss and some cash may be lost during that period in trading operations. Such loss of cash in trading is called cash lost in operations and is shown as an outflow of cash in Cash Flow Statement.

B. **Decrease in or Discharge of Liabilities.** Decrease in or discharge of any liability, fixed or current, results in outflow of cash either actual or notional. For example, when redeemable preference shares are redeemed and loans are repaid, it will amount to an outflow of actual cash. But when a liability is converted into another, such as issue of shares for debentures, there will be a notional flow of cash into the business.

C. **Increase in or Purchase of Assets.** Just like decrease in or sale of assets is a source or inflow of cash, increase or purchase of any assets is a outflow or application of cash.

D. **Non-Trading Payments.** Payment of any non-trading expenses also constitute outflow of cash. For example, payment of dividends, payment of income-tax, *etc.*

HUMAN RESOURCE ACCOUNTING

Human resources are considered as important assets and are different from the physical assets. Physical assets do not have feelings and emotions, whereas human assets are subjected to various types of feelings and emotions. In the same way, unlike physical assets human assets never gets depreciated.

Therefore, the valuations of human resources along with other assets are also required in order to find out the total cost of an organization. In 1960s, Rensis Likert along with other social researchers made an attempt to define the concept of human resource accounting (HRA).

1. The American Association of Accountants (AAA) defines HRA as follows: 'HRA is a process of identifying and measuring data about human resources and communicating this information to interested parties'.
2. Flamhoitz defines HRA as 'accounting for people as an organizational resource. It involves measuring the costs incurred by organizations to recruit, select, hire, train, and develop human assets. It also involves measuring the economic value of people to the organization'.

3. According to Stephen Knauf, 'HRA is the measurement and quantification of human organizational inputs such as recruiting, training, experience and commitment'.

Need for HRA

The need for human asset valuation arose as a result of growing concern for human relations management in the industry.

Behavioural scientists concerned with management of organizations pointed out the following reasons for HRA:

1. Under conventional accounting, no information is made available about the human resources employed in an organization, and without people the financial and physical resources cannot be operationally effective.
2. The expenses related to the human organization are charged to current revenue instead of being treated as investments, to be amortized over a period of time, with the result that magnitude of net income is significantly distorted. This makes the assessment of firm and inter-firm comparison difficult.
3. The productivity and profitability of a firm largely depends on the contribution of human assets. Two firms having identical physical assets and operating in the same market may have different returns due to differences in human assets. If the value of human assets is ignored, the total valuation of the firm becomes difficult.
4. If the value of human resources is not duly reported in profit and loss account and balance sheet, the important act of management on human assets cannot be perceived.
5. Expenses on recruitment, training, etc. are treated as expenses and written off against revenue under conventional accounting. All expenses on human resources are to be treated as investments, since the benefits are accrued over a period of time.

Objectives of HRA

Rensis Likert described the following objectives of HRA:

1. Providing cost value information about acquiring, developing, allocating and maintaining human resources.
2. Enabling management to monitor the use of human resources.
3. Finding depreciation or appreciation among human resources.
4. Assisting in developing effective management practices.
5. Increasing managerial awareness of the value of human resources.
6. For better human resource planning.
7. For better decisions about people, based on improved information system.
8. Assisting in effective utilization of manpower.

METHOD OF VALUATION OF HUMAN RESOURCES

There are certain methods advocated for valuation of human resources. These methods include historical method, replacement cost method, present value method, opportunity cost method and standard cost method. All methods have certain benefits as well as limitations.

Benefits of HRA

There are certain benefits for accounting of human resources, which are explained as follows:

1. The system of HRA discloses the value of human resources, which helps in proper interpretation of return on capital employed.
2. Managerial decision-making can be improved with the help of HRA.
3. The implementation of human resource accounting clearly identifies human resources as valuable assets, which helps in preventing misuse of human resources by the superiors as well as the management.
4. It helps in efficient utilization of human resources and understanding the evil effects of labour unrest on the quality of human resources.
5. This system can increase productivity because the human talent, devotion, and skills are considered valuable assets, which can boost the morale of the employees.
6. It can assist the management for implementing best methods of wages and salary administration.

Limitations of HRA

HRA is yet to gain momentum in India due to certain difficulties:

1. The valuation methods have certain disadvantages as well as advantages; therefore, there is always a bone of contention among the firms that which method is an ideal one.
2. There are no standardized procedures developed so far. So, firms are providing only as additional information.
3. Under conventional accounting, certain standards are accepted commonly, which is not possible under this method.
4. All the methods of accounting for human assets are based on certain assumptions, which can go wrong at any time. For example, it is assumed that all workers continue to work with the same organization till retirement, which is far from possible.
5. It is believed that human resources do not suffer depreciation, and in fact they always appreciate, which can also prove otherwise in certain firms.
6. The lifespan of human resources cannot be estimated. So, the valuation seems to be unrealistic.

INFLATION ACCOUNTING

Inflation Accounting is a technique of accounting which helps to understand the financial position of a company or country when the country is experiencing a high inflation. High inflation causes a wrong projection and hence this technique is used.

Using this technique, a company's financial position can be evaluated even during a period of hyperinflation. The true profits should be shown in P&L along with the correct assets and liabilities in the balance sheet. Since inflation affects the costs of business, the overall picture is different and hence this technique has to be adopted.

Methods

1. **Current Purchasing Power (CPP) Method.** The financial statements are converted into figures at current purchasing price. However the values of only the non-monetary items are converted.
   Conversion Factor = Price index at the time of conversion / Price index at the date of transaction
2. Each and every item under the financial statements is restated at its current value.
3. **Hybrid Method.** Mix of both CPP method and CCA method.

Advantage

By converting figures of financial statements at current prices the statements become more relevant to the current economic and financial conditions.

Disadvantage

The price level is general price level and not for the individual items. Also the depreciation charged might not be adequate for replacing all types of assets.

ENVIRONMENTAL ACCOUNTING

Environmental accounting is an attempt to broaden the scope of the accounting frameworks used to assess economic performance, to take stock of elements that are not recorded in public or private accounting books. These gaps occur because the various costs of using nature are not captured, being considered, in many cases, as externalities that can be forwarded to others or postponed. Positive externalities—the natural resource—are depleted with no recording in National Accounts (while companies do record them as depreciation elements). Depletion of renewable resource results in degradation of the environment, which adds to negative externalities resulting from pollution and fragmentation of cyclic and living systems. Degradation, or its financial counterpart in depreciation, is not recorded at all. Therefore, the indicators of production, income, consumption, saving, investment, and debts on which many economic decisions are taken are flawed, or at least incomplete and sometimes misleading, when immediate benefits are in fact losses in the long run, when we consume the reproductive functions of our capital. Although national accounting has been an important driving force in change, environmental accounting encompasses all accounting frameworks including national accounts, financial accounting standards, and accounts established to assess the costs and benefits of plans and projects.

There are several approaches to economic environmental accounting at the national level. Of these approaches, one purpose is the calculation of *genuine* economic welfare by taking into account losses from environmental damage caused by economic activity and gains from unrecorded services provided by Nature. Here, particular attention is given to the calculation of a "Green GDP" or "Adjusted National Income" and/or "Genuine Savings" as well as natural assets value and depletion. A different view considers the damages caused to renewable natural capital and the resulting maintenance and restoration costs. Besides approaches based on benefits and costs, more descriptive accounts in physical units are produced with the purpose of assessing resource use efficiency. With regard to natural assets, the focus can be on assets directly used by the economy, or more broadly, on ecosystem capacity to deliver services, ecosystem resilience, and its possible degradation. These different approaches are not necessarily contradictory, although controversies can be noted in the literature.

The discussion focuses on issues such as the legitimacy of combining values obtained with shadow prices (needed to value the elements that are not priced by the market) with the transaction values recorded in the national accounts, the relative importance of accounts in monetary vs. physical units, and ultimately, the goals for environmental accounting. These goals include assessing the sustainability of the economy in terms of conservation (or increase) of the net income flow and total economic wealth (the *weak sustainability* paradigm), in relation to the sustainability of the ecosystem, which supports livelihoods and well-being in the broader sense (*strong sustainability*).

In 2012, the UN Statistical Commission adopted an international statistical standard called, the "System of Environmental-Economic Accounting Central Framework" (SEEA CF). The SEEA CF covers only items for which enough experience exists to be proposed for implementation by national statistical offices. A second volume on SEEA-Experimental Ecosystem Accounting (SEEA-EEA) was added in

2013 to supplement the SEEA CF with a research agenda and the development of tests. Experiments of the SEEA-EEA are developing at the initiative of the World Bank (WAVES), UN Environment Programme (VANTAGE, ProEcoServ), or the UN Convention on Biological Diversity (CBD) (SEEA-Ecosystem Natural Capital Accounts-Quick Start Package [ENCA-QSP]).

INDIAN ACCOUNTING STANDARDS

Sub Section (3A) to section 211 of Companies Act, 1956 requires that every Profit/Loss Account and Balance Sheet shall comply with the Accounting Standards. 'Accounting Standards' means the standard of accounting recommended by the ICAI and prescribed by the Central Government in consultation with the National Advisory Committee on Accounting Standards (NACAs) constituted under section 210(1) of Companies Act, 1956.

Indian Accounting Standards Issued by the Institute of Chartered Accountants of India are as below:

Ind AS-101 – First Time Adoption of Indian Accounting Standards

This standard ensures that an entity's first Ind AS financial statements and its interim financial reports for part of the period covered by those financial statements, contain high quality information that is transparent for users and comparable over all periods presented. An entity shall prepare and present an opening Ind AS Balance Sheet at the date of transition to Ind AS. This is the starting point for its accounting in accordance with Ind AS.

Ind AS-102 – Share Based Payments

This standard specifies the financial reporting by an entity when it undertakers a share-based payment transaction. An entity shall recognise the goods or services acquired or received in a share based payment transaction when it obtains the goods or as the services are received. For cash-settled share-based payment transactions, the entity shall measure the goods or services acquired and the liability incurred at the fair value of the liability.

Ind AS-103 – Business Combinations

A business combination is a transaction or other event in which a reporting entity, i.e. the acquires obtains control of one or more businesses, i.e. the acquire.

Ind AS 103 does not apply to the following:

- The formation of a joint arrangement.
- The acquisition of an asset or group of assets that is not a business.

Ind AS-104 – Insurance Contracts

This standard specifies the financial reporting for insurance contracts by an entity that issues, such contracts. It requires limited improvements to accounting by insurers for insurance contracts. An insurance contract is a contract under which one party, i.e., the insurer accepts significant insurance risk from another party by agreeing to compensate the policyholder if a specified uncertain future event adversely affects the policyholder.

Ind AS-105 – Non-current Assets held for Sale and Discontinued Operations

This standard specifies the accounting for assets held for sale and the presentation and disclosure of discontinued operations. It requires assets that meet the criteria to be classified or held for sale, to be measured at the lower of carrying amount and fair value less costs to sell and depreciation on such assets to cease.

Here, a discontinued operation is a component of an entity that either has been disposed of or is classified as held for sale and represents a separate (major) line of business or geographical area of operations.

Ind AS-106 – Exploration for and Evaluation of Mineral Resources

This standard specifies the financial reporting for the exploration for and evaluation of mineral resources. Here, exploration and evaluation expenditure refers to those, which are incurred by an entity in connection with the exploration for and evaluation of mineral resources before the technical feasibility. An entity shall disclose information that identifies and explains the amounts recognised in its financial statements arising from the exploration for and evaluation of mineral resources.

Ind AS-104 – Financial Instruments Disclosures

This standard requires entities to provide disclosures in their financial statements that enable users to evaluate the significance of financial instruments for the financial position and performance of an entity. This standard applies to all entities, including entities that have few financial instruments and those that have many financial instruments.

Ind AS-108 – Operating Segments

This standard requires an entity to report financial and descriptive information about its reportable segments. Reportable segments are operating segments or aggregations of operating segments that meet specified criteria. This standard requires an entity to report a measure of operating segment profit or loss and of segment assets.

Ind AS-109 – Financial Instruments

This standard establishes principles for the financial reporting of financial assets and liabilities that will present relevant and useful information to users of financial statements for their assessment of the amounts, timing and uncertainty of an entity's future cash flow.

Ind AS-110 – Consolidated Financial Statements

The objective of this statement is to present financial statements of a parent and its subsidiary(ies) as a single economic entity. In other words, the holding company and its subsidiary(ies) are treated as one entity for the preparation of these consolidated financial statements.

Consolidated profit/loss account and consolidated balance sheet are prepared for disclosing the total profit/loss of the group and total assets and liabilities of the group. As per this Accounting Standard, the consolidated balance sheet, if prepared, should be prepared in the manner prescribed by this statement. A holding company has to prepare its financial statement consolidated with its all subsidiary companies as per AS-21. Both balance sheet and profit and loss account has to be consolidated for the holding and subsidiary companies.

Ind AS-111 – Joint Arrangements

This standard establishes principles for financial reporting by entities that have an interest in (joint) arrangements. This standard shall be applied by all entities that are a party to a joint arrangement. Joint arrangement is an arrangement of which two or more parties have joint control. It is either a joint operation or a joint venture.

Ind AS-112 – Disclosure of Interests in other Entities

This standard requires an entity to disclose information that enables users of its financial statements to evaluate the nature of and risks associated with, its interests in other entities and the effects of those interests on its financial position and performance.

Ind AS-113 – Fair Value Measurement

This standard applies when another Ind AS requires or permits fair value measurements or disclosures about fair value measurements. Here, fair value refers to the price that would be received to sell an asset or paid to transfer a liability in an orderly transaction between market participants at the measurement date.

Ind AS-114 – Regulatory Deferral Accounts

This standard specifies the financial reporting requirements for regulatory deferral account balances that arise when an entity provides goods or services to customers at a price or rate that is subject to rate regulation.

Ind AS-115 – Revenue from Contracts with Customers

This standard establishes .the principles that an entity shall apply to report useful information to users of financial statements about the nature, amount, timing of revenue etc.

This standard applies to all contracts with customers, except:

- The lease contracts' (within the scope of Ind AS 17).
- Insurance contracts (within the scope of AS 104).

Ind AS-1 – Presentation of Financial Statements

This standard prescribes the basis for preparation of financial statements to ensure comparability both with the entity's financial statements of previous period and with the financial statements of other entities. It requires an entity to present a complete set of financial statements (at least annually) with comparative amounts for the preceding year.

A complete set of financial statements includes:

- A balance sheet as at the end of the period.
- A statement of profit and loss for the period.
- A statement of changes in equity for the period.
- A statement of cash flow for the period.
- Notes and other explanatory information.

Ind AS-2 – Inventories Accounting

The objective of this standard is to formulate the method of computation of cost of inventories/ stock, determine the value of closing stock/ inventory, at which the inventory is to be shown in balance sheet till it is not sold and recognised as revenue. Stock, to be valued at cost or market value, whichever is lower. Quantity of the stock should be verified physically.

Ind AS-7 – Statement of Cash Flow

Cash flow statement is additional information to user of financial statement. This statement exhibits the flow of incoming and outgoing cash. This statement assesses the ability of the enterprise to generate cash and to utilise the cash. This statement is one of the tools for assessing the liquidity and solvency of the enterprise.

Cash flow is divided into three activities which are as follows:

Operating Activity. It includes:

- Current year profit
- Changes in working capital
- Non-cash expenses
- Extraordinary cash inflows or outflows

Financing Activity. It includes:

- Issue of equity or preference shares or debentures
- Loan taken
- Repayment of loan
- Redemption of shares and debentures

Investing Activity. It includes:

- Purchase of fixed assets or investments
- Sales of fixed assets or investment
- Dividend, interest or rental received on fixed assets or investments.

Ind AS-8 – Accounting Policies, Changes in Accounting Estimate and Errors

This standard prescribes the criteria for selecting and changing accounting policies, together with the accounting treatment and disclosure of changes in accounting policies, changes in accounting estimates and corrections of errors. Accounting policies are the specific principles, bases, conventions, rules and practices applied by an entity in preparing and presenting financial statements. This standard is intended to enhance the relevancy and reliability of an entity's financial statements.

Ind AS-10 – Events after the Reporting Period

This standard states that an entity should adjust its financial statements for events after the reporting period. Here 'events after the reporting period' are those events, that occur between the end of the reporting period and the date when the financial statements are approved by the BOD (in case of company) or by the corresponding approving authority (in other case). This standard requires that an entity should not prepare its financial statements on a going concern basis if events after the reporting period indicate that the going concern assumption is not appropriate.

Ind AS-11 – Construction Contracts

Accounting for long-term construction contracts involves question as to, when revenue should be recognised and how to measure the revenue in the books of contractor. As the period of construction contract is long, work of construction starts in l year and is completed in another year or after 4-5 years or so. Therefore, question arises how the profit or loss of construction contract by contractor should be determined. There may be following two ways to determine profit or loss. On year-to-year basis based on percentage of completion or on completion of the contract.

Ind AS-12 – Income Taxes

This Accounting Standard prescribes the accounting treatment for taxes on income. Traditionally, amount of tax payable is determined on the profit/loss computed as per Income Tax Laws. According to this Accounting Standard, tax on income is determined on the principle of accrual concept. According to this concept, tax should be accounted in the period, in which corresponding revenue and expenses are accounted. In simple words, tax shall be accounted on accrual basis, not on liability to pay basis.

Ind AS-16 – Property, Plant and Equipment

The objective of this standard is to prescribe the accounting treatment for property, plant and equipment, so that users of the financial statements can discern information about investment made by an enterprise in its property, plant and equipment and the changes in such investment.

Ind AS-17 – Leases

Lease is an arrangement, by which the lessor gives the right to use an asset for given period of time to the lessee on rent. It involves two parties, a lessor and a lessee and an asset, which is to be leased. The lessor who owns the asset, agrees to allow the lessee to use it for a specified period of time in return of periodic rent payments.

There are two types of lease agreements:

- Operating lease
- Finance lease

Ind AS-18 – Revenue

It explains as to, when the revenue should be recognised in profit and loss account and also states the circumstances, in which revenue recognition can be postponed. Revenue means gross inflow of cash receivable or other consideration arising in the course of ordinary activities of an enterprise such as the sale of goods, rendering of services and use of enterprises resources by other yielding interest, dividend and royalties. In other words, revenue is a charge made to customers/clients for goods supplied and services rendered.

Ind AS-19 – Employee Benefits

This Accounting Standard has been revised by ICAI and is applicable in respect of accounting period commencing on or after 1st April, 2006. The scope of the Accounting Standard has been enlarged, to include accounting for short-term employee benefits and termination benefits.

Ind AS-20 – Accounting for Government Grants and Disclosure of Government Assistance

Government grants are assistance by the government in the form of cash or kind to an enterprise in return for past or future compliance with certain conditions. Government assistance, which cannot be valued reasonably, is excluded from government grants. Those transactions with government, which cannot be distinguished from the normal trading transactions of the enterprise are not considered as government grants.

Government assistance is action by government designed to provide an economic benefit specific to an entity or range of entities qualifying under certain criteria.

Ind AS-21 – The Effects of Changes in Foreign Exchange Rates

Effect of changes in foreign exchange rate shall be applicable in respect of accounting period commencing on or after 1st April, 2004 and is mandatory in nature. This Accounting Standard is applicable to accounting for transactions in foreign currencies in translating in the financial statement of foreign operation, integral as well as non-integral and also accounting for forward exchange.

Effects of changes in Foreign Exchange Rate, an enterprises should disclose following aspects:

- Amount exchange difference included in net profit or loss.
- Amount accumulated in foreign exchange translation reserve.
- Reconciliation of opening and closing balance of Foreign Exchange Translation Reserve.

Ind AS-23 – Borrowing Costs

Enterprises are borrowing the funds to acquire, build and install the fixed assets and other assets, these assets take time to make them usable or saleable, therefore the enterprises incur the interest (cost on borrowing) to acquire and build these assets. The objective of the Accounting Standard is to prescribe the treatment of borrowing cost (interest + other cost) in accounting, whether the interest and other cost, i.e., borrowing cost related to a qualifying assets must be capitalised into the cost of that assets rather than transferring it into the profit and loss account.

Qualifying asset is an asset, which takes a period of 12 months or more to be constructed or manufactured longer or shorter period may be considered as per the conditions.

Ind AS-24 – Related Party Disclosure

Sometimes business transactions between related parties lose the feature and character of the arms length transactions. Related party relationship affects the volume and decision of business of one enterprise for the benefit of the other enterprise. Hence, disclosure of related party transaction is essential for proper understanding of financial performance and financial position of enterprise.

Ind AS-27 – Separate Financial Statements

This standard prescribes the accounting and disclosure requirement for investments in joint ventures, subdiaries etc. When an entity prepares separate financial statements, it shall account for investments in subsidiaries, joint ventures and associates either at cost or, in accordance with Ind AS 109, i.e., financial instruments.

Ind AS-28 – Investments in Associates and Joint Ventures

This standard prescribes the accounting for investments in associates and joint ventures. This standard shall be applied by all entities that are investors with joint control of or significant influence over an investee.

If an entity holds, directly or indirectly, 20% or more of the voting power of the investee, it is presumed that the entity has significant influence. An associate is an entity over which the investor has significant influence.

Joint venture is defined as a contractual arrangement, whereby two or more parties carry on an economic activity under 'joint control'. Control is the power to govern the financial and operating policies of an economic activity so as to obtain benefit from it. Joint control is the contractually agreed sharing of control over economic activity.

Ind AS-29 – Financial Reporting in Hyper-inflationary Economies

This standard is applied to the financial statements, including the consolidated financial statements, if entity whose functional currency is the "currency of a Hyper-inflationary economy. Appendix of Ind AS-29 prescribes that in the reporting period in which an entity identifies the existence of hyperinflation in the economy of its functional currency, not having been Hyper-inflationary in the prior period, the entity shall apply the requirements of this standard, as if the economy had always been Hyper-inflationary.

Ind AS-32 – Financial Instruments: Presentation

The objective of this standard is to establish principles for presenting financial instruments as liabilities or equity and for offsetting financial assets and financial liabilities. It applies to the classification of financial instruments, from the perspective of the issuer, into financial assets, financial liabilities and equity instruments; the classification of related interest, dividends, losses and gains and the circumstances, in which financial assets and financial liabilities should be offset. The principles in this standard complement the principles for recognising and measuring financial assets and financial liabilities in Accounting Standard financial instruments.

Ind AS-34 – Interim Financial Reporting

Interim financial reporting is the reporting for periods of less than a year generally for a period of 3 months. As per clause 41 of listing agreement, the companies are required to publish the financial results on a quarterly basis.

Ind AS-36 – Impairment of Assets

'Impairment of asset' means weakening in value of asset. In other words, when the value of asset decreases, it may be called impairment of an asset. As per this AS, asset is said to be impaired, when carrying amount of asset is more than its recoverable amount.

Ind AS-37 – Provisions, Contingent Liabilities and Contingent Assets

This standard prescribes the accounting for provisions, contingent liabilities, contingent assets, provision for restructuring cost.

Provision. It is a liability, which can be measured only by using a substantial degree of estimation.

Contingent Liability. A liability is present obligation of the enterprise arising from past events, the settlement of which is expected to result in an outflow from the enterprise of resources embodying economic benefits.

Ind AS-38 – Intangible Assets

An intangible asset is an identifiable non-monetary asset without physical substance, held for use in the production or supplying of goods or services for rentals to others or for administrative purpose. A self-generated intangible asset can not be recognised into the balance sheet.

Ind AS-40 – Investment Property

This standard prescribes the accounting treatment for investment property and related disclosure requirements. An investment property is a property (either land or building), which is held by the owner or lessee to earn rentals or for capital appreciation, or both. However, investment property shall be recognised as an asset when it is probable that the future economic benefits that are associated with the investment property will flow to the entity and the cost of the investment property can be measured reliably.

Ind AS-41 – Agriculture

This standard prescribes the accounting treatment and disclosures related to agricultural activity. Here, agriculture activity refers to the management by an entity of the biological transformation and harvest of biological assets for sale or for conversion into agricultural produce or into additional biological assets. A biological asset shall be measured on initial recognition and at the end of each reporting period at its fair value less costs to sell.

EXISTING ACCOUNTING STANDARDS (AS)

Accounting standards are the existing accounting standards which are issued under Companies (accounting standard) Rules, 2006. The list of AS is as follows:

AS No.	Title
AS 1	Disclosure of Accounting Policies
AS 2	Valuation of Inventories
AS 3	Cash Flow Statements
AS 4	Contingencies and Events occurring after the Balance Sheet date
AS 5	Net profit or loss for the period, prior period items and changes in Accounting Policies
AS 7	Construction Contracts
AS 9	Revenue Recognition
AS 10	Property, Plant and Equipment
AS 11	The Effects of Changes in Foreign Exchange Rates
AS 12	Accounting for Government Grants
AS 13	Accounting for Investment
AS 14	Accounting for Amalgamations
AS 15	Employee Benefits
AS 16	Borrowing Costs
AS 17	Segment Reporting
AS18	Related Party Disclosures
AS 19	Leases
AS 20	Earnings per Share
AS 21	Consolidated Financial Statements
AS 22	Accounting for Taxes on Income
AS 23	Accounting for investments in Associates
AS 24	Discontinuing Operations
AS 25	Interim Financial Reporting
AS 26	Intangible Assets
AS 27	Financial Reporting of Interests in Joint Venture
AS 28	Impairment of Assets »
AS 29	Provisions, Contingent Liabilities and Contingent Assets

Now, India have two sets of accounting standards viz. existing accounting standards under Companies (Accounting Standard) Rules, 2006 and IFRS converged Indian Accounting Standards (Ind AS).

INTERNATIONAL FINANCIAL REPORTING STANDARDS (IFRS)

These are issued by International Accounting Standard Board (IASB). IASB replaced International Accounting Standard Committee (IASC) in 2001. IASC was formed in 1973 to develop International, Accounting Standards (IAS) which had global acceptance and made different accounting statements of different countries similar and comparable. These IAS are applicable up to date along with IFRS.

OBJECTIVES OF IFRS

The IFRS foundation is an independent, not for profit private sector organisation working in public interest.

Its principal objectives are:

- To develop a single set of high quality, understandable, enforceable and globally accepted international financial reporting standards, through its standard body, the IASB.
- To promote the use and application of those standards.
- To take account of the financial reporting needs of emerging economies and small and medium-sized entities.
- To bring about convergence of national accounting standards and International Financial Reporting Standards to high quality solutions.

IFRS ISSUED BY THE IASB

IFRS-1 – First-time Adoption of International Financial Reporting Standards

This standard sets out the procedures that an entity must follow when it adopts IFRSs for the first time as the basis for preparing its general purpose financial statements.

Here, first time adoption means making an explicit and unreserved statement, for the first time, that its general purpose financial statements comply with IFRSs.

IFRS-2 – Share Based Payment

This standard requires an entity to recognise share based payment transactions (such as granted shares, share options, or share appreciation rights) in its financial statements, including transactions with employees or other parties to be settled in cash, other assets, or equity instruments of the entity. Specific requirements are included for equity settled and cash settled share based payment transactions, as well as those where the entity or supplier has a choice of cash or equity instruments. IFRS-2 was originally issued in February, 2004 and first applied to annual periods beginning on or after 1st January, 2005.

IFRS-3 – Business Combinations

This standard outlines the accounting when an acquirer obtains control of a business, i.e., an acquisition or merger. Such business combinations are accounted for using the 'acquisition method', which generally requires assets acquired and liabilities assumed to be measured at their fair values at the acquisition date.

A revised version of IFRS-3 was issued in January, 2008 and applies to business combinations occurring in an entity's first annual period beginning on or after 1st July, 2009.

IFRS-4 – Insurance Contracts

This standard applies, with limited exceptions, to all insurance contracts that an entity issues and to reinsurance contracts that it holds. This standard requires disclosure of information that helps users:

- to understand the I amounts in the insurer's financial statements that arise from insurance contracts.
- to evaluate the nature and extent of risks arising from insurance contracts.

IFRS-4 was issued in March, 2004 and applies to annual periods beginning on or after 1st January, 2005.

IFRS-5 – Non-current Assets held for Sale and Discontinued Operations

This standard outlines how to account for non-current assets held for sale (or for distribution to owner). In general terms, assets (or disposal groups) held for sale are not depreciated but are measured at the lower of carrying amount and fair value less costs to sell and are presented separately in the statement of financial position. Specific disclosures are also required for discontinued operations and disposals of non-current assets.

IFRS-5 was issued in March, 2004 and applies to annual periods beginning on or after 1st January, 2005.

IFRS-6 – Exploration for an Evaluation of Mineral Resources

This standard has the effect of allowing entities adopting the standard for the first time to use accounting policies for exploration and evaluation assets that were applied before adopting IFRS. It also modifies impairment testing of I exploration and evaluation assets by introducing different impairment indicators and allowing the carrying amount to be tested at an aggregate level.

IFRS-6 was issued in December, 2004 and applies to annual periods beginning on or after 1st January, 2006.

IFRS-7 – Financial Instruments: Disclosures

This standard requires disclosure of information about the significance of financial instruments to an entity and the nature and extent of risks arising from those financial instruments both in qualitative and quantitative terms. Specific disclosures are required in relation to transferred financial assets and a number of other matters.

IFRS-7 was originally issued in August, 2005 and applies to annual periods beginning on or after 1st January, 2007.

IFRS-8 – Operating Segments

This standard requires particular classes of entities (essentially those with publicly traded securities) to disclose information about their operating segments, products and services, the geographical areas in which they operate and their major customers. Information is based on internal management reports both in the identification of operating segments and measurement of disclosed segment information.

IFRS-8 was issued in November, 2006 and applies to annual periods beginning on or after 1st January, 2009.

IFRS-9 – Financial Instruments

This standard includes requirements for recognition and measurement, impairment, derecognition and general hedge accounting. The IASB completed its project to replace IAS 39 in phases, adding to the standard as it completed each phase. This standard does not replace the requirements for portfolio fair value hedge accounting for interest rate risk.

IFRS-10 – Consolidated Financial Statements

This standard outlines the requirements for the preparation and presentation of consolidated financial statements, requiring entities to consolidate entities, it controls. Control requires exposure or rights to variable returns and the ability to affect those returns through power over an investee.

IFRS-10 was issued in May, 2011 and applies to annual periods beginning on or after 1st January, 2013.

IFRS-11 – Joint Arrangements

This standard outlines the accounting by entities that jointly control an arrangement. Joint control involves the contractually agreed sharing of control and arrangement subject to joint control which are classified as either a joint venture (representing a share of net assets and equity accounted) or a joint operation (representing rights to assets and obligations for liabilities, accounted for accordingly).

IFRS-11 was issued in May, 2011 and applies to annual reporting periods beginning on or after 1st January, 2013.

IFRS-12 – Disclosure of Interest in other Entities

This standard requires a wide range of disclosures about an entity's interests in subsidiaries, joint arrangements, associates and unconsolidated 'structured entities'. Disclosures are presented as a series of objectives, with detailed guidance on satisfying those objectives.

IFRS-12 was issued in May, 2011 and applies to annual periods beginning on or after 1st January, 2013.

IFRS-13 – Fair Value Measurement

This standard requires or permits fair value measurements or disclosures and provides a single IFRS framework for measuring fair value and requires disclosures about fair value measurement. The standard defines fair value on the basis of an 'exit price' notion and uses a 'fair value hierarchy', which results in a market based rather than entity specific measurement.

IFRS-13 was issued in May, 2011 and applies to annual periods beginning on or after 1st January, 2013.

IFRS-14 – Regulatory Deferral Accounts

This standard permits an entity which is a first time adopter of International Financial Reporting Standards (IFRS) to continue to account, with some limited changes 'for regulatory deferral account balances' in accordance with its previous GAAP, both on initial adoption "of IFRS and in subsequent financial statements.

IFRS-14 was originally issued in January, 2014 and applies to an entity's first annual IFRS financial statements for a period beginning on or after 1st January, 2016.

IFRS-15 – Revenue from Contracts with Customers

This standard specifies how and when an IFRS reporter will recognise revenue as well as requiring such entities to provide users of financial statements with more informative, relevant disclosures. This standard provides a single, principles based five step model to be applied to all contracts with customers.

IFRS-15 was issued in May, 2014 and applies to an annual reporting period beginning on or after 1st January, 2018.

IFRS-16 – Leases

This standard specifies how an IFRS reporter will recognise, measure, present and disclose leases. The standard provides a single lessee accounting model, requiring lessees to recognise assets and liabilities for all leases unless the lease term is 12 months or less or the underlying asset has a low value. Lessors continue to classify leases as operating or finance, with IFRS 16's approach to lessor accounting substantially unchanged from its predecessor, IAS 17.

IFRS-16 was issued in January, 2016 and applies to annual reporting periods beginning on or after 1st January, 2019.

IFRS-17 – Insurance Contracts

This standard establishes the principles for the recognition, measurement, presentation and disclosure of insurance contracts within the scope of the standard. The objective of this standard is to ensure that an entity provides relevant information that faithfully represents those contracts. This information gives a basis for users of financial statements to assess the effect that insurance contracts have on the entity's financial position, financial performance and cash flows.

IFRS-17 was issued in May, 2017 and applies to annual reporting periods beginning on or after 1st January, 2020.

AUDITING

INDEPENDENT FINANCIAL AUDIT

For any foreign executive operating in India, it is beneficial to have a basic understanding of audit procedures in the country. We have previously introduced audit in India for non-auditors. In this article, we provide an overview of the different types of audit and audit reporting in India.

Audits are generally classified into two types: (i) Statutory audits; and (ii) Internal audits.

Statutory audits are conducted in order to report the state of a company's finances and accounts to the Indian government. Such audits are performed by qualified auditors who are working as external and independent parties. The audit report of a statutory audit is made in the form prescribed by the government department.

Internal audits are conducted at the bequest of internal management in order to check the health of a company's finances and analyze the operational efficiency of the organization. Internal audits may be performed by an independent party or by the company's own internal staff.

As per India's Companies Act, 2013, the following companies must have an internal auditing system.

1. Every company whose shares are registered on the stock exchange.
2. Companies whose shares are not listed on the stock exchange and have:

   Paid up share capital of Rs 500 million (US$6.7 million) or more during the preceding financial year; Turnover of Rs 2 billion (US$26.9 million) or more during the preceding financial year; Outstanding loans or borrowings from banks or public financial institutions exceeding Rs 1 billion (US$13.4 million) or more at any point in time during the preceding financial year; or Outstanding deposits of Rs 250 million (US$3.3 million) or more at any point in time during the preceding financial year.
3. Every private company with:

   Turnover of Rs 2 billion (US$26.9 million) or more during the preceding financial year; or

   Outstanding loans or borrowings from banks or public financial institutions exceeding Rs 1 billion (US$13.4 million) or more at any point in time during the preceding financial year.

   The statutory auditor of the company must report on the internal auditing system of the company in the audit report.

Statutory Audits in India

In India, statutory audits are conducted for each fiscal year (April 1 to March 31) and not the calendar year. The two most common types of statutory audits in India are: Tax audits and Company audits.

(A) Tax Audits

Tax audits are required under Section 44AB of India's Income Tax Act 1961. This section mandates that every person whose business turnover exceeds Rs 10 million (US$ 134,508) in any previous year, and every person working in a profession with gross receipts exceeding Rs 5 million (US$ 67,254) must have their accounts audited by an independent chartered accountant.

It should be noted that the provision of tax audits are applicable to everyone, be it an individual, a partnership firm, a company or any other entity. The tax audit report is to be obtained by September 30 after the end of the previous fiscal year. Non-compliance with the tax audit provisions may attract a penalty of 0.5 percent of turnover or Rs 100,000 (US$1,345), whichever is lower.

There are no specific rules regarding the appointment or removal of a tax auditor.

(B) Company Audits

The provisions for a company audit are contained in the Companies Act, 2013. Every company, irrespective of its nature of business or turnover, must have its annual accounts audited each financial year. For this purpose, the company and its directors have to first appoint an auditor at the outset.

Thereafter, at each annual general meeting (AGM), an auditor is appointed by the shareholders of the company who will hold the position from one AGM to the conclusion of the next AGM.

The Companies (Amendment) Act, 2017 provides that auditors can be appointed for a term of five consecutive AGMs and their appointment need not be ratified in each of the AGMs. Individuals and partnership firms, auditors cannot be appointed for more than one or two terms, respectively. After the completion of the term, the auditor must be changed.

Only an independent chartered accountant or a partnership firm of chartered accountants can be appointed as the auditor of a company. The following persons are specifically disqualified from becoming an auditor per the Companies Act:

- A body corporate;
- An officer or employee of the company;
- A person who is a partner with an employee of the company or employee of an employee of the company;

Audits are conducted to express a true and fair view of a company's financial statements. Therefore, the auditor's opinion expressed in the ultimate report is based on the information reviewed and analyzed during the verification of financial statements. Upon completing the report, the auditor may express one of the following four opinions:

- Unqualified opinion;
- Qualified opinion;
- Disclaimer of opinion; and
- Adverse opinion.

1. Unqualified Opinion

When an independent auditor concludes that the financial records and statements of a company are present fairly and appropriately, in accordance with the financial reporting framework, the judgment is called an unqualified opinion.

An unqualified opinion generally indicates the following points:

- Generally accepted accounting principles (GAAP) are consistently applied in the preparation of financial statements;

- Financial statements comply with the relevant statutory requirements and regulations;
- There is adequate disclosure of all material matters relevant to the proper presentation of financial information (subject to statutory requirements); and
- If there are any changes in the accounting principles or in the application method, then it has been properly checked and determined in the financial statement of the company.

2. Qualified Opinion

An auditor expresses a qualified opinion when according to him or her, the financial statements of the company – as a whole – are not free from material misstatements, and the misstatements are material but not pervasive in nature.

The effect of misstatement is material when information with such misstatement can affect the decisions of the users of the financial statements.

The effect of misstatement is pervasive when such misstatement is not confined to one element, account or item of financial statement and reflects the widespread effect of misstatement.

Pervasive effects on the financial statements are those that, in the auditor's judgment:

- Are not confined to specific elements, accounts or items of the financial statements;
- If so confined, represent or could represent a substantial proportion of the financial statements; or
- In relation to disclosures, are fundamental to users' understanding of the financial statements.

3. Disclaimer of Opinion

A disclaimer of opinion is expressed when the possible effect of a limitation on scope is material and pervasive to the extent that the auditor is unable to obtain sufficient appropriate audit evidence.

As a result, the auditor is unable to express an opinion on the financial statements.

4. Adverse Opinion

An adverse opinion is issued when there are limitations on the scope of the auditor's work.

It is also issued when there is disagreement with management regarding the acceptability of the accounting policies selected, the method of their application, or the adequacy of the financial statement disclosure.

When an auditor expresses an adverse opinion, a clear description of all the substantive reasons is included in the audit report.

VOUCHING

The term vouching is the core thing of auditing which refers to the inspecting of documentary evidence by an auditor to support and substantiate a transaction. The main objective of this practice is to establish the authenticity and accuracy of the transactions that are written in the primary books of account. Vouching involves verification of a transaction which is recorded in the books of account by checking it with the appropriate authority and documentary evidence based on which they have made the entry. It also involves confirming and checking whether the amount that has been stated in the voucher is posted to a right account that would reveal the transaction's nature when it is included in final statements of accounts. Valuation is not included in vouching.

Vouching may be considered as the essence or the most important thing of auditing, because an audit's success is dependent on the accurateness with which vouching is performed. Auditing can begin only when all vouchers are entered. Vouching is verification and confirmation of entries that are recorded in the books of account by checking of vouchers or documentary evidence like debit and credit notes, invoices, receipts, statements, etc. The main objective of vouching is to find that the transactions that are recorded in the books of accounts are properly recorded and they are in proper order and are correctly authorized. Vouching is different from simple routine checking as vouching is much more accurate than the latter.

In case of routine checking, the entries that are recorded in the books of account reflect only the information that the book keeper wishes to reveal, the entries can even be untrue without any vouchers or vouching. When a company uses vouching, it has proper documentation and evidence of capital, expenses and written evidence in audits. For auditing, vouching is very important as an auditor needs proper evidence of all transactions while doing audit. If vouching is not done then the claims of the auditor will not be considered to be accurate and fair. By using vouching, frauds that are difficult to detect can be discovered. Therefore, vouching must be performed with great care and importance; otherwise the auditor can face charges of negligence.

VERIFICATION AND VALUATION OF ASSETS AND LIABILITIES

The processes of routine checking and vouching would only substantiate transactions as they occur from day to day and confirm the acquisition of assets or assumption of liabilities at the first instance but the value thereof may change by the end of a financial period when the balance sheet is prepared.

Evidently, in the last analysis, variation in the inter-relation assets and liabilities is the most important factor determining profit or loss through its influence on the difference between capitals at the commencement and at the close of a particular financial period.

Such variation may be the result of genuine factors operating in course of normal business activities or it may be intentionally engineered by manipulation or falsification of accounts. Besides, any inappropriate valuation of assets and liabilities, whether inadvertently or fraudulently done, would vitiate the financial state of affairs of a business by exhibiting a wrong picture in the balance sheet.

Basis of Valuation of Assets

In view of the importance of valuation an auditor should always be careful to see whether assets are valued on some reasonable and appropriate basis.

The standard methods of valuation that are usually followed in respect of different classes of assets are enumerated below:

Nature and Purpose of Acquisition

1. **Fixed.** Stable in nature. Acquired for permanent or long-term retention and use in the business for earning income.
2. **Intangible.** Semi-Stable in nature. Acquired as a non-monetary identifiable asset, for use in business to augment earnings or as a class of fixed assets with no physical or tangible existence but valuable all the same, e.g., goodwill intellectual property, or license rights.
3. **Fictitious.** Semi-stable or temporary assets without any tangible form, usually expenditure or losses of unusual nature not realisable in cash, e.g., preliminary expenses, loss on issue of securities or special advertisement cost.
4. **Floating.** Subject to constant movement or changes. Acquired for temporary retention and conversion into cash as early as possible.

Basis of Valuation

1. **Fixed.** Going concern value, i.e., historical cost or original cost of acquisition (including adjustments for additions including all expenses of bringing an asset into a reasonable condition or disposals) minus proper depreciation on a consistent basis irrespective of the market value.
2. **Intangible.** Usually on the same basis as fixed assets, i.e., written down value according to the policy on amortisation or fair value of benefits enjoyable on future. As per new norms from ICA, intangible assets will have to be written-off in a maximum of 10 years.
3. **Fictitious.** Cost/expenditure incurred or balance thereof less amount written-off from year to year depending on financial policy.
4. **Floating.** Realisable value, i.e., market value (net realisable value) or cost price whichever is lower.

REVALUATION OF ASSETS

There may be periodical revaluation of assets (i.e., revision of book values) by a systematic assessment so as to show a more realistic value of assets based on the physical condition and estimated future working life of assets, trend of market prices, etc. It may be noted that reserve created on revaluation, if any, would not be available for distribution.

Revaluation may be done on basis of:

(a) A number of factors like technical up gradation, replacement cost, productivity and efficiency of the assets; or

(b) Historical cost, which does not reflect a true and fair view of the affairs, suitably revised to indicate realistic value.

Revaluation is made on the basis of: (a) replacement cost (net realisable value having regard to market trends) as reduced by accumulated depreciation; or (b) indexation method based on industrial indices; or (c) appraisal method i.e. valuation by expert valuers or appraisers like architects, engineers, certified valuers.

Accounting Standard AS 10 issued by the Institute of Chartered Accountants of India provides that the revalued amount of a fixed asset should be shown in the financial statement by restating both the gross book value and the accumulated depreciation to give the net revised book value, or by restating the net book value by adding the net increase thereof.

The selective revaluation processes as above are not available under instructions for making out assets contained in Schedule VI to the Companies Act, 1956, which require that in case of any writing up of the asset(s) it must be shown at its increased figure in the Balance Sheet subsequent to such writing up.

Auditor's Duty towards Valuation of Assets

An auditor should inquire into the basis of valuation of all assets and liabilities used or adopted by client with the greatest care before finally passing any item.

He should be thoroughly satisfied that they have been properly valued or revalued on scientific principles so as to represent their true and fair worth to the business at the date of the balance sheet. It is, however, no part of an auditor's normal duty to value assets or liabilities himself.

That work is usually done either by a responsible officer of the business or by some independent and expert valuer and, in such circumstances, an auditor's responsibility is confined to the acceptance of certificates of value from the management or the valuer, as the case may be, subject, of course, to suitable personal inquiries made by himself to establish that the values appear to be reasonable having regard to the nature of the business and of the assets or liabilities concerned.

In any case, an auditor is not responsible for valuation of assets and liabilities provided he exercises reasonable skill and care in scrutinising the basis of valuation (London & General Bank case; Kingston Cotton Mills case; Westminster Road Construction Co. case.

VERIFICATION OF ASSETS AND LIABILITIES OF A BUSINESS

Verification of assets means substantiation of the actual existence of assets under the legal ownership and/or possession of the clients on the date of balance sheet. This is as important as valuation of assets, if not more; because the balance sheet should include only such items as are genuinely owned by the clients and an auditor should never pass an asset unless he is fully satisfied about the bona fide ownership of the same by his clients.

VERIFICATION OF LIABILITIES

Generally liabilities are valued at face value. Verification of liabilities is as important as that of assets because any understatement or omission thereof would vitally affect the result of business and also the financial state of affairs. Usually liabilities are small in number and more or less fixed in nature and, as such, they offer less difficulties to an auditor than assets.

An auditor should see that all liabilities or obligations genuinely outstanding on the closing date even those omitted accidentally or deliberately are duly accounted for, that all credit balances shown by books are real liabilities and that there is no manipulation in regard thereto.

An auditor must be satisfied that liabilities recorded in books are real, omission, if any, of liabilities are accounted for and duly disclosed. In fact, an auditor would be liable for negligence if he fails to detect omission of liabilities Westminster Road Construction Co. case. Auditor's report should be qualified for any omission of liability.

Important points regarding verification of liabilities are enumerated below. It may, however, be noted that a major portion of such verification would have already been done at the time of routine checking and vouching of the books of account. As an additional safeguard the auditor may obtain a certificate from some responsible officer stating that all liabilities have been fully taken into account.

CONTINGENT LIABILITIES

A contingent liability is an incidence which is conditional or contingent on the happening' of certain events. There is an element of uncertainty about this group of liabilities, which may or may not occur. Such a liability, if it eventually arises, involves payment of money in future.

The following are the main types of contingent liabilities:

(i) Liability in respect of bills discounted or accepted on behalf of other parties, but not matured.
(ii) Liability under guarantee or surety arrangements in favour of others.
(iii) Liability under incomplete contracts for which compensation may or may not have to be paid under forward contracts.
(iv) Liability under pending law suits, claims or taxation appeals.
(v) Liability in respect of unpaid calls on partly paid shares held.
(vi) Liability for accumulated arrear dividends on cumulative preference shares.
(vii) Liability for claims not acknowledged as debts.

(viii) Liability of members of a company limited by guarantee.

(ix) Possible personal liabilities of partners in a firm.

(x) Liability under guarantee(s) for loans taken by others.

(xi) Other uncertain financial liability.

If any liability under the aforesaid heads does not actually accrue on the date of the balance sheet it should be mentioned by way of a separate note on the liabilities side of the balance sheet, compulsorily in case of a company and preferably in other cases also—but the figures should not be extended to the money column.

The maturity of any contingent liability may arise from either acquisition of asset or incurring of loss. If, however, any of these liabilities is expected to cause an actual loss, adequate reserve should be provided for the same.

These items would usually be discovered in course of routine checking and vouching. It is also useful to check contracts, notices, lawyers' bills, minute books, bank letters, correspondence etc. and to hold discussions with clients.

As additional measure an auditor may secure from the client's solicitors, legal advisers or tax consultants particulars of pending suits, claims, appeals etc. and obtain a schedule of contingent liabilities certified by a responsible officer to the effect that all probable liabilities under this head have been taken into account, as it may not be possible for the auditor to gain in the normal course of audit knowledge of all items of contingent liabilities. An auditor should see that proper notes re: contingent liabilities are incorporated in the balance sheet.

The above exercise by an auditor would ensure disclosure of 'true and fair view' of the profit or loss and of the state of affairs of an enterprise by the Profit and Loss Account and the Balance Sheet.

AUDIT OF FINANCIAL STATEMENTS

A financial statement audit is the examination of an entity's financial statements and accompanying disclosures by an independent auditor. The result of this examination is a report by the auditor, attesting to the fairness of presentation of the financial statements and related disclosures. The auditor's report must accompany the financial statements when they are issued to the intended recipients.

The purpose of a financial statement audit is to add credibility to the reported financial position and performance of a business. The Securities and Exchange Commission requires that all entities that are publicly held must file annual reports with it that are audited. Similarly, lenders typically require an audit of the financial statements of any entity to which they lend funds. Suppliers may also require audited financial statements before they will be willing to extend trade credit (though usually only when the amount of requested credit is substantial).

Audits have become increasingly common as the complexity of the two primary accounting frameworks, Generally Accepted Accounting Principles and International Financial Reporting Standards, have increased, and because there have been an ongoing series of disclosures of fraudulent reporting by major companies.

The primary stages of an audit are:

1 **Planning and risk assessment.** Involves gaining an understanding of the business and the business environment in which it operates, and using this information to assess whether there may be risks that could impact the financial statements.

2. **Internal controls testing.** Involves the assessment of the effectiveness of an entity's suite of controls, concentrating on such areas as proper authorization, the safeguarding of assets,

and the segregation of duties. This can involve an array of tests conducted on a sampling of transactions to determine the degree of control effectiveness. A high level of effectiveness allows the auditors to scale back some of their later audit procedures. If the controls are ineffective (i.e., there is a high risk of material misstatement), then the auditors must use other procedures to examine the financial statements. There are a variety of risk assessment questionnaires available that can assist with internal controls testing.

3. **Substantive procedures.** Involves a broad array of procedures, of which a small sampling are:
   - *Analysis*. Conduct a ratio comparison with historical, forecasted, and industry results to spot anomalies.
   - *Cash*. Review bank reconciliations, count on-hand cash, confirm restrictions on bank balances, issue bank confirmations.
   - *Marketable securities*. Confirm securities, review subsequent transactions, verify market value.
   - *Accounts receivable*. Confirm account balances, investigate subsequent collections, test year-end sales and cutoff procedures.
   - *Inventory*. Observe the physical inventory count, obtain confirmation of inventories held at other locations, test shipping and receiving cutoff procedures, examine paid supplier invoices, test the computation of allocated overhead, review current production costs, trace compiled inventory costs to the general ledger.
   - *Fixed assets*. Observe assets, review purchase and disposal authorizations, review lease documents, examine appraisal reports, recalculate depreciation and amortization.
   - *Accounts payable*. Confirm accounts, test year-end cutoff.
   - *Accrued expenses*. Examine subsequent payments, compare balances to prior years, recompute accruals.
   - *Debt*. Confirm with lenders, review lease agreements, review references in board of directors minutes.
   - *Revenue*. Examine documents supporting a selection of sales, review subsequent transactions, recalculate percentage of completion computations, review the history of sales returns and allowances.
   - *Expenses*. Examine documents supporting a selection of expenses, review subsequent transactions, confirm unusual items with suppliers.

An audit is the most expensive of all the types of examination of financial statements. The least expensive is a compilation, followed by a review. Due to its cost, many companies attempt to downgrade to a review or compilation, though this is only an option if it is acceptable to the report recipients. Publicly held entities must have their quarterly financial statements reviewed, in addition to the annual audit.

Audits are more expensive for publicly-held firms, for auditors must adhere to the stricter audit standards of the Public Company Accounting Oversight Board (PCAOB), and so will pass their increased costs through to their clients.

COST AUDIT

Cost Audit is a critical review undertaken to verify the correctness of Cost Accounts and to check that cost accounting principles and planning have been efficiently followed. It is noteworthy that

India is the only country which has introduced statutory cost audit to regulate about 45 vital industries of the country. Cost Audit has been defined by the Chartered Institute of Management Accountants (CIMA) of Landon as "the verification of cost accounts and a check on the adherence to the cost accounting plan."

This definition implies the following:

(i) The objects of cost accounting with reference to which the cost accounting plan must have been drawn up have to be kept in mind to see whether or not the plan itself and the figures collected will lead to the achievement of the goal or objective set. For instance, if the objective is to achieve maximum efficiency, the plan and the analysis of data will be different from the case where the only objective is to fix prices.

(ii) It has to be examined whether the methods laid down for ascertaining costs and other relevant decisions are being implemented. Treatment and determination of abnormal losses of gains or treatment of certain expenses as direct or indirect are cases in point.

(iii) The correctness of the figures has to be vouched.

'Statutory Cost Audit is a system of audit introduced by the Government of India for the review examination and appraisal of the cost accounting record and added information required to be maintained by specified industries' (ICWA of India).

The concept of cost audit has been elaborated by ICWA as 'an audit of efficiency of minute details of expenditure, while the work is in progress and not a post mortem examination. Financial audit is a 'fait accompli', cost audit is mainly a preventive measure, a guide for management policy and decision in addition, to being a barometer of performance'.

Cost Audit can be called efficiency audit. It is evidenced by amendment in section 209 which reads. 'The object of the amendment of the section is to ensure specified company proper records relating to utilisation of material labour are available which would make efficiency audit (cost- audit) possible'.

Management Auditing is the process of "auditing the quality of managers through appraising them as individual managers and appraising the quality of the total system of managing in an enterprise." Thus management audit aims at assessing how managers perform different functions of management, e.g., planning, coordinating, motivating, etc.

ADVANTAGES OF COST AUDIT

The chief advantage of a cost audit will be that management will be sure to get reliable data for its objectives — price fixing, decision-making, control, etc. Existence of such a system of audit will also be of great use for maintaining internal check and control and will be of great help to even financial audit. But it must be understood that the aims of financial and cost audit are different.

The former aims at prevention of frauds and errors and with presentation of Profit and Loss Account and Balance Sheet which exhibit a true and fair view of the state of affairs (of profit earned during the year and of financial position at the end of the year).

It is concerned with totality of expenditure and revenue rather than its functional analysis. Cost Audit will establish the accuracy of cost of each product, job, activity, etc., and is concerned with proper analysis of information and its estimation so that management gets the necessary information promptly. Apart from reliability of data, cost audit should afford certain incidental advantages. Rather, it should be said that cost audit will help consolidate and realize advantages expected from a system of costing. Following statement of the HR Gokhale Ex-minister of Law, Justice and Company Affairs emphasizes the social advantage of cost audit.

'The objective of this measure (cost audit) is to protect consumers from unwarranted increase in prices. Reasonableness of the prices charged can only be ensured by correct determination of costs and the margin charged by producers and their retailers. Another object underlying this step is to make the industries covered by such rules alert and efficient and also to make them know their rational cost with a view to reducing it to the extent possible. Thus by resorting to this method, the interest of consumer is safeguarded and it is definite step towards removal of social injustice'.

The advantages, briefly, are as follows:

(i) A close check will be maintained on all wastages—materials in store, labour, etc.—and they will be promptly located and reported.

(ii) Inefficiencies in production (or efficiencies) will be located and converted into monetary terms.

(iii) Through fixation of individual responsibility, management by exception will be possible.

(iv) The system of budgetary control and standard costing will be greatly facilitated with cost audit at the hands of a qualified cost accountant.

(v) Records will be up-to-date and information for various purposes will be available.

(vi) Cost audit may unearth a number of errors and frauds which may not be revealed otherwise. This is because a cost auditor examines expenditure minutely and compares it with standards and ascertains exact reasons for discrepancy.

Cost audit offers many advantages to management, cost accountant, shareholders, statutory auditor, consumers and the government.

These advantages are summarized below:

Advantages to Management

(i) Errors in following costing principles and techniques are detected. Inconsistencies and frauds can also be detected. This keeps everyone alert and promotes efficiency.

(ii) Cost audit can serve to measure performance of managers and better performance can be rewarded.

(iii) It helps to prepare accurate cost reports and this business planning can be more accurate.

(iv) Inter-firm comparisons can be made with ease and this might be a very useful proposition if industrial intelligence is good.

(v) Cost audit can give an idea about the comparative operational efficiency of each department of division; and may thus pin-point deficiencies and also encourage to operate in a competitive spirit.

Advantages to Management/Cost Accountant

Important advantages are:

(i) His task is facilitated since errors, deficiencies, etc., are pointed out. Costing plans can be prepared to take care of these things.

(ii) Cost audit may help in easier reconciliation of cost and financial accounts.

(iii) If the cost auditor is an outsider and is an expert, he can certainly give some practical and sound advice to streamline costing systems and organisation.

(iv) Cost audit helps to focus attention of management on the problems faced by the cost accountant. This helps him to realize his goals and objectives with ease.

Advantages to Statutory Auditor

Important advantages are:

(i) Audited cost data helps him to determine the value of stocks, remuneration of managerial personnel, etc., with ease and accuracy.

(ii) Data and statements of cost audit help him to prepare his audit programme and plan so that he concentrates more on those aspects which have not been adequately covered by cost audit.

Advantages to Consumers

(i) The direct benefit accrues where a statutory cost audit has been done to fix a reasonable price for the consumers.

(ii) Since cost audit aims at ensuring efficiency in the organisation, this may also get reflected in reduced prices to the consumers.

Advantages to Labour

(i) If cost audit is done thoroughly labour also stands to gain through increased profitability in the shape of bonus and other benefits.

(ii) Also it brings into focus the role of labour in improving efficiency in term of increased productivity.

Advantages to Shareholders

(i) There is correct valuation of all kinds of inventories. This may project a true picture of the organisation before shareholders and other investors and help them to assess its performance.

(ii) External cost audit highlights efficiency or inefficiency, utilisation of manpower and other resources, adequacy of return, etc.

Advantages to Government and Economy

(i) It helps the government to settle accounts where cost-plus contracts have been made.

(ii) The government can intervene to protect the interests of the consumers, labour, shareholders and investors from exploitage or inefficient managements.

(iii) At the national level, cost audit promotes cost consciousness and overall efficiency. This means that every rupee invested produces the maximum quantity of goods and services.

Types of Cost Audit

The main types of Cost audit are the following:

(i) **Cost Audit as an Aid to Management.** The aim is to see that all information placed before management is relevant, reliable and prompt so that management can discharge its duties well. It must also be seen that no relevant or pertinent information is suppressed.

(ii) **Cost Audit on Behalf of a Customer.** Often contracts are placed on "Cost Plus" basis. In other words, the customer will determine the final price to be paid on the basis of exact cost plus an agreed margin of profit. The customer, in such a case, usually gets cost accounts of the product concerned audited to establish correct cost and, therefore, price.

(iii) **Cost Audit on Behalf of Government.** Sometimes the Government is approached with request for financial help or protection. Before taking a decision on the request, the Government may choose to get cost accounts of the applicant audited to establish whether the need for help is genuine or is a result of mere inefficiency.

(iv) **Cost Audit under Statute.** The Amendment Act of 1965 has inserted a new section, 233B, in the Companies Act, 1956 whereby the Central Government may order that certain classes of companies will get their cost accounts audited by a member of the Institute of Cost and Works Accounts of India. Only such companies as are required to maintain proper records regarding materials consumed, labour and other expenses under Section 209 (as amended to date) and may be required to get their cost accounts audited. The powers and duties and manner of appointment of the cost auditor are the same as that of external financial auditor and the same disqualifications will apply. The cost auditor will submit his report to the Company Law Board with a copy to the company. The right to investigate all aspects of cost accounts is presumably granted to the cost auditor.

The aim of cost audit under statute seems to be that the Government wishes to know, as an instrument of control, the costs of various goods. Government has the power to prescribe the forms in which cost audit reports are to be made out. These are designed not only to verify information, but also to convey good deal of information to Government.

(v) **Cost Audit on Behalf of the Trade Association.** Sometimes trade associations seek to maintain prices at a certain level. For this purpose, the accuracy of costing information submitted by various concerns has to be checked. The trade associations may seek to have full information about production capacity and the relative efficiency of productive processes.

RECENT TRENDS IN AUDITING

Robotic process automation (RPA) is the use of software to perform rules-based tasks in a virtual environment by mimicking user actions to obtain the same or enhanced results. Cognitive intelligence (CI)—a step beyond RPA—includes natural language processing and generation, artificial intelligence, and machine learning.

As functions adopt RPA, CI, and similar technologies, internal audit should support them in identifying, assessing, and monitoring the risks that come along with these technologies. Internal audit should consider using RPA to automate repetitive controls testing and internal reporting tasks.

Internal audit plans should address the effects of RPA and CI on processes, management, and the organization. To provide sound assurance, internal audit should become involved early. In audit planning, use key risk themes to assess the risks of digital programs, processes, and products. And review the digital strategy and road map to decide where to focus, given the risk themes.

Digital poses the usual cyber risks, plus new strategic, reputational, and third-party risks—in a fast-paced environment. Internal audit should aim to understand the tools used to automate processes and controls and then assess the integrity of those tools.

In recent years, cybersecurity audits have often focused on regulatory compliance—areas such as data privacy, information technology (IT) security, and business continuity. Companies should continue to focus on assurance while understanding that compliance with existing regulations hardly guarantees high, or even adequate, cyber risk management.

Internal auditors accustomed to providing compliance-related assurance need new mind-sets and methods—start by thinking broadly. Then challenge management on risk identification, monitoring, and management in those areas.

Beyond-the-basics analytics is the single most powerful booster of internal audit efficiency and effectiveness available. Yet internal audit's adoption of analyticshas been relatively uneven and slow.

Analytics should be integral to all of internal audit's planning, execution, and reporting, and it should be reflected in methods and skills accordingly. Set your sights on "Digital IA," an integrated set of analytical capabilities geared to using and auditing advanced technologies.

Business leaders want—and need—a more holistic picture of third-party risks and their management. This calls for internal audit to understand the organization's entire approach to third-party relationships.

When planning your internal audits, start with an assessment of third-party contracts on the basis of spend and risk. For vendor spend assurance, promote adoption of automated tools for analyzing spend and vendor performance. An overall extended enterprise risk management framework can help uncover key areas of risk, specifically those that are embedded within the third-party ecosystem.

An organization's culture plays a major role in business performance and marketplace reputation. As the third line of defense, internal audit plays a vital role in culture risk management.

Internal audit should engage in broader organizational-level culture risk management efforts—providing assurance and advice on culture as appropriate and validating risk management activities. A culture risk assessment can provide insight into intangible drivers of risk, controls effectiveness, compliance failures, and potential misconduct. It can also direct audit fieldwork and analysis to where it matters most.

A crisis management plan provides a framework and contingency plans for senior executives should the need arise. Responsibility for crisis management sits with senior leaders, which means that internal audit is the logical—and perhaps only—source of assurance and advice.

An organization needs a crisis management program encompassing governance, process, and risks. Go beyond regulatory guidance and checklists. Audit not just the existence of plans, but their likely effectiveness. Also consider industry-specific issues and evolving regulations.

Principles and practices of agile development are being applied to audits and projects by forward-thinking internal audit groups. Agile methods foster rapid response to emerging issues, closer collaboration with stakeholders, faster delivery cycles, and streamlined reporting. Agile has the power to revolutionize internal audit by making audits and reviews more relevant, risk based, and real time.

Good candidates for Agile Internal Auditing are areas with a need for more responsive and relevant reporting, high-stakes projects like IT installations or merger integrations, and where internal audit groups need to do more with less. Learn about Agile Internal Audit.

Management Audit

Management Audit is the systematic and dispassionate examination, analysis and appraisal of management's overall performance. It is a form of appraisal of the total performance of the management by means of an objective and comprehensive examination of the organization structure, its components such as department, its plans and policies, methods of process or operation and controls, and its use of physical facilities and human resources.

Management Audit is an important tool for the continuous appraisal and evaluation of the methods and performance of an enterprise. The prime objective of Management Audit is to locate defects of irregularities in the areas covered by the audit and to suggest possible improvements. It assists the management in managing the operations of an undertaking in the most efficient manner practicable.

Economic outlook, the adequacy of the organization structure, compliance with policies and procedures, reliability of the system of control, adequate protective methods, causes of variances, effective utilization of manpower and equipment, efficiency of the method of operation etc., all come under the purview of management audit.

Thus Management Audit is concerned with evaluation and appraisal of the control system and information in the entire or in various segments of the organizations. Its scope has been widened to appraise in detail the systems and subsystems, procedures, job separation, authorization, accountability, quality of personnel, quality of information generation etc.

Objective of Management Audit

The main objectives of Management Audit are:

(a) To ensure optimum utilization of human resources and available physical facilities.
(b) To point out deficiencies in objectives, policies, procedures and planning.
(c) To suggest improved methods of operations.
(d) To point out weak links in organizational structure and in internal control system and suggesting improvements.
(e) To help management by providing early signals of sickness, ways and means to avoid the same; and
(f) To anticipate problems and suggest remedies to solve them in time.

Scope of Management Audit

The scope of Management Audit has no limitations. The areas of review depend on the objectives of the business.

Accordingly, the scope of Management Audit may include:

(a) The suitability, practicability and present compliance or otherwise of the organization with its designated objects and aims.
(b) The current reputation of the organization in relation to the general public and within its own particular industrial or commercial field.
(c) The rate of return on investors' capital – whether poor, adequate or above average.
(d) Relationship of the business with its own shareholders and the investing public in general.
(e) The ratios of operating returns and the rate of return on capital projects.
(f) The relationship between management and staff within the business.
(g) The aims and effectiveness of management at its various levels such as top level, middle level and operational level.
(h) Financial policies and control relating to production, sales and distribution and in other functions of the organization.

Weaknesses Revealed by Management Audit

The weaknesses that a Management Audit might reveal may include:

(a) Weaknesses among the members of the Board of Directors.
(b) A lack of awareness among directors and managers of the objectives of the organization and the extent to which these are being achieved, failure to define clearly the objectives and responsibilities of individual managers.
(c) Inadequate steps taken to provide adequate finance.
(d) Lack of technical competence of managers.
(e) Retaining authority by managers for matters which ought to have been delegated.
(f) Lack of clear and identifiable management style in the organization.
(g) Lack of proper staff/management training.
(h) Failure on the part of managers to measure and assess the performance of their subordinates.
(i) Inadequacy of the management information system.
(j) Lack of enforcement of procedures and too much wastage of time in enforcing such procedures.

Weaknesses revealed by Management Audit should be studied in detail to ascertain the real causes and proper remedial action may be taken by the top management to eliminate such weaknesses.

ENERGY AUDIT

Energy today has become a key factor in deciding the product cost at micro level as well as in dictating the inflation and the debt burden at the macro level. Energy cost is a significant factor in economic activity at par with factors of production like capital, land and labor. The imperatives of an energy shortage situation calls for energy conservation measure, which essentially mean using less energy for the same level of activity. Energy Audit attempts to balance the total energy inputs with its use and serves to identify all the energy streams in the systems and quantifies energy usage's according to its discrete function. Energy Audit helps in energy cost optimization, pollution control, safety aspects and suggests the methods to improve the operating & maintenance practices of the system. It is instrumental in coping with the situation of variation in energy cost availability, reliability of energy supply, decision on appropriate energy mix, decision on using improved energy conservation equipment's, instrumentation's and technology

Objectives of Energy Audit

The Energy Audit provides the vital information base for overall energy conservation program covering essentially energy utilization analysis and evaluation of energy conservation measures. It aims at:

- Identifying the quality and cost of various energy inputs.
- Assessing present pattern of energy consumption in different cost centers of operations.
- Relating energy inputs and production output.
- Identifying potential areas of thermal and electrical energy economy.
- Highlighting wastage's in major areas.
- Fixing of energy saving potential targets for individual cost centers.
- Implementation of measures for energy conservation & realization of savings.

Detailed Energy Audit

The detailed audit goes beyond quantitative estimates of costs and savings. It includes engineering recommendations and well-defined project, giving due priorities. Approximately 95% of all energy is accounted for during the detailed audit. The detailed energy audit is conducted after the preliminary energy audit. Sophisticated instrumentation including flow meter, flue gas analyzer and scanner are use of compute energy efficiency.

Scope of work for detailed Energy Audit

- **Review of Electricity Bills, Contract Demand and Power Factor.** For the last one year, in which possibility will be explored for further reduction of contract demand and improvement of power factor
- **Electrical System Network.** Which would include detailed study of all the Transformer operations of various Ratings / Capacities, their operational pattern, Loading, No Load Losses, Power Factor Measurement on the Main Power Distribution Boards and scope for improvement if any. The study would also cover possible improvements in energy metering systems for better control and monitoring.

- **Study of Motors and Pumps Loading.** Study of motors (above 10 kW) in terms of measurement of voltage (V), Current (I), Power (kW) and power factor and thereby suggesting measures for energy saving like reduction in size of motors or installation of energy saving device in the existing motors. Study of Pumps and their flow, thereby suggesting measures for energy saving like reduction in size of Motors and Pumps or installation of energy saving device in the existing motors / optimization of pumps.
- **Study of Air conditioning plant.** w.r.t measurement of Specific Energy consumption i.e. kW / TR of refrigeration, study of Refrigerant Compressors, Chilling Units, etc. Further, various measures would be suggested to improve its performance.
- **Cooling Tower.** This would include detailed study of the operational performance of the cooling towers through measurements of temperature differential, air/water flow rate, to enable evaluate specific performance parameters like approach, effectiveness etc.
- **Performance Evaluation of Boilers.** This includes detailed study of boiler efficiency, Thermal insulation survey and flue gas analysis.
- **Performance Evaluation of Turbines.** This includes detailed study of Turbine efficiency, Waste heat recovery.
- **Performance Evaluation of Air Compressor.** This includes detailed study of Air compressor system for finding its performance and specific energy consumption
- **Evaluation of Condenser performance.** This includes detailed study of condenser performance and opportunities for waste heat recovery.
- **Performance Evaluation of Burners / Furnace.** This includes detailed study on performance of Furnace / Burner, thermal insulation survey for finding its efficiency
- **Windows / Split Air Conditioners.** Performance shall be evaluated as regards, their input power vis-a-vis TR capacity and performance will be compared to improve to the best in the category
- **Illumination.** Study of the illumination system, LUX level in various areas, area lighting etc. and suggest measures for improvements and energy conservation opportunity wherever feasible.
- **DG Set.** Study the operations of DG sets to evaluate their average cost of Power Generation, Specific Energy Generation and subsequently identify areas wherein energy savings could be achieved after analysing the operational practices etc. of the DG sets.

The entire recommendations would be backed up with techno-economic calculations including the estimated investments required for implementation of the suggested measures and simple payback period. Measurement would be made using appropriate instrumentation support for time lapse and continuous recording of the operational parameters.

ENVIRONMENT AUDIT

Environmental audit is defined as basic management tool which comprises a systematic, documented, periodic and objective evaluation of how well organization, management systems and equipments are performing. A good environment management policy requires that there should be a constant effort to analyze and monitor various industrial working system and processes to generate and transmit this information for the inspecting authority such as exercise which generates necessary information on analysis of pollution being generated or will be generated and completion of annual estimate has been termed as environmental audit. Generally following are the 3 phases when an environmental audit is taken up for an industry:

- Pre-audit activity- pertaining to collection of information.
- Activity at site pertaining to evaluation of information collected.
- Post audit activity pertaining to drawing conclusion and identifying areas of improvement if any.

Objectives

- Environment audit needs for an industry are internal as well as external value
- External needs serve to achieve compliance standards and establish a report with regulatory bodies for implementation of environment management policies.
- Internal need serves the industry as well as self evaluation tool for the process and technology.
- It helps in pollution control, improves production safety and health conservations of nocturnal resources by the way of ensuring waste prevention and reduction, assessing compliance with regulatory requirement, placing environmental information to the public.

Advantages

- EA report provides the necessary information on how well the management systems are performing to keep place with sustainable level of development.
- It provides performance evaluation of industrial working facilities and its possible effect in the surrounding.
- It refers to compliance with local, regional and national laws and regulation
- Potential areas for reduction in raw material consumption leads to cost saving
- Provide an upto date environmental data to the inspecting authority.

SYSTEMS AUDIT

An information systems audit performed by RMAS is a comprehensive examination of a given targeted system. The audit consists of an evaluation of the components which comprise that system, with examination and testing in the following areas:

High-level systems architecture review

Business process mapping (e.g. determining information systems dependency with respect to user business processes)

End user identity management (e.g. authentication mechanisms, password standards, roles limiting or granting systems functionality)

Operating systems configurations (e.g. services hardening)

Application security controls

Database access controls (e.g. database configuration, account access to the database, roles defined in the database)

Anti-virus/Anti-malware controls

Network controls (e.g. running configurations on switches and routers, use of Access control lists, and firewall rules)

Logging and auditing systems and processes

IT privileged access control (e.g. System Administrator or root access).

IT processes in support of the system (e.g. user account reviews, change management).

Backup/Restore procedures

The general mechanics of the audit consist of sampling configuration and log files, with subsequent interviews with key personnel. Additionally, RMAS performs testing with regard to identified key controls, and may require the creation of user accounts such that RMAS auditors may more thoroughly peruse the system and determine the efficacy of implemented controls. Further, a subset of integration testing may be performed against test or staging environments to assure controls that the general user may experience are in place and functioning as described and expected.

While much of the evaluation performed in an information systems audit is heavily focused on the IT general control environment for the given system, interviews with primary the primary users or information owners may be conducted. Inquiry into the user community would be performed to determine general user acceptance of the system and to determine service expectations with regard to the system.

SAFETY AUDIT

A safety audit is a structured process whereby information is collected relating to the efficiency, effectiveness, and reliability of a company's total health and safety management system.

Safety audits serve two broad purposes:

1. They are routinely conducted in order to determine whether the company is in compliance with safety legislation. These can be performed by representatives of a regulatory body or by the company itself.
2. They are used to identify weaknesses in their safety programs and processes. These audits are then used as a guide for designing safety plans or to identify corrective actions that should be undertaken.

A safety audit is a more thorough process than technical inspections or spot-check inspections.

In addition to ensuring compliance, safety audits also review the company's safety documentation and determine whether their record-keeping systems are adequate or need to be more robust. They will also look beyond the current activity in the workplace and evaluate the company's safety training.

A safety audit can involve a walk-through of the facility, interviewing management or employees, and reviewing company documentation.

Safety audits are beneficial because they:

- Promote constant review of systems to ensure that they do not become weakened by habit.
- Facilitate planned improvements to programs, policies, and procedures.
- Help to identify weaknesses in human resources departments.
- Help to demonstrate management's dedication to employee health and safety.

MULTIPLE CHOICE QUESTIONS

1. What is the primary purpose of financial accounting?
   (1) To provide information to internal users
   (2) To facilitate decision-making
   (3) To communicate financial information to external users
   (4) To control and monitor business operations
2. Which accounting principle requires businesses to record transactions at their original cost?
   (1) Going Concern Principle
   (2) Cost Principle
   (3) Matching Principle
   (4) Revenue Recognition Principle
3. What is the basic accounting equation?
   (1) Assets = Liabilities + Equity
   (2) Assets = Revenue – Expenses
   (3) Liabilities = Assets – Equity
   (4) Equity = Assets + Liabilities
4. According to the Consistency Principle, what should remain consistent in financial reporting?
   (1) Accounting methods and principles
   (2) Financial performance
   (3) Management decisions
   (4) External audit procedures
5. Which financial statement reports a company's revenues and expenses over a specific period?
   (1) Balance Sheet
   (2) Income Statement
   (3) Statement of Cash Flows
   (4) Statement of Retained Earnings
6. What does the Matching Principle state?
   (1) Revenue should be recognised when earned, not when cash is received
   (2) Expenses should be recorded when incurred, not necessarily when paid
   (3) All transactions should be recorded at their historical cost
   (4) Financial statements should be prepared consistently each accounting period
7. The concept of materiality in accounting suggests that
   (1) All transactions, regardless of size, should be recorded
   (2) Only significant transactions need to be recorded
   (3) Financial statements should always be audited
   (4) Internal users have priority over external users in financial reporting
8. Which accounting concept assumes that a business will continue to operate indefinitely?
   (1) Business Entity Concept
   (2) Going Concern Concept
   (3) Monetary Unit Concept
   (4) Time Period Concept
9. The principle of conservatism suggests that
   (1) Assets should be recorded at their market value
   (2) Liabilities should be understated to avoid financial risk
   (3) Revenue should be recognised when cash is received
   (4) Anticipate no profit but recognise all losses
10. Which of the following is an example of an intangible asset?
    (1) Buildings
    (2) Inventory
    (3) Patents
    (4) Accounts Receivable
11. The principle of objectivity in accounting emphasizes
    (1) The use of subjective judgment in financial reporting
    (2) The need for personal opinions in decision-making
    (3) The importance of reliable, verifiable evidence in recording transactions
    (4) The emphasis on financial projections over historical data

12. What is the purpose of the statement of cash flows?
    (1) To report the company's financial position at a specific point in time
    (2) To provide information about a company's liquidity and cash flow activities
    (3) To disclose changes in equity during a specific period
    (4) To present a summary of a company's revenue and expenses
13. Under the Accrual Basis of Accounting, when is revenue recognised?
    (1) When cash is received
    (2) When goods are delivered or services are performed
    (3) When expenses are incurred
    (4) At the end of the accounting period
14. What is the purpose of the Accounting Equation?
    (1) To verify the accuracy of accounting records
    (2) To determine the net income of a company
    (3) To calculate the ending balance in a specific account
    (4) To record adjusting entries
15. The concept of the Monetary Unit Assumption implies that
    (1) All transactions should be recorded in monetary terms
    (2) Only significant transactions need to be recorded
    (3) The financial statements should be prepared consistently each accounting period
    (4) All transactions should be reported at their historical cost
16. Which financial statement reports a company's retained earnings over a specific period?
    (1) Income Statement
    (2) Balance Sheet
    (3) Statement of Cash Flows
    (4) Statement of Retained Earnings
17. What does the term "Going Concern" imply in accounting?
    (1) The business will operate indefinitely
    (2) The company will only sell goods
    (3) The need for periodic audits
    (4) All transactions should be reported at fair value
18. When is revenue recognised under the Cash Basis of Accounting?
    (1) When goods are delivered or services are performed
    (2) When cash is received
    (3) At the end of the accounting period
    (4) When an invoice is issued
19. What is the purpose of the Balance Sheet?
    (1) To report the company's revenues and expenses
    (2) To provide information about cash flow activities
    (3) To present the financial position of a company at a specific point in time
    (4) To disclose changes in equity during a specific period
20. In double-entry accounting, every transaction affects at least
    (1) One account
    (2) Two accounts
    (3) Three accounts
    (4) Four accounts
21. What is the purpose of a Trial Balance?
    (1) To verify the accuracy of accounting records
    (2) To determine the net income of a company
    (3) To calculate the ending balance in a specific account
    (4) To record adjusting entries
22. The principle of consistency in accounting suggests that
    (1) Financial statements should always be audited
    (2) Management decisions should be consistent
    (3) All transactions should be recorded at historical cost
    (4) The company should follow the same accounting methods and principles consistently
23. What is the purpose of the Statement of Retained Earnings?
    (1) To report the company's revenues and expenses
    (2) To provide information about cash flow activities
    (3) To disclose changes in equity during a specific period

(4) To summarise a company's net income and expenses

24. According to the Conservatism Principle, how should uncertainties and risks be treated?
(1) Overstate assets and liabilities
(2) Understate assets and liabilities
(3) Recognise potential gains but not potential losses
(4) Recognise potential losses but not potential gains

25. What is the purpose of adjusting entries in accounting?
(1) To verify the accuracy of accounting records
(2) To record transactions at their historical cost
(3) To update accounts to reflect the accrual basis of accounting
(4) To calculate the ending balance in a specific account

26. According to the Business Entity Concept, what distinguishes the finances of a business from those of its owners?
(1) Assets
(2) Liabilities
(3) Equity
(4) The owner's personal transactions

27. What does the term "Materiality" refer to in accounting?
(1) The size and significance of a financial transaction
(2) The accuracy of financial statements
(3) The need for external audits
(4) The consistency in accounting methods

28. When are expenses recognised under the Accrual Basis of Accounting?
(1) When cash is paid
(2) When goods are delivered or services are performed
(3) At the end of the accounting period
(4) When an invoice is issued

29. What does the Time Period Concept in accounting emphasize?
(1) The need for accurate financial records
(2) The relevance of financial information over a specific period
(3) The importance of materiality in financial reporting
(4) The need for consistency in accounting methods

30. Under the Matching Principle, when should expenses be recognised?
(1) When cash is paid
(2) When goods are delivered or services are performed
(3) At the end of the fiscal year
(4) When an invoice is issued

31. What is the purpose of the Statement of Cash Flows?
(1) To report the company's financial position at a specific point in time
(2) To provide information about cash flow activities
(3) To disclose changes in equity during a specific period
(4) To present a summary of a company's revenue and expenses

32. According to the Business Entity Concept, why should the personal transactions of the owner be kept separate from the business transactions?
(1) To maintain consistency in accounting methods
(2) To adhere to the principle of materiality
(3) To provide a clear picture of the financial position of the business
(4) To facilitate external audits

33. When is revenue recognised under the Cash Basis of Accounting?
(1) When goods are delivered or services are performed
(2) When cash is received
(3) At the end of the accounting period
(4) When an invoice is issued

34. What is the purpose of the Adjusted Trial Balance?
(1) To verify the accuracy of accounting records
(2) To determine the net income of a company
(3) To calculate the ending balance in a specific account
(4) To prepare financial statements

35. According to the principle of Conservatism, how should the valuation of assets be approached?
(1) At their historical cost

(2) At their market value
(3) At their book value
(4) At their fair value

36. In a partnership firm, who is a 'partner by estoppel'?
(1) Incoming Partner
(2) Outgoing Partner
(3) Partner whose authority is not known to outsiders
(4) Partner whose authority is known to outsiders

37. What is the share of profits or losses usually based on in a partnership?
(1) Capital contribution
(2) Time devoted to the business
(3) Sales generated
(4) Fixed ratio agreed upon by partners

38. In a partnership, what does 'goodwill' represent?
(1) Total assets of the firm
(2) Partners' personal assets
(3) Reputation and customer relations of the business
(4) Liabilities of the firm

39. What happens to the share of a deceased partner in the partnership?
(1) Transferred to the remaining partners
(2) Returned to the deceased partner's family
(3) Distributed among all partners including the deceased partner's legal heirs
(4) Transferred to the government

40. When a partner retires, what is the treatment of goodwill in the accounts?
(1) It is written off
(2) It is distributed among the remaining partners
(3) It is transferred to the retiring partner
(4) It is retained in the books

41. In case of insolvency of a partner, who has the first claim on the partner's estate?
(1) The firm's creditors
(2) The partner's personal creditors
(3) The remaining partners
(4) The government

42. What is the minimum number of partners required to form a partnership firm in many jurisdictions?
(1) 1 (2) 2
(3) 3 (4) 4

43. What is a 'partner's loan' in a partnership firm?
(1) Money invested by a partner in the business
(2) Money borrowed by a partner from the firm
(3) Money borrowed by the firm from a partner
(4) Money owed by the firm to a partner

44. When a partner is unable to pay off their debts, what is the legal status called?
(1) Retirement (2) Insolvency
(3) Dissolution (4) Admission

45. What is the purpose of a partner's capital account in a partnership firm?
(1) To record the partner's share of profits
(2) To track the partner's personal investments and withdrawals
(3) To calculate interest on loans provided by the partner
(4) To account for the partner's salary

46. In the event of a partner's retirement, what term is used for the amount paid to the retiring partner over and above their capital balance?
(1) Bonus (2) Interest
(3) Salary (4) Commission

47. What does 'joint and several liability' mean in the context of partnership?
(1) Each partner is liable for their own actions only
(2) Partners are liable for the firm's debts collectively
(3) Partners are liable for their individual shares of debts
(4) One partner is solely responsible for all the debts

48. In a partnership, what is the role of a sleeping partner?
(1) Active involvement in daily operations
(2) Limited liability without active involvement
(3) Managing the financial accounts
(4) Making all major decisions

49. What happens to the assets of a partnership firm in the event of its dissolution?
(1) Distributed among partners
(2) Sold and the proceeds used to pay off debts

(3) Transferred to the government
(4) Given to the remaining partner

50. What is the purpose of a revaluation account in a partnership firm?
(1) To record changes in the value of assets and liabilities
(2) To calculate the interest on partner's loans
(3) To distribute profits among partners
(4) To close the books at the end of the financial year

51. How is the salary of a working partner usually treated in the partnership accounts?
(1) Deducted from the partner's capital account
(2) Treated as a liability
(3) Shown as an expense
(4) Added to the partner's capital account

52. In a partnership, what is the purpose of the statement of affairs?
(1) To declare the firm's profits
(2) To disclose the firm's financial position in case of insolvency
(3) To calculate partner's drawings
(4) To announce the retirement of a partner

53. What is the primary reason for preparing a revaluation account during the admission of a new partner?
(1) To distribute profits among partners
(2) To adjust the value of assets and liabilities
(3) To calculate interest on partner's loans
(4) To determine the partner's salary

54. What is the purpose of a partner's current account in a partnership firm?
(1) To track the partner's personal investments
(2) To record changes in the value of assets
(3) To account for partner's salary
(4) To track withdrawals and deposits made by the partner

55. In the dissolution of a partnership, what is the order in which the claims are settled?
(1) Liabilities, Capital, Current Accounts
(2) Current Accounts, Capital, Liabilities
(3) Capital, Liabilities, Current Accounts
(4) Capital, Current Accounts, Liabilities

56. How are profits or losses shared in a partnership firm?
(1) Equally among all partners
(2) According to the capital contribution of each partner
(3) Based on the length of time each partner has been in the business
(4) According to the agreed-upon ratio among partners

57. What is the term used for the process of settling the accounts of a partner who wants to leave the partnership?
(1) Admission (2) Retirement
(3) Dissolution (4) Insolvency

58. What is the minimum number of partners required to form a partnership firm in some jurisdictions?
(1) 1 (2) 2
(3) 3 (4) 4

59. What is the term used for the withdrawal of a partner from an ongoing partnership?
(1) Admission (2) Retirement
(3) Dissolution (4) Insolvency

60. In case of insolvency of a partner, who has the first claim on the partner's estate?
(1) The firm's creditors
(2) The partner's personal creditors
(3) The remaining partners
(4) The government

61. What is the share of profits or losses usually based on in a partnership?
(1) Capital contribution
(2) Time devoted to the business
(3) Sales generated
(4) Fixed ratio agreed upon by partners

62. When a partner is unable to pay off their debts, what is the legal status called?
(1) Retirement (2) Insolvency
(3) Dissolution (4) Admission

63. What happens to the assets of a partnership firm in the event of its dissolution?
(1) Distributed among partners
(2) Sold and the proceeds used to pay off debts
(3) Transferred to the government
(4) Given to the remaining partner

64. When a partner retires, what is the treatment of goodwill in the accounts?
(1) It is written off
(2) It is distributed among the remaining partners

(3) It is transferred to the retiring partner
(4) It is retained in the books

65. What is the purpose of a revaluation account in a partnership firm?
(1) To record changes in the value of assets and liabilities
(2) To calculate the interest on partner's loans
(3) To distribute profits among partners
(4) To close the books at the end of the financial year

66. What is a 'partner's loan' in a partnership firm?
(1) Money invested by a partner in the business
(2) Money borrowed by a partner from the firm
(3) Money borrowed by the firm from a partner
(4) Money owed by the firm to a partner

67. What is the purpose of a partner's current account in a partnership firm?
(1) To track the partner's personal investments
(2) To record changes in the value of assets
(3) To account for partner's salary
(4) To track withdrawals and deposits made by the partner

68. In a partnership, what is the role of a sleeping partner?
(1) Active involvement in daily operations
(2) Limited liability without active involvement
(3) Managing the financial accounts
(4) Making all major decisions

69. When a partner is unable to pay off their debts, what is the legal status called?
(1) Retirement (2) Insolvency
(3) Dissolution (4) Admission

70. In a partnership firm, who is a 'partner by estoppel'?
(1) Incoming Partner
(2) Outgoing Partner
(3) Partner whose authority is not known to outsiders
(4) Partner whose authority is known to outsiders

71. What is the term used for the conversion of shares into stock?
(1) Forfeiture (2) Reissue
(3) Conversion (4) Consolidation

72. When a company cancels the unpaid calls on forfeited shares, it is known as
(1) Forfeiture (2) Calls in Advance
(3) Calls in Arrears (4) Reissue

73. In the context of shares, what does "forfeiture" refer to?
(1) Issuing new shares
(2) Canceling shares
(3) Taking back shares
(4) Converting shares to stock

74. What is the process of returning the amount received on application and allotment to unsuccessful applicants?
(1) Refund of shares
(2) Forfeiture of shares
(3) Reissue of shares
(4) Liquidation of shares

75. When a company buys back its own shares from the market, it is known as
(1) Reissue (2) Forfeiture
(3) Buyback (4) Liquidation

76. Which financial statement reflects the financial position of a company at a specific point in time?
(1) Income Statement
(2) Cash Flow Statement
(3) Statement of Changes in Equity
(4) Balance Sheet

77. What is the primary purpose of a company's liquidation?
(1) To merge with another company
(2) To cease operations and distribute assets to stakeholders
(3) To issue new shares
(4) To reissue forfeited shares

78. In the context of mergers and acquisitions, what is the term for the company that is acquiring another company?
(1) Acquirer (2) Target
(3) Merger (4) Amalgamation

79. When two companies combine to form a new entity, it is called
(1) Merger (2) Acquisition
(3) Amalgamation (4) Reconstruction

80. What is the accounting term for the excess of the purchase consideration over the fair value of identifiable net assets acquired?

(1) Goodwill (2) Amortisation
(3) Depreciation (4) Capitalisation

81. Which of the following is a reason for the reconstruction of a company?
(1) Profitable operations
(2) Financial distress
(3) Expansion of business
(4) Shareholder activism

82. What happens to the shareholders of a company that undergoes amalgamation?
(1) They become shareholders of the amalgamating company
(2) They receive cash in exchange for their shares
(3) They become shareholders of the new entity
(4) They lose their shares

83. In the context of shares, what does "reissue" refer to?
(1) Issuing new shares
(2) Selling forfeited shares to new shareholders
(3) Converting shares to stock
(4) Canceling shares

84. What is the term for the process of reducing the nominal value of a company's share capital?
(1) Consolidation
(2) Subdivision
(3) Forfeiture
(4) Conversion

85. Which statement is true regarding the liquidation of a company?
(1) Creditors are paid before shareholders
(2) Shareholders are paid before creditors
(3) Both creditors and shareholders are paid simultaneously
(4) Liquidation only involves the distribution of assets to shareholders

86. What is the primary purpose of the statement of changes in equity?
(1) To show the sources and uses of cash
(2) To explain the changes in shareholders' equity during a period
(3) To report the company's profitability
(4) To disclose the company's assets and liabilities

87. In the context of mergers, what is a horizontal merger?
(1) A merger between a supplier and a customer
(2) A merger between companies at different stages of the supply chain
(3) A merger between competitors in the same industry
(4) A merger between unrelated companies

88. What is the accounting treatment for the reissue of forfeited shares at a price higher than their forfeited value?
(1) Gain on Reissue account
(2) Share Premium account
(3) Loss on Reissue account
(4) Forfeited Shares Suspense account

89. Which document represents a promise to pay a specific amount at a specified future date and is considered a liability for a company?
(1) Common stock
(2) Preferred stock
(3) Debenture
(4) Retained earnings

90. What is the term for the process of combining two or more companies to form a single entity?
(1) Liquidation
(2) Reconstruction
(3) Amalgamation
(4) Acquisition

91. In the context of acquisitions, what is due diligence?
(1) The process of negotiating the terms of the acquisition
(2) The investigation and evaluation of a target company's financial and operational information
(3) The announcement of the acquisition to the public
(4) The legal process of transferring ownership of the target company

92. What is the primary purpose of a company's memorandum of association?
(1) To outline the company's day-to-day operations
(2) To specify the company's capital structure
(3) To detail the roles and responsibilities of employees

(4) To describe the company's products and services

93. Which type of reconstruction involves the creation of a new company to take over the assets and liabilities of the existing company?

(1) Amalgamation
(2) Merger
(3) External Reconstruction
(4) Internal Reconstruction

94. What is the accounting term for the process of allocating the cost of an intangible asset over its useful life?

(1) Amortisation (2) Depreciation
(3) Impairment (4) Accretion

95. What is the purpose of a resolution in the context of corporate actions?

(1) To express the company's financial performance
(2) To declare dividends to shareholders
(3) To formalise decisions made by the company's board or shareholders
(4) To issue new shares

96. When a company issues new shares to existing shareholders in proportion to their existing holdings, it is known as

(1) Rights Issue
(2) Private Placement
(3) Bonus Issue
(4) Preferential Allotment

97. What is the purpose of the Securities and Exchange Board of India (SEBI) in the context of corporate accounting?

(1) To regulate the issuance of financial statements
(2) To regulate the stock market and protect the interests of investors
(3) To set accounting standards for companies
(4) To conduct audits of public companies

98. In the context of share capital, what is the term for the amount per share that is credited to the share capital account?

(1) Face Value (2) Premium
(3) Discount (4) Calls in Arrears

99. What is the accounting term for the process of allocating the cost of a tangible asset over its useful life?

(1) Amortisation (2) Depreciation
(3) Impairment (4) Accretion

100. Which financial statement reports a company's revenues and expenses during a specific period?

(1) Balance Sheet
(2) Income Statement
(3) Cash Flow Statement
(4) Statement of Changes in Equity

Directions: Each of the following items consists of two statements, one labelled as Assertion (A) and other labelled as Reason (R). You are to examine these two statements carefully and decide if the (A) and the (R) are individually true and if so, whether (R) is the correct explanation of (A). Select your answers to these items using the codes given below:

(1) Both (A) and (R) are true, and (R) is the correct explanation of (A).
(2) Both (A) and (R) are true, but Reason is NOT the correct explanation of (A)
(3) (A) is true, but the (R) is false.
(4) Both (A) and (R) are false.

101. Assertion (A): Forfeited shares are considered as the property of the company.
Reason (R): The company has the right to sell forfeited shares to new shareholders.

102. Assertion (A): Goodwill is considered an intangible asset.
Reason (R): Goodwill arises when the purchase consideration is higher than the fair value of the identifiable net assets acquired.

103. Assertion (A): Liquidation involves the orderly winding up of a company's affairs.
Reason (R): Liquidation always results in the distribution of assets to shareholders.

104. Assertion (A): Rights issue allows existing shareholders to purchase additional shares at a discounted price.
Reason (R): Rights issue helps the company raise additional capital without diluting existing shareholders' ownership significantly.

105. Assertion (A): External reconstruction involves the creation of a new legal entity.
Reason (R): Internal reconstruction involves changes within the existing legal framework of the company.

106. What is a holding company?

(1) A company that holds a small percentage of shares in another company
(2) A company that holds a significant percentage of shares in another company

(3) A company that is owned by another company
(4) A company that holds only debt securities

107. In consolidated financial statements, how are the accounts of subsidiaries treated?
(1) Kept separate from the holding company's accounts
(2) Consolidated with the holding company's accounts
(3) Ignored in financial reporting
(4) Disclosed in the footnotes only

108. What is the term for a subsidiary company that is wholly owned by the holding company?
(1) Associate
(2) Joint venture
(3) Minority interest
(4) Wholly-owned subsidiary

109. What is goodwill in the context of holding company accounts?
(1) The positive reputation of the holding company
(2) The excess of the cost of investment over the fair value of net assets acquired
(3) The market value of the subsidiary's assets
(4) The holding company's total assets

110. What is the method used to account for an investment in a subsidiary where the holding company controls the subsidiary?
(1) Equity method
(2) Cost method
(3) Market value method
(4) Liquidation method

111. How does a holding company usually report its investments in subsidiaries in its individual financial statements?
(1) At cost
(2) At fair value
(3) Using the equity method
(4) At market value

112. In consolidated financial statements, what is minority interest?
(1) The interest of the holding company in its subsidiaries
(2) The interest of external parties in the consolidated entity
(3) The interest of the subsidiary in the holding company
(4) The interest of the government in the consolidated entity

113. How is the dividend income from a subsidiary accounted for in the books of the holding company?
(1) As revenue
(2) As a reduction of investment cost
(3) As a liability
(4) As a gain on disposal

114. What is the purpose of preparing consolidated financial statements for a group of companies?
(1) To show the financial position of each company separately
(2) To comply with legal requirements
(3) To present the financial position of the group as a single economic entity
(4) To compare the financial performance of different subsidiaries

115. How is intercompany transactions treated in consolidated financial statements?
(1) Ignored in the consolidation process
(2) Eliminated to avoid double counting
(3) Treated as revenue for the subsidiary
(4) Shown separately in the consolidated financial statements

116. What is the purpose of the non-controlling interest (NCI) section in consolidated financial statements?
(1) To show the interest of the holding company in subsidiaries
(2) To disclose the interest of minority shareholders in subsidiaries
(3) To represent the interest of the government in subsidiaries
(4) To indicate the interest of employees in subsidiaries

117. How is the share capital of a subsidiary accounted for in consolidated financial statements?
(1) Excluded from the consolidated financial statements
(2) Treated as a liability
(3) Combined with the share capital of the holding company
(4) Shown separately under minority interest

118. What is the primary reason for a holding company to acquire subsidiaries?
(1) To increase competition in the industry
(2) To diversify its business operations

(3) To gain control over other companies
(4) To reduce its own risk

119. How is the consolidation of financial statements affected when a holding company owns less than 100% of a subsidiary?
(1) The consolidation is not affected; it remains the same.
(2) Only the assets of the subsidiary are consolidated.
(3) Only the liabilities of the subsidiary are consolidated.
(4) A portion representing minority interest is included in the consolidated financial statements.

120. In consolidated financial statements, how are unrealised profits on intra-group transactions treated?
(1) Ignored
(2) Deferred
(3) Recognised in full
(4) Recognised only if material

121. What is the accounting treatment for goodwill arising from the acquisition of a subsidiary?
(1) Amortised over a fixed number of years
(2) Written off immediately
(3) Impaired if necessary
(4) Subjected to an annual impairment test

122. When preparing consolidated financial statements, how are dividends received from a subsidiary accounted for?
(1) As revenue
(2) As a reduction in investment cost
(3) As a liability
(4) As an expense

123. What is the term for the process of combining the financial statements of a holding company and its subsidiaries?
(1) Aggregation
(2) Amalgamation
(3) Consolidation
(4) Merger

124. In consolidated financial statements, how are intra-group balances treated?
(1) Excluded from the consolidated financial statements
(2) Consolidated and eliminated
(3) Shown as separate line items
(4) Treated as liabilities only

125. What is the term for a situation where a holding company and its subsidiaries use different accounting policies?
(1) Harmonisation
(2) Divergence
(3) Convergence
(4) Uniformity

Directions: Each of the following items consists of two statements, one labelled as Assertion (A) and other labelled as Reason (R). You are to examine these two statements carefully and decide if the (A) and the (R) are individually true and if so, whether (R) is the correct explanation of (A). Select your answers to these items using the codes given below:
(1) Both (A) and (R) are true, and (R) is the correct explanation of (A).
(2) Both (A) and (R) are true, but Reason is NOT the correct explanation of (A)
(3) (A) is true, but the (R) is false.
(4) Both (A) and (R) are false.

126. Assertion (A): Consolidated financial statements are prepared to provide a comprehensive view of the economic entity.
Reason (R): Holding companies and their subsidiaries are considered a single economic entity for financial reporting purposes.

127. Assertion (A): The equity method is commonly used by holding companies to account for their investments in subsidiaries.
Reason (R): The equity method reflects the holding company's influence over the financial and operating policies of the subsidiary.

128. Assertion (A): The non-controlling interest (NCI) in consolidated financial statements represents the share of profits attributable to minority shareholders.
Reason (R): NCI reflects the portion of a subsidiary that is not owned by the holding company.

129. Assertion (A): Goodwill arising from the acquisition of a subsidiary is amortised over a fixed period.
Reason (R): Goodwill is considered an intangible asset with a finite useful life.

130. Assertion (A): Intra-group transactions and balances are eliminated in the consolidation process.
Reason (R): Eliminating intra-group transactions ensures that they are not double-counted in the consolidated financial statements.

131. What is the primary focus of marginal costing?
(1) Fixed costs
(2) Variable costs
(3) Total costs
(4) Semi-variable costs

132. In break-even analysis, the point where total revenue equals total cost is known as
(1) Profit point
(2) Break-even point
(3) Margin of safety
(4) Target point

133. What happens to the profit when sales exceed the break-even point?
(1) There is a loss
(2) Profit is zero
(3) There is a profit
(4) Contribution margin decreases

134. If the contribution margin ratio increases, what will happen to the break-even point?
(1) Increase
(2) Decrease
(3) Remain unchanged
(4) Cannot be determined

135. Which of the following is not considered a variable cost in marginal costing?
(1) Direct materials
(2) Direct labour
(3) Rent on factory building
(4) Variable manufacturing overhead

136. What is the formula for calculating the contribution margin?
(1) Sales – Variable Costs
(2) Fixed Costs – Variable Costs
(3) Sales – Fixed Costs
(4) Variable Costs/Sales

137. What is the purpose of standard costing?
(1) To control costs by setting predetermined standards
(2) To maximise profits
(3) To minimise variable costs
(4) To eliminate fixed costs

138. Variances in standard costing are the differences between
(1) Actual costs and standard costs
(2) Fixed costs and variable costs
(3) Budgeted costs and actual costs
(4) Historical costs and forecasted costs

139. A favorable variance indicates that
(1) Actual costs are higher than standard costs
(2) Actual costs are lower than standard costs
(3) Actual costs equal standard costs
(4) There is no need for cost control

140. What is the primary advantage of using standard costing?
(1) It simplifies the accounting process
(2) It helps in performance evaluation and cost control
(3) It eliminates the need for budgeting
(4) It reduces the need for cost analysis

141. What is the purpose of a master budget?
(1) To provide a historical record of financial transactions
(2) To control and coordinate business activities
(3) To calculate the cost of goods sold
(4) To assess the profitability of a company

142. Which budget focuses on expected cash receipts and cash disbursements?
(1) Sales budget
(2) Cash budget
(3) Production budget
(4) Direct materials budget

143. A flexible budget is useful because it
(1) Is easy to prepare
(2) Adjusts for changes in activity levels
(3) Eliminates the need for cost analysis
(4) Ignores variances

144. What is the primary purpose of a variance analysis in budgetary control?
(1) To identify the causes of variances
(2) To ignore budget deviations
(3) To eliminate all variances
(4) To increase budgeted amounts

145. In process costing, how are costs allocated to products?
(1) Individually for each unit
(2) On a batch basis
(3) Over a specific time period
(4) Equally among all units produced

146. Which industry is most likely to use process costing?
(1) Custom furniture manufacturing
(2) Automobile manufacturing

(3) Custom jewelry production
(4) Boutique clothing production

147. What is the primary focus of activity-based costing (ABC)?
(1) Allocating costs based on direct labour hours
(2) Allocating costs based on machine hours
(3) Allocating costs based on activities that drive costs
(4) Allocating costs based on sales revenue

148. In ABC, what is the purpose of assigning costs to activities?
(1) To increase the total cost of products
(2) To simplify cost allocation
(3) To identify the cost drivers of each activity
(4) To eliminate all costs

149. What is relevant costing?
(1) Considering all costs, both variable and fixed
(2) Ignoring all costs
(3) Considering only costs that will change as a result of a decision
(4) Considering historical costs

150. What is the opportunity cost?
(1) The actual cost incurred
(2) The cost of an alternative foregone when a decision is made
(3) The variable cost
(4) The sunk cost

151. What is life cycle costing?
(1) A cost accounting technique focused on the entire life cycle of a product
(2) A method to reduce costs during the production phase
(3) A method that considers only the initial cost of a product
(4) A method used in process costing

152. What is target costing?
(1) Setting a cost that companies must achieve to earn a desired profit margin
(2) Setting a budget without considering profit margins
(3) Ignoring cost considerations in the decision-making process
(4) Setting prices without considering costs

153. What is Kaizen costing?
(1) A cost accounting method that focuses on continuous improvement
(2) A method to maximise profits
(3) A method to eliminate all costs
(4) A method to reduce costs during economic downturns

154. What does JIT stand for in the context of cost accounting?
(1) Just-in-Time
(2) Job-In-Transit
(3) Joint Inventory Tracking
(4) Joint Investment Technique

Directions: Each of the following items consists of two statements, one labelled as Assertion (A) and other labelled as Reason (R). You are to examine these two statements carefully and decide if the (A) and the (R) are individually true and if so, whether (R) is the correct explanation of (A). Select your answers to these items using the codes given below:
(1) Both (A) and (R) are true, and (R) is the correct explanation of (A).
(2) Both (A) and (R) are true, but Reason is NOT the correct explanation of (A)
(3) (A) is false, but (R) is true.
(4) Both (A) and (R) are false.

155. Assertion (A): Break-even analysis is a static concept and is not useful for decision-making.
Reason (R): Break-even analysis provides insights into the level of activity needed to cover costs and make a profit.

156. Assertion (A): Standard costing is used primarily for historical cost reporting.
Reason (R): Standard costing is a tool for setting cost expectations and controlling performance.

157. Assertion (A): A favorable variance is always a positive outcome for a company.
Reason (R): A favorable variance indicates that actual costs are lower than standard costs.

158. Assertion (A): Process costing is suitable for industries with continuous mass production.
Reason (R): In process costing, products move through production processes with little or no differentiation between units.

159. Assertion (A): Activity-Based Costing (ABC) always leads to higher product costs compared to traditional costing methods.
Reason (R): ABC assigns overhead costs based on the actual consumption of resources by activities.

160. The current ratio is calculated as
(1) Current Assets/Current Liabilities
(2) Total Assets/Total Liabilities
(3) Net Income/Total Assets
(4) Current Assets – Current Liabilities

161. The debt-to-equity ratio is a measure of
(1) Liquidity (2) Solvency
(3) Profitability (4) Efficiency

162. The return on equity (ROE) is calculated as
(1) Net Income/Average Total Assets
(2) Net Income/Average Shareholders' Equity
(3) Operating Income/Total Assets
(4) Gross Profit/Sales

163. The quick ratio excludes which of the following from the current assets?
(1) Inventory
(2) Accounts Receivable
(3) Prepaid Expenses
(4) Cash

164. Earnings per share (EPS) is calculated as
(1) Net Income/Average Total Assets
(2) Net Income/Average Shareholders' Equity
(3) Net Income/Weighted Average Number of Shares
(4) Gross Profit/Sales

165. The inventory turnover ratio is calculated as
(1) Cost of Goods Sold / Average Inventory
(2) Sales / Average Inventory
(3) Net Income / Average Inventory
(4) Average Inventory / Cost of Goods Sold

166. The price-earnings ratio (P/E ratio) is calculated as
(1) Market Price per Share / Earnings per Share
(2) Earnings per Share / Market Price per Share
(3) Total Assets / Earnings per Share
(4) Total Liabilities / Earnings per Share

167. A high receivables turnover ratio indicates
(1) Efficient management of receivables
(2) Inefficient management of receivables
(3) High liquidity
(4) Low profitability

168. Funds flow statement helps in analyzing changes in
(1) Cash flows
(2) Profitability
(3) Financial position
(4) Market share

169. In funds flow analysis, an increase in working capital is represented by a
(1) Positive item
(2) Negative item
(3) Both positive and negative items
(4) Neutral item

170. The source of funds in funds flow statement is
(1) Increase in liabilities
(2) Decrease in assets
(3) Decrease in liabilities
(4) Increase in assets

171. Cash flow from operating activities includes
(1) Cash receipts from the sale of long-term assets
(2) Cash payments for interest
(3) Cash payments for dividends
(4) Cash receipts from the issue of common stock

172. Free cash flow is calculated as
(1) Operating Cash Flow – Investing Cash Flow
(2) Operating Cash Flow + Investing Cash Flow
(3) Operating Cash Flow – Financing Cash Flow
(4) Operating Cash Flow + Financing Cash Flow

173. Cash flow from financing activities includes
(1) Cash payments for interest
(2) Cash receipts from the sale of goods and services
(3) Cash payments to acquire treasury stock
(4) Cash payments for operating expenses

Directions: Each of the following items consists of two statements, one labelled as Assertion (A) and other labelled as Reason (R). You are to examine these two statements carefully and decide if the (A) and the (R) are individually true and if so, whether (R) is the correct explanation of (A). Select your answers to these items using the codes given below:
(1) Both (A) and (R) are true, and (R) is the correct explanation of (A).
(2) Both (A) and (R) are true, but Reason is NOT the correct explanation of (A)
(3) (A) is false, but (R) is true.
(4) (A) is true, but (R) is false

174. Assertion (A): The debt-to-equity ratio provides insights into a company's long-term solvency.

Reason (R): A higher debt-to-equity ratio indicates a lower financial risk for the company.

175. Assertion (A): A high current ratio always indicates efficient management.

Reason (R): An excessively high current ratio may suggest that the company is not utilising its current assets effectively.

176. Assertion (A): Funds flow analysis focuses on the sources and uses of funds during a specific period.

Reason (R): Funds flow analysis helps in assessing the liquidity position of a company.

177. Assertion (A): Cash flow from operating activities is a better indicator of a company's ability to generate cash.

Reason (R): Cash flow from operating activities includes adjustments for non-cash expenses.

178. Assertion (A): Free cash flow is a measure of a company's ability to pay dividends and reduce debt.

Reason (R): Free cash flow is calculated as operating cash flow minus capital expenditures.

179. Human Resources Accounting involves the
(1) Measurement of physical assets
(2) Measurement of human capital value
(3) Valuation of land and buildings
(4) Assessment of technology assets

180. Which of the following is a limitation of Human Resources Accounting?
(1) Difficulty in assigning a monetary value to human skills
(2) Inability to measure physical assets
(3) Lack of relevance in the business environment
(4) Ease of accounting for intangible assets

181. Human Resources Accounting includes the measurement of
(1) Financial assets only
(2) Tangible assets only
(3) Intellectual and human capital
(4) Only physical assets

182. The concept of Human Resources Accounting is based on the assumption that
(1) Human resources have no economic value
(2) Human capital can be accurately measured in monetary terms
(3) Intellectual assets cannot be accounted for
(4) Only tangible assets contribute to the organisation's success

183. What is the primary objective of Human Resources Accounting?
(1) To depreciate human capital
(2) To assign a monetary value to human resources
(3) To ignore the value of human skills
(4) To focus on physical assets only

184. Inflation Accounting is used to adjust financial statements for the impact of
(1) Changing market conditions
(2) Variations in exchange rates
(3) Changes in the general price level
(4) Fluctuations in interest rates

185. What is the primary purpose of restating financial statements under Inflation Accounting?
(1) To increase the reported profits
(2) To maintain the historical cost of assets
(3) To reflect the true economic value of assets and liabilities
(4) To eliminate the impact of foreign exchange fluctuations

186. Which method is commonly used in Inflation Accounting to adjust historical costs to current costs?
(1) Historical cost accounting
(2) Current purchasing power accounting
(3) Cash flow accounting
(4) Accrual accounting

187. In the context of Inflation Accounting, what is the "restatement" of financial statements?
(1) Adjusting for changes in market conditions
(2) Recasting financial statements to reflect changes in the general price level
(3) Ignoring the impact of inflation on financial reporting
(4) Eliminating foreign exchange effects

188. Inflation Accounting is particularly relevant in economies with
(1) Stable prices
(2) Hyperinflation
(3) Deflation
(4) Constant interest rates

189. Environmental Accounting involves the
(1) Measurement of human capital value

(2) Evaluation of ecological impacts on financial statements
(3) Assessment of technology assets
(4) Valuation of land and buildings

190. What is the primary focus of Environmental Accounting?
(1) Assessing the impact of inflation on financial statements
(2) Evaluating the environmental performance of a business
(3) Measuring human resources in monetary terms
(4) Ignoring the ecological footprint of a company

191. The Triple Bottom Line concept includes considerations for
(1) Profits, people, and politics
(2) Profits, people, and planet
(3) Profits, products, and partnerships
(4) Profits, processes, and philanthropy

192. Environmental Accounting aims to integrate
(1) Social and economic aspects
(2) Economic and political aspects
(3) Environmental and social aspects
(4) Financial and marketing aspects

193. The main purpose of incorporating environmental costs in financial statements is to
(1) Minimise reported profits
(2) Reflect the true cost of doing business
(3) Ignore the impact of environmental factors
(4) Eliminate the need for sustainable practices

194. Assertion (A): Human Resources Accounting provides a precise and universally accepted method for valuing human capital.
Reason (R): Valuing human skills in monetary terms is subjective and involves several challenges.

195. Assertion (A): Inflation Accounting is essential for presenting financial statements that reflect the economic reality of a business.
Reason (R): Inflation Accounting adjusts for changes in the purchasing power of money over time.

196. Assertion (A): Environmental Accounting focuses solely on financial aspects related to environmental performance.
Reason (R): Environmental Accounting integrates environmental and social aspects into financial reporting.

197. Assertion (A): Current purchasing power accounting is a method used in Inflation Accounting to adjust financial statements for the impact of inflation.
Reason (R): Under current purchasing power accounting, historical costs are adjusted based on changes in the general price level.

198. Assertion (A): The Triple Bottom Line concept considers three aspects: profits, people, and the planet.
Reason (R): Environmental Accounting is a key component of the Triple Bottom Line approach.

199. Which body in India is responsible for the formulation of Indian Accounting Standards (Ind AS)?
(1) Ministry of Finance
(2) Reserve Bank of India (RBI)
(3) Institute of Chartered Accountants of India (ICAI)
(4) Securities and Exchange Board of India (SEBI)

200. Ind AS 1 prescribes the presentation of
(1) Income Statement
(2) Cash Flow Statement
(3) Statement of Changes in Equity
(4) Balance Sheet

201. Ind AS 16 deals with the accounting for
(1) Leases
(2) Revenue from Contracts with Customers
(3) Property, Plant, and Equipment
(4) Financial Instruments

202. Ind AS 109 is related to the accounting for
(1) Leases
(2) Financial Instruments
(3) Revenue from Contracts with Customers
(4) Inventories

203. Ind AS 38 focuses on the accounting treatment for
(1) Leases
(2) Intangible Assets
(3) Inventories
(4) Financial Instruments

204. As per Ind AS 17, the lessee recognises a lease liability and
(1) An intangible asset
(2) A financial liability
(3) A tangible asset
(4) A contingent liability

205. The International Accounting Standards Board (IASB) is the independent standard-setting body responsible for developing
(1) Indian Accounting Standards (Ind AS)
(2) Generally Accepted Accounting Principles (GAAP)
(3) International Financial Reporting Standards (IFRS)
(4) US Generally Accepted Accounting Principles (US GAAP)

206. IFRS 9 is related to the accounting for
(1) Leases
(2) Financial Instruments
(3) Revenue from Contracts with Customers
(4) Inventories

207. IFRS 15 provides guidance on the recognition of
(1) Leases
(2) Financial Instruments
(3) Revenue from Contracts with Customers
(4) Intangible Assets

208. IFRS 16 is associated with the accounting for
(1) Leases
(2) Financial Instruments
(3) Revenue from Contracts with Customers
(4) Intangible Assets

209. IFRS 5 focuses on the accounting treatment for
(1) Leases
(2) Discontinued Operations
(3) Revenue Recognition
(4) Financial Instruments

210. IFRS 3 addresses the accounting treatment for
(1) Leases
(2) Business Combinations
(3) Financial Instruments
(4) Revenue from Contracts with Customers

Directions: Each of the following items consists of two statements, one labelled as Assertion (A) and other labelled as Reason (R). You are to examine these two statements carefully and decide if the (A) and the (R) are individually true and if so, whether (R) is the correct explanation of (A). Select your answers to these items using the codes given below:
(1) Both (A) and (R) are true, and (R) is the correct explanation of (A).
(2) Both (A) and (R) are true, but Reason is NOT the correct explanation of (A)
(3) (A) is false, but (R) is true.
(4) (A) is true, but (R) is false

211. Assertion (A): The adoption of Ind AS in India aligns the accounting practices with global standards.
Reason (R): Ind AS is converged with International Financial Reporting Standards (IFRS).

212. Assertion (A): IFRS provides a common language for business affairs so that company accounts are understandable and comparable across international boundaries.
Reason (R): IFRS is widely adopted by countries around the world, promoting consistency and comparability.

213. Assertion (A): Ind AS 115, Revenue from Contracts with Customers, provides a comprehensive framework for recognising revenue.
Reason (R): The core principle of Ind AS 115 is to recognise revenue when control of goods or services transfers to the customer.

214. Assertion (A): IFRS 16 brings significant changes to lease accounting by requiring lessees to recognise most leases on their balance sheets.
Reason (R): IFRS 16 eliminates the distinction between finance leases and operating leases for lessees.

215. Assertion (A): Ind AS 109, Financial Instruments, introduces an expected credit loss model for the impairment of financial assets.
Reason (R): The expected credit loss model is more forward-looking compared to the incurred loss model under the previous standard.

216. What is the primary objective of an independent financial audit?
(1) Detecting fraud
(2) Providing assurance on financial statements
(3) Maximising profits
(4) Preparing tax returns

217. Which of the following is a characteristic of an external auditor?
(1) Employed by the company
(2) Independent from the client

(3) Responsible for daily operations
(4) Involved in decision-making

218. The concept of audit independence means
(1) The auditor is financially dependent on the client
(2) The auditor is objective and impartial
(3) The auditor is responsible for the client's internal controls
(4) The auditor has a personal relationship with the client

219. Which of the following is an inherent limitation of an audit?
(1) Detection of all frauds
(2) Possibility of material misstatement due to error or fraud
(3) Unlimited scope of audit procedures
(4) Independence of the auditor

220. What is the purpose of an auditor's report?
(1) To provide financial advice to the client
(2) To express an opinion on the financial statements
(3) To prepare the financial statements
(4) To perform internal control procedures

221. Vouching is the process of
(1) Tracing transactions from financial statements to source documents
(2) Tracing transactions from source documents to financial statements
(3) Verifying bank balances
(4) Confirming accounts receivable

222. The main objective of vouching is to
(1) Detect errors in financial statements
(2) Ensure compliance with tax regulations
(3) Verify the accuracy of source documents
(4) Confirm cash balances

223. Which document is commonly used in vouching for the verification of sales transactions?
(1) Purchase order
(2) Sales invoice
(3) Bank statement
(4) Credit memo

224. In vouching, the auditor is primarily concerned with
(1) Checking the arithmetic accuracy of financial statements
(2) Tracing transactions to supporting documents
(3) Confirming balances with external parties
(4) Reviewing internal controls

225. The objective of vouching is to ensure that
(1) All transactions are recorded in the financial statements
(2) Financial statements are prepared in accordance with tax regulations
(3) There are no internal control weaknesses
(4) Transactions recorded in the financial statements are valid and supported by evidence

226. Verification is concerned with
(1) Checking the accuracy of financial statements
(2) Confirming balances with external parties
(3) Examining the existence and ownership of assets and liabilities
(4) Evaluating internal control procedures

227. Which of the following is an example of verification of assets?
(1) Confirming accounts payable
(2) Inspecting title deeds of property
(3) Examining bank reconciliations
(4) Reviewing depreciation policies

228. What is the primary concern in the valuation of liabilities?
(1) Existence
(2) Completeness
(3) Measurement
(4) Presentation and disclosure

229. The auditor's responsibility in relation to the valuation of assets and liabilities is to
(1) Determine the fair value of all assets and liabilities
(2) Assess the reasonableness of management's estimates
(3) Ignore management's estimates and use historical cost
(4) Perform a detailed examination of all transactions

230. The auditor's verification procedures for investments may include
(1) Confirming the existence of investments with the company's bankers
(2) Reviewing the minutes of board meetings
(3) Tracing transactions to supporting documents
(4) Inspecting property title deeds

231. The audit of financial statements involves
(1) Preparing financial statements
(2) Expressing an opinion on the fairness of financial statements
(3) Confirming accounts receivable
(4) Detecting fraud in the company

232. The concept of materiality in auditing refers to
(1) The size of the financial statements
(2) The significance of an item in the financial statements
(3) The completeness of audit procedures
(4) The existence of internal controls

233. Which of the following statements is true regarding the auditor's responsibility for fraud detection?
(1) Auditors are responsible for detecting all instances of fraud
(2) Auditors are only responsible for detecting fraud if it significantly affects the financial statements
(3) Auditors have no responsibility for fraud detection
(4) Auditors are responsible for preventing fraud in the company

234. The audit report is addressed to
(1) Shareholders of the company
(2) Management of the company
(3) Regulatory authorities
(4) All of the above

235. The phrase "present fairly, in all material respects" in the auditor's report indicates
(1) Absolute assurance on the financial statements
(2) A reasonable assurance on the financial statements
(3) An absolute guarantee of the company's future performance
(4) A guarantee of the company's stock price

236. The primary focus of cost audit is on the examination of
(1) Financial statements
(2) Costing systems and cost accounts
(3) Internal controls
(4) Tax returns

237. The objective of cost audit is to
(1) Ensure compliance with tax regulations
(2) Identify areas for cost reduction
(3) Detect fraud in financial statements
(4) Verify the accuracy of cash transactions

238. Which of the following is a benefit of cost audit for a company?
(1) Higher tax liabilities
(2) Increased production costs
(3) Improved cost control and efficiency
(4) Lower profitability

239. Cost audit is mandatory for certain companies as per the regulations of
(1) International Accounting Standards (IAS)
(2) Generally Accepted Auditing Standards (GAAS)
(3) Cost Audit Rules
(4) International Financial Reporting Standards (IFRS)

240. The cost auditor's responsibility is to express an opinion on the
(1) Fair presentation of financial statements
(2) Adequacy and accuracy of cost accounting records
(3) Existence of internal controls
(4) Market value of company assets

Directions: Each of the following items consists of two statements, one labelled as Assertion (A) and other labelled as Reason (R). You are to examine these two statements carefully and decide if the (A) and the (R) are individually true and if so, whether (R) is the correct explanation of (A). Select your answers to these items using the codes given below:
(1) Both (A) and (R) are true, and (R) is the correct explanation of (A).
(2) Both (A) and (R) are true, but Reason is NOT the correct explanation of (A)
(3) (A) is false, and (R) is true.
(4) (A) is false, and (R) is false

241. **Assertion (A):** The primary responsibility of the auditor is to detect all instances of fraud in the company.
Reason (R): Auditors have a responsibility for the prevention of fraud.

242. **Assertion (A):** The audit report is only addressed to the shareholders of the company.
Reason (R): The audit report is a public document and is accessible to regulatory authorities.

243. **Assertion (A):** Materiality is a concept in auditing that refers to the size of the financial statements.

Reason (R): Materiality is the concept of determining the significance of an item in the financial statements.

244. **Assertion (A):** The auditor's opinion is an absolute guarantee of the future performance of the company.

Reason (R): The auditor's opinion provides reasonable assurance about the fairness of the financial statements.

245. **Assertion (A):** The cost audit is mandatory for all companies, irrespective of their size and nature of business.

Reason (R): Cost audit is required only for companies specified in the Cost Audit Rules.

246. What is the primary focus of a management audit?
(1) Reviewing financial statements
(2) Assessing the effectiveness of management policies and procedures
(3) Verifying the accuracy of source documents
(4) Conducting internal control evaluations

247. In a management audit, the auditor evaluates
(1) Financial reporting accuracy
(2) Employee training programs
(3) Compliance with tax regulations
(4) Supplier relationships

248. Which of the following is a characteristic of a management audit?
(1) Focused solely on financial performance
(2) Emphasises compliance with external regulations
(3) Evaluates the efficiency of organisational processes
(4) Primarily concerned with detecting fraud

249. A management audit is often initiated by
(1) External auditors
(2) Regulatory authorities
(3) Shareholders
(4) Internal management

250. The outcome of a management audit is typically communicated through
(1) An audit report
(2) Financial statements
(3) A tax return
(4) Board meeting minutes

251. What is the primary goal of an energy audit?
(1) Maximising profits
(2) Reducing energy consumption and costs
(3) Ensuring compliance with accounting standards
(4) Evaluating internal controls

252. In an energy audit, the auditor assesses
(1) Financial statements
(2) Energy usage patterns and efficiency
(3) Employee training programs
(4) Compliance with tax regulations

253. Which sector is likely to benefit the most from an energy audit?
(1) Technology
(2) Healthcare
(3) Manufacturing
(4) Legal services

254. The main output of an energy audit is
(1) A financial report
(2) A recommendation for energy-efficient practices
(3) A tax return
(4) An internal control assessment

255. An energy audit contributes to
(1) Increasing carbon emissions
(2) Reducing the company's environmental footprint
(3) Ignoring sustainability practices
(4) Maximising energy consumption

256. What is the primary objective of an environmental audit?
(1) Maximising profits
(2) Assessing employee performance
(3) Evaluating the company's impact on the environment
(4) Verifying compliance with tax regulations

257. In an environmental audit, the auditor examines
(1) Financial statements
(2) Waste disposal practices
(3) Employee training programs
(4) Board meeting minutes

258. Which of the following is a key focus area in an environmental audit?
(1) Employee salaries
(2) Environmental conservation efforts

(3) Tax evasion
(4) Customer satisfaction

259. The primary stakeholders interested in the outcomes of an environmental audit include
(1) Shareholders
(2) Regulatory authorities
(3) Suppliers
(4) All of the above

260. An environmental audit promotes
(1) Increased pollution
(2) Sustainable business practices
(3) Ignoring environmental regulations
(4) Maximising resource consumption

261. What is the primary focus of a systems audit?
(1) Reviewing financial statements
(2) Assessing the effectiveness of internal controls
(3) Verifying compliance with tax regulations
(4) Evaluating information systems and technology infrastructure

262. In a systems audit, the auditor examines
(1) Financial reporting accuracy
(2) Data security measures
(3) Employee training programs
(4) Board meeting minutes

263. The objective of a systems audit is to ensure
(1) Maximum profits
(2) Compliance with external regulations
(3) The efficiency and security of information systems
(4) A higher tax liability

264. Which of the following is a potential risk area addressed in a systems audit?
(1) Quality of customer service
(2) Accuracy of financial statements
(3) Unauthorised access to sensitive data
(4) Supplier relationships

265. A systems audit contributes to
(1) Ignoring technological advancements
(2) Enhancing information systems reliability
(3) Maximising data breaches
(4) Ignoring the need for cybersecurity measures

266. What is the primary goal of a safety audit?
(1) Maximising profits
(2) Reducing workplace accidents and injuries
(3) Evaluating internal controls
(4) Ensuring compliance with accounting standards

267. In a safety audit, the auditor assesses
(1) Financial statements
(2) Compliance with tax regulations
(3) Employee training programs on safety
(4) Supplier relationships

268. The main focus of a safety audit is on
(1) Environmental impact
(2) Employee well-being and workplace safety
(3) Financial performance
(4) Tax liabilities

269. The primary stakeholders interested in the outcomes of a safety audit include
(1) Shareholders
(2) Regulatory authorities
(3) Employees
(4) All of the above

270. A safety audit contributes to
(1) Ignoring workplace safety practices
(2) Minimising the importance of employee well-being
(3) Promoting a safe and healthy work environment
(4) Maximising workplace accidents

Directions: Each of the following items consists of two statements, one labelled as Assertion (A) and other labelled as Reason (R). You are to examine these two statements carefully and decide if the (A) and the (R) are individually true and if so, whether (R) is the correct explanation of (A). Select your answers to these items using the codes given below:
(1) Both (A) and (R) are true, and (R) is the correct explanation of (A).
(2) Both (A) and (R) are true, but Reason is NOT the correct explanation of (A)
(3) (A) is false, but (R) is true.
(4) (A) is false, and (R) is false

271. Assertion (A): The primary focus of an energy audit is on reducing energy consumption and costs.
Reason (R): An energy audit evaluates the efficiency of organisational processes.

272. **Assertion (A):** An environmental audit primarily evaluates the financial performance of a company.

Reason (R): The key focus of an environmental audit is to assess the company's impact on the environment.

273. **Assertion (A):** The main goal of a systems audit is to Maximise profits for the company.

Reason (R): A systems audit evaluates the efficiency and security of information systems.

274. **Assertion (A):** The outcome of a safety audit is primarily communicated through financial statements.

Reason (R): A safety audit focuses on employee well-being and workplace safety.

275. **Assertion (A):** Management audits are typically initiated by external auditors.

Reason (R): Management audits assess the effectiveness of management policies and procedures.

ANSWERS

1. (3)	2. (2)	3. (1)	4. (1)	5. (2)	6. (2)	7. (2)	8. (2)	9. (4)	10. (3)
11. (3)	12. (2)	13. (2)	14. (1)	15. (1)	16. (4)	17. (1)	18. (2)	19. (3)	20. (2)
21. (1)	22. (4)	23. (3)	24. (4)	25. (3)	26. (4)	27. (1)	28. (2)	29. (2)	30. (2)
31. (2)	32. (3)	33. (2)	34. (4)	35. (1)	36. (4)	37. (4)	38. (3)	39. (2)	40. (3)
41. (2)	42. (2)	43. (3)	44. (2)	45. (2)	46. (1)	47. (2)	48. (2)	49. (2)	50. (1)
51. (4)	52. (2)	53. (2)	54. (4)	55. (1)	56. (4)	57. (2)	58. (2)	59. (2)	60. (2)
61. (4)	62. (2)	63. (2)	64. (3)	65. (1)	66. (3)	67. (4)	68. (2)	69. (2)	70. (4)
71. (3)	72. (1)	73. (3)	74. (1)	75. (3)	76. (4)	77. (2)	78. (1)	79. (3)	80. (1)
81. (2)	82. (3)	83. (2)	84. (1)	85. (1)	86. (2)	87. (3)	88. (2)	89. (3)	90. (3)
91. (2)	92. (2)	93. (3)	94. (1)	95. (3)	96. (1)	97. (2)	98. (1)	99. (2)	100. (2)
101. (1)	102. (1)	103. (3)	104. (1)	105. (1)	106. (2)	107. (2)	108. (4)	109. (2)	110. (1)
111. (1)	112. (2)	113. (1)	114. (3)	115. (2)	116. (2)	117. (1)	118. (3)	119. (4)	120. (2)
121. (4)	122. (2)	123. (3)	124. (2)	125. (2)	126. (1)	127. (3)	128. (1)	129. (4)	130. (1)
131. (2)	132. (2)	133. (3)	134. (2)	135. (3)	136. (1)	137. (1)	138. (1)	139. (2)	140. (2)
141. (2)	142. (2)	143. (2)	144. (1)	145. (4)	146. (2)	147. (3)	148. (3)	149. (3)	150. (2)
151. (1)	152. (1)	153. (1)	154. (1)	155. (2)	156. (3)	157. (2)	158. (1)	159. (3)	160. (1)
161. (2)	162. (2)	163. (1)	164. (3)	165. (1)	166. (1)	167. (1)	168. (3)	169. (1)	170. (1)
171. (2)	172. (1)	173. (3)	174. (4)	175. (3)	176. (2)	177. (1)	178. (1)	179. (2)	180. (1)
181. (3)	182. (2)	183. (2)	184. (3)	185. (3)	186. (2)	187. (2)	188. (2)	189. (2)	190. (2)
191. (2)	192. (3)	193. (2)	194. (3)	195. (1)	196. (3)	197. (1)	198. (1)	199. (3)	200. (3)
201. (3)	202. (2)	203. (2)	204. (3)	205. (3)	206. (2)	207. (3)	208. (1)	209. (2)	210. (2)
211. (1)	212. (1)	213. (1)	214. (1)	215. (1)	216. (2)	217. (2)	218. (2)	219. (2)	220. (2)
221. (2)	222. (3)	223. (2)	224. (2)	225. (4)	226. (3)	227. (2)	228. (3)	229. (2)	230. (1)
231. (2)	232. (2)	233. (2)	234. (1)	235. (2)	236. (2)	237. (2)	238. (3)	239. (3)	240. (2)
241. (4)	242. (2)	243. (3)	244. (3)	245. (3)	246. (2)	247. (2)	248. (3)	249. (4)	250. (1)
251. (2)	252. (2)	253. (3)	254. (2)	255. (2)	256. (3)	257. (2)	258. (2)	259. (4)	260. (2)
261. (4)	262. (2)	263. (3)	264. (3)	265. (2)	266. (2)	267. (3)	268. (2)	269. (4)	270. (3)
271. (1)	272. (3)	273. (3)	274. (3)	275. (3)					

UNIT 3

BUSINESS ECONOMICS

SYLLABUS

- Meaning and scope of business economics
- Objectives of business firms
- Demand analysis: Law of demand; Elasticity of demand and its measurement; Relationship between AR and MR
- Consumer behavior: Utility analysis; Indifference curve analysis
- Law of Variable Proportions: Law of Returns to Scale
- Theory of cost: Short-run and long-run cost curves
- Price determination under different market forms: Perfect competition; Monopolistic competition; Oligopoly- Price leadership model; Monopoly; Price discrimination
- Pricing strategies: Price skimming; Price penetration; Peak load pricing

Meaning of Business Economics

Everyday a number of decisions are made by us as individuals or entrepreneurs. Almost all such decisions, directly or indirectly, relate to economic variables like demand, supply, stock, price, input, output, profit, financials etc. Business economics is providing solution to these problems faced by business firms. It provides a tool-box of analysis and a technique of thinking for business firms, enriching the conceptual and technical skills of managers facing decision problems. It is that branch of economics which links abstract theory and business practice by identifying problems, organising information & evaluation all feasible alternatives to choose the best three from.

Characteristics of Business Economics

Managerial Decision. Business economics is an applied subject, which helps in taking managerial decision to formulate business policies. It helps in decision-making to maximise output with minimum cost.

Applied Nature of Economic Theory. In economic theory, different laws are formulated but the applied part of economics is used in business economics. The nature of business economics is applied and not theoretical.

Problems and Solutions Business economics helps in studying the complicated and different types of problems related to business and suggests policy implications, so that the problems can be easily solved. .

Economics of a Firm. The aim of a firm is to get maximum profit, which is possible only by effective policy adoption and decision-making to minimise the cost of production.

Coordinating Nature. Business economics coordinates between the theoretical and practical aspects necessarily required for running a firm. It uses micro as well as macro models.

NATURE AND USES OF BUSINESS ECONOMICS

All human activities can be divided into two categories *i.e.* economic and non-economic. Economic activities are related to the production of wealth. Every human being undertakes some kind of work with a view to earn his living. All these activities create utilities. Non-economic activities are not undertaken with economic motives, these may be in the form of religious, cultural or social activities. The element of profit which is prevalent in economic activities distinguishes them from non-economic activities.

Uses of Business Economics

1. **Activities Related to Distribution of Goods and Services.** In business economics, the goods are produced to satisfy the needs of consumers. The goods are to be transferred from the place of production to the place of consumption. All those activities which facilitate this transfer are a part of commerce.

   Noel Branton "Commerce is concerned with a group of activities, which, directly and indirectly are involved in the distribution of goods between the places where they come into existence and the persons who finally uses them.

   Noel Branton includes, in the purview of Commerce, all those activities which help in taking goods from the producers to the consumers.

   Distribution of goods and services may be the primary activity of commerce but it involves many more things. A number of hindrances or obstacles come in the way of taking goods from producers to consumers. Commerce has to tackle all those hindrances so that activities are carried on smoothly.

G. K. Bucknall "The business of distribution is called commerce. It includes not merely the buying and selling of goods but also their transport, methods of financing and insurance."

E.E. Clark "Marketing consists of those effects which effect either transfer in ownership of goods and care for their physical distribution." By *American Marketing Society*, "Marketing is the performance of business activities that direct the flow of goods and services from producer to consumer to user". In this approach of marketing the focus is on product. Producers are of the view that if they have a good product then consumers will always respond favourably and there is a little need of promotional efforts. The production oriented philosophy of marketing is no longer valid and this approach cannot help in modern marketing. Commerce is no longer confined to distribution of goods rather it also deals with aspects like accounting and finance.

2. **Activities Related to Exchange of Goods.** Business economics is concerned with exchange of goods. It refers to all those activities and effects which bring buyers and sellers together.

   James Stephenson, "Commerce is concerned with the exchange of goods; with all that is involved in the buying and selling of goods at any stage in their progress from raw materials to finished goods in the consumers' hands. It covers not only the function of buying and selling and handling goods but also many services which must be provided to finance, insure, store and transport goods in the course of these exchanges." According to this view commerce is an organised system for the exchange of goods and services between the members of the business world. The producers and consumers are brought closer. The process of exchange encounters many hindrances. Commerce ensures the removal of various obstacles in the flow of goods and services between producers and consumers.

3. **Activities Related to Distribution and Exchange.** Business economics is used in the study of activities related to both distribution and exchange.

   G.M. Whitehead, "Commerce is the distribution and exchange of all surplus goods produced in the fields, mines, seas, forests and factories of the earth so that they reach the final consumer in the right place, and the right condition, at the right time, in the right quantity."

   Whitehead emphasised the following things in his definition:

   (i) There are surplus goods which can be exchanged. The producers and others who have produced for others send them in the channel of distribution and exchange.

   (ii) The goods should reach the place of final consumers.

   (iii) The quantity and quality of goods reaching the consumers should be proper and as per their needs. This has to be ensured by the intermediaries between the producers and ultimate consumers.

   (iv) Though production may be on a large scale but the consumer will be supplied only the quantity required by him. This is possible by using warehouses for storing goods and releasing quantities as and when needed and in right quantity.

4. **Activities Related to Business Operations.** It is the study of business and its operations.

   Evelyn Thomas, "Commerce seeks to show how the business world operates. It is not concerned with the basic problems that confront the economists. It is not for the student to reason why he takes the existing system for granted and proceeds to discover how it works."

   P. Sargent, "The word is certainly of wider connotation than Business Administration which refers exclusively to the internal management and direction of any firm. The case is strong, therefore, not only for distinguishing a course of studies and research wider than economics, which will integrate relevant studies in law, sociology, accounting and statistical methods, but for stressing the word commerce as wider than Business Administration."

In the words of *F.C. Hooper*, business is the "whole complex field of commerce and industry, the basic industries, processes and manufacturing and the network of ancillary services, distribution, banking, insurance, transport and so on which serve and inter-penetrate the world of business as a whole".

5. **As a Study of Human Beings.** Business economics is also thought of as a study of human beings as producers and consumers. It gives a very wide view of commerce.

   Swift, "It is a study of all of us engaged in production of goods and services, in distribution and in professions and study of us as consumers learning to plan and buy wisely in age when shopping is becoming a technical matter." Swift has taken the view that commerce is a study of human beings engaged in production of goods and services and also as consumers of those goods. This view equates commerce with economics. Commerce is a part of economics, rather practical aspect of it. Equating commerce with economics will be stretching the limits too much.

OBJECTIVES OF BUSINESS FIRMS

A firm is a unit engaged in the production and/or distribution of goods and services. All firms (e.g., sole proprietorship, joint stock firm, cooperative, public sector firms, etc.,) operating under perfectly competitive framework or monopoly or monopolistically competitive or oligopoly aim at profit maximization, just as all students of all countries appearing at all kinds of examinations aim only at maximizing marks.

As all firms—from perfect competition to oligopoly—aim at profit-maximization, their marginal costs become equal to marginal revenues. In other words, price-output determination of this kind of marginal approach or standard approach suggests that when marginal cost equals marginal revenue, profit is maximized. Profit-maximization may be considered as a basic objective of a business firm.

But the attainment of such goal does not take into account the complexities of the real world and, hence, involves several obstacles. It is indeed true that a firm may not be able to maximize profit because of uncertainty in business conditions.

Further, profit maximization objective may change if the firm's behaviour changes. Our standard neoclassical approach may fit within the perfectly competitive model and monopoly model. But, modern business firms are mostly characterized by monopolistic competition and oligopoly.

In this real business world, one finds mutual interdependence among firms. Profit- maximization, then, is not accepted as the primary goal. Again, in recent times, one finds changing organizational structure of firms where we find different groups and sub-groups having different as well as conflicting goals.

In this complex world, no one aims at maximizing anything—everyone simply aims to **'satisfy'** a range of objectives. For all these reasons, today we face supplement to the profit-maximizing goal.

Alternatives to profit maximization model are grouped into two:

- Managerial theories, and behavioural theories.

  Do Firms Really Maximize only Profit?
- It is said that the sole objective of a firm is the maximization of profit.

This is what traditional economics believes since, apparently this objective is not only simple but also easily quantifiable. But, in today's world, such profit-maximization goal has come in for sharp criticisms. New teachers of economics argue that all men involved in production are social animals whose aims are not only multifarious but also conflicting and complicated.

In view of this, one finds lack of unanimity among the managers-directors relating to business decision. All these cannot really be summed up in the profit-maximizing goal. Rather, disillusionment with the goal of profit-maximization has led to the emergence of some other competing goals that firms want to attain.

Doubts in the goal of profit-maximization arose due to the following reasons:

Firstly, managers of today's business are quite different from their predecessors. Earlier, it was the entrepreneur who owned and managed the entire business firm, who took all the business decisions. Naturally, profit – a special category of income – must go to this gentleman. But today the style of business has undergone a sea-change.

Here we find separation between ownership and management. These two functions of a joint stock company are performed separately by two distinct classes having divergent motivations. Today's decision-makers are interested in maximizing their salaries and other forms of job satisfaction, rather than profit. Obviously, these people aim at maximizing their own welfare.

Only shareholders—the owners of a joint stock company—are concerned with the goal of profit-maximization. These two goals seem to be in conflicting terms. In view of this, a question may be posed in this way: Who will be maximizing whose profit? It is virtually impossible to give any a priori answer to this question.

Secondly, at least perfectly competitive model suggests that even if firms do not go for profit-maximization, they would be forced to sacrifice this goal in the long run due to the pressure of free entry and free exit. In the midst of this freedom of entry, no firm can enjoy more than normal profit.

In the ultimate analysis, only the fittest will survive due to the pressure of market forces. But due to the variety of factors, entry in any industry is not an easy one in today's world. There are various barriers to entry. If so, then the argument of market forces loses its potency.

In view of these limitations, the goal of profit-maximization is now being replaced by a wardrobe of theories. Here we won't go into the jungle of theories which may sometimes be confusing. Here we will present, in brief, two important alternative goals to profit- maximization. First is Nobel Laureate W. J. Baumol's **'Sales Maximization'** goal and the second is H. A. Simon's **'Satisfying Theory of Profit'**.

Sales Maximization Goal

According to Baumol, managers of modern business are more interested in maximizing their sales rather than profits. Baumol has suggested that firms maximize sales revenue subject to a minimum profit constraint. This minimum profit constraint is specified at that minimum level that is just enough to keep shareholders happy.

Again, for survival, managers also consider a minimum level of profit. When this constrained maximization problem is solved by the choice of output level, Baumol has shown that output is higher under the sales maximization model than under profit- maximization model.

Some economists have suggested an alternative to maximizing the value of sales. To them, maximization of output is the most accepted goal.

Satisficing Theory of Profit

According to Simon, business firms strive for **'satisfactory'** rate of profit, rather than maximum profit.

He argues that often managers fail to estimate the desired volume of profit or sales due to the imperfection in information or data. In view of this, instead of maximizing the goal of profit, Simon argues that firms aspire to a satisfactory level or rate of profit. Simon quotes **"Cost-plus pricing"** as a form of satisficing which has empirical backing.

Despite these, the goal of profit-maximization seems to be uppermost in the mind of the businessmen. Profit is the ultimate incentive to firms.

Even the public sector enterprises which often run on a no-profit-no-loss basis also want to maximize profit. It is true also those private firms are also conscious of their social responsibility. Still then, no one has shirked the goal of profit-maximization at the altar of other alternative goals to profit maximization.

DEMAND ANALYSIS

Concept of Demand

In managerial economics, we are concerned with demand for a commodity faced by the firm. This depends upon the size of the total market or industry demand for the commodity, k, which in turn is the sum of the demands for the commodity of the individual consumers in the market. Thus we begin by examining the theory of consumer demand in order to learn about the market demand on which the demand for the product faced by a particular firm depends.

Demand is one of the crucial requirements for the existence of any business enterprise. A firm is interested in its own profit and/or sales, both of which depend partially upon the demand for its product. The decision which management makes with respect to production, advertising, cost allocation, pricing etc., call for an analysis of demand.

Demand for a commodity refers to the quantity of the commodity which an individual household is willing to purchase per unit of time at a particular price.

Demand for a commodity implies:

- Desire to acquire it,
- Willingness to pay for it, and
- Ability to pay for it.

Mere desire to buy a product is not demand. A miser's desire for and his ability to pay for a car is not demand because he does not have the necessary will to pay for it. Similarly, poor man's desire for and his willingness to pay for a car is not demand because he lacks the necessary purchasing power. One can also conceive of a person who possesses both the will and purchasing power to pay for a commodity, yet this is not demand for that commodity if he does not have desire to have that commodity.

Demand for a commodity has to be stated with reference to time, its price and that of related commodities, consumer's income and taste etc. Demand varies with fluctuations in these factors. Further it also depends on quality because if the quality changes it can be deemed as another commodity.

Determinants of Demand

Factors determining demand

- General factors
  - Price of the product itself
  - Income of the consumer
  - Tastes and preferences of the consumer
  - Prices of related goods (which include prices of substitutes and complements)
- Additional factors related to luxury goods and durables
  - Consumer's expectations of future prices
  - Consumer's expectations of future income
- Additional factors related to market demand
  - Size of Regional Distribution of population
  - Composition of Population
  - Distribution of Income

Let us discuss these demand determinants.

(i) **Price of the Commodity.** We often find that a consumer buys more of a commodity when its price declines, and vice-versa. Thus, we can say that for a normal good the price of a commodity and its demand vary inversely, determinants other than the price of the commodity remaining constant. A fall in the price of a normal good leads to rise in consumer's purchasing power. He can, therefore, buy more of it (*Substitution effect*). Similarly, an increase in price will reduce his purchasing power and, thereby reducing demand for the commodity (*Income Effect*).

(ii) **Income of the Consumer.** With an increase in income, a household buys increased amount of most of the commodities in his consumption bundle though the extent of the increase may differ between commodities. Normally both the quantity demanded of a good and income of the household move in the same direction. However, in case of certain commodities like foods, fruits, vegetables, etc., the amount demanded increases with an increase in income, but beyond a certain level of income the amount demanded of the good remains unchanged even when income changes . There are still some other commodities in whose case, beyond a point, the amount demanded even starts decreasing with further increase in income. Such commodities in case of which amount demanded decreases with an increase in income and increases with a decrease in income after a particular level of income, are called *inferior goods.* The term inferior is not used here in the context of the quality of the commodity; it simply refers to the case of an exception to the normal income-demand relationship.

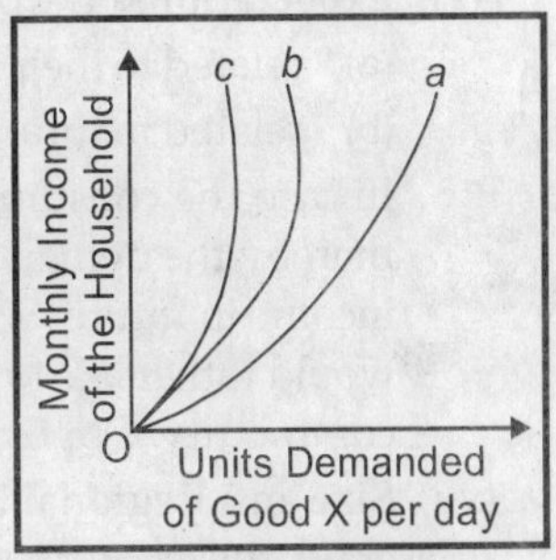

Income-Demand Relationship.

(iii) **Prices of Related Goods.** When a change in the price of one commodity influences the demand of the other commodity, we say that the two commodities are related. These related commodities are of two types : substitutes and complements. When the price of one commodity and the quantity demanded of the other commodity move in the same direction (i.e., both increase together or decrease together), the two goods are called substitutes, e.g., apple and pears, tea and coffee, rail and road transport services, etc.

On the other hand, when price of one commodity and quantity demanded of the other commodity move in opposite direction, then the two commodities are said to be complementary to each other, e.g., bread and butter, pen and ink, petrol and automobiles, tea and sugar, etc.

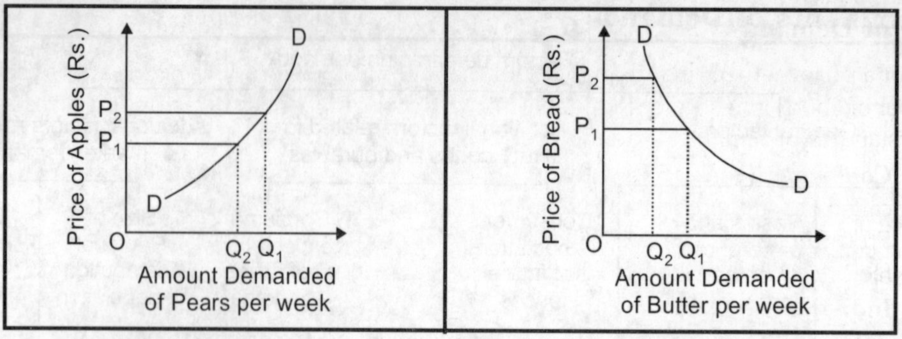

Substitute Goods Case. **Complementary Goods case.**

(iv) **Tastes and Preferences.** We know it quite well that the change in tastes and preferences of a consumer in favour of a commodity results in greater demand for the commodity, while if this change is against the commodity it results in smaller demand for the commodity. For example, if jeans catch the fancy of consumers, the firms selling jeans will have greater demand now than before. Opposite will be the case if jeans go out of fashion. Modern business firms not only try to adjust to changes in market trends and fancies, they also try to influence the market demand with the help of their sales campaigns.

(v) **Advertisement.** A lot of money is spent on advertisement to influence the tastes and preferences of the consumers in their favour. This increases their sales.

(vi) **Expectations.** The consumers make two kinds of expectations :

(a) related to their future income; and

(b) related to future prices of the good and its related goods.

In case the consumer expects a higher income in future, he spends more at present, and thereby the demand for the good increases. Opposite will be the case, if he expects lower income in future. Similarly, if the consumer expects future prices of the good to increase, he would rather like to buy the commodity now than later. This will increase the demand for the commodity. Opposite holds good when it is expected that prices in future will come down.

(vii) **Size and Regional Distribution of Population.** The greater is the number of consumers of a good, the greater is the market demand for it. Thus, the demand for a commodity is directly related with the population, which is determined by birth & death rates. Population is also affected by migration and immigration. Regional distribution of the population also affects the demand.

(viii) **Composition of population.** If there are more children, demand fur baby food, toys, biscuits, sweets, etc. will be more. Similarly, if there are more old people, spectacles, artificial teeth, sticks, tonics, fruits, etc. will be more in demand. Predominance of young people in the population will raise the demand for cosmetics, sport goods, jeans, etc. Similarly, sex composition also affects the demand for a number of commodities.

(ix) **Distribution of Income.** If income is equally distributed among the different sections of the society, all of them will be in a position to demand goods. But, there will be more demand for goods purchased by relatively poorer people, like wheat, rice, fans, etc. But, if the income is unevenly distributed, majority of the people will get small portion of the national income and so the demand for commodity will be limited. Most of the demand in this case will come from rich people for luxuries. Further, in this case, relatively greater proportion of the income will be saved (by rich people).

Type of Demand

For a purposeful demand analysis for managerial decisions, it is necessary to classify the large number of goods and services available in every economy. Policy decisions are also facilitated by an understanding of demand at various levels of aggregation. A classification in these respects is as follows:

1. **Consumer goods and producer goods.** Goods and services used for final consumption are called consumer goods. These include, those consumed by human-beings, animals, birds etc. Producer goods refers to the goods used for production of other goods, like plant and machines, factory buildings, services of employees, raw materials etc.
2. **Individual demand and market demand.** Market demand is the summation of demand for a good by all individual buyers in the market. For example, if the market of good X has, say only three buyers, then individual and market demand (monthly) could be as follows :

Demand of X.

Price of X	Buyer 1	Buyer 2	Buyer 3	All Buyers Market Demand
8	5	10	0	15
7	8	12	4	24
6	12	15	7	34
5	20	19	12	51
4	30	25	20	75
3	45	30	30	105

This can be shown by a graph as:

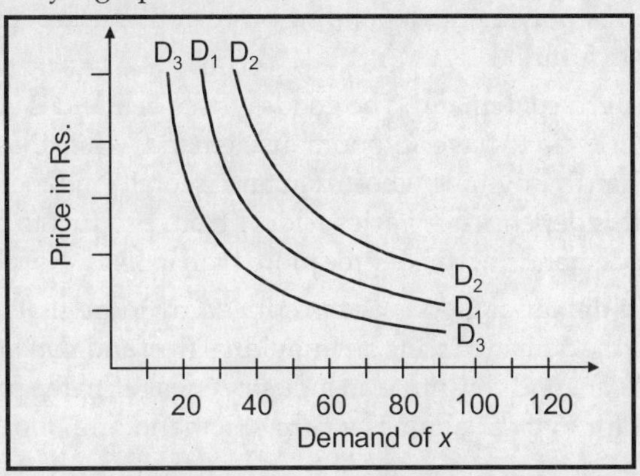

Individual Demand and Market Demand.

In above figure D_1D_1 represents demand curve of buyer 1, D_2D_2 of buyer 2, D_3D_3 of buyer 3 and DD that of all three of them called the market demand curve. The market demand curve is thus the horizontal summation of individual demand curves. A firm would be interested in the market demand for its products while each consumer would be concerned basically with only his own individual demand.

Market Demand Curve. This curve is the horizontal summation of the individual demand curves. This come graphically shows different quantities of a particular commodity demanded by all the consumer at different possible price at a point of time. The figure given below shows graphical presentation of market demand schedule P and Q are tow consumers in the market.

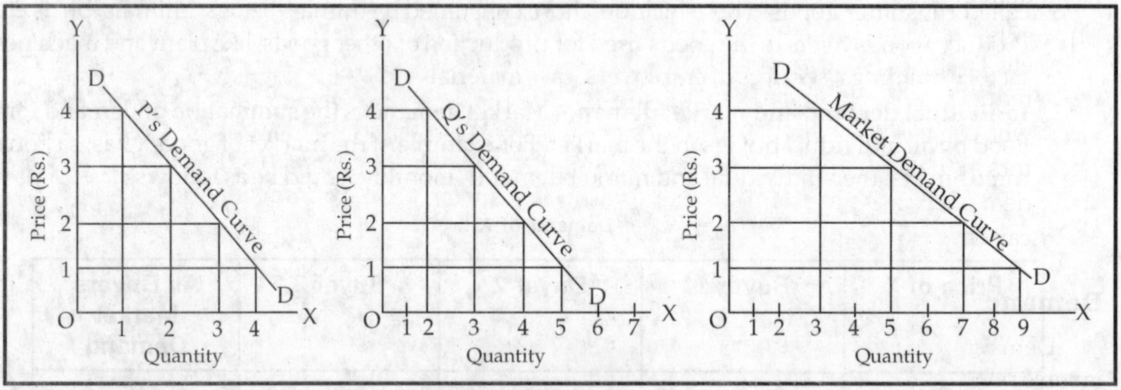

Market Demand Curve

3. **Perishable and durable goods.** Perishable goods become unusable after sometime, others are durable goods. Precisely, perishable goods are those which can be consumed only once while in case of durable goods, their services are only consumed. Durable goods pose more complicated problems for demand analysis than non-durables. Sales of non-durables are made largely to meet current demand which depends on current conditions. In contrast, sales of durable goods go partly to satisfy new demand and partly to replace old items. Further, the latter set of goods are generally more expensive than the former set, and their demand alone is subject to preponement and postponement, depending on current market conditions vis-à-vis expected market conditions in future.
4. **Autonomous and derived demand.** The goods whose demand is not tied with the demand for some other goods are said to have autonomous demand, while the rest have derived demand. However, there is hardly anything whose demand is totally independent of any other demand. But the degree of this dependence varies widely from product to product. Thus, the autonomous and derived demand vary in degree more than in kind.
5. **Firm and industry demand.** Goods are produced by more than one firm and so there is a difference between the demand facing an individual firm and that facing an industry. (All firms producing a particular good constitute an industry engaged in the production of that good). For example, demand for Fiat car alone is a firm's demand and demand for all kinds of cars is industry's demand.
6. **Demand by market segments and by total market.** If the market is large in terms of geographical spread, product uses, distribution channels, customer sizes or product varieties, and if any one or more of these differences were significant in terms of product price, profit margins, competition, seasonal patterns or cyclical sensitivity, then it may be worthwhile to distinguish the market by specific segments for a meaningful analysis. In that case, the total demand would mean the total demand for the product from all market segments while a particular market segment demand would refer to demand for the product in that specific market segment.

7. **Short Run Demand and Long Run Demand.** This distinction is important from the view point of control and management of demand. Short-run demand refers to the existing demand for substitutes, element of competition, seasonal patterns and cyclical sensitivity. When the differences are great, demand analysis must be done segmentwise. Accordingly, different market strategies should be formulated. Further, long-run demand refers to the size and pattern of demand, that will prevail ultimately, when enough time has been allowed to let the market adjust itself to the changes in technology, tastes, products improvement, promotional efforts, etc. For example, suppose a firm makes substantial improvements in its products features & reduces the price. In short run, the existing buyers will raise the demand. Howards the product, who come to know about these changes after some time. It may invite entry of potential competitors in the industry with close substitutes of the product in question. Projections of long run demand trends are useful to business firms in planning production, inventory, investment and capacity expansion.

Demand Curve

Demand curve considers only the price-demand relation, other factors remaining the same. The inverse relationship between the price and the quantity demanded for the commodity per time period is the **demand schedule** for the commodity and the plot of the data (with price on the vertical axis and quantity on the horizontal axis) gives the **demand curve** of the individual.

An individual's demand schedule for commodity X.

Price of x (per Unit) P_x	Quantity of x Demanded (in Units) D_x
2.0	1.0
1.5	2.0
1.0	3.0
0.5	4.5

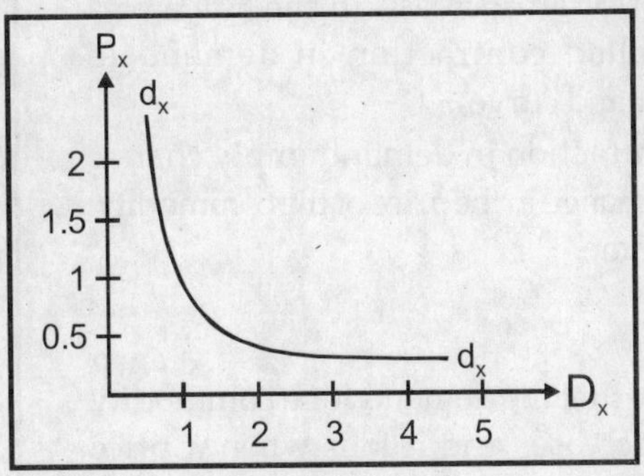

Demand Curve.

The Demand curve is negatively sloped, indicating that the individual purchases more of the commodity per time period at lower prices (other factors being constant).

The inverse relationship between the price of the commodity and the quantity demanded per time period is referred to as the law of demand.

A fall in P_x leads to an increase in D_x (so that the slope is negative) because of the substitution effect and income effect.

Shifts in the Demand Curve

If any of the things held constant in drawing a demand curve change, there is a shift in the demand curve. It is of two types:

(a) **Increase in Demand.** The demand curve shifts upwards or to the right, when the individual demands more of the commodity at each commodity price, if the price of a substitute commodity increases or the price of a complimentary commodity falls, and if the consumer's taste for the commodity changes.

(b) **Decrease in demand.** With opposite changes in factors affecting demand, the demand curve shifts to d_{x2}.

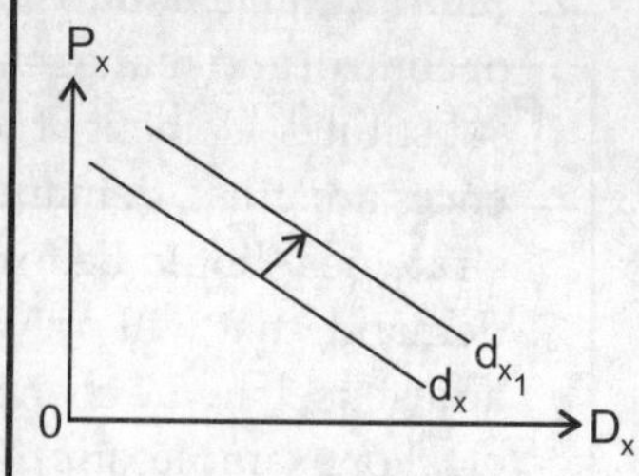

Increase in Demand

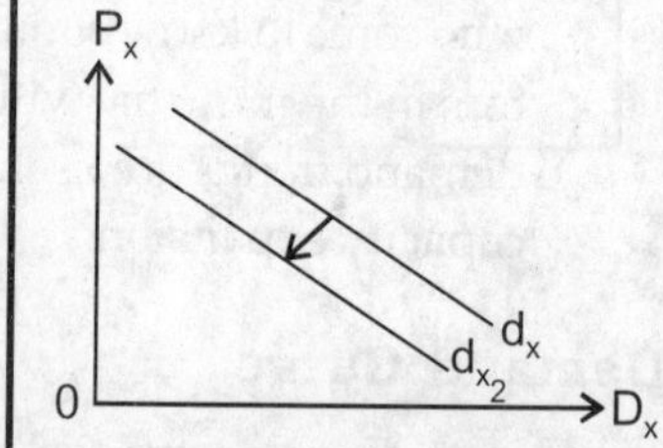

Decrease in Demand

To clearly distinguish between a movement along a given demand curve (as a result of change in price) from a shift in demand (as a result of change in income, price of related commodities and tastes), the first is known as *a change in quantity demanded* and the second one is known as *a change in demand.*

Movement along Demand Curve :

Law of demand states that other things remaining the same, if price of a commodity rises, its demand decrease and if price of the commodity falls, its demand increase. Extension and contraction in demand are represented by a movement (moving down & up respectively) along the same demand curve.

(a) **Extension in demand.** When quantity demanded of a commodity increases as a result of the fall in the price, it is called extension (or expansion) in demand (a movement down the demand curve).

(b) **Contraction in demand.** When the quantity demanded decreases as a result of an increase in the price of a commodity, it is called contraction in demand (a movement up the demand curve).

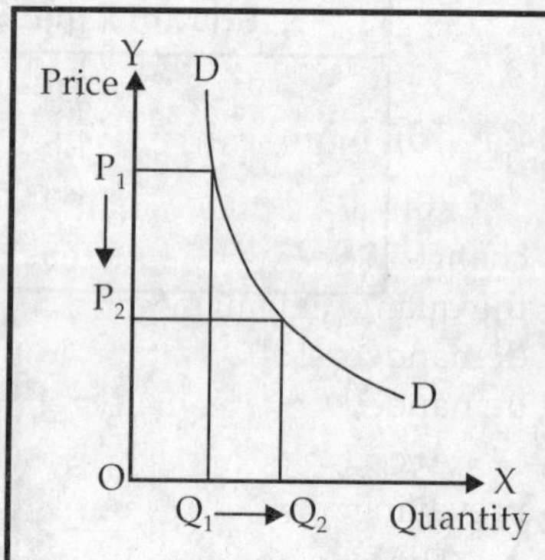

Extension in Demand

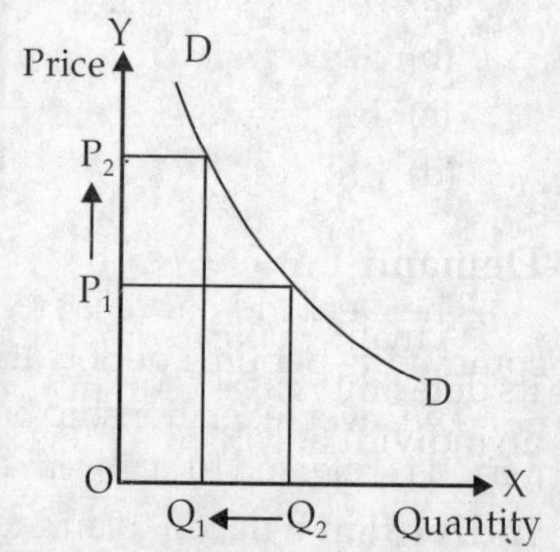

Contraction in Demand

Thus, extension and contraction in demand imply change in quantity demanded due to change in the price of the commodity, other things remaining the same.

Demand Schedule

The law of demand states that the demand for a commodity increases when its prices decreases and it falls when it price rises, other things remaining constant. The law of demand can be presented through a demand schedule. Demand schedule is a series of prices placed in ascending or descending order and the corresponding quantities which consumers would like to buy per unit of time. Based on the logic of demand curve, a hypothetical demand schedule for a commodity (Wheat) is shown in the given table.

Demand Schedule for Wheat.

Price per kg of Wheat (Rs)	Wheat demanded by a family per day (in kg)	Points representing price quantity combination
20	1	A
19	2	B
18	3	C
17	4	D
16	5	E
15	6	F
14	7	G

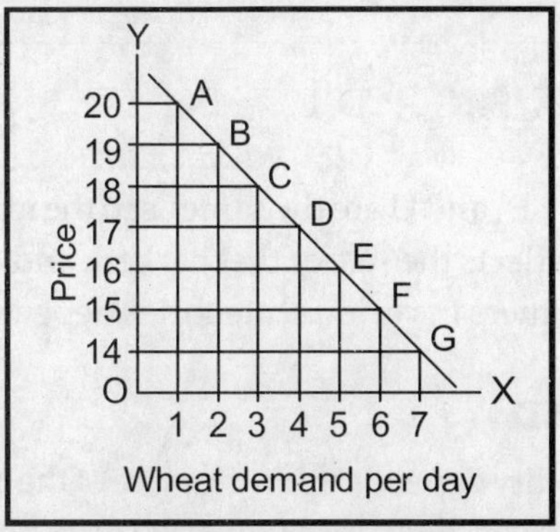

Demand Curve for Wheat.

Law of Demand

Law of demand is an important law in economics which explains the relationship between change in quantity demanded and change in price. It states that higher the price, the lower would be the quantity demanded in the market, and the lower the price, the higher would be the quantity demanded in the market. In other words, the law of demand says that the price and the quantity demanded are negatively related, all other things being equal.

According to *Prof. Thomas*, "At any given time, the demand for a commodity or service at the prevailing price is greater than it would be at a higher price and less than it would be at a lower price".

The law is applicable only when other things remain the same. This means that:

(a) Income of consumers should remain the same.

(b) The commodity should not be an item of conspicuous consumption.

(c) Tastes and preferences of consumers should not change.

(d) Price of other related goods should remain the same.

Demand Function

A mathematical expression of the relationship between quantity demanded of the commodity and its determinants is known as the demand function. When this relationship relates to the demand by an individual consumer it is known as individual demand function.

Individual Demand Function

$Q_{dx} = f(P_x, Y, P_1, \ldots P_{n-1}, T, A, E_y, E_p, U)$

where

Q_{dx} is quantity demanded of product X

P_x is price of product X

Y is household income

$P_1, ..., P_{n-1}$ is prices of all the other 'related' products in economy (related products include substitutes and complements)

T is tastes of consumer

A is advertising

E_y is consumer's expected future income

E_p is consumer's expectations about future prices

U is those determinants which are not covered in the list of determinants given above.

Market Demand Function

$Q_{dx} = f(P_x, Y, P_1, ... P_{n-1}, T, A, E_y, E_p, P, D, U)$

where

$Q_{dx}, P_x, Y, P_1, ... P_{n-1}, T, A, E_y, E_p$ and U are the same as in the individual's demand function while

P is population (which reflects the size of the market), and

D is distribution of consumers in various categories depending on income, age, sex etc.

ELASTICITY OF DEMAND

The demand for any commodity depends upon the price of the commodity, with the condition that other things remain equal. Whenever there is a change in price, there is also a change in the quantity demanded. The change in quantity demanded as a result of change in price is known as elasticity of demand.

Measurement of Elasticity of Demand

Prof. Marshall suggested a mathematical method for measuring elasticity of demand. The formula for this method is given as follows :

$$E = \frac{\text{Percentage change in demand for a product}}{\text{Percentage change in the price of the product}}$$

Symbolically, it may be stated as $E = \frac{\Delta Q / Q}{\Delta Z / Z} = \frac{\Delta Q}{\Delta Z} \cdot \frac{Z}{Q}$

E refers to elasticity of demand

Δ refers to change

Q refers to quantity demanded

Z refers to price.

The formula states that the elasticity of demand refers to the percentage change in demand as a result of a percentage change in price. The percentage change in demand for a product is expressed as

$$\frac{\text{Change in Demand}}{\text{Original Demand}} \times 100$$

Likewise, the percentage change in price for product is expressed as :

$$\frac{\text{Change in Price}}{\text{Original Price}} \times 100$$

The elasticity formula is thus rewritten as follows :

$$E = \frac{\dfrac{\text{Change in Demand}}{\text{Original Demand}} \times 100}{\dfrac{\text{Change in Price}}{\text{Original Price}} \times 100}$$

$$E = \frac{\text{Change in Demand}}{\text{Original Demand}} \times \frac{\text{Original Price}}{\text{Change in Price}}$$

By re-arranging this formula, we will get

$$E = \frac{\text{Change in Demand}}{\text{Change in Price}} \times \frac{\text{Original Price}}{\text{Original Demand}}$$

Factors Determining Elasticity of Demand

The Elasticity of demand is based on :

(1) Nature of commodity
(2) Extent of use
(3) Range of substitutes
(4) Income level
(5) Proportion of income spent on the commodity
(6) Urgency of demand
(7) Durability of the commodity
(8) Influence of price
(9) Joint demand
(10) Government policy

ARC and Point Elasticity Measurements

There are two kinds of elasticity measurement :

(1) Point elasticity; (2) Arc elasticity.

Point elasticity of demand relates to the elasticity at a particular point on the demand curve, while arc elasticity of demand is the average elasticity over a segment of the demand curve, *i.e.*, average of the demand curve.

Point Elasticity. The formula of elasticity of demand for point elasticity is

$$\varepsilon = \frac{\Delta Q}{\Delta Z} \cdot \frac{Z}{Q}$$

If ΔZ is taken as very small, $\Delta Q/\Delta Z$ approximates to the slope of the demand curve in the neighbourhood of original Z and Q. In other words, when ΔZ approaches its limit of zero, then $\lim_{\Delta Z \to 0} \frac{\Delta Q}{\Delta Z}$ becomes $\frac{dQ}{dZ}$. Thus

$$\varepsilon = \frac{dQ}{dZ} \cdot \frac{Z}{Q}$$

Arc Elasticity. If instead of measuring elasticity by taking $\Delta Z \to 0$ (as we do in case of point elasticity), we measure it over larger segment of the demand curve, we get arc elasticity measure. The arc elasticity is the measure of average elasticity, *i.e.*, it is the elasticity at the mid-point of the chord that connects the initial and new point on the demand curve. In the figure the end points of the arc are (P_1, Q_1) and (P_2, Q_2).

Coordinates of mid-point would, therefore, be $\left(\frac{P_1 + P_2}{2}, \frac{Q_1 + Q_2}{2}\right)$. The change between the end points would be ΔP and ΔQ. The elasticity at the mid-point of the arc (*i.e.*, Arc Elasticity) would be :

$$E = \frac{\Delta Q}{\left(\frac{Q_1+Q_2}{2}\right)} \div \frac{\Delta P}{\left(\frac{P_1+P_2}{2}\right)} = \frac{\Delta Q}{(Q_1+Q_2)} \cdot \frac{(P_1+P_2)}{\Delta P}$$

$$= \frac{\Delta Q}{\Delta P} \cdot \frac{P_1+P_2}{Q_1+Q_2}$$

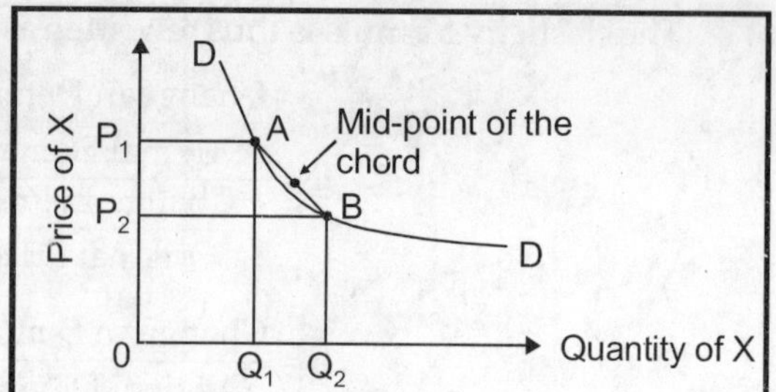

(Arc Elasticity)

Types of Elasticity of Demand

1. Price Elasticity of Demand. The elasticity (or responsiveness) of demand in a market is great or small, as the amount demanded increases more or less for a given fall in price and diminishes much or less for a given rise in price. It can be computed by :

$$e_p = \frac{\frac{\text{Change in the Quantity Demand}}{\text{Quantity Demand}}}{\frac{\text{Change in Price}}{\text{Price}}}$$

$$= -\frac{(Q_2 - Q_1)/Q_1}{(P_2 - P_1)/P_1}$$

$$= -\frac{\Delta Q/Q_1}{\Delta P/P_1} = -\frac{\Delta Q}{Q_1} \cdot \frac{P_1}{\Delta P} = -\frac{\Delta Q}{\Delta P} \cdot \frac{P_1}{Q_1}$$

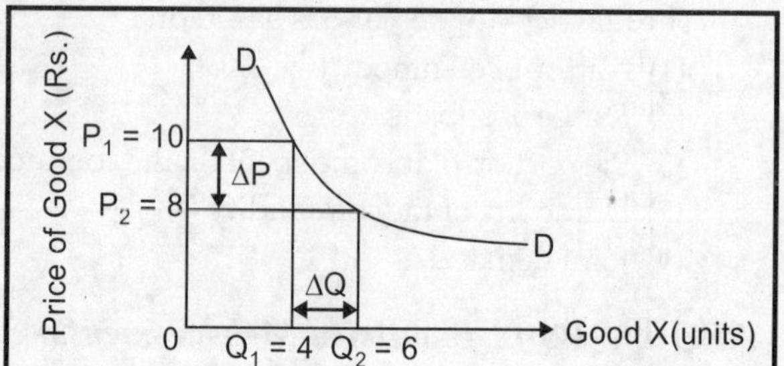

(Elasticity Measurement)

In figure, DD is the demand curve for a consumer for good X. At price = Rs. 10, 4 units of good X are demanded. When price goes down to Rs 8, quantity demanded increases to 6. So $\Delta P = 8 - 10 = -2$, and $\Delta Q = 6 - 4 = 2$, and

$$E = -\frac{\Delta Q}{\Delta P} \cdot \frac{P}{Q} = -\left(\frac{2}{-2}\right)\left(\frac{10}{4}\right) = 2.5$$

Higher the elasticity of demand, greater will be the percentage change in quantity demanded for every percentage change in price.

(i) **Perfectly Elastic Demand ($E = \infty$).** This is a situation where no reduction in price is needed to cause an increase in demand.

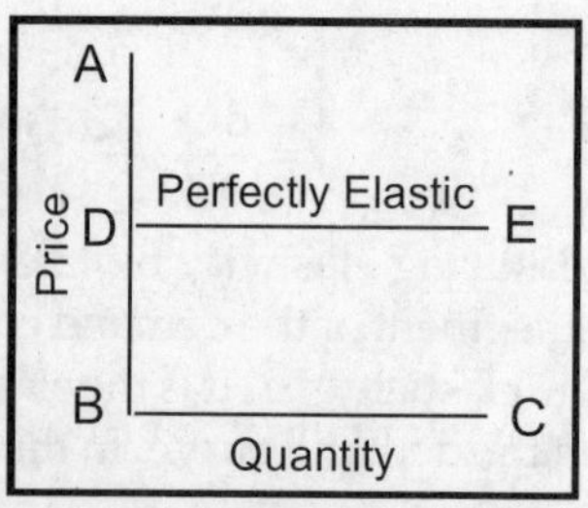

Perfect Elastic Demand.

(ii) **Perfectly Inelastic Demand ($E = 0$).** In this situation a change in price causes no change in quantity demanded. When the quantity demanded of a commodity remains the same, irrespective of any rise or fall in price of a commodity, then the demand is perfectly inelastic.

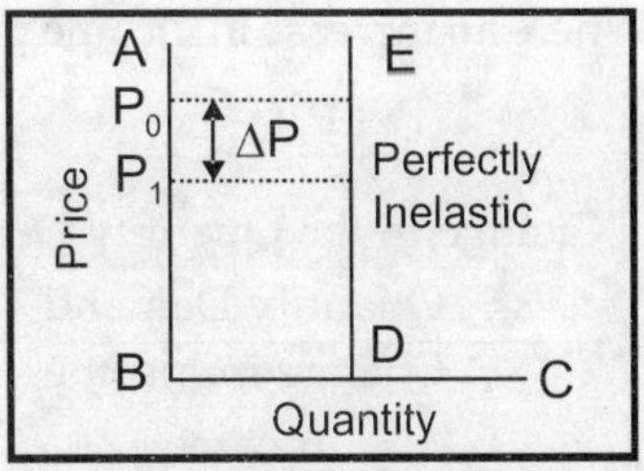

Perfect Inelastic Demand.

(iii) **Unit Elastic Demand (E = 1).** This is a situation when a given proportionate change in price causes equal proportionate change in the quantity demanded. If the price of commodity A goes up by 20%, and if it results in the contraction of demand by exactly 20%, demand curve slopes from left to right.

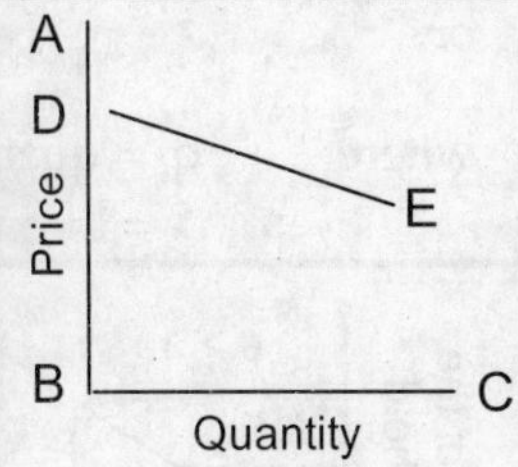

Unity of Elasticity Demand.

(iv) **Relatively More Elastic Demand (E > 1).** This is a situation when reduction in a price leads to more than proportionate change in demand. A proportionate fall in price accompanied by a relatively large proportionate increase in the quantity demanded and vice-versa.

Demand is more sensitive to price changes and change in price brings about a large distortion in demand. The demand curve would be more inclined to appear like horizontal curve.

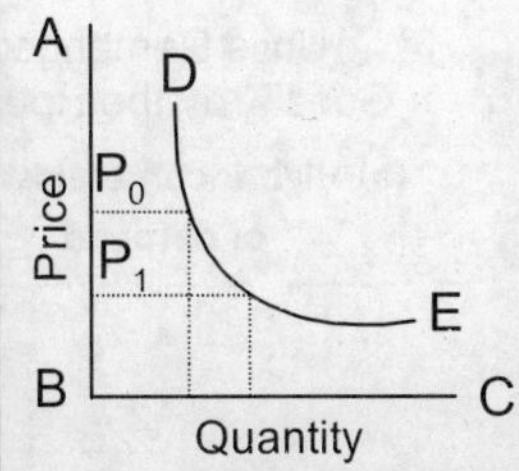

Relatively More Elastic Demand.

(v) **Relatively Inelastic Demand (E < 1).** This is a situation when a reduction in price leads to less than proportionate change in demand. Demand is in elastic when a given proportionate fall in the price of a commodity causes a relatively small proportionate increase in the quantity demanded and vice-versa. In such a situation, the demand curve would be inclined to look vertical and look more parallel to AB axis.

If the prices go-up by 50%, the demand reduces by less than 50%.

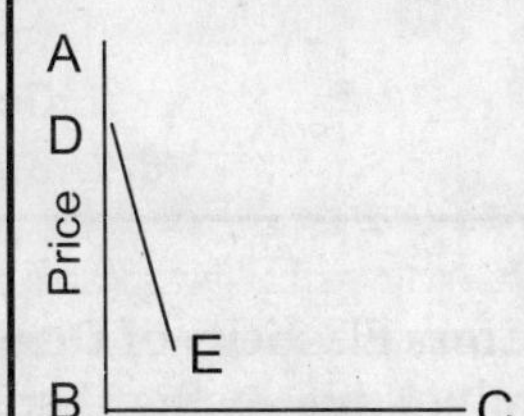

Relatively Inelastic Demand.

2. Income Elasticity of Demand. Income elasticity of demand means the ratio of the percentage change in the quantity demanded to the percentage change in income. The income elasticity measures the responsiveness of demand to changes in income.

Income elasticity of demand for a commodity shows the extent to which a consumer's demand for the commodity changes as a result of the change in his income.

(i) **Zero Income Elasticity.** When a change in income has no effect on the quantity demanded.

(ii) **Positive Income Elasticity.** Where an increase in income may lead to an increase in quantity demanded and vice versa.

(a) **Unit Elasticity.** When the increase in income brings about a proportionate change in the quantity demanded.

(b) **More than unit Elasticity.** When an increase in income brings about more than proportionate increase in the quantity demanded.

(c) **Less than unit Elasticity.** When an increase in income brings about less than proportionate change in quantity demanded.

(iii) **Negative Income Elasticity.** Where an increase in income may lead to a reduction in the quantity demanded.

It can be expressed as :

$$e_y = \frac{\frac{\text{Change in the Quantity Demand}}{\text{Quantity Demand}}}{\frac{\text{Change in Income}}{\text{Income}}}$$

or, $$e_y = \frac{\Delta q_x}{q_x} / \frac{\Delta y}{y} = \frac{\Delta q_x}{\Delta y} / \frac{y}{q_x}$$

where q_x = quantity demanded of X, and
y = income level of consumer

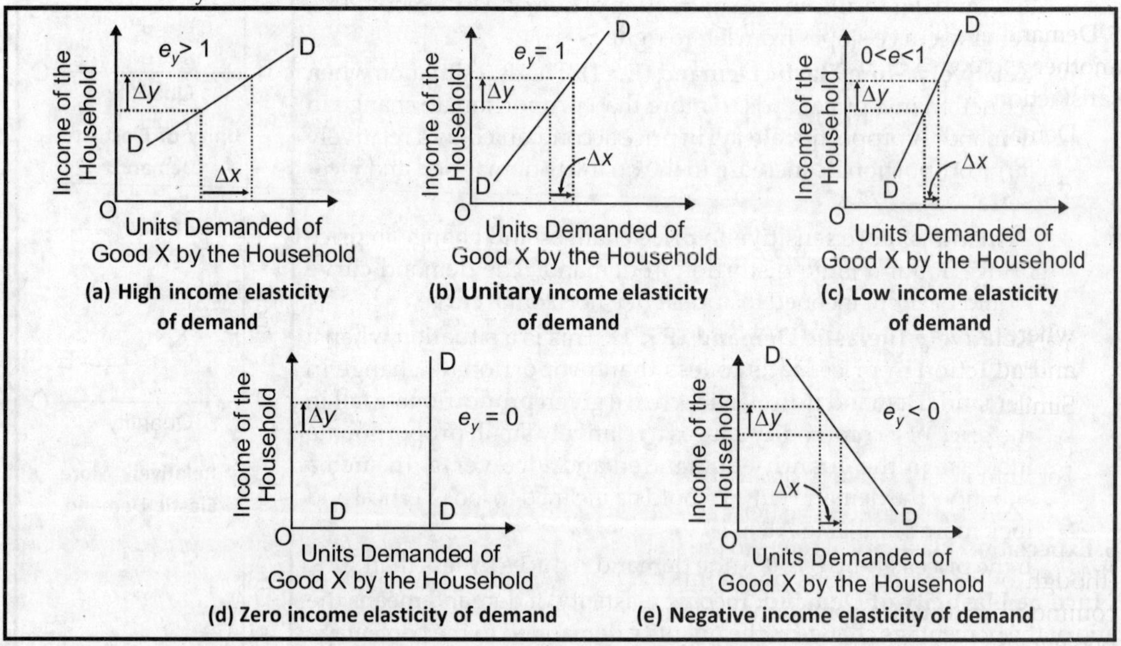

Types of Income Elasticities of Demand.

3. Cross Elasticity of Demand. The cross elasticity of demand refers to a change in the demand for a product due to the changes in the price of a related product (which could be a substitute or complementary). If the cross elasticity is positive, the related commodity is a "substitute" and if the cross elasticity is negative the related commodity is 'complementary'. Thus, the price of one commodity is the independent variable, where as the quantity of another commodity is a dependent variable.

It is defined as the ratio of the percentage change in demand for one good due to a change in the price of some other related good. Once we assume that two commodities X and Y are related, the expression of cross elasticity of demand would be

$$e_{xy} = \frac{\Delta q_x}{q_x} \div \frac{\Delta p_y}{p_y} = \frac{\Delta q_x}{\Delta p_y} \times \frac{p_y}{q_x}$$

e_{xy} will have +ve sign if two goods are substitutes
e_{xy} will have –ve sign if two goods are substitutes
For substitutes $0 < e_{xy} < \infty$
For complements $-\infty < e_{xy} < 0$

4. Advertising Elasticity. The responsiveness of demand to change in advertising or rather promotional expenses is known as advertising elasticity. It can be expressed as :

$$e_a = \frac{\dfrac{\text{Change in Sales}}{\text{Sales}}}{\dfrac{\text{Change in Advertisment Expenditure}}{\text{Advertisment Expenditure}}}$$

$$e_a = \frac{\Delta Q}{\Delta A} \cdot \frac{A}{Q}$$

where Q = quantity of good X sold, and A = units of advertising expenditure on good X.

The Arc elasticity formula in this case can be written as $e_a = \frac{(Q_2 - Q_1)(A_2 + A_1)}{(Q_2 + Q_1)(A_2 - A_1)}$

5. Demand Elasticity of Substitution. It is defined as the degree to which one good can be substituted for another as a consequence of a given change in their price ratio, if the consumer is to enjoy the same satisfaction.

Demand elasticity of substitution is defined as

$$\sigma = \frac{\text{Proportionate change in the quantity ratios of goods X and Y}}{\text{Proportionate change in the price ratios of goods X and Y}}$$

$$= \frac{\Delta(Q_x / Q_y)}{(Q_x / Q_y)} \div \frac{\Delta(P_x / P_y)}{(P_x / P_y)}$$

where, (Q_x/Q_y) is the ratio of the quantities of goods Q_x and Q_y and $\Delta(Q_x/Q_y)$ is the change in the quantity ratio.

Similarly, (P_x/P_y) is the price ratio of the two goods and $\Delta(P_x/P_y)$ is the change in the price ratio.

For Infinite substitution elasticity $(\sigma = \infty)$

Zero substitution elasticity $(\sigma = 0)$; High and low substitution elasticity $(0 < \sigma_s < \infty)$

6. Expectation Elasticity. It refers to the responses of observed current price to future price expectations (though other expectations about future income, future availability, outlays prices of related commodities, future promotional outlays, etc. can also be thought of). It is defined as the ratio of percentage change in the level of expected future prices (P_{t+1}) to the percentage change in the level of current price (P_t). Thus.

$$e_{pe} = \frac{dP_{t+1}}{dP_t} \cdot \frac{P_t}{P_{t+1}}$$

Expectation elasticity is unitary, when a rise in current price is expected to result in an equiproprotional rise in future price. If rise in expected future price is more than/less than proportional to current price rise, expectation elasticity is greater / less than one.

Demand Forecasting

"Demand forecasting is an estimate of sales in monetary or physical units for a specified future period under a proposed marketing plan or programme and under an assumed set of economic and other forces outside the unit for which the forecast is made."

Steps Involved in Forecasting

The following steps are necessary to have an efficient forecast of demand :

Step I. ***Identification of objective.*** It is necessary to be clear about what does one want to get from the forecast. The purpose of the exercise may be the estimation of one or more than one aspect, like quantity and composition of demand, price to be quoted, sales planning, inventory control, etc. The approach to the problem will accordingly differ.

Step II. ***Determining the nature of goods under consideration.*** Different category of goods have their own distinctive demand patterns. It is, therefore, necessary to determine the class in which the good falls; these being broadly classified as the capital goods, consumer durables and non-durables. This will help us in identifying the approach of the forecasting exercise and in determining the variables to be considered for forecasting.

Step III. ***Selecting a proper method of forecasting.*** The selection of an appropriate method of forecasting is related to the objective of forecasting, type of data available, period for which the forecast is to be made, etc. For example, if the data shows cyclic fluctuations, the use of linear trend will not be suitable. Similarly, general trend may be more useful for long-run forecasting, while seasonal patterns will be more important for the short-run forecasts.

Step IV. ***Interpretation of results.*** Mere preparation of forecasts does not lead the management anywhere. Interpretation of results is of equal importance. Efficiency of a forecast depends, to a large extent, upon the efficiency in the interpretation of its results. Most of the times, the forecasted results are to be well-supported by the background factors (like government policy, general business environment, international economic and political scene, etc.), which have not entered the exercise of forecasting. Further, we need to frequently revise the forecasts in the light of changing circumstances because forecasts are, in the first instance, made on the assumption of continuation of past events.

Factors Affecting Demand Forecasting

(1) Period of estimating
(2) Level of forecasting
(3) Adjustment
(4) Specific factors
(5) Age of commodity
(6) Nature of commodity

Methods of Demand Forecasting

(1) Evolutionary Method
(2) Substitute Method
(3) Growth Curve Method
(4) Opinion Polling Method
(5) Sales Experience Approach
(6) Correlation Method
(7) Controlled Experiments
(8) Economic Indicators Method

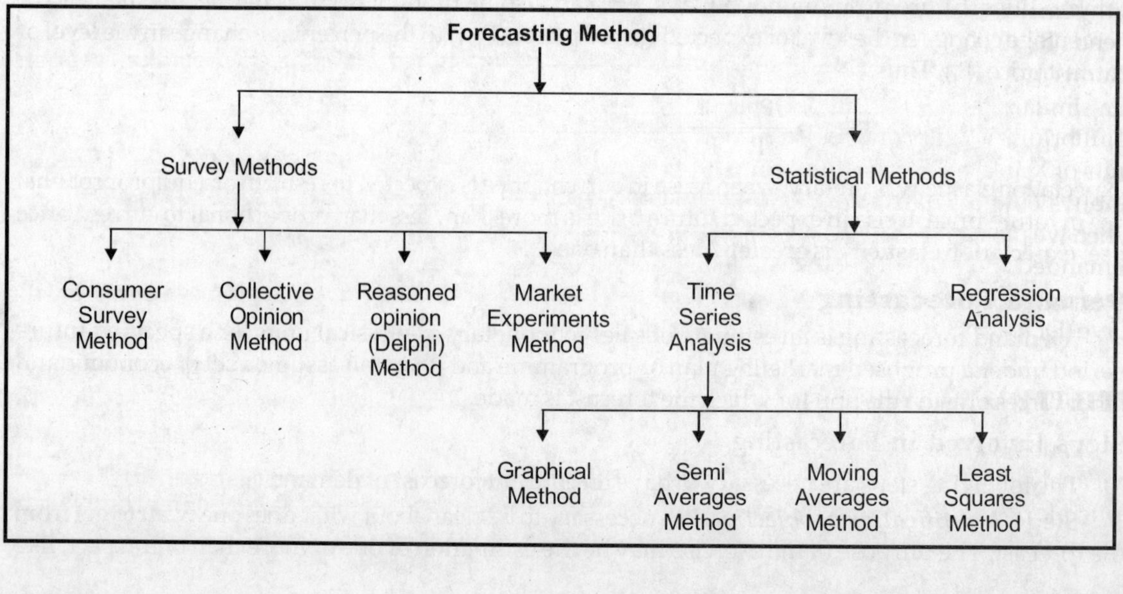

CURVE ANALYSIS

An indifference curve is defined as a curve showing different combinations of two goods which represents equal satisfaction to the consumer. The consumer is indifferent in his choice out of the different points on the same curve.

Properties of indifference Curves

(i) Indifference curves slope downward from the left to the right.
(ii) Indifference curves are convex to the origin.
(iii) Indifference curves never intersect each other i.e., they are parallel to one another.
(iv) The higher the indifference curve, the greater the satisfaction.
(v) Indifference curve never touch any axis.
(vi) Indifference curves need not to be parallel to each other.

Indifference Curve Analysis

This approach has been developed by the economists like Hicks and Allen. Assuming ordinal measurement of utility and relatedness of goods and relaxing the assumption of constant marginal utility of money, the technique of indifference analysis has been developed.

Derivation of the Demand Curve using Indifference Curve

Let us assume that there is only a single good X and that the consumer has an income of Rs 500 which he can spend on this good. So, the consumer has a choice to spend the entire or a part of his income on good X. As he spends less income he consumes lesser amount of X but saves some money. In the limit, when he spends nothing he gets no X at all. By joining all such combinations of money income and good X, we can get a budget line.

As the price of X declines the budget line shifts outwards from A_1B_1 to A_2B_2 and to A_3B_3. With every shift in the budget line we get a new equilibrium point (E_1, E_2 and E_3). At E_1 the consumer buys 40 units of X and has Rs 100 left with him. In other words, the consumer spends Rs 400 (= Rs 500 – Rs 100) to buy 40 units of X *i.e.*, P_x = Rs 400/40 = Rs 40. In a similar manner we can find that at equilibrium E_2 the consumer buys 50 units of X at P_x = Rs 7; at equilibrium E_3 he buys 60 units of X at price of Rs 5. When we plot combinations of quantity demanded and price of good X and join these points by a line, we get a demand curve (DD).

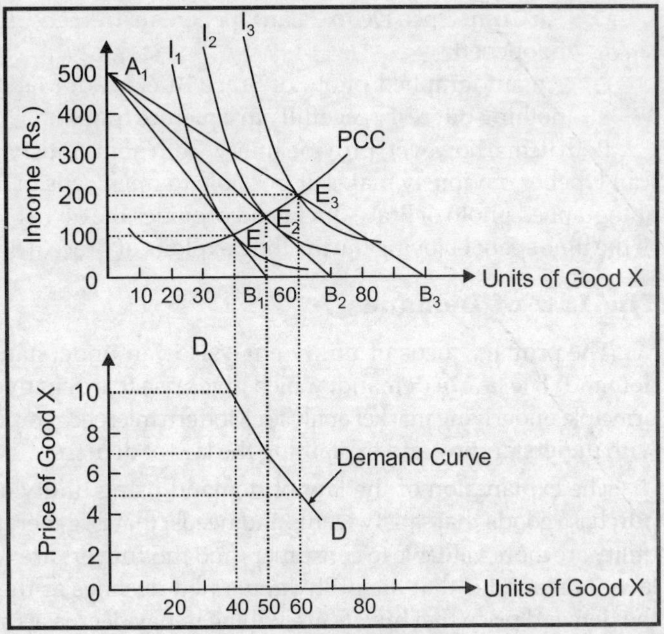

Derivation of a Demand Curve.

UTILITY ANALYSIS

A subset of consumer demand theory that analysis consumer behavior and market demand using total utility and marginal utility. The key principle of utility analysis is the law of diminishing marginal utility, which offers an explanation for the law of demand and the negative slope of the demand curve.

Utility analysis, a subset of consumer demand theory, provides insight into an understanding of market demand and forms a cornerstone of modern microeconomics. In particular, this analysis investigates consumer behavior, especially market purchases, is based on the satisfaction of wants and needs (that is, utility) generated from the consumption of a good.

Utility analysis is primarily taught in introductory courses. A more sophisticated version of consumer demand theory relies on the analysis of indifference curves and is more commonly found at the intermediate course level and above.

Utility and Satisfaction

The primary focus of utility analysis is on the satisfaction of wants and needs obtained by the consumption of goods. This is technically termed as utility. The utility generated from consumption affects the decision to purchase and consume a good.

When used in the analysis of consumer behavior, utility assumes a very precise meaning, which differs from the everyday use of the term. In common use, the term utility means "useful." For example, a "utility" knife is one with many uses, something that is handy to have around. In baseball, a "utility" player can perform quite well at several different positions and is thus useful to have in the team. Moreover, a public "utility" is a company that supplies a useful product, such as electricity, natural gas, or trash collection.

In contrast, the specific economic use of the term utility in the study of consumer behavior means the satisfaction of wants and needs obtained from the consumption of a commodity. The good consumed need not be "useful" in the everyday sense of the term. It only needs to provide satisfaction.

In other words, a frivolous good that has little or no practical use, can provide as much utility as a more useful good.

- An Omni Open Deluxe Can Opener is extremely useful, especially when a sealed can needs to be opened.
- An autographed photo of Brace Brickhead, Medical Detective, is not very useful. It does nothing but rest peacefully in a picture frame.

Both items, however, provide utility. Both items satisfy wants and needs. The Omni Open Deluxe Can Opener obviously makes it possible to open cans of food which satisfy the hunger need. The autographed photo of Brace Brickhead provides the owner with a warm, fuzzy feeling and a reminder of the time spent enjoying the thrilling exploits of Brace Brickhead, Medical Detective.

The Law of Demand

The primary focus of utility analysis is an understanding of market demand and the law of demand. The law of demand, which gives rise to a negatively-sloped demand curve, is an essential principle underlying market analysis. Modern microeconomic theory, among other topics, is concerned with understanding and explaining the law of demand.

The explanation of the law of demand using utility analysis is relatively simple. Consumers purchase goods that satisfy wants and needs, that is, generate utility. Those goods that generate more utility are more valuable to consumers and thus buyers are willing to pay a higher price. The key to the law of demand is that the utility generated declines as the quantity consumed increases. As such, the demand price that buyers are willing to pay decreases as the quantity demanded increases.

Total Utility

Utility analysis begins with the total utility derived from the consumption of different quantities of a good. Total utility is simply a measure of the total satisfaction of wants and needs obtained from the consumption or use of a good or service. It is often convenient to present total utility for a range of quantities in a table such as the one displayed below.

Total Utility

Rides	Total Utility (Utils)
0	0
1	11
2	20
3	27
4	32
5	35
6	36
7	35
8	32

Utility analysis is based on the presumption that the amount of utility generated from the consumption of a good can be explicitly measured. The standard hypothetical measurement unit is "utils."

Suppose, for example, that Sikhar Kumar spends a day riding the Monster Loop Death Plunge roller coaster at the Shady Valley Amusement Park, then records the amount of total utility achieved at the end of each ride. The two columns presented in the table measure the number of rides and the total utility accumulated by Sikhar at the end of each ride (in utils).

- Before his first ride, Sikhar receives no utility. No activity, no utility.
- Sikhar's first ride generates 11 utils of utility.
- The total utility generated if Sikhar takes 8 rides is 32 utils.
- Sikhar's utility increases for the first 6 rides, reaching a high of 36 utils, before declining back to 32 utils for the 8th ride.
- Presumably Sikhar's utility continues to decline after the 8th ride.
- Sikhar obtains the highest total utility from 6 rides on the roller coaster.

The motivation that guides Sikhar's roller coaster riding is to maximize utility, that is, to consume the quantity of the good that generates the highest level of utility. In this example, utility is maximized at 6 rides.

In many situations, however, the consumption of a good faces constraints. Sikhar, for example, might face a time constraint because he plans to attend a live concert of the rock-and-roll group, Live Headless Squirrels, that prevents him from riding more than 4 times. Or he might face an income constraint because the amusement park charges Rs 1 per ride and he has only Rs 5 in his pocket.

In these situations Sikhar, as well as other consumers, might pursue constrained utility maximization. This means achieving the highest possible utility, given certain restrictions that prevent the highest overall level of utility from being achieved.

Marginal Utility

Total utility is used as a starting point for utility analysis. However, a great deal of additional insight is gained from marginal utility. Marginal utility is the additional utility, or extra satisfaction of wants and needs, obtained from the consumption or use of an additional unit of a good or service. Marginal utility is, in other words, the extra satisfaction gained from an extra unit of good.

Marginal utility is specified as:

$$\text{marginal utility} = \frac{\text{change in total utility}}{\text{change in quantity}}$$

If, for example, total utility increases from 20 to 27 utils, then marginal utility is 7 utils.

Marginal Utility

Rides	Total Utility (Utils)	Marginal Utility (Utils)
0	0	
1	11	11
2	20	9
3	27	7
4	32	5
5	35	3
6	36	1
7	35	–1
8	32	–3

The far right column of this table presents marginal utility values derived from each ride Sikhar undertakes. Marginal utility from the first ride is 11 utils. The extra utility generated by the second ride is 9 utils. The third ride provides another 7 utils. The remaining numbers in the right column are interpreted in a similar manner.

Marginal utility provides a direct link between utility analysis and demand. The demand price a buyer is willing to pay for a given good is based on the marginal utility derived from consuming the good. In this example, Sikhar is most likely willing to pay more for the first ride than the fifth ride, in that the first ride generates 11 utils of satisfaction, but the fifth ride generates only 3 utils.

The Law of Diminishing Marginal Utility

A clear pattern is displayed by the marginal utility values in the far right column. Marginal utility decreases as Sikhar takes more rides. This decreasing marginal utility reflects the law of diminishing marginal utility. The law of diminishing marginal utility states that marginal utility, or the extra utility obtained from consuming a good, decreases as the quantity consumed increases. In essence, each additional good consumed is less satisfying than the previous one. This law is particularly important for insight into market demand and the law of demand.

If each additional unit of a good is less satisfying, then a buyer is willing to pay less. As such, the demand price declines. This inverse law of demand relation between demand price and quantity demanded is a direct implication of the law of diminishing marginal utility.

UTILITY MAXIMIZATION

The process or goal of obtaining the highest level of utility from the consumption of goods or services. The goal of maximizing utility is a key assumption underlying consumer behavior studied in consumer demand theory. Consumers are assumed to make choices, especially concerning the purchase of goods, such that they obtain the highest possible level of satisfaction. Utility maximization can be achieved at the peak of the total utility curve.

Utility maximization is the guiding notion underlying consumer choices analyzed with consumer demand theory and utility analysis. It makes sense to think that people are generally motivated to do what is best for them, to purchase the most satisfying goods, to make the decisions that do more good than harm, to improve their overall living standards and well-being, that is, to maximize their utility.

Working through the logical consequences of this assumption, when combined with other principles of consumer behavior especially the law of diminishing marginal utility, makes it possible to gain insight into such things: market demand and the law of demand.

Utility Analysis

Roller Coaster Utility

Rides	Total Utility (Util)
0	0
1	11
2	20
3	27
4	32
5	35
6	36
7	35
8	32

The accompanying table can be used to illustrate utility maximization. The numbers indicate the total utility obtained by Sikhar Kumar while riding the Monster Loop Death Plunge roller coaster at the Shady Valley Amusement Park. The right-hand column is the accumulated satisfaction Sikhar receives from riding the Monster Loop Death Plunge roller coaster 8 times during his day at the amusement park.

The numbers indicate that Sikhar receives the greatest total utility, 36 utils, by riding the Monster Loop Death Plunge roller coaster 6 times. Taking 5 trips around the Monster Loop Death Plunge roller coaster track generates only 35 utils. Likewise, 7 rides generate only 35 utils. Maximum utility comes from 6 rides and only 6 rides. Anything else comes in less.

The Peak of the Curve

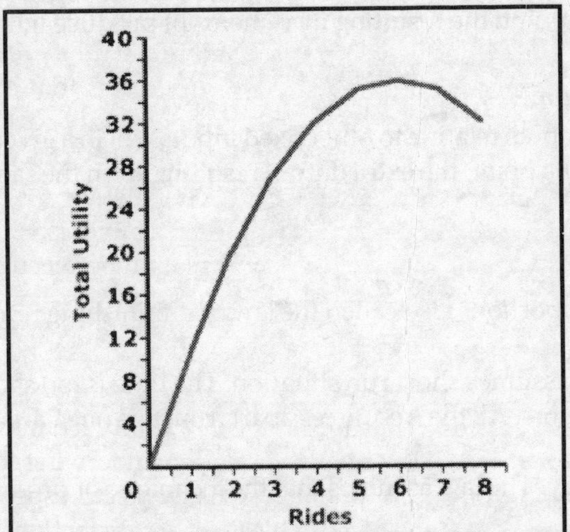

Total Utility Curve

Utility maximization can be visually identified with a total utility curve, such as the one presented in this exhibit. In this case the maximum level of utility obtained by Sikhar riding the Monster Loop Death Plunge roller coaster is relatively obvious. The total utility curve reaches its highest point for 6 roller coaster rides. The curve increases up to the sixth ride, then declines for subsequent rides.

UTILITY MEASUREMENT

A quantification of the satisfaction of wants and needs achieved through the consumption of goods and services. In principle, utility measurement can take one of two forms: (1) cardinal, which is based on numerical values (1, 2, 3, etc.) and (2) ordinal which is based on rankings (first, second, third, etc.). While the hypothetical instructional analysis of utility relies on cardinal utility, ordinal utility is a more realistic way to measure satisfaction.

Utility measurement provides a basis for discussing the satisfaction of wants and needs derived from consumption, which then enables an understanding of the role utility plays in market demand.

However, as the study of consumer demand theory progressed, economists realized that cardinal utility was both unlikely and unneeded. Ordinal utility, the ranking or preferences, was not only more realistic, it also provided a sufficient theoretical basis for analyzing the connection between utility and market demand.

LAW OF VARIABLE PROPORTIONS

There were three laws of returns mentioned in the history of economic thought up till Alfred Marshall's time. These laws were the laws of increasing returns, diminishing returns and constant returns. Dr. Marshall was of the view that the law of diminishing returns applies to agriculture and the law of increasing returns to industry. Much time was wasted in discussion of this issue. However, it was later on recognized that there are not three laws of production. It is only one law of production which has three phases, increasing, diminishing and negative production. This general law of production was named as the ***Law of Variable Proportions or the Law of Non-Proportional Returns.***

The Law of Variable Proportions which is the new name of the famous ***law of Diminishing Returns*** has been defined by **Stigler** in the following words:

"As equal increments of one input are added, the inputs of other productive services being held constant, beyond a certain point, the resulting increments of produce will decrease *i.e.*, the marginal product will diminish".

According to **Samuelson**

"An increase in some inputs relative to other fixed inputs will in a given state of technology cause output to increase, but after a point, the extra output resulting from the same addition of extra inputs will become less".

Assumptions

The law of variable proportions also called the law of diminishing returns holds good under the following assumptions:

(i) **Short run.** The law assumes short run situation. The time is too short for a firm to change the quantity of fixed factors. All the, resources apart from this one variable, are held unchanged in quantity and quality.

(ii) **Constant technology.** The law assumes that the technique of production remains unchanged during production.

(iii) **Homogeneous factors.** Each factor unit is assumed to be identical in amount and quality.

Explanation and Example

The law of variable proportions is, now explained with the help of table and graph.

Schedule:

Fixed Inputs (Land & Capital)	Variable Resource (labor)	Total Produce (TP Quintals)	Marginal (Quintals)	Product MP Stage or Phase	(Average Product (AP Quintals)
30	1	10	10	Increasing marginal	10
30	2	25	15	return	12.5
30	3	37	12	Diminishing marginal	12.3
30	4	47	10	returns	11.8
30	5	55	8		11.0
30	6	60	5		10.0
30	7	63	3		9.0
30	8	63	0	Negative marginal	7.9
30	9	62	–1	returns	6.8

In the table above, it is assumed that a farmer has only 30 acres of land for cultivation. The investment on it in the form of tubewells, machinery etc., (capital) is also fixed. Thus land and capital with the farmer is fixed and labor is the variable resource.

As the farmer increases units of labor from one to two to the amount of other fixed resources (land and capital), the marginal as well as average product increases. The total product also increase at an increasing rate from 10 to 25 quintals. It is the stage of increasing returns.

The stage of increasing returns with the employment of more labor does not last long. It is shown in the table that with the employment of 3rd labor at the farm, the marginal product and the average product (AP) both fall but marginal product (MP) falls more speedily than the average product (AP). The fall in MP and AP continues as more men are put on the farm.

The decrease, however, remains positive up to the 7th labor employed. On the employment of 7th worker, the total production remains constant at 63 quintals. The marginal product is zero, if more men are employed the marginal product becomes negative. It is the stage of negative returns. We here find the behavior of marginal product (MP), it shows three stages. In the first stage, it increases, in the 2nd it continues to fall and in the 3rd stage it becomes negative.

Three Stages of the Law:

There are three phases or stages of production, as determined by the law of variable proportions: (i) Increasing returns (ii) Diminishing returns (iii) Negative returns

Graph. These stages can be explained with the help of graph below:

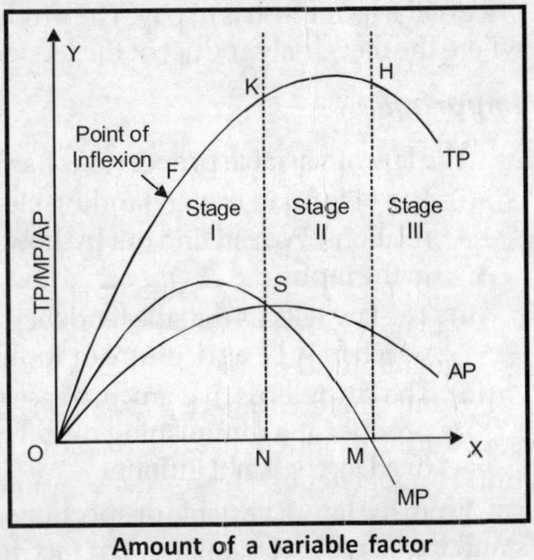

Amount of a variable factor

(i) **Stage of Increasing Returns.** The first stage of the law of variable proportions is generally called the stage of increasing returns. In this stage as a variable resource (labor) is added to fixed inputs of other resources, the total product increases up to a point at an increasing rate as is shown in figure.

The total product from the origin to the point K on the slope of the total product curve increases at an increasing rate. From point K onward, during the stage II, the total product no doubt goes on rising but its slope is declining. This means that from point K onward, the total product increases at a diminishing rate. In the first stage, marginal product curve of a variable factor rises in a part and then falls. The average product curve rises throughout and remains below the MP curve.

Causes of Initial Increasing Returns:

The phase of increasing returns starts when the quantity of a fixed factor is abundant relative to the quantity of the variable factor. As more and more units of the variable factor are added to the constant quantity of the fixed factor, it is more intensively and effectively used. This causes the production to increase at a rapid rate. Another reason of increasing returns is that the fixed factor initially taken is indivisible. As more units of the variable factor are employed to work on it, output increases greatly due to full and effective utilization of the variable factor.

(ii) **Stage of Diminishing Returns.** This is the most important stage in the production function. In stage 2, the total production continues to increase at a diminishing rate until it reaches its maximum point (H) where the 2nd stage ends. In this stage both the marginal product (MP) and average product of the variable factor are diminishing but are positive.

Causes of Diminishing Returns:

The 2nd phase of the law occurs when the fixed factor becomes inadequate relative to the quantity of the variable factor. As more and more units of a variable factor are employed, the marginal and average product decline. Another reason of diminishing returns in the production function is that the fixed indivisible factor is being worked too hard. It is being used in non-optimal proportion with the variable factor, Mrs. J. Robinson still goes deeper and says that the diminishing returns occur because the factors of production are imperfect substitutes of one another.

(iii) **Stage of Negative Returns.** In the 3rd stage, the total production declines. The TP, curve slopes downward (From point H onward). The MP curve falls to zero at point M and then is negative. It goes below the X axis with the increase in the use of variable factor (labor).

Causes of Negative Returns:

The 3rd phase of the law starts when the number of a variable factor becomes too excessive relative to the fixed factors. A producer cannot operate in this stage because total production declines with the employment of additional labor.

A rational producer will always seek to produce in stage 2 where MP and AP of the variable factor are diminishing. At which particular point, the producer will decide to produce depends upon the price of the factor he has to pay. The producer will employ the variable factor (say labor) up to the point where the marginal product of the labor equals the given wage rate in the labor market.

Importance

The law of variable proportions has vast general applicability, briefly explained below :

(i) It is helpful in understanding clearly the process of production. It explains the input output relations. We can find out by-how much the total product will increase as a result of an increase in the inputs.

(ii) The law tells us that the tendency of diminishing returns is found in all sectors of the economy which may be agriculture or industry.

(iii) The law tells us that any increase in the units of variable factor will lead to increase in the total product at a diminishing rate. The elasticity of the substitution of the variable factor for the fixed factor is not infinite.

From the law of variable proportions, it may not be understood that there is no hope for raising the standard of living of mankind. The fact, however, is that we can suspend the operation of diminishing returns by continually improving the technique of production through the progress in science and technology.

RETURNS TO SCALE OR LAW OF RETURNS TO SCALE

It is a long run law that studies the changes in output, when all the factors of production or inputs are increased together. The study of changes in output as a result of changes in the scale forms the subject matter of 'returns to scale'.

The law of return to scale has certain assumptions:

- Technique of production is unchanged.
- All units 'of factors are homogenous.
- Returns are measured in physical terms.

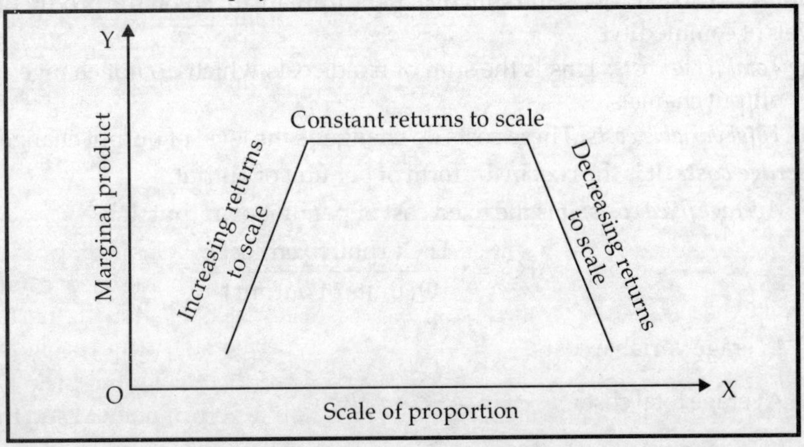

The Laws of Returns to Scale

It also has the following three stages:

1. **Stage of Increasing Returns to Scale (IRS).** If the increase in all the factors leads to more than proportionate increase in output, returns to scale are said to be increasing.

   Mathematically,

   Initial Production $(Q_x) = f(L, K)$

   New Production, $(3Q_x) > f(2L, 2K)$

   Here, f = Functional relationship

   L = Units of labour

   K = Units of capital

   Q_x = Quantity of good X

2. **Stage of Constant Returns to Scale (CRS).** If all the factors of production are increased in a given proportion and the output increases in the same proportion, returns to scale are said to be constant.

   Mathematically,

   Initial Production $(Q) = f(L, K)$

   New Production $(2Q_x) = f(2L, 2K)$

3. **Stage of Diminishing or Decreasing Returns to Scale (DRS).** If the increase in all the factors leads to a less than proportionate increase in output, returns to scale are decreasing.

Mathematically,

Initial Production $(Q_x) = f(L, K)$ {DRS}

New Production $(1.5Q_x) < f(2L, 2K)$

THEORY OF COST

The quantity of output supplied in the market at a certain price will depend upon its cost of production. So many factors of production like labourer, building, machinery etc. are required for the production of any commodity, the inputs are not available for use in the production process unless they are paid their price, the price is paid in the form of rent, wages, interest. The sum total of these payments is called the cost of production.

1. **Short run costs:**

   (i) ***Total Cost.*** Total cost is the sum of expenditure incurred on the production of various levels of commodity.

   (a) *Total fixed costs:* This is the sum of fixed costs which do not change as the level of output changes.

   (b) *Total variable costs:* These costs do change as the level of output changes.

   (ii) ***Average costs.*** It is the cost in the form of per unit of output.

   (a) *Average fixed costs:* It is the fixed cost of per unit of output. It is

$$AFC = \frac{TFC(\text{Total fixed cost})}{Q(\text{units of output})}$$

   (b) Average variable costs $= \dfrac{TVC}{Q}$

   (c) Average total costs $= AFC + AVC$

   or $ATC = \dfrac{TC}{Q}$

   (iii) ***Marginal costs*** = It is the change in the total cost resulting from change in the level of output by one unit.

2. **Long run costs:**

   (i) ***Long run total cost:*** It is the least possible cost of production at any given level of output when all factors are variable.

   (ii) ***Long run average cost*** $= \dfrac{LTC}{Q} = \dfrac{\text{Long run total cost}}{\text{Output}}$

   (iii) ***Long run Marginal Cost*** – It is the addition to total cost caused by producing one more unit of output.

REVENUE

We know that price is determined by the interaction of demand and supply. The market forces of demand and supply determine the output of an individual firm. The market demand for a product determines the receipts of the firm from selling its output. These receipts are known as 'revenue' of the firm. According to Dooley, 'the revenue of a firm is its sales, receipts or income."

Concepts

1. **Total revenue.** The total income received by seller from selling a given amount of output is called total revenue.

$$TR = P \times Q$$

where,

TR = Total Revenue

P = Price

Q = No. of units sold.

2. **Average revenue.** It is the revenue per unit of the commodity sold.

$$AR = \frac{TR}{Q}$$

where,

AR = Average Revenue

TR = Total Revenue

Q = No. of units sold

3. **Marginal Revenue.** It is the addition of total revenue made by the addition of one unit to the total output.

$$MR = TR_n - TR_{n-1}$$

SHORT-RUN AND LONG-RUN COST CURVES

Short-run Cost Curves

In the short-run, a firm will adjust output to demand by varying the variable factors. If all the factors of production can be used in varying proportions, it means that the scale of operations of the firm can be changed. Each time, the scale of operations is changed, a new short-run cost curve will have to be drawn for the firm such as SAC', SAC" and SAC" in the next diagram (Fig. A).

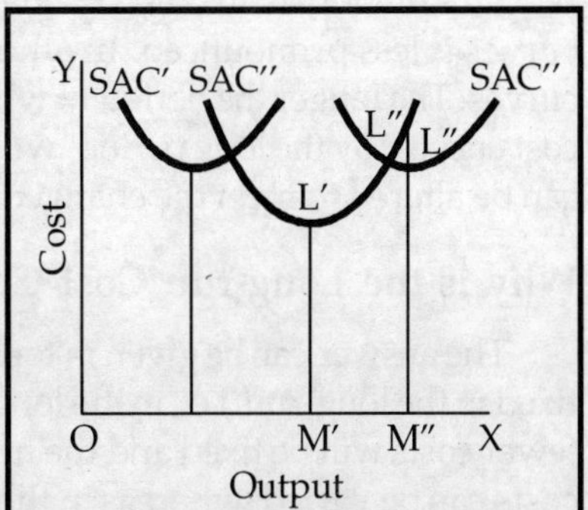

Fig. A Short-run Cost Curves

To begin with, let us suppose that the firm has the short-run cost curve SAC ". In this case, the optimum output will be OM'. Now, if it is desired to increase the output to OM" in the short-run, it can be obtained at the average cost M"L" along the short-run cost curve SAC", because in the short-run, the scale of operations is fixed. But, in the long run, a new and bigger plant can be built on which OM " is the optimum output. That is, the firm has now a short-run average cost curve SAC "', and by increasing the scale of its operations, the firm can produce the OM" output at a cost of M "L"' instead of M "L".

Thus, it will be seen that, at any scale of operations in the short-run, a firm will have regions of rising and falling costs. But, in the long-run, the firm can produce on a completely different cost curves to the left (i.e., SAC') or right (i.e., SAC"') of the original cost curve (i.e., SAC"). For each different scale represented by a different short-run cost curve, there will be an output where the average cost is the minimum. This is the optimum output.

Long-run Average Cost Curve

In the diagram (Fig. B), SAC, SAC, and SAC, are the short-run cost curves corresponding to the different scales of operations. In each case, the firm in question will be producing the desired output at the lowest cost. For example, OM "output is produced at PM" in the scale of operations represented by the curve SAC OM will be produced on SAC, and so on.

It should be clearly understood that only in the long-run can the scale of operations be altered; in the short-run, it will be fixed, and the average cost of output above or below the optimum level will necessarily rise along the short-run cost curve in question, whether it be SAC, SAC2 and SAC3. A long-run average cost will show what the long-run cost of producing each output will be. It will be seen, in the Fig. B that the short-run average cost curve SAC, has a lower minimum point than either the curves SAC, and SAC3. The optimum output of the firm is obtained at OM.

The long-run average cost curve LAC is a tangent to all the short-run cost curves SAC, SAC2 and SAC. The LAC curve will, therefore, be U-shaped like the short-run cost curves, but its U-shape will be less pronounced than that of the short-run cost curves. It will be flatter. That is why the long-run cost curve is called an 'Envelope', because it envelops all the short-run cost curves.

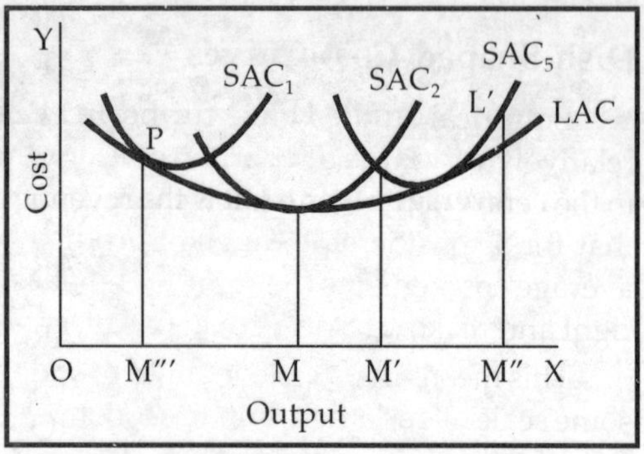

Fig. B LAC Curve: An Envelope

The cost curves, whether short-run or long-run, are U-shaped because the cost of production first starts falling as output is increased owing to the various economies of scale. But after touching the lowest point at the optimum output level, it starts rising, and goes on rising if production is continued beyond the optimum level.

This obviously makes a U-shape. But, as we have said already, the U-shape of the long-run cost curves is less pronounced. In other words, the long-run average costs are flatter than the short-run curves. The longer the period to which the curve relates, the less pronounced will be the U-shape of the cost curves. By the long period, we mean the period during which the size and organisation of the firm can be altered to meet the changed conditions.

Why is the Long-run Cost Curves Flatter?

The answer can be given in terms of fixed and variable costs. We have said before that no costs are fixed in the long-run, i.e., in the long run all costs are variable. In other words, the longer the period, the fewer costs will be fixed and the more costs will be variable. That is, in the long period, the total fixed costs can be varied, whereas in the short period, this amount is fixed absolutely.

In the short-run, if output is reduced, average cost will rise because the fixed costs will work out at a higher figure. But, in the long-run, fixed costs can be reduced if the output is continued at the low level. Hence, average fixed cost will be lower in the long than in the short run.

The variable costs will not rise as sharply in the long-run as in the short-run, because in the long-run, the size of the firm can be increased to deal more economically with an increased output. Thus, LAC curves are flatter than the short-run cost curves, because, in the long-run, the average fixed cost will be lower, and variable costs will not rise to sharply as in the short period.

Why are Long-Run Cost Curves U-Shaped?

We have explained above that the long-run cost-curves are U-Shaped. That is, as output is increased, the cost per unit falls, then it reaches a minimum after which it starts ascending so that it takes the shape of U.

How do we account for this U-shape?

The reason is that the cost curve falls on account of the various economies of scale. But when the firm has expanded too much, economies are changed into diseconomies and the cost curve starts rising.

Dish-Shaped Cost Curves

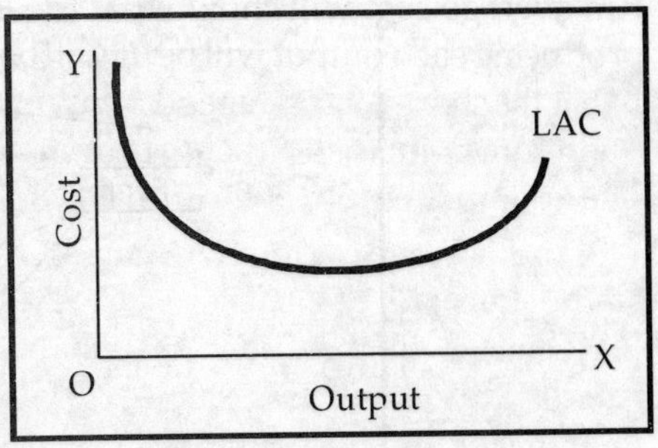

Dish-Shaped LAC Curves

Empirical studies have further revealed that there is relatively very large flat portion or a large horizontal region in the centre of the long-run average cost curve. This means that for a considerable range of production, the long-run average cost remains the same and then it moves up at the right and making a sort of dish or saucer.

This means that the economies of scale are exhausted at some scale of operation, but diseconomies do not occur yet. But after the scale is enlarged beyond a point, dis-economies emerge and bring about a rise in the long-run average cost and thus give the curve a saucer or dish shape.

L-shaped Cost Curves

Recently some economists have put forward the view based on recent empirical studies that the cost curves take the shape of 'L' and not 'U'. According to them, the shape of the long-run cost curve will be something as is given in Fig. C.

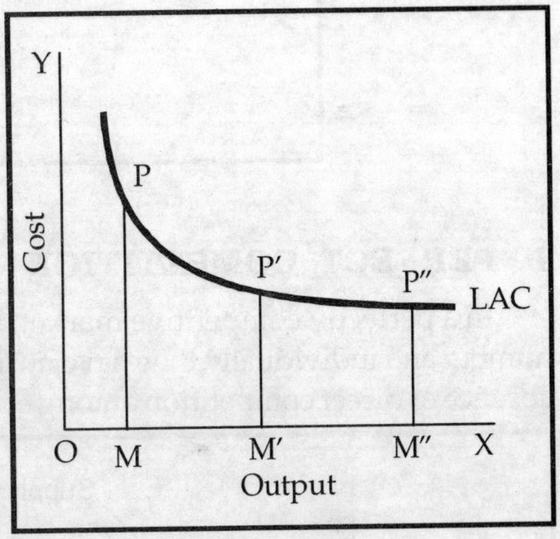

Fig. C L-shaped Cost Curves

In this diagram (Fig. C), first OM is output produced and PM is the average cost of production including both the fixed and variable costs. When the output is expanded to OM", the cost is P'M', and when output is further increased to OM", the cost is P"M" which is almost equal to P'M'.

From this point onwards, the cost per unit is stabilized so that, whatever the output, the cost per unit remains practically the same and the LAC comes to have L-shape. This means that the cost first falls over a range of output, and then it neither rises nor falls but remains flat.

The following two reasons are given in support of the L-shape:

(i) Rapid technical progress brings about a sharp decline in unit cost up to a certain point and then stabilizes it.

(ii) With lapse of time the producer learns to produce at lower cost.

PRICE DETERMINATION IN DIFFERENT MARKET SITUATIONS

According to Prof. Sidgwick, "A market is a body of persons in such commercial relations that each can easily acquaint himself with the rate at which certain kinds of exchange of goods and services are from time to time made by the other."

Market structure refers to the number and size distribution of buyers and sellers in the market for goods or services.

A market consists of all firms and individuals who are willing and able to buy or sell a particular product. This includes firms and individuals currently engaged in buying and selling and potential entrants. Markets are traditionally divided into four basic classifications, namely :

(1) Perfect competition
(2) Perfect monopoly
(3) Monopolistic competition
(4) Oligopoly

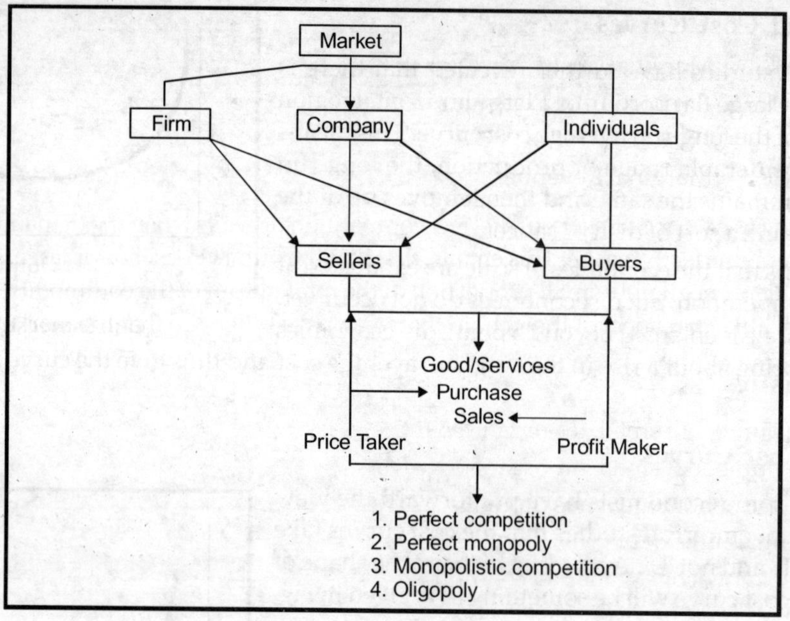

Market Structure

1. PERFECT COMPETITION

In a perfectly competitive market, the buyers and sellers have no rivalry since they are in large number and individually they have no influence over the price of the commodity. There is a complete absence of direct competition among economic group. In this market, the seller is a price taker.

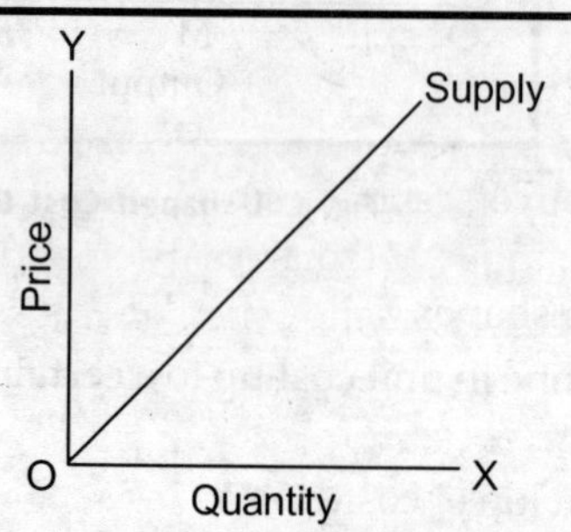

Supply Curve in Perfect Competition.

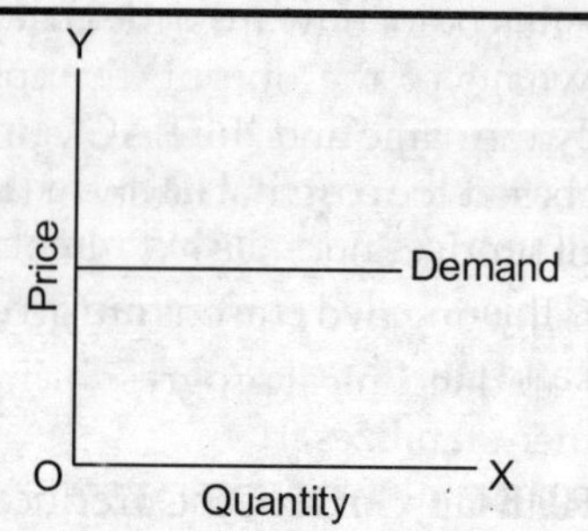

Demand Curve in Perfect Competition.

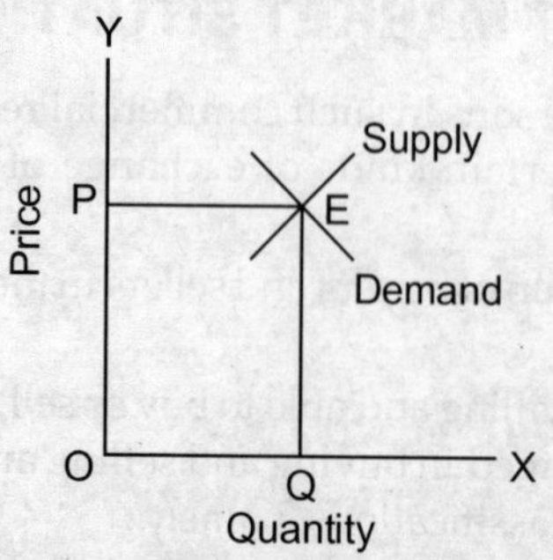

Market Price determination under Perfect Competition.

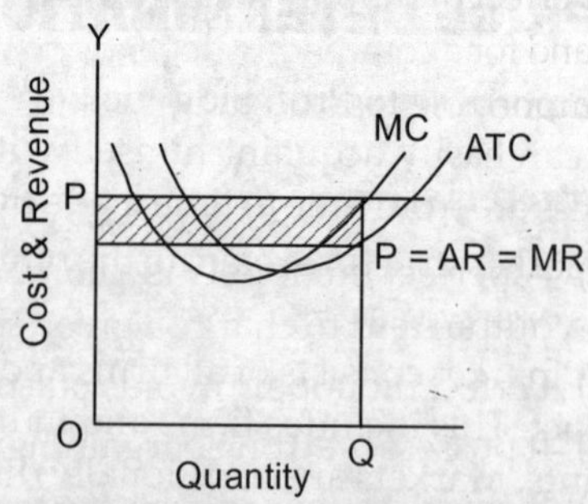

Price Output Competition.

where

MC = Marginal Cost
ATC = Average Total Revenue
P = Price
MR = Marginal Revenue

According to *Mrs. Joan Robinson*, "Perfect competition prevails when the demand for the output of each producer is perfectly elastic. This entails, first that the number of sellers is large, so that the output of any one seller is negligibly small proportion of the total output of the commodity, and second, that buyers are all alike in respect of their choice between rival sellers, so that the market is perfect."

Characteristics

(i) Large number of small, un-organised firms
(ii) Large number of small, un-organised buyers.
(iii) Existence of homogeneous products
(iv) Free entry and exit of firms.
(v) Perfect knowledge of market conditions.
(vi) The goods and services as well as resources are to be perfectly mobile between firms.
(vii) All the firms should enjoy easy access to the market.
(viii) There should be absence of government or artificial restriction on the working of the firms.

Pricing under Perfect Competition

Price under perfect competition is determined by the laws of supply and demand. The action and the inter-action of the forces of demand and supply determine price under perfect competition. Prices will be fixed at a point where the supply and demand are at an equilibrium, and this equilibrium will change by changes in the forces of supply and demand. The demand side is governed by the law of demand based on marginal utility of the commodity to the buyers; and the supply side is governed by the cost of production. So to say, the interaction of marginal supply and marginal demand decides the price and this is called equilibrium price and at this point, the buyers and sellers are satisfied and the demand and supply are equal.

2. PERFECT MONOPOLY

Perfect monopoly means absence of competition. Under monopoly the cross elasticity is zero. The demand for a commodity depends on the prices of related goods, which are substitutes and complements. The monopolist is said to be the king of the market. He rules the market with his price.

Characteristics

(i) A perfect monopoly is a combination of several producers and they agree to produce a given output and to charge a given price.
(ii) Perfect monopoly avoids cut-throat competition and its attendant evils.
(iii) It possesses strong bargaining powers to purchase commodities at low prices.
(iv) It enjoys the benefit of large scale marketing.

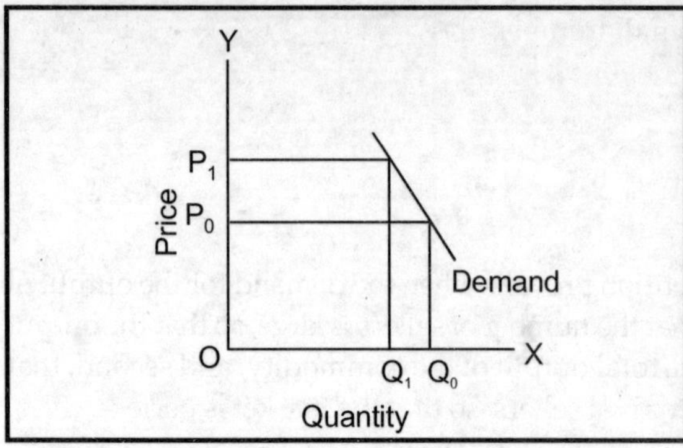

The Firm's Demand Curve under Monopoly

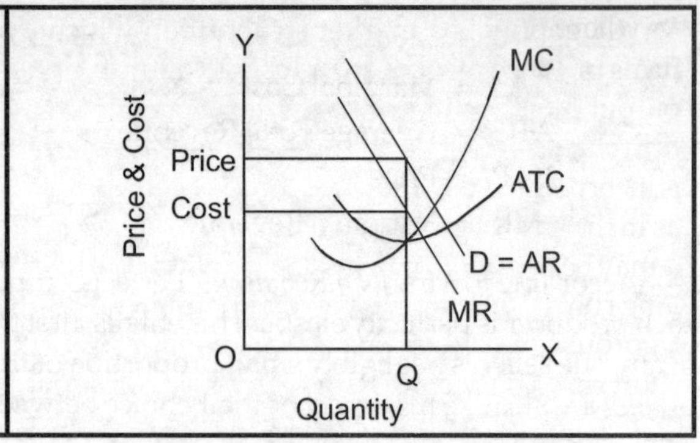

Price Output Decision under Monopoly

3. MONOPOLISTIC COMPETITION

Monopolistic competition refers to markets in which there are a large number of firms competing supplying product which consumers believe are close but not complete substitutes. Monopolistic competition is analogous to perfect competition except for the element of product differentiation.

According to Leftwithch, " Monopolistic competition is a market situation in which there are many sellers of a particular product but the product of each seller is in some way differentiated in the minds of consumers from the product of every other seller."

Monopolistic competition is a market structure quite similar to pure competition but distinguished from it by the fact that consumers perceive difference among the products of different firms. Firms have some control over the prices at which they sell their products. As in pure competition, above normal profit are attainable only in the short run.

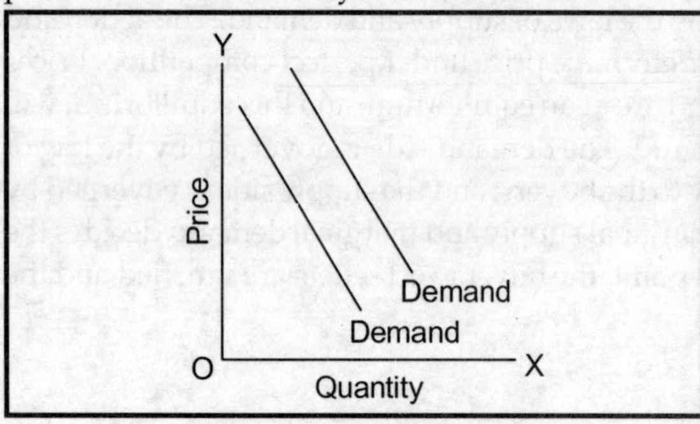

Relationship between Product Cost and Marginal Revenue.

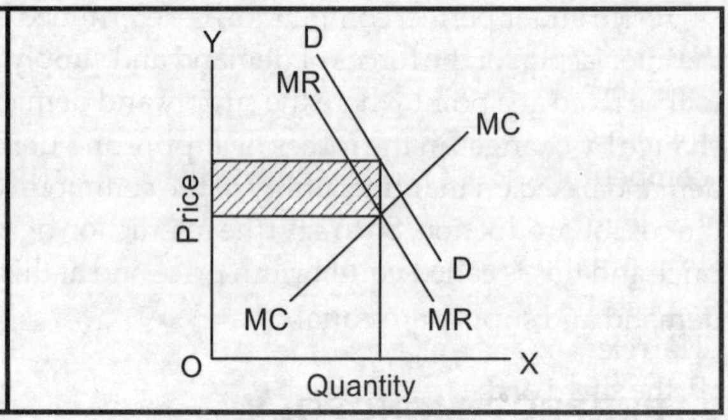

Equality of Marginal Cost and Marginal Revenue.

Characteristics

(1) Existence of large number of firms

(2) No close substitutes

(3) Freedom of entry and exit

(4) Sales promotion or selling cost.

(5) Inelastic demand curve

(6) Complete control over the supply of commodity

(7) Profit in the long period

(8) A large number of buyers

4. OLIGOPOLY

Monopolistic competition requires a large number of competitors and free entry and exit. Many real-world markets today, however are made up of a small number of suppliers and entry into and exit from the industry are restricted. Oligopoly is the term used to describe such markets.

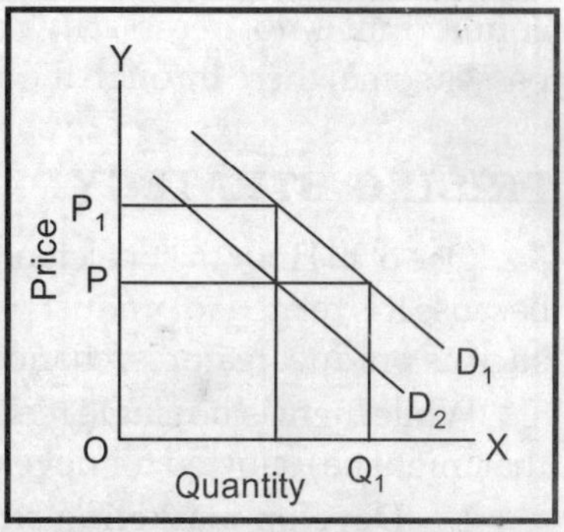

Demand Curve under Oligopoly.

Oligopoly is a market structure in which a small number of firms produce most of an industry's output. Under oligopoly, price output decisions of firms are interdependent in the sense that if one firm changes its price, the other firms may react, and this knowledge is incorporated into the price/output decision problem. In oligopoly, as in the case of monopoly, barriers to entry can be substantial and it may be possible for firms to earn above normal profits, even in the long run. In other instances, competition among a few firms can be rigorous, and above normal profits may only be observed in the short run. The demand curve under oligopoly is given in the figure.

Characteristics

(1) Few sellers
(2) Homogeneous or Differentiated products
(3) Conflicting attitudes of firms
(4) Indeterminatedness of demand curve
(5) Mutual Interdependence
(6) Advertisement
(7) Sale promotion
(8) Price rigidity
(9) Elements of monopoly
(10) Earriers to entry.

Sweezy's Kinky Demand Model

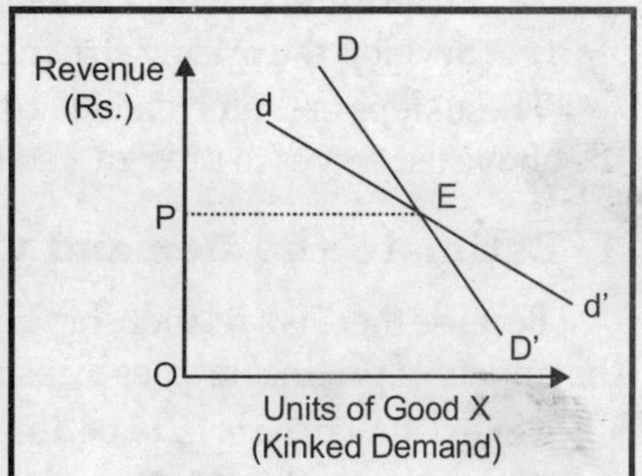

The assumption behind the theory of kinked demand is that each oligopolist will act and react in a way that keeps conditions tolerable for all members of the industry. Such a situation is most likely to occur where products are quite similar and, therefore, their prices also the same. If one firm is selling at a price lower than that of its competitors, these competitors will be compelled to reduce their prices to match this firm's price on the other hand, if one firm decides to sell at a higher price its competitors do not react by raising their prices.

Figure shows the individual demand curve dd′ and the firm's market share curve DD′ intersecting at E. It is believed that if an oligopolist reduces his price he expects his competitors to follow suit, while no competitor will follow him when he raises the price. The relevant demand curve for the firm is, therefore, dED′ (with a kink at E). For price reduction below P, the share of the market-demand curve, D′E, is relevant as the countermoves by the rivals will keep the market share of the firm constant. And, for price increases above P, the firm goes alone and, therefore, the relevant demand curve for the firm is its own demand curve dE. Such a kinked demand curve is shown in second figure. The upper part of the demand curve has a higher price elasticity than the lower part. Due to the kink in the demand curve of the oligopolist, his MR curve is discontinuous at the level of output corresponding to the kink. The MR curve in second figure has two parts : the part dA corresponding to the upper part of the demand curve (dE) and BMR corresponding to the lower part of demand curve, ED′.

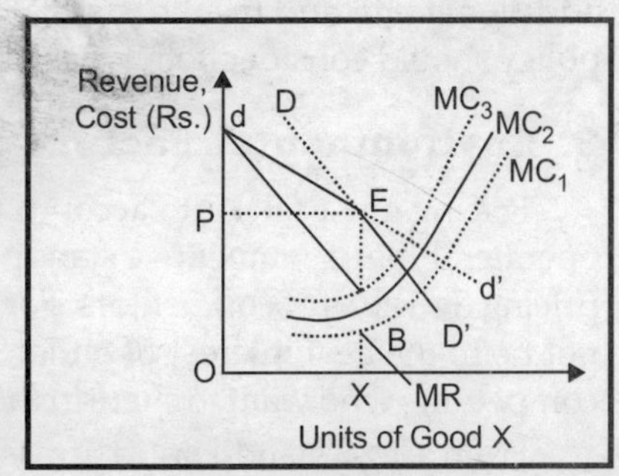

Stickiness of Price.

In second figure, equilibrium is defined by the point at the kink (E), because at any point to the left of the kink MC is below MR, while to the right of the kink MC is higher than MR. Thus, total profit is maximised at the point of the kink. However, the equilibrium is not necessarily defined by the intersection of the MC and MR curves. In general MC passes somewhere through the discontinuous section AB of the MR curve.

PRICING STRATEGY

One of the four major elements of the marketing mix is price. Pricing is an important strategic issue because it is related to product positioning. Furthermore, pricing affects other marketing mix elements such as product features, channel decisions, and promotion.

While there is no single recipe to determine pricing, the following is a general sequence of steps that might be followed for developing the pricing of a new product:

1. **Develop marketing strategy** - perform marketing analysis, segmentation, targeting, and positioning.
2. **Make marketing mix decisions** - define the product, distribution, and promotional tactics.
3. **Estimate the demand curve** - understand how quantity demanded varies with price.
4. **Calculate cost** - include fixed and variable costs associated with the product.
5. **Understand environmental factors** - evaluate likely competitor actions, understand legal constraints, etc.
6. **Set pricing objectives** - for example, profit maximization, revenue maximization, or price stabilization (status quo).
7. **Determine pricing** - using information collected in the above steps, select a pricing method, develop the pricing structure, and define discounts.

These steps are interrelated and are not necessarily performed in the above order. Nonetheless, the above list serves to present a starting framework. Some of these factors are explained below :

1. Estimate the Demand Curve

Because there is a relationship between price and quantity demanded, it is important to understand the impact of pricing on sales by estimating the demand curve for the product.

For existing products, experiments can be performed at prices above and below the current price in order to determine the price elasticity of demand. Inelastic demand indicates that price increases might be feasible.

2. Calculate Costs

If the firm has decided to launch the product, there is likely at least a basic understanding of the costs involved, otherwise, there might be no profit to be made. The unit cost of the product sets the lower limit of what the firm might charge, and determines the profit margin at higher prices.

The total unit cost of a producing a product is composed of the variable cost of producing each additional unit and fixed costs that are incurred regardless of the quantity produced. The pricing policy should consider both types of costs.

3. Environmental Factors

Pricing must take into account the competitive and legal environment in which the company operates. From a competitive standpoint, the firm must consider the implications of its pricing on the pricing decisions of competitors. For example, setting the price too low may risk a price war that may not be in the best interest of either side. Setting the price too high may attract a large number of competitors who want to share in the profits.

From a legal standpoint, a firm is not free to price its products at any level it chooses. For example, there may be price controls that prohibit pricing a product too high. Pricing it too low may be considered predatory pricing or "dumping" in the case of international trade. Offering a different price for different consumers may violate laws against price discrimination. Finally, collusion with competitors to fix prices at an agreed level is illegal in many countries.

4. Pricing Objectives

The firm's pricing objectives must be identified in order to determine the optimal pricing. Common objectives include the following:

(i) **Current profit maximization** - seeks to maximize current profit, taking into account revenue and costs. Current profit maximization may not be the best objective if it results in lower long-term profits.

(ii) **Current revenue maximization** - seeks to maximize current revenue with no regard to profit margins. The underlying objective often is to maximize long-term profits by increasing market share and lowering costs.

(iii) **Maximize quantity** - seeks to maximize the number of units sold or the number of customers served in order to decrease long-term costs as predicted by the experience curve.

(iv) **Maximize profit margin** - attempts to maximize the unit profit margin, recognizing that quantities will be low.

(v) **Quality leadership** - use price to signal high quality in an attempt to position the product as the quality leader.

(vi) **Partial cost recovery** - an organization that has other revenue sources may seek only partial cost recovery.

(vii) **Survival** - in situations such as market decline and overcapacity, the goal may be to select a price that will cover costs and permit the firm to remain in the market. In this case, survival may take a priority over profits, so this objective is considered temporary.

(viii) **Status quo** - the firm may seek price stabilization in order to avoid price wars and maintain a moderate but stable level of profit.

For new products, the pricing objective often is either to maximize profit margin or to maximize quantity (market share). To meet these objectives, skim pricing and penetration pricing strategies often are employed. Joel Dean discussed these pricing policies in his classic HBR article entitled, Pricing Policies for New Products.

Skim pricing attempts to "skim the cream" of the top of the market by setting a high price and selling to those customers who are less price sensitive. Skimming is a strategy used to pursue the objective of profit margin maximization.

Skimming is most appropriate when:

- Demand is expected to be relatively inelastic; that is, the customers are not highly price sensitive.
- Large cost savings are not expected at high volumes, or it is difficult to predict the cost savings that would be achieved at high volume.
- The company does not have the resources to finance the large capital expenditures necessary for high volume production with initially low profit margins.

Penetration pricing pursues the objective of quantity maximization by means of a low price. It is most appropriate when:

- Demand is expected to be highly elastic; that is, customers are price sensitive and the quantity demanded will increase significantly as price declines.

- Large decreases in cost are expected as cumulative volume increases. The product is of the nature of something that can gain mass appeal fairly quickly.
- There is a threat of impending competition.

As the product lifecycle progresses, likely there will be changes in the demand curve and costs. As such, the pricing policy should be re-evaluated over time.

The pricing objective depends on many factors including production cost, existence of economies of scale, barriers to entry, product differentiation, rate of product diffusion, the firm's resources, and the product's anticipated price elasticity of demand.

5. Pricing Methods

To set the specific price level that achieves their pricing objectives, managers may make use of several pricing methods. These methods include:

- **Cost-plus pricing** - set the price at the production cost plus a certain profit margin.
- **Target return pricing** - set the price to achieve a target return-on investment.
- **Value-based pricing** - base the price on the effective value to the customer relative to alternative products.
- **Psychological pricing** - base the price on factors such as signals of product quality, popular price points, and what the consumer perceives to be fair.

In addition to setting the price level, managers have the opportunity to design innovative pricing models that better meet the needs of both the firm and its customers. For example, software traditionally was purchased as a product in which customers made a one-time payment and then owned a perpetual license to the software. Many software suppliers have changed their pricing to a subscription model in which the customer subscribes for a set period of time, such as one year. Afterwards, the subscription must be renewed or the software no longer will function. This model offers stability to both the supplier and the customer since it reduces the large swings in software investment cycles.

6. Price Discounts

The normally quoted price to end users is known as the list price. This price usually is discounted for distribution channel members and some end users. There are several types of discounts, as outlined below.

(i) **Quantity discount** - offered to customers who purchase in large quantities.

(ii) **Cumulative quantity discount** - a discount that increases as the cumulative quantity increases. Cumulative discounts may be offered to resellers who purchase large quantities over time but who do not wish to place large individual orders.

(iii) **Seasonal discount** - based on the time when the purchase is made and designed to reduce seasonal variation in sales. For example, the travel industry offers much lower off-season rates. Such discounts do not have to be based on time of the year; they also can be based on day of the week or time of the day, such as pricing offered by long distance and wireless service providers.

(iv) **Cash discount** - extended to customers who pay their bill before a specified date.

(v) **Trade discount** - a functional discount offered to channel members for performing their roles. For example, a trade discount may be offered to a small retailer who may not purchase in quantity but nonetheless performs the important retail function.

(vi) **Promotional discount** - a short-term discounted price offered to stimulate sales.

MULTIPLE CHOICE QUESTIONS

1. What is the primary focus of business economics?

(1) Social welfare
(2) Maximising profit
(3) Environmental sustainability
(4) Political stability

2. Which of the following best describes the scope of business economics?

(1) Limited to microeconomics only
(2) Limited to macroeconomics only
(3) Encompasses both microeconomics and macroeconomics
(4) Limited to accounting principles

3. In business economics, what does the term "demand" refer to?

(1) Quantity of goods and services demanded by consumers
(2) Quantity of money in circulation
(3) Quantity of goods and services supplied by producers
(4) Quantity of resources available in the market

4. What is the significance of elasticity in business economics?

(1) Measures the responsiveness of quantity demanded to changes in price
(2) Measures the quantity demanded at a specific point in time
(3) Indicates the total demand in the market
(4) Measures the quantity supplied by producers

5. Which of the following is an example of a microeconomic decision?

(1) Government budget allocation
(2) Pricing strategy of a firm
(3) National unemployment rate
(4) Inflation rate in the country

6. What does the term "opportunity cost" mean in business economics?

(1) The cost of production
(2) The cost of forgoing the next best alternative
(3) The total cost of a product
(4) The cost of raw materials

7. Which of the following is a macroeconomic indicator?

(1) Consumer price index (CPI)
(2) Price elasticity of demand
(3) Marginal utility
(4) Production cost

8. What role does business economics play in decision-making for a firm?

(1) It doesn't impact decision-making
(2) Provides a theoretical framework with no practical application
(3) Helps in making informed decisions to Maximise profits
(4) Focuses only on social welfare

9. What is the main goal of a firm in the context of business economics?

(1) Maximising shareholder wealth
(2) Maximising social welfare
(3) Minimising profits
(4) Maximising government revenue

10. Which of the following is a feature of a perfectly competitive market in business economics?

(1) Few sellers
(2) Product differentiation
(3) Barriers to entry
(4) Homogeneous products

Directions: Each of the following items consists of two statements, one labelled as Assertion (A) and other labelled as Reason (R). You are to examine these two statements carefully and decide if the (A) and the (R) are individually true and if so, whether (R) is the correct explanation of (A). Select your answers to these items using the codes given below:

(1) Both (A) and (R) are true, and (R) is the correct explanation for (A).
(2) Both (A) and (R) are true, but (R) is not the correct explanation for (A).
(3) (A) is true, but (R) is false.
(4) Both (A) and (R) are false.

11. **Assertion (A):** Business economics is primarily concerned with profit Maximisation.
Reason (R): Profit is the sole objective of firms in a market economy.

12. **Assertion (A):** Microeconomics deals with individual economic units.
Reason (R): Macroeconomics focuses on the overall economic performance of a country.

13. **Assertion (A):** Elasticity of demand measures the percentage change in quantity demanded for a good in response to a percentage change in its price.
Reason (R): Elasticity helps businesses understand how sensitive consumer demand is to price changes.

14. **Assertion (A):** Opportunity cost is the value of the next best alternative forgone in order to pursue the chosen option.
Reason (R): Opportunity cost is not a relevant concept in business decision-making.

15. **Assertion (A):** Macroeconomic indicators provide insights into the overall health of an economy.
Reason (R): Microeconomic decisions have a negligible impact on the overall economy.

16. What is the primary objective of a business firm?
(1) Maximising social welfare
(2) Maximising profits
(3) Minimising costs
(4) Achieving market share

17. Which of the following is a financial objective of a business firm?
(1) Employee satisfaction
(2) Environmental sustainability
(3) Maximising shareholder wealth
(4) Social responsibility

18. In the context of business objectives, what does the term "market share" refer to?
(1) The total profit earned by a firm
(2) The percentage of the total market sales held by a firm
(3) The number of employees in a firm
(4) The diversity of products offered by a firm

19. What is the significance of the objective of "customer satisfaction" for a business firm?
(1) It ensures environmental sustainability
(2) It attracts government subsidies
(3) It leads to repeat business and loyalty
(4) It Maximises short-term profits

20. Which of the following is a long-term objective of a business firm?
(1) Meeting quarterly profit targets
(2) Maximising sales in the current year
(3) Building a strong brand image
(4) Minimising production costs in the short run

21. What is the social responsibility objective of a business firm?
(1) Maximising shareholder wealth
(2) Contributing to the well-being of society
(3) Minimising production costs
(4) Achieving economies of scale

22. Which of the following is an example of an operational objective for a business firm?
(1) Increasing employee satisfaction
(2) Reducing the carbon footprint
(3) Improving production efficiency
(4) Engaging in philanthropic activities

23. Why do businesses pursue the objective of "innovation"?
(1) To Minimise costs
(2) To gain a competitive edge
(3) To avoid legal issues
(4) To Maximise social welfare

24. What does the term "stakeholder satisfaction" imply for a business firm?
(1) Maximising profits for shareholders only
(2) Balancing the interests of various stakeholders
(3) Ignoring the concerns of employees
(4) Focusing solely on customer satisfaction

25. Which of the following is an environmental objective for a business firm?
(1) Maximising sales
(2) Minimising waste production
(3) Reducing employee turnover
(4) Expanding market share rapidly

Directions: Each of the following items consists of two statements, one labelled as Assertion (A) and other labelled as Reason (R). You are to examine these two statements carefully and decide if the (A) and the (R) are individually true and if so, whether (R) is the correct explanation of (A). Select your answers to these items using the codes given below:

(1) Both (A) and (R) are true, and (R) is the correct explanation for (A).
(2) Both (A) and (R) are true, but (R) is not the correct explanation for (A).

(3) (A) is true, but (R) is false.
(4) Both (A) and (R) are false.

26. **Assertion (A):** Maximising shareholder wealth is the sole objective of a business firm.
Reason (R): Shareholders are the primary owners of the firm, and their wealth reflects the success of the business.

27. **Assertion (A):** Long-term survival is not a significant objective for a business firm.
Reason (R): Firms focus more on short-term gains to satisfy immediate stakeholder demands.

28. **Assertion (A):** Corporate social responsibility is an optional objective for a business firm.
Reason (R): Profit Maximisation should always take precedence over social responsibility.

29. **Assertion (A):** Achieving cost leadership is a strategic objective for business firms.
Reason (R): Cost leadership helps firms gain a competitive advantage by offering lower prices.

30. **Assertion (A):** Ethical considerations are irrelevant to the objectives of a business firm.
Reason (R): Ethical behaviour may conflict with profit Maximisation and shareholder wealth.

31. According to the Law of Demand, what is the relationship between price and quantity demanded?
(1) Directly proportional
(2) Inversely proportional
(3) Unrelated
(4) Constant

32. What is the reason behind the Law of Demand?
(1) Changes in consumer preferences
(2) Income effect and substitution effect
(3) Government regulations
(4) Producer expectations

33. If the price of a good decreases and its quantity demanded increases, what is this phenomenon called?
(1) Elasticity (2) Substitution effect
(3) Inferior good (4) Law of Demand

34. Elastic demand is characterised by:
(1) Large percentage change in quantity demanded for a small percentage change in price
(2) Small percentage change in quantity demanded for a large percentage change in price
(3) No change in quantity demanded for any change in price
(4) Constant demand curve

35. What is the formula for price elasticity of demand?
(1) (Change in Quantity Demanded / Change in Price)
(2) (Percentage Change in Quantity Demanded/Percentage Change in Price)
(3) (Change in Price / Change in Quantity Demanded)
(4) (Percentage Change in Price / Percentage Change in Quantity Demanded)

36. If the price elasticity of demand is greater than 1, the demand is
(1) Elastic (2) Inelastic
(3) Unitary elastic (4) Perfectly elastic

37. In a perfectly competitive market, how does Marginal Revenue (MR) compare to Average Revenue (AR)?
(1) MR is always equal to AR
(2) MR is greater than AR
(3) MR is less than AR
(4) The relationship between MR and AR depends on the market structure

38. If a firm is experiencing diminishing Marginal Revenue (MR), what is happening to Average Revenue (AR)?
(1) AR is increasing
(2) AR is decreasing
(3) AR is constant
(4) AR is irrelevant to MR

39. In a monopolistic market, how does the demand curve look in relation to the Marginal Revenue (MR) curve?
(1) Demand curve is above MR curve
(2) Demand curve is below MR curve
(3) Demand curve coincides with MR curve
(4) No relationship between the two curves

Directions: Each of the following items consists of two statements, one labelled as Assertion (A) and other labelled as Reason (R). You are to examine these two statements carefully and decide if the (A) and the (R) are individually true and if so, whether (R) is the correct explanation of (A). Select your answers to these items using the codes given below:
(1) Both (A) and (R) are true, and (R) is the correct explanation for (A).

(2) Both (A) and (R) are true, but (R) is not the correct explanation for (A).
(3) (A) is true, but (R) is false.
(4) Both (A) and (R) are false.

40. **Assertion (A):** According to the Law of Demand, as the price of a good decreases, the quantity demanded increases.
Reason (R): Consumers tend to substitute a cheaper good for a more expensive one.

41. **Assertion (A):** Elasticity of demand measures how much quantity demanded changes in response to a change in price.
Reason (R): If demand is elastic, a small change in price will result in a large change in quantity demanded.

42. **Assertion (A):** In a perfectly competitive market, Marginal Revenue is equal to Average Revenue.
Reason (R): Each additional unit sold in a perfectly competitive market is sold at the same price.

43. **Assertion (A):** If the price elasticity of demand is less than 1, the demand is considered elastic.
Reason: Elasticity values are always expressed in percentages.

44. **Assertion (A):** In a monopolistic market, the Marginal Revenue curve lies below the Demand curve.
Reason (R): Monopolistic firms can sell more units only by lowering the price.

45. What is utility in the context of consumer behaviour?
(1) The total satisfaction derived from consuming a good or service
(2) The price of a good or service
(3) The quantity of a good or service demanded by consumers
(4) The cost of production for a firm

46. According to the Law of Diminishing Marginal Utility, what happens to the additional satisfaction as the consumption of a good increases?
(1) It increases continuously
(2) It remains constant
(3) It decreases
(4) It becomes negative

47. What is the relationship between total utility and marginal utility?
(1) Total utility is always equal to marginal utility
(2) Total utility is greater than marginal utility
(3) Total utility is the sum of all marginal utilities
(4) Total utility and marginal utility are unrelated

48. In indifference curve analysis, what does an indifference curve represent?
(1) The combination of goods that gives the consumer maximum satisfaction
(2) The budget constraint faced by the consumer
(3) The demand curve for a single good
(4) The production possibilities of a firm

49. What is the slope of an indifference curve?
(1) The price of one good in terms of the other
(2) The ratio of the marginal utility of one good to the other
(3) The quantity of one good in terms of the other
(4) The budget constraint faced by the consumer

50. If an indifference curve is concave to the origin, what does it imply about the consumer's preferences?
(1) The consumer has perfect substitutes
(2) The consumer has perfect complements
(3) The consumer experiences diminishing marginal rate of substitution
(4) The consumer has constant marginal rate of substitution

Directions: Each of the following items consists of two statements, one labelled as Assertion (A) and other labelled as Reason (R). You are to examine these two statements carefully and decide if the (A) and the (R) are individually true and if so, whether (R) is the correct explanation of (A). Select your answers to these items using the codes given below:
(1) Both (A) and (R) are true, and (R) is the correct explanation for (A).
(2) Both (A) and (R) are true, but (R) is not the correct explanation for (A).
(3) (A) is true, but (R) is false.
(4) Both (A) and (R) are false.

51. **Assertion (A):** The Law of Diminishing Marginal Utility explains why the demand for a good decreases as its price rises.
Reason (R): Consumers are willing to pay more for goods that provide higher marginal utility.

52. **Assertion (A):** Indifference curves cannot intersect with each other.
Reason (R): If two indifference curves intersect, it implies that the consumer is indifferent between different combinations of goods.

53. **Assertion (A):** A consumer will always choose a point on the highest possible indifference curve.
Reason (R): Indifference curves represent different levels of satisfaction, and consumers aim to Maximise their satisfaction.

54. **Assertion (A):** Indifference curves are always downward-sloping from left to right.
Reason (R): The Law of Diminishing Marginal Utility ensures that consumers prefer a diverse combination of goods.

55. **Assertion (A):** A higher indifference curve represents a lower level of satisfaction for the consumer.
Reason (R): Indifference curves represent different levels of satisfaction, and a higher curve indicates a higher level of satisfaction.

56. What does the Law of Variable Proportions explain?
(1) The relationship between output and input in the short run
(2) The relationship between output and input in the long run
(3) The impact of government regulations on production
(4) The impact of technology on input costs

57. According to the Law of Variable Proportions, what happens to output if one input is increased while other inputs are held constant?
(1) Output increases at an increasing rate
(2) Output increases at a decreasing rate
(3) Output remains constant
(4) Output decreases

58. In the short run, what is the stage where total product increases at a decreasing rate as additional units of the variable input are added?
(1) Stage of increasing returns
(2) Stage of diminishing returns
(3) Stage of constant returns
(4) Stage of negative returns

59. What is the shape of the total product curve in the stage of diminishing returns?
(1) Linear (2) Concave
(3) Convex (4) Vertical

60. Which factor is assumed to be fixed in the short run when analyzing the Law of Variable Pro portions?
(1) Land (2) Labour
(3) Capital (4) Entrepreneurship

61. What does the Law of Returns to Scale focus on?
(1) The impact of variable inputs on production
(2) The impact of fixed inputs on production
(3) The relationship between output and all inputs in the short run
(4) The relationship between output and all inputs in the long run

62. If all inputs are increased by a certain percentage and output increases by the same percentage, the production exhibits:
(1) Increasing returns to scale
(2) Constant returns to scale
(3) Decreasing returns to scale
(4) Negative returns to scale

63. In the Law of Returns to Scale, what does it mean when output increases more than proportionately to an increase in all inputs?
(1) Increasing returns to scale
(2) Constant returns to scale
(3) Decreasing returns to scale
(4) Negative returns to scale

64. What is the characteristic of constant returns to scale?
(1) Output increases at an increasing rate
(2) Output increases at a decreasing rate
(3) Output increases at the same rate as the increase in inputs
(4) Output remains constant

65. In the long run, if a doubling of all inputs leads to less than a doubling of output, the production exhibits:
(1) Increasing returns to scale
(2) Constant returns to scale
(3) Decreasing returns to scale
(4) Negative returns to scale

Directions: Each of the following items consists of two statements, one labelled as Assertion (A) and other labelled as Reason (R). You are to examine these two statements carefully and decide if the (A) and the (R) are individually true and if so, whether (R) is the correct explanation of (A). Select your answers to these items using the codes given below:

(1) Both (A) and (R) are true, and (R) is the correct explanation for (A).
(2) Both (A) and (R) are true, but (R) is not the correct explanation for (A).
(3) (A) is true, but (R) is false.
(4) Both (A) and (R) are false.

66. **Assertion (A):** In the Law of Variable Proportions, the stage of diminishing returns occurs when the marginal product of the variable input is negative.
Reason (R): Diminishing returns set in when the marginal product of the variable input decreases.

67. **Assertion (A):** The Law of Returns to Scale is concerned with the impact of changes in all inputs on the scale of production.
Reason (R): Returns to scale refer to the percentage change in output resulting from a percentage change in all inputs.

68. **Assertion (A):** Increasing returns to scale imply that doubling all inputs will result in more than a doubling of output.
Reason (R): Increasing returns to scale occur when the scale of production leads to greater efficiency.

69. **Assertion (A):** In the stage of diminishing returns in the Law of Variable Proportions, the total product reaches its maximum.
Reason (R): Diminishing returns occur when the additional output from an additional unit of the variable input is declining.

70. **Assertion (A):** Constant returns to scale imply that doubling all inputs will result in exactly a doubling of output.
Reason (R): Constant returns to scale occur when the scale of production has no impact on efficiency.
(1) Both Assertion and Reason are true, and Reason is the correct explanation for Assertion.
(2) Both Assertion and Reason are true, but Reason is not the correct explanation for Assertion.
(3) Assertion is true, but Reason is false.
(4) Both Assertion and Reason are false.

71. In the short run, which cost is considered a fixed cost?
(1) Total cost (2) Variable cost
(3) Marginal cost (4) Fixed cost

72. What is the relationship between average variable cost (AVC) and marginal cost (MC) in the short run when AVC is at its minimum?
(1) AVC = MC
(2) AVC < MC
(3) AVC > MC
(4) No relationship between AVC and MC

73. What does the short-run average total cost (ATC) curve look like when marginal cost (MC) is below ATC?
(1) ATC is rising
(2) ATC is falling
(3) ATC is constant
(4) ATC is at its minimum point

74. In the short run, which cost curve is U-shaped?
(1) Average total cost (ATC)
(2) Average variable cost (AVC)
(3) Marginal cost (MC)
(4) Total fixed cost (TFC)

75. What is the distinguishing feature of the long-run cost curve?
(1) All costs are variable
(2) All costs are fixed
(3) Some costs are fixed, and some are variable
(4) No costs are incurred

76. In the long run, what is the shape of the long-run average total cost (LRATC) curve when increasing returns to scale are experienced?
(1) U-shaped
(2) Downward-sloping
(3) Upward-sloping
(4) Constant

77. If a firm experiences constant returns to scale in the long run, what happens to the long-run marginal cost (LRMC) curve?
(1) It is U-shaped
(2) It is downward-sloping
(3) It is upward-sloping
(4) It is horizontal

78. What does the long-run average cost curve look like when there are diseconomies of scale?
(1) U-shaped
(2) Downward-sloping
(3) Upward-sloping
(4) Constant

79. Which cost concept is irrelevant in the long run?
(1) Average variable cost (AVC)

(2) Total fixed cost (TFC)
(3) Marginal cost (MC)
(4) Average total cost (ATC)

Directions: Each of the following items consists of two statements, one labelled as Assertion (A) and other labelled as Reason (R). You are to examine these two statements carefully and decide if the (A) and the (R) are individually true and if so, whether (R) is the correct explanation of (A). Select your answers to these items using the codes given below:

(1) Both (A) and (R) are true, and (R) is the correct explanation for (A).
(2) Both (A) and (R) are true, but (R) is not the correct explanation for (A).
(3) (A) is true, but (R) is false.
(4) Both (A) and (R) are false.

80. Assertion (A): In the short run, total fixed cost (TFC) remains constant regardless of the level of production.
Reason (R): Fixed costs are incurred even when production is zero.

81. Assertion (A): Average variable cost (AVC) may continue to fall even when marginal cost (MC) is rising in the short run.
Reason (R): AVC is influenced by the variable cost per unit, while MC is influenced by the additional cost of producing one more unit.

82. Assertion (A): Long-run average total cost (LRATC) is always lower than short-run average total cost (SRATC).
Reason (R): In the long run, firms can adjust all inputs and achieve greater efficiency compared to the short run.

83. Assertion (A): Diseconomies of scale occur when a firm becomes too large, leading to higher per-unit production costs.
Reason (R): Diseconomies of scale result in an upward-sloping long-run average cost curve.

84. Assertion (A): Long-run marginal cost (LRMC) is always equal to short-run marginal cost (SRMC).
Reason (R): Marginal cost remains constant regardless of the time horizon.

85. In perfect competition, what is the number of firms in the market?
(1) Few large firms
(2) One dominant firm
(3) Many small firms
(4) Only one firm

86. What type of product does a firm in perfect competition produce?
(1) Differentiated product
(2) Homogeneous product
(3) Unique product
(4) Luxury product

87. In perfect competition, how does a firm determine its price?
(1) By setting its own price
(2) By observing market price
(3) By negotiating with competitors
(4) By government regulations

88. What is a key characteristic of monopolistic competition?
(1) Few sellers in the market
(2) Identical products
(3) Perfect knowledge among buyers
(4) Product differentiation

89. In monopolistic competition, how does a firm set its price?
(1) By observing market price
(2) By setting its own price
(3) By following a price leader
(4) By government regulations

90. In oligopoly, what is the role of a price leader?
(1) To compete aggressively
(2) To set the price for the entire industry
(3) To collude with other firms
(4) To follow the market price

91. What is the primary motive behind the price leadership model in oligopoly?
(1) To Maximise profits
(2) To Minimise competition
(3) To increase market share
(4) To create barriers to entry

92. In a monopoly, how is price determined?
(1) By market forces
(2) By government regulations
(3) By the demand and supply interaction
(4) By the monopolist

93. What is the characteristic of the demand curve faced by a monopoly?
(1) Perfectly elastic
(2) Perfectly inelastic
(3) Downward-sloping
(4) Horizontal

94. What is the goal of price discrimination?
(1) To Maximise consumer surplus
(2) To Minimise profits
(3) To charge different prices to different consumers
(4) To promote fair competition

95. What is a necessary condition for successful price discrimination?
(1) Homogeneous market
(2) Perfect competition
(3) Market power
(4) Identical consumer preferences

Directions: Each of the following items consists of two statements, one labelled as Assertion (A) and other labelled as Reason (R). You are to examine these two statements carefully and decide if the (A) and the (R) are individually true and if so, whether (R) is the correct explanation of (A). Select your answers to these items using the codes given below:
(1) Both (A) and (R) are true, and (R) is the correct explanation for (A).
(2) Both (A) and (R) are true, but (R) is not the correct explanation for (A).
(3) (A) is true, but (R) is false.
(4) Both (A) and (R) are false.

96. Assertion (A): In perfect competition, individual firms have no control over the market price.
Reason (R): In perfect competition, each firm is a price taker and cannot influence the market price.

97. Assertion (A): Monopolistic competition is characterised by product differentiation.
Reason (R): Firms in monopolistic competition produce identical products.

98. Assertion (A): Oligopoly firms may engage in collusion to set prices collectively.
Reason (R): Collusion helps oligopoly firms Maximise individual profits.

99. Assertion (A): A monopoly can charge any price it desires for its product.
Reason (R): A monopoly faces a perfectly elastic demand curve.

100. Assertion (A): Price discrimination is only possible in markets with identical consumer preferences.
Reason (R): Price discrimination relies on charging different prices to different groups of consumers based on their willingness to pay.

101. What is the primary objective of price skimming?
(1) Maximising market share
(2) Attracting cost-conscious consumers
(3) Quickly recovering production costs
(4) Capturing consumer surplus

102. When is price skimming often employed in the product life cycle?
(1) Introduction stage
(2) Growth stage
(3) Maturity stage
(4) Decline stage

103. How does price skimming affect early adopters and innovators?
(1) They pay higher prices initially
(2) They pay lower prices initially
(3) They pay the same price as later consumers
(4) They receive the product for free

104. What is the primary objective of price penetration?
(1) Maximising short-term profits
(2) Attracting a large market share quickly
(3) Recovering production costs slowly
(4) Catering to high-income consumers

105. In price penetration, what is the typical pricing strategy during the initial stages of product introduction?
(1) High initial prices
(2) Low initial prices
(3) Dynamic pricing
(4) Auction pricing

106. When is peak load pricing commonly applied?
(1) During periods of low demand
(2) During periods of high demand
(3) Throughout the entire day
(4) Only on weekends

107. What is the goal of peak load pricing?
(1) To encourage off-peak consumption
(2) To Maximise profits during peak hours
(3) To Minimise variable costs
(4) To establish a price floor

108. Which industry often uses peak load pricing?
(1) Grocery stores
(2) Public transportation
(3) Libraries
(4) Gas stations

109. What pricing strategy involves initially setting a high price and then gradually lowering it over time?

(1) Price skimming
(2) Price penetration
(3) Dynamic pricing
(4) Bundle pricing

110. Which pricing strategy combines elements of both high and low pricing?

(1) Penetration skimming
(2) Dynamic pricing
(3) Hybrid pricing
(4) Elastic pricing

Directions: Each of the following items consists of two statements, one labelled as Assertion (A) and other labelled as Reason (R). You are to examine these two statements carefully and decide if the (A) and the (R) are individually true and if so, whether (R) is the correct explanation of (A). Select your answers to these items using the codes given below:

(1) Both (A) and (R) are true, and (R) is the correct explanation for (A).
(2) Both (A) and (R) are true, but (R) is not the correct explanation for (A).
(3) (A) is true, but (R) is false.
(4) Both (A) and (R) are false.

111. Assertion (A): Price skimming is most effective when there is limited competition and high demand for the product.
Reason (R): Price skimming allows firms to capture consumer surplus from early adopters.

112. Assertion (A): Price penetration is often associated with high initial prices to signal product quality.
Reason (R): Consumers may perceive products with higher prices as being of higher quality.

113. Assertion (A): Peak load pricing is used to manage congestion during peak hours and encourage off-peak consumption.
Reason (R): Peak load pricing involves charging higher prices during periods of high demand.

114. Assertion (A): Mixed pricing strategies are designed to cater to different segments of the market.
Reason (R): Mixed strategies help firms capture both early adopters willing to pay high prices and price-sensitive consumers.

115. Assertion (A): Peak load pricing is more effective in industries where consumers have limited flexibility in adjusting their consumption patterns.
Reason (R): Peak load pricing relies on the inelasticity of demand during peak hours.

ANSWERS

1. (2)	**2.** (3)	**3.** (1)	**4.** (1)	**5.** (2)	**6.** (2)	**7.** (1)	**8.** (3)	**9.** (1)	**10.** (4)
11. (3)	**12.** (1)	**13.** (1)	**14.** (3)	**15.** (2)	**16.** (2)	**17.** (3)	**18.** (2)	**19.** (3)	**20.** (3)
21. (2)	**22.** (3)	**23.** (2)	**24.** (2)	**25.** (2)	**26.** (3)	**27.** (4)	**28.** (4)	**29.** (1)	**30.** (4)
31. (2)	**32.** (2)	**33.** (4)	**34.** (1)	**35.** (2)	**36.** (1)	**37.** (1)	**38.** (2)	**39.** (1)	**40.** (1)
41. (1)	**42.** (1)	**43.** (3)	**44.** (1)	**45.** (1)	**46.** (3)	**47.** (3)	**48.** (1)	**49.** (2)	**50.** (3)
51. (2)	**52.** (2)	**53.** (1)	**54.** (2)	**55.** (3)	**56.** (1)	**57.** (2)	**58.** (2)	**59.** (2)	**60.** (3)
61. (4)	**62.** (2)	**63.** (1)	**64.** (3)	**65.** (3)	**66.** (3)	**67.** (1)	**68.** (1)	**69.** (3)	**70.** (2)
71. (4)	**72.** (1)	**73.** (2)	**74.** (1)	**75.** (1)	**76.** (2)	**77.** (4)	**78.** (3)	**79.** (2)	**80.** (1)
81. (1)	**82.** (1)	**83.** (1)	**84.** (4)	**85.** (3)	**86.** (2)	**87.** (2)	**88.** (4)	**89.** (2)	**90.** (2)
91. (1)	**92.** (4)	**93.** (3)	**94.** (3)	**95.** (3)	**96.** (1)	**97.** (3)	**98.** (3)	**99.** (4)	**100.** (3)
101. (3)	**102.** (1)	**103.** (1)	**104.** (2)	**105.** (2)	**106.** (2)	**107.** (2)	**108.** (2)	**109.** (1)	**110.** (3)
111. (1)	**112.** (3)	**113.** (1)	**114.** (1)	**115.** (1)					

UNIT 4

BUSINESS FINANCE

SYLLABUS

- Scope and sources of finance; Lease financing
- Cost of capital and time value of money
- Capital structure
- Capital budgeting decisions: Conventional and scientific techniques of capital budgeting analysis
- Working capital management; Dividend decision: Theories and policies
- Risk and return analysis; Asset securitization
- International monetary system
- Foreign exchange market; Exchange rate risk and hedging techniques
- International financial markets and instruments: Euro currency; GDRs; ADRs
- International arbitrage; Multinational capital budgeting

SCOPE AND SOURCES OF FINANCE

Financial management is an organic function of any business. Any organization needs finances to obtain physical resources, carry out the production activities and other business operations, pay compensation to the suppliers, etc. There are many theories around financial management:

1. Some experts believe that financial management is all about providing funds needed by a business on terms that are most favorable, keeping its objectives in mind. Therefore, this approach concerns primarily with the procurement of funds which may include instruments, institutions, and practices to raise funds. It also takes care of the legal and accounting relationship between an enterprise and its source of funds.
2. Another set of experts believe that finance is all about cash. Since all business transactions involve cash, directly or indirectly, finance is concerned with everything done by the business.
3. The third and more widely accepted point of view is that financial management includes the procurement of funds and their effective utilization. For example, in the case of a manufacturing company, financial management must ensure that funds are available for installing the production plant and machinery. Further, it must also ensure that the profits adequately compensate the costs and risks borne by the business.

In a developed market, most businesses can raise capital easily. However, the real problem is the efficient utilization of the capital through effective financial planning and control.

Further, the business must ensure that it deals with tasks like ensuring the availability of funds, allocating them, managing them, investing them, controlling costs, forecasting financial requirements, planning profits and estimating returns on investment, assessing working capital, etc.

The Scope of Financial Management

The introduction to financial management also requires you to understand the scope of financial management. It is important that financial decisions take care of the shareholders' interests.

Further, they are upheld by the maximization of the wealth of the shareholders, which depends on the increase in net worth, capital invested in the business, and plowed-back profits for the growth and prosperity of the organization.

Core Financial Management Decisions

In organizations, managers in an effort to minimize the costs of procuring finance and using it in the most profitable manner, take the following decisions:

Investment Decisions: Managers need to decide on the amount of investment available out of the existing finance, on a long-term and short-term basis. They are of two types:

- Long-term investment decisions or Capital Budgeting mean committing funds for a long period of time like fixed assets. These decisions are irreversible and usually include the ones pertaining to investing in a building and/or land, acquiring new plants/machinery or replacing the old ones, etc. These decisions determine the financial pursuits and performance of a business.
- Short-term investment decisions or Working Capital Management means committing funds for a short period of time like current assets. These involve decisions pertaining to the investment of funds in the inventory, cash, bank deposits, and other short-term investments. They directly affect the liquidity and performance of the business.

Financing Decisions: Managers also make decisions pertaining to raising finance from long-term sources (called Capital Structure) and short-term sources (called Working Capital).

They are of two types:

- Financial Planning decisions which relate to estimating the sources and application of funds. It means pre-estimating financial needs of an organization to ensure availability of adequate finance. The primary objective of financial planning is to plan and ensure that the funds are available as and when required.
- Capital Structure decisions which involve identifying sources of funds. They also involve decisions with respect to choosing external sources like issuing shares, bonds, borrowing from banks or internal sources like retained earnings for raising funds.

Dividend Decisions. These involve decisions related to the portion of profits that will be distributed as dividend. Shareholders always demand a higher dividend, while the management would want to retain profits for business needs. Hence, this is a complex managerial decision.

Classification of Sources of Finance

Classification on the Basis of Period

- **Long-term Sources.** These sources provide finance to business firms for a period exceeding five years. e.g. Equity shares, retained earnings etc.
- **Medium-term Sources.** These sources provide finance to business firms for a period exceeding one year but less than five years. e.g. Loan from banks, public deposits etc.
- **Short-term Sources.** These sources provide finance to business firms for less than one year. e.g. Trade credit, factoring etc.

Classification on the Basis of Ownership

- **Owner's Funds.** Funds or finance provided by the owners of the business is referred to as owners funds. Being the recipient of the profit earned by the business, they have the incentive to invest in the business. The funds provided by they owners are not required to be paid back during the life of the business, therefore they are a permanent source of finance. e.g. Equity shares, GDR/ADR etc.
- **Borrowed Funds.** The funds that are raised by way of loans and credit from the public, banks and financial institutions are termed as borrowed funds. These funds are raised from external source and are required to be paid back after a stipulated period. A fixed rate of interest is also required to be paid on amount raised from these sources. e.g. Debentures, lease financing etc.

Classification on the Basis of Source of Generation

- **Internal Sources.** These include all those funds which are generated from within a business, such as, from collection of receivables, disposing off surplus inventories and ploughing back of profit. These sources can however, fulfil only limited needs. e.g. Equity shares, retained earnings etc.
- **External Sources.** These include all those funds which are generated from outside a business. These sources carry a cost/but large amounts can be raised through these sources. Also, in some cases, business is required to mortgage its assets for raising finance from these sources. e.g. Debentures, public deposits etc.

LEASE FINANCING

Lease financing is one of the important sources of medium- and long-term financing where the owner of an asset gives another person, the right to use that asset against periodical payments. The owner of the asset is known as lessor and the user is called lessee.

The periodical payment made by the lessee to the lessor is known as lease rental. Under lease financing, lessee is given the right to use the asset but the ownership lies with the lessor and at the end of the lease contract, the asset is returned to the lessor or an option is given to the lessee either to purchase the asset or to renew the lease agreement.

Different Types of Lease

Depending upon the transfer of risk and rewards to the lessee, the period of lease and the number of parties to the transaction, lease financing can be classified into two categories. Finance lease and operating lease.

a. **Finance Lease.** It is the lease where the lessor transfers substantially all the risks and rewards of ownership of assets to the lessee for lease rentals. In other words, it puts the lessee in the same condition as he/she would have been if he/she had purchased the asset. Finance lease has two phases: The first one is called primary period. This is non-cancellable period and in this period, the lessor recovers his total investment through lease rental. The primary period may last for indefinite period of time. The lease rental for the secondary period is much smaller than that of primary period.

b. **Features of Finance Lease.** From the above discussion, following features can be derived for finance lease:
   1. A finance lease is a device that gives the lessee a right to use an asset.
   2. The lease rental charged by the lessor during the primary period of lease is sufficient to recover his/her investment.
   3. The lease rental for the secondary period is much smaller. This is often known as peppercorn rental.
   4. Lessee is responsible for the maintenance of asset.
   5. No asset-based risk and rewards is taken by lessor.
   6. Such type of lease is non-cancellable; the lessor's investment is assured.

c. **Operating Lease.** Lease other than finance lease is called operating lease. Here risks and rewards incidental to the ownership of asset are not transferred by the lessor to the lessee. The term of such lease is much less than the economic life of the asset and thus the total investment of the lessor is not recovered through lease rental during the primary period of lease. In case of operating lease, the lessor usually provides advice to the lessee for repair, maintenance and technical knowhow of the leased asset and that is why this type of lease is also known as service lease.

d. **Features of Operating Lease.** Operating lease has following features:
   1. The lease term is much lower than the economic life of the asset.
   2. The lessee has the right to terminate the lease by giving a short notice and no penalty is charged for that.
   3. The lessor provides the technical knowhow of the leased asset to the lessee.
   4. Risks and rewards incidental to the ownership of asset are borne by the lessor.
   5. Lessor has to depend on leasing of an asset to different lessee for recovery of his/her investment.

Advantages and Disadvantages of Lease Financing

At present leasing activity shows an increasing trend. Leasing appears to be a cost-effective alternative for using an asset. However, it has certain advantages as well as disadvantages.

i. **Advantages:**

Lease financing has following advantages:

a. **To Lessor.** The advantages of lease financing from the point of view of lessor are summarized below

Assured Regular Income:

Lessor gets lease rental by leasing an asset during the period of lease which is an assured and regular income.

Preservation of Ownership: In case of finance lease, the lessor transfers all the risk and rewards incidental to ownership to the lessee without the transfer of ownership of asset hence the owner-ship lies with the lessor.

Benefit of Tax :As ownership lies with the lessor, tax benefit is enjoyed by the lessor by way of depreciation in respect of leased asset.

High Profitability :The business of leasing is highly profitable since the rate of return based on lease rental, is much higher than the interest payable on financing the asset.

High Potentiality of Growth :The demand for leasing is steadily increasing because it is one of the cost efficient forms of financing. Economic growth can be maintained even during the period of depression. Thus, the growth potentiality of leasing is much higher as compared to other forms of business.

Recovery of Investment :In case of finance lease, the lessor can recover the total investment through lease rentals.

b. **To Lessee.** The advantages of lease financing from the point of view of lessee are discussed below:

Use of Capital Goods. A business will not have to spend a lot of money for acquiring an asset but it can use an asset by paying small monthly or yearly rentals.

Tax Benefits. A company is able to enjoy the tax advantage on lease payments as lease payments can be deducted as a business expense.

Cheaper. Leasing is a source of financing which is cheaper than almost all other sources of financing.

Technical Assistance. Lessee gets some sort of technical support from the lessor in respect of leased asset.

Inflation Friendly. Leasing is inflation friendly, the lessee has to pay fixed amount of rentals each year even if the cost of the asset goes up.

Ownership. After the expiry of primary period, lessor offers the lessee to purchase the assets— by paying a very small sum of money.

ii. **Disadvantages:**

Lease financing suffers from the following disadvantages:

a. **To Lessor.** Lessor suffers from certain limitations which are discussed below:

Unprofitable in Case of Inflation: Lessor gets fixed amount of lease rental every year and they cannot increase this even if the cost of asset goes up.

Double Taxation: Sales tax may be charged twice: First at the time of purchase of asset and second at the time of leasing the asset.

Greater Chance of Damage of Asset: As ownership is not transferred, the lessee uses the asset carelessly and there is a great chance that asset cannot be usable after the expiry of primary period of lease.

b. **To Lessee.** The disadvantages of lease financing from lessee's point of view are given below:

Compulsion. Finance lease is non-cancellable and even if a company does not want to use the asset, lessee is required to pay the lease rentals.

Ownership. The lessee will not become the owner of the asset at the end of lease agreement unless he decides to purchase it.

Costly. Lease financing is more costly than other sources of financing because lessee has to pay lease rental as well as expenses incidental to the ownership of the asset.

Understatement of Asset. As lessee is not the owner of the asset, such an asset cannot be shown in the balance sheet which leads to understatement of lessee's asset.

CAPITAL STRUCTURE

In order to run and manage a company, funds are needed. Right from the promotional stage upto end, finances play an important role in a company's life. If funds are inadequate, the business suffers and if funds are not properly managed, the entire organisation suffers. It is therefore, necessary that correct estimate of the current and future need of capital be made to have an optimum capital structure which shall help the organisation to run its work smoothly and without any stress.

"Capital structure of a company refers to the composition or make up of its capitalisation and it includes all long-term capital resources viz., loans, reserves, shares and bonds." The capital structure is made up of debt and equity securities and refers to permanent finance of a firm. It is composed of long term debt, preference share capital and shareholders funds. For raising long-term finances, a company can issue three type of securities viz., equity shares, preference shares and debentures. A decision about the proportions among these types of securities refers to the capital structure of an enterprise.

Financing the firm's assets is a very crucial problem in every business and as a general rule, there should be a proper mix of debt and equity capital in financing the firm's assets. The use of long-term fixed interest bearing debt and preference share capital along with equity shares is called financial leverage or trading on equity.

Thus, optimum capital structure is that combination of debt and equity that leads to the maximum value of the firm and hence the wealth of its owners and minimises the company's cost of capital.

Theories of Capital Structure

1. **Net Income Approach.** According to this approach, a firm can minimise the weighted average cost of capital and increase the value of the firm as well as market price of equity shares by using debt financing to the maximum possible extent. The theory propounds that a company can increase its value and reduce the overall cost of capital by increasing the proportion of debt in its capital structure. This approach is based upon the following assumptions:

   (i) The cost of debt is less than the cost of equity.

   (ii) There are no taxes.

   (iii) The risk perception of investors is not changed by the use of debt.

   The line of argument in favour of net income approach is that as the proportion of debt financing in capital structure increases, the proportion of a cheaper source of funds increases. This results in the decrease in overall (weighted average) cost of capital leading to an increase in the value of the firm. The reasons for assuming cost of debt to be less than the cost of equity are that interest rates are usually lower than dividend rates due to element of risk and the benefit of tax as the interest is a deductible expense.

2. **Net Operating Income Approach.** This theory as suggested by Durand is another extreme of the effect of leverage on the value of the firm. According to this approach, change in the capital structure of a company does not affect the market value of the firm and the overall cost of capital remains constant irrespective of the method of financing. It implies that the overall cost of capital remains the same whether the debt-equity mix is 50:50 or 20:80 or 0:100. Thus, there is nothing as an optimal capital structure and every capital structure is the optimum capital structure. This theory presumes that
   (i) the market capitalises the value of the firm as a whole and
   (ii) the business risk remains constant at every level of debt equity mix.

   The reasons propounded for such assumptions are that the increased use of debt increases the financial risk of the equity shareholders and hence the cost of equity increases. On the other hand, the cost of debt remains constant with the increasing proportion of debt as the financial risk of the lenders is not affected.

   Thus, the advantage of using the cheaper source of funds, *i.e.*, debt is exactly offset by the increased cost of equity.

3. **The Traditional Approach.** The traditional approach, also known as Intermediate approach, is a compromise between the two extremes of net income approach and net operating income approach. According to this theory, the value of the firm can be increased initially or the cost of capital can be decreased by using more debt as the debt is a cheaper source of funds than equity. Thus, optimum capital structure, can be reached by a proper debt-equity mix. Beyond a particular point, the cost of equity increases because increased debt increases the financial risk of the equity shareholders. The advantage of cheaper debt at this point of capital structure is offset by increased cost of equity. After this there comes a stage, when the increased cost of equity cannot be offset by the advantage of low-cost debt. Thus, overall cost of capital, according to this theory, decreases upto a certain point, remains more or less unchanged for moderate increase in debt thereafter; and increases or rises beyond a certain point. Even the cost of debt may increase at this stage due to increased financial risk.

4. **Modigliani and Miller Approach.** M & M hypothesis is identical with the Net Operating Income approach if taxes are ignored. However, when corporate taxes are assumed to exist, their hypothesis is similar to the Net Income Approach.

   (a) ***In the absence of taxes.*** The theory proves that the cost of capital is not affected by changes in the capital structure or say that the debt-equity mix is irrelevant in the determination of the total value of a firm. The reason argued is that though debt is cheaper to equity, with increased use of debt as a source of finance, the cost of equity increases. This increase in cost of equity offsets the advantage of the low cost of debt. Thus, although the financial leverage affects the cost of equity, the overall cost of capital remains constant. The theory emphasises the fact that a firm's operating income is a determinant of its total value. The theory further propounds that beyond a certain limit of debt, the cost of debt increases (due to increased financial risk) but the cost of equity falls thereby again balancing the two costs. In the opinion of Modigliani & Miller, two identical firms in all respects except their capital structure cannot have different market values or cost of capital because of arbitrate process. In case two identical firms except of their capital structure have different market values or cost of capital, arbitrate will take place and the investors will engage in 'personal leverage' (*i.e.*, they will buy equity of the other company in preference to the company having lesser value) as against the 'corporate leverage'; and this will again render the two firms to have the same total value.

The M & M approach is based upon the following assumptions:

(i) There are no corporate taxes.
(ii) There is a perfect market.
(iii) Investors act rationally.
(iv) The expected earnings of all the firms have identical risk characteristics.
(v) The cut-off point of investment in a firm is capitalisation rate.
(vi) Risk to investors depends upon the random fluctuations of expected earnings and the possibility that the actual value of the variables may turn out to be different from their best estimates.
(vii) All earnings are distributed to the shareholders.

(b) ***When the corporate taxes are assumed to exist.*** Modigliani and Miller, in their article of 1963 have recognised that the value of the firm will increase or the cost of capital will decrease with the use of debt on account of deductibility of interest charges for tax purpose. Thus, the optimum capital structure can be achieved by maximising the debt mix in the equity of a firm.

According to the M & M approach, the value of a firm unlevered can be calculated as:

$$\text{Value of unlevered firm } (V_u) = \frac{\text{Earnings Before Interest and tax}}{\text{Overall cost of capital}}$$

i.e. $\frac{\text{EBIT}}{K_o}$ (l – t) and, the value of a levered firms is:

$V_L = V_u + tD$

where, V_u is value of unlevered firm

and tD is the discounted present value of the tax savings resulting from the tax deductibility of the interest charges, t is the rate of tax and D is the quantum of debt used in the mix.

COST OF CAPITAL

The cost of capital of a firm is the minimum rate of return expected by its investors. It is the weighted average cost of various sources of finance used by a firm. The capital used by a firm may be in the form of debt, preference capital, retained earnings and equity shares. Cost of capital for a firm may be defined as the cost of obtaining funds, *i.e.*, the average rate of return that the investors in a firm would expect for supplying funds to the firm.

According to **Hampton, John J** "*cost of capital is the rate of return the firm requires from investment in order to increase the value of the firm in the market place.*"

Basic aspects of the cost of capital:

(i) Cost of capital is not a cost as such - In fact, it is the rate of return that a firm requires to earn from its projects.
(ii) It is the minimum rate of return-cost of capital of a firm is that minimum rate of return which will at least maintain the market value of the shares.
(iii) It comprises of three components:
    (a) the expected normal rate of return at zero risk level, say the rate of interest allowed by banks.

(b) the premium of business risk.

(c) the premium for financial risk on account of pattern of capital structure.

Cost of capital may be represented as :

$$K = r_0 + b + f$$

where,

K = cost of capital, r_0 = normal rate of return at zero risk level,

b = premium for business risk, f = premium for financial risk.

Classification of Cost

1. **Historical Cost and Future Cost.** Historical costs are book costs which are related to the past. Future costs are estimated costs for the future. In financial decisions future costs are more relevant than the historical costs. However, historical costs act as guide for the estimation of future costs.
2. **Specific Cost and Composite Cost.** Specific cost refers to the cost of specific source of capital while composite cost is combined cost of various sources of capital. It is the weighted average cost of capital. In case more than one form of capital is used in the business, it is the composite cost which should be considered for decision-making and not the specific cost. But where only one type of capital is employed, the specific cost of that type of capital may be considered. In capital structure decisions, it is the weighted average cost of capital which should be given consideration.
3. **Explicit Cost and Implicit Cost.** An explicit cost is the discount rate which equates the present value of cash inflows with the present value of cash outflows. In other words, it is the internal rate of return. The explicit cost of a specific sources of finance may be determined with the help of the following formula:

$$I_0 = \frac{O_1}{(1+k)} + \frac{O_2}{(1+k)^2} \ldots\ldots \frac{O_n}{(1+k)^n}$$

$$= \sum_{t=1}^{n} \frac{O_t}{(1+k)^t}$$

where, I_0, is the net cash inflow at zero point of time,

O_t is the outflow of cash in periods 1, 2 and *n*.

k is the explicit cost of capital.

Implicit cost also known as the opportunity cost is the cost of the opportunity foregone in order to take up a particular project. For example, the implicit cost of retained earnings is the rate of return available to shareholders by investing the funds elsewhere.

4. **Average Cost and Marginal Cost.** An average cost refers to the combined cost of various sources of capital such as debentures, preference shares and equity shares. It is the weighted average cost of the costs of various sources of finance. Marginal cost of capital refers to the average cost of capital which has to be incurred to obtain additional funds required by a firm.

Computation of Cost of Capital

Computation of overall cost of capital of a firm involves:

A. Computation of cost of specific source of finance and

B. Computation of weighted average cost of capital.

A. Computation of Specific Source of Finance

Computation of each specific source of finance, viz., debt, preference share capital, equity share capital and retained earnings is discussed as below:

1. **Cost of Debt.** The cost of debt is the rate of interest payable on debt. For example, a company issues Rs. 1,00,000 for 10% debentures at par; the before-tax cost of this debt issue will also be 10%. By way of a formula, before-tax-cost of debt may be calculated as:

$$K_{db} = \frac{I}{P}$$

where,

K_{db} = Before tax cost of debt

I = Interest

and P = Principal

In case the debt is raised at premium or discount, we should consider P as the amount of net proceeds received from the issue and not the face value of securities. The formula may be changed to

$$K_{db} = \frac{1}{NP}(1-t)$$

where,

NP = Net Proceeds

Further, when debt is used as a source of finance, the firm saves a considerable amount in payment of tax as interest is allowed as a deductible expense in computation of tax. Hence, the effective cost of debt is reduced. The After-tax cost of debt may be calculated with the help of following formula:

$$K_{da} = K_{db}(1-t) = \frac{D}{MP}$$

where,

K_{da} = After-tax cost of debt

t = Rate of tax.

Cost of Redeemable Debt. Usually, the debt is issued to be redeemed after a certain period during the life time of a firm. Such a debt issue is known as Redeemable debt. The cost of redeemable debt capital may be computed as:

Before-tax cost of debt:

$$K_{db} = \frac{1+\frac{1}{n}(P-NP)}{\frac{1}{2}(P+NP)}$$

where,

I = Interest

N = Number of years in which debt is to be redeemed

P = Proceeds at par

NP = Net Proceeds

After-tax cost of debt,

$$K_{da} = K_{db}(1-t)$$

$$K_{da} = \frac{1+\frac{1}{n}(P-NP)}{\frac{1}{2}(P+NP)}(1-t)$$

2. **Cost of Preference Capital.** A fixed rate of divided is payable on preference shares. Though dividend is payable at the discretion of the Board of directors and there is no legal binding to pay dividend, yet it does not mean that preference capital is cost free. The cost of preference capital is a function of dividend expected by its investors, *i.e.*, its stated dividend. In case dividends are not paid to preference shareholders, it will affect the fund raising capacity of the firm. Hence, dividends are usually paid regularly on preference share except when there are no profits to pay dividends. The cost of preference capital which is perpetual can be calculated as:

$$K_p = \frac{D}{P}$$

where,

K_p = Cost of Preference Capital

D = Annual Preference Dividend

P = Preference Share Capital (Proceeds).

Further, if preference shares are issued at Premium or Discount or when costs of floatation are incurred to issue preference shares, the nominal or par value of preference share capital has to be adjusted to find out the net proceeds from the issue of preference shares. In such a case, the cost of preference capital can be computed with the following formula:

$$K_p = \frac{D}{NP}$$

It may be noted that as dividends are not allowed to be deducted in computation of tax, no adjustment is required for taxes.

Sometimes Redeemable Preference Shares are issued which can be redeemed or cancelled on maturity date. The cost of redeemable preference share capital can be calculated as:

$$K_{pr} = \frac{D + \frac{MV-NP}{n}}{\frac{1}{2}(MV+NP)}$$

where,

K_{pr} = Cost of Redeemable Preference Shares

D = Annual Preference Dividend

MV = Maturity Value of Preference Shares

NP = Net Proceeds of Preference Shares.

3. **Cost of Equity Share Capital.** The cost of equity is the maximum rate of return that the company must earn on equity financed portion of its investments in order to leave unchanged the market price of its stock. The cost of equity capital is a function of the expected return by its investors. The cost of equity is not the out-of-pocket cost of using equity capital as the equity shareholders are not paid dividend at a fixed rate every year. Moreover, payment of dividend is not a legal binding. It may or may not be paid. But it does not mean that equity share capital is a cost free capital. Shareholders invest money in equity shares on the expectation of getting

dividend and the company must earn this minimum rate so that the market price of the shares remains unchanged. Whenever a company wants to raise additional funds by the issue of new equity shares, the expectations of the shareholders have to be evaluated. The cost of equity share capital can be computed in the following ways:

(a) ***Dividend Yield Method or Dividend Price Ratio Method.*** According to this method, the cost of equity capital is the discount rate that equates the present value of expected future dividends per share with the net proceeds (or current market price) of a share. Symbolically.

$$K_e = \frac{D}{NP} \text{ or } \frac{D}{MP}$$

where,

K_e = Cost of Equity Capital

D = Expected dividend per share

NP = Net proceeds per share and

MP = Market Price per share

The basic assumptions underlying this method are that the investors give prime importance to dividends and risk in the firm remains unchanged. The dividend price ratio method does not seem to consider the growth in dividend, (i) it does not consider future earnings or retained earnings, and (ii) it does not take into account the capital gains. This method of computing cost of equity capital is suitable only when the company has stable earnings and stable dividend policy over a period of time.

(b) ***Dividend yield plus growth in dividend method.*** When the dividends of the firm are expected to grow at a constant rate and the dividend-pay-out ratio is constant, this method may be used to compute the cost of equity capital. According to this method the cost of equity capital is based on the dividends and the growth rate.

$$K_e = \frac{D}{NP} + G$$

where,

K_e = Cost of Equity Capital

D = Expected dividend per share

NP = Net proceeds per share

G = Rate of growth in dividends.

Further, in case cost of existing equity share capital is to be calculated, the NP should be changed with MP (market price per share) in the above equation.

$$K_e = \frac{D}{NP} + G$$

(c) ***Earning Yield Method.*** According to this method, the cost of equity capital is the discount rate that equates the present values of expected future earnings per share with the net proceeds (or, current market price) of a share. Symbolically:

$$K_e = \frac{\text{Earnings per share}}{\text{Net Proceeds}}$$

$$= \frac{EPS}{NP}$$

where, the cost of existing capital is to be calculated:

$$K_e = \frac{\text{Earnings per share}}{\text{Market Price per share}}$$

$$= \frac{\text{EPS}}{\text{MP}}$$

This method of computing cost of equity capital may be employed in the following cases:

(i) When the earnings per share are expected to remain constant.

(ii) When the dividend pay-out-ratio is 100 per cent, *i.e.* all the available profits are distributed as dividends.

(iii) When a firm is expected to earn an amount on new equity share capital, which is equal to the current rate of earning.

(iv) The market price of the share is influenced only by earnings per share.

(d) ***Realised Yield Method.*** One of the serious limitations of using dividend yield method or earnings yield method is the problem of estimating the expectations of the investors regarding future dividends and earnings. It is not possible to estimate future dividends and earnings correctly; both of these depend upon so many uncertain factors. To remove this drawback, realised yield method, which takes into account the actual average rate of return realised in the past, may be applied to compute the cost of equity share capital. To calculate the average rate of return realised, dividends received in the past alongwith the gain realised at the time of sale of shares should be considered. The cost of equity capital is said to be the realised rate of return by the shareholders. This method of computing cost of equity share capital is based upon the following assumption:

(i) The firm will remain in the same risk class over the period;

(ii) The shareholders' expectations are based upon the past realised yield;

(iii) The investors get the same rate of return as the realised yield even if they invest elsewhere and

(iv) The market price of shares does not change significantly.

4. **Cost of Retained Earnings.** It is sometimes argued that retained earnings do not involve any cost because a firm is not required to pay dividends on retained earnings. However, the shareholders expect a return on retained profits. Retained earnings accrue to a firm only because of some sacrifice made by the shareholders in not receiving the dividends out of the available profits.

The cost of retained earnings may be considered as the rate of return which the existing shareholders can obtain by investing the after-tax dividends in alternative opportunity of equal qualities. It is thus the opportunity cost of dividends foregone by the shareholders. Cost of retained earnings can be computed with the help of following formula:

$$K_r = \frac{D}{NP} + G$$

where,

K_r = Cost of retained earnings

D = Expected dividend

NP = Net proceeds of share issue

G = Rate of growth.

Further, it is important to note that shareholders, usually, cannot obtain the entire amount of retained profits by way of dividends even if there is 100 percent pay out ratio. It is so because the shareholders are required to pay tax on their dividend income. So, some adjustment has to be made for tax. However, tax adjustment in determining the cost of retained earnings is a difficult problem because all shareholders do not fall under the same tax bracket. Moreover, if the shareholders wish to invest their after-tax dividend income in alternative securities, they may have to incur some costs of purchasing the securities, such as brokerage. Hence, the effective rate of return realised by the shareholders from the new investment will be somewhat lesser than their present return from the firm. To make adjustment in the cost of retained earnings for tax and costs of purchasing new securities, the following formula may be adopted

$$K_r = \left(\frac{D}{NP} + G\right) \times (1-t) \times (1-b)$$

or

$$K_r = K_e (1-t)(1-b)$$

where,

K_r = Cost of retained earnings
D = Expected dividend
G = Growth Rate
NP = Net Proceeds of Equity Issue
t = Tax rate
b = Cost of purchasing new securities or brokerage costs
K_e = Rate of return available to shareholders.

B. *Computation of Weighted Average Cost of Capital*

Weighted average cost of capital is the average cost of various sources of financing. Weighted average cost of capital is also known as composite cost of capital, overall cost of capital or average cost of capital. Once the specific cost of individual sources of finance is determined, we can compute the weighted average cost of capital by putting weights to the specific costs of capital in proportion of the various sources of funds to the total. The weights may be given either by using the book value of the source or marked value of the source. The cost of capital calculated according to the market value weights is usually higher than the book value weights and market value weights are sometimes preferred to the book value weights because the market value represents the true value of the investors. However, the market value weights suffer from the following limitations:

(i) It is very difficult to determine the market values because of frequent fluctuations.
(ii) With the use of market value weights, equity capital gets greater importance.

For the above limitations, it is better to use book value which is readily available. Weighted average cost of capital can be computed as follows:

$$K_w = \frac{\Sigma XW}{\Sigma W}$$

where,

K_w = Weighted average cost of capital
X = Cost of specific source of finance
W = Weight, proportion of specific source of finance.

TIME VALUE OF MONEY (TVM)

There is no reason for any rational person to delay taking an amount owed to him or her. More than financial principles, this is basic instinct. The money you have in hand at the moment is worth more than the same amount you 'may' get in future. One reason for this is inflation and another is possible earning capacity. The fundamental code of finance maintains that, given money can generate interest, the value of a certain sum is more if you receive it sooner. This is why it is called as the present value.

Basically, the time value of money validates that it is more beneficial to have cash now than later. Say, if you invest a Rs. 100 today - the returns will be more compared to the same investment made 2 months from now. Moreover, there is always a risk that the borrower might delay even more or not pay at all in the future.

TVM with an Example

The relevance of TVM depends on how much returns you can generate from the capital available. Money has immense growth potential and the more you delay employing this potential, the more you lose the chance to earn on it. For instance, if a friend or lender gives you two options - to take Rs. 10,000 today or to take Rs, 10,500 next year.

Now, even if this promise is from someone or an entity you trust implicitly, chances are more that the second option is a raw deal. With more and more schemes ranging from low-risk to high-risk - tax-saving FDs, ELSS et. - there is a high chance that you can make at least 7% on this sum, which is Rs. 10,700. But if the interest rate offered is less than 5%, then you may consider taking the money next year. So, it depends on the possible returns as per the RBI guidelines or the market.

Present Value and Future Value

Present Value is the same as Time Value as elaborated above. It is the money you have currently that is equal to a future one-time disbursal or several part-payments - discounted by a suitable rate of interest.

Future Value is the sum of money that any saving scheme with a compounded interest will build to by a pre-decided future date. It applies to both lumpsum as well as recurring investments like SIP.

Basic TVM Formula

Based on your financial circumstances at the time, the TVM formula can vary to some extent. Example, in the case of annuity (income) or perpetuity (until death) pension payments, the general formula can have more components. But as a whole, the basic TVM formula is as shown:

$FV = PV \times [1 + (I/N)] (N*T)$

Where,

FV is Future value of money,

PV is Present value of money,

I is the interest rate,

N is the number of compounding periods annually and

T is the number of years in the tenure.

For instance, if you invest Rs. 1 lakh for 5 years at 10% interest, the future value of this one lakh will be Rs. 161,051 as per the formula. This formula can help you to analyze different investments over different time periods, enabling you to make optimal and informed financial decisions.

TVM and Compounding Periods

How often the invested amount compounds too has a huge impact on future value. See how increasing the compounding frequency in the above example make a difference to the earnings.

Monthly:	Rs. 164530.89
Quarterly:	Rs. 163,861.64
Semi-annually:	Rs. 162889.46
Annually:	Rs. 161,051

This is where the power of compounding works. It proves that TVM is dependent on interest rate, tenure as well as the number of compounding periods per financial year.

CAPITAL BUDGETING

Capital budgeting is the process of making investment decisions in capital expenditures. A capital expenditure is an expenditure the benefits of which are expected to be received over period of time exceeding one year. Capital budgeting is the process of deciding whether or not to commit resources to a particular long term project whose benefits are to be realised over a period of time, longer than one year.

According to **Charles T. Horngreen**, *'Capital budgeting is long term planning for making and financing proposed capital outlays.*

Features of Capital Budgeting

1. Capital budgeting decisions involve the exchange of current funds for the benefits to be achieved in future.
2. The future benefits are expected to be realised over a series of years.
3. The funds are invested in non-flexible and long term activities.
4. They have a long term and significant effect on the profitability of the concern.
5. They involve, generally, huge funds.
6. They are irreversible decisions.
7. They are 'strategic investment decisions', involving large sums of money.

Methods of Capital Budgeting

A. Traditional Methods

1. **Pay-Back Period Method.** The 'Pay-back' sometimes called as pay out or pay off period method represents the period in which the total investment in permanent assets pays back itself. This method is based on the principle that every capital expenditure pays itself back within a certain period out of the additional earnings generated from the capital assets. Thus, it measures the period of time for the original cost of a project to be recovered from the additional earnings of the project itself. Under this method, various investments are ranked according to the length of their pay back period in such a manner that the investment with a shorter pay back period is preferred to the one which has longer pay back period.

   In case of evaluation of a single project, it is adopted if it pays back for itself within a period specified by the management and if the project does not pay back itself within the period specified by the management then it is rejected.

   The pay-back period can be ascertained in the following manner:

(i) Calculate annual net earnings (profits) before depreciation and after taxes; these are called annual cash inflows.

(ii) Divide the initial outlay (cost) of the project by the annual cash inflow, where the project generates constant annual cash inflows.

Thus, where the project generates constant cash inflows:

$$\text{Pay-back period} = \frac{\text{Cash outlay of the project or Original cost of the asset}}{\text{Annual cash inflows}}$$

(iii) Where the annual cash inflows (Profit before depreciation and after taxes) are unequal, the pay-back period can be found by adding up the cash inflows until the total is equal to the initial cash outlay of project or original cost of the asset.

2. **Improvements in traditional approach to pay back period method**

(i) ***Post Pay-back Profitability Method.*** One of the serious limitations of Pay-back period method is that it does not take into account the cash inflows earned after pay-back period and hence the true profitability of the project cannot be assessed. Hence, improvement over this method can be made by taking into account the returns receivable beyond the pay-back period. These returns are called post pay-back profits.

$$\text{Post Pay-back Profitability Index} = \frac{\text{Post Pay-back Profits}}{\text{Investment}} \times 100$$

(ii) ***Pay-back Reciprocal Method.*** Sometimes, Pay-back Reciprocal method is employed to estimate the internal rate of return generated by a project. Pay-back Reciprocals can be calculated as under:

$$\text{Pay back Reciprocal} = \frac{\text{Annual Cash Inflow}}{\text{Total Investment}}$$

(This can also be calculated in percentage by multiplying the above by 100). However, this method should be used only when the following two conditions are satisfied:

(a) Equal cash inflows are generated every year.

(b) The project under consideration has a long life which must be at least twice the pay-back period.

(iii) ***Post Pay-back Period Method.*** One of the limitations of the pay-back period method is that is it ignores the life of the project beyond the pay-back period. Post Pay-back Period method takes into account the period beyond the pay-back method. This method is also known as Surplus Life over Pay-back method. According to this method, the project which gives the greatest post pay-back period may be accepted. The method can be employed successfully where the various projects under consideration do not differ significantly as to their size and the expected cash inflows are even throughout the life of the project.

(iv) ***Discounted Pay-back Method.*** Another serious limitation of the pay-back period method is that it ignores the time value of money. Hence, an improvement over this method can be made by employing the discounted pay-back period method. Under this method the present values of all cash outflows and inflows are computed at an appropriate discount rate. The present values of all inflows are cumulated in order of time. The time period at which the cumulated present value of cash inflows equals the present value of cash outflows is known as Discounted Pay-back Period. The project which gives a shorter discounted pay-back period is accepted.

3. **Rate of Return Method.** This method takes into account the earnings expected from the investment over their whole life. It is known as Accounting Rate of Return method for the reason that under this method, the accounting concept of profit (net profit after tax and depreciation) is used rather than cash inflows. According to this method, various projects are ranked in order of the rate of earnings or rate of return. The project with the higher rate of return is selected as compared to the one with lower rate of return. This method can also be used to make decision as to accepting or rejecting a proposal. The expected return is determined and the project which has a higher rate of return than the minimum rate specified by the firm called the cut off rate, is accepted and the one which gives a lower expected rate of return than the minimum rate is rejected.

   The return on investment method can be used in several ways as follows:

   (a) ***Average Rate of Return Method***: Under this method average profit after tax and depreciation is calculated and then it is divided by the total capital outlay or total investment in the project. In other words, it establishes the relationship between average annual profits to total investments.

   Thus,

$$\text{Average Rate of Return} = \frac{\text{Total Profits (after depreciation and taxes)}}{\text{Net investment in the project} \times \text{No. of years of profits}} \times 100$$

or

$$= \frac{\text{Average annual profits}}{\text{Net investment in the project}} \times 100$$

   (b) ***Return per unit of Investment Method.*** This method is small variation of the average rate of return method. In this method the total profit after tax and depreciation is dividend by the total investment, *i.e.*,

$$\text{Return per unit of Investment} = \frac{\text{Total Profit (after depreciation and taxes)}}{\text{Net investment in the project}} \times 100$$

   (c) ***Return on Average Investment Method.*** In this method the return on average investment is calculated. Using of average investment for the purpose of return on investment is preferred because the original investment is recovered over the life of the asset on account of depreciation charges. For example:

$$\text{The Return on Average Investment} = \frac{\text{Total Profit after depreciation and taxes}}{\frac{\text{Total Net investment}}{2}} \times 100$$

   (d) ***Average Return on Average Investment Method.*** This is the most appropriate method of rate of return on investment. Under this method, average profit after depreciation and taxes is divided by the average amount of investment;

   thus,

   Average Return on Average Investment

$$= \frac{\text{Average Annual Profit after dep. and taxes}}{\text{Average Investment}} \times 100$$

$$= \frac{\text{Average Annual Profit}}{\frac{\text{Net Investment}}{2}} \times 100$$

B. Time-adjusted or discounted cash flow methods

The traditional methods of capital budgeting *i.e.*, pay-back method as well as accounting rate of return method, suffer from the serious limitations that give equal weight to present and future flow of incomes. These methods do not take into consideration the time value of money, the fact that a rupee earned today has more value than a rupee earned after five years. The time-adjusted or discounted cash flow methods take into account the profitability and also the time value of money. These methods also called modern methods of capital budgeting are becoming increasingly popular day by day. Following are the discounted cash flow methods:

1. **Net present value method.** The net present value method is a modern method of evaluating investment proposals. This method takes into consideration the time value of money and attempts to calculate the return on investments by introducing the factor of time element. It recognises the fact that a rupee earned today is worth more than the same rupee earned tomorrow. The net present values of all inflows and outflows of cash occurring during the entire life of the project is determined separately for each year by discounting these flows by the firm's cost of capital or a pre-determined rate. The following are the necessary steps to be followed for adopting the net present value method of evaluating investment proposals:

   (i) First of all determine an appropriate rate of interest that should be selected as the minimum required rate of return called 'cut-off rate or discount rate'. The rate should be a minimum rate of return below which the investor considers that it does not pay him to invest. The discount rate should be either the actual rate of interest in the market on long-term loans or it should reflect the opportunity cost of capital of the investor.

   (ii) Compute the present value of total investment outlay, *i.e.* cash outflows at the determined discount rate. If the total investment is to be made in the initial year, the present value shall be the same as the cost of investment.

   (iii) Compute the present values of total investment proceeds, *i.e.*, cash inflows, (profit before depreciation and after tax) at the above determined discount rate.

   (iv) Calculate the net present value of each project by subtracting the present value of cash inflows from the present value of cash outflows for each project.

   (v) If the net present value is positive or zero, *i.e.*, when present value of cash inflows either exceeds or is equal to the present value of cash outflows, the proposal may be accepted. But in case the present value of inflows is less than the present value of cash outflows, the proposal should be rejected.

   (vi) To select between mutually exclusive projects, projects should be ranked in order of net present values, *i.e.* the first preference should be given to the project having the maximum positive net present value.

   The present value of Re. 1 due in any number of years can be found with the use of the following mathematical formula:

$$PV = \frac{1}{(1+r)^n}$$

where, PV = present value

r = rate of interest/discount rate

n = number of years

The present value for all the cash inflows for a number of years is thus found as follows:

$$PV = \frac{A_1}{(1+r)} + \frac{A_2}{(1+r)^2} + \frac{A_3}{(1+r)^3} + \cdots\cdots + \frac{A_n}{(1+r)^n}$$

$A_1, A_2, A_3, \ldots\ldots A_n$ = Future net cash flows (profit after tax but before depreciation)

r = rate of interest

1, 2, 3,................., and n = numbers of years

However as n becomes large, the calculations of $(1+r)^n$ becomes difficult. Present value can also be found by the use of Present value Tables.

2. **Internal Rate of Return Method.** The internal rate of return method is also a modern technique of capital budgeting that takes into account the time value of money. It is also known as 'time adjusted rate of return', 'discounted cash flow', 'discounted rate of return', 'yield method' and 'trial and error yield method'. In the net present value method the net present value is determined by discounting the future cash flows of a project at a predetermined or specified rate called the cut-off rate. But under the internal rate of return method, the cash flows of a project are discounted at a suitable rate by hit and trial method, which equates the net present value so calculated to the amount of the investment. Under this method, since the discount rate is determined internally, this method is called as the internal rate of return method. The internal rate of return can be defined as that rate of discount at which the present value of cash-inflows is equal to the present value of cash outflows. It can be determined with the help of the following mathematical formula.

$$C = \frac{A_1}{(1+r)} + \frac{A_2}{(1+r)^2} + \frac{A_3}{(1+r)^3} + \cdots + \frac{A_n}{(1+r)^n}$$

where,

C = Initial outlay at time zero.

$A_1, A_2, A_3, \ldots\ldots A_n$ = Future net cash flows at different periods.

1, 2, 3, ..., n = numbers of years.

r = rate of discount of internal rate of return.

The internal rate of return can also be determined with the help of present value tables. The following steps are required to practice the internal rate of return method.

(i) Determine the future net cash flows during the entire economic life of the project. The cash inflows are estimated for future profits before depreciation but after taxes.

(ii) Determine the rate of discount at which the value of cash inflows is equal to the present value of cash outflows. This may be determined as explained after step (4).

(iii) Accept the proposal if the internal rate of return is higher than or equal to the minimum required rate of return. *i.e.* ,the cost of capital or cut off rate and reject the proposal if the internal rate of return is lower than the cost of cut-off rate.

(iv) In case of alternative proposals select the proposal with the highest rate of return as long as the rates are higher than the cost of capital or cut-off-rate.

Determination of Internal Rate of Return (IRR)

(a) **When the annual net cash flows are equal over the life of the assets.** Firstly, find out present value factor by dividing initial outlay (cost of the investment) by annual cash flow, *i.e.*,

$$\text{Present Value Factor} = \frac{\text{Initial Outlay}}{\text{Annual Cash Flow}}$$

(b) **When the annual cash flows are unequal over the life of the asset.** In case annual cash flows are unequal over the life of the asset, the internal rate of return cannot be determined according to the technique suggested above. In such cases, the internal rate of return is calculated by hit and trial and that is why this method is also known as hit and trial yield method. We may start with any assumed discount rate and find out the total present value of cash outflows which is equal to the cost of the initial investment where total investment is to be made in the beginning. The rate, at which the total present value of all cash inflows equals the initial outlay, is the internal rate of return. Several discount rates may have to be tried until the appropriate rate is found. The calculation process may be summed up as follows:

(i) Prepare the cash flow table using an arbitrary assumed discount rate to discount the net cash flows to the present value.

(ii) Find out the Net Present Value by deducting from the present value of total cash flows calculated in (i) above the initial cost of the investment.

(iii) If the Net Present Value (NPV) is positive, apply higher rate of discount.

(iv) If the higher discount rate still gives a positive net present value, increase the discount rate further until the NPV becomes negative.

(v) If the NPV is negative at this higher rate, the internal rate of return must be between these two rates.

3. Profitability Index Method or Benefit Cost Ratio

It is also a time – adjusted method of evaluating the investment proposals. Profitability index also called as Benefit - Cost Ratio (B/C) or 'Desirability factor' is the relationship between present value of cash inflows and the present value of cash outflows. Thus,

$$\text{Profitability Index} = \frac{\text{Present value of cash inflows}}{\text{Present value of cash outflows}}$$

or

$$\text{P.I.} = \frac{\text{PV of cash inflows}}{\text{Initial cash outlay}}$$

The profitability index may be found for net present values of inflows.

$$\text{P.I. (Net)} = \frac{\text{NPV (Net Present Value)}}{\text{Initial cash outlay}}$$

The net profitability index can also be found as profitability index (gross) minus one.

The proposal is accepted if the profitability index is more than one and is rejected in case the profitability index is less than one. The various projects are ranked under this method in order of their profitability index, in such a manner that one with higher profitability index is ranked higher than the other with lower profitability index.

WORKING CAPITAL MANAGEMENT

Capital required for a business can be classified under two main categories *i.e.*,

(i) Fixed capital

(ii) Working capital

Every business needs funds for two purposes for its establishment and to carry out its day-to-day operations. Long term funds are required to create production facilities through purchase of fixed assets such as plant and machinery, land, building, furniture etc. Investments in these assets represent that part of firm's capital which is blocked on a permanent or fixed basis and is called fixed capital. Funds are also needed for short-term purposes for the purchase of raw materials, payment of wages and other day-to-day expenses, *etc.* these funds are known as working capital.

Working capital, in general practice, refers to the excess of current assets over current liabilities. Management of working capital is therefore concerned with the problems that arise in attempting to manage the current assets, the current liabilities and the inter-relationship that exists between them.

The basic goal of working capital management is to manage the current assets and current liabilities of a firm in such a way that a satisfactory level of working capital is maintained *i.e.* it is neither inadequate nor excessive. Working capital management is three dimensional in nature:

(i) Dimension I is concerned with the formulation of policies with regard to profitability, risk and liquidity.

(ii) Dimension II is concerned with the decisions about the composition and level of current assets.

(iii) Dimension III is concerned with the decisions about the composition and level of current liabilities.

Concepts of Working Capital

There are two concepts of working capital:

(i) Gross working capital

(ii) Net working capital

In the broad sense, the term working capital refers to the gross working capital and represents the amount of funds invested in current assets. Thus, *the gross working capital is the capital invested in total current assets of the enterprise.* Current assets are those assets which in the ordinary course of business can be converted into cash within a short period of normally one accounting year. Examples of current assets are given as under:

Constituents of Current Assets

1. Cash in hand and bank balances.
2. Bills Receivables.
3. Sundry Debtors (less provision for bad debts).
4. Short-term loans and advances.
5. Inventories of stocks, as:
   (a) Raw materials, (b) Work-in-process
   (c) Stores and spares, (d) Finished goods.
6. Temporary investments of surplus funds.
7. Prepaid Expenses.
8. Accrued Incomes.

In a narrow sense, the term working capital refers to the net working capital. *Net working capital is the excess of current assets over current liabilities*, or say:

Net working capital = *Current Assets* – *Current liabilities*

Net working capital may be positive or negative. When the current assets exceed the current liabilities the working capital is positive and the negative working capital results when the current liabilities are more than the current assets. Current liabilities are those liabilities which are intended to be paid in the ordinary course of business within a short period of normally one accounting year out of the current assets or the income of the business. Examples of current liabilities are given as under:

Constituents of Current Liabilities

1. Bills Payable.
2. Sundry Creditors or Accounts Payable.

3. Accrued or Outstanding Expenses.
4. Short-term loans, advances and deposits.
5. Dividends Payable.
6. Bank Overdraft.
7. Provision for taxation, if it does not amount to appropriation of profits.

The gross working capital concept is financial or going concern concept whereas net working capital is an accounting concept of working capital. These two concepts of working capital are not exclusive, rather both have their own merits. The gross concept is sometimes preferred to the net concept of working capital for the following reasons:

1. It enables the enterprise to provide correct amount of working capital at the right time.
2. Every management is more interested in the total current assets with which it has to operate than the sources from where it is made available.
3. The gross concept takes into consideration the fact that every increase in the funds of the enterprise would increase its working capital.
4. The gross concept of working capital is more useful in determining the rate of return on investments in working capital.

The net working capital concept, however, is also important for the following reasons:

1. It is a qualitative concept which indicates the firm's ability to meet its operating expenses and short-term liabilities.
2. It indicates the margin of protection available to the short-term creditors, *i.e.*, the excess of current assets over current liabilities.
3. It is an indicator of the financial soundness of an enterprise.
4. It suggests the need for financing a part of the working capital requirements out of permanent sources of funds.

To conclude, it may be said that, both gross and net, concepts of working capital are important aspects of the working capital management. The net concept of working capital may be suitable only for proprietary form of organisations such as sole-trader or partnership firms. But the gross concept is very suitable to the company form of organisation where there is a divorce between ownership, management and control.

However, it may be made clear that *as per the general practice, net working capital is referred to simply as working capital*. In the words of Hoagland, "Working capital is descriptive of that capital which is not fixed. But the more common use of the working capital is to consider it as the difference between the book value of the current assets and current liabilities."

Classification or Kinds of Working Capital

1. **Permanent or Fixed Working Capital.** Permanent or fixed working capital is the minimum amount which is required to ensure effective utilisation of fixed facilities and for maintaining the circulation of current assets. There is always a minimum level of current assets which is continuously required by the enterprise to carry out its normal business operations. For example, every firm has to maintain a minimum level of raw materials, work-in-process, finished goods and cash balance. This minimum level of current assets is called permanent or fixed working capital as this part of capital is permanently blocked in current assets. As the business grows, the requirements of permanent working capital also increase due to the increase in current assets. The permanent working capital can further be classified as regular working capital and reserve working capital required to ensure circulation of current assets from cash to inventories, from inventories to receivables and from receivables to cash and so on. Reserve working capital is the excess amount over the requirement for regular working

capital which may be provided for contingencies that may arise at unstated periods such as strikes, rise in prices, depression, *etc*.

2. **Temporary or Variable Working Capital.** Temporary or variable working capital is the amount of working capital which is required to meet the seasonal demands and some special exigencies. Variable working capital can be further classified as seasonal working capital and special working capital. Most of the enterprises have to provide additional working capital to meet the seasonal and special needs. The capital required to meet the seasonal needs of the enterprise is called seasonal working capital. Special working capital is that part of working capital which is required to meet special exigencies such as launching of extensive marketing campaigns, for conducting research, *etc*.

   Temporary working capital differs from permanent working capital in the sense that it is required for short periods and cannot be permanently employed gainfully in the business. Figures given below illustrate the difference between permanent and temporary working capital.

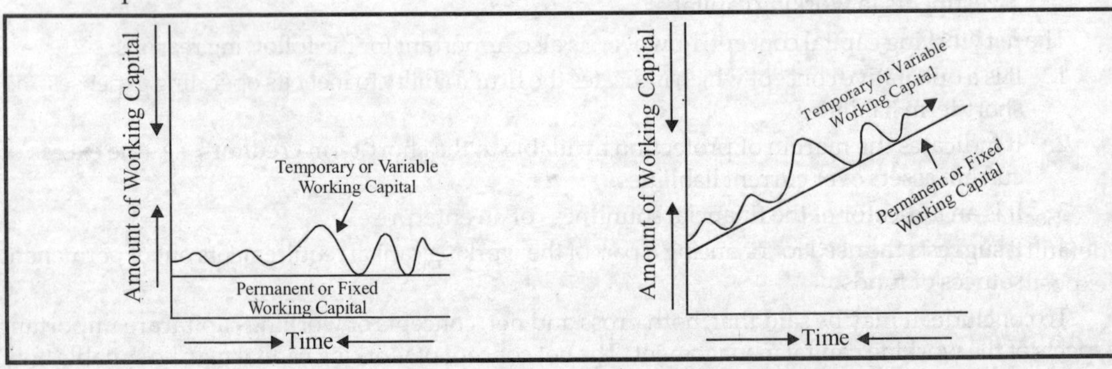

Fig. 1. Fig. 2

In Fig. 1, permanent working capital is stable or fixed over time while the temporary or variable working capital fluctuates. In Fig. 2, permanent working capital is also increasing with the passage of time due to expansion of business but even then it does not fluctuate as variable working capital which sometimes increases and sometimes decreases.

DIVIDEND POLICY

The term dividend refers to that part of profits of a company which is distributed by the company among its shareholders. It is the reward of the shareholders for investments made by them in the shares of the company. The investors are interested in earning the maximum return on their investments and to maximise their wealth. A company, on the other hand, needs to provide funds to finance its long-term growth. If a company pays out as dividend most of what it earns, then for business requirements and further expansions it will have to depend upon outside resources such as issue of debt or new shares. Dividend policy of a firm, thus affects both the long-term financing and wealth of shareholders.

Types of Dividend Policy

1. **Regular Dividend Policy.** Payment of dividend at the usual rate is termed as regular dividend. The investors such as retired persons, widows and other economically weaker persons prefer to get regular dividends.
2. **Stable Dividend Policy.** The term stability of dividend's means consistency or lack of variability in the stream of dividend payments. It may be established in three forms:

(a) ***Constant dividend per share.*** Some companies follow a policy of paying fixed dividend per share irrespective of the level of earnings year after year. Such firms usually create a 'Reserve for Dividend Equalisation', to enable them pay the fixed dividend even in the year when the earnings are not sufficient.

(b) ***Constant pay out ratio.*** It means payment of a fixed percentage of net earnings as dividends every year. The amount of dividends in such a policy fluctuates in direct proportion to the earnings of the company.

(c) ***Stable rupee dividend plus extra dividend.*** Some companies follow a policy of paying constant low dividend per share plus an extra dividend in the years of high profits.

3. **Irregular Dividend Policy.** Some companies follow irregular dividend payments on account of the following:
   (a) Uncertainty of earnings. (b) Unsuccessful business operations.
   (c) Lack of liquid resources.
   (d) Fear of adverse effects of regular dividends on the financial standing of the company.
4. **No Dividend Policy.** A company may follow a policy of paying no dividends presently because of its unfavourable working capital position or on account of requirements of funds for future expansion and growth.

RISK AND RETURN ANALYSIS: ASSET SECURITIZATION

Securitization is a risk management tool used to reduce idiosyncratic risk associated with the default of individual assets. Banks and other financial institutions use securitization to lower their exposure to risk and reduce the size of their overall balance sheet.

The Securitization Process

Securitization can be best described as a two-step process:

Step 1: Packaging. The bank (or financial institution) combines multiple assets into a single "compound asset." The return offered by the compound asset is some weighted average of the return offered by the individual assets that make up the "compound asset."

Step 2: Sale. The bank (or financial institution) sells the "compound asset" to global capital market investors.

How Securitization Works

Securitization works on the assumption that the probability of several assets defaulting is lower than the probability of a single asset defaulting. It assumes that the default probability of different assets is independently distributed. The logic underlying the practice of securitization can be best described using an example.

Asset	Return	Default Probability
A	40%	0.2
B	48%	0.3
C	64%	0.35

Three investors invested \$1,000 in three separate assets: Asset A, Asset B, and Asset C. They sell the assets to a bank. The expected return from the investment is $(40\% \times 1000 \times 0.8) + (48\% \times 1000 \times 0.7) + (64\% \times 1000 \times 0.65) = 320 + 336 + 416 = \$1072 = 35.73\%$ return. However, the variance associated with the above investments is very high.

Therefore, the bank wants to remove the assets from its balance sheet. The bank creates a Compound Asset X by combining Simple Assets A, B, and C. Consider an investor who purchases $100 worth of X. The investor will receive a 50.66% rate of return. However, the investor faces considerable less risk than an individual investor who only owns one of the assets A, B, or C.

Situation	Probability	Returns
None Fail	0.364	+1520
A Fails	0.2	+120
B Fails	0.3	+40
C Fails	0.35	−120
A and B Fails	0.06	−1360
A and C Fails	0.07	−1520
B and C Fails	0.105	−1600
All Fail	0.021	−3000

History of Securitization

Banks in the US first started securitizing home mortgages in the 1970s. The initial "mortgage-backed securities" were seen as relatively safe and allowed banks to give out more mortgage loans to prospective home owners. The practice created a housing boom in the US and resulted in a tremendous increase in house prices across the country.

In the 1980s, Wall Street investment banks extended the idea of the mortgage-backed securities to other types of assets. They realized that securitization drastically increased the number of securities available in the market without the need to raise any real economic variable. The increase in the number of securities available raised the number of potential transactions the banks could make (most banks were paid according to the number of transactions they were involved in).

The rapid deterioration in the quality of the underlying assets within the market for asset-backed securities and a general lack of government regulation was one of the key reasons for the 2008 recession.

INTERNATIONAL MONETARY SYSTEM

International monetary system refers to a system that forms rules and standards for facilitating international trade among the nations.

It helps in reallocating the capital and investment from one nation to another.

It is the global network of the government and financial institutions that determine the exchange rate of different currencies for international trade. It is a governing body that sets rules and regulations by which different nations exchange currencies with each other.

With the growing complexity in the international trade and financial market, the international monetary system is necessary to assign a standard value of the international currencies. The rules and regulations set by the international monetary system to regulate and control the exchange value of the currencies are agreed upon by the respective governments of the nations. Thus, the government's stand may affect the decision making of the international monetary system. For example, change in the trade policy of a government may affect the international trade of goods and services.

International monetary system motivates and encourages the nations to participate in the international trade to improve their BOP and minimize the trade deficit. It has grown over the years as a single architectural body with a vision to integrate the global economy. Some of the important achievements of the international monetary system over the years have been the establishment of World Bank and International Monetary Fund in the year 1944.

The establishment of IMF and World Bank is the result of the agreement among nations to set a body, which promotes and supports the international trade. Now, let's discuss the evolution of international monetary system. Earlier in 1870 to 1914, trade was carried with the help of gold and silver without any institutional support. At that time, monetary system was decentralized and market based and money played a minor role as compared to gold in international trade.

The use of gold declined after World War I as war increased expenditure and inflation. In such a scenario, countries planned to revive the standard of gold but failed due to great depression. Thus, in 1944, 730 representatives of 44 nations met at Bretton Woods, New Hampshire, United States to create a new international monetary system.

This was called as the Bretton Woods system, which became a turning point in the history of international trade. The aim of new international monetary system is to create a stabilized international currency system and ensure a monetary stability for all the nations.

It was decided that since the United States held most of the world's gold, thus all the nations would determine the values of their currencies in terms of dollar. The central banks of nations were given the task of maintaining fixed exchange rates with respect to dollar for each currency.

The Bretton Woods system ended in 1971 as the trade deficit and growing inflation undermined the value of dollar in the whole world. In 1973, the floating exchange rate system, also known as flexible exchange rate system was developed that was market based.

FOREIGN EXCHANGE MARKET

The foreign exchange market is an over-the-counter (OTC) marketplace that determines the exchange rate for global currencies. Participants are able to buy, sell, exchange and speculate on currencies. Foreign exchange markets are made up of banks, forex dealers, commercial companies, central banks, investment management firms, hedge funds, retail forex dealers and investors.

Forex Market Basics

Understanding the Foreign Exchange Market

The foreign exchange market - also called forex, FX, or currency market - was one of the original financial markets formed to bring structure to the burgeoning global economy. In terms of trading volume it is, by far, the largest financial market in the world. Aside from providing a venue for the buying, selling, exchanging and speculation of currencies, the forex market also enables currency conversion for international trade settlements and investments. According to the Bank for International Settlements (BIS), which is owned by central banks, trading in foreign exchange markets averaged $5.1 trillion per day in April 2016.

Currencies are always traded in pairs, so the "value" of one of the currencies in that pair is relative to the value of the other. This determines how much of country A's currency country B can buy, and vice versa. Establishing this relationship (price) for the global markets is the main function of the foreign exchange market. This also greatly enhances liquidity in all other financial markets, which is key to overall stability.

The value of a country's currency depends on whether it is a "free float" or "fixed float". Free floating currencies are those whose relative value is determined by free market forces, such as supply / demand relationships. A fixed float is where a country's governing body sets its currency's relative value to other currencies, often by pegging it to some standard. Free floating currencies include the U.S. Dollar, Japanese Yen and British Pound, while examples of fixed floating currencies include the Chinese Yuan and the Indian Rupee.

One of the most unique features of the forex market is that it is comprised of a global network of financial centers that transact 24 hours a day, closing only on the weekends. As one major forex hub closes, another hub in a different part of the world remains open for business. This increases the liquidity available in currency markets, which adds to its appeal as the largest asset class available to investors.

The most liquid trading pairs are, in descending order of liquidity:

1. EUR/USD 2. USD/JPY 3. GBP/USD

KEY TAKEAWAYS

- The foreign exchange market is an over-the-counter (OTC) marketplace that determines the exchange rate for global currencies.
- It is, by far, the largest financial market in the world and is comprised of a global network of financial centers that transact 24 hours a day, closing only on the weekends.
- Currencies are always traded in pairs, so the "value" of one of the currencies in that pair is relative to the value of the other.

Forex Leverage

The leverage available in FX markets is one of the highest that traders and investors can find anywhere. Leverage is a loan given to an investor by their broker. With this loan, investors are able to increase their trade size, which could translate to greater profitability. A word of caution, though: losses are also amplified.

For example, investors who have a \$1,000 forex market account can trade \$100,000 worth of currency with a margin of 1 percent. This is referred to as having a 100:1 leverage. Their profit or loss will be based on the \$100,000 notional amount.

Benefits of Using the Forex Market

There are some key factors that differentiate the forex market from others, like the stock market.

- There are fewer rules, which means investors aren't held to the strict standards or regulations found in other markets.
- There are no clearing houses and no central bodies that oversee the forex market.
- Most investors won't have to pay the traditional fees or commissions that you would on another market.
- Because the market is open 24 hours a day, you can trade at any time of day, which means there's no cut-off time to be able to participate in the market.
- Finally, if you're worried about risk and reward, you can get in and out whenever you want and you can buy as much currency as you can afford.

FOREIGN EXCHANGE RISK MANAGEMENT

1. **Identification and quantification of exposure.** Business cycle of the company is analyzed to identify where foreign exchange risk exists. Future cash flow which are confirm to arise out of contracts already entered and future foreign currency cash flows which are not confirm over the time period are forecasted and measured to get the foreign exchange exposure. After measuring the level of exposure of the company, decision is to be made regarding what magnitude of risk is to be hedged and how much risk is to be covered.
2. **Policy formulation.** Effective FERM requires well-framed policies, clear objectives and parameters within which the strategy is to be controlled. These policies should clearly mention

the principles which is to be followed and extent of hedging (risk coverage) which are needed. Objectives should set standard for bank's exposure to foreign exchange risk; and personnel are appointed who have the authority to trade in foreign exchange on behalf of company; and should mention the different currencies, which have been approved for transaction within the company. There should be some stop loss arrangements to prevent the firm from abnormal losses if the forecasts turn out wrong. There should be monitoring systems to detect critical levels in the foreign exchange rates where appropriate measure is required.

3. **Hedging.** After formulating policies, the firms then decides about an appropriate hedging strategies keeping in mind the principles and objectives and extent of exposure coverage. There are various financial instruments available for the firm to mitigate its risk- futures, forwards, options and swaps and issue of foreign debt. Hedging strategies and instruments are explained later.
4. **Reporting and Review.** Risk management policies are periodically reviewed based on periodic reports prepared. These periodic reports measure the effectiveness of hedging strategy adopted by the company to mitigate its foreign exchange exposure. The review of risk management policies are done to judge the validity of benchmarks set; whether they are effective in controlling the exposures; what the market trends are and whether the overall strategy is enough or change is required in it.

Hedging Tools and Techniques

External Techniques

1. **Forward Contracts.** Forward contracts involve an agreement between two parties to buy/sell a specific quantity of an underlying asset at a fixed price on a specified date in the future. In other words, Forward contracts are those where counterparty agrees to exchange a specified quantity of an asset at a future date for a price agreed today. These are the most commonly used foreign exchange risk management tools. The corporations can enter into forward contracts for the foreign currencies which it need for payment or which it will receive in future. Since the rate of exchange is already fixed for the future transaction, there will be no variability in the cash flows. Hence, changes that take place between the contract date and the actual transaction date does not make any impact. This will eliminate the foreign exchange exposure. The future settlement date can be an exact date or any time between two agreed dates.
2. **Currency Futures.** Currency futures contract involves a standardized contract between two parties to buy/sell an amount of currency at a fixed price on a specified date in the future and are traded on organized exchanges. Futures contracts are more liquid than forward contracts as they are traded in an organized exchange. A depreciation of currency can be hedged by selling futures and currency appreciations can be hedged by buying futures. Thus, inflow and outflow of different currencies with respect to each other can be fixed by selling and buying currency futures, eliminating the Foreign Exchange Exposure.
3. **Currency Options.** Currency options are contracts which provides the holder the right to buy or sell a specified amount of currency for a specified price over a given time period. Currency options give the owner of the agreement the right to buy or sell but not an obligation. The owner of the agreement has a choice whether to use or not to use the option based on the exchange rates. He/she can choose to sell or buy the currency or let the option lapse. The writer of the option gets a price for granting this option. The price payable is known as premium. The fixed price at which the owner can sell or buy the currency is called as strike price or the exercise price. Options giving the holder a right to buy are called call options and Options giving the holder a right to sell is called put options. It is possible to take advantage

of the potential gains through currency options. For example, If an Indian business firm has to purchase capital goods from the USA in US$ after three months, the company should buy a currency call option. There are two possibilities. First, if the dollar depreciates, then the exchange rates will be favorable as spot rate will be less than the strike price and the company can buy the US$ at the prevailing spot rate, as it will cost less. Second, if the dollar appreciates, then the exchange rates will be unfavorable as spot rate will be more than the strike price and the company can opt to use its right and buy the US$ at the strike price. Hence, in both the cases the company will be paying the less to buy the dollar to pay for the goods.

4. **Currency Swaps.** A currency swap involves an agreement between two parties to exchange a series of cash flows in one currency for a series of cash flows in another currency, at agreed intervals over an agreed period is done to convert a liability in one currency to some other currency. Its purpose is to raise funds denominated in other currency. One party holding one currency swaps it for another currency held by other party. Each party would pay the interest for the exchanged currency at regular interval of time during the term of the loan. At maturity or at the termination of the loan period each party would re-exchange the principal amount in two currencies.
5. **Foreign Debt.** Foreign debts are an effective way to hedge the foreign exchange exposure. This is supported by the International Fischer Effect relationship. For example, a company is expected to receive a fixed amount of Euros at a future date. There is a possibility that the company can experience loss if the domestic currency appreciates against the Euros. To hedge this, company can take a loan in Euros for the same time period and convert the foreign currency into domestic currency at the spot exchange rate. And when the company receives Euros, it can pay off its loan in Euros. Hence the company can completely eliminate its foreign exchange exposure.
6. **Cross Hedging.** Cross Hedging means taking opposing position in two positively correlated currencies. It can be used when hedging of a particular foreign currency is not possible. Even though hedging is done in a different currency, the effects would remain the same and hence cross hedging is an important technique that can be used by companies.
7. **Currency Diversification.** Currency Diversification means investing in securities denominated in different currencies. Diversification reduces the risk even if currencies are non-correlated. It will give the company global exposure, minimize foreign exchange exposure and capitalize on exchange rate disparities.

Internal Techniques

A. **Netting.** Netting implies offsetting exposures in one currency with exposure in the same or another currency, where exchange rates are expected to move high in such a way that losses or gains on the first exposed position should be offset by gains or losses on the second currency exposure. It is of two types of bilateral netting & multilateral netting. In bilateral netting, each pair of subsidiaries nets out their own positions with each other. Flows are reduced by the lower of each company's purchases from or sales to its netting partner.

B. **Matching.** Matching refers to the process in which a company matches its currency inflows with its currency outflows with respect to amount and timing. When a company has receipts and payments in same foreign currency due at same time, it can simply match them against each other. Hedging is required for unmatched portion of foreign currency cash flows. This kind of operation is referred to as natural matching. Parallel matching is another possibility. When gains in one foreign currency are expected to be offset by losses in another, if the movements in two currencies are parallel is called parallel matching.

C. **Leading and Lagging.** These involve adjusting the timing of the payment or receivables. Leading is accelerating payment of strengthening currencies and speeding up the receipt of weakening currencies. Lagging is delaying payment of weakening currencies and postponing receipt of strengthening currencies. In these the payable or receivable of the foreign currency is postponed in order to benefit from the movements in exchange rates.

D. **Pricing Policy.** There can be two types of pricing tactics: price variation and currency of invoicing policy. Price variation can be done as increasing selling prices to offset the adverse effects of exchange rate fluctuations. However, it may affect the sales volume. So proper analysis should be done regarding customer loyalty, market position, competitive position before increasing price. Secondly, foreign customers can be insisted to pay in home currency and paying all imports in home currency.

E. **Government Exchange Risk Guarantee.** Government agencies in many countries provide insurance against export credit risk and introduce special export financing schemes for exporters in order to promote exports. In recent years a few of these agencies have begun to provide exchange risk insurance to their exporters and the usual export credit guarantees. The exporter pays a small premium on his export sales and for this premium the government agency absorbs all exchange losses and gains beyond a certain level.

INTERNATIONAL FINANCIAL MARKETS

International financial markets consist of mainly international banking services and international money market. The banking services include the services such as trade financing, foreign exchange, foreign investment, hedging instruments such as forwards and options, etc. All these banking services are provided by international banks. International money market includes the Euro currency markets, Euro credits, Euro notes, Euro commercial Paper etc.

International financial markets, as we saw, can broadly be classified into international banking and international money market. International markets are accessed by multinational corporations more than anybody else. Traders or businesses having import and export transaction also have frequent access to these markets.

International Banking

International banking is quite different from the domestic banking as there are several services which are required only in an international environment and are provided by international banks. Following are such services:

Trade Financing. Several trade financing services are required by importers and exporters. An importer importing goods from outside may wish to open a letter of credit to be given to the exporter from another country. The importer is not known to the exporter and therefore the deal is routed through the banks.

Documentary collection is another in which the exporter of goods provides the bank with all the documents required for releasing the goods under shipment. They are handed over to the importer only after the payment is made to the bank.

A trader who is not a place invest a lot of money into his debtors can avail factoring and forfeiting services. Under this service, the trader hands over his accounts receivables into a bank or third party's hand for collection. The trader effectively sells his debtors at a discount and frees his money.

Foreign Exchange. International businesses have frequent transactions in foreign currencies and therefore have payables or receivables in those currencies. To close such transactions the businesses need foreign exchange which is provided by international banks and institutions. These institutions have their bid and ask rates for such currency buying and deposits. They buy or accept currencies at a bid price which is less than their ask price at which they sell. These banks have the privilege to trade foreign exchange in international markets.

Foreign Investments. We all know that the banks are no more doing traditional banking. They have a gamut of services to be provided to their clients both domestic and international. Foreign investment is one of such services being provided by multinational banks to their clients. Since these banks have the presence in many countries; they are better positioned to provide consulting services to their clients for their investing requirements.

Hedging Exchange Rate Risk. It is known fact that the dealing in foreign currency is risky. The risk is assumed because the prices of currencies are very fluctuating. The price at which a deal is struck may not remain constant till all the transactions are over. Here is where the hedging plays an important role. With the help of hedging instruments such as forwards and options, such risk can be mitigated and planned profits may be attained. Such instruments are the contracts which lock the prices of currency on a particular day in future.

International Money Market. International money market mainly deals in Euro currency deposits, Euro credits, Euro notes, Euro commercial Papers etc. All these involve foreign currencies. Euro currency deposits are deposits of foreign currency in a bank situated in a country which is different from the country of that foreign currency. An Indian depositing US dollars in Chinese bank situated in China is called Euro currency deposit.

Euro credits are a kind of loan extended to corporations in a currency other than the home currencies. These are normally short term to the medium term loan and are extended by a syndicate of banks because the quantum of loan is too big and the risk cannot be assumed just by one bank.

Likewise, the other money market instruments include euro notes, euro commercial papers etc.

In essence, the international financial market is even bigger a market available for multinational and other domestic companies. A growing business when reaches international heights also has a lot of services to be offered by international banks and financial institutions. These markets provide a business with a platform to take their businesses to a different height.

EUROPEAN AND GLOBAL DEPOSITARY RECEIPT

Most international investors are familiar with American Depositary Receipts (ADRs) that make it easy to purchase foreign companies on U.S. stock exchanges. But, there are several other types of depositary receipts that investors may come across.

What are Depositary Receipts?

Depositary receipts are simply financial instruments trading on a local exchange that represent a foreign company's publicly-traded securities.

Depositary receipts are issued by investment banks in a process that involves purchasing shares in a foreign company, grouping them into packets (usually 10 shares per packet), and issuing each packet as a depositary receipt on a local stock exchange. The shares issued on the stock exchange are priced in a local currency and pay dividends in a local currency, which simplifies that process for domestic investors looking to buy shares in foreign stock.

The prices of depositary receipts are based on the value of the underlying shares, but they are independently traded and settled. For example, Roche Holdings Ltd. (VTX: ROG) on the SIX Swiss Exchange won't have the same valuation as the Roche Holdings Ltd. (OTC: RHHBY) ADR. Traders may even find arbitrage opportunities between the shares where they can simultaneously buy a foreign stock and sell an ADR for a marginal profit.

Types of Depositary Receipts

Depositary receipts work the same regardless of their region with the exception of the stock exchange and underlying currency. That said, there are different terms used by investors for depositary receipts in different regions, that are important to know.

American Depositary Receipts (ADRs) may be the most familiar to U.S. international investors. An ADR represents a set number of shares of a foreign stock and trades on a U.S. stock exchanges, such as the New York Stock Exchange (NYSE) or NASDAQ.

European Depositary Receipts (EDRs) provide European investors with locally-traded shares in non-European companies. While EDRs may be issued in any European currency, the most common currency is the euro, since it's the most widely used in the region.

Global Depositary Receipts (GDRs) are the generalized form of an ADR or EDR. In other words, they represent non-American and non-European depositary receipts. They are most commonly used by developed markets to invest in frontier or emerging markets.

Depositary Receipt Trading

The most popular issuers of GDRs include J.P. Morgan, Citigroup, Deutsche Bank, and the Bank of New York Mellon, but there are countless banks that issue these kinds of securities around the world. These banks generate revenue when the ADRs are sold into the market by charging a commission on the trade-just like any other trade. Banks may also charge fees on dividends issued and pass on any expenses related to currency conversions.

These ADRs are listed on stock exchanges like the Frankfurt Stock Exchange, Luxembourg Stock Exchange, and the London Stock Exchange. At these exchanges, ADRs trade on the International Order Book-or IOB-that serves as an electronic order book for international securities.

Investors trading ADRs, EDRs, or GDRs should also be aware of several unique risk factors that could influence their profitability:

- **Currency Risk.** Depositary Receipts must be converted into the home currency at some point, which means that currency dynamics can make a big difference on pricing and dividend yields. Investors should keep these factors in mind.
- **Political Risk.** Depositary Receipts represent ownership in international shares, which means that they may be subject to international risk factors, such as political risks, especially because they typically target emerging markets.
- **Liquidity Risk.** Depositary Receipts may not trade as frequently as the foreign stock, which means that investors could have a hard time buying or selling at a fair price, particularly when a market is moving sharply lower.

The Bottom Line

Most international investors are familiar with American Depositary Receipts (ADRs) that make it easy to purchase foreign companies on U.S. stock exchanges. But, there are several other types of depositary receipts that investors may come across, including European Depositary Receipts (EDRs) and Global Depositary Receipts (GDRs). It's important for international investors to understand these terms to fully understand the best ways to buy and sell shares, as well as the unique risk factors that may be involved in the process.

INTERNATIONAL ARBITRAGE

Arbitrage can be loosely defined as capitalizing on a discrepancy in quoted prices by making a riskless profit. In many cases, the strategy does not require an investment of funds to be tied up for a length of time and does not involve any risk.

Locational Arbitrage

Commercial banks providing foreign exchange services normally quote about the same rates on currencies, so shopping around may not necessarily lead to a more favorable rate. If the demand and supply conditions for a particular currency vary among banks, the banks may price that currency at different rates, and market forces will force realignment. When quoted exchange rates vary among locations, participants in the foreign exchange market can capitalize on the discrepancy. Specifi cally, they can use locational arbitrage, which is the process of buying a currency at the location where it is priced cheap and immediately selling it at another location where it is priced higher

Triangular Arbitrage

Cross exchange rates represent the relationship between two currencies that are different from one's base currency. In the United States, the term cross exchange rate refers to the relationship between two nondollar currencies.

Covered Interest Arbitrage

The forward rate of a currency for a specified future date is determined by the interaction of demand for the contract (forward purchases) versus the supply (forward sales). Forward rates are quoted for some widely traded currencies (just below the respective spot rate quotation) in the Wall Street Journal. Financial institutions that offer foreign exchange services set the forward rates, but these rates are driven by the market forces (demand and supply conditions). In some cases, the forward rate may be priced at a level that allows investors to engage in arbitrage. Their actions will affect the volume of orders for forward purchases or forward sales of a particular currency, which in turn will affect the equilibrium forward rate. Arbitrage will continue until the rate is aligned where it should be, and at that point arbitrage will no longer be feasible. This arbitrage process and its effects on the forward rate are described next. Covered interest arbitrage is the process of capitalizing on the interest rate differential between two countries while covering your exchange rate risk with a forward contract. The logic of the term covered interest arbitrage becomes clear when it is broken into two parts: "interest arbitrage" refers to the process of capitalizing on the difference between interest rates between two countries; "covered" refers to hedging your position against exchange rate risk. Covered interest arbitrage is sometimes interpreted to mean that the funds to be invested are borrowed locally. In this case, the investors are not tying up any of their own funds. In another interpretation, however, the investors use their own funds. In this case, the term arbitrage is loosely defined since there is a positive dollar amount invested over a period of time. The following discussion is based on this latter meaning of covered interest arbitrage; under either interpretation, however, arbitrage should have a similar impact on currency values and interest rates.

MULTINATIONAL CAPITAL BUDGETING

1. **Complexities of Regulatory Environment.** The differences exist between the parent's cash flow and the project's cash flow because of tax laws and other regulatory environment. For parent, the cash flows to the parent are relevant because the shareholders expect higher rate of return. Therefore, it is necessary to make a distinction between parent's cash flow from that of the project.

2. **Complexities Due to Type of Financing.** Parent's cash flows depend on the form of financing that parent adopts to finance the project (debt versus equity). Thus the parent's cash flows cannot be separated from the financing decisions.
3. **Difficulty in Recognizing the Exact Remittances.** Remittances to the parent must be explicitly recognized. The differences in tax laws, and political systems, differences in financial markets and institutions function, the cash flows to the parent tend to vary. These aspects are also required to be considered while determining parent's cash flows.
4. **Difficultly in Anticipating Inflation Rates.** The rate of inflation in host country and parent country must also be anticipated to decide the real return and exchange rate forecasts. Inflation also changes the competitive positron of the product or service to be marketed. If the cash flows are in different currencies, the expected inflation rates are required to be forecasted for evaluating a project.
5. **Difficulty in Anticipating Changes in Exchange Rate.** The cash flow of the parent firm going to be affected on account of change in the exchange rate between parent firm's currency and foreign subsidiary unit's currency. Such changes in the exchange rate also affect the competitive position of the parent firm, and in turn impact the long term cash flow of the project.
6. **Segmented Capital Markets.** Since the project is being implemented in a different country, therefore the capital markets are segmented by space. Use of segmented capital markets may provide an opportunity or may involve higher costs. The financing aspect has to be carefully examined, by considering the regulating framework in respective countries.
7. **Subsidized Loans and Cost of Capital.** Uses of subsidized loans complicate both the capital structure and the ability to calculate weighted average cost of capital for discounting purposes.
8. **Evaluation of Political Risk.** For each project political risk must be evaluated, because the cash flows can be severely affected by the changes in political environment. The changes in the government would change the political philosophy thereby leading to new economic environment.

   Extreme form of risk is the 'risk of expropriation' and repatriation. In the case of expropriation, the projects and the parent's cash flows tend to change drastically because in this case the funds are blocked in the country of the project.
9. **Cash Flow Determination.** Like domestic capital budgeting decisions, foreign investment decisions require to be evaluated on the basis of their cash flow requirements and their cash flow after taxation (CFAT) generating capacity in the future years.

A: At the Level of Subsidiary:

Assume that the subsidiary is an independent company and calculations are to be performed in the local currency where the subsidiary is located, determination of cash outflows as well as cash inflows related to the project is a simple exercise. In fact, it is similar to domestic investment decisions.

B: At the Level of Parent:

The parent firm makes investment in the form of FDI; hence the interested value would be availability of prospective cash flow to be remitted to the parent firm. The cash flow after taxation available to the foreign subsidiary will not have importance.

The difference between above two cash flows arises on account of tax regulations, exchange controls, inflation and currency fluctuations. It is often customary to charge fees for technology transfer, management or supervisory fees and royalties from the subsidiary unit. Though they are treated as project expenses by the subsidiary, they in fact constitute returns (cash inflows) to the parent MNC.

Above all, a difference may also crop up if the project involves local production of products hitherto exported by parent company to the host country. The difference may be favourable to parent MNC, if the project can augment or promote sales of its other product(s), in host country.

The parent firm requires specific forecasts regarding the amounts and time period when such remittances are expected to be received from the foreign subsidiary or affiliates. In addition, to the financial other benefits are available in the indirect form to the parent firm, like acquiring the better knowledge about taste, fashion, and attitude of market, habits and willingness to consume of foreigners, etc.

Such knowledge and exposure supports the parent firm in future, to diversify in different product groups, or to enter in to new market. It also supports them to strengthen their research and developmental activities. For instance, some companies like to enter first into South-East Asia before trying to establish a subsidiary in Japan or China.

Thus, evaluation of cash flows from the perspective of the parent firm should reckon factors such as taxes, restrictions on repatriation of income, exchange rate risk, country risk (political and economic risk) and so on.

The effect of government priorities and other factors on APV of a project, being in a sector which is in a high priority area for the foreign government may result in one or more of the following:

1. A higher amount of blocked funds getting activated.
2. More profits being allowed to be repatriated to the foreign parent company.
3. Lower taxes (which would affect the profitability of a project only if these rates are still higher than the domestic tax rates faced by the parent company).
4. A higher depreciation allowance leading to a higher depreciation tax shield,
5. A larger concessionary loan and / or a lower interest rate charged on the loan.

Such factors would result in an increase in the APV, and hence, the economic viability of a project. In such a scenario, if two different projects with similar commercial viability are being considered by a firm, the fact that one of them is in a sector which is a priority sector for the foreign government, may tilt the decision in its favour.

MULTIPLE CHOICE QUESTIONS

1. What is the scope of finance in business?
   (1) Only focusing on accounting transactions
   (2) Limited to budgeting and forecasting
   (3) Extending beyond raising funds and managing them
   (4) Solely concerned with marketing strategies
2. Which financial decision involves determining the appropriate mix of debt and equity for a firm?
   (1) Capital budgeting
   (2) Working capital management
   (3) Financing decision
   (4) Dividend decision
3. What is the primary objective of financial management?
   (1) Maximising shareholder wealth
   (2) Maximising sales revenue
   (3) Minimising expenses
   (4) Achieving break-even
4. Which source of finance involves obtaining funds by issuing shares to the public?
   (1) Debt financing
   (2) Equity financing
   (3) Internal financing
   (4) Lease financing
5. What does working capital management primarily involve?
   (1) Deciding the capital structure
   (2) Managing short-term assets and liabilities
   (3) Determining dividend policy
   (4) Assessing long-term investment opportunities
6. What is a financial lease?
   (1) A lease that transfers ownership of the asset to the lessee
   (2) A short-term lease arrangement
   (3) A lease that does not transfer ownership of the asset to the lessee
   (4) A lease with variable lease payments
7. In a finance lease, who bears the risk of obsolescence?
   (1) Lessor (2) Lessee
   (3) Shared by both parties
   (4) Government
8. What is an advantage of lease financing for lessees?
   (1) Lower cost of capital
   (2) Full ownership of the asset
   (3) Flexibility in adjusting lease terms
   (4) Tax deductibility of lease payments
9. What is an operating lease?
   (1) A lease for manufacturing equipment
   (2) A lease that transfers ownership at the end of the lease term
   (3) A short-term lease with cancelation options
   (4) A lease for real estate
10. What is the primary motivation for a firm to choose lease financing over traditional debt financing?
    (1) Tax advantages
    (2) Lower interest rates
    (3) Easier documentation
    (4) Greater control over the asset
11. What is the cost of capital?
    (1) The total expenses incurred by a company
    (2) The cost associated with the company's equity
    (3) The cost of raising funds for a particular project
    (4) The cost of debt only
12. Which component of the cost of capital is often considered the cost of equity?
    (1) Dividend yield (2) Capital gains
    (3) Dividend payout ratio
    (4) Risk-free rate plus a risk premium
13. What is the Weighted Average Cost of Capital (WACC)?
    (1) The average cost of all sources of capital, weighted by their proportion in the capital structure
    (2) The cost of capital for debt financing only
    (3) The cost of equity financing only
    (4) The average cost of retained earnings

14. How does a company determine its optimal capital structure?
(1) By Maximising the debt component
(2) By Minimising the equity component
(3) By Minimising the overall cost of capital
(4) By Maximising the cost of debt

15. What is the relationship between the cost of capital and risk?
(1) Inverse relationship
(2) Direct relationship
(3) No relationship
(4) Unpredictable relationship

16. What is the time value of money?
(1) The concept that money loses value over time
(2) The idea that a sum of money has different values at different points in time
(3) The interest earned on money over time
(4) The cost associated with borrowing money

17. What does the present value represent in the context of time value of money?
(1) The future value of a sum of money
(2) The current value of a future sum of money
(3) The interest earned on an investment
(4) The discount rate

18. In time value of money calculations, what does the discount rate represent?
(1) The rate of inflation
(2) The rate of return on an investment
(3) The opportunity cost of capital
(4) The risk-free rate

19. How does compounding affect the future value of money?
(1) Increases it (2) Decreases it
(3) Has no effect on it
(4) Makes it unpredictable

20. What is the formula for calculating the future value of a single sum of money?
(1) $FV = PV \times (1+r)t$ (2) $FV = PV/(1+r)t$
(3) $FV = PV + r \times t$ (4) $FV = PV'' r \times t$

Directions: Each of the following items consists of two statements, one labelled as Assertion (A) and other labelled as Reason (R). You are to examine these two statements carefully and decide if the (A) and the (R) are individually true and if so, whether (R) is the correct explanation of (A). Select your answers to these items using the codes given below:
(1) Both (A) and (R) are true, and (R) is the correct explanation for (A).
(2) Both (A) and (R) are true, but (R) is not the correct explanation for (A).
(3) (A) is true, but (R) is false.
(4) Both (A) and (R) are false.

21. **Assertion (A):** The cost of capital is the rate of return required by an investor to invest in a particular project.
Reason (R): The cost of capital represents the opportunity cost of using funds in a specific project rather than in an alternative investment.

22. **Assertion (A):** The Weighted Average Cost of Capital (WACC) is used as the discount rate in capital budgeting decisions.
Reason (R): WACC represents the average cost of all sources of capital used by a company.

23. **Assertion (A):** The time value of money implies that a sum of money today is worth more than the same sum in the future.
Reason (R): The time value of money is based on the principle that individuals prefer to receive a sum of money sooner rather than later.

24. **Assertion (A):** Compounding leads to an increase in the future value of money.
Reason (R): Compounding involves earning interest on both the principal amount and the accumulated interest.

25. **Assertion (A):** The present value is the value of a future sum of money discounted at a predetermined rate.
Reason (R): The present value represents the current worth of a future sum of money, considering the time value of money.

26. What is capital structure?
(1) The makeup of a firm's physical assets
(2) The composition of a firm's equity
(3) The mix of a firm's long-term debt and equity financing
(4) The proportion of cash and cash equivalents

27. What is the primary goal of determining an optimal capital structure?
(1) Minimising the cost of debt
(2) Maximising shareholder wealth
(3) Eliminating financial risk
(4) Minimising the cost of equity

28. What is financial leverage in the context of capital structure?
(1) The use of debt to increase the return on equity

(2) The use of equity to increase the return on debt
(3) The issuance of preferred stock to finance operations
(4) The reliance on internal sources of funds

29. Which financial ratio measures a company's financial leverage?
(1) Current ratio (2) Debt-to-equity ratio
(3) Return on assets
(4) Price-to-earnings ratio

30. What is the impact of financial leverage on a firm's earnings per share (EPS)?
(1) Increases EPS (2) Decreases EPS
(3) No impact on EPS
(4) Makes EPS unpredictable

31. What is the key consideration in the Modigliani-Miller Proposition with taxes?
(1) Taxes do not affect the value of a leveraged firm
(2) Taxes increase the cost of equity
(3) Taxes decrease the cost of debt
(4) Taxes have no impact on capital structure decisions

32. What does the pecking order theory suggest about capital structure decisions?
(1) Firms prefer equity over debt
(2) Firms prefer debt over equity
(3) Firms prefer internal financing over external financing
(4) Firms prefer retained earnings over debt and equity

33. Which type of risk is associated with a high level of financial leverage?
(1) Market risk (2) Business risk
(3) Financial risk (4) Operational risk

34. What is the cost of equity in the weighted average cost of capital (WACC) formula?
(1) The risk-free rate
(2) The expected return on market portfolio
(3) The dividend yield
(4) The capital asset pricing model (CAPM)

35. What does the term "homemade leverage" refer to?
(1) Individuals adjusting their own leverage by investing in leveraged or unleveraged assets
(2) Leverage created by personal borrowing
(3) Leverage created by adjusting a company's capital structure
(4) Leveraging personal assets to invest in the stock market

Directions: Each of the following items consists of two statements, one labelled as Assertion (A) and other labelled as Reason (R). You are to examine these two statements carefully and decide if the (A) and the (R) are individually true and if so, whether (R) is the correct explanation of (A). Select your answers to these items using the codes given below:
(1) Both (A) and (R) are true, and (R) is the correct explanation for (A).
(2) Both (A) and (R) are true, but (R) is not the correct explanation for (A).
(3) (A) is true, but (R) is false.
(4) Both (A) and (R) are false.

36. **Assertion (A):** The use of debt in a firm's capital structure increases financial risk.
Reason (R): Financial risk is the variability in earnings before interest and taxes (EBIT) due to changes in interest costs.

37. **Assertion (A):** According to the Modigliani-Miller Proposition, in the absence of taxes, the value of a leveraged firm is equal to the value of an unleveraged firm.

38. **Assertion (A):** The pecking order theory suggests that firms prefer debt over equity when making capital structure decisions.
Reason (R): Firms follow a hierarchy in financing, preferring internal financing over external financing and debt over equity.

39. **Assertion (A):** Financial risk is higher for a company with a higher level of financial leverage.
Reason (R): Financial risk is the risk that a company may be unable to meet its financial obligations.

40. **Assertion (A):** The cost of equity in the WACC formula is based on the dividend yield.
Reason: The cost of equity represents the return required by shareholders, which includes dividends and capital gains.

41. Which of the following is a conventional technique of capital budgeting?
(1) Net Present Value (NPV)
(2) Sensitivity Analysis
(3) Internal Rate of Return (IRR)
(4) Payback Period

42. In capital budgeting, what does the Payback Period measure?
(1) The time it takes to recover the initial investment

(2) The discounted cash flows over the project's life
(3) The profitability index of the project
(4) The rate of return on the investment

43. What is a limitation of the Payback Period as a capital budgeting tool?
(1) It considers the time value of money
(2) It ignores the cash flows beyond the payback period
(3) It is complex and time-consuming
(4) It is not widely used in practice

44. Which scientific technique considers the present value of cash inflows and outflows over the project's life?
(1) Net Present Value (NPV)
(2) Payback Period
(3) Accounting Rate of Return (ARR)
(4) Profitability Index

45. What is the main advantage of using the Internal Rate of Return (IRR) as a capital budgeting tool?
(1) It considers the time value of money
(2) It provides a clear cutoff for project acceptance
(3) It is easy to calculate
(4) It is not affected by changes in interest rates

46. What does the Profitability Index (PI) represent in capital budgeting?
(1) The ratio of the present value of cash inflows to the initial investment
(2) The internal rate of return of the project
(3) The payback period of the project
(4) The accounting rate of return on the project

47. Which method assumes that cash inflows are reinvested at the project's cost of capital?
(1) Net Present Value (NPV)
(2) Profitability Index (PI)
(3) Internal Rate of Return (IRR)
(4) Payback Period

48. Which technique accounts for the risk associated with future cash flows?
(1) Payback Period
(2) Sensitivity Analysis
(3) Net Present Value (NPV)
(4) Accounting Rate of Return (ARR)

49. What is Sensitivity Analysis used for in capital budgeting?
(1) Identifying the sensitivity of project cash flows to changes in interest rates
(2) Assessing the impact of changes in a single variable on project profitability
(3) Calculating the payback period of the project
(4) Determining the accounting rate of return

Directions: Each of the following items consists of two statements, one labelled as Assertion (A) and other labelled as Reason (R). You are to examine these two statements carefully and decide if the (A) and the (R) are individually true and if so, whether (R) is the correct explanation of (A). Select your answers to these items using the codes given below:
(1) Both (A) and (R) are true, and (R) is the correct explanation for (A).
(2) Both (A) and (R) are true, but (R) is not the correct explanation for (A).
(3) (A) is true, but (R) is false.
(4) Both (A) and (R) are false.

50. **Assertion (A):** Net Present Value (NPV) is considered a superior capital budgeting technique compared to the Payback Period.
Reason: NPV accounts for the time value of money and considers cash flows over the entire project life.

51. **Assertion (A):** The Payback Period is more useful for projects with quick returns.
Reason (R): Payback Period considers the time required to recover the initial investment.

52. **Assertion (A):** Internal Rate of Return (IRR) is the discount rate that makes the Net Present Value (NPV) zero.
Reason (R): IRR is a measure of the profitability of an investment and is used to evaluate the attractiveness of a project.

53. **Assertion (A):** Profitability Index (PI) is calculated as the ratio of the present value of cash inflows to the initial investment.
Reason (R): PI provides a measure of the project's profitability per unit of investment.

54. **Assertion (A):** Sensitivity Analysis helps assess the impact of changes in multiple variables on project profitability.
Reason (R): Sensitivity Analysis is used to evaluate the project's sensitivity to variations in key input parameters.

55. What is the primary objective of working capital management?
(1) Maximising long-term investments
(2) Minimising short-term liabilities
(3) Maximising shareholder wealth

(4) Ensuring the smooth operation of day-to-day activities

56. Which ratio measures a company's ability to meet short-term obligations with its short-term assets?

(1) Debt-to-Equity Ratio
(2) Current Ratio
(3) Quick Ratio (4) Return on Assets

57. What is the Cash Conversion Cycle?

(1) The time taken to convert accounts payable into cash
(2) The time taken to convert inventory into accounts receivable
(3) The time taken to convert raw materials into finished goods and then into cash
(4) The time taken to pay off long-term debt

58. How does aggressive working capital management impact liquidity?

(1) Increases liquidity
(2) Decreases liquidity
(3) Has no impact on liquidity
(4) Makes liquidity unpredictable

59. What is the purpose of inventory turnover ratio in working capital management?

(1) To measure how quickly inventory is sold
(2) To assess the level of inventory financing
(3) To determine the average age of inventory
(4) To calculate the cost of holding inventory

60. According to the Modigliani-Miller Proposition, what is the impact of dividend policy on the value of the firm?

(1) Dividend policy increases the firm's value
(2) Dividend policy has no impact on the firm's value
(3) Dividend policy decreases the firm's value
(4) Dividend policy is inversely related to the firm's value

61. Which dividend policy suggests that dividends are paid out of the company's earnings and not from its retained earnings?

(1) Residual Dividend Policy
(2) Stable Dividend Policy
(3) Regular Dividend Policy
(4) Irregular Dividend Policy

62. What is the primary assumption of the Dividend Irrelevance Theory proposed by Modigliani and Miller?

(1) Investors prefer high dividends
(2) Investors are indifferent to dividends
(3) Investors prefer low dividends
(4) Investors are risk-averse

63. Which theory argues that investors prefer a steady stream of dividends and value the certainty of income?

(1) Bird-in-the-Hand Theory
(2) Modigliani-Miller Proposition
(3) Tax Preference Theory
(4) Residual Dividend Theory

64. What does the Dividend Payout Ratio measure?

(1) The proportion of profits reinvested in the business
(2) The proportion of profits paid out as dividends
(3) The proportion of retained earnings
(4) The proportion of common equity

Directions: Each of the following items consists of two statements, one labelled as Assertion (A) and other labelled as Reason (R). You are to examine these two statements carefully and decide if the (A) and the (R) are individually true and if so, whether (R) is the correct explanation of (A). Select your answers to these items using the codes given below:

(1) Both (A) and (R) are true, and (R) is the correct explanation for (A).
(2) Both (A) and (R) are true, but (R) is not the correct explanation for (A).
(3) (A) is true, but (R) is false.
(4) Both (A) and (R) are false.

65. Assertion (A): The Cash Conversion Cycle is a measure of a company's efficiency in managing its working capital.

Reason (R): The Cash Conversion Cycle reflects the time taken to convert resources into cash flows.

66. Assertion (A): Aggressive working capital management may lead to lower carrying costs but can increase the risk of stockouts.

Reason (R): Aggressive working capital management involves Minimising the level of inventory and accounts receivable.

67. Assertion (A): According to the Dividend Irrelevance Theory, investors are indifferent to the firm's dividend policy.

Reason (R): Investors can create their desired cash flows by selling shares if the firm does not pay dividends.

68. Assertion (A): The Dividend Payout Ratio is a measure of the proportion of profits paid out as dividends.

Reason (R): A higher Dividend Payout Ratio indicates that a company is reinvesting more in its business.

69. **Assertion (A):** The Bird-in-the-Hand Theory suggests that investors prefer a higher dividend payout due to the certainty of income.

Reason (R): This theory is based on the belief that investors view dividends as more certain than capital gains.

70. What is the relationship between risk and return in investments?
(1) Inverse relationship
(2) No relationship
(3) Direct relationship
(4) Unpredictable relationship

71. Which investment carries the highest level of risk?
(1) U.S. Treasury Bonds
(2) Blue-chip stocks
(3) Corporate bonds with a high credit rating
(4) Small-cap stocks

72. What is systematic risk in the context of investments?
(1) Unpredictable market fluctuations
(2) Risks associated with a specific industry
(3) Risks specific to a particular company
(4) Market-related risks that cannot be diversified away

73. Which measure assesses the volatility of an investment compared to the overall market?
(1) Beta (2) Alpha
(3) Standard Deviation (4) Sharpe Ratio

74. How does diversification impact the risk of an investment portfolio?
(1) Increases risk
(2) Has no impact on risk
(3) Decreases risk
(4) Makes risk unpredictable

75. What is asset securitisation?
(1) The process of converting physical assets into financial assets
(2) The process of pooling financial assets and converting them into tradable securities
(3) The process of converting financial liabilities into physical assets
(4) The process of diversifying financial assets

76. What is the purpose of asset securitisation for financial institutions?
(1) To increase liquidity
(2) To decrease liquidity
(3) To reduce the credit risk associated with loans
(4) To simplify financial reporting

77. Which financial assets are commonly securitised?
(1) Corporate bonds
(2) Mortgage-backed securities
(3) Treasury bills
(4) Preferred stocks

78. What role do Special Purpose Vehicles (SPVs) play in asset securitisation?
(1) They represent the regulatory authority overseeing securitisation
(2) They issue the securities backed by the pooled assets
(3) They originate the loans being securitised
(4) They act as intermediaries between investors and issuers

79. What is the key benefit of asset securitisation for issuers?
(1) Increased control over assets
(2) Lower financing costs
(3) Reduced liquidity
(4) Higher credit risk

Directions: Each of the following items consists of two statements, one labelled as Assertion (A) and other labelled as Reason (R). You are to examine these two statements carefully and decide if the (A) and the (R) are individually true and if so, whether (R) is the correct explanation of (A). Select your answers to these items using the codes given below:
(1) Both (A) and (R) are true, and (R) is the correct explanation for (A).
(2) Both (A) and (R) are true, but (R) is not the correct explanation for (A).
(3) (A) is true, but (R) is false.
(4) Both (A) and (R) are false.

80. **Assertion (A):** The Sharpe Ratio measures the excess return per unit of risk.

Reason (R): A higher Sharpe Ratio indicates better risk-adjusted performance.

81. **Assertion (A):** Systematic risk is also known as diversifiable risk.

Reason (R): Systematic risk is the risk that affects the entire market and cannot be eliminated through diversification.

82. **Assertion (A):** Asset securitisation is a process that involves pooling and repackaging financial assets into securities.

Reason (R): The goal of asset securitisation is to transform illiquid assets into tradable securities.

83. **Assertion (A):** Special Purpose Vehicles (SPVs) are used in asset securitisation to originate loans.

Reason (R): SPVs are entities created to isolate financial risk and protect investors in securitised assets.

84. **Assertion (A):** Asset securitisation lowers credit risk for issuers by spreading risk across a broader investor base.

Reason (R): Asset securitisation involves the creation of securities backed by a pool of diversified assets.

85. What is the primary function of the International Monetary System (IMS)?
(1) Facilitate international trade and investment
(2) Regulate domestic monetary policies
(3) Stabilize exchange rates
(4) Manage global inflation rates

86. Which organisation is responsible for overseeing the international monetary system and promoting global monetary cooperation?
(1) International Monetary Fund (IMF)
(2) World Trade Organization (WTO)
(3) Bank for International Settlements (BIS)
(4) World Bank

87. What is the role of Special Drawing Rights (SDRs) in the IMF?
(1) A form of international currency issued by the IMF
(2) A tool for controlling inflation rates globally
(3) A mechanism for balancing trade deficits
(4) A form of gold reserves held by member countries

88. Which system allows exchange rates to fluctuate based on market forces without significant government intervention?
(1) Fixed Exchange Rate System
(2) Gold Standard
(3) Floating Exchange Rate System
(4) Bretton Woods System

89. What was the key feature of the Bretton Woods System established in 1944?
(1) Gold-backed currency for all member countries
(2) Fixed exchange rates with the U.S. dollar as the primary reserve currency
(3) Flexible exchange rates among member countries
(4) Barter-based trade system

90. In a pegged exchange rate system, what determines the value of a country's currency?
(1) Market forces and supply-demand dynamics
(2) The gold reserves held by the country
(3) The central bank's commitment to a fixed rate against another currency
(4) The inflation rate of the country

91. Which exchange rate system allows currencies to fluctuate within a specified range around a central rate?
(1) Fixed Exchange Rate System
(2) Floating Exchange Rate System
(3) Managed Float Exchange Rate System
(4) Currency Board System

92. What is a currency crisis?
(1) A sudden devaluation of a country's currency
(2) A rapid increase in the value of a country's currency
(3) The introduction of a new currency in a country
(4) A stable exchange rate between two currencies

93. How does a country implement sterilized intervention in the foreign exchange market?
(1) By intervening in the market without affecting its domestic money supply
(2) By allowing its currency to float freely
(3) By tying its currency to a commodity like gold
(4) By maintaining a fixed exchange rate

94. What event marked the end of the Bretton Woods System in 1971?
(1) The signing of the Plaza Accord
(2) The collapse of the gold standard
(3) The establishment of the European Monetary System
(4) The adoption of the euro as a common currency

95. What is the primary feature of the current international monetary system?
(1) The return to the gold standard
(2) A managed float exchange rate system
(3) A fixed exchange rate system
(4) The dominance of a single global currency

Directions: Each of the following items consists of two statements, one labelled as Assertion (A) and other labelled as Reason (R). You are to examine these two statements carefully and decide if the (A) and the (R) are individually true and if so, whether (R) is the correct explanation of (A). Select your answers to these items using the codes given below:

(1) Both (A) and (R) are true, and (R) is the correct explanation for (A).
(2) Both (A) and (R) are true, but (R) is not the correct explanation for (A).
(3) (A) is true, but (R) is false.
(4) Both (A) and (R) are false.

96. Assertion (A): The gold standard was characterised by fixed exchange rates backed by gold reserves.
Reason (R): Under the gold standard, countries agreed to exchange their currencies for a fixed amount of gold.

97. Assertion (A): The Plaza Accord was aimed at depreciating the U.S. dollar to address trade imbalances.
Reason (R): The Plaza Accord involved coordinated intervention in the foreign exchange market to influence currency values.

98. Assertion (A): Special Drawing Rights (SDRs) serve as a supplementary international reserve asset.
Reason (R): SDRs are allocated to IMF member countries based on their relative economic size and need for reserves.

99. Assertion (A): Sterilized intervention involves buying or selling foreign currency without affecting the domestic money supply.
Reason (R): Sterilized intervention is a monetary policy action aimed at influencing the exchange rate while offsetting its impact on domestic money supply.

100. Assertion (A): The Plaza Accord was a response to the appreciation of the U.S. dollar.
Reason (R): The accord aimed to devalue the U.S. dollar to make U.S. exports more competitive in global markets.

101. What is the primary function of the foreign exchange market?
(1) Facilitate international trade
(2) Control domestic interest rates
(3) Regulate inflation rates
(4) Monitor stock market activities

102. Which of the following is a major participant in the foreign exchange market?
(1) Central banks
(2) Local grocery stores
(3) Small retail investors
(4) Non-profit organisations

103. In the foreign exchange market, what is the base currency in the currency pair EUR/USD?
(1) Euro (2) U.S. Dollar
(3) Japanese Yen (4) British Pound

104. What is the significance of bid and ask prices in the foreign exchange market?
(1) They indicate the opening and closing prices of a currency
(2) They represent the highest and lowest prices in a trading session
(3) Bid is the buying price, and ask is the selling price
(4) They determine the currency supply and demand

105. What is the role of forex brokers in the foreign exchange market?
(1) Execute buy and sell orders on behalf of clients
(2) Set interest rates for central banks
(3) Issue new currencies for circulation
(4) Regulate exchange rate policies

106. What is exchange rate risk?
(1) The risk of a country's currency depreciating in value
(2) The risk of a country's currency appreciating in value
(3) The risk of fluctuation in currency values impacting financial results
(4) The risk of a fixed exchange rate system collapsing

107. Which of the following is a transaction exposure to exchange rate risk?
(1) Translation exposure
(2) Economic exposure
(3) Operating exposure
(4) Accounting exposure

108. What is translation exposure in the context of exchange rate risk?
(1) The risk of changes in future cash flows due to exchange rate fluctuations
(2) The risk of misinterpreting financial statements due to currency differences
(3) The risk of changes in the value of foreign subsidiaries on the balance sheet

(4) The risk of currency depreciation impacting export prices

109. What is a forward contract used for in foreign exchange?

(1) To buy or sell a specified amount of currency at a future date at a predetermined rate

(2) To immediately exchange one currency for another in the spot market

(3) To speculate on short-term currency movements

(4) To invest in foreign stock markets

110. What is the primary purpose of using currency options as a hedging instrument?

(1) To guarantee a fixed exchange rate for future transactions

(2) To provide the right, but not the obligation, to buy or sell a currency at a specified price

(3) To eliminate all exchange rate risk

(4) To ensure immediate settlement of foreign transactions

Directions: Each of the following items consists of two statements, one labelled as Assertion (A) and other labelled as Reason (R). You are to examine these two statements carefully and decide if the (A) and the (R) are individually true and if so, whether (R) is the correct explanation of (A). Select your answers to these items using the codes given below:

(1) Both (A) and (R) are true, and (R) is the correct explanation for (A).

(2) Both (A) and (R) are true, but (R) is not the correct explanation for (A).

(3) (A) is true, but (R) is false.

(4) Both (A) and (R) are false.

111. Assertion (A): Translation exposure is concerned with the impact of exchange rate fluctuations on future cash flows.

Reason (R): Translation exposure arises when a firm's foreign currency-denominated assets and liabilities are translated into the home currency.

112. Assertion (A): A forward contract allows a firm to lock in a future exchange rate for a specified amount of currency.

Reason (R): Forward contracts are standardized agreements to exchange currencies at a future date at a predetermined rate.

113. Assertion (A): Currency options provide the holder the right, but not the obligation, to buy or sell a currency at a predetermined rate.

Reason (R): Currency options are financial derivatives that can be used to hedge against unfavorable exchange rate movements.

114. Assertion (A): Transaction exposure is related to the impact of exchange rate fluctuations on future cash flows.

Reason (R): Transaction exposure arises when a firm has existing contractual commitments denominated in a foreign currency.

115. Assertion (A): Hedging with forward contracts eliminates all risks associated with exchange rate fluctuations.

Reason (R): Hedging with forward contracts helps to fix future exchange rates, reducing uncertainty in cash flows.

116. What is Eurocurrency?

(1) Currency used exclusively in European Union countries

(2) European Union's official currency

(3) Currency deposited in banks outside its country of origin

(4) Digital currency used for international trade

117. Which of the following is a key feature of Eurocurrency markets?

(1) Strict government regulations

(2) High level of transparency

(3) Limited accessibility to non-European entities

(4) Absence of a central regulatory authority

118. In Eurocurrency terminology, what does "Eurodollar" refer to?

(1) European Union's official dollar currency

(2) U.S. dollars deposited in banks outside the United States

(3) Digital dollars used for international transactions

(4) U.S. dollars exclusively used in European markets

119. What is the primary purpose of Global Depository Receipts (GDRs)?

(1) To facilitate cross-border currency exchanges

(2) To represent ownership of shares in a foreign company

(3) To standardize international accounting practices

(4) To regulate Eurocurrency markets

120. How are GDRs typically denominated?

(1) In the currency of the issuing company

(2) In the currency of the depository bank
(3) In the currency of the home country
(4) In U.S. dollars only

121. Which institution typically issues GDRs?
(1) World Bank
(2) International Monetary Fund (IMF)
(3) Multinational corporations
(4) Central banks of European countries

122. What is an American Depository Receipt (ADR)?
(1) A document certifying ownership of U.S. dollars held in foreign banks
(2) A financial instrument representing ownership of shares in a foreign company, traded on U.S. stock exchanges
(3) A regulatory document required for foreign companies to operate in the U.S.
(4) A currency issued by the U.S. Treasury for international trade

123. How are ADRs different from GDRs?
(1) ADRs are only issued for European companies
(2) GDRs are traded on U.S. stock exchanges, while ADRs are not
(3) GDRs are denominated in U.S. dollars, while ADRs can be denominated in any currency
(4) ADRs represent ownership of shares in a U.S. company

Directions: Each of the following items consists of two statements, one labelled as Assertion (A) and other labelled as Reason (R). You are to examine these two statements carefully and decide if the (A) and the (R) are individually true and if so, whether (R) is the correct explanation of (A). Select your answers to these items using the codes given below:
(1) Both (A) and (R) are true, and (R) is the correct explanation for (A).
(2) Both (A) and (R) are true, but (R) is not the correct explanation for (A).
(3) (A) is true, but (R) is false.
(4) Both (A) and (R) are false.

124. Assertion (A): Eurocurrency markets are subject to strict government regulations.
Reason (R): Eurocurrency markets operate outside the jurisdiction of the country's domestic regulations.

125. Assertion (A): GDRs are a means for foreign companies to raise capital in international markets.
Reason (R): GDRs allow foreign companies to issue shares in international markets without directly listing on local stock exchanges.

126. Assertion (A): ADRs can only be denominated in U.S. dollars.
Reason (R): ADRs represent ownership of shares in a foreign company and can be traded in multiple currencies.

127. Assertion (A): GDRs are issued by central banks to facilitate international trade.
Reason (R): GDRs are typically issued by multinational corporations to raise capital from international investors.

128. Assertion (A): Eurodollars are U.S. dollars deposited in European banks.
Reason (R): Eurodollars are exclusively used in European countries for financial transactions.

129. What is international arbitrage?
(1) A legal process for resolving international disputes
(2) The simultaneous buying and selling of assets in different markets to take advantage of price differentials
(3) An international treaty to regulate financial markets
(4) A form of international taxation

130. What is covered interest arbitrage?
(1) Taking advantage of interest rate differentials between two countries to profit from currency exchange
(2) Settling international trade disputes through arbitration
(3) Investing in stocks listed on multiple international exchanges
(4) Speculating on changes in commodity prices

131. In covered interest arbitrage, what would an arbitrageur do if the forward rate is higher than the calculated future spot rate?
(1) Borrow in the domestic currency and invest in the foreign currency
(2) Borrow in the foreign currency and invest in the domestic currency
(3) Keep the funds in a domestic bank account
(4) Convert all funds to a stable cryptocurrency

132. What is the primary challenge in multinational capital budgeting?
(1) Exchange rate fluctuations

(2) Regulatory compliance
(3) Taxation issues
(4) Availability of skilled labour

133. How does the use of a higher discount rate in the capital budgeting process affect the evaluation of multinational projects?
(1) It increases the present value of future cash flows
(2) It decreases the present value of future cash flows
(3) It has no impact on the present value of future cash flows
(4) It makes the project less sensitive to exchange rate changes

134. What is the significance of the Adjusted Present Value (APV) approach in multinational capital budgeting?
(1) It considers the impact of exchange rate fluctuations on project cash flows
(2) It accounts for the volatility of the stock market
(3) It adjusts the discount rate based on regulatory changes
(4) It focuses on the net present value of projects

Directions: Each of the following items consists of two statements, one labelled as Assertion (A) and other labelled as Reason (R). You are to examine these two statements carefully and decide if the (A) and the (R) are individually true and if so, whether (R) is the correct explanation of (A). Select your answers to these items using the codes given below:

(1) Both (A) and (R) are true, and (R) is the correct explanation for (A).
(2) Both (A) and (R) are true, but (R) is not the correct explanation for (A).
(3) (A) is true, but (R) is false.
(4) Both (A) and (R) are false.

135. Assertion (A): International arbitrage ensures that exchange rates remain stable.
Reason (R): Arbitrageurs take advantage of price differentials in different markets, aligning exchange rates.

136. Assertion (A): The covered interest arbitrage strategy involves taking advantage of interest rate differentials to make risk-free profits.
Reason (R): The forward rate reflects the expected future spot rate, and arbitrageurs exploit any discrepancies.

137. Assertion (A): Multinational capital budgeting faces challenges due to exchange rate fluctuations.
Reason (R): Changes in exchange rates can impact the cash flows of multinational projects and their present values.

138. Assertion (A): The Adjusted Present Value (APV) approach is particularly useful in evaluating multinational projects with complex cash flow structures.
Reason (R): The APV approach allows for separate consideration of the impact of financing decisions on project value.

ANSWERS

1. (3)	**2.** (3)	**3.** (1)	**4.** (2)	**5.** (2)	**6.** (1)	**7.** (2)	**8.** (4)	**9.** (3)	**10.** (1)
11. (3)	**12.** (4)	**13.** (1)	**14.** (3)	**15.** (2)	**16.** (2)	**17.** (2)	**18.** (3)	**19.** (1)	**20.** (1)
21. (1)	**22.** (1)	**23.** (1)	**24.** (1)	**25.** (1)	**26.** (3)	**27.** (2)	**28.** (1)	**29.** (2)	**30.** (1)
31. (3)	**32.** (3)	**33.** (3)	**34.** (4)	**35.** (1)	**36.** (3)	**37.** (3)	**38.** (4)	**39.** (1)	**40.** (3)
41. (4)	**42.** (1)	**43.** (2)	**44.** (1)	**45.** (1)	**46.** (1)	**47.** (1)	**48.** (2)	**49.** (2)	**50.** (1)
51. (1)	**52.** (1)	**53.** (1)	**54.** (3)	**55.** (4)	**56.** (2)	**57.** (3)	**58.** (2)	**59.** (1)	**60.** (2)
61. (3)	**62.** (2)	**63.** (1)	**64.** (2)	**65.** (1)	**66.** (1)	**67.** (1)	**68.** (3)	**69.** (1)	**70.** (3)
71. (4)	**72.** (4)	**73.** (1)	**74.** (3)	**75.** (2)	**76.** (1)	**77.** (2)	**78.** (2)	**79.** (2)	**80.** (1)
81. (3)	**82.** (1)	**83.** (3)	**84.** (1)	**85.** (1)	**86.** (1)	**87.** (1)	**88.** (3)	**89.** (2)	**90.** (3)
91. (3)	**92.** (1)	**93.** (1)	**94.** (2)	**95.** (2)	**96.** (1)	**97.** (1)	**98.** (1)	**99.** (1)	**100.** (1)
101. (1)	**102.** (1)	**103.** (1)	**104.** (3)	**105.** (1)	**106.** (3)	**107.** (3)	**108.** (3)	**109.** (1)	**110.** (2)
111. (3)	**112.** (3)	**113.** (1)	**114.** (1)	**115.** (3)	**116.** (3)	**117.** (4)	**118.** (2)	**119.** (2)	**120.** (4)
121. (3)	**122.** (2)	**123.** (2)	**124.** (3)	**125.** (1)	**126.** (3)	**127.** (3)	**128.** (3)	**129.** (2)	**130.** (1)
131. (2)	**132.** (1)	**133.** (2)	**134.** (1)	**135.** (1)	**136.** (1)	**137.** (1)	**138.** (1)		

UNIT 5

BUSINESS STATISTICS AND RESEARCH METHODS

SYLLABUS

- Measures of central tendency
- Measures of dispersion
- Measures of skewness
- Correlation and regression of two variables
- Probability: Approaches to probability; Bayes' theorem
- Probability distributions: Binomial, poisson and normal distributions
- Research: Concept and types; Research designs
- Data: Collection and classification of data
- Sampling and estimation: Concepts; Methods of sampling - probability and non-probability methods; Sampling distribution; Central limit theorem; Standard error; Statistical estimation
- Hypothesis testing: z-test; t-test; ANOVA; Chi-Vsquare test; Mann-Whitney test (U-test); Kruskal-Wallis test (H-test); Rank correlation test
- Report writing

MEASURES OF CENTRAL TENDENCY

We have studied how to collect raw data, its classification and tabulation in a useful form, which contributes in solving many problems of statistical concern. Yet, this is not sufficient, because practical purposes, there is need for further condensation, particularly when we want to compare two or more different distributions. We may reduce the entire distribution to one number which represents the distribution.

A single value which can be considered as typical or representative of a set of observations and around which the observations can be considered as centered is called an 'Average' (or average value) or a center of location. Since such typical values tends to lie centrally within a set of observations when arranged according to magnitudes, averages are called measures of central tendency.

In fact the distribution have a typical value (average) about which, the observations are more or less symmetrically distributed. This is of great importance, both theoretically and practically. Dr. A.L. Bowley correctly stated, "Statistics may rightly be called the science of averages."

The word average is commonly used in day-to-day conversations. For example, we may say that Vinod is an average boy of my class; we may talk of an average Indian, average income, etc. When it is said, "Vinod is an average student," it means is that he is neither very good nor very bad, but a mediocre student. However, in statistics the term average has a different meaning.

The fundamental measures of tendencies are:

(1) Arithmetic mean
(2) Median
(3) Mode
(4) Geometric mean
(5) Harmonic mean
(6) Weighted averages

However, the most common measures of central tendencies or Locations are Arithmetic mean, median and mode.

Arithmetic Mean

This is the most commonly used average which you have also studied and used in lower grades. Here are two definitions given by two great masters of statistics.

Horace Sacrist. "Arithmetic mean is the amount secured by dividing the sum of values of the items in a series by their number."

W.I. King. "The arithmetic average may be defined as the sum of aggregate of a series of items divided by their number."

Thus, the students should add all observations (values of all items) together and divide this sum by the number of observations (or items).

Ungrouped Data

Suppose, we have 'n' observations (or measures) $x_1, x_2, x_3, \ldots\ldots, x_n$ then the Arithmetic mean is obviously $\frac{x_1 + x_2 + x_3 + \ldots + x_n}{n}$.

We shall use the symbol x (pronounced as x bar) to denote the Arithmetic mean. Since, we have to write the sum of observations very frequently, we use the usual symbol 'Σ' (pronounced as sigma) to denote the sum. The symbol x_i will be used to denote, in general the 'ith' observation. Then the sum, $x_1 + x_2 + x_3 + \ldots\ldots + x_n$ will be represented by $\sum_{i=1}^{n} x_i$ or $\sum x_i$ simply.

Therefore, the Arithmetic Mean of the set $x_1 + x_2 + x_3 + \ldots\ldots + x_n$ is given by,

$$\bar{x} = \frac{\sum x_i}{n} = \frac{x_1 + x_2 + x_3 + \ldots + x_n}{n}$$

This method is known as the "Direct Method".

Indirect Method (Assumed Mean Method)

The assumed mean is used to compute the arithmetic mean and standard deviation for a grouped data. In other words, by assuming the mean for the grouped data, the actual mean can be obtained easily. Thus, the method of calculating the mean by assuming the mean is known as assumed mean method.

$$\bar{u} = \frac{\sum u_i}{n} \quad \text{where } u = x_i - A$$

A = Assumed Mean = A + $\bar{u}$

Short-cut Method

Sometimes the values of x are very big and in that case, to simplify the calculation the short-cut method is used. For this, first you assume a mean (called as the assumed mean). Let it be A. Now find the deviations of all the values of x from A. We now get a new variable $u_i = x_i - A$

Now find

$$\bar{u} = \frac{\sum u_i}{n} \quad \text{then} \quad \bar{x} = \frac{\sum u_i}{n}$$

or $\quad \bar{x} = A + \bar{u}$

Discrete Series

There is a difference in the methods for finding the arithmetic means of the individual series and a discrete series. In the discrete series, every term (*i.e.* value of x) is multiplied by its corresponding frequency ($f_i x_i$) and then their total (sum) is found ($\Sigma f_i x_i$). The arithmetic mean is then obtained by dividing the total frequency (Σf) by the above sum so obtained.

Therefore, if the observations $x_1 + x_2 + x_3 + \ldots\ldots + x_n$ are repeated $f_1 + f_2 + f_3 + \ldots\ldots + f_n$ times, then we have:

$$\text{Arithmetic mean } (\bar{x}) = \frac{\sum f_i x_i}{\sum f_i} \quad i.e. \quad \frac{f_1 x_1 + f_2 x_2 + f_3 x_3 + \ldots + f_n x_n}{f_1 + f_2 + f_3 + \ldots + f_n}$$

The formula for arithmetic mean by direct method and by the short-cut methods are as follows:

Direct Method Short-cut Method

$$\bar{x} = \frac{\sum f_i x_i}{\sum f_i} \Rightarrow \bar{x} = A + \bar{u} \quad \text{where } \bar{u} = \frac{\sum f_i u_i}{\sum f_i}$$

and $u = x_i - A$

Therefore, $\bar{x} = A + \frac{\sum f_i u_i}{\sum f_i}$

Arithmetic Mean for Grouped Data

Continuous Series. The procedure of finding the arithmetic mean in this series, is the same as we have used in the discrete series. The only difference is that in this series, we are given class-intervals, whose mid-values (class-marks) are to be calculated first.

Formula, Arithmetic mean $(\bar{x}) = \frac{\sum f_i x_i}{\sum f_i}$

where x = mid-value

Step-Deviation Method. Here, all class intervals are of the same width say 'c'. This method is employed in place of the Short-cut method. We measure all the class-marks (mid values) from some convenient value, say 'A', which generally should be taken as the class-mark of a class of maximum frequency or of a class which is the middle one. All the class marks happen to be multiples of c, since all class intervals are equal. We consider class frequencies as if they are centered at the corresponding class-marks.

Theorem. If $x_1, x_2, x_3, ..., x_n$ are n values of the class marks with frequencies $f_1, f_2, f_3, ...f_n$ respectively and if each x_i is expressed in terms of the new variable u_i by the relation $x_i = A + cu_i$ then, with the usual notation, we have $\bar{x} = A + c\bar{u}$

where, $\bar{u} = \frac{\sum f_i u_i}{\sum f_i}$ and $u_i = \frac{x_i - A}{c}$

This method is also known as the "Coding method."

Properties of Arithmetic Mean

1. The sum of the deviations, of all the values of x, from their arithmetic mean, is zero.

   Justification: $\sum f_i(x_i - \bar{x}) = \sum f_i x_i - \bar{x}\sum f_i = 0$

   Since $\bar{x}$ is a constant, $\bar{x} = \frac{\sum f_i x_i}{\sum f_i}$ $\quad \therefore \sum f_i x_i = \bar{x}\sum f_i$

2. The product of the arithmetic mean and the number of items gives the total of all items.

   Justification: $\bar{x} = \frac{\sum f_i x_i}{\sum f_i} \Rightarrow \sum f_i x_i = \bar{x}\sum f_i$

   or $\bar{x} = \frac{\sum x_i}{N} \Rightarrow \bar{x} \cdot N = \sum x_i$

3. If $\bar{x}_1$ and $\bar{x}_2$ are the arithmetic mean of two samples of sizes n_1 and n_2 respectively then, the arithmetic mean $\bar{x}$ of the distribution combining the two can be calculated as

   $$\bar{x} = \frac{n_1\bar{x}_1 + n_2\bar{x}_2}{n_1 + n_2}$$

   This formula can be extended for more groups or samples.

$$\bar{x}_1 = \frac{\sum x_{1i}}{n_1} \Rightarrow \sum x_{1i} = n_1\bar{x}_1$$

Justification: $\bar{x}_1 = \dfrac{\sum x_{1i}}{n_1} \Rightarrow \sum x_{1i} = n_1\bar{x}_1 =$ total of the observations of the first sample

Similarly, $\sum x_{2i} = n_2\bar{x}_2 =$ total of the observations of the first sample

The combined mean of the two samples

$$= \frac{\text{combined mean}}{n_1 + n_2}$$

$$\bar{x} = \frac{n_1\bar{x}_1 + n_2\bar{x}_2}{n_1 + n_2}$$

Merits

1. It is rigidly defined. Its value is always definite.
2. It is easy to calculate and easy to understand. Hence, it is very popular.
3. It is based on all the observations; so that it becomes a good representative.
4. It can be easily used for comparison.
5. It is capable of further algebraic treatment such as finding the sum of the values of the observations, if the mean and the total number of the observations are given; finding the combined arithmetic mean when different groups are given etc.
6. It is not affected much by sampling fluctuations.

Demerits

1. It is affected by outliers or extreme values. For example, the average (A.) mean of 10, 15, 25 and 500 is $\bar{x} = \dfrac{10 + 15 + 25 + 500}{4} = 137.5$

   Now, observe first three values whose arithmetic. mean is $\dfrac{10 + 15 + 25}{3} = 16.67$ (approx.)

   Due to the outlier 500 the arithmetic. mean of the four numbers is raised to 137.5. In such a case arithmetic. mean is not a good representative of the given data.
2. It is a value which may not be present in the given data.
3. Many a times it gives absurd results like 4.4 children per family.
4. It is not possible to take out the average of ratios and percentages.
5. We cannot calculate it when open-end class intervals are present in the data.

MEDIAN

It is the value of the size of the central item of the arranged data (data arranged in the ascending or the descending order). Thus, it is the value of the middle item and divides the series in to equal parts.

In **Connor's words** – "The median is that value of the variable which divides the group into two equal parts, one part comprising all values greater and the other all values lesser than the median." For example, the daily wages of 7 workers are 5, 7, 9, 11, 12, 14 and 15 dollars. This series contains 7 terms. The fourth term *i.e.* 11 is the median.

Median in Individual Series (Ungrouped Data)

Steps

1. Set the individual series either in the ascending (increasing) or in the descending (decreasing) order, of the size of its items or observations.
2. If the total number of observations be 'n' then

A. If 'n' is odd,

$$\text{The median} = \text{size of} \left(\frac{n+1}{2}\right)^{th} \text{observation}$$

B. If 'n' is even, the median

$$= \frac{1}{2}\left[\begin{array}{l}\text{size of} \left(\frac{n}{2}\right)^{th} \text{observations} \\ + \text{size of} \left(\frac{n+1}{2}\right)^{th} \text{observations}\end{array}\right]$$

Median in Discrete Series

Steps:

1. Arrange the data in ascending or descending order of magnitude.
2. Find the cumulative frequencies
3. Apply the formula:

A. If'n' = $\sum f_i$ (odd) then,

$$\text{Median} = \text{size of} \left(\frac{n+1}{2}\right)^{th} \text{item}$$

B. If 'n' = $\sum f_i$ (even) then,

$$\text{Median} = \frac{1}{2}\left[\begin{array}{l}\text{size of} \left(\frac{n}{2}\right)^{th} \text{item} \\ + \text{size of} \left(\frac{n+2}{2}\right)^{th} \text{item}\end{array}\right]$$

Median in Continuous Series (Grouped Data)

Steps:

1. Determine the particular class in which the value of the median lies. Use $n/2$ as the rank of the median and not $\left(\frac{n+1}{2}\right)$.
2. After ascertaining the class in which median lies, the following formula is used for determining the exact value of the median.

$$\text{Median} = l_1 + \left(\frac{N/2 - c.f.}{f}\right)(l_2 - l_1)$$

where, l_1 = lower limit of the median class, the class in which the middle item of the distribution lies.

l_2 – upper limit of the median class

c.f. = cumulative frequency of the class preceding the median class

f = sample frequency of the median class

It should be noted that while interpolating the median value of frequency distribution it is assumed that the variable is continuous and that there is an orderly and even distribution of items within each class.

> The median is the value that is the mid-point of a group of values, having an equal number of items in the group above and below it. For instance, in a room with five people aged 23, 25, 37, 44 and 87, the median age is 37, as there are an equal number of persons older and younger than 37. The median is used where strong outliers may skew the representation of the group, such as with incomes. If you have one person who earns $1 billion a year and nine other people who earn under $100,000 a year, the mean income for people in the group would be around $100 million, a gross distortion. The median income would be under $100,000, more closely representing the situation of the majority of the group.

Note that, while calculating the median of a series, it must be put in the 'exclusive class-interval' form. If the original series is in inclusive type, first convert it into the exclusive type and then find its median.

Merits

1. It is rigidly defined.
2. It is easy to calculate and understand.
3. It is not affected by extreme values like the arithmetic mean. For example, 5 persons have their incomes Rs 2000, Rs 2500, Rs 2600, Rs 3000, Rs 5000. The median would be Rs 2600 while the arithmetic mean would be Rs 3020.
4. It can be found by mere inspection.
5. It is fully representative and can be computed easily.
6. It can be used for qualitative studies.
7. Even if the extreme values are unknown, median can be calculated if one knows the number of items.
8. It can be obtained graphically.

MODE

It is the size of that item which possesses the maximum frequency. According to Professor Kenney and Keeping, the value of the variable which occurs most frequently in a distribution is called the mode.

It is the most common value and point of maximum density.

Ungrouped Data (Individual Series)

The mode of this series can be obtained by mere inspection. The number which occurs most often is the mode.

Grouped Data

Steps :

1. Determine the modal class which as the maximum frequency.
2. By interpolation the value of the mode can be calculated as -

$$\text{Mode} = l_1 - \left(\frac{f_1 - f_0}{2f_1 - f_0 - f_2}\right)(l_2 - l_1)$$

where

l_1 = lower limit of the modal class

l_2 = upper limit of the modal class

f_1 = frequency of the modal class

f_0 = frequency of the class preceding to the modal class

f_2 = frequency of the class succeeding the modal class

Merits

1. It is simple to calculate.
2. In an individual or discrete distribution it can be located by mere inspection.
3. It is easy to understand. Everyone is used to the idea of average size of a garment, an average American etc.
4. It is not isolated like the median as it is the most common item.
5. Like the Average mean, it is not a value which cannot be found in the series.
6. It is not necessary to know all the items. What we need in the point of maximum density frequency.
7. It is not affected by sampling fluctuations.

Demerits

1. It is ill defined.
2. It is not based on all observations.
3. It is not capable of further algebraic treatment.
4. It is not a good representative of the data.
5. Sometimes there are more than one values of mode.

EMPIRICAL RELATION BETWEEN MEAN, MEDIAN AND MODE

A distribution in which the values of mean, median and mode coincide (*i.e.* mean = median = mode) is known as a symmetrical distribution. Conversely, when values of mean, median and mode are not equal the distribution is known as asymmetrical or skewed distribution. In moderately skewed or asymmetrical distribution a very important relationship exists among these three measures of central tendency. In such distributions the distance between the mean and median is about one-third of the distance between the mean and mode. Karl Pearson expressed this relationship as:

Mode = mean – 3 [mean – median]

Mode = 3 median – 2 mean

and Median = mode + $\frac{2}{3}$ [mean – mode]

Knowing any two values, the third can be computed.

GEOMETRIC MEAN

Geometric Mean is a measure of central tendency which is generally used to compare two set of values. It is evaluated by finding product of all the numbers and then taking their n^{th} root. Geometric mean is different from arithmetic mean because it uses product of the observations rather than sum.

Formula for evaluating geometric mean is as follows, if we have n number of observations, then

$$\text{Geometric Mean} = \sqrt[n]{x_1 x_2 x_3 \ldots x_n}$$

HARMONIC MEAN

Harmonic Mean is also one of the different kinds of average and it is applied for the situations when you have a desired rate of average.

The reciprocal of the arithmetic mean is called as Harmonic Mean. It is calculated by dividing the number of observations by the sum of reciprocal of the observation.

The formula to find the harmonic mean is given by:

$$\text{Harmonic Mean (H)} = \frac{n}{\frac{1}{x_1} + \frac{1}{x_2} + \frac{1}{x_3} + \ldots \frac{1}{x_n}}$$

where, n = Total number of numbers or terms.

$x_1, x_2, x_3, \ldots x_n$ = Individual terms or individual values.

WEIGHTED MEAN (AVERAGES)

Weighted Mean is a measurement of central tendency. It represents the average of a given data. Weighted mean is similar to arithmetic mean or sample mean. Weighted mean is calculated when data is given in a different way than in arithmetic mean or sample mean.

Sometimes, there are frequencies assigned to each term in the given data, then we can no longer use simple arithmetic mean formula. Few values may occur more frequently than others, therefore corresponding frequencies are allotted to each value. These frequencies are often referred as weights . In this case, weighted mean formula is used.

Weighted mean formula is as follows:

$$\bar{x} = \frac{\sum f_i x_i}{\sum f_i}$$

Where, $\bar{x}$ = weighted mean.

$x_i = x_1, x_2, x_3, \ldots$ = Items given.

and $f_i = f_1, f_2, f_3, \ldots$ = Frequencies corresponding to the given items

MEASURES OF DISPERSION

RANGE

In any statistical series, the difference between the largest and the smallest values is called as the range.

$$\text{Thus Range (R)} = L - S \quad \begin{cases} L = \text{Largest value of the series} \\ S = \text{Smallest value of the series} \end{cases}$$

Coefficient of Range

The relative measure of the range. It is used in the comparative study of the dispersion co-efficient of

$$\text{Range} = \frac{L - S}{L + S}$$

Mean Deviation

Average deviations (mean deviation) is the average amount of variations (scatter) of the items in a distribution from either the mean or the median or the mode, ignoring the signs of these deviations by Clark and Senkade.

INDIVIDUAL SERIES

Steps :

(1) Find the mean or median or mode of the given series.

(2) Using and one of three, find the deviations (differences) of the items of the series from them. *i.e.* $x_i - x$, $x_i - \text{Me}$ and $x_i - \text{Mo}$.
Me = Median and Mo = Mode.

(3) Find the absolute values of these deviations *i.e.* ignore there positive (+) and negative (–) signs.
i.e. $|x_i - x|$, $|x_i - \text{Me}|$ and $|x_i - \text{Mo}|$.

(4) Find the sum of these absolute deviations.
i.e. $\Sigma\ |x_i - x| +$, $\Sigma\ |x_i - \text{Me}|$, and $\Sigma\ |x_i - \text{Mo}|$.

(5) Find the mean deviation using the following formula.
$\text{M.D} = (\partial x) = \Sigma\ x_i - x,\ \partial(\text{Me}) = \Sigma\ x_i - \text{Me}$
or $\partial(\text{Mo}) = x_i \text{Mo}$

Note that :

(i) generally M. D. obtained from the median is best for the practical purpose.

(ii) co-efficient of M. D. $= \dfrac{\partial \overline{x}}{x} = \dfrac{\partial(\text{Me})}{\text{Me}} = \dfrac{\partial(\text{Mo})}{\text{Mo}}$

VARIANCE

The term variance was used to describe the square of the standard deviation R.A. Fisher in 1913. The concept of variance is of great importance in advanced work where it is possible to split the total into several parts, each attributable to one of the factors causing variations in their original series. Variance is defined as follows:

$$\text{Variance} = \frac{\Sigma(x_i - \overline{x})^2}{n}.$$

STANDARD DEVIATION (S.D.)

It is the square root of the arithmetic mean of the square deviations of various values from their arithmetic mean. It is denoted by s.d. or σ.

Thus, s.d. $(\sigma_x) = \sqrt{\dfrac{\Sigma(x_i - \overline{x})^2}{n}}$ for the ungrouped data

$= \sqrt{\dfrac{\Sigma f_i(x_i - \overline{x})^2}{n}}$ for the grouped data

where $n = \Sigma f_i$

Merits

(1) It is rigidly defined and based on all observations.
(2) It is amenable to further algebraic treatment.
(3) It is not affected by sampling fluctuations.
(4) It is less erratic.

Demerits

(1) It is difficult to understand and calculate.
(2) It gives greater weight to extreme values.

Note that variance $V(x) = \dfrac{\Sigma(x_i - \overline{x})^2}{n}$ and

and s. d. (σ_x) = and $\sqrt{\dfrac{\Sigma(x_i - \overline{x})^2}{n}}$ and $\sqrt{\dfrac{\Sigma f_i(x_i - \overline{x})^2}{n}}$

Then $V(x) = \sigma_x{}^2$

COEFFICIENT OF VARIATION (C.V.)

To compare the variations (dispersion) of two different series, relative measures of standard deviation must be calculated. This is known as coefficient of variation or the coefficient of s.d. It's formula is

$$\text{C.V.} = \frac{\sigma_x}{\overline{x}} \times 100$$

Thus it is defined as the ratio s. d. to its mean.

Remark: It is given as a percentage and is used to compare the consistency or variability of two more series. The higher the C.V., the higher the variability and lower the C.V., the higher is the consistency of the data.

Combined Standard Deviation. If two sets containing n_1 and n_2 items having means x_1 and x_2 and standard deviations 1 and 2 respectively are taken together then,

(1) Mean of the combined data is $\overline{x} = \dfrac{n_1\overline{x}_1 + n_2\overline{x}_2}{n_1 + n_2}$

(2) s.d. of the combined set is $\sigma = \sqrt{\dfrac{n_1(\sigma_1^2 + d_1^2) + n_2(\sigma_2^2 + d_2^2)}{n_1 + n_2}}$

where $d_1 = \overline{x}_1 - \overline{x}$ and $d_2 = \overline{x}_2 - \overline{x}$

PERCENTILE

The nth percentile is that value (or size) such that n% of values of the whole data lies below it. For example, a score of 7% from the topmost score would be 93th percentile as it is above 93% of the other scores.

000 111111 222222 4444 55 666 7777 8 999 | (10) 11 11 etc.
← 93% of scores →
93th percentile

Percentile Range

It is used as one of the measure of dispersion. It is a set of data and is defined as $= P_{90} - P_{10}$ where P_{90} and P_{10} are the 90th and 10th percentile respectively. The semi - percentile range, i.e. $\left(\frac{P_{90} - P_{10}}{2}\right)$ can also be used but it is not common in use.

Quartiles and Interquartile Range

If we concentrate on two extreme values (as in the case of range), we don't get any idea about the scatter of the data within the range (*i.e.* the two extreme values). If we discard these two values the limited range thus available might be more informative. For this reason the concept of interquartile range is developed. It is the range which includes middle 50% of the distribution. Here 1/4 (one quarter) of the lower end and 1/4 (one quarter) of the upper end of the observations are excluded.

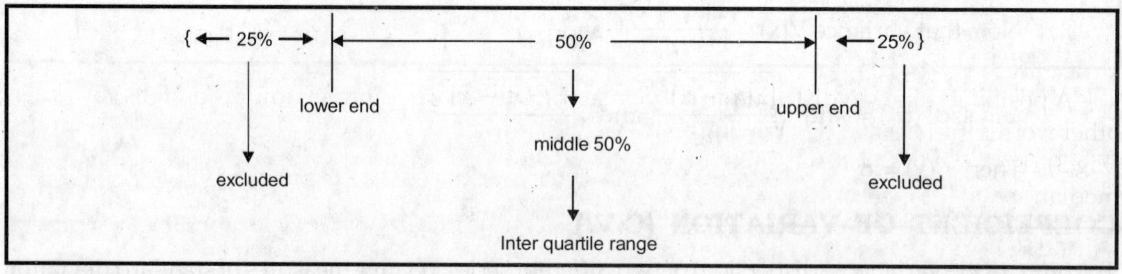

Now, the lower quartile (Q_1) is the 25th percentile and the upper quartile (Q_3) is the 75th percentile. It is interesting to note that the 50th percentile is the middle quartile (Q_2) which is in fact what you have studied under the title ' Median ". Thus, symbolically

Inter quartile range = $Q_3 - Q_1$

If we divide ($Q_3 - Q_1$) by 2 we get what is known as Semi-Inter quartile range.

i.e. $\frac{Q_3 - Q_1}{2}$. It is known as Quartile deviation (Q. D or SI QR).

Therefore Q. D. (SI QR) = $\frac{Q_3 - Q_1}{2}$.

MEASURES OF SKEWNESS, MOMENTS AND KURTOSIS

The voluminous raw data cannot be easily understood. Hence, we calculate the measures of central tendencies and obtain a representative figure. From the measures of variability, we can know that whether most of the items of the data are close to our away from these central tendencies. But these statical means and measures of variation are not enough to draw sufficient inferences about the data. Another aspect of the data is to know its symmetry. For "Graphic display" a frequency may be symmetrical about mode or may not be. This symmetry is well studied by the knowledge of the "Skewness." Still one more aspect of the curve that we need to know is its flatness or otherwise its top. This is understood by what is known as " Kurtosis."

SKEWNESS

It may happen that two distributions have the same mean and standard deviations. For an example, see the below diagram.

Although the two distributions have the same means and standard deviations they are not identical. Where do they differ ?

They differ in symmetry. The left-hand side distribution is symmetrical one where as the distribution on the right-hand is asymmetrical or skewed. For a symmetrical distribution, the values, of equal distances on either side of the mode, have equal frequencies. Thus, the mode, median and mean - all coincide. Its curve rises slowly, reaches a maximum (peak) and falls equally slowly (Fig. 1). But for a skewed distribution, the mean, mode and median do not coincide. Skewness is positive or negative as per the positions of the mean and median on the right or the left of the mode.

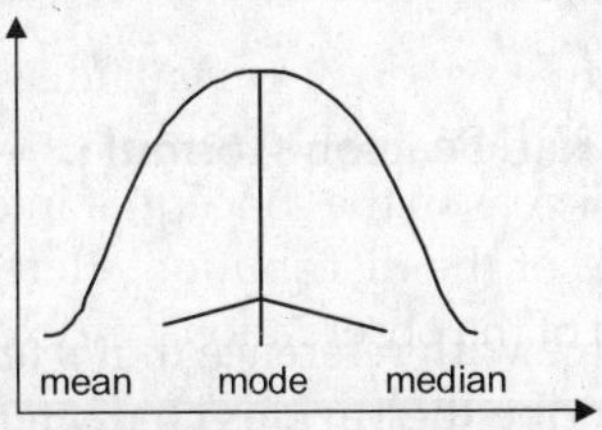

Fig. (1)

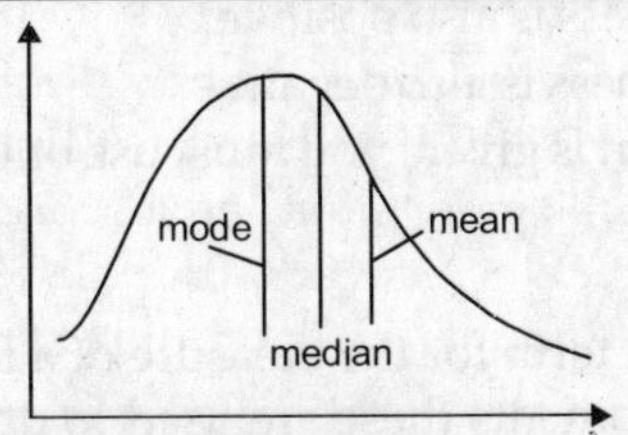

Fig. (2)

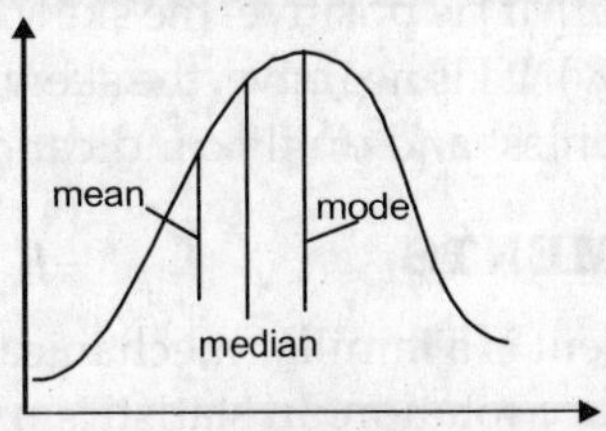

Fig. (3)

A positively skewed distribution curve rises rapidly, reaches the maximum and falls slowly. In other words, the tail as well as median on the right-hand side. A negatively skewed distribution curve (Fig.3) rises slowly reaches its maximum and falls rapidly. In other words, the tail as well as the median are on the left-hand side.

Size	Frequency	Size	Frequency	Size	Frequency
1	12	1	4	1	3
2	13	2	6	2	7
3	14	3	12	3	8
4	15	4	10	4	10
5	14	5	8	5	12
6	13	6	7	6	6
7	12	7	3	7	4

Tests of Skewness

1. The values of mean, median and mode do not coincide. The more the difference between them, the more is the skewness.
2. Quartiles are not equidistant from the median, *i.e.* $(Q_3 - Me)$ $(Me - Q_1)$.
3. The sum of positive deviations from the median are not equal to the sum of the negative deviations.
4. Frequencies are not equally distributed at points of equal deviation from the mode.
5. When the data is plotted on a graph they do not give the normal bell-shaped form.

Measure of Skewness

First measure of skewness has been given by Karl Pearson.

Co-efficient of skewness

$$S_{kp} = \text{Mean} - \text{Mode} \quad J = \frac{\overline{x} - Mo}{\overline{x}}$$

i.e. $S_{kp} = - Mo$

Pearson has suggested the use of this formula if it is not possible to determine the mode (Mo) of any distribution,

(Mean – Mode) = 3 (mean – median)

$$S_{kp} = 3\,(-Mo) \text{ Thus } J = \frac{3(\overline{x} - Me)}{\sigma_{\overline{x}}}$$

Note :

(i) Although the co-efficient of skewness is always within ± 1, but Karl Pearson's co-efficient lies within ± 3.

(ii) If J = 0, then there is no skewness

(iii) If J is positive, the skewness is also positive.

(iv) If J is negative, the skewness is also negative.

Unless and until no indication is given, you must use only Karl Pearson's formula.

MOMENTS

Moment is a familiar mechanical term for the measure of a force with reference to it's tendency to produce rotation. In statistics moments these are used to describe the various characteristics of a frequency distribution like center tendency, variation, skewness and kurtosis.

Moments are calculated using the arithmetic mean. According to Waugh, the arithmetic mean of the various powers of these deviations in any distribution are called the moments of the distribution. Let ' x ' be the deviation of any item in a distribution from the arithmetic mean of that distribution. The arithmetic mean of the various powers of these deviations is the moments of the distribution. If we take the mean of the 1st power of the deviations, we get the 1st moment about the mean, the mean of the squares of the deviations gives the second moment about the mean, the mean of the cubes gives the third moment about the mean and so on. The moments about mean are called the "central moment" and are denoted by $\mu_1, \mu_2, \mu_3, \mu_4$....

Symbolically, $\mu_1 = \frac{\Sigma(x-\bar{x})}{n}$ or $\frac{\Sigma x}{n}$ ..... 1st central moment = 0

Since, sum of deviations of items from the arithmetic mean is always zero.

$$\mu_2 = \frac{\Sigma f(x-\bar{x})^2}{n} \text{ or } \frac{\Sigma x^2}{n} \quad (\mu_2 = \sigma^2 \text{ or } \sigma = \sqrt{\mu_2})$$

$$\mu_3 = \frac{\Sigma(x-\bar{x})^3}{n} \text{ or } \frac{\Sigma x^3}{n} \text{ and so on}$$

For frequency distribution,

$$\mu_1 = \frac{\Sigma f(x-\bar{x})}{n} \text{ or } \frac{\Sigma fx}{n}$$

$$\mu_2 = \frac{\Sigma f(x-\bar{x})^2}{n} \text{ or } \frac{\Sigma fx^2}{n}$$

$$\mu_3 = \frac{\Sigma f(x-\bar{x})^3}{n} \text{ or } \frac{\Sigma fx^3}{n}$$

$$\mu_4 = \frac{\Sigma f(x-\bar{x})^4}{n} \text{ or } \frac{\Sigma fx^4}{n} \text{ where } n = \Sigma f \text{ and so on}$$

In many cases it is very difficult to calculate moments about actual moment, particularly when actual mean is in fractions. In such case we first compute moments about an arbitrary origin 'A' and then convert these moments into moments about actual mean. These are called ' raw moments ' which are denoted by v.

Thus we have

$$v_1 = \frac{\Sigma f(x-A)}{n}, \quad v_2 = \frac{\Sigma f(x-A)^2}{n}$$

$$\nu_3 = \frac{\Sigma f(x-A)^3}{n}, \quad \nu_4 = \frac{\Sigma f(x-A)^4}{n} \text{ and so on.}$$

For frequency distribution

$$\nu_1 = \frac{\Sigma f_i(x-A)}{n}, \quad \nu_2 = \frac{\Sigma f_i(x-A)^2}{n}$$

$$\nu_3 = \frac{\Sigma f_i(x-A)^3}{n}, \quad \nu_4 = \frac{\Sigma f_i(x-A)^4}{n} \text{ and so on}$$

Now, to obtain the central moment as

$$\mu = \nu - \nu = \sigma$$

$$\mu = \nu - 3\nu.\nu + 2\,\nu$$

$$\mu = \nu - 4\nu.\nu + 6\,\nu - 3\,\nu$$

Pearson's β and ν coefficients. Karl Pearson defined the following four coefficients, based upon four moments about the mean:

β coefficients
$$\beta_1 = \frac{\mu_3^3}{\mu_2^3} = \frac{\mu_3^2}{\sigma^6}$$
$$\beta_2 = \frac{\mu_4}{\mu_2^2} = \frac{\mu_4}{\sigma^4}$$

ν coefficient
$$\nu_1 = \sqrt{\beta_1} = \frac{\mu_3}{\sigma^3}$$
$$\nu_2 + \beta_2 - 3 = \frac{\mu_4}{\mu^2} - 3 = \frac{\mu_4 - 3\sigma^2}{\sigma^4}$$

These are pure numbers and they provide information about the shape of the curve obtained from the frequency distribution.

For symmetrical distribution, the moments of odd order about the mean vanish and therefore $\beta_3 = 0$ rendering $\beta_1 = 0$ thus β_1 gives the measure of departure from symmetry and also defines a measure of skewness. Also $\beta_2 = \frac{\mu_4}{\mu^2}$ gives the measure of flatness of the mode and also defines the measure of Kurtosis or convexity of the curve.

Note :

(1) If $\beta_2 = 3$ *i.e.* $\nu_2 = 0$ then the curve is normal which is neither flat nor peaked *i.e.* Meso kurtic.

(2) If $\beta_2 > 3$ *i.e.* $\nu_2 > 0$ then the curve is more peaked than a normal curve and is called Lepto kurtic.

(3) If $\beta_2 < 3$ *i.e.* $\nu_2 <> 0$ then curve is flatter than a normal curve and is called Platy kurtic.

KURTOSIS

It has its origin in the Greek word "Bulginess." In statistics it is the degree of flatness or 'peakedness' in the region of mode of a frequency curve. It is measured relative to the 'peakedness' of the normal curve. It tells us the extent to which a distribution is more peaked or flat-topped than the normal curve. If the curve is more peaked than a normal curve it is called 'Lepto Kurtic.' In this case items are more clustered about the mode. If the curve is more flat-topped than the more normal curve, it is Platy-Kurtic. The normal curve itself is known as "Meso Kurtic."

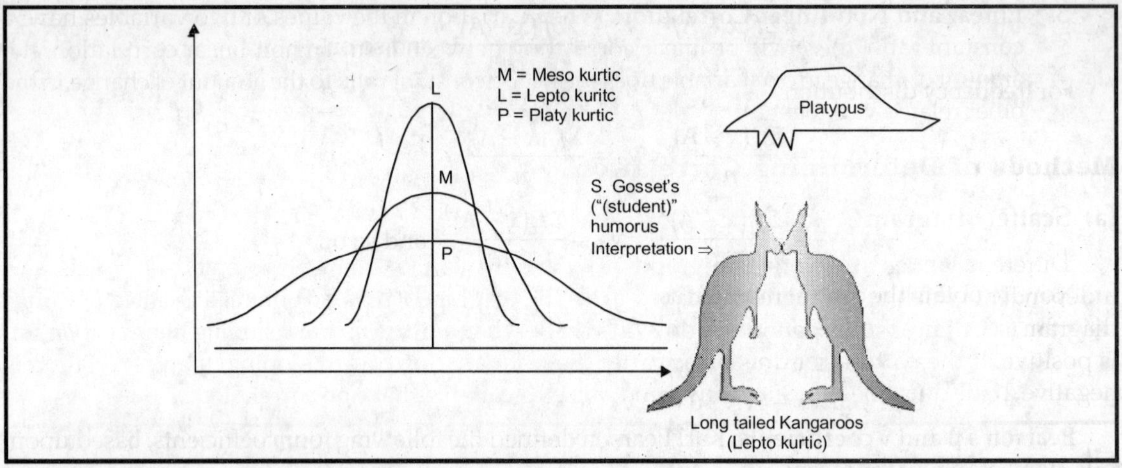

CORRELATION AND REGRESSION OF TWO VARIABLES

It is a statistical method to determine the relationship between two or more variables. Its values can lie between +1 and –1. The direction of the relation is determined by sign. If increase in one variable leads to increase in dependent variable, then relation is positive. On the other hand, if increase in one variable leads to decrease in dependent variable, then value will be negative. In case no relation exists between two variables, correlation will be zero.

Uses of Correlation

1. Decision maker will come to know the nature of relationship between variables and the degree of the relation.
2. Getting a quantitative figure for correlation makes the decision making process objective.
3. It helps in forecasting and planning because changes in variables and its impact can be estimated beforehand.
4. It helps the researcher in identifying such factors which can stabilize the economy.

Precautions in Applying Correlation

1. It is difficult to distinguish between dependent variables and independent variables.
2. Both the correlated variables are affected by a third variable, which has not been taken into consideration by the researcher.
3. The correlation may be due to chance.
4. Very high degree of correlation between two variables does not necessarily indicate a cause and effect relationship between them.

Types of Correlation

1. **Single and Multiple Correlation.** Only two variables are considered in single correlation, *i.e.*, one independent and another dependent variable. In case of multiple correlation, the relation between more than two variables is judged.
2. **Partial and Total Correlation.** In the case of partial correlation, relation of the two or more variables are considered assuming other variables to be constant. Total correlation is based on all the variables without assuming any variable to be constant.

3. **Linear and Non-linear Correlation.** When variation in the values of two variables have a constant ratio, there will be linear correlation between them. In non-linear correlation, the amount of change in one variable does not bear a constant ratio to the amount of change in the other related variable.

Methods of Determining Correlation

(a) Scatter diagram

Different values are plotted in graphs. Dependent variables are represented on y-axis and independent variables are represented on x-axis. The diagram of dots, so obtained is called a scatter diagram (see figure). If the patterns of dots on a scatter diagram are upward sloping, then correlation is positive. If the patterns of dots on a scatter diagram are downward sloping, then correlation is negative. If the dots does not show any trend, the two variables have no correlation.

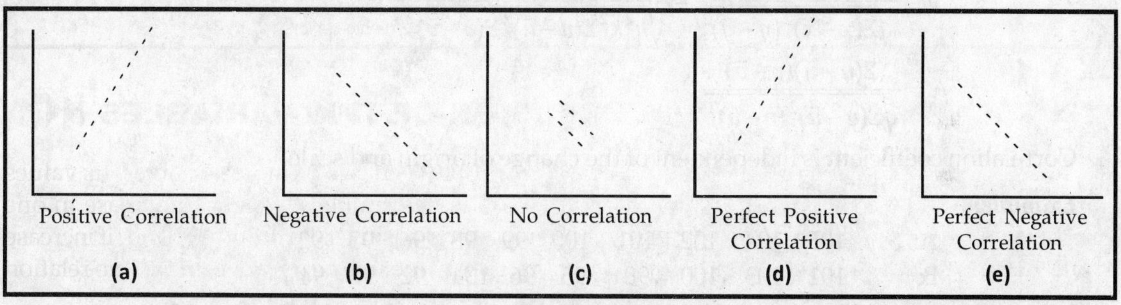

Scatter diagram

(i) **Merits of Scatter Diagram.** Scatter diagram is easy to understand. Even a layman who is not trained in mathematics or statistics can understand scattered diagram. If the relation is fairly apparent, then it can be shown through scattered diagram rather than by calculating through mathematical formula.

(ii) **Demerits of Scattered Diagram.** This method does not give any quantitative figure of the degree of correlation. Hence comparison of different data and their correlation are not possible. Scattered diagram is not an objective method of measuring correlation.

(b) Karl Pearson's Coefficient of Correlation

(i) **Measure from Mean**

$$r = \frac{\sum(x-\bar{x})(y-\bar{y})}{\sqrt{\sum(x-\bar{x})^2\sum(y-\bar{y})^2}}$$

where x and y are the values of the variates.

If σx and σy denotes the standard deviation of the variates then r will be

$$r = \frac{\frac{1}{n}\sum(x-\bar{x})(y-\bar{y})}{\sqrt{\frac{1}{n}\sum(x-\bar{x})^2}\sqrt{\frac{1}{n}\sum(y-\bar{y})^2}}$$

$$= \frac{cov\,(x,y)}{\sigma_x\sigma_y}$$

where,

$$\text{Cov}(x, v) = \frac{1}{n}\Sigma(y-\overline{y})(x-\overline{x})$$

$$= \frac{1}{n}\Sigma xy - \overline{x}\frac{\Sigma y}{n} - \overline{y}\frac{\Sigma x}{n} + \overline{x}\,\overline{y}$$

(ii) **Change of Origin and Scale**

Let $u = \dfrac{x-a}{h}$, $v = \dfrac{y-b}{k}$

So that $x = a + hu$, $y = b + kv$

$\overline{x} = a + h\overline{u}$, $\overline{y} = b + k\overline{v}$

$$r = \frac{\Sigma(x-\overline{x})(y-\overline{y})}{\sqrt{\Sigma(x-\overline{x})^2(y-\overline{y})^2}} = \frac{\Sigma(hu-h\overline{u})(kv-k\overline{v})}{\sqrt{h^2k^2\Sigma(u-\overline{u})^2\Sigma(v-\overline{v})^2}}$$

$$= \frac{\Sigma(u-\overline{u})(v-\overline{v})}{\sqrt{\Sigma(u-\overline{u})^2(v-\overline{v})^2}}$$

Correlation coefficient is independent of the change of origin and scale.

Example:

A:	105	104	102	101	100	99	98	96	93	92
B:	101	103	100	98	95	96	104	92	97	94

Let x and y denote the values in the series A and B respectively and let $u = x - 100$, $v = y - 96$.

Sl. No.	x	y	u	v	uv	u^2	v^2
1	105	101	5	5	25	25	25
2	104	103	4	7	28	16	49
3	102	100	2	4	8	4	16
4	101	98	1	2	2	1	4
5	100	95	0	–1	0	0	1
6	99	96	–1	0	0	1	0
7	98	104	–2	8	–16	4	64
8	96	92	–4	–4	16	16	16
9	93	97	–7	+1	–7	49	1
10	92	94	–8	–2	16	64	4
N = 10			–10	20	72	180	180

$$r = \frac{72 - \frac{1}{10}(-10)20}{\sqrt{180 - \frac{(-10)^2}{10}}\sqrt{180 - \frac{(20)^2}{10}}} = 0.596$$

(iii) **Short-cut Method**

$$\frac{\Sigma dx \cdot dy - \frac{\Sigma dx \cdot dy}{N}}{\sqrt{\left[\Sigma dx^2 - \frac{(\Sigma dx)^2}{N}\right] \times \left[\Sigma dy^2 - \frac{(\Sigma dy)^2}{N}\right]}}$$

In the formula,

$\sum dx$ and $\sum dy$ are sum of deviations from the assumed mean of x and y respectively.

$\sum dx^2$ and $\sum dy^2$ are sum of square of the deviations from the assumed mean in x and y series respectively.

(iv) **Correlation with Frequency Distribution**

$$r = \frac{N\sum fdx.df - \sum fdx.df.\sum fdf}{\sqrt{\left[N\sum fdx^2 (\sum fdx)^2\right].\left[N\sum fdy^2(\sum f.dy)^2\right]}}$$

Properties of the coefficient of correlation

1. The 'value of r' will lie between +1 and –1.
2. The 'value of r' is independent of change of scale and origin of the variable x and y.
3. The ' value of r' is the geometric mean of two regression coefficients.

   $$r = \sqrt{b_{xy}.b_{yx}}$$

4. Probable error can be calculated

   $$\text{P.E.} = 0.6745\frac{1-r^2}{\sqrt{N}}$$

   where 0.6745 is a constant number

   r is Pearson coefficient of correlation

   N is number of items.

5. Standard error can be calculated

   $$\text{SE} = \frac{1-r^2}{\sqrt{N}}$$

Merits of Coefficient of Correlation

1. In one figure of r, both the degree of correlation and its direction can be calculated.
2. It can be derived from the use of standard deviation.
3. It is closely related to regression analysis.
4. Probable error and standard error can be calculated from coefficient of correlation.

Limitations of Coefficient of Correlation

1. It assumes a linear relationship between independent and dependent variables, which may not always be true.
2. It is applicable only if the distribution is normal.
3. The value of the coefficient is unduly affected by the extreme items.
4. It is difficult to calculate.
5. It is difficult to understand.

(c) Spearman's Rank Difference Method

Under this method, original values are not taken into account. Instead, the values are ranked.

(i) **Formula.** Formula of Spearman's rank-correlation coefficient is

$$r = 1 - \frac{6\sum d^2}{n(n^2-1)}$$

Where 'd' is the difference between the ranks of paired items of x and y variables.

(ii) **Correction for tied ranks.** In Spearman's rank-correlation method, the biggest item gets the first rank, the next to it gets second rank and so on. But, difficulty may be encountered where two or more items are of equal value. In such cases, correction has to be applied. $\frac{m(m^2-1)}{12}$ has to be added to $\sum d^2$. 'm' is the number of times a particular value of x and y has been repeated. Separate correction has to be applied for each separate case of repetition of ranks.

(iii) **Values of Spearman's Rank-Correlation.** If the value of d is zero for each individual, then the correlation is positive and will be equal to one.

If $6\sum d^2 = n(n^2-1)$ or, $\sum d^2 = \frac{n(n^2-1)}{6}$ then the correlation is zero, which means that there is no correlation at all between the two variables.

Example:

			Rank			
Sl. No.	**x**	**y**	**x**	**y**	**d**	Σd^2
1	105	101	1	3	–2	4
2	104	103	2	2	0	0
3	102	100	3	4	–1	1
4	101	98	4	5	–1	1
5	100	95	5	8	–3	9
6	99	96	6	7	–1	1
7	98	104	7	1	+6	36
8	96	92	8	10	-2	4
9	93	97	9	6	+3	9
10	92	94	10	9	+1	1
					0	$\Sigma d^2 = 66$

$$r = 1 - \frac{6\Sigma d^2}{n(n^2-1)} = 1 - \left[\frac{6(66)}{990}\right] = 1 - \frac{396}{990}$$

$$r = 1 - 0.4 = 0.6$$

REGRESSION ANALYSIS

Regression analysis is based on the relation-ship between two or more variables. The known variable is called as 'independent variable' and the variable we are trying to predict is called as 'dependent variable'. Regression analysis shows us how to determine both the nature and the strength of a relationship between independent variable and dependent variable.

According to M. M. Blair, "Regression analysis is a mathematical measure of the average relationship between two or more variables in terms of the original units of the data."

The term 'Regression' was first used by Sir Francis Galton in 1877 in the study of heredity. Galton made a study that showed that the height of sons born to tall parents will tend to move back, or 'Regress' towards the mean height of the population. In statistics the term 'Regression' is used to denote backward tendency which means going back to average. In Economics regression analysis is used as the basic technique for measuring or estimating the relationship among economic variables that constitute the essence of economic theory and economic life.

Before developing the methods of regression it is necessary to distinguish between two types of relationships, linear and non-linear :

1. If the relationships between two (or more) variables is best described by means of a straight line (or a plane), it is called linear. Linear relationship implies a constant change in the dependent variable with respect to changes in the independent variables. It is extensively used for predictive purposes.
2. If the underlying relationship between two (or more) variables is best described by a curve the relationship is called non-linear. A non-linear relationship implies a varying absolute change in the dependent variable with respect to changes in the independent variable. Its predictive value is limited.

Types of Regression

1. **Simple Regression.** The regression analysis for studying only two variables at a time, is called the Simple Regression.
2. **Multiple Regression.** The regression analysis for studying more than two variables at a time is known as Multiple Regression.
3. **Linear Regression.** The task of bringing out linear relationships consists of developing methods of fitting a straight line or the regression line, as is often called, to the data on two variables.
4. **Non-linear Regression.** If the curve of regression is not a straight line, then it is called a Non-linear Regression.

Utility of Regression Analysis

Today, the regression analysis technique plays a vital role in managerial decisions. The importance of this technique can be stated through the following points:

1. This technique helps in determining the coefficient of correlation.
2. This technique establishes the rate of change in one variable, in terms of the changes in another variable.
3. Regression analysis helps prediction and thus it can estimate the value of unknown quantities.
4. This technique helps in economic and business investigations.
5. The study of regression analysis indicates the cause and effect relationship.

Difference between Correlation and Regression Analysis

1. In correlation, we cannot say that one variable is the cause and other the effect. While in regression analysis one variable is taken as dependent and the other is independent—thus making it possible to study the cause and effect relationship.

2. Correlation coefficient is independent of change of scale and origin but regression coefficients are independent of change of origin but not of scale.
3. Correlation indicates the quantity of relation between to variables but regression analysis indicate the nature of two variables.

Precautions in the Use of Regression Analysis

As the regression analysis has a predictive value, its limitations must be recognised and it must be used with caution. Regression Analysis suffers from the following limitations :

1. A value of Y cannot be predicted if the value of X is beyond the values on which the regression equation is based. For example, if the various values of X range from 200 to 1400, then a value of Y corresponding to X = 1500 should not be estimated.
2. In case of a time series, the value of Y which involves the prediction of a result for 'X', a future event, may not be relevant. For example, if the data relate to years 1971 to 1979 and a prediction for 1980 or any later date is desired, regression analysis may not be used satisfactorily.
3. The analysis is confined to data where the distribution of Y is normal.

ELEMENTARY THEORY OF PROBABILITY

The theory of probability was developed towards the end of the 18th century and its history suggests that it developed with the study of games and chance, such as rolling a dice, drawing a card, flipping a coin etc. Apart from these, uncertainty prevailed in every sphere of life. For instance, one often predicts: "It will probably rain tonight." "It is quite likely that there will be a good yield of cereals this year" and so on. This indicates that, in layman's terminology the word 'probability' thus connotes that there is an uncertainty about the happening of events. To put 'probability' on a better footing we define it. But before doing so, we have to explain a few terms."

Trial

A procedure or an experiment to collect any statistical data such as rolling a dice or flipping a coin is called a trial.

Random Trial or Random Experiment

When the outcome of any experiment can not be predicted precisely then the experiment is called a random trial or random experiment. In other words, if a random experiment is repeated under identical conditions, the outcome will vary at random as it is impossible to predict about the performance of the experiment. For example, if we toss a honest coin or roll an unbiased dice, we may not get the same results as our expectations.

Sample Space

The totality of all the outcomes or results of a random experiment is denoted by Greek alphabet Ω or English alphabets and is called the sample space. Each outcome or element of this sample space is known as a sample print.

Event

Any subset of a sample space is called an event. A sample space S serves as the universal set for all questions related to an experiment 'S' and an event A w.r.t. It is a set of all possible outcomes favourable to the event A.

For example,

A random experiment :- flipping a coin twice

Sample space : Ω or S = {(HH), (HT), (TH), (TT)}

The question : "both the flipps show same face"

Therefore, the event A : { (HH), (TT) }

Equally Likely Events

All possible results of a random experiment are called equally likely outcomes and we have no reason to expect any one rather than the other. For example, as the result of drawing a card from a well shuffled pack, any card may appear in draw, so that the 52 cards become 52 different events which are equally likely.

Mutually Exclusive Events

Events are called mutually exclusive or disjoint or incompatible if the occurrence of one of them precludes the occurrence of all the others. For example in tossing a coin, there are two mutually exclusive events viz turning up a head and turning up of a tail. Since both these events cannot happen simultaneously. But note that events are compatible if it is possible for them to happen simultaneously. For instance in rolling of two dice, the cases of the face marked 5 appearing on one dice and face 5 appearing on the other, are compatible.

Exhaustive Events

Events are exhaustive when they include all the possibilities associated with the same trial. In throwing a coin, the turning up of head and of a tail are exhaustive events assuming of course that the coin cannot rest on its edge.

Independent Events

Two events are said to be independent if the occurrence of any event does not affect the occurrence of the other event. For example in tossing of a coin, the events corresponding to the two successive tosses of it are independent. The flip of one penny does not affect in any way the flip of a nickel.

Dependent Events

If the occurrence or non-occurrence of any event affects the happening of the other, then the events are said to be dependent events. For example, in drawing a card from a pack of cards, let the event A be the occurrence of a king in the 1st draw and B be the occurrence of a king in the 1st draw and B be the occurrence of a king in the second draw. If the card drawn at the first trial is not replaced then events A and B are independent events.

Note:

(1) If an event contains a single simple point *i.e.* it is a singleton set, then this event is called an elementary or a simple event.

(2) An event corresponding to the empty set is an "impossible event."

(3) An event corresponding to the entire sample space is called a 'certain event'.

Complementary Events

Let S be the sample space for an experiment and A be an event in S. Then A is a subset of S. Hence $\bar{A}$, the complement of A in S is also an event in S which contains the outcomes which are not favourable to the occurrence of A *i.e.* if A occurs, then the outcome of the experiment belongs to A, but if A does not occur, then the outcomes of the experiment belongs to $\bar{A}$.

It is obvious that A and $\bar{A}$ are mutually exclusive. $A \cap \bar{A} = \phi$ and $A \cup \bar{A} = S$.

If S contains n equally likely, mutually exclusive and exhaustive points and A contains m out of these n points then $\bar{A}$ contains $(n - m)$ sample points.

Mathematical (or A Priori or Classic) Definition

If there are 'n' exhaustive, mutually exclusive and equally likely cases and m of them are favourable to an event A, the probability of A happening is defined as the ratio m/n

Expressed as a formula:

$$P(A) = \frac{m}{n} = \frac{\text{Number of favourable outcomes}}{\text{Total number of possible outcomes}}$$

$$P(A) = \frac{n(A)}{n(S)}$$

This definition is due to 'Laplace.' Thus probability is a concept which measures numerically the degree of certainty or uncertainty of the occurrence of an event.

For example, the probability of randomly drawing taking from a well-shuffled deck of cards is 4/52. Since 4 is the number of favourable outcomes (*i.e.* 4 kings of diamond, spade, club and heart) and 52 is the number of total outcomes (the number of cards in a deck).

If A is any event of sample space having probability P, then clearly, P is a positive number (expressed as a fraction or usually as a decimal) not greater than unity. $0 \leq P \leq 1$ *i.e.* 0 (no chance or for impossible event) to a high of 1 (certainty). Since the number of cases not favourable to A are $(n - m)$, the probability q that event A will not happen is, $\frac{n-m}{n} = q$ or $q = 1 - m/n$ or $q = 1 - p$.

Now note that the probability q is nothing but the probability of the complementary event A *i.e.* $\bar{A}$

Thus $p(\bar{A}) = 1 - p$ or $p(\bar{A}) = 1 - p(\bar{A})$

so that $p(A) + p(\bar{A}) = 1$ *i.e.* $p + q = 1$

Relative Frequency Definition

The classical definition of probability has a disadvantage *i.e.* the words 'equally likely' are vague. In fact, since these words seem to be synonymous with "equally probable". This definition is circular as it is defining (in terms) of itself. Therefore, the estimated or empirical probability of an event is taken as the relative frequency of the occurrence of the event when the number of observations is very large.

Van Mise's Statistical (or Empirical) Definition

If trials are to be repeated a great number of times under essentially the same condition then the limit of the ratio of the number of times that an event happens to the total number of trials, as the number of trials increases indefinitely is called the probability of the happening of the event.

It is assumed that the limit exists and finite uniquely. Symbolically $p(A) = p = \lim_{n \to \infty} \frac{m}{n}$ provided it is finite and unique.

The two definitions are apparently different but both of them can be reconciled the same sense.

THE LAWS OF PROBABILITY

So far we have discussed probabilities of single events. In many situations we come across two or more events occurring together. If event A and event B are two events and either A or B or both occurs, is denoted by $A \cap B$ or $(A + B)$ and the event that both A and B occurs is denoted by $A \cap B$ or AB. We term these situations as compound event or the joint occurrence of events. We may need probability that A or B will happen.

It is denoted by $P(A \cap B)$ or $P(A + B)$. Also we may need the probability that A and B (both) will happen simultaneously. It is denoted by $P(A \cap B)$ or $P(AB)$.

Consider a situation, you are asked to choose any 3 or any diamond or both from a well shuffled pack of 52 cards. Now you are interested in the probability of this situation.

Now see the following diagram.

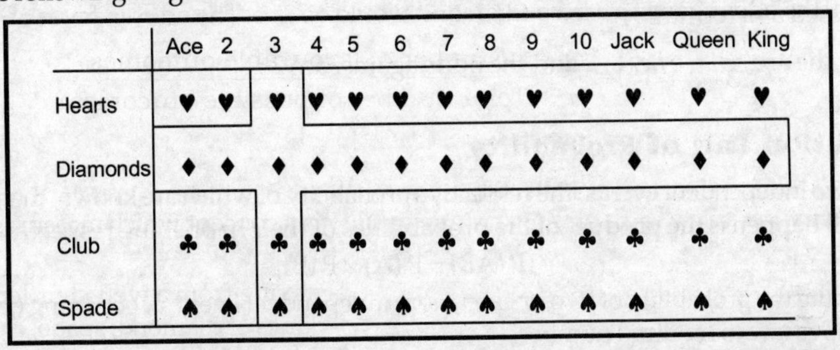

It is denoted by $P(A \cup B)$ or $P(A + B)$. Also we may need the probability that A and B (both) will happen simultaneously. It is denoted by $P(A \cap B)$ or $P(AB)$.

Consider a situation, you are asked to choose any 3 or any diamond or both from a well shuffled pack of 52 cards. Now you are interested in the probability of this situation.

Now count the dots in the area 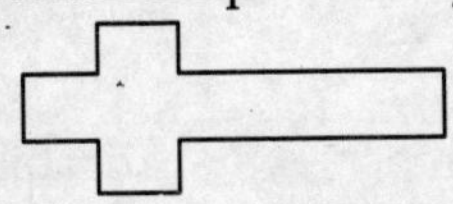 which fulfills the condition any 3 or any diamond or both. They are 16.

Thus the required probability

$$= \frac{\text{No. of favourable outcomes}}{\text{Total no. of outcomes}}$$

$$= \frac{16}{52} \text{ or } 0.31$$

In the language of set theory, the set any 3 or any diamond or both is the union of the sets 'any 3 which contains 4 cards' and 'any diamond' which contains 15 cards. The number of cards in their union is equal to the sum of these numbers minus the number of cards in the space where they overlap. Any points in this space, called the intersection of the two sets, is counted here twice (double counting), once in each set. Dividing by 52 we get the required probability.

$$= P(\text{any } 3) + P(\text{any diamond}) - P(3 \text{ of diamond})$$

$$= \frac{4}{52} + \frac{13}{52} - \frac{1}{52} = \frac{16}{52} \text{ or } 0.31$$

Thus P (any 3 or any diamond or both)

In general, if the letters A and B stands for any two events, then

$$\left.\begin{array}{c} (P \cup B) = P(A) + P(B) - P(A \cap B) \\ \text{or} \\ P(A + B) = P(A) + P(B) - P(AB) \end{array}\right\} \text{Addition Law}$$

Clearly, the outcomes of both A and B are non-mutually exclusive.

Odds in Favour and Against

If P is the probability that an event will occur and $q\ (= 1 - p)$ is the probability of the non-occurrence of the event; then we say that the odds in favour of the event occurring are $p : q$ (p to q) and the odds against its occurring are $q : p$.

For example, if the event consists of drawing a card if club from the deck of 52 cards, then the odds in favor are $\frac{13}{52} : \frac{39}{52}$ *i.e.* $\frac{1}{4} : \frac{3}{4}$ *i.e.* 1 : 3.

Similarly the odds against a card of diamond would be 3 : 1. The odds in favor of 4 or 6 in a single toss of a fair die are $\frac{1}{3} : \frac{2}{3}$; *i.e.* 1 : 2 and the odds against are 2 : 1.

Multiplication Law of Probability

If there are two independent events; the respective probability of which are known, then the probability that both will happen is the product of the probabilities of their happening respectively

$$P(AB) = P(A) \times P(B)$$

To compute the probability of two or even more independent event all occurring (joint occurrence) extent the above law to required number.

For example, first flip a penny, then the nickle and finally flip the dime.

On landing, probability of heads is $\frac{1}{2}$ for a penny

probability of heads is $\frac{1}{2}$ for a nickle

probability of heads is $\frac{1}{2}$ for a dime

Thus the probability of landing three heads will be $\frac{1}{2} \times \frac{1}{2} \times \frac{1}{2} = \frac{1}{8}$ or 0.125. (Note that all three events are independent)

Conditional Probability

In many situations you get more information than simply the total outcomes and favourable outcomes you already have and, hence you are in position to make yourself more informed to make judgements regarding the probabilities of such situations. For example, suppose a card is drawn at random from a deck of 52 cards. Let B denotes the event 'the card is a diamond' and A denotes the event 'the card is red'. We may then consider the following probabilities.

(i) $P(B) = \frac{^{13}C_1}{^{52}C_1} = \frac{13}{52}$

(ii) $P(A) = \frac{^{26}C_1}{^{52}C_1} = \frac{26}{52}$

(iii) P(AB) = The probability that the card is both a diamond and a red card

$$= \frac{^{13}C_1}{^{52}C_1} = \frac{13}{52}$$

(iv) The probability that the card is a diamond knowing that it is red.

Since there are 26 red cards of which 13 are diamonds, the probability that the card is diamond is $\frac{13}{26}$. In other words the probability of event B knowing that A has occurred is $\frac{13}{26}$.

The probability of B under the condition that A has occurred is known as condition probability and it is denoted by P (B/A). Thus $P(B/A) = \frac{13}{26}$. It should be observed that the probability of the event B is increased due to the additional information that the event A has occurred.

Conditional probability found using the formula $P(B/A) = \frac{P(AB)}{P(A)}$

Justification :- $P(A/B) = \frac{P(AB)}{P(A)} = \frac{13}{26} = \frac{13/52}{26/52} = \frac{P(AB)}{P(B)}$

Similarly $P(A/B) = \frac{P(AB)}{P(A)}$

In both the cases if A and B are independent events then P (A/B) = P (A) and P(B/A) = P(B)

Therefore $P(A) = \frac{P(AB)}{P(B)} \Rightarrow P(AB) = P(A) . P(B)$

or $P(B) = \frac{P(AB)}{P(A)} \Rightarrow P(AB) = P(A) . P(B)$

Propositions

(1) If A and B are independent events then A and B' are also independent where B' is the complementary event B.

(2) If A and B are independent events then A' and B' are also independent events.

(3) Two independent events cannot be mutually exclusive.

(4) De Morgan's Laws : $P(A \cup B)' = P(A' \cap B')$

$P(A \cap B)' = P(A' \cup B')$

THEORETICAL DISTRIBUTIONS

Random Variables

When we assign a number to each point of a sample space, we have a function which is defined on the sample space. This function is called a random variable (or stochastic variable).

It is usually denoted by bold letters like **X** or **Y**.

Consider two independent tosses of a fair coin

$\therefore$ S = { (HH), (HT), (TH), (TT) }

Let X denote the number of heads.

Then X (HH) = 2, X (HT) = 1, X(TH) = 1 and X(TT) = 0

i.e. X = 0, 1, 2. Here X is known as a random variable. Thus a random variable is one, which denotes the numerical value of an outcome, of a random experiment.

(1) If the random variable X takes only finite values or countably infinite values, then X is known as a 'discrete variable'.

(2) If the random variable takes the uncountably infinite values between a specified range or limit, it is called as 'continuous random variable'.

For example: X denotes the age of a person.

Discrete Probability Distribution

Return to the above given example of tossing of a fair coin twice.

$$S = \{ (HH), (HT), (TH), (TT) \}$$

Then X (HH) = 2, X (HT) = 1, X (TH) = 1 and X(TT) = 0

Also $P(HH) = \frac{1}{4}$, $P(HT) = \frac{1}{4}$, $P(TH) = \frac{1}{4}$ and $P(HH) = \frac{1}{4}$

The probability distribution: Number of Heads

X P(x)

$$0 \rightarrow \frac{1}{4} \text{ or } 0.25$$

$$1 \rightarrow \frac{1}{4} + \frac{1}{4} = \frac{1}{2} \text{ or } 0.50$$

$$2 \rightarrow \frac{1}{4} \text{ or } 0.25$$

The probability graph can be obtained by using a bar chart as shown in figure (i) or a Histogram as shown in figure (ii).

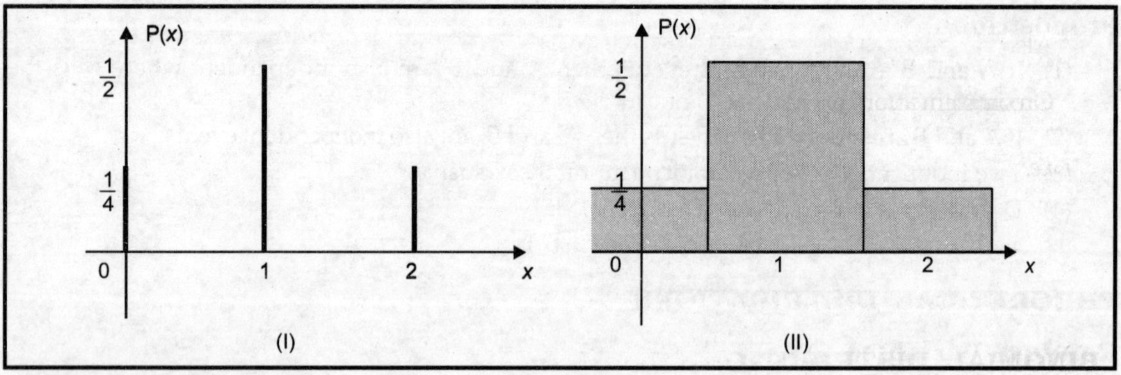

Total of Probabilities of Discrete Random Variables

As you have noted from the probability distribution table or from the bar chart (in which the sum of ordinates *i.e.* heights of bar is:

(1) and from the Histogram (in which sum of the rectangular area is 1), the sum (total) of probabilities of all values of X always equal to 1.

Thus, if the random variable $X = X_1, X_2, X_3, ...X_i, ...X_n$ and X_i each is associated with a number P_i *i.e.* X_1 with P_1, X_2 with P_2 ...., $X_n = P_n$. Then P_i is called probabilities of X_i and is denoted by $P(X_i)$ or simply P(X) which satisfies (1) $P(X_i) > 0$

(2) $\sum_{i=1}^{n} P(X_i) = 1$ then $P(X_i)$ or P(X) is called the probability mass function of the discrete random variable X.

i.e. $X \; X_1 \; X_2 \; X_3 \; .... \; X_n$

$P(X) \; P_1 \; P_2 \; P_3 \; .... \; P_n$

Mathematical Expression of a Discrete Random Variable

If $X = x_i$ is a discrete random variable.

Taking $X = x_1, x_2, ..., x_n$ with respective probabilities

$P_i = P_1, P_2, ..., P_n$ then

The mathematical expression of X is denoted by E(X) and denoted by,

$$E(X) = P_1X_1 + P_2X_2 + ... + P_nX_n = \sum_{i=1}^{n} P_i X_i$$

Mean and Standard Deviation. If the random variable X, assumes the values $x_1, x_2, ..., x_n$ with associated probabilities as $P_1, P_2, ... P_n$ respectively then,

$$\text{Mean (X or } \mu) = \frac{\sum_{i=1}^{n} P_i X_1}{\sum_{i=1}^{n} P_i}$$

$$\text{Therefore } \bar{X} \text{ or } \mu = \sum_{i=1}^{n} P_i X_i = E(X)$$

i.e. Mean = E(X) = Expected value.

$$\text{Also variance (X)} = \sigma_x 2 = \sum_{i=1}^{n} (X_i - \bar{X})^2 \ P_i$$

On simplification, we get, the standard deviation,

$$\textit{i.e.} \quad \sigma_x 2 = \sqrt{\sum_{i=1}^{n} P_i X_i^2 = (\bar{X})^2}$$

PROBABILITY DISTRIBUTIONS

BINOMIAL DISTRIBUTION

Bernoulli's trials. A series of independent trials which can be resulted in one of the two mutually exclusive possibilities 'successes' or 'failures' such that the probability of the success (or failures) in each trials is constant, then such repeated independent trials are called as "Bernoulli's trials".

A discrete variable which can result in only one of the two outcomes (success or failure) is called Binomial.

For example, a coin flip, the result of an examination success or failures, the result of a game - win or loss etc. The Binomial distribution is also known as Bernoulli's distribution, which expresses probabilities of events of dichotomous nature in repeated trials.

When do we get a Binomial distribution ?

The following are the conditions in which probabilities are given by binomial distribution.

1. A trial is repeated 'n' times where n is finite and all 'n' trials are identical.
2. Each trial (or you can call it an event) results in only two mutually exclusive, exhaustive but not necessarily equally likely possibilities, success or failure.
3. The probability of a "success" outcome is equal to some percentage which is identified as proportion 'p'.
4. This proportion 'p', remains constant throughout all events (or trials). It is defined as the ratio of the number of successes to the number of trials.

5. The events (or trials) are independent.
6. If probability of success is 'p', then the probability of failures is $1 - p$ this is denoted by q. Thus, $p + q = 1$.

Suppose a coin is flipped twice. Let 'p' be the probability of getting heads and q the probability of tails, such that $p + q = 1$ (note that $p = q = 1/2$ if the coin is fair) Then there are three possible outcomes which are given below.

Sr. no.	First Flip	Second Flip	Probability
1.	Tail	Tail	$q \times q = q^2$
2.	Head or Tail	Tail	$p \times q$ or $q \times p$ $= 2pq$
3.	Head	Head	$p \times p = p^2$

The sum of all these probabilities is $q^2 + 2pq + p^2 = (q + p)^2$. The terms of $(q + p)^2$ in its expansion gives the probabilities of getting 0, 1, 2 heads.

The result obtained above can be generalized to find the probability of getting 'r' heads in flipping n coins simultaneously.

The probabilities of getting 0, 1, 2, 3, ..., r, ...n heads in a flip of 'n' coins are the terms of the expansion $(q + p)^n$. Since, the expansion is given by the Binomial Theorem, the distribution is called Binomial Distribution.

Thus the Binomial formula is,

$$p\,(x = r) = {}^nC_r\, q^{n-r} \,.\, p^r$$

i.e.

$$p\,(x = r) = \frac{n!}{r!(n-r)!} q^{n-r} . p^r$$

or

$$p\,(x = r) = \frac{n!}{r!(n-r)!} (1-p)^{n-r} . p^r$$

where $n! = n\,(n-1)\,(n-2)$ ....3 . 2. 1

Properties of the Binomial Distribution

We get below some important properties of the Binomial distribution without derivations.

1. If x denotes the Binomial variation, expression of x *i.e.* the mean of the distribution is given by,

$$\boxed{E(x) = \mu = np}$$

2. The standard deviation of the Binomial distribution is determined by,

$$\boxed{\sigma = \sqrt{npq}} \text{ or } \boxed{\sigma = \sqrt{np(1-p)}}$$

3. If in experiment, each of n trials, is repeated N times then expression of r successes *i.e.* the expected frequency of r successes in N experiment is given by,

$$\boxed{\text{Frequency} = N\,{}^nC_r q^{n-r} . p^r}$$

POISSON DISTRIBUTION

A Poisson distribution is the probability distribution that results from a Poisson experiment.

A Poisson random variable is the number of successes that result from a Poisson experiment. The probability distribution of a Poisson random variable is called a Poisson distribution.

Given, the mean number of successes (μ) that occur in a specified region, we can compute the Poisson probability based on the following formula:

Poisson Formula. Suppose, we conduct a Poisson experiment, in which the average number of successes within a given region is μ. Then, the Poisson probability is:

$$P(x; \mu) = (e^{-\mu}) (\mu^x) / x!$$

where x is the actual number of successes that result from the experiment, and e is approximately equal to 2.71828.

The Poisson distribution has the following properties:

- The mean of the distribution is equal to μ.
- The variance is also equal to μ.

Attributes of a Poisson Experiment

A Poisson experiment is a statistical experiment that has the following properties:

- The experiment results in outcomes that can be classified as successes or failures.
- The average number of successes (μ) that occurs in a specified region is known.
- The probability that a success will occur is proportional to the size of the region.
- The probability that a success will occur in an extremely small region is virtually zero.

Note that the specified region could take many forms. For instance, it could be a length, an area, a volume, a period of time, etc.

Notation

The following notation are helpful, when we talk about the Poisson distribution.

- ***e***: A constant equal to approximately 2.71828. (Actually, e is the base of the natural logarithm system.)
- **μ**: The mean number of successes that occur in a specified region.
- ***x***: The actual number of successes that occur in a specified region.
- **P(*x*; μ)**: The Poisson probability that exactly x successes occur in a Poisson experiment, when the mean number of successes is μ.

NORMAL DISTRIBUTION

The normal distribution developed by Gauss is a continuous distribution of maximum utility.

If we know a curve such that the area under the curve from $x = a$ to $x = b$ is equal to the probability that x will take a value between a and b and that the total area under the curve is unity, then the curve is called the probability curve.

If the curve is described by the relation $y = \phi(x)$ then $y = \phi(x)$ is called a probability density or simply probability function.

Among all the probability curves, the normal curve is the most important one. The corresponding function is called the normal probability function and the probability distribution is called the normal distribution. The normal distribution can be considered as the limiting form of the Binomial Distribution, however n, the number of trials, is very large and neither P nor q is very small.

The normal distribution is given by

$$y = \frac{1}{\sigma\sqrt{2\pi}} \cdot e^{-(x-\mu)^2/2\sigma^2}$$

where y = ordinate, x = abscissa of a point on the curve, u = the mean of x, σ = S. D. of x.
x = a constant = 3.1416 and e = a constant = 2.7183.

The Normal Curve

The shape of a normal curve is like a bell. It is symmetrical about the maximum ordinate if P and Q are two points on the x-axis, the shaded area PQRS, bounded by the portion of the curve RS, the ordinates at P and Q and the x-axis is equal to the probability that the variate x lies between $x = a$ and $x = b$ at P and Q respectively. We have already seen that the total area under a normal curve is unity. Any probability distribution, defined this way is known as the normal distribution. The distribution can be completely known if we know the values of μ and σ. Therefore, μ and σ are known as the parameters of the distribution. The normal distribution with mean μ and standard deviation σ is denoted by N (μ, σ).

Properties of the Normal Distribution (Normal Curve)

1. The normal curve is bell-shaped and symmetrical about the maximum ordinate at $x = \mu$, the mean. This ordinate divides the curve into two equal parts. The part on one side is the mirror image of the other side. It has the maximum height at $x = \mu$. Thus, the mode of the distribution is also μ. The ordinate $x = \mu$ divides the whole area under the curve into two equal parts. Hence, the median is also $x = \mu$. Thus for the normal distribution, the mean, mode and median coincide *i.e.* mean = median = mode = μ.
2. We know that the area under the normal curve is equivalent to the probability of randomly drawing a value in the given range. The area is the greatest in the middle, where the "hump" (where mean, mode and median coincide) and then thin out towards on the either sides of the curve, *i.e.* tails, but never becomes zero. In other words, the curve never intersects x-axis at any finite point. *i.e.* x-axis is its Asymptote.
3. Since the curve is symmetrical about mean. The first quartile Q_1 and the third quartile Q_3 lie at the same distance on the two sides of the mean μ. The distance of any quartile from μ is 0.6745 σ units. Thus,

   $Q_1 = \mu - 0.6745\,\sigma$ or $\mu - \frac{2}{3}\sigma$ and

   $Q_3 = \mu + 0.67566$ or $\mu + \frac{2}{3}\sigma$

   Hence, middle 50% observations lie between

   $\mu - \frac{2}{3}\sigma$ and $\mu + \frac{2}{3}\sigma$
4. Since the normal curve is symmetrical its Skewness is zero and kurtosis is 3. The curve is meso Kurtic.
5. The mean deviation is approximately.
6. As discussed earlier, the probability for the variable to lie in any interval (a, b) in the range of variable is given by the are under the normal curve, the two ordinates $x = a$ and $x = b$, and the x-axis

The area under the normal curve is distributed as follows :

1. The area between $x = \mu - \sigma$ and $x = \mu + \sigma$ is 18.27%
2. The area between $x = \mu - 2\sigma$ and $x = \mu + 2\sigma$ is 95.45%
3. The area between $x = \mu - 3\sigma$ and $x = \mu + 3\sigma$ is 99.73%

These areas are shown in the following figure.

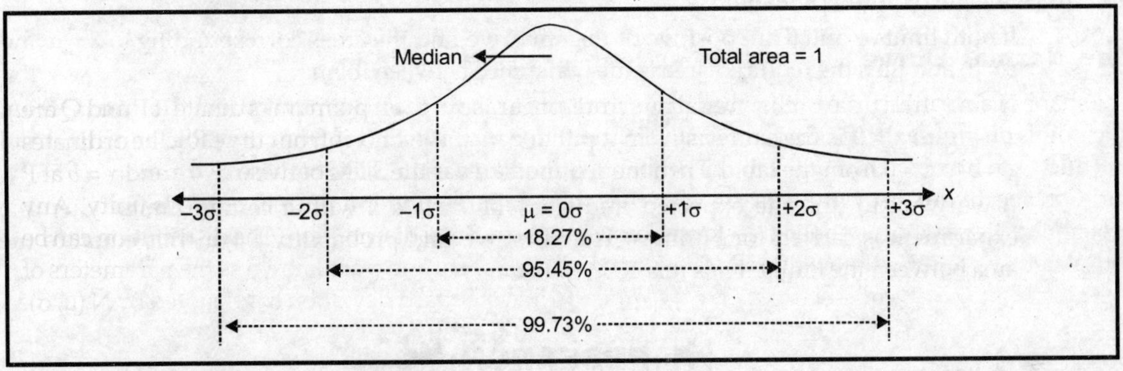

i.e. $P(\mu - \sigma < x < \mu + \sigma) = 18.27\%$

$P(\mu - 2\sigma < x < \mu + 2\sigma) = 95.45\%$

$P(\mu - 3\sigma < x < \mu + 3\sigma) = 99.73\%$

7. $\mu \pm 1$ are points of inflexons

The Standard Normal Variate (Z-Score)

The problem of finding the probability reduces to finding the area between the two ordinates. For different values and we get different normal curves, which multiplies it into too many problems if we are to find the area between the given values for different curves with different μ and σ.

All such problems can be reduced to a single one by reducing all normal distributions to a single normal distribution called 'Standardized Normal Distribution' or to what is known as the Z-score.

To convert a value to a Z-score is to express it in terms of how many standard deviations it is above or below the mean. This actually amounts to the shifting of the origin to μ and reducing its scale by σ.

Thus,

$$z = \frac{x - \mu}{\sigma}$$

where x = the value to be converted, μ = the population mean and σ = the population standard deviation obviously the $\mu = 0$ and $\sigma = 1$ for the Normal standard distribution. It is denoted by N (0,1).

The areas under the curve between $x = 0$ and various ordinate $x = a$ are in a table of standard normal probabilities. This area is equal to the probability that x will assume a value between $x = 0$ and $x = a$.

How to use Table?

The table gives the areas from the ordinate $x = 0$ to $x = 3.09$ which covers more than 0.499 units of area on one side *i.e.* more than 0.99 units of area on both sides, the total area being 1, and it is 0.5 on both sides.

If the variate is not standardized first then convert it into a standardized normal variate *i.e.* z-score, using $z = \frac{x-\mu}{\sigma}$ and find the limits of z-score corresponding to the given limits of the variate.

If we want to find the probability of x between $x = a$, and $x = b$, we find z from $z = \frac{x-\mu}{\sigma}$.

Suppose the values are a and b. Then referring to the table we find the area between $z = \alpha$ and $z = \beta$. This is the required probability.

1. If both limits α and β are positive or negative, we find the areas corresponding to $z = \alpha$ and $z = \beta$ and then the required area is the Difference between them.
2. If one limit say α is negative and other say β is positive then the areas from $z = -\alpha$ to $z = 0$ is the same as from $z = 0$ to $z = \alpha$. We find it from the table and also from $z = 0$ to $z = \beta$ from the table. Then the required area is the SUM of these two areas.
3. If we want to find the expected frequency of variate x within certain limits when the experiment is carried for N times. Then first we find probability P which is equal to the area between the limits. Thus it is NP.

RESEARCH

1. **Basic Research.** This research is conducted largely for the enhancement of knowledge, and is a research which does not have immediate commercial potential. The research which is done for human welfare, animal welfare and plant kingdom welfare. It is called basic, pure, fundamental research. The main motivation here is to expand man's knowledge, not to create or invent something. According to Travers, "Basic Research is designed to add to an organized body of scientific knowledge and does not necessarily produce results of immediate practical value." Such a research is time and cost intensive (Example: An experimental research that may not be or will be helpful in the human progress). It is used to solve a problem by adding to the field of application of a discipline.
2. **Applied Research.** Applied research is designed to solve practical problems of the modern world, rather than to acquire knowledge for knowledge's sake. The goal of applied research is to improve the human condition. It focuses on analysis and solving social and real life problems. This research is generally conducted on a large scale basis and is expensive. As such, it is often conducted with the support of some financing agency like the national government, public corporation, world bank, UNICEF, UGC, Etc. According to Hunt, "applied research is an investigation for ways of using scientific knowledge to solve practical problems" for example:- improve agriculture crop production, treat or cure a specific disease, improve the energy efficiency of homes, offices, how can communication among workers in large companies be improved. to all growth calculation help in short sample to this method.
3. **Problem Oriented Research.** Research is done by industry apex body for sorting out problems faced by all the companies. E.g. WTO does problem oriented research for developing countries, in India agriculture and processed food export development authority (APEDA) conduct regular research for the benefit of agri-industry.
   - As the name indicates, problem identifying researches are undertaken to know the exact nature of problem that is required to be solved.
   - Here, one clarification is needed when we use the term 'Problem', it is not a problem in true sense. It is usually a decision making dilemma or it is a need to tackle a particular business situation.

- It could be a difficulty or an opportunity.

  For e.g. Revenue of Mobile company has decreased by 25% in the last year. The cause of the problem can be any one of the following:

  Poor quality of the product. • Lack of continuous availability. • Not so effective advertising campaign. • High price. • Poor calibre / lack of motivation in sales people/marketing team. • Tough competition from imported brands. • Depressed economic conditions

  In the same case, suppose the prime cause of problem is poor advertising campaign & secondary cause is higher pricing. • To tackle the problem of poor advertising, we have to answer questions like, what can be the new advertising campaign, who can be the brand ambassador, which media, which channel, at what time & during which programme advertisements will be broadcast.

4. **Quantitive Research.** This research is based on numeric figures or numbers. Quantitative research aims to measure the quantity or amount and compares it with past records and tries to project for future period. In social sciences, "quantitative research refers to the systematic empirical investigation of quantitative properties and phenomena and their relationships". The objective of quantitative research is to develop and employ mathematical models, theories or hypothesis pertaining to phenomena.

   The process of measurement is central to quantitative research because it provides fundamental connection between empirical observation and mathematical expression of quantitative relationships. Statistics is the most widely used branch of mathematics in quantitative research. Statistical methods are used extensively with in fields such as economics and commerce.

   In sum, the research using the normative approach conducts why it may called quantitative research as the inferences from it are largely based on quantitative data. Moreover, objectivity is the primary guard so that the research may be replicated by others, if necessary.

5. **Qualitative Research.** Qualitative research presents a non-quantitative type of analysis. Qualitative research is collecting, analyzing and interpreting data by observing what people do and say. Qualitative research refers to the meanings, definitions, characteristics, symbols, metaphors, and description of things. Qualitative research is much more subjective and uses very different methods of collecting information,mainly individual, in-depth interviews and focus groups.

The nature of this type of research is exploratory and open ended. Small number of people are interviewed in depth and or a relatively small number of focus groups are conducted. Qualitative research can be further classified in the following types:

I. **Phenomenology** is a form of research in which the researcher attempts to understand how one or more individuals experience a phenomenon. Eg:-we might interview 20 victims of Bhopal tragedy.

II. **Ethnography** is a type of research which focuses on describing the culture of a group of people. A culture is the shared attributes, values, norms, practices, language, and material things of a group of people. Eg:-the researcher might decide to go and live with the tribal in Andaman Island and study the culture and the educational practices.

III. **Case study** is a form of qualitative research that is focused on providing a detailed account of one or more cases. E.g. we may study a classroom that was given as new curriculum for technology use.

IV. **Grounded theory** is an inductive type of research,based or grounded in the observations of data from which it was developed; it uses a variety of data sources, including quantitative data, review of records, interviews, observation and surveys.

V. **Historical research** allows one to discuss past and present events in the context of the present condition, and allows one to reflect and provide possible answers to current issues and problems. E.g. the lending pattern of business in the 19th century.

DATA

A data type is a type of data. Of course, that is rather circular definition, and also not very helpful. Therefore, a better definition of a data type is a data storage format that can contain a specific type or range of values.

When computer programs store data in variables, each variable must be assigned a specific data type. Some common data types include integers, floating point numbers, characters, strings, and arrays. There may also be more specific types, such as dates, timestamps, boolean values, and varchar (variable character) formats.

Some programming languages require the programmer to define the data type of a variable before assigning it a value. Other languages can automatically assign a variable's data type when the initial data is entered into the variable. For example, if the variable "var1" is created with the value "1.25," the variable would be created as a floating point data type. If the variable is set to "Hello world!," the variable would be assigned a string data type. Most programming languages allow each variable to store a single data type. Therefore, if the variable's data type has already been set to an integer, assigning string data to the variable may cause the data to be converted to an integer format.

Data types are also used by database applications. The fields within a database often require a specific type of data to be input. For example, a company's record for an employee may use a string data type for the employee's first and last name. The employee's date when hire would be stored in a date format, while his or her salary may be stored as an integer. By keeping the data types uniform across multiple records, database applications can easily search, sort, and compare fields in different records.

The most common data types include boolean, integer, floating-point number, character, and alphanumeric string. There are many other data types in programming languages, each serving a specific function and storing data in a particular way. Understanding the different data types allows programmers to design computer applications more efficiently and accurately.

Collecting and Analyzing Data

Essentially, collecting data means putting your design for collecting information into operation. You've decided how you're going to get information – whether by direct observation, interviews, surveys, experiments and testing, or other methods – and now you and/or other observers have to implement your plan. There's a bit more to collecting data. If you are conducting observations, for example, you'll have to define what you're observing and arrange to make observations at the right times, so you actually observe what you need to. You'll have to record the observations in appropriate ways and organize them so they're optimally useful.

Recording and organizing data may take different forms, depending on the kind of information you're collecting. The way you collect your data should relate to how you're planning to analyze and use it. Regardless of what method you decide to use, recording should be done concurrent with data collection if possible, or soon afterwards, so that nothing gets lost and memory doesn't fade.

Some of the things you might do with the information you collect include:

- Gathering together information from all sources and observations.
- Making photocopies of all recording forms, records, audio or video recordings, and any other collected materials, to guard against loss, accidental erasure, or other problems.

- Entering narratives, numbers, and other information into a computer program, where they can be arranged and/or worked on in various ways.
- Performing any mathematical or similar operations needed to get quantitative information ready for analysis. These might, for instance, include entering numerical observations into a chart, table, or spreadsheet, or figuring the mean (average), median (midpoint), and/or mode (most frequently occurring) of a set of numbers.
- Transcribing (making an exact, word-for-word text version of) the contents of audio or video recordings.
- Coding data (translating data, particularly qualitative data that isn't expressed in numbers, into a form that allows it to be processed by a specific software program or subjected to statistical analysis).
- Organizing data in ways that make them easier to work with. How you do this will depend on your research design and your evaluation questions. You might group the observations by the dependent variable (indicator of success) they relate to, by individuals or groups of participants, by time, by activity, etc. You might also want to group observations in several different ways, so that you can study interactions among different variables.

Analyzing Data

Analyzing information involves examining it in ways that reveal the relationships, patterns, trends, etc. that can be found within it. That may mean subjecting it to statistical operations that can tell you not only what kinds of relationships seem to exist among variables, but also to what level you can trust the answers you're getting. It may mean comparing your information to that from other groups (a control or comparison group, statewide figures, etc.), to help draw some conclusions from the data. The point, in terms of your evaluation, is to get an accurate assessment in order to better understand your work and its effects on those you're concerned with, or in order to better understand the overall situation.

There are two kinds of data you're apt to be working with, although not all evaluations will necessarily include both. **Quantitative data** refer to the information that is collected as, or can be translated into, numbers, which can then be displayed and analyzed mathematically. **Qualitative data** are collected as descriptions, anecdotes, opinions, quotes, interpretations, etc., and are generally either not able to be reduced to numbers, or are considered more valuable or informative if they are left as narratives. As you might expect, quantitative and qualitative information needs to be analyzed differently.

1. **Quantitative data.** As we've discussed, quantitative data are typically collected directly as numbers. Some examples include:
   - The frequency (rate, duration) of specific behaviors or conditions.
   - Test scores (*e.g.*, scores/levels of knowledge, skill, etc.)
   - Survey results (*e.g.*, reported behavior, or outcomes to environmental conditions; ratings of satisfaction, stress, etc.)
   - Numbers or percentages of people with certain characteristics in a population (diagnosed with diabetes, unemployed, Spanish-speaking, under age 14, grade of school completed, etc.).

   Data can also be collected in forms other than numbers, and turned into quantitative data for analysis. Researchers can count the number of times an event is documented in interviews or records, for instance, or assign numbers to the levels of intensity of an observed event or behavior. For instance, community initiatives often want to document the amount and intensity of environmental changes they bring about – the new programs and policies that result from their efforts. Whether or not this kind of translation is necessary or useful depends on the nature of what you're observing and on the kinds of questions your evaluation is meant to answer.

Quantitative data is usually subjected to statistical procedures such as calculating the mean or average number of times an event or behavior occurs (per day, month, year). These operations, because numbers are "hard" data and not interpretation, can give definitive, or nearly definitive, answers to different questions. Various kinds of quantitative analysis can indicate changes in a dependent variable related to – frequency, duration, timing (when particular things happen), intensity, level, etc. They can allow you to compare those changes to one another, to changes in another variable, or to changes in another population. They might be able to tell you, at a particular degree of reliability, whether those changes are likely to have been caused by your intervention or program, or by another factor, known or unknown. And they can identify relationships among different variables, which may or may not mean that one causes another.

2. **Qualitative data.** Unlike numbers or "hard data", qualitative information tends to be "soft," meaning it can't always be reduced to something definite. That is in some ways a weakness, but it's also a strength. A number may tell you how well a student did on a test; the look on her face after seeing her grade, however, may tell you even more about the effect of result on her. That look can't be translated to a number, nor can a teacher's knowledge of student's history, progress, and experience, all of which go into the teacher's interpretation of that look. And that interpretation may be far more valuable in helping that student succeed than knowing her grade or numerical score on the test.

As explained above, qualitative data can sometimes be changed into numbers, usually by counting the number of times specific things occur in the course of observations or interviews, or by assigning numbers or ratings to the dimensions (*e.g.*, importance, satisfaction, ease of use).

Qualitative data can sometimes tell you things that quantitative data can't. It may reveal why certain methods are working or not working, whether part of what you're doing conflicts with participants' culture, what participants see as important, etc. It may also show you patterns – in behaviour, physical or social environment, or other factors – that the numbers in your quantitative data don't, and occasionally even identify variables that researchers weren't aware of.

Quantitative analysis is considered to be objective – without any human bias attached to it – because it depends on the comparison of numbers according to the mathematical computations. Analysis of qualitative data is generally accomplished by methods more subjective – dependent on people's opinions, knowledge, assumptions, and inferences (and therefore biases) – than that of quantitative data. The identification of patterns, the interpretation of people's statements or other communication, the spotting of trends – all of these can be influenced by the way the researcher sees the world. Be aware, however, that quantitative analysis is influenced by a number of subjective factors as well. What the researcher chooses to measure, the accuracy of the observations, and the way the research is structured to ask only particular questions it can all influence the results, as can the researcher's understanding and interpretation of the subsequent analyses.

SAMPLING AND ESTIMATION

Most of the researches are based on samples rather than population. The reason is that it is impracticable to observe the total population or to apply a questionnaire or any other tool on the total population under controlled condition. Shortage of time or money is another problem. Study of the total population is neither possible nor needed because if sample is representative to the population, it will give the same result. We study only a sample and then generalize the results to the population.

Meaning of Sampling

Sampling is the process by which a relatively small number of individuals, objects or events is selected and analysed to find out something about the total population from which the sample was drawn. It helps to reduce expenditure, time and energy of the researcher and can produce greater precision and accuracy due to better controlling.

Steps in Sampling

Defining the population. A population refers to any collection of specified group of humans and non humans, such as object, institution, time units, geographical area or events. It is also called universe.

The population may be finite or infinite both. Population need to be existent and hypothetical both.

Exact definition of the population is necessary before selecting any sample. For example, if we want to survey the achievement of students in mathematics, the researcher will have to specify the following things:

I. Age and grade of students.
II. Type of school—public or government.
III. Place of the population.
IV. Socio-economic status of the students.
V. Academic year for which data is to be collected.

Exact definition of the population will help the researcher to select truly representative sample.

Listing the population. After defining the population, a comprehensive and accurate list of the population is also prepared. It is technically called sampling frame. It is very difficult to prepare a perfect sampling frame in large scale surveys.

Selecting a representative sample. After preparing a list, sample is selected from the frame. A sample must have at least the following characteristics:

(i) It must be unbiased and true representative of the population.
(ii) It must be adequate enough to provide statistical treatment of the data.
(iii) It must provide all the informations about the population from which the sample is drawn.
(iv) Sample must adequately represent all the units or groups of populations from which it is drawn.
(v) It must be adequate enough to represent the entire population.

Obtaining an adequate sample. If population is homogeneous, a relatively small sample may serve the purpose. Large sample is needed when the differences between variables **under study** are small and variables are not highly correlated. The size of the sample will also depend upon the methods used in drawing the sample.

Objectives of Sampling

Sampling is used in practice for attaining the following objectives :

(i) Sampling enables us to get accurate measurements of possible values of the parameters and the precision of estimate and the degree of reliability of estimate.

(ii) Sampling is the only choice when a test involves the destruction of the item under study. For example for testing of different types of fruits, wheat and rice by their respective dealers, sampling method is used.

(iii) The most important aim of sampling studies is to obtain maximum information about the phenomena under study with the minimum sacrifice in terms of money, time and energy.

Some Concepts of Sampling/Fundamentals of Sampling

1. **Universe or Population.** In statistics, the term universe means the total of the items or units in any field of inquiry whereas the concept of population refers to the total of items about which information is obtained. Generally we use both universe and population as interchangeable terms. But a researcher has to define both the terms precisely. Broadly speaking, population or universe can be of two types-finite and infinite. Finite universe means the population which contain a definite number of units. For example, the population of Indian Union, the number of workers in a factory are studied under finite universe. The symbol 'N' is generally used to indicate how many items have been included in case of a finite population. The measurement of the units in infinite universe is not possible. It shows us an approximation of a very large finite population. The probabilities of various events can be better estimated if we have selected the infinite universe.

   Universes can also be classified as hypothetical and existent. Hypothetical universe does not consist of concrete objects. For example, throwing of the dice a large number of times and the results are recorded. Such a universe consists of an infinite number of items. In case of the hypothetical universe the values of p and q remain constant in various trials where, p stands for the happening of an event and q stands for not happening of an event.

2. **Sampling Frame.** The group or the elementary units or cluster of such units form the very basis of sampling process in which case they are called sampling units. If the population or universe is finite and the time frame is in the present or past then there is a possibility for such a frame to be identical with the population. As such, the sampling frame is either constructed by an investigator for the purpose of his study or may be based on the existing list of the population. For example telephone directory may form the basis for conducting opinion survey in Darbhanga city.

3. **Sampling Design.** A sampling design deals with a definite plan for obtaining a sample from the sampling frame. It is a technique or the procedure which is adopted by the researcher for selecting some sampling units from which inference about the population or universe are drawn.

4. **Statistics and Parameters.** Statistics deals with the characteristics of a sample whereas a parameter is a characteristics of a population or universe. The word parameter is used to indicate various statistical measures like mean, standard deviation, correlation etc. in the universe whereas the term statistics refers to the statistical measures relating to the sample. But when such statistical measures describe the characteristics of a population, they are known as parameters.

5. **Sampling Error.** If the sample is representative, the data will be reliable and there does not arise any error. Otherwise, there is a part of the population since its results may not be exactly equal to the true value of the population. Sampling errors are those errors which arise on account of sampling and they generally happen to be random variations in the sample estimates around the true population values. Sampling errors occur randomly and are equally likely to be in either direction and as such their expected value is zero. The sampling errors are of two types: (a) biased and (b) non-biased. The biased error arises due to the bias in selection process while the second due to chance of differences between the units of population included in the sample and those not included. The bias may arise due to faulty process of selection, faulty work during the collection of data and faulty methods of analysis.

   As opposed to sampling errors, we may have non-sampling errors which arise from one or more of the following factors :

   (a) Lack of trained and experienced investigators.
   (b) Errors due to non-sampling.
   (c) Errors committed during presentation of results.
   (d) Inadequate and inconsistent data.
   (e) Lack of adequate inspection and supervision of primary staff.
   (f) Inadequate method of interview.

   Statisticians have not provided us any measure of non-sampling error.

6. **Precision.** The theory of sampling makes an attempt to indicate the degree of reliance that can be placed on various estimates obtained from sampling studies. These limits vary with the degree of confidence which we wish to achieve in our assertions. Thus, precision is the range within which the population average will lie in accordance with the reliability specified in the confidence level as a percentage of the estimate or it indicates the numerical quantity.

7. **Confidence Level and Significance Level.** The confidence level or reliability means the expected percentage of times that the actual value will fall within the given precision limits. Thus if we take a confidence level of 80%, then we mean that there are 80 chances in 100 or 0.8 in 1, that the sample results represent the true condition of the population within a specified precision range against 20 chances in 100 or 0.2 in 1; that it does not whereas the significance level indicates the likelihood that the answer will fall outside the range.

8. **Sampling Distribution.** We are generally concerned with sampling distribution in sampling analysis. We take samples from the universe and in each sample we compute various statistical measures like mean, standard deviation and then find out that each sample may give its own value for the statistic under consideration. Thus, the mean of the sampling distribution can be taken as the mean of the universe.

Important Sampling Distribution

In statistics of variables generally the question of finding out the values of p and q does not arise and as such it is very difficult to obtain the expected frequencies. If say 100 samples are taken and if the mean value of each sample is found out, we shall have a series relating to the mean of 100 samples. Similarly we can have a series of standard deviation of 100 samples. Such series relating to the values of a function are called sampling distributions. The most important characteristic of all sampling distribution is that they give a more or less normal distribution. The following are some of the important sampling distributions :

1. **Sampling Distribution of Mean.** Sampling distribution of mean refers to the probability distribution of all the possible means of random samples of a given size that are taken from a population.
2. **Sampling Distribution of Proportion.** Like sampling distribution of mean, we can have a sampling distribution of proportion also. It is found in case of statistics of attributes. If the probability of the happening of an event in one trial is known, we can find the probability of its happening *r* times in *n* trials by the expansion of a binomial. The mean and standard deviation of such series are given by the following rules :

   $$M = np$$

   $$\sigma = \sqrt{npq}$$

   If instead of recording the number of success we record the proportion of success or $1/n^{th}$ of the number in each sample the mean proportion of success is

   $$m = p$$

   and standard deviation (σ) would be = $\sqrt{\frac{pq}{n}}$

   If there is some difference between observed values of the mean and standard deviation and their expected values. These differences may be due to what we have been calling fluctuations of sampling. As we are well aware of the fact that in a normal frequency distribution 99.73% of the items lie within the limits given by mean ±3 standard deviation. In other words, $np \pm 3\sqrt{npq}$ would cover a very large majority of cases.
3. **Student's t-Distribution.** Series of means or standard deviations of the small samples may or may not be normally distributed and similarly it is not possible to substitute the mean or the standard deviation of a small sample in place of the parameter mean or standard deviation for the calculation of standard error.

   When population standard deviation (σ_p) is not known and the sample is of a small size, say less than 50, then we use t-distribution for the sampling distribution of mean and work out t-variables. The following methods are used for the calculation of mean and standard deviation. When the sampling variables are small:

   $$t = \frac{x - m}{\sigma}\sqrt{n}$$

   where, x represents the mean of the sample, *m* the mean of the universe, σ the standard deviation of the sample and *n* the number of observations.

   $$\sigma = \sqrt{\frac{\Sigma d^2}{n-1}}$$
4. **F-distribution.** The square of the standard deviation or the squares of deviation taken from the mean is called variance. If σ^{21} and $(\sigma^{21})^2$ are the variances of the independent samples of size n_1 and n_2 respectively taken from two independent normal populations, having the same variance $(\sigma_p{}^1)^2$

   $(\sigma_p{}^2)^2$ = The ratio $F = \frac{(\sigma_s^1)^2}{(\sigma_s^2)^2}$

   where, $(\sigma_1)^2 = \frac{\Sigma \bar{X}_1 i - (x_1)^2}{n_1 - 1}$

and $$(\sigma_p^2) = \frac{\Sigma \bar{X}_2 i - (x_2)^2}{n_2 - 1}$$

as an F distribution with $n_1 - 1$ and $n_2 - 1$ degrees of freedom. F value is calculated on the basis of the following formula :

$$F = \frac{\text{Variance between Samples } (V_2)}{\text{Variance within Samples } (V_1)}$$

5. **Chi-square (χ^2) distribution.** The chi-square distribution is used to study the divergence of actual and expected frequencies and from this value coefficient of contingency is calculated to find out if there is any association between the attributes in study. Thus it is a measure of actual divergence of the observed and expected frequencies. If the calculated value of chi-square is very small as compared to its table value, it indicates that the divergence between actual and expected frequencies is very little and consequently the fit is good. If, on the other hand, the calculated value is greater than its table value it clearly shows that the divergence between expected and observed frequencies is very great and consequently the fit is poor. The value of χ^2 is calculated with the formula

$$\chi^2 = \Sigma \left[\frac{(O - E)^2}{E} \right]$$

Where, O stands for the observed frequency and E for the corresponding expected frequency.

Error

Sampling Errors

In a sample survey, since, only a small portion of the population is studied, its results are bound to differ from the census results and thus, have a certain amount of error. This error would always be there no matter that the sample is drawn at random and that it is highly representative. This error is attributed to fluctuations of sampling and is called *sampling error*. Sampling error is due to the fact that only a subset of the population (*i.e.* sample) has been used to estimate the population parameters and draw inferences about the population. Thus, sampling error is present only in sample survey and is completely absent in census method.

Sampling errors are primarily due to the following reasons :

1. ***Faulty selection of the sample.*** Some of the bias are introduced by the use of defective sampling technique for the selection of a sample *e.g.*, purposive or judgement sampling in which the investigator deliberately selects a representative sample to obtain certain results. This bias can be overcomed by strictly adhering to a simple random sample or by selecting a sample at random subject to restrictions which, while, improving the accuracy are of such nature that they do not introduce bias in the results.
2. ***Substitution.*** If difficulties arise in enumerating a particular sampling unit included in the random sample, the investigators usually substitute a convenient member of the population. This obviously leads to some bias since, the characteristics possessed by the substituted unit will usually, be different from those possessed by the unit originally included in the sample.
3. ***Faulty demarcation of sampling units.*** Bias due to defective demarcation of sampling units is particularly significant in area surveys such as agricultural experiments in the field or crop cutting surveys, *etc.* In such surveys, while, dealing with border line cases, it depends more or less on the discretion of the investigator whether to include them in the sample or not.

4. ***Error due to bias in the estimation method.*** Sampling method consists in estimating the parameters of the population by appropriate statistics computed from the sample. Improper choice of the estimation techniques might introduce the error. For example, in simple random sampling, if $x_1, x_2, ..., x_n$ are observations on the n sampled units, then the sample variance

$$s^2 = \frac{1}{n}\sum_{i=1}^{n}(x_i - \bar{x})^2$$

is a biased estimator of the population variance σ^2 while, an unbiased estimate of σ^2 is given by

$$s^2 = \frac{1}{n-1}\sum_{i=1}^{n}(x_i - \bar{x})^2$$

5. ***Variability of the population.*** Sampling error also depends on the variability or heterogeneity of the population to be sampled.

Non-Sampling Errors

Non-sampling errors are not attributed to chance and are consequence of certain factors which are within human control. In other words, they are due to certain causes which can be traced and may arise at any stage of the enquiry, viz., planning and execution of the survey and collection, processing and analysis of the data. Non-sampling errors are thus, present both in census surveys as well as sample surveys. Obviously, non-sampling errors will be of large magnitude in a census survey than in a sample survey because, they increase with the increase in the number of units to be examined and enumerated. It is very difficult to prepare an exhaustive list of all the sources of non-sampling errors. We enumerate below some of the important factors responsible for non-sampling errors in any survey (census or sample).

1. Faulty planning, including vague and faulty definitions of the population or the statistical units to be used, incomplete list of population-members (*i.e.* incomplete frame in case of sample survey).
2. Vague and imperfect questionnaire which might result in incomplete or wrong information.
3. Defective methods of interviewing and asking questions.
4. Vagueness about the type of the data to be collected.
5. Exaggerated or wrong answers to the questions which appeal to the pride or prestige or self-interest of the respondents. For example, a person may overstate his education or income or understate his age or he may give wrong statements to safeguard his self-interest.
6. Personal bias of the investigator.
7. Lack of trained and qualified investigators and lack of supervisory staff.
8. Failure of respondents' memory to recall the events or happenings in the past.
9. Non-response and Inadequate or Incomplete Response, bias due to non-response results if in a house-to-house survey the respondent is not available in spite of repeated visits by the investigator or, if the respondent refuses to furnish the information. Incomplete response error is introduced, if the respondent is unable to furnish information on certain questions or, if he is unwilling or even refuses to answer certain questions.
10. Improper Coverage, if the objectives of the survey are not precisely stated in clear cut terms, this may result in (i) the inclusion in the survey of certain units which are not to be included or (ii) the exclusion of certain units which were to be included in the survey under the objectives. For example, in a census to determine the number of individuals in the age group, say, 15

years to 55 years, more or less serious errors may occur in deciding whom to enumerate unless particular community or area is not specified and also, the time at which the age is to be specified.

11. Compiling Errors, *i.e.* wrong calculations or entries made during the processing and analysis of the data. Various operations of data processing such as editing and coding of the responses, punching of cards, tabulation and summarising the original observations made in the survey are a potential source of error. Compilation errors are subject to control through verification, consistency checks, etc.
12. Publication errors, *i.e.* the errors committed during presentation and printing of tabulated results are basically due to two sources. The first one refers to the mechanics of publication-the proofing error and the like. The other, which is of a more serious nature, lies in the failure of the survey organisation to point out the limitations of the statistics.

Methods of Sampling

(1) Non Probability Method

In this method, sample is selected by the discretion of the researcher and no theoretical basis is taken into consideration here. While selecting the sample, the researcher only thinks from where he will get the required data to serve his purpose. That is why it is also called *purposive sample.*

Other types of non-probability sample are as follows:

(a) **Quota or chunk sample.** In this method, quota of sample from different units of the population is fixed and thus, total sample is selected.

(b) **Incidental sample.** In this method, whosoever is available to cooperate for providing information is selected and thus, the required number of sample is obtained.

Advantages of non probability sample

These methods are very useful in the situation when:

(i) The researcher wants to understand the problem by contacting with only informed people.

(ii) The sample to be selected is small and researcher wants to get some idea about the population characteristics in a very short period of time.

(iii) Different units of the populations have total characteristics of their respective units, then selection of few units out of so many is considered sufficient.

Limitations of non-probability methods

(i) Such sample can be biased and hence, generalization of results for the entire population may be misleading.

(ii) Such samples depend on uncontrolled factors and researcher's insight which cannot be relied on all the time.

(iii) Sampling errors in these samples cannot be determined because they can affect variance within the group as well as between the groups.

(iv) Such sampling frame does not adequately cover the population.

(2) Probability Methods

In this method of sampling, each unit of the population has equal chance of being selected. That is why they are also called **random samples**.

Probability samples have the following characteristics:

(i) Each unit in the sample has some known probability of entering the sample.

(ii) Weights appropriate to the probabilities are used in the analysis of the sample.

(iii) The process of sampling is automatic in one or more steps of selection of units in the sample.

In probability sampling, a researcher designs the sample in a way that ensures that each unit in the population has a fair chance of being selected and numerical value of that chance can also be calculated.

These methods can help the researcher in the following ways:

(i) The researcher can know the size of the sample which is needed for a desired level of accuracy.

(ii) He can tell the chance for each of unit being selected.

(iii) He can calculate sampling error.

(iv) He can determine the level of confidence.

Types of Random Methods

(A) Simple or Unrestricted Random Sampling

In this type of sampling, each unit of the population has equal chance of being selected. Several devices are used here to draw samples from population.

(a) **Lottery method.** If there are X numbers in a population, each unit is assigned numbers from one to last. Then they are properly mixed up. After that required numbers of units are taken out from the lot one by one.

(b) **Use of random table.** Fisher and Yates have prepared a random table. After assigning consecutive numbers to all units of the population the investigator starts from any point on the random table and reads consecutive numbers in any direction; horizontally, vertically or diagonally. If the number of population is less than 999 (of three digits only) investigator takes only three digits of the random table from the left and matches the numbers of the table to the number given to different units of the population.

Limitations

(i) Simple random sampling procedure is an ideal plan theoretically but practically it is very tough job if number of units of population is very large.

(ii) Simple random sampling procedure fails when lists of units of the population are not available.

(iii) This procedure fails when population is infinite.

(iv) It is again not good to use this method when different units of the population is very much heterogeneous in characteristics.

(B) Stratified Random Sampling

This method is used to overcome the above four problems. Here, the researcher first divides his whole population into different stratum on the basis of certain characteristics and random sample is drawn from each stratum. This stratification of the population makes different small homogenous groups of the population and simple random sampling technique can be applied to each group to select required number of sample. This makes the sample more representative to the population.

A population can be stratified on many grounds such as age, sex, grade, economic condition, place of residing, occupation, castes etc. The efficiency of stratified random sample depends on the allocation of sample size to stratum. Percentage method is the best method of allocating sample size among stratums.

Advantages

(i) This method is especially useful in opinion surveys when we have to cover a large and scattered population.

(ii) It can be used when lists of all units of the population is not available.

(iii) It can make different units of population homogeneous and small and thus, we can use lottery method for each stratum very easily.

(C) Systematic Sampling

When a population is finite and can be properly listed, this method is used. Here, all the units of the population are listed in an alphabetical order first. Then, if we have to select 100 units out of 1000 units of a population, we will keep interval of 10 units throughout the population.

If population is homogeneous this method of sampling is as good as simple random method and researcher cannot apply his own bias here.

Limitations. This method will not work properly in two situations.

(a) If population is showing some trend in its characteristics, then trend will not change from beginning to end and thus, sample may be biased to a particular trend.

(b) This method will also not work in case of cyclic variables. If attendance of students of a school is generally very low on Monday due to certain reasons, and we select only Monday of the week for the whole year as a sample for studying the attendance of students, our sample will not give the correct result.

(D) Cluster Sampling

This method is used when :

I. Population is infinite.

II. List of all units of population is not available.

III. Population is scattered over a wide geographical area.

IV. Individuals have to be studying as a group.

V. Individual units cannot be sampled due to administrative reasons.

(E) Multistage Sampling

It is used in large scale surveys for making the study more comprehensive. Sampling here is done in two, three or four stages. In large scale surveys we generally use mailed questionnaire to collect data. The missing data due to incomplete response or non return of the questionnaire might introduce a bias. The researcher draws a second sample randomly from non respondent and contacts them personally to collect the required information with the help of interview. One more example is that if we want to study the attitude of teachers across the country towards a particular text book, we will first sample states from across the country. Finally sample of few schools will be selected from each district and thus, survey will be undertaken.

SAMPLING DISTRIBUTION

A sampling distribution is a probability distribution of a statistic obtained through a large number of samples drawn from a specific population. The sampling distribution of a given population is the distribution of frequencies of a range of different outcomes that could possibly occur for a statistic of a population.

Understanding Sampling Distribution

A lot of data drawn and used by academicians, statisticians, researchers, marketers, analysts, etc. are actually samples, not populations. A sample is a subset of a population. For example, a medical researcher that wanted to compare the average weight of all babies born in North America from 1995 to 2005 to those born in South America within the same time period cannot within a reasonable amount of time draw the data for the entire population of over a million childbirths that occurred over the ten-year time frame. He will instead only use the weight of, say, 100 babies, in each continent to make a conclusion. The weight of 200 babies used is the sample and the average weight calculated is the sample mean.

Now suppose that instead of taking just one sample of 100 newborn weights from each continent, the medical researcher takes repeated random samples from the general population, and computes the sample mean for each sample group. So, for North America, he pulls up data for 100 newborn weights recorded in the US, Canada and Mexico as follows: four 100 samples from select hospitals in the US, five 70 samples from Canada and three 150 records from Mexico, for a total of 1200 weights of newborn babies grouped in 12 sets. He also collects a sample data of 100 birth weights from each of the 12 countries in South America.

Each sample has its own sample mean and the distribution of the sample means is known as the sample distribution.

The average weight computed for each sample set is the sampling distribution of the mean. Not just the mean can be calculated from a sample. Other statistics, such as the standard deviation, variance, proportion, and range can be calculated from sample data. The standard deviation and variance measure the variability of the sampling distribution.

The number of observations in a population, the number of observations in a sample and the procedure used to draw the sample sets determine the variability of a sampling distribution. The standard deviation of a sampling distribution is called the standard error. While the mean of a sampling distribution is equal to the mean of the population, the standard error depends on the standard deviation of the population, the size of the population and the size of the sample.

Knowing how spread apart the mean of each of the sample sets are from each other and from the population mean will give an indication of how close the sample mean is to the population mean. The standard error of the sampling distribution decreases as the sample size increases.

Special Considerations

A population or one sample set of numbers will have a normal distribution. However, because a sampling distribution includes multiple sets of observations, it will not necessarily have a bell-curved shape.

Following our example, the population average weight of babies in North America and in South America has a normal distribution because some babies will be underweight (below the mean) or overweight (above the mean), with most babies falling in between (around the mean). If the average weight of newborns in North America is seven pounds, the sample mean weight in each of the 12 sets of sample observations recorded for North America will be close to seven pounds as well.

However, if you graph each of the averages calculated in each of the 1,200 sample groups, the resulting shape may result in a uniform distribution, but it is difficult to predict with certainty what the actual shape will turn out to be. The more samples the researcher uses from the population of over a million weight figures, the more the graph will start forming a normal distribution.

- A sampling distribution is a probability distribution of a statistic obtained through a large number of samples drawn from a specific population.

- The sampling distribution of a given population is the distribution of frequencies of a range of different outcomes that could possibly occur for a statistic of a population.
- A lot of data drawn and used by academicians, statisticians, researchers, marketers, and analysts are actually samples, not populations.

STATISTICAL ESTIMATION

The method of statistically drawing an inference on data is called the statistical inference. Thus, the testing of hypothesis and the inference are the most important factors involved. The theory of estimation is a part of statistics that extracts parameters from observations that are corrupted with noise.

Estimation is a division of statistics and signal processing that determines the values of parameters through measured and observed empirical data. The process of estimation is carried out in order to measure and diagnose the true value of a function or a particular set of populations. It is done on the basis of observations on the samples, which are a combined piece of the target population or function. Several statistics are used to perform the task of estimation.

There are two very important terms that are used in estimation: the estimator and the estimate. To understand the concept of the estimator and estimate in detail, we will use an example. Let's say that a1, a2, a3 and so on is a collection of samples from some group of a certain population with 'x' as its parameter. Here, if T= T (a) is a statistic, then E (T(a)) = x. From these equations we can realize that an estimation of the statistic has been carried out, where the statistic T is an estimator and the parameter 'x' is the estimator.

Estimation has many important properties for the ideal estimator. These properties include unbiased nature, efficiency, consistency and sufficiency.

The estimators that are unbiased while performing estimation are those that have 0 bias results for the entire values of the parameter. Going by statistical language and terminology, unbiased estimators are those where the mathematical expectation or the mean proves to be the parameter of the target population. In the above mentioned example for estimation, T is going to be the unbiased estimator only if its estimate comes out to be equal to 'x.'

In estimation, the estimators that give consistent estimates are said to be the consistent estimators. As the number of random variables increase, the degree of concentration should be higher and higher around the estimate in order to make the estimator of estimation the consistent estimator. If the estimator gives an unbiased estimate and the variance of the estimator comes out to be zero, then the estimator of estimation is called the consistent estimator. These two conditions need to be fulfilled only if the numbers of random variables reach infinity.

In estimation there are many estimators that have ample incidences of consistent estimators, and according to the property of efficiency in estimation, the consistent estimators should be normally distributed. This kind of property was taken into account in the theory of estimation, because there were incidents of the estimators having ample consistent estimations but were not the efficient estimators.

An estimator is known as the sufficient estimator only when the joint conditional distribution function of the sample/observation has the condition of T1 T2 T3 T4 (and so on and so forth), and are the values under the given estimator function 'T'. Thus, the resultant joint conditional estimation has to be absolutely sovereign of the parameter 'x'. While carrying out the task of estimation, a researcher should always know that the best estimator is the one that is the minimum variance unbiased estimator (MVUE). This means that the estimator has the minimum variability when it is compared to other estimators.

HYPOTHESIS TESTING

A statistical hypothesis is an assumption about a population parameter. This assumption may or may not be true. Hypothesis testing refers to the formal procedures used by statisticians to accept or reject statistical hypotheses.

Statistical Hypotheses

The best way to determine whether a statistical hypothesis is true would be to examine the entire population. Since that is often impractical, researchers typically examine a random sample from the population. If sample data are not consistent with the statistical hypothesis, the hypothesis is rejected.

There are two types of statistical hypotheses.

- **Null hypothesis.** The null hypothesis, denoted by H0, is usually the hypothesis that sample observations result purely from chance.
- **Alternative hypothesis.** The alternative hypothesis, denoted by H1 or Ha, is the hypothesis that sample observations are influenced by some non-random cause.

For example, suppose we wanted to determine whether a coin was fair and balanced. A null hypothesis might be that half the flips would result in Heads and half in Tails. The alternative hypothesis might be that the number of Heads and Tails would be very different. Symbolically, these hypotheses would be expressed as

$$H0: P = 0.5$$
$$Ha: P = 0.5$$

Suppose we flipped the coin 50 times, resulting in 40 Heads and 10 Tails. Given this result, we would be inclined to reject the null hypothesis. We would conclude, based on the evidence, that the coin was probably not fair and balanced.

Hypothesis Tests

Statisticians follow a formal process to determine whether to reject a null hypothesis, based on sample data. This process, called hypothesis testing, consists of four steps.

- **State the hypotheses.** This involves stating the null and alternative hypotheses. The hypotheses are stated in such a way that they are mutually exclusive. That is, if one is true, the other must be false.
- **Formulate an analysis plan.** The analysis plan describes how to use sample data to evaluate the null hypothesis. The evaluation often focuses around a single test statistic.
- **Analyze sample data.** Find the value of the test statistic (mean score, proportion, t-score, z-score, etc.) described in the analysis plan.
- **Interpret results.** Apply the decision rule described in the analysis plan. If the value of the test statistic is unlikely, based on the null hypothesis, reject the null hypothesis.

Decision Errors

Two types of errors can result from a hypothesis test :

- **Type I error.** A Type I error occurs when the researcher rejects a null hypothesis when it is true. The probability of committing a Type I error is called the significance level. This probability is also called alpha, and is often denoted by α.
- **Type II error.** A Type II error occurs when the researcher fails to reject a null hypothesis that is false. The probability of committing a Type II error is called Beta, and is often denoted by β. The probability of not committing a Type II error is called the Power of the test.

Decision Rules

The analysis plan includes decision rules for rejecting the null hypothesis. In practice, statisticians describe these decision rules in two ways - with reference to a P-value or with reference to a region of acceptance.

- **P-value.** The strength of evidence in support of a null hypothesis is measured by the P-value. Suppose the test statistic is equal to S. The P-value is the probability of observing a test statistic as extreme as S, assuming the null hypothesis is true. If the P-value is less than the significance level, we reject the null hypothesis.
- **Region of acceptance.** The region of acceptance is a range of values. If the test statistic falls within the region of acceptance, the null hypothesis is not rejected. The region of acceptance is defined so that the chance of making a Type I error is equal to the significance level.

  The set of values outside the region of acceptance is called the region of rejection. If the test statistic falls within the region of rejection, the null hypothesis is rejected. In such cases, we say that the hypothesis has been rejected at the level of significance.

These approaches are equivalent. Some statistics texts use the P-value approach; others use the region of acceptance approach. In subsequent lessons, this tutorial will present examples that illustrate each approach.

One-Tailed and Two-Tailed Tests

A test of a statistical hypothesis, where the region of rejection is on only one side of the sampling distribution, is called a one-tailed test. For example, suppose the null hypothesis states that the mean is less than or equal to 10. The alternative hypothesis would be that the mean is greater than 10. The region of rejection would consist of a range of numbers located on the right side of sampling distribution; that is, a set of numbers greater than 10.

A test of a statistical hypothesis, where the region of rejection is on both sides of the sampling distribution, is called a two-tailed test. For example, suppose the null hypothesis states that the mean is equal to 10. The alternative hypothesis would be that the mean is less than 10 or greater than 10. The region of rejection would consist of a range of numbers located on both sides of sampling distribution; that is, the region of rejection would consist partly of numbers that were less than 10 and partly of numbers that were greater than 10.

ANALYSIS AND INTERPRETATION OF DATA

Data analysis and interpretation is the process of assigning meaning to the collected information and determining the conclusions, significance, and implications of the findings. The steps involved in data analysis are a function of the type of information collected, however, returning to the purpose of the assessment and the assessment questions will provide a structure for the organization of the data and a focus for the analysis.

The analysis of *NUMERICAL (QUANTITATIVE) DATA* is represented in mathematical terms. The most common statistical terms include:

- **Mean.** The mean score represents a numerical average for a set of responses.
- **Standard deviation.** The standard deviation represents the distribution of the responses around the mean. It indicates the degree of consistency among the responses. The standard deviation, in conjunction with the mean, provides a better understanding of the data. For example, if the mean is 3.3 with a standard deviation of 0.4, then two-thirds of the responses lie between 2.9 (3.3 – 0.4) and 3.7 (3.3 + 0.4).

- **Frequency distribution.** Frequency distribution indicates the frequency of each response. For example, if respondents answer a question using an agree/disagree scale, the percentage of respondents who selected each response on the scale would be indicated. The frequency distribution provides additional information beyond the mean, since it allows for examining the level of consensus among the data.

Higher levels of statistical analysis (*e.g.*, t-test, factor analysis, regression, ANOVA) can be conducted on the data, but these are not frequently used in most program/project assessments.

The analysis of *NARRATIVE (QUALITATIVE) DATA* is conducted by organizing the data into common themes or categories. It is often more difficult to interpret narrative data since it lacks the built-in structure found in numerical data. Initially, the narrative data appears to be a collection of random, unconnected statements. The assessment purpose and questions can help direct the focus of the data organization. The following strategies may also be helpful when analyzing narrative data.

Focus groups and Interviews:

- **Read and organize the data from each question separately.** This approach permits focusing on one question at a time (*e.g.*, experiences with tutoring services, characteristics of tutor, student responsibility in the tutoring process).
- **Group the comments by themes, topics, or categories.** This approach allows for focusing on one area at a time (*e.g.*, characteristics of tutor – level of preparation, knowledge of content area, availability).

Documents

- Code content and characteristics of documents into various categories (*e.g.*, training manual – policies and procedures, communication, responsibilities).

Observations

- Code patterns from the focus of the observation (*e.g.*, behavioral patterns – amount of time engaged/not engaged in activity, type of engagement, communication, interpersonal skills).

The analysis of the data via statistical measures and/or narrative themes should provide answers to the assessment questions. Interpreting the analyzed data from the appropriate perspective allows for determination of the significance and implications of the assessment.

Central Limit Theorem

The Central Limit Theorem (CLT) is a statistical theory which states that given a sufficiently large sample size from a population with a finite level of variance, the mean of all samples from the same population will be approximately equal to the mean of the population.

It tells us that,

The Central Limit Theorem is exactly what the shape of the distribution of means will be when we draw repeated samples from a given population. Specifically, as the sample sizes get larger, the distribution of means calculated from repeated sampling will approach normality.

As the sample size increases, the sampling distribution of the mean, X-bar, can be approximated by a normal distribution with mean μ and standard deviation $\alpha/\sqrt{n}$ where:

- μ is the population mean
- σ is the population standard deviation
- n is the sample size

In other words, if we repeatedly take independent random samples of size n from any population, then when n is large, the distribution of the sample will approach a normal distribution.

Redefining it more ahead,

The central limit theorem states that when an infinite number of successive random samples are taken from a population, the sampling distribution of the means of those samples will become approximately normally distributed with mean μ and standard deviation $\alpha/\sqrt{N}$ as the sample size (N) becomes larger, irrespective of the shape of the population distribution.

Let us understand CLT by following illustration:

Suppose we draw a random sample of size n ($x_1, x_2, x_3, \ldots x_{n-1}, x_n$) from a population random variable that is distributed with mean μ and standard deviation σ.

Do this repeatedly, drawing many samples from the population, and then calculate the x of each sample.

We will treat the x values as another distribution, which we will call the sampling distribution of the mean ($\bar{x}$).

Given a distribution with a mean μ and variance σ_2, the sampling distribution of the mean approaches a normal distribution with a mean (μ) and a variance σ_2/n as n, the sample size, increases and the amazing and very interesting intuitive thing about the central limit theorem is that no matter what the shape of the original (parent) distribution, the sampling distribution of the mean approaches a normal distribution.

A normal distribution is approached very quickly as n increases, note that n is the sample size for each mean and not the number of samples

Remember, in a sampling distribution of the mean the number of samples is assumed to be infinite.

Three different components of the central limit theorem

(1) Successive sampling from a population

(2) Increasing sample size

(3) Population distribution.

Standard Error

Standard error is the standard deviation of the sampling distribution of a statistic. It can be abbreviated as S.E.

Standard error plays a very crucial role in the large sample theory. It also may form the basis for the testing of a hypothesis. The statistical inference involved in the construction of the confidence interval is mainly based on standard error.

The magnitude of the standard error gives an index of the precision of the estimate of the parameter. It is inversely proportional to the sample size, meaning that smaller samples tend to produce greater standard errors.

The standard deviation of a sample is generally designated by the Greek letter sigma (σ). It can also be defined as the square root of the variance present in the sample.

Statistical Estimation

The method of statistically drawing an inference on data is called the statistical inference. Thus, the testing of hypothesis and the inference are the most important factors involved. The theory of estimation is a part of statistics that extracts parameters from observations that are corrupted with noise.

Estimation is a division of statistics and signal processing that determines the values of parameters through measured and observed empirical data. The process of estimation is carried out in order to measure and diagnose the true value of a function or a particular set of populations. It is done on the basis of observations on the samples, which are a combined piece of the target population or function. Several statistics are used to perform the task of estimation.

There are two very important terms that are used in estimation: the estimator and the estimate. To understand the concept of the estimator and estimate in detail, we will use an example. Let's say that a_1, a_2, a_3 and so on is a collection of samples from some group of a certain population with 'x' as its parameter. Here, if T= T (a) is a statistic, then E (T(a)) = x. From these equations we can realize that an estimation of the statistic has been carried out, where the statistic T is an estimator and the parameter 'x' is the estimator.

Estimation has many important properties for the ideal estimator. These properties include unbiased nature, efficiency, consistency and sufficiency.

The estimators that are unbiased while performing estimation are those that have 0 bias results for the entire values of the parameter. Going by statistical language and terminology, unbiased estimators are those where the mathematical expectation or the mean proves to be the parameter of the target population. In the above mentioned example for estimation, T is going to be the unbiased estimator only if its estimate comes out to be equal to 'x.'

In estimation, the estimators that give consistent estimates are said to be the consistent estimators. As the number of random variables increase, the degree of concentration should be higher and higher around the estimate in order to make the estimator of estimation the consistent estimator. If the estimator gives an unbiased estimate and the variance of the estimator comes out to be zero, then the estimator of estimation is called the consistent estimator. These two conditions need to be fulfilled only if the numbers of random variables reach infinity.

In estimation, there are many estimators that have ample incidences of consistent estimators, and according to the property of efficiency in estimation, the consistent estimators should be normally distributed. This kind of property was taken into account in the theory of estimation, because there were incidents of the estimators having ample consistent estimations but they were not the efficient estimators.

An estimator is known as the sufficient estimator only when the joint conditional distribution function of the sample/observation has the condition of T_1, T_2, T_3, T_4 (and so on and so forth), and are the values under the given estimator function 'T.' Thus, the resultant joint conditional estimation has to be absolutely sovereign of the parameter 'x.' While carrying out the task of estimation, a researcher should always know that the best estimator is the one that is the minimum variance unbiased estimator (MVUE). This means that the estimator has the minimum variability when it is compared to other estimators.

SMALL SAMPLE TEST

t–test

When size of the sample is less than 30, theory of sampling is called as small sample. In Z test we assumed that sample statistics is distributed normally.

If size of sample is small, normality cannot be applied. As a result a separate test or new test to deal with small samples is t-test.

Prof. Gosset developed 't' test under his pen name student. Therefore, it is also known as student's 't' test.

It is defined as :

If from a normal population with $\overline{x} = \mu$ the sample of size n is drawn, t is defined as

$$t = \frac{\overline{x} - \mu}{\frac{\sigma_s}{\sqrt{n-1}}}$$

where $\overline{x} = \frac{\Sigma x}{N}$

$$\sigma_s = \sqrt{\frac{\Sigma(x-\overline{x})^2}{n}}$$

or $t = \frac{\overline{x} - \mu}{\frac{s}{\sqrt{n}}}$ where $\overline{x} = \frac{\Sigma x}{N}$, $s = \sqrt{\frac{\Sigma(x-\overline{x})^2}{n-1}}$

where s is called as unbiased estimate of population standard deviation.

Assumptions

1. Parent population is normal in nature.
2. Sample is random in nature.
3. Population standard deviation is not given.

Uses of 't' test

1. To test hypothesis related with population mean:

H_0 : Population mean = μ

H_1 : Population mean $\neq \mu$.

If we are to test the hypothesis that the population mean equal to μ or not. For this purpose, we will prepare the following set of hypothesis.

H_0 : pop. mean = μ.

H_1 : pop mean $\neq \mu$

and t is calculated as

$$t = \frac{\overline{x} - \mu}{\frac{\sigma_s}{\sqrt{n-1}}}$$

Calculated value of 't' is compared with its tabulated value at a given level of significance for n-1 degrees of freedom. If 't' calculated is greater than 't' tabulated, null hypothesis may be rejected otherwise accepted.

2. ***To test hypothesis related with difference of population means :***

Ist case – Non Paired samples. To test whether the difference between two population means is significant or not. Following is the SET of hypothesis

$H_0 : \mu_1 = \mu_2$ or $\mu_1 - \mu_2 = 0$

or Difference is insignificant

$H_1 : \mu_1 \neq \mu_2$

or $\mu_1 - \mu_2 \neq 0$

or Difference is significant

Suppose $\overline{x}_1$ = mean of sample from 1st population

$\overline{x}_2$ = mean of sample from 2nd population

$$\therefore \quad t = \frac{\bar{x}_1 - \bar{x}_2}{\sqrt{s^2\left[\frac{1}{n_1}+\frac{1}{n_2}\right]}}$$

n_1 = size of 1st sample

n_2 = size of 2nd sample

$$s^2 = \text{compiled pooled variance} = \frac{n_1\sigma_{s_1}^2 + n_2\sigma_{s_2}^2}{n_1+n_2-2}$$

$$s^2 = \frac{n_1\left[\frac{\Sigma(x_1-\bar{x}_1)^2}{n_1}\right] + n_2\left[\frac{\Sigma(x_2-\bar{x}_2)^2}{n_2}\right]}{n_1+n_2-2}$$

Cancelling n_1 by n_1, n_2 by n_2, we get

$$s^2 = \frac{\Sigma(x_1-\bar{x}_1)^2 + \Sigma(x_2-\bar{x}_2)^2}{n_1+n_2-2}$$

Calculated value of t is compared with its critical value at a given LOS for $n_1 + n_2 - 2$ degree of freedom and the decision is taken.

IInd case – Paired Samples. If the various observations of the two samples are paired together, we apply paired 't' test.

$H_0 : \mu_1 = \mu_2$

or $\mu_1 - \mu_2 = 0$

or $\bar{D} = 0$ [on the average difference is equal to 0]

$H_1 : \mu_1 \neq \mu_2$

or $\mu_1 - \mu_2 = 0$ or $\bar{D} \neq 0$

$$\therefore \quad t = \frac{\bar{d}}{\frac{\sigma d}{\sqrt{n-1}}} \quad \text{where d = is the differences between paired values}$$

$d = x_1 - x_2$

or $d = x_2 - x_1$

$$\bar{d} = \frac{\Sigma d}{n}$$

$$\sigma_d = \sqrt{\frac{\Sigma(d-\bar{d})^2}{n}}$$

n = no. of pairs

Calculated value of 't' is compared with its tabulated value at LOS for n – 1 degree of freedom.

F-Test

F- test is a small sample test given by Prof. Snedicor. It is defined as, if from two normal populations with equal variance, we draw independent random samples of sizes n_1 and n_2 respectively and $s_1^2 = \frac{\Sigma(x_1-\bar{x}_1)^2}{n_1 - 1}$ is the unbiased estimate of variance of Ist population and $s_2^2 = \frac{\Sigma(x_2-\bar{x}_2)^2}{n_2 - 1}$ is the unbiased estimate of variance of 2nd population, then statistic 'F' is defined as

$$F = \frac{s_1^2}{s_2^2} \text{ if } s_1^2 > s_2^2$$

$$\text{or} \quad F = \frac{s_2^2}{s_1^2} \text{ if } s_2^2 > s_1^2$$

Assumptions

1. Parent population from which samples are drawn are normal in nature
2. Both the population have same variance.
3. Samples are random and independent.

Uses

To test the significance of the difference between the two population variance - we can check that whether the populations from which samples are drawn have some variance or not. Following is the set of hypothesis.

$H_0 = \sigma_1^2 = \sigma_2^2$ or difference in two population variances is insignificant.

$H_1 = \sigma_1^2 \neq \sigma_2^2$ or difference is significant. Suppose, from the two population, we draw two samples of sizes n_1 and n_2 the unbiased estimates of population variances will be calculated as below.

$$s_1^2 = \frac{\Sigma(x_1 - \bar{x}_1)^2}{n_1 - 1}, \; s_2^2 = \frac{\Sigma(x_2 - \bar{x}_2)^2}{n_2 - 1}$$

$$\text{Then } F = \frac{s_1^2}{s_2^2} \text{ if } s_1^2 > s_2^2 \qquad v_1 = n_1 - 1; v_2 = n_2 - 1$$

$$\text{or } F = \frac{s_2^2}{s_1^2} \text{ if } s_2^2 > s_1^2 \qquad v_1 = n_2 - 1; v_2 = n_1 - 1$$

Calculated value of 'F' is compared with its critical value at a given LOS for v_1, v_2 degree of freedom and decision is taken.

F Test makes basis of ANOVA

Analysis of variance is that technique of data analysis which is used for analysing total variations in the variable under study. Total variations are divided into variations because of chance factor. In the end by calculating 'F' ratio it is decided whether variations because of different treatments are significantly higher than variations because of chance factor.

The concept of ANOVA was developed by Prof. Fisher and is based upon 'F' test. Students 't' test can be used to study the difference of means if number of samples is two. If no. of samples is 3 or more, 't' test fails to study the significance of the difference between population means. In such cases, we apply ANOVA.

Chi-square Test

If 'E_{of}' denotes observed frequencies and 'E_f' denotes expected frequencies, chi square is defined as

$$\chi^2 = \frac{\left(E_{of} - E_f\right)^2}{E_f}$$

Uses

1. To test the significance of difference or to test the goodness of fit.
2. To test the association of attributes or characteristics.

Applications

(i) In two by two table if any cell frequency is less than 5, it will make the applicability of χ^2 test impossible. In the process of pooling degree of freedom will be lost. In '2×2' contingency table degree of freedom (2–1) (2–1) = 1. After pooling is done degree of freedom will be lost and correct degree of freedom will be zero for which χ^2 distribution does not exist. Hence χ^2 test cannot be applied. For this purpose Prof. F.C. Yates has given a correction called as Yates correction for continuity. After the application of this correction χ^2 is calculated as below.

$$\chi^2 = \frac{N\left[(ad-bc)-\frac{1}{2}N\right]^2}{(a+c)(b+d)(a+b)(c+d)}$$

Pooling will not be required and therefore χ^2 test can be applied.

(ii) Suppose we are to test hypothesis related with population variance. For this purpose we shall frame the following set of hypothesis.

H_0 : Population variance = σ^2

H_1 : Population variance ≠ σ^2

The value of χ^2 is calculated as below

$$\chi^2 = \frac{(n)(\sigma_s^2)}{\sigma_0^2}$$

where n = size of the sample

$$\sigma_s^2 = \frac{\Sigma(x-\bar{x})^2}{n}$$

σ_0^2 = Population variance claimed under null hypothesis.

Calculated value of χ^2 is compared with its critical value at a given level of significance for n–1 degree of freedom. If χ^2 (calculated) is greater than χ^2 (tab) null hypothesis may be rejected or otherwise accepted.

Z-Test

There are different types of Z-test each for different purpose. Some of the popular types are outlined below:

1. Z-test for single proportion is used to test a hypothesis on a specific value of the population proportion.

   Statistically speaking, we test the null hypothesis $H_0: p = p_0$ against the alternative hypothesis $H_1: p >< p_0$ where p is the population proportion and p_0 is a specific value of the population proportion we would like to test for acceptance.

   The example on tea drinkers explained above requires this test. In that example, $p_0 = 0.5$. Notice that in this particular example, proportion refers to the proportion of tea drinkers.

2. Z-test for difference of proportions is used to test the hypothesis that two populations have the same proportion.

   For example suppose one is interested to test if there is any significant difference in the habit of tea drinking between male and female citizens of a town. In such a situation, Z-test for difference of proportions can be applied.

One would have to obtain two independent samples from the town- one from males and the other from females and determine the proportion of tea drinkers in each sample in order to perform this test.

3. Z -test for single mean is used to test a hypothesis on a specific value of the population mean.

   Statistically speaking, we test the null hypothesis H_0: $\mu = \mu_0$ against the alternative hypothesis H_1: $\mu >< \mu_0$ where μ is the population mean and μ_0 is a specific value of the population that we would like to test for acceptance.

   Unlike the t-test for single mean, this test is used if $n \geq 30$ and population standard deviation is known.

4. Z-test for single variance is used to test a hypothesis on a specific value of the population variance.

   Statistically speaking, we test the null hypothesis H_0: $\sigma = \sigma_0$ against H_1: $\sigma >< \sigma_0$ where σ is the population mean and Ã0 is a specific value of the population variance that we would like to test for acceptance.

   In other words, this test enables us to test if the given sample has been drawn from a population with specific variance σ_0. Unlike the chi square test for single variance, this test is used if $n \geq 30$.

5. Z-test for testing equality of variance is used to test the hypothesis of equality of two population variances when the sample size of each sample is 30 or larger.

ANOVA

Analysis of Variance (ANOVA) is a parametric statistical technique used to compare data sets. This technique was invented by R.A. Fisher, and is thus often referred to as Fisher's ANOVA, as well. It is similar in application to techniques such as t-test and z-test, in that it is used to compare means and the relative variance between them. However, analysis of variance (ANOVA) is best applied where more than 2 populations or samples are meant to be compared.

Statistics Solutions is the country's leader in Analysis of Variance (ANOVA) and dissertation statistics. Contact Statistics Solutions today for a free 30-minute consultation.

The use of this parametric statistical technique involves certain key assumptions, including the following:

1. **Independence of case.** Independence of case assumption means that the case of the dependent variable should be independent or the sample should be selected randomly. There should not be any pattern in the selection of the sample.
2. **Normality.** Distribution of each group should be normal. The Kolmogorov-Smirnov or the Shapiro-Wilk test may be used to confirm normality of the group.
3. **Homogeneity.** Homogeneity means variance between the groups should be the same. Levene's test is used to test the homogeneity between groups.

If particular data follows the above assumptions, then the analysis of variance (ANOVA) is the best technique to compare the means of two, or more, populations.

Analysis of variance (ANOVA) has three types:

One way analysis. When we are comparing more than three groups based on one factor variable, then it said to be one way analysis of variance (ANOVA). For example, if we want to compare whether or not the mean output of three workers is the same based on the working hours of the three workers.

Two way analysis. When factor variables are more than two, then it is said to be two way analysis of variance (ANOVA). For example, based on working condition and working hours, we can compare whether or not the mean output of three workers is the same.

K-way analysis. When factor variables are *k*, then it is said to be the *k*-way analysis of variance (ANOVA).

Key Terms and Concepts

Sum of square between groups. For the sum of the square between groups, we calculate the individual means of the group, then we take the deviation from the individual mean for each group. And finally, we will take the sum of all groups after the square of the individual group.

Sum of squares within group. In order to get the sum of squares within a group, we calculate the grand mean for all groups and then take the deviation from the individual group. The sum of all groups will be done after the square of the deviation.

F-ratio. To calculate the F-ratio, the sum of the squares between groups will be divided by the sum of the square within a group.

Degree of freedom. To calculate the degree of freedom between the sums of the square group, we will subtract one from the number of groups. The sum of the square within the group's degree of freedom will be calculated by subtracting the number of groups from the total observation.

BSS $df = (g-1)$ for BSS is between the sum of squares, where g is the group, and df is the degree of freedom.

WSS $df = (N-g)$ for WSS within the sum of squares, where N is the total sample size.

Significance. At a predetermine level of significance (usually at 5%), we will compare and calculate the value with the critical table value. Today, however, computers can automatically calculate the probability value for F-ratio. If p-value is lesser than the predetermined significance level, then group means will be different. Or, if the p-value is greater than the predetermined significance level, we can say that there is no difference between the groups' mean.

Analysis of variance (ANOVA) in SPSS. In SPSS, analysis of variance (ANOVA) can be performed in many ways. We can perform this test in SPSS by clicking on the option "one way ANOVA," available in the "compare means" option. When we are performing two ways or more than two ways analysis of variance (ANOVA), then we can use the "univariate" option available in the GLM menu. SPSS will give additional results as well, like the partial eta square, Power, regression model, post hoc, homogeneity test, etc. The post hoc test is performed when there is significant difference between groups and we want to know exactly which group has means that are significantly different from other groups.

MANN-WHITNEY TEST (U-TEST)

Mann-Whitney U test is the non-parametric alternative test to the independent sample t-test. It is a non-parametric test that is used to compare two sample means that come from the same population, and used to test whether two sample means are equal or not. Usually, the Mann-Whitney U test is used when the data is ordinal or when the assumptions of the t-test are not met.

Sometimes understanding the Mann-Whitney U is difficult interpret because the results are presented in group rank differences rather than group mean differences.

Assumptions of the Mann-Whitney

Mann-Whitney U test is a non-parametric test, so it does not assume any assumptions related to the distribution of scores. There are, however, some assumptions that are assumed

1. The sample drawn from the population is random.
2. Independence within the samples and mutual independence is assumed. That means that an observation is in one group or the other (it cannot be in both).
3. Ordinal measurement scale is assumed.

Use of Mann-Whitney

Mann-Whitney U test is used for every field, but is frequently used in psychology, healthcare, nursing, business, and many other disciplines. For example, in psychology, it is used to compare attitude or behavior, etc. In medicine, it is used to know the effect of two medicines and whether they are equal or not. It is also used to know whether or not a particular medicine cures the ailment or not. In business, it can be used to know the preferences of different people and it can be used to see if that changes depending on location.

Administration, Analysis, and Reporting

Statistics Solutions consists of a team of professional methodologists and statisticians that can assist the student or professional researcher in administering the survey instrument, collecting the data, conducting the analyses and explaining the results.

KRUSKAL-WALLIS TEST (H-TEST)

The Kruskal-Wallis test is a nonparametric (distribution free) test, and is used when the assumptions of one-way ANOVA are not met. Both the Kruskal-Wallis test and one-way ANOVA assess for significant differences on a continuous dependent variable by a categorical independent variable (with two or more groups). In the ANOVA, we assume that the dependent variable is normally distributed and there is approximately equal variance on the scores across groups. However, when using the Kruskal-Wallis Test, we do not have to make any of these assumptions. Therefore, the Kruskal-Wallis test can be used for both continuous and ordinal-level dependent variables. However, like most non-parametric tests, the Kruskal-Wallis Test is not as powerful as the ANOVA.

Null hypothesis. Null hypothesis assumes that the samples (groups) are from identical populations.

Alternative hypothesis. Alternative hypothesis assumes that at least one of the samples (groups) comes from a different population than the others.

Example questions answered:

- How do test scores differ between the different grade levels in elementary school?
- Do job satisfaction scores differ by race?

The distribution of the Kruskal-Wallis test statistic approximates a chi-square distribution, with k-1 degrees of freedom, if the number of observations in each group is 5 or more. If the calculated value of the Kruskal-Wallis test is less than the critical chi-square value, then the null hypothesis cannot be rejected. If the calculated value of Kruskal-Wallis test is greater than the critical chi-square value, then we can reject the null hypothesis and say that at least one of the samples comes from a different population.

Assumption

1. We assume that the samples drawn from the population are random.
2. We also assume that the observations are independent of each other.
3. The measurement scale for the dependent variable should be at least ordinal.

RANK CORRELATION TEST

The Spearman's Rank Correlation Coefficient is used to discover the strength of a link between two sets of data. This example looks at the strength of the link between the price of a convenience item (a 50 cl bottle of water) and distance from the Contemporary Art Museum in El Raval, Barcelona.

Spearman's Rank Correlation Coefficient

A correlation can easily be drawn as a scatter graph, but the most precise way to compare several pairs of data is to use a statistical test - this establishes whether the correlation is really significant or if it could have been the result of chance alone.

Spearman's Rank correlation coefficient is a technique which can be used to summarise the strength and direction (negative or positive) of a relationship between two variables.

The result will always be between plus 1 and minus 1.

Method - Calculating the Coefficient

- Create a table from your data.
- **Rank the two data sets.** Ranking is achieved by giving the ranking '1' to the biggest number in a column, '2' to the second biggest value and so on. The smallest value in the column will get the lowest ranking. This should be done for both sets of measurements.
- **Tied scores are given the mean (average) rank.** For example, the three tied scores of 1 euro in the example below are ranked fifth in order of price, but occupy three positions (fifth, sixth and seventh) in a ranking hierarchy of ten. The mean rank in this case is calculated as (5+6+7) ÷ 3 = 6.
- **Find the difference in the ranks (*d*).** This is the difference between the ranks of the two values on each row of the table. The rank of the second value (price) is subtracted from the rank of the first (distance from the museum).

  Square the differences (d^2) To remove negative values and then sum them (Σ^2)

REPORT WRITING

Mostly, research work is presented in a written form. The practical utility of research study depends heavily on the way it is presented to those who are expected to act on the basis of research findings. Research report is a written document containing key aspects of research project.

Research report is a medium to communicate research work with relevant people. It is also a good source of preservation of research work for the future reference. Many times, research findings are not followed because of improper presentation. Preparation of research report is not an easy task. It is an art. It requires a good deal of knowledge, imagination, experience, and expertise. It demands a considerable time and money.

Definitions:

1. In simple words:
   Research report is the systematic, articulate, and orderly presentation of research work in a written form.
2. We can also define the term as:
   Research report is a research document that contains basic aspects of the research project.
3. In the same way, we can say:
   Research report involves relevant information on the research work carried out. It may be in form of hand-written, typed, or computerized.

Report Format

There is no one best format for all reports. Format depends on several relevant variables. One must employ a suitable format to create desirable impression with clarity. Report must be attractive. It should be written systematically and bound carefully. A report must use the format (often called structure) that best fit the needs and wants of its readers. Normally, following format is suggested as a basic outline, which has sufficient flexibly to meet the most situations.

Research report is divided into three parts as:

I. First Part (Formality Part):
   - (i) Cover page
   - (ii) Title page
   - (iii) Certificate or statement
   - (iv) Index (brief contents)
   - (v) Table of contents (detailed index)
   - (vi) Acknowledgement
   - (vii) List of tables and figures used
   - (viii) Preface/forwarding/introduction
   - (ix) Summary report

II. Main Report (Central Part of Report):
   - (i) Statement of objectives
   - (ii) Methodology and research design
   - (iii) Types of data and its sources
   - (iv) Sampling decisions
   - (v) Data collection methods
   - (vi) Data collection tools
   - (vii) Fieldwork
   - (viii) Analysis and interpretation (including tables, charts, figures, etc.)
   - (ix) Findings
   - (x) Limitations
   - (xi) Conclusions and recommendations
   - (xii) Any other relevant detail

III. Appendix (Additional Details):
   - (i) Copies of forms used
   - (ii) Tables not included in findings
   - (iii) A copy of questionnaire
   - (iv) Detail of sampling and rate of response
   - (v) Statement of expenses

(vi) Any other relevant information
(vii) Bibliography – list of books, magazines, journals, and other reports

Key Considerations/Factors:

While preparing research report, following issues must be considered:

(i) Objectives
(ii) Type of problem/subject
(iii) Nature and type of research
(iv) Audience or users of research work
(v) Size of report
(vi) Time and cost
(vii) Form of writing – handwritten, typed, or computerized.
(viii) Language
(ix) Contents of report
(x) Order of contents
(xi) Number of copies
(xii) Format – type and size of paper; lengths width, and depth of report; and pattern of writing including paragraph, indent, numbering, font size and type, colouring, etc.
(xiii) Binding (for soft, and, particularly, for hard copy) – type, quality of material, colour, etc., related issues.

MULTIPLE CHOICE QUESTIONS

1. What is the purpose of measures of central tendency in statistics?
   (1) To measure the spread of data
   (2) To identify outliers in a dataset
   (3) To summarize the main characteristics of a dataset
   (4) To assess the skewness of data distribution
2. Which measure of central tendency is most affected by extreme values in a dataset?
   (1) Mean (2) Median
   (3) Mode (4) Range
3. If a dataset has a symmetric distribution, which measure of central tendency is usually the best choice?
   (1) Mean (2) Median
   (3) Mode (4) Standard Deviation
4. Which of the following is not a measure of central tendency?
   (1) Geometric Mean
   (2) Harmonic Mean
   (3) Interquartile Range
   (4) Trimmed Mean
5. In a positively skewed distribution, how are the mean, median, and mode related?
   (1) Mean > Median > Mode
   (2) Mode > Median > Mean
   (3) Median > Mean > Mode
   (4) Mode > Mean > Median
6. Calculate the mean of the following dataset: 12, 18, 22, 26, 30.
   (1) 18 (2) 22
   (3) 24 (4) 26
7. Find the median of the dataset: 15, 20, 25, 30, 35.
   (1) 20 (2) 25
   (3) 27.5 (4) 30
8. If the mode of a dataset is 12 and the median is 15, what can you infer about the distribution?
   (1) Positively skewed
   (2) Symmetric
   (3) Negatively skewed
   (4) Bimodal

Directions: Each of the following items consists of two statements, one labelled as Assertion (A) and other labelled as Reason (R). You are to examine these two statements carefully and decide if the (A) and the (R) are individually true and if so, whether (R) is the correct explanation of (A). Select your answers to these items using the codes given below:
(1) Both (A) and (R) are true, and (R) is the correct explanation for (A).
(2) Both (A) and (R) are true, but (R) is not the correct explanation for (A).
(3) (A) is true, but (R) is false.
(4) Both (A) and (R) are false.

9. **Assertion (A):** The median is a resistant measure of central tendency.
   Reason (R): The median is not influenced by extreme values in a dataset.
10. **Assertion (A):** The mean is the most appropriate measure of central tendency for a dataset with a normal distribution.
    Reason (R): The mean provides a balance point that Minimises the sum of squared deviations from each data point.
11. **Assertion (A):** The mode is not always a unique value in a dataset.
    Reason (R): A dataset may have more than one mode, making it multimodal.
12. **Assertion (A):** The mean is sensitive to extreme values in a dataset.
    Reason (R): Outliers or extreme values have a significant impact on the mean.
13. **Assertion (A):** In a perfectly symmetrical dataset, the mean and median are always equal.
    Reason (R): Symmetrical distributions have a balanced shape, making the mean and median coincide.
14. What is the range of the data set {3, 7, 10, 15, 20}?
    (1) 17 (2) 18
    (3) 17.5 (4) 20
15. Which of the following is not a measure of dispersion?
    (1) Mean (2) Range

(3) Variance
(4) Standard Deviation

16. The interquartile range is the:
(1) Range of the middle 50% of the data
(2) Range of the entire data set
(3) Difference between the largest and smallest values in the data set
(4) Average of the data set

17. Which measure of dispersion is affected most by extreme values?
(1) Range
(2) Interquartile Range
(3) Variance
(4) Standard Deviation

18. The formula for calculating variance is
(1) $\sqrt{(\Sigma(xi - \overline{x})^2/n)}$
(2) $\sqrt{(xi - \overline{x})^2/n)}$
(3) $\sqrt{\Sigma(xi - \overline{x})^2/n)}$
(4) $\Sigma(xi - \overline{x})^2/n)$

19. The coefficient of variation is a measure of dispersion that is used to
(1) Compare the dispersion of two or more data sets with different units
(2) Measure the spread of data around the mean
(3) Measure the range of the data set
(4) Calculate the standard deviation

20. Which measure of dispersion is not affected by extreme values?
(1) Range
(2) Interquartile Range
(3) Variance
(4) Standard Deviation

21. The mean absolute deviation is calculated by
(1) Taking the average of the absolute deviations from the mean
(2) Squaring the deviations from the mean and then taking the square root
(3) Taking the median of the absolute deviations from the mean
(4) Adding all the deviations from the mean

22. The formula for calculating the coefficient of variation is
(1) (Standard Deviation / Mean) × 100
(2) (Mean / Standard Deviation) × 100
(3) (Range / Mean) × 100
(4) (Mean / Range) × 100

23. Which measure of dispersion is the square root of the variance?
(1) Range
(2) Interquartile Range
(3) Standard Deviation
(4) Mean Absolute Deviation

24. The variance of a data set is always
(1) Positive (2) Negative
(3) Zero (4) Undefined

25. The sum of the deviations from the mean is always:
(1) Zero (2) Positive
(3) Negative (4) Undefined

26. The coefficient of variation is expressed in
(1) Percentage (2) Ratio
(3) Both (1) and (2) (4) Neither (1) nor (2)

27. The measure of dispersion that uses all the observations in its calculation is
(1) Range
(2) Interquartile Range
(3) Variance
(4) Mean Absolute Deviation

28. The measure of dispersion that is not affected by the presence of outliers is
(1) Range
(2) Interquartile Range
(3) Variance
(4) Standard Deviation

29. The range of a data set is
(1) The difference between the largest and smallest values
(2) The average of the data set
(3) The middle 50% of the data
(4) The spread of data around the mean

30. The measure of dispersion that is most commonly used in statistical analysis is
(1) Range
(2) Interquartile Range
(3) Variance
(4) Standard Deviation

31. The measure of dispersion that is not affected by the order of the data is
(1) Range
(2) Interquartile Range
(3) Variance
(4) Mean Absolute Deviation

32. The measure of dispersion that is the most diffi cult to calculate by hand is
(1) Range (2) Interquartile Range
(3) Variance (4) Standard Deviation

33. The measure of dispersion that is not commonly used in practice is:
(1) Range
(2) Interquartile Range
(3) Variance
(4) Mean Absolute Deviation

34. The measure of dispersion that is not affected by the units of measurement is:
(1) Range
(2) Interquartile Range
(3) Coefficient of Variation
(4) Standard Deviation

35. The measure of dispersion that is not a resistant measure is
(1) Range
(2) Interquartile Range
(3) Variance
(4) Mean Absolute Deviation

36. The measure of dispersion that is not a measure of spread is
(1) Range
(2) Interquartile Range
(3) Variance
(4) Mean Absolute Deviation

37. The measure of dispersion that is not a measure of variability is
(1) Range
(2) Interquartile Range
(3) Variance
(4) Mean Absolute Deviation

38. The measure of dispersion that is not a measure of central tendency ism
(1) Range (2) Interquartile Range
(3) Variance
(4) Mean Absolute Deviation

Directions: Each of the following items consists of two statements, one labelled as Assertion (A) and other labelled as Reason (R). You are to examine these two statements carefully and decide if the (A) and the (R) are individually true and if so, whether (R) is the correct explanation of (A). Select your answers to these items using the codes given below:

(1) Both (A) and (R) are true, and (R) is the correct explanation for (A).
(2) Both (A) and (R) are true, but (R) is not the correct explanation for (A).
(3) The (A) is true, but the (R) is false.
(4) Both (A) and (R) are false.

39. **Assertion (A):** The interquartile range is a robust measure of dispersion.
Reason (R): It is not affected by extreme values or outliers.

40. **Assertion (A):** Standard deviation is preferred over variance for describing the spread of data.
Reason: Standard deviation is in the same unit as the data.

41. **Assertion (A):** If the mean absolute deviation is zero, all data points in the set are equal.
Reason (R): Mean absolute deviation is the average of the squared differences from the mean.

42. **Assertion (A):** Coefficient of variation is a relative measure of dispersion.
Reason (R): It compares the standard deviation to the mean of the data set.

43. **Assertion (A):** The range is sensitive to extreme values.
Reason (R): The range is the difference between the maximum and minimum values in a dataset.

44. What does a positive skewness value indicate?
(1) Left-skewed distribution
(2) Symmetric distribution
(3) Right-skewed distribution
(4) Normal distribution

45. Which measure is used to quantify the degree of skewness in a distribution?
(1) Mean (2) Median
(3) Mode
(4) Skewness coefficient

46. In a perfectly symmetrical distribution, the skewness coefficient is:
(1) 0 (2) 1
(3) –1 (4) Undefined

47. A negative skewness value indicates
(1) Left-skewed distribution
(2) Symmetric distribution
(3) Right-skewed distribution
(4) Normal distribution

48. Which measure of skewness is based on the third moment of a distribution?
(1) Pearson's first coefficient of skewness
(2) Pearson's second coefficient of skewness

(3) Bowley's coefficient of skewness
(4) Karl Pearson coefficient of skewness

49. What does a correlation coefficient of 0 indicate?
(1) Perfect positive correlation
(2) No correlation
(3) Perfect negative correlation
(4) Undefined correlation A

50. The correlation coefficient ranges between:
(1) –1 and 1 (2) 0 and 1
(3) $-\infty$ and ∞ (4) 0 and 100

51. In regression analysis, the variable being predicted is called the
(1) Independent variable
(2) Dependent variable
(3) Explanatory variable
(4) Control variable

52. The coefficient of determination is also known as
(1) R-squared
(2) Beta coefficient
(3) Correlation coefficient
(4) Standard error

53. In simple linear regression, the relationship between the independent and dependent variables is assumed to be
(1) Linear (2) Non-linear
(3) Exponential (4) Logarithmic

54. The least squares method Minimises the:
(1) Sum of absolute errors
(2) Sum of squared errors
(3) Sum of cubed errors
(4) Sum of errors

55. The regression line is also known as the
(1) Line of best fit
(2) Correlation line
(3) Trend line
(4) Fitted line

56. The formula for the correlation coefficient is based on
(1) Covariance and standard deviations
(2) Mean and median
(3) Range and variance
(4) Skewness and kurtosis

57. The coefficient of determination measures the proportion of
(1) Total variation explained by the independent variable
(2) Total variation explained by the dependent variable
(3) Total variation explained by the regression line
(4) Total variation explained by the correlation

58. In regression analysis, the residual represents the
(1) Difference between the observed and predicted values
(2) Difference between the independent and dependent variables
(3) Difference between the mean and median
(4) Difference between the correlation and covariance Answer:
(1) Difference between the observed and predicted values

Directions: Each of the following items consists of two statements, one labelled as Assertion (A) and other labelled as Reason (R). You are to examine these two statements carefully and decide if the (A) and the (R) are individually true and if so, whether (R) is the correct explanation of (A). Select your answers to these items using the codes given below:
(1) Both (A) and (R) are true, and the (R) is the correct explanation of the (A).
(2) Both (A) and (R) are true, but the (R) is not the correct explanation of the (A).
(3) (A) is true, but the (R) is false.
(4) (A) is false, but the (R) is true.

59. Assertion (A): A positive correlation coefficient indicates a strong linear relationship between two variables.
Reason (R): A positive correlation coefficient means that as one variable increases, the other variable also tends to increase.

60. Assertion (A): The coefficient of determination can range from 0 to 1.
Reason (R): The coefficient of determination measures the proportion of the total variation in the dependent variable that is predictable from the independent variable.

61. Assertion (A): A negative skewness value indicates a left-skewed distribution.
Reason (R): In a left-skewed distribution, the tail on the left side is longer or fatter than the right side.

62. Assertion (A): The correlation coefficient measures the strength and direction of the linear relationship between two variables.

Reason (R): The correlation coefficient ranges from –1 to 1, where –1 indicates a perfect negative linear relationship and 1 indicates a perfect positive linear relationship.

63. Assertion (A): In regression analysis, the residual represents the difference between the observed and predicted values.

Reason (R): The residual is used to assess the accuracy of the regression model in predicting the dependent variable.

64. What is the classical approach to probability based on?

(1) Relative frequency of an event
(2) Subjective judgment
(3) Prior knowledge
(4) Equally likely outcomes

65. In the frequentist approach to probability, how is the probability of an event defined?

(1) Based on subjective judgment
(2) Based on prior knowledge
(3) Based on the relative frequency of an event
(4) Based on equally likely outcomes

66. Which approach to probability considers the likelihood of an event based on personal judgment or experience?

(1) Classical approach
(2) Frequentist approach
(3) Subjective approach
(4) Empirical approach

67. What does Bayes' theorem describe?

(1) The probability of an event based on prior knowledge
(2) The probability of an event based on relative frequency
(3) The probability of an event based on equally likely outcomes
(4) The probability of an event based on subjective judgment

68. In Bayes' theorem, what does $P(A \mid B)$ represent?

(1) The probability of event A given event B has occurred
(2) The probability of event B given event A has occurred
(3) The joint probability of events A and B
(4) The conditional probability of events A and B

69. What is the formula for Bayes' theorem?

(1) $P(A \mid B) = P(B \mid A) * P(A) / P(B)$
(2) $P(A \mid B) = P(A) * P(B \mid A) / P(B)$
(3) $P(A \mid B) = P(A) * P(B) / P(A \cap B)$
(4) $P(\cup A \mid B) = P(A \cap B) / P(B)$

70. In the context of Bayes' theorem, what does $P(B \mid A)$ represent?

(1) The probability of event A given event B has occurred
(2) The probability of event B given event A has occurred
(3) The joint probability of events A and B
(4) The conditional probability of events A and B

71. What is the denominator in Bayes' theorem?

(1) $P(A)$ (2) $P(B)$
(3) $P(A \cap B)$ (4) $P(B \mid A)$

72. Which approach to probability is based on the relative frequency of an event in the long run?

(1) Classical approach
(2) Frequentist approach
(3) Subjective approach
(4) Empirical approach

73. What is the joint probability of two events A and B?

(1) $P(A) * P(B)$ (2) $P(A \mid B) * P(B \mid A)$
(3) $P(A \cap B)$ (4) $P(A \cup B)$

74. In the context of probability, what does $P(A \cap B)$ represent?

(1) The probability of event A given event B has occurred
(2) The probability of event B given event A has occurred
(3) The joint probability of events A and B
(4) The conditional probability of events A and B Answer:
(3) The joint probability of events A and B

75. What is the union of two events A and B?

(1) $P(A) + P(B)$ (2) $P(A \mid B) + P(B \mid A)$
(3) $P(A \cap B)$ (4) $P(A \cup B)$

76. What is the conditional probability of events A and B?

(1) $P(A) * P(B)$ (2) $P(A \mid B) * P(B \mid A)$
(3) $P(A \cap B)$ (4) $P(A \mid B)$

77. In the context of probability, what does $P(A \mid B) * P(B)$ represent?

(1) The probability of event A given event B has occurred
(2) The joint probability of events A and B
(3) The conditional probability of events A and B
(4) The probability of event B

78. What is the probability of event A given that event B has occurred?
(1) $P(A|B)$ (2) $P(B|A)$
(3) $P(A \cap B)$ (4) $P(A \cup B)$

Directions: Each of the following items consists of two statements, one labelled as Assertion (A) and other labelled as Reason (R). You are to examine these two statements carefully and decide if the (A) and the (R) are individually true and if so, whether (R) is the correct explanation of (A). Select your answers to these items using the codes given below:
(1) Both (A) and (R) are true, and the (R) is the correct explanation of the (A).
(2) Both (A) and (R) are true, but the (R) is not the correct explanation of the (A).
(3) (A) is true, but the (R) is false.
(4) (A) is false, but the (R) is true.

79. **Assertion (A):** Bayes' theorem allows us to update the probability of an event based on new information.
Reason (R): Bayes' theorem incorporates prior knowledge about the event and updates the probability based on new evidence.

80. **Assertion (A):** The classical approach to probability assumes that all outcomes are equally likely.
Reason (R): In the classical approach, the probability of an event is calculated as the ratio of favorable outcomes to the total number of outcomes.

81. **Assertion (A):** The frequentist approach to probability is based on the relative frequency of an event in the long run.
Reason (R): In the frequentist approach, the probability of an event is defined as the limit of the relative frequency of the event as the number of trials approaches infinity.

82. **Assertion (A):** The subjective approach to probability considers the likelihood of an event based on personal judgment or experience.
Reason (R): In the subjective approach, the probability of an event is determined subjectively based on an individual's beliefs, opinions, or experience.

83. **Assertion (A):** The joint probability of two events A and B is the probability that both events occur simultaneously.
Reason (R): The joint probability of events A and B is denoted as $P(A \cap B)$ and represents the intersection of events A and B.

84. In a binomial distribution, each trial has
(1) Two possible outcomes
(2) Three possible outcomes
(3) Multiple possible outcomes
(4) Infinite possible outcomes

85. The mean of a binomial distribution is calculated as
(1) $n * p$ (2) $n + p$
(3) n / p (4) $n - p$

86. The variance of a binomial distribution is calculated as
(1) $n * p$ (2) $n + p$
(3) n / p (4) $n - p$

87. The Poisson distribution is used to model
(1) Continuous random variables
(2) Discrete random variables
(3) Both continuous and discrete random variables
(4) None of the above

88. The mean and variance of a Poisson distribution are
(1) Equal (2) Not related
(3) Mean is greater than variance
(4) Variance is greater than mean

89. In a Poisson distribution, the parameter λ represents
(1) The mean (2) The variance
(3) The standard deviation
(4) The mode

90. In a normal distribution, the mean, median, and mode are
(1) Always equal (2) Always different
(3) Equal only in specific cases
(4) Equal for discrete variables

91. In a standard normal distribution, the mean is:
(1) 0 (2) 1
(3) –1 (4) Undefined

92. The area under the curve of a normal distribution between any two points is equal to
(1) The mean (2) The variance
(3) The standard deviation
(4) The probability of the variable falling between those two points

Directions: Each of the following items consists of two statements, one labelled as Assertion (A) and other labelled as Reason (R). You are to examine these two statements carefully and decide if the (A) and the (R) are individually true and if so, whether (R) is the correct explanation of (A). Select your answers to these items using the codes given below:

(1) Both (A) and (R) are true, and the (R) is the correct explanation of the (A).
(2) Both (A) and (R) are true, but the (R) is not the correct explanation of the (A).
(3) (A) is true, but the (R) is false.
(4) (A) is false, but the (R) is true.

93. **Assertion (A):** The binomial distribution is used to model the number of successes in a fixed number of independent trials with the same probability of success.
Reason (R): The binomial distribution assumes a fixed number of trials and each trial has two possible outcomes.

94. **Assertion (A):** The Poisson distribution is a limiting case of the binomial distribution when the number of trials becomes large and the probability of success becomes small.
Reason (R): The Poisson distribution is used to model the number of events occurring in a fixed interval of time or space.

95. **Assertion (A):** In a normal distribution, approximately 68% of the data falls within one standard deviation from the mean.
Reason (R): The empirical rule states that for a normal distribution, about 68% of the data falls within one standard deviation from the mean.

96. **Assertion (A):** The variance of a binomial distribution is equal to the product of the number of trials and the probability of success.
Reason (R): The variance of a binomial distribution measures the spread or dispersion of the distribution.

97. **Assertion (A):** The Poisson distribution is used to model the number of rare events occurring in a fixed interval of time or space.
Reason (R): The Poisson distribution is characterised by a single parameter », which represents the average rate of occurrence of the events.

98. What is research?
(1) A process of memorization
(2) A systematic investigation to discover new knowledge
(3) A form of entertainment
(4) A method of storytelling

99. Which of the following is NOT a characteristic of good research?
(1) Replicability (2) Randomness
(3) Precision (4) Objectivity

100. What is the purpose of exploratory research?
(1) To test hypotheses
(2) To gain insights and familiarity with a topic
(3) To establish causation
(4) To generalize findings to a population

101. Which type of research design involves the collection of data at a single point in time?
(1) Longitudinal design
(2) Cross-sectional design
(3) Experimental design
(4) Descriptive design

102. In experimental research, what is the variable that the researcher manipulates called?
(1) Independent variable
(2) Dependent variable
(3) Control variable
(4) Extraneous variable

103. A hypothesis is
(1) A fact (2) A random guess
(3) A testable prediction
(4) An observation

104. Which of the following is an example of a qualitative research method?
(1) Survey (2) Experiment
(3) Case study (4) Observation

105. What is the main goal of causal research?
(1) To describe a phenomenon
(2) To explore relationships between variables
(3) To determine cause and effect relationships
(4) To generate new theories

106. Which of the following is an example of a non-probability sampling method?
(1) Random sampling
(2) Stratified sampling
(3) Convenience sampling
(4) Systematic sampling

107. What is a population in research terms?
(1) The entire group of people or things being studied
(2) The sample chosen for the study
(3) The variable being measured
(4) The research hypothesis

108. Which research design involves the study of a phenomenon within its natural context?
(1) Experimental design

(2) Cross-sectional design
(3) Longitudinal design
(4) Descriptive design

109. What is a case study in research?
(1) A type of descriptive research that involves studying a single case in depth
(2) An experimental design with multiple groups
(3) A method for collecting survey data
(4) A type of longitudinal research

110. What is the purpose of a pilot study in research?
(1) To test the reliability of the measurement instruments
(2) To collect data for analysis
(3) To draw final conclusions
(4) To recruit participants for the main study

111. What is the difference between primary and secondary research?
(1) Primary research is original research conducted firsthand, while secondary research involves analyzing existing data.
(2) Primary research is less reliable than secondary research.
(3) Secondary research is conducted in a laboratory setting, while primary research is conducted in the field.
(4) Primary research is less expensive than secondary research.

112. What does a null hypothesis state in research?
(1) There is a significant relationship between variables
(2) There is no significant relationship between variables
(3) The researcher has no hypothesis
(4) The sample size is null

113. Which of the following is a characteristic of a good research question?
(1) It is vague and unclear
(2) It is too specific
(3) It is testable and specific
(4) It is unrelated to the research topic

114. In survey research, what is a sampling frame?
(1) The sample selected for the study
(2) The population of interest
(3) The list from which the sample is drawn
(4) The research instrument used to collect data

115. What is a control group in experimental research?
(1) The group that receives the experimental treatment
(2) The group that is not exposed to the independent variable
(3) The group that is randomly selected for the study
(4) The group that is observed in a natural setting

116. Which of the following is a disadvantage of using secondary data in research?
(1) It is expensive
(2) It is time-consuming
(3) It may not be specific to the researcher's needs
(4) It is more reliable than primary data

117. What is a double-blind study in experimental research?
(1) Neither the researcher nor the participants know who is in the control group.
(2) Only the researcher knows who is in the experimental group.
(3) Only the participants know if they are in the control or experimental group.
(4) Both the researcher and the participants are aware of group assignments.

Directions: Each of the following items consists of two statements, one labelled as Assertion (A) and other labelled as Reason (R). You are to examine these two statements carefully and decide if the (A) and the (R) are individually true and if so, whether (R) is the correct explanation of (A). Select your answers to these items using the codes given below:
(1) Both (A) and (R) are true, and (R) is the correct explanation for (A).
(2) Both (A) and (R) are true, but (R) is not the correct explanation for (A).
(3) (A) is true, but (R) is false.
(4) Both (A) and (R) are false.

118. **Assertion (A):** Cross-sectional research is more suitable for studying changes over time.
Reason (R): Cross-sectional research involves studying a group of participants at a single point in time.

119. **Assertion (A):** Exploratory research is often conducted when the topic is poorly understood.
Reason: The goal of exploratory research is to test hypotheses.

120. **Assertion (A):** Longitudinal research design is suitable for studying the effects of an intervention.

Reason (R): Longitudinal research involves the collection of data at multiple points in time.

121. Assertion (A): Convenience sampling is a random sampling method.

Reason: In convenience sampling, participants are chosen based on their availability and accessibility.

122. Assertion (A): Correlational research can establish cause-and-effect relationships between variables.

Reason (R): Correlational research examines the relationship between two or more variables without manipulating them.

123. What is the first step in the data collection process?

(1) Data analysis (2) Data interpretation
(3) Data cleaning (4) Defining the problem

124. Which of the following is a method of primary data collection?

(1) Survey (2) Literature review
(3) Observing secondary sources
(4) Census

125. What is a disadvantage of using open-ended questions in surveys?

(1) They provide limited information
(2) Respondents may provide biased answers
(3) They are time-consuming to analyze
(4) They limit the creativity of respondents

126. In statistical terms, what is a population?

(1) The sample selected for the study
(2) The entire group of people or things being studied
(3) The variable being measured
(4) The research hypothesis

127. Which of the following is an example of quantitative data?

(1) Colors of cars (2) Height of students
(3) Types of fruits (4) Categories of movies

128. What is the purpose of a pilot study in data collection?

(1) To recruit participants for the main study
(2) To test the reliability of the measurement instruments
(3) To draw final conclusions
(4) To analyze data

129. What is the difference between a population and a sample?

(1) A population is a subset of a sample
(2) A sample is a subset of a population
(3) The terms are used interchangeably
(4) A population and a sample are the same thing

130. Which of the following is a measure of central tendency?

(1) Range (2) Variance
(3) Median (4) Standard deviation

131. In stratified sampling, how are the strata defined?

(1) Randomly
(2) According to some characteristic relevant to the study
(3) Alphabetically
(4) Based on convenience

132. What is the purpose of random sampling in research?

(1) To ensure that every individual in the population has an equal chance of being selected
(2) To select the most convenient participants
(3) To oversample certain groups
(4) To eliminate bias in the sample

133. Which of the following is an example of non-sampling error in data collection?

(1) Sampling bias
(2) Measurement error
(3) Random sampling
(4) Stratified sampling

134. What is the purpose of coding in data processing?

(1) To conduct statistical tests
(2) To enter data into a computer
(3) To assign numerical values to data for analysis
(4) To collect primary data

135. Which of the following is an example of a secondary data source?

(1) Survey responses (2) Census data
(3) Experiment results
(4) Observations made by a researcher

136. What is the main advantage of using a convenience sample in data collection?

(1) It is cost-effective
(2) It is time-efficient
(3) It ensures a representative sample
(4) It eliminates bias

137. What is the purpose of a frequency distribution in data analysis?

(1) To summarize the characteristics of a sample
(2) To organise data into categories
(3) To determine the range of a dataset
(4) To conduct hypothesis testing

138. Which of the following is a measure of variability in a dataset?
(1) Mean (2) Mode
(3) Range (4) Median

139. What is the advantage of using a Likert scale in surveys?
(1) It is easy to analyze
(2) It provides a wide range of responses
(3) It limits respondents' choices
(4) It is suitable for open-ended questions

140. Which of the following is an example of a categorical variable?
(1) Age (2) Height
(3) Gender (4) Weight

141. What is a histogram used for in data representation?
(1) To show the relationship between two variables
(2) To display the distribution of a single variable
(3) To compare means of different groups
(4) To show trends over time

142. What is the purpose of the mode in data analysis?
(1) To measure the average
(2) To identify the most frequent value in a dataset
(3) To measure variability
(4) To determine the range

Directions: Each of the following items consists of two statements, one labelled as Assertion (A) and other labelled as Reason (R). You are to examine these two statements carefully and decide if the (A) and the (R) are individually true and if so, whether (R) is the correct explanation of (A). Select your answers to these items using the codes given below:
(1) Both (A) and (R) are true, and the (R) is the correct explanation of the (A).
(2) Both (A) and (R) are true, but the (R) is not the correct explanation of the (A).
(3) (A) is true, but the (R) is false.
(4) (A) is false, but the (R) is true.

143. **Assertion (A):** Data cleaning is necessary before data analysis to ensure accuracy.
Reason (R): Data cleaning involves removing outliers, which are irrelevant to the study.

144. **Assertion (A):** A census is always preferable to a sample in research.
Reason (R): A census provides more accurate results as it includes the entire population.

145. **Assertion (A):** A Likert scale is a type of ordinal data.
Reason (R): Likert scales measure the intensity of agreement or disagreement with statements.

146. **Assertion (A):** The range is sensitive to extreme values in a dataset.
Reason (R): The range is the difference between the maximum and minimum values.

147. **Assertion (A):** Coding in data processing involves encrypting data for security.
Reason (R): Coding is the process of assigning numerical values to data for analysis.

148. What is sampling in statistics?
(1) The process of analyzing data
(2) The process of collecting data from the entire population
(3) The process of selecting a subset of individuals or items from a population
(4) The process of organising data

149. What is the advantage of probability sampling over non-probability sampling?
(1) It is less time-consuming
(2) It ensures every individual in the population has an equal chance of being selected
(3) It is more cost-effective
(4) It eliminates bias

150. Which of the following is an example of a non-probability sampling method?
(1) Simple random sampling
(2) Stratified sampling
(3) Convenience sampling
(4) Systematic sampling

151. What is stratified sampling?
(1) Dividing the population into subgroups and then randomly selecting samples from each subgroup
(2) Selecting every nth individual from a list after a random start
(3) Randomly selecting individuals from the entire population
(4) Dividing the population into clusters and then randomly selecting entire clusters

152. What is the central limit theorem?
(1) The theorem that establishes a relationship between the mean and median of a distribution
(2) The theorem that states that as the sample size increases, the sampling distribution of the sample mean approaches a normal distribution
(3) The theorem that describes the spread of a distribution
(4) The theorem that establishes the relationship between the mode and median of a distribution

153. What is the purpose of the standard error in statistics?
(1) To measure the variability within a sample
(2) To measure the variability between samples
(3) To estimate the variability in the population
(4) To calculate the range of a distribution

154. Which of the following is a point estimate?
(1) Confidence interval (2) Standard error
(3) Sample mean (4) Margin of error

155. What is the margin of error in statistical estimation?
(1) The range of values within which the population parameter is likely to fall
(2) The standard deviation of the population
(3) The amount by which the sample mean may deviate from the population mean
(4) The probability of obtaining a sample mean within a specific range

156. Which of the following is a characteristic of a good estimator?
(1) High bias and low precision
(2) Low bias and low precision
(3) High bias and high precision
(4) Low bias and high precision

157. What is a confidence interval?
(1) A range of values that estimates the variability in the population
(2) A range of values within which the sample mean is likely to fall
(3) A measure of variability within a sample
(4) A range of values that estimates the margin of error

158. Which of the following is a non-probability sampling method?
(1) Simple random sampling
(2) Systematic sampling
(3) Purposive sampling
(4) Stratified sampling

159. What is the primary disadvantage of convenience sampling?
(1) It is time-consuming
(2) It is expensive
(3) It may lead to biased results
(4) It ensures representation from all subgroups in the population

160. In systematic sampling, what is the sampling interval?
(1) The range of values within the sample is likely to fall
(2) The probability of selecting a particular individual
(3) The number of individuals between the selected individuals
(4) The measure of variability within a sample

161. What is the purpose of cluster sampling?
(1) To ensure every individual in the population has an equal chance of being selected
(2) To divide the population into subgroups based on characteristics
(3) To randomly select entire clusters of individuals
(4) To select individuals based on convenience

162. What is the formula for standard error in statistics?
(1) $\frac{s}{\sqrt{n}}$ (2) $\frac{s}{n}$
(3) $\sqrt{\frac{s^2}{n}}$ (4) $\sqrt{\frac{n}{s}}$

163. Which of the following is an example of a probability sampling method?
(1) Snowball sampling
(2) Convenience sampling
(3) Quota sampling
(4) Simple random sampling

164. What is the primary purpose of the central limit theorem in statistical analysis?
(1) To estimate the margin of error
(2) To describe the distribution of a single variable
(3) To establish a relationship between the mean and median
(4) To provide a foundation for statistical inference

165. What is the main advantage of quota sampling?
(1) It ensures every individual in the population has an equal chance of being selected
(2) It is cost-effective
(3) It guarantees representation from all subgroups in the population
(4) It eliminates sampling bias

166. What is the relationship between sample size and standard error?
(1) As sample size increases, standard error decreases
(2) As sample size increases, standard error increases
(3) Sample size and standard error are unrelated
(4) Standard error is not affected by sample size

167. Which of the following is a measure of variability in a sampling distribution?
(1) Mean (2) Mode
(3) Standard deviation (4) Median

Directions: Each of the following items consists of two statements, one labelled as Assertion (A) and other labelled as Reason (R). You are to examine these two statements carefully and decide if the (A) and the (R) are individually true and if so, whether (R) is the correct explanation of (A). Select your answers to these items using the codes given below:
(1) Both (A) and (R) are true, and the (R) is the correct explanation of the (A).
(2) Both (A) and (R) are true, but the (R) is not the correct explanation of the (A).
(3) (A) is true, but the (R) is false.
(4) (A) is false, but the (R) is true.

168. Assertion (A): In simple random sampling, every individual in the population has an equal chance of being selected.
Reason: Simple random sampling is a non-probability sampling method.

169. Assertion (A): The standard error decreases as the sample size increases.
Reason (R): The standard error is a measure of the variability within a sample.

170. Assertion (A): Stratified sampling is useful when the population has distinct subgroups.
Reason (R): In stratified sampling, individuals are randomly selected from the entire population.

171. Assertion (A): Quota sampling ensures a representative sample from all subgroups in the population.
Reason (R): Quota sampling is a probability sampling method.

172. Assertion (A): The margin of error is inversely related to the confidence level in a confidence interval.
Reason (R): Increasing the confidence level widens the range of values in the confidence interval.

173. What is the purpose of hypothesis testing in statistics?
(1) To summarize data
(2) To make predictions
(3) To draw conclusions about population parameters based on sample data
(4) To collect data

174. Which of the following is used for hypothesis testing when the population standard deviation is known?
(1) t-test (2) ANOVA
(3) z-test (4) Chi-square test

175. In hypothesis testing, the null hypothesis is often denoted by:
(1) H_1 (2) H_{alt}
(3) H_0 (4) H_{test}

176. What does a p-value represent in hypothesis testing?
(1) The probability of making a Type I error
(2) The probability of rejecting a true null hypothesis
(3) The probability of obtaining the observed results by chance alone
(4) The level of significance

177. When is a two-tailed test used in hypothesis testing?
(1) When the null hypothesis is directional
(2) When the alternative hypothesis is non-directional
(3) When the sample size is large
(4) When the population standard deviation is known

178. Which statistical test is used to compare the means of two independent groups?
(1) t-test (2) ANOVA
(3) Chi-square test
(4) Mann-Whitney test (U-test)

179. What is the critical region in hypothesis testing?
(1) The region where the null hypothesis is accepted
(2) The region where the alternative hypothesis is accepted
(3) The region beyond the critical value(s) where the null hypothesis is rejected
(4) The region where the p-value is less than 0.05

180. Which of the following is used for hypothesis testing when the population standard deviation is unknown?
(1) z-test (2) t-test
(3) ANOVA (4) Chi-square test

181. What is a Type II error in hypothesis testing?
(1) Incorrectly rejecting a true null hypothesis
(2) Incorrectly accepting a false null hypothesis
(3) Correctly rejecting a true null hypothesis
(4) Correctly accepting a false null hypothesis

182. Which statistical test is used to compare the means of more than two groups?
(1) t-test (2) ANOVA
(3) Mann-Whitney test (U-test)
(4) Rank correlation test

183. In ANOVA, what does the F-statistic compare?
(1) Means of different groups
(2) Variances within and between groups
(3) Medians of different groups
(4) Proportions in different groups

184. When do you reject the null hypothesis in a t-test for independent samples?
(1) When the observed p-value is less than the level of significance
(2) When the observed p-value is greater than the level of significance
(3) When the sample mean is close to the population mean
(4) When the sample size is small

185. What does the chi-square test assess?
(1) Difference in means
(2) Difference in proportions
(3) Difference in variances
(4) Association between categorical variables

186. Which statistical test is used to compare the medians of two independent groups?
(1) t-test (2) ANOVA
(3) Mann-Whitney test (U-test)
(4) Rank correlation test

187. What is the Kruskal-Wallis test used for?
(1) Comparing means of more than two groups
(2) Comparing variances within and between groups
(3) Comparing medians of more than two groups
(4) Assessing the correlation between two variables

188. What is the purpose of the Mann-Whitney test (U-test)?
(1) Comparing means of two independent groups
(2) Comparing variances within and between groups
(3) Comparing medians of more than two groups
(4) Assessing the correlation between two variables

189. What does the rank correlation test assess?
(1) Association between two variables
(2) Difference in means
(3) Difference in proportions
(4) Variance within a group

190. Which of the following is true regarding the p-value in hypothesis testing?
(1) A smaller p-value indicates stronger evidence against the null hypothesis
(2) A larger p-value indicates stronger evidence against the null hypothesis
(3) The p-value is independent of the level of significance
(4) The p-value is always equal to 0.05

191. When is a one-tailed test appropriate in hypothesis testing?
(1) When the alternative hypothesis is non-directional
(2) When the sample size is small
(3) When the null hypothesis is non-directional
(4) When a specific direction of the effect is hypothesized

192. What is the critical value in hypothesis testing?
(1) The value beyond which the null hypothesis is rejected
(2) The value that is equal to the population mean

(3) The value that ensures a p-value greater than 0.05
(4) The value that is always 0.05

Directions: Each of the following items consists of two statements, one labelled as Assertion (A) and other labelled as Reason (R). You are to examine these two statements carefully and decide if the (A) and the (R) are individually true and if so, whether (R) is the correct explanation of (A). Select your answers to these items using the codes given below:

(1) Both (A) and (R) are true, and the (R) is the correct explanation of the (A).
(2) Both (A) and (R) are true, but the (R) is not the correct explanation of the (A).
(3) The (A) is true, and the (R) is false.
(4) The (A) is false, and the (R) is true.

193. **Assertion (A):** The chi-square test is used to compare the means of two independent groups.
Reason (R): The chi-square test is suitable for comparing categorical variables.

194. **Assertion (A):** The t-test is used for comparing the means of more than two groups.
Reason (R): ANOVA is the appropriate test for comparing means of more than two groups.

195. **Assertion (A):** A p-value of 0.03 is stronger evidence against the null hypothesis than a p-value of 0.10.
Reason (R): The level of significance is usually set at 0.10.

196. **Assertion (A):** The F-statistic is used in t-tests for independent samples.
Reason (R): The F-statistic compares variances within and between groups in ANOVA.

197. **Assertion (A):** A non-directional hypothesis can only be tested using a two-tailed test.
Reason (R): A one-tailed test is appropriate when a specific direction of the effect is hypothesized.

198. What is the purpose of a report in a professional context?
(1) To express personal opinions
(2) To share personal experiences
(3) To communicate information and findings
(4) To entertain the audience

199. Which of the following is a key element of a well-structured report?
(1) Unorganised content
(2) Ambiguous language
(3) Clarity and coherence
(4) Excessive use of jargon

200. What is the typical structure of a formal report?
(1) Introduction, body, and conclusion
(2) Only the body section
(3) Appendices only
(4) No specific structure

201. Which tense is commonly used in a report's findings and conclusions?
(1) Past tense (2) Present tense
(3) Future tense (4) A mix of tenses

202. What is the purpose of an executive summary in a report?
(1) To provide a detailed analysis of findings
(2) To summarize key information for busy readers
(3) To present raw data
(4) To offer personal opinions

203. Which of the following is a characteristic of formal language in report writing?
(1) Informal tone and colloquial expressions
(2) Technical jargon without explanation
(3) Precision and clarity
(4) Humorous anecdotes

204. What is the purpose of including visuals (charts, graphs) in a report?
(1) To make the report longer
(2) To confuse the readers
(3) To present data in a clear and visually appealing manner
(4) To fill empty spaces on the page

205. What should be the tone of a report in a professional setting?
(1) Casual and friendly
(2) Formal and objective
(3) Sarcastic and humorous
(4) Emotional and subjective

206. Which of the following is a common mistake in report writing?
(1) Providing clear recommendations
(2) Using technical terms without explanation
(3) Including personal opinions
(4) Using a formal tone

207. What is the primary purpose of the conclusion section in a report?
(1) To introduce the report's topic
(2) To provide recommendations
(3) To summarize key findings
(4) To present raw data

208. Which of the following is true about the use of headings and subheadings in a report?
(1) They should be avoided to maintain a formal tone
(2) They help organise and structure the content
(3) They are only necessary in lengthy reports
(4) They distract readers from the main content

209. What is the role of proofreading in the report-writing process?
(1) To draft the initial content
(2) To add more information to the report
(3) To check for errors in grammar, punctuation, and spelling
(4) To create the executive summary

210. Which of the following is a recommendation for writing an effective report?
(1) Use complex language to impress the audience
(2) Include all possible details, even if not directly relevant
(3) Keep the report concise and focused on key information
(4) Avoid using visuals and graphics

211. What is the purpose of the introduction section in a report?
(1) To present the main findings
(2) To provide background information and context
(3) To offer personal opinions
(4) To list recommendations

212. Which of the following is a guideline for using technical terms in a report?
(1) Use technical terms without providing explanations
(2) Avoid using technical terms to ensure clarity
(3) Use technical terms sparingly and provide explanations when necessary
(4) Assume that the audience is familiar with all technical terms

213. What is the purpose of citations and references in a report?
(1) To increase the word count
(2) To provide evidence and credit to sources
(3) To confuse the readers
(4) To showcase the writer's knowledge

214. Which of the following is a key component of the body section in a report?
(1) Executive summary
(2) Recommendations
(3) Introduction
(4) Conclusion

215. What is the significance of using an appropriate style guide in report writing?
(1) It restricts creativity
(2) It ensures consistency and professionalism
(3) It is only necessary for academic reports
(4) It doesn't impact the quality of the report

216. How should one handle data that is not central to the report's main findings?
(1) Include it in the executive summary
(2) Omit it from the report
(3) Present it in a separate appendix
(4) Highlight it in the conclusion

217. What is the purpose of a table of contents in a lengthy report?
(1) To provide detailed recommendations
(2) To summarize key findings
(3) To help readers navigate the report
(4) To present raw data

Directions: Each of the following items consists of two statements, one labelled as Assertion (A) and other labelled as Reason (R). You are to examine these two statements carefully and decide if the (A) and the (R) are individually true and if so, whether (R) is the correct explanation of (A). Select your answers to these items using the codes given below:
(1) Both (A) and (R) are true, and the (R) is the correct explanation of the (A).
(2) Both (A) and (R) are true, but the (R) is not the correct explanation of the (A).
(3) The (A) is true, and the (R) is false.
(4) The (A) is false, and the (R) is true.

218. **Assertion (A):** The executive summary should include personal opinions and anecdotes.
Reason (R): The executive summary is meant to provide a brief overview of the report's key findings.

219. **Assertion (A):** The use of visuals in a report is optional and does not contribute to its effectiveness.
Reason (R): Visuals, such as charts and graphs, help present complex information in a clear and concise manner.

ANSWERS

1. (3)	2. (1)	3. (1)	4. (3)	5. (1)	6. (3)	7. (2)	8. (1)	9. (1)	10. (1)
11. (1)	12. (1)	13. (1)	14. (1)	15. (1)	16. (1)	17. (1)	18. (4)	19. (1)	20. (2)
21. (1)	22. (1)	23. (3)	24. (1)	25. (1)	26. (1)	27. (3)	28. (2)	29. (1)	30. (4)
31. (3)	32. (4)	33. (4)	34. (3)	35. (1)	36. (4)	37. (4)	38. (1)	39. (1)	40. (1)
41. (3)	42. (1)	43. (1)	44. (3)	45. (4)	46. (1)	47. (1)	48. (4)	49. (2)	50. (1)
51. (2)	52. (1)	53. (1)	54. (2)	55. (1)	56. (1)	57. (1)	58. (1)	59. (2)	60. (1)
61. (1)	62. (1)	63. (1)	64. (4)	65. (3)	66. (3)	67. (1)	68. (1)	69. (1)	70. (2)
71. (2)	72. (2)	73. (3)	74. (3)	75. (4)	76. (4)	77. (2)	78. (1)	79. (1)	80. (1)
81. (1)	82. (1)	83. (1)	84. (1)	85. (1)	86. (1)	87. (2)	88. (1)	89. (1)	90. (1)
91. (1)	92. (4)	93. (1)	94. (2)	95. (1)	96. (4)	97. (1)	98. (2)	99. (2)	100. (2)
101. (2)	102. (1)	103. (3)	104. (3)	105. (3)	106. (3)	107. (1)	108. (4)	109. (1)	110. (1)
111. (1)	112. (2)	113. (3)	114. (3)	115. (2)	116. (3)	117. (1)	118. (4)	119. (3)	120. (1)
121. (4)	122. (4)	123. (4)	124. (1)	125. (3)	126. (2)	127. (2)	128. (2)	129. (2)	130. (3)
131. (2)	132. (1)	133. (2)	134. (3)	135. (2)	136. (1)	137. (2)	138. (3)	139. (1)	140. (3)
141. (2)	142. (2)	143. (2)	144. (4)	145. (1)	146. (1)	147. (4)	148. (3)	149. (2)	150. (3)
151. (1)	152. (2)	153. (2)	154. (3)	155. (1)	156. (4)	157. (1)	158. (3)	159. (3)	160. (3)
161. (3)	162. (1)	163. (4)	164. (4)	165. (3)	166. (1)	167. (3)	168. (3)	169. (2)	170. (3)
171. (3)	172. (4)	173. (3)	174. (3)	175. (3)	176. (3)	177. (2)	178. (1)	179. (3)	180. (2)
181. (2)	182. (2)	183. (2)	184. (1)	185. (4)	186. (3)	187. (3)	188. (1)	189. (1)	190. (1)
191. (4)	192. (1)	193. (4)	194. (4)	195. (1)	196. (4)	197. (1)	198. (3)	199. (3)	200. (1)
201. (1)	202. (2)	203. (3)	204. (3)	205. (2)	206. (2)	207. (3)	208. (2)	209. (3)	210. (3)
211. (2)	212. (3)	213. (2)	214. (2)	215. (2)	216. (3)	217. (3)	218. (4)	219. (4)	

UNIT 6

BUSINESS MANAGEMENT AND HUMAN RESOURCE MANAGEMENT

SYLLABUS

- Principles and functions of management
- Organization structure: Formal and informal organizations; Span of control
- Responsibility and authority: Delegation of authority and decentralization
- Motivation and leadership: Concept and theories
- Corporate governance and business ethics
- Human resource management: Concept, role and functions of HRM; Human resource planning; Recruitment and selection; Training and development; Succession planning
- Compensation management: Job evaluation; Incentives and fringe benefits
- Performance appraisal including 360 degree performance appraisal
- Collective bargaining and workers' participation in management
- Personality: Perception; Attitudes; Emotions; Group dynamics; Power and politics; Conflict and negotiation; Stress management
- Organizational Culture: Organizational development and organizational change

Definitions of Management

One widely quoted definition of management is 'Management is the art of getting things done through others."

Some more definitions of management are given below :

- According to Harold Koontz, "Management is the art of getting things done through and with people in formally organized groups.
- According to D.J. Clough, "Management is the arts and science of decision-making and leadership."
- According to Peter F. Drucker, "Management is a multi-purpose organ that manages a business and manages managers and manages worker and work."
- According to E.F.L. Brech, "Management is a social process entailing responsibility for the effective (or efficient) planning and regulation of the operations of an enterprise."

PRINCIPLES OF MANAGEMENT

A principle means a fundamental truth on the basis of reasoning, a primary element of general law. Principles of management are not like principle of physical sciences. Management principles are fundamental truths of general validity which have value in predicting the results of managerial action. They are such guidelines which come to the help of managers.

Henri Fayol gave the following fourteen principles of management :

1. **Division of Work.** The work is divided in such a way that it promotes specialisation and one person does only one thing rather than doing everything himself.
2. **Parity between Authority and Responsibility.** Authority and responsibility go side by side and should be commensurate to each other.
3. **Discipline.** is essential in all levels of management. Discipline is obtained through judicial application of penalties. Limits of acceptable behaviour are absolutely necessary to define, if that everyone in the organization knows what can and cannot be done.
4. **Unity of Command.** One person should receive orders from one superior only.
5. **Unity of Direction.** There should be one head and one plan for a group of activities having the same objectives.
6. **Subordination of Individual Interest to General Interest.** Fayol was of the opinion that the interest of one *employee or a group of employees should not prevail the interest of the enterprise* as a whole. Management should make efforts to reconcile individual interests with common interests.
7. **Fair Remuneration to Workers.** Fayol wanted the remuneration to be paid to employees to be just and fair and should afford maximum satisfaction to both employees and the employer.
8. **Effective Centralisation.** Fayol favoured centralisation of powers with the top management.
9. **Scalar Chain.** Fayol was of the opinion that a hierarchic channel called the scalar chain is necessary to ensure unity of command and effective communication. However, a gang plank may be created by passing the established line of authority, to facilitate quick communication.
10. **Order.** It means the right man in the right job and right material in the right place. Material order means a proper place for everything and everything in its right place.
11. **Equity.** It means justice and kindness. Fayol was of the opinion that to encourage workers to fulfil their duties with devotion and loyalty, management should deal with the workers with equity – based on kindness and justice.

12. **Stability in Tenure.** Fayol felt that instability of personnel is both the cause and effect of bad management so there should be a stability in tenure.
13. **Initiative.** Employees should be given the chance and opportunity in taking initiative in deciding and implementing the plans.
14. **Esprit de corps.** It refers to harmony and mutual understanding among the member of the organisations.

Classification of Managerial Functions

The elements of management process (planning, organising, staffing, directing and controlling) are known as functions of management. There is however, no single list of functions acceptable to all various authors have classified these functions differently. Henri Fayol has classified them into planning, organising, commanding, coordinating and controlling. Luther Gullick has given Keyword 'POSDCORB' which stands for Planning (P), Organising (O), Staffing (S), Directing (D), Controlling (CO), Reporting (R) and Budgeting (B). These functions of management have been discussed in detail below :

⏭ PLANNING ⏮

Planning helps in determining the course of action to be followed for achieving various organisational objectives. It is a decision in advance; what to do, when to do, how to do and who will do a particular task. Planning is a process which involves 'thinking before doing.'

Louis A. Allen. Management planning involves "the development of forecasts, objectives, policies, programmes, procedures, schedules and budgets." According to him, planning is essentially deciding about future. The ways and means required to achieve organisational goals form the essential part of planning.

George B. Galloway. In simple words, it is organised foresight plus corrective hindsight... "conceived as a process," planning embraces a series of steps:

(i) the determination of objectives to be sought;
(ii) research to understand the problem;
(iii) the discovery of alternative solutions;
(iv) policy making .... Choosing between alternatives, including the frequent choice of doing nothing;
(v) the detailed execution of the chosen alternative known in physical planning as layout or design."

Objectives

Objectives are the end results which an organisation tries to achieve. McFarland has defined objectives in terms of goals, aims, or purposes. He says that:

"Objectives are the goals, aims, or purposes that organisations wish to achieve over varying periods of time."

According to Louis Allen, "objectives are goals established to guide the efforts of management and each of its components."

Concepts of Objectives

1. Organisations or groups are created basically for certain objectives. Members in the organisation or group try to achieve these objectives.
2. Objectives may be broad or they may be specifically mentioned. They may pertain to a wide or narrow part of the organisation. They may be set either for the long term or for the short term.

3. Objectives may be clearly defined because they provide clear direction for managerial action.
4. Objectives have hierarchy. At the top level, it may be broad organisational purpose which can be broken into specific objectives at the departmental level. From departmental objectives, units of the department may derive their own objectives.
5. Organisational objectives have social sanction, since organisations are social units, their objectives must conform to the general needs of the society.
6. An organisation may have multiple objectives.

PRINCIPLES OF MANAGEMENT BY HENRI FAYOL

Henri Fayol is claimed to be the real father of modern management. He was a Frenchman born in 1841 and was working as an engineer with a mining company. He improved the condition of the company from virtual bankruptcy to high success. From his practical experience, he developed some techniques. He brought out some 14 basic management principles, which he felt, could be used in all management situations, irrespective of the organizational framework.

He wrote a book entitled, General and Industrial Management, in French that was later on translated into English. It is now considered as one of the classics of management literature. The book mainly covers the aspects of the immutable and repetitive character of the management process and the concept that management can be taught in the classroom or the workplace. He also laid down the principles of management, which he deemed important for any organization.

Henri Fayol's 14 Principles of Management

Henri Fayol suggested the following 14 principles as the general principles management:

- **Division of Work.** This is the principle of specialization, which is very well expressed by economists as being a necessary factor for efficiency in the utilization of labor.
- **Authority and Responsibility.** In this principle, Fayol conceives authority as a combination of official authority deriving from a manager's official position and personal authority, which is compounded of intelligence, experience, moral worth, past services etc.
- **Discipline.** Holding the notion that discipline is 'respect for agreements which are directed as achieving obedience, application, energy and the outward marks of respect', Fayol declares that discipline requires good superiors at all levels, clear and fair agreements and judicious application of penalties.
- **Unit of Command.** This is the principle, which states that on employee should receive orders from one superior only.
- **Unity of Direction.** According to Fayol, the unity of direction principle implies that each group of activities having the some objectives must have one head and one plan. As distinguished from the principle of unity of command, Fayol perceives unity of direction as related to the functioning of personnel.
- **Subordination of Individual Interest to General Interest.** In any group, the interest of the group should supersede that of the individual. When the interests differ, it is the function of the management to reconcile them.
- **Remuneration of Personnel.** Fayol perceives that remuneration and methods of payment should be fair and also should be able to afford the maximum satisfaction to employee and employer.
- **Centralization.** Although Fayol does not use the term, Centralization of Authority, his principle definitely refers to the extent to which authority is concentrated or dispersed in on enterprise.

Individual circumstances determine the degree of centralization that gives the best over all yields.

- **Scalar Chain.** Fayol thinks of the scalar chain as a line of authority, a chain of superiors from the highest to the lowest ranks. And, because it is an error of a subordinate to depart needlessly from the lines of authority, the chain should be short-circuited.
- **Order.** Breaking this principle into material order and social order, Fayol thinks of it as a simple edge for everything. This organization is the principle, which refers to arrangement of things and persons in an organization.
- **Equity.** Fayol perceives this principle as one of eliciting loyalty and devotion from personnel with a combination of kindliness and justice in managers while dealing with subordinates.
- **Stability of Tenure of Personnel.** Finding that instability is both the cause and effect of bad management, Fayol points out the dangers and costs of unnecessary turnover.
- **Initiative.** Initiative is conceived as the process of thinking out and executing a plan. Since it is one of the keenest satisfactions for an intelligent man to experience, Fayol exhorts managers to sacrifice personal vanity in order to permit subordinates to exercise it.
- **Esprit de corps.** This principle implies that union is strength and an extension of the principle of unity of command. Fayol here emphasizes on the need for teamwork and the importance of communication in obtaining it.

5 Principles of Scientific Management: Propounded by Taylor

Principles of scientific management propounded by Taylor are:

1. **Science, Not Rule of Thumb.** In order to increase organisational efficiency, the 'Rule of Thumb' method should be substituted by the methods developed through scientific analysis of work.

   Rule of Thumb means decisions taken by manager as per their personal judgments. According to Taylor, even a small production activity like loading iron sheets into box cars can be scientifically planned. This will help in saving time as well as human energy. Decisions should be based on scientific enquiry with cause and effect relationships.

   This principle is concerned with selecting the best way of performing a job through the application of scientific analysis and not by intuition or hit and trial methods.

   The work assigned to any employee should be observed and analyzed with respect to each element or part thereof and the time involved therein so as to decide the best way of performing that the work and to determine the standard output for same.

2. **Harmony, Not Discord.** Taylor emphasized that there should be complete harmony between the workers and the management since if there is any conflict between the two, it will not be beneficial either for the workers or the management.

   Both the management and the workers should realize the importance of each other. In order to achieve this state, Taylor suggested complete mental revolution on the part of both management and workers.

   It means that there should be complete change in the attitude and outlook of workers and management towards each other. It should always be kept in mind that prosperity for an employer cannot exist for a long time unless it is accompanied by the prosperity of the employees of that organisation and vice versa.

   It becomes possible by: (a) sharing a part of surplus with workers (b) training of employees, (c) division of work (d) team spirit (e) positive attitude (f) sense of discipline (g) sincerity etc.

Management should always be ready to share the gains of the company with the workers and the latter should provide their full cooperation and hard work for achieving organizational goals. Group action with mutual-trust and understanding should be perfect understanding the focus of working.

This principle requires that there should be perfect understanding between the management and workers and both should feel that they are part of same family. It helps to produce synergy effect since both management and workers work in unison.

For example, in most of the Japanese companies, paternalistic style of management is in practice and there is complete openness between workers and the management. Usually, workers don't go on the strike but, if at all they do so, they just wear a black badge and work even more than the normal hours just to impress upon the management that their focus is on their demands as well as organisational objectives.

3. **Mental Revolution.** The technique of Mental Revolution involves a change in the attitude of workers and management towards each other. Both should realize the importance of each other and should work with full cooperation. Management as well as the workers should aim to increase the profits of the organisation.

   For this the workers should put in their best efforts so that the company makes profit and on the other hand management should share part of profits with the workers. Thus, mental revolution requires a complete change in the outlook of both management and workers. There should be a spirit of togetherness between workers and management.

4. **Cooperation, Not Individualism.** This principle is an extension of principle of 'Harmony, not discord' and lays stress on mutual cooperation between workers and the management. Cooperation, mutual confidence, sense of goodwill should prevail among both, managers as well as workers. The intention is to replace internal competition with cooperation.

   Both 'Management' and 'Workers' should realize the importance of each other. Workers should be considered as part of management and should be allowed to take part in decision making process of the management. Management should always welcome their suggestions and should also reward them if their suggestions prove to be beneficial for the organisation viz. reduction of costs or increase in production etc.

   At the same time, workers should also resist from going on strike or making unnecessary demands from management. Workers should be treated as integral part of organisation and all important decisions should be taken after due consultation with workers. Both of them should visualize themselves as two pillars whose soundness alone can ensure achievement of common goals of the organisation.

   Taylor also suggested that there should be proper division of work and responsibility between the two. Management should always guide, encourage and help the workers.

5. **Development of each and every person to his or her greatest efficiency and prosperity.** Efficiency of any organisation also depends on the skills and capabilities of its employees to a great extent. Thus, providing training to the workers was considered essential in order to learn the best method developed through the use of scientific approach. To attain the efficiency, steps should be taken right from the process of selection of employees. Employees should be scientifically selected.

   The work assigned to each employee should suit his/her physical, mental and intellectual capabilities. Efficient employees produce more to earn more. This ultimately helps to attain efficiency and prosperity for both organisation and the employees.

Decision Making

A decision is the selection from among alternatives. In the words of MacFarland, "A decision is an act of choice wherein an executive forms a conclusion about what must be done in a given situation. A decision represents a course of behaviour chosen from a number of possible alternatives." The way an executive acts or decides the course of action from among various alternatives is an act of decision-making.

Characteristics

Following are the characteristics of decision-making:

1. Decision-making is based on rational thinking. The manager tries to foresee various possible effects of a decision before taking a particular one.
2. It is a process of selecting the best from among alternatives available.
3. It involves the evaluation of various alternatives available. The selection of best alternative will be made only when pros and cons of all of them are discussed and evaluated.
4. Decision making is the end product because it is preceded by discussions and deliberations.
5. Decision-making is aimed to achieve organisational goals.
6. It also involves certain commitment. Management is committed to every decision it takes.

Types of Decisions

The Managerial decisions may be classified as follows:

1. **Organisational and Personal Decisions.** When a person takes a decision in the organisation as an executive it will be an organisational decision.

   An executive can also take decisions about himself. Such decisions are known as personal decisions.
2. **Routine and Strategic Decisions.** Routine decisions are made repetitively following certain established rules, procedures, policies etc. These are taken at middle and lower level management.

   Strategic decisions relate to policy matters and need the development and analysis of alternatives and are taken by top management.
3. **Programmed and Non-programmed Decisions.** Programmed decisions are of a routine nature and are taken within the specified procedures.

   Non-repetitive decisions are on the other hand non-programmed decisions.
4. **Policy and Operative Decisions.** Policy decisions determine the basic policies of the organisation and are taken at the top level management.

   Operative decisions, on the other hand, are less important and are related with day-to-day operations of the business. These decisions are taken in the light of policies decided by the top management.
5. **Individual and Group Decisions.** If the decision is taken by one person it is known as individual decision. In small concerns only the owner takes all important decisions.

   Group decisions are taken by a group of persons. The decisions of Board of Directors or Committees come under this category. These are, generally, important decisions and relate to policy matters.

Theories of Decision-Making

Following theories are used in decision-making:

1. **Marginal Theory.** This theory stresses on profit maximisation. The economists who propounded this theory say that profits will be maximum only when marginal costs of inputs are equal to marginal revenues. Marginal cost represents the additional cost of producing an additional unit and marginal revenue is the extra revenue from that product. When the marginal costs and revenues differ, the profits cannot be maximum. Either more additional revenues will be earned at less additional costs or *vice versa*. In practice, it is very difficult to locate the marginal point for each factor of production because these are carried on with the co-operation of everyone in the organisation.
2. **Psychological Theory.** The thrust of this theory is on the maximisation of customer satisfaction. The manager acts as an "administrative man" rather than 'economic man'. A good manager will try to protect economic interest of the enterprise besides maximising consumer satisfaction. Those alternatives may be selected which will help the consumers. According to this theory the consumer's interests should be a top priority in the mind of the decision-maker.
3. **Mathematical Theory.** This theory is based on the use of models. This is also known as operations research theory. The techniques generally used include linear programming, theory of probability, simulation models, monte carlo technique, germs theory, network theory, etc. The analyst defines the problem area, uses symbols for unknown data and then tries to solve it. This theory is more systematic as compared to other theories.

Techniques of Decision-Making

Following techniques of decision making are generally employed :

1. **Intuition.** Decisions are taken by the inner feeling of the person. The past knowledge, training and experience of the decision-maker plays an important role in intuitive decisions.
2. **Facts.** Sound and proper decisions are taken on the basis of factual data.
3. **Experience.** In this technique, past experiences play an important role in making new decisions in similar situation.
4. **Considered Opinions.** In this technique, some things are discussed and these which are considered by more persons becomes the basis for decision-making. These decisions are logical and sound.
5. **Operations Research.** This is modern technique. It helps managers by providing scientific basis for solving organisational problems involving interaction of components of the organisation.
6. **Linear Programming.** This technique is used to determine the best use of limited resources for achieving given objectives. This method is based on the assumption that there exists a linear relationship between variables and that the limits of variations could be ascertained. Linear programming can be used for solving problems in areas like production, transportation, warehousing, etc.

Steps in Decision-Making

Decision-making involves the following steps :

1. Defining the problem;
2. Analysis of problem;
3. Alternative courses of action;
4. Evaluation of alternatives;
5. Experience;
6. Experimentation; and
7. Implementation and follow up.

ORGANIZING

Organisation is a systematic arrangement of people to accomplish some specific purpose. Every organisation is composed of three elements i.e. people, goals and system. Each organisation has a distinct purpose. This purpose is expressed as goals generally.

According to Louis Allen. "Organising is the process of identifying and grouping work to be performed, defining and delegating responsibility and authority and establishing relationships for the purpose of enabling people to work most effectively together in accomplishing objectives." In the words of Allen, organisation is an instrument for achieving organisational goals. The work of each and every person is defined and authority and responsibility is fixed for accomplishing the same.

According to George Terry. "Organising is the establishing of effective authority relationships among selected work, persons, and work places in order for the group to work together efficiently." According to Terry organisation is the creation of relationship among persons and work so that it may be carried on in a better and efficient way. Organizing is the process of arranging and allocating work, authority, and resources among an organization's members so they can achieve the organization's goals.

Different goals require different structures. An organization that aims to develop computer software, for example, needs a different structure than does a manufacturer of blue jeans. Producing a standardized product like blue jeans requires efficient assembly-line techniques, whereas producing software requires organizing teams of professionals such as system analysts and programmers. Although these professionals must interact effectively, they cannot be organized like assembly-line workers. Thus, managers must match an organization's structure to its goals and resources, a process called *organizational design*.

Relationships and time are central to organizing activities. Organizing produces a structure for the relationships in an organization, and it is through these structured relationships that future plans will be pursued. For instance, Natalie Anderson coordinates the work of various people and structures time in organizing the production process for the Pankovsky book. Another aspect of relationships that is part of organizing is seeking new people to join the structure of relationships. This search is called staffing.

Organisational Structure

Organisation structure is a basic framework within which the managers' decision-making behaviour takes place.

In a simple term, structure is the pattern in which various parts or components are inter-related or inter-connected. Thus organisation structure is the pattern of relationships among various components or parts of the organisation. This prescribes the relationships among various activities and positions.

Organisation Structure requires various activities in sequence:

1. **Identification of Activities.** In designing the structure, managers must identify the various necessary activities that must be performed in order to achieve the organisational objectives. It should be kept in mind that:
   (a) all the necessary activities are performed;
   (b) there is no unnecessary duplication in performing various necessary activities; and
   (c) the various activities are performed in a synchronised or coordinated way.
2. **Grouping of Activities.** Closely related and similar activities are grouped together to form departments, divisions, or sections because coordination of numerous activities can best be achieved by grouping them into basic and derivative departments.
3. **Delegation of Authority.** Since the assignment of the job to an individual creates responsibility on his part, he must have corresponding authority to discharge his obligations.

Formal and Informal Organization

Formal Organization

Formal organization is a fixed set of rules of intra-organization procedures and structures. As such, it is usually set out in writing, with a language of rules that ostensibly leave little discretion for interpretation. In some societies and in some organizations, such rules may be strictly followed; in others, they may not be followed properly.

Informal Organization

Informal organization is the interlocking social structure that governs how people work together in practice. It is the aggregate of behaviors, interactions, norms, personal and professional connections through which work gets done and relationships are built among people who share a common organizational affiliation or cluster of affiliations. It consists of a dynamic set of personal relationships, social networks, communities of common interest, and emotional sources of motivation. The informal organization evolves organically and spontaneously in response to changes in the work environment, the flux of people through its porous boundaries, and the complex social dynamics of its members. Tended effectively, the informal organization complements the more explicit structures, plans, and processes of the formal organization: it can accelerate and enhance responses to unanticipated events ,foster innovation, enable people to solve problems that require collaboration across boundaries, and create footpaths showing where the formal organization may someday need to pave a way.

Functions of Informal Organization

1. They perpetuate the cultural and social values that the group holds dear,
2. They provide social status and satisfaction that may not be obtained from the formal organization,
3. They promote communication among members,
4. They provide social control by influencing and regulating behavior inside and outside the group.

Disadvantage of Informal Groups

1. Resistance to change.
2. Role conflict
3. Rumor
4. Conformity

Benefits of the Informal Organization

1. Blend with formal system
2. Lighten management work load
3. Fill gaps in management abilities
4. Act as a safety valve
5. Encourage improved management practice

The Informal Organization and the Formal Organization

The nature of the informal organization becomes more distinct when its key characteristics are juxtaposed with those of the formal organization. Formal rules are often adapted to subjective interests — social structures within an enterprise and the personal goals, desires, sympathies and behaviors of the individual workers — so that the practical everyday life of an organization becomes *informal*. Practical experience shows no organization is ever completely rule-bound: instead, all real organizations represent some mix of formal and informal. Consequently, when attempting to legislate for an organization and to create a formal structure, it is necessary to recognize informal organization in order to create workable structures. However, informal organization can fail, or, if already set in order, can work against mismanagement.

Formal organizations are typically understood to be systems of coordinated and controlled activities that arise when work is embedded in complex networks of technical relations and boundary-spanning exchanges. But in modern societies, formal organizational structures arise in highly institutional contexts.

Comparison between formal and Informal Organisation

Point of Comparison	Formal Organisation	Information Organisation
1. Origin	Created deliberately	Arise spontaneously
2. Nature	Planned and official	Unplanned and unofficial
3. Size	Large	Small
4. Continuity	Stable	Instable and dynamic
5. Focus	Builts around jobs	Build around people and their roles.
6. Structure	Definite structure mechanical & rational	Structureless impersonal and emotional
7. Goals	Profits & service to society	Satisfaction of memories.
8. Charting	Shown on organisational Chart.	Not shown on organisation chart
9. Control process	Rigid rules & regulations	Group norms & values.
10. Influence processes	Legitimate authority	Power
11. Authority	Positional flows, top town	Personal flows, bottom up
12. Communication	Official and well-defined paths. One way & slow flow of information	Unspecified channels. Two-way and fast flow of information, grapevine.

Key Characteristics of the Informal Organization:

- evolving constantly
- dynamic and responsive
- requires insider knowledge to be seen
- flat and fluid
- grass roots
- excellent at motivation
- treats people as individuals
- cohered by trust and reciprocity
- difficult to pin down
- essential for situations that change quickly or are not yet fully understood

Key Characteristics of the Formal Organization:

- enduring, unless deliberately altered
- static
- plain to see
- hierarchical
- top-down
- excellent at alignment
- equates "person" with "role"
- bound together by codified rules and order
- easily understood and explained
- critical for dealing with situations that are known and consistent

Historically, some have regarded the informal organization as the by product of insufficient formal organization—arguing, for example, that "it can hardly be questioned that the ideal situation in the business organization would be one where no informal organization existed." However, the contemporary approach—one suggested as early as 1925 by Mary Parker Follett, the pioneer of community centers and author of influential works on management philosophy—is to integrate the informal organization and the formal organization, recognizing the strengths and limitations of each.

SPAN OF CONTROL

The larger an organisation, the more management layers it has. As a result, a hierarchy is born. Multiple people in a department deal with a single superior. Some departments might only have ten people, while others consist of over a hundred employees. In both cases, span of control is present to properly manage all layers of the organisation.

The Span of Control is the number of employees a manager can supervise as effectively as possible. The addition of new hierarchical layers makes the organisational structure steeper.

A large Span of Control leads to a flatter organisational structure, which results in lower costs. A small span of control creates a steeper organisational structure, which requires more managers and which will consequently be more expensive for the organisation. It is therefore useful for an organisation if its managers have a large span of control.

Two Dimensions

The Span of Control always involves two dimensions:

- **Horizontal dimension.** This is the number of direct subordinates a manager actually supervises. This is also referred to as Span of Control.
- **Vertical dimension.** This is the number of levels that are (in)directly managed. It refers to the extent to which the manager's wishes trickle down to the lowest levels of the organisation. This is also known as Depth of Control. It is mainly aimed at the extent of communication between a manager and his subordinates in the levels he is responsible for. Without a good leader, downward communication can be impaired.

Factors

Good leadership partially has to do with a manager's innate talents. In addition, there are several other factors that play a role. One example would be the size of the Span of Control and the number of subordinates.

It also has to do with:

- A manager's experience and expertise.
- A manager's personality and people skills.
- Employees' experience, expertise and their behaviour towards each other.
- The nature of the work and the complexity of the assigned tasks.
- The nature of the organisation and the level of communication, delegating and interaction.

Assigned Tasks

Initially, it is about assigning tasks, authority and responsibilities. The more authority and responsibility an employee has, the higher his position in the hierarchy of the organisation. The number of tasks an employee has, however, has no bearing on their hierarchical position. It is vital to distinguish between compound tasks and singular tasks.

Compound tasks are primarily intended for inexperienced employees just starting out. They still require a lot of supervision and instruction and need to be monitored frequently by their managers.

Although the employee strives to achieve a specific result within the allotted time, there are sub-tasks (compound) that have to be completed along the way. The supervisor spends a lot of time guiding the employee. The more of these inexperienced employees there are in a team, the harder a supervisor's job gets.

The singular task is meant for experienced employees. He knows the objective, when the task needs to be completed and he is also responsible for the entire process. He requires little or no supervision by his superior.

At most, he might benefit from some instruction beforehand and an interim and final evaluation. It is easier for a manager to supervise a large group of such employees, because everyone knows what is expected of them.

Harmony

Span of Control is indicative of the quality of leadership. It is also a well-known fact that a manager with a large Span of Control has a lot of people under him. The smaller a manager's Span of Control, the less subordinates he can lead.

It is therefore very important for Span of Control and scope of control to be in harmony with each other. When one is larger or smaller than the other, problems arise in leadership method, employee instruction and teamwork.

Increasing Span of Control

When a manager supervises a large number of employees, he often has little time to align activities and monitor the quality of how activities are executed.

Every situation needs to be assessed individually based on factors that determine the span of control. If a situation arises in which a supervisor manages too many employees, there are several ways for finding a solution to increase the Span of Control:

- Training the manager, teaching him management skills such as delegating and clear communication.
- Training employees, teaching them to work independently and make better use of their time.
- Delegation by the manager, decreasing his work load and improving the division of labour.
- Improving procedures and systems; when procedures take up a lot of time, it is a good idea to find efficient solutions with the help of the management team.
- Involving HR, who will unburden the manager by taking over certain specialist tasks such as the department's HR policy.
- Assigning a personal assistant, who can take over routine activities, reducing the manager's work load.
- Appointing an assistant-manager who reports to the manager, but in the perception of the subordinates is fully qualified in terms of executive and policy tasks and can act as manager when needed.

Span of Control Example

Here are two examples to illustrate the harmony between Scope of control and Span of Control.

First is a situation with a manager with years of experience leading a team of approximately 40 people. Problems arise when his team is reduced to 20 people as a result of cutbacks. At first, everything still seems to be okay. Everyone knows what is expected of them, but as time goes by, the manager starts feeling uneasy. He wants to have more control and make things go his way.

Employees start to feel the manager is constantly looking over their shoulder and see his presence as a hindrance. It is likely that the manager will start to get bored and will no longer be able to find intrinsic motivation in his work. Conflicts may arise and small problems become big ones very easily. In some cases, the manager can feel he is not sufficiently stimulated, which can have very negative consequences.

The second situation involves a manager who is used to leading a team of about five employees. He will experience stress when he is made responsible for a group of 20 people. If the employees are able to function on their own, things might be al-right at first. But when problems or conflicts arise, the manager needs to be there for all 20 of his subordinates. He will find it difficult to delegate tasks, because he is used to working one-on-one with only about five employees.

The situation becomes more complicated for the manager when the majority of the 20 employees are not able to function independently. The manager will be confronted with his own lack of delegating skills. In both cases it is important to identify the problem and offer practical solutions.

LEADING

Meaning of Leading

Leading is the managerial function of guiding, inspiring, instructing and harnessing people towards the accomplishment of desired results. If is that part of the management process which actuates the members of an organisation to work effectively and efficiently for the achievement of the goals.

Motivation

Motivation has come from motives which are the expression of human needs by a human being. Motivation is the process of inducing persons to experience needs for certain desired behaviour so that organisational efficiency is achieved.

Scott has defined it as: "Motivation means a process of stimulating people to action to accomplish desired goals."

McFarland has defined it as: "Motivation refers to the way in which urges, drives, desires, aspirations, strivings, needs, direct, control, or explain the behaviour of human beings."

Characteristics of Motivation

1. Motivation is an internal feeling. Motivation is a psychological phenomenon which generates within an individual.
2. Person in totality, not in part, is motivated. Each individual in the organisation is a self-contained and inseparable unit and his all needs are interrelated.
3. Motivation is the product of anticipated values from an action and the perceived probability that these values will be achieved by the action.

Thus, motivation is one of the most important factors determining organisational efficiency. All organisational facilities will go waste in the lack of motivated people to utilise these facilities effectively. Every superior in the organisation must motivate his subordinates for the right types of behaviour.

Leadership

Leadership is an essential ingredient for successful organisation. The successful organisation has one major attribute that sets it apart from unsuccessful organisation that is dynamic and effective leadership.

Leadership has been defined by Davis as follows:

"Leadership is the ability to persuade others to seek defined objectives enthusiastically. It is the human factor which binds a group together and motivates it towards goals." Thus, leadership is the process of influencing the activities of an individual or a group for goal achievement in a given situation. Leadership process comprises of three factors-leader, the follower, and other variable.

Characteristics of Leadership

1. Leadership is basically personal quality. This quality motivates the individuals to be with leaders.
2. Leader, by exercising his leadership, tries to influence the behaviour of individuals around him to fulfil certain pre-determined objectives.
3. Leader tries to influence the individual to behave in a particular way.
4. There is a relationship between leader and individuals (followers) which arises out of functioning for a common goal.
5. Leadership is a continuous process of influencing behaviour.
6. Leadership is exercised in a particular situation. The situation variables also affect the effectiveness of leadership.

AUTHORITY AND RESPONSIBILITY

Authority

Authority, in simple words, is the right way of commanding subordinates, issuing orders and instructions, and exacting obedience from the team. It is also the right of the manager to make decisions. Also, to act or not to act depends on how he perceives the objectives of the organization.

Henri Fayol, who designed the administrative theory of 14 principles of management, defined authority as 'the right to give orders and exact obedience'. He also recognized that any official authority vested in the job was often ineffective.

He further added that the presence of leadership qualities and traits like intelligence, experience, etc., usually, enhance authority. However, as an important key to the manager's job, authority is the power to command others and decide to act or refrain from acting to achieve the organization's goals. A manager needs authority. It makes his position real and gives him the power to order his subordinates and get them to comply. When there is a chain of superior-subordinate relations in an organization, it is the authority which binds and provides a basis for responsibility.

James Mooney specified that coordination is the primary principle of an organization. Therefore, it must have its own principle and foundation in Authority or the supreme coordinating power.

Coordination is the all-inclusive principle of organization, it must have its own principle and foundation in Authority or the supreme coordinating power.

Always, in every form of organization, this supreme coordinating authority must rest somewhere, else there would be no directive for any truly coordinated effort. Without authority, there will be no relations between subordinates and superiors and the organization will be in chaos.

Official and Personal Authority

The authority that a manager enjoys due to his position is the official authority or authority of position. Apart from the official authority, a manager might influence the behavior of other people in the organization.

This is the personal authority of the manager. A manager with both official and personal authority is very effective. Authority is not unlimited power and consists of specific rights and permissions to act for the organization in specified areas.

Responsibility

Responsibility has different meanings in management. The most common description is the obligation on the manager to perform the task himself. The essence of responsibility is 'obligation'.

Anyone who accepts a task must be held responsible for its performance too. In the context of hierarchical relations in an organization, responsibility is the obligation of a subordinate to perform the tasks assigned.

Therefore, responsibility is relative to the person. Also, it emanates from the subordinate-superior relations in an organization. Hence, the manager can get the assigned duty done by his subordinate.

He also needs to ensure a proper discharge of the duty. Therefore, in an organization, authority and responsibility move as follows - authority flows downwards, whereas responsibility is exacted upwards.

Sometimes, informal leadership emerges in an organization. This can create problems in the clear definition of responsibilities of the subordinates. However, the responsibility towards the seniors does not change.

Accountability

Every employee is answerable to his superior for the accomplishment of the task assigned to him. This is accountability. When a manager delegates a task, he assigns duties and delegates the required authority so that his subordinates can accomplish the task.

However, the process is not complete unless the subordinate is answerable to the superior for his functioning. Therefore, authority goes downward and makes everyone accountable for the duties assigned.

Authority and Power

In order to explain the limits to formal authority, many experts make a distinction between authority and power. According to some theories, authority is the right to command in the official hierarchical sense.

On the other hand, power is the capacity to influence the behavior of others. However, in the real world, many managers also have the power to exact obedience from their subordinates.

The proportion in which they are divided can vary according to the role of the manager. While the head of a division in the Army will have a more complete combination of authority and power, as assistant manager of a call center might not be able to use power to that extent.

In an ideal scenario, authority and responsibility along with power and accountability are equal to each other in every position of the organization. If the balance between them gets disturbed, problems arise.

For example, if an employee is given authority but does not have enough power, he can't do his job effectively. This is because lacking power, he is unable to use punishments and rewards for enforcing authority.

Even is he has equal power and authority, it is important to equate them with responsibility and accountability. Else, he will pass the responsibility to some other employee the moment problems start surfacing.

DELEGATION OF AUTHORITY

The Delegation of Authority is an organizational process wherein, the manager divides his work among the subordinates and give them the responsibility to accomplish the respective tasks. Along with the responsibility, he also shares the authority, i.e., the power to take decisions with the subordinates, such that responsibilities can be completed efficiently.

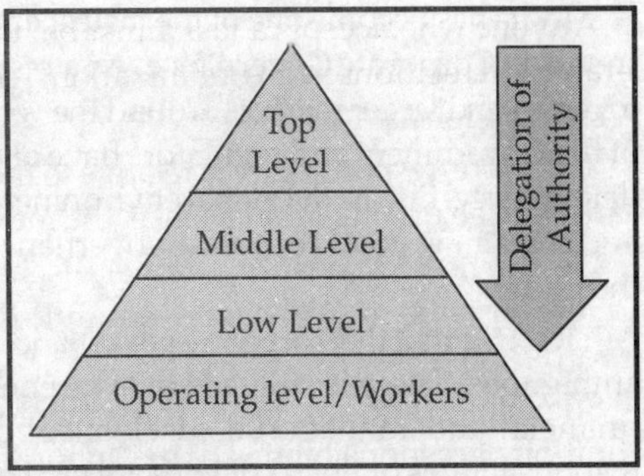

In other words, a delegation of authority involves the sharing of authority downwards to the subordinates and checking their efficiency by making them accountable for their doings. In an organization, the manager has several responsibilities and work to do. So, in order to reduce his burden, certain responsibility and authority are delegated to the lower level, i.e. to the subordinates, to get the work done on the manager's behalf.

Under the delegation of authority, the manager does not surrender his authority completely, but only shares certain responsibility with the subordinate and delegates that much authority which is necessary to complete that responsibility.

Features of Delegation of Authority

1. Delegation means giving power to the subordinate to act independently but within the limits prescribed by the superior. Also, he must comply with the provisions of the organizational policy, rules, and regulations.
2. Delegation does not mean that manager give up his authority, but certainly he shares some authority with the subordinate essential to complete the responsibility entrusted to him.
3. Authority once delegated can be further expanded, or withdrawn by the superior depending on the situation.
4. The manager cannot delegate the authority which he himself does not possess. Also, he can not delegate his full authority to a subordinate.
5. The delegation of authority may be oral or written, and may be specific or general.
6. The delegation is an art and must comply with all the fundamental rules of an organization.

DECENTRALIZATION

Decentralization refers to a company's top management delegating authority to subunits of the company. Subunits include divisions, subsidiaries, profit centers, investment centers, and so on.

The extent of decentralization varies. For example, a profit center is likely to have authority to make decisions involving revenues and expenses, but will not have authority to make investment decisions or enter into banking relationships.

A benefit of decentralization is having the decision makers closer to the markets in order to make better and faster decisions. Another benefit of decentralization is having more individuals share the work involved in decision making. This in turn provides excellent training and development of future leaders of the company.

A disadvantage of decentralization occurs if a subunit makes a decision that is good for the subunit's financial results, but it means less than optimal results for the company as a whole.

CORPORATE GOVERNANCE AND BUSINESS ETHICS

Corporate Governance

The issues of governance, accountability and transparency in the affairs of the company, as well as about the rights of shareholders and role of Board of Directors have never been so prominent as it is today. The corporate governance has come to assume a centre stage in the Board room discussions.

India has become one of the fastest emerging nations to have aligned itself with the international trends in Corporate Governance. As a result, Indian companies have increasingly been able to access to newer and larger markets around the world; as well as able to acquire more businesses. The response of the Government and regulators have also been admirably quick to meet the challenges of corporate delinquency. But, as the global environment changing continuously, there is a greater need of adopting and sustaining good corporate governance practices for value creation and building corporations of the future.

It is true that the 'corporate governance' has no unique structure or design and is largely considered ambiguous. There is still lack of awareness about its various issues, like, quality and frequency of financial and managerial disclosure, compliance with the code of best practice, roles and responsibilities of Board of Directories, shareholders rights, etc. There have been many instances of failure and scams in the corporate sector, like collusion between companies and their accounting firms, presence of weak or ineffective internal audits, lack of required skills by managers, lack of proper disclosures, non-compliance with standards, etc. As a result, both management and auditors have come under greater scrutiny.

But, with the integration of Indian economy with global markets, industrialists and corporates in the country are being increasingly asked to adopt better and transparent corporate practices. The degree to which corporations observe basic principles of good corporate governance is an increasingly important factor for taking key investment decisions. If companies are to reap the full benefits of the global capital market, capture efficiency gains, benefit by economies of scale and attract long term capital, adoption of corporate governance standards must be credible, consistent, coherent and inspiring.

Quality of corporate governance primarily depends on following factors, namely:- integrity of the management; ability of the Board; adequacy of the processes; commitment level of individual Board members; quality of corporate reporting; participation of stakeholders in the management; etc. Since this is an important element affecting the long-term financial health of companies, good governance framework also calls for effective legal and institutional environment, business ethics and awareness of the environmental and societal interests.

Hence, in the years to come, corporate governance will become more relevant and a more acceptable practice worldwide. This is easily evident from the various activities undertaken by many companies in framing and enforcing codes of conduct and honest business practices; following more stringent norms for financial and non-financial disclosures, as mandated by law; accepting higher and appropriate accounting standards; enforcing tax reforms coupled with deregulation and competition; etc.

However, inapt application of corporate governance requirements can adversely affect the relationship amongst participants of the governance system. As owners of equity, institutional investors are increasingly demanding a decisive role in corporate governance. Individual shareholders, who usually do not exercise governance rights, are highly concerned about getting fair treatment from controlling shareholders and management. Creditors, especially banks, play a key role in governance systems, and serve as external monitors over corporate performance. Employees and other stakeholders also play an important role in contributing to the long term success and performance of the corporation. Thus, it is necessary to apply governance practices in a right manner for better growth of a company

Business Ethics

Ethics refers to a system of moral principles–a sense of right and wrong and goodness and badness of actions and their motives and consequences. Business Ethics refers to the application of ethics to business. It is the study of good and evil, right and wrong and just and unjust actions of businessmen.

Business ethics does not differ from generally accepted norms of good or bad. If dishonesty is considered to be unethical and immoral in society, then any businessman who is dishonest with employees, customers, shareholders or competitors is acting unethically and immorally. If protecting others from any harm is considered to be ethical then a company that recalls a defective and harmful product from the market is acting ethically.

"Ethics deals with the right actions of individual; Business ethics is related with the test of values or social values."

– **Peter F. Drucker**

Sources of Business Ethics

(i) **Religion.** One of the oldest sources of ethical inspiration is religion. More than 100, 000 different religions exist across the globe. But despite doctrinal differences, the major religions coverage on the belief that ethics is an expression of divine will that reveals the nature of right and wrong in business and other areas of life. The world's great religions are also in agreement on fundamental principles which are similar to the building blocks of secular ethical doctrine. The principle of reciprocity towards one's fellow human beings is found in all major religions such as Hinduism, Buddhism, Christianity, Islam, Judaism and Confucianism. The great religions preach the necessity for an orderly social system and emphasise social responsibility in such a way so as to contribute to the general welfare. Built upon such varieties there are many other rules of conduct.

(ii) **Cultural Experience.** Culture refers to a set of values, rules and standards transmitted among generations and acted upon to produce behaviours that fall within acceptable limits. These rules and standards always play an important part in determining values, because individuals anchor their conduct in the culture of the group.

(iii) **The Legal System.** Laws are rules of conduct, approved by legislatures, that guide human behaviour in any society. They codify ethical expectations and keep changing as new evils emerge. But laws cannot cover all ethical expectations of society. Law is reactive; new statutes and enforcement always lag behind the opportunity for corporate expediency.

Whatever ethics that law codifies, it is binding on business. Society expects business to abide by law and obeying law is presumed to be ethical behaviour.

Importance of Business of Ethics

Ethics is important to business for several reasons as stated below:

(i) **Ethics corresponds to basic human needs.** It is a human trait that man desires to be ethical, not only in his private life but also in his business affairs where, being a manager, he knows his decisions may affect the lives of thousands of employees. Moreover, most people want to be part of an organisation which they can respect and be publicly proud of, because they perceive its purpose and activities to be honest and beneficial to the society. Most top managers would like to respond to this need of their employees; and they (managers) themselves feel an equal need to be genuinely proud of the company they are directing. These basic ethical needs compel the organisations to be ethically oriented.

(ii) **Values create credibility with the public.** A company perceived by the public to be ethically and socially responsive will be honoured and respected even by those who have no intimate knowledge of its actual working. There will be an instinctive prejudice in favour of its products, since people believe that the company offers value for money. Its public issues will attract an immediate response.

(iii) **Values give management credibility with employees.** Values are supposed to be a common language to bring leaderships and its people together. Organisational ethics, when perceived by employees as genuine, create common goals, values and language. The management has credibility with its employees precisely because it has credibility with the public. Neither sound business strategy, nor a generous compensation policy and fringe benefits can win employee credibility; but perceived moral and social uprightness can.

(iv) **Values help better decision making.** Another point of great importance is that an ethical attitude helps the management make better decisions, *i.e.*, decisions which are in the interest of the public, their employees and the company's own long term good, even though decision making is slower. This is so because respect for ethics will force a management to take various aspects-economic, social, and ethical-in making decisions.

(v) **Ethics and profit go together.** A company which is inspired by ethical conduct is also profitable one. Value driven companies are sure to be successful in the long run, though in the short run, they may lose money.

(vi) **Law cannot protect society, ethics can.** Ethics is important because the government, law and lawyers cannot do everything to protect society. Technology develops faster than the government can regulate. People in an industry often know the dangers in a particular technology better than the regulatory agencies. Further, government cannot always regulate all activities which are harmful to society. Where law fails, ethics can succeed. An ethical oriented management takes measures to prevent pollution and protect workers' health even before being mandated by law.

Two theories are pertinent when one talks about the matter of ethics.

1. The theory of moral unity essentially advocates the principle that business actions should be judged by the general ethical standards of society. There exists only one ethical standard which applies to business and to non-business situations.
2. Opposed to the theory of moral unity is the theory of amorality, which argues that business can be amoral, and the actions of businessmen need not be guided by general ethical standards. Managers may act selfishly because the market mechanism distills their actions into benefits to shareholders and society at large.

However, the theory of amorality is not acceptable to anybody. Everyone agrees that business actions should be subject to the same ethical standards as the one applicable to the society in general.

HUMAN RESOURCE MANAGEMENT

Human Resource Management is a management function involving procurement of suitable human resources, train and develop their competencies, motivate them, reward them effectively and create in them an urge to be part of the management team whose aim should be rendered, dedicated, committed service for the success and growth of the organization. It applies to all types of organizations, industry, business, Government, education, health or social welfare of the people.

Scope of HRM

All major activities in the working life of the employee from the time of his entry into the organization until he leaves, retires, come under the purview of human resource management:

The most important activities undertaken are

1. Planning, job design, job analysis, procurement, recruitment, selection, induction, placement, training and development.
2. Compensation, rewards, benefits, retirement benefits, medical and health care.
3. Motivation, Motivational aids, bonus, incentives, career development, growth, decision making, delegation of authority and power, promotion *etc.*
4. Employee Relations-Grievance handling participation, collective bargaining and other aspects of cordial relations conducive to mutual understanding and trust.

5. Employee evaluation and performance improvement, Human Resource Audit and Human Resource Accounting.

Objectives of HRM

The objectives of Human Resource Management are:

(a) To provide attractive, equitable incentives, rewards, benefits, social security measures, to ensure retention of competent employees.

(b) To provide, create, utilize and motivate employees to accomplish organizational goals.

(c) To maintain high morale, encourage value system and create environment of trust, mutuality of interests.

(d) To create opportunities, to provide facilities, necessary motivation to individuals and groups for their growth with the growth of the organization by training and development and fair compensation.

(e) To secure integration of individuals and groups in securing organizational effectiveness.

(f) To ensure that, there is no threat of unemployment, inequalities, adopting a policy recognizing merit and employee contribution and conditions for stability of employment.

(g) To provide opportunities for communication, expression, participation, appreciation, recognition and provide fair efficient leadership.

(h) To create a sense and feeling of belongingness, team spirit and encourage suggestions from employees.

HUMAN RESOURCE PLANNING

Human Resource Planning is the process by which a management determines how an organization should move from its current manpower position to its desired manpower position. Through planning, a management strives to have the right number and the right kind of people at the right places, at the right time, to do things which result in both the organization and the individual receiving the maximum long range benefits. Of all the M's in management (*i.e.*, the management of materials, machines, methods, money, motive) the most important is "M" for men or human resources. It is the most valuable asset of an organization. It is in fact an important economic resource, covering all human resources - organized or unorganized, employed or capable of employment, working at all levels supervisors, executives; Government employees, "blue" and "white" collar workers, managerial, scientific, engineering, technical, skilled or unskilled persons, who are employed in creating, designing, developing, managing and operating productive and service enterprises and other economic activities.

Process of Human Resource Planning

The process of human resource planning is one of the most crucial, complex and continuing managerial functions which embraces organizational development, management development, career planning and succession planning. The process has gained importance in India with the increase in the size of business enterprises, complex production technology and the adoption of professional management technique. It may be rightly regarded as a multi-step process, including various steps such as:

A. Objectives of Human Resource Planning

Human resources planning fulfils individual, organizational and national goals, but the ultimate mission or purpose is to relate future human resources to future enterprise needs so as to maximize the future return on investment in human resources. In fact, the main purpose is one of matching or fitting employee abilities to enterprise requirements, with an emphasis on future instead of present arrangements. The objectives may be laid down for a short term (*i.e.*, for one year). For example, the short-term objective may be to hire 25 persons from Scheduled Tribes or Backward Classes for purpose of training. The long-term objective may be to start a new industry, to expand the market share, to produce a new product, to develop its own sales force rather than depend on distributors or to have minority group members eventually in position of middle and upper management cadres.

B. Estimating the Future Organizational Structure or Forecasting the Manpower Requirements

The management must estimate the structure of the organization at a given point of time. For this estimate, the number and type of employees needed have to be determined. Many environmental factors affect this determination. They include business forecasts, expansion and growth, design and structural changes, management philosophy, government policy, product and human skills mix, and competition.

Forecasting provides the basic premises on which the manpower planning is built. In determining the requirements of human resources, the expected losses which are likely to occur through labour turnover — retirement, death, transfers, promotions, demotions, dismissals, disability, resignations, lay-offs and other separations — should be taken into account.

It may be noted that for purpose of manpower planning, the main dimensions to be taken into consideration are

(i) The total number of personnel available, this could be obtained from the pay-rolls and other personnel records, such as the applications for employment.

(ii) The job-family, *i.e.*, a detailed job-description for each position.

(iii) Age distribution of the employees available in the present departments.

(iv) Qualification and experience desired, such as a person with 5 years or 10 years experience in a particular branch/job.

(v) The salary range *etc.*

C. Auditing Human Resources

Once the future human resource needs are estimated, the next step is to determine the present supply of manpower resources. This is done through what is called "Skills Inventory." A skills inventory contains data about each employee's skills, abilities, work preference and other items of information which indicate his overall value to the company.

Some organizations do not compile a skills inventory but prepare organization charts to determine "how many people, at what level, in what position and what kind of experience and training would be required to meet the objectives." These charts show a person's age, the number of years he has been in a particular position and his fitness for promotion. These Charts or Skills Inventories help in determining and evaluating the quantity and quality of the present human resources of an organization. They tell us 'what exists in stock' and 'what is needed to be added to that stock', taking into account the capability, qualifications, experience, skill, knowledge and promotional potential of employees. Some companies maintain a Manning Table, which lists all the jobs in the unit and the number of workers holding each job. Other companies also use manpower replacement charts, which show the present performance of each position holder and the promotional potential of possible replacements.

D. Job Analysis

After having decided how many persons would be needed, it is necessary to prepare a job analysis, which records details of training, skills, qualifications, abilities, experience and responsibilities, *etc.*, which are needed for a job. Job analysis includes the preparation of job descriptions and job specifications.

E. Developing a Human Resource Plan

This step refers to the development and implementation of the human resource plan, which consists of finding out the sources of labour supply with a view to make an effective use of these sources. The first thing, therefore, is to decide on the policy — should the person be hired from within through promotional channels or should it be obtained from an outside source. The best policy which is followed by most organizations is to fill up higher vacancies by promotion and lower level positions by recruitment from the labour market.

RECRUITMENT

The first step in the development of a concern's personnel activity is to employ the right type of persons to operate the organisation. If the organisation does not possess right kind of people, it leads to lowered production and employee morale and increased absenteeism and labour turnover.

Recruitment is the process of searching for prospective employees and stimulating them to apply for jobs in the concern. It develops and maintains adequate manpower to run an organisation efficiently.

Methods of Recruiting

1. From within the company
   - By promotion
   - By transfer
   - Former employees who had good service records when they left.
2. From outside the company
   - Friends and relatives of present employees duly recommended by them.
   - Through press and other advertisements.
   - Through employment agencies.
   - Through schools, colleges, universities.
   - Through labour unions.
   - From waiting lists.
   - From unsolicited applications received from both at the gate and through the mail.
   - From labour contractors with the help of notices exhibited at the factory gates.

Procedure for Recruitment and Selection. The main purpose of a proper procedure of recruitment and selection is to find the right man for each job, the exact procedure will depend upon the job for which appointment is to be made. For ordinary workers in a factory, the procedure would be rather simple. The old practice of entrusting the task of selection to the foreman or some other official who is not well versed in the techniques of scientific vocational selection is now being gradually replaced by a more efficient system of selection by a central employment department. The employment department should be manned by psychologists and technical experts and should select workers and employees for all departments.

(a) **Requisition.** The first step in the direction of employing people is requisitioning of workers by the supervisor in whose department vacancies arise. A requisition should state clearly the number of workers required and should be accompanied by the relevant job specification.

(b) **Recruitment.** The next step will be for the employment department to write to the employment exchange or advertise the vacancy in the newspapers asking the candidates to send applications giving their qualifications or tap some other source of labour. On receipt of applications from candidates or names from the employment exchange, the recruitment office should eliminate the candidates who are obviously unqualified for the job and prepare a list of candidates who are eligible for the job.

(c) **Application Blanks.** The selection of workers is the next step involving a more careful screening of the potential candidates from the lists already prepared. For this purpose, a form is sent to the candidates who are qualified. The form must be designed to elicit full information about the candidate particularly with regard to his educational qualifications, his experience, his interests, *etc.* It should ask for definite information. A candidate should be asked to state how he has been employed during the past five or ten years with reasons for any change of jobs. This will show whether this candidate is of a type who sticks to one job or is one likely to give up a job on a flimsy ground. Some concerns have the practice of asking candidates to come for interview and fill up 'blanks' then and there. When forms are filled up in this way, they have one important advantage. The candidate may give information which is contrary to what he gave in his original application. An explanation of the discrepancy will probably throw some light on his character and personality. Filling up the application blank provides fair opportunity to those who do not feel at ease in the interview but can write down their answers without any hesitation. A few candidates are generally invited for a personal interview.

(d) **Trade Tests.** In case of jobs which involve technical work, a trade test is generally required. For recruitment of a stenographer in an office, a test can be given to check up his speed both at dictation and typing. Workers for a factory can be given similar tests (*i.e.* trade tests) to find out their capabilities for the type of job for which they are being considered.

(e) **Psychological Tests.** Acting on the principle that individuals differ from one another by degree though not in kind, industrial psychologists have devised certain tests which seek to measure the psychological characteristics of individual applicants for a position. A psychological test is an objective and standard measure of a sample of human behaviour. It consists of giving to the applicant a task which is representative of the job for which he is being considered. His performance on the task is evaluated relative to that of the other candidates. There are different types of tests standardized for jobs at different levels. Some of the important tests used in industry are:

(i) *Intelligence Tests, i.e.* tests which measure the mental capacity of a person to graph and put together the elements of a novel or abstract situation.

(ii) *Aptitude Tests, i.e.*, tests to measure the aptitude of applicants which is their capacity to learn the skills required on a particular job.

(iii) *Interests Tests, i.e.* tests to determine the preferences of an applicant for occupations of different kinds.

(iv) *Exterity tests, i.e.* to determine an individual's capacity to use his fingers and hands in industrial work.

(v) *Achievement Tests, i.e.* tests of the level of knowledge and proficiency in certain skills already achieved by the applicants.

(vi) *Personality test, i.e.* tests designed to judge the emotional balance, maturity and temperamental qualities of a person.

(f) **Interview.** The purpose of the employment interview is to find out that the candidate's mental and social make-up and to know whether the qualities possessed by him make him suitable for a job in the concern. The purpose of the interview is definitely not to confuse the candidate. Therefore, it must be conducted in a friendly atmosphere and the candidate must be made to feel at ease. At the interview, questions should better be asked on the basis of job specifications, although questions arising out of the candidate's answers should not be ruled out. Matters like hours of work, rest period, work on holidays and overtime should be carefully explained. So far, the employment interview is considered to be the most satisfactory way of judging temperamental qualities of the candidates. In fact, in some concerns, it is the only tool of selection.

(g) **Medical Test.** No worker should be selected without a medical test. This is important because a person of poor health may generally be absent and the training given to him may go waste. A person suffering from any diseases may spread it amongst other workers. In any case even if a person does not suffer from any disease, the requirements of a job may be so exacting that a person of poor physique may not be able to handle it properly. For example, if a worker is required to handle heavy materials, he must possess sufficient physical strength to do that.

(h) **On-the-job Test and Selection.** It is one of the basis of the results of these various tests that the candidate would be finally selected but before he is given a job on permanent basis it would be better to try him out for a few weeks in the factory itself. This is because no procedure of selection can find out the whole reality about the personality of the selected candidates. It is only by observing workers actually at work that one can find out how they behave with their fellow-workers and supervisors. By observing a candidate at work it will be known whether he can do his job properly or not. Therefore, it is only after a trial for a few weeks that the person concerned should be treated as finally selected. If a person is not found suitable, the management may transfer him to some other job. If an unsuitable person is made permanent, it will be a cause of dissatisfaction both to the management and to the employee in time to come. The management will be dissatisfied because the person cannot do his job well and the employee will be dissatisfied because he will not get any further promotion.

SELECTION

After attracting a number of applicants through various sources, the next stage is the selection process., *i.e.* to select the persons most appropriate for the organization. The different procedural steps involved in the selection process are:

(a) **Job descriptions.** The first step is to develop job descriptions for the positions to be advertised and filled. A job description is a combination of short statements that describe both the work to be performed and the essential requirements of the particular job. It includes job title, job responsibilities, job knowledge, physical activities *etc*.

(b) **Application forms.** An application form is the most universal mechanism used to screen the applicants to be called for interview and other tests for selection purposes.

(c) **Employment tests.** A test is a rapid method of obtaining samples of behaviour to help the interviewer to form judgement to hire or not to hire a given applicant.

(d) **Interviewing.** An interview is a conversation between an applicant and the interviewer and much of the interaction between these two is carried on by gestures, postures, facial expressions and other communicative behaviour.

(e) **Physical examination.** Many jobs require unusual stamina, strength or tolerance in unpleasant conditions. The physical examination reveals whether or not an applicant is fit for a particular job.

(f) **Induction and orientation.** It has been reported by many concerns that over half of the employee quits over within the first six months on the job and a large portions of this is because workers are introduced to their jobs in a haphazard manner. Induction implies introducing or orienting a man/employee to the organisation.

Model Procedure for Effective Personnel Selection

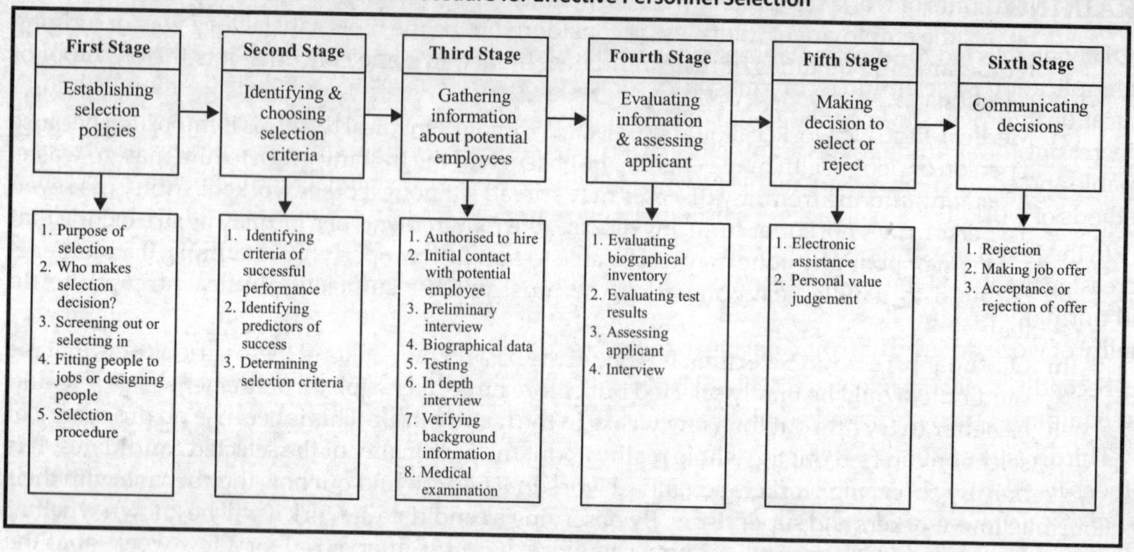

Steps in Selection procedure

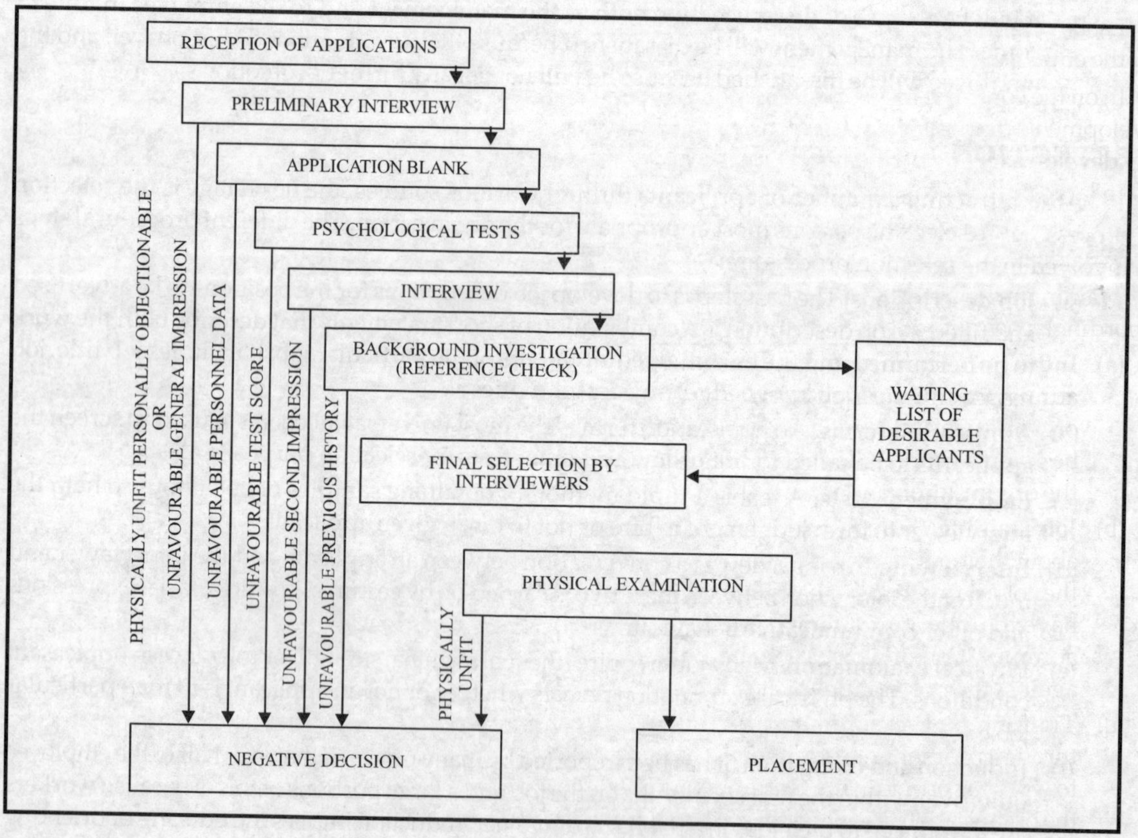

TRAINING

Having selected the most suitable persons for the various categories of jobs in the concern through the application of scientific techniques, it becomes necessary to arrange for their training. While education improves the knowledge and understanding of employees in a general way, training aims at increasing the aptitudes, skills and abilities of the workers to perform specific job. A person, however capable and competent, cannot do his best at a job unless he is systematically trained in the correct methods of work. The advantages of a training programme are obviously numerous.

In the first place, training brings about an improvement of the quality and quantity of output by increasing the skill of the employees. A novice, who has just started working without proper training, will normally produce less than another person who has been systematically trained. In fact, the quality of work done by him may not be up to the mark for lack of proper training.

Secondly, trained personnel will be able to make much better and more economical use of materials and equipment than untrained employees, thus reducing the cost of production.

Thirdly, since trained personnel will commit very few mistakes, the management can well afford to focus its attention on planning the work and encourage expert workers.

Fourthly, training also helps in spotting out promising men and in locating mistakes in selection. The promising trainee will naturally be discovered from his quick understanding of instruction. An unsuitable trainee, on the other hand, will show absolutely no interest in training for the job concerned.

Lastly, training will create a feeling among the workers that they are being properly cared for and that the employer is sincere to them. This will improve relations between the employers and employees.

If, on the contrary, the workers are not fully trained in the correct methods of work, unwholesome developments may follow. The level of output and the quality of work may be poor. Untrained workers may develop a feeling of dissatisfaction towards their jobs and may leave the concern quite frequently and in large numbers, making for a high percentage of labour turnover with its attendants evils.

Types of Training

Training programmes may be arranged by industrial concerns for different specific purposes. Accordingly, training of workers may be of the following type:

(a) **Induction Training.** Induction refers to the initial training provided to workers on their admission to an organisation. The object of such training is to introduce the workers to the organisation and familiarise him with it. Under such a programme, therefore, the worker may be given a general idea about the products manufactured by the organisation, the history of the organisation and its rules, working conditions, *etc*.

(b) **Job Training**: Such training is provided to workers with the object of increasing their knowledge about their respective jobs as also of enhancing their efficiency. It enables the workers to know the correct methods of handling the equipment and materials at their jobs. Since the workers have to undergo training in all the processes connected with their job, they can avoid the accumulation of work at vital points (*i.e.*, bottlenecks) and can take necessary precautions against the possibilities of accidents.

(c) **Training for Promotion.** In most of the organisations, at least some of the vacancies are filled through promotion from amongst existing workers. This provides encouragement to workers to work for promotion. Before, however, workers are promoted to occupy superior positions in the organisation, it is necessary to provide some training to them so that they are well prepared to shoulder their new responsibilities.

(d) **Refresher Training.** Workers may be formally trained for their jobs in the beginning when they are put to work. But with the passage of time, many of the methods and instructions may be lost sight of or forgotten. Refresher training is meant for reviving them in the minds of the workers through short term courses.

Methods of Training

The following methods are usually adopted by industrial concerns to provide training to their employees:

(i) **On-the-job Training.** Under this method, the worker puts on a machine or a specific job in the factory. He is instructed by an experienced employee or a special supervisor. No special school has to be opened for the trainees and in the course of their training, they continue to add to the output. Usually, the experienced workers acting as instructors have neither the time or inclination nor the competence to provide suitable instruction to the trainees. The method can therefore, be successful only if the trainers are well qualified and show enough interest in the trainees.

(ii) **Vestibule Training.** A vestibule is a fore court or entrance-hall through which one has to pass before entering the main rooms in a house. In vestibule training, therefore, the "workers are trained on specific jobs in a special part of the plant." An attempt is made to create working conditions which are similar to the actual workshop conditions. This enables the workers to secure training in the best methods of work and to get rid of initial nervousness.

(iii) **Apprenticeship Training.** This method of training is in vogue in those trades, crafts and technical fields in which a long period is required for gaining proficiency. The trainees serve as apprentices to experts for long periods, say, seven years. They have to work in direct association with and also under the direct supervision of their masters. The object of such training is to make the trainees all-round craftsmen. The apprentices are paid their remuneration according to the apprenticeship agreements.

(iv) **Internship Training.** This method of training refers to a joint programme of training in which the technical institutions and business houses co-operate. The object of such co-operation is to provide such training that will bring about a balance between theory and practice. For this purpose students may be sent to factories for practical training in between their terms at schools.

(v) **Learner Training.** The "learners" are those who join industry for semi-skilled jobs without any prior knowledge about the elements of industrial engineering. They have, therefore, to undergo a programme of education and training. For this purpose, it may become necessary to send them to vocational schools for some time for the study of arithmetic, workshop mathematics and learning operation of machines. After this they may be assigned regular production jobs.

Training and Development

In a rapidly changing society, employee's training and development are not only an activity that is desirable but also an activity that an organization must commit resources to if it has to maintain a viable and knowledgeable work force.

Training is a process of learning a sequence of programmed behaviour. It is application of knowledge. It gives people an awareness of the rules and procedures to guide their behaviour. It attempts to improve their performance on the current job or prepare them for an intended job. *Development* is a related process. It covers not only those activities which improve job performance but also those which bring about growth of their personality; help individuals in the progress towards maturity and actualization of their potential capacities. In organizational terms, it is intended to equip persons to earn promotion and hold greater responsibility. Training a person for a bigger and higher job is development.

Distinction Between Training and Development

"*Training*" is short-term process utilizing a systematic and organized procedure by which non-managerial personnel learn technical knowledge and skills for a definite purpose. On the other hand, "*Development*" is a long-term educational process utilising a systematic and organized procedure by which managerial personnel learn conceptual and theoretical knowledge for general purpose.

"*Training*" refers only to instruction in technical and mechanical operations, while "*development*" refers to philosophical and theoretical educational concepts. Training is designed for non-managers, while development involves managerial personnel.

Training and development differ in four ways:

(a) "What" is learned;

(b) "Who" is learning;

(c) "Why" such learnings take place; and

(d) "When" learning occurs.

The difference may be stated as

Learning Dimensions	Training	Development
Who ?	Non-managerial personnel	Managerial personnel
What?	Technical and mechanical operation	Theoretical, conceptual ideas
Why?	Specific job-related purpose	General knowledge
When ?	Short-term	Long-term

Steps in Training Programs

1. **Discovering or Identifying Training Needs.** A training program should be established only when it is felt that it would assist in the solution of specific operational problems. The most important step, in the first place, is to make a thorough analysis of the entire organization, its operations and manpower resources available in order to find out "The trouble spots" where training may be needed.
2. **Getting Ready for the Job.** Under this step, it is to be decided who is to be trained — the newcomer or the old employee, or the supervisory staff or all of them selected from different departments.

   The trainer has to be prepared for the job, because he is the key figure in the entire program.
3. **Preparation of the Learner.** This step consists:

   (i) In putting the learner at ease;

   (ii) In stating the importance and ingredients of the job and its relationship to work flow;

   (iii) In explaining why he is being taught;

   (iv) In creating interest and encouraging questions. Finding out what the learner already knows about his job or other jobs;

   (v) In explaining the 'why' of the whole job and relating it to some other job, the worker already knows;

   (vi) In placing the learner as close to his normal working position as possible; and

   (vii) In familiarising him with the equipments, materials, tools and trade terms.

4. **Presentation of Operation and Knowledge.** The trainer should clearly *tell, show, illustrate* and *question* in order to put over the new knowledge and operations. The learner should be told of the sequence of the entire job and why each step in its performance is necessary. Instructions should be given clearly, completely and patiently; there should be an emphasis on key points and one point should be explained at a time. For this purpose, the trainer should demonstrate or make use of audio-visual aids and should ask the trainee to repeat the operations. He should also be encouraged to ask questions in order to indicate that he really knows and understands the job.
5. **Performance Try out.** Under this, the trainee is asked to go through the job several times slowly, explaining him each step. Mistakes are corrected and if necessary, some complicated steps are done for the trainee the first time. The trainee is asked to do the job, gradually building up skill and speed. As soon as the trainee demonstrates that he can do the job in a right way, he is put on his own, but not abandoned.
6. **Follow-up.** This step is undertaken with a view to test the effectiveness of training efforts. This consists of:
   (a) Putting a trainee "on his own."
   (b) Checking frequently to be sure that he has followed instructions; and
   (c) Tapering off extra supervision and close follow-up until he is qualified to work with normal supervision.

Exit Policy and Its Implications

The government of India adopted a new economic policy and one of the important aspects of the liberalised economic policy is the Exit Policy.

Under this policy, the govt. has allowed business and industrial establishment, to reduce their excess staff and employers. The reduction of excess staff is a result of restructuring of organizations due to modernising, applying new technology and new methods of operation so that the industrial organizations could operate economically and withstand the competition with companies and organizations which have accepted foreign collaborations, innovative methods and technology upgradation, rendering some employees' services.

SUCCESSION PLANNING

Exit Policy

Voluntary Retirement Schemes - have been legally found to be giving no problem to employers, employees and their unions. The essence of the voluntary retirement scheme which is approved by the government, involves voluntary separation of employees who are above the age of 40 years or have served the company or establishment for minimum 10 years. The company, may offer different separation benefits to employees in different age groups subject to overall benefits which are tax exempted upto a limit of Rs. 5 lakhs. Public sector undertakings, however, have to obtain prior approval of the Government before offering and implementing the voluntary retirement schemes.

The Reasons for Proposing V.R.S.

(i) Recession in business.
(ii) Intense competition which makes the establishment unviable unless downsizing is resorted to.
(iii) Changes in technology, production process, innovation, new product line.
(iv) Re-alignment of business - due to market conditions.

(v) Joint-ventures with foreign collaborations.
(vi) Takeovers and mergers.
(vii) Business re-engineering process.
(viii) Product/Technology obsolencences.

Procedure for Voluntary Retirement Scheme

The employer has to issue a circular communicating of his decisions to offer voluntary retirement scheme - mentioning therein.

(a) The reasons for downsizing.
(b) Eligibility *i.e.*, who are eligible to apply for voluntary retirement.
(c) The age limit and the minimum service period of employees who can apply (Employees who are 40 and above and those who have completed minimum 10 years of service in the establishment).
(d) The benefits that are offered.
(e) The right of an employer to accept or reject any application for voluntary retirement.
(f) The circular may indicate income tax incidence on any voluntary retirement benefits which are in excess of Rs. 5 lacs, which is maximum tax free benefit under such schemes.
(g) It should also indicate that those employees who opt for voluntary retirement and accept the benefits under such scheme shall not be eligible in future for employment in the establishment.

Steps to be taken for introducing and implementing Voluntary Retirement Scheme

(i) If the company is public sector undertaking obtaining approval of the Government is necessary.
(ii) Identify departments/employees to whom V.R.S. is to be offered (Target group of employees - age above 40 years and employees with more than 10 years of service in the company).
(iii) If there is a union of employees in the establishment, involve the union by communicating to them the reasons, the target group and the benefits to be offered to those who opt for the scheme.
(iv) Formulate the terms of V.R.S. and benefits to be offered are to be mentioned in the circular and decide the period during which the scheme is to be kept open.
(v) Motivate the managers through counselling.
(vi) Counselling employees is an essential part of implementing the scheme. The counselling should include what the retiring employee can do in future *i.e.*, rehabilitation, how to manage the funds received under the scheme.
(vii) After receipt of applications for accepting V.R.S., scrutinise, decide whose applications are to be accepted and those whose are not to be accepted.
(viii) For those whose applications are to be accepted prepare a worksheet showing the benefits, each will receive including other dues like provident fund, gratuity and earned leave wages for the balance unveiled earned leave and tax incidence on any V.R.S. amount that exceed Rs. 5 lakhs.

Induction

Induction is a technique by which a new employee is rehabilited into his surroundings and introduced to the practices, policies and purposes of the organization. In other words, the idea is to welcome a newcomer, make him feel at home and generate in him a feeling that his own job, however small, is meaningful and has a significance as a part of the total organisation.

The purpose of induction is to introduce the new employee and the organization to each other, to help them become acquainted and to help them accommodate each other. The newcomer is explained what is expected of him and for this, he has explained the rules, regulations, policies and procedures that directly affect him. He is made aware of how his job fits into the overall operation of the organization, his own duties and responsibilities and to whom he should look for when he has any problem.

Induction Procedure

Each industry develops its own procedures as per its needs. The procedure should basically follow these steps:

First, the new person needs time and a place for report to work.

Second, it is very important that the supervisor or the immediate boss meet and welcome the employee to the organization.

Third, administrative work should be completed. Such items as vacations, probationary period, medical absences, suggestion systems should be covered.

Fourth, the departmental orientation can be conducted. This should include a get-acquainted talk, introduction to the department, explanation of the functions of the department and job instruction and to whom he should look for help when he has any problem.

Fifth, verbal explanations are supplemented by a wide variety of printed material, employee hand books, flyers, employee manuals, house-journals, picture stories, comics and cartoons, pamphlets, *etc.* alongwith short guided tour around the plant.

Typical Techniques of Induction Programs

A typical induction program should consist primarily of three steps:

(a) General orientation by the staff of the personnel department;

(b) Specific orientation by the job supervisor, or his representative; and

(c) Follow-up orientation by either the personnel department or the supervisor.

The first phase of the programme should ordinarily be conducted by the personnel department. This type of induction is general, because it gives the necessary general information about the history and operations of the firm-*the purpose of which is to help an employee to build up some pride and interest in the organisation*. Information is also given on specific employee services, such as pension, health and welfare plans, safety programmes *etc. The better policy is not to give everything in one day, but to administer smaller doses over a long period.*

At the second stage, induction should be conducted by the job supervisor. *Induction is specific and requires skill on the part of the foreman.* The employee is shown the department and his place of work, introduced to other employees, informed of the locations of the bathrooms, lavatories, canteens and time clock; and told about the organization's specific practices and customs. *The purpose of specific induction is to enable an employee to adjust himself to his work and environment.*

Follow-up induction takes place within one week to six months from the time of the initial hiring and orientation. It is conducted either by a foreman or a specialist. *Its purpose is to find out whether the employee is reasonably well-satisfied with him.*

COMPENSATION MANAGEMENT

The workmen's compensation Act, 1923 (Amended upto 1986)

- The Workmen's Compensation Act came into force in 1924. Before this act, it was a lengthy and costly process for a worker who had got injured in the course of employment to get proper compensation from the employer.
- Originally the act covered workers of certain specified industries, not drawing more than Rs. 300 p.m.
- The Act was amended subsequently in 1933, 1938, 1939, 1946, 1958, 1962, 1976 and 1986.

The details of this act are as follows:

Main Features of the Act

- The worker (or his dependents) can claim compensation if the injury has been caused by an accident in the course of the employment; provided he was not under the influence of drink or drug and the accident was not due to his wilful disobedience of the rules.
- The amount of compensation depends upon the result of the injury and the nature of disablement.
- All fatal accidents are to be brought to the notice of the commissioner and the employer shall deposit the amount of compensation with him (i.e. the commissioner) within 30 days.

Important Definitions

1. **Dependent mean**
   - A widow, a minor son, unmarried daughter or a widowed mother, and
   - If wholly or in part dependent on the earnings of the worker at the time of his or her death,
     (i) a widower, a minor brother and unmarried sister;
     (ii) a widowed daughter-in-law and
     (iii) a minor child of predeceased daughter, *etc.*
2. **Minor.** A person below 18 years of age.
3. Partial disablement means disablement of temporary nature and which reduces the earning capacity of a workman.
4. Total disablement implies such disablement which (temporarily or permanently) incapacitates a workman for all work and he cannot earn at all (for a period or forever).
5. Workman means a person (other than one whose employment is of casual nature and who is employed otherwise than for the purpose of the employer's trade or business) who is
   (i) a railway servant and not permanently employed in any administrative capacity;
   (ii) getting wages not exceeding
   Rs. 500– as per Act of 1923
   Rs. 1000–As per Act modified in 1976.

Employer's Liability for Compensation

- The employer is liable to compensate if
  (i) injury has been caused by accident;
  (ii) during the course of employment; and
  (iii) has resulted in workman's death; permanent or temporary, total or partial disablement.

- The employer is not liable to pay compensation if
  (i) the injury disables a workman for less than 3 days;
  (ii) the injury is caused by an accident which occurred while the workman was under the influence of drink or drugs;
  (iii) the injury is caused due to wilful disobedience of the rules by the workman or
  (iv) the injury is caused owing to the wilful removal of any safety guard by the workman.

Employer's Liability in Case of Occupational Diseases

If the disease contracted is an occupational disease peculiar to the employment (such as silicosis to foundry workers), the employer shall give compensation to the workman.

Amount of Compensation

(a) Where death results from the injury	An amount equal to 40% of the monthly wages of the deceased workman multiplied by the relevant factor. or An amount of 20,000 rupees, whichever is more.
(b) Where permanent total disablement results from the injury	An amount equal to 50% of the monthly wages of the injured workman multiplied by the relevant factor or An amount of 24000 rupees, whichever is more.

Where the monthly wages of a workman exceed one thousand rupees, the monthly wages for the purpose of classes (a) and (b) above shall be deemed to be 1000 rupees only.

(c) Where temporary disablement whether total or partial results from the injury, a half monthly payment of the sum equivalent to 25% of monthly wages of the workman, to be paid.

Distribution of Compensation

- Payment of compensation in respect of death of a workman or under legal disability shall be deposited by the employer with the commissioner. Employer should not make payment of compensation directly.
- An employer of course can give advance to any dependent on account of compensation not exceeding Rs. 100.
- The commissioner, after deducting this advance, may allot the entire amount of the compensation to anyone dependent.

Notice and Claims of Accident

- A workman injured in an accident should first of all give in writing a notice of the accident to the employer. The purpose of giving a notice is to enable the employer to check the facts of the accident and also to enable the workman to take steps to mitigate the consequences of the accident.
- The notice should contain particulars of the workman, date of accident and cause of accident.
- A claim for compensation must be made within two years of the occurrence of the accident or within two years of the date of death.
- In case of occupational diseases the period of two years is counted from the day the workman gives notice of the disablement to his employer.

- Where the commissioner receives an information about fatal accident, he may send a notice to workman's employer asking the circumstances which led to workman's death, about deposition of compensation, etc.

Medical Examination

- An injured workman who has submitted a notice, shall present himself for the medical examination, if the employer wants.
- Such an offer by the employer must be free of charge and within 3 days from the time at which service of notice has been affected.
- If a workman does not present himself for the medical examination, his right for compensation shall be suspended for the period of refusal and he will get full compensation only after he provides sufficient cause for not presenting himself for the medical examination.
- If a workman whose right to compensation has been suspended, dies without presenting himself for the medical examination, the commissioner, if he thinks fit, may direct the amount of compensation to the dependents of the deceased workman.

Appointment of Commissioner

The State Government may, by notification in his Official Gazette appoint any person to be commissioner for workmen's compensation for such areas as may be specified in this notification. Every commissioner is deemed to be a public servant within the meaning of the Indian Penal Code.

WAGES AND SALARY ADMINISTRATION

For the worker, wages constitute the income by which he lives. Wages include both money and non-money payments. Non-money payments may also he called as Fringe benefits. Fair wage is a wage paid to a worker which is fair as regards to the work accomplished by him and which is sufficient to fulfil his basic necessities of life.

Systems of Wage Payment

There are two fundamental methods of remunerating labour for its services to an industrial concern:

(i) a man may be paid on the basis of the time that he spends on his job or
(ii) he may be paid for the quantity of work that he performs.

Most of the wage systems in vogue in industry are modifications or combinations of the primary principles of payment by time and payment by results. In its simple form, time wage system adopts time as the basis of labour remuneration without specifically taking the output into account. On the other hand, in the simplest type of payment by results, wages are calculated on the basis of production irrespective of time spent on work.

Time Wage System

The time wage system is by far the simplest and historically the oldest method of wage payment. It is also referred to as the 'day work' system of wages – a name which dates back to the time when a day was considered to be a convenient unit for the calculation of a workman's wages. In its present form, it refers to the arrangement whereby the employer buys the time of the worker in units which may vary from one hour to one month in duration. In other words, the worker is paid on the basis of the time that he devotes to his work at the work place. Thus, if a worker is paid at the rate of Rs. 2

per day, his wages for 15 days of work would be equal to Rs. 2 × 15 = Rs. 30. Hence time wage = T × R where 'T' is the time spent at the work place and 'R' is the rate of pay per unit of time. The quantity of output turned out by him is not specifically considered while remunerating labour under this system.

JOB EVALUATION

Time wage system offers the following advantages:

(i) It gives the workers a sense of security which is so important for sustaining their interest in work. The remuneration under this system is certain and the worker has not to suffer a cut even when his efficiency is temporarily impaired by an injury or sickness.

(ii) In those lines of production, where skill of the worker and quality of product matter more than speed or quantity of output, workers can devote themselves to their jobs with greater care and attention if they are assured of a fixed time rate.

(iii) It follows from above that the workers will avoid over speeding and the consequent damage to equipment if they are paid a fixed time-rate independent of production.

(iv) The calculation of wages is simplified by this system. The cost of operating a time wage scheme is almost negligible because the only record that has to be maintained is that of the time for which a worker has been at his work.

(v) In those cases where the production is not standardized, the productivity of a worker cannot be accurately measured. In such instances, time wage is the only just method of wage payment.

(vi) In modern factories, production is carried on a mass scale, usually on the assembly-line. Under such a set-up, a particular worker cannot perform his work faster than the other members of his group. If a worker performs his part of the job more quickly than others, he may have to be idle till he receives more work from the workers preceding him on the assembly-line.

Ultimately, therefore, his output will be the same as that of the group as a whole. The wages of the workers in such manufacturing organisations are paid on time basis rather than on piece basis.

(vii) Trade unions accept this system of wage payment quite willingly because it does not create any distinctions in the ranks of workers on account of differences in efficiency.

Drawbacks

The time wage system is found lacking in following respects:

(i) It does not distinguish between the efficient and inefficient and between the honest worker and the shirker. In other words, it offers no positive inducement to the worker to improve his performance.

(ii) The superior workers are repressed under this system because they are paid at par with the inferior workers.

(iii) From the point of view of the employer, it creates difficulties in the calculation of the labour cost and the cost of production per unit. The output may be fluctuating for same amount of wages.

(iv) It offers too much of security to workers.

(v) It follows from above that the efficient use of this system can be made only when there is adequate provision for effective supervision so that workers do not waste their time. This also adds to the cost of production.

Modified Time Rate

Wages may also be paid according to some modifications of time wage system. Under the Time Rate at High Wage Levels Plan, the workers, whose output remains below a specified standard, get a time rate which is lower than that given to those who are able to attain or exceed the standard. This method has the advantage of offering the necessary incentive to the high-class labour which is important for obtaining a high production level. But it can be applied only where the work can be graded according to skill and where a worker can be kept at the job, operation or machine demanding the same degree of skill. This plan is also called the 'multiple time plan.' Another modification of the time wage system is the 'Graduated Time Rate Plan'. Under such a plan, time rates are adjusted to suit general or particular economic circumstances or to allow for different personal qualities in the workers. Thus, the time rate may be suitably adjusted by the cost of living index or awards for the merits of the individual workers.

Piece Wage System

Under this system a worker is paid for the amount of work performed rather than for the time spent on the job. A specified rate of wage may be fixed per unit of output measured in terms of tonnes of coal, number of pieces of garments or pounds of yarn. The basis of pay in this case is the output or production and the wages are paid independent of time. If, the worker takes an unreasonably long time to do a particular job or produce a particular product, the employer, of course, will naturally ask him to improve his speed or quit, in fact, the worker will himself realise that it will not be financially worthwhile for him to work on a job if he cannot work with some speed and produce enough to earn a wage that will meet his personal requirements.

The wage payable to a worker under this plan is calculated by multiplying the number of products by piece-rate. In other words, the wages of a worker = N × R where 'N' is the number of units of a product produced and 'R' is the wage rate per unit of product. If a worker produces 15 units when the piece-rate is Rs. 2 per unit, the total wages will be Rs. 15 × 2 = Rs. 30.

Evaluation

The piece-wage system can be commended on the basis of the following advantages that it offers:

(i) It distinguishes between the efficient and less efficient workers and offers direct and positive encouragement to the superior workers to realise their ambitions.

(ii) It ensures fairness to everyone by relating wages to results. People with poor performance are penalised.

(iii) The cost can easily be calculated for the preparation of estimates, *etc.*, because the cost of labour per unit is constant.

(iv) Since the workers are themselves interested in the maximization of wages through the maximization of output, they have not to be goaded by foremen. Strict supervision is not necessary under this system.

Drawbacks

The system suffers from the following drawbacks:

(i) It makes the workers feel insecure because the wages are paid on the basis of output. If, therefore, the worker's efficiency is temporarily reduced because of a factor beyond his control, wages will be lower than otherwise.

(ii) It lays so much stress on the quantity of production that the quality is quite often lost sight of. To ensure proper quality of production, rigid inspection and quality control become necessary.

(iii) Labour unions oppose it on ethical grounds, because it creates greed and unhealthy rivalries born out of suspicion and jealousy among the workers. Politically too, piece rates weaken labour unions.

(iv) In their zeal to maximize output, the workers may work at excessive speeds and may mishandle and damage machinery. In the process of over-speeding, they may injure their health and efficiency.

(v) If workers are not able to maximize production due to some fault on the part of management (say, defective production control, *etc.*), they are likely to develop dissatisfaction which may affect the employer-employee relations adversely.

(vi) The setting of piece-rates may itself become a controversial issue which may spoil industrial relations.

(vii) It involves the maintenance of elaborate production records and pay rolls.

The Standard Hour System

A variation of the piece wage system known by this title (also known as the One Hundred Per Cent Gain Sharing System) has the following features:

(i) A standard time is allowed to complete a particular job (say 10 hours).

(ii) A time rate in the form of a specified rate per hour is set for each class of work (*e.g.*, Re. 1 per hour).

(iii) If the worker, completes the job in standard time or less, the worker is paid for his standard time at the specified rate per hour (say, if the work is finished in 8 hours, the worker will be paid for 10 hours at the rate of Re. 1 an hour, *i.e.*, Rs. 10).

(iv) If the worker takes more than the standard time to complete the job, he may be paid at the guaranteed time rate for the time he actually spent on the job.

(v) If there is no guaranteed time rate, he will be paid only for standard time.

Incentive Plans

Both time wage and piece wage plans have their own strong points and drawbacks. As has already been observed, the time wage plan assigns the gains or losses arising from variations in workers' productivity to the employer; the piece-wage system, on the other hand, offers no guarantee of a consistently reasonable wage and passes on the gains or losses owing to changes in worker's productivity to them. Under the incentive plans of wage payment, however, both the basic systems are blended together in such a manner that the workers are induced to increase their productivity and the employer happily parts with a part of his increased revenue to encourage the workers towards this end. Under such systems, both time and speed form the basis of wage payment.

The following are few Incentive plans:

1. **Halsey Plan.** It is an American plan originated by F. A. Halsey to encourage efficiency amongst workers as well as to guarantee them wages according to time basis. The standard time required for a job is determined beforehand on the basis of time and motion studies and/or from past records. Workers who perform the job in less than the standard time and thus save time are rewarded with a bonus, but the worker who takes longer than the standard time is not punished, and is paid wages according to time wage system. The total earnings of a worker under this is equal to the money value of $33\frac{1}{3}$ per cent of the time saved in case of standard time set on previous experience and 50 per cent of the time saved when the standards are scientifically set. Thus, if a job requiring 20 hours is done in 16 hours, the workers will be paid wages for 16 hours + wage for 50 per cent of the time saved, namely, 2 hours. In all, therefore, the worker will get wages for 18 hours. If a worker is paid at the rate of 50 p. per hour, his wages will be calculated as follow: 16 x .50 + 4/2 x .50 *i.e.*, Rs. 8.00 + 1.00 = Rs. 9.00.
2. **Rowan plan.** Introduced in 1901, by James Rowan of David Rowan and Sons, Glasgow, this plan is quite popular in England. Wages, according to time basis, are guaranteed and the slow worker is not made to suffer. A standard time is determined beforehand and a bonus is

paid according to time save. The only difference between Halsey Plan and Rowan Plan relates to the calculation of the bonus. Under this plan, bonus is based on that proportion of the time saved which the time taken bears to the standard time. It can be expressed as follows:

$$\text{Bonus} = \text{Time saved} \times 16 \times 80\text{ P} + 4 \times \frac{16}{20} \times 80 \times \text{Hourly rate}$$

Thus, if a 20-hour job is done in 16 hours and if the hourly rate is 80 paise, the total earnings of the worker will be

$$16 \times 80\text{ P} + 4 \times \frac{16}{20} \times 80\text{ P}$$

or Rs. 12.80 + 2.56 = Rs. 15.36 in all.

3. **Taylor's Differential Piece Wage Plan.** F.W. Taylor, the founder of scientific management, devised this system in 1880. He was opposed to the payment of wages on time basis and, therefore, under his system there was no guarantee of wages. On the other hand, Taylor was firmly of the view that the standard of performance in terms of a fair day's work can be fixed quite accurately through careful time study. Under Taylor's plan, standard of output is fixed per hour or per day and two piece wage rates are laid. Those exceeding the standard or even just attaining it, are entitled to the higher rate and those, whose output is less than the standard output, are paid at a lower rate. For example, the standard may be fixed at 40 units per day and the piece rates may be 30 P. and 25 P. per unit. If a worker produces 40 units, he should get wages at the rate of 30 P. *i.e.*, Rs. 12.00 , but if he produces only 39 units he would be paid at the rate of 25 P. per unit only and his wages would come to Rs. 9.75. This shows that the penalty of the output being less than the standard output is too severe that the worker would be prompted to try to produce as much as the standard output.
4. **Merric Differential or Multiple Piece-rate plan.** It is a modification of the Taylor's scheme. While Taylor prescribes two-rates–one, for the slow and the inefficient workers and the second, for the efficient ones, this plan lays down three rates: one for the beginners, the second for the developing workers and the third for the highly skilled and efficient workers. Like Taylor's plan, it lays down a standard output through time studies and expects the workers to attain it. No guaranteed time rate is set. Those who are able to produce upto 83% of the standard output become entitled to the first and the lowest piece rate. Those whose output exceeds 83% of the standard but does not reach the standard are paid the second higher rate which includes an increase of 10%. Those who attain or exceed the standard get the third, *i.e.*, the highest piece rate on their output which includes a further increase of 10% in the basic rate.
5. **Emerson's Efficiency Plan.** Emerson was also a proponent of scientific management and he devised this system of wages to encourage efficiency amongst workers. Under this system, wages on the time basis are guaranteed even to those workers whose output is below the standard. The workers who prove efficient are paid a bonus. For the purpose of determining efficiency, either the standard output per unit of time is fixed, or the standard time for a job is determined and efficiency is determined on the basis of a comparison of actual performance against the standard.
6. **Gantt's Task and Bonus Plan.** Under it, wages on time basis are guaranteed to every worker. On the basis of careful study of workers and conditions of work, a good standard of performance under the best conditions is determined. Bonus is paid to those workers who show cent per cent efficiency. No bonus is payable to a worker if his efficiency is less than 100%. Thus, if a 10-hour job is done in 10½ hours showing an efficiency of 95 per cent, the worker concerned will get wages on time basis for 10 ½ hours without any bonus. But at 100 per cent efficiency a bonus of 20 per cent is paid, so that if a 10-hour job is done in 10 hours

and if the hourly rate is 50 P, the worker would get wages for 10 hours, namely, Rs. 5.00 plus a bonus of 20 per cent, namely, Re. 1.00 making a total of Rs. 6.00. If the output reaches the standard task in less than the time set for it, the piece rate will be paid. This system is therefore, essentially a piece rate system with a guarantee of wages on time basis.

7. **Bedeaux Point Premium Plan.** The chief novelty of this plan is that the value of time saved is divided between workers and foreman, three-fourths to workers and one-fourth to foreman. This is done on the basis that a worker cannot show good results if his foreman does not fully co-operate with him; therefore, the foreman is also entitled to an incentive. The wages payable to the worker under this plan can also be expressed as wages for the actual time worked plus 75 per cent of the time saved.
8. **Hayne's Plan.** Under this plan, the standard time of a job is fixed in terms of MANT which is the short form of man-minutes. The worker is paid wages on time basis in any case but if the standard time of various jobs done by him exceeds the actual time, that is to say, if there is a saving of time, the worker will be paid a share of it. The saving is naturally calculated in terms of mants (as in case of Bedeaux's plan). The results saving is divided by 60 to convert it into hours. By multiplying hours so calculated by the time rate, the total value of the time saved is determined.

   The benefit of time saved is divided as follows:

   (a) If the work is standardized, 5/6th to the workers and 1/6th to the foreman,

   (b) if the work is non-standardised 5/10th to the worker, 1/10th to the foreman and 4/10 th to management.

   Standardised work means work which is of a repetitive nature and non-standardised work means work of different nature every time. The bonus payable to the foreman is credited to a fund. If the worker loses time due to a fault of the foreman, the foreman will lose his bonus to the extent the workers has to be paid wages for idle time. No mants are credited to the worker for a product that does not pass inspection.
9. **Priestman Bonus System.** This is a plan which takes the productivity of all workers as a whole into account. If, during a year, the output rises either above the standard output or the output of the previous year, the wages of the workers are increased in the same ratio. Thus, if in 1968 the output per worker per hour came to 10 units while in 1969, the hourly output per worker is, on the average, 11 units, the wages in 1969 would be 10 per cent higher than in 1968. Since this system does not take into account individual efficiency, it will not have a good effect upon individual initiative though workers as a whole may begin to feel that there is some benefit from increased output.
10. **Barth Variable Sharing Plan.** This plan is similar to the Halsey and Rowan plans because it is also based on standard time set for the completion of a job. Unlike those plans, however, it does not guarantee a time rate. Wages under this plan are calculated according to the following formula:

$$\sqrt{\text{Standard hours} \times \text{actual hours}} \times \text{rate per hour}$$

11. **Group Incentive Plans.** The plans which have been discussed above represent incentive plans for individual workers but certain pieces of work can be done only by groups of workers. Group incentive plans are, therefore, necessary for efficient completion of such tasks. But it should be remembered that, as far as possible, group-work should be avoided because all the members of a group would receive bonus on the same basis even if some of them did not contribute effectively to the completion of the job. This has an undesirable effect on other members of the group and generally, it is found that group-work is not done efficiently. But, if

there is group-work and incentive is to be provided, it is generally done by fixing a piece rate for the entire job for all the workers. Care should be taken to divide the piece rate bonus amongst the members of the group according to their skill and to the time devoted by them. For this purpose, the wages of various workers should be calculated first according to time basis and then the extra wage which the group might earn on piece basis should be divided amongst the members in the ratio of wages calculated on time basis.

12. **The Scanlon Plan.** The plan which bears the name of Mr. Joseph Scanlon of the United Steel works of America is among the most popular plans for sharing the gains from improvements in productivity. According to this formula, for each 1% of increase in productive efficiency, a 1 % participating bonus is paid to each employee covered by the plan. All employees except the top management share in the bonus. Thus, foremen, superintendents, engineers and other managerial staff have a recognised part in the plan. The workers who were previously working on piece rates were guaranteed their regular hourly rate plus their average incentive earnings before the operation of the plan. One-half of the first 15% of any bonus earned in any month is set aside as a reserve. Such a reserve fund is to be used to meet fluctuations in labour costs. Any "unused portion" of this reserve by November of the given year is paid out in December and a new reserve fund is created.

PERFORMANCE APPRAISAL

Appraisal is the evaluation of worth, quality or merit. Performance appraisal is a systematic evaluation of personnel by superiors or others familiar with their performance. It is also described as merit rating in which one individual is ranked as better or worse in comparison to others. It is a systematic and objective way of judging the relative work or ability of an employee in performing his job. Performance appraisal has two basis:

(i) appraisal of employers according to traits, attributes and general behaviour on the job.
(ii) appraisal of results, work and goals achieved by the employees.

Methods of Performance Appraisal

1. **Ranking.** In this method a person is ranked against others on the basis of certain traits and characteristics.
2. **Paired Comparison.** In this method, each person is compared with other persons taking only one at a time. Usually only one trait, over all suitability to perform the job, is considered.
3. **Grading.** In this method certain categories of abilities or performance are defined well in advance and persons are put in particular category depending on their traits and characteristics.
4. **Forced-choice method.** This method contains a series of groups of statements and the rater checks how effectively the statement describes each individual being evaluated.
5. **Critical Incident Method.** In this method, only critical incidents and behaviour associated with these incidents are taken for evaluation.
6. **Graphic Rating Scale.** This method assesses the degree of certain qualities required for a job. The central idea behind this scaling is to provide the rater with a continuum representing various degrees of a particular quality.

INDUSTRIAL RELATIONS IN INDIA

The term 'Industrial Relations' is used to refer to the relations between the parties concerned with industry. Under the present-day factory system of industrial production, the two parties which come into direct contact with each other are the workers and the management representing the employer. Cordial and peaceful Industrial Relations between the employees and the employer are highly essential for increasing productivity and the economic growth of the country. Industrial relationship is the composite result of the attitudes and approaches of the employees towards each other with regard to planning supervision, direction and co-ordination of the activities of an organisation with a minimum of human effort, spirit of co-operation and with proper regard for the genuine well being of all the members of the organisation.

The basic requirements of an industrial relation programme are:

(i) To have the support of top management.
(ii) To be leased on second personnel policy.
(iii) To follow proper practices.
(iv) To follow up and evaluate the pattern of employee action.

The important functions of industrial relations are as follows:

(i) Employee relations
(ii) Labour relations
(iii) Public relations

PERFORMANCE APPRAISAL INCLUDING 360 DEGREE PERFORMANCE APPRAISAL

PERFORMANCE APPRAISAL

The 360 degrees Performance Appraisal method was first used in the 1940s. Analogous to the multiple points on a compass, the 360 method provides each employee the opportunity to receive performance feedback from his or her supervisor, peers, staff members, co-workers and customers.

360-degree feedback or multi-source feedback is an appraisal or performance assessment tool that incorporates feedback from all who observe and are affected by the performance of a candidate.

For which Category of Employees is this Tool Used?

Usually, this tool is used for employees at middle and senior level. The complexity of their roles enables the organisation to generate sufficient data from all stakeholders for a meaningful assessment.

Which Organisations use 360 Degree to Assess Employee Performance?

Most organisations that focus on employee development use the 360-degree tool to assess performance and potential of staff and enable the employees to map their career path based on the feedback. Organisations take 360-degree feedback about an employee before taking a major decision about the professional's career.

The results from 360-degree feedback are often used by the person receiving the feedback to plan training and development. Results are also used by some organizations in making administrative decisions, such as pay or promotion. When this is the case, the 360 assessment is for evaluation purposes, and is sometimes called a "360-degree review."

360 degree feedback is the most comprehensive appraisal where the feedback about the employees' performance comes from all the sources that come in contact with the employee on his job. this method is being used in the (MARUTHI SUZUKI Motors and HCL)

Who are the Stakeholders in Doing 360-Degree Assessment?

360 degree respondents for an employee can be his/her peers, managers (i.e. superior), subordinates, team members, customers, suppliers/ vendors - anyone who comes into contact with the employee and can provide valuable insights and information or feedback regarding the "on-the-job" performance of the employee.360 degree appraisal has four integral components:

Self-appraisal gives a chance to the employee to look at his/her strengths and weaknesses, his achievements, and judge his own performance. Superior's appraisal forms the traditional part of the 360 degree appraisal where the employees' responsibilities and actual performance is rated by the superior.

Subordinates appraisal gives a chance to judge the employee on the parameters like communication and motivating abilities, superior's ability to delegate the work, leadership qualities etc. Also known as internal customers, the correct feedback given by peers can help to find employees' abilities to work in a team, co-operation and sensitivity towards others.

Self-assessment is an indispensable part of 360 degree appraisals and therefore 360 degree Performance appraisal have high employee involvement and also have the strongest impact on behavior and performance. It provides a "360-degree review" of the employees' performance and is considered to be one of the most credible performance appraisal methods.

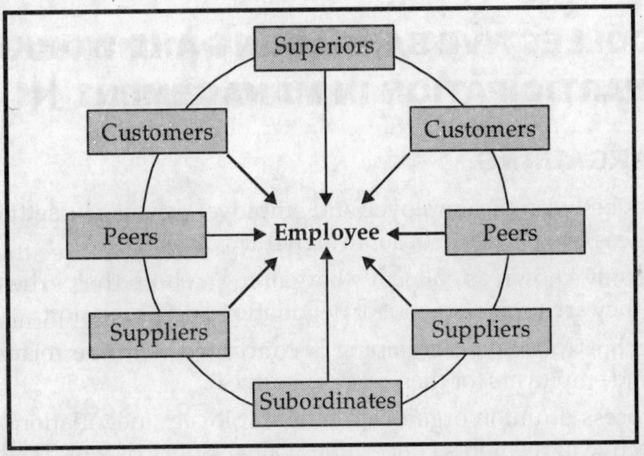

360 degree appraisal is also a powerful developmental tool because when conducted at regular intervals (say yearly) it helps to keep a track of the changes others' perceptions about the employees. A 360 degree appraisal is generally found more suitable for the managers as it helps to assess their leadership and managing styles. This technique is being effectively used across the globe for performance appraisals. Some of the organizations following it are Wipro, Infosys, and Reliance Industries etc.

Advantages of 360 Degree Appraisal

- Offer a more comprehensive view towards the performance of employees.
- Improve credibility of performance appraisal.
- Such colleague's feedback will help strengthen self-development.
- Increases responsibilities of employees to their customers.
- The mix of ideas can give a more accurate assessment.
- Opinions gathered from lots of staff are sure to be more persuasive.

- Not only manager should make assessments on its staff performance but other colleagues should do, too.
- People who undervalue themselves are often motivated by feedback from others.
- If more staff takes part in the process of performance appraisal, the organizational culture of the company will become more honest.

Disadvantages of 360 Degree Appraisal

- Taking a lot of time, and being complex in administration.
- Extension of exchange feedback can cause troubles and tensions to several staff.

Who should Conduct 360 Degree Performance Appraisal?

- Subordinates
- Peers
- Managers (i.e. superior)
- Team members
- Customers
- Suppliers / vendors
- Anyone who comes into contact with the employee and can provide valuable insights and information.

COLLECTIVE BARGAINING AND WORKERS' PARTICIPATION IN MANAGEMENT

COLLECTIVE BARGAINING

Industrial disputes between the employee and employer can also be settled by discussion and negotiation between these two parties in order to arrive at a decision.

This is also commonly known as collective bargaining as both the parties eventually agree to follow a decision that they arrive at after a lot of negotiation and discussion.

According to **Beach**, "Collective Bargaining is concerned with the relations between unions reporting employees and employers (or their representatives).

It involves the process of union organization of employees, negotiations administration and interpretation of collective agreements concerning wages, hours of work and other conditions of employees arguing in concerted economic actions dispute settlement procedures".

According to **Flippo**, "Collective Bargaining is a process in which the representatives of a labor organization and the representatives of business organization meet and attempt to negotiate a contract or agreement, which specifies the nature of employee-employer union relationship".

"Collective Bargaining is a mode of fixing the terms of employment by means of bargaining between organized body of employees and an employer or association of employees acting usually through authorized agents. The essence of Collective Bargaining is bargaining between interested parties and not from outside parties".

According to an **ILO Manual in 1960**, the Collective Bargaining is defined as:

"Negotiations about working conditions and terms of employment between an employer, a group of employees or one or more employers organization on the other, with a view to reaching an agreement."

It is also asserted that "the terms of agreement serve as a code defining the rights and obligations of each party in their employment relations with one another, if fixes large number of detailed conditions of employees and during its validity none of the matters it deals with, internal circumstances give grounds for a dispute counseling and individual workers".

Collective Bargaining Involves

(i) Negotiations
(ii) Drafting
(iii) Administration
(iv) Interpretation of documents written by employers, employees and the union representatives
(v) Organizational Trade Unions with open mind.

Forms of Collective Bargaining

The working of collective bargaining assumes various forms. In the first place, bargaining may be between the single employer and the single union, this is known as single plant bargaining. This form prevails in the United States as well as in India.

Secondly, the bargaining may be between a single firm having several plants and workers employed in all those plants. This form is called multiple plants bargaining where workers bargain with the common employer through different unions.

Thirdly, instead of a separate union bargaining with separate employer, all the unions belonging to the same industry bargain through their federation with the employer's federation of that industry. This is known as multiple employer bargaining which is possible both at the local and regional levels. Instances in India of this industry-wide bargaining are found in the textile industry.

The common malady of union rivalry, small firms and existence of several political parties has given rise to a small unit of collective bargaining. It has produced higher labour cost, lack of appreciation, absence of sympathy and economic inefficiency in the realm of industrial relationships. An industry-wide bargaining can be favourable to the economic and social interests of both the employers and employees.

Essential Pre-Requisites for Collective Bargaining:

Effective collective bargaining requires the following pre-requisites:

(i) Existence of a strong representative trade union in the industry that believes in constitutional means for settling the disputes.
(ii) Existence of a fact-finding approach and willingness to use new methods and tools for the solution of industrial problems. The negotiation should be based on facts and figures and both the parties should adopt constructive approach.
(iii) Existence of strong and enlightened management which can integrate the different parties, i.e., employees, owners, consumers and society or Government.
(iv) Agreement on basic objectives of the organisation between the employer and the employees and on mutual rights and liabilities should be there.
(v) In order that collective bargaining functions properly, unfair labour practices must be avoided by both the parties.
(vi) Proper records for the problem should be maintained.
(vii) Collective bargaining should be best conducted at plant level. It means if there are more than one plant of the firm, the local management should be delegated proper authority to negotiate with the local trade union.
(viii) There must be change in the attitude of employers and employees. They should realise that differences can be resolved peacefully on negotiating table without the assistance of third party.

(ix) No party should take rigid attitude. They should enter into negotiation with a view to reaching an agreement.

(x) When agreement is reached after negotiations, it must be in writing incorporating all term of the contract.

WORKERS PARTICIPATION IN MANAGEMENT

For higher productivity and sound industrial relations, it is extremely important to give the workers the place of partners in industry. The workers must be increasingly associated with the management of industrial undertakings so that they develop an awareness of the problems of industry and begin to feel that they have a positive contribution to make to the operation of their units. Such association with management should gradually give place to labour participation in management. The principle of participation seeks to meet the psychological needs of the workers, brings them closer to the management, promotes their interest in self-education, gives them an insight into the economic and technical conditions and purposes of the undertaking where they work and serves to bridge the gulf between the management and the workers.

Methods of Securing Worker's Participation in Management

1. **Co-partnership.** Co-partnership makes the workers shareholders in the company for which they are working. In this way, the workers become part-owners of the concern and acquire some hand in its internal management. They may be able to elect their representatives to the Board of Directors and participate in the management of the concern.
2. **Suggestions Scheme.** To arouse and maintain employees interest in the problems of their concern and its management, suggestions scheme can be used with advantage. The management may invite suggestions from the workers for improvement in the existing set-up and agree to pay suitable sums of money by way of rewards to the workers whose suggestions prove really useful. The payment may bear some proportion to the value of the suggestions in terms of improvement brought about or profit reaped. Such schemes are useful because they provide not only some new ideas to the management but also feeling of importance to the workers. Experience has shown that many of the suggestions thus made by the workers prove quite useful.
3. **Joint Consultation.** Joint consultation involves the setting up of joint committees comprising the representatives of management and workers to discuss various matters concerning working conditions of the workers. The decisions of such joint committees are usually advisory in character though the management will have little reason to reject the advice because it is the outcome of deliberations between the representatives of the management and labour. Generally, questions relating to wages, bonus and piece-rates are excluded from the scope of the committees. These matters are considered to be the subject-matter of collective bargaining. The long list of matters dealt with by joint committees includes accident prevention, management of canteens and other questions of physical welfare like meals, drinking water, safety, first-aid, issue and revision of work rules, avoidance of waste of time and materials, absenteeism and lateness, questions of discipline, training of apprentices, improvements in the production set-up, removal of grievances, adjustment of festival and national holidays, administration of welfare and fine funds, *etc.*
4. **Employee Representation on the Board of Directors.** The measures which have been outlined in the foregoing pages imply some measure of participation in and association with a limited parts of the management of the affairs of an industrial undertaking. Ultimately, however, full-fledged participation of workers in management can be ensured only through their

participation in the chief organ of management. In the long run, the workers would be satisfied with nothing short of their representation-on the body responsible for managing the affairs of the concern in all aspects, *i.e.*, the Board of Directors. The practice of allowing workers' elected representatives to sit on the Board of Directors has been adopted in several countries of the world. On the other hand, many others believe that the workers' representatives of the Board of Directors can serve to create an understanding of the problems of a going concern. It is claimed that the management will be able to inspire confidence in the minds of the workers in this way.

PERSONALITY

Personality and personality development are one of the key concepts in HRD. By personality, we mean the traits and characteristics that make up an individual's psyche and determine how he or she interacts with their environment.

Personality is determined by a number of factors including the traits that one is endowed with as a result of genetic factors and characteristics that have been developed due to his or her interactions with the environment. This is the variation of the so-called nature vs. nurture debate that revolves around whether an individual's personality is determined because of genes or whether the personality is a product of the environment. Without going into the specifics of the debate, it would suffice to say here that personality is a product of both characteristics that have been acquired as well as some natural abilities. The point here is that all of us are good at something and hence it is up to each one of us to select the profession or calling that suits us best.

Continuing in the same vein, some individuals have higher IQ levels whereas others have higher EQ levels (IQ refers to Intelligence Quotient and EQ refers to Emotional Intelligence Quotient). Further, we usually fare well at some tasks and not that well at other tasks. Hence, the aspect that should determine which profession or role in an organization suits us should be done according to our determination of which role suits us better.

The HRD function has a crucial role to play in matching individuals traits with job roles and determining whether an individual's personality attributes measure up to the requirements of the job that he or she is expected to do. This is the aspect of the skills and job description matrix where at the time of hiring, the HRD function maps the individual's skills against the traits necessary for the job and then assigns the individual to the role accordingly.

Further, personality is a function of the environment and is determined according to a "social mirror" where each of us are molded and shaped by the environmental influences. In turn, our personality determines how the environment is shaped. So, this symbiotic relationship between an individual's personality and the environment determines to a great extent whether the relationship between the individual and the environment is smooth or is characterized by friction.

In many technology and financial services companies where personality is important for the success of the individual in the chosen role, managers and people managers often spend a great deal of time with the employees to assess the "fit" between the individual and the job. They are assisted by the HRD function in this endeavor where the individual is deemed suitable for some roles and unsuitable for other roles. Only when there is a determination of the strategic fit between the individual and the role can there be job fulfillment and job satisfaction. Indeed, employees are consulted during their appraisals and 1:1 with the managers to determine this fit.

Finally, as discussed elsewhere, there is no point in having the right person for the wrong job and the wrong person for the right job. Hence, there has to be a rational assessment of the fit and then only can organizations achieve the balance that is needed for optimal performance.

PERCEPTION

Perception means perceiving, i.e., giving meaning to the environment around us. It can be defined as a process which involves seeing, receiving, selecting, organising, interpreting and giving meaning to the environment.

Nature of Perception

(1) Perception is the intellectual process.
(2) Perception is the basic cognitive or psychological process.
(3) Perception becomes a subjective process and different people may perceive the same event differently.

Perception and Sensation

There is a distinction between sensation and perception. Sensation is the response of a physical sensory organ. The physical senses are vision, hearing, tough, smell and taste. These senses are bombarded by stimuli and reactions in particular sense organ take place because of these, e.g., of sensation may be reaction of eye to colour, ear to sound and so on. Sensation percedes perception. Perception is much more than sensation. Perception depends upon the sensory raw data. The perceptual process adds to or/and subtracts from the sensory world. Perception is determined by both physiological and psychological characteristics, of the organism. However, sensation only activates the organs of the body and is not affected by such psychological factors as learning and motives. Activation of eyes to see an object is sensation and the inference what is being seen is perception. For managerial action, it is the latter which is important.

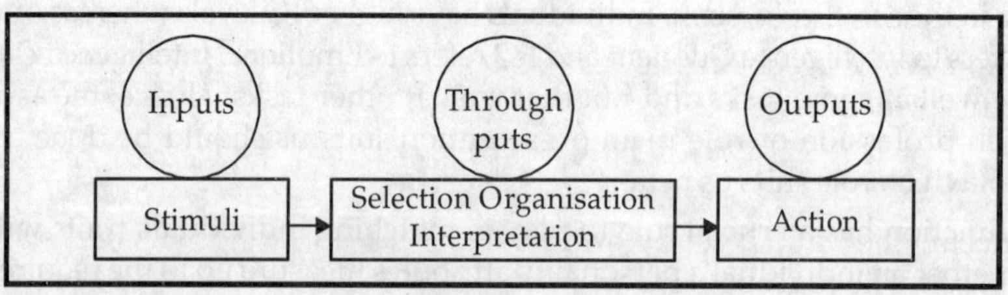

Perceptual Process

Perceptual Process

Perception is a process of receiving, selecting, organising, interpreting, checking and reacting to stimuli. This is like an input-through put-output process in which the stimuli can be considered as 'inputs' transformation of 'input' through selection, organization and interpretation as 'through puts' and the ultimate behaviour/action as 'output'. The whole perceptional process can be presented as follows : These are explained one by one

1. **Receiving Stimuli.** The first process in the perception is the presence of stimuli. The stimuli are received from the various sources. Through the five organs. It is a physiological aspect of perception process. Stimuli may be external to us (such as sound waves) and inside us (such as energy generation by muscles).
2. **Selection of Stimuli.** After receiving the stimuli or data, some are selected. Others are screened out. Two types of factors affect selection of stimuli for processing : external and internal factors. External factors relate to stimuli such as intensity of stimuli, its size, movement, repetition, etc. Internal factors, relate to the perceiver such as his/her age, learning, interest, etc. Normally, he will select the objects which interest him and will avoid that for which he is indifferent. This is also called 'selective perception'.

3. **Organization of Stimuli.** Organising the bits of information into a meaningful whole is called "organization". There are three ways by which the selected data, i.e., inputs are organised. These are : (i) Grouping, (ii) Closure and (iii) Simplification.
   (i) *Grouping.* In grouping, the perceiver groups the various stimuli on the basis of their similarity or proximity. For example, all the workers coming from the same place may be perceived as similar on the basis of proximity.
   (ii) *Closure.* When faced with incomplete information, people fill up the gaps themselves to make the information meaningful. This may be done on the basis of past experience, past data, or hunches. For example, in many advertisement, alphabets are written by putting electric bulbs indicating the shape of the concerned alphabets but broken lines. In such cases, people tend to fill up the gap among different bulbs to get meaning out of these.
   (iii) *Simplification.* People identify main stimulus features and assesses how they are organized. He interprets a stimulus situation, the perceiver simples the information.

Factors Influencing Perceptual Set External Factors

1. **Size.** Bigger size attracts the attention of the perceiver
2. **Intensity.** A loud sound, strong odor or bright light is noticed more as compared to a soft sound, weak odour or dimlight.
3. **Repetition.** A repeated external stimulus is more attention getting than a single one. Advertisers use this principle.
4. **Novelty and Familiarity.** A novel or a familiar external situation can serve as attention getter.
5. **Contrast.** It is a kind of uniqueness which can be used for attention getting. Letters of bold types, persons dressed differently than others, etc., get more attention.
6. **Motion.** A moving object draws more attention as compared to a stationary object. Advertisers use this principle.

Internal Factors

Self-concept. The way a person views the world depends a great deal on the concept or image he has about himself. The concept plays an internal role in perceptual selectivity.

Beliefs. A person's beliefs have profound influence on his perception. Thus, a fact is conceived not on what it is but what a person believes it to be.

Expectations. These affect what a person perceives. A technical manager may expect ignorance about the technical features of a product from non-technical people.

Inner Needs. The need is a feeling of tension or discomfort, when one thinks he is missing something. People with different needs experience different stimuli. According to Freud, wishful thinking is the means by which the Id attempts to achieve tension reduction.

Response Disposition. It refers to a person's tendency to perceive familiar stimuli rather than unfamiliar ones.

Response Salience. It is the set of disposition which are determined not by the familiarity of the stimulus situations, but by the person's own cognitive predispositions. Thus, a particular problem may be viewed as a marketing problem by marketing personnel, a control problem by accounting people and human relations problem by personnel people.

Perceptual Defence. It refers to the screening of those elements which create conflict and threatening situation in people.

1. Denying the existence or importance of conflicting information.

2. Distorting the new information to match the old one.
3. Acknowledging the new information but treating it as a non-representation exception. The factors that influence perception may be broadly divided into three categories :
   a. Factors that reside in the 'Perceiver' (i.e., attitude, motives, interests, past experiences and personality, expectations)
   b. Factors of the 'situation' and-factors connected with the 'Target'.
   c. Factors that determine the preferred location of a brand on each of the relevant dimension in perceptive mapping.

Attitudes

Respect for Others

Respect in the workplace doesn't solely extend to the way employees interact with management. People who have self-respect don't do managers' biding no matter what; they think for themselves and present alternative ideas at times, but respectfully. Employees should also have a respectful attitude when interacting with clients and customers as well as co-workers. Those with this type of attitude are willing to treat other people politely and professionally, even if they disagree with the other person's point of view.

Infectious Enthusiasm

Someone who is enthusiastic about life in general radiates a positive energy that rubs off on everyone around her. She dives into every project with interest, eagerly learns new skills and ideas and quickly applies them to her work. Some people are born with positive energy, but it can also be developed. Teach your staff to approach every situation, positive or negative, as a challenge and an opportunity. Adopt a "glass half full" attitude in the company and encourage employees to build on it. Soon they'll extend an enthusiastic attitude toward co-workers, customers and everything they do.

Commitment to the Job

Small businesses need employees who are not only committed to the goals and initiatives that affect the bottom line, but who also are committed to their particular positions. Employees project a committed attitude by showing a willingness to do whatever it takes to fulfill the duties of their positions and via the development of new ideas to make the company even better. When committed individuals work together as a team towards company goals, everyone benefits.

Innovative Ideas

Employees with an innovative attitude don't shy away from trying something new or finding a different way to do things. Small businesses need employees who can think outside of the box and innovate new ways to accomplish existing tasks and approach goals. Employees with this type of attitude know their ideas might not work out to be the best way to do something, but that the biggest failure is not at least giving new ideas a shot.

Helpfulness

It is important to have a helpful attitude at work, whether that means assisting clients and customers with their needs or helping co-workers accomplish overall company goals. The more helpful an attitude employees have, the more people want to be around them at work and the more willing they are to partner with those employees on key projects and initiatives.

Emotions

Being 'emotional' and 'professional' are often misunderstood as being two polar opposites. It is assumed that an individual who is able to discharge their duties without showing any emotion is what a true professional is. The truth, however, is that emotions affect people, and people, in turn, affect the organization's emotional climate.

For the longest time, we were told that the key to a good work-life balance and subsequent professional success was the ability to keep 'personal' and 'professional' domains of our lives separate. The reasoning that is often offered to justify this adage is the fact that one cannot afford to 'take it personally' when it comes to work, as this is a place where decisions are purely pragmatic and business-oriented in nature. On the other hand, we are encouraged to let our emotions, and not our reasoning guide our decision making on the personal front, especially when it comes to something that affects our loved ones. In reality, however, segregating the personal from the professional is futile, at best, as both are integral parts of our daily experiences. Similarly, we often mistake that being emotional and rational are mutually exclusive.

Research on Emotional Intelligence, one of the latest buzz words in the corporate circle, over the last three decades has done well to bust the myth that emotions have no place in the professional setting. If anything, evidence suggests the opposite! When people come to work, they don't leave behind their emotions at work, they bring them with them. And the experiences that they have at and outside work affects the feelings they express at work. Emotions affect everything we do at work – right from the relationships we share with our workmates and bosses, to how we negotiate our deadlines, to how we share the workload, and how we give and receive feedback. Since emotions are such a key variable affecting a wide range of outcomes at the workplace, it only makes sense that those who are better able to navigate emotions, both that of others and their own, in different situations are more likely to be successful at the workplace.

Masking emotions, especially negative ones also come with significant emotional labour, or in other words the exhaustion one experiences as a result of spending substantial emotional energy. When we 'put-on' an emotion to cover for what we are actually experiencing; like avoiding sharing negative news with your colleagues, and instead pretending that everything is fine, it is not only likely to take a toll on our own emotional well-being (as constantly being 'in character' that everything is going well is tiring), it is also equally likely that your behaviour will be seen as odd or suspicious by your colleagues, thereby prompting speculation of the worst. Instead, if one were to acknowledge that things were challenging at the moment, but that a solution was being actively worked on, this would allow others to stop speculating, and take comfort in your honesty and reassurance.

While managing emotions while at no point suggests that only negative emotions need to be managed (or in other words, repressed), there is evidence to show that positive approaches to situations are in fact advantageous from the point-of-view of cognitive processing. Positive thinking helps one do better, simply because processing negative thoughts takes a lot of our mental resources. It, therefore, does indicate that being to shake-off a negative mood and bring oneself back to a positive mood allows us to take in information which we would otherwise miss as our focus would be on negative emotions instead.

Lastly, in an organization's context, creating an Emotionally Intelligent workforce, leads to an innovative culture, full of positive conflict and energy. An emotionally intelligent workforce can moderate their behaviour and reactions as per the requirements of the customer, peer, supervisor or subordinate leading to optimal output. Given, the current context of diverse culture and educational background of the workforce, it increasingly becomes the responsibility of the Organization (or the Human Resource function) to build this culture and the competency.

What can HR managers and people managers do to make the workplace and employees 'Emotionally Intelligent'?

1. Enabling a culture of openness at the workplace: Enabling employees share concerns, appreciations, and feedback openly, without fear of a backlash
2. Training Managers and Employees for milestone events: Providing training to Managers for handling milestone events like Appraisals, Layoffs, Developmental Feedback, Coaching / Mentoring to enable institutionalization of the culture across employee groups
3. Train employees on Self Awareness / Emotional Intelligence: Identifying an emotion accurately, and early, enables individuals to manage it effectively. Being in touch with one's emotions and being able to accurately distinguish one emotion from another allows them to identify a negative emotion – using both bodily, as well as mental cues.
4. Identify role models: Identify role models who are champions at managing emotions in the workplace. Explain how this has helped them become successful, both personally and professionally.

GROUP DYNAMICS

Groups versus Teams

- All teams are groups
- Some groups are just people assembled together
- Teams have task interdependence whereas some groups do not (e.g., group of employees enjoying lunch together)

Reasons for group formation

- Personal characteristics (beliefs, attitudes, values, age, sex, hobbies)
- Interests and goals
- Opportunity for interaction
- Influence power

Why do we join groups?

- Satisfy social needs
- Source approval
- Knowledge
- Goal attainment and task performance
- Social identity

Types of Groups

- Informal: Natural formation in work environment in response to the need for social contact
- Interest Group: who have a mutual interest e.g., working mothers
- Friendship Group: who have common characteristics e.g., marital status, sports
- Reference Group: any group with whom an individual identifies for the purpose of forming opinions or making decisions
- Formal: Deliberately created to perform a specific task e.g., R/d lab, mgmt team
- Standing Task Group: consists of a supervisor who exercises formal authority over subordinates
- Task Group: a temporary formal group that is created to solve specific problem

- Open: constant change of members
- Closed: members are stable
- In: the groups to which we belong
- Out: the groups to which we don't belong

Life Cycle of a Group/Stages of Group Development

FORMING: (Awareness)

Lot of uncertainty, focus on understanding the goal, work out procedures for performing the task, decides on structure, leadership

STORMING: (Conflict)

Mixture of expressions, conflicts regarding priorities of goals, responsibilities of each member

NORMING: (COOPERATION)

Group Cohesiveness, share info, shows acceptance, compromising decisions

PERFORMING: (Productivity)

Group is fully operational, high productivity & helps each other

ADJOURNING: (SEPARATION)

Group disbandon after the task, fulfillment of task performance, feeling of sadness at the loss of friendship

Power and Politics

SOURCES OF POWER

- Knowledge as power
- Resources as power
- Decision as power

OTHER SOURCES OF POWER

- Number of people as power
- Reward Power: Ability to reward others
- Coercive Power: Ability to influence others behavior by punishing their undesirable behavior
- Referent Power: By being respected & admired
- Legitimate Power: Power by position & authority
- Information Power: Access to and/control of information
- Expert Power: The ability to control another person's behavior through the possession of knowledge, experience or judgment that the other person does not have

POLITICS

It is the way that people gain & use power in the organisations

Organisational politics –

- Attempts to influence others using discretionary behaviours to promote personal objectives
- discretionary behaviours neither explicitly prescribed nor prohibited
- Politics may be good or bad for the organisation

Causes of Political Behaviour

- Lust for power
- Competition or command over resources

- Protection of self-interests
- Unequal distributional of authority
- Need for inter-department coordination
- Discretionary authority
- Saturation in career

Handling Organisational Politics

- Clearly defined jobs
- Effective communication
- Proper managerial behaviour
- Fair evaluation system

STONEWALLING. The practice of willingly hiding information by being secretive & deceitful which occurs when organisations punish individuals who are honest & reward those who are unethical.

BOTTOM LINE THINKING. The belief that an organisations financial success is the only thing that matters.

CONFLICT AND NEGOTIATION

Conflict and negotiation are aspects of running a business. Business owners face conflict with partners, managers, employees and the general public. Negotiation is often necessary to create an amicable solution for all parties involved in the conflict. Many small or home-based businesses avoid internal conflict and negotiation because owners are primarily responsible for completing business functions. However, external conflict and negotiation occur for most companies in the business environment.

Conflict often occurs when individuals have different ideas, beliefs or theories regarding business operations. Business owners may also find conflict when bargaining with individuals or other businesses. Acquiring economic resources or other business assets often involves bargaining. Negotiation is the process of discussing each individual's position about a topic and attempting to reach a solution that benefits both parties. Conflicts and negotiation are usually more prevalent in larger business organizations since more individuals are involved in the company's operations.

Conflict and negotiation may result in several options being created to resolve difficult situations. Business owners might follow a few steps when processing discussion options and solutions: identifying the problem, analyzing the issue, creating different strategies or approaches, and acting on outcomes or ideas. These steps provide a logical process to follow when solving conflict and negotiation issues.

Business owners can use conflict negotiation to create a more favorable outcome when dealing with a stronger party. Small businesses often have lower purchasing power or negotiating positions than larger organizations. Lower purchasing power often drives business owners to create the best situations for saving their company money while improving product quality and production output. Business owners ought to use negotiation to create relationships that provide their company with a competitive advantage over other businesses in the economic marketplace.

According to the book "Getting to Yes," business owners should develop their BATNA—"best alternative to negotiated agreement." Many business owners realize they cannot obtain all their requests during a conflict and negotiation process. Having a best alternative to negotiated agreement on hand ensures business owners receive as many concessions as possible during the negotiation process. However, these alternatives might create more conflict if they continually require the other party to give up more benefits.

The conflict and negotiation process can result in one party engaging in unethical behavior. Small business owners may get caught up in this situation if they have little experience in conflict and negotiation. They must have the resolve to walk away from conflicts or negotiations that will result in unfavorable conditions for their company. Refusing to negotiate or reconcile conflicts can be difficult for many small businesses looking to improve or advance business operations.

Stress Management

A healthy job is likely to be one where the pressures on employees are appropriate in relation to their abilities and resources, to the amount of control they have over their work, and to the support they receive from people who matter to them. As health is not merely the absence of disease or infirmity but a positive state of complete physical, mental and social well-being (WHO, 1986), a healthy working environment is one in which there is not only an absence of harmful conditions but an abundance of health-promoting ones.

These may include continuous assessment of risks to health, the provision of appropriate information and training on health issues and the availability of health promoting organisational support practices and structures. A healthy work environment is one in which staff have made health and health promotion a priority and part of their working lives.

- Work-related stress is the response people may have when presented with work demands and pressures that are not matched to their knowledge and abilities and which challenge their abilities to cope.
- Stress occurs in a wide range of work circumstances but is often made worse when employees feel they have little support from supervisors and colleagues, as well as little control over work processes.
- There is often confusion between pressure or challenge and stress and sometimes it is used to excuse bad management practice.

Pressure at the workplace is unavoidable due to the demands of the contemporary work environment. Pressure perceived as acceptable by an individual, may even keep workers alert, motivated, able to work and learn, depending on the available resources and personal characteristics. However, when that pressure becomes excessive or otherwise unmanageable it leads to stress. Stress can damage an employees' health and the business performance.

Work-related stress can be caused by poor work organisation (the way we design jobs and work systems, and the way we manage them), by poor work design (for example, lack of control over work processes), poor management, unsatisfactory working conditions, and lack of support from colleagues and supervisors.

Research findings show that the most stressful type of work is that which values excessive demands and pressures that are not matched to workers' knowledge and abilities, where there is little opportunity to exercise any choice or control, and where there is little support from others.

Employees are less likely to experience work-related stress when - demands and pressures of work are matched to their knowledge and abilities - control can be exercised over their work and the way they do it - support is received from supervisors and colleagues - participation in decisions that concern their jobs is provided.

What are stress-related hazards at work?

Stress related hazards at work can be divided into work content and work context.

Work contents includes - job content (monotony, under-stimulation, meaningless of tasks, lack of variety, etc) - work load and work pace (too much or too little to do, work under time pressure, etc.) - working hours (strict or inflexible, long and unsocial, unpredictable, badly designed shift systems) - Participation and control (lack of participation in decision-making, lack of control over work processes, pace, hours, methods, and the work environment)

Work context includes - career development, status and pay (job insecurity, lack of promotion opportunities, under- or over-promotion, work of 'low social value', piece rate payment schemes, unclear or unfair performance evaluation systems, being over- or under-skilled for a job) - role in the organization (unclear role, conflicting roles) - interpersonal relationships (inadequate, inconsiderate or unsupportive supervision, poor relationships with colleagues, bullying/harassment and violence, isolated or solitary work, etc) -organizational culture (poor communication, poor leadership, lack of behavioural rule, lack of clarity about organizational objectives, structures and strategies) - work-life balance (conflicting demands of work and home, lack of support for domestic problems at work, lack of support for work problems at home, lack of organizational rules and policies to support work-life balance)

ORGANISATIONAL CULTURE

ORGANISATIONAL DEVELOPMENT

Organisational development (OD) is concerned with facilitating change in organisations through a holistic and humanistic approach that puts people at the heart of the process.

We define Organisational Development as the work of facilitating organisational success, by aligning structural, cultural and strategic realities of work to respond to the needs of an ever-evolving business climate.

At the heart of good organizational development is the deep connection between the best business processes and structures on the one hand, and the people working within the organization on the other. In short, it is to create great organisations!

There are significant differences between organisational development and 'culture change', 'change management' and 'business transformation'. Find out more about the definition of OD here.

To achieve high performance and competitive advantage, organisations are often in the midst of significant learning and change.

In traditional organisation and leadership theory, the inspirational, top-down vision for the organisation is supposedly created by a few and thrust upon the many.

Such change initiatives may result in a successful change of procedures and structures (the easier bit), but rarely trigger sustainable change in working methods, culture and organisational effectiveness which is at the root of real return on investment, profitability and long-term transformation. Organisational Development (OD) is an area of expertise which addresses this challenge with decades of internationally tried and tested research and practice, spanning thousands of professionals.

Organization Development (OD) is the work of facilitating organisational success, by aligning structural, cultural and strategic realities of work to respond to the needs of an ever-evolving business climate.

Characteristics of OD include

- Changes to the structure, culture, strategy and processes of an individual job through to an entire organisation.
- The application of behavioural science knowledge and practice to facilitate transformation within an organisation.
- The improvement of organisational effectiveness by involving members of the organisation in understanding the challenge whilst enabling in them new skills, knowledge and ways of thinking.
- The promotion of high productivity, performance, quality products, financial performance and continuous improvement.

- The facilitation of change in a flexible, adaptive and often participative way.
- Sustainability, so consistent change in the right direction continues beyond the life of the initial change initiative.

OD also operates from a particular set of values that shape how the work is done. Key to this is the valuing of human potential and therefore the importance of understanding the systemic challenges from a range of stakeholders and to then engage those stakeholders directly in shaping the change, partly so that change is well conceived of but also so that, through broad ownership, its chance of being understood and implemented are maximised.

The roots of Organisational Development can be found in the USA, in the work of Kurt Lewin (1898-1947). Seen as the founding father of OD, he founded the 'Research Center for Group Dynamics' at MIT, experimented with collaborative change processes, and proposed the first concepts of group dynamics and action research, which underpin OD. Lewin found that using participative methods in small groups led to positive changes in attitude and greater commitment from the people in organisations. A parallel interest in what happens in individuals and groups in work also arose in Europe and the UK over a similar period, with Roffey Park founded in 1946 and The Tavistock Institute in 1947.

Abraham Maslow (1908-1970), a psychology professor most famous for his 'hierarchy of needs', and another important figure in the history of Organisational Development, believed that when an individual's needs were met, it led to 'self-actualisation'. When an organisation was open, and the individual's contributions were recognised, this was more likely to occur. Other theorists advocated participation as a means of motivating employees and achieving a greater performance, and leadership styles that were democratic and involving were shown to lead to better organisational performance and employee satisfaction.

In 1969, Warren Bennis introduced the concept of organisational culture, identifying that OD is 'a complex educational strategy intended to change beliefs, attitudes, values, and structures of organizations so that they can better adapt to new technologies, markets, and challenges, and the dizzying rate of change itself'.

at the start of the 1980's, developed this idea of 'organisational culture', using metaphors of the cultural iceberg and lily pad. With the iceberg, Schein shows how difficult it is to see what underlies the behaviours of an organisation, as most is hidden below the surface. With his lily pad analogy, he proposes that we can easily see the flowers on the water (the behaviours explicit in an organisation), however unless we drop down to the stems (the values supporting those behaviours) and then the partly hidden roots (the assumptions behind these values and behaviours), we cannot truly understand what drives the organisation's actions and thoughts of the people within the organisation.

Behavioural sciences, including anthropology, economics, psychology, and sociology have all had their impact in the evolution of Organisational Development, and as a result, in 2002, Toby Egan identified there had been 27 definitions of OD between the period 1969 and 2003.

Organisational Development is adaptive, flexible and evolving. It puts people at the heart of change, emphasises creativity and innovation, and positively affects the bottom line.

- OD creates a continuous cycle of improvement, from strategy, through to implementation, evaluation and further change.
- OD increases communication across all levels of the organisation, aligning employees to shared values and manifesting change from employee feedback
- OD increases innovation through employee development and engagement and an effective analysis of the market.

- OD increases profit by improved productivity and creativity, reducing costs, minimising staff turnover and creating a culture of openness and adaptive and ongoing change

ORGANISATIONAL CHANGE

Organisational change refers to any alteration that occurs in total work environment. Organisational change is an important characteristic of most organisations. An organisation must develop adaptability to change otherwise it will either be left behind or be swept away by the forces of change. Organisational change is inevitable in a progressive culture. Modern organizations are highly dynamic, versatile and adaptive to the multiplicity of changes.

Organisational change refers to the alteration of structural relationships and roles of people in the organization. It is largely structural in nature. An enterprise can be changed in several ways. Its technology can be changed, its structure, its people and other elements can be changed too. Organisational change calls for a change in the individual behaviour of the employees.

Organizations survive, grow or decay depending upon the changing behaviour of the employees. Most changes disturb the equilibrium of situation and environment in which the individuals or groups exist. If a change is detrimental to the interests of individuals or groups, they will resist the change.

Causes of Organisational Change

(A) External Pressures:

i. **Change in Technology and Equipment.** Advancements in technology is the major cause (i.e., external pressure) of change. Each technological alternative results in new forms of organization to meet and match the needs.

ii. **Market Situation.** Changes in market situation include rapidly changing goals, needs and desires of consumers, suppliers, unions etc. If an organization has to survive, it has to cope with changes in market situations.

iii. **Social and Political Changes.** Organisational units literally have no control over social and political changes in the country. Relations between government and business or drive for social equality are some factors which may compel for organisational change.

(B) Internal Pressures (Pressures for Change from Within the Organisation):

i. **Changes in the Managerial Personnel.** One of the most frequent reasons for major changes in the organisation is the change of executives at the top. No two managers have the same style, skills or managerial philosophies.

ii. **Deficiencies in the Existing Organization.** Many deficiencies are noticed in the organisations with the passage of time. A change is necessary to remove such deficiencies as lack of uniformity in the policies, obstacles in communication, any ambiguity etc.

iii. **Other Factors.** Certain other factors such as listed below also demand a change in the organisation:

- Employee's desire to share in decision-making
- Employee's desire for higher wage rate
- Improvement in working conditions, etc.

Response to Organisational Change

Every change is responded by the people working in the organisation. These responses may be positive or negative depending upon the fact as how they affect people.

Before introducing a change, the manager should study and understand employee's attitudes so as to create a positive response. Three sets of factors-psychological, personal and social- govern the attitude of people.

Process of Organisational Change

Unless the behavioural patterns of the employees change, the change will have a little impact on the effectiveness of the organisation.

(1) **Unfreezing.** The essence of unfreezing phase is that the individual is made to realize that his beliefs, feelings and behaviour are no longer appropriate or relevant to the current situation in the organisation. Once convinced, people may change their behaviour. Reward for those willing to change and punishment for others may help in this matter.

(2) **Changing.** Once convinced and ready to change, an individual, under this phase, learns to behave in new ways. He is first provided with the model in which he is to identify himself. Gradually he will accept that model and behave in the manner suggested by the model. In another process (known as internalisation), the individual is placed in a situation where new behaviour is demanded of him if he is to operate successfully.

(3) **Refreezing.** During this phase, a person has to practice and experiment with the new method of behaviour and see that it effectively blends with his other behavioural attitudes. Reinforcement, for creating a permanent set in the individual, is provided through either continuous or intermittent schedules.

Resistance to Organisational Change

Resistance to change is perhaps one of the baffling problems a manager encounters because it can take many shapes. People may resign, they may show tardiness, loss of motivation to work, increased absenteeism, request for transfer, wild-cat strikes, shoddy work, reduction in productivity etc.

Classification of Resistance to Change

Resistance to change may be classified as:

1. Industrial Resistance:

Individual resistance may be there because of the following reasons:

A. Economic Reasons:

(a) **Obsolescence of Skills.** When a person feels that with the introduction of newer processes, his skills will just become obsolete, he will resist the change. For example, a twenty years experienced accountant is quite likely to resist the introduction of a computer for preparing the wage bills because he feels that might affect his pay and position.

(b) **Fear of Economic Loss.** People resist change if it opens the possibility of lowering their income directly or indirectly.

B. Personal Reasons:

(a) **Ego Defensiveness.** A sales manager may turn down the suggestions of a salesman simply because the manager perceives that his ego may be deflated by accepting the suggestion.

(b) **Status Quo.** Most of the people feel comfortable with status quo and strongly resist change as it may involve uncertainty and risk.

(c) **Fear of Unknown.** Change presents unknown and unknown poses a constant threat and sores people. For fear of unknown, a manager may refuse promotion that requires his relocating in another state.

C. **Social Reasons:**

(a) **Social Displacement.** Introduction of change (e.g., relocating) may result in breaking up of work groups and thus result in disturbance of the existing social relationships of people.

(b) **Peer Pressure.** Whenever change is unwilling to the peers, they force the individual subordinate employees who are bent of accepting the change, to resist it.

2. *Organizational Resistance:*

Resistance may also be present at organizational level. Some organizations are so designed that they resist innovations.

Some of the reasons of organizational resistance are:

(a) **Threats to Power and Influence.** Some people (especially sitting at the top levels) resist change because they feel that a change might affect their position, power and influence in the organization.

(b) **Organizational Structure.** Some organization structures (e.g., bureaucratic structure) have inbuilt mechanism for resistance to change.

(c) **Resource Constraints.** Non-availability of financial, material and human resources may also act as a resistance to change.

(d) **Sunk Cost.** In some companies, heavy capital is blocked in the fixed or permanent assets. If such an organization wishes to introduce change, then difficulty arises because of these sunk costs.

Overcoming Resistance to Organisational Change

Change creates tension and emotional turmoil in the mind of employees. Change thus results in resistance quite frequently, negative reactions doom the success of the change program especially when a manager is unable to handle it properly.

Some of the techniques to handle the change properly and to deal with resistance to change are:

(a) **Education and Communication.** One of the easiest techniques to overcome resistance to change is to educate the people who resist it. In many cases, people do not properly understand the change and hence become afraid of its consequences and resist change.

(b) **Participation and Involvement.** If subordinates are allowed to participate and involve themselves in the change process (decision-making regarding the implementation of the change), their misunderstandings about the consequences of change are cleared, they generally feel satisfied and do not oppose change.

(c) **Support.** Support may be facilitative and emotional. Managers sometimes deal with potential resistance by being supportive. This includes listening, providing emotional support, providing training in new skills etc.

(d) **Incentives.** Offering incentive is another fruitful way to overcome resistance to change.

(e) **Manipulation.** Managers generally indulge in manipulation when all other tactics have failed to overcome resistance to change.

(f) **Coercion.** At times, there is no way except to deal with resistance coercively. People are forced to accept change by threatening them with loss of their jobs, promotion possibilities and so forth.

MULTIPLE CHOICE QUESTIONS

1. What is the primary focus of management?
   (1) Profit Maximisation
   (2) Employee satisfaction
   (3) Goal attainment
   (4) Innovation
2. Which of the following is a principle of management proposed by Henri Fayol?
   (1) Hierarchy of needs
   (2) Unity of command
   (3) Theory X and Theory Y
   (4) Maslow's hierarchy of needs
3. What is the purpose of the planning function in management?
   (1) To control day-to-day operations
   (2) To organise resources for goal achievement
   (3) To set organisational objectives and determine the means to achieve them
   (4) To motivate employees
4. Which function of management involves assigning tasks, grouping tasks into departments, and allocating resources?
   (1) Planning (2) Organizing
   (3) Leading (4) Controlling
5. Who is known for the classical management theory and the five functions of management?
   (1) Peter Drucker
   (2) Frederick Taylor
   (3) Elton Mayo
   (4) Henri Fayol
6. Which management function involves monitoring activities to ensure they are on the right track toward goal attainment?
   (1) Planning (2) Organizing
   (3) Leading (4) Controlling
7. What does the principle of equity in management emphasize?
   (1) Equal pay for equal work
   (2) Fair treatment of employees
   (3) Employee motivation
   (4) Efficiency in operations
8. Which management function involves influencing and guiding employees toward the achievement of organisational goals?
   (1) Planning (2) Organizing
   (3) Leading (4) Controlling
9. Who developed the concept of Theory X and Theory Y in management?
   (1) Peter Drucker
   (2) Frederick Taylor
   (3) Elton Mayo
   (4) Douglas McGregor
10. Which of the following is an example of an interpersonal role of a manager, as identified by Henry Mintzberg?
    (1) Decisional role
    (2) Informational role
    (3) Figurehead role
    (4) Resource allocator role
11. Which management function involves selecting and training employees, as well as developing and maintaining a positive organisational culture?
    (1) Planning (2) Organizing
    (3) Leading (4) Controlling
12. What is the focus of the controlling function in management?
    (1) Setting goals
    (2) Allocating resources
    (3) Monitoring and adjusting activities to ensure goal attainment
    (4) Assigning tasks
13. Who is known for the concept of the scalar chain in management?
    (1) Peter Drucker (2) Frederick Taylor
    (3) Elton Mayo (4) Henri Fayol
14. Which of the following is a characteristic of the autocratic style of leadership?
    (1) Employee empowerment
    (2) Shared decision-making
    (3) Centralized decision-making
    (4) Participative decision-making

15. Which management function involves setting objectives, identifying methods to achieve them, and making decisions on the allocation of resources?
(1) Planning (2) Organizing
(3) Leading (4) Controlling

16. According to Frederick Taylor, what is the focus of scientific management?
(1) Employee satisfaction
(2) Employee empowerment
(3) Efficiency and productivity
(4) Organizational culture

17. Which of the following is a principle of management suggested by Mary Parker Follett?
(1) Unity of command
(2) Scalar chain
(3) Division of labor
(4) Coordination through direct communication

18. What is the focus of the human relations approach in management?
(1) Employee empowerment
(2) Efficiency and productivity
(3) Employee satisfaction and social needs
(4) Centralized decision-making

19. Which of the following is a disadvantage of the autocratic leadership style?
(1) Promotes employee empowerment
(2) Encourages creativity and innovation
(3) May lead to employee dissatisfaction and low morale
(4) Facilitates shared decision-making

20. What does the principle of unity of command in management emphasize?
(1) The need for clear reporting relationships
(2) The importance of employee empowerment
(3) The coordination of activities
(4) The delegation of authority

Directions: Each of the following items consists of two statements, one labelled as Assertion (A) and other labelled as Reason (R). You are to examine these two statements carefully and decide if the (A) and the (R) are individually true and if so, whether (R) is the correct explanation of (A). Select your answers to these items using the codes given below:
(1) Both (A) and (R) are true, and the (R) is the correct explanation of the (A).
(2) Both (A) and (R) are true, but the (R) is not the correct explanation of the (A).
(3) The (A) is true, and the (R) is false.
(4) The (A) is false, and the (R) is true.

21. **Assertion (A):** Planning is a one-time activity and does not require ongoing attention in the management process.
Reason (R): Planning involves setting objectives and determining the means to achieve them.

22. **Assertion (A):** The principle of unity of command suggests that an employee should receive orders from only one supervisor.
Reason (R): Unity of command promotes clear reporting relationships and avoids confusion.

23. **Assertion (A):** The controlling function in management is focused on punishing employees for mistakes.
Reason (R): Controlling involves monitoring and adjusting activities to ensure goal attainment.

24. **Assertion (A):** The autocratic leadership style promotes employee empowerment and shared decision-making.
Reason (R): Autocratic leadership involves centralized decision-making by the leader.

25. **Assertion (A):** The human relations approach in management emphasizes the importance of employee satisfaction and social needs.
Reason (R): The human relations approach is primarily concerned with efficiency and productivity.

26. What is the primary purpose of formal organisation structure?
(1) Encouraging socialization among employees
(2) Facilitating informal communication
(3) Providing a framework for achieving organisational goals
(4) Promoting flexibility and adaptability

27. Which term refers to the arrangement of tasks, responsibilities, and authority in an organisation?
(1) Organisation culture
(2) Organisation structure
(3) Organisation climate
(4) Organisation behaviour

28. In a functional organisational structure, how are employees grouped?
(1) Based on geography

(2) Based on product lines
(3) Based on functions or roles
(4) Based on customer segments

29. What is an advantage of a flat organisational structure?
(1) Increased efficiency in communication
(2) Clearly defined hierarchy
(3) Centralized decision-making
(4) Greater specialisation of tasks

30. In which organisational structure is decision-making authority concentrated at the top levels of management?
(1) Flat structure (2) Tall structure
(3) Matrix structure (4) Network structure

31. What is a characteristic of a matrix organisational structure?
(1) Clear lines of authority
(2) Division of employees based on functions
(3) Dual reporting relationships
(4) Low employee specialisation

32. In an informal organisation, how is communication typically facilitated?
(1) Through formal channels and procedures
(2) Through established reporting relationships
(3) Through informal networks and relationships
(4) Through written documents only

33. What is the purpose of an organisational chart?
(1) To showcase employee achievements
(2) To display the organisation's financial performance
(3) To represent the formal structure of an organisation
(4) To outline employee benefits

34. Which term refers to the number of subordinates a manager can efficiently manage?
(1) Hierarchy
(2) Span of control
(3) Chain of command
(4) Division of labour

35. What is a characteristic of a decentralized organisational structure?
(1) Centralized decision-making
(2) Clear lines of authority
(3) Greater decision-making authority at lower levels
(4) Limited employee autonomy

36. In a network organisational structure, how are tasks and projects coordinated?
(1) Through a hierarchical chain of command
(2) Through formal reporting relationships
(3) Through a flexible and informal network of relationships
(4) Through centralized decision-making

37. What is the primary focus of an informal organisation?
(1) Achieving organisational goals
(2) Adhering to formal policies and procedures
(3) Meeting financial targets
(4) Social interactions among employees

38. What is a disadvantage of a narrow span of control?
(1) Reduced communication complexity
(2) Limited flexibility and adaptability
(3) Increased managerial workload
(4) Efficient decision-making

39. What is an informal organisation also referred to as?
(1) Hidden organisation
(2) Shadow organisation
(3) Invisible organisation
(4) Social organisation

40. What is the primary benefit of a wide span of control?
(1) Increased managerial workload
(2) Efficient communication and decision-making
(3) Limited employee autonomy
(4) Greater specialisation of tasks

Directions: Each of the following items consists of two statements, one labelled as Assertion (A) and other labelled as Reason (R). You are to examine these two statements carefully and decide if the (A) and the (R) are individually true and if so, whether (R) is the correct explanation of (A). Select your answers to these items using the codes given below:
(1) Both (A) and (R) are true, and the (R) is the correct explanation of the (A).
(2) Both (A) and (R) are true, but the (R) is not the correct explanation of the (A).
(3) The (A) is true, but the (R) is false.
(4) (A) is false, but the (R) is true.

41. **Assertion (A):** Informal organisations play a crucial role in fostering social interactions among employees.

Reason (R): Formal organisations focus solely on achieving organisational goals.

42. **Assertion (A):** A matrix structure is characterised by dual reporting relationships.
Reason (R): Matrix structures are rigid and do not allow for flexibility.

43. **Assertion (A):** Decentralized organisational structures encourage greater autonomy at lower levels.
Reason (R): Centralized structures promote decision-making authority at all levels of the organisation.

44. **Assertion (A):** A narrow span of control is advantageous for increased flexibility.
Reason (R): A narrow span of control may lead to excessive managerial workload.

45. **Assertion (A):** A flat organisational structure promotes efficient communication and decision-making.
Reason (R): A flat structure has fewer hierarchical levels, reducing the complexity of communication.

46. What is authority in an organisational context?
(1) The number of employees in a department
(2) The power to give orders and enforce obedience
(3) The level of responsibility assigned to an employee
(4) The size of the organisational structure

47. What is the primary purpose of delegation in management?
(1) To increase the workload of managers
(2) To centralize decision-making
(3) To empower employees and distribute tasks
(4) To reduce employee autonomy

48. In the process of delegation, what does the delegator transfer to the delegatee?
(1) Accountability
(2) Authority
(3) Responsibility
(4) All of the above

49. What is the relationship between authority and responsibility in delegation?
(1) They are unrelated concepts
(2) They are inversely proportional
(3) They are directly proportional
(4) They are interchangeable terms

50. What is a potential disadvantage of over-delegation?
(1) Increased employee empowerment
(2) Reduced managerial workload
(3) Loss of control and coordination
(4) Improved decision-making efficiency

51. Which term refers to the process of entrusting a task or responsibility to a subordinate?
(1) Decentralisation
(2) Authorisation
(3) Delegation
(4) Centralisation

52. What is the primary benefit of decentralization in an organisation?
(1) Increased control at the top levels
(2) Efficient decision-making at lower levels
(3) Reduced employee autonomy
(4) Centralized authority

53. What does the principle of scalar chain emphasize in delegation?
(1) Horizontal communication
(2) Vertical communication
(3) Centralized decision-making
(4) Formal authority

54. In a decentralized organisation, where is decision-making authority distributed?
(1) Only at the top levels
(2) Only at the middle levels
(3) Only at the lower levels
(4) Across various levels of the organisation

55. What is the purpose of a delegation of authority?
(1) To concentrate decision-making at the top
(2) To empower employees and distribute responsibilities
(3) To limit employee autonomy
(4) To increase managerial workload

56. What is a characteristic of a centralized organisation in terms of decision-making?
(1) Decision-making authority is concentrated at the top
(2) Decision-making authority is distributed across various levels
(3) Decision-making is absent
(4) Decision-making authority is limited to lower levels

57. Which of the following is a key element of effective delegation?
(1) Overloading employees with tasks
(2) Providing clear instructions and expectations
(3) Avoiding communication with subordinates
(4) Retaining all decision-making authority

58. What does the term "chain of command" refer to in delegation?
(1) A linear reporting structure
(2) A decentralized structure
(3) A flat organisational structure
(4) An absence of reporting relationships

59. In a decentralised organisation, what is the role of lower-level managers in decision-making?
(1) Limited role with no decision-making authority
(2) Full decision-making authority
(3) No role in decision-making
(4) Limited role in specific areas only

60. What is the primary difference between delegation and decentralization?
(1) Delegation involves distributing tasks, while decentralization involves concentrating authority.
(2) Delegation involves concentrating authority, while decentralization involves distributing tasks.
(3) Delegation and decentralization are synonymous terms.
(4) Delegation and decentralization have no relationship.

61. What is a potential disadvantage of under-delegation?
(1) Increased employee empowerment
(2) Reduced managerial workload
(3) Inefficient use of employee skills
(4) Improved decision-making efficiency

62. What is the role of a delegatee in the delegation process?
(1) To assign tasks to superiors
(2) To supervise the delegator
(3) To receive and complete delegated tasks
(4) To avoid taking on additional responsibilities

63. In a centralized organisation, what is the flow of decision-making authority?
(1) Bottom-up (2) Top-down
(3) Lateral (4) Circular

64. What is an advantage of delegation in terms of employee development?
(1) Stifling employee growth and learning
(2) Limiting exposure to new tasks and challenges
(3) Providing opportunities for skill development and growth
(4) Discouraging career advancement

65. What does the term "line authority" refer to in delegation?
(1) The authority to make decisions and issue orders within a specific department
(2) The authority to communicate horizontally across departments
(3) The authority to make decisions at the top level
(4) The absence of decision-making authority

Directions: Each of the following items consists of two statements, one labelled as Assertion (A) and other labelled as Reason (R). You are to examine these two statements carefully and decide if the (A) and the (R) are individually true and if so, whether (R) is the correct explanation of (A). Select your answers to these items using the codes given below:
(1) Both (A) and (R) are true, and the (R) is the correct explanation of the (A).
(2) Both (A) and (R) are true, but the (R) is not the correct explanation of the (A).
(3) The (A) is true, but the (R) is false.
(4) The (A) is false, and the (R) is true.

66. **Assertion (A):** Delegation of authority is a process that only occurs in centralised organisations.
Reason (R): Centralized organisations do not distribute decision-making authority.

67. **Assertion (A):** Decentralization leads to more efficient decision-making at lower levels of the organisation.
Reason (R): In decentralized organisations, decision-making authority is concentrated at the top.

68. **Assertion (A):** Over-delegation can lead to a loss of control and coordination in an organisation.
Reason (R): Effective delegation involves providing clear instructions and expectations.

69. **Assertion (A):** Under-delegation can result in the inefficient use of employee skills.
Reason (R): Under-delegation involves empowering employees with excessive tasks.

70. **Assertion (A):** Decentralization involves the concentration of decision-making authority at the top levels of management.
Reason (R): In decentralized organisations, decision-making authority is distributed across various levels.

71. What is motivation in the context of organisational behaviour?
(1) Employee supervision
(2) The force that drives individuals to achieve their goals
(3) The punishment for low performance
(4) Strict rules and regulations

72. Which theory of motivation emphasizes the role of physiological needs in driving behaviour?
(1) Expectancy theory
(2) Maslow's hierarchy of needs
(3) Herzberg's two-factor theory
(4) Equity theory

73. According to Herzberg's two-factor theory, which factors are associated with job satisfaction?
(1) Hygiene factors (2) Motivators
(3) Intrinsic factors (4) Extrinsic factors

74. Which motivation theory suggests that individuals are motivated by the expectation of a reward that will follow their actions?
(1) Expectancy theory
(2) Equity theory
(3) Theory X and Theory Y
(4) Hierarchy of needs theory

75. What does the concept of "equity" in motivation theory refer to?
(1) Fair and just treatment of employees
(2) Providing employees with excessive rewards
(3) Promoting employees based on seniority
(4) Creating a competitive work environment

76. According to Douglas McGregor, what is the assumption of Theory X regarding employees?
(1) Employees are self-motivated and seek responsibility.
(2) Employees inherently dislike work and will avoid it if possible.
(3) Employees are motivated by social needs.
(4) Employees are primarily motivated by higher-order needs.

77. Which leadership style is characterised by a leader who makes decisions without consulting the team members?
(1) Autocratic leadership
(2) Democratic leadership
(3) Transformational leadership
(4) Laissez-faire leadership

78. What is the focus of transactional leadership?
(1) Building strong interpersonal relationships
(2) Inspiring and motivating followers
(3) Exchanging rewards and punishments for performance
(4) Encouraging creativity and innovation

79. In the context of the expectancy theory, what is expectancy?
(1) The belief that effort will lead to performance
(2) The anticipation of rewards
(3) The perception of fairness
(4) The hierarchy of needs

80. Which motivation theory suggests that individuals are motivated by a desire for fairness and equality in the workplace?
(1) Expectancy theory
(2) Equity theory
(3) Maslow's hierarchy of needs
(4) Herzberg's two-factor theory

81. What is the focus of transformational leadership?
(1) Transactional exchanges
(2) Charismatic behaviour
(3) Extrinsic rewards
(4) Inspiring and motivating followers to achieve their full potential

82. According to Maslow's hierarchy of needs, which needs are considered higher-order needs?
(1) Physiological needs
(2) Safety needs
(3) Esteem needs
(4) Social needs

83. Which theory of motivation suggests that individuals are motivated by the belief that their efforts will lead to good performance and that good performance will be rewarded?

(1) Equity theory
(2) Hierarchy of needs theory
(3) Expectancy theory
(4) Two-factor theory

84. What is the main idea behind Herzberg's two-factor theory?
(1) Employees are motivated by physiological needs.
(2) Job satisfaction and dissatisfaction are influenced by different factors.
(3) Employees are motivated by social needs.
(4) Job satisfaction is solely influenced by extrinsic factors.

85. Which leadership style encourages team members to participate in decision-making and values their input?
(1) Laissez-faire leadership
(2) Autocratic leadership
(3) Democratic leadership
(4) Transactional leadership

86. According to Theory Y, what is the assumption regarding employees?
(1) Employees are inherently lazy and avoid work.
(2) Employees seek responsibility and can be creative.
(3) Employees are motivated by extrinsic rewards.
(4) Employees are motivated by physiological needs.

87. What is the primary focus of a laissez-faire leadership style?
(1) Controlling and directing every aspect of the team's work
(2) Empowering team members to make decisions
(3) Inspiring and motivating through charisma
(4) Exchanging rewards and punishments for performance

88. In the context of motivation, what does the term "valence" refer to?
(1) The anticipation of rewards
(2) The belief that effort will lead to performance
(3) The perceived value of the rewards
(4) The hierarchy of needs

89. Which leadership style involves a leader who inspires and motivates followers through charisma and vision?
(1) Autocratic leadership
(2) Laissez-faire leadership
(3) Transformational leadership
(4) Transactional leadership

90. According to Maslow's hierarchy of needs, which needs must be satisfied before higher-order needs can be addressed?
(1) Esteem needs
(2) Safety needs
(3) Physiological needs
(4) Social needs

Directions: Each of the following items consists of two statements, one labelled as Assertion (A) and other labelled as Reason (R). You are to examine these two statements carefully and decide if the (A) and the (R) are individually true and if so, whether (R) is the correct explanation of (A). Select your answers to these items using the codes given below:
(1) Both (A) and (R) are true, and the (R) is the correct explanation of the (A).
(2) Both (A) and (R) are true, but the (R) is not the correct explanation of the (A).
(3) The (A) is true, but the (R) is false.
(4) The (A) is false, and the (R) is true.

91. Assertion (A): Expectancy theory suggests that individuals are motivated by the anticipation of rewards.
Reason (R): According to expectancy theory, individuals must believe that their efforts will lead to good performance and that good performance will be rewarded.

92. Assertion (A): Autocratic leadership involves empowering team members to make decisions collectively.
Reason (R): Autocratic leadership is characterised by a leader who makes decisions without consulting the team.

93. Assertion (A): Transformational leadership focuses on exchanging rewards and punishments for performance.
Reason (R): Transformational leadership involves inspiring and motivating followers to achieve their full potential.

94. Assertion (A): Equity theory suggests that individuals are motivated by the belief that their efforts will lead to good performance.
Reason (R): Equity theory emphasizes the perception of fairness in the distribution of rewards.

95. **Assertion (A):** According to Theory X, employees are inherently motivated and seek responsibility.
Reason (R): Theory X assumes that employees inherently dislike work and must be coerced or directed to perform.

96. What is the primary purpose of corporate governance?
(1) Maximising shareholder wealth
(2) Increasing employee satisfaction
(3) Achieving social responsibility
(4) Enhancing customer loyalty

97. Which of the following is a key element of corporate governance?
(1) Employee training programs
(2) Stakeholder conflict resolution
(3) Board oversight and accountability
(4) Marketing strategies

98. What is the role of the board of directors in corporate governance?
(1) Day-to-day management of operations
(2) Representing the interests of employees
(3) Setting the strategic direction of the company
(4) Conducting market research

99. In the context of corporate governance, what does the term "stakeholder" refer to?
(1) Shareholders only
(2) Employees only
(3) Individuals or groups with an interest in the company
(4) Customers only

100. Which principle of corporate governance emphasizes transparency and openness in decision-making?
(1) Fairness
(2) Accountability
(3) Transparency
(4) Responsibility

101. What is the purpose of an audit committee in corporate governance?
(1) Conducting marketing research
(2) Evaluating employee performance
(3) Ensuring financial reporting accuracy and compliance
(4) Managing day-to-day operations

102. What is the primary focus of business ethics?
(1) Maximising profits at any cost
(2) Balancing stakeholder interests
(3) Achieving social responsibility
(4) Enhancing employee satisfaction

103. Which of the following is a potential consequence of unethical business practices?
(1) Enhanced corporate reputation
(2) Increased customer loyalty
(3) Legal and regulatory issues
(4) Improved employee morale

104. What is the purpose of a code of ethics in business?
(1) Maximising shareholder wealth
(2) Ensuring compliance with legal requirements
(3) Balancing stakeholder interests
(4) Enhancing employee training programs

105. In the context of corporate governance, what does the term "fiduciary duty" refer to?
(1) A legal obligation to act in the best interest of stakeholders
(2) Prioritizing shareholder interests over employee interests
(3) A commitment to Maximise profits at any cost
(4) Avoiding social responsibility

106. Which of the following is a characteristic of effective corporate governance?
(1) Lack of transparency in decision-making
(2) Weak board oversight and accountability
(3) Inadequate stakeholder engagement
(4) Strong ethical leadership

107. What is the focus of social responsibility in business ethics?
(1) Maximising profits without consideration for societal impact
(2) Balancing the interests of employees and shareholders
(3) Contributing to the well-being of society
(4) Ignoring the impact of business on the environment

108. What is the purpose of a whistleblower protection policy in business ethics?
(1) Encouraging unethical behaviour
(2) Discouraging employees from reporting misconduct

(3) Providing a mechanism for reporting unethical behaviour without fear of retaliation
(4) Promoting transparency in financial reporting

109. In the context of business ethics, what does the term "conflict of interest" refer to?
(1) Ethical decision-making
(2) Balancing stakeholder interests
(3) A situation in which personal interests interfere with professional duties
(4) Maximising shareholder wealth

110. What is the primary goal of corporate social responsibility (CSR)?
(1) Maximising shareholder wealth
(2) Achieving legal compliance
(3) Balancing stakeholder interests
(4) Contributing to the well-being of society

111. What does the "triple bottom line" concept in corporate social responsibility (CSR) involve?
(1) Maximising profits, Minimising costs, and optimising shareholder wealth
(2) Balancing the interests of employees, customers, and shareholders
(3) Focusing on financial, social, and environmental performance
(4) Ignoring social and environmental considerations for economic gains

112. Which of the following is an example of an ethical leadership behaviour?
(1) Ignoring conflicts of interest
(2) Encouraging employees to engage in unethical practices
(3) Promoting transparency and openness in decision-making
(4) Avoiding stakeholder engagement

113. What is the purpose of a corporate ethics training program?
(1) Encouraging unethical behaviour
(2) Discouraging reporting of unethical conduct
(3) Providing employees with guidance on ethical decision-making
(4) Promoting a culture of secrecy

114. What is the focus of the "whistleblower" protection laws?
(1) Discouraging employees from reporting unethical behaviour
(2) Protecting individuals who report illegal or unethical activities from retaliation
(3) Encouraging unethical behaviour
(4) Prioritising the interests of shareholders over other stakeholders

115. What is the role of a corporate ethics officer in an organisation?
(1) Encouraging unethical behaviour
(2) Discouraging transparency in decision-making
(3) Promoting ethical conduct and ensuring compliance with ethical standards
(4) Ignoring the impact of business on the environment

Directions: Each of the following items consists of two statements, one labelled as Assertion (A) and other labelled as Reason (R). You are to examine these two statements carefully and decide if the (A) and the (R) are individually true and if so, whether (R) is the correct explanation of (A). Select your answers to these items using the codes given below:
(1) Both (A) and (R) are true, and the (R) is the correct explanation of the (A).
(2) Both (A) and (R) are true, but the (R) is not the correct explanation of the (A).
(3) The (A) is false, and the (R) is true.
(4) Both (A) and (R) are false.

116. **Assertion (A):** Corporate governance focuses solely on maximising shareholder wealth.
Reason (R): Corporate governance also involves considering the interests of other stakeholders.

117. **Assertion (A):** A code of ethics is unnecessary in organisations that prioritise maximising profits.
Reason (R): A code of ethics ensures legal compliance but has no impact on profit maximisation.

118. **Assertion (A):** Social responsibility in business ethics involves contributing to the well-being of society.
Reason (R): Social responsibility is limited to legal compliance and profitability.

119. **Assertion (A):** Whistleblower protection policies discourage employees from reporting unethical behaviour.
Reason (R): Whistleblower protection policies provide a mechanism for reporting unethical behaviour without fear of retaliation.

120. Assertion (A): The "triple bottom line" concept in CSR involves focusing on financial, social, and environmental performance.

Reason (R): CSR is exclusively concerned with financial and economic performance.

121. What is the primary focus of Human Resource Management (HRM)?
(1) Maximising shareholder wealth
(2) Enhancing customer satisfaction
(3) Managing and developing people within organisations
(4) Implementing marketing strategies

122. What is the role of HRM in recruitment and selection?
(1) Developing marketing campaigns
(2) Managing financial resources
(3) Attracting and hiring suitable employees
(4) Implementing technology solutions

123. Which HRM function involves assessing employee performance and providing feedback for improvement?
(1) Compensation and benefits
(2) Training and development
(3) Performance management
(4) Employee relations

124. What is the purpose of employee orientation in HRM?
(1) Determining compensation packages
(2) Introducing new employees to the organisation and its policies
(3) Managing employee relations
(4) Conducting job analysis

125. In HRM, what does the term "talent management" refer to?
(1) Attracting and retaining high-potential employees
(2) Implementing technology solutions
(3) Conducting market research
(4) Developing financial strategies

126. What is the goal of employee training and development in HRM?
(1) Determining compensation packages
(2) Improving employee satisfaction
(3) Enhancing employee skills and capabilities
(4) Managing financial resources

127. What is the purpose of a job analysis in HRM?
(1) Determining compensation packages
(2) Assessing employee performance
(3) Identifying the duties and responsibilities of a job
(4) Conducting market research

128. Which HRM function is responsible for managing employee relations, conflicts, and grievances?
(1) Compensation and benefits
(2) Employee engagement
(3) Employee relations
(4) Talent management

129. In HRM, what does the term "compensation" encompass?
(1) Employee training programs
(2) Financial performance analysis
(3) All the financial and non-financial rewards provided to employees
(4) Employee relations management

130. What is the primary goal of employee engagement in HRM?
(1) Maximising shareholder wealth
(2) Enhancing employee satisfaction
(3) Fostering a positive and productive work environment
(4) Conducting market research

131. Which HRM function involves determining fair and competitive wages for employees?
(1) Performance management
(2) Employee engagement
(3) Compensation and benefits
(4) Talent management

132. What is the purpose of succession planning in HRM?
(1) Assessing employee performance
(2) Developing strategies for employee retention
(3) Identifying and preparing future leaders within the organisation
(4) Conducting job analysis

133. In HRM, what is the significance of diversity and inclusion initiatives?
(1) Determining compensation packages
(2) Enhancing employee satisfaction
(3) Fostering a diverse and inclusive workplace culture
(4) Implementing technology solutions

134. What is the role of HRM in the performance appraisal process?
(1) Conducting market research
(2) Determining compensation packages
(3) Assessing employee performance and providing feedback
(4) Managing financial resources

135. Which HRM function involves designing and implementing programs to improve employee well-being?
(1) Compensation and benefits
(2) Employee engagement
(3) Employee wellness programs
(4) Talent management

136. What is the primary focus of HRM in employee retention?
(1) Conducting market research
(2) Managing financial resources
(3) Developing strategies to retain valuable employees
(4) Implementing technology solutions

137. In HRM, what does the term "workforce planning" involve?
(1) Determining compensation packages
(2) Developing strategies for employee engagement
(3) Ensuring the organisation has the right number and types of employees
(4) Managing financial resources

138. What is the purpose of an exit interview in HRM?
(1) Assessing employee performance
(2) Conducting market research
(3) Identifying reasons for employee turnover and gathering feedback
(4) Managing financial resources

139. What is the significance of HRM in legal compliance?
(1) Maximising shareholder wealth
(2) Ensuring the organisation complies with employment laws and regulations
(3) Conducting market research
(4) Developing financial strategies

140. In HRM, what is the purpose of a career development program?
(1) Developing financial strategies
(2) Determining compensation packages
(3) Enhancing employee skills and capabilities for future roles
(4) Managing employee relations

Directions: Each of the following items consists of two statements, one labelled as Assertion (A) and other labelled as Reason (R). You are to examine these two statements carefully and decide if the (A) and the (R) are individually true and if so, whether (R) is the correct explanation of (A). Select your answers to these items using the codes given below:
(1) Both (A) and (R) are true, and the (R) is the correct explanation of the (A).
(2) Both (A) and (R) are true, but the (R) is not the correct explanation of the (A).
(3) The (A) is false, and the (R) is true.
(4) The (A) is true, and the (R) is false.

141. Assertion (A): The primary focus of HRM is to maximise shareholder wealth.
Reason (R): HRM is concerned with managing and developing people within organisations.

142. Assertion (A): Employee engagement in HRM is solely about maximising profits for the organisation.
Reason (R): Employee engagement involves fostering a positive and productive work environment.

143. Assertion (A): Talent management in HRM is limited to attracting high-potential employees.
Reason (R): Talent management also involves retaining and developing key employees within the organisation.

144. Assertion (A): Compensation and benefits in HRM cover only financial rewards provided to employees.
Reason (R): Compensation and benefits encompass both financial and non-financial rewards.

145. Assertion (A): Workforce planning in HRM involves developing strategies for employee engagement.
Reason (R): Workforce planning is about ensuring the organisation has the right number and types of employees.

146. What is the primary goal of Human Resource Planning (HRP)?
(1) Maximising shareholder wealth
(2) Determining compensation packages
(3) Ensuring the organisation has the right number and types of employees
(4) Conducting market research

147. Which factor is considered in demand forecasting for HRP?
(1) Current employee turnover
(2) Employee engagement levels
(3) Historical financial performance
(4) Marketing strategies

148. What does the term "succession planning" involve in HRP?
(1) Identifying and preparing future leaders within the organisation
(2) Determining compensation packages
(3) Conducting job analysis
(4) Managing employee relations

149. How does HRP contribute to organisational efficiency?
(1) Maximising shareholder wealth
(2) Reducing employee engagement
(3) Aligning workforce supply with organisational demand
(4) Ignoring employee turnover rates

150. What is the purpose of a skills inventory in HRP?
(1) Assessing employee performance
(2) Identifying and cataloging employee skills and qualifications
(3) Conducting market research
(4) Developing strategies for employee engagement

151. Which of the following is a source of external recruitment?
(1) Employee referrals
(2) Internal job postings
(3) Promotions within the organisation
(4) Campus hiring

152. What is the primary goal of a job description in the recruitment process?
(1) Determining compensation packages
(2) Attracting suitable candidates
(3) Conducting market research
(4) Managing employee relations

153. What is the purpose of a selection interview in the recruitment process?
(1) Identifying and cataloging employee skills
(2) Assessing employee performance
(3) Determining compensation packages
(4) Evaluating the suitability of candidates for a job

154. Which recruitment method is typically used for filling higher-level positions within an organisation?
(1) Internal job postings
(2) Employee referrals
(3) Campus hiring
(4) Executive search firms

155. What is the significance of a realistic job preview in the recruitment process?
(1) Determining compensation packages
(2) Providing candidates with an accurate preview of the job and organisation
(3) Conducting market research
(4) Managing employee relations

156. What is the goal of on-the-job training methods?
(1) Maximising shareholder wealth
(2) Enhancing employee satisfaction
(3) Developing specific job-related skills while working
(4) Conducting market research

157. Which training method involves learning from experienced employees in a one-on-one setting?
(1) Job rotation
(2) Coaching and mentoring
(3) Classroom training
(4) E-learning

158. What is the purpose of a needs assessment in the training and development process?
(1) Assessing employee performance
(2) Determining compensation packages
(3) Identifying gaps between current and desired skills and knowledge
(4) Managing employee relations

159. Which training method is effective for teaching complex technical skills?
(1) Classroom training
(2) On-the-job training
(3) E-learning
(4) Simulations and role-playing

160. What is the focus of leadership development programs in training and development?
(1) Determining compensation packages
(2) Developing the skills and abilities of potential leaders within the organisation
(3) Conducting market research
(4) Managing employee relations

161. What is the purpose of identifying high-potential employees in succession planning?
(1) Determining compensation packages
(2) Preparing individuals for leadership roles within the organisation
(3) Conducting market research
(4) Managing employee relations

162. What is the role of a development plan in succession planning?
(1) Assessing employee performance
(2) Identifying and preparing future leaders within the organisation
(3) Determining compensation packages
(4) Conducting job analysis

163. What is the purpose of a talent review meeting in succession planning?
(1) Conducting market research
(2) Assessing employee performance
(3) Identifying high-potential employees and discussing their development
(4) Managing employee relations

164. How does succession planning contribute to organisational sustainability?
(1) Maximising shareholder wealth
(2) Developing a pool of qualified individuals for key roles
(3) Conducting market research
(4) Ignoring employee turnover rates

165. What is the primary focus of a talent management strategy in succession planning?
(1) Determining compensation packages
(2) Attracting and retaining high-potential employees
(3) Managing employee relations
(4) Conducting job analysis

Directions: Each of the following items consists of two statements, one labelled as Assertion (A) and other labelled as Reason (R). You are to examine these two statements carefully and decide if the (A) and the (R) are individually true and if so, whether (R) is the correct explanation of (A). Select your answers to these items using the codes given below:
(1) Both (A) and (R) are true, and the (R) is the correct explanation of the (A).
(2) Both (A) and (R) are true, but the (R) is not the correct explanation of the (A).
(3) The (A) is false, and the (R) is true.
(4) The (A) is true, and the (R) is false.

166. **Assertion (A):** Human Resource Planning (HRP) is solely concerned with determining compensation packages.
Reason: HRP is focused on ensuring the organisation has the right number and types of employees.

167. **Assertion (A):** A realistic job preview is used in the recruitment process to maximise shareholder wealth.
Reason: A realistic job preview provides candidates with an accurate preview of the job and organisation.

168. **Assertion (A):** On-the-job training methods aim to develop specific job-related skills while employees are working.
Reason: On-the-job training is only effective for theoretical learning and not for practical skill development.

169. **Assertion (A):** Succession planning involves ignoring employee turnover rates within an organisation.
Reason: Succession planning focuses on developing a pool of qualified individuals for key roles.

170. **Assertion (A):** A talent management strategy in succession planning aims to determine compensation packages.
Reason: Talent management in succession planning involves attracting and retaining high-potential employees.

171. What is the primary purpose of job evaluation in compensation management?
(1) Determining employee turnover rates
(2) Assessing employee performance
(3) Establishing the relative worth of different jobs
(4) Conducting employee training programs

172. In the context of compensation management, what does the term "pay structure" refer to?
(1) Determining compensation packages
(2) The hierarchy of jobs within an organisation based on their relative worth
(3) Conducting market research
(4) Assessing employee performance

173. What is the purpose of a salary survey in compensation management?
(1) Determining compensation packages
(2) Assessing employee performance

(3) Conducting market research on salary levels in the industry
(4) Establishing job hierarchies

174. In the context of job evaluation, what is the role of a job description?
(1) Determining employee turnover rates
(2) Assessing employee performance
(3) Describing the duties and requirements of a job
(4) Conducting employee training programs

175. What is the significance of a compensation philosophy in compensation management?
(1) Determining employee turnover rates
(2) Providing a framework for making compensation decisions aligned with organisational goals
(3) Conducting market research
(4) Assessing employee performance

176. Incentive plans in compensation management are designed to:
(1) Establish job hierarchies
(2) Encourage and reward employee performance
(3) Determine compensation packages
(4) Assess employee turnover rates

177. What is the purpose of a bonus in compensation management?
(1) Determining employee turnover rates
(2) Encouraging and rewarding exceptional performance
(3) Assessing employee performance
(4) Establishing job hierarchies

178. In the context of incentives, what is profit sharing?
(1) Determining employee turnover rates
(2) Employees receive a share of the company's profits
(3) Conducting market research
(4) Establishing job hierarchies

179. What is the primary goal of fringe benefits in compensation management?
(1) Determining employee turnover rates
(2) Enhancing employee satisfaction and well-being
(3) Conducting market research
(4) Assessing employee performance

180. In the context of fringe benefits, what does the term "health insurance" encompass?
(1) Providing employees with guidance on ethical decision-making
(2) Offering medical coverage, including hospitalisation and medication
(3) Conducting market research
(4) Determining employee turnover rates

181. What is the significance of a flexible benefits plan in compensation management?
(1) Determining compensation packages
(2) Allowing employees to choose from a menu of benefits to meet their individual needs
(3) Assessing employee performance
(4) Conducting market research

182. In the context of compensation management, what is the purpose of a salary range?
(1) Determining employee turnover rates
(2) Providing a range of acceptable salaries for a particular job
(3) Assessing employee performance
(4) Establishing job hierarchies

183. What is the primary focus of a merit-based compensation system?
(1) Determining compensation packages
(2) Linking pay increases to individual performance
(3) Conducting market research
(4) Assessing employee turnover rates

184. In the context of incentive plans, what is the purpose of a commission-based system?
(1) Determining employee turnover rates
(2) Rewarding employees based on a percentage of sales or revenue generated
(3) Assessing employee performance
(4) Establishing job hierarchies

185. What is the role of a job evaluation committee in compensation management?
(1) Determining compensation packages
(2) Assessing employee performance
(3) Evaluating the relative worth of different jobs within the organisation
(4) Conducting market research

186. What is the purpose of a cost-of-living adjustment (COLA) in compensation management?
(1) Determining employee turnover rates

(2) Adjusting salaries to account for changes in the cost of living
(3) Assessing employee performance
(4) Conducting market research

187. In the context of incentives, what is the purpose of a recognition program?
(1) Determining compensation packages
(2) Acknowledging and rewarding employees for their contributions and achievements
(3) Assessing employee performance
(4) Establishing job hierarchies

188. What is the significance of a deferred compensation plan in compensation management?
(1) Determining employee turnover rates
(2) Providing employees with guidance on ethical decision-making
(3) Delaying the payment of a portion of an employee's compensation to a future date
(4) Conducting market research

189. In the context of compensation management, what is the purpose of a sign-on bonus?
(1) Determining employee turnover rates
(2) Attracting new employees to the organisation
(3) Assessing employee performance
(4) Establishing job hierarchies

190. What is the role of a salary survey in job evaluation?
(1) Determining compensation packages
(2) Conducting market research on salary levels in the industry
(3) Assessing employee performance
(4) Establishing job hierarchies

Directions: Each of the following items consists of two statements, one labelled as Assertion (A) and other labelled as Reason (R). You are to examine these two statements carefully and decide if the (A) and the (R) are individually true and if so, whether (R) is the correct explanation of (A). Select your answers to these items using the codes given below:
(1) Both (A) and (R) are true, and the (R) is the correct explanation of the (A).
(2) Both (A) and (R) are true, but the (R) is not the correct explanation of the (A).
(3) The (A) is false, and the (R) is true.
(4) The (A) is true, and the (R) is false.

191. Assertion (A): Job evaluation is focused on determining employee turnover rates.
Reason (R): Job evaluation establishes the relative worth of different jobs within an organisation.

192. Assertion (A): A bonus in compensation management is primarily designed to enhance employee satisfaction.
Reason (R): Bonuses are used to encourage and reward exceptional performance.

193. Assertion (A): Fringe benefits play a minimal role in enhancing employee satisfaction and well-being.
Reason (R): Fringe benefits are designed to enhance employee satisfaction and well-being.

194. Assertion (A): A salary range in compensation management provides flexibility in determining compensation packages.
Reason (R): A salary range offers a range of acceptable salaries for a particular job.

195. Assertion (A): Incentive plans in compensation management are solely focused on determining compensation packages.
Reason (R): Incentive plans are designed to encourage and reward employee performance.

196. What is the primary goal of performance appraisal?
(1) Determining compensation packages
(2) Assessing employee turnover rates
(3) Evaluating and improving employee performance
(4) Conducting market research

197. In the context of performance appraisal, what does the term "360-degree feedback" involve?
(1) Feedback provided by the supervisor only
(2) Feedback from multiple sources, including peers, subordinates, and supervisors
(3) Assessing employee turnover rates
(4) Conducting market research

198. What is the purpose of setting performance goals in the performance appraisal process?
(1) Determining compensation packages
(2) Providing a benchmark for evaluating employee performance
(3) Assessing employee turnover rates
(4) Conducting market research

199. What is the role of a performance appraisal form in the evaluation process?
(1) Determining compensation packages

(2) Providing a structured framework for assessing and documenting employee performance
(3) Assessing employee turnover rates
(4) Conducting market research

200. What is the purpose of self-assessment in performance appraisal?
(1) Determining compensation packages
(2) Allowing employees to evaluate their own performance
(3) Assessing employee turnover rates
(4) Conducting market research

201. In the context of performance appraisal, what is the significance of regular feedback sessions?
(1) Determining compensation packages
(2) Providing ongoing communication and guidance on performance
(3) Assessing employee turnover rates
(4) Conducting market research

202. What is the primary focus of the graphic rating scale method in performance appraisal?
(1) Determining compensation packages
(2) Assessing employee turnover rates
(3) Using a scale to rate various performance factors
(4) Conducting market research

203. In performance appraisal, what does the critical incident method involve?
(1) Assessing employee turnover rates
(2) Focusing on specific events that demonstrate exceptional or poor performance
(3) Determining compensation packages
(4) Conducting market research

204. What is the purpose of the forced ranking method in performance appraisal?
(1) Determining compensation packages
(2) Assessing employee turnover rates
(3) Ranking employees based on their performance in comparison to others
(4) Conducting market research

205. What is the significance of the Management by Objectives (MBO) method in performance appraisal?
(1) Determining compensation packages
(2) Setting performance goals and objectives collaboratively between employees and managers
(3) Assessing employee turnover rates
(4) Conducting market research

206. In the context of performance appraisal, what is the purpose of a performance improvement plan?
(1) Determining compensation packages
(2) Providing employees with guidance on ethical decision-making
(3) Assessing employee turnover rates
(4) Outlining steps for employees to enhance their performance

207. What is the role of peer reviews in 360-degree performance appraisal?
(1) Determining compensation packages
(2) Assessing employee turnover rates
(3) Gathering feedback from coworkers to evaluate an employee's performance
(4) Conducting market research

208. What is the purpose of a performance appraisal interview?
(1) Determining compensation packages
(2) Assessing employee turnover rates
(3) Discussing and reviewing an employee's performance
(4) Conducting market research

209. In performance appraisal, what does the term "halo effect" refer to?
(1) Assessing employee turnover rates
(2) Allowing positive perceptions in one area to influence overall performance ratings
(3) Determining compensation packages
(4) Conducting market research

210. What is the primary focus of the behaviourally anchored rating scale (BARS) method in performance appraisal?
(1) Determining compensation packages
(2) Assessing employee turnover rates
(3) Using specific examples of behaviour to rate performance
(4) Conducting market research

211. What is the purpose of the narrative appraisal method in performance appraisal?
(1) Determining compensation packages
(2) Assessing employee turnover rates
(3) Providing a written account of an employee's performance
(4) Conducting market research

212. In 360-degree performance appraisal, who typically provides feedback?
   (1) Only the supervisor
   (2) Multiple sources, including peers, subordinates, customers, and supervisors
   (3) Assessing employee turnover rates
   (4) Conducting market research

213. What is the purpose of a performance rating scale in 360-degree performance appraisal?
   (1) Determining compensation packages
   (2) Assessing employee turnover rates
   (3) Providing a standardised method for rating various performance factors
   (4) Conducting market research

214. What is the role of a feedback facilitator in 360-degree performance appraisal?
   (1) Determining compensation packages
   (2) Assessing employee turnover rates
   (3) Assisting in the collection and dissemination of feedback
   (4) Conducting market research

215. In performance appraisal, what is the purpose of a performance rating scale with numerical scores?
   (1) Determining compensation packages
   (2) Assessing employee turnover rates
   (3) Providing a quantitative measure of performance
   (4) Conducting market research

Directions: Each of the following items consists of two statements, one labelled as Assertion (A) and other labelled as Reason (R). You are to examine these two statements carefully and decide if the (A) and the (R) are individually true and if so, whether (R) is the correct explanation of (A). Select your answers to these items using the codes given below:
   (1) Both (A) and (R) are true, and the (R) is the correct explanation of the (A).
   (2) Both (A) and (R) are true, but the (R) is not the correct explanation of the (A).
   (3) The (A) is false, and the (R) is true.
   (4) The (A) is true, and the (R) is false.

216. **Assertion (A):** Performance appraisal is primarily concerned with determining compensation packages.
   Reason (R): The main goal of performance appraisal is to evaluate and improve employee performance.

217. **Assertion (A):** 360-degree feedback involves obtaining performance feedback only from supervisors.
   Reason (R): 360-degree feedback includes feedback from multiple sources, including peers, subordinates, and supervisors.

218. **Assertion (A):** The forced ranking method in performance appraisal involves ranking employees based on their performance in comparison to others.
   Reason (R): Forced ranking aims to assess individual performance in isolation, without comparing it to others.

219. **Assertion (A):** The Management by Objectives (MBO) method is focused on assessing employee turnover rates.
   Reason (R): MBO involves setting performance goals and objectives collaboratively between employees and managers.

220. **Assertion (A):** The halo effect in performance appraisal refers to allowing negative perceptions in one area to influence overall performance ratings.
   Reason (R): The halo effect occurs when positive perceptions in one area influence overall performance ratings.

221. What is collective bargaining?
   (1) Individual negotiation between employees and management
   (2) A group of employees forming a union
   (3) A process of negotiation between employers and a group of employees aimed at agreements on working conditions
   (4) Determining compensation packages

222. What is the primary goal of collective bargaining?
   (1) Determining compensation packages
   (2) Establishing a labour union
   (3) Negotiating agreements on employment conditions
   (4) Conducting market research

223. In collective bargaining, what does the term "bargaining unit" refer to?
   (1) A group of management representatives
   (2) A group of employees represented by a union for negotiations
   (3) Determining compensation packages
   (4) Conducting market research

224. What is the purpose of a collective bargaining agreement (CBA)?
(1) Establishing a labour union
(2) Determining compensation packages
(3) Providing a written contract specifying terms and conditions of employment
(4) Conducting market research

225. In the context of collective bargaining, what is the role of a mediator?
(1) A representative of the management
(2) A neutral third party facilitating negotiations between employers and employees
(3) Determining compensation packages
(4) Conducting market research

226. What is a lockout in the context of collective bargaining?
(1) A situation where employees refuse to work
(2) A decision by management to prevent employees from working during a labour dispute
(3) Establishing a labour union
(4) Determining compensation packages

227. What is a strike in the context of collective bargaining?
(1) Establishing a labour union
(2) A situation where employees refuse to work
(3) Determining compensation packages
(4) Conducting market research

228. What is the significance of workers' participation in management?
(1) Determining compensation packages
(2) Involving employees in decision-making processes and organisational matters
(3) Establishing a labour union
(4) Conducting market research

229. What is the primary goal of workers' participation in management?
(1) Determining compensation packages
(2) Enhancing employee engagement
(3) Ensuring employees have a voice in organisational decisions
(4) Conducting market research

230. In workers' participation, what does the term "joint consultation" involve?
(1) Employees making decisions without management input
(2) Collaborative discussions and sharing of information between management and employees
(3) Determining compensation packages
(4) Conducting market research

231. What is the purpose of a works council in workers' participation?
(1) Determining compensation packages
(2) A formal structure for employees to communicate and negotiate with management
(3) Establishing a labour union
(4) Conducting market research

232. In workers' participation, what is the role of a shop steward?
(1) A representative of the management
(2) An employee who leads union activities
(3) Determining compensation packages
(4) A representative elected by union members to address workplace issues

233. What is the purpose of a grievance procedure in collective bargaining?
(1) Determining compensation packages
(2) A process for addressing and resolving disputes between employees and management
(3) Establishing a labour union
(4) Conducting market research

234. In collective bargaining, what is the significance of "good faith bargaining"?
(1) Employees negotiating without genuine intent
(2) Employers negotiating without genuine intent
(3) A requirement for both parties to negotiate honestly and with a sincere desire to reach an agreement
(4) Determining compensation packages

235. What is the role of a conciliator in collective bargaining?
(1) A representative of the management
(2) A neutral third party facilitating negotiations between employers and employees
(3) Establishing a labour union
(4) Determining compensation packages

236. What is the purpose of a collective bargaining process?
(1) Determining compensation packages

(2) Negotiating agreements on employment conditions
(3) Establishing a labour union
(4) Conducting market research

237. What is the role of a strike vote in collective bargaining?
(1) Determining compensation packages
(2) A formal vote by union members to authorise a strike if necessary
(3) Establishing a labour union
(4) Conducting market research

238. What is the purpose of a picket line in collective bargaining?
(1) Determining compensation packages
(2) A line formed by striking workers to protest and discourage others from entering the workplace
(3) Establishing a labour union
(4) Conducting market research

239. What is the role of a conciliation board in collective bargaining?
(1) A representative of the management
(2) A neutral third party facilitating negotiations between employers and employees
(3) Determining compensation packages
(4) A board appointed to help resolve disputes and make recommendations

240. In workers' participation, what is the purpose of a quality circle?
(1) Determining compensation packages
(2) A small group of employees who meet regularly to identify and solve workplace problems
(3) Establishing a labour union
(4) Conducting market research

Directions: Each of the following items consists of two statements, one labelled as Assertion (A) and other labelled as Reason (R). You are to examine these two statements carefully and decide if the (A) and the (R) are individually true and if so, whether (R) is the correct explanation of (A). Select your answers to these items using the codes given below:
(1) Both (A) and (R) are true, and the (R) is the correct explanation of the (A).
(2) Both (A) and (R) are true, but the (R) is not the correct explanation of the (A).
(3) The (A) is true, but the (R) is false.
(4) The (A) is false, and the (R) is true.

241. Assertion (A): The primary goal of collective bargaining is to establish a labour union.
Reason (R): Collective bargaining is a process of negotiation between employers and a group of employees aimed at agreements on working conditions.

242. Assertion (A): A lockout is a situation where employees refuse to work during a labour dispute.
Reason (R): A lockout is a decision by management to prevent employees from working during a labour dispute.

243. Assertion (A): Workers' participation in management focuses on determining compensation packages.
Reason (R): Workers' participation involves involving employees in decision-making processes and organisational matters.

244. Assertion (A): Joint consultation in workers' participation means employees making decisions without management input.
Reason (R): Joint consultation involves collaborative discussions and sharing of information between management and employees.

245. Assertion (A): Good faith bargaining is a requirement for both parties in collective bargaining to negotiate honestly and with a sincere desire to reach an agreement.
Reason (R): In good faith bargaining, either party can negotiate with deceptive intentions.

ANSWERS

1. (3)	**2.** (2)	**3.** (3)	**4.** (2)	**5.** (4)	**6.** (4)	**7.** (2)	**8.** (3)	**9.** (4)	**10.** (3)
11. (3)	**12.** (3)	**13.** (4)	**14.** (3)	**15.** (1)	**16.** (3)	**17.** (4)	**18.** (3)	**19.** (3)	**20.** (1)
21. (3)	**22.** (1)	**23.** (4)	**24.** (4)	**25.** (3)	**26.** (3)	**27.** (2)	**28.** (3)	**29.** (1)	**30.** (2)
31. (3)	**32.** (3)	**33.** (3)	**34.** (2)	**35.** (3)	**36.** (3)	**37.** (4)	**38.** (2)	**39.** (4)	**40.** (2)
41. (1)	**42.** (3)	**43.** (3)	**44.** (4)	**45.** (1)	**46.** (2)	**47.** (3)	**48.** (2)	**49.** (3)	**50.** (3)
51. (3)	**52.** (2)	**53.** (2)	**54.** (4)	**55.** (2)	**56.** (1)	**57.** (2)	**58.** (1)	**59.** (2)	**60.** (3)
61. (3)	**62.** (3)	**63.** (2)	**64.** (3)	**65.** (1)	**66.** (4)	**67.** (3)	**68.** (1)	**69.** (3)	**70.** (4)
71. (2)	**72.** (2)	**73.** (2)	**74.** (1)	**75.** (1)	**76.** (2)	**77.** (1)	**78.** (3)	**79.** (1)	**80.** (2)
81. (4)	**82.** (3)	**83.** (3)	**84.** (2)	**85.** (3)	**86.** (2)	**87.** (2)	**88.** (3)	**89.** (3)	**90.** (3)
91. (1)	**92.** (4)	**93.** (4)	**94.** (4)	**95.** (4)	**96.** (1)	**97.** (3)	**98.** (3)	**99.** (3)	**100.** (3)
101. (3)	**102.** (2)	**103.** (3)	**104.** (2)	**105.** (1)	**106.** (4)	**107.** (3)	**108.** (3)	**109.** (3)	**110.** (4)
111. (3)	**112.** (3)	**113.** (3)	**114.** (2)	**115.** (3)	**116.** (4)	**117.** (4)	**118.** (3)	**119.** (3)	**120.** (3)
121. (3)	**122.** (3)	**123.** (3)	**124.** (2)	**125.** (1)	**126.** (3)	**127.** (3)	**128.** (3)	**129.** (3)	**130.** (3)
131. (3)	**132.** (3)	**133.** (3)	**134.** (3)	**135.** (3)	**136.** (3)	**137.** (3)	**138.** (3)	**139.** (2)	**140.** (3)
141. (3)	**142.** (3)	**143.** (3)	**144.** (3)	**145.** (3)	**146.** (3)	**147.** (1)	**148.** (1)	**149.** (3)	**150.** (2)
151. (4)	**152.** (2)	**153.** (4)	**154.** (4)	**155.** (2)	**156.** (3)	**157.** (2)	**158.** (3)	**159.** (4)	**160.** (2)
161. (2)	**162.** (2)	**163.** (3)	**164.** (2)	**165.** (2)	**166.** (3)	**167.** (4)	**168.** (4)	**169.** (3)	**170.** (4)
171. (3)	**172.** (2)	**173.** (3)	**174.** (3)	**175.** (2)	**176.** (2)	**177.** (2)	**178.** (2)	**179.** (2)	**180.** (2)
181. (2)	**182.** (2)	**183.** (2)	**184.** (2)	**185.** (3)	**186.** (2)	**187.** (2)	**188.** (3)	**189.** (2)	**190.** (2)
191. (3)	**192.** (2)	**193.** (3)	**194.** (1)	**195.** (4)	**196.** (3)	**197.** (2)	**198.** (2)	**199.** (2)	**200.** (2)
201. (2)	**202.** (3)	**203.** (2)	**204.** (3)	**205.** (2)	**206.** (4)	**207.** (3)	**208.** (3)	**209.** (2)	**210.** (3)
211. (3)	**212.** (2)	**213.** (3)	**214.** (3)	**215.** (3)	**216.** (4)	**217.** (4)	**218.** (4)	**219.** (3)	**220.** (3)
221. (3)	**222.** (3)	**223.** (2)	**224.** (3)	**225.** (2)	**226.** (2)	**227.** (2)	**228.** (2)	**229.** (3)	**230.** (2)
231. (2)	**232.** (4)	**233.** (2)	**234.** (3)	**235.** (2)	**236.** (2)	**237.** (2)	**238.** (2)	**239.** (4)	**240.** (2)
241. (4)	**242.** (4)	**243.** (4)	**244.** (4)	**245.** (3)					

UNIT 7

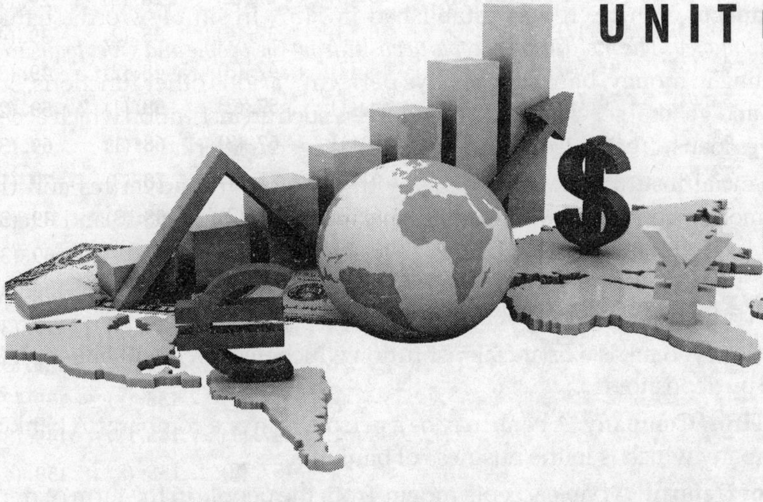

BANKING AND FINANCIAL INSTITUTIONS

SYLLABUS

- Overview of Indian financial system
- Types of banks: Commercial banks; Regional Rural Banks (RRBs); Foreign banks; Cooperative banks
- Reserve Bank of India: Functions; Role and monetary policy management
- Banking sector reforms in India: Basel norms; Risk management; NPA management
- Financial markets: Money market; Capital market; Government securities market
- Financial Institutions: Development Finance Institutions (DFIs); Non-Banking Financial Companies (NBFCs); Mutual Funds; Pension Funds
- Financial Regulators in India
- Financial sector reforms including financial inclusion
- Digitisation of banking and other financial services: Internet banking; mobile banking; Digital payments systems
- Insurance: Types of insurance- Life and Non-life insurance; Risk classification and management; Factors limiting the insurability of risk; Re-insurance; Regulatory framework of insurance- IRDA and its role

OVERVIEW OF INDIAN FINANCIAL SYSTEM

The term Bank is being used since long time but there is no clear conception regarding its beginning. Origin of the word bank belongs to the word **Banchi** or to the Greek word **Banque**. Both these words refer to some kind of banking. *Casa De San Giorgio* was the first bank to be established in 1148. The first public bank was **Bank of Venice**. It was established in 1157. In simple words, bank *refers to an institution that deals in money. The institution accepts deposits from the people and gives loans to those who are in need.* Besides dealing in money, banks these days perform various other functions, such as credit creation, agency job and general service. Bank, therefore, is such an institution which accepts deposits from the people, gives loans, creates credit and undertakes agency work.

A bank is a financial institution which deals with deposits and advances and other related services. It receives money from those who want to save in the form of deposits and it lends money to those who need it.

Characteristics/Features of a Bank

1. **Dealing in Money.** Bank is a financial institution which deals with other people's money i.e. money given by depositors.
2. **Individual / Firm / Company.** A bank may be a person, firm or a company. A banking company means a company which is in the business of banking.
3. **Acceptance of Deposit.** A bank accepts money from the people in the form of deposits which are usually repayable on demand or after the expiry of a fixed period. It gives safety to the deposits of its customers. It also acts as a custodian of funds of its customers.
4. **Giving Advances.** A bank lends out money in the form of loans to those who require it for different purposes.
5. **Payment and Withdrawal.** A bank provides easy payment and withdrawal facility to its customers in the form of cheques and drafts. It also brings back money in circulation. This money is in the form of cheques, drafts, etc.
6. **Agency and Utility Services.** A bank provides various banking facilities to its customers. They include general utility services and agency services.
7. **Profit and Service Orientation.** A bank is a profit seeking institution having service oriented approach.
8. **Ever increasing Functions.** Banking is an evolutionary concept. There is continuous expansion and diversification as regards the functions, services and activities of a bank.
9. **Connecting Link.** A bank acts as a connecting link between borrowers and lenders of money. Banks collect money from those who have surplus money and give the same to those who are in need of money.
10. **Banking Business.** A bank's main activity should be to do business of banking which should not be subsidiary to any other business.
11. **Name Identity.** A bank should always add the word "bank" to its name to enable people to know that it is a bank and that it is dealing in money.

TYPES OF BANKS

Banks may be classified on various basis, as under:

Classification on the Basis of Ownership

On the basis of ownership, banks are of the following types:

(i) **Public Sector Banks.** Public Sector Banks are those banks which are owned by the government. The Government runs these banks. In India 20 banks (14+ 6) were nationalised in 1969 and 1980 respectively. All these banks now belong to the public sector category. Social welfare is their principal objective.

(ii) **Private Sector Banks.** These are the banks which are owned and run by the private sector. Various banks in the country such as Vijaya Bank belong to this category. An individual has control over these banks in proportion to the shares of the banks held by him.

(iii) **Co-operative Banks.** Co-operative Banks are those banks which are jointly run by a group of individuals. Each individual has an equal share in these banks. The affairs of the bank are managed by its shareholders. Profits are equally distributed among the shareholders. Mutual help from the members of co-operative banks is the principal objective of these banks.

Classification According to Law

Banks are classified into the following two categories on the basis of Reserve Bank Act, 1934:

(i) **Scheduled Banks.** These are the banks having paid up capital of at least Rs. 5 lacs. These are like a joint stock company or a cooperative organisation. These banks find their mention in the second schedule of the Reserve Bank.

(ii) **Non-Scheduled Banks.** These banks are not mentioned in the second schedule of Reserve Bank. Paid-up capital of these banks is less than Rs. 5 lacs. The number of such banks is gradually falling in India. There are only '3' such banks at present.

Classification according to Functions

On the basis of their functions, banks are classified as under:

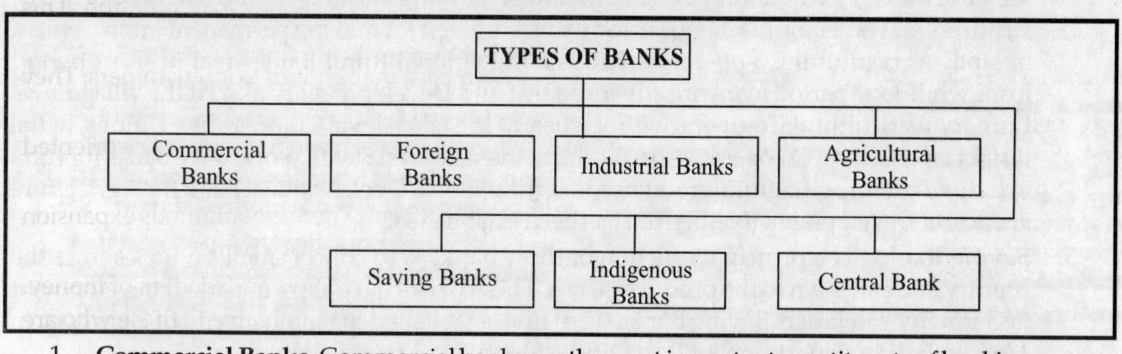

1. **Commercial Banks.** Commercial banks are the most important constituents of banking system. These are the banks which do banking business to earn profit. According to **Goldfield** and **Chandler** the term *'Commercial' with regard to these banks refers to Commercial Loan Theory.* According to this theory, in the assets of banks are included short term loans in addition to cash. Hence, Commercial Banks are those banks which advance loans for short period. In the words of **Culbertson**, *'Commercial Banks are the institutions that make short term loans to business and in the process create money'*. According to **Reed** and **Gill**, *'A commercial bank is a financial institution that accepts demand deposits and makes commercial loans and is regulated by a bank regulatory agency"*.

According to **Goldfield** and **Chandler** it is wrong as well as confusing to call these banks as commercial banks. This is because of two reasons. First, these banks also give long period loans to agriculture and industry. Second, many other institutions have also come up which give only short-period loans. The principal function of these banks is that the credit created by these banks is accepted and functions like money as a medium of exchange. These banks do not issue notes but create credit on the basis of their cash deposits. Credit creation is the principal function of these banks. **Chandler** therefore, maintains that it would be more appropriate to call these banks as **Cheque Deposits Banks**. But their current and popular name is Commercial Banks. Thus, a commercial bank is a bank which deals in money and credit for the purpose of earning profit. The State Bank of India, Punjab National Bank, Indian Bank, Canara Bank are some of the examples of Commercial Banks.

2. **Foreign Banks.** Foreign Banks are those banks which are incorporated in a foreign country. They have set up their branches in India. Their principal function is to make credit arrangement for the exports and imports of the country and these banks deal in foreign exchange. These banks convert the country's currency into currencies of other countries, and likewise foreign currencies are converted into domestic currency. To perform this function of currency-conversion, these banks have to keep with them currencies of the various countries. These banks have their head offices in foreign countries.

   Most of the exchange banks in India are foreign banks; *Grindlays Bank, Chartered Bank, Hong-Kong Bank, Bank of America* are examples of these banks in India.
3. **Industrial Banks.** Industrial Banks are those banks which offer long term and medium term loans to the industries and also work for their development. These banks help industries in the sale of their debentures, bonds and shares. Banks themselves purchase the shares as well as underwrite the debentures of the industries. Industrial Banks give loans to the industries for the purchase of land and machinery. In India many industrial banks have been established after independence, viz. *Industrial Development Bank of India, Industrial Finance corporation, State Finance Corporations and others.*
4. **Agricultural Banks.** Agricultural Banks are those banks which give credit to agricultural sector of the economy. Short period loans are given to the farmers for the purchase of seeds, fertilizers and other inputs. Long period loans are given for making permanent improvement of land. Agricultural Co-operative Banks and Regional Rural Banks deal in short period loans while long period loans are advanced by Land Development Banks. At the village level Primary Agricultural Co-operative Societies, at the tehsil level Co-operative Unions, at the district level Central Co-operative Banks and at the state level State Co-operative Banks function in India. To fulfil agricultural credit needs at the national level, National Bank for Agriculture and Rural Development (NABARD) has been established.
5. **Saving Banks.** The principal function of these banks is to collect small savings across the country and put them to the productive use. These Banks have shown marked development in Germany and Japan. Saving Banks were first established in Hamberg city of Germany in 1765. In India a department of Post Offices functions as Saving Banks.
6. **Indigenous Banks.** These Banks found their origin in India. These banks made a significant contribution to the development of agriculture and industry before independence. *Mahajans*, rural money lenders and jewellers have been the fore-runners of these banks in India. These agencies do their banking business with their own funds. Even these days nearly 40% of agricultural loans are offered by the indigenous banks in India.
7. **Central Bank.** Central Bank is the Apex bank of the banking system of the country. It issues currency notes and acts as banker's bank. It controls credit and regulates the banking system of the country. Central Bank occupies an important status in monetary and banking system of a country. Economic stability is the principal function of these banks. The Central Bank issues

all types of currency, controls all other banks in the country and functions as a bank of the Government. This Bank also controls and regulates the flow of credit. The Reserve Bank of India, Bank of England and Federal Reserve System are the Central Banks respectively of India, England and U.S.A. Though the first Central bank in the world was established in 1668 in Sweden, but the true beginning of Central banking system is marked with the establishment of Bank of England in 1694. In short, Central Bank is an institution that controls and regulates the banking system of a country.

History and Growth of Banking System in India

The Indian banking system traces sack its history to 1786, when the first bank general bank of India was established.

From that year till today, the journey of growth of the Indian banking system can he divided into three phases:

Phase I (Early Phase from 1786 to 1969 of Indian Banks)

- In the mid 19th century, the East India Company established the Bank of Bengal in 1809, the Bank of Bombay in 1840 and the Bank of Madras in 1843.
  These were initially , independent units and were referred as the Presidency Banks. These three were later merged in 1920, as Imperial Bank of India, which had European shareholders.
- Later in 1865, Allahabad Bank was established followed by Punjab National Bank in 1894. Between 1906 and 1913, Bank of India, Central Bank of India, Bank of Baroda, Canara Bank, Indian Bank and Bank of Mysore were set-up.
- Reserve Bank of India came into being in 1935.

Phase II (Nationalisation of Indian Banks and upto 1991 prior to Indian Banking Sector Reforms)

- In 1949, Banking Regulation Act enacted.
- After independence, the Imperial Bank of India was nationalised under the State Bank of India Act of 1955 and became known as the State Bank of India for handling Central and State Government Banking transactions and functioning as the principal agent of RBI.
- In 1959, seven subsidiaries of SBI were also nationalised.
- In 1961, insurance cover extended to deposits.
- With effect from the midnight of 19th July, 1969, 14 major banks were nationalised.
- In 1971, credit guarantee corporation was created.
- Regional Rural Bank was introduced in 1975.
- In 1980, 6 banks with deposits over Rs 200 crore were nationalised.

Phase III (New Phase of Indian Banking System with the advent Indian Financial and Banking Sector Reforms after, 1991)

- Prior to 1991, all banks were state owned. In 1991, government opened the gate of liberalisation of banking practices as per the report of a banking committee set-up under the chairmanship of Mr. M. Narasimham.
- Later on, in the year 1993, the government merged New Bank of India with Punjab National Bank. It was the only merger between nationalised banks and resulted in the reduction of the number of nationalised banks from 20 to 19.

- Till now, banking industry has changed tremendously with retail banking shifting to universal banking, E-banking and has customer satisfaction as the highest priority.

Classification of Commercial Banks on the basis of their Organisation

On the basis of their organisation, commercial banks may be classified as under:

(a) **Unit Banking.** According to **Kent**, '*Under unit banking system, the banking operations are carried through a single banking office rather than through a net work of branches. Each* banking company is a separate company, separately licensed, having its own capital, Board of Directors and shareholders.'

In this banking system a particular bank functions in a limited area. Bank is of small size and generally it has no branch office. Such a bank deposits its money in some big bank, called Correspondent Bank. The control and ownership of these banks is generally in the hands of local individuals. This banking system is popular in U.S.A.

(b) **Branch Banking.** Branch banking refers to that system of banking in which a bank establishes its head office in some big city and operates the various branches all over the country. Some of its branches may also be in foreign countries. Branch Banking System is popular in India, Britain, Canada, France, Germany and various other countries. In the words of **Goldfield** and **Chandler**, '*A branch bank is a banking corporation that directly owns two or more banking agencies.*'

Branch Banking is a system in which:

(i) a bank renders its banking services at two or more places

(ii) head office has the overall control over the working of various branches

(iii) branches can be opened in the same town, state or the country in which the concerned head office is located or at different places

(iv) overall control of all the branches is done by one central authority, viz. Board of Directors.

(c) **Group Banking.** Group Banking is that banking system is which two or more banks operate under the control of a holding company. In the words of **Goldfield** and **Chandler**, 'Group Banking refers to the system in which a corporation or a holding company operates two or more banks simultaneously. These banks are known as **subsidiaries** of the corporation or the holding company. These banks may be unit banks or branch banks.' Group banking system is most popular in the United States of America. According to Bank Holding Company Act, 1956 (U.S.A.) 'A holding company is the one which has at least 25% equity of the concerned group of banks. There can be more than one or many banks under the control and management of the holding company. The holding company is popularly known as parent company and the group of banks operating under it are called operating companies or subsidiary companies. Each bank in the group is controlled by the parent company.' Presently there are nearly 500 group banks in America.

(d) **Chain Banking.** Chain Banking is a banking system where the same individual or group of individuals control two or more banks. In this system an undivided or a group of individuals buy the bulk of shares of two or more banks and thus happen to control and manage them. This system of banking became popular in U.S.A. in 1920. In this system every bank in the banking chain has its own identity as well as independent board of management. However, it is possible that one individual is the member of various management boards.

(e) **Correspondent Banking.** Reed and Gill states that, '*Correspondent Banking is an arrangement that exists among banks throughout the country based on the practice of smaller banks carrying deposits with larger banks in exchange for the performance of various services.*' Services rendered by the larger banks include cheque clearing, sale and purchase of securities, making advances for big loans and the like. These larger banks are called Correspondent Banks.

Correspondent banking system has developed owing to the facts that: (a) Smaller Banks can generally not afford funds for rendering certain major banking services such as the sale and purchase of securities and (b) Smaller banks find it difficult to function as clearing agents.

Correspondent banks perform the following principal functions:

(i) to procure currency and coins from the Central Bank for distribution among smaller banks.

(ii) to facilitate clearing and collection of cheques for their member banks.

(iii) to facilitate domestic as well as foreign payments on behalf of the member banks.

(iv) to render such agency services on behalf of the member banks as sale and purchase of securities, issuing bank drafts and the like. Correspondent banking is fairly popular in countries like USA.

Classification of Scheduled Banks

Scheduled hanks can further he categorised as follows:

Public Sector Banks. Public sector banks are banks, in which the government and RBI has major holding. They are managed and operated by the government. They can be further sub-divided into SBI and its associate banks, other nationalised banks and regional rural banks. These are as follows:

SBI and Associate Banks. State Bank of India (SBI) is the country's largest commercial bank in terms of assets, deposits and employees. It is a government—owned corporation which offers a wide range of general banking services from loans and advances to corporates and individuals in India and abroad.

Note. All subsidiary banks of SBI and Bhartiya Mahila Bank have been merged into SBI in April 2017.

Nationalised Banks. In 1955, the Imperial Bank of India was nationalised and was given the name 'State Bank of India'. On 19th July, 1969, major 14 Indian commercial banks were nationalised.

In 1980, another 6 banks were nationalised. Till the year 1980, approximately 80% of the banking segment in India was under government's ownership.

The following is the list of all nationalised hanks:

- Allahabad Bank
- Andhra Bank
- Bank of Baroda
- Bank of India
- Bank of Maharashtra
- Canara Bank
- Central Bank of India
- Corporation Bank
- Indian Bank
- Indian Overseas Bank
- Oriental Bank of Commerce
- Punjab and Sind Bank
- Punjab National Bank
- Syndicate Bank
- UCO Bank
- Union Bank of India
- United Bank of India
- Dena Bank and Vijaya Bank have been merged into Bank of Baroda in April, 2019

Objectives Behind Nationalisation of Banks in India. Following are the objectives behind nationalisation of banks in India

- Minimising regional imbalance.
- Expansion of bank branches, especially in rural areas.
- Controlling private monopolies.
- Speed-up economic growth.

- Priority sector lending.
- Developing banking habits.
- Provide better credit: facility for agriculture.
- Using bank as tool of social welfare.

Regional Rural Banks. To liquidate rural indebtedness by stages and to dispense institutional credit facilities to farmers and artisans in rural areas, the Government of India promulgated on 26th

September, 1975, the regional rural banks ordinance, 1975, to set-up regional rural banks throughout the country. Banks has started working from 2nd October, 1975. Regional rural banks came to be established under the Regional Rural Banks Act, 1976. Initially, 5 RRBs were set-up at Moradabad, Gorakhpur (UP), Bhiwani, Jaipur and Malda (W.B.). As on 31st March, 2019, there are 56 regional rural banks.

Regional rural banks in India penetrated every corner of the country and extended a helping hand in the growth process of the country.

These banks provide institutional credit to the weaker sections of the society at the concessional rate of interest, mobilise rural savings and channelise for supporting the productive activities in the rural areas.

The RRB is governed by a Board of Directors, who exercises all the powers and discharges all the functions of RRB. It consists of a chairman and 3 directors appointed by the Central Government for 5 years, 2 directors nominated by the concerned State Government and 3 directors nominated by the sponsor banks. Reserve Bank of India has brought RRB's under the ambit of priority sector lending on par with the commercial banks.

The National Bank for Agricultural and Rural Development (NABARD) is vested with powers of inspection of RRBs and to call for any data from them. It also provides refinance at concessional interest rate to the RRBs.

National Bank for Agricultural and Rural Development (NABARD)

It is an apex development financial institution of India. It was established on 12th July, 1982 with an initial capital of Rs 100 crore under National Bank for Agricultural and Rural Development Act, 1981 .

Later, its capital was enhanced to Rs 2,000 crore by the Government of India and RBI. It replaced the Agricultural Credit Department (ACD) and Rural Planning and Credit Cell (RPCC) of Reserve Bank of India and Agricultural Refinance and Development Corporation (ARDC). It is one of the premiere agencies to provide credit in rural areas. The amendment to NABARD Act in 2001, classify it as a 'Development Bank', which have 'permitted it to enhance its capital, subject to the minimum holding of 51% by the GOI and RBI. NABARD provides long-term refinance for minor irrigation, plantation, horticulture, land development, animal husbandry, fisheries etc. It also provide short-term loan assistance for financing of seasonal agricultural operations, marketing of crops etc. It also offers medium-term loan facilities for approved agricultural purposes.

Functions of NABARD

The functions of NABARD have been divided into three categories:

- **Credit Distribution.** Take measures towards institutions building for improving capacity of the credit delivery system, including monitoring, formulation of rehabilitation schemes, restructuring of credit institutions, training of personnel etc.
- **Development Coordinates.** The rural financing activities of all institutions engaged in development work at the field level and maintain coordination with Government of India,

State Governments, Reserve Bank of India and other national level institutions concerned with policy formations.

- **Regulatory.** It inspects the working of RRBs and cooperative banks of all types except the primary cooperative banks. All RRBs and cooperative banks submitting returns to the RBI are required to furnish a copy of return to the NABARD. It is empowered to obtain any information or statement from the RRBs and cooperative banks.

Private Sector Banks

After the nationalisation of 14 larger banks in 1969, no banks were allowed to be set-up in the private sector. Global Trust Bank was, thus, the first private bank after liberalisation; it was later amalgamated with Oriental Bank of Commerce (OBC). Then Housing Development Finance Corporation Limited (HDFC) became the first (still existing) to receive an 'in principle' approval from the Reserve Bank of India (RBI) to set-up a bank in the private sector. These banks are registered as companies with limited liability. They are formed as joint stock company under the Indian Companies Act and are governed by Banking Regulation Act, 1949.

The list of major private sector banks working in India are as follows:

- Axis Bank
- City Union Bank
- HDFC Bank
- ICICI Bank
- South Indian Bank
- Yes Bank

Foreign Banks in India

Foreign banks are those banks which are registered in foreign country. They have set-up their branches in India and their headquarter is set-up in foreign country. Now, foreign banks in India are permitted to set-up local subsidiaries and they are treated equally under the Banking Regulation Act. The policy conveys that foreign banks in India may not acquire Indian ones (except for weak banks identified by the RBI, on its terms) and their Indian subsidiaries will not be able to open branches freely. It was made compulsory for these banks to deal in Indian currency.

Foreign Banks Operating in India

Few of these hanks are as follows:

- Abu Dhabi Commercial Bank
- American Express Banking Corp.
- Bank of America
- HSBC Ltd.

NON-SCHEDULED BANK

It means a banking company as defined in clause (c) of Section 5 of the Banking Regulation Act, 1949 (10 of 1949), which is not a scheduled bank. Banks with reserve capital of less than Rs 5 lakh qualify as 'non-scheduled banks, these banks are not governed according to the RBI Act and they receive no benefits from the RBI. These banks can avail remittance facilities from the RBI.

COOPERATIVE BANKS

Cooperative banks are registered under the Cooperative Societies Act and are governed by the Banking Regulations Act, 1949 and Banking Laws (Cooperative Societies) Act, 1955. People who come together to jointly serve their common interest often from a cooperative society under the Cooperative Societies Act.

When a cooperative society engages itself in banking business, it is called a cooperative bank. They generally give credit facilities to small farmers, salaried employees, small-scale industries etc. Cooperative banks are available in rural as well as in urban areas. Such banks can be categorised into Central Cooperative Banks and State Cooperative Banks. These are as follows:

Central Cooperative Bank. These are the federations of primary credit societies in a district and are of two types, i.e. those having a membership of primary societies only and those having a membership of societies as well as individual. The funds of the banks consists of share capital, deposits, loan and overdrafts from State Cooperative Banks and joint stocks. These banks provide finance to member societies within the limits of borrowing capacity of societies. They also conduct all the business of a joint stock bank.

State Cooperative Bank. These banks, also known as apex banks, from the apex of the cooperative credit structure in each state. Its funds are obtained from their own share capital, deposits, loans and overdrafts from the Reserve Bank of India. 50-90% of working capital of SCBs are contributed by the Reserve Bank.

Characteristics of Good Banking System

Banking System of a country contributes a great deal in the process of its economic development. It therefore becomes essential that a country has a good banking system. Following are the characteristic features of a good banking system:

1. **Conducive to Country's Economic Conditions.** Banking system of a country should be conducive to its economic conditions. Indian economy is an underdeveloped agricultural economy. It needs a banking system that identifies various sources of credit and generates suitable credit facilities for agricultural and related sectors of the economy.
2. **Sound Financial Basis.** A good banking system should have sound financial basis. It should generate public faith for which it should be mandatory for the banks to obtain license from the Govt. Banks should have enough of minimum reserves to retain their credibility. Also, credit-related risks should be minimised.
3. **Mobilisation of Savings.** A good banking system should facilitate mobilisation of savings. People should be encouraged to save more and assured of suitable investment prospects.
4. **Controlled Credit.** A good banking system underlines the importance of controlled credit. Flow of credit is so channelised that it conforms to the development needs of the nation. Central bank of the country should have quantitative as well as qualitative control over the flow of credit.
5. **Uniformity of Policies.** A good banking system should exhibit uniformity of policies. If dear-money policy is needed during periods of inflation, it must be uniformly adopted across all sectors of the economy. In case of finance-crunch, the whole banking system of the nation should adhere to the required monetary discipline. There should be no loopholes in the system. Monetary System should be conducive to growth programmes of the nation.
6. **A Co-ordinated System.** A good banking system should be a well co-ordinated system of banking. There can be diverse categories of banking institutions in the country, but all should be complementary to each other in conformity with the overall programmes of growth and development. There should only be a healthy competition across different banking institutions that only promotes the efficiency and productivity of the Banking System as a whole. Thus, a fairly high degree of complementarily is expected across industrial banks, rural development banks, Mutual Fund, Financial Institutions and other financial intermediaries. The whole structure of financial intermediaries should efficiently cater to diverse financial needs of various sectors of the economy.

7. **Trained and Progressive Administration.** Trained and progressive administration is yet another characteristic of a good banking system. Administrative set of the banking structure must conform to the standard norms of efficiency and productivity. And these norms of efficiency should not only yield high profitability but also ensure efficient consumer service. Central Bank of the country and the Government should have fair degree of control over the banking system with a view to ensure progressive banking administration.
8. **Modernisation.** A good banking system should be exposed to modernisation with a view to stimulating dynamism in its functioning. It must be integrated with the banking system of developed nations as a part of overall globalisation of diverse economic structures in different countries of the world.

In short, a good banking system should be friendly to overall programmes of growth and development of a nation and should be modern as well as flexible to function as an integrated unit of the global financial market structure.

Functions of Commercial Banks

Functions of commercial banks can be divided into three parts:

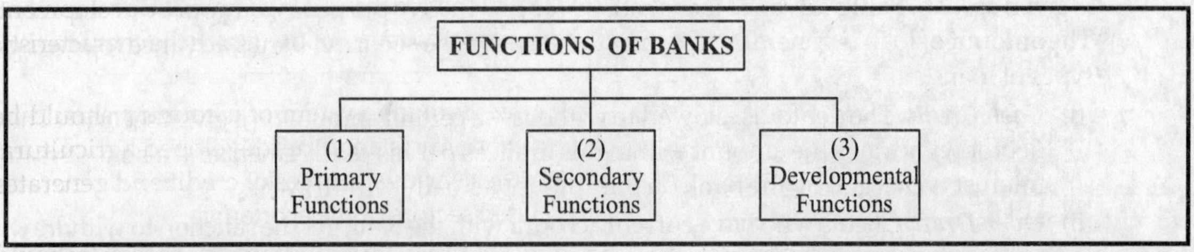

A. Primary Functions

Commercial Banks perform two primary functions:

1. **Accepting of Deposits.** A bank accepts deposits from the public. People can deposit their cash balances in either of the following accounts as per their convenience:
   (i) ***Fixed or Time Deposit Account.*** Cash is deposited in this account for a fixed period. The depositor gets receipts for the amount deposited. It is called Fixed Deposit Receipt. It comprises the name of the depositor, amount of the deposit, rate of interest and the period of deposit. This receipt is not transferable. If the depositor stands in need of the amount before the expiry of the fixed period, he can withdraw the same after paying the discount to the bank. This type of deposit attracts high rate of interest. Longer the period of deposit higher is the rate of interest. It is so because bank can use this amount for a longer period. It is also called *Time Liability of the bank.*
   (ii) ***Current or Demand Deposit Account.*** A depositor can deposit his funds any number of times he likes and can also withdraw the same any number of times he wishes. Ordinarily, businessmen deposit their funds in this account. Generally, no interest is paid by the bank on the demand deposit account. Rather the bank demands some charges from the depositors if the amount lying in account falls below the minimum limit. The amount from this account is withdrawn through cheques. This type of account is also called *Demand Liability*. In America, it is called Chequing Account.
   (iii) ***Saving Deposit Account.*** This account is meant for encouraging small savings. Restrictions are imposed by the bank on the amount to be withdrawn by the depositor. If the latter wants to withdraw more money than is allowed then he has to give prior notice to the

bank. Bank pays interest on this account although its rate is less than the rate of interest paid on fixed account.

(iv) ***Home Safe Saving Account.*** This account has been introduced recently by the banks. A small portable safe is provided to the depositor at his place. Key of the safe is kept by Bank. Depositor puts his small savings in it as convenient to him and after sometime hands the same over to bank and gets it entered in his account. Many banks collect the saved amount by deputing an agent to the place of the depositor. Interest paid on this account is less than the one paid on saving account.

(v) ***Recurring Deposit Account.*** Under this account a specified amount is deposited every month for a specific period, say 12, 24, 36 or 60 months. This amount cannot be withdrawn before the expiry of the given period except under exceptional circumstances. Interest on the amount deposited is also credited to the account of the depositor. Like time-deposit account, interest paid on this account is higher than other accounts.

2. **Advancing of Loans.** Another primary function of the commercial banks is to advance loans. A certain part of the cash received by the banks as deposits is kept in the reserve and the rest is given as loan. Banks advance loans mostly for productive purposes, on approved security. The amount of loan is generally less than the value of the security. Banks advance following types of loans:

(i) ***Cash Credit.*** The debtor is allowed to withdraw a certain amount on a given security. The debtor withdraws the amount within this limit, as per his requirement and also repays it. Interest is charged by the bank on the amount actually withdrawn.

(ii) ***Over-Draft.*** Clients who have current account with the bank get the sanction to withdraw more money than is lying in the said account. It is called over draft. This facility is available for short-term to reliable persons. Supposing a person has Rs. 10,000 lying in current account. If the bank allows him to issue cheques upto Rs. 12,000, then the amount of Rs. 2,000 will be called over- draft.

(iii) ***Loans and Advances.*** These loans are given in the form of a fixed amount. Bank enters the amount of loan in the account books of the debtor. The latter can withdraw it any time. The interest is chargeable on the whole amount from the day the loan is sanctioned irrespective of the fact that the debtor withdraws the whole amount or part of it.

(iv) ***Discounting of the Bill of Exchange.*** It is another method of giving advance by the banks. Under this method, banks give advance to their clients on the basis of their bills of exchange before the maturity of such bills. A deduction is made out of the face value of the bill for the period the bill is yet to run. This deduction is called discounting of the bill. The banks discount only the trade bills. The bills are discounted at the market rate of interest. On the expiry of the maturity period, the amount mentioned in the bill is collected from the party concerned by the bank.

(v) ***Investment in Government Securities.*** Purchasing of Government securities by the banks tantamount to advancing loans by them to the Government. Banks prefer to buy Government securities as these are considered to be the safest investment.

3. **Credit Creation.** One of the main functions of banks these days is to create credit. Banks create credit by giving more loans than their primary deposits.

B. Secondary Functions

Besides the above primary functions, banks also perform many secondary functions such as agency functions, general utility and social functions.

1. **Agency Functions.** Banks act as agents to their customers in different ways:
   (i) ***Collection and Payment of Various Items.*** Banks collect cheques, rent, interest etc. on behalf of their customers and also make payment of taxes, insurance premium etc. on their behalf.
   (ii) ***Purchase and Sale of Securities.*** Banks normally are more knowledgeable with regard to stock and share business. As such they buy, sell and keep in safe custody the securities on behalf of their customers.
   (iii) ***Trustee and Executor.*** Banks also act as trustees and executors of the property of their customers on their advice.
   (iv) ***Remitting of Money.*** Banks also remit money from one place to the other through bank drafts.
   (v) ***Purchase and Sale of Foreign Exchange.*** Banks buy and sell foreign exchange and thus promote international trade. This function is mainly discharged by Foreign Exchange Banks.
   (vi) ***Letter of References.*** Banks also give information about economic position of their customers to domestic and foreign traders and likewise provide information about economic position of domestic and foreign traders to their customers.
2. **General Utility Services.** Commercial banks also provide certain services of general utility to the society:
   (i) ***Locker Facilities.*** Banks provide locker facilities to their customers. People can keep their gold or silver jewellery or other important documents in these lockers. Their annual rent is very nominal.
   (ii) ***Traveller's Cheque and Letters of Credit.*** Banks issue traveller's cheque and letters of credit to their customers so that they may be spared from the risk of carrying cash during their journey.
   (iii) ***Business Information and Statistics.*** Being familiar with the economic situation of the country, the banks give advice to their customers on financial matters on the basis of business information and statistical data collected by them.
   (iv) ***Help in Transportation of Goods.*** Big businessmen or industrialists after consigning goods to their retailers send the Railway Receipt (Consignment Note) to the bank. The retailers get this Receipt from the bank on payment of the value of the consignment to it. Having obtained the Railway Receipt from the bank they get delivery of the consignment from the Railway Goods Office. In this way banks help in the transportation of goods from the production centres to the consumption centres.

C. Developmental Functions

In modern times, banks also perform following significant functions relating to economic development and social welfare of the country.

1. Banks collect idle savings of the people and invest the same in productive activities. Thus, they help in accelerating the rate of capital formation.
2. Banks are also taking part in capital market. They have been giving long-term advances to industry, agriculture, small-scale industry, traders, transporters *etc.* They also finance export trade.
3. Banks give loans to weaker sections of the society on low rate of interest. Small artisans, landless agricultural labourers and poor classes get cheap loans from the banks.

4. Commercial banks have opened their branches in rural areas and small towns to provide banking facilities to the people living therein.
5. Since banks do not give loans for speculative and unproductive activities, bank credit can be used productively.
6. Banks also give credit at low rate of interest to finance such programmes as are meant for rural development and removal of unemployment.
7. The commercial banks either of their own or through their subsidiaries, perform several financial functions. These include mutual funds, Merchant banking, Housing Finance, Factory Leasing, factoring, Stock Investment *etc.*

In short, a modern bank performs several functions which are of great significance to the economic growth of a country. A bank is no longer an institution required to accept deposits and advance loans. It plays a significant role in the economic development and social welfare of a country.

Role of Commercial Bank in Economic Development

Commercial banks play a significant role in economic development of less developed countries like India. Commercial Banks are a nerve-centre of the country's capital market, industrial as well as trading activity. In the words of **Thirlwall** "*Banks can encourage thrift and allocate savings more productively than otherwise by offering a return on savings to be used outside the sector in which they may operate. Banks can help to breakdown sectoral bottlenecks and to unit interest rates*".

Following observations highlight the role of commercial banks in economic development:

1. **Helpful in Mobilisation of Savings and Capital Formation.** Commercial banks offer facilities of deposits, and that too on lucrative terms. This stimulates thrift as well as attracts idle savings into organised capital market of the country. By extending credit facility to the investors and entrepreneurs, banks convert savings into capital formation which is an instrumental variable of growth and development of less developed countries.
2. **Helpful in Innovations.** Also, commercial banks are helpful in innovations, yet another vital parameter of growth and development. Innovations stimulate the process of growth through new technology, discovery of new markets for the existing products as well as new products for the existing markets. Innovations are the off-shoots of Research and Development Divisions of different producing units in the country. And these divisions are lucratively financed by the commercial banks. But for the patronization by commercial banks of the country, research and development activity would remain to be a far cry. Offering judicious financial assistance, banks facilitate the percolation of new technology across different sectors of the economy.
3. **Helpful in the Effective Implementation of Monetary Policy.** Without active cooperation of commercial banks, it would not be possible to carry out effective implementation of any monetary policy in the country. In fact commercial banks constitute the centre-stage of any monetary programme of the Government or the Central Bank of the country. An organised system of commercial banking is almost a pre-condition for any monetary discipline sought to be achieved through any type of monetary policy. Greater the intensive expansion of commercial banking system of a nation, savings broaden, is the base of deposits and accordingly greater is the responsiveness of Banking System of a country to the various instruments of monetary policy. This facilitates control of credit in accordance with credit needs of diverse sectors of the economy.
4. **Banks Influence Interest Rates.** Banks influence the rate of interest as well as structure of interest rates by means of credit creation. Accordingly, the banks influence the volume and pattern of investment, so very vital in the context of growth and development in less developed countries like India.

5. **Helpful in the Development of Priority Sectors.** Commercial Banks contribute their might in the development of priority sectors of the economy. The banks help achieve this objective by means of its selective credit policy. Banks in less developed countries are often engaged in fostering the enterprising interest of farmers and small scale industrialists with a view to improving the rate of production, attaining self-sufficiency in foodgrain production and achieving equitable distribution of income and property.
6. **Helpful in Productive activities and Exports.** Commercial Banks are helpful in stimulating economic activity and expanding exports in less developed countries. Productive activity both in agricultural as well as industrial sectors of these economy can be sustained and stimulated only when credit needs of the sectors are judiciously fulfilled at reasonably low rate of interest. Also export-base can be expanded only when exporters are offered easy finance facility. Commercial banks are expected to play a constructive role in this context.

Thus, commercial banks play a crucial role in the context of growth and development—in less developed countries by offering a well organised credit market catering to all the financial needs of various sectors of the economy.

RESERVE BANK OF INDIA

Central Bank occupies a significant status in the context of monetary and banking system of a country. Reserve Bank of India is country's Central Bank. On the recommendations of Hilton Young Commission, it was established on April 1, 1935. To begin with, both the Govt. as well as individuals had shares in the Reserve Bank. It's total capital of Rs. 5 crores was divided in 5 lacs shares of Rs. 100 each. After independence, Reserve Bank was nationalized in 1949. Shares of the individuals were purchased by the government at the rate of Rs. 118 and Rs. 10 only per share.

Reserve Bank performs all the function of a central bank viz, issue of notes, banker to the state, regulation of banking system in the country, exchange control, credit control etc. It advises the government on the formulation of monetary policy. It meets the financial needs of agriculture, industry, trade, transport, small industries in the interest of the economic development of the country. It helps in alleviating poverty, removing regional inequalities and unemployment. In short, it performs both banking and developmental functions.

Organisation and Management

Reserve Bank of India is managed by the **Central Board of Directors.** Presently this Board consists of 20-members. Besides Governor and Four Deputy Governors, '4' Directors are nominated, each by the Four Local Boards. These Boards are established, respectively, in Mumbai, Calcutta, Chennai and New Delhi. According to the Reserve Bank of India Act, the nominated members term is of four-year duration. Governor and Deputy Governors are appointed by the government for a period of 5-years. Central Board of Directors must hold at least '6' meetings in a year and at least one meeting in 3-months. Bank's Head Office is located in Mumbai. The bank has 14 branch offices.

FUNCTIONS OF THE RESERVE BANK

The principle function of Reserve Bank of India is to regulate the monetary system of the country (in accordance with the overall economic policy of the government) in such a way that the balanced economic growth of the country is achieved alongwith economic stability. According to the Preamble of Reserve Bank of India Act, 1934, 'The main functions of the bank are to regulate the issue of bank notes and keeping of reserves with a view to securing monetary stability in India and generally to operate the currency and credit system of the country to its advantage.'

Functions of the Reserve Bank may be classified into two parts:

1. Traditional Functions and
2. Developmental Functions

Traditional Functions of the Reserve Bank

Traditional functions of Reserve Bank may be classified as under;

Table 1

(i) Central Banking Functions	(ii) General Banking Functions	(iii) Prohibitory Functions
1. Note Issuing	1. To Accept Deposits	1. Neither to participate in business, nor to provide economic assistance.
2. Regulation of Credit	2. To deal in bills	2. Neither to purchase share nor to give loans against it.
3. Bank of Banks	3. Lending of money	3. Neither to purchase immovable wealth nor to lend loans against it.
4. Banker of the Government	4. To deal in foreign securities	4. Not to deal in time bill.
5. Regulation of Exchange	5. To deal in costly metals	5. Not to give interest on private savings.
6. Other Functions (a) Clearing house Functions (b) Change of currency (c) Transfer of currency (d) Publication of Information (e) Control over Nationalized Banks	6. To deal with the banks of the other countries 7. Miscellaneous Functions	6. Not to advance loans without securities.

Central Banking Functions of the Reserve Bank

Reserve Bank is the Central Bank of India. Its Central Banking functions are as under:

1. **Issue of Paper Currency.** Reserve Bank of India has the monopoly right of Note-Issue. It issues notes of the denomination of Rs. 2, 5, 10, 20, 50, 100 and 500. The bank has its separate department for note issuing. This is known as Issue Department. In accordance with the Reserve Bank of India Act, this bank is required to maintain Reserve Fund for note-issuing. This is to maintain confidence of the people in the country's currency. Since 1956, note-issuing is based on Minimum Reserve System. Presently, a Minimum Reserve of Rs. 200 crores is to be maintained for issuing-notes upto any limit. This comprises of gold worth Rs. 115 crores and foreign securities worth Rs. 85 crores.
2. **Regulation of Credit.** Regulation of credit implies control over the credit policy of the commercial banks. Being the Central Bank, the Reserve Bank controls the creation of credit by the Commercial Banks. According to the Reserve Bank of India Act, this bank can adopt several measures to control credit creation, viz, changing the Bank Rate, Open market

operations, change in the Reserve Requirement of the Commercial Banks *etc.* Reserve Bank also controls the loan policy, interest policy and investment policy of the Commercial banks.

3. **Bank of Banks.** Being the Central Bank, Reserve Bank of India is the bank of all the Banks in the country. In this context the Reserve Bank acts as a guide of the Commercial Banks, besides controlling and regulating their affairs. During times of emergency, it is lender of the last resort for the Commercial Banks. That is, it gives loans to the Commercial Banks during times of emergency. Banking Companies Act, (1949), has conferred various rights on the Reserve Bank, such as to issue licenses to the banks, regulate the number and branches of commercial banks, examine the plans and accord sanctions for the merger of banks, obtain reports from the banks, examine the credit policy of the banks and give advice and suggestions.

4. **Banker of the Government.** Reserve Bank is the banker of the Central and State Government. All banking functions of the Government are handled by the Reserve Bank of India. Thus,

   (i) The Reserve Bank keeps cash balances of the Central and State Governments and makes payment out of these balances on the advice of the Government. No interest is paid to the Government on these balances.

   (ii) The bank arranges public loans for the Governments.

   (iii) It sells and purchases Government securities.

   (iv) It also sells Treasury Bills on behalf of the Government by issuing Tenders.

   (v) The bank also gives loans to the Government. It is called Ways and Means Advances. These loans are returned within 90 days.

   (vi) On the basis of experience of the monetary system, the bank advices the government on the monetary and economic policies.

   (vii) Reserve Bank also has the right to function on behalf of foreign governments .

   (viii) The Bank functions for the success of monetary and economic policies of the government.

5. **Regulation of Foreign Exchange.** Being the Central Bank of the Country, Reserve Bank of India also regulates exchange rate of rupee in terms of foreign currencies. It tries to maintain stability of exchange rate. For this, the Reserve Bank deals in foreign exchange only at fixed rates right from the beginning. Earlier, entire business of foreign exchange was done through the medium of sterling. But after India became member of the International Monetary Fund in 1947, Sterling System was given up in favour of the IMF system of exchange. Reserve Bank deals in the currencies of those countries only which are members of IMF.

6. **Other Functions.** Besides the above stated specific functions, the Reserve Bank of India performs the following other functions:

   (i) ***Export Assistance.*** Reserve Bank gives loans to the export industries. These loans are given directly as well as indirectly by refinancing the loans given by other banks.

   (ii) ***Clearing House Functions.*** Being Central Bank of the country, the Reserve Bank also functions as Clearing House. Inter-banking obligations are conveniently settled through this house.

   (iii) ***Change of Currency.*** The bank changes big notes into small ones and small notes into coins.

   (iv) ***Transfer of Currency.*** The bank also facilitates the transfer of currency. It also issues demand hundies on its branches.

(v) ***Publication of Statistics and Other Information.*** Reserve Bank publishes data on the various parameters, such as money, credit, finance, agricultural and industrial output. Reports on these data are also periodically published.

(vi) ***Training in Banking.*** The Reserve Bank has opened various Training Centres to produce talented bankers:

(a) Bankers Training College
(b) College of Agricultural Banking, Pune
(c) Reserve Bank Staff College, Chennai
(d) National Institute of Bank Management
(e) Zonal Training Centres.

7. **Supervisory Functions.** The Reserve Bank performs certain non- monetary functions of the nature of supervision of banks and promotion of efficient banking in India. The Reserve Bank has been given wide powers of supervision and control over commercial, co-operative and regional banks. The various aspects of supervisory functions are as follows :

(i) No bank can be established in India without obtaining a licence from Reserve Bank.

(ii) The Reserve bank supervises branch expansion, liquidity of the assets, management, amalgamation and liquidation of the banking institutions in India.

(iii) An inspection directorate has been established in 1995 to make vigorous inspection of the working of the banking institutions.

(iv) The nationalised banks and regional rural banks are directly controlled and supervised by the Reserve Bank.

General Banking Functions of the Reserve Bank

Reserve Bank is not a commercial bank. Yet, being the Central Bank, it performs certain general banking functions as well. These functions are as follows:

1. **To Accept Deposits.** The bank accepts deposits of the central government, state governments, Port-Trust and private individuals. But no interest is paid on these deposits.
2. **To Deal in Bills.** Reserve Bank buys, sells and rediscounts the Bills, Promissory Notes and Hundies. However, these bills should not be of the duration exceeding 90-days and should be payable within the country.
3. **Lending of Money.** As a Central Bank, the Reserve Bank of India gives loans to the central and state Governments. These loans are of the duration of not more than 90-days. The loans are given against securities, credit notes of the banks and gold or silver.
4. **To Deal in Agricultural Bills.** Reserve Bank also buys, sells and discounts agricultural bills. These bills should be payable in India and should not be of the duration exceeding 15-months.
5. **To Deal in Foreign Securities.** The bank deals in all such foreign securities which are encashable within '10' years from the date of purchase.
6. **To Deal in Costly Metals.** Reserve Bank deals in the sale and purchase of gold, silver as well as the coins of these metals.
7. **To Deal with the Banks of Others Countries.** Being a member of IMF, Reserve Bank establishes business relations with the banks of other member countries. It can open accounts with those banks, act as their agent or handle IMF dealings.

Prohibitory Functions of the Reserve Bank

Reserve Bank of India Act prohibits this bank from performing certain activities. This is with a view to avoid competition of this bank with its member banks. The prohibitory functions of the bank are:

(i) The bank cannot participate in trade, commerce or industrial activity of the country. It can only control a particular business for sometime with a view to realize the loans.

(ii) The bank cannot buy its own shares or that of any other bank or a company. Also it cannot give loan on the basis of such shares.

(iii) It cannot give loan against the security of any immovable property. Also it cannot buy immovable property beyond its needs.

(iv) The bank can neither stop nor accept such bills which are payable on demand.

(v) It cannot pay interest on its deposits.

(vi) The bank cannot give loans without securities.

Developmental Functions of the Reserve Bank

India adopted the strategy of planned development programme with a view to accelerate the rate of growth. In these programmes the contribution of Reserve Bank of India cannot be over-emphasized. Economic progress of a country depends upon the growth and development of its industry, agriculture, trade and commerce, as well as the stability of domestic price level and foreign exchange rate. The Reserve Bank of India has very actively catered to the financial needs of industries over the last 50 years. It has been encouraging exports also. In the field of agriculture, the Reserve Bank of India has been actively engaged in the provision of agricultural credit, fertilizers and machinery. Research, Statistics and Publication Division of the Reserve Bank of India has been providing useful information to the planners. It has appreciably contributed to the growth process of the economy. It has indeed succeeded as a central bank of the country. Following points should bring out the contribution of the Reserve Bank of India to the process of economic growth.

1. **Promotion of Agricultural Finance.** Right from the beginning, Reserve Bank of India has an Agricultural Credit Department. The principal function of this department is to conduct research regarding various problems of agricultural credit. Besides this, the bank advises the central government, state governments and co-operative societies on the various aspects of agricultural growth. It also helps the central governments and state governments in establishing godowns and warehouses in different parts of the country. Contribution of the Reserve Bank in the field of agricultural credit is notable. However, the bank does not fulfil credit needs of the farmers directly.

   Contribution of the Reserve Bank to the field of agricultural credit may be described as under:

   (i) **Short term Agricultural Credit.** Reserve Bank arranges short-period credit for the State Co-operative Banks for the sale of agricultural produce and other seasonal agricultural operations, at less than 2% rate of interest. The Bank offers credit to State Co-operative Banks on the sureties or the securities of state governments.

   (ii) **Medium Term Agricultural Credit.** Medium term credit is generally offered for a period ranging between 3 to 5 years. The Reserve Bank did not have the right to offer medium-term loans till the Year 1953. But from 1953 onwards, medium term loans could be advanced on the securities of the State Governments to Agricultural Co-operatives for agricultural purposes. This type of credit is given for the following purposes :

   (a) Irrigation, purchase of pumpsets, boring of tubewell and digging of wells,

(b) Land Reclamation,

(c) Purchase of agricultural implements and cattle.

(d) 'Gobar' Gas Plants,

(e) Purchase of shares of the Co-operative Sugar Mills. In 1956, the Reserve Bank established National Agricultural Credit (Stabilization) Fund. When crop productivity suffers due to certain reasons, farmers are not in a position to pay back their loans to the co-operatives, in turn the cooperatives fail to return their short-period loans. In such situations, the co-operatives can seek loans from National Agricultural Credit (Stabilisation) Fund and get their short term loans converted into medium term loans.

(iii) **Long Term Credit.** National Agricultural Credit (Long Term Operations) Fund caters to the long period credit requirements of the agricultural sector. Reserve Bank used so advance loans to the state Governments for the purchase of shares of Co- operatives. It also used to buy debentures of Land Development Banks. Joint efforts of the Reserve Bank and the Government of India led to the establishment of National Bank for Agriculture and Rural Development (NABARD). Now all functions of the Reserve Bank relating to agricultural sector of the economy are handled by this bank. Authorized capital of this bank has been fixed to be Rs. 500 crs., and it's paid-up capital is Rs. 100 crs. Of this, shares worth Rs. 50 crores have been purchased each by the Government of India and Reserve Bank of India. Thus, National Bank for Agriculture and Rural Development is in fact the joint venture of the Government of India and Reserve Bank. This bank can raise capital from within the country and abroad, by selling debentures. All assets and liabilities of National Agricultural Credit (Stabilization) Fund and National Agriculture Credit (Long Term Operations) Fund have been transferred to the National Bank for Agriculture and Rural Development.

In short, Reserve Bank has made an important contribution in the field of agricultural credit. Besides arranging credit for agricultural operations, the Bank also performs various related activities:

(a) It inspects Co-operative Banks,

(b) Standing Advisory Committees on Agriculture have been established to render advice on matters of agricultural credit. Since 1982-83 all functions of the Reserve Bank relating to agricultural sector have been entrusted to National Bank for Agriculture and Rural Development (NABARD).

2. **Promotion of Industrial Finance.** Reserve Bank provides significant financial assistance for the industrial development of the country. It established Industrial Finance Department in 1957. This department executes all plans of the Reserve Bank regarding industrial finance. The following observations should bring out the contribution of Reserve Bank in the field of industrial finance.

(i) ***Establishment of Specialized Institutions.*** To cope with the growing need of industrial finance in India, Reserve Bank has established various specialised institutes. Industrial Finance Corporation of India, Industrial Development Bank of India, State Finance Corporations and Industrial Credit and Investment Corporation and Small Industries Development Bank of India are some of the notable names in this regard.

(ii) ***National Industrial Credit (Long Term Operations) Fund.*** With a view to satisfy credit needs of the large scale industries, Reserve Bank started National Industrial Credit (Long-Term Operations) Fund in 1964. This Fund was started with Rs. 10 crores in the first year, and Rs. 5 crores were to be added to it annually. This Fund is used for several purposes:

(a) To give loan to Industrial Development Bank for the purchase of shares and debentures of Finance Corporation of India and State Finance Co-operations.

(b) To buy Debentures issued by the Development Bank.

(iii) ***Credit Guarantee Scheme for Small Scale Industries.*** From July 1, 1960 onwards, Reserve Bank has arranged for guaranteeing the credit raised by small scale industries. Credit Guarantee Organisation of the Reserve Bank looks after this scheme. Under this scheme 75% of the standing loans of the small industries are guaranteed by Credit Guarantee Organisation.

(iv) ***Help to Sick Industrial Units.*** Reserve Bank also arranges for financial assistance to the sick industrial units. Sick Industrial Unit Division of the Reserve Bank looks after this function of the bank. This Division identifies sick units of large, medium and small industries and arranges loans for them from the Nationalized Banks.

(v) ***Export Assistance.*** Export Houses get financial assistance from the Reserve Bank, both directly as well as indirectly by way of 'Refinance' of the loans given by other financial institutes. In 1963 Export Credit Bill Plan was also started. And, in 1982 it was with the assistance of Reserve Bank that the Government established Export-Import Bank. This Bank avails of the credit facility from Reserve Bank.

3. **Promotion of Export Finance.** The Reserve Bank has adopted several measures for promotion of export finance.

(i) ***Special Schemes.*** Reserve banks has been offering special refinance facilities to banks to encourage them for providing larger credit for exports. Several schemes has been introduced from time to time to achieve this objective. Some of the notable schemes are:

(a) Export Bill Credit Scheme,

(b) Pre-shipment Credit Scheme,

(c) Duty Drawback Credit Scheme,

(d) Concessional Rates of Interest on Bank Credit for Exports.

(ii) ***Export-Import Bank of India.*** The Reserve Bank helped in setting up Export-Import Bank of India on 1st January, 1982. The main objective of this bank is to provide financial facilities to export import trade.

4. **Promotion of Banking.** The Reserve Bank has undertaken several measures to promote the banking structure of the country. The main steps undertaken in this direction are:

(i) **Strengthening of Banking Structure.** The Reserve Bank has strengthened the banking structure of the country. A large number of weak, unsound or improperly managed banks have been eliminated or reconstructed. Amalgamation have been brought about either voluntarily or compulsorily.

(ii) ***Extension of Banking Facilities.*** The banking facilities have been extended throughout the country, especially in small towns and rural areas so as to improve the geographical coverage of banks. The relatively unbanked states have been given preference in the matter of setting up new offices.

(iii) ***Extension of Functional Coverage.*** The functional coverage of the banks has also been extended. The sectoral distribution of banks credit in favour of the priority sectors such as agriculture, small scale industries etc. has been improved. Now, more credit is available to small borrowers. Regional rural banks have been set up to meet the credit requirements of small farmers, artisans and other persons of small means in rural areas.

(iv) ***Deposit Insurance.*** To inspire greater public confidence in bank deposits and thereby, spread banking habit in the country, insurance of deposits with commercial banks was introduced in 1962. *The Deposit Insurance and Credit Guarantee Corporation* has been set up to provide protection to depositors and guarantee cards to eligible institutions.

(v) ***Development of Bill Market.*** The Reserve Bank has introduced several schemes with a view to encourage the growth of a bill market in India. It has been helpful in meeting genuine credit needs of the trade and industry and in strengthening the banking system in the country.

(vi) ***Training in Banking.*** The Reserve Bank has also arranged the education and training of the different categories of banking personnel. Several institutions like Banker's Training College at Mumbai, College of Agricultural Banking, Staff Training College and Indira Gandhi Institute of Development Research *etc.*, have been started. The Reserve Bank of India took the initiative in establishing the **National Institute of Bank Management** at Mumbai to serve as an apex institution.

We can conclude that the Reserve Bank has been doing valuable work in aiding development and promoting saving and banking habits. The Bank pursues a variety of developmental and promotional functions to accelerate the rate of growth.

MONETARY POLICY OF THE RESERVE BANK

One of the important functions of the Reserve Bank as a central bank of the country is to formulate and administer the monetary policy.

1. **Meaning.** Monetary policy refers to the Policy through which the central bank of the country controls:
   (i) the supply of money,
   (ii) availability of money and
   (iii) cost of money or rate of interest, in order to attain a set of objectives oriented towards the growth and stability of the economy. According to D.C. Rowan, 'The monetary policy is defined as discretionary action undertaken by the authorities designed to influence:
   (a) the supply of money,
   (b) cost of money or rate of interest and
   (c) the availability of money.

   Thus, the monetary policy of the Reserve Bank refers to the use of instruments of credit control by the Reserve Bank so as to regulate the amount of credit creation by banks. It also aims at varying the cost and availability of credit with a view of influencing level of aggregate demand in the economy.

2. **Objectives.** The main objectives of the monetary policy of the Reserve Bank are:
   (a) ***Controlled Expansion of the Total Quantity of Money.*** This policy is the outcome of the conflicting interests of economic development and control of inflation.
   (i) Expansion of money supply was needed to finance the process of economic development.
   (ii) Control of money supply was required to check inflationary pressure generated in the economy as a result of the vast developmental and non-developmental expenditure. Expansion of money supply was needed to meet the increased demand of funds for the development process. Reserve Bank recognised the need for expansion of credit and money supply for carrying out the rapid development and diversification

of the economy. At the same time, the control over the expansion of money supply was needed to restrain the inflationary forces of the economy. Thus, expansion of money supply was needed to finance the development process and control of money supply was deemed essential to combat inflation or rise in prices. Thus, controlled expansion of money supply was essential for growth with stability.

(b) *Sectoral Employment of Credit.* The second objective of monetary policy was to allocate funds to predetermined sectors. The Reserve Bank has determined the allocation of funds to various sectors and also the rates at which these are made available. This allocation is being made according to the priorities laid down in the plans and requirements of day-to -day development.

3. **Measures of Monetary Policy.** In order to carry out its monetary policy of controlled expansion the RBI has adopted the following measures:

(a) *Measures for expansion of Currency and Credit.* In India, the Reserve Bank has sole right to issue currency. It can issue any amount of currency against the minimum security of Rs. 200 crores comprising of gold and foreign securities. Since the inception of planning in 1914, there is vast expansion of currency. In 1951, notes worth Rs. 1407 crores were issued but in 2014, the value increased to Rs. 4,63,823 crores. Besides tremendous increase in the issue of the notes, the following measures were also adopted to expand the money supply:

(i) Supplying of additional funds to commercial banks.
(ii) Supplying credit to such special groups like agricultural cooperatives, and regional rural banks.
(iii) providing finance and discounting facilities for food procurement, export credit etc.
(iv) Setting up of special institutions to provide credit to industry, agriculture, foreign trade, like IDBI, IFCI, SIDBI, NABARD, EXIM and so on.

(b) *Measures for Controlling of Credit.* The Reserve Bank has also adopted traditional methods of credit control for controlling credit. The credit control was deemed essential to restraint the inflationary trends of the economy. The RBI has to adopt both the quantitative and qualitative methods of credit control. These methods have been discussed in detail under the heading control of credit by the Reserve Bank.

4. **Control of Credit by the Reserve Bank.** Control of Credit by the Reserve Bank of India

Credit control is most important function of Reserve Bank of India. Credit control in the economy is required for the smooth functioning of the economy. By using credit control methods RBI tries to maintain monetary stability. There are two types of methods:

1. **Quantitative methods:**

A. *Manipulation of Bank Rate.* Bank rate is the rate at which the reserve bank is prepared to buy or re discount bills of exchange or other commercial paper eligible for purchase under the act. Increase in the bank rate reduces the credit creation power of banks and decrease in bank rate increases the credit creation power of the banks.

Difference between Bank Rate and Repo Rate. Bank Rate and Repo Rate seem to be similar terms because in both of them RBI lends to the banks. However, Repo Rate is a short-term measure and it refers to short-term loans and used for controlling the amount of money in the market. On the other hand, Bank Rate is a long-term measure and is governed by the long-term monetary policies of the RBI. In broader term, bank rate is the rate of interest which a central bank charges on the loans and advances that it extends to commercial banks and other financial intermediaries. RBI uses this tool to control the money supply.

B. **Open market operations.** Open Market Operations refer to the purchase and sale of the Government securities (G-Secs) by RBI from / to market. The objective of Open Market Operations is to adjust the rupee liquidity conditions in the economy on a durable basis. When RBI sells government security in the markets, the banks purchase them. When the banks purchase Government securities, they have a reduced ability to lend to the industrial houses or other commercial sectors. This reduced surplus cash, contracts the rupee liquidity and consequently credit creation / credit supply. When RBI purchases the securities, the commercial banks find them with more surplus cash and this would create more credit in the system. Thus, in the case of excess liquidity, RBI resorts to sale of G-secs to suck out rupee from system. Similarly, when there is a liquidity crunch in the economy, RBI buys securities from the market, thereby releasing liquidity. It's worth note here that the market for government securities is not well developed in India but still OMO plays very important role.

C. **Manipulation of Cash reserve ratio.** The Cash Reserve Ratio is the amount of funds that the banks are bound to keep with Reserve bank of India as a portion of their Net Demand and Time Liabilities (NDTL). The objective of CRR is to ensure the liquidity and solvency of the Banks. The CRR is maintained fortnightly average basis.

Impacts of Increasing CRR. When RBI increases the CRR, less funds are available with banks as they have to keep larger portions of their cash in hand with RBI. This means that banks will now have less money to play with. Moreover, Reserve Bank does not pay any interest on the CRR balances. Since commercial banks don't earn any interest, the banks are left with an option than to increase the interest rates. If RBI hikes this rate substantially, banks will have to increase the loan interest rates. The home loans, car loans and EMI of floating Rate loans increase. Thus hike in CRR leads to increase of interest rates on Loans provided by the Banks.

Reduction in CRR sucks money out of the system causing to decrease in money supply. When money supply decreases, the inflation comes down.

2. **Qualitative Methods:**

A. ***Selective Qualitative Credit controls.*** With the help of selective credit control methods the central bank can control and direct the flow of credit in the country. Rationing of credit is involved in this. These control regulates the use of credit by discriminating between essential and non essential purposes.

B. ***Moral persuasion and direct action.*** Central bank may refuse to grant further loans or re discount of bill for the banks to control their credit creation ability. The central bank may request banks not to use the accommodation of obtained for financing speculative or non essential transactions.

Qualitative credit is used by the RBI for selective purposes. Some of them are

Margin requirements. This refers to difference between the securities offered and amount borrowed by the banks.

Consumer Credit Regulation. This refers to issuing rules regarding down payments and maximum maturities of installments credit for purchase of goods.

RBI Guidelines. RBI issues oral, written statements, appeals, guidelines, warnings etc. to the banks.

Rationing of credit. The RBI controls the Credit granted / allocated by commercial banks.

Moral Suasion. Psychological means and informal means of selective credit control.

Direct Action. This step is taken by the RBI against banks that don't fulfil conditions requirements. RBI may refuse to rediscount their papers or may give excess credits or charge a penal rate of interest over and above the Bank rate, for credit demanded beyond a limit.

(II). **Selective Credit Control.** This refers to the control of specific credit meant for certain specific objectives. For example, if the government wants to check the rising prices of wheat in India, the Reserve Bank may instruct the member banks not to give loans against the security of wheat. Traders will not get credit for the purchase of wheat and, therefore, they will not be able to buy large quantities of wheat. This would bring down wheat prices as the credit squeeze is directed towards wheat alone. It is thus, called 'Selective Control'.

Banking Companies Act, 1949 has conferred upon the Reserve Bank many rights of selective credit control. These rights are being frequently exercised by the Reserve Bank particularly since 1956 onwards. Following techniques of selective credit control are generally adopted.

(i) ***Change in Margin Requirements on Loans.*** Reserve Bank directs the member banks to change their margin requirement from time to time. First such direction was given by the Reserve Bank in May and September 1956 regarding rice-trade. In 1957, margin requirement for wheat was fixed at 40%. In 1958, it was raised to 80 percent. In 1970, it was again brought down to 40 percent. In 2013, it was raised to 53 percent. Likewise, margin requirement has been varied regarding various commodities from time to time.

(ii) ***Rationing of Credit.*** Rationing of credit is yet another technique of selective credit control. Under this programme, the Reserve Bank fixed credit quota for member banks as well as their limits for the payment of Bills. Quota system was introduced in 1960. If the member banks seek more loans than their fixed quota, they will have to pay higher interest charges to the Reserve Bank than the prevailing bank rate.

(iii) ***Credit Authorisation Scheme (CAS).*** This scheme was introduced by RBI in November 1965. Under this scheme, the banks were to attain the authorization of the Reserve Bank before sanctioning any fresh limit of Rs. 1 crore or more to any single party. The amount of the limit has been changed from time to time. It was raised in 1986, to Rs. 6 crore. Since 1987, Credit Authorisation Scheme has been liberalised to allow large amount of loans to meet genuine demands of production sector without the prior sanction of the Reserve Bank. However, in such cases a system of post sanction scrutiny called **Credit Monetary Arrangements** (CMA) has been introduced by the Reserve Bank.

(iv) ***Loan System for Delivery of Bank Credit.*** The '**Loan System**' for delivery of bank credit has been introduced with effect from April 21, 1995. The objective of the loan system is to bring about discipline in the utilisation of bank credit by large borrowers and gain better control over credit fund. As per the loan system, it is mandatory for banks to restrict the cash credit component to 75 per cent of the maximum permissible bank finance (MPBF) for the borrowers with assessed MPBF of Rs. 20 crore and above. The balance of 25 percent of MPBF mostly sanctioned by way of short term loans for working capital purposes. It is to be sanctioned as a demand loan for a minimum period of one year.

(v) ***Ceiling on Term Loans.*** In October 1994, the ceiling for term loans for any project of Rs. 50 crore for each bank was abolished and the limit of Rs. 200 crore for the banking system as a whole was raised to Rs. 500 crores for any project.

Features of Monetary Policy

The following are the main features of the monetary policy of the Reserve Bank of India:

1. **Active Policy.** Before the advent of planning in India in 1951, the monetary policy of the Reserve Bank was a passive, cheap and easy policy. It means that Reserve Bank did not use the measures of monetary policy to regulate the economy. For example, from 1935 to 1951, the bank rate remained stable at 3%. But since 1951, the Reserve Bank has been following an active monetary policy. It has been using all the measures of credit control.
2. **Overall Expansion.** An important feature of Reserve Bank's monetary policy is that of overall expansion of money supply. In the words of **S.L.N. Sinha** '*The Reserve Bank's responsibility is not merely one of credit restriction. In a growing economy there has to be continuous expansion of money supply and bank credit and the central bank has the duty to see that if legitimate credit requirements are met*'. In fact, the overall trend of money supply has been one of the expansion along with an almost continuous rise in the price level.
3. **Seasonal Variations.** The monetary policy is characterised by the changing behaviour of busy and slack seasons. These seasons are tied to the agricultural seasons. In the busy season, there is an expansion of funds on account of the seasonal needs of financing production, and inventory building of agricultural commodities. On the other hand, the slack season is characterised by the contraction of funds due to the return flow. It may be pointed out that aggregate contraction of funds during the slack season has tended to fall far short of expansion in the preceding busy season. Thus, during busy season the Reserve Bank adopts an expansionary credit policy and tightens the liquidity pressures during the slack season.
4. **Tight and Dear Monetary Policy.** In order to restrain inflation the Reserve Bank has often adopted a tight and dear monetary policy. A tight monetary policy implies that the rate of growth of money supply is lowered. A dear money policy refers to increase in bank rate. This increase in bank rate leads to an increase in the interest rates charged by the banks.
5. **Investment and Saving Oriented.** The monetary policy adopted by the Reserve Bank is both investment and saving oriented. To encourage investment, adequate funds were made available for productive purposes at reasonable rates of interest. The Reserve Bank has also kept the interest on deposits at a reasonable rate to attract the savings.
6. **Imbalance in Credit Allocation.** The monetary policy is biased towards industrial sector. Agriculture does not get the required institutional finances. Consequently, it has to depend upon money lenders to a considerable extent for its credit needs. The agricultural sector has to pay high rate of interest and even then does not get required amount of capital. A large part of funds flows to large industries. Even small scale industries suffer from the inadequacy of finances. Thus monetary policy has resulted in imbalances in credit allocation.
7. **Wide Range of Methods of Credit Control.** The Reserve Bank have used a wide range of instruments of credit control. It has adopted all the measures of quantitative and qualitative credit control to meet the needs of a complex and varying economic situation. Since, the objective has been to achieve economic growth with stability, the policy of monetary management has gone beyond the traditional regulatory function. It has adopted a more positive role of channelling credit to desired sectors.
8. **Guiding Factors.** According to **Shri. C. Rangarajan** the following three factors have essentially guided the conduct of monetary policy:
   (i) Monetary policy measures have generally been a response to fiscal policy.
   (ii) While monetary policy has been primarily acting through availability of credit, the cost of credit has also been adjusted upwards sometimes very sharply to meet effectively the inflationary situations.

(iii) The area of operation of monetary policy did not remain confined to those related to regulation of monetary authority in the allocation of credit to the non-government sector because of an important element of national economic policy, specially after the nationalisation of banks.

Limitations or Evaluation of Monetary Policy

The following are the main limitations of the monetary policy adopted by the Reserve Bank:

1. **Restricted Scope of Monetary Policy in Economic Development.** In reality the monetary policy has been assigned only a minor role in the process of economic development. The monetary policy is not given any predominant role in the process of economic development. The role assigned to the Reserve Bank is minor indeed. The Reserve Bank is expected to see that the process of economic development should not be hindered for want of availability of adequate funds.
2. **Limited Role in Controlling Prices.** The monetary policy of Reserve bank has played only a limited role in controlling the inflationary pressure. It has not succeeded in achieving the objective of growth with stability. The former Governor of Reserve Bank, **I.G. Patel** states, '*the role of monetary policy in combating inflation is strictly limited and that monetary policy can be effective only if it is a part of an overall framework of policy which includes not only fiscal and foreign exchange policy but also what is described as an income policy'. In India, however*, the monetary policy of the Reserve Bank is not appropriately integrated with fiscal, foreign exchange and income policies.
3. **Unfavourable Banking Habits.** An important limitation of the monetary policy is unfavourable banking habits of Indian masses. People in India prefer to make use of cash rather than cheque. This means that a major portion of the cash generally continues to circulate in the economy without returning to the banks in the form of deposits. This reduces the credit creation capacity of the banks. Moreover, in India there is predominance of currency in the money supply. This hampers the credit creating capacity of the banks. Due to high proportion of currency in money supply, banks have to face the problem of large withdrawals of currency every time they create credit. Fortunately, the recent trend is increasing deposit ratio in money supply. It is expected to make money policy more effective.
4. **Underdeveloped Money Market.** Another limitation of monetary policy in India is underdeveloped money market. The weak money market limits the coverage, as also the efficient working of the monetary policy. The money market comprises of the parts, the organised money market and unorganised money market. The money policy works only in organised money market. It fails to achieve the desired results in unorganised money market.
5. **Existence of Black Money.** The existence of black money in the economy limits the working of the monetary policy. The black money is not recorded since the borrowers and lenders keep their transactions secret. Consequently the supply and demand of money also not remain as desired by the monetary policy. In the words of **V. Pandit**, '*Black money is rightly regarded as a threat to the official money credit policy mechanism to manage demand and price in several sectors of the economy*'.
6. **Conflicting Objectives.** An important limitation of monetary policy arises from its conflicting objectives. To achieve the objective of economic development the monetary policy is to be expansionary but contrary to it to a curb on inflation can be realised by contracting the money supply. The monetary policy generally fails to achieve a proper coordination between these two objectives.

7. **Influence of Non-Monetary Factors.** An important limitation of monetary policy is its ignorance of non-monetary factors. The monetary policy can never be the primary factor in controlling inflation originating in real factors, deficit financing and foreign exchange resources. The Reserve Bank has no control over deficit financing. It cannot regulate the deficit financing, which affects money supply considerably.
8. **Limitations of Monetary Instruments.** An important limitation of monetary policy is related to the inherent limitations in the various instruments of credit control. There are limitations regarding frequent and sharp changes in the bank rate, as these are supposed to conflict with the development objectives. Most bank rates are virtually fixed and mutually unrelated so that the scope for adjustment is very limited. The margin requirements have tended to be so high for most of the time due to prolonged inflation, that the scope for further increase in them is limited. The CRR and SLR have also been fixed very high locking most of the funds in low yielding assets. These limitations of monetary instruments hampers the smooth working of monetary policy.
9. **Not Proper Implementation of the Monetary Policy.** Successful application of monetary policy is not merely a question of availability of instruments of credit control. It is also a question of judgement with regard to timing and the degree of restraint employed or relaxation allowed. However, past experience shows that Reserve Bank's credit restrictions have always fallen short of the required extent of restraint. The bank has adopted a hesitant attitude in the field of monetary control.

In short, the monetary policy of the Reserve Bank suffers from many limitations. It requires improvements in many directions.

Reform Measures of Financial Sector and More Control over Banks

The Reserve Bank is playing an important role in reinforcing the reform measures in the financial sector undertaken in accordance with the New Economic Policy. The Bank also took initiative to support the revival of the economy price stability. The **Janakiraman committee** appointed after the security scam submitted its report in 1993. In the light of the findings of Janakiraman committee and its recommendation the Bank undertook several corrective measures to restore financial credibility, and to plug existing loopholes and to bring about overall qualitative improvement in the entire financial sector. The following are some of the important measures undertaken by the Reserve Bank to achieve this objective:

1. **Strengthening of Market Intelligence.** The committee recommended that the Reserve Bank should strengthen its market intelligence to supplement its own information. The Reserve Bank has set up recently a Market Intelligence Cell (MIC) within the bank. Banking intelligence in the supervisory wing is also being strengthened.
2. **Mechanisation and Computerization.** The other recommendation of the committee is in respect of mechanisation and computerization of the entire financial system. The Reserve Bank has a major role to play in implementing this recommendation. The Janakiraman Committee has commented that the major lacuna for not detecting sufficiently early the irregularities in securities transaction by banks was the absence of Electronic Data Processing (EDP) system in the operations that deal with recording clearing settlement and finally related securities. In November 1992, the Bank introduced a system of **Electronic Clearance Settlement and Depository (ECSD)** for the purpose.
3. **Establishment of Internal Debt Management Cell (IDMC).** A beginning has been made to move from direct to indirect instrument of monetary control, with the launching of an active internal debt management policy. For strengthening the internal debt management policies,

the Bank has created an **Internal Debt Management Cell** (I.D.M.C) as an independent unit with effect from October 1, 1992. A decision has been taken to set up a new institution to be called **Securities Trading Corporation of India**, dedicated to the development of a separate market for Government Securities.

4. **Gold Management Division.** The Reserve Bank has set up a Gold Management Division. The main function of this division is to explore the possible use of gold in economic adjustment and growth by mobilizing gold from the public and strengthening the **international reserve position** of the country.

5. **Establishment of Committees.** The Reserve Bank has set up two committees viz.
   (i) ***Sundaraman Committee.*** This committee has been set up under the chairmanship of Dr. G. Sundaraman to examine the structure of export credit and
   (ii) ***Nayar Committee.*** This committee was set up under the chairmanship of Shri P. R. Nayar to examine the Adequacy of Institutional credit to the small scale industries sector and related aspects.

   These committees have submitted reports and the bank has already started action on their recommendations.

6. **Inspection of Commercial Banks.** Inspection of the banks by the Reserve Bank has assumed a critical role in the light of the large scale irregularities of banks in the securities transaction. A committee was appointed under the chairmanship of **Shri S. Padmanabhan** to suggest measures in this regard. The main recommendations of this committee are concerned with on site supervisory process of the Reserve Bank. These comprise of:
   (i) Annual Financial Inspection (AFI)
   (ii) Audit of Select items by statutory auditors
   (iii) Management Audit to be conducted by the Reserve Bank's senior and experienced executives once in two years.
   (iv) Scrutiny of social lending and development aspects by the Reserve Bank's staff, independent of the main annual financial inspection and
   (v) Special Inspections and investigations as and when needed.

7. **More Control over Frauds in Banks.** The Reserve Bank appointed a committee on Frauds and Malpractices in Banks under the Chairmanship of Shri A. Ghosh. The committee recommended that all bank should review their instruction manuals and evolve adequate systems and procedures to strengthen internal control, monitoring and vigilance mechanism, particularly in the area of preventive vigilance with a view to ensuring strict compliance of the various systems.

   In short, Reserve Bank has started strict inspection of the banks to avoid further fraud and malpractices.

8. **Control of Non-Banking Financial Companies.** On the basis of the recommendations of **Shah Commission** regarding control of the functions of NBFC, Reserve Bank Act, was amended in 1997. As per the amended Act, registration of non-banking financial companies with the RBI has been made obligatory. Reserve Bank has been authorised to prevent these companies from accepting deposits from public. The RBI has also been conferred with statutory power to control the working of these companies.

NABARD

NABARD is set up as an apex Development Bank with a mandate for facilitating credit flow for promotion and development of agriculture, small-scale industries, cottage and village industries, handicrafts and other rural crafts. It also has the mandate to support all other allied economic activities in rural areas, promote integrated and sustainable rural development and secure prosperity of rural areas. In discharging its role as a facilitator for rural prosperity NABARD is entrusted with:

1. Providing refinance to lending institutions in rural areas
2. Bringing about or promoting institutional development and
3. Evaluating, monitoring and inspecting the client banks.

Besides this pivotal role, NABARD also:

- Acts as a coordinator in the operations of rural credit institutions.
- Extends assistance to the government, the Reserve Bank of India and other organizations in matters relating to rural development.
- Offers training and research facilities for banks, cooperatives and organizations working in the field of rural development.
- Helps the state governments in reaching their targets of providing assistance to eligible institutions in agriculture and rural development.
- Acts as regulator for cooperative banks and RRBs.

Objectives

NABARD was established in terms of the Preamble to the Act, "for providing credit for the promotion of agriculture, small scale industries, cottage and village industries, handicrafts and other rural crafts and other allied economic activities in rural areas with a view to promote IRDP and securing prosperity of rural areas and for matters connected with incidental thereto".

The main objectives of the NABARD as stated in the statement of objectives while placing the bill before the Lok Sabha were categorized as under :

1. The National Bank will be an apex organisation in respect of all matters relating to policy, planning operational aspects in the field of credit for promotion of Agriculture, Small Scale Industries, Cottage and Village Industries, Handicrafts and other rural crafts and the allied economic activities in rural areas.
2. The Bank will serve as a refinancing institution for institutional credit such as long-term, short-term for the promotion of activities in the rural areas.
3. The Bank will also provide direct lending to any institution as may approved by the Central Government.
4. The Bank will have organic links with the Reserve Bank and maintain a close link with in.

Role and Functions

- NABARD is an apex institution accredited with all matters concerning policy, planning and operations in the field of credit for agriculture and other economic activities in rural areas.
- It is an apex refinancing agency for the institutions providing investment and production credit for promoting the various developmental activities in rural areas.
- It takes measures towards institution building for improving absorptive capacity of the credit delivery system, including monitoring, formulation of rehabilitation schemes, restructuring of credit institutions, training of personnel, etc.
- It co-ordinates the rural financing activities of all the institutions engaged in developmental work at the field level and maintains liaison with Government of India, State Governments, Reserve Bank of India and other national level institutions concerned with policy formulation.

- It prepares, on annual basis, rural credit plans for all districts in the country; these plans form the base for annual credit plans of all rural financial institutions.
- It undertakes monitoring and evaluation of projects refinanced by it.
- It promotes research in the fields of rural banking, agriculture and rural development.

RURAL BANKS IN INDIA

The economic development in India followed socialist-inspired policies for most of its independent history, including state-ownership of many sectors; India's per capita income increased at only around 1% annualized rate in the three decades after Independence. Since the mid-1980s, India has slowly opened up its markets through economic liberalization. After more fundamental reforms since 1991 and their renewal in the 2000s, India has progressed towards a free market economy.

India lives in its villages, and while the cities have grown immensely over the last 20 years, rural areas have not seen that kind of development. For India's economy to be strong, the rural economy needs to grow. Rural areas are still plagued by problems of malnourishment, illiteracy, unemployment and lack of basic infrastructure like schools, colleges, hospitals, sanitation, etc. Our villages need to grow in tandem with cities and standard of life has to improve there for inclusive growth to happen. If rural India is poor, India is poor.

Rural development is not merely development of rural areas but also the development of the rural people into self reliant and self-sustaining modern little communities. Rural development in the country is designed to enhance the socio-economic living conditions for the people living in rural India while conserving their culture and rich tradition. The government seeks to achieve higher targets related to rural production, employment and higher living standards which will pave the way for all round economic development of the country. This includes setting up basic infrastructure and facilities such as medical facilities, schools, and transport facilities, apart from scheme implementation related to improving rural employment, agricultural productivity and rural industrialization.

The rural population in India suffers from a great deal of indebtedness and is subject to exploitation in the credit market due to high interest rates and the lack of convenient access to credit. Rural households need credit for investing in agriculture and smoothening out seasonal fluctuations in earnings. Rural households need access to financial institutions that can provide them with credit at lower rates and at reasonable terms than the traditional money-lender and thereby help them avoid debt-traps that are common in rural India.

The Regional Rural Banks have been growing in importance since their inception in 1975 as special institutions playing a catalyst role in the development of rural areas. They have been playing a significant role in financing the weaker sections of the community in the rural areas and also in inculcating banking habit among rural masses.

The RRBs' were established, "with a view to develop the rural economy by providing for the purpose of development of agriculture, trade, commerce, industry and other productive activities in the rural areas, credit and other facilities, particularly to small and marginal farmers, agricultural labourers, artisans and small entrepreneurs and for matters connected therewith and incidental thereto." (The RRB Act, 1996)

It can be affirmed that the RRBs were established as a new set of State sponsored, rural-oriented, region-based, low cost banks, having the ethos of cooperatives and business acumen of commercial banks for providing credit in rural areas, particularly to the relevant weaker sections of the society. It would be fair to say that RRBs have succeeded in spreading the banking services to far flung rural areas, mobilizing rural savings, opening up new avenues for rural poor through institutional credit and generating employment opportunities. However, the mandate of financing only their target group borrowers, coupled with an administered interest rate structure, poor recovery performance, increasing establishment cost, and low level of operational efficiency have resulted in RRBs incurring losses and losing their financial viability from their inception.

India Lives in Villages

India Rural Development Report highlights that the growth rate of rural per capita consumption rose exponentially in the last seven years. However, according to the report, rural India still battles with poverty and lack of basic infrastructure.

1. 30% population of the country lives Below Poverty Line (BPL)
2. 80% of BPL population lives in rural areas
3. Nearly 50% of the rural poor lived in seven states – Jharkhand, Bihar, Assam, Odissa, Chattisgarh, MP and UP
4. This rose to 65% though states like Bihar, Chattisgarh and Uttar Pradesh have reduced poverty significantly
5. 44% of the rural poor in come under scheduled castes and scheduled tribes.
6. 18% of rural households have access to all three basic services – drinking water within premises, sanitation and electricity
7. 45% of rural households lack electricity connections
8. 70% of rural households lack sanitation facilities
9. 20% have none of the three basic services
10. 18% of rural families rely on non-farm employment as major source of their livelihood
11. Income from farm livelihood not sufficient for households
12. Encourage new crop models, revive traditional crops like millet
13. Various types of collective farming help small farmers overcome problems of scale, insecure land tenancy and poor access to credit, modern supply chains and storage.

Regional Rural Banks (RRBs) were established in the year 1975 as a low cost financial intermediation structure in the rural areas to ensure sufficient flow of institutional credit for agriculture and other rural sectors. The global financial crisis and the current Euro zone crisis have affected the banks in the advanced economies; the spill over is reflecting on banks in emerging economies including India.

Some of the features of this type of banking are :

(i) **The Operational Area of RRB.** The area of operation of RRBs is limited to the area as notified by Government of India covering one or more districts in the State.

(ii) **Structure of Regional Rural Banks.** In RRBs, there are three share holders namely Government of India (50% share), Sponsor bank (35% share), and State Government (15% share). Thus, we can say RRBs are jointly owned by Government of India, Sponsor Bank and respective State Government.

(iii) **Special Facilities Given by RBI and Other Institutions to RRBs so that they Can Manage Competition from Stronger Banks like Commercial Banks.** With a view to facilitate RRBs operations, the RBI gave RRBs direct access to refinance assistance at a concessional rate of three per cent below the bank rate.

(iv) **Regulatory Control.** NABARD is the regulatory authority of Regional Rural Banks.

(v) **Organizational Structure.** Organizational Structure for RRB's varies from branch to branch and depends upon the nature and size of business done by the branch. The Head Office of an RRB normally had three to seven departments. The following is the decision making hierarchy of officials in a Regional Rural Bank: (a) Board of Directors, (b) Chairman & Managing Director, (c) General Manager, (d) Chief Manager / Regional Managers, (e) Senior Manager, (f) Manager, (g) Officer / Assistant Manager, (h) Assistants.

Role of RRB's. The importance of the rural banking in the economic development of a country cannot be overlooked. As Gandhiji said "Real India lives in villages," and village economy is the backbone of Indian economy. Without the development of the rural economy, the objectives of economic planning cannot be achieved. Reserve Bank of India in association with the other commercial banks has taken various initiatives to establish the equipped financial system in the rural India by offering various loans facilities for Crops (Short-term Loans) and Agriculture and Allied Activities (Term-Loans). In order to smoothen the system, RRB plays the key role by providing the following services:

Opening of no-frills accounts. Basic banking no-frills account with nil or very low minimum balance & banking charges that make such accounts accessible to vast sections of the rural population. RRBs are providing small overdrafts in such accounts. Relaxation on know-your-customer (KYC) norms: Since August 2005, KYC requirements for opening bank accounts were relaxed for small accounts. RRBs are now permitted to take any evidence as to the identity and address of the customer to their satisfaction.

General Credit Cards (GCCs). With a view to helping the poor and the disadvantaged rural people with access to easy credit, RRBs introduced general purpose credit card facility up to 15,000 at their rural and semi-urban branches.

The objectives of RRBs can be summarized as follows:

To provide cheap and liberal credit facilities for small and marginal farmers, agriculture Laborers, artisans, small entrepreneurs and other weaker sections.

- To save the rural poor from the moneylenders. To act as a catalyst element and thereby, accelerate the economic growth in the particular region.
- To cultivate the banking habits among the rural people and mobilize savings for the economic development of rural areas.
- To increase employment opportunities by encouraging trade and commerce in rural areas.
- To encourage entrepreneurship in rural areas.
- To cater the needs of the backward areas which are not covered by the other efforts of the Government.
- To develop underdeveloped regions and thereby, strive to remove economic disparity between regions.

Challenges for the RRB'S

Although RRBs had a rapid expansion of branch network and increase in volume of business, these institutions went through a very difficult evolutionary process due to the following problems:

Heavy reliance on sponsor banks for investment avenues with low returns barring exceptions, step-motherly treatment from sponsor banks.

1. Chairman of RRBs under the direction of Regional Managers appointed as Board of Directors by sponsor banks
2. Burden of government subsidy schemes and inadequate knowledge of customers leading to low quality assets

3. Unionized staff with low commitment to profit orientation and functional efficiency.
4. Inadequate skills in treasury management for profit orientation.
5. Inadequate exposure and skills to innovate products limiting the lending portfolios.

Inadequate effort to achieve desired levels of excellence in staff competence for managing the affairs and business as an independent entity.

Serious undermining of the Board by compulsions to look up to sponsor banks, GOI, NABARD and RBI for most decisions.

RRB hampered by an across the board ban on recruitment of staff.

Suggestions for Improvement of RRBs

Government should encourage and support banks to take appropriate steps in rural development. Efforts should be made to ensure that the non-interest cost of credit to small borrowers is kept as low as possible.

Productivity can be improved by controlling the costs and increasing the income.

Government should take firm action against the defaulters and shouldn't make popular announcements like waiving of loans.

The RRBs have to make an important change in their decision making with regard to their investments:

1. The RRBs have to be very careful and reduce the operating expenses, because it has been found from our study that these expenses have increased the total expenditure of the banks.
2. The RRBs have to give due preference to the micro credit scheme and encourage in the formation of self help group.
3. Cooperative societies may be allowed to sponsor or co-sponsor with commercial banks in the establishment of the RRB.
4. A uniform pattern of interest rate structure should be devised for the rural financial agencies.
5. The RRB must strengthen effective credit administration by way of credit appraisal, monitoring the progress of loans and their efficient recovery.

Scenario in (2018) and Future Plans for Regional Rural Banks

As per reports of June, 2018, Government of India has put on hold further amalgamation of RRBs. As per newspaper reports (June 2018), GoI has conveyed to the sponsor banks that no fresh proposal of amalgamation of RRBs should be taken up at present.

A Bill to amend the RRB Act is being considered by the parliamentary standing committee on finance. The amendments are aimed at increasing the pool of investors to tap capital for RRBs. Thus, A Bill to amend the RRB Act is being considered by the parliamentary standing committee on finance. The amendments are aimed at increasing the pool of investors to tap capital for RRBs. Thus, Government is exploring a new class of investors to raise capital for these banks. In a communiqué to the heads of public sector banks, the finance ministry said there was a need to tap other sources of capital for RRBs. Government of has been making various effort to make RRBs a profitable institution by infusing fresh capital, by allowing RRBs .to lend commercial projects, consortium finance, foreign currency, insurance business on referral basis. RRBs are also fast moving towards core banking solution for effectiveness and to increase customer base. Over 20 RRBs are already on CBS platform.

BANKING SECTOR REFORMS IN INDIA

An efficient banking structure can promote greater amount of investment which can help achieve a faster growth rate of the economy, worldwide experience confirms that countries with well developed and market -oriented banking systems grow faster and more consistently than those with weaker and strictly regulated systems. Banking system in many of the underdeveloped countries are strictly regulated. They have been plagued by poor performance, low profitability and in many cases even insolvency. Such problems have necessitated move towards the development of a more efficient and well functioning banking system. The Indian banking system has been no exception in these respects.

Economic Reforms of the Banking Sector In India

Indian banking sector has undergone major changes and reforms during economic reforms. Though, it was a part of overall economic reforms, it has changed the very functioning of Indian banks. These reforms have not only influenced the productivity and efficiency of many of the Indian Banks, but has left everlasting footprints on the working of the banking sector in India.

Let us get acquainted with some of the important reforms in the banking sector in India.

1. **Reduced CRR and SLR.** The Cash Reserve Ratio (CRR) and Statutory Liquidity Ratio (SLR) are gradually reduced during the economic reforms period in India. By Law in India the CRR remains between 3-15% of the Net Demand and Time Liabilities. It is reduced from the earlier high level of 15% plus incremental CRR of 10% to current 4% level. Similarly, the SLR is also reduced from early 38.5% to current minimum of 25% level. This has left more loanable funds with commercial banks, solving the liquidity problem.
2. **Deregulation of Interest Rate.** During the economic reforms period, interest rates of commercial banks were deregulated. Banks now enjoy freedom of fixing the lower and upper limit of interest on deposits. Interest rate slabs are reduced from Rs.20 Lakhs to just Rs. 2 Lakhs. Interest rates on the bank loans above Rs.2 lakhs are fully decontrolled. These measures have resulted in more freedom to commercial banks in interest rate regime.
3. **Fixing prudential Norms.** In order to induce professionalism in its operations, the RBI fixed prudential norms for commercial banks. It includes recognition of income sources. Classification of assets, provisions for bad debts, maintaining international standards in accounting practices, etc. It helped banks in reducing and restructuring Non-performing assets (NPAs).
4. **Introduction of CRAR.** Capital to Risk Weighted Asset Ratio (CRAR) was introduced in 1992. It resulted in an improvement in the capital position of commercial banks, almost all the banks in India has reached the Capital Adequacy Ratio (CAR) above the statutory level of 9%.
5. **Operational Autonomy.** During the reforms period commercial banks enjoyed the operational freedom. If a bank satisfies the CAR then it gets freedom in opening new branches, upgrading the extension counters, closing down existing branches and they get liberal lending norms.
6. **Banking Diversification.** The Indian banking sector was well diversified during the economic reforms period. Many of the banks have started new services and new products. Some of them have established subsidiaries in merchant banking, mutual funds, insurance, venture capital, etc. which has led to diversified sources of income for them.
7. **New Generation Banks.** During the reforms period many new generation banks have successfully emerged on the financial horizon. Banks such as ICICI Bank, HDFC Bank, UTI Bank have given a big challenge to the public sector banks leading to a greater degree of competition.

8. **Improved Profitability and Efficiency.** During the reform period, the productivity and efficiency of many commercial banks has improved. It has happened due to the reduced Non-performing loans, increased use of technology, more computerization and some other relevant measures adopted by the government.

Reforms in Banking Sector in India

The Indian banking sector is an important constituent of the Indian financial system. The banking sector plays a vital role for promoting business in urban as well as in rural areas in recent years. Without a sound and effective banking system, India cannot be considered as a healthy economy. For the past three decades India's banking system has several outstanding achievements to its credit. It is no longer confined to only metropolitans or cosmopolitans in India. In fact, Indian banking system has reached even to the remote corners of the country. This is one of the main reasons of India's growth process. With total deposits of over Rs. 22 lakh crores in 2007-08, the Indian commercial banking sector is one of the largest in the world. Over the decades, the Indian banking sector has grown steadily in size, measured in terms of total deposits, at a fairly uniform average annual growth rate of about 22%.

Committees on Reforms in the Banking Sector

It was in response to the growing inefficiencies of the banking system that the government of India set up two committees.

A. Narasimham Committee on Financial System in 1991.

B. Narasimham Committee on the Banking Sector Reforms in 1998.

It may be noted that the Chairman of both the committees was the same person, Mr. Narasimham, Deputy Chairman, Reserve Bank of India. The main recommendations of these committees may be summarised as follows:

A. Report of the committee to Review the Financial System or Narasimham Committee

A high level committee was appointed by the Government of India under the Chairmanship of Shri M. Narasimham in August 1991 to examine all aspects relating to the structure, organisation, functions and procedures of the financial system. The committee's report was tabled in Parliament on December 17, 1991: The main recommendations of the committee are as follows:

1. **Reduction in Liquidity Ratio.** The committee recommended phased reduction in the Statutory Liquidity Ratio (SLR) to 25 percent over a period of five years. It also recommended the progressive reduction in Cash Reserve Ratio (CRR) from the present high level.
2. **Abolition of Directed Credit Programmes.** The directed credit programmes should be abolished gradually. The priority sector should be redefined.
3. **Free Determination of Interest Rates.** The rate of interest should be determined freely without the intervention of the Reserve Bank of India. Attempts should be made to achieve a minimum 4 percent capital adequacy ratio in relation to risk weighted assets by March 1993.
4. **Improvements in Accounting Systems of the Banks.** The committee recommended for the adoption of uniform accounting practices particularly in regard to income recognition and provisioning against doubtful debts. It also recommended imparting for transparency to bank balance sheets and making full disclosures in them.
5. **Establishment of Special Tribunals.** The special tribunals should be set up to speed up the process of the recovery of loans. An **Assets Reconstruction Fund** (ARF) should be established to take over from banks and financial institutions a portion of their bad and doubtful debts at a discount.

6. **Reconstitution of Banking System.**
   (i) The banking system should be restructured so as to have 3 or 4 large banks which could become international in character.
   (ii) There should be 8 to 10 national banks with network of branches throughout the country engaged in universal banking.
   (iii) There should be local banks whose operation would be generally confined to specific region.
   (iv) There should be rural banks whose operation would be confined to rural areas and whose business would be to finance agriculture and allied activities. It recommended setting up of one or more rural banking subsidiary by each public sector bank to take over all its rural branches.
   (v) The Regional Rural Banks should be permitted to engage in all types of banking business.
7. **Abolition of Branch Licensing.** The committee has recommended abolition of branch licensing and leaving the matter of opening or closing of branches to the commercial judgement of individual banks.
8. **Foreign Banking.** The committee recommended for liberalizing the policy with regard to allowing foreign banks to open offices in India as branches or as subsidiaries. The foreign operations of Indian banks should be rationalised.
9. **More Freedom to Banks.** Banks be given freedom to recruit officers. The banks be inspected on the basis of internal inspection report.
10. **Ending of Dual Control.** The dual control over the banking system of the Finance Ministry and Reserve Banks should be ended. The Reserve Bank should establish a separate quasi-autonomous body to take over the supervisory function over the banks.
11. **Financial Institutions.** The committee made the following recommendations regarding financial institutions :
   (i) Transferring of direct lending function of IDBI to a separate institution while retaining to IDBI apex and refinancing role.
   (ii) The Reserve Bank should set up a new agency to supervise financial institutions such as merchant banks, mutual funds, leasing companies, venture capital companies and factor companies.
   (iii) Capital market be liberalized.
   (iv) An appropriate legal structure be organised and operate mutual funds on the basis of experience of other countries.

In short, the recommendations by the Narasimham committee would have far reaching implications on the working of banking and financial system in the years to come.

B. Narasimham Committee Report on Banking Sector Reforms

The United Front Government appointed Narasimham Committee to review the progress of reforms in the banking sector. The committee submitted its report to the Finance Minister on April 23, 1998. The main objective of the Banking Sector Reforms Committee was to establish strong, efficient and profitable banking system of the global standard.

The main recommendations of the committee are as follows:

1. **Strengthening the Banking System**
   The following recommendations are made to strengthen the banking system:
   (i) Capital Adequacy Requirements should take into consideration **market risks** in addition to **credit risks**.

(ii) Risk weight on a Government guaranteed advance should be the same as other advances.

(iii) Minimum Capital to Risk Assets Ratio (CRAR) be increased from the existing 8 percent to 10 percent. There should be penal provisions for bank that do not maintain CRAR.

(iv) Public sector bank in a position to access the capital market at home or abroad be encouraged.

2. **Asset Quality**

The following recommendations have been made to improve asset quality:

(i) The ratio of non-performing assets to the total assets should be reduced.

(ii) For evaluating the quality of assets portfolio, advanced covered by government guarantees, which have turned sticky, be treated as Non-performing Assets.

(iii) For banks with a high NPA portfolio, the following two alternative approaches could be adopted.

(a) All loan assets in the doubtful and loss categories, should be identified and their realisable value determined. The assets could be transferred to an Asset Reconstruction Company (ARC) which would issue NPA Scrap Bonds.

(b) The banks with high ratio of Non-Performing Assets (NPA) should issue bonds backed by government guarantee.

(iv) The interest subsidy element in credit for the private sector should be totally eliminated. Interest rate on loans under Rs. 2 lakhs should be deregulated.

3. **System and Methods in Banks**

The committee made the following recommendations to improve the systems and methods in banks:

(i) There should be an independent loan review mechanism specially for large borrowed accounts and systems to identify potential Non-performing Assets (NPA).

(ii) Banks and Financial institutions should have a system of recruiting skilled manpower from the open market.

(iii) Public sector banks should be given flexibility to determine managerial remuneration levels taking into account market trends.

(iv) There may be need to redefine the scope of external vigilance and investigation agencies with regard to banking business.

(v) There is need to develop information and control system in several areas concerning the banking operations.

4. **Structural Issues**

The following recommendations have been made regarding structural issues of the banks:

(i) With the conversion of activities between banks and Developmental Financial Institution DFI it is said that should over a period of time convert themselves to bank.

(ii) Banking system should be reconstituted:

(a) 2 or 3 banks with an international status should be established.

(b) 8 or 10 large banks should be established. These banks should take care of the needs of the large and medium corporate sectors and the larger of the small enterprises.

(c) There should be merger of large number of local banks.

(iii) There should be merger of large banks only with the large banks. The large bank should not be merged with weaker banks.

(iv) Weak banks should be either nutrised into healthy units or closed down.

(v) The minimum share of holding by Government Reserve Bank in the equity of the nationalised banks and the state Bank should be brought down to 33%.

(vi) The Reserve Bank of India should not be the owner of any other bank.

(vii) There is need for a reform of the deposit insurance scheme.

(viii) Reserve Bank of India should totally withdraw from the primary market in 91 day treasury bills.

(ix) Necessary changes should be made in banking and debt recovery legislation.

(x) A high level of professionalism needs to be introduced as much in the Board level as in Management. The Board of Directors should include efficient and professional persons. There should be rapid computerisation of the banking. There should be modernisation and technology upgradation of the banking operations.

In short according to **Narasimham Committee**, '*A strong and efficient banking system functionally diverse and geographically widespread, is critical to the attainment of the objectives of creating a market driven, productive and competitive economy. The reforms in the banking sector has been receiving major emphasis.*'

Banking Sector Reforms

Among the recommendations of the Narasimham Committee that have been implemented by Government of India till date are:

1. **Deregulation of Entry of Private Sector Banks.** In 1992-93, the entry of private sector banks both domestic and foreign have been deregulated. At present there are 34 domestic and 42 foreign private sector banks. The policy of deregulation has been implemented with the objective of generating increased competition for incumbent public sector banks and increased allocational efficiency of the banking system. The Reserve Bank of India has sought to ensure that the new entrants are professionally managed, financially viable and technologically strong. Capital norms of foreign banks have also been substantially liberalised, *joint ventures between foreign and Indian banks have been permitted for the first time since independence.*
2. **Liberalised Branch Expansions.** The branch licensing policy has been liberalised. The banks are allowed more freedom to plan branch expansion in response to market needs. However, the permission for branch expansion is subject to certain minimum performance requirements.
3. **Deregulation of Interest Rates.** After the reforms interest rates have been deregularised . Prior to 1992, interest rates were completely administered by the RBI and were highly complex and rigid. The RBI would stipulate maximum deposit rates on both savings and time deposits for all maturities as well as minimum lending rates on loans of different sizes and maturities. This system guaranteed banks a minimum interest rate spread and measure of protection against mounting losses. Moreover the same rates were charged by all banks. Since 1992, interest rates have been deregulated in a phased manner and by July 1996, banks were allowed to set interest rates on all term deposits and on all advances greater than Rs. 2 lakh. Each bank is required to announce its own Prime Lending Rates (PLR). The Prime Lending Rate is that rate which a bank charges from its prime borrowers. It was decided with effect from April 29,1998, that the interest rates on loans upto Rs. 2 lakh should not exceed the prime lending rate (PLR) of the concerned bank. However the lending rates on export are still prescribed.
4. **Introduction of Capital Adequacy Norms.** Narasimham Committee recommended the introduction of prudential norms, to meet international standards. **Prudential Norms** are controls and limits imposed by the Central Bank on the activities of the banks. Most common Prudential Norms are related to Capital Adequacy norms and Asset classification. Narasimham Committee recommended the introduction of capital adequacy norm of 8 percent

in tune with the norms set by the **Bank for International Settlement** (BIS). The capital adequacy ratio expresses the real capital as a percentage of total weighted risks. It indicates the margin of protection available to both depositors and creditors against unanticipated losses that may be experienced by a bank. A bank's real capital is the worth evaluated after taking into account the riskiness of its assets. If all the assets of a bank were riskless, then a bank's real capital is equal to the book value of the capital. However if the riskiness of assets are taken into account to evaluate them the value of a bank's risk weighted assets and hence its capital will be less than the book value. This recommendation has been implemented. All commercial banks are required to maintain a Capital to Risk Assets Ratio (CRAR) of not less than 8 percent in tune with BIS norms. This sought to minimize the problems of inadequacy of capital compared to risk exposure that has persistently plagued public sector banks. It was hoped that introduction of BIS norms would provide Indian Banks with a comfortable cushion against insolvency thereby ensuring market stability. In pursuance of Narasimham Committee on Bank Reforms recommendation, the Government of India proposed to raise the minimum Capital to Risk-Weighted Asset Ratio (CRAR) from the existing level of 8 percent to 10 percent in phases. Out of 27 public sector banks, 26 banks attained the stipulated 8 percent CRAR by March 1998. By this date 19 PSB's attained CRAR exceeding 10 percent.

5. **Introduction of Internationally Accepted Norms of Income Recognition.** Along with the introduction of capital adequacy norms, new norms of income recognition asset classification and provising has also been introduced. Asset classification means that the assets of a bank are classified for making provisions.

   Assets can be: (i) Standard or (ii) Non Performing Assets (NPA).

   In India:

   (i) Standard Assets are defined as credit facilities with respect to which interest or principal or both are paid by due date, or within 30 days of due date. On the other hand,

   (ii) Non-Performing Assets (NPA) is that asset which is not paid for a periods of two quarters.

   New Norms of Income Recognition asset classification has been introduced to reflect more accurately the quality of loan portfolios and to obtain a true picture of the financial situation of each bank. For example, the profits of 27 public sector banks were reduced by 45 percent due to a switch to the new accounting norms.

6. **Permission to Public Sector Banks to sale their Shares.** Narasimham Committee's recommendation to allow public sector banks to access the capital market to raise equity has been accepted. In order to enable banks to take care of their additional needs of capital the Government of India decided to allow some of the stronger public sector banks to approach the capital market to directly mobilise the equity funds from the public. The public is allowed to subscribe upto 49 percent of the capital of public sector banks. State Bank of India was the first public sector bank to sale its share in the market. Till now, 8 Public Sector banks have issued their shares amounting Rs. 6015 crore to the public.

7. **Reduction of Cash Reserve Ratio (CRR) and Statutory Liquidity Ratio (SLR).** Narasimham Committee recommended that CRR and SLR should be gradually reduced. The Reserve Bank has reduced Cash Reserve Ratio to 10 percent and statutory liquidity ratio to 25 percent. The CRR obligates a bank to hold a certain fraction of its total deposits as reserves with the Central Bank in order to ensure liquidity of the banking system. CRR imposes an effective loss of income to the banks since the interest earned on these reserves is significantly low (around 5 percent) compared to the return that can be earned in loans. In India CRR had increased from a low 3 percent as of May 1973 to as high as 15 percent in 1989. Now it has been reduced to 10 percent. It will release more funds to the banks to lend them at a higher rate of interest.

The Statutory Liquidity Ratio (SLR) requires banks to invest a predetermined proportion of their total demand and time liabilities in Government and other approved securities. Since the interest rate on such securities were significantly below market rates, the SLR requirement negatively affects the income earning capacity of banks. The SLR was 31.5% in 1996 but it has now been reduced to 25 percent.

Note: Around 63 committees have been formed in banking sector.

Impact of the Reforms

Impact of the reforms in the banking sector may be discussed as follows:

1. **Impact of Reforms on Performance of Banks.** It is important to evaluate the impact of reforms on comparative performance of Major Bank Groups. Thus, impact can be studied under the following heads:

   (i) ***Impact on Structure of Banking Sector.*** The structure of the Indian banking system has undergone significant changes in terms of private sector bank operations. Since, the advent of reforms the number of domestic as well as foreign private sector banks have increased substantially.

   (ii) ***Impact on Growth Rates of Deposits and Advances.*** The rate of growth of deposits for public sector banks in the Reforms period are slightly lower than those prevailing in the pre-reforms period. The deposit growth rates of foreign banks declined but of domestic private banks increased. One of the main reasons behind the overall sluggist growth rate of bank deposits in the Reforms period is the growth of non-bank financial intermediaries including mutual funds, finance companies and stock market. The growth rate of advances of public sector banks declined but that of private sector banks increased.

   The better performance of private sector banks in the advance market is linked to their ability to attract some of the corporate clients of the public sector banks by providing them better service and better packages.

   (iii) ***Non-Interest Income of Banks.*** Non-interest income of a bank comes from different service based activities such as credit card transactions, merchant banking, leasing etc. Before Reforms, Foreign Banks have the highest proportion of non-interest income to their total income. However since reforms the proportion of non-interest income out of the total income of the Public Sector banks and domestic banks have increased from 9 percent to 11 percent. On the other hand the share of non-interest income in the case of Foreign Banks have declined from 24 percent to 18 percent. The trends in non-interest income indicate that the domestic banks are diversifying away from their core business and are providing increased competition to the foreign banks in the provision of fee based services.

   (iv) ***Non-Performing Assets and Capital Adequacy.*** Since Reforms, percentage of the non-performing assets as percentage of total loans is declining for all the bank groups. However in case of foreign banks it is the least of all other banking groups. None of the new domestic banks showed any non performing assets as yet. In the post-reform period mostly the banks have attained the capital adequacy ratio of 8 percent. In case of public sector banks, the Government has infused new capital worth Rs. 20046 crore to enable them to attain the capital adequacy ratio.

   (v) ***Profitability.*** In the post reform period, all the banks showed a significant improvement in their profitability with certain exceptions. In 1995-96, the nationalised banks reported net losses. However, in 1997-98 all the banking groups showed increase in profitability.

2. **Availability of Credit.** Availability of credit to the private sector as a proportion of the total deposits of the banking sector is indicated by the credit-deposit ratio. Following the reforms

the credit deposit ratio (CDR) of commercial banks as a whole declined substantially from 60.6 percent in 1991-92 to 54.9 percent in 1997-98. It is partly because of the recession over the period and partly because of the banks were learning to adjust to the new lending norms under the reforms. The decrease in CDR since the reforms has been accompanied by a corresponding increase in the proportion of risk-free Government securities in Bank's major earning assets *i.e.* loans and advances and investments. In other words, during post reform period, the banks are investing more in government securities compared to advancing in the form of loans.

3. **Interest Rate Trends.** The structure of deposit rates in the reforms period points to increasing attempt by RBI to liberalise the term deposit rate structure and boost the mobilization of both short term and long term deposits. Such attempts have been made with a view to augment the resources of the banking system to prevent a liquidity 'crunch' and a consequent upward pressure on nominal lending rates. While rates for smaller advances of less term Rs. 2 lakh continue to be fixed and subsidized by the RBI rates for advances over Rs. 2 lakh were deregulated.
4. **Banks Vs. Non-Bank Intermediation.** Since, the financial sector reforms started in India, commercial banks have been facing increasing competition from term lending institutions like Industrial Development Bank of India, ICICI, Mutual Funds, Chit Funds and the Capital market. Such competition was practically absent until recent years owing to various RBI and Government of India regulations which favoured banks in the mobilization of deposits by regulating private sector entry into financial services and due to an underdeveloped capital market.

   With the financial sector reforms, non-bank financial intermediaries and the capital market have experienced impressive growth in recent years. Such growth greatly increased the confidence of the small investor in non bank deposits and investments. The share of non-bank deposits in household savings increased and of the banks decreased. The share of bank in project loans to private sector has also declined. This was primarily due to the growth of development banks and the capital market.
5. **Competition.** The liberalised entry of private sector banks including foreign banks has an impact in the competition of the banking sector. Evidence of increased competition in the post reform era emerges from three indicators:
   (i) There has been a change in the market share of public and private sector banks. It is a sign of increased competition since any changes in favour of private and foreign banks signal the extent to which these banks have been successful by offering lower prices and better services. The market share of public sector banks in both the deposits and advances have fallen while those of private banks have improved.
   (ii) Another signal of growing competition between public sector and private sector banks is non - bank concentration ratio. This ratio gives the total market share of the largest banks in the industry. It is used to measure the extent of competition in a market. Trends in the estimates of four-bank concentration ratio reveal a decline in the post reforms period. It is due to the slower growth of the largest banks, all of which are in the public sector. It is also due to the increased competition from private sector banks.
   (iii) The third indicator of competition is the quality and range of customer services. There are indications that the scope and intensity of such competition has certainly increased since the reforms. This is manifested in rapidly increasing use of computer and telecommunication technology by public sector bank in order to provide improved and faster banking services, similar to those provided by private sector and foreign banks.

Greater emphasis is also now being paid on value added services such as credit cards and merchant banking. As a manifestation of increased competition, a number of public and private banks have been setting up ATM's introducing tele-banking, providing specialised services and introducing credit card operations. An additional indication of increased quality competition is in the attempt of banks to seek quality certification ISO 9000 from International Standards organisation.

6. **Efficiency.** The following indicators are used to judge the extent of improvement in efficiency of the banks:
   (i) The first efficiency indicator is the **proportion of operating cost to working funds**. It measures a bank's ability to economise on total costs. With respect to this indicator while the domestic private banks have registered a significant improvement in lowering costs in the reforms period, the cost of both public sector banks and foreign banks have registered an increase.
   (ii) The second efficiency indicator is the **proportion of staff expenditure to working funds**. With respect to this indicator the foreign banks have the lowest expenditure while the public sector banks have the highest expenditure. The domestic private sector banks have registered a significant reduction in such expenditure in the reforms period.
   (iii) Another efficiency indicator is **spread** or Net Interest margin as percentage of working funds. Spread (Net Interest Margin) is the difference between interest income and interest expenditure by a bank. A higher spread may indicate the fact that a bank may be more capable of mobilizing deposits at low rate of interest or advancing credit at higher interest rates. Foreign banks have the highest spread followed by domestic private banks and then by public sector banks. Such differences could signify dynamic efficiency differences. However, the comparison is not entirely fair because the public sector banks carry a greater burden of lending to the priority sector at subsidised interest rates.

NON-PERFORMING ASSET

Identification

NPA is a classification used by financial institutions that refer to loans that are in jeopardy of default. Once the borrower has failed to make interest or principal payments for 90 days the loan is considered to be a non-performing asset. Non-performing assets are problematic for financial institutions since they depend on interest payments for income. Troublesome pressure from the economy can lead to a sharp increase in non-performing loans and often results in massive write-downs.

With a view to moving towards international best practices and to ensure greater transparency, it has been decided to adopt the '90 days overdue' norm for identification of NPA, from the year ending March 31, 2004. Accordingly, with effect from March 31, 2004, a non-performing asset (NPA) shall be a loan or an advance where;

- Interest and/or installment of principal remain overdue for a period of more than 90 days in respect of a term loan,
- The account remains 'out of order' for a period of more than 90 days, in respect of an Overdraft/ Cash Credit (OD/CC),
- The bill remains overdue for a period of more than 90 days in the case of bills purchased and discounted,

- Interest and/or installment of principal remains overdue for two harvest seasons but for a period not exceeding two half years in the case of an advance granted for agricultural purposes, and
- Any amount to be received remains overdue for a period of more than 90 days in respect of other accounts.

Classification

Banks are required to classify non-performing assets further into the following three categories based on the period for which the asset has remained non-performing and the realisability of the dues:

1. **Sub-standard assets.** A sub standard asset is one which has been classified as NPA for a period not exceeding 12 months.
2. **Doubtful Assets.** A doubtful asset is one which has remained NPA for a period exceeding 12 months.
3. **Loss assets.** Where loss has been identified by the bank, internal or external auditor or central bank inspectors but the amount has not been written off, wholly or partly.

Sub-standard asset is the asset in which bank have to maintain 15% of its reserves. All those assets which are considered as non-performing for period of more than 12 months are called as Doubtful Assets. All those assets which cannot be recovered are called as Loss Assets.

CAPITAL ADEQUACY RATIO (BASEL'S NORMS)

The Committee on Banking Regulations and Supervisory Practices (Basel Committee) had released the guidelines on capital measures and capital standards in July 1988 which were been accepted by Central Banks in various countries including RBI. In India it has been implemented by RBI w.e.f. 1.4.92.

Objectives of CAR. The fundamental objective behind the norms is to strengthen the soundness and stability of the banking system.

Capital Adequacy Ratio or CAR or CRAR. It is ratio of capital fund to risk weighted assets expressed in percentage terms i.e.

Minimum requirements of capital fund in India:

- Existing Banks 09%
- New Private Sector Banks 10%
- Banks undertaking Insurance business 10%
- Local Area Banks 15%

Tier I Capital should at no point of time be less than 50% of the total capital. This implies that Tier II cannot be more than 50% of the total capital.

Capital Fund

Capital Fund has two tiers - Tier I capital include

- paid-up capital
- statutory reserves
- other disclosed free reserves
- capital reserves representing surplus arising out of sale proceeds of assets.

Minus

- equity investments in subsidiaries,
- intangible assets, and
- losses in the current period and those brought forward from previous periods

To work out the Tier I capital, Tier II capital consists of:

- Un-disclosed reserves and cumulative perpetual preference shares:
- Revaluation Reserves (at a discount of 55 percent while determining their value for inclusion in Tier II capital)
- General Provisions and Loss Reserves upto a maximum of 1.25% of weighted risk assets
- Investment fluctuation reserve not subject to 1.25% restriction
- Hybrid debt capital Instruments (say bonds)
- Subordinated debt (long term unsecured loans)

Risk weighted assets - Fund Based. Risk weighted assets mean fund based assets such as cash, loans, investments and other assets. Degrees of credit risk expressed as percentage weights have been assigned by RBI to each such assets.

Non-funded (Off-Balance sheet) Items. The credit risk exposure attached to off-balance sheet items has to be first calculated by multiplying the face amount of each of the off-balance sheet items by the credit conversion factor. This will then have to be again multiplied by the relevant weightage.

Reporting Requirements

Banks are also required to disclose in their balance sheet the quantum of Tier I and Tier II capital fund, under disclosure norms.

An annual return has to be submitted by each bank indicating capital funds, conversion of off-balance sheet/non-funded exposures, calculation of risk-weighted assets, and calculations of capital to risk assets ratio.

FINANCIAL MARKETS

MONEY MARKET

Money Market can be understood as the market for short term funds, wherein lending and borrowing of funds varies from overnight to a year. It is an important part of the financial system that helps in fulfilling the short term and very short term requirements of the companies, banks, financial institution, government agencies and so forth.

Salient Features of Money Market

- It is a wholesale market, as the transaction volume is large.
- Trading takes place over the telephone, after which written confirmation is done by way of e-mails.
- Participants include banks, mutual funds, investment institutions and Central Banks.
- There is an impersonal relationship between the participants in the money market, and so, pure competition exists.
- Money market operations focuses on a particular area, which serves a region or an area. On the basis of the market size and needs, the area may differ.

There are five major segments of money market which are Certificate of Deposits (CD), Commercial Paper, Swaps, Repo and Government treasury securities.

Money Market Instruments

In this market, only those financial instruments are traded which are immediate substitutes for money, which includes:

1. **Call/Notice Money.** When the money raised or borrowed on demand for a very short term which ranges from one day to 14 days, then it is be called as notice money, and when it exceeds 14 days it is termed as call money.
2. **Treasury Bills.** These are short term, negotiable financial assets issued by the central bank, on behalf of the government, for overcoming liquidity shortfalls.
3. **Commercial Bills.** A commercial bill is a negotiable, self-liquidating instrument that is less risky in nature. When goods are bought on credit, these bills improve the liability to make payment at the specified date.
4. **Commercial Paper.** It alludes to an unsecured promissory note, issued by large and creditworthy companies, at a discount on its face value and redeemable on its face value.
5. **Certificate of Deposit.** It is an unsecured, negotiable financial instrument which a bank and financial institution issues to individuals, corporation, trust, funds etc. at a discount on its face value and its maturity vary from 15 days to one year.

The financial assets dealt in the money market possess high liquidity, low transaction cost, less risky and no loss in value. And so, it acts as a whole sale debt market for such instruments.

Functions of Money Market

The three basic functions of money market are:

- It provides a balancing tool for equating the demand for and supply of short term funds.
- It provides a centre for the intervention of central bank, for controlling liquidity and general interest rate level.
- It provides a proper reach to the suppliers and users of the short term funds, to fulfil their requirements, at a reasonable market clearing price.

Money market plays a vital role in equating the short term liquidity imbalances within the country. Indeed, with the help of this market, the central bank controls liquidity and interest rate level in the country.

CAPITAL MARKET

"Capital Markets" refers to activities that gather funds from some entities and make them available to other entities needing funds. The core function of such a market is to improve the efficiency of transactions so that each individual entity doesn't need to do search and analysis, create legal agreements, and complete funds transfer.

Capital markets consist of suppliers and users of funds. Suppliers of funds include households and institutions serving them, such as pension funds; life insurance companies; charitable foundations such as colleges, hospitals, and religious institutions; and nonfinancial companies generating cash beyond their needs for investment. Users of funds include home and motor vehicle purchasers; nonfinancial companies; and governments financing infrastructure investment and operating expenses.

Markets include primary markets, where new equity stock and bond issues are sold to investors, and secondary markets, which trade existing securities.

Capital Markets in Context

Broadly, capital markets can refer to markets for any financial asset.

In the context of corporate finance, the term refers to venues for obtaining investable capital for nonfinancial companies. Here, "investable capital" includes the external funds included in a weighted average cost of capital calculation – common and preferred equity, public bonds, and private debt – that are also used in a return on invested capital calculation.

In a more limited corporate finance context, it refers to only equity funding, excluding debt.

In a financial services industry context, it refers to financial companies involved primarily in private markets, as opposed to public ones. In this sense, it is referring to investment banks, private equity, and venture capital firms in contrast to broker-dealers and public exchanges. In this case, capital markets are considered primary offerings of debt and equity (initial public offering) supported by investment banks through underwriting. This contrasts with the time after the initial public offering when the offering is publicly trading on exchanges in a secondary market. In the U.S., the primary regulator for an exchange is the Securities and Exchange Commission (SEC). This industry context is often meant when "capital markets" are contrasted with "financial markets."

In the context of public markets operated by a regulated exchange, "capital markets" can refer to equity markets in contrast to debt/bond/fixed income, money, derivatives, and commodities markets. Mirroring the corporate finance context, "capital markets" can also mean equity and debt/bond/ fixed income markets.

In a tax context, capital markets might refer to investments intended to be held for over one year for capital gains tax treatment. This is often related to transactions arranged privately through investment banks or private funds (such as private equity or venture capital).

GOVERNMENT SECURITIES MARKET

A government security is a bond issued by a government authority with a promise of repayment upon maturity. Government securities such as savings bonds, treasury bills and notes also promise periodic coupon or interest payments. These securities are considered as low-risk, since they are backed by the taxing power of the government.

The Treasury Department issues government securities through auctions to institutional investors for buying and selling. Retail investors buy government securities directly from the Treasury Department's website, banks or brokers. Since, most government securities are backed by the full faith and credit of the U.S. government, default is unlikely.

Rates on government bonds affect the entire U.S. economy. The government's sale or repurchase of its bonds affect the money supply and influence interest rates. For example, when the Federal Reserve repurchases Treasuries, sellers deposit proceeds in banks, which lend money to customers, who deposit the loan proceeds in bank accounts, and use the money for various purposes. Therefore, every dollar of repurchased Treasuries increases the money supply by several dollars.

Examples of Government Securities

Savings bonds offer a fixed interest rate over a certain period of time. When an investor buys and holds a savings bond until maturity, he receives the bond's face value plus accrued interest. Savings bonds are not redeemable for the first 12 months when they are outstanding. Redeeming a bond in the first five years means forfeiting the last three months of interest.

Treasury notes (T-notes) are intermediate-term bonds maturing in two, three, five or 10 years. They provide semiannual interest payments at fixed coupon rates. T-Notes typically have a $1,000 face value; those with two- or three-year maturities have a $5,000 face value.

Treasury bonds (T-Bonds) are long-term bonds maturing in 10 to 30 years. T-Bonds provide semiannual interest payments and have $1,000 face values. The bonds fund shortfalls in the federal budget, regulate the nation's money supply, and execute U.S. monetary policy.

Pros and Cons of Government Securities

Government securities are exempt from state and local taxes, making government bonds advantageous for investors in high tax brackets. The bonds are very liquid, but have low rates of return. The securities rarely protect against inflation and have little or no capital gains opportunity.

Many investors hold government securities through mutual funds. The funds offer diversification among all types and maturities of bonds, which is difficult for retail investors to achieve without investing more cash than mutual funds require. However, fund-management fees lower investors' overall returns.

Although government securities carry little risk of default, they carry interest rate risk. When interest rates rise or fall, bond prices react inversely. Fortunately, when interest rates rise, T-Note prices typically fall less than with other bonds. With their steady income streams, government securities are a conservative choice in a fluctuating market.

FINANCIAL INSTITUTIONS

DEVELOPMENT FINANCIAL INSTITUTIONS (DFI)

Development Financial Institutions are specialized institutions set up primarily to provide development/ project finance especially in developing countries. These development banks are usually majority-owned by national governments. The source of capital of these banks is national or international development funds. This ensures their creditworthiness and their ability to provide project finance in a very competitive rate.

DFIs differentiates itself from commercial banks as it strikes a balance between commercial operational norms as followed by commercial banks on one hand, and developmental responsibilities on the other. They provide long-term loans, guarantees and underwriting functions. DFIs provide long term finance to fund the activities to those sectors where the risk is higher for the commercial banks to finance. So, DFIs are not just plain lenders like commercial banks but they act as companions in the development of significant sectors of the economy. After independence, as the role of commercial banks were limited to providing working capital financing for short periods, the DFIs were set up to finance the development on long term basis for the significant sectors of the economy like infrastructure sector.

The Development Finance Institutions can be classified into four categories:

- National Development Banks Ex: IDBI, SIDBI, ICICI, IFCI, IRBI,
- IDFC Sector specific financial institutions Ex: TFCI, EXIM Bank, NABARD, HDFC, NHB
- Investment Institutions Ex: LIC, GIC and UTI
- State level institutions Ex: State Finance Corporations and SIDCs.

In India, the role of DFIs is to support long term infrastructures of industry and agriculture. The DFIs were set up under the full control of both Central and State Governments. These institutions were used by the government for spurring economic growth and aid social development. The DFIs provide finance to all those entities which are not adequately served by the banks and capital markets like households, SMEs, and private corporations.

In India, the first DFI was operationalised in 1948 with the setting up of the Industrial Finance Corporation (IFCI). After the passage of state Financial corporations (SFCs) Act, 1951, state level small and medium-sized financial corporations were established. It was succeeded by the establishment of industrial Finance Corporation of India (IFCI). In 1955, the first DFI in private sector, the Industrial Credit and Investment Corporation of India (ICICI), was set up with the backing of the World Bank. In 1958, Refinance Corporation for Industry, which was taken over by the Industrial Development Bank of India (IDBI) was established. In 1963, Agriculture Refinance Corporation was established.

The major development in the institution building was the establishment of IDBI as an apex term-lending institution, and that of the Unit Trust of India (UTI), as subsidiaries of the Reserve Bank of India (RBI) in 1964. Similarly, in 1960s, State Industrial Development Corporations (SIDCs) were developed in the states.

Industrial Finance Corporation of India (IFCI), Industrial Development Bank of India (IDBI), National Bank for Agriculture and Rural Development (NABARD), National Housing Board (NHB) and Small Industry Development Bank of India (SIDBI) were all launched with majority ownership of the Reserve Bank of India (RBI).

After 2000-2001, the prominence of development banking has started to decline as many firms from development banking had quit post liberalization. During 2002-2004, ICICI and IDBI were turned into commercial banks. From then, the share of the development banks fell down to just 30% from two-thirds. The government found that the DFIs failed miserably to provide credits to small scale sector and rural farm sectors for long term. Also, they do not have low cost deposits in the form of current and savings accounts similar to that of commercial banks. Until reforms in 1991, the DFIs had access to state funding. But after 1991 reforms, reduced public spending in DFIs resulted in their decline. So, the DFIs had to rely on a variety of methods to fill the gap created by the reduced state funding. There were growing reliance on bank credit, private equity in corporate financing and external commercial borrowing (ECBs).

At present the line between the role of DFIs and commercial banks have blurred due to overlapping of their functions. Nowadays, the commercial banks are actively involved in developmental financing similar to that of the DFIs, especially after the merger of ICICI and IDBI within the banking system. So, nowadays the commercial banks are often called as the universal banks as it provides all types of financial services.

The DFIs role of industrialization and the developmental finance till the onset of liberalization cannot be denied. They were crucial to realize the larger developmental goals as prescribed by the Five Year Plans. Though, as of now, the commercial banks have largely taken the place of DFIs in developmental financing, they are unlikely to emphasize environmental and social concerns while making investment decisions and lending, especially if they result in reduction in profitability. In India, it has been observed that the greater private participation in developmental banking has often resulted in accumulation of private profit rather than social benefit. Hence, it would be wise to revive the concept of DFI if the government wishes to keep societal, cultural, regional, rural and environmental concerns intact while financing long term developmental projects.

NON-BANKING FINANCIAL COMPANIES (NBFC)

A Non-Banking Financial Company is a company registered under the Companies Act, 1956 engaged in the business of loans and advances, acquisition of shares/stocks/bonds/debentures/securities issued by government or local authority or other marketable securities of a like nature, leasing, hire-purchase, insurance business, chit business but does not include any institution whose principal business is that of agriculture activity, industrial activity, purchase or sale of any goods (other than securities) or providing any services and sale/purchase/construction of immovable property. A non-banking institution which is a company and has principal business of receiving deposits under any scheme or arrangement in one lump sum or in installments by way of contributions or in any other manner, is also a non-banking financial company (Residuary non-banking company).

NBFCs lend and make investments and hence, their activities are akin to that of banks; however there are a few differences as given below:

- NBFC cannot accept demand deposits;
- NBFCs do not form part of the payment and settlement system and cannot issue cheques drawn on itself;
- deposit insurance facility of Deposit Insurance and Credit Guarantee Corporation is not available to depositors of NBFCs, unlike in case of banks.

NBFCs are categorized:

- in terms of the type of liabilities into Deposit and Non-Deposit accepting NBFCs,
- non deposit taking NBFCs by their size into systemically important and other non-deposit holding companies (NBFC-NDSI and NBFC-ND) and
- by the kind of activity they conduct.

Within this broad categorization the different types of NBFCs are as follows:

1. **Asset Finance Company (AFC) .** An AFC is a company which is a financial institution carrying on as its principal business the financing of physical assets supporting productive/economic activities, such as automobiles, tractors, lathe machines, generator sets, earth moving and material handling equipments, moving on own power and general purpose industrial machines. Principal business for this purpose is defined as aggregate of financing real/ physical assets supporting economic activity and income arising therefrom is not less than 60% of its total assets and total income respectively.
2. **Investment Company (IC) .** IC means any company which is a financial institution carrying on as its principal business the acquisition of securities,
3. **Loan Company (LC).** LC means any company which is a financial institution carrying on as its principal business, the providing of finance whether by making loans or advances or otherwise for any activity other than its own but does not include an Asset Finance Company.
4. **Infrastructure Finance Company (IFC).** IFC is a non-banking finance company a) which deploys at least 75 per cent of its total assets in infrastructure loans, b) has a minimum Net Owned Funds of Rs 300 crore, c) has a minimum credit rating of 'A 'or equivalent d) and a CRAR of 15%.
5. **Systemically Important Core Investment Company (CIC-ND-SI).** CIC-ND-SI is an NBFC carrying on the business of acquisition of shares and securities.
6. **Infrastructure Debt Fund: Non- Banking Financial Company (IDF-NBFC).** IDF-NBFC is a company registered as NBFC to facilitate the flow of long term debt into infrastructure projects. IDF-NBFC raise resources through issue of Rupee or Dollar denominated bonds of minimum 5 year maturity. Only Infrastructure Finance Companies (IFC) can sponsor IDF-NBFCs.
7. **Non-Banking Financial Company - Micro Finance Institution (NBFC-MFI).** NBFC-MFI is a non-deposit taking NBFC having not less than 85% of its assets in the nature of qualifying assets which satisfy the following criteria:
    - loan disbursed by an NBFC-MFI to a borrower with a rural household annual income not exceeding Rs 1,00,000 or urban and semi-urban household income not exceeding Rs 1,60,000;
    - loan amount does not exceed Rs 50,000 in the first cycle and Rs 1,00,000 in subsequent cycles;
    - total indebtedness of the borrower does not exceed Rs 1,00,000;
    - tenure of the loan not to be less than 24 months for loan amount in excess of Rs 15,000 with prepayment without penalty;

- loan to be extended without collateral;
- aggregate amount of loans, given for income generation, is not less than 50 per cent of the total loans given by the MFIs;
- loan is repayable on weekly, fortnightly or monthly instalments at the choice of the borrower

8. **Non-Banking Financial Company – Factors (NBFC-Factors).** NBFC-Factor is a non-deposit taking NBFC engaged in the principal business of factoring. The financial assets in the factoring business should constitute at least 50 percent of its total assets and its income derived from factoring business should not be less than 50 percent of its gross income.
9. **Mortgage Guarantee Companies (MGC).** MGC are financial institutions for which at least 90% of the business turnover is mortgage guarantee business or at least 90% of the gross income is from mortgage guarantee business and net owned fund is Rs 100 crore.
10. **NBFC.** Non-Operative Financial Holding Company (NOFHC) is financial institution through which promoter/promoter groups will be permitted to set up a new bank .It's a wholly-owned Non-Operative Financial Holding Company (NOFHC) which will hold the bank as well as all other financial services companies regulated by RBI or other financial sector regulators, to the extent permissible under the applicable regulatory prescriptions.

It is illegal for any financial entity or unincorporated body to make a false claim of being regulated by the Reserve Bank to mislead the public for collecting deposits and it is liable for penal action under the Indian Penal Code. Information in this regard may be forwarded to the nearest office of the Reserve Bank and the Police.

MUTUAL FUNDS

Mutual funds are created when several people who wish to earn wealth (investors) combine their resources to create a huge investable amount (corpus). This large corpus is then invested into various companies across industries, operating in different sectors of the economy - depending on the type of fund chosen. All the investors of a mutual fund share in its profits, losses, incomes, and expenses in direct proportion to their level of investment.

Companies that create mutual fund schemes are called Fund Houses or Asset Management Companies (AMCs). The professionals who study the markets and pick companies to invest in are called Fund Managers. Fund managers spend a great deal of time analysing markets and studying different sectors of the economy to figure out which companies are most likely to turn a profit - in different time frames - and choose the best option.

There are thousands of mutual funds in India, under different categories, offered by hundreds of AMCs and Fund Houses. For fairness and transparency, global agencies exist that analyse and rate the performance of funds over time and make sure that investors are well informed before investing. It is mandatory for AMCs to declare a standard against which the performance of any given fund can be measured - this is called a benchmark. There are also regulatory bodies like AMFI and SEBI that ensure no investor ever gets scammed.

Mutual funds allow individuals to make their money work for them - meaning that they do not need to actively perform tasks for monetary gain. Any amount invested in mutual funds will either grow or shrink depending on market performance and the skill of the fund manager.

There are many different types of mutual funds available today, and can be categorised based on investment objective, structure and asset class. Apart from this, there are also specialised mutual funds.

Mutual funds are an investment tool that pools money from several investors and invests it in company stocks, bonds, government instruments, etc. in order to generate a profit for investors. This profit may be paid out as dividends to investors (dividend plans) or reinvested by the fund for capital appreciation (growth plan). There are different types of mutual funds based on various characteristic differences. Most mutual funds try to diversify their investments as many different companies and industries as possible, and some invest in only specific industries and sectors of the economy. Some funds aim for high-risk-high-reward strategies, while some opt for low-risk-regular-income strategies. There's a huge variety of funds to choose from, and a large number of Asset Management Companies (AMCs)/fund houses. that offer excellent schemes for all types of investors. Some banks and financial distributors also sell mutual funds.

Different types of mutual funds operate slightly different from one another, but they all have some basic principles on which they operate that define them as mutual funds.

The most basic ways in which mutual funds operate are explained below:

1. An asset management company (AMC)/fund house identifies a potential earning possibility in the market and calculates the risk and potential reward involved in this particular investment.
2. The AMC studies other related investment opportunities that could boost the value of - or ensure the success of - the main opportunity.
3. The fund manager working for the AMC picks and chooses different investments in order to balance out the risk and total earning potential - balancing the right high risk reward equities with high safety-relatively consistent income securities.
4. All the details about the fund including risk factors are well documented and presented to the industry body SEBI for regulatory approval and to the public for consideration.
5. The fund scheme is made available to the public, who then buy into the fund by purchasing fund units. The more fund units are purchased, larger the investment, and thus greater the proportion of potential income.
6. The investments are made and, depending on the fund's structure, the fund will either be passively or actively managed by a fund manager.
7. Under the dividend option, declared dividends are proportionally distributed amongst investors. Under the growth option, dividends are reinvested for capital appreciation.
8. At the end of the fund's tenure, capital gains are paid out to the investors.

Now let's understand basic mutual fund operation with an example:

Let's say, that there's a huge national demand for 50 lakh units of bottled water per month, but the water bottling plant can only produce 1 lakh units per month. Suppose that the bottling plant can meet this demand if it has a new bottling machine - it can earn a massive profit from supplying the demand. Unfortunately, the bottling plant does not have the funds to purchase this new machine - so it seeks investment. This is an opportunity for a win-win situation for any investor who has enough wealth to help the bottling plant purchase the machine. In most cases, individual investors won't have the requisite funds to purchase large machinery, so, a few investors get together and pool their funds to buy the machine, and will split all profits equally amongst themselves, or in proportion of the amount they've invested.

Once the machine has been purchased, the investors must wait for the bottling plant to integrate the new technology and start producing enough units to meet the demand.

Now that the bottling plant has met the demand of 50 lakh bottles per month - which is a 50x increase in supply - it will obviously be earning a lot more income for the sale of its product. Since the expansion of this bottling plant was enabled by the purchase of a machine, which was enabled by the foresight of certain investors - the investors will get to claim a share of the new profits enjoyed by the bottling company.

This basically explains how an investment helps a company grow, but mutual funds take it a step further. Mutual funds don't just invest in one or two companies, but in hundreds of companies across different sectors of the economy. In addition to the bottling plant, the same mutual fund scheme may have invested in a transportation company, enabling quicker movement of bottled water from the factory to the distribution centres. In addition to the transportation company, the same mutual fund scheme could also have invested in an advertising agency that promotes the sale of this particular brand of bottled water - ensuring smooth sales from distribution centre to end customer. In this way, a mutual fund takes care of most aspects of its investment and tries to ensure its success.

Now since it's a mutual fund, it can have two options by which investors can enjoy their profits - growth or dividend. Under the growth option, all earnings made by the fund are reinvested in the fund itself, and the capital invested is allowed to grow until the tenure of the investment is completed or the investor chooses to redeem the investment. Under the dividend option, the bottling plant will declare income, and dividends will be distributed amongst the investors.

Now, suppose that the demand for water suddenly dropped from 50 lakh units to 10 lakh units, but the machine had already been purchased and is now running on lower capacity, or the machine purchased was faulty, or there's a labour strike preventing water from being bottled – the profits generated will not be as high as expected, and returns for investors will be low, and investors could also lose money. This is called a risk factor, and is one of the major defining characteristics of any mutual fund scheme. Risk must be thoroughly studied in order to mitigate it, and even then, great care must be taken to invest the right amount at the right time in the right place.

This is basically how a mutual fund works - large amounts of money are pooled together to invest in companies/ government instruments that can generate a profit as a result of increased capacity, capability, etc. enabled by investments.

PENSION FUNDS

In India, pension plans have two stages – the accumulation stage and the vesting stage. In the former, the investors pay annual premiums until the time they reach the age of retirement. On reaching the retirement age; the second stage, the vesting stage begins. During this stage of the pension plan, the retiree will start receiving annuities until the time of their death or the death of their nominee.

The contributions that are made to a pension plan, under section 80CCC, are tax-exempt up to a maximum ceiling of INR 1 lakh. The withdrawals, however, are not tax-free. Only one-third of the corpus that is distributed to the retiree (soon after reaching the retirement age) by the pension plan is tax-free. The rest of the money is distributed as an annuity and is subject to taxation depending on the retiree's tax rate at the time of retirement.

There are different kinds of pension plans which are described below:

- plans that are sponsored by an insurer where the investment is solely in debt and are best suited for investors who are conservative.
- plans that are unit linked and invest in both equity and debt.
- the National Pension Scheme which invests in either in 100 percent government securities, 100 percent debt securities (other than government securities) or in a maximum of 50 percent equity.

There is no doubt that pension plans are a much safer form of investment with multiple classifications which are based on the benefits of the plan and its structure.

The classification of pension funds can be based on the following:

a. **National Pension Scheme.** The Government of India introduced a new Pension Scheme for people who wanted to build up their pension amount. With the scheme, your savings will be invested in debt and equity market, based on your preference. It allows you to withdraw 60 percent of the funds at the time of retirement and the remaining 40 percent is used for the purchase of the annuity. The maturity amount is subject to tax.

b. **Deferred Annuity.** With the deferred annuity plan, you can accumulate a corpus through a single premium or regular premiums over the term of the policy. The pension begins once the policy term gets over. This deferred annuity plan has tax benefits wherein no tax is charged on the money invested until you plan to withdraw it. This scheme can be bought by either making regular contributions, or by a one-time payment. This way it works for you whether you want to invest the entire amount at one time or want to invest systematically.

c. **Pension Funds.** The government body, Pension Fund Regulatory and Development Authority (PFRDA), has authorized six companies to operate as fund managers. These plans offer comparatively better returns at the time of maturity and remain in force for a substantial amount of time.

d. **Immediate Annuity.** In this type of scheme, the pension beings right away. As soon as you deposit a lump-sum amount, your pension starts. This is based on the amount the policyholder invests. You can choose from a range of annuity options. In accordance with the Income Tax Act of 1961, the premiums of the immediate annuity plans are tax exempt. Post the death of the policyholder, it is the nominee who is entitled to the money.

e. **Guaranteed Period Annuity.** Regardless of whether the holder survives the duration, this annuity option is given for periods like 5 years to 10, 15 or 20 years.

f. **Pension Plans with and without cover.** Pension plans with cover include life cover which means that at the death of the policyholder, the family members are paid a lump sum amount. This amount may not be a very large amount. The without-cover plan as the name suggests, does not have life cover. If the policyholder passes away, the nominee gets the corpus. At present, the immediate annuity plans are without cover, while the deferred plans are with cover.

g. **Annuity certain.** In this scheme, the annuitant is paid the annuity for a certain number of years. This period can be picked by the annuitant and in case of their death, the beneficiary receives the annuity.

h. **Life Annuity.** The life annuity scheme pays the annuity amount to the annuitant until the time of death. If the annuitant dies and they had chosen the option "with spouse", the spouse receives the pension amount.

Want to know more about which pension fund to invest in? Visit ClearTax to choose from a list of hand-picked funds that are curated to suit your finances.

Advantages of Pension Plans

a. **Option in Investment.** Pension funds give investors the option to invest in either the safe government securities or take some risk and invest in debt and equity investments depending on their risk profile. The risk is balanced by the prospect of higher returns that are generated by the investment.

b. **Long-term savings.** These plans serve as a long-term savings scheme regardless of whether you opt for a lump sum payments or multiple payments of small amounts, the savings is assured. Pension plans create an annuity which can be invested further and give rise to a steady flow of cash post your retirement.

c. **Choose how you want to get paid.** Depending on what your age or what your plans are, you can either invest a lump sum amount and get annuity payments right away or you may choose a deferred annuity plan which will let your corpus earn more interest until the payouts begin.

d. **Works as a life insurance cover.** There are pension plans that give the investor the lump sum amount when they retire or in the case of the death of the individual, whichever scenario occurs earlier. This means that your pension policy also serves as a life insurance cover.

e. **Negates the effect of Inflation.** It is a good way of negating the effects of inflation, by investing in pension plans. These plans pay a lump sum amount during your retirement which amounts to a maximum of S! of the corpus that is accumulated and the remaining T! of the corpus is used in generating a steady cash flow.

f. **Access a lump sum amount during an emergency.** You may make adjustments to your pension policy to access the lump sum payout in case of an emergency. This can be done to cover one's long-term health care as well.

Disadvantages of Pension Plans

a. **Limited amount of deduction allowed.** Though pension plans qualify you to a tax deduction, the maximum allowed deduction on life insurance premiums is INR 1 lakh under the Income Tax Act.

b. **Taxation on the annuity.** When you receive the annuity after your retirement, it is taxable as on that date.

c. **High returns require high-risk taking.** To make sure that the payout at the time of your retirement is adequate, you may have to seek high-risk options in order to obtain higher returns. The traditional non-risky investment options may not be enough to override the effects of inflation.

d. **Best suited for early investors.** If you are not an early investor, this investment option may be a little late for you. As the returns earned by someone who invests at age 21 as opposed to someone aged 30 or 35 years, will get a substantially larger return.

FINANCIAL REGULATORS IN INDIA

In India, the financial system is regulated with the help of independent regulators, associated with the field of insurance, banking, commodity market, and capital market and also the field of pension funds. On the other hand, the Indian government is also known for playing a significant role in controlling the field of financial security and also influencing the roles of such mentioned regulators. You must be aware of the regulatory bodies and their functions, before a final say. The most prominent of all is RBI or Reserve Bank of India. Let us look in detail about various Financial Regulatory Bodies in India.

RBI – Reserve Banks of India

Reserve Bank of India is the apex monetary Institution of India. It is also called as the central bank of the country.

The Reserve Bank of India was established on April 1, 1935 in accordance with the provisions of the Reserve Bank of India Act, 1934. The Central Office of the Reserve Bank was initially established in Calcutta but was permanently moved to Mumbai in 1937. The Central Office is where the Governor sits and where policies are formulated. Though originally private owned, since nationalization in 1949, the Reserve Bank is fully owned by the Government of India.

The Central Office is where the Governor sits and is where policies are formulated. Though originally privately owned, since nationalization in 1949, the Reserve Bank is fully owned by the Government of India.

SEBI – Securities and Exchange Board of India

Apart from RBI, SEBI also forms a major part under the financial body of India. This is a regulator associated with the security markets in Indian Territory. Established in the year 1988, the SEBI Act came into power in the year 1992, 12th April. The board comprises of a Chairman, Whole time members, Joint secretary, member appointed, Deputy Governor of RBI, secretary of corporate affair ministry and also part time member. There are three groups, which fall under this category, and those are the investors, the security issuers and market intermediaries.

PFRDA – Pension Fund Regulatory and Development Authority

Pension Fund regulatory is a pension related authority, which was established in the year 2003 by the Indian Government. It is authorized by the Finance Ministry, and it helps in promoting income security of old age by regulating and also developing pension funds. On the other hand, this group can also help in protecting the interest rate of the subscribers, associated with the schemes of pension money along with the related matters. PFRDA is also responsible for the appointment of different other intermediate agencies like Pension fund managers, CRA, NPS Trustee Bank and more.

FMC – Forward Markets Commission

Other than the financial bodies mentioned above, FMC also plays a major role. It is the chief regulator of the commodity (MCX, NCDEX, NMCE, UCX etc) of the Indian futures market. As per the latest news feed, it has regulated the amount of Rs. 17 trillion, under the commodity trades. Headquarter is located in Mumbai, and the financial regulatory agency is working in collaboration with the Finance Ministry. The chairman of FMC works together with the Members of the same organization to meet the required ends. The main aim of this body is to advise the Central Government on matters of the Forwards Contracts Act, 1952.

IRDA – Insurance Regulatory and Development Authority

Lastly, it is better to mention the name of IRDA or insurance regulatory and Development authority, as a major part of the financial body. This company is going to regulate the apex statutory body, which will regulate and at the same time, develop the insurance industry. It comprised of the Indian Parliamentary act and was passed duly by the Indian Government. Headquarter of this group is in Hyderabad, and it was shifted from Delhi to Hyderabad. These are some of the best-possible points, which you can try and focus at, while dealing with financial bodies of India.

FINANCIAL SECTOR REFORMS INCLUDING FINANCIAL INCLUSION

Financial sector is the mainstay of any economy and it contributes immensely in the mobilisation and distribution of resources. Financial sector reforms have long been viewed as significant part of the program for policy reform in developing nations. Earlier, it was thought that they were expected to increase the efficiency of resource mobilization and allocation in the real economy to generate higher rates of growth. Recently, they are also seen to be critical for macroeconomic stability. It was due to the repercussion of the East Asian crisis, since weaknesses in the financial sector are broadly regarded as one of the major causes of collapse in that region.

The elements of the financial sector are Banks, Financial Institutions, Instruments and markets which mobilise the resources from the surplus sector and channelize the same to the different needy sectors in the economy. The process of accumulative capital growth through institutionalisation of savings and investment fosters economic growth. Reform of the financial sector was recognized, from the very beginning, as an integral part of the economic reforms initiated in 1991. The economic reform process occurred amidst two serious crisis involving the financial sector the balance of payments crisis that endangered the international credibility of the country and pushed it to the edge of default;

and the grave threat of insolvency confronting the banking system which had for years concealed its problems with the help of faulty accounting strategies. Furthermore, some deep rooted problems of the Indian economy in the early nineties were also strongly related to the financial sector such as large scale pre-emption of resources from the banking system by the government to finance its fiscal deficit. Excessive structural and micro regulation that inhibited financial innovation and increased transaction costs. Relatively inadequate level of prudential regulation in the financial sector. Poorly developed debt and money markets. And outdated (often primitive) technological and institutional structures that made the capital markets and the rest of the financial system highly inefficient.

Major aims of the financial sector reforms are to allocate the resources proficiently, increasing the return on investment and hastened growth of the real sectors in the economy. The processes introduced by the Government of India under the reform process are intended to upturn the operational efficiency of each of the constituent of the financial sector.

The major delineations of the financial sector reforms in India were found as under:

- Removal of the erstwhile existing financial repression.
- Creation of an efficient, productive and profitable financial sector.
- Enabling the process of price discovery by the market determination of interest rates that improves allocate efficiency of resources.
- Providing operational and functional autonomy to institutions.
- Preparing the financial system for increasing international competition.
- Opening the external sector in a calibrated manner.
- Promoting financial stability in the wake of domestic and external shocks.

At global level, financial sector reforms have been driven by two apparently contrary forces. The first is a thrust towards liberalization, which seeks to decrease, if not eliminate a number of direct controls over banks and other financial market participants. The second is a thrust in favour of strict regulation of the financial sector. This dual approach is also apparent in the reforms tried in India.

Financial and banking sector reforms are in following areas:

Financial Markets

- Regulators
- Non-banking finance companies
- Mutual funds
- Deregulation of banking system
- Consolidation imperative
- The banking system
- The capital market
- Overall approach to reforms
- Capital market developments

Regulators

The Finance Ministry constantly formulated major strategies in the field of financial sector of the country. The Government acknowledged the important role of regulators. The Reserve Bank of India (RBI) has become more independent. Securities and Exchange Board of India (SEBI) and the Insurance Regulatory and Development Authority (IRDA) became important institutions. Some opinions are also there that there should be a super-regulator for the financial services sector instead of multiplicity of regulators.

Indian Banking Sector and Financial Reforms

The main intent of banking sector reforms was to uphold a diversified, efficient and competitive financial system with the aim of improving the allocative efficiency of resources through operational flexibility, improved financial viability and institutional solidification.

In August 1991, the government selected a high level Committee on the Financial System (the Narasimham Committee) to look into all facets of the financial system and make comprehensive recommendations for improvements. The Committee submitted its report in November 1991, making several recommendations for reforms in the banking sector and also in the capital market. Soon thereafter, the government announced broad acceptance of the approach of the Narasimham Committee and a process of gradualist reform in the banking sector and in the capital market was set in motion, a process that has now been under way for more than six year.

In India, around 80% of businesses are regulated by public sector banks. PSBs are still governing the commercial banking system. The RBI has given license to new private sector banks as part of the liberalization process. The RBI has also been granting licenses to industrial houses. Many banks are effectively running in the retail and consumer segments but are yet to deliver services to industrial finance, retail trade, small business and agricultural finance. Major change observed by individuals is many transformation in policies of the banking sector. The reforms have focussed on eliminating financial repression through reductions in statutory pre-emptions, while stepping up prudential regulations at the same time. Additionally, interest rates on both deposits and lending of banks have been gradually deregulated.

The major reforms relating to the banking system were:

- Capital base of the banks were strengthened by recapitalization, public equity issues and subordinated debt.
- Prudential norms were introduced and progressively tightened for income recognition, classification of assets, provisioning of bad debts, marking to market of investments.
- Pre-emption of bank resources by the government was reduced sharply.
- New private sector banks were licensed and branch licensing restrictions were relaxed.

Similarly, several operational reforms were introduced in the area of credit policy:

- Detailed regulations relating to Maximum Permissible Bank Finance were abolished.
- Consortium regulations were relaxed substantially.
- Credit delivery was shifted away from cash credit to loan method.

Many reports signified that the initial steps have been taken in the form of allowing new banks to set up shop. Private Corporates, public sector entities and Non-Banking Finance Companies with a strong track record can now apply to set up new banks and the Reserve bank of India will consider these applications in the coming months. The addition of new banks will mean more competition for this sector in the country and it will lead to a development in services for the end customer. It is anticipated to increase financial enclosure as more and more people across the country will be able to access banking facilities. In reforms for the existing banks the public sector banks have been allowed to increase or decrease the authorised capital without the presence of an overall ceiling. This will provide greater flexibility to the banks to conduct their fund raising activities as per the requirements. The strict restriction of voting rights in banks will also be relaxed and this will aid the banking sector to develop, as large investors will be able to get a bigger voice in the coming days in the banks and the manner in which they operate.

When evaluating banking sector reform, it can be identified that banks have experienced strong balance sheet growth in the post-reform period in an environment of operational flexibility. Enhancement in the financial health of banks, reflected in noteworthy improvement in capital adequacy and improved asset quality, is distinctly observable. It is striking that this progress has been realised despite the espousal of international best practices in prudential norms. Competitiveness and productivity gains have also been enabled by proactive technological deepening and flexible human resource management. These significant gains have been achieved even while renewing goals of social banking viz. maintaining the wide reach of the banking system and directing credit towards important but underprivileged sectors of civilisation.

Forex market reform

Forex market reform took place in 1993 and the successive adoption of current account convertibility were the acmes of the forex reforms introduced in the Indian market. Under these reforms, authorised dealers of foreign exchange as well as banks have been given greater sovereignty to perform in the activities and numerous operations. Additionally, the entry of new companies have been allowed in the market. The capital account has become effectively adaptable for non-residents but still has some reservations for residents.

Impact on the Reform Measures

The broader objectives of the financial sector reform process are to articulate the policy to enhance the financial condition and to reinforce the institutions. As part of the reforms process, many private banks were granted licence to operate in India. This has resulted into a competitive environment in the banking industry which in turn has assisted in using the resources more competently. Conventionally, the industrial units were sanctioned term loan by the development banks and working capital by the commercial banks. The reform process has transformed the pattern of financing and now both the institutions are willing to extend long term loan as well as working capital loan. But there is some differences in the mode of operation. This has empowered the industrial units to avail credit facilities from a single institution. Despite the fact that the banks provide both the term loan and the working capital loans, the industrial units prefer the development banks for the following reasons.

It provides equal support to the new as well as existing industries.

The period of repayment of loan is comparatively longer.

Besides providing financial backing, it acts as the implementing agency for the different government sponsored schemes. Hence, the industrial units can avail of both the financial assistance as well as the incentives offered under various development schemes through a Single Window System. As lending is the main activity of these institutions, it acquires specialisation in this field and can share its expertise with the industrial units.

Capital Market Reform

Capital market is defined as a financial market that works as a channel for demand and supply of debt and equity capital. It channels the money provided by savers and depository institutions (banks, credit unions, insurance companies, etc.) to borrowers and investees through a variety of financial instruments (bonds, notes, shares) called securities. A capital market is not a compact unit, but a highly decentralized system made up of three major parts that include stock market, bond market, and money market. It also works as an exchange for trading existing claims on capital in the form of shares. The Capital Market deals in the long-term capital Securities such as Equity or Debt offered by the private business companies and also governmental undertakings of India.

In the agenda of financial sector reforms, Improvement of the capital market is important area and action has been taken parallel with reforms in banking. India has experienced functioning in capital markets the Bombay Stock Exchange (BSE) for over a hundred years but until the 1980s, the volume of activity in the capital market was relatively limited. Capital market activity extended rapidly in the 1980s and the market capitalization of companies registered in the BSE rose from 5 per cent of GDP in 1980 to 13 per cent in 1990. It is observed that the Indian capital market has perceived major reforms in the decade of 1990s and thereafter. It is on the edge of the growth. Thus, the Government of India and SEBI took numerous measures in order to improve the working of the Indian stock exchanges and to make it more progressive and energetic. The Securities and Exchange Board of India (SEBI) was well-known in 1988. It got a legal status in 1992. SEBI was principally set up to control the activities of the commercial banks, to control the operations of mutual funds, to work as a promoter of the stock exchange activities and to act as a regulatory authority of new issue activities of companies. The SEBI was established with the vital objective, "to protect the interest of investors in securities market and for matters connected therewith or incidental thereto." The main functions of SEBI are as follows:

- To control the business of the stock market and other securities market.
- To promote and regulate the self-regulatory organizations.
- To forbid fraudulent and unfair trade practices in securities market.
- To promote awareness among investors and training of intermediaries about safety of market.
- To prohibit insider trading in securities market.
- To regulate huge acquisition of shares and takeover of companies.

However, the stock market remained primeval and poorly controlled. Companies who want to access the capital market needed prior permission of the government which also had to approve the price at which new equity could be raised. While new issues were strictly controlled, there was insufficient regulation of stock market activity and also of various market participants including stock exchanges, brokers, mutual funds, etc. The domestic-capital market was also closed to portfolio investment from abroad except through a few closed ended mutual funds floated abroad by the Unit Trust of India (UTI) which were committed to Indian investment.

The practice of reform of the capital market was started in 1992 along the lines recommended by the Narasimham Committee. It was intended to remove direct government control and replacing it by a regulatory framework based on transparency and disclosure supervised by an independent regulator. The first step was taken in 1992 when the Securities and Exchange Board of India (SEBI), which was initially established as a non-statutory body in 1988, was raised to a complete capital market regulator with statutory powers in 1992. The requirement of prior government permission for accessing capital markets and for prior approval of issue pricing was stopped and companies were permissible to access markets and price issues freely, subject only to disclosure norms laid down by SEBI.

The Regulatory Framework

As the time passed, SEBI has implemented a modern regulatory framework with rules and regulations to control the behaviour of major market participants such as stock exchanges, brokers, merchant bankers, and mutual funds. It has also sought to control activities such as takeovers and insider trading which have implications for investor protection. The governing structure of stock exchanges has been changed to make the boards, of the exchanges more broad based and less dominated by brokers. The new regulatory framework intended to support investor protection by ensuring disclosure and transparency rather than through direct control. SEBI acts as a supervisor of the system undertaking supervision of the activities of various participants including stock exchange and mutual funds and violations of the rules are punishable by SEBI.

The regulatory framework is new and there is a need to be advanced with experience gained and also as gaps and insufficiencies are identified. SEBI needs to be further strengthened in some areas and its disciplinary powers.

Opening the Capital Market to Foreign Investors

Significant policy initiative in 1993 was the opening of the capital market to foreign institutional investors (FIIs) and allowing Indian companies to raise capital abroad by issue of equity in the form of global depository receipts (GDRs).

Modernization of Trading and Settlement Systems

Major developments occurred in trading methods which were highly antiquated earlier. The National Stock Exchange (NSE) was established in 1994 as an automated electronic exchange. It empowered brokers in 220 cities all over the country to link up with the NSE computers via VSATs and trade in a unified exchange with automatic matching of buy and sell orders with price time priority, thus ensuring maximum transparency for investors. The initiation of electronic trading by the NSE generated competitive pressure which forced the BSE to also introduce electronic trading in 1995.

The settlement system was old-fashioned which involved physical delivery of share certificates to the buyer who then had to deliver them to a company registrar to record change of ownership after which the certificates had to be returned to the buyer. This process was consuming and also had significant risks for investors. The first step towards paperless trading was put in place by enacting legislation which allowed dematerialization of share certificates with settlement by electronic transfer of ownership from one account to another within a depository. The National Securities Depository Ltd (NSDL) opened for business in 1996.

Future Trading

Currently, an important gap in India's capital market is future markets. Good market in index futures would help in risk management and provide greater liquidity to the market. A decision to present futures trading has been taken and the legislative changes needed to implement this decision have been submitted to parliament.

Several Problems in the Capital Market

Though, there are numerous reforms made in the regulatory framework and trading and settlement systems, the functioning of the capital market in the post-reform period has been heavily criticized. Investors, particularly small investors who entered the market in the early stages of liberalization, did not get good value of their investments. It was perceived that many dishonest companies took advantage of the exclusion of government control over issue prices to raise capital at inflated prices, at the expense of inexperienced investors. Merchant bankers and underwriters involved in these issues.

Issuers of capital must also understand that the capital market should not be viewed, as a passive source of equity capital which can be tapped by companies at will to raise equity on favourable terms. Cross-country studies have revealed that stock markets in developing countries have been an important source for financing of new investments through IPOs than in developed countries where financing of new investment has relied mainly on internal generation of surpluses. New companies raising funds have typically relied on venture capital or private placement rather than public issues.

Mutual Funds

Presently, the mutual funds industry is controlled under the SEBI (Mutual Funds) Regulations, 1996 and amendments thereto. With the issuance of SEBI rules, the industry had a framework for the setting up of many more companies, both Indian and foreign firms. The Unit Trust of India is biggest mutual fund controlling a quantity of nearly Rs.70,000 crores, but its share is going down. With the growth in the securities markets and tax advantages granted for investment in mutual fund units, mutual funds became widespread. The foreign owned AMCs are the ones which are now setting the pace for the industry. They are introducing new products, setting new standards of customer service, improving disclosure standards and experimenting with new types of distribution.

Reform of the Insurance Sector

The Insurance sector in India directed by Insurance Act, 1938, the Life Insurance Corporation Act, 1956 and General Insurance Business (Nationalisation) Act, 1972, Insurance Regulatory and Development Authority (IRDA) Act, 1999 and other related Acts. The basis of liberalizing the banking system and encouraging competition among the three major participants' viz. public sector banks, Indian private sector banks, and foreign banks, applies equally to insurance. There is a strong case for ending the public sector monopoly in insurance and opening it up to private sector participants subject to suitable prudential regulation.

Cross-country data advocates that contractual savings institutions are highly significant determinant of the aggregate rate of savings and insurance and pension schemes are the most important form of contractual savings in this reference. A competitive insurance industry providing diversified insurance products to fulfil differing customer needs, can help increase savings in this situation and allocate them efficiently. The insurance and pensions industry has long-term liabilities which it seeks to match by investing in long-term secure assets. A healthy insurance is an important source of long-term capital in domestic currency which is especially for infrastructure financing. Improvements in insurance will strengthen the capital market at the long-term end by adding new companies in this section of the market, giving it greater depth or liquidity.

The Malhotra Committee had suggested opening up the insurance sector to new private companies as early as 1994. It took five years to build an agreement on this issue and legislation to open up insurance, allowing foreign equity up to 26 per cent was finally submitted to Parliament in 1999.

Overall Approach to Reforms

It is assessed that since last years, there have seen major improvements in the working of various financial market contributors. The government and the regulatory authorities have followed a step-by-step approach. The entry of foreign companies has helped in the start of international practices and systems. Technology developments have enhanced customer service. Some gaps however remain such as lack of an inter-bank interest rate benchmark, an active corporate debt market and a developed derivatives market. In general, the cumulative effect of the developments since 1991 has been quite encouraging. An indication of the strength of the reformed Indian financial system can be seen from the way India was not affected by the Southeast Asian crisis.

To summarize, the financial sector is main element of the Indian economic system. Financial experts suggested that there is a need for effective reforms to ensure that this remains competitive and attractive for investors from across the world. The economic reforms have preferred the need for changing the policy objective to promotion of industries and the formation of more integrated infrastructural facilities. Financial sector reforms are centre point of the economic liberalization that was introduced in India in mid-1991. It was witnessed that national financial liberalisation has brought about the deregulation of interest rates, dismantling of directed credit, improving the banking system, enhancing the functioning of the capital market that include the government securities market. Regulators and economic experts put more emphasis on banking reforms to enhance economy and enable people to access numerous facilities. Fundamental objective of financial sector reforms in the 1990s was to create an effectual, competitive and steady that could contribute in greater measure to inspire progression.

DIGITISATION OF BANKING AND OTHER FINANCIAL SERVICES

INTERNET BANKING

Online banking allows a user to execute financial transactions via the internet. Online banking is also known as "internet banking" or "web banking." An online bank offers customers just about every service traditionally available through a local branch, including deposits, which is done online or through the mail, and online bill payment.

Online banks do not provide direct ATM access, but they make provisions for consumers to use ATMs at other banks and retail stores, and they may reimburse consumers for some of the ATM fees charged by other financial institutions. Reduced overhead costs associated with not having physical branches typically allow online banks to offer consumers significant savings on banking fees; they also offer higher interest rates on accounts. Online banks handle customer service by phone, email or online chat. Online banking is frequently performed on mobile devices as Wi-Fi and 4G networks have become widely available. In the United States, prominent online banks include Ally Bank, Bank5 Connect, Discover Bank, GE Capital Bank and Synchrony Bank.

Advantages of Online Banking

Convenience is a major advantage of online banking. Basic banking transactions such as paying bills and transferring funds between accounts can easily be performed at times convenient to consumers. In effect, consumers can perform banking transactions 24 hours-a-day, seven-days a week. Online banking is fast and efficient. Funds can be transferred between accounts almost instantly, especially if the two accounts are held at the same banking institution. Banking accounts can be monitored more closely thanks to online banking. This allows consumers to keep their accounts safe. Around-the-clock access to banking information provides early detection of fraudulent activity that has the potential to cause financial loss. Online banking allows for the opening and closing of fixed deposit and recurring deposit accounts that typically offer higher rates of interest.

Disadvantages of Online Banking

For a novice online banking customer, using systems for the first time may present challenges that prevent transactions from being processed. Although, online banking security is continually improving, such accounts are still vulnerable when it comes to hacking. Consumers are advised to use their data plans, rather than public Wi-Fi networks when using online banking, to prevent unauthorized access. Additionally, online banking is dependent on a reliable internet connection. Connectivity issues from time-to-time may make it difficult to determine if banking transactions have been successfully processed. On occasion, consumers may prefer face-to-face interactions for more complex banking issues.

MOBILE BANKING

Mobile banking is the act of making financial transactions on a mobile device (cell phone, tablet, etc.). This activity can be as simple as a bank sending fraud or usage activity to a client's cell phone or as complex as a client paying bills or sending money abroad. Advantages of mobile banking include the ability to bank anywhere and at any time. Disadvantages includes security concerns and a limited range of capabilities when compared to banking in person or on a computer.

Mobile banking is very convenient in today's digital age with many banks offering impressive apps. The ability to deposit a check, to pay for merchandise, to transfer money to a friend or to find an ATM instantly are reasons why people choose to use mobile banking. However, establishing a secure connection before logging into a mobile banking app is important or else a client might risk his personal information being compromised.

Mobile Banking and Cybersecurity

Cybersecurity has become increasingly important in many mobile banking operations. Cybersecurity encompasses a wide range of measures taken to keep electronic information private and avoid damage or theft. It is also used to make data is not misused, extending from personal information to complex government systems.

Three main types of cyber attacks can occur. These are:

- Backdoor attacks, in which thieves exploit alternate methods of accessing a system that don't require the usual means of authentication. Some systems have backdoors by design; others result from error.
- Denial-of-service attacks prevent the rightful user from accessing the system. For example, thieves might enter a wrong password enough times that the account is locked.
- Direct-access attack includes bugs and viruses, which gain access to a system and copy its information and/or modify it.

Steps financial advisors can take to protect their clients against cyber attacks include:

- Helping to educate clients about the importance of strong, unique passwords (i.e. not reusing the same one for every password-protected site), along with how a password manager like Valt or LastPass can add an extra layer of security.
- Never accessing client data from a public location — and being sure the connection is always private and secure.

Mobile Banking and Remittances

Remittances are funds that an expatriate sends to his or her country of origin via wire, mail, or mobile banking (online transfer). These peer-to-peer transfers of funds across borders have enormous economic significance for many of the countries that receive them – so much so that the World Bank and the Gates Foundation have set up complex tracking mechanisms. They estimate that remittances to developing countries amounted to $429 billion in 2016, down 2.4 percent from the $440 billion recorded in 2015.

DIGITAL PAYMENTS SYSTEMS

Digital payment is a way of payment which is made through digital modes. In digital payments, payer and payee both use digital modes to send and receive money. It is also called electronic payment. No hard cash is involved in digital payments. All the transactions in digital payments are completed online. It is an instant and convenient way to make payments.

If we talk about cash payments, you have to first withdraw cash from your account. Then you use this cash to pay at shops. Shopkeeper goes to the bank to deposit the cash which he got from you. This process is time-consuming for you and also for the shopkeeper. But in digital payments, the money transfers from your account to the shopkeeper's account immediately. This process is automatic and neither you nor the shopkeeper is required to visit the bank.

Digital payments save you from long queues of ATMs and banks. Because, if you pay digitally, you won't need to withdraw cash from your account.

From commonly used cards to newly launched UPI, digital payments has many types of payment. Some modes meant for tech-savvies and some for less-technical persons. Below are the different modes of digital payments.

UPI Apps

UPI or unified payment interface is a payment mode which is used to make fund transfers through the mobile app. You can transfer funds between two accounts using UPI apps. You will have to register for mobile banking to use UPI apps. Currently, this service is only available for android phone users. Hence, you can use UPI only when you have an android phone.

You need to download a UPI app and create a VPA or UPI ID. There are too many good UPI apps available such as BHIM, SBI UPI app, HDFC UPI app, iMobile, PhonePe app etc. It is not mandatory to use the UPI app from your bank to enjoy UPI service. You can download and use any UPI app.

UPI apps are a faster solution to send money using VPA or even IFSC and account number. But they have some limitations also. If you do not have an android phone you cannot use UPI app, It is not for you. Lack of stable internet connection can also cause trouble for these apps.

AEPS

AEPS is an Aadhaar based digital payment mode. The term AEPS stands for Aadhaar Enabled Payment Service. Customer needs only his or her Aadhaar number to pay any merchant. AEPS allows bank for bank transactions. It means the money you pay will be deducted from your account and credited to the payee's account directly.

You need to link your Aadhaar number to your bank account to use AEPS. Unlike Debit cards and USSD, AEPS does not have any charges on transactions. You can use AEPS with the help of PoS (Point of sale) machines. You can withdraw or deposit cash, send money to another Aadhar linked account with it. The good thing about AEPS is that it doesn't need your signature, bank account details or any password. It uses your fingerprint as a password. No one can forge your fingerprints, thus it is the most secure digital payment mode.

USSD

USSD banking or *99# banking is a mobile banking based digital payment mode. You do not need to have a smartphone or internet connection to use USSD banking. You can easily use it with any normal feature phone. USSD banking is as easy as checking your mobile balance. You can use this service for many financial and non-financial operations such as checking balance, sending money, changing MPIN and getting MMID.

The *99# code works as a bridge between your telecom operator's server and your bank's server. It uses your registered mobile number to connect with your bank account. Hence, dial *99# with your registered number only. USSD banking has a transaction limit of Rs. 5000 per day per customer. RBI has also set a maximum charge of Rs. 2.5 per operation.

Cards

Cards are provided by banks to their account holders. These have been the most used digital payment modes till now. Many of us use cards for transferring funds and making digital payments. Credit cards, debit cards and prepaid cards are the main types of cards. You can also use Rupay debit card for digital payments.

Credit cards are issued by banks and some other entities authorized by RBI. These cards give you the ability to withdraw or use extra money. Credit cards are used for domestic as well as international payments.

Debit cards are issued by the bank where you have your account. You can use these cards for the money in your account. The payments you make with these cards debit from your account and credit immediately to the payee's account. You can use these cards to make payments to one bank account to another.

Prepaid cards are another type of cards which you use to pay digitally. You must have to recharge these cards before using just like prepaid SIM cards.

Cards are one of the best modes when you pay at portals or E-commerce sites. But if we talk about paying to merchants it is not the most suitable way. It charges 0.75% – 2.0% on transactions. Also, you cannot use cards to pay if the merchant does not have a PoS (swipe) machine.

E-Wallets

E-Wallet or mobile wallet is the digital version of your physical wallet with more functionality. You can keep your money in an E-wallet and use it when needed. Use the E-Wallets to recharge your phone, pay at various places and send money to your friends. If you have a smartphone and a stable internet connection, you can use E-wallets to make payments. These E-wallets also give additional cashback offers. Some of the most used E-wallets are State bank buddy, ICICI Pockets, Freecharge, Paytm etc.

E-wallets are an easy and faster way to make payments but have some limitations. These apps are good if you send money to a wallet to another. But if you want to send money to a bank account these apps are not suitable. Also, you have to be extra careful with these apps. These apps do not ask for any PIN or password when you perform a transaction using your wallet money. If you do not lock your phone, anyone can use the money in your wallet. I suggest you must lock your phone if you want to use E-Wallet apps.

Advantages of Digital Payments

Easy and convenient. Digital payments are easy and convenient . You do not need to take loads of cash with you. All you need is your mobile phone or Aadhaar number or a card to pay. UPI apps and E-Wallets made digital payments easier.

Pay or send money from anywhere. With digital payment modes, you can pay from anywhere anytime. Suppose your close friend's mother fell ill at night. He called you at midnight and asked some money. Don't worry, you can send money to your friend using digital payment modes such as UPI apps, USSD or E-Wallets.

Discounts from taxes. Government has announced many discounts to encourage digital payments. If you use digital modes to make a payment up to Rs. 2000, you get full exemption from service tax. You also get 0.75% discounts on fuels and 10% discount on insurance premiums of government insurers.

Written record. You often forget to note down your cash spendings. Or even if you note, it takes a lot of time. But you do not need to note your spendings every time with digital payments. These are automatically recorded in your passbook or inside your E-Wallet app. This helps to maintain your record, track your spendings and budget planning.

Less Risk. Digital payments have less risk if you use them wisely. If you lose your mobile phone or debit/credit card or Aadhar card you don't have to worry a lot. No one can use your money without MPIN, PIN or your fingerprint in the case of Aadhar. But it is advised that you should get your card blocked if you lost it. Also call the helpline of your E-wallet to suspend the wallet account to prevent anyone from using your wallet money.

DRAWBACKS OF DIGITAL PAYMENTS

Every coin has two sides so as the digital payments. Despite many advantages, digital payments have a few drawbacks also.

Difficult for a non-technical person: As most of the digital payment modes are based on mobile phone, the internet and cards. These modes are somewhat difficult for non-technical persons such as farmers, workers etc.

The risk of data theft: There is a big risk of data theft associated with the digital payment. Hackers can hack the servers of the bank or the E-Wallet you are using and easily get your personal information. They can use this information to steal money from your account.

Overspending: You keep limited cash in your physical wallet. Hence, you think twice before buying anything. But if you use digital payment modes, you have all your money with you always. This can result in overspending .

Future of Digital Payments

The future of digital payments is very bright. India is experiencing a remarkable growth in digital payments. In 2015-16, a total of Rs. 4018 billion transacted through mobile banking as compared to Rs. 60 billion in 2012-13. The percentage of the digital payments through other modes is also increasing in a significant speed.

Digital Revolution

Digital revolution has provided an easy way to go for digital payments. India has more than 100 crore active mobile connections and more than 22 crore smartphone users as of March 2016. This number is going to increase further with a faster internet speed. The reach of mobile network, Internet and electricity is also expanding digital payments to remote areas. This will surely increase the number of digital payments.

Government's Support

The government is supporting digital payments a lot. It has reduced some taxes and announced incentives for digital payments. It has launched Lucky Grahak Yojna for customers and Digi Dhan Vyapar Yojna for shopkeepers. You can get cash prizes up to 1 crore if you pay digitally. Due to these incentives and waivers, more people are showing interest in digital payments.

A convenient way to pay

Digital payments are more convenient than cash payments. You do not need to carry a lot of cash with you all the time. You can make digital payments in seconds. The change is not a concern for digital payments when you can pay the exact amount. You will also have all your payments recorded automatically. We all love simplicity and ease. Hence, we can say that Digital payments is the future of fund transfer and money transactions.

INSURANCE

Life insurance is a contract that offers financial compensation in case of death or disability. Some life insurance policies even offer financial compensation after retirement or a certain period of time. Life insurance, thus, helps you secure your family's financial security even in your absence. You either make a lump-sum payment while purchasing a life insurance policy or make periodic payments to the insurer. These are known as premiums. In exchange, your insurer promises to pay an assured sum to your family in the event of death, disability or at a set time.

Life insurance can help you support your family even after retirement. Depending on what it covers, Life insurance can be classified into various types:

Term Insurance

- It is the most basic type of insurance.
- It covers you for a specific period.
- Your family gets a lump-sum amount in the case of your death.- If, however, you survive the term, no money will be paid to you or your family.

Whole Life Insurance

- It covers you for a lifetime.
- Your family receives a certain sum of money after your death.
- They will also be entitled to a bonus that often accrues on such amount.

Endowment Policy

– Like a term policy, it is also valid for a certain period.
– A lump-sum amount will be paid to your family in the event of your death.
– Unlike a term plan, you get the maturity proceeds after the term period.

Money-back Policy

– A certain percentage of the sum assured will be paid to you periodically throughout the term as survival benefit.
– After the expiry of the term, you get the balance amount as maturity proceeds.
– Your family gets the entire sum assured in case of death during the policy period. This is regardless of the survival benefit payments made.

Unit-linked Insurance Plans (ULIPs)

– Such products double up as investment tools.
– A part of your premium goes towards your insurance cover.
– The remaining amount is invested in Debt and Equity.
– A lump-sum amount will be paid to your family in the event of your death.

Child Plan

– This ensures your child's financial security.
– In the event of your death, your child gets a lump-sum amount.
– The insurer pays the premium amounts after your death.
– Your child will continue to get a certain sum of money at specific intervals.

Pension Plans

– This helps build your retirement fund.
– You can get a regular pension amount after retirement.
– In the case of your death, your family can claim the sum assured.

Tax Benefits

- Life insurance not only ensures the well-being of your family, it also brings tax benefits.
- The amount you pay as premium can be deducted from your total taxable income.
- However, this is subject to a maximum of Rs 1.5 lakh, under Section 80C of the Income Tax Act.
- The premium amount used for tax deduction should not exceed 10% of the sum assured.

What is General Insurance?

A general insurance is a contract that offers financial compensation on any loss other than death. It insures everything apart from life. A general insurance compensates you for financial loss due to liabilities related to your house, car, bike, health, travel, etc. The insurance company promises to pay you a sum assured to cover damages to your vehicle, medical treatments to cure health problems, losses due to theft or fire, or even financial problems during travel.

Simply put, a general insurance offers financial protection for all your assets against loss, damage, theft, and other liabilities. It is different from life insurance.

Let us help you understand better:

Situation 1

– You plan to propose to your girlfriend on the Eiffel Tower.
– You already finalised the deal with a jeweller in Paris.

- But, things don't go as planned and you meet with an accident there.
- Your treatment requires Rs. 50,000. But, still paid for that dainty piece of jewellery.
- Your travel insurance made you ready for emergencies.
- It paid for the expenses related to your accident. You could, thus, go ahead and surprise your partner with a diamond ring without worrying about the treatment costs.

Situation 2

- You cannot stop celebrating your new car. You hit the roads with your latest possession.
- Everything goes well until a car suddenly tries to overtake you. It leaves huge dents and dislocates your left mirror.
- Your new baby on the block needs repairs worth Rs. 30,000. Yet, you have a smile on your face.
- The dent in your car didn't cause a dent in your pocket.
- Your motor insurance' own damage cover paid for your car's damages caused by the accident. In fact, the insurer settled the bill directly at the garage.

Situation 3

- Your daughter wants to become a pilot.
- You have saved all your disposable income to fund her dreams.
- Unfortunately, you fall severely ill.
- You need Rs. 2 lakh for your treatment immediately. Yet, you also easily pay your daughter's course fees.
- You didn't face a dilemma of choosing one over the other and compromise your daughter's future. Your health insurance took care of your treatment costs. Your savings, thus, remained unaffected by your sudden illness.

As you can see, general Insurance can be the answer to life's various problems. But, for that, you need to select the right insurances from the myriad ones available.

What are the types of general insurance available? / What all can be insured?

You can get almost anything and everything insured. But there are five key types available:

Health Insurance

This type of general insurance covers the cost of medical care. It pays for or reimburses the amount you pay towards the treatment of any injury or illness.

It usually covers:

- Hospitalisation
- The treatment of critical illnesses
- Medical bills prior to or post hospitalisation
- Day care procedures like cataract operations

You can also opt for add-on benefits like:

- Maternity cover: Your health insurance covers you for the costs related to childbirth. This includes pre-delivery check-ups, hospitalisation during delivery, and post-natal care.
- Pre-existing diseases cover: Your health insurance takes care of the treatment of diseases you may have before buying the health insurance policy.
- Accident cover: Your health insurance can pay for the medical treatment of injuries caused due to accidents and mishaps.

Your health insurance can also help you save tax. Your premium payment can reduce your taxable income.

For	Tax deduction on the premium amount	Total
Self	Rs. 25,000 (Rs. 30,000 if you are a senior citizen)	Rs. 25,000 (or Rs. 30,000)
Parents, who are senior citizens		Rs. 30,000 Rs. 55,000 (or Rs. 60,000)

Senior citizen = Individual aged 60 or over

Home Insurance

Home insurance is a cover that pays or compensates you for damage to your home due to natural calamities, man-made disasters or other threats.

It cover liabilities due to fire, burglary, theft, flood, earthquakes, and sabotage. It not only offers financial protection to your home, but also takes care of the valuables inside the property.

Some of the common types of home insurance are:

Standard fire and special perils policy. This covers your home against fire outbreaks and special perils. The dangers covered are:

- Natural calamities like lightening, flood, storm, earthquake, etc.
- Damage caused due to overflowing or bursting of water tanks, pipes, etc.
- Damage caused due to man-made activities such as riots, strikes, etc.

Home structure insurance.

- This protects the structure of your home from any kinds of risks and damages.
- The cover is also extended to the permanent fixtures within the house such as kitchen and bathroom fittings.

Public liability coverage. The damage caused to other person or their property inside the insured home can also be compensated.

Content Insurance. This covers the content inside the insured home. What's commonly covered: television, refrigerator, portable equipment, etc.

Fire Insurance

Fire insurance pays or compensates for the damages caused to your property or goods due to fire.

It covers the replacement, reconstruction or repair expenses of the insured property as well as the surrounding structures.

It also covers the damages caused to a third-party property due to fire.

In addition to these, it takes care of the expenses of those whose livelihood has been affected due to fire.

Types of Fire Insurance

Some of the common types are:

Valued policy	The insurer firsts value the property and then undertakes to pay compensation up to that value in the case of loss or damage.
Floating policy	It covers the damages to properties lying at different places.
Comprehensive policy	This is known as an all-in-one policy. It has a wide coverage and includes damages due to fire, theft, burglary, etc.
Specific policy	This covers you for a specific amount which is less than the real value of the property.

RISK CLASSIFICATION AND MANAGEMENT

Insurance Risk Management is the assessment and quantification of the likelihood and financial impact of events that may occur in the customer's world that require settlement by the insurer; and the ability to spread the risk of these events occurring across other insurance underwriter's in the market. Risk Management work typically involves the application of mathematical and statistical modelling to determine appropriate premium cover and the value of insurance risk to 'hold' vs 'distribute'.

Insurance Risk Management: Value

- Alignment of the pricing market strategy and reinsurance arrangements to the organisation's risk appetite as well as optimising the goals of the organisation
- Assist clients to recognise risk events and changes to claim rates earlier, so as to move towards a more market responsive, risk-based pricing approach which ensures the efficient deployment of capital and a reduction in extreme risk event losses.
- Enhance the feedback mechanism from claims function to underwriting and product development processes to improve the performance and profitability of these processes.

Insurance Risk Management: Core Services

Enhanced Risk Strategies Frameworks. Create the right risk strategies to achieve the enterprises strategic aims and implements the optimum frameworks to ensure risk is appropriately managed.

Work Undertaken

- Assessment, design and implementation of insurance strategies
- Assessment, design, implementation of insurance risk frameworks
- Assessment, design and implementation of insurance risk related risk portfolios and assessment methodologies
- Assessment, design and implementation of insurance risk appetite statements
- Claims function KPI design
- Commodity sector strategy Input
- Insurance product pricing
- Underwriting Function KPI Design
- Reinsurance Program Design

Example: Put in place an enhanced risk framework following an acquisition.

Enhanced Risk Performance

Putting words into action – delivering risk performance within agreed tolerances at the sharp end – day after day.

Work Undertaken

- Insurance Risk Analysis – Trend analysis
- Insurance Risk Analysis – Exposure Measurement
- Insurance Risk Exposure Management
- Risk capital Reserving
- Claims Result Analysis
- Reinsurance Effectiveness
- Insurance Risk Aggregation and concentration risk measurement and management
- Peer review Actuarial Services
- Audit review of liabilities, capital etc

- Insurance Needs Assessment and/or Insurance Selection recommendations for non-insurance clients
- Risk Management Software Systems - Insurance Risk Underwriting Software Design, Specifications, Testing, Review
- Mergers and Acquisitions assistance

Example: Assisted in the development of an enhanced Risk Appetite process for a general insurer.

Enhanced Risk Management Functions Capabilities

Create the optimum organisational solutions and equips the enterprise with the right skills and capabilities to manage risk to achieve strategic aims.

Work Undertaken

- Assessment, design and implementation of Insurance Risk Management functions
- Claims Function – Assessment
- Underwriting Function Assessment
- Appointed Actuary Services
- Interim management solutions: Insurance Risk Officers and other professionals

Example: Deployment of an experienced PWC Partner to act an interim CRO for the Wealth Business of a 'Big 4 Bank'.

FACTORS LIMITING THE INSURABILITY OF RISK

Because private insurance companies are businesses that want to make a profit, there are only certain risks—known as insurable risks—that private insurers are willing to cover. Almost all risks insured by insurance companies are pure risks, which are risks where there is no possibility of profit. Additionally, since insurable losses can only be compensated by the payment of money, only risks involving financial loss are insurable. Insurance companies also do not insure against predictable losses, such as wear and tear, and inherent vice, which is the self-destruction of property caused by the nature of the thing itself, such as the rotting of fruit.

So that an insurance company can remain a viable concern, any risks that it chooses to cover must have a predictable payout and an affordable premium that will cover the costs of the payout and the insurance company's operating expenses, and still yield a reasonable profit.

Losses must be accidental and unintentional. If they were not, then a moral hazard would be created, where many people would cause losses to collect insurance. This would raise premiums to unaffordable levels, and make payouts by the company unpredictable, since the losses would not occur by chance. People would stop paying premiums if they knew that the premiums were used to enrich dishonest people. For instance, one reason why insurance companies rarely cover mental illness is because it is easily feigned, and thus, it would be difficult to prevent dishonesty.

Another requirement to keep premiums affordable is that the loss must be determinable and measurable. The loss must be determinable because an insurance company will only pay for a loss if the loss was for a covered reason. The loss must be measurable to know how much to pay, because an insurance company will only pay to cover the actual loss, and no more. If the insurance company paid more than the actual loss, then the insured could make a profit by causing partial losses, then collecting the entire amount from the insurance company, thereby violating the principle of indemnity. This would not only increase premiums because of the larger payout, but it would also create a moral hazard by motivating some people to cause losses to profit from insurance, raising premiums even more.

RE-INSURANCE

Reinsurance, also known as insurance for insurers or stop-loss insurance, is the practice of insurers transferring portions of risk portfolios to other parties by some form of agreement to reduce the likelihood of paying a large obligation resulting from an insurance claim. The party that diversifies its insurance portfolio is known as the ceding party. The party that accepts a portion of the potential obligation in exchange for a share of the insurance premium is known as the reinsurer.

Reinsurance allows insurers to remain solvent by recovering some or all of the amounts paid to claimants. Reinsurance reduces net liability on individual risks and catastrophe protection from large or multiple losses. It also provides ceding companies the capacity to increase their underwriting capabilities in terms of the number and size of risks.

By covering the insurer against accumulated individual commitments, reinsurance gives the insurer more security for its equity and solvency and more stable results when unusual and major events occur. Insurers may underwrite policies covering a larger quantity or volume of risks without excessively raising administrative costs to cover their solvency margins. In addition, reinsurance makes substantial liquid assets available for insurers in case of exceptional losses.

Facultative coverage protects an insurer for an individual or a specified risk or contract. If several risks or contracts need reinsurance, each is negotiated separately. The reinsurer has all rights for accepting or denying a facultative reinsurance proposal.

A reinsurance treaty is effective for a set time period rather than on a per-risk or contract basis. The reinsurer covers all or a portion of the risks that the insurer may incur.

Under proportional reinsurance, the reinsurer receives a prorated share of all policy premiums sold by the insurer. When claims are made, the reinsurer bears a portion of the losses based on a pre-negotiated percentage. The reinsurer also reimburses the insurer for processing, business acquisition, and writing costs.

With non-proportional reinsurance, the reinsurer is liable if the insurer's losses exceed a specified amount, known as the priority or retention limit. As a result, the reinsurer does not have a proportional share in the insurer's premiums and losses. The priority or retention limit may be based on one type of risk or an entire risk category.

Excess-of-loss reinsurance is a type of non-proportional coverage in which the reinsurer covers the losses exceeding the insurer's retained limit. This contract is typically applied to catastrophic events, covering the insurer either on a per-occurrence basis or for the cumulative losses within a set time period.

Under risk-attaching reinsurance, all claims established during the effective period are covered, regardless of whether the losses occurred outside the coverage period. No coverage is provided for claims originating outside the coverage period, even if the losses occurred while the contract was in effect.

IRDA

Insurance Regulatory Development and Authority (IRDA) is the statutory, independent and apex body that governs and supervise the Insurance Industry in India.

It was constituted by Parliament of India Act called Insurance Regulatory and Development Authority of India (IRDA of India) after the formal declaration of Insurance Laws (Amendment) Ordinance 2014, by the President of India Pranab Mukherjee on December 26,2014.

Establishment

- IRDA Act was passed upon the recommendations of Malhotra Committee report (7 Jan,1994), headed by Mr R.N. Malhotra (Retired Governor, RBI)

- Main Recommendations - Entrance of Private Sector Companies and Foreign promoters & An independent regulatory authority for Insurance Sector in India
- In April, 2000, it was set up as statutory body, with its headquarters at New Delhi.
- The headquarters of the agency were shifted to Hyderabad, Telangana in 2001.

Objectives of IRDA

- To promote the interest and rights of policy holders.
- To promote and ensure the growth of Insurance Industry.
- To ensure speedy settlement of genuine claims and to prevent frauds and malpractices
- To bring transparency and orderly conduct of in financial markets dealing with insurance.

Organisational Setup of IRDA

IRDA is a ten member body consists of :

- One Chairman (For 5 Years & Maximum Age - 60 years)
- Five whole-time Members (For 5 Years and Maximum Age- 62 years)
- Four part-time Members (Not more than 5 years)

The chairman and members of IRDA are appointed by Government of India

Functions And Duties of IRDA

Section 14 of IRDA Act,1999 lays down the duties and functions of IRDA:

- It issues the registration certificates to insurance companies and regulates them.
- It protects the interest of policy holders.
- It provides license to insurance intermediaries such as agents and brokers after specifying the required qualifications and set norms/code of conduct for them.
- It promotes and regulates the professional organisations related with insurance business to promote efficiency in insurance sector.
- It regulates and supervise the premium rates and terms of insurance covers.
- It specifies the conditions and manners, according to which the insurance companies and other intermediaries have to make their financial reports.
- It regulates the investment of policyholder's funds by insurance companies.
- It also ensures the maintenance of solvency margin (company's ability to pay out claims) by insurance companies.

Role of IRDA

- To protect the interest of and ensure just treatment to insurance policyholder.
- To encourage and ensure the systematic growth of the insurance industry so as to benefit the common man and help in bringing economic growth.
- To set, promote, monitor, apply high standard of integrity, fair, dealing financial viability and capability of those it regulates.
- Bringing economic growth.
- To provide dispute resolution mechanism and ensure speedy settlement of genuine claims.
- To take suitable steps against circumstances, where set standards do not prevail or inappropriately enforced.
- To bring about the optimal amount of self-regulation in day-to-day, activities of the industry reliable with the requirement of the prudential regulation.

MULTIPLE CHOICE QUESTIONS

1. What is the primary regulatory body overseeing the Indian financial system?
   (1) Securities and Exchange Board of India (SEBI)
   (2) Reserve Bank of India (RBI)
   (3) Insurance Regulatory and Development Authority of India (IRDAI)
   (4) Ministry of Finance
2. Which institution is responsible for regulating and supervising the capital markets in India?
   (1) Reserve Bank of India (RBI)
   (2) Securities and Exchange Board of India (SEBI)
   (3) Insurance Regulatory and Development Authority of India (IRDAI)
   (4) Ministry of Finance
3. What is the primary function of the Reserve Bank of India (RBI)?
   (1) Regulating the stock markets
   (2) Conducting monetary policy and regulating the money supply
   (3) Supervising insurance companies
   (4) Managing the country's fiscal policy
4. Which entity is responsible for regulating and overseeing the insurance sector in India?
   (1) Reserve Bank of India (RBI)
   (2) Securities and Exchange Board of India (SEBI)
   (3) Insurance Regulatory and Development Authority of India (IRDAI)
   (4) Ministry of Finance
5. What is the purpose of the National Stock Exchange (NSE) in India?
   (1) Regulating banks
   (2) Facilitating trading in equities and derivatives
   (3) Supervising mutual funds
   (4) Managing foreign exchange reserves
6. Which organisation plays a key role in promoting financial inclusion in India?
   (1) National Stock Exchange (NSE)
   (2) Small Industries Development Bank of India (SIDBI)
   (3) National Bank for Agriculture and Rural Development (NABARD)
   (4) Industrial Development Bank of India (IDBI)
7. What is the function of the Small Industries Development Bank of India (SIDBI)?
   (1) Regulating the insurance sector
   (2) Promoting and financing small-scale industries
   (3) Conducting monetary policy
   (4) Regulating foreign direct investment
8. Which financial institution provides long-term finance for industrial projects in India?
   (1) Industrial Finance Corporation of India (IFCI)
   (2) National Bank for Agriculture and Rural Development (NABARD)
   (3) Export-Import Bank of India (EXIM Bank)
   (4) Small Industries Development Bank of India (SIDBI)
9. The term "Repo Rate" is associated with which financial institution in India?
   (1) National Stock Exchange (NSE)
   (2) Reserve Bank of India (RBI)
   (3) Securities and Exchange Board of India (SEBI)
   (4) National Payments Corporation of India (NPCI)
10. What is the primary function of the Securities and Exchange Board of India (SEBI)?
    (1) Regulating the insurance sector
    (2) Regulating and supervising the capital markets
    (3) Conducting monetary policy
    (4) Providing agricultural credit
11. Which organisation is responsible for promoting and regulating foreign trade in India?
    (1) Reserve Bank of India (RBI)
    (2) Export-Import Bank of India (EXIM Bank)

(3) National Bank for Agriculture and Rural Development (NABARD)
(4) Ministry of Commerce and Industry

12. What is the main objective of the National Payments Corporation of India (NPCI)?
(1) Regulating banks
(2) Facilitating electronic payments and settlements
(3) Promoting agricultural and rural development
(4) Regulating the stock markets

13. Which financial institution in India focuses on providing credit to the agricultural sector?
(1) Small Industries Development Bank of India (SIDBI)
(2) National Bank for Agriculture and Rural Development (NABARD)
(3) Export-Import Bank of India (EXIM Bank)
(4) Industrial Finance Corporation of India (IFCI)

14. The term "CRR" (Cash Reserve Ratio) is associated with which institution?
(1) National Stock Exchange (NSE)
(2) Reserve Bank of India (RBI)
(3) Securities and Exchange Board of India (SEBI)
(4) National Payments Corporation of India (NPCI)

15. What is the primary role of the Export-Import Bank of India (EXIM Bank)?
(1) Providing credit to small-scale industries
(2) Promoting and financing foreign trade
(3) Conducting monetary policy
(4) Regulating the insurance sector

16. Which organisation regulates and supervises the pension funds in India?
(1) Reserve Bank of India (RBI)
(2) Pension Fund Regulatory and Development Authority (PFRDA)
(3) Insurance Regulatory and Development Authority of India (IRDAI)
(4) Ministry of Finance

17. The term "Nifty" is associated with which stock market index in India?
(1) BSE Sensex (2) NSE Nifty
(3) CNX Midcap (4) NSE Bank Index

18. What is the main function of the Employees' Provident Fund Organisation (EPFO) in India?
(1) Regulating the insurance sector
(2) Providing credit to small-scale industries
(3) Managing employees' provident funds and pension schemes
(4) Regulating foreign direct investment

19. Which institution regulates and supervises the credit information companies in India?
(1) Reserve Bank of India (RBI)
(2) Securities and Exchange Board of India (SEBI)
(3) Insurance Regulatory and Development Authority of India (IRDAI)
(4) Credit Information Bureau (India) Limited (CIBIL)

20. What is the primary function of the National Housing Bank (NHB) in India?
(1) Regulating banks
(2) Providing credit to small-scale industries
(3) Promoting and regulating housing finance institutions
(4) Conducting monetary policy

21. Which financial institution provides refinance facilities for institutional and developmental activities in rural areas?
(1) Small Industries Development Bank of India (SIDBI)
(2) National Bank for Agriculture and Rural Development (NABARD)
(3) Export-Import Bank of India (EXIM Bank)
(4) Industrial Finance Corporation of India (IFCI)

22. What is the primary objective of the Banking Codes and Standards Board of India (BCSBI)?
(1) Regulating the insurance sector
(2) Promoting and regulating housing finance institutions
(3) Ensuring banks adhere to codes and standards for fair banking practices
(4) Managing foreign exchange reserves

23. Which institution issues and regulates the use of the Indian Rupee currency notes in the country?
(1) Reserve Bank of India (RBI)
(2) Securities and Exchange Board of India (SEBI)
(3) Ministry of Finance
(4) National Payments Corporation of India (NPCI)

24. The term "Sovereign Gold Bond" is associated with which financial instrument in India?
(1) Equity shares
(2) Government securities backed by gold
(3) Mutual funds
(4) Corporate bonds

25. What is the primary function of the Forward Markets Commission (FMC) in India?
(1) Regulating banks
(2) Regulating and supervising commodity futures markets
(3) Conducting monetary policy
(4) Regulating foreign direct investment

Directions: Each of the following items consists of two statements, one labelled as Assertion (A) and other labelled as Reason (R). You are to examine these two statements carefully and decide if the (A) and the (R) are individually true and if so, whether (R) is the correct explanation of (A). Select your answers to these items using the codes given below:
(1) Both (A) and (R) are true, and the (R) is the correct explanation of the (A).
(2) Both (A) and (R) are true, but the (R) is not the correct explanation of the (A).
(3) The (A) is false, and the (R) is true.
(4) The (A) is false, and the (R) is false.

26. **Assertion (A):** The Reserve Bank of India (RBI) is responsible for regulating and supervising commodity futures markets in India
Reason (R): The RBI oversees all financial markets, including commodities.

27. **Assertion (A):** The Securities and Exchange Board of India (SEBI) regulates and supervises the insurance sector in India.
Reason (R): SEBI is the primary regulatory body for the capital markets, not insurance.

28. **Assertion (A):** The Employees' Provident Fund Organisation (EPFO) manages employees' provident funds and pension schemes in India.
Reason (R): EPFO primarily deals with the regulation and supervision of banks.

29. **Assertion (A):** The National Housing Bank (NHB) regulates and supervises the credit information companies in India.
Reason (R): NHB focuses on promoting and regulating housing finance institutions.

30. **Assertion (A):** The term "Nifty" is associated with the BSE Sensex in India.
Reason (R): Nifty and Sensex are two different stock market indices in India.

31. What is the primary function of commercial banks?
(1) Regulating monetary policy
(2) Providing credit to small-scale industries
(3) Accepting deposits and offering loans
(4) Supervising insurance companies

32. Which regulatory body oversees the functioning of commercial banks in India?
(1) Securities and Exchange Board of India (SEBI)
(2) Reserve Bank of India (RBI)
(3) Insurance Regulatory and Development Authority of India (IRDAI)
(4) Ministry of Finance

33. What is the main source of income for commercial banks?
(1) Trading in securities
(2) Fees and commissions
(3) Interest on loans and advances
(4) Dividends from investments

34. Which type of account is considered a liability for a commercial bank?
(1) Savings account
(2) Fixed deposit account
(3) Current account
(4) Loan account

35. What is the function of a demand draft issued by a commercial bank?
(1) Providing credit to small-scale industries
(2) Facilitating electronic payments and settlements
(3) Promoting agricultural and rural development
(4) Providing a secure means of transferring funds

36. What is the primary focus of Regional Rural Banks (RRBs) in India?
(1) Providing services in urban and metropolitan areas
(2) Regulating monetary policy
(3) Promoting agricultural and rural development
(4) Facilitating international trade

37. Who sponsors Regional Rural Banks (RRBs) in India?
(1) State Governments

(2) Foreign banks
(3) Private individuals
(4) Central Government

38. Which of the following is a characteristic feature of Regional Rural Banks (RRBs)?
(1) Operating only in urban areas
(2) Providing a wide range of financial services
(3) Having a limited area of operation
(4) Focusing on international banking

39. What is the primary objective of establishing Regional Rural Banks (RRBs)?
(1) Maximising profits for shareholders
(2) Promoting financial inclusion in rural areas
(3) Providing services exclusively to urban populations
(4) Regulating monetary policy

40. Which regulatory body supervises and monitors the functioning of Regional Rural Banks (RRBs) in India?
(1) Reserve Bank of India (RBI)
(2) National Bank for Agriculture and Rural Development (NABARD)
(3) Securities and Exchange Board of India (SEBI)
(4) Ministry of Finance

41. What is a key characteristic of foreign banks operating in India?
(1) Limited to providing services only to foreign nationals
(2) Regulated by the central bank of their home country
(3) Providing services exclusively in rural areas
(4) Subject to the same regulations as domestic banks

42. Which of the following is a function of foreign banks in India?
(1) Providing services exclusively to Indian citisens
(2) Facilitating international trade and finance
(3) Promoting agricultural and rural development
(4) Regulating monetary policy

43. What distinguishes foreign banks from domestic banks in terms of their origin?
(1) Operating only in urban areas
(2) Headquartered in a foreign country
(3) Providing services exclusively in rural areas
(4) Subject to different regulatory frameworks

44. Which regulatory body oversees the operations of foreign banks in India?
(1) Reserve Bank of India (RBI)
(2) National Bank for Agriculture and Rural Development (NABARD)
(3) Securities and Exchange Board of India (SEBI)
(4) Ministry of Finance

45. What is the significance of correspondent banking relationships for foreign banks?
(1) Offering credit to small-scale industries
(2) Facilitating international trade and fund transfers
(3) Providing services exclusively to urban populations
(4) Regulating monetary policy

46. What is the primary objective of cooperative banks?
(1) Maximising profits for shareholders
(2) Promoting financial inclusion in rural areas
(3) Providing services exclusively to foreign nationals
(4) Regulating monetary policy

47. What distinguishes cooperative banks from commercial banks in terms of ownership?
(1) Owned by private individuals or corporations
(2) Owned and operated by the government
(3) Owned by their members who are also their customers
(4) Owned by foreign investors

48. Which type of customers are the primary members of cooperative banks?
(1) Foreign nationals
(2) Urban residents
(3) Farmers and small-scale entrepreneurs
(4) Corporate entities

49. What is the role of cooperative banks in promoting agricultural and rural development?
(1) Offering credit to large corporations
(2) Providing services exclusively to foreign nationals
(3) Extending credit to farmers and rural communities
(4) Regulating monetary policy

50. Which regulatory body oversees the functioning of cooperative banks in India?
(1) Reserve Bank of India (RBI)
(2) National Bank for Agriculture and Rural Development (NABARD)
(3) Securities and Exchange Board of India (SEBI)
(4) Ministry of Finance

Directions: Each of the following items consists of two statements, one labelled as Assertion (A) and other labelled as Reason (R). You are to examine these two statements carefully and decide if the (A) and the (R) are individually true and if so, whether (R) is the correct explanation of (A). Select your answers to these items using the codes given below:
(1) Both (A) and (R) are true, and the (R) is the correct explanation of the (A).
(2) Both (A) and (R) are true, but the (R) is not the correct explanation of the (A).
(3) The (A) is false, and the (R) is false.
(4) The (A) is true, and the (R) is false.

51. **Assertion (A):** Commercial banks focus primarily on promoting agricultural and rural development.
Reason (R): Providing credit to small-scale industries is the main function of commercial banks.

52. **Assertion (A):** Foreign banks in India are not subject to the same regulatory frameworks as domestic banks.
Reason (R): Foreign banks operate independently of any regulatory oversight.

53. **Assertion (A):** Regional Rural Banks (RRBs) have a broader area of operation compared to commercial banks.
Reason (R): RRBs operate exclusively in urban and metropolitan areas.

54. **Assertion (A):** Cooperative banks are owned and operated by the government.
Reason (R): Cooperative banks are owned by their members who are also their customers.

55. **Assertion (A):** The primary objective of cooperative banks is to Maximise profits for shareholders.
Reason (R): Cooperative banks focus on promoting financial inclusion in rural areas.

56. What is the primary function of the Reserve Bank of India (RBI)?
(1) Regulating stock markets
(2) Conducting monetary policy
(3) Providing credit to small-scale industries
(4) Supervising insurance companies

57. Which department of the RBI is responsible for issuing and regulating the Indian Rupee currency notes?
(1) Currency Management Department
(2) Banking Regulation Department
(3) Financial Stability Unit
(4) External Investments and Operations Department

58. What is the purpose of the Banking Regulation Department in the RBI?
(1) Issuing and regulating currency notes
(2) Supervising and regulating banks and financial institutions
(3) Managing the country's foreign exchange reserves
(4) Conducting monetary policy

59. Which unit of the RBI focuses on maintaining the stability and resilience of the financial system?
(1) Currency Management Department
(2) Banking Regulation Department
(3) Financial Stability Unit
(4) External Investments and Operations Department

60. The RBI acts as a banker to the government. What does this entail?
(1) Issuing currency notes
(2) Providing loans to the government
(3) Regulating stock markets
(4) Managing foreign exchange reserves

61. What is the primary objective of the External Investments and Operations Department in the RBI?
(1) Regulating banks
(2) Managing the country's foreign exchange reserves
(3) Conducting monetary policy
(4) Providing credit to small-scale industries

62. Which function of the RBI involves controlling the supply of money and credit in the economy?
(1) Currency management
(2) Monetary policy
(3) Banking regulation
(4) Financial stability

63. The RBI acts as the custodian of foreign exchange reserves. What is the purpose of this role?
   (1) Issuing and regulating currency notes
   (2) Promoting financial inclusion in rural areas
   (3) Managing the country's foreign exchange reserves
   (4) Conducting monetary policy

64. Which unit of the RBI is responsible for regulating and supervising non-banking financial companies (NBFCs)?
   (1) Currency Management Department
   (2) Banking Regulation Department
   (3) Financial Stability Unit
   (4) Department of Non-Banking Regulation

65. What is the purpose of the Inspection Department in the RBI?
   (1) Conducting monetary policy
   (2) Regulating stock markets
   (3) Supervising and inspecting banks
   (4) Managing the country's foreign exchange reserves

66. The Monetary Policy Committee (MPC) of the RBI is responsible for:
   (1) Issuing currency notes
   (2) Regulating stock markets
   (3) Formulating monetary policy
   (4) Providing credit to small-scale industries

67. What is the primary role of the Financial Stability and Development Council (FSDC) in coordination with the RBI?
   (1) Managing the country's foreign exchange reserves
   (2) Promoting financial inclusion in rural areas
   (3) Ensuring financial stability in the economy
   (4) Regulating banks

68. Which unit of the RBI is responsible for implementing the government's monetary policies?
   (1) Currency Management Department
   (2) Banking Regulation Department
   (3) Department of Government and Bank Accounts
   (4) External Investments and Operations Department

69. What is the purpose of the Department of Government and Bank Accounts in the RBI?
   (1) Conducting monetary policy
   (2) Regulating stock markets
   (3) Managing the government's accounts and transactions
   (4) Providing credit to small-scale industries

70. Which function of the RBI involves the regulation and supervision of payment systems in the country?
   (1) Currency management
   (2) Monetary policy
   (3) Banking regulation
   (4) Department of Payment and Settlement Systems

71. What is the repo rate in the context of the RBI's monetary policy?
   (1) The rate at which banks borrow from each other
   (2) The rate at which banks borrow from the RBI
   (3) The rate at which banks lend to the RBI
   (4) The rate at which the RBI borrows from the government

72. How does the RBI use the repo rate to influence the economy?
   (1) By controlling inflation
   (2) By promoting agricultural and rural development
   (3) By regulating foreign exchange reserves
   (4) By managing government accounts

73. What is the reverse repo rate in the context of the RBI's monetary policy?
   (1) The rate at which banks borrow from each other
   (2) The rate at which banks borrow from the RBI
   (3) The rate at which banks lend to the RBI
   (4) The rate at which the RBI borrows from the government

74. How does the RBI use the reverse repo rate to influence the economy?
   (1) By controlling inflation
   (2) By promoting agricultural and rural development
   (3) By regulating foreign exchange reserves
   (4) By managing government accounts

75. What is the Cash Reserve Ratio (CRR) in the RBI's monetary policy?
   (1) The ratio of currency in circulation to total deposits
   (2) The ratio of cash reserves to total assets

(3) The ratio of deposits to loans and advances
(4) The ratio of cash reserves to total deposits

76. How does the RBI use the Cash Reserve Ratio (CRR) to influence the economy?
(1) By controlling inflation
(2) By promoting agricultural and rural development
(3) By regulating foreign exchange reserves
(4) By managing government accounts

77. What is the Statutory Liquidity Ratio (SLR) in the RBI's monetary policy?
(1) The ratio of currency in circulation to total deposits
(2) The ratio of cash reserves to total assets
(3) The ratio of deposits to loans and advances
(4) The ratio of liquid assets to net demand and time liabilities

78. How does the RBI use the Statutory Liquidity Ratio (SLR) to influence the economy?
(1) By controlling inflation
(2) By promoting agricultural and rural development
(3) By regulating foreign exchange reserves
(4) By managing government accounts

79. What is the Marginal Standing Facility (MSF) in the context of the RBI's monetary policy?
(1) A facility for banks to borrow long-term funds
(2) A facility for banks to borrow short-term funds
(3) A facility for banks to invest in government securities
(4) A facility for banks to lend to the RBI

80. How does the RBI use the Marginal Standing Facility (MSF) to influence the economy?
(1) By controlling inflation
(2) By promoting agricultural and rural development
(3) By regulating foreign exchange reserves
(4) By managing government accounts

Directions: Each of the following items consists of two statements, one labelled as Assertion (A) and other labelled as Reason (R). You are to examine these two statements carefully and decide if the (A) and the (R) are individually true and if so, whether (R) is the correct explanation of (A). Select your answers to these items using the codes given below:
(1) The (A) is true, and the (R) is false.
(2) The (A) is false, and the (R) is false.
(3) The (A) is false, and the (R) is true.
(4) The (A) is true, and the (R) is true.

81. Assertion (A): The Reserve Bank of India (RBI) is responsible for issuing and regulating currency notes.
Reason (R): The RBI has a dedicated department known as the Currency Management Department.

82. Assertion (A): The Financial Stability Unit in the RBI is primarily focused on regulating banks.
Reason (R): Financial Stability Unit is responsible for maintaining stability and resilience in the financial system.

83. Assertion (A): The Department of Payment and Settlement Systems in the RBI is responsible for formulating monetary policy.
Reason (R): The Department of Payment and Settlement Systems regulates and supervises payment systems.

84. Assertion (A): The RBI's Monetary Policy Committee (MPC) formulates monetary policy independently of the government.
Reason (R): The government has the sole authority to formulate and implement monetary policy in India.

85. Assertion (A): The repo rate set by the RBI influences inflation in the economy.
Reason (R): The repo rate affects the cost of borrowing for banks, which, in turn, influences lending rates and spending in the economy.

86. What are the Basel Norms in the context of banking?
(1) Guidelines for marketing strategies
(2) Standards for financial reporting
(3) Regulatory framework for banking supervision
(4) Rules for customer service

87. Which committee introduced the Basel Committee on Banking Supervision (BCBS) and the Basel Norms?
(1) Narasimham Committee
(2) Rangarajan Committee
(3) Hilton Young Committee
(4) Basel Committee

88. Under Basel III, what is the minimum Common Equity Tier 1 (CET1) capital requirement for banks?
(1) 4% (2) 6%
(3) 8% (4) 10%

89. What is the purpose of the Basel III framework?
(1) Enhancing risk management practices
(2) Increasing interest rates
(3) Reducing customer services
(4) Promoting marketing strategies

90. Which risk does the Basel II framework primarily aim to address?
(1) Credit risk (2) Market risk
(3) Operational risk (4) Liquidity risk

91. What is the focus of the Basel III framework in comparison to Basel II?
(1) Addressing market risk
(2) Strengthening capital requirements
(3) Managing operational risk
(4) Minimising liquidity risk

92. What is the purpose of the Capital Adequacy Ratio (CAR) under Basel III?
(1) Ensuring profitability
(2) Managing customer complaints
(3) Assessing a bank's capital adequacy in relation to its risk
(4) Controlling marketing strategies

93. Which component of the Basel III framework focuses on the leverage ratio to prevent excessive leverage?
(1) Common Equity Tier 1 (CET1)
(2) Tier 1 Capital
(3) Tier 2 Capital
(4) Capital Conservation Buffer

94. What is the objective of the Liquidity Coverage Ratio (LCR) under Basel III?
(1) Encouraging high-risk investments
(2) Ensuring banks have sufficient high-quality liquid assets to cover short-term liabilities
(3) Minimising customer services
(4) Promoting marketing strategies

95. Which committee recommended the adoption of the Basel II norms in India?
(1) Narasimham Committee
(2) Rangarajan Committee
(3) Malegam Committee
(4) Hilton Young Committee

96. What is the primary purpose of risk management in the banking sector?
(1) Maximising profits
(2) Minimising customer complaints
(3) Identifying and mitigating potential risks
(4) Promoting marketing strategies

97. Which type of risk is associated with fluctuations in interest rates and market prices?
(1) Credit risk (2) Market risk
(3) Operational risk (4) Liquidity risk

98. What is credit risk in the context of banking?
(1) Risk of losses due to changes in market prices
(2) Risk of default by borrowers
(3) Risk of fraud and misconduct
(4) Risk of insufficient liquidity

99. Which risk is associated with the day-to-day operations of a bank, including technology and human factors?
(1) Credit risk (2) Market risk
(3) Operational risk (4) Liquidity risk

100. What does the term "ALM" stand for in the context of risk management in banks?
(1) Asset Liability Management
(2) Advanced Liquidity Monitoring
(3) Aggressive Loan Management
(4) Adequate Liability Measurement

101. What does NPA stand for in the banking sector?
(1) Non-Performing Asset
(2) Net Profit Analysis
(3) New Product Assessment
(4) Non-Permissible Account

102. How is an asset classified as a Non-Performing Asset (NPA)?
(1) When it fails to generate profits
(2) When it is not actively marketed
(3) When it becomes overdue for a specified period
(4) When it is not part of the bank's investment portfolio

103. What is the impact of NPAs on a bank's financial health?
(1) Improves profitability
(2) Increases customer satisfaction
(3) Deteriorates financial health and profitability
(4) Boosts marketing strategies

104. What is the purpose of the Insolvency and Bankruptcy Code (IBC) in managing NPAs?
(1) Promoting marketing strategies

(2) Identifying potential customers
(3) Resolving and liquidating stressed assets
(4) Increasing customer services

105. Which committee recommended the establishment of Asset Reconstruction Companies (ARCs) in India?
(1) Narasimham Committee
(2) Rangarajan Committee
(3) Tandon Committee
(4) Malegam Committee

106. What is the role of Asset Reconstruction Companies (ARCs) in managing NPAs?
(1) Promoting marketing strategies
(2) Acquiring and resolving distressed assets from banks
(3) Offering high-risk loans
(4) Boosting customer complaints

107. What is the significance of the Prompt Corrective Action (PCA) framework in managing NPAs?
(1) Encourages high-risk investments
(2) Restricts banking operations for weak banks to prevent further deterioration
(3) Maximises customer satisfaction
(4) Promotes marketing strategies

108. Which regulatory body oversees the implementation of the Prompt Corrective Action (PCA) framework?
(1) Reserve Bank of India (RBI)
(2) Securities and Exchange Board of India (SEBI)
(3) Insurance Regulatory and Development Authority of India (IRDAI)
(4) Ministry of Finance

109. What is the purpose of the SARFAESI Act in managing NPAs?
(1) Facilitates customer complaints
(2) Empowers banks to take possession and sell assets of defaulting borrowers
(3) Regulates marketing strategies
(4) Boosts liquidity risk

110. Which measure is used to assess a bank's asset quality and NPA management?
(1) Capital Adequacy Ratio (CAR)
(2) Return on Investment (ROI)
(3) Gross NPA Ratio
(4) Current Ratio

Directions: Each of the following items consists of two statements, one labelled as Assertion (A) and other labelled as Reason (R). You are to examine these two statements carefully and decide if the (A) and the (R) are individually true and if so, whether (R) is the correct explanation of (A). Select your answers to these items using the codes given below:
(1) The (A) is true, and the (R) is false.
(2) The (A) is false, and the (R) is false.
(3) The (A) is false, and the (R) is true.
(4) The (A) is true, and the (R) is true.

111. Assertion (A): The Basel Norms focus on enhancing risk management practices in banks.
Reason (R): Basel III strengthens capital requirements and introduces measures to address liquidity risk.

112. Assertion (A): Operational risk in banking is associated with fluctuations in interest rates.
Reason (R): Operational risk includes risks arising from internal processes, systems, and human factors.

113. Assertion (A): The Prompt Corrective Action (PCA) framework restricts banking operations for weak banks.
Reason (R): PCA is designed to intervene and take corrective measures to prevent the financial health of banks from deteriorating further.

114. Assertion (A): The SARFAESI Act empowers banks to resolve NPAs by facilitating customer complaints.
Reason (R): The SARFAESI Act enables banks to take possession and sell assets of defaulting borrowers.

115. Assertion (A): The Gross NPA Ratio is a measure used to assess a bank's liquidity risk.
Reason (R): The Gross NPA Ratio indicates the proportion of a bank's assets that have turned non-performing.

116. What is the primary characteristic of the money market?
(1) Long-term securities
(2) High-risk instruments
(3) Short-term instruments
(4) Speculative trading

117. Which of the following is a typical participant in the money market?
(1) Venture capitalists
(2) Individual investors
(3) Commercial banks (4) Stockbrokers

118. What is the purpose of the money market?
(1) Funding long-term projects
(2) Facilitating speculative trading
(3) Meeting short-term borrowing and lending needs
(4) Investing in real estate

119. Which instrument is commonly traded in the money market?
(1) Corporate bonds
(2) Treasury bills
(3) Common stock
(4) Mortgage-backed securities

120. What is the maturity period of instruments in the money market?
(1) Over 10 years (2) 1 to 10 years
(3) Less than 1 year (4) No fixed maturity

121. Which of the following is not a money market instrument?
(1) Certificate of Deposit (CD)
(2) Commercial paper
(3) Corporate bonds
(4) Repurchase agreements (repos)

122. What is the key characteristic of a Certificate of Deposit (CD)?
(1) No fixed maturity period
(2) High liquidity
(3) Long-term instrument
(4) Issued only by the government

123. Who issues Treasury bills in the money market?
(1) Commercial banks
(2) Corporate entities
(3) Government
(4) Non-profit organisations

124. What is the interest rate on Treasury bills called?
(1) Coupon rate (2) Dividend rate
(3) Discount rate (4) Yield rate

125. What is the primary function of the money market in the financial system?
(1) Capital formation
(2) Risk management
(3) Providing short-term liquidity
(4) Long-term investment

126. What is the primary characteristic of the capital market?
(1) Short-term securities
(2) Low-risk instruments
(3) Long-term securities
(4) Speculative trading

127. Which of the following is a typical participant in the capital market?
(1) Central banks
(2) Individual investors
(3) Commercial banks
(4) Money market mutual funds

128. What is the purpose of the capital market?
(1) Meeting short-term borrowing and lending needs
(2) Facilitating speculative trading
(3) Funding long-term projects
(4) Investing in real estate

129. Which instrument is commonly traded in the capital market?
(1) Treasury bills
(2) Common stock
(3) Commercial paper
(4) Certificate of Deposit (CD)

130. What is the typical maturity period of instruments in the capital market?
(1) Less than 1 year
(2) 1 to 10 years
(3) Over 10 years
(4) No fixed maturity

131. Which of the following is a long-term debt instrument issued by corporations?
(1) Treasury bills
(2) Commercial paper
(3) Corporate bonds
(4) Repurchase agreements (repos)

132. What is the key characteristic of a corporate bond?
(1) No fixed maturity period
(2) High liquidity
(3) Issued only by the government
(4) Represents a loan to the issuing corporation

133. Who regulates the capital market in many countries, including the U.S.?
(1) Securities and Exchange Commission (SEC)
(2) Federal Reserve System (Fed)
(3) Central banks
(4) Commercial banks

134. What is the function of an investment bank in the capital market?

(1) Issuing currency notes
(2) Facilitating short-term borrowing
(3) Underwriting and trading securities
(4) Managing government accounts

135. What is an Initial Public Offering (IPO) in the context of the capital market?
(1) Sale of government bonds
(2) First-time sale of a company's shares to the public
(3) Issuance of Treasury bills
(4) Redemption of corporate bonds

136. What are government securities?
(1) Equity shares issued by the government
(2) Debt instruments issued by the government
(3) Preferred stock issued by the government
(4) Mutual funds managed by the government

137. Which government agency is responsible for issuing and managing government securities in the U.S.?
(1) Federal Reserve System (Fed)
(2) Securities and Exchange Commission (SEC)
(3) Department of Treasury
(4) Internal Revenue Service (IRS)

138. What is the purpose of government securities in the financial market?
(1) Providing short-term liquidity
(2) Funding long-term projects
(3) Regulating stock markets
(4) Facilitating speculative trading

139. What is the key advantage of investing in government securities?
(1) High-risk
(2) High returns
(3) Low-risk
(4) Short-term maturity

140. Which type of government security pays periodic interest to the bondholder?
(1) Treasury bills (2) Treasury notes
(3) Treasury bonds (4) Savings bonds

Directions: Each of the following items consists of two statements, one labelled as Assertion (A) and other labelled as Reason (R). You are to examine these two statements carefully and decide if the (A) and the (R) are individually true and if so, whether (R) is the correct explanation of (A). Select your answers to these items using the codes given below:
(1) The (A) is true, and the (R) is false.
(2) The (A) is false, and the (R) is false.
(3) The (A) is false, and the (R) is true.
(4) The (A) is true, and the (R) is true.

141. Assertion (A): The money market primarily deals with long-term securities.
Reason (R): The money market is focused on providing short-term liquidity to meet borrowing and lending needs.

142. Assertion (A): Individual investors are typical participants in the money market.
Reason (R): The money market is mainly composed of institutional participants like banks and financial institutions.

143. Assertion (A): The capital market primarily deals with short-term instruments.
Reason (R): The capital market is designed for funding long-term projects and issuing long-term securities.

144. Assertion (A): Government securities are considered low-risk instruments.
Reason (R): Government securities are backed by the creditworthiness of the government.

145. Assertion (A): Corporate bonds are short-term debt instruments.
Reason (R): Corporate bonds represent long-term debt issued by corporations.

146. What is the primary objective of Development Finance Institutions (DFIs)?
(1) Maximising shareholder wealth
(2) Funding long-term infrastructure projects
(3) Facilitating short-term loans
(4) Speculative trading

147. Which sector do DFIs primarily focus on for financing?
(1) Retail (2) Agriculture
(3) Manufacturing (4) Services

148. Which financial institution in India was initially set up as a DFI but later transformed into a bank?
(1) ICICI Bank (2) HDFC Bank
(3) IDBI Bank (4) Axis Bank

149. What role do DFIs play in economic development?
(1) Short-term financing
(2) Facilitating speculative trading
(3) Fostering long-term industrial growth
(4) Managing government accounts

150. Which government agency is responsible for promoting and regulating DFIs in India?

(1) SEBI (2) RBI
(3) NABARD (4) SIDBI

151. What distinguishes NBFCs from traditional banks?
(1) Ability to accept demand deposits
(2) Focus on short-term lending
(3) Inability to issue debentures
(4) Limited regulatory oversight

152. Which of the following is a common type of NBFC in India?
(1) Commercial banks
(2) Insurance companies
(3) Microfinance institutions
(4) Credit unions

153. What is the primary source of funding for NBFCs?
(1) Customer deposits
(2) Government grants
(3) Equity shares
(4) Borrowings from banks and financial institutions

154. What is the primary business activity of an Asset Finance Company (AFC) among NBFCs?
(1) Providing short-term loans
(2) Financing the purchase of physical assets
(3) Offering insurance products
(4) Facilitating international trade

155. What regulatory body oversees the functioning of NBFCs in India?
(1) RBI (2) SEBI
(3) IRDAI (4) NABARD

156. What is the basic structure of a mutual fund?
(1) Limited Liability Company (LLC)
(2) Partnership
(3) Trust
(4) Sole proprietorship

157. How do mutual funds generate returns for their investors?
(1) Issuing debentures
(2) Investing in government securities
(3) Trading in stock markets
(4) Managing customer complaints

158. What is the role of a fund manager in a mutual fund?
(1) Accepting customer deposits
(2) Making investment decisions on behalf of investors
(3) Issuing insurance policies
(4) Facilitating short-term loans

159. Which type of mutual fund primarily invests in stocks?
(1) Equity fund (2) Debt fund
(3) Hybrid fund (4) Money market fund

160. What is the Net Asset Value (NAV) of a mutual fund?
(1) Total assets minus total liabilities
(2) Total liabilities minus total assets
(3) Total market value of assets divided by the number of units
(4) Total number of units multiplied by the market value of assets

161. What is the primary purpose of pension funds?
(1) Short-term lending
(2) Facilitating speculative trading
(3) Providing insurance products
(4) Accumulating funds for retirement benefits

162. How do pension funds invest the accumulated funds?
(1) Only in government securities
(2) Only in stocks
(3) In a diversified portfolio of assets
(4) In short-term loans

163. What distinguishes a defined benefit pension plan from a defined contribution plan?
(1) Fixed contributions by employees
(2) Fixed contributions by employers
(3) Fixed retirement benefits
(4) No fixed retirement benefits

164. Which regulatory body oversees pension funds in India?
(1) RBI (2) SEBI
(3) PFRDA (4) IRDAI

165. What is the Employee Provident Fund (EPF) in India?
(1) A pension fund
(2) A mutual fund
(3) A government bond
(4) A provident fund for employees

Directions: Each of the following items consists of two statements, one labelled as Assertion (A) and other labelled as Reason (R). You are to examine these two statements carefully and decide if the (A) and the (R) are individually true and if so, whether (R) is the correct explanation of (A). Select your answers to these items using the codes given below:

(1) The (A) is true, and the (R) is false.
(2) The (A) is false, and the (R) is false.
(3) The (A) is false, and the (R) is true.
(4) The (A) is true, and the (R) is true.

166. Assertion (A): Development Finance Institutions primarily focus on short-term financing.
Reason (R): DFIs play a crucial role in funding long-term infrastructure projects.

167. Assertion (A): Non-Banking Financial Companies (NBFCs) can accept demand deposits.
Reason (R): NBFCs are financial institutions that cannot accept demand deposits.

168. Assertion (A): Mutual funds are regulated by the Securities and Exchange Board of India (SEBI).
Reason (R): SEBI has the authority to regulate and oversee the functioning of mutual funds in India.

169. Assertion (A): Pension funds operate only in the stock market.
Reason (R): Pension funds typically invest in a diversified portfolio of assets to accumulate funds for retirement benefits.

170. Assertion (A): Defined contribution pension plans offer fixed retirement benefits.
Reason (R): In defined contribution plans, the retirement benefits are based on the contributions made and the returns generated on those contributions.

171. Which is the central banking institution in India responsible for monetary policy?
(1) SEBI (2) RBI
(3) IRDAI (4) PFRDA

172. What is the main function of RBI in the financial system?
(1) Regulating the stock market
(2) Regulating insurance companies
(3) Issuing currency notes
(4) Managing pension funds

173. Who is the current Governor of the Reserve Bank of India (as of the knowledge cutoff date in January 2022)?
(1) Shaktikanta Das (2) Raghuram Rajan
(3) Urjit Patel (4) Subbarao

174. What is the primary tool used by RBI to control inflation and money supply in the economy?
(1) Fiscal policy
(2) Open Market Operations (OMO)
(3) Foreign exchange reserves
(4) Repo rate

175. Which committee recommended the establishment of the Reserve Bank of India?
(1) Narasimham Committee
(2) Rangarajan Committee
(3) Hilton Young Committee
(4) Chakravarty Committee

176. What is the primary regulatory body for the securities market in India?
(1) RBI (2) SEBI
(3) IRDAI (4) PFRDA

177. Which of the following is under the purview of SEBI's regulation?
(1) Banking services
(2) Insurance companies
(3) Mutual funds
(4) Pension funds

178. What is the primary objective of SEBI?
(1) Regulating currency circulation
(2) Protecting the interests of investors in securities
(3) Issuing currency notes
(4) Managing pension funds

179. Who appoints the chairman of SEBI?
(1) President of India
(2) Prime Minister of India
(3) Ministry of Finance
(4) RBI Governor

180. What is the key initiative of SEBI to promote financial literacy and investor education?
(1) Operation Red Alert
(2) Operation Blue Chip
(3) Operation Green Revolution
(4) Operation Safeguard

181. Which regulatory body oversees the insurance sector in India?
(1) RBI (2) SEBI
(3) IRDAI (4) PFRDA

182. What is the primary function of IRDAI?
(1) Regulating the stock market
(2) Regulating banking services
(3) Regulating insurance companies
(4) Managing pension funds

183. Who appoints the chairman of IRDAI?
(1) President of India
(2) Prime Minister of India

(3) Ministry of Finance
(4) RBI Governor

184. Which committee recommended the establishment of IRDAI?
(1) Chakravarty Committee
(2) Malhotra Committee
(3) Rangarajan Committee
(4) Narasimham Committee

185. What is the minimum solvency margin required for insurance companies in India?
(1) 100% (2) 150%
(3) 200% (4) 300%

186. Which regulatory body oversees the pension sector in India?
(1) RBI (2) SEBI
(3) IRDAI (4) PFRDA

187. What is the primary function of PFRDA?
(1) Regulating currency circulation
(2) Regulating mutual funds
(3) Regulating pension funds
(4) Managing insurance companies

188. Who appoints the chairman of PFRDA?
(1) President of India
(2) Prime Minister of India
(3) Ministry of Finance
(4) RBI Governor

189. Which committee recommended the establishment of PFRDA?
(1) Chakravarty Committee
(2) Malhotra Committee
(3) Rangarajan Committee
(4) Narasimham Committee

190. What is the flagship pension scheme launched by PFRDA for unorganised sector workers?
(1) Atal Pension Yojana (APY)
(2) Pradhan Mantri Jeevan Jyoti Bima Yojana (PMJJBY)
(3) Pradhan Mantri Suraksha Bima Yojana (PMSBY)
(4) Employees' Provident Fund (EPF)

Directions: Each of the following items consists of two statements, one labelled as Assertion (A) and other labelled as Reason (R). You are to examine these two statements carefully and decide if the (A) and the (R) are individually true and if so, whether (R) is the correct explanation of (A). Select your answers to these items using the codes given below:
(1) The (A) is true, and the (R) is false.
(2) The (A) is false, and the (R) is false.
(3) The (A) is false, and the (R) is true.
(4) The (A) is true, and the (R) is true.

191. Assertion (A): RBI issues currency notes and coins in India.
Reason (R): RBI is the sole authority for the issue and supply of currency notes.

192. Assertion (A): SEBI regulates insurance companies in India.
Reason (R): SEBI is primarily responsible for regulating and developing the securities market.

193. Assertion (A): IRDAI sets the solvency margin for insurance companies.
Reason (R): Solvency margin is determined by the Ministry of Finance, not IRDAI.

194. Assertion (A): PFRDA regulates the pension sector and oversees the functioning of EPF.
Reason (R): PFRDA focuses on pension funds, and EPF is managed by the Ministry of Labour and Employment.

195. Assertion (A): SEBI has the authority to protect the interests of investors in securities.
Reason (R): Protecting investor interests is one of the primary objectives of SEBI.

196. Which committee recommended the establishment of the National Stock Exchange (NSE) in India?
(1) Narasimham Committee
(2) Rangarajan Committee
(3) Bimal Jalan Committee
(4) Rajan Committee

197. What is the primary objective of the Goods and Services Tax (GST) in India?
(1) Promoting exports
(2) Simplifying taxation
(3) Reducing inflation
(4) Managing fiscal deficit

198. Which regulatory framework aimed at the liberalization of the Indian financial sector?
(1) LPG Reforms
(2) Green Revolution
(3) White Revolution
(4) Black Money Act

199. What is the purpose of the Insolvency and Bankruptcy Code (IBC) in India?
(1) Regulating stock markets
(2) Facilitating financial inclusion

(3) Resolving and liquidating stressed assets
(4) Managing pension funds

200. What is the primary focus of the Financial Stability and Development Council (FSDC)?
(1) Regulating currency circulation
(2) Managing mutual funds
(3) Ensuring financial stability and development
(4) Facilitating short-term loans

201. What is the objective of financial inclusion?
(1) Excluding certain individuals from the financial system
(2) Promoting access to financial services for all segments of society
(3) Restricting the growth of banks
(4) Encouraging speculative trading

202. Which program was launched by the Government of India to promote financial inclusion in rural areas?
(1) Pradhan Mantri Jan Dhan Yojana (PMJDY)
(2) Swachh Bharat Abhiyan
(3) Make in India (4) Skill India

203. What is the primary goal of the Jan Dhan Yojana (PMJDY)?
(1) Providing employment opportunities
(2) Enhancing agricultural productivity
(3) Promoting financial inclusion
(4) Regulating stock markets

204. Which financial product is a part of the Jan Dhan Yojana (PMJDY)?
(1) Mutual funds
(2) Pension plans
(3) Zero-balance bank accounts
(4) Fixed deposits

205. What is the purpose of the Micro Units Development and Refinance Agency (MUDRA) Bank?
(1) Regulating insurance companies
(2) Facilitating short-term loans
(3) Promoting financial inclusion by providing loans to micro-enterprises
(4) Issuing currency notes

206. What is the concept of "Aadhaar-enabled Payment System (AePS)" in India?
(1) Using Aadhaar for obtaining passports
(2) Using Aadhaar for making digital payments
(3) Using Aadhaar for accessing healthcare services
(4) Using Aadhaar for voting in elections

207. Which platform facilitates the transfer of money using a mobile phone, even without having a bank account?
(1) UPI (Unified Payments Interface)
(2) NEFT (National Electronic Funds Transfer)
(3) RTGS (Real Time Gross Settlement)
(4) SWIFT (Society for Worldwide Interbank Financial Telecommunication)

208. What is the role of the Bharat Bill Payment System (BBPS) in digital financial inclusion?
(1) Facilitating international trade
(2) Regulating insurance companies
(3) Providing a one-stop solution for various bill payments
(4) Managing pension funds

209. Which initiative aims to provide financial services to the unbanked and underprivileged through digital means?
(1) Ujjwala Yojana
(2) Pradhan Mantri Jeevan Jyoti Bima Yojana (PMJJBY)
(3) Jan Dhan Yojana (PMJDY)
(4) Bharat Net Project

210. What is the primary goal of the Digital India initiative?
(1) Promoting financial inclusion
(2) Simplifying taxation
(3) Facilitating short-term loans
(4) Enhancing digital infrastructure and literacy

211. What is the purpose of the Financial Literacy Centers (FLCs) in India?
(1) Regulating currency circulation
(2) Providing financial education and counseling
(3) Issuing currency notes
(4) Managing mutual funds

212. Which organisation is responsible for promoting financial literacy in India?
(1) RBI (2) SEBI
(3) IRDAI
(4) National Institute of Financial Management (NIFM)

213. What is the significance of the "Dhan Gyan" initiative?
(1) Promoting financial inclusion
(2) Enhancing digital infrastructure
(3) Providing financial literacy in rural areas
(4) Regulating insurance companies

214. Which scheme focuses on providing financial education to school children in India?
(1) Pradhan Mantri Jan Dhan Yojana (PMJDY)
(2) Ujjwala Yojana
(3) Pradhan Mantri Vaya Vandana Yojana (PMVVY)
(4) National Institute of Financial Management (NIFM)

215. What is the role of the Banking Codes and Standards Board of India (BCSBI) in promoting financial literacy?
(1) Issuing currency notes
(2) Regulating insurance companies
(3) Setting standards for banking practices and promoting financial literacy
(4) Managing mutual funds

Directions: Each of the following items consists of two statements, one labelled as Assertion (A) and other labelled as Reason (R). You are to examine these two statements carefully and decide if the (A) and the (R) are individually true and if so, whether (R) is the correct explanation of (A). Select your answers to these items using the codes given below:
(1) The (A) is true, and the (R) is false.
(2) The (A) is false, and the (R) is false.
(3) The (A) is false, and the (R) is true.
(4) The (A) is true, and the (R) is true.

216. **Assertion (A):** Financial inclusion aims to exclude certain individuals from the financial system.
Reason (R): Financial inclusion focuses on providing access to financial services for all segments of society.

217. **Assertion (A):** Jan Dhan Yojana (PMJDY) offers zero-balance bank accounts to promote financial inclusion.
Reason (R): The Jan Dhan Yojana initiative aims to encourage people to open bank accounts, even with no initial deposit.

218. **Assertion (A):** Digital India initiative focuses solely on promoting digital payments.
Reason (R): Digital India aims to enhance digital infrastructure and literacy across various sectors.

219. **Assertion (A):** UPI (Unified Payments Interface) allows money transfer without a bank account.
Reason (R): UPI is a digital payments system that facilitates fund transfers between bank accounts using a mobile phone.

220. **Assertion (A):** Financial Literacy Centers (FLCs) provide financial counseling and education.
Reason (R): The primary purpose of FLCs is to offer financial education and counseling to individuals.

221. What is Internet banking?
(1) Traditional branch banking
(2) Banking services offered through physical branches
(3) Banking services accessed online
(4) Mobile banking services

222. Which of the following is a common feature of Internet banking?
(1) In-person transactions
(2) Writing physical checks
(3) Online fund transfers
(4) Safe deposit boxes

223. What is the primary advantage of Internet banking for customers?
(1) Limited access to account information
(2) Convenience of 24/7 access
(3) Dependence on physical branches
(4) Restricted transaction options

224. Which security measure is commonly used in Internet banking for user authentication?
(1) Physical tokens
(2) Written signatures
(3) Telephone PINs
(4) Face recognition

225. What is the role of firewalls in Internet banking security?
(1) Facilitating unauthorised access
(2) Blocking legitimate transactions
(3) Preventing unauthorised access and protecting data
(4) Managing physical branches

226. What is Mobile banking?
(1) Banking services accessed online
(2) Banking services offered through physical branches
(3) Banking services accessed via mobile devices
(4) In-person transactions

227. Which of the following is a common feature of Mobile banking?
(1) Physical checkbooks
(2) In-person visits to branches

(3) SMS alerts
(4) Manual record-keeping

228. What is the primary advantage of Mobile banking for customers?
(1) Limited access to account information
(2) Dependence on physical branches
(3) Convenience of banking on the go
(4) Restricted transaction options

229. Which security measure is commonly used in Mobile banking for user authentication?
(1) Physical tokens
(2) Biometric authentication
(3) Written signatures
(4) Fax verification

230. What is the role of encryption in Mobile banking security?
(1) Facilitating unauthorised access
(2) Blocking legitimate transactions
(3) Securing data during transmission
(4) Managing physical branches

231. What is a Digital Payment System?
(1) Traditional barter system
(2) Physical currency transactions
(3) Electronic methods for financial transactions
(4) Written promissory notes

232. Which of the following is a characteristic of Digital Payment Systems?
(1) Cash transactions only
(2) Limited access to banking services
(3) Real-time electronic transactions
(4) In-person visits to branches

233. What is the primary advantage of Digital Payment Systems for users?
(1) Delayed transaction processing
(2) Dependence on physical currency
(3) Convenience and speed of transactions
(4) Restricted transaction options

234. Which type of Digital Payment System involves using a physical card for transactions?
(1) UPI (Unified Payments Interface)
(2) Mobile Wallets
(3) Debit and Credit Cards
(4) NEFT (National Electronic Funds Transfer)

235. What is the role of biometric authentication in Digital Payment Systems?
(1) Securing data during transmission
(2) Preventing unauthorised access to physical branches
(3) Verifying identity using fingerprints or facial recognition
(4) Issuing physical currency notes

236. What is a Mobile Wallet in the context of digital payments?
(1) Physical wallet made of leather
(2) Electronic wallet accessed via mobile devices
(3) Bank statement
(4) In-person wallet transactions

237. Which of the following is a commonly used Mobile Wallet?
(1) UPI (2) Google Pay
(3) NEFT (4) SWIFT

238. What does UPI stand for in the context of digital payments?
(1) Unified Payment Instruction
(2) Uniform Payment Interface
(3) Unified Payments Integration
(4) Unified Payments Interface

239. Which feature is common to both Mobile Wallets and UPI for transactions?
(1) Cash transactions
(2) Physical branch visits
(3) Real-time electronic transactions
(4) Written promissory notes

240. How does UPI simplify digital transactions?
(1) By adding complexity to the process
(2) By requiring physical documentation
(3) By using a single identifier for transactions
(4) By restricting access to banking services

Directions: Each of the following items consists of two statements, one labelled as Assertion (A) and other labelled as Reason (R). You are to examine these two statements carefully and decide if the (A) and the (R) are individually true and if so, whether (R) is the correct explanation of (A). Select your answers to these items using the codes given below:
(1) The (A) is true, and the (R) is false.
(2) The (A) is false, and the (R) is false.
(3) The (A) is false, and the (R) is true.
(4) The (A) is true, and the (R) is true.

241. **Assertion (A):** Internet banking allows customers to access banking services only during business hours.

Reason (R): Internet banking provides 24/7 access to banking services.

242. **Assertion (A):** Mobile banking requires physical visits to bank branches for transactions.
Reason (R): Mobile banking allows users to perform transactions using mobile devices.

243. **Assertion (A):** Biometric authentication is commonly used in both Internet banking and Mobile banking.
Reason (R): Biometric authentication enhances the security of online transactions.

244. **Assertion (A):** Digital Payment Systems involve physical transactions with written promissory notes.
Reason (R): Digital Payment Systems primarily use electronic methods for financial transactions.

245. **Assertion (A):** Both Mobile Wallets and UPI allow real-time electronic transactions.
Reason (R): Mobile Wallets and UPI are digital payment methods that enable instantaneous transactions.

246. What type of insurance provides coverage for a specified period and pays a benefit if the policyholder dies during that period?
(1) Health insurance
(2) Property insurance
(3) Life insurance
(4) Liability insurance

247. Which of the following is an example of Non-life insurance?
(1) Term life insurance
(2) Health insurance
(3) Property insurance
(4) Whole life insurance

248. What does "underwriting" in insurance refer to?
(1) Calculating premiums
(2) Assessing risks and deciding on coverage
(3) Claim settlement process
(4) Marketing insurance products

249. Which type of insurance provides coverage for damage or loss to property, such as homes and cars?
(1) Health insurance
(2) Property insurance
(3) Liability insurance
(4) Travel insurance

250. In insurance, what is "indemnity" related to?
(1) The insured party
(2) The insurance premium
(3) Compensation for losses
(4) Insurance agents

251. What is risk classification in insurance?
(1) Categorizing insurance agents
(2) Assessing the financial health of insurance companies
(3) Categorizing risks to determine appropriate premiums
(4) Calculating insurance profits

252. What is the purpose of risk management in insurance?
(1) Maximising profits for insurance companies
(2) Minimising losses and ensuring financial stability
(3) Setting insurance premiums
(4) Marketing insurance products

253. Which of the following is a risk management technique used by insurance companies?
(1) Risk avoidance
(2) Risk retention
(3) Risk transfer
(4) All of the above

254. What is "moral hazard" in insurance?
(1) A situation where the insured intentionally causes a loss
(2) A situation where the insured is unaware of potential risks
(3) A situation where insurance agents manipulate premiums
(4) A situation where the insured is overcharged for premiums

255. Which risk management technique involves spreading the risk among multiple policyholders?
(1) Risk avoidance (2) Risk retention
(3) Risk transfer (4) Risk reduction

256. What is an example of a factor limiting the insurability of risk?
(1) Existence of multiple risks
(2) Unpredictable events
(3) High premium rates
(4) Low probability of loss

257. Which of the following is a reason for a risk to be considered uninsurable?

(1) Low probability of loss
(2) Lack of financial resources
(3) Existence of multiple risks
(4) Predictable events

258. What is "adverse selection" in insurance?
(1) Insured party intentionally causing a loss
(2) Selection of insurance policies based on the insured party's unfavorable characteristics
(3) Inadequate insurance coverage
(4) Unpredictable events

259. Why might an insurance company refuse coverage for a particular risk?
(1) To Maximise profits
(2) Due to adverse selection
(3) To attract more customers
(4) To comply with regulatory requirements

260. What is a key consideration in determining the insurability of risk?
(1) Existence of multiple risks
(2) Predictable events
(3) Probability of loss
(4) Low premium rates

261. What is re-insurance in the insurance industry?
(1) Insuring the same risk with multiple policies
(2) Transferring risk from the insured to the insurer
(3) Insuring against losses caused by the insured party
(4) Insurance purchased by insurance companies to limit their risks

262. What is the primary purpose of re-insurance?
(1) To increase premiums
(2) To Minimise losses and protect against catastrophic events
(3) To avoid risk transfer
(4) To discourage risk retention

263. Which party is the reinsurer in a re-insurance arrangement?
(1) The primary insurer
(2) The insured party
(3) The regulatory authority
(4) The insurance agent

264. What is "catastrophe reinsurance" used for?
(1) Covering losses caused by intentional acts of the insured party
(2) Covering losses due to unpredictable catastrophic events
(3) Covering routine and predictable losses
(4) Transferring risk to multiple insurers

265. What is the effect of re-insurance on the primary insurer's exposure to risk?
(1) Increases exposure
(2) Decreases exposure
(3) Has no impact on exposure
(4) Shifts exposure to the reinsurer

266. What does IRDA stand for in the context of insurance regulation in India?
(1) Indian Regulatory Development Authority
(2) Insurance Regulatory and Development Authority
(3) Insurance Reinsurance and Development Agency
(4) Indian Risk and Development Authority

267. What is the role of IRDA in the insurance sector?
(1) Setting insurance premiums
(2) Marketing insurance products
(3) Regulating and overseeing insurance companies
(4) Calculating insurance profits

268. Which of the following is a function of IRDA?
(1) Assessing risk for insurance policies
(2) Approving insurance claims
(3) Marketing insurance products
(4) Formulating and enforcing regulations for insurance companies

269. How does IRDA contribute to consumer protection in the insurance sector?
(1) By Maximising insurance company profits
(2) By ensuring fair claim settlements and preventing fraudulent practices
(3) By setting high premium rates
(4) By encouraging adverse selection

270. What is the significance of the regulatory framework provided by IRDA?
(1) Maximising profits for insurance companies
(2) Ensuring a level playing field among insurance companies
(3) Setting insurance premiums
(4) Marketing insurance products

ANSWERS

1. (2)	**2.** (2)	**3.** (2)	**4.** (3)	**5.** (2)	**6.** (3)	**7.** (2)	**8.** (1)	**9.** (2)	**10.** (2)
11. (4)	**12.** (2)	**13.** (2)	**14.** (2)	**15.** (2)	**16.** (2)	**17.** (2)	**18.** (3)	**19.** (1)	**20.** (3)
21. (2)	**22.** (3)	**23.** (1)	**24.** (2)	**25.** (2)	**26.** (4)	**27.** (3)	**28.** (2)	**29.** (3)	**30.** (3)
31. (3)	**32.** (2)	**33.** (3)	**34.** (4)	**35.** (4)	**36.** (3)	**37.** (1)	**38.** (3)	**39.** (2)	**40.** (2)
41. (4)	**42.** (2)	**43.** (2)	**44.** (1)	**45.** (2)	**46.** (2)	**47.** (3)	**48.** (3)	**49.** (3)	**50.** (1)
51. (3)	**52.** (3)	**53.** (3)	**54.** (3)	**55.** (3)	**56.** (2)	**57.** (1)	**58.** (2)	**59.** (3)	**60.** (2)
61. (2)	**62.** (2)	**63.** (3)	**64.** (4)	**65.** (3)	**66.** (3)	**67.** (3)	**68.** (3)	**69.** (3)	**70.** (4)
71. (2)	**72.** (1)	**73.** (3)	**74.** (1)	**75.** (4)	**76.** (1)	**77.** (4)	**78.** (1)	**79.** (2)	**80.** (1)
81. (4)	**82.** (3)	**83.** (3)	**84.** (1)	**85.** (4)	**86.** (3)	**87.** (4)	**88.** (2)	**89.** (1)	**90.** (1)
91. (2)	**92.** (3)	**93.** (3)	**94.** (2)	**95.** (1)	**96.** (3)	**97.** (2)	**98.** (2)	**99.** (3)	**100.** (1)
101. (1)	**102.** (3)	**103.** (3)	**104.** (3)	**105.** (1)	**106.** (2)	**107.** (2)	**108.** (1)	**109.** (2)	**110.** (3)
111. (4)	**112.** (3)	**113.** (4)	**114.** (3)	**115.** (3)	**116.** (3)	**117.** (3)	**118.** (3)	**119.** (2)	**120.** (3)
121. (3)	**122.** (2)	**123.** (3)	**124.** (3)	**125.** (3)	**126.** (3)	**127.** (2)	**128.** (3)	**129.** (2)	**130.** (2)
131. (3)	**132.** (4)	**133.** (1)	**134.** (3)	**135.** (2)	**136.** (2)	**137.** (3)	**138.** (2)	**139.** (3)	**140.** (2)
141. (3)	**142.** (3)	**143.** (3)	**144.** (4)	**145.** (3)	**146.** (2)	**147.** (3)	**148.** (1)	**149.** (3)	**150.** (2)
151. (4)	**152.** (3)	**153.** (4)	**154.** (2)	**155.** (1)	**156.** (3)	**157.** (3)	**158.** (2)	**159.** (1)	**160.** (3)
161. (4)	**162.** (3)	**163.** (3)	**164.** (3)	**165.** (4)	**166.** (3)	**167.** (3)	**168.** (4)	**169.** (3)	**170.** (3)
171. (2)	**172.** (3)	**173.** (3)	**174.** (4)	**175.** (3)	**176.** (2)	**177.** (3)	**178.** (2)	**179.** (3)	**180.** (4)
181. (3)	**182.** (3)	**183.** (3)	**184.** (2)	**185.** (2)	**186.** (4)	**187.** (3)	**188.** (3)	**189.** (3)	**190.** (1)
191. (3)	**192.** (3)	**193.** (1)	**194.** (3)	**195.** (4)	**196.** (1)	**197.** (2)	**198.** (1)	**199.** (3)	**200.** (3)
201. (2)	**202.** (1)	**203.** (3)	**204.** (3)	**205.** (3)	**206.** (2)	**207.** (1)	**208.** (3)	**209.** (3)	**210.** (4)
211. (2)	**212.** (1)	**213.** (3)	**214.** (1)	**215.** (3)	**216.** (3)	**217.** (4)	**218.** (3)	**219.** (3)	**220.** (4)
221. (3)	**222.** (3)	**223.** (2)	**224.** (1)	**225.** (3)	**226.** (3)	**227.** (3)	**228.** (3)	**229.** (2)	**230.** (3)
231. (3)	**232.** (3)	**233.** (3)	**234.** (3)	**235.** (3)	**236.** (2)	**237.** (2)	**238.** (4)	**239.** (3)	**240.** (3)
241. (3)	**242.** (3)	**243.** (4)	**244.** (3)	**245.** (4)	**246.** (3)	**247.** (3)	**248.** (2)	**249.** (2)	**250.** (3)
251. (3)	**252.** (2)	**253.** (4)	**254.** (1)	**255.** (3)	**256.** (2)	**257.** (2)	**258.** (2)	**259.** (2)	**260.** (3)
261. (4)	**262.** (2)	**263.** (1)	**264.** (2)	**265.** (2)	**266.** (2)	**267.** (3)	**268.** (4)	**269.** (2)	**270.** (2)

UNIT 8

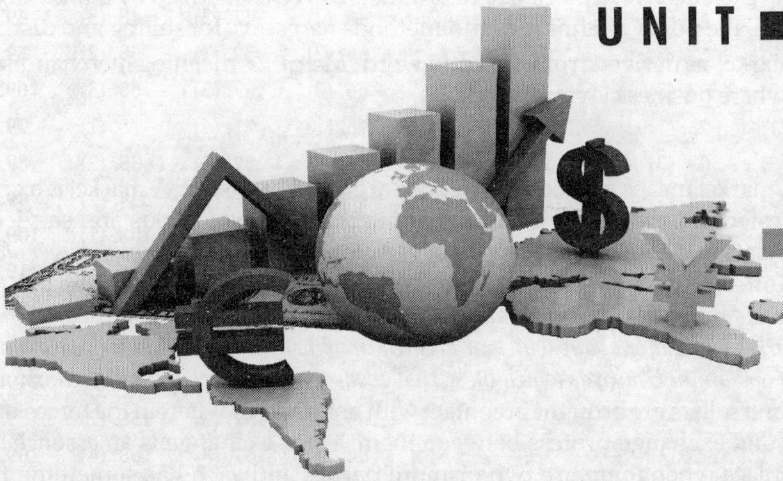

MARKETING MANAGEMENT

SYLLABUS

- Marketing: Concept and approaches; Marketing channels; Marketing mix; Strategic marketing planning; Market segmentation, targeting and positioning
- Product decisions: Concept; Product line; Product mix decisions; Product life cycle; New product development
- Pricing decisions: Factors affecting price determination; Pricing policies and strategies
- Promotion decisions: Role of promotion in marketing; Promotion methods - Advertising; Personal selling; Publicity; Sales promotion tools and techniques; Promotion mix
- Distribution decisions: Channels of distribution; Channel management
- Consumer Behaviour; Consumer buying process; factors influencing consumer buying decisions
- Service marketing
- Trends in marketing: Social marketing; Online marketing; Green marketing; Direct marketing; Rural marketing; CRM
- Logistics management

MARKETING

THE EVOLUTION OF MARKETING

Marketing has its origin in the fact that man is a creature of needs and wants. Needs and wants create a sense of discomfort in persons and they tend to get objects (*i.e.* products) those satisfy these needs and wants. The word marketing has been derived from market which may be looked upon as an arena for potential exchange, *i.e.* a place where products can be exchanged by money or anything else. Marketing includes the policy, techniques and methods necessary for selling and distribution.

The word 'Market' is derived from the Latin word '*Marcatus*' meaning merchandise ware traffic, trade or a place where business is conducted.

Concepts

To a layman, market means a place where goods are brought or sold. A market is a group of buyers and sellers interested in negotiating the terms of purchase/sale of goods and services. **American Marketing Association** defines *'market as the aggregate demand of the potential buyers for a product or service.'* **Philip Kotler** defines market *'as an area for potential exchanges'*. According to **Pyle** *'Marketing includes both place and region in which buyers and sellers are in free competition with one another'*. **Clark** and **Clark** state, *a market is a center about which or an area in which the forces leading to exchange of title to a particular product operate and towards which the actual goods tend to travel*. Broadly, market is any region in which buyers and sellers are brought in contact with one another wherein the forces of demand and supply facilitate and exchange profess between them. Thus, exchange is an essence of marketing. Exchange takes place when there are two or more parties and each has something they desire to exchange for something else. Therefore, a market consists of a group of person or persons on one side having the goods they want to sell and on the other a group of prospective buyers who want to pay for and buy. It means that three points are interlinked namely, place, area and demand.

1. **Place.** A market is a convenient meeting place for buyers and sellers to gather together to effect the exchange of goods and services.
2. **Area.** A market develops in any area, where, there are:
   (i) Two or more individuals having unsatisfied wants,
   (ii) They have product(s) to exchange and
   (iii) They have some means of communication such as phone, teller, correspondence *etc.* With the means of communication, the forces of demand and supply freely operate and the informed buyers and sellers can strike the dealing without formal face to face meeting.
3. **Demand.** A market consists of people with needs to satisfy money to spend and the will to spend money to satisfy their wants.

The process of exchange represents the market where buyers (demand) and sellers (supply) exchange the product against money/other products. The means of communication assists the free flow of demand and supply which determines the price. Usually money acts as the medium of exchange. The act of exchange leads to transfer of ownership and possession from a seller to a buyer in the market. Feedback information indicates buyer's post purchase behaviour. If satisfied, buyer makes repeated purchases otherwise he switches to other brands.

Concepts of Marketing

A. Old Concept

This concept of marketing was popular when business was done on small scale and there was little or no competition. According to this concept, marketing consists of merely buying and selling activities that effect the transfer of ownership of goods and services.

According to **Clark** and **Clark** – *Marketing consists of those efforts which effect transfer in the ownership of goods and services and which provide for physical distribution*

According to American. Marketing Association – *'Marketing is the performance of business activities that direct the flow of goods and services from producer to consumer or user.*

Characteristics of Old Concept of Marketing

1. It consists of only production, purchases and sales activities.
2. It is product oriented, *i.e.*, it focuses attention only on product to be sold ignoring, consumer's interest and tastes.
3. Its activities come to an end on sale, *i.e.*, it does not provide after sale services.
4. It does not give importance to consumer satisfaction.
5. It aims at earning maximum profits.

Criticism

1. It focuses only on production, purchases and sale activities and ignores other activities of marketing. 2. It ignores consumer research. 3. It is a product oriented concept. 4. It ignores after-sale activities. 5. Consumer satisfaction and social responsibility has no place in this concept. 6. It fails to point out close inter-relationship between product (supply) and market (demand).

B. New Concept

New concept of marketing is a broader concept which considers marketing as a continuous process of discovering and converting consumer wants into appropriate products and services by developing a product on the basis of marketing research, creating demand for these products through promotion and serving the demand through transport and storage with the help of channels of distribution such as wholesalers and retailers.

Marketing concept states that consumers want satisfaction is the economic and social justification of a firm's existence. Therefore, all the firm's activities in the areas of production, engineering, finance as well as marketing must be directed primarily to determine what the consumer's wants are and then satisfy these wants, though making a reasonable profits.

The new concept is **consumer oriented**. It considers consumer as the '*King*' around which all business activities rotate. The concept is also founded on **consumer satisfaction**.

The concept says all business activities are integrated, i.e., marketing management cannot be an independent function. The management's functional areas are interdependent and not independent. The marketing function influences production, finance, personnel and in turn is influenced by these functions. This modern concept allows earning **reasonable profits through consumer satisfaction**.

According to **William Stanton**, *'Marketing is a total system of interacting business activities designed to plan, price, promote and distribute want satisfying products and services to present and potential customers'.*

According to **Council of Institute of Marketing**, *'Marketing is the management function which organizes and directs all those activities involved in assessing and converting customer purchasing power into effective demand for a specific product or service and in moving the product or service to the final consumer or use so as to achieve the profit target or other objectives set by a company'.*

According to **Cundiff**, **Still** and **Govani**, *'Marketing is the managerial process by which products are matched with markets and through which transfers of ownership are affected'.*

Characteristics of New Concept of Marketing

1. It recognizes the consumer's supremacy as it is consumer oriented. Creation of satisfied customers is the main aim of marketing.

2. Modern marketing begins with consumers and it ends also with the consumers. Marketing research is starting point of marketing in-order to secure adequate information of current consumer needs. Offer of complete service and satisfaction including post-purchase satisfaction is the ending step of marketing.
3. Modern marketing begins before production as well as it succeeds production. Discovery of consumer needs and desires takes place before production with the help of marketing research. Product planning and development is undertaken before actual production. These are important marketing functions. Other marketing functions such as pricing, promotion, distribution, succeed production.
4. Modern marketing adopts the systematic approach to marketing. Such an approach provides a good basis for orderly and integrated analysis and planning of all business activities relating to product, pricing, promotion and distribution.
5. It aims at earning profit only by satisfying consumers.
6. It provides after sale services such as home delivery, guarantee *etc.*

This concept can be illustrated as under:

Consumer Research → Purchase → Production → Storage

Transport → Pricing → Promotion →Selling → After Sale Services

Merchandising, Selling and Marketing

Merchandising is only product planning. It aims at the internal planning relation to products or services for marketing at the right time, right price and in proper colour, qualities and sizes. Thus it is only a part of marketing study.

Selling is pre-occupied with the seller's need to convert his product into cash. It focuses on the needs of the seller. It seeks profits by '**pushing**' the products on the buyers.

Selling is certainly a part of marketing. To quote **Levitt**, '*the difference between selling and marketing is more than semantic*'.

Various Views Regarding Marketing Concept

(a) **Distribution of Goods and Services Concept.** According to this concept, marketing includes only those activities that assist in distribution of goods and services from the producer to the final consumer.

According to **Tousley**, **Clark** and **Clark**, '*Marketing consists of those efforts which effect transfers in the ownership of goods and services and which provide for physical (distribution)*'.

According to **American Marketing Association**, '*Marketing is the performance of business activities that direct the flow of goods and services from producer to consumer or users.*'

This concept has lost its significance in today's changed scenario. It is an indication of old concept and as such includes only three activities in marketing i.e., purchase, production and selling. Therefore, this concept is also criticized on some issues as the old concept.

(b) **Creation of Utilities Concept.** According to this concept, marketing is an activity concerned with generating utilities. According to Economists, marketing is a system which creates value in products by generating utilities in them. These utilities, according to **Converse, Huegy** and **Mitchell** are of three types – place, time and possession. But **Richard Buskirk** has added form utility also and therefore, according to him, there are four utilities. In fact, all the four utilities are effected by marketing activities. When the product is planned and developed and then this marketing activity creates from utility. When the products are sent to various places for sale through various means, *place utility* is created. Similarly, when the goods are stored by middleman much before its demand, there is creation of *time utility*. The marketing activity relating to advertisement and sales promotion creates *possession utility* where the consumer influenced by such promotion measures comes to purchase the product resulting in change of possession of ownership of product from producer to consumer. According to **Richard Buskirk**, *'Marketing is an integrated system of action that creates value in goods through its creation of form, place, time and ownership utilities'*.

(c) **Delivery of Standard of Living Concept.** According to this concept, marketing is concerned with providing standard of living to the society. It is consumer oriented concept and it emphasizes on satisfying the desires. Therefore, product planning comes under its scope. In order, to provide the desired standard of living, it is necessary to make arrangements for the development of goods desired by society and to include all the features desired by them.

(d) **System Approach Concept.** According to this concept marketing refers to the total process by means of which goods and services are exchanged. It involves all business activities because these activities are mutually inter-related. Today the business environment is faced with mass production, stiff competition and complex channels of distribution, so there is need for proper system or process which will help the producer as well as consumer to overcome all the obstacles in the exchange of goods and services.

According to **Stanton**, *'Marketing system is an interacting set of institutions, activities and flows designed to facilitate exchange transactions between an organization (business or nonbusiness) and its market'*.

Philip Kotler says, *'The exchanges that take place in a society along with the facilitating institutions, make up its marketing system'*.

In fact, the concept is based on new concept of marketing and as such it includes all the activities that start before production and continues even after sales. The first process of marketing process is **assembling** wherein inputs are gathered at a central place either for further processing or for sale. Then the goods are **dispersed** to consumers through wholesalers and retailers at profitable and reasonable price. But before dispersion, **equalisation process** is done to balance demand and supply through storage and transportation.

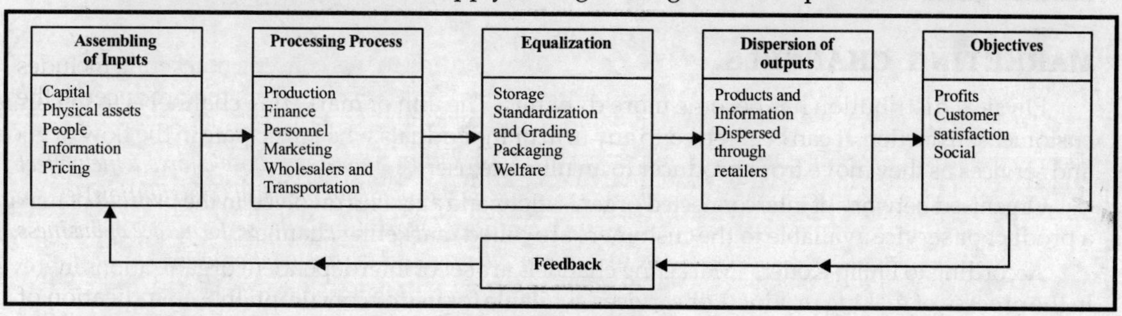

The System Approach

(e) **Societal Marketing Concept.** This concept concentrates on producing goods and services, which are beneficial to the society. It says that firm's task is to determine the needs and desires of consumers and to satisfy them more effectively than the competitors in a way that is beneficial both to the consumer and the society. It aims at balancing profits, consumer satisfaction and public interest. The marketing process is regarded as a means by which society meets its consumption needs. Here, the firm realizes its social responsibilities.

MARKETING APPROACHES

Product Approach. The study relates to the flow of a certain commodity and its movement from the producer to the ultimate customer, comes under this approach. The system claims that it is simple and gives good result over the marketing of each product, but at the same time this approach is time consuming and repetitive process.

Institutional Approach. This approach is also known as middleman approach. In this approach, emphasise is given to understand and analyse the functions of institutions, who are discharging their marketing functions.

Functional Approach. In this approach, marketing splits into many functions like buying, selling, pricing, standardisation, advertising, packing etc. Here, each function is studied in detail in order to understand and analyse the nature, need and importance of each function.

Management Approach. This approach is mainly concerned with, how managers handle specific problems and situations. It aims through evaluation of current market practices to achieve specific marketing objectives.

System Approach. Systems focus on inter-relations and interconnections among the functions of marketing. The system examines marketing connections inside as well as outside the firm.

Societal Approach. This system gives no importance as to how the business meets the consumer's needs. Therefore, attention is paid to ecological factors' like sociological, cultural, legal etc. and marketing decisions and their impact on the society's well being.

Legal Approach. Under this approach, the study is concentrated only on legal aspects, leaving other important aspects. This approach does not benefit in giving any idea of marketing.

Economical Approach. This approach deals with only the problems of supply, demand and price which are important from the economic point of view.

MARKETING MIX

Marketing involves a number of functions in order to achieve its target of consumer satisfaction. These functions are independent in themselves. Their effective coordination is often described as **marketing mix**.

MARKETING CHANNELS

Physical distribution has become more dynamic. The aim of marketing channel is to maximise customer satisfaction. It can be referred to any firm or individuals who participate in the flow of goods and services as they move from producer to an ultimate user.

Organised network of interconnected organisations and agencies involved in the process of making a product or service available to the customers are called marketing channels.

According to Philip Kotler, "Marketing channels are set of interdependent organisations involved in the process of making products or services available for use or consumption."

Types of Marketing Channels

Non-integrated Channel

In this channel, each enterprise is separately owned and operated concern. Manufacturers, wholesalers and retailers bargain with each other, negotiate over terms of sale and otherwise behave autonomously. The other name for non-integrated channel is individualistic or conventional market channel. In this marketing channel, there are following two types of channels:

Direct Channel. When the manufacturer instead of selling the goods to the intermediary, sells it directly to the consumer, then it is known as direct channel or zero level channel. Retail outlets, mail order selling and internet selling are some of its examples.

Following are the main types of indirect channel:

One Level Channel. In this method, an intermediary is used. Here, a manufacturer sells the goods directly to the retailer, instead of selling it to agents or wholesalers. This method is used for expensive products.

Two Level Channel. In this method, a manufacturer sells the material to a wholesaler, the wholesaler to the retailer and then, the retailer to the consumer. This medium is mainly used to sell soap, tea, salt etc.

Three Level Channel. Under this, one more level is added to two level channel in the form of agent. An agent facilitates to reduce the distance between the manufacturer and the wholesaler. Some big companies do not directly contact the wholesaler, they take the help of agents.

Indirect Channel. When the manufacturer gets the help of one or more middlemen to move goods from the production place to the place of consumption, then the distribution channel is called indirect channel.

Integrated Channel

Integrated channels are the networks in which channel components participate in a coordinated manner. Integrated channel is classified into following two types:

Vertical Distribution Channel. These channels are professionally managed and centrally programmed networks, pre-engineered to achieve operating economies and maximum market impact.

Its main types are as follows:

Administered Vertical Channel. In administered vertical channels, one of a limited number of firms use developed programmes to achieve the coordination of marketing activities. A manufacturer controls the marketing of a particular line of merchandise.

Contractual Vertical Channel. Under contractual vertical distribution channel, independent firms are employed on a voluntary basis to develop a more efficient system on a contractual basis, be as to achieve systematic economies and increased market impact.

Corporate Vertical Channel Under corporate vertical distribution channel, channel components are owned and operated by one organisation. The firms own both production and distribution facilities. E.g. Bata, Tata etc.

Horizontal Distribution Channel

A horizontal marketing system is a distribution channel arrangement, whereby two or more organisations at the same level join together for marketing purposes to capitalise on a new dictionary. In other words, horizontal marketing system is the merger of two unrelated companies who have come together to exploit the market opportunities. Generally, this type of marketing system is followed by companies who lack V in capital, human resources, production techniques, marketing programmes and are afraid of incurring the huge losses.

Functions of Marketing Channels

Helps in Production Function The producer can concentrate on the production function leaving the marketing problem to middlemen, who is specialised in the profession.

Promotion. Promoting the products in their territories is another function that middlemen perform. Many of them design their own sales incentive programmes, aimed at building customers traffic at the other outlets.

Information Provider. Middlemen have a role in providing information about the market to the manufacturer. Developments like change in customer demography, psychography, media, habits and the entry of a new competitor etc. are some of the information that all manufacturers want.

Pricing. The middlemen can give suggestions to the producer, regarding paying habits of different users. Pricing may be different for different markets or products depending upon the distribution channel.

Price Stability. Maintaining price stability in the market is the main function of the middlemen. In many situations, the middlemen absorb an increase in the price of the products and try to charge old price from the users. This helps in maintaining price stability.

Financing. Middlemen provide necessary working capital in the form of advance payments for goods and services for financing manufacturer's operation.

Matching Demand and Supply. Intermediaries assemble the goods from many producers, in such a manner that a customer can affect purchases with ease. The goal of marketing is the matching of segments of supply and demand.

Matching the Needs of Buyers and Sellers. Marketing channel members helps to match the needs of buyers and sellers. Normally, most sellers want to reach the potential buyers and in the same way, buyers also want to know about the potential sellers.

Standardisation of Transactions. By standardising transactions, marketing channel automate most of the stages in the flow of products from the manufacturer to the customers.

Consolidation and Distribution. Consumers often prefer to buy a wide variety of consumer goods at one time and place. Retail stores enable consumers to do just that because they stock and display a great number of different products.

The idea of 'mix' of marketing functions was conceived by **Prof. N. H. Border** of Harvard Business School. According to him, '*the marketing mix refers to the apportionment of effort, the combination, the designing and the integration of elements of marketing into a programme or* '**mix**' *which on the basis of an appraisal of the market forces, will best achieve the objectives of an enterprise at a given time*'. **Philip Kotler** states, '*the firm task is to find the best solution for its marketing decision variables, the setting constitutes its marketing mix*'. According to **Mc. Carthy**, '*Marketing is the pack offer sets of variables namely product, price, promotion and place variables*'.

The Marketing mix is made up of four elements namely Product, Price, Promotion and Place that constitute the marketing decisions from marketers view point. However, these can be four C's from the angle of consumers. This can be illustrated as follows:

'Product' for marketer – Consumer's 'needs and wants' for customer.
'Price' for marketer – 'Cost' to the customer.
'Promotion' for marketer – 'Communication' for the customer.
'Place' for marketer – 'Convenience' for the customer.

In brief, marketing mix is the master mix of sub mixes namely, product mix, price mix, promotion mix and place mix. These are the elements of marketing decisions on which the firm has control. Hence, marketing mix signifies internal controllable forces.

Elements of Marketing Mix

(i) **Product.** Quality, Features, Design, Brand, Package, Service.
(ii) **Place.** Transportation, Warehousing storage, Inventory, Wholesaler, Retailer.
(iii) **Price.** Price differentials, Credit terms, Discount, Payment period.
(iv) **Promotion.** Personal Selling, Advertising, Sale Promotion, Public relations.

Forces Affecting Changes in Marketing Mix

The marketing mix is dynamic in nature. It must be changed with time to cope with the demands of the environment. The following are the reasons that require the change in marketing mix:

1. **Consumer's Buying Behaviour.** Consumer's buying behaviour is affected by buying habits, living standard, social environment, technological changes *etc*. The change in any of these factors, changes the buying behaviour of consumer and as such the marketer must make necessary changes in his marketing mix in order to satisfy his customers.

2. **Competitor's Behaviour.** With the entry of new firms, competition intensifies. To face this, the marketer need to make actual or psychological changes in his marketing mix.
3. **Intermediaries' Behaviour.** The behaviour of intermediaries—wholesalers or retailers and their attitudes, practices, commission rate etc. effect the marketing of the products. If at a certain point of time, certain chain of distribution becomes less effective, the marketer must go in for another channel. Thus, it makes a change in his marketing mix.
4. **Governmental Behaviour.** The government frames rules and regulations in respect of products, pricing, competitive practices, advertising etc. Any change in such rules will force the marketer to make necessary changes in his marketing mix.
5. **Product Improvement Policy.** Consumers must be satisfied in a better way through improvements in quality, design, size, *etc.* This requires modification of products, introduction of new products and elimination of unprofitable products. All this brings out change in the existing marketing mix.
6. **Branding Policy.** Brand creates a particular image in the minds of the consumer. Decisions of change in brand considering the objectives and economies make a change in marketing mix. Similar change is affected if the change in packaging is desired.
7. **Physical Distribution Policy.** It includes channels of distribution, transportation, warehousing, inventory control etc. The marketer aims at providing products at the right time and right place. To fulfill this objectives he may need to make the necessary changes.
8. **Pricing Policy.** Price effects the volume of sales. Price alterations maybe made by the marketer in order to attract the buyers. This may be in the form of discount, allowances, credit sales *etc.*
9. **Promotion Policy.** Firms undertake promotion work—advertising, personal selling, sales promotion *etc.* to inform and persuade the customers. Any change in message or technique of promotion brings about change in marketing mix.

The four P's model of marketing mix has gained acceptances because it must be cleared that what is suitable mix for one company may not be suitable for another. Hence each and every situation must be carefully analyzed before allocating the companies resources.

STRATEGIC MARKETING PLAN COMPONENTS AND BENEFITS

Successful businesses create and rely on business plans to help guide them and to clarify priorities. Business plans spell out ways companies intends to rationalize their resources, engage in production, and even handle their clients. Most importantly, sound business plans include strategic marketing plans.

Strategic marketing planning is considered a creative process in its own right. Management and operations teams strive to come up with and implement practical marketing strategies that can guarantee a stable flow of business for a company.

Strategic marketing plans revolve around the kind of environment an entity desires to establish for clients in the quest to make sales. Plans include concepts such as geographical and demographic target markets as well as market segmentation.

Components of a Marketing Plan

The specifics of strategic marketing plans will vary from business to business and industry to industry, but all plans should include five key components:

1. **Company positioning.** Outline the current position of the firm financially. Such an analysis allows the planning team to identify the strategies that were previously put in place and assess the success of the overall plan against the financial results. In the end, a SWOT analysis

reveals the current situation of the company by examining strengths, weaknesses, opportunities, and threats.

2. **Goals and strategies.** The strategic marketing plan is never complete without listing the organizational goals and strategies to be implemented. The goals inform the rationalization of resources in production, distribution, and marketing while the strategies discuss the conversion of targets into realities. For instance, a goal may state the intention to improve brand recognition and image while the corresponding plan defines the most appropriate media or promotion method to achieve desired results.
3. **Market opportunities.** The plan always should assess emerging or existing market opportunities that may be harnessed in the short and long term. By so doing, the planners easily can dedicate resources to the most promising opportunity.
4. **Target market defined.** It is important to define the target groups for all your products and services. This step allows you to conduct more research on their needs, demands, and even preferences to capitalize on sales. Also, define the demographic and geographic stratification of these groups.
5. **Marketing budget.** Last and most importantly, a strategic marketing plan is considered complete due to the inclusion of a realistic marketing budget and the dedication of an implementation period. Tough decisions have to be made at this point. These include the division of duties and responsibilities.

Benefits of Strategic Marketing Planning

The process of creating a plan facilitates a common understanding among all stakeholders in an organization. The plan informs management decisions, the behavior of the employees towards institutional goals, and also the response among current and potential clients. The plan also is subjected to changes over a period of time to meet changing demands.

A sound marketing plan allows a corporate entity to grow its market share which results in more revenue and profits. As a firm expands, it can enjoy large economies of scale and thus fewer operational costs. Overall, the strategic marketing planning process connects the production engine to consumption.

MARKET SEGMENTATION

Market segmentation is a strategy that sub divides the target market into sub-groups of consumer with distinct and homogeneous characteristics so as to have different marketing programme for each sub-group in order to provide satisfaction to consumers and profit to the marketer.

For example, Lakme company concentrates on women segment, whereas Leo Toys concentrates on children segment.

According to **Stanton**, *'Market segmentation consists of taking the total heterogeneous market for a product and dividing it into several sub markets or segments each of which tends to be homogeneous in all significant aspects'*.

According To **Philip Kotler**, *'Market segmentation is the sub dividing of a market into homogeneous sub-sects of customers where any sub-sect may conceivably be selected as a market target to be reached within a distinct marketing mix'*.

According to **Cundiff** and **Still**, *'Market segments are grouping of consumers according to such characteristics as income, age, degree of urbanization, race or ethnic classification, geographic location or education'*.

Objectives of Market Segmentation

The main objective of market segment is to know about the varying buying behaviour of the consumers so that target consumers can be reached easily by framing various marketing programmes based on such differences of the consumers.

'The purpose of market segment is to determine difference among buyers which may be consequential in choosing among them or marketing to them', **Philip Kotler.**

Requirements for an Effective Segmentation

Segmenting the market can be beneficial when these segments are used to make separate marketing programmes for each segment and implementing them. The following factors must be considered so that effective market segment can be created.

1. **Identifiable and Measurable.** The markets must be able to identify the members of the segment, *i.e.*, knowing whether an individual is or is not the member of a segment. The members can be identified on the basis of certain common characteristics like demographic, social, cultural *etc*. Moreover, its size should also be measurable because if the informations are not sufficient to enable to know the size of the segment, the markets cannot be properly segmented.
2. **Accessible.** It must be possible to reach different segments in regard to both promotion and distribution. The firms must be able to make them aware of products or services and they must also make the products available to them through distribution system at a reasonable cost.
3. **Substantiable.** The segment must be large enough to justify a separate marketing programme. This depends not only on the number of actual or potential buyers but also on their purchasing power. A small number of buyers as in case of luxuries with high purchasing value are considered feasible.

Methods of Market Segmentation

1. **Each Buyer A Separate Market.** Under this method, there are as many segments as many there are consumers. It is based on the principle that each consumer is in itself a market because each consumer varies in his tastes and likings. Such classification is possible for the goods whose buyers are limited, *e.g.*, ships, aircrafts. But where the number of buyers is large, it is not possible to treat each buyer a separate market.
2. **Broad Classes of Buyers.** This is more acceptable method of segmentation. Under this buyers with similar characteristics are grouped under one segment and thus, each segment is treated as a separate market, *e.g.*, a marketer may make classification as– men, ladies and children. Thus, a lady belonging to any age, culture or social class will come under the ladies segment. Same rule applies to men and children.

Basis for Market Segmentation

The broadest basis for segmenting market is separating the final consumer from industrial users. Final consumer differ significantly from industrial users and as such separate marketing programmes are required for each of the two segments.

Segmenting the Consumer Market

The consumer market can be segmented on the basis of consumer characteristics like geographic, demographic and psychographics or on the basis of consumer responses such as benefits sought, use occasions and brand loyalties.

I. **Geographic Segmentation.** The market is divided into different geographic areas such as nations, states, regions, cities, or neighbourhoods. The variations in consumption pattern among buyers living in different geographical areas make it necessary to segment the market on this basis. The retailers may distinguish between nearby and distant customer. A local dealer may group as – urban and rural. A regional manufacturer may segment into zones –

North, South, East, West. Whereas, national manufacturer may classify in terms of States, Districts – Cities – Towns etc.

The variations in consumption patterns may be due to:

(a) ***Cultural Heritage.*** The persons with different cultural backgrounds differ in their buying patterns *e.g.*, an Indian because the culture prefers sarees, suits instead of shirts and jeans which are more preferred by a western customer. It is due to culture of Punjab the people over there prefer suit instead of sarees which are more preferred in U.P. Similar differences are found in food, furniture, housing *etc. e.g.*, South Indian prefers rice whereas North Indians prefer chapattis.

(b) ***Urbanization.*** Urbanization is whether buyers live in urban, sub-urban or rural areas. The urban people are well educated with high incomes and have mobility while the rural people are less educated with low incomes and low rate of mobility. The urban population prefers to buy a variety products ranging from kitchenwares to furniture, to cosmetics, to electrical appliances *etc., e.g.*, they now-a-days prefer to buy wrought iron furniture, instead of traditional wooden furniture or cooking range instead of stoves whereas the rural clientele do not easily switch to new products. The demand over there is more of seeds, fertilizers and daily necessities of life.

(c) ***Population Density.*** Due to high population density levels certain products may not have demand at such places, *e.g.*, because of the space problem there may be very less demand for grass cutting machine in metropolitan cities whereas the demand for lifts, excalators may be high ovér there.

(d) ***Climate.*** The climatic differences have great impact over the purchase decisions, *e.g.*, due to the cold climatic conditions of Mussoorie, people over there demand woolen garments, heaters etc. whereas people living in plains like Delhi demand cotton clothes, ACs etc.

II. **Demographic Segmentation.** This is the most purposeful and commonly used base. The consumers are grouped in terms of following similarities:

(a) ***Age.*** The need and desires change with age. For example, a child may need toys, sweets, milk bottles *etc.* while a teenager may demand not only books, clothes, shoes but also cosmetics, cassettes, artificial jewellery etc. The older people may need nutritious food, medicines, religious books etc. Thus, the manufacturer can classify his customers on age basis and concentrate on one or all the age groups. The textile manufacturer may produce clothing of various designs and colours to suit each age group or he may concentrate only on children but he can easily further break them into gaps like 0 – 1 year old, 1 year – 4 years old, 4 years – 10 years old and the like. He can thus, manufacture various garments to suit and satisfy all children groups.

(b) ***Income.*** The income of an individual determines to a great extent the type and quantity of products he buys. A person with low income is more concerned with purchasing necessities like food, clothing, rent etc. With increase in income the purchase pattern starts changing and they buy more of comforts and luxury items. For example, a person with low income may first decide to buy a fan but as his income increases he may buy cooler or even an air conditioner. The availability of products in large, medium and small packs is also to influence buying by all income groups. The decision to sell on credit is also due to the differences in income of consumers.

(c) ***Education.*** The level of individuals education plays an important role in purchase of many goods specially books. Certain books are aimed at school children whereas others at college students and still others at highly educated class *e.g.*, circus and carnivals may be seen by less educated population whereas more educated persons may prefer to go to light music concert or watch shakespeare drama at the theatre.

(d) *Family Life Cycle.* This concept refers to the various stages in the life of an ordinary family.

Consumption patterns are affected to some extent by the marital status of a person. Married people pay more attention to buying goods like furniture, home products, kitchenwares *etc.* whereas bachelors who are more carefree, spendthrift and fashion conscious purchase latest and recreational products like cassettes, fashionable clothes, junk food, foreign tours *etc.* Similarly, family with small kids will be more interested in purchasing labour saving appliances and children products. Whereas older couple with no or adult children will spend on comfort providing products.

(e) *Sex.* Physical differences require variations in the design and styling of certain products like bicycle, scooters, clothing, perfumes *etc.* Purchase decisions are dominated either by men or women *e.g.*, women may make purchases of food, ornaments and household items while men often take decisions regarding furniture, electrical appliances or vehicles.

(f) *Religion.* It also effects the purchase decision, e.g., some religions prohibit the use of meat and liquor whereas others do not put any objection on its use. Thus, religion affects the demand of such products. Another example is regarding the religion book. A Sikh will demand Guru Granth Sahib whereas a Hindu will look for Gita or Ramayana.

(g) *Occupation.* It is an important base for segmentation of products consumed in job related ways e.g., a doctor will demand medical equipments, medicines *etc.* whereas a teacher will demand books, pens *etc.*

III. **Psychographic Segmentation.** It describes the human characteristics of consumer. It segments the market on how people act. Though, it is difficult to measure but they provide a useful basis for segmenting.

(a) *Personality.* It effects the consumption of many goods especially those which are consumed publicly. The differences for product preference is so wide that it is not possible to serve the same product to all the consumers. To judge personality traits of an individual is a difficult task but if the important personality types are recognized, then the management can easily select the most profitable segment or segments. This aspect plays a significant role in products like clothing, furniture, automobiles, cosmetics, cigarettes, liquor *etc.* For example, Digjam usually promotes its clothing as *Suiting For Connoisseur*. Similarly, Raymonds advertisement says **Raymonds** '*The Complete Man*'.

(b) *Life Style.* Goods consumed by consumers express their life style. In other words, interests of people in various goods is influenced by life style. Thus, the consumers can be grouped as **swingers** who seek up-to date goods, **status seekers** who try to buy goods that will reflect a high status and **plain joes** who seek ordinary, simple goods. Marketers are realizing the implications of this aspect and are segmenting their marketers by consumer styles, *e.g.*, televisions in different models, furniture of various styles and design, telephone of various models – cordless and pagers.

(c) *Social Class.* The society is divided into various classes and a consumer belonging to a particular class purchases according to its class features. The society is generally divided into 3 classes – upper, middle and lower. Upper class demands expensive and superior products *e.g.*, antiques, A/Cs, mobile phone, and other luxurious items. Middle class demand for comfortable products, *e.g.*, cooler, scooter etc., whereas lower class demand necessities, are food, clothing and housing. Therefore, many companies design products for specific social classes, incorporating those features that will appeal to the target social class.

IV. **Behavioural Segmentation.** Here, the buyers are divided into groups on the basis of their knowledge, use or response. The behavioural variables are believed to be the best starting point for segmenting the market.

(a) ***Occasions.*** Buyers need for a product, change according to the occasion for which he is buying, e.g., ordinarily, a buyer may purchase cotton clothes but to attend a special occasion, say, a marriage, he may like to purchase silk clothing. Similarly for daily consumption ordinary plain biscuits can be used but for special occasions cream milky biscuits with some toppings may be preferred. Thus, the marketers look for the major occasions and study the consumer needs for that occasion and make sure that the product meets that need. The occasions include marriage, birthday, acquisition of home, job promotions, illness, death of a family members etc.

(b) ***Benefits.*** When consumers buy a particular product they have their expectation. Such expectations differ for product to product and from consumer to consumer. These benefits can be durability, economy, efficiency, prestige *etc.*, *e.g.*, a shampoo market may have 4 benefits – cleanliness, economy, protection (protein, enriched and anti dandruff) and cosmetic (long silky hairs) benefits. Each segment favours certain brand. The company can study these features and decide to which segment they want to comply and know the characteristics of that segment and the major existing competitive brands. The company can also search for a new benefit and launch a brand that delivers it. Benefit segmentation usually implies that a company should focus on satisfying one benefit group.

Colgate and Palmolive promotes its Colgate toothpaste as offering 3 benefits – **cavity protection, better breath** and **whiter teeth**.

(c) ***User Status.*** The users can be distinguished as non-users, ex-users, potential-users, first time-users and regular users of the product. Companies concentrate on regular users and aim at converting potential users into regular users and they also try to attract users of competitive brands. Even the non-users should not be ignored because through extensive information, their resistance to use the product can be removed.

(d) ***Usage Rate.*** Markets can be segmented into light, medium and heavy user groups of the product. Though the heavy users are small in number but they show a high percentage of total consumption. Therefore, company likes to attract heavy users.

(e) ***Loyalty Status.*** The consumers create brand preference according to their likings and thus rate the competitive brands. Sometimes they become so addicted to a particular brand that they do not want to buy any other brand. Thus we may classify the consumers **as most loyal, moderately loyal and switchers. Most loyal** are the ones who in no case will buy any other brand as they have developed loyalty towards one specific brand. They are not ready to purchase any substitute. For example, a person using Kissan sauce will always use this brand only. **Moderately loyal** are the ones who do not stick to one particular brand rather they can easily choose between 2 or 3 brands. For example, a consumer may either buy Kissan sauce or Maggi sauce or Noga sauce. Switchers are the ones who are not loyal to any brand. They rather, purchase the brands which are conveniently available and are low priced. Such consumers do not decide in advance the brand to be purchased rather they decide on the spot what to purchase. They neither have a specific choice nor a range of choice.

However, it is very difficult to measure loyality correctly as it depends on the availability of competing products.

(f) ***Attitude.*** People's reaction for the product is an important factor in deciding what types of people are and what are their attitudes towards the product. People's attitude can be enthusiastic, positive, indifferent, negative and hostile. The firms thank enthusiastic consumers, pay peculiar attention to consumers having positive attitude, try to win indifferent consumers, aim at changing the attitudes of negative and hostile consumers.

The marketer can thus, segment the market in many ways and choose the most profitable segment to deal with. The choice of the segment helps in making decisions regarding product, price, promotion and place.

Segmenting the Industrial Market Demographic Variables

(a) **Industry** – Which industries that buy the product should be focused.
(b) **Company size** – What size of the company is to be focused.
(c) **Location** – What geographical area should be focused.

Operating Variables

(a) **User/non user Status** – the focus should be on heavy, medium, light users or non users.
(b) **Customer Capabilities** – the focus should be on industry producing many customer services or few services.

Purchasing Variables

(a) **Purchasing Function Organization** – the focus should be on companies with centralized or decentralized purchasing organization.
(b) **General Purchase Policies** – the focus should be on companies that prefer leasing, service contracts, sealed bidding.
(c) **Purchasing Criteria** – the focus should be on companies that are seeking quality, service, price.

Situational Variables

(a) **Urgency** – the focus should be on companies that need quick delivery.
(b) **Size of Order** – should the focus be on large or small orders.

Personal Variables

(a) **Buyer – Seller Similarity** – the focus should be on company size whose attitude and values are similar to own.
(b) **Risk Bearing** – the focus should be on companies taking risk or avoiding risk.
(c) **Loyality** – the focus should be on companies that are more loyal to their suppliers.

In general, industrial companies do not focus on one segment variable but apply multi attribute segmentation.

Segmentation and Marketing Strategy

As no two consumers are identical, therefore, a marketer can adopt different marketing strategies. Such difference is based on market segment. He can adopt any of the following three strategies:

1. **Undifferentiated Marketing Strategy.** This strategy ignores the varying demands and puts forward one single product for the whole market. It focuses on common needs of the people and thus designs a product that satisfies the maximum number of buyers. Such a strategy needs a single marketing programme. It relies on mass production, mass distribution and mass advertising. It portrays a superior image of the product and tries to protect itself from competition. The best example can be of Coco Cola, which for many years produced a single flavour, packed in one bottle size for all consumers. Similarly. Cigarettes, regardless of brands, were of same size wrapped in white paper and packed in a same soft container with aluminium foil.

This strategy offers cost economies in the areas of production, inventory, administration, selling and distribution and research and development. Such economies are due to narrow product line and large scale production. Inspite of this, the strategy, raises doubts. As all the firms offer single product market programme for the entire market, competition becomes intense resulting in reduced profit.

2. **Differentiated Marketing Strategy.** This strategy considers the varying needs and, therefore, designs various products. The firm may operate in several or all segments of the market. Under this strategy the firm develops different marketing programmes for each segment. Thus, it multiplies its sales by providing increased consumer satisfaction. It also hopes at greater brand loyalty and repeat sales because it is able to position its product according to the customers desire. Now a days most of the firms have adopted this strategy. In India, Hindustan Uni Lever Ltd., Godrej Ltd., Nestle and many other companies have used this strategy effectively. Even Coca Cola company now produces drink of varying flavour like orange (Fanta), lemon (sprite), strong cola flavour (Thums up) and packs in bottles of different sizes and cans.

   This strategy, no doubt increases production cost, product modification costs, administration costs, inventory costs, promotion cost, research and development costs, but at the same time it is a sales oriented strategy.

3. **Concentrated Strategy.** This strategy instead of focusing on total market, considers only one particular part of market. It instead of going for a smaller share in whole market, looks for larger share in one or few sub markets. This alternative becomes necessary when the firm's resources are limited, *e.g.*, Johnson & Johnson Ltd. concentrates only on baby products. Similarly, Digjam Company manufactures only men's clothing.

The strategy makes the organization specialized in the needs of the selected segment which results in better positioning of the product. Due to specialization, the firm can enjoy production, distribution and promotion economies. But, it also hinders the growth of the firm because the firm gets tied up to one segment only. This also puts the firm to more risk because if that segment stops purchasing or a competitor enters the same segment its market share will be greatly effected. Moreover, the firm may neglect other segments that are otherwise profitable.

Selection of a Marketing Strategy

1. **Financial Resources.** The financial resources of the company plays an important role in choosing the strategy. If its financial resources are ample, it may either adopt differentiated or undifferentiated strategy. On the other hand, if financial resources are limited, it is forced to go in for concentrated marketing.
2. **Product Homogeneity.** If the product manufactured by various producers it do not differ such as salt, gasoline, steel, etc. then undifferentiated marketing strategy is more appropriate. But if variations are possible, e.g., clothing, T.V., watches, etc. then differentiated or concentrated marketing strategy is more suited.
3. **Product Life Cycle Stage.** When the firm introduces a new product the firm's aim is to develop primary demand. The company at this stage brings out one or few products only, therefore, undifferentiated marketing strategy seems to be more suitable. It may also decide to concentrate on one segment and thus follow the concentrated marketing strategy. In the mature stage it may pursue with differentiated strategy and offer various versions of the product which will help to maintain or increase the sales level.
4. **Customers Homogeneity.** If the buyers have same tastes, desires, needs and are alike in other characteristics, a strategy of undifferentiated marketing is appropriate. On the other hand, if

the market is heterogeneous, either concentrated or differentiated marketing strategy will work.

5. **Government Policy.** The government frames various policies from time to time to protect the interests of the masses. For instance, the government follows public distribution system in order to make available the necessities at reasonable prices. In such cases, the marketer has to accept the guidelines issued by government.

Thus, we see that marketer cannot rely on any particular strategy because marketing is dynamic and with the change in circumstances, the strategy has to be changed.

Benefits of Market Segmentation

1. **To Know the Marketing Opportunities.** Market segmentation helps the marketer to know the marketing opportunities well in time. It helps him to stand at a position where he can understand the needs of each segment against the products offered by competitors and thus position his product in a better way and satisfy the consumers. Segments with low level of satisfaction from current offerings may represent excellent marketing opportunities.
2. **To Prepare Effective Marketing Programme.** In the absence of segmentation, a single marketing programme will be framed which may not be effective for all consumer groups. But because of segmentation the seller can create separate marketing programs to market the need of different buyers. He can make better adjustments of his products and marketing appeals.
3. **Helpful in Competition.** Market segmentation helps to know the level of competition in each segment. If the competitor has strong hold on one segment, there is no use in wasting resources on such segment. However, where competitor's product fail to satisfy the target group, the management can penetrate in it.
4. **Best Allocation of Resources.** The different marketing response of the various market segments helps in allocating the limited resources of the concern. A low marketing budget will be allocated to the segment where marketing opportunities are less and thus wasteful expenditure of the resources will be prevented.
5. **Knowledge of Customer's Satisfaction.** All marketing activities are directed towards the satisfaction of consumer. Market segmentation helps to know the needs and preferences of each segment so as to make the adjustment in the product and the marketing programme accordingly. With the help of segmentation it becomes much easy to measure the level of satisfaction in each segment and also to make improvements in the satisfaction level.

TARGETING

Once the marketer creates different segments within the market, he then devises various marketing strategies and promotional schemes according to the tastes of the individuals of particular segment. This process is called targeting. Once market segments are created, organization then targets them.

Targeting is the second stage and is done once the markets have been segmented.

Organizations with the help of various marketing plans and schemes target their products amongst the various segments.

Nokia offers handsets for almost all the segments. They understand their target audience well and each of their handsets fulfils the needs and expectations of the target market.

Tata Motors launched Tata Nano especially for the lower income group.

Positioning

Positioning is the last stage in the Segmentation Targeting Positioning Cycle.

Once the organization decides on its target market, it strives hard to create an image of its product in the minds of the consumers. The marketers create a first impression of the product in the minds of consumers through positioning.

Positioning helps organizations to create a perception of the products in the minds of target audience.

Ray Ban and Police Sunglasses cater to the premium segment while Vintage or Fastrack sunglasses target the middle income group. Ray Ban sunglasses have no takers amongst the lower income group.

Garnier offers wide range of merchandise for both men and women.

Each of their brands has been targeted well amongst the specific market segments. (Men, women, teenagers as well as older generation)

Men - Sunscreen lotions, Deodorant

Women - Daily skin care products, hair care products

Teenagers - Hair colour products, Garnier Light (Fairness cream)

Older Generation - Cream to fight signs of ageing, wrinkles

A female would never purchase a sunscreen lotion meant for men and vice a versa. That's brand positioning.

PRODUCT DECISIONS

PRODUCT

Alderson defines – '*A product is bundle of utilities consisting of various product features and accompanying services.*'

According to Philip Kotler – '*A product is anything that can be offered to a market for attention, acquisition, use or consumption that might satisfy a want or need it includes physical objects, services, persons, places; organization and ideas*'.

According to Stanton – '*A product is a set of tangible and intangible attributes including packaging, colour, price, manufacturer's prestige, retailer's prestige and manufacturer's and retailer's services which the buyer may accept as offering satisfaction or wants or needs.*'

Explicit Characteristics of Products

According to Prof. *Sturdivant* and his associates explicit characteristics of products are:

(a) **Physical Appearance.** Product is viewed as bundle of physical attributes made up of glass, wood, metal *etc.* having a particular shape, size, colour, design, weight, length, taste, fragrance etc.

(b) **Associated Services.** It is generally understood that the seller will offer certain before and after sale services on the purchase of product. Before actual purchase, the seller offers services like credit facilities, display etc. and after the purchase delivery, installation, free repairs, guarantee etc. are given.

(c) **Package and Brand Name.** Package is part of product as it is sometimes difficult to separate the contents from its package *e.g.*, face wash, perfume, antiseptic cream *etc.* Similarly brand is intrinsic to product. The brand gives identification to the product even without naming the product, *e.g.*, 'Dalda' automatically stands for the product 'ghee' even though the word ghee is not used. Similarly 'Maruti' for cars, 'Air-tel' for mobile phone services, 'Bata' for shoes.

(d) **Product Mix.** It is the entire range of products of a company for sale. It need not consist of related products. Thus, a given product is the part of a set of products offered for sale by the seller.

(e) **Product Life Cycle.** The PLC consists of 4 stages – Introduction, growth, maturity and decline. Each product is at some stage of its existence. The various stages have different implications for the producer and the consumer.

Implicit Characteristics of Products

According to Prof. *Sturdivant*, implicit characteristics of products are:

(a) **Product Symbolism.** Every product symbolizes certain size, colour, shape, design, texture etc. It communicates certain level of performances – like durability, speed, breaking strength, resistances to water, light, heat *etc.*, economy, status *etc.*

(b) **Communication Media.** The Product gives information regarding its contents, usefulness, availability and the like.

(c) **Product Perception.** The consumer has certain perceptions about the product regarding its quality, usefulness, price etc. When he purchases the product, he compares it with his perceptions. Therefore, the seller must try to find what consumers think of a certain product so that he can come out with a product according to their expectations.

(d) **Product Evaluation.** The consumer evaluates the functional psychological benefits of products mainly with regard to its price. Such evaluation differs from person to person and time to time in case of same individuals.

Kind of Products

1. **Durable Goods.** Durable goods are tangible goods that have long life. They can be used again and again. *e.g.*, T.V., furniture, computer, vacuum cleaner *etc.* They are generally highly priced and require guarantee services. Personal selling method of promotion is more suitable for selling such products.
2. **Non – Durable Goods.** Non-durable goods are tangible goods that have a short life. They usually get consumed in one or few uses, *e.g.*, eatables, soap, *etc.* Such goods are lowly priced and frequently purchased, therefore, advertising is the best way to promote them.
3. **Services.** Services are intangible benefits that meet the needs of the buyer. They are inseparable from the provider. They cannot be stored and as such are perishable in nature. Its sale is depended on quality as well as the goodwill of the provider *e.g.*, services of chartered accountant, services of hotel, services of insurance company *etc.*
4. **Consumer Goods.** Consumer goods are the goods which can be directly used by the final user without further processing *e.g.*, Telephone, shampoo, biscuits *etc.* They are meant for personal use.

   Prof. Melvin T. Copeland of Harvard Business School classified consumer goods on the basis of buying habits into three classes – **convenience, shopping** and **speciality**. This is the traditional product classification and it is the most widely used classification.

   (a) **Convenience Goods.** Such goods are purchased from convenient places frequently in small quantities without making much comparisons regarding their price and quality *e.g.*, toothpaste, soap, eatables magazines *etc.* These are non-durables. Buyers purchase them generally on the basis of brand preferences but sometimes trial purchases of alternative brands may be made after perceiving the advertisement.

   (b) **Shopping Goods.** Such goods are purchased after making careful comparisons regarding quality, prices and style at various shops. These goods get used up slowly and therefore, they are infrequently purchased. The comparisons regarding price are more dominant in case of homogeneous shopping goods whereas, in case of heterogeneous shopping goods, quality is more emphasized *e.g.*, clothing, shoes, kitchen appliances, jewelleries.

   (c) **Specialty Goods.** Such goods have certain unique feature because of which the consumers are ready to put in special purchasing efforts. They are generally highly priced and branded. The consumers do not compare the desired speciality good with others, *e.g.*, to purchase Ray Ban sun glasses, the consumer will be ready to search the shop where it is available and go there even if it is far off. The other example are – Titan watches, Videocon washing machine, Santro car *etc.*

5. **Industrial Goods.** Industrial goods are the goods which are used for further production of goods and services *e.g.*, machinery, raw materials, component parts *etc.* These are used as input in producing other products. Its buyers are limited in number but their purchasing power is high. Such products are usually of technical nature.
   (a) ***Installations.*** These are immovable capital items involving high investment. These are purchased only after the approval by top management and on detailed analysis of the product *e.g.*, building, plants, computers and other fixed equipments. Such goods get depreciated on use. Personal selling is more suitable for such products.
   (b) ***Neccessory Equipments.*** These consist of movable factory equipments, which help in production process, *e.g.*, lift trucks, hand tools, drills etc. or office equipments like desks, typewriters, *etc.* They do not become part of finished product. They are inexpensive and have short life. Buying procedure of such goods is of routine nature.
   (c) ***Raw Material.*** These are the basic products that become the part of finished product. They are either farm products, *e.g.*, wheat, sugar cane, cotton, fish or natural products like crude oil, iron ore, petroleum etc. If the cost of raw material to the total cost of production is small the buying process is of routine basis but if raw material's cost forms a considerable part of total production cost, the purchase decisions are taken by top executives.
   (d) ***Fabricating Parts.*** These are manufactured goods that, without any substantial change in form, are incorporated into the finished goods, *e.g.*, tyres, tubes, bulks, batteries etc. but certain component materials like iron, cement etc. require further processing. Such goods are generally purchased on contract basis after making careful analysis of the seller regarding to his reliability with regard to time, prices and service.
   (e) ***Supplies.*** It includes the items which are necessary to run the business but they do not become part of the final product. They are of two kinds – factory supplies such as grease, paints, nails, coal, oil and office supplies like papers, pens, pencils, inks, carbons, tags *etc.* They are in-expensive. Routine purchase procedure through intermediates is followed without much interference of top executives.

READ & DIGEST

A. Major Characteristics of Consumer Goods

Convenience Goods	Shopping Goods	Speciality Goods
1. Frequently purchased.	1. Purchases can be postponed.	1. Infrequently purchased.
2. Low priced	2. Highly priced.	2. Available at speciality shop.
3. Purchased in small quantities	3. Available at certain shops only.	3. Special purchase effort required.
4. Available at nearest convenient places.	4. Comparison on the basis of quality, style, price etc. required.	4. Costly luxury goods.
5. Minimum time and comparison efforts required.	5. Purchased from central market.	5. Durable.
6. High replacement rate.	6. Durable.	
7. Perishable.		

B. Comparison between Convenience Goods, Shopping Goods and Speciality Goods

Convenience Goods	Shopping Goods	Speciality Goods
1. Available at numerous outlets.	1. Available at limited . outlets.	1. Available at exclusive outlets.
2. Wide distribution.	2. Selective distribution.	2. Exclusive distribution.
3. Sale through wholesaler and retailer.	3. Direct sale to retailer.	3. Direct sale to retailer.
4. High sales turnover.	4. Medium sales turnover.	4. Low sales turnover.
5. Advertising as main tool of promotion	5. Personal selling and sales promotion techniques as main tool of promotion.	5. Personal selling as main tool of promotion.
6. Lowly priced.	6. Medium priced.	6. Highly priced.

(f) ***Services.*** This includes the services of various specialists that are required in business such as services of engineers, chartered accountants, financial consultants, etc. It also includes maintenance and repair services. Services are intangible, expensive and, therefore, they are usually undertaken on contract basis.

READ & DIGEST

Difference between Consumer Products and Industrial Products

Consumer Products	Industrial Products
1. **Nature of Customers:**	
Customers of consumer product are final users.	Customers of industrial products are Industrialists or producers.
2. **Number of Customers:**	
Customers of consumer products are large in number.	Customers of industrial products are in limited number.
3. **Nature of Demand:**	
Demand for consumer products is direct demand, *i.e.,* it is Autonomous Demand.	Demand for industrial products is indirect demand *i.e.,* it is Derived Demand.
4. **Product Analysis:**	
Buyers of consumer products are not aware of the merits and demerits of the product.	Buyers of industrial products are well versed. They go with the merits and demerits of the product.
They do not make detailed analysis of the product before buying.	They make detailed analysis of the product before buying.
5. **Expansion of Market:**	
The market of consumer product is wide.	Market of industrial products is not very wide
6. **Marketing Strategies:**	
Emphasis is laid on advertising for selling consumer products.	Emphasis is laid on personal selling for increasing the sale of industrial products.

PRODUCT PLANNING

According to **Stanton**, '*Product planning embraces all activities which enable producer and middlemen to determine what should constitute a company's line of products*'.

According to **Johnson**, '*Product planning determines the characteristics of product, best meeting the consumer's numerous desires, characteristics that add saleability to products and incorporates these characteristics into the finished products*'.

According to **Mason** and **Rath**, '*The planning, direction and control of all stages in the life of a product from the time of its creation to the time of its removal from the company's line of product is known as product planning*'.

According to professor **Dale Littler**, '*Product planning involves devising procedures to evaluate the performance of products and planning the modification, 'where necessary of existing products aimed at extending their lives, the deletion of those products which have reached the terminal stage of their lives, and the development and marketing of new products*'.

Thus, product planning is concerned with determining which products will be produced and marketed by the company, which products need modifications and which ones should be eliminated.

Elements of Product Planning

1. **Marketing Research.** Before producing a new product, marketing research is carried out to know the desired need of the consumers so that product's size, colour, design, features, package, price *etc.* are according to their requirements.
2. **Technical Research:** After knowing the product features desired by the consumers, it is important to know whether such features can be incorporated in product or not. For this, technical and engineering tests are done.
3. **Modification in Existing Products.** If the existing product needs certain modification so that it gets according to the demand, then collection of necessary facts and making changes in the product accordingly is also a part of product planning.
4. **Elimination of the Product.** If a product looses demand or its competition intensifies or it results in declining profits, the decision to eliminate the product is also the function of product planning.

Product planning is a comprehensive activity. It includes all the activities from the time of its creation to the time of its elimination from the company's product line.

Product Development

According to **Stanton**, '*Product development encompasses the technical activities of product research, engineering and designing*'.

According to **Tietjan**, '*It is an art of marketing out and supervising the search, screening, development and commercialization of new products, the modification of existing lines and the discontinuance of marginal or unprofitable items*'.

New product development consists of generating new ideas and screening them to know their sales potential, profitability, financial and product requirements. The various models are then developed after careful research, which are then tested to know the need for any modifications. If test results are successful, decision to produce it on mass scale is taken.

Principles of Product Development

1. **Principle of Standardisation.** Standardization with regard to development of products refers to standards regarding its size, shape, colour, quantity, quality and physical and other

attributes of the product. In India, Bureau of Indian Standards have established certain standards. The use of standards is optional. A company desiring to conform to standards has to obtain a license.

2. **Principle of Simplification.** This principle refers to eliminating unnecessary product differentiations, sizes and shapes, quality, design, *etc*. It helps to make marketing programme simpler and reducing production and storing costs.
3. **Principle of Specialization.** This principle aims at avoiding unnecessary product diversifications and establishing position in some specified field. This helps in increasing the efficiency of employees and results in economies in costs.

The above principles though quite varied in nature, are closely related to each other. Without simplification, there can neither be standardization nor simplification. Therefore, all the above three principles should be followed in developing the product.

Scope of Product Planning and Product Development

The scope of product planning and product development is very wide. It includes everything relating to product such as size, shape, design, price, colour, brand etc. It also includes all those factors, which affect the market of the product. The following aspects are included in the scope of product planning and development.

1. **Product Decision.** Before developing a product, the management has to decide which product it wants to produce. This helps in getting together the necessary resources for the production.
2. **Design and Size of the Product.** Design refers to the structure, shape, colour combination, flavour, fragrance etc. of the product. Size is the capacity or quantity or weight of the product. The product normally has three sizes – small, medium or large.
3. **Name of the Product.** The product planning and development also includes the decision regarding the name of the product. The name should be such, which can be easily pronounced, remembered and which relates to the product.
4. **Colour of the Product.** The colour aspect is not very important for industrial product but it greatly helps in selling in case of consumer products. The colour combination should be decided keeping in view the target consumers.
5. **Price of the Product.** Price is one of the important element of product planning. Price should be determined after analyzing the demand, competition level, paying capacity of buyers, type of product, distribution system, Govt. regulations *etc.* Any carelessness in fixing the right price on the part of the manufacture can give disastrous results.
6. **Brand, Package and Label of the Product.** While planning the product, decision regarding products brand, package and label has also to be taken.

   Brand is a name, symbol or design, which distinguishes the product from those of the competitors and helps in easy recognition. Brand decision involves decision regarding such name, symbol or design.

   Packaging protects the product from spoilage, ensures freshness, prevents adulteration and provides easy transportation and storage. Product planning involves decision regarding package material, package size, design and shape.

   Label is the information tag attached to the product, which gives details regarding quantity, ingredients, date of manufacture and expiry date *etc.* of the product.
7. **New Uses of the Product.** Product planning also involves search regarding the new uses to which the product can be put to.

8. **Guarantee and Service of the Product.** Product planning also involves decision regarding guarantee and other after sale services to be provided. Guarantee gives satisfaction to the customer that if the product gets damaged before the specified period, either the product will be changed or free repair services will be provided.

Product Change Decision

1. **Product Modification Decision.** Product modification involves either change in the product itself or repositioning it by changing its promotional focus. According to **Philip Kotler**, '*A product modification is any deliberate alteration in the physical attributes of a product or its packaging*'. The main reason for product modification is either to stimulate new sales or attract new customers. Modification may facilitate:
   (i) satisfying the additional needs of the buyers,
   (ii) satisfying all customers—rich or poor by grading up or grading down the quality of the product and
   (iii) making the product more attractive by changing the design, colour, shape *etc.*

Need for Product Modification

1. **Competition.** To face competition, the modifications in the product may become necessary.
2. **Technical Progress.** The technical improvements make it necessary to upgrade the product *e.g.*, ordinary washing machines are now being replaced by semi-automatic or automatic machines which washes, rinses and dries the clothes.
3. **Sale Decline.** The decline in sales level can be prevented by making necessary modifications in the product.

Strategies of Product Modification

The product may be modified through the following ways:

1. **Quality Changes.** The quality of the product is either improved or degraded either by changing the material from which it is prepared or by involving changes in the engineering process. Improved product helps in making the product attractive and inducing the higher class of customer to purchase. Degradation on the other hand lowers the price of the product and helps in attracting the next layer of price sensitive customers.
2. **Style Changes.** The style improvements enhance the appearance of the product. The launching of new models of cars, TVs, fridge, phones *etc.* are the outcomes of style. Changes. Such a change helps the manufacturer to have permanent share in the market.
3. **Functional Changes.** This policy aims at improving the working of the product or adding of additional features to the product to make the product more efficient, convenient and secure.

Though, the above strategies are independent of each other but normally all three strategies are adopted simultaneously to achieve better response.

Product Elimination Decision

When there is no possibility of improving or modifying the product, the management may be forced to withdraw it from the market. The process of withdrawal or removal or deletion of the product from the product-line is known as **product elimination**. The continuation of such product adversely affects the profits and reputation of the company. The decision to eliminate the product from the product line must be taken only after careful analysis of related factors. A proper systematic approach should be followed for eliminating the product.

Reasons of Product Elimination

1. **Declining Sales.** When the sales of the product are continuously falling and there is no scope of any improvement, the manufacturer may decide to eliminate the product.
2. **Declining Profits.** If there is continuous fail in the profits of the product without any scope of increase, the manufacturer may decide to eliminate the product.
3. **Declining Price.** If the prevailing market conditions show a tendency of consistent fall in the price of the product without any possibility of raise to maintain sales , the manufacturer may decide to withdraw the product.
4. **Life Cycle of the Product.** Once the product reaches the saturation point in its life cycle, it will soon enter the declining stage where the sales as well as the profits will fall. Thus, it forces the manufacture to discontinue the product.
5. **Managerial Time.** If the product requires greater percentage of managerial time as compared to other products due to which the profitability of other products is adversely affected, the manufacturer may like to stop the production of such a product.
6. **Reduction in Product's Effectiveness.** If the product fails to fulfill its objectives for which it is included in the company's product line, the manufacturer may eliminate it. Sometimes, product's effectiveness fails as a consequence of aging process due to which the product usually dies a natural death.
7. **Substitute Product.** Emergence of superior substitute product either necessitates modification or elimination of the product.
8. **Promotional Budget.** If there is consistent need to increase the promotional budget to maintain the sales of the product, the manufacturer may be required to eliminate the product.

Reasons for not taking Elimination Decision

1. **Change in Factors.** It is often assumed that sales fall is due to outside factor. As the economic and market situations will become favourable, the sales will rise.
2. **Encouragement through Product Modification.** Management feels the sales can be enhanced by product modification.
3. **Change in Marketing Programme.** The product sometimes fails to recognize the shortcomings in the product. He rather, blames the marketing programme and assumes that by making changes in the promotional budget, promotional message and motivating dealers, the sales can be increased.
4. **Helpful in Sale of other Products.** If the product acts as a bait for increasing the sale of other products, the manufacturer may continue to include it in the product line inspite of the low sales.
5. **Interest of Personnel.** The person engaged in the production and management of such products prefers its continuation as their livelihood depends on it. Sometimes due to emotional or psychological reasons the product is not eliminated.
6. **Hiding of Defects.** The person responsible for the success of product, tries to hide its drawbacks. The management thus remains unaware of the product failure and the production remains continued.

Product Abandonment Practice

One of the following methods is adopted for the elimination of the product from the product line:

1. **On a Piecemeal Basis.** Instead of eliminating the product instantly, it is done slowly and slowly. This practice is followed when there is constant fall in the value of the product.

2. **On a Crisis Basis.** The sales are constantly falling or cost is constantly increasing or stock is piling up in godowns, the decision to eliminate the product should be taken and production should be immediately stopped.
3. **Periodic Product Review Method.** The most systematic method is to make periodic checks of the products whose average profits are falling. This prevents the unnecessary continuance of weak products. It enables timely modification or withdrawal of products.

Stages of Product Elimination Decision

The Decision to eliminate the product, in a small firm is taken by the proprietor himself. In large concerns, a separate committee consisting of specialists from production, marketing, finance and controlling department is constituted. Such a committee decides the procedure to be followed for elimination after considering the objective of elimination.

Product elimination procedure consists of two stages creative stage and operational stage. The creative stage consists of constituting the committee and determining the procedure to be followed for elimination. The operational stage actually conducts the process of elimination.

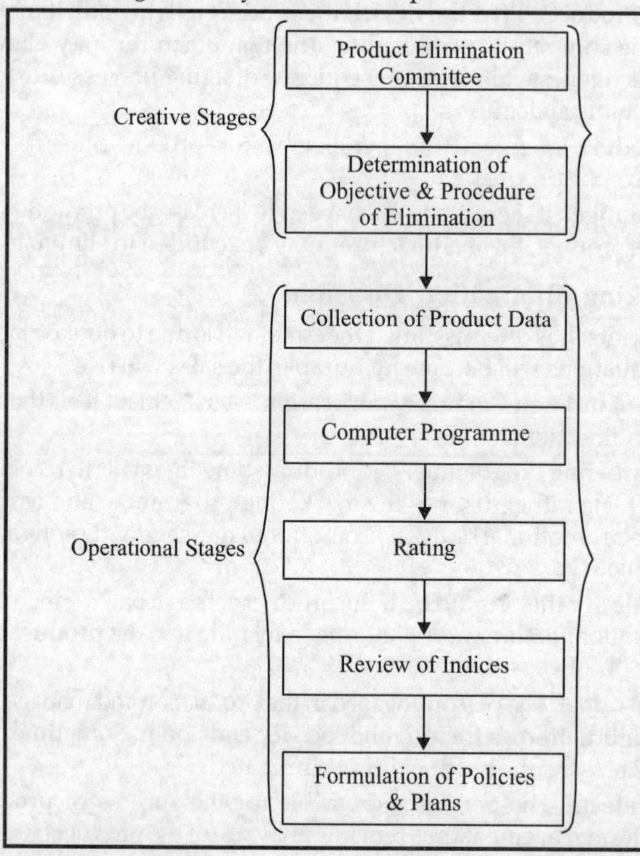

1. **Collection of Product Data.** The data is collected regarding the product whose sales and profits are falling or the stock is getting piled up. The data relates to sales, cost, price *etc.* of past many years.
2. **Computer Programme.** The above data is fed into the computer who analyse it.
3. **Rating.** The results of data are then studied by the product elimination committee. The committee rates the result and prepares the list.

4. **Review of Indices.** The committee review the indices prepared and takes the decision of elimination on its basis.
5. **Formation of Policies and Plans.** The committee makes plans and policies regarding the elimination.

NEW PRODUCT DEVELOPMENT

The concern develops the new product to be undertaken by it. The procedure of development of new product is :

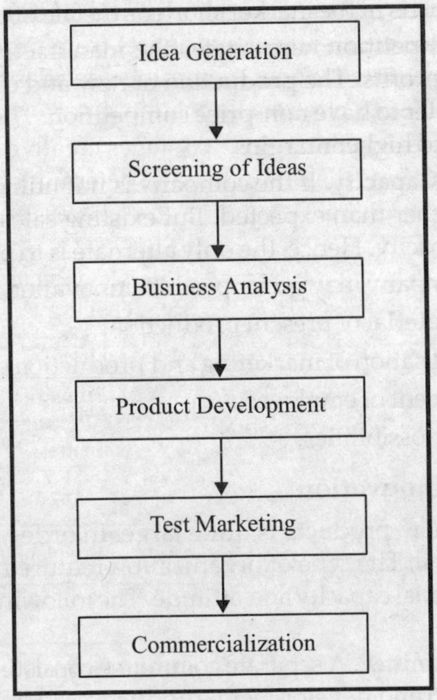

Development of New Products.

Product Innovation

Any product, which the consumers perceive as an addition to the already available choices is a new product. Innovation in product planning is newness. New products may be a result of:

(i) major modifications to the existing products, *e.g.*, coffee choc recently introduce by Nescafe as a new flavour of coffee with chocolate, flat T.V.'s introduced by T.V. companies,

(ii) duplication of competitor's products *e.g.*, new brands of soaps and

(iii) innovative original products, e.g., computers, Robots, solar energy, nuclear power, microwave ovens, vaccum-cleaners.

Product innovation is necessary due to the following factors:

(a) **Market Changes.** The market is dynamic. The desires and likings of consumers keep changing. To cope with buyer's demand, the marketer must make adequate changes in his existing producer. With the development of communication system, transport and exchange facilities, the information and fashion spread at a rapid pace. This necessitates the marketer to make innovations in his product.

(b) **Technological Changes.** Technological researches have opened wide markets both for the existing products and new products. Due to technological developments, consumer demand new improved technically advanced products. The marketers who do not make such necessary changes in their products and product lines are bound to fail. For example, due to availability of cassette and C.D. players there is less demand for record players and radio.

(c) **Diversification of Risk.** The products popular today eventually become outdated and obsolete. This risk can be avoided by making necessary changes in existing products and providing the consumer with wide variety. Thus, it makes the marketer to undertake continuous innovations.

(d) **Company Growth.** In order to grow and expand, the company introduces new products. The incoming of new products in the market shortens the life of existing products.

(e) **Competition.** The competition necessitates the manufacturer to indulge in new product planning to maintain profits. The production of new and differentiated products makes it possible for the marketer to have non-price competition. The marketers can innovate better products and command higher margins.

(f) **Utilisation of Excess Capacity.** If the company is not utilizing its full capacity, the cost of production will be higher than expected. But existing sales may act as a limiting factor in utilizing the excess capacity. Hence, the only alternate is to produce new product.

(g) **Other Factors.** The company may go for product innovation due to the following reasons:

(i) To utilize waste material of present production.

(ii) To make better utilisation of marketing and production skills.

(iii) To avoid retrenchment of employees.

(iv) To enhance profit possibilities.

Organisation for Product Innovation

The chances of failure of new products is quite large. In order to ensure its success, a proper organizational set up is essential. The type of organization required in any concern depends on its size, nature of products, managerial capacity and attitude. The following various forms of organization can be adopted:

1. **Product Planning Committee.** A separate committee consisting of persons representing from various fields– research and development, production, marketing, engineering, accounting and finance is formed. The committee either takes the full responsibility for product innovation or it assists the product manager in his work. This committee, is in-fact responsible for analyzing the position of existing products and giving its acceptance to new product planning.
2. **New Product Department.** The industries that grow at a rapid pace such as electronics and computer manufacturing, form a separate department. The head of the department has great many powers. He is directly linked with the top management. This department takes new product development as a full time activity. This department screens the various ideas regarding new product, develops product, tests it and ensures its commercial viability.
3. **Product Managers.** Certain concerns have separate product managers for each kind of product. The product manager is responsible for planning the complete marketing programme for his group of products. He sets marketing goods and strategies, prepare budgets, price the products, develop advertising and sales promotion plans, secure dealer co-operation, maintains adequate stock and do other related activities. He also keeps an eye on competitor's product. As he has in depth knowledge of his products, he is often entrusted with the responsibility of innovating new products or modifying existing products, so as to maintain adequate marketability in future.

4. **Product Consultants.** The concerns instead of forming a separate department or hiring a new product manager, takes the services of product consultants. Such consultants are not the employees of the concern. They provide advice on charging fees. Such persons are specialized in their field. The product consultants are usually adopted under following conditions:
   (i) The company is very small and it cannot afford full time manager.
   (ii) Detailed information is required regarding possibilities of all new products.
   (iii) Technically related information regarding competitor's product is required.

Essential for the Success of Product Innovation

Development of new product involves risk and uncertainty. Proper managerial practices can help reduce risk to a greater extent. **Philip Kotler** gives the following three essentials for successful product-innovation :

1. **Effective Organizational Arrangements.** Effective organizational structure is essential for proper conduct of new product development. A proper organization clearly specifies the responsibility of each person. The concern can either have a new product manager or product committee or separate product department or hire the services of consultants.
2. **Experienced and Professional Personnel.** A concern requires not only effective organization but also experienced and professional personnel. The personnel must have technical knowledge and skill. Keen interest in product development, creative marketing ability, leadership qualities, risk-taking and corrective decision-making ability. In addition to this he must be able, to undertake research work as various researches regarding market potentiality, product viability, economy, performance, packaging, promotion, competitive strength and the like are needed.
3. **Sound Procedures.** A proper product development procedure should be followed. Minimum of six stages are involved in product innovation namely, idea generation — screening — business analysis — product development-test marketing and commercialization. Each stage gives critical decision of whether the product should go to the next stage or should it be abandoned or should more facts be gathered. Any such decision should be taken only after careful analysis and logical thinking.

Product Policy Decision

The producer takes certain important decisions regarding his product, which are known as product related decisions. Today, the manufacturer instead of producing only one product, manufacturers a variety of products to satisfy all consumers and to maximize his profits.

The firm producing various products takes production decision at the following three levels:

1. **Product Item.** The detailed description of one product in manufacturers list is known as product item. According to **Philip Kotler** – *product item is a specific version of a product that has a separate designation in the seller's list*, *e.g.*, Johnson & Johnson's Clean & Clear Moisturiser is a product item.
2. **Product Line.** A broad group of products, which are meant for essentially similar uses and possess reasonably similar physical characteristics constitute product base line *e.g.*, range of chocolates is a product line as it satisfies one need of different consumers. Similarly range of electronics is a product line that satisfies different but inter related needs of a segment.

   It may be defined as '*a group of products that are closely related because they function in a similar manner, are sold to the same customer groups, are marketed through the same types of outlets or fall within given price ranges*'.

According to **Stanton**, '*A broad group of products interested for essentially similar uses and possessing reasonably similar physical characteristics constitute a product like*'.

Thus Amul's product line includes ghee, butter, cheese, milk, ice-cream, chocolate *etc.* Videocon's electronic product line includes T.V., music system, refrigerator, A.C., washing machine etc.

3. **Product Mix.** It is the full list of all products offered for sale by a company. It need not consist of related products.

   It may be defined as — '*the set of all product lines and terms that a particular seller offers for sale to buyers*'.

According to American Marketing Association '*Product mix is the composite of products offered for sale by a firm or a business unit.*'

Thus, Manikchand's Tea, Flour, electrical accessories, construction, packaging, greeting and wedding cards, power projects and mineral water are its product mix.

A product mix has certain length, width, depth and consistency.

Length of product mix refers to the total number of items in its product mix.

Width or breadth of product mix refers to the number of different product lines offered by the company *e.g.*, Hindustan Uni Lever Ltd. produces soaps, shampoos, creams, moisturisers, talcum powder, deodorants and many other cosmetic products. The greater the number of different classes of products the greater the width of product line.

Depth of product mix refers to the average number of items offered by the company under each product line *i.e.*, quality, sizes, colours, models offered within each product line *e.g.*, Hindustan Lever Ltd.'s soap line consist of Hamam, Lux, Liril, Lifebuoy, Pears *etc.* Greater the number of brands in any product class, greater is the depth of product line.

Consistency of product mix refers to how closely related the various product lines are in terms of production requirement, consumer behaviour, distribution channel or in some other way, *e.g.*, the various toiletries offered by Hindustan Lever Ltd. have consistency as most of the products enhance beauty in one way or the other.

This can be illustrated as:

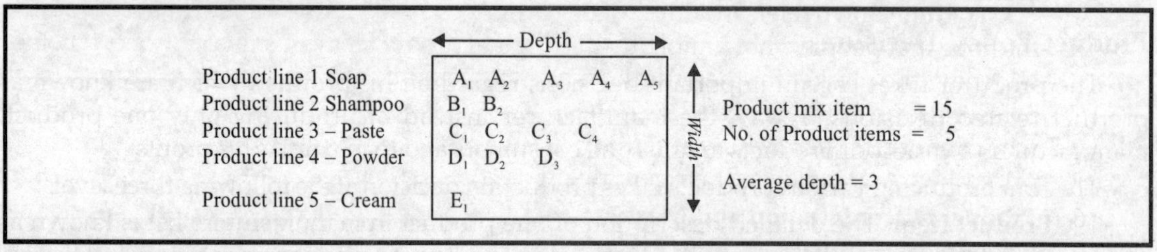

PRODUCT LINE

The concept of Product line is a dynamic concept because the company has to adopt different product lines at different point of line and in different circumstance. This requires a modification or change in the existing product line. Modification of product line implies contraction, expansion, changing models and quality standards.

1. **Contraction of Product Mix.** It implies either to (i) eliminate a product line or (ii) reduce the number of products within the product line and thus reducing the sizes, styles, colours and varieties. It is generally done when the competition intensifies and it is difficult to sell those products at a profit or when the product has reached its declining stage of life cycle or when its costs exceed its price and make it impossible to sell them at a profit. Such a decision is more

difficult to act on because money has already been invested. Therefore, products are allowed to stay for long until they fail.

2. **Expansion of Product Mix.** It implies either to
   (i) add a product line or
   (ii) increase the number of products within the product line. It is done to exploit market opportunities and to add more profitable products, *e.g.*, Godrej recently added a new product – Fair glow soap in its soap line. The new lines undertaken may be related or unrelated to the present products. For example, Nestle group recently added a new product line -Mineral water even Coca Cola company and Pepsi Cola have recently added mineral water product line in their business. LG has launched healthcare and household product line to its existing product lines of consumer durables and IT products.
3. **Alteration of Existing Products.** Instead of launching a new product, the company may make changes in its existing products with regard to size, colour, design, package, flavours or texture. Such an alteration is less risky. It has no effect on width and depth of the product mix *e.g.*, Nescafe launched new flavour of coffee – Choc Coffee.
4. **Development of New Uses for Existing Products.** The company may promote new uses for the existing products, *e.g.*, Surf detergent can be promoted not only to clean clothes but also for cleaning utensils and floor.
5. **Trading Up and Trading Down.** It implies an expansion of product lines. The company comes out with changed version of a product and it also alters the promotional strategies.

   Trading Up refers to adding of high priced prestigious products to their existing line, in the hope of increasing the sales of existing low priced products. The marketer who has attained a good reputation in his low priced products may introduce high priced products. The seller though, continues to depend for large portion of sales on low priced products. He gradually makes a shift in his promotional strategies to emphasise new products and thus ultimately increases the sale of new products, *e.g.*, Godrej Washing Powder added Ezee for delicate clothes. Maruti Udyog traded up and launched 'Baleno' luxurious car. Frost-free refrigerators introduced by companies manufacturing refrigerators is another example of trading up.

   Trading Down refers to adding of the low priced products to its line of quality product in the hope that people who cannot buy the original product may buy this new one. It helps in widening the market for the product. The manufacture of single tub washing machine by Samsung is an example of trading down wherein the company has tried to persuade those who cannot offer to buy fully automatic washing machine. Others are manufacturer of low priced TVs, Audio players, Refrigerators *etc.*
6. **Product Differentiation and Market Segmentation.** Product differentiation is a strategy wherein the manufacturer tries to promote that his product is different and better than the competitor's. The difference may be in quality, design, shape, colour, brand, package *etc*. This strategy protects the company from price competition.

Market segmentation on the other hand, is a strategy wherein the manufacturer concentrates on one or more homogeneous part of the total hetrogeneous market. He tries to make the product according to the requirements of a particular segment.

Factor Influencing Change in Product Mix

1. **Change in Demand.** The change in demand of a product effects the product mix of the manufacture. Demand changes due to change in population, their purchasing power and nature, *e.g.*, if the income of people increase they may not prefer to buy low priced product &

thus it affects its demand. As a result of this the product will have to eliminate the product or bring a change in its quality and thus his product mix change.

2. **Production.** As large scale production results in diminishing per unit cost. Therefore, the manufacturer may like to change his product mix to get cost economics. Sometimes, the producer may also undertake to manufacture by-product and thus brings about a change in his product mix.
3. **Competition.** Competition also affects the product mix of the company. If leader manufacturer makes a change in his product and present it in a new form then the followers too have to make the alterations and thus their product mix gets changed.
4. **Finance.** The company may adopt modification policy and change its product mix in order to make better use of its financial resources. If the company is continuously running into losses, it may change its product mix and manufacture a new product and eliminate the older one. The company may even change its product mix to reduce the effects of depression period.
5. **Marketing.** The company may change its product mix to make more effective use of the marketing capacity. For instance if certain branch of company has less work, it may change its product mix and produce some new product instead.
6. **Manufacturer's Image.** The manufacturer of low priced product may like to improve his image and thus change his product mix by producing better product.
7. **Government Control Image.** The manufacturer has to follow the rules and regulations framed by government. Any change in such rules will force the producer to change his product mix accordingly.

Thus we see that a manufacturer keeps changing his product mix to attain his objective of maximizing profit as well as sales. He infact strives to attain optimal product mix. According to **Philip Kotler** '*The current product mix is said to be optimal if no adjustment would enhance the company's chances of achieving the objectives.*'

PRICING DECISIONS

'Price' is the amount of money to be paid in return for a bundle of utilities.

The term **'price'** need not be confused with the term **'pricing'**. Pricing is the function of translating into quantitative terms the value of the product or service or idea by the marketing manager before it is offered for sale to consumers. Pricing is the process of setting objectives, identifying the factors governing the price, formulating price policies and strategies setting prices, implementing them and controlling them. Pricing as a marketing function has great importance. Its importance can be summarized as:

1. **Means of Allocating Resources.** Price generates revenues which are made available for the firm's expansion and development. Price influences the factors of production land, labour, capital and entrepreneurship. It allocates the resources for the optimum output and distribution.
2. **Price Affects Demand.** Price has an inverse relation with demand. Increase in price leads to fall in demand and vice versa. But, sometimes, higher prices help the firm to advertise extensively and thus push up its demand.
3. **Price is Competitive Weapon.** The company has to decide whether its prices will be above, equal or below its competitors. It must also decide its prices at various stages of product's life cycle considering the prevailing competitive conditions.
4. **Price Determines Profitability.** The impact of price rise or fall is instantly reflected in the resulting profits, provided other variables remain constant. Price can be used as a mean to

cover weaknesses in other elements of marketing mix and thus it can be easily used for defensive and offensive strategies.

Factors Affecting Pricing Policy

Pricing decisions should be consistent with company's objectives. Such decisions are influenced by numerous factors. Some of these factors are internal over which the manufacturer has control to a certain extent whereas, others are the external factors which are beyond manufacturer's control. Therefore, the marketer faces great difficulty in determining the actual price.

Internal Factors

1. **Organisational Factors.** Pricing decision can be centralized or decentralized. Generally it is the top management, which sets the guidelines within which the price is to be administered. The top management determines the price range, while the actual price is dealt at lower level. Thus, the nature and type of organization effects the pricing decisions.
2. **Marketing Mix.** All the elements of marketing mix — product, price, place promotion effect each other. Thus, any change in price will have an immediate effect on other three elements. The firm may either decide to cut down its price in order to attract price sensitive customers or it may raise its price to build up its image. But, any such decision must be taken after considering the total marketing strategy.
3. **Product Differentiation.** The more different a product is from that of the competitor, the more is the freedom the company enjoys in setting the prices. Product differentiation is a technique by which the producer makes his product distinct from that of competitors. Such distinctiveness may be real or imaginary. It can be by means of design, colour, shape, fragrance, brand name or advertising messages. For example, bathing soap though same may be highlighted for difference either in colour or fragrance.
4. **Product Costs.** The cost of product plays a vital role in deciding the price. Every producer will like to set a price, which will cover the cost so that the firm has a chance of earning surplus. But the price must not be set without considering the demand and competition levels.
5. **Product Life Cycle.** The stage of the product life cycle decides the price policy to be followed. In the introduction stage the prices are kept low so that the product can easily penetrate the market. As the sales increase and the product reaches the growth stage, the prices can be raised to a certain extent. During the maturity stage, the prices are, either kept at same level or lowered to face competition. In the Decline stage, prices are reduced to maintain demand.
6. **Pricing Objectives.** The objectives set for pricing affects the decision regarding fixation of price for a particular product. The objectives can be — skim the cream, price stability, profit maximization, targeted return on sale or investment *etc.*

External Factors

1. **Product Demand.** Demand has a great impact on pricing. If the demand increases, the price of the product can be raised. On the contrary, if the product has low demand, the price of the product will also decrease. The company should also keep the elasticity demand factor in mind while fixing the price of a product. If the demand of the product is inelastic, high price may be fixed but if demand is elastic, firm should fix lower prices than that of the competitors.
2. **Competition.** Competition is a crucial factor in price determination. The company must know the pricing policies and strategies, objectives strengths and weaknesses of the competitors. This helps to know the possibilities for raising or lowering the prices. Even in monopolistic

conditions, the manufacturer has to consider the competition with that of substitute products before fixing the price of his products.

3. **Distribution Channel.** A number of intermediaries exist between the manufacturer and the final consumer. Each of them charges for their services, which ultimately add up to the cost of the product. Therefore, longer the distribution channel, higher will be the prices of the product and vice versa.
4. **Suppliers.** Suppliers of inputs, especially raw materials and fabricated parts that can have great impact on the price of a product. If the suppliers raise the price, it will lead the manufacturer to increase the price of the product, which will ultimately affect the consumers. The scarcity or abundance of the raw material also has considerable influences on the final pricing decisions.
5. **Economic Conditions.** The inflationary or deflationary tendency affects pricing. In boom period, high prices may be fixed in-order to cover the increasing cost of production. Whereas, in recession period, prices are reduced considerably so as to maintain the level of turnover of the product.
6. **Buyer Behaviour.** Buyers may be business buyers or final consumers. The composition and behaviour of these buyers have great impact on the pricing decisions. Generally, if the buyers are small users though large in number as in case of daily consumer items, they do not have much influence on pricing decisions. On the other hand, few buyers but large users have considerable influence on the pricing decisions. Again, the pricing decision is affected by the fact whether the consumer is industrial user or final user. The firm cannot have the same price policy for both the classes of consumers.
7. **Government Regulation.** The government of the nation influences the pricing policies in a number of ways. It regulates the prices of the products it makes available and services it renders to the community like postal, telegraph, gas, transport, electricity *etc.* Many laws and acts have been framed to restrict price hikes, artificial scarcity and consumer exploitation. These are MRTP Act, Essential Commodities Act, Consumer Protection Act and so on.

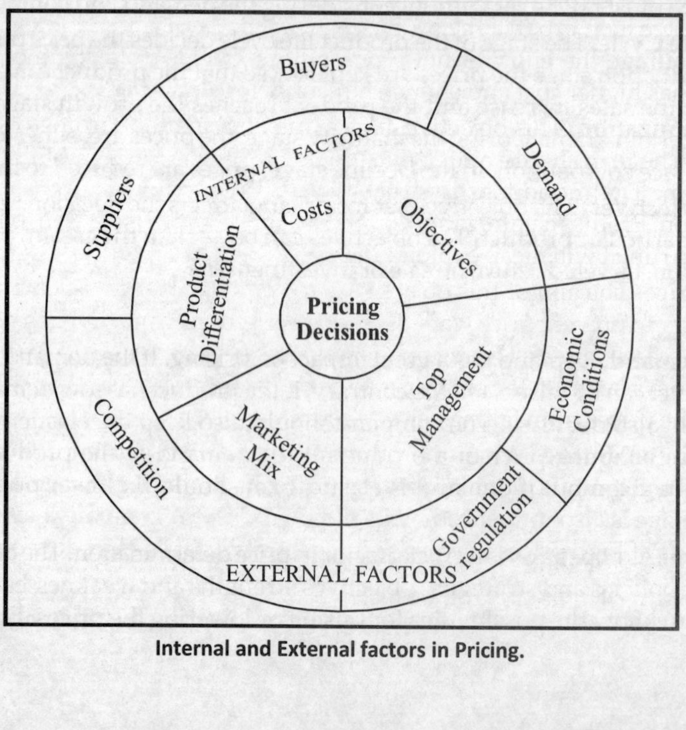

Internal and External factors in Pricing.

Pricing Objectives

Pricing objectives provide basis for formulating price policies, framing pricing strategies and setting actual prices. The price objectives must be consistent with internal organizational atmosphere and compatible with the external environment. They should aim at achieving the firm's objectives. The main goal in pricing may be classified as follows:

1. **Survival.** It is the most fundamental objective. In order to exist, the firms tolerate short run losses, reductions in size of operation and many other difficulties. When the firm faces survival crisis, it prices its product at a level, which will at least cover the organizations expenses. However, survival objective is a short-term goal. Once, the position of the firm improves, it shifts to other price objectives.
2. **Target Return on Investment or Net Sale.** The firm expects a certain return on its investment. The price is so fixed that it includes the pre-determined average return, *i.e.* sales price covers all the costs and leave desired margin, e.g., a firm may set a target at 10% or 20% return on investment. This target may be for a long term or short term. Target ROI pricing is usually adopted by the firms who are industry leaders because they can set the standards to be followed by the followers. It is also commonly used by companies selling in established market where there are no substitutes. Wholesalers and retailers adopt it on short-term basis. They set the target on net sales.
3. **Market Share.** Target market share means that portion of the industry sale, which a company aspires to attain. The firm may adopt this as an objective either to maintain or to improve the market share. When the market has growth potential, market share is a better indicator of firm's progress. A firm may be earning good returns but its share of market might be negative. The firm may lower the price than that of competitors in order to capture the market. This may bring down the profit margins but it will certainly discourage the competitors from entering the market.
4. **To Meet or Prevent Competition.** Meeting of competition implies keeping price equal to that of the competitors. Generally, companies that are price followers adopt this policy. Sometimes, companies price their products below the price of the competitors in order to fight competition and to discourage the entry of new competitors. Such a policy is more successful if the competitor has higher cost and as such he cannot lower his prices.
5. **Profit Maximization.** This objective aims at maximizing the earnings under given market conditions. The firm should aim at maximizing profits on total output rather than on each product item. The monopolistic situation or scarcity condition give chances for profit maximization. Profits maximization should be adopted as a long-term objective. If adopted during short run, it will mean exploitation of consumers.
6. **Stabilize Price.** The aim of this objective is to even out cyclical fluctuations in prices. The companies try to prevent price wars. They do not indulge in maximizing profits during boom period or in scarcity times. During boom period, they increase their supply and thus, prevent the prices from rising. On the contrary, during depression period, they decrease their supply to prevent the prices from falling below a certain level.
7. **To Maintain an Image.** When the company comes into existence, it develops a certain impression in the minds of the people regarding its product, package, brand name and the like. This image is also influenced by its pricing policy. A company having a image of high quality goods at high prices may loose its customers if it goes for low quality goods at low prices.

PRICE POLICIES

The price policies can be divided into following four categories:

I. **On the Basis of Flexibility.**

(i) ***One Price Policy.*** Under this policy, all the customers who are purchasing a particular quantity at a particular time are charged the same price, *i.e.*, the price is fixed and no changes are made in it.

(ii) ***Flexible Price Policy.*** Under this policy different buyers are charged different prices for the same quantity purchased. The difference in pricing depends on bargaining power of buyer, his paying capacity, personal relationship between buyer and seller and many other such factors.

II. **On the Basis of Price Level.**

(i) **Meeting Competition Policy.** The companies adopting this policy adjust their prices according to that of the competitors. If the competitors lower their prices, they too do the same. On the other-hand, if the competitors increase their price, they also follow suit. Such a policy is adopted in case of highly competitive goods.

(ii) **Under the Market Policy.** It is a policy in which the company always keeps its prices less than those prevailing in the market. It is adopted when a company wants to enter the market or it wants to expand. If a company adopts the policy when its product is at the initial stage of its life cycle, it can easily enter the market and if it continues to follow this policy, it can later easily expand.

(iii) **Above the Market Policy.** Under this policy, the company keeps its prices more than those prevailing in the market. It is adopted by companies who either enjoy a good reputation in the market or offer unique product. The customers get attracted to the company because of its prestigious brand name. Such a company spends highly on advertisement.

III. **On the Basis of Specialty.**

(i) ***Bait Pricing Policy.*** The marketer keeps low priced and high priced goods. He attracts the consumer by showing low priced goods. Once the customer gets attracted towards the low priced goods, he is told about its drawbacks and is encouraged to purchase the other high priced product. Thus, low priced goods act as **'Bait'** for attracting the buyer.

(ii) ***Price Lining Policy.*** The various products are priced according to their quality standards. The products may be classified as good, better and best. The first price stands for economy choice, the second for the medium quality and the third for the best quality products are highly priced. It assists the buyer in making choice according to his budget.

(iii) ***Full-line Pricing Policy.*** When a manufacturer producing various products, is unable to calculate the fixed expenses incurred on each product separately, he prices his products according to their demand. By doing so price of certain products are fixed high, while others are priced less. This helps to recover the total fixed cost.

(iv) ***Skimming Pricing Policy.*** It is a policy, which aims at extracting maximum profits from the market, and as such the manufacturer keeps high prices. This policy is, therefore, known as skimming the cream of demand. It is generally adopted at the time of introducing the product in the market, till there is no competition.

(v) ***Penetration Pricing Policy.*** This policy aims at capturing the market as soon as possible, therefore, the prices are kept at low level. It is adopted at the time of introduction of new product. It helps in developing brand preference and keeping out competitors.

(vi) *Leader Pricing.* This is generally adopted in **oligopolistic** market conditions where there are few sellers, each of whom tries for large market share. No seller has control over the price. Any one firm may take initiative in fixing the price and others follow it.

(vii) *Loss Leader Pricing.* Under this policy, few popular products are temporarily offered at low prices with a view to attract customers. Such products are termed as loss leaders. The rationale behind this is to induce the customers to purchase other products when they come to purchase the popular advertised terms and thus increase the overall sales.

(viii) *Psychological Pricing Policy.* When prices are fixed in such a manner that they have some psychological effect on buyers, it is known as psychological pricing.

IV. **On the Basis of Geographical Conditions.**

The transport cost acts as an important element in pricing. Because of the wide geographical distances between the production center and consumption center, it is necessary to decide whether the transit charges will be borne by the buyer or the seller. The following are the major ways of charging transit

(i) ***Uniform Delivery Pricing Policy.*** It is one in which the firm bears full transportation cost irrespective of location of buyers. Thus, all the buyers are to pay a uniform price. The expenses necessary for the movement of goods from the point of origin to the point of consumption are borne by the firm. Such a policy helps in capturing distant marketers. The firms actually add in full or part the average of the total freight charges for all the customers to the price quoted. It is also known as **F.O.R.** (Free on rail), 'Destination price' or 'Postage stamp.'

(ii) ***Production Point Pricing Policy.*** It is one in which the firm quotes ex-factory price. It does not bear the transportation cost. Such a policy may be **'ex-factory'** or **'free on rail'** (F.O.R). In case of ex-factory price, the buyer bears the freight charges from the factory point. Whereas in case of F.O.R price, the firm bears the freight charges upto the railway station or the transport agency. After that the buyer has to meet freight.

(iii) ***Zonal Delivery Pricing Policy.*** It is one where the firm divides the country into different zones and quotes uniform prices for each zone. These prices differ from zone to zone. The company adds average transportation cost to the basic price to arrive at the zonal price. Such a price benefits the buyer living at a distant place within a zone.

(iv) ***Base Point Pricing.*** It implies partial absorption of the transport cost by the company. One or more geographical locations are selected as points from which the transportation costs are calculated. The buyers pay ex-factory price plus freight calculated from the nearest base point. This price policy is normally the collective decision of all the firms.

Price Determination Procedure

There is no specific procedure applicable to all firms for price determination., Usually, the following steps are adopted:

1. **Select Target Market.** The very first step is to select the segment or segments in which the company will pursue. The demographic and psychographic characteristics of the selected segment will affect the pricing decision. The buying motives, price sensitivity, paying capacity, location etc. have considerable affect on price.
2. **Determine Demand for the Product.** Each price level gives different levels of demand. Higher the price, lower will be the demand. Estimating the demand for an established product is easier than for a new product. There are two steps in demand estimation:
   (a) Knowing the expected price.
   (b) Determining sales volume at various prices.

Expected price refers to the price range. Surveys may be conducted of potential buyers or competitors' prices may be studied or the product may be tested in limited area to know the expected price. After knowing the price range, sales volume at different prices are estimated. The product with elastic demand is usually priced lower than the product with an inelastic demand.

3. **Anticipate and Analyze the Competitive Reaction.** The competition has great influence on price. Competition may come from:
   (i) Similar products;
   (ii) Close substitute or even from:
   (iii) Unrelated products seeking the same consumer income.

   The marketer should study the competitor's product. Price, promotional strategies and other marketing policies. The company tries to avoid potential competition by keeping prices as low as possible.
4. **Establish Expected Share of the Market.** The company intending to capture large market share, will opt for low prices. Large share of the market can also be captured by adopting promotional techniques and by going for non-price competition strategy. The company must consider its production capacity, plant extension cost etc. before deciding on market share.
5. **Select Pricing Strategy.** Normally, for pricing a new product, two alternatives are available:
   (a) Skimming price policy and
   (b) Penetration price policy.

   Skimming price policy is one in which prices are kept high with a view to skim the cream, of demand. It is possible when the product has distinctive features or when there is no competition and the consumers are not price-sensitive. The firm can later, easily lower the prices and attract other segments of the market.

   Penetration price policy on the other hand, is one in which prices are kept low with a view to capture large market share. This policy makes sense when buyers are price sensitive, there is fear of competition and the company's cost of production goes down with increase in scale of production.
6. **Consider Company's Marketing Policies.** The company's policies regarding product distribution and promotion affects the price:
   (i) ***Product Policies.*** The composition of product, its quality, durability, resistance to heat, light, water, breaking strength, shrinkage etc. affects its price. Perishable products which cannot be stored for long periods are priced low to facilitate its easy disposal. The change in fashion also forces the seller to price the products at a level so that they get disposed off before the fashion changes.
   (ii) ***Distribution Policies.*** The manufacturer may either sell the products directly or through intermediaries. The length and complexity of the distribution channel greatly influence the price. The long and more complex the channel, high will be the price in order to compensate the persons involved in it.
   (iii) ***Promotion Policies.*** The more the promotional activities undertaken, higher will be price. The price is set to cover all the promotional cost.
7. **Select the Specific Price.** After considering all the above facts ultimately a specific price is selected. The procedures used for setting specific prices vary under different market conditions. The prices may be determined through the forces of Demand and Supply or by cost of production or on the basis of competitor's prices.

DISTRIBUTION DECISIONS

Distribution is concerned with various activities such as movement of goods, storage of goods, the legal promotional and financial activities involved in the transfer of good's ownership from producer to consumer. Hence it can be said that the channel of distribution involves those activities through which goods pass by producer to the consumer. The channel of distribution serves as a link between producer and consumers. It is the distribution channel through which a producer puts his product in the hands of actual users.

Every producer reaches to the consumer with the help of intermediates and it makes possible the movement of goods and services. It means the participants in the channels of distributions are — producers, intermediaries and the consumer.

Definitions

1. *'Every producer seeks to link together the set of marketing intermediaries that best fulfill the firm's objectives. The set of marketing intermediaries is called the marketing channel or trades channel or channel distribution'.*
   – Philip Kotler
2. *'A channel of distribution for the product is the route taken by the title to the goods as they move from the producer to the ultimate consumer or industrial user.'*
   – Stanton
3. *'A channel of distribution may be defined as a path traced in the direct or indirect transfer of the title to a product, as it moves from the producer to ultimate consumers or industrial users'*
   – Cundiff and Still

Functions of Distribution Channels

1. **Products Flow to the Market.** Distribution channels are the network which provide flow of the products to the market, *i.e.*, availability according to need or demand.
2. **Time and Place Utility.** Distribution channels create time and place utility by providing goods to the consumer at proper place and at proper time, taking into consideration the season and requirements of consumers.
3. **Satisfaction to the Consumers.** Distribution channels provide satisfaction to the consumer by providing services to them and by supplying goods in different varieties, colours and according to fashion.
4. **Contact between Consumer and Producer.** Through distribution channels producer comes into the contact with the consumer, which is useful to collect some important information regarding product and behaviour of the consumer.
5. **Other functions.** Other functions performed by distribution channels are — fixing price, reutilization of decisions, managing finances, promotional activities, aiding communication *etc.*

Types of Distribution Channels

The distribution channels can be classified into three parts:

(i) Direct distribution channel
(ii) Indirect distribution channel
(iii) Dual distribution channel

(i) Direct Distribution Channel. It is the system of distribution channel in which producer can sell the goods directly to the consumer without the help of intermediaries.

Producer → Consumer

Following methods can be used in direct distribution:

(a) ***By Own Sales Shops.*** A producer of consumer goods of daily necessity can open shops at different parts of city or some times in different cities also. e.g., Liberty shoes company has a number of shops scattered all over the country and sells their products directly to the consumers. By this manufacturers have control over distribution channel and have first hand information regarding customers preferences.

(b) ***By Mail Order.*** By mail order a producer can also sell his product. He sends his catalogue to the different present and potential consumers and receives the order by mail. The goods ordered are despatched through mail and payments are also received through mail (VPP). This method is of great benefit to customers living at remote and far away places. Usually this method is used for books *etc*. However, mail order is not suitable in case of perishable goods. The example of mail order business in India is Mail order Sales limited, Bombay.

(c) ***By Travelling Sales Representatives.*** The travelling sales representative contacts the prospective buyers with samples and literature, the orders are taken by them from the customers and are executed by the producer directly. This type of sale is very popular now-a-days and is used for common items like kitchen articles, domestic use items like vacuum cleaners.

(d) ***By Telephone.*** Telephone is also acting as a direct channel. Order can be taken on telephone and then goods are despatched to the person's house who ordered for it. It is sale by retailers, Asian Sky Shops *etc*.

The direct channel of distribution has some advantages as well as some disadvantages which are as follows:

Advantages

1. **To the Customers**
   (i) Consumers get the goods in their pure form.
   (ii) The price of goods are reasonable because of less cost.
   (iii) Goods can be purchased at fixed price.
2. **To the Producer**
   (i) It is economical method because nothing has to be paid to the middlemen.
   (ii) Consumer's demand can be estimated directly by the manufacturers.
   (iii) This method leads to reputation of concern because manufacturer does not depend on middlemen.
   (iv) Sales are done on cash basis. The motto of these shops is 'cash and carry'. This reduces the risk of bad debts.

Disadvantages

1. **To the Consumer**
   (i) He has to pay a price fixed by the manufacturer, he cannot negotiate.
   (ii) Once, a good purchased there is no provision to change it.
   (iii) Credit benefit cannot be achieved by consumer as manufacturer always makes cash sales.
2. **To the Producer**
   (i) This method is not suitable in case of high level competition.
   (ii) All the risk and losses lie with the producer.
   (iii) It is not suitable in case of mass production and sales at large scale.

(iv) When the consumers are widely scattered, it is very difficult to establish direct contact with them.

(ii) Indirect Channels of Distribution. It is the system in which the manufacturer sells his goods with the help of intermediaries. The whole process of indirect channel of distribution looks like a chain. It includes agents, wholesaler and retailer.

(1) Producer → Retailer → Consumer
(2) Producer → Wholesaler → Consumer
(3) Producer → Wholesaler → Retailer → Consumer
(4) Producer → Agent → Wholesaler → Retailer → Consumer.

The first two channels are known as one level channels of distribution.

Producer → Wholesaler → Retailer → Consumer is two level channel.

Producer → Agent → Wholesaler → Retailer → Consumer is three level channel.

Advantages.

1. **To the Consumers.**
   (1) The consumer can avail credit facility.
   (2) They have choice of selection because the intermediaries have different brands of product.
   (3) They can compare the different brands of product.
2. **To the Producer.**
   (1) Competition can be faced easily.
   (2) Through Indirect channel expansion of business is possible
   (3) Increase in sale is possible because intermediaries make each possible or to get more profit.

Disadvantages.

1. To the Consumer.
   (1) Consumer has to pay more price because cost of product now includes remuneration of middlemen.
   (2) Consumers are not satisfied because goods provided by the wholesalers and retailers are not in pure form in certain situation.
   (3) No direct relation with the producer, they cannot put their grievances directly before producers.
2. To the Producer.
   (1) He can access the market demand properly because he has to depend upon middlemen..
   (2) Increase in cost of product because of remuneration paid to middlemen.
   (3) No direct relation with the consumers, which causes lack of information regarding the tasks, fashion and interest of consumer.

(iii) Dual Distribution Channel.

When a manufacturer opts both the channels, *i.e.* direct and indirect channel then this combined channel is known as dual distribution channel.

In this channel manufacturer can take advantages of both the system. Now-a-days it is very much useful and necessary for each manufacturer.

Main objective to opt this system is to increase in scope of sales distribution. But the main problem to opt this channel is related to distribution ratio. It is difficult to find out that at which place direct channel is to be adopted and at which indirect channel.

PROMOTION DECISIONS

Promotion is *'any marketing effort whose function is to inform or persuade actual or potential consumers about the merits of a (given) product or service for the purpose of introducing a consumer either to continue or to start purchasing the firm's 'product or service at some (given) price'*. Promotion intents to inform, persuade and influence people through communication.

Promotion is defined as, *'the co-ordination of all seller-initiated efforts to set up channels of information and persuasion to facilitate the sale of goods or services or the acceptance of an idea'*.

Need of Promotional Activities

1. The increasing distance between the producer and consumer and the growth in number of consumers have made it necessary for the producer to undertake promotional activities. It makes the potential consumer to know from where, how, when and at what price the product would be available.
2. The widening of market area due to development of physical distribution facilities, have made communication necessary.
3. The increase in number of middlemen, have necessitated that the middlemen should be well communicated so that he can pass on the desired information to the consumers.
4. Stiff competition compels to have specialized promotion techniques to restore the demand.
5. Promotion activities are essential to maintain the falling demand either due to entry of new product or because of change in likings of consumer.

Communication Process

Promotional strategy is closely related to the process of communication and therefore, it is also known as marketing communication. Marketing communication is the message that deals with the buyer-seller relationship. The seller provides the buyer the relevant information in a persuasive language.

'Communication' is derived from the Latin word 'communis' meaning common, *i.e.* the receiver understands the message in same sense in which it is communicated either verbally or non-verbally. Thus, communication can be oral or written, personal or public, with words, figures, symbols or combination thereof.

According to **Newman**, **Summer** and **Warren**, *'Communication is an exchange of facts, ideas, opinions or emotions by two or more persons'*. According to **Keith Davis**, *'Communication is the process of passing information and understanding from one person to another'*.

Communication attempts to share understanding by two or more persons. It involves transmission of information. It is conceived with who says what to whom, through which channel and with what effect.

Marketing communication involves exchange of message regarding **product** – uses, benefits, ingredients, durability, strength regarding breakage, shrinkage, resistance to water, light, heat, *etc.* **brand name** 'quality, prestige and standard; **package** 'ensuring freshness and care taken by manufacturer; **price**' index of quality.

Elements of Communication

(i) **Sender or Source.** The source is the person or party desiring to communicate. The party sends the message through some channels such as advertisement to the receiver. The communication is effective if the receiver understands it in the same sense as is intended by the source.

(ii) **Encoding.** The idea to be communicated is translated in a language or medium of expression suitable for transmission, *i.e.*, the thought is put into symbolic form such as words, signs, picture, charts, sales manuals, copy, artwork *etc.*

(iii) **Message.** It is the subject-matter of any communication. The message may either be visual or verbal.

(iv) **Media/Channel.** It refers to the medium by which the message can be carried or delivered. Channels may include any form of promotion such as advertisement, sales promotion, personal selling or publicity. The message may be communicated through newspapers, magazines, television, radio *etc.*

(v) **Decoding.** Decoding is the receiver's interpretation of the message which depends upon his past experience. It is the process by which the receiver assigns meaning to the symbols transmitted by the sender.

(vi) **Receiver.** The receiver is the party receiving the message, also called as audience or destination. Communication aims at influencing the audience, which is the target link in the message. The message should be framed according to the psychographic, demographic and geographic characteristics of the audience.

(vii) **Feedback.** The receiver's response is known as feedback. He may make further communication or accept and take action on it. It gives an idea what the audience has learned and how they have behaved. It in fact, gives cue as to when and how the message should be altered to be most effective. Feedback may be in the form of— a nod, an expression of interest or anger, or a smile or acceptance of the message by conduct.

One more component—noise is also normally present in the communication system, which creates obstacles and distorts the communication process. It can arise due to faulty transmission, faulty reception or interference. It changes the message received from the source from which it was sent and thus reduces the effectiveness of communication process.

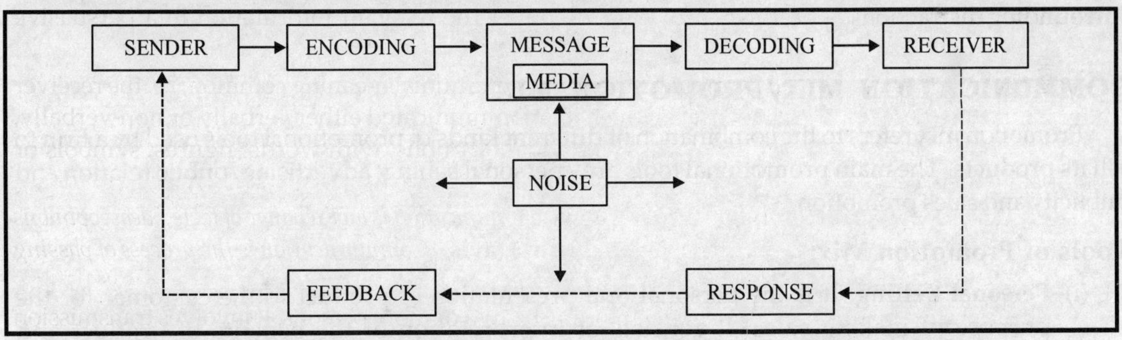

Apart from noise, there are other reasons for not receiving the intended message:

(i) **Selective Attention.** The prospect does not notice all the stimuli that is intended to reach him. People are exposed to several hundred commercial messages a day. It is not possible for them to receive all the messages. It is for this reason that headlines are given in bold eye catching manner.

(ii) **Selective Distortion.** The prospect twists the message to hear what they want to hear. They often add things to the message that are not there and fail to notice other things that are there. Therefore, the communication should give simple, clear and interesting messages. He should also repeat them.

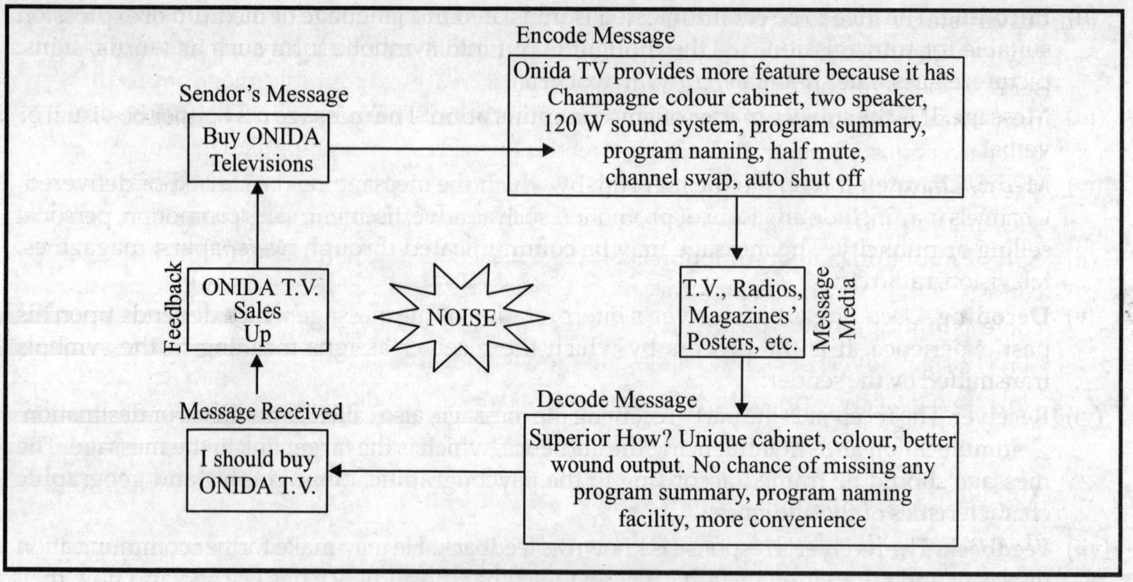

The Communication Process

(*Source: The Tribune*)

(iii) **Selective Recall.** People are able to retain only a small portion of messages that reach them, in their permanent memory. If the receiver's initial attitude towards the message is positive, the message is likely to be accepted and have high recall. If his initial attitude is negative, the message will be rejected but it will stay in his long term memory.

The challenge to the communicator is to develop a message that will attract attention in spite of surrounding distractions.

COMMUNICATION MIX/PROMOTION MIX

Promotion mix refers to the combination of different kinds of promotional tools used by a firm to sell its products. The main promotional tools are - personal selling, advertising, public relation and publicity and sales promotion.

Tools of Promotion Mix

(i) **Personal Selling.** It is the personal oral presentation of product to the customer for the purpose of making sales. It consists of interpretation of the benefits of product and services to the buyer and persuading him to buy right kind of the product. It aims at individual thus the sales person to tailor-make their messages according to the characteristics and need of the buyer. The sales person can also get immediate feedback. It helps to develop a personal relationship between the customer and salesman resulting in better understanding. It allows for demonstration of the product thereby enables the buyer to get intensive information.

The American Marketing Association defines personal selling as 'oral presentation in a conversation with one more prospective purchases for the purpose of making sales.'

The tools of personal selling include – sales-presentation, sales meetings, salesman samples and Tele-marketing.

(ii) **Advertising.** Advertising is a non-personal form of communication regarding goods and services from an identified source to large number of potential customers. It aims to sell goods and services, help the concern to face competition and create a favourable image of products and firm. The various media of advertising are- newspapers, magazines, catalogues, radio, T.V., billboards signs, posters *etc*. The recent trend is towards sponsorships like close-up Antakshri. The American Marketing Association defines advertisement as, 'any paid form of non personal presentation and promotion of goods, services or ideas by an identified sponsor.'

(iii) **Sales Promotion.** Sales promotion is the device used to stimulate demand for the product. It consists of short term and temporary incentives to induce sales such as displays, demonstration, contests, gifts, premium packs, off season discounts, sampling, coupons, *etc.*, For example,

(a) Fa soap advertises – Buy three soaps and get one free.

(b) Get 50*gm* close up toothpaste free with 160*ml* clinic plus shampoo.

(c) Get 100*gm* Pepsodent paste free with 200 *gm* Pepsodent paste

(*Source: Times of India*)

American Marketing Association defines sales promotion as , *those marketing activities, other than personal selling, advertising and publicity that stimulate consumer purchasing and dealer effectiveness, such as displays, shows and demonstrations, expositions and various non current selling efforts, not in ordinary routine'*.

(iv) **Publicity and Public Relations.** Publicity is form of communication promoting to the mass market. It is not paid for. The tools of publicity include press conferences, speeches, annual reports, publication, donations and sponsorships (only that part which is not paid for).

Public relations is the firm's relationship with the public, *e.g.*, customers, suppliers, stockholders, employees, Government, general public and society. The purpose of such communication is to develop a favourable image of the product and the organization.

Factor Influencing Promotional or Communication Mix

To accomplish promotion and marketing objectives usually, combination of two or more promotional methods are applied for one product. This constitutes the promotion mix for that product. There is no ideal promotion mix for any firm. It depends largely on intention and judgment of the marketing manager because it is hard to measure the effect of one medium at a particular time for a particular product. The managerial decision about the promotional mix of a firm is influenced by the following factors:

1. **Nature of Product.** The selection of promotional method depends upon the nature of product. For example, industrial goods being highly complex and technical in nature require personal selling. Though, advertising and publicity may also have influence but just to provide general information. Whereas convenience goods depend on advertising and display as they are lowly priced and frequently purchased. For shopping goods the consumer does not require much of prior knowledge. He purchases it after careful consideration of quality, price and durability therefore, the main emphasis is on personal selling together with advertising. Whereas in case of specialty goods the consumer must have full knowledge. Such goods have high unit value and infrequently purchase therefore, here the emphasis is on advertising, personal selling as well as sales promotion.
2. **Product Life Cycle.** In the introduction stage, the consumers are unaware of the product, therefore, advertising is extensively used so as to stimulate primary demand. In addition to advertising emphasis is also placed on personal selling, trade shows, demonstrations,

exhibitions publicity *etc*. In the growth stage, consumer is aware of the uses and attributes of the product. Advertising is done to promote selective demand and to keep the buyer away from competitor's brand. During the maturity stage, creating brand preference and maintaining brand loyalty becomes utmost important. Therefore, emphasis is placed an advertising and sales promotion. In the decline stage promotional efforts are reduced to minimum. Only few concerns try to push up sales with high promotional advertisement. Aggressive personal selling programme may be taken at segments where demand for the product exists. In the obsolescence stage all-promotional efforts are stopped as the product is withdrawn from the market.

3. **Nature of the Market.**

   (a) ***Kinds of Customers.*** Final consumer – advertisement, personal selling and sales promotion.
   Industrial consumers – personal selling.
   Wholesalers personal selling
   Retailers – advertisement in trade magazines and newspaper, sales promotion.

   (b) ***Geographical Area.*** If it is local Market – personal selling is possible. But if it is National/International market – advertisement and other promotional tools are applied.

   (c) ***Concentration of Market.*** If the customers are concentrated at one place personal selling is possible but if they are widely spread then advertisement and sales promotion is adopted.

4. **Size of budget.** Selection depends on cost of media and availability of funds. A firm with huge promotional budget can undertake all promotional activities. Firm with low budget depends mainly on local newspapers, outdoor advertisements, wall writings etc.,4 because other means of promotion such as personal selling, discounts, free gifts advertisement in trade magazines etc., involve high cost.

5. **Nature of Competition.** The promotional efforts must match the level of competition. There is a general tendency to go for high advertising, sales promotion and personal selling when there is highly competitive environment.

6. **Promotional Strategy.** The choice of promotional tools depends whether a company adopts push or pull strategy. In case of push strategy, dealer is asked to promote the product line aggressively, for which they are granted high margins and exclusive dealership. Thus, here personal selling and sales promotion play a vital role. On the other hand, pull strategy stimulates demand of end-consumer so that they may ask retailers for the product.

ELEMENTS OF CONSUMER BEHAVIOUR

Consumer behaviour is psychological, social and physical behaviour of potential consumers. According to **Walter** and **Paul**, '*Consumer behaviour is the process whereby individuals decide whether what, when, where, how and from whom to purchase goods and services.*'

The consumer behaviour can be studied with the help of stimulus response model. The buying process is made up of following stages, input-process-output-feedback. The potential consumers are subjected to various stimuli (input). Responding to these stimuli, they make certain purchases (output). After consumption, they convey their positive or negative responses.

Stimulus-Response Model

Outside Stimuli		Buyer's Black Box		Buyer's Purchase Decision
Marketing	**Environment**	**Buyer's Characteristics**	**Buyer s Decision**	
1. Product	1. Economic	1. Cultural	1. Problem recognition	1. Product choice.
2. Price	2. Technological →	2. Social recognition	2. Information research →	2. Brand choice
3. Place	3. Political	3. Personal	3. Evaluation	3. Dealer choice
4. Promotion	4. Cultural	4. Psychological	4. Decision.	4. Purchase timing
			5. Post Purchase behaviour	5. Purchase amount
Stimuli (Inputs)		Process (Processing)		Response (Output)

Stages in Buying Process

The buying process comprises of five stages :

1. **Need Recognition.** The decision to buy start with recognizing the need or desire for something which will give satisfaction on consumption. Such desire may arise either due to internal stimulus (*i.e.* desire for comfort, safety, prestige, conformity, curiosity etc.) Such stimulus acts as a cue for the marketer. The intensity of need determines the priority list of the consumer. He will make immediate purchases for the most urgent need and postpone other purchases because his means are limited. The marketer must search to know what aroused the need or desire of the consumer and how he proceeded to satisfy it.
2. **Information Search.** The recognized need can be satisfied promptly only when it is known what product or brand will best satisfy it and where is that product available. The consumer gathers such information either by recalling the relevant information stored in memory or by topping sources like friends, family, neighbour, colleagues or salespersons, dealers, advertisements, packaging, displays or mass media like newspaper, radio, television and consumer information centers.
3. **Evaluation of Alternatives.** The consumer assesses various alternative products or services and judges their want satisfying potential. In evaluating the alternatives many aspects are taken into consideration such as product attributes, utility function of each attribute, brand image, trade-off, concessions, convenience and facilities.

   As pointed in the above example, the consumer who wishes to buy a product may not be aware of the total number of product varieties available in the market. He may further not consider all the varieties that he is aware of because of the limitation of time, income, availability etc. Out of the consideration set, he lists out certain varieties on the basis of certain criteria. He then ultimately makes a decision regarding particular brand.

The Matiz 'Total Spice' Advantage

Price	Matiz SG E2	Santro LS E2	Santro LE E2	Zen VX E2	Zen LX E2	Wagon R LX E2	Wagon R LXI E2	Alto VX E2
Ex showroom price (Rs) Chandigarh	3,41,000	3,75,000	3,34,000	3,73,000	3,34,000	3,31,000	3,56,000	3,57,000
Price difference (Rs)	–	34,000	7,000	32,000	7,000	10,000	15,000	16,000
Power Stearing	√	√	X	X	X	X	√	X
Warranty								
Comparison	4 years	2 years				1 year		

(*Source – The Tribune March*, 17th 2001)

4. **Purchase Decision.** After evaluating the alternatives, the buyer buys the brand he likes the most. But, sometimes, his intention to purchase a particular brand is intervened by variables like – attitude of others, change in income, change in priority, dealer terms, availability and other unexpected situational factors. He may also postpone, modify or avoid a purchase due to perceived risk. The consumers are not certain about the purchase outcome and, therefore, they hesitate to take purchase action. The marketer should try to reduce the risk factor by providing sufficient information, popularizing brands and giving warranties. Such actions on behalf of the marketer will boast up the confidence of the buyer.
5. **Post Purchase Reaction.** The consumer has certain expectations from the product. Such expectations are framed on the basis of message received from seller, friends and other sources. If the product performances match the expectations, the consumer feels satisfied and go for repeated purchase. He even speaks positive for it in public. But, if the product fails to come up to his expectations, he feels dissatisfied. He may then either simply stop buying the product or he may take action like talking negative about the product or launching complaint to the company or seeking help of other agencies that might help him or take legal action. It is for this reason that marketer should never exaggerate about product benefits. The marketer can minimize dissatisfaction by giving evidences of satisfied brand users, entertain customer suggestions, provide instructions of use and or communicate with buyers.

Types of Buying Behaviour

Buying behaviour vary with the type of product to be purchased. The more expensive and complex the product, more the efforts involved in its purchase. The buying behaviour can be classified as:

(a) **Complex Buying Behaviour.** Such behaviour on the part of consumers is found while purchasing an expensive, risky and infrequently product. The consumers are required to put in extra effort and time to compare brand differences. The buyer usually do not have much knowledge about the product and existing brands. He, therefore, first gathers information on the basis of which he develops his beliefs and attitudes and then after careful analysis makes the purchase choice. The marketer in-order to build brand preference must provide detailed information on product attributes and its competitive superiority.

(b) **Dissonance – Reducing Buying Behaviour.** When a consumer though highly involved in purchasing the product does not find much differences in brands, may take the decision quickly. He may either go for a price or convenient location or dealer relation as all the brands in the particular price range are more or less same. But after purchase he may find certain dissatisfying features or learn about better features of other brands or low price of apparently expensive product. The buyer feels restless and tends to reduce dissonance by either changing or justifying his views or altering his behaviour.

(c) **Habitual Buying Behaviour.** Such behaviour is found for inexpensive, frequently purchased product. The consumer do not make much effort in comparing brands. They usually purchase it on the basis of information received through advertisements without evaluating it on any significant aspect. The repetition of advertisement creates familiarity Of the brand name, which makes it easy for the consumer to select. The marketer of such products find price and sales promotion incentive as an effective tool in developing demand. They use catchy slogans and attractive pictures to make it easy for the consumer to recognize and remember the brand name.

(d) **Variety Seeking Buying Behaviour.** Such a behaviour is found for products characterizing low involvement on the part of consumer but having significant brand differences. The consumer purchases the product without much comparisons. They evaluate the product on use. Next time the consumer goes for change of brand just to have a variety and not due to dissatisfaction from the previous brand. The marketer of new brand encourages the consumer to seek variety by offering discounts, contest coupons, free samples, promoting as choice of new generation *etc.* whereas the marketer of existing brand promotes habitual buying by giving reminder advertisements, putting pressure on experienced trusted name in the field and ensuring continuous availability.

Determinants of Consumer Behaviour

The behaviour of consumers with regard to purchases are influenced by various uncontrollable variables. Most of these factors are interdependent and interrelated. The variables affect each consumer differently leading to different behaviour by consumers. Therefore, each of these factors should be analysed in detail.

(a) Economic	(b) Social	(c) Cultural	(d) Personal	(e) Psychological
1. Personal income	1. Family	1. Culture and subculture	1. Age and Life Cycle stage	1. Motivation
2. Family income	2. Reference groups	2. Social class	2. Occupation	2. Perception
3. Income expectations	3. Opinion leaders	3. Caste	3. Income	3. Learning
4 Liquid assets	4. Roles & status		4. Life-style	4. Beliefs & attitudes
5. Consumer credit			5. Personality	
6. Govt. policy				

Importance of Marketing to Consumers

1. **Increase in Knowledge to Consumers.** Marketing through various means of promotion – advertising, publicity, salesmanship, inform the consumers about the various kinds of products available and thus increases their knowledge.
2. **Facilitates Choice.** The availability of products in different varieties, sizes, design, colours, shapes etc. helps the consumer to make choice.
3. **Availability of Good Quality Products.** Marketing undertakes R & D activities which helps in improving the quality. Thus, the consumers get better quality products.
4. **Stable Prices.** Marketing equalises demand and supply. It helps in movement of goods from area of surplus to area of deficit and thus stabilizes the prices.

SERVICE MARKETING

The world economy nowadays is increasingly characterized as a service economy. This is primarily due to the increasing importance and share of the service sector in the economies of most developed and developing countries. In fact, the growth of the service sector has long been considered as indicative of a country's economic progress.

Economic history tells us that all developing nations have invariably experienced a shift from agriculture to industry and then to the service sector as the main stay of the economy.

This shift has also brought about a change in the definition of goods and services themselves. No longer are goods considered separate from services. Rather, services now increasingly represent an integral part of the product and this interconnectedness of goods and services is represented on a goods-services continuum.

Definition and characteristics of Services

The American Marketing Association defines services as - "Activities, benefits and satisfactions which are offered for sale or are provided in connection with the sale of goods."

The defining characteristics of a service are:

Intangibility: Services are intangible and do not have a physical existence. Hence services cannot be touched, held, tasted or smelt. This is most defining feature of a service and that which primarily differentiates it from a product. Also, it poses a unique challenge to those engaged in marketing a service as they need to attach tangible attributes to an otherwise intangible offering.

1. **Heterogeneity/Variability.** Given the very nature of services, each service offering is unique and cannot be exactly repeated even by the same service provider. While products can be mass produced and be homogenous the same is not true of services. e.g; All burgers of a particular flavor at McDonalds are almost identical. However, the same is not true of the service rendered by the same counter staff consecutively to two customers.
2. **Perishability.** Services cannot be stored, saved, returned or resold once they have been used. Once rendered to a customer the service is completely consumed and cannot be delivered to another customer. eg: A customer dissatisfied with the services of a barber cannot return the service of the haircut that was rendered to him. At the most he may decide not to visit that particular barber in the future.
3. **Inseparability/Simultaneity of production and consumption.** This refers to the fact that services are generated and consumed within the same time frame. Eg: a haircut is delivered to and consumed by a customer simultaneously unlike, say, a takeaway burger which the customer may consume even after a few hours of purchase. Moreover, it is very difficult to separate a service from the service provider. Eg: the barber is necessarily a part of the service of a haircut that he is delivering to his customer.

Types of Services

1. Core Services: A service that is the primary purpose of the transaction. Eg: a haircut or the services of lawyer or teacher.
2. Supplementary Services: Services that are rendered as a corollary to the sale of a tangible product. Eg: Home delivery options offered by restaurants above a minimum bill value.

Difference between Goods and Services

Given below are the fundamental differences between physical goods and services:

Goods	Services
A physical commodity	A process or activity
Tangible	Intangible
Homogenous	Heterogeneous
Production and distribution are separation from their consumption	Production, distribution and consumption are simultaneous processes
Can be stored	Cannot be stored
Transfer of ownership is possible	Transfer of ownership is not possible

TRENDS IN MARKETING

SOCIAL MARKETING

Social marketing is an approach used to develop activities aimed at changing or maintaining people's behaviour for the benefit of individuals and society as a whole.

Combining ideas from commercial marketing and the social sciences, social marketing is a proven tool for influencing behaviour in a sustainable and cost-effective way.

It helps you to decide:

- Which people to work with
- What behaviour to influence
- How to go about it
- How to measure it

Social marketing is not the same as social media marketing.

Approach

Social marketing is a systematic and planned process. It follows six steps:

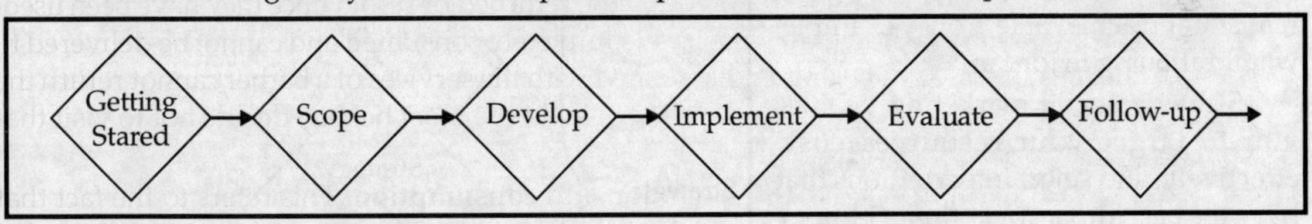

Behaviour

The goal of social marketing is always to change or maintain how people behave - not what they think or how aware they are about an issue. If your goal is only to increase awareness or knowledge, or change attitudes, you are not doing social marketing.

Benefits People and Society

This is the value - perceived or actual - as it is defined by the people who are targeted by a social marketing intervention. It is not what is assumed to benefit them by the organisation that is trying to encourage the behaviour change.

A Social Marketing Approach

Even if you don't take social marketing any further, just considering these four questions will add value to your projects and policies.

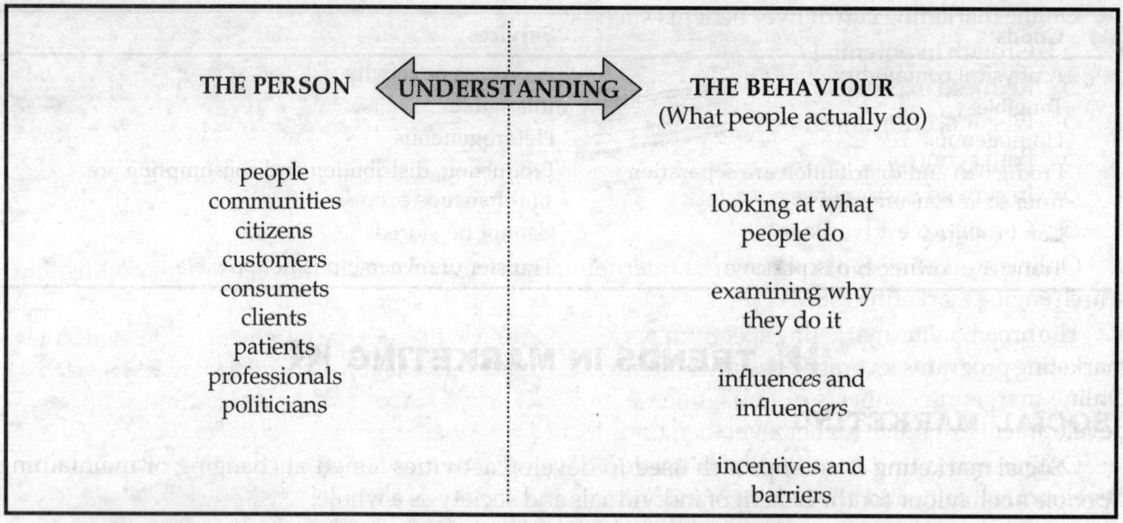

1. Do I really understand my target audience and see things from their perspective?
2. Am I clear about what I would like my target audience to do?
3. For my target audience, do the benefits of doing what I would like them to do outweigh the costs or barriers to doing it?
4. Am I using a combination of activities in order to encourage people to achieve the desired action?

How Social Marketing Helps

Policy social marketing helps to ensure policy is based on an understanding of people's lives, making policy goals realistic and achievable. Policy example: water rationing in Jordan.

Strategy social marketing enables you to target your resources cost-effectively, and select interventions that have the best impact over time. Strategy example: lung disease strategy in England

Implementation and delivery social marketing enables you to develop products, services and communications that fit people's needs and motivations. Delivery example: child car seats in Texas.

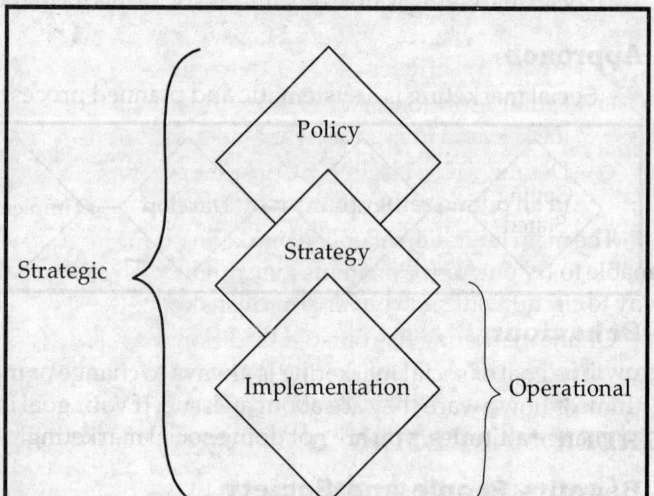

ONLINE MARKETING

Online marketing is a set of tools and methodologies used for promoting products and services through the internet. Online marketing includes a wider range of marketing elements than traditional business marketing due to the extra channels and marketing mechanisms available on the internet.

Online marketing can deliver benefits such as:

- Growth in potential
- Reduced expenses
- Elegant communications
- Better control
- Improved customer service
- Competitive advantage

Online marketing is also known as internet marketing, web marketing, digital marketing and search engine marketing (SEM).

The broad online marketing spectrum varies according to business requirements. Effective online marketing programs leverage consumer data and customer relationship management (CRM) systems. Online marketing connects organizations with qualified potential customers and takes business development to a much higher level than traditional marketing.

Online marketing combines the internet's creative and technical tools, including design, development, sales and advertising, while focusing on the following primary business models:

- E-commerce
- Lead-based websites
- Affiliate marketing
- Local search

Online marketing has several advantages, including:

- Low costs: Large audiences are reachable at a fraction of traditional advertising budgets, allowing businesses to create appealing consumer ads.
- Flexibility and convenience: Consumers may research and purchase products and services at their leisure.
- Analytics: Efficient statistical results are facilitated without extra costs.
- Multiple options: Advertising tools include pay-per-click advertising, email marketing and local search integration (like Google Maps).
- Demographic targeting: Consumers can be demographically targeted much more effectively in an online rather than an offline process.

The main limitation of online marketing is the lack of tangibility, which means that consumers are unable to try out, or try on items they might wish to purchase. Generous return policies are the main way to circumvent such buyer apprehension.

Online marketing has outsold traditional advertising in recent years and continues to be a high-growth industry.

GREEN MARKETING

Green marketing is the marketing of environmentally friendly products and services. It is becoming more popular as more people become concerned with environmental issues and decide that they want to spend their money in a way that is kinder to the planet.

Green marketing can involve a number of different things, such as creating an eco-friendly product, using eco-friendly packaging, adopting sustainable business practices, or focusing marketing efforts on messages that communicate a product's green benefits.

This type of marketing can be more expensive, but it can also be profitable due to the increasing demand. For example, products made locally in North America tend to be more expensive than those made overseas using cheap labor, but they have a much smaller carbon footprint because they don't have to fly across the globe to get here. For some consumers and business owners, the environmental benefit outweighs the price difference.

LOHAS

Consumers who prefer to purchase green products even though they might be more expensive fall into the 'LOHAS' category. LOHAS stands for Lifestyles of Health and Sustainability. According to Wikipedia:

"LOHAS describes an integrated, rapidly growing market for goods and services that appeal to consumers whose sense of environmental and social responsibility influences their purchase decisions."

These consumers are active supporters of environmental health and are the heaviest purchasers of green and socially responsible products. They also have the power to influence other consumers.

Green Marketing Methods

Beyond making an environmentally friendly product, business owners can do other things as part of their green marketing efforts. The following can all be part of a green marketing strategy:

- Using eco-friendly paper and inks for print marketing materials.
- Skipping the printed materials altogether and option for electronic marketing.
- Having a recycling program and responsible waste disposal practices.
- Using eco-friendly product packaging.
- Using efficient packing and shipping methods.
- Using eco-friendly power sources.
- Taking steps to offset environmental impact.

Greenwashing

Some marketers try to capitalize on the growing number of green consumers by simply taking a green marketing approach to products that might not otherwise be considered green. They try to position their products as a better choice for the environment when they're really not. An example of this is when a company uses the color green in their packaging, or the word green somewhere in their messaging, when there isn't anything particularly eco-friendly about their product, nor it's not more eco-friendly than competing products. Greenwashing is not only misleading, but it can also be damaging to a company's reputation.

If consumers want to be certain they are indeed buying a green product, they should look for official certifications listed on the product packaging.

DIRECT MARKETING

Direct marketing is a promotional method that involves presenting information about your company, product, or service to your target customer without the use of an advertising middleman. It is a targeted form of marketing that presents information of potential interest to a consumer that has been determined to be a likely buyer.

For example, subscribers to teen magazines might be presented with Facebook ads for acne medication which, based on their age, they are likely to need. Or members of the United States Equestrian Federation might all receive an email promotion offering special pricing on horse gear. Current residents of Wilmington, Delaware might receive a flyer announcing the arrival of Wegmans supermarket to their area. Conversely, people in Wilmington, Ohio would not.

Forms of Direct Marketing

Common forms of direct marketing include:

- Brochures
- Catalogs
- Fliers
- Newsletters
- Post cards
- Coupons
- Emails
- Targeted online display ads
- Phone calls
- Text messages

The Goal

While some marketing techniques aim to increase awareness or to educate markets about a company's products or services, direct marketing's sole goal is to persuade the recipient to take action. While getting a sale is the ultimate goal, some customers will not be ready to buy on-the-spot. But they might:

- Visit a website
- Call for more information
- Return a postcard requesting a quote
- Enter their name and email address
- Make a purchase

Reasons it's Successful

Unlike mass advertising, which is presented to everyone, direct marketing is presented only to people who are suspected to have an interest or need in your company's product, based on information gathered about them.

For example, graduates of Princeton University might be sent an email announcing a new cashmere sweater now available for sale with the school's logo on it. Only students, graduates, and their parents are likely to be interested in owning such a piece of clothing, so by limiting who receives the announcement, the manufacturer saves money on distribution costs and increases the odds of reaching people who might make a purchase.

Other reasons direct marketing is more successful are:

- You can make the message personal, making the recipient feel it is meant just for them.
- It is more cost-effective to market to buyers who have been identified as likely to buy.
- For that reason it also has a higher return on investment, since the likelihood of making a sale to a targeted customer list is higher to begin with.
- It is measurable. Direct marketing uses a number of built-in ways to track the success of each campaign, allowing you to improve with each mail or email cycle.

RURAL MARKETING

Rural marketing is a process of developing, pricing, promoting, and distributing rural specific goods and services leading to desired exchange with rural customers to satisfy their needs and wants, and also to achieve organizational objectives.

The emergence of rural markets as highly untapped potential emphasizes the need to explore them. Marketers over the past few decades, with innovative approaches, have attempted to understand and tap rural markets. Some of their efforts paid off and many markets still an enigma. Rural marketing is an evolving concept, and as a part of any economy, has untapped potential; marketers have realized the opportunity recently. Improvement in infrastructure and reach, promise a bright future for those intending to go rural. Rural consumers are keen on branded goods nowadays, so the market size for products and services seems to have burgeoned.

The rural population has shown a trend of moving to a state of gradual urbanization in terms of exposure, habits, lifestyles, and lastly, consumption patterns of goods and services. So, there are dangers on concentrating more on the rural customers. Reducing the product features in order to lower prices is a dangerous game to play. Rural buyers like to follow the urban pattern of living. Astonishingly, as per the census report 2003-04, there are total 638365 villages in India in which nearly 70% of total population resides; out of them 35 % villages have more than 1000 population.

Rural per capita consumption expenditure grew by 11.5 per cent while the urban expenditure grew by 9.6 per cent. There is a tremendous potential for consumer durables like two-wheelers, small cars, television sets, refrigerators, air-conditioners and household appliances in rural India.

CONCEPT OF RURAL MARKETING

The concept of Rural Marketing in India Economy has always played an influential role in the lives of people. In India, leaving out a few metropolitan cities, all the districts and industrial townships are connected with rural markets. The rural market in India generates bigger revenues in the country as the rural regions comprise of the maximum consumers in this country. The rural market in Indian economy generates almost more than half of the country's income. Rural marketing in Indian economy can be classified under two broad categories.

These are:

(i) The market for consumer goods that comprise of both durable and non-durable goods.

(ii) The market for agricultural inputs that include fertilizers, pesticides, seeds, and so on.

The concept of rural marketing in India is often been found to forms ambiguity in the mind of people who think rural marketing is all about agricultural marketing. However, rural marketing determines the carrying out of business activities bringing in the flow of goods from urban sectors to the rural regions of the country as well as the marketing of various products manufactured by the non-agricultural workers from rural to urban areas.

To be precise, rural marketing in India Economy covers two broad sections, namely:

(i) Selling of agricultural products in the urban areas.

(ii) Selling of manufactured products in the rural regions.

The rural market in India is not a separate entity in itself and it is highly influenced by the sociological and behavioural factors operating in the country. The rural population in India accounts for around 627 million, which is exactly 74.3 percent of the total population.

Conceptually, rural marketing is not significantly different to urban marketing. Marketing manager has to perform the same tasks, but differently in rural marketing. It can be said that marketing is not different, but markets (buyers and users).

In rural marketing, a firm has to undergo marketing efforts to satisfy rural segments, which notably differ from urban segments in some aspects. At the same time, we must note that increasing literacy rate, improved sources of income, awareness due to improved and increased means of communication and transportation, high rate of mobility within and between countries due to liberalization and globalization, and many other such reasons, some customers are likely to be identical.

Even, a few rural customers seem cosmopolitan! So, one can find customers of different behaviour patterns within a village or a town. In the same way, most of products are commonly used in both urban and rural areas. In some aspects, both rural and urban customers behave in homogeneous pattern. Some Indian customers have become global and cosmopolitan!

'Rural marketing' is similar to simply 'marketing.' Rural marketing differs only in terms of buyers. Here, target market consists of customers living in rural areas. Thus, rural marketing is an application of marketing fundamentals (concepts, principles, processes, theories, etc.) to rural markets.

1. Let us define the term in simple way as: Rural marketing concerns with planning and implementing marketing programmes (often referred as marketing strategies or simply 4P's) for rural markets to achieve marketing goals.
2. In more specific words: Rural marketing is a process of developing, pricing, promoting, and distributing rural specific goods and services leading to desired exchange with rural customers to satisfy their needs and wants, and also to achieve organizational objectives.
3. Marketing efforts remain same, only important aspect is type of buyers. So, the term can be defined as: When marketing activities are undertaken for rural segments, it is turned as rural marketing and the management is called rural marketing management.
4. Since marketing manager has to carry out similar tasks. So, definition of marketing stated by American Marketing Association can be equally applicable in relation to rural segments. We will add only specific word 'rural' to define the term: Rural marketing is a process of planning, and executing the conception, pricing, promotion, and distribution of ideas, goods, and services to create exchange (for rural segments) that satisfy individual and organizational objectives.

   (Only the word 'rural' has been added to the definition adopted by the AMA. The word implies that marketing activities are undertaken in rural areas to satisfy rural segments.)
5. More specifically, it can be said: Rural Marketing means to produce products (goods and services) for the rural customers and to make necessary arrangement to supply them.
6. At last, we can say: Rural marketing is the marketing for the customers residing in rural areas. It involves designing marketing programme (4P's) to arrive at desired exchange with the rural customers that satisfies their needs and wants.

LOGISTICS MANAGEMENT

Logistics management is a supply chain management component that is used to meet customer demands through the planning, control and implementation of the effective movement and storage of related information, goods and services from origin to destination. Logistics management helps companies reduce expenses and enhance customer service.

The logistics management process begins with raw material accumulation to the final stage of delivering goods to the destination.

By adhering to customer needs and industry standards, logistics management facilitates process strategy, planning and implementation.

Logistics management involves numerous elements, including:

- Selecting appropriate vendors with the ability to provide transportation facilities.
- Choosing the most effective routes for transportation.

- Discovering the most competent delivery method.
- Using software and IT resources to proficiently handle related processes.

In logistics management, unwise decisions create multiple issues. For example, deliveries that fail or are delayed lead to buyer dissatisfaction. Damage of goods due to careless transportation is another potential issue. Poor logistics planning gradually increases expenses, and issues may arise from the implementation of ineffective logistics software. Most of these problems occur due to improper decisions related to outsourcing, such as selecting the wrong vendor or carrying out delivery tasks without sufficient resources.

To resolve these issues, organizations should implement best logistic management practices. Companies should focus on collaboration rather than competition. Good collaboration among transportation providers, buyers and vendors helps reduce expenses. An efficient and safe transportation provider is also vital to business success.

MULTIPLE CHOICE QUESTIONS

1. What is the primary focus of marketing?
   (1) Maximising profits
   (2) Satisfying customer needs and wants
   (3) Reducing production costs
   (4) Expanding market share
2. Which marketing approach emphasizes building long-term relationships with customers?
   (1) Transactional marketing
   (2) Relationship marketing
   (3) Mass marketing
   (4) Niche marketing
3. What is the core idea of the societal marketing concept?
   (1) Maximising shareholder wealth
   (2) Satisfying customer needs at a profit
   (3) Meeting customer needs while enhancing societal well-being
   (4) Competing solely on price
4. Which marketing orientation focuses on understanding and meeting the specific needs of a target market?
   (1) Product orientation
   (2) Sales orientation
   (3) Market orientation
   (4) Production orientation
5. In the marketing mix, what does the term "promotion" refer to?
   (1) Pricing strategy
   (2) Product development
   (3) Advertising and communication efforts
   (4) Distribution channels
6. What is the purpose of marketing channels (distribution channels) in the marketing process?
   (1) Maximising production efficiency
   (2) Creating brand awareness
   (3) Facilitating the movement of goods and services from producers to consumers
   (4) Setting pricing strategies
7. What is a direct channel in marketing?
   (1) Involves intermediaries between producers and consumers
   (2) Bypasses intermediaries, selling directly to consumers
   (3) Utilizes multiple intermediaries
   (4) Focuses on international distribution
8. Which type of distribution strategy involves using multiple channels to reach different customer segments?
   (1) Exclusive distribution
   (2) Intensive distribution
   (3) Selective distribution
   (4) Horizontal distribution
9. What role do intermediaries play in marketing channels?
   (1) Creating products
   (2) Consuming products
   (3) Facilitating the exchange process between producers and consumers
   (4) Setting pricing strategies
10. Which marketing channel function involves gathering and distributing information about the market and consumers?
    (1) Transactional function
    (2) Facilitating function
    (3) Logistical function
    (4) Matching function
11. What are the traditional 4 Ps of the marketing mix?
    (1) Product, Price, Promotion, Place
    (2) Production, Profit, People, Placement
    (3) Promotion, Positioning, Price, Production
    (4) People, Product, Place, Promotion
12. Which element of the marketing mix refers to the range of products or services offered by a company?
    (1) Price (2) Promotion
    (3) Product (4) Place
13. What is the role of the "price" element in the marketing mix?
    (1) Creating brand awareness
    (2) Communicating with customers
    (3) Determining the cost of production

(4) Capturing the value of the product or service for the customer

14. What does the "promotion" element of the marketing mix involve?
(1) Setting product prices
(2) Communicating with target customers
(3) Developing new products
(4) Establishing distribution channels

15. In the marketing mix, what does the term "place" refer to?
(1) Pricing strategy
(2) Product development
(3) Distribution channels and logistics
(4) Advertising and promotion

16. What is strategic marketing planning?
(1) Short-term tactical decisions to boost sales
(2) Long-term process of defining the company's direction and making decisions on allocating its resources
(3) Day-to-day operational decisions
(4) Ad hoc decision-making without a clear plan

17. What is a SWOT analysis in strategic marketing planning?
(1) Analyzing customer preferences
(2) Evaluating a company's strengths, weaknesses, opportunities, and threats
(3) Setting promotional strategies
(4) Estimating production costs

18. What is the purpose of setting marketing objectives in strategic planning?
(1) To Maximise short-term profits
(2) To guide decision-making and provide a clear direction
(3) To focus solely on cost reduction
(4) To limit market expansion

19. What is the role of a marketing strategy in strategic planning?
(1) Maximising production efficiency
(2) Setting short-term goals
(3) Outlining the overall approach for reaching marketing objectives
(4) Creating brand awareness

20. What is the significance of market segmentation in strategic marketing planning?
(1) Focusing on mass marketing
(2) Ignoring customer needs
(3) Dividing the market into distinct groups with similar needs and characteristics
(4) Reducing product variety

21. What is market segmentation?
(1) Offering the same product to all customers
(2) Dividing the market into smaller groups with similar needs and characteristics
(3) Focusing solely on mass marketing
(4) Maximising production efficiency

22. What is demographic segmentation based on?
(1) Geographic location
(2) Age, gender, income, and education
(3) Behavioral characteristics
(4) Psychographic factors

23. Which targeting strategy involves offering different products to different market segments?
(1) Undifferentiated targeting
(2) Concentrated targeting
(3) Differentiated targeting
(4) Mass targeting

24. What is the purpose of positioning in marketing?
(1) Reducing production costs
(2) Creating brand awareness
(3) Establishing a distinctive image in the minds of consumers
(4) Focusing solely on short-term goals

25. What is the primary focus of market targeting?
(1) Minimising market share
(2) Maximising short-term profits
(3) Selecting specific market segments to serve
(4) Ignoring customer needs

Directions: Each of the following items consists of two statements, one labelled as Assertion (A) and other labelled as Reason (R). You are to examine these two statements carefully and decide if the (A) and the (R) are individually true and if so, whether (R) is the correct explanation of (A). Select your answers to these items using the codes given below:
(1) The (A) is true, and the (R) is false.
(2) The (A) is false, and the (R) is false.
(3) The (A) is false, and the (R) is true.
(4) The (A) is true, and the (R) is true.

26. **Assertion (A):** Relationship marketing focuses on short-term transactions.
Reason (R): Relationship marketing emphasizes building long-term relationships with customers.

27. **Assertion (A):** Promotion in the marketing mix involves setting product prices.
Reason (R): Promotion is primarily concerned with advertising and communication efforts.

28. **Assertion (A):** SWOT analysis is a tool used in strategic marketing planning.
Reason (R): SWOT analysis evaluates a company's strengths, weaknesses, opportunities, and threats.

29. **Assertion (A):** Market segmentation involves offering the same product to all customers.
Reason (R): Market segmentation divides the market into smaller groups with similar needs and characteristics.

30. **Assertion (A):** Positioning in marketing is focused on Minimising production costs.
Reason (R): Positioning aims to establish a distinctive image in the minds of consumers.

31. What is a product in a marketing context?
(1) Only physical goods
(2) Anything offered in a market for attention, use, or consumption
(3) Only tangible items
(4) Only services

32. What is the core component of a product that provides value to customers?
(1) Branding
(2) Packaging
(3) Core benefit or core customer value
(4) Pricing strategy

33. Which of the following is an example of a durable product?
(1) Newspaper (2) Smartphone
(3) Soft drink (4) Fast food

34. What is the purpose of product augmentation in marketing?
(1) Adding features and benefits to differentiate the product
(2) Reducing production costs
(3) Eliminating competitors
(4) Focusing solely on core product features

35. What is a convenience product?
(1) A product that consumers purchase frequently and with minimal effort
(2) A high-priced luxury item
(3) A product with a long life cycle
(4) A specialised industrial product

36. What is a product line?
(1) The total range of products offered by a company
(2) A single product
(3) The average selling price of products
(4) The number of units sold

37. What does the term "product mix" refer to?
(1) The variety of product lines offered by a company
(2) The total number of products in a product line
(3) The average selling price of products
(4) The distribution channels used for products

38. Which of the following is an example of a product mix decision?
(1) Setting the price of a single product
(2) Introducing a new product line
(3) Choosing a brand name
(4) Creating advertising copy

39. What is the significance of having a well-balanced product mix?
(1) Reducing production costs
(2) Minimising competition
(3) Catering to different customer needs and segments
(4) Focusing solely on core products

40. What is the primary objective of product line extension?
(1) Eliminating competitors
(2) Reducing production costs
(3) Increasing market share within the same product category
(4) Lowering prices

41. What stage of the product life cycle is characterised by slow sales growth and a lack of profits?
(1) Introduction stage
(2) Growth stage
(3) Maturity stage
(4) Decline stage

42. What is the primary focus in the growth stage of the product life cycle?
(1) Maximising profits
(2) Creating awareness and promoting the product
(3) Managing declining sales
(4) Reducing production costs

43. Which stage of the product life cycle is characterised by intense competition and the need for differentiation?
(1) Introduction stage (2) Growth stage
(3) Maturity stage (4) Decline stage

44. What is the primary challenge in the decline stage of the product life cycle?

(1) Maximising profits
(2) Maintaining market share
(3) Managing declining sales
(4) Introducing new features

45. What strategy is appropriate in the decline stage of the product life cycle?
(1) Harvesting
(2) Rapid growth
(3) Introduction of new features
(4) Intensive promotion

46. What is the first stage in the new product development process?
(1) Commercialisation
(2) Idea generation
(3) Concept testing
(4) Product development

47. What is concept testing in the new product development process?
(1) Launching the product in the market
(2) Assessing consumer reactions to a product idea before its development
(3) Developing prototypes
(4) Determining pricing strategies

48. What is the purpose of product development in the new product development process?
(1) Testing market reactions
(2) Finalizing the marketing mix
(3) Bringing the product concept to reality
(4) Conducting concept testing

49. What is the significance of test marketing in new product development?
(1) Rapidly introducing the product to the market
(2) Obtaining feedback on how the product performs in a real market environment
(3) Setting the final price of the product
(4) Eliminating competitors

50. What is the last stage in the new product development process?
(1) Commercialization (2) Idea generation
(3) Concept testing
(4) Product development

Directions: Each of the following items consists of two statements, one labelled as Assertion (A) and other labelled as Reason (R). You are to examine these two statements carefully and decide if the (A) and the (R) are individually true and if so, whether (R) is the correct explanation of (A). Select your answers to these items using the codes given below:

(1) The (A) is true, and the (R) is false.
(2) The (A) is false, and the (R) is false.
(3) The (A) is false, and the (R) is true.
(4) The (A) is true, and the (R) is true.

51. Assertion (A): A well-balanced product mix is essential for Minimising competition.
Reason (R): A well-balanced product mix caters to different customer needs and segments.

52. Assertion (A): The growth stage of the product life cycle is characterised by slow sales growth.
Reason (R): The growth stage involves creating awareness and promoting the product.

53. Assertion (A): The maturity stage of the product life cycle requires intense competition and differentiation.
Reason (R): In the maturity stage, products often face declining sales.

54. Assertion (A): The decline stage of the product life cycle involves the introduction of new features.
Reason (R): The decline stage is characterised by managing declining sales.

55. Assertion (A): Concept testing is the final stage in the new product development process.
Reason (R): Concept testing involves assessing consumer reactions to a product idea before its development.

56. What is a key internal factor affecting price determination?
(1) Customer demand
(2) Production costs
(3) Competitor pricing
(4) Economic conditions

57. How does customer perception influence pricing decisions?
(1) It has no impact on pricing decisions
(2) Customers are not concerned about prices
(3) Customer perceptions affect the perceived value of a product
(4) It only affects premium products

58. What is the relationship between demand elasticity and pricing decisions?
(1) Inelastic demand allows for higher prices
(2) Elastic demand allows for higher prices
(3) Elastic demand requires lower prices
(4) Inelastic demand requires lower prices

59. How do competitor prices influence pricing decisions?
(1) Competitor prices have no impact

(2) Prices are set independently of competitors
(3) Competitor prices are a key consideration in setting prices
(4) Competitor prices only matter for new products

60. What is the purpose of considering the stage of the product life cycle in price determination?
(1) To Minimise competition
(2) To focus solely on cost reduction
(3) To Maximise short-term profits
(4) To align pricing with the product's position in the market

61. Which pricing strategy involves setting a high initial price to capitalize on early adopters?
(1) Skimming pricing
(2) Penetration pricing
(3) Discount pricing
(4) Psychological pricing

62. What is the objective of penetration pricing?
(1) To Maximise short-term profits
(2) To capture a large market share quickly
(3) To cater exclusively to premium customers
(4) To align prices with production costs

63. What is the primary advantage of psychological pricing?
(1) Maximising profits
(2) Simplifying pricing decisions
(3) Appealing to customer emotions and perceptions
(4) Focusing solely on cost reduction

64. Which pricing policy involves setting prices based on the perceived value to the customer?
(1) Cost-plus pricing
(2) Value-based pricing
(3) Skimming pricing
(4) Penetration pricing

65. What is the purpose of using a price bundling strategy?
(1) Reducing production costs
(2) Simplifying pricing decisions
(3) Offering discounts for bulk purchases
(4) Minimising competition

66. What is the goal of dynamic pricing?
(1) Offering consistent prices over time
(2) Adjusting prices based on real-time demand and supply
(3) Maximising short-term profits
(4) Ignoring competitor prices

67. What is a disadvantage of using cost-plus pricing as the sole pricing strategy?
(1) It ignores customer perceptions and demand
(2) It is too complex for implementation
(3) It Maximises short-term profits
(4) It simplifies pricing decisions

68. Which pricing strategy is often used for new products with high development costs?
(1) Penetration pricing
(2) Skimming pricing
(3) Psychological pricing
(4) Cost-plus pricing

69. What does a price skimming strategy aim to achieve in the long run?
(1) Maintaining a consistent market share
(2) Gradually lowering prices to capture more customers
(3) Maximising short-term profits
(4) Encouraging price competition

70. Which pricing strategy involves setting a price that covers production costs and provides a desired level of profit?
(1) Cost-plus pricing
(2) Value-based pricing
(3) Skimming pricing
(4) Psychological pricing

71. What is the goal of premium pricing?
(1) Capturing a large market share quickly
(2) Offering the lowest prices in the market
(3) Positioning the product as high-quality and exclusive
(4) Ignoring competitor prices

72. What pricing strategy is suitable for products with a short product life cycle?
(1) Skimming pricing
(2) Penetration pricing
(3) Psychological pricing
(4) Temporary discount pricing

73. What does a loss leader pricing strategy involve?
(1) Setting prices that cover production costs
(2) Offering low prices to attract customers and stimulate other profitable sales
(3) Ignoring competitor prices
(4) Focusing solely on cost reduction

74. What is the purpose of a freemium pricing strategy?
(1) Maximising short-term profits

(2) Capturing a large market share quickly
(3) Offering a basic product for free and charging for premium features
(4) Ignoring customer perceptions

75. In what situation would a company use a competitive pricing strategy?
(1) When it wants to Maximise short-term profits
(2) When it aims to offer the lowest prices in the market
(3) When it is the only player in the market
(4) When it focuses solely on cost reduction

Directions: Each of the following items consists of two statements, one labelled as Assertion (A) and other labelled as Reason (R). You are to examine these two statements carefully and decide if the (A) and the (R) are individually true and if so, whether (R) is the correct explanation of (A). Select your answers to these items using the codes given below:
(1) The (A) is true, and the (R) is false.
(2) The (A) is false, and the (R) is false.
(3) The (A) is false, and the (R) is true.
(4) The (A) is true, and the (R) is true.

76. Assertion (A): Value-based pricing considers only production costs.
Reason (R): Value-based pricing focuses on the perceived value to the customer.

77. Assertion (A): Psychological pricing is primarily concerned with cost reduction.
Reason (R): Psychological pricing appeals to customer emotions and perceptions.

78. Assertion (A): Dynamic pricing involves adjusting prices based on real-time demand and supply.
Reason (R): Dynamic pricing simplifies pricing decisions.

79. Assertion (A): A loss leader pricing strategy aims to Maximise short-term profits.
Reason (R): A loss leader pricing strategy involves offering low prices to attract customers and stimulate other profitable sales.

80. Assertion (A): Freemium pricing involves offering a basic product for free and charging for premium features.
Reason (R): Freemium pricing aims to capture a large market share quickly.

81. What is the primary role of promotion in marketing?
(1) Maximising production efficiency
(2) Reducing product variety
(3) Communicating value and information to target customers
(4) Setting product prices

82. Which of the following is a promotional objective?
(1) Minimising competition
(2) Focusing solely on cost reduction
(3) Creating awareness, interest, and desire among customers
(4) Ignoring customer perceptions

83. What is the significance of integrated marketing communications (IMC)?
(1) Ignoring customer perceptions
(2) Maximising short-term profits
(3) Coordinating all promotional activities to provide a unified message
(4) Setting product prices

84. What does the AIDA model represent in the context of promotion?
(1) Attention, Interest, Desire, Action
(2) Awareness, Interest, Decision, Action
(3) Attention, Inquiry, Decision, Acceptance
(4) Awareness, Inquiry, Desire, Acceptance

85. Which promotional element focuses on creating a favorable image for a company or its products?
(1) Advertising (2) Personal selling
(3) Publicity (4) Sales promotion

86. What is the primary purpose of advertising?
(1) Maximising production efficiency
(2) Creating personal connections with customers
(3) Communicating a message to a large audience through mass media
(4) Ignoring customer perceptions

87. Which advertising medium is considered a form of paid, non-personal communication?
(1) Public relations (2) Social media
(3) Television (4) Word-of-mouth

88. What is the advantage of online advertising over traditional forms of advertising?
(1) Limited reach to a global audience
(2) Lower cost and precise targeting options
(3) Longer production time for advertisements
(4) Lower audience engagement

89. What is the purpose of reminder advertising?
(1) Creating awareness of a new product
(2) Encouraging immediate purchase

(3) Reinforcing previous knowledge of a product
(4) Ignoring customer perceptions

90. What is native advertising?
(1) Advertising in international markets only
(2) A form of advertising that blends with the content and context of the platform
(3) Exclusively online advertising
(4) Word-of-mouth advertising

91. What is the key characteristic of personal selling?
(1) Mass communication through various channels
(2) Direct communication between a salesperson and a potential customer
(3) Creating a favorable image for a company
(4) Ignoring customer perceptions

92. What is the primary goal of personal selling?
(1) Maximising production efficiency
(2) Building long-term relationships with customers
(3) Creating mass awareness through mass media
(4) Ignoring customer perceptions

93. What is consultative selling?
(1) Focusing solely on cost reduction
(2) Providing information and advice to help customers make informed decisions
(3) Creating a favorable image for a company
(4) Mass communication through various channels

94. Which stage of the personal selling process involves identifying and qualifying potential customers?
(1) Closing (2) Prospecting
(3) Pre-approach (4) Follow-up

95. What is the purpose of the closing stage in personal selling?
(1) Building rapport with customers
(2) Identifying potential customers
(3) Obtaining a commitment or agreement from the customer
(4) Ignoring customer perceptions

96. What is the key characteristic of publicity?
(1) Paid communication
(2) Controlled by the company
(3) Non-personal communication
(4) Focused on creating immediate purchase

97. What is the primary source of publicity?
(1) Word-of-mouth
(2) Mass media
(3) Sales promotions
(4) Direct marketing

98. What distinguishes publicity from advertising?
(1) Limited reach
(2) Lack of control by the company
(3) Paid communication
(4) Word-of-mouth

99. What is the potential impact of negative publicity on a company?
(1) Enhancing the company's reputation
(2) Creating immediate purchase
(3) Damaging the company's reputation
(4) Ignoring customer perceptions

100. What is guerrilla marketing?
(1) Traditional advertising in mainstream media
(2) Unconventional and low-cost marketing efforts to create buzz
(3) Personal selling focused on high-end products
(4) Word-of-mouth advertising

101. What is the purpose of sales promotions?
(1) Building long-term relationships with customers
(2) Creating awareness through mass media
(3) Encouraging immediate purchase or sales of a product
(4) Ignoring customer perceptions

102. Which sales promotion tool involves offering a free product with the purchase of another product?
(1) Discounts (2) Samples
(3) Premiums (4) Contests

103. What is the primary objective of a contest as a sales promotion technique?
(1) Building long-term relationships with customers
(2) Maximising short-term profits
(3) Encouraging immediate purchase
(4) Creating awareness through mass media

104. Which sales promotion tool involves reducing the normal selling price of a product?
(1) Premiums (2) Discounts
(3) Samples (4) Contests

105. What is the purpose of a loyalty program as a sales promotion technique?
(1) Building long-term relationships with customers
(2) Encouraging immediate purchase
(3) Maximising short-term profits
(4) Creating awareness through mass media

106. What is the promotion mix?
(1) A single promotional method used by companies
(2) The combination of various promotional elements used by a company
(3) Focusing solely on personal selling
(4) Ignoring customer perceptions

107. Which promotional element is considered a short-term incentive to encourage the purchase or sale of a product?
(1) Publicity (2) Personal selling
(3) Advertising (4) Sales promotion

108. What is the role of direct marketing in the promotion mix?
(1) Creating mass awareness through mass media
(2) Building long-term relationships with customers
(3) Focusing solely on cost reduction
(4) Communicating directly with individual customers

109. Which promotional element is most effective in building brand awareness?
(1) Personal selling (2) Advertising
(3) Publicity (4) Direct marketing

110. What is the **primary** characteristic of integrated marketing communications (IMC)?
(1) Focusing solely on personal selling
(2) Coordinating all promotional activities to provide a unified message
(3) Ignoring customer perceptions
(4) Maximising short-term profits

Directions: Each of the following items consists of two statements, one labelled as Assertion (A) and other labelled as Reason (R). You are to examine these two statements carefully and decide if the (A) and the (R) are individually true and if so, whether (R) is the correct explanation of (A). Select your answers to these items using the codes given below:
(1) The (A) is true, and the (R) is false.
(2) The (A) is false, and the (R) is false.
(3) The (A) is false, and the (R) is true.
(4) The (A) is true, and the (R) is true.

111. **Assertion (A):** Publicity is a paid form of communication controlled by the company.
Reason (R): Publicity is non-personal communication that lacks control by the company.

112. **Assertion (A):** Personal selling is suitable for creating mass awareness.
Reason (R): Personal selling involves direct communication between a salesperson and a potential customer.

113. **Assertion (A):** Sales promotions are focused on building long-term relationships with customers.
Reason (R): Sales promotions are aimed at encouraging immediate purchase or sales of a product.

114. **Assertion (A):** Direct marketing involves mass communication through various channels.
Reason (R): Direct marketing communicates directly with individual customers.

115. **Assertion (A):** The promotion mix involves a combination of various promotional elements used by a company.
Reason (R): The promotion mix focuses solely on personal selling.

116. Which of the following is not a channel of distribution?
(1) Wholesaler (2) Retailer
(3) Consumer (4) Manufacturer

117. What is the main advantage of using a direct channel of distribution?
(1) Cost savings
(2) Better control over pricing
(3) Greater reach to customers
(4) Exclusivity

118. Which of the following is an indirect channel of distribution?
(1) Manufacturer to consumer
(2) Manufacturer to retailer to consumer
(3) Manufacturer to wholesaler to retailer to consumer
(4) Manufacturer to government to consumer

119. Which of the following is a benefit of using intermediaries in distribution?
(1) Lower prices for the end consumer
(2) Greater control over product quality
(3) Higher profit margins for the manufacturer
(4) Shorter lead times to market

120. Which of the following is not a type of retailer?
(1) Department store

(2) Specialty store
(3) Discount store
(4) Manufacturer

121. Which of the following is an example of a vertical marketing system?
(1) A manufacturer sells to a wholesaler who sells to a retailer who sells to the end consumer
(2) A manufacturer owns a retailer that sells its products exclusively
(3) A manufacturer sells directly to the end consumer through its website
(4) A manufacturer sells to multiple retailers who compete with each other to sell the most of its products

122. Which of the following is the most common type of distribution channel used in the consumer goods industry?
(1) Direct selling (2) Retailing
(3) Wholesaling (4) Franchising

123. Which of the following is a disadvantage of using a multi-channel distribution strategy?
(1) Higher costs
(2) Lower customer satisfaction
(3) Limited reach to customers
(4) Increased complexity in managing inventory

124. Which of the following is an example of a horizontal marketing system?
(1) A manufacturer sells to multiple retailers who compete with each other to sell the most of its products
(2) A manufacturer owns a retailer that sells its products exclusively
(3) A manufacturer sells to a wholesaler who sells to a retailer who sells to the end consumer
(4) A manufacturer sells directly to the end consumer through its website

125. Which of the following is an example of a push strategy in distribution?
(1) Offering discounts to end consumers who purchase products online
(2) Running television ads to create demand for a new product
(3) Offering incentives to retailers who order large quantities of a product
(4) Setting up pop-up stores to sell products in high-traffic areas

126. Which of the following is an example of a pull strategy in distribution?
(1) Offering discounts to end consumers who purchase products online
(2) Running television ads to create demand for a new product
(3) Offering incentives to retailers who order large quantities of a product
(4) Setting up pop-up stores to sell products in high-traffic areas

127. Which of the following is an example of a specialty store?
(1) Walmart (2) Best Buy
(3) Sephora (4) Macy's

128. Which of the following is an example of a general merchandise retailer?
(1) Walmart (2) Best Buy
(3) Sephora (4) Macy's

129. Which of the following is an example of a cognitive objective in distribution channel management?
(1) To understand the benefits and drawbacks of various distribution channels
(2) To be able to sell products effectively through e-commerce channels
(3) To be able to negotiate favorable terms with wholesalers and retailers
(4) To be able to analyze sales data to determine the most effective channels for a product

130. Which of the following is an example of a psychomotor objective in distribution channel management?
(1) To understand the benefits and drawbacks of various distribution channels
(2) To be able to sell products effectively through e-commerce channels
(3) To be able to negotiate favorable terms with wholesalers and retailers
(4) To be able to handle and display products effectively in a retail environment

131. Which of the following is an example of a affective objective in distribution channel management?
(1) To understand the benefits and drawbacks of various distribution channels
(2) To be able to sell products effectively through e-commerce channels
(3) To be able to negotiate favorable terms with wholesalers and retailers

(4) To develop a positive attitude towards the role of intermediaries in distribution

132. Which of the following is not a goal of channel management?
(1) Maximising sales
(2) Minimising costs
(3) Maximising customer satisfaction
(4) Minimising competition

133. Which of the following is a key function of channel management?
(1) Developing new products
(2) Managing human resources
(3) Managing supply chain logistics
(4) Negotiating with intermediaries

134. Which of the following is an example of a channel conflict?
(1) Two retailers compete to sell the most of a manufacturer's product
(2) A retailer and a wholesaler have a disagreement over pricing
(3) A manufacturer opens its own retail store, competing with its existing retailers
(4) An intermediary refuses to carry a manufacturer's product

135. Which of the following is not a strategy for managing channel conflict?
(1) Offering exclusive distribution agreements
(2) Offering volume discounts to all intermediaries
(3) Providing training and support for intermediaries
(4) Offering higher profit margins to preferred intermediaries

136. Which of the following is a benefit of using exclusive distribution agreements?
(1) Greater control over pricing
(2) Greater reach to customers
(3) Higher profit margins
(4) Lower costs

137. Which of the following is a disadvantage of using exclusive distribution agreements?
(1) Higher costs
(2) Limited reach to customers
(3) Lower profit margins
(4) Limited control over pricing

138. Which of the following is a benefit of using a franchise distribution system?
(1) Greater control over pricing
(2) Greater reach to customers
(3) Lower costs
(4) Higher profit margins

139. Which of the following is a disadvantage of using a franchise distribution system?
(1) Higher costs
(2) Limited control over pricing
(3) Limited reach to customers
(4) Lower profit margins

140. Which of the following is an example of a horizontal conflict in distribution?
(1) A manufacturer and a retailer have a disagreement over pricing
(2) Two retailers compete to sell the most of a manufacturer's product
(3) A manufacturer opens its own retail store, competing with its existing retailers
(4) An intermediary refuses to carry a manufacturer's product

141. Which of the following is an example of a vertical conflict in distribution?
(1) A manufacturer and a retailer have a disagreement over pricing
(2) Two retailers compete to sell the most of a manufacturer's product
(3) A manufacturer opens its own retail store, competing with its existing retailers
(4) An intermediary refuses to carry a manufacturer's product

142. Which of the following is a benefit of using a multi-channel distribution strategy?
(1) Lower costs
(2) Greater control over product quality
(3) Higher profit margins
(4) Greater reach to customers

143. Which of the following is a disadvantage of using a multi-channel distribution strategy?
(1) Higher costs
(2) Lower customer satisfaction
(3) Limited reach to customers
(4) Increased complexity in managing inventory

144. Which of the following is a benefit of using a push strategy in distribution?
(1) Greater control over pricing
(2) Higher profit margins
(3) Quicker time-to-market
(4) Greater reach to customers

145. Which of the following is a benefit of using a pull strategy in distribution?

(1) Lower costs
(2) Lower inventory levels
(3) Greater reach to customers
(4) Greater control over pricing

146. Which of the following is not a benefit of using intermediaries in distribution?
(1) Greater reach to customers
(2) Lower costs
(3) Shorter lead times to market
(4) Greater control over pricing

147. Which of the following is a key component of effective channel management?
(1) Maximising profits for the manufacturer
(2) Minimising costs for the manufacturer
(3) Maximising customer satisfaction
(4) Minimising competition

148. Which of the following is a disadvantage of using a direct channel of distribution?
(1) Higher costs
(2) Limited reach to customers
(3) Greater complexity in managing inventory
(4) Lower profit margins

149. Which of the following is a benefit of using a direct channel of distribution?
(1) Lower costs
(2) Greater control over pricing
(3) Greater reach to customers
(4) Exclusivity

150. Which of the following is an example of a franchisor?
(1) Starbucks (2) Subway
(3) McDonald's (4) All of the above

151. Which of the following is an example of a franchising model where the franchisee buys the right to use the franchisor's brand and system?
(1) Product distribution franchise
(2) Management consulting franchise
(3) Business format franchise
(4) Manufacturing franchise

152. Which of the following is an example of a product distribution franchise?
(1) McDonald's (2) Coca-Cola
(3) Holiday Inn (4) Ford

153. Which of the following is an example of a horizontal marketing system?
(1) A manufacturer sells to a wholesaler who sells to a retailer who sells to the end consumer
(2) A manufacturer owns a retailer that sells its products exclusively
(3) A manufacturer sells to multiple retailers who compete with each other to sell the most of its products
(4) A manufacturer sells directly to the end consumer through its website

154. Which of the following is an example of a vertical marketing system?
(1) A manufacturer sells to multiple retailers who compete with each other to sell the most of its products
(2) A manufacturer owns a retailer that sells its products exclusively
(3) A manufacturer sells to a wholesaler who sells to a retailer who sells to the end consumer
(4) A manufacturer sells directly to the end consumer through its website

155. Which of the following is a benefit of using a franchise distribution system?
(1) Lower costs
(2) Greater control over pricing
(3) Greater reach to customers
(4) Lower risk for the franchisee

Directions: Each of the following items consists of two statements, one labelled as Assertion (A) and other labelled as Reason (R). You are to examine these two statements carefully and decide if the (A) and the (R) are individually true and if so, whether (R) is the correct explanation of (A). Select your answers to these items using the codes given below:
(1) Both (A) and (R) are true and the (R) is a correct explanation of the (A).
(2) Both (A) and (R) are true, but the (R) is not a correct explanation of the (A).
(3) The (A) is true, but the (R) is false.
(4) The (A) is false, but the (R) is true.

156. **Assertion (A):** Wholesalers are intermediaries that buy products from manufacturers and sell them to retailers and other businesses.
Reason: Wholesalers provide a valuable service to manufacturers by handling large quantities of product and reducing the costs of distribution.

157. **Assertion (A):** Indirect channels of distribution are less expensive than direct channels of distribution.
Reason: Indirect channels of distribution involve fewer intermediaries and lower distribution costs.

158. Assertion (A): Specialty stores typically offer a larger selection of products and services than general merchandise retailers.

Reason: Specialty stores target a specific category of products or customer, and therefore have a more focused product offering.

159. Assertion (A): Conflict in distribution channels can arise due to differences in goals or objectives between different members of the channel.

Reason: Effective channel management involves optimizing the interests of all members of the channel to achieve common goals.

160. Assertion (A): Franchising is a distribution model that involves a franchisor who provides a branded product or service to a franchisee who operates a business using the franchisor's system.

Reason: Franchising is a type of vertical marketing system where the franchisor owns the brand and the franchisee operates using the franchisor's system and processes.

161. Which of the following is not a stage in the consumer buying process?

(1) Information search
(2) Purchase decision
(3) Post-purchase evaluation
(4) Product design

162. Which of the following is not an external factor influencing consumer buying decisions?

(1) Culture (2) Family
(3) Personal income (4) Social class

163. Which of the following is an example of a product attribute that can influence consumer buying decisions?

(1) Price (2) Culture
(3) Personal income (4) Social class

164. Which of the following is not a psychological factor influencing consumer buying decisions?

(1) Motivation (2) Perception
(3) Culture (4) Attitude

165. Which of the following is an example of a situational factor influencing consumer buying decisions?

(1) Personality (2) Social class
(3) Time (4) Culture

166. Which of the following is an example of a post-purchase action that a consumer might take after buying a product?

(1) Researching other products to buy
(2) Telling a friend about the product
(3) Returning the product for a refund
(4) All of the above

167. What is the main difference between a want and a need in consumer behaviour?

(1) A want is something a consumer must have to survive, while a need is something they desire but do not require.
(2) A need is something a consumer must have to survive, while a want is something they desire but do not require.
(3) A want and a need are the same thing in consumer behaviour.
(4) A want is something a consumer desires but cannot obtain, while a need is something they require and can obtain.

168. Which of the following is not a type of decision-making process that consumers might use when making a purchase?

(1) Routine (2) Limited
(3) Extensive (4) Quick

169. Which of the following is an example of a high involvement purchase for a consumer?

(1) A pack of gum
(2) A new car
(3) A ream of printer paper
(4) A coffee at Starbucks

170. Which of the following is an example of an internal search for information during the consumer buying process?

(1) Reading reviews online
(2) Asking friends for recommendations
(3) Visiting a store to check out a product
(4) All of the above

171. Which of the following is an example of an external search for information during the consumer buying process?

(1) Using a product regularly and becoming familiar with its features
(2) Asking friends for recommendations
(3) Visiting a store to check out a product
(4) All of the above

172. Which of the following is not a type of perceived risk that can affect consumer buying decisions?

(1) Financial risk (2) Performance risk
(3) Social risk (4) Health risk

173. Which of the following is a type of social influence that can affect consumer buying decisions?

(1) Income level

(2) Personal values
(3) Family structure
(4) Peer pressure

174. Which of the following is an example of a reference group that can influence consumer buying decisions?
(1) Friends (2) Family
(3) Celebrities (4) All of these

175. Which of the following is an example of a cultural factor that can influence consumer buying decisions?
(1) Language (2) Age
(3) Education level (4) All of these

176. Which of the following is an example of a personal factor that can influence consumer buying decisions?
(1) Occupation (2) Social class
(3) Culture (4) Reference groups

177. Which of the following is an example of a psychological factor that can influence consumer buying decisions?
(1) Social class (2) Culture
(3) Attitudes (4) Family structure

178. Which of the following is not a stage in the traditional consumer buying process model?
(1) Need recognition
(2) Attitude formation
(3) Evaluation of alternatives
(4) Purchase decision

179. Which of the following is an example of a post-purchase evaluation a consumer might make after buying a product?
(1) Deciding whether to buy the same product again
(2) Researching other products to buy
(3) Telling a friend about the product
(4) All of the above

180. Which of the following is an example of a situational factor that can influence consumer buying decisions?
(1) Perception (2) Attitudes
(3) Time (4) Culture

181. Which of the following is not a type of decision-making process that consumers might use when making a purchase?
(1) Habitual (2) Limited
(3) Extensive (4) Perceptual

182. Which of the following is not a challenge faced by global logistics managers?
(1) Language barriers
(2) Currency exchange rates
(3) Supply chain visibility
(4) Limited access to real-time data

183. Which of the following is an example of a product attribute that can influence consumer buying decisions?
(1) Personal values (2) Reference groups
(3) Advertising (4) Price

184. Which of the following is not a type of perceived risk that can affect consumer buying decisions?
(1) Physical risk (2) Performance risk
(3) Financial risk (4) Personal risk

185. Which of the following is an example of a social influence that can affect consumer buying decisions?
(1) Attitudes (2) Personal values
(3) Family structure (4) Culture

186. Which of the following is an example of a reference group that can influence consumer buying decisions?
(1) Celebrities
(2) Personal values
(3) Social class
(4) Attitudes

187. Which of the following is an example of a cultural factor that can influence consumer buying decisions?
(1) Age (2) Perception
(3) Attitudes (4) Language

188. Which of the following is an example of a personal factor that can influence consumer buying decisions?
(1) Attitudes (2) Reference groups
(3) Income level (4) Culture

189. Which of the following is an example of a psychological factor that can influence consumer buying decisions?
(1) Social class (2) Culture
(3) Perception (4) Reference groups

190. Which of the following is a type of perceived risk that can affect consumer buying decisions?
(1) Financial risk (2) Time risk
(3) Social risk (4) All of the above

191. Which of the following is a type of situational factor that can influence consumer buying decisions?
(1) Attitudes (2) Personality
(3) Social class (4) Time

192. Which of the following is a type of decision-making process that consumers might use when making a purchase?
(1) Unplanned (2) Limited
(3) Extensive (4) All of these

193. Which of the following is not an example of a logistics function?
(1) Sales forecasting
(2) Transportation management
(3) Inventory management
(4) Supply chain management

194. Which of the following is not a stage in the traditional consumer buying process model?
(1) Need recognition
(2) Information search
(3) Attitude formation
(4) Purchase decision

195. Which of the following is an example of an external search for information during the consumer buying process?
(1) Using a product regularly and becoming familiar with its features
(2) Reading reviews online
(3) Visiting a store to check out a product
(4) All of the above

196. Which of the following is an example of a high involvement purchase for a consumer?
(1) A sandwich for lunch
(2) A new phone charger
(3) A new car
(4) A pack of gum

197. Which of the following is a type of situational factor that can influence consumer buying decisions?
(1) Personal values
(2) Age
(3) Culture
(4) Income level

198. Which of the following is an example of a psychological factor that can influence consumer buying decisions?
(1) Social class
(2) Culture
(3) Attitudes
(4) Personal values

199. Which of the following is an example of a personal factor that can influence consumer buying decisions?
(1) Personal values (2) Reference groups
(3) Income level (4) Culture

200. Which of the following is a type of situational factor that can influence consumer buying decisions?
(1) Social class (2) Personality
(3) Time (4) Perception

Directions: Each of the following items consists of two statements, one labelled as Assertion (A) and other labelled as Reason (R). You are to examine these two statements carefully and decide if the (A) and the (R) are individually true and if so, whether (R) is the correct explanation of (A). Select your answers to these items using the codes given below:
(1) Both (A) and (R) are true and the (R) is a correct explanation of the (A).
(2) Both (A) and (R) are true, but the (R) is not a correct explanation of the (A).
(3) The (A) is true, but the (R) is false.
(4) The (A) is false, but the (R) is true.

201. **Assertion (A):** Consumer buying behaviour is the study of the processes consumers use to choose, purchase, and use products.
Reason: Factors that influence consumer buying decisions include internal psychological factors, external factors like culture and social class, and situational factors like time and urgency.

202. **Assertion (A):** Perception is the process by which people select, organise, and interpret information from the world around them.
Reason: Perception is not influenced by external factors and is solely determined by a person's internal biases and beliefs.

203. **Assertion (A):** A consumer's culture can influence their values, beliefs, and behaviours related to purchasing.
Reason: Culture is a situational factor that can affect consumer buying decisions.

204. **Assertion (A):** The consumer buying process is characterised by several distinct stages that must be completed in sequence.
Reason: External factors like family, culture, and social class are the most important factors in consumer buying decisions.

205. **Assertion (A):** Situational factors like time, location, and social environment are important influences on consumer buying decisions.
Reason: These situational factors are largely independent of a consumer's personal values and beliefs.

206. Which of the following is not a characteristic of services?
(1) Tangibility (2) Perishability
(3) Variability (4) Intangibility

207. Which of the following is not a type of service encounter?
(1) Remote encounter
(2) Phone encounter
(3) Face-to-face encounter
(4) Text encounter

208. Which of the following is not a component of the service experience?
(1) Personal interaction
(2) Service environment
(3) Service delivery process
(4) Product features

209. Which of the following is not a factor that can influence service quality?
(1) Reliability (2) Responsiveness
(3) Price (4) Empathy

210. Which of the following is not a benefit of a strong service culture?
(1) Improved employee satisfaction
(2) Increased customer retention
(3) Reduced marketing costs
(4) Lower employee turnover

211. Which of the following is not a stage in the service delivery process?
(1) Pre-service (2) Service encounter
(3) Post-service (4) Product design

212. Which of the following is not a type of service encounter employee?
(1) Provider (2) Facilitator
(3) Enabler (4) Coordinator

213. Which of the following is not a type of customer participation in service delivery?
(1) Essential (2) Optional
(3) Extraneous (4) Forced

214. Which of the following is not a benefit of effective service recovery?
(1) Increased customer loyalty
(2) Improved service quality
(3) Reduced costs
(4) Positive word-of-mouth communication

215. Which of the following is not an example of a physical environment factor that can impact service quality?
(1) Lighting (2) Noise level
(3) Employee attitude (4) Temperature

216. Which of the following is an example of an intangible aspect of service quality?
(1) Price (2) Employee attitude
(3) Wait time (4) Product features

217. Which of the following is not a component of service reliability?
(1) Consistency (2) Timeliness
(3) Responsiveness (4) Dependability

218. Which of the following is an example of a personalized service encounter?
(1) Banking online
(2) Ordering food at a fast food restaurant
(3) Having a wedding planner
(4) Buying a product from a vending machine

219. Which of the following is not a reason why service marketing is different from product marketing?
(1) Services are intangible
(2) Services cannot be stored or transported
(3) Services are not subject to supply and demand
(4) Services are perishable

220. Which of the following is not a strategy for managing customer expectations in service delivery?
(1) Communicating clear service promises
(2) Over-promising to ensure customer satisfaction
(3) Providing realistic wait times
(4) Managing customer feedback and complaints

221. Which of the following is not an example of a potential service failure?
(1) Long wait times
(2) Incompetent or uncaring employees
(3) Inconsistent service quality
(4) Availability of a wide range of products

222. Which of the following is not a reason why customer participation is important in service delivery?
(1) It can reduce costs for the service provider
(2) It can improve customer satisfaction
(3) It can enhance the customer's understanding of the service
(4) It can increase product features

223. Which of the following is not an example of a moment of truth in service delivery?
(1) Booking a hotel room online
(2) Checking into a hotel
(3) Ordering food at a restaurant
(4) Receiving a bill at a restaurant

224. Which of the following is not a benefit of effective service recovery?
(1) Improving brand reputation
(2) Generating new customers
(3) Reducing marketing costs
(4) Increasing employee satisfaction

225. Which of the following is an example of a service recovery strategy?
(1) Ignoring the customer's complaint
(2) Blaming the customer for the problem
(3) Apologizing and offering a solution
(4) Denying responsibility for the problem

226. Which of the following is not a type of brand personality that can be associated with services?
(1) Excitement (2) Competence
(3) Sincerity (4) Confidence

227. Which of the following is not a characteristic of a strong service culture?
(1) Customer focus
(2) Employee empowerment
(3) Lack of teamwork
(4) Continuous improvement

228. Which of the following is not an example of a service guarantee?
(1) Money-back guarantee
(2) Price matching guarantee
(3) Satisfaction guarantee
(4) Availability guarantee

229. Which of the following is not a factor that can influence customer perceptions of service quality?
(1) Culture (2) Personal values
(3) Income level (4) Time of day

230. Which of the following is not a component of service delivery process design?
(1) Job design
(2) Service facility design
(3) Service quality measurement
(4) Employee rewards and recognition

231. Which of the following is not an example of a personalized service encounter?
(1) Making a purchase through an online retailer
(2) Ordering fast food via drive-through
(3) Having a personal shopper at a department store
(4) Meeting with a financial advisor

232. Which of the following is not a key challenge faced in service delivery?
(1) Ensuring consistent service quality
(2) Managing the physical environment
(3) Understanding customer perceptions and expectations
(4) Limiting customer participation

233. Which of the following is not an example of a service encounter employee?
(1) Provider (2) Manager
(3) Enabler (4) Facilitator

234. Which of the following is not a type of service delivery system?
(1) Self-service
(2) Employee-delivered service
(3) Partner-delivered service
(4) Automated-delivery service

235. Which of the following is not an example of a moment of truth in service delivery?
(1) Checking out of a hotel
(2) Ordering food for delivery
(3) Applying for a loan at a bank
(4) Calling a customer service hotline

236. Which of the following is an example of a physical environment factor that can influence customer perceptions of service quality?
(1) Employee attitude
(2) Wait time
(3) Lighting
(4) Knowledge of the service provider

237. Which of the following is not an example of a service recovery strategy?
(1) Apologizing and offering a solution
(2) Ignoring the customer's complaint
(3) Offering a discount on future services
(4) Providing compensation for the issue

238. Which of the following is not a factor that can influence customer expectations in service delivery?
(1) Advertising
(2) Personal experiences
(3) Prior knowledge of the service
(4) Customer participation

239. Which of the following is not a characteristic of effective customer participation in service delivery?
(1) It reduces costs for the service provider
(2) It results in higher levels of customer satisfaction
(3) It can lead to higher levels of loyalty
(4) It eliminates the need for employees in the service delivery process

240. Which of the following is an example of a service encounter that involves high customer participation?
(1) Making a purchase through an online retailer
(2) Ordering a meal at a fast food restaurant
(3) Meeting with a financial advisor
(4) Taking a shuttle bus to the airport

241. Which of the following is not a reason why services are difficult to evaluate in terms of quality?
(1) They are intangible
(2) They are not easily duplicated
(3) Their value is subjective
(4) They are not affected by customer perceptions

242. Which of the following is not a stage in the service delivery process?
(1) Pre-service
(2) Service encounter
(3) Post-service
(4) Product design

243. Which of the following is an example of a type of service delivery system?
(1) Employee-delivered service
(2) Vending machine-delivered service
(3) Salesperson-delivered service
(4) All of the above

244. Which of the following is an example of a moment of truth in service delivery?
(1) Searching for a product online
(2) Making a purchase through a self-service kiosk
(3) Calling a customer service hotline
(4) None of the above

245. Which of the following is not a factor that can influence customer perceptions of service quality?
(1) Personal values
(2) Social influence
(3) Wait time
(4) Employee job satisfaction

Directions: Each of the following items consists of two statements, one labelled as Assertion (A) and other labelled as Reason (R). You are to examine these two statements carefully and decide if the (A) and the (R) are individually true and if so, whether (R) is the correct explanation of (A). Select your answers to these items using the codes given below:
(1) Both (A) and (R) are true and the (R) is a correct explanation of the (A).
(2) Both (A) and (R) are true, but the (R) is not a correct explanation of the (A).
(3) The (A) is true, but the (R) is false.
(4) The (A) is false, but the (R) is true.

246. **Assertion (A):** Services are intangible and cannot be stored for later use.
Reason: Unlike physical products, services cannot be manufactured in advance and stored for later use.

247. **Assertion (A):** Customer participation is an important factor in service delivery and can impact both service quality and customer satisfaction.
Reason: Customer participation is always optional and does not affect service quality in any significant way.

248. **Assertion (A):** Effective service recovery can help service providers retain customers and enhance service quality.
Reason: Service recovery always involves compensating the customer monetarily for any problems or issues they faced during service delivery.

249. **Assertion (A):** Service quality can impact a customer's perception of a brand and can result in positive or negative word-of-mouth communication.
Reason: A customer's perception of service quality is not influenced by factors like wait time or employee attitude, which are outside of the service provider's control.

250. **Assertion (A):** Logistics management involves managing the entire supply chain from raw materials to the end consumer.
Reason: Effective logistics management leads to increased shipping costs for a company.

251. **Assertion (A):** The physical environment can impact a customer's perception of service quality and can be managed by service providers to enhance the service experience.

Reason: The physical environment is not a significant factor in a customer's perception of service quality and is largely outside of the service provider's control.

252. Social marketing is focused on
(1) Maximising profits for the company
(2) Creating social change and promoting positive behaviours
(3) Increasing market share
(4) Maximising shareholder value

253. Green marketing focuses on:
(1) Selling products and services to urban customers
(2) Selling environmentally friendly products and services
(3) Promoting direct and personalized communication with customers
(4) Building relationships with customers through loyalty programs

254. Which of the following is not a type of direct marketing?
(1) Telemarketing (2) Direct mail
(3) Email marketing (4) TV advertising

255. Which of the following is not a benefit of implementing a CRM system?
(1) Increased customer loyalty
(2) Improved customer satisfaction
(3) Reduced marketing costs
(4) Increased employee job satisfaction

256. Which of the following is an example of a social marketing campaign?
(1) A restaurant promoting a new menu item on social media
(2) A company offering a loyalty card to customers
(3) A non-profit organisation promoting healthy eating habits
(4) An e-commerce website offering a discount code to customers

257. Which of the following is not a component of green marketing?
(1) Promoting environmentally friendly products
(2) Educating customers on environmental issues
(3) Focusing only on expected financial returns
(4) Encouraging sustainable manufacturing practices

258. Which of the following is not a benefit of using online marketing?
(1) Increased reach to customers
(2) Lower marketing costs
(3) Greater control over message delivery
(4) Limited targeting options

259. Which of the following is not a type of direct mail marketing?
(1) Catalogs
(2) Coupon mailings
(3) Fax marketing
(4) Social media posts

260. Which of the following is not a component of successful rural marketing?
(1) Understanding the rural mindset and values
(2) Offering a range of products suited to rural customers
(3) Using traditional media for advertising
(4) Focusing on personalized communication with customers

261. Which of the following is an example of a CRM system?
(1) A loyalty card program
(2) An online banner ad
(3) A billboard
(4) A targeted email campaign

262. Which of the following is not a benefit of using green marketing?
(1) Increased market share
(2) Improved brand reputation
(3) Lower marketing costs
(4) Increased customer loyalty

263. Which of the following is not a type of social marketing campaign?
(1) Promoting healthy eating habits
(2) Encouraging people to recycle
(3) Selling a new clothing line on social media
(4) Discouraging drug use among teens

264. Which of the following is not a factor to consider when implementing an online marketing strategy?
(1) Target audience
(2) Budget
(3) Social media platform
(4) Employee job satisfaction

265. Which of the following is not an example of green marketing?
(1) Promoting the use of biodegradable products

(2) Using recycled materials in manufacturing
(3) Offering exclusive discounts to customers
(4) Encouraging sustainable sourcing practices

266. Which of the following is an example of direct mail marketing?
(1) A targeted email campaign
(2) Telemarketing
(3) A social media post
(4) A coupon mailing

267. Which of the following is not a benefit of using rural marketing strategies?
(1) Greater reach to rural customers
(2) Increased customer loyalty
(3) Lower marketing costs
(4) Increased market share among urban customers

268. Which of the following is not a type of social marketing campaign targeting public health concerns?
(1) Anti-tobacco campaigns
(2) Anti-drug campaigns
(3) Mental health awareness campaigns
(4) Promoting new clothing lines

269. Which of the following is not a benefit of using online marketing?
(1) Greater targeting options
(2) Higher marketing costs
(3) Increased reach to customers
(4) Real-time tracking of marketing campaigns

270. Which of the following is not an example of green marketing?
(1) Using solar energy to power manufacturing facilities
(2) Promoting the use of single-use plastics
(3) Recycling materials in manufacturing
(4) Using materials from sustainable sources

271. Which of the following is not a component of direct marketing?
(1) Personalized communication with customers
(2) Use of traditional media for advertising
(3) Focus on targeted audience
(4) Direct response mechanisms

272. Which of the following is not a key factor in effective CRM implementation?
(1) Data collection and management
(2) Employee job satisfaction
(3) Effective use of technology
(4) Customer feedback and analysis

273. Which of the following is not a benefit of effective green marketing?
(1) Increased customer loyalty
(2) Improved brand reputation
(3) Lower costs
(4) Increased market share

274. Which of the following is not an example of a rural marketing strategy?
(1) Using traditional media for advertising
(2) Offering a range of products suited to rural customers
(3) Focusing on personalized communication with customers
(4) Offering virtual reality shopping experiences

275. Which of the following is not a benefit of social marketing?
(1) Increased customer retention
(2) Positive social change
(3) Lower marketing costs
(4) Greater control over message delivery

276. Which of the following is an example of an online marketing tool?
(1) A flyer (2) A billboard
(3) A website (4) A print ad

277. Which of the following is not a component of successful green marketing?
(1) Promoting environmental protection
(2) Educating customers on environmental issues
(3) Offering a range of products suited to green customers
(4) Encouraging sustainable manufacturing practices

278. Which of the following is not an example of direct marketing?
(1) Email marketing
(2) Billboard advertising
(3) Telemarketing (4) Direct mail

279. Which of the following is not a strategy for effective rural marketing?
(1) Offering a range of products to suit rural customers
(2) Using personalized communication with customers
(3) Focusing only on urban customers
(4) Using traditional media for advertising

280. Which of the following is not a benefit of implementing a CRM system?

(1) Improved customer satisfaction
(2) Increased customer loyalty
(3) Lower costs
(4) Increased employee job satisfaction

281. Which of the following is not a characteristic of successful green marketing?
(1) Promoting environmentally friendly products
(2) Implementing sustainable manufacturing practices
(3) Focusing on expected short-term profits
(4) Educating customers on environmental issues

282. Which of the following is not an example of a social marketing campaign?
(1) Promoting healthy eating habits
(2) Encouraging people to recycle
(3) Offering a new line of clothing on social media
(4) Discouraging drug use among teens

283. Which of the following is not a key consideration when implementing an online marketing strategy?
(1) Target audience
(2) Budget
(3) Social media platform
(4) Physical location of the company

284. Which of the following is an example of a direct mail marketing campaign?
(1) A targeted email campaign
(2) A billboard ad
(3) A TV ad
(4) A coupon mailing

285. Which of the following is not a factor to consider when implementing a green marketing strategy?
(1) Expected short-term profits
(2) Use of environmentally friendly products
(3) Recycling materials in manufacturing
(4) Educating customers on environmental issues

286. Which of the following is not a component of successful rural marketing?
(1) Offering a range of products suited to rural customers
(2) Using personalized communication with customers
(3) Focusing solely on urban customers
(4) Using traditional media for advertising

287. Which of the following is an example of a customer interaction that can be tracked using a CRM system?
(1) A customer calling to complain about a product
(2) A customer browsing a company's website
(3) A customer visiting a retail store
(4) A customer filling out a paper feedback form

288. Which of the following is not a benefit of effective social marketing?
(1) Increased customer loyalty
(2) Positive social change
(3) Reduced marketing costs
(4) Greater control over message delivery

289. Which of the following is not a component of successful green marketing?
(1) Promoting the use of environmentally friendly products
(2) Educating customers on environmental issues
(3) Using traditional media for advertising
(4) Encouraging sustainable sourcing practices

290. Which of the following is an example of direct mail marketing?
(1) A TV ad
(2) A targeted email campaign
(3) A social media post
(4) A catalog mailing

Directions: Each of the following items consists of two statements, one labelled as Assertion (A) and other labelled as Reason (R). You are to examine these two statements carefully and decide if the (A) and the (R) are individually true and if so, whether (R) is the correct explanation of (A). Select your answers to these items using the codes given below:
(1) Both (A) and (R) are true and the (R) is a correct explanation of the (A).
(2) Both (A) and (R) are true, but the (R) is not a correct explanation of the (A).
(3) The (A) is true, but the (R) is false.
(4) The (A) is false, but the (R) is true.

291. **Assertion (A):** Social marketing campaigns are aimed at promoting social change and positive behaviours.
Reason: Social marketing campaigns are always aimed at increasing market share for a company.

292. **Assertion (A):** Green marketing is focused on selling environmentally friendly products and services.

Reason: Green marketing has no connection to environmental protection or sustainable manufacturing practices.

293. **Assertion (A):** CRM systems are designed to increase employee job satisfaction.

Reason: CRM systems can help companies better understand customers and improve customer satisfaction.

294. **Assertion (A):** Rural marketing focuses on promoting products and services to urban customers.

Reason: Rural marketing strategies are focused on understanding the rural mindset and values and building relationships with rural customers.

295. **Assertion (A):** Online marketing offers greater control over message delivery compared to traditional marketing methods.

Reason: Online marketing is more expensive and difficult to implement than traditional marketing methods.

296. Which of the following is not a key function of logistics management?

(1) Transportation
(2) Inventory management
(3) Forecasting
(4) Financial accounting

297. Which of the following is an example of a logistics service provider?

(1) A manufacturer
(2) A retailer
(3) A third-party logistics (3PL) provider
(4) A wholesaler

298. Which of the following is not a challenge faced by logistics managers?

(1) Limited access to real-time data
(2) Demand forecasting
(3) Weather conditions
(4) Supply chain disruption

299. Which of the following is an example of a transportation mode in logistics management?

(1) Warehousing (2) Stock control
(3) Transit (4) Production planning

300. Which of the following is not a metric used to measure logistics performance?

(1) Cost per unit
(2) Customer satisfaction
(3) Employee satisfaction
(4) On-time delivery

301. Which of the following is an example of a document used in logistics management?

(1) Purchase order
(2) Balance sheet
(3) Income statement
(4) Marketing plan

302. Which of the following is not a benefit of effective logistics management?

(1) Increased customer satisfaction
(2) Lower costs
(3) Higher employee turnover
(4) Improved speed of shipments

303. Which of the following is not a factor to consider when selecting a transportation mode in logistics management?

(1) Availability (2) Cost
(3) Color (4) Transit time

304. Which of the following is an example of a logistics activity?

(1) Sales forecasting
(2) Designing a new product
(3) Managing inventory levels
(4) Setting prices for products

305. Which of the following is an example of a performance indicator used in logistics management?

(1) Sales revenue
(2) Employee job satisfaction
(3) Warehouse size
(4) Customer satisfaction

306. Which of the following is not a factor to consider when managing inventory in logistics management?

(1) Carrying costs (2) Demand forecasting
(3) Transit time (4) Stockouts

307. Which of the following is not an example of a logistics operation?

(1) Supply chain management
(2) Sales forecasting
(3) Transportation management
(4) Inventory management

308. Which of the following is not a challenge faced by e-commerce logistics management?

(1) Managing product returns
(2) Ensuring data security
(3) Limited access to real-time data
(4) Meeting customer expectations for delivery speed

309. Which of the following is an example of a warehouse operation in logistics management?
(1) Designing a new product
(2) Managing sales forecasts
(3) Picking and packing orders
(4) Setting prices for products

310. Which of the following is an example of a logistics procedure?
(1) Setting marketing goals
(2) Hiring new employees
(3) Conducting a customer satisfaction survey
(4) Conducting quality checks on incoming inventory

311. Which of the following is not a factor to consider when selecting a warehouse location in logistics management?
(1) Availability (2) Cost
(3) Color (4) Accessibility

312. Which of the following is not a key component of supply chain management?
(1) Logistics management
(2) Marketing management
(3) Operations management
(4) Procurement management

313. Which of the following is an example of a logistics technology?
(1) A sales report
(2) A balance sheet
(3) A transportation management system (TMS)
(4) A marketing plan

314. Which of the following is not a benefit of using logistics technology?
(1) Lower costs
(2) Improved visibility into the supply chain
(3) Increased complexity in managing the supply chain
(4) Quicker decision-making

315. Which of the following is an example of a logistics cost?
(1) Salaries of marketing staff
(2) Cost of raw materials
(3) Transportation costs
(4) Cost of office supplies

316. Which of the following is not a responsibility of a logistics manager?
(1) Ensuring compliance with regulations
(2) Designing new products
(3) Managing inventory levels
(4) Coordinating transportation activities

317. Which of the following is not a type of inventory in logistics management?
(1) Raw materials inventory
(2) Work-in-progress inventory
(3) Finished goods inventory
(4) Employee inventory

318. Which of the following is not a factor to consider when determining shipment frequency in logistics management?
(1) Cost
(2) Availability of transportation
(3) Customer demand
(4) Employee scheduling preferences

319. Which of the following is an example of a logistics network design decision?
(1) Setting prices for products
(2) Selecting a transportation mode
(3) Hiring new employees
(4) Conducting market research

320. Which of the following is not a benefit of using a transportation management system (TMS) in logistics management?
(1) Lower costs
(2) Improved visibility into the supply chain
(3) Increased complexity in managing the supply chain
(4) Quicker decision-making

321. Which of the following is an example of a logistics metric that measures efficiency?
(1) Customer satisfaction
(2) Cost per unit
(3) Employee job satisfaction
(4) Brand recognition

322. Which of the following is not a key factor to consider when designing a logistics network?
(1) Cost (2) Lead time
(3) Manufacturing process
(4) Customization requirements

323. Which of the following is not an example of a logistics network?
(1) Manufacturer to retailer to end consumer
(2) Manufacturer to end consumer
(3) Manufacturer to wholesaler to retailer to end consumer
(4) Retailer to end consumer

324. Which of the following is a component of inbound logistics?

(1) Warehousing (2) Transportation
(3) Stock control (4) Customer service

325. Which of the following is an example of a logistics technology that can be used to track inventory levels?
(1) A production report
(2) A balance sheet
(3) Radio frequency identification (RFID) tags
(4) A marketing plan

326. Which of the following is not a benefit of using electronic data interchange (EDI) in logistics management?
(1) Higher costs
(2) Improved accuracy of data
(3) Quicker decision-making
(4) Reduced paperwork and administrative tasks

327. Which of the following is not a characteristic of an agile logistics system?
(1) Dynamic (2) Flexible
(3) Fast (4) High in cost

328. Which of the following is not a factor to consider when selecting a logistics service provider?
(1) Availability
(2) Cost
(3) Color
(4) Level of service quality

329. Which of the following is an example of a logistics process?
(1) Conducting market research
(2) Designing a new product
(3) Managing inventory levels
(4) Posting on social media

330. Which of the following is not a factor to consider when selecting a warehouse in logistics management?
(1) Location (2) Cost
(3) Size (4) Color

331. Which of the following is an example of a logistics metric that measures effectiveness?
(1) Cost per unit
(2) Customer satisfaction
(3) Transit time
(4) Employee job satisfaction

332. Which of the following is not a type of supply chain?
(1) Closed-loop supply chain
(2) Reverse supply chain
(3) Open-loop supply chain
(4) Customer satisfaction supply chain

Directions: Each of the following items consists of two statements, one labelled as Assertion (A) and other labelled as Reason (R). You are to examine these two statements carefully and decide if the (A) and the (R) are individually true and if so, whether (R) is the correct explanation of (A). Select your answers to these items using the codes given below:
(1) Both (A) and (R) are true and the (R) is a correct explanation of the (A).
(2) Both (A) and (R) are true, but the (R) is not a correct explanation of the (A).
(3) The (A) is true, but the (R) is false.
(4) The (A) is false, but the (R) is true.

333. **Assertion (A):** Logistics management is focused on managing the movement and storage of goods and services.
Reason: Effective logistics management leads to increased costs for a company.

334. **Assertion (A):** Transportation is a critical component of logistics management.
Reason: Transportation modes have no impact on the speed of product delivery.

335. **Assertion (A):** Inventory management is focused on managing the flow of goods into and out of a company's warehouses and distribution centers.
Reason: Effective inventory management can help reduce costs and improve customer satisfaction.

ANSWERS

1. (2) **2.** (2) **3.** (3) **4.** (3) **5.** (3) **6.** (3) **7.** (2) **8.** (4) **9.** (3) **10.** (2)
11. (1) **12.** (3) **13.** (4) **14.** (2) **15.** (3) **16.** (2) **17.** (2) **18.** (2) **19.** (3) **20.** (3)
21. (2) **22.** (2) **23.** (3) **24.** (3) **25.** (3) **26.** (1) **27.** (1) **28.** (4) **29.** (2) **30.** (3)
31. (2) **32.** (3) **33.** (2) **34.** (1) **35.** (1) **36.** (1) **37.** (1) **38.** (2) **39.** (3) **40.** (3)
41. (1) **42.** (2) **43.** (3) **44.** (3) **45.** (1) **46.** (2) **47.** (2) **48.** (3) **49.** (2) **50.** (1)
51. (4) **52.** (3) **53.** (1) **54.** (3) **55.** (3) **56.** (2) **57.** (3) **58.** (1) **59.** (3) **60.** (4)
61. (1) **62.** (2) **63.** (3) **64.** (2) **65.** (3) **66.** (2) **67.** (1) **68.** (2) **69.** (2) **70.** (1)
71. (3) **72.** (1) **73.** (2) **74.** (3) **75.** (2) **76.** (3) **77.** (3) **78.** (1) **79.** (3) **80.** (4)
81. (3) **82.** (3) **83.** (3) **84.** (1) **85.** (3) **86.** (3) **87.** (3) **88.** (2) **89.** (3) **90.** (2)
91. (2) **92.** (2) **93.** (2) **94.** (2) **95.** (3) **96.** (3) **97.** (2) **98.** (2) **99.** (3) **100.** (2)
101. (3) **102.** (3) **103.** (3) **104.** (2) **105.** (1) **106.** (2) **107.** (4) **108.** (4) **109.** (4) **110.** (2)
111. (2) **112.** (3) **113.** (3) **114.** (3) **115.** (1) **116.** (3) **117.** (1) **118.** (3) **119.** (4) **120.** (4)
121. (2) **122.** (2) **123.** (4) **124.** (1) **125.** (3) **126.** (2) **127.** (3) **128.** (1) **129.** (1) **130.** (4)
131. (4) **132.** (4) **133.** (4) **134.** (3) **135.** (2) **136.** (1) **137.** (2) **138.** (2) **139.** (2) **140.** (2)
141. (1) **142.** (4) **143.** (1) **144.** (3) **145.** (2) **146.** (4) **147.** (3) **148.** (2) **149.** (2) **150.** (4)
151. (3) **152.** (4) **153.** (3) **154.** (2) **155.** (3) **156.** (1) **157.** (4) **158.** (3) **159.** (1) **160.** (1)
161. (4) **162.** (3) **163.** (1) **164.** (3) **165.** (3) **166.** (4) **167.** (2) **168.** (4) **169.** (2) **170.** (4)
171. (2) **172.** (4) **173.** (4) **174.** (4) **175.** (4) **176.** (1) **177.** (3) **178.** (2) **179.** (4) **180.** (3)
181. (4) **182.** (4) **183.** (4) **184.** (4) **185.** (3) **186.** (1) **187.** (4) **188.** (3) **189.** (3) **190.** (4)
191. (4) **192.** (4) **193.** (1) **194.** (3) **195.** (2) **196.** (3) **197.** (4) **198.** (3) **199.** (3) **200.** (3)
201. (1) **202.** (3) **203.** (3) **204.** (4) **205.** (3) **206.** (1) **207.** (4) **208.** (4) **209.** (3) **210.** (3)
211. (4) **212.** (4) **213.** (3) **214.** (3) **215.** (3) **216.** (2) **217.** (3) **218.** (3) **219.** (3) **220.** (2)
221. (4) **222.** (4) **223.** (1) **224.** (3) **225.** (3) **226.** (4) **227.** (3) **228.** (2) **229.** (3) **230.** (3)
231. (1) **232.** (4) **233.** (2) **234.** (4) **235.** (2) **236.** (3) **237.** (2) **238.** (4) **239.** (4) **240.** (3)
241. (4) **242.** (4) **243.** (4) **244.** (3) **245.** (4) **246.** (1) **247.** (3) **248.** (3) **249.** (3) **250.** (3)
251. (3) **252.** (2) **253.** (2) **254.** (4) **255.** (4) **256.** (3) **257.** (3) **258.** (4) **259.** (4) **260.** (4)
261. (1) **262.** (3) **263.** (3) **264.** (4) **265.** (3) **266.** (4) **267.** (4) **268.** (4) **269.** (2) **270.** (2)
271. (2) **272.** (2) **273.** (3) **274.** (4) **275.** (1) **276.** (3) **277.** (3) **278.** (2) **279.** (3) **280.** (4)
281. (3) **282.** (3) **283.** (4) **284.** (4) **285.** (1) **286.** (3) **287.** (1) **288.** (4) **289.** (3) **290.** (4)
291. (3) **292.** (3) **293.** (3) **294.** (4) **295.** (3) **296.** (4) **297.** (3) **298.** (2) **299.** (3) **300.** (3)
301. (1) **302.** (3) **303.** (3) **304.** (3) **305.** (4) **306.** (3) **307.** (2) **308.** (2) **309.** (3) **310.** (4)
311. (3) **312.** (2) **313.** (3) **314.** (3) **315.** (3) **316.** (2) **317.** (4) **318.** (4) **319.** (2) **320.** (3)
321. (2) **322.** (3) **323.** (4) **324.** (2) **325.** (3) **326.** (1) **327.** (4) **328.** (3) **329.** (3) **330.** (4)
331. (2) **332.** (4) **333.** (3) **334.** (3) **335.** (1)

UNIT 9

LEGAL ASPECTS OF BUSINESS

SYLLABUS

- Indian Contract Act, 1872: Elements of a valid contract; Capacity of parties; Free consent; Discharge of a contract; Breach of contract and remedies against breach; Quasi contracts
- Special contracts: Contracts of indemnity and guarantee; contracts of bailment and pledge; Contracts of agency
- Sale of Goods Act, 1930: Sale and agreement to sell; Doctrine of Caveat Emptor; Rights of unpaid seller and rights of buyer
- Negotiable Instruments Act, 1881: Types of negotiable instruments; Negotiation and assignment; Dishonour and discharge of negotiable instruments
- The Companies Act, 2013: Nature and kinds of companies; Company formation; Management, meetings and winding up of a joint stock company
- Limited Liability Partnership: Structure and procedure of formation of LLP in India
- The Competition Act, 2002: Objectives and main provisions
- The Information Technology Act, 2000: Objectives and main provisions; Cyber crimes and penalties
- The RTI Act, 2005: Objectives and main provisions
- Intellectual Property Rights (IPRs) : Patents, trademarks and copyrights; Emerging issues in intellectual property
- Goods and Services Tax (GST): Objectives and main provisions; Benefits of GST; Implementation mechanism; Working of dual GST

INDIAN CONTRACT ACT, 1872

The Indian Contract Act, 1872 prescribes the law relating to contracts in India. The Act was passed by British India and is based on the principles of English Common Law. It is applicable to all the states of India except the state of Jammu and Kashmir. It determines the circumstances in which promises made by the parties to a contract shall be legally binding and the enforcement of these rights and duties. DEFINITION : Under Section 2(h), Indian Contract act defines Contract as an agreement which is enforceable by law.

The Act as enacted originally had 266 Sections, it had wide scope and included.

- General Principles of Law of Contract- Sections 01 to 75.
- Contract relating to Sale of Goods- Sections 76 to 123.
- Special Contracts- Indemnity, Guarantee, Bailment & Pledge- Sections 124 to 238.
- Contracts relating to Partnership- Sections 239 to 266.

Indian Contract Act embodied the simple and elementary rules relating to sale of goods and Partnership. The developments of modern business world found the provisions contained in the Indian Contract Act inadequate to deal with the new regulations or give effect to the new principles. Subsequently, the provisions relating to the Sale of Goods and Partnership contained in the Indian Contract Act were repealed respectively in the year 1930 and 1932 and new enactments namely Sale of Goods and Movables Act 1930 and Indian Partnership act 1932 were reenacted.

At present the Indian Contract Act may be divided into two parts:

a. Part 1: deals with the General Principles of Law of Contract Sections 1 to 75

b. Part 2: deals with Special kinds of Contracts such as:

   (1) Contract of Indemnity and Guarantee

   (2) Contract of Bailment and Pledge

   (3) Contract of Agency.

1. **Offer 2(a).** When one person signifies to another his willingness to do or to abstain from doing anything, with a view to obtaining the assent of that other to such act or abstinence, he is said to make a proposal.
2. **Acceptance 2(b).** When the person to whom the proposal is made, signifies his assent there to, the proposal is said to be accepted.
3. **Promise 2(b).** A Proposal when accepted becomes a promise. In simple words, when an offer is accepted it becomes promise.
4. **Promisor and promisee 2(c).** When the proposal is accepted, the person making the proposal is called as promisor and the person accepting the proposal is called as promisee.
5. **Consideration 2(d).** When at the desire of the promisor, the promisee or any other person has done or abstained from doing or does or abstains from doing or promises to do or to abstain from doing something such act or abstinence or promise is called a consideration for the promise. Price paid by one party for the promise of the other Technical word meaning QUID-PRO-QUO i.e. something in return.
6. **Agreement 2(e).** Every promise and set of promises forming the consideration for each other. In short,
7. **Contract 2(h).** An agreement enforceable by Law is a contract.
   Therefore, there must be an agreement and it should be enforceable by law.
8. **Reciprocal Promises 2(f).** Promises which form the consideration or part of the consideration for each other are called 'reciprocal promises'.

9. **Void agreement 2(g).** An agreement not enforceable by law is void.
10. **Voidable contract 2(i).** An agreement is a voidable contract if it is enforceable by Law at the option of one or more of the parties there to (i.e. the aggrieved party), and it is not enforceable by Law at the option of the other or others.
11. **Void contract 2(j).** A contract which ceases to be enforceable by Law becomes void when it ceases to be enforceable.

According to Section 2(b), "When the person to whom the proposal is made, signifies his assent thereto, the proposal is said to be accepted. A proposal, when accepted, becomes a promise."

Rules

1. Acceptance should be absolute and unqualified. If the parties are not in ad idem on all matters concerning the offer and acceptance, there is no valid contract. For example, "A" says to "B" "I offer to sell my car for Rs.50,000/-. "B" replies "I will purchase it for Rs.45,000/-". This is not acceptance and hence it amounts to a counter offer.
2. It should be Communicated to the offeror. To conclude a contract between parties, the acceptance must be communicated in some prescribed form. A mere mental determination on the part of offeree to accept an offer does not amount to valid acceptance.
3. Acceptance must be in the mode prescribed. If the acceptance is not according to the mode prescribed or some usual and reasonable mode (where no mode is prescribed) the offeror may intimate to the offeree within a reasonable time that acceptance is not according to the mode prescribed and may insist that the offer be accepted in the prescribed mode only. If he does not inform the offeree, he is deemed to have accepted the offer. For example, "A" makes an offer to "B" says to "B" that "if you accept the offer, reply by voice. "B" sends reply by post. It will be a valid acceptance, unless "A" informs "B" that the acceptance is not according to the prescribed mode.
4. Acceptance must be given within a reasonable time before the offer lapses. If any time limit is specified, the acceptance must be given within the time, if no time limit is specified it must be given within a reasonable time.
5. It cannot precede an offer. If the acceptance precedes an offer it is not a valid acceptance and does not result in contract. For example, in a company shares were allotted to a person who had not applied for them. Subsequently, when he applied for shares, he was unaware of the previous allotment. The allotment of share previous to the application is not valid.
6. Acceptance by the way of conduct.
7. Mere silence is no acceptance.

Silence does not per-se amounts to communication- Bank of India Ltd. Vs. Rustom Cowasjee- AIR 1955 Bom. 419 at P. 430; 57 Bom. L.R. 850- Mere silence cannot amount to any assent. It does not even amount to any representation on which any plea of estoppel may be found, unless there is a duty to make some statement or to do some act free and offer must be consent

1. Acceptance must be unambiguous and definite.
2. Acceptance cannot be given before communication of an offer.

According to Section 2(d), Consideration is defined as: "When at the desire of the promisor, the promisee or any other person has done or abstained from doing, or does or abstains from doing, or promises to do or abstain from doing something, such act or abstinence or promise is called consideration for the promise". Consideration means 'something in return'.

In short, Consideration means *quid pro quo* i.e. something in return.

The consideration or object of an agreement is lawful, unless and until it is:

1. **Forbidden by law.** If the object or the consideration of an agreement is for doing an act forbidden by law, such agreement are void, for example, "A" promises "B" to obtain an employment in public service and "B" promises to pay Rs one lakh to "A". The agreement is void as the procuring government job through unlawful means is prohibited.
2. **If it involves injury to a person or property of another.** For example, "A" borrowed Rs.100/- from "B" and executed a bond to work for "B" without pay for a period of 2 years. In case of default, "A" owes to pay the principal sum at once and huge amount of interest. This contract was held void as it involved injury to the person.
3. **If courts regards it as immoral.** An agreement in which consideration in object of which is immoral is void. For example, An agreement between husband and wife for future separation is void.
4. Is of such nature that, if permitted, it would defeat the provisions of any law.
5. Is fraudulent, or involves or implies injury to the person or property of another.
6. **Is opposed to public policy.** An agreement which tends to be injurious to the public or against the public good is void. For example, agreements of trading with foreign enemy, agreement to commit crime, agreements which interfere with the administration of justice, agreements which interfere with the course of justice, stifling prosecution, maintenance and champerty.
7. **Agreements in restrained of legal proceedings.** This deals with two category. One is, agreements restraining enforcement of rights and the other deals with agreements curtailing period of limitation.
8. **Trafficking in public offices and titles:** Agreements for sale or transfer of public offices and title or for procurement of a public recognition like Padma Vibhushan or Padma Shri etc. for monetary consideration is unlawful, being opposed to public policy.
9. **Agreements restricting personal liberty.** Agreements which unduly restricts the personal liberty of parties to it are void as being opposed by public policy.
10. **Marriage brokerage contact.** Agreements to procure marriages for rewards are void under the ground that marriage ought to proceed with free and voluntary decisions of parties.
11. Agreements interfering marital duties: Any agreement which interfere with performance of marital duty is void being opposed to public policy. An agreement between husband and wife that the wife will never leave her parental house.
12. Consideration may take in any form-money, goods, services, a promise to marry, a promise to forbear etc.

Contract Opposed to Public Policy can be Repudiated by the Court of law even if that contract is beneficial for all of the parties to the contract- What considerations and objects are lawful and what not-Mewar Marble Industries Pvt. Ltd. Vs. Rajasthan State Electricity Board, Jaipur, 1993 Cr. L.J. 1191 at 1197, 1198 [Raj.]- Agreement of which object or consideration was opposed to public policy, unlawful and void-- What better and what more can be an admission of the fact that the consideration or object of the compounding agreement was abstention by the board from criminally prosecuting the petitioner-company from offense under Section 39 of the act and that the Board has converted the crime into a source of profit or benefit to itself. This consideration or object is clearly opposed to public policy and hence the compounding agreement is unlawful and void under Section 23 of the Act. It is unenforceable as against the Petitioner-Company.

Section 11 of The Indian Contract Act specifies that every person is competent to contract provided:

1. He should not be a minor i.e. an individual who has not attained the age of majority i.e. 18 years in normal case and 21 years if guardian is appointed by the Court.

2. He should be of sound mind while making a contract. A person who is usually of unsound mind, but occasionally of sound mind, can make a contract when he is of sound mind. Similarly, if a person is usually of sound mind, but occasionally of unsound mind, may not make a valid contract when he is of unsound mind.
3. He is not disqualified from contracting by any other law to which he is subject.

There are other laws of the land that disqualify certain persons from contracting. They are:

- Alien enemy
- Foreign sovereigns, diplomatic staff etc.
- Artificial persons i.e. corporation, companies etc.
- Insolvents
- Convicts
- Pardanashin Women

According to Section 13, " two or more persons are said to be in consent when they agree upon the same thing in the same sense (*Consensus-ad-idem*). According to Section 14,

"Consent is said to be free when it is not caused by coercion or undue influence or fraud or misrepresentation or mistake."

ELEMENTS OF A VALID CONTRACT

1. **Coercion (Section 15).** "Coercion" is the committing, or threatening to commit, any act forbidden by the Indian Penal Code under (45, 1860), or the unlawful detaining, or threatening to detain, any property, to the prejudice of any person whatever, with the intention of causing any person to enter into an agreement. For example, "A" threatens to shoot "B" if he doesn't release him from a debt which he owes to "B". "B" releases "A" under threat. Since the release has been brought about by coercion, such release is not valid.
2. **Undue influence (Section 16).** "Where a person who is in a position to dominate the will of another enters into a contract with him and the transaction appears on the face of it, or on the evidence, to be unconscionable, the burden of proving that such contract was not induced by undue influence shall lie upon the person in the position to dominate the will of the other." (Section 16(2)) States that "A person is deemed to be in a position to dominate the will of another;
   - Where he holds a real or apparent authority over the other. For example, an employer may be deemed to be having authority over his employee an income tax authority over to the assessee.
   - Where he stands in a fiduciary relationship to other, For example, the relationship of Solicitor with his client, spiritual advisor and devotee.
   - Where he makes a contract with a person whose mental capacity is temporarily or permanently affected by the reason of age, illness or mental or bodily distress"
3. **Fraud (Section 17).** "Fraud" means and includes any act or concealment of material fact or misrepresentation made knowingly by a party to a contract, or with his connivance, or by his agent, with intent to deceive another party thereto of his agent, or to induce him to enter into the contract. Mere silence is not fraud. A contracting party is not obliged to disclose each and everything to the other party. There are two exceptions where even mere silence may be fraud, one is where there is a duty to speak, then keeping silence is fraud or when silence is in itself equivalent to speech, such silence is fraud.
4. **Misrepresentation (Section 18).** "Causing, however innocently, a party to an agreement to make a mistake as to the substance of the thing which is the subject of the agreement".

5. **Mistake of fact (Section 20).** "Where both the parties to an agreement are under a mistake as to a matter of fact essential to the agreement, the agreement is void". A party cannot be allowed to get any relief on the ground that he had done some particular act in ignorance of law. Mistake may be bilateral mistake where both parties to an agreement are under mistake as to the matter of fact. The mistake must relate to a matter of fact essential to the agreement.

The process of concluding a contract through an agent involves a twofold relationship. On the one hand, the law of agency is concerned with the external business relations of an economic unit and with the powers of the various representatives to affect the legal position of the principal. On the other hand, it rules the internal relationship between principal and agent as well, thereby imposing certain duties on the representative (diligence, accounting, good faith, etc.).

Under section 201 to 210 an agency may come to an end in a variety of ways:

(i) **By the principal revoking the agency.** However, principal cannot revoke an agency coupled with interest to the prejudice of such interest. Such Agency is coupled with interest. An agency is coupled with interest when the agent himself has an interest in the subject-matter of the agency, e.g., where the goods are consigned by an upcountry constituent to a commission agent for sale, with poor to recoup himself from the sale proceeds, the advances made by him to the principal against the security of the goods; in such a case, the principal cannot revoke the agent's authority till the goods are actually sold, nor is the agency terminated by death or insanity. (Illustrations to section 201)

(ii) By the agent renouncing the business of agency;

(iii) By the business of agency being completed;

(iv) By the principal being adjudicated insolvent (Section 201 of The Indian Contract Act. 1872)

The principal also cannot revoke the agent's authority after it has been partly exercised, so as to bind the principal (Section 204), though he can always do so, before such authority has been so exercised (Sec 203).

Further, as per section 205, if the agency is for a fixed period, the principal cannot terminate the agency before the time expired, except for sufficient cause. If he does, he is liable to compensate the agent for the loss caused to him thereby. The same rules apply where the agent, renounces an agency for a fixed period. Notice in this connection that want of skill continuous disobedience of lawful orders, and rude or insulting behavior has been held to be sufficient cause for dismissal of an agent. Further, reasonable notice has to be given by one party to the other; otherwise, damage resulting from want of such notice, will have to be paid (Section 206). As per section 207, the revocation or renunciation of an agency may be made expressly or impliedly by conduct. The termination does not take effect as regards the agent, till it becomes known to him and as regards third party, till the termination is known to them (Section 208). Sub-agent who is appointed by an agent for participate on behalf of his work.

Type of Offer

- General Offer
- Specified offer
- Cross offer
- Counter Offer.

When an agent's authority is terminated, it operates as a termination of subagent also. (Section 210).

QUASI CONTRACTS

The word 'Quasi' means pseudo. Hence, a Quasi contract is a pseudo-contract. When we talk about a valid contact we expect it to have certain elements like offer and acceptance, consideration, the capacity to contract, and free will. But there are other types of contracts as well.

There are cases where the law implies a promise and imposes obligations on one party while conferring rights to the other even when the basic elements of a contract are not present. These promises are not legal contracts, but the court recognizes them as relations resembling a contract and enforces them like a contract. These promises/ relations are Quasi contracts. These obligations can also arise due to different social relationships which we will look at in this article.

The core principles behind a Quasi Contract are justice, equity and good conscience. It is based on the maxim: "No man must grow rich out of another persons' loss."

Let's look at an example of a Quasi contract: Peter and Oliver enter a contract under which Peter agrees to deliver a basket of fruits at Oliver's residence and Oliver promises to pay Rs 1,500 after consuming all the fruits. However, Peter erroneously delivers a basket of fruits at John's residence instead of Oliver's. When John gets home he assumes that the fruit basket is a birthday gift and consumes them.

Although, there is no contract between Peter and John, the court treats this as a Quasi-contract and orders John to either return the basket of fruits or pay Peter.

Features of a Quasi Contract

1. It is usually a right to money and is generally (not always) to a liquated sum of money
2. The right is not an outcome of an agreement but is imposed by law.
3. The right is not available against everyone in the world but only against a specific person(s). Hence it resembles a contractual right.

Sections 68 – 72 of the Indian Contract Act, 1872 detail five circumstances under which a Quasi contract comes to exist. Remember, there is no real contract between the parties and the law imposes the contractual liability due to the peculiar circumstances.

Section 68 – Necessaries Supplied to Persons Incapable of Contracting

Imagine a person incapable of entering into a contract like a lunatic or a minor. If a person supplies necessaries suited to the condition in life of such a person, then he can get reimbursement from the property of the incapable person.

John is a lunatic. Peter supplies John with certain necessaries suited to his condition in life. However, John does not have the money or sanity and fails to pay Peter. This is termed as a Quasi contract and Peter is entitled to reimbursement from John's property.

However, to establish his claim, Peter needs to prove two things:

1. John is a lunatic
2. The goods supplied were necessary for John at the time they were sold/ delivered.

Section 69 – Payment by an Interested Person

If a person pays the money on someone else's behalf which the other person is bound by law to pay, then he is entitled to reimbursement by the other person.

Peter is a zamindar. He has leased his land to John, a farmer. However, Peter fails to pay the revenue due to the government. After sending notices and not receiving the payment, the government releases an advertisement for sale of the land (which is leased to John). According to the Revenue law, once the land is sold, John's lease agreement is annulled.

John does not want to let go of the land since he has worked hard on the land and it has started yielding good produce. In order to prevent the sale, John pays the government the amount due from Peter. In this scenario, Peter is obligated to repay the said amount to John.

Section 70 – Obligation of Person enjoying the benefits of a Non-Gratuitous Act

Imagine a person lawfully doing something or delivering something to someone without the intention of doing so gratuitously and the other person enjoying the benefits of the act done or goods delivered. In such a case, the other person is liable to pay compensation to the former for the act, or goods received. This compensation can be in money or the other person can, if possible, restore the thing done or delivered.

However, the plaintiff must prove that:

- The act that is done or thing delivered was lawful
- He did not do so gratuitously
- The other person enjoyed the benefits

Section 71 – Responsibility of Finder of Goods

If a person finds goods that belong to someone else and takes them into his custody, then he has to adhere to the following responsibilities:

- Take care of the goods as a person of regular prudence
- No right to appropriate the goods
- Restore the goods to the owner (if found)

Peter owns a flower shop. Olivia visits him to buy a bouquet but forgets her purse in the shop. Unfortunately, there are no documents in the purse to help ascertain her identity. Peter leaves the purse on the checkout counter assuming that she would return to take it.

John, an assistant at Peter's shop finds the purse lying on the counter and puts it in a drawer without informing Peter. He finished his shift and goes home. When Olivia returns looking for her purse, Peter can't find it. He is liable for compensation since he did not take care of the purse which any prudent man would have done.

Section 72 – Money paid by Mistake or Under Coercion

If a person receives money or goods by mistake or under coercion, then he is liable to repay or return it.

Let us see an example. Peter misunderstands the terms of the lease and pays municipal tax erroneously. After he realizes his mistake, he approached the municipal authorities for a reimbursement. He is entitled to be reimbursed since he had paid the money by mistake.

Similarly, money paid by coercion which includes oppression, extortion or any such means, is recoverable.

SPECIAL CONTRACTS

CONTRACTS OF INDEMNITY AND GUARANTEE

The term Indemnity literally means "Security against loss". In a contract of indemnity one party – i.e. the indemnifier promise to compensate the other party i.e. the indemnified against the loss suffered by the other.

The English law definition of a contract of indemnity is – "it is a promise to save a person harmless from the consequences of an act". Thus it includes within its ambit losses caused not merely by human agency but also those caused by accident or fire or other natural calamities.

The definition of a contract of indemnity as laid down in Section 124 – "A contract by which one party promises to save the other from loss caused to him by the conduct of the promisor himself, or by the conduct of any other person, is called a contract of indemnity.

The definition provided by the Indian Contract Act confines itself to the losses occasioned due to the act of the promisor or due to the act of any other person.

Under a contract of indemnity, liability of the promisor arises from loss caused to the promisee by the conduct of the promisor himself or by the conduct of other person. [Punjab National Bank v Vikram Cotton Mills].

Every contract of insurance, other than life insurance, is a contract of indemnity. The definition is restricted to cases where loss has been caused by some human agency. [Gajanan Moreshwar v Moreshwar Madan]

Section 124 deals with one particular kind of indemnity which arises from a promise made by an indemnifier to save the indemnified from the loss caused to him by the conduct of the indemnifier himself or by the conduct of any other person, but does not deal with those classes of cases where the indemnity arises from loss caused by events or accidents which do not depend upon the conduct of indemnifier or any other person. [Moreshwar v Moreshwar]

"Contract of indemnity" defined.-A contract by which one party promises to save the other from loss caused to him by the conduct of the promisor himself, or by the conduct of any other person, is called a "contract of indemnity".

Illustration

A contracts to indemnify B against the consequences of any proceedings which C may take against B in respect of a certain sum of 200 rupees. This is a contract of indemnity.

Nature of Contract of Indemnity

A contract of indemnity may be express or implied depending upon the circumstances of the case, though Section 124 of the Indian Contract Act does not seem to cover the case of implied indemnity.

A broker in possession of a government promissory note endorsed it to a bank with forged endorsement. The bank acting in good faith applied for and got a renewed promissory note from the Public Debt Office. Meanwhile the true owner sued the Secretary of State for conversion who in turn sued the bank on an implied indemnity. It was held that – it is general principle of law when an act is done by one person at the request of another which act is not in itself manifestly tortious to the knowledge of the person doing it, and such act turns to be injurious to the rights of a third person, the person doing it is entitled to an indemnity from him who requested that it should be done. [Secretary of State v Bank of India].

The Indian Contract Act also deals with special cases of implied indemnity –

1. U/s 69 if a person who is interested in payment of money which another is bound by law to pay and therefore pays it, he is entitled to be indemnified. For instance – if a tenant pays certain electricity bill to be paid by the owner, he is entitled to be indemnified by the owner.
2. Section 145 provides for right of a surety to claim indemnity from the principal debtor for all sums which he has rightfully paid towards the guarantee.
3. Section 222 provides for liability of the principal to indemnify the agent in respect of all amounts paid by him during the lawful exercise of his authority.

The plaintiff, an auctioneer, acting on the instruction of the defendant sold certain cattle which subsequently turned out to belong to someone else other than the defendant. When the true owner sued the auctioneer for conversion, the auctioneer in turn sued the defendant for indemnity. The Court held that the plaintiff having acted on the request of the defendant was entitled to assume that, if it would turned out to be wrongful, he would be indemnified by the defendant. [Adamson v Jarvis].

Validity of Indemnity Agreement

A contract of indemnity is one of the species of contracts. The principles applicable to contracts in general are also applicable to such contracts so much so that the rules such as free consent, legality of object, etc., are equally applicable.

Where the consent to an agreement is caused by coercion, fraud, misrepresentation, the agreement is voidable at the option of the party whose consent was so caused. As per the requirement of the Contract Act, the object of the agreement must be lawful. An agreement, the object of which is opposed to the law or against the public policy, is either unlawful or void depending upon the provision of the law to which it is subject.

Contract of Indemnity when Enforceable

The question whether the liability of indemnifier commences only when the indemnified has actually suffered loss or when there is an apprehension that the indemnified by all chances is likely to suffer it.

The former view was held in cases like – Shankar Nimbaji v Laxman Sapdu / Chand Bibi v Santosh Kumar Pal.

The plaintiff filed a suit to recover Rs. 5,000/- and interest from defendant by the sale of a mortgaged property and, in case of deficit, for a decree against the estate of defendant 2 which was in the hands of his sons, the defendant 2 died during the pendency of the suit. It was held that plaintiff cannot sue the defendant in anticipation that the proceeds realized by the sale of the mortgaged property would be insufficient and there would be some deficit. [Shankar Nimbaji v Laxman Sapdu]

The defendant's father while purchasing certain property covenanted to pay off mortgage debt incurred by the plaintiff and also promised to indemnify him if they were made liable for the mortgage debt. The defendant's father failed to pay off the mortgage debt and plaintiff filed an action to enforce the covenant. It was held as the plaintiff had not yet suffered any damage, the suit was premature so far as the cause of action on indemnity was concerned. [Chand Bibi v Santosh Kumar Pal]

A different point of view was held by the Courts in the following cases –

Plaintiff company agreed to act as commission agent for the defendant firm for purchase and sale of "Hessian" and "Gunnies" and charge commission on all such purchases and the defendant firm agreed to indemnify the plaintiff against all losses in respect of such transactions. The plaintiff company purchased certain Hessian from one Maliram Ramjidas. The defendant firm failed to pay for or take delivery of the Hessian. Then Maliram Ramjidas resoled it at lesser price and claimed the difference as damages from the plaintiff company. The plaintiff company went into liquidation and the liquidator filed a suit to recover the amount claimed by Maliram from the defendant firm under the indemnity. The defendant argued that in as much as the plaintiff had not yet paid any amount to Maliram in respect of their liability they were not entitled to maintain the suit under indemnity. It was held negative and decided in plaintiff's favour with a direction that the amount when recovered from the defendant firm should be paid to Maliram Ramjidas. [Osmal Jamal & Sons Ltd. v Gopal Purushotham]

After the landmark decision in the case of Gajanan Moreshwar v Moreshwar Madan Mantri it has been well established that the liability of the indemnifier commences as soon as the loss of the indemnified becomes absolute, certain or imminent. It is not necessary that the promisee should pay for the loss.

Rights of the indemnity holder – (Section 125)

An indemnity holder (i.e. indemnified) acting within the scope of his authority is entitled to the following rights –

1. Right to recover damages – he is entitled to recover all damages which he might have been compelled to pay in any suit in respect of any matter covered by the contract.
2. Right to recover costs – He is entitled to recover all costs incidental to the institution and defending of the suit.
3. Right to recover sums paid under compromise – he is entitled to recover all amounts which he had paid under the terms of the compromise of such suit. However, the compensation must

not be against the directions of the indemnifier. It must be prudent and authorized by the indemnifier.

4. Right to sue for specific performance – he is entitled to sue for specific performance if he has incurred absolute liability and the contract covers such liability. The promisee in a contract of indemnity, acting within the scope of his authority, is entitled to recover from the promisor:
   a. all damages which he may be compelled to pay in any suit in respect of any matter to which the promise to indemnify applies;
   b. all costs which he may be compelled to pay in any such suit if, in bringing or defending it, he did not contravene the orders of the promisor, and acted as it would have been prudent for him to act in the absence of any contract of indemnity, or if the promisor authorized him to bring or defend the suit;
   c. all sums which he may have paid under the terms of any compromise of any such suit, if the compromise was not.

It is important to note here that the right to indemnity cannot be claimed of dishonesty, lack of good faith and contravention of the promisor's request. However, the right cannot be negatived in case of oversight. [Yeung v HSBC]

Right of Indemnifier

Section 125 of the Act only lays down the rights of the indemnified and is quite silent of the rights of indemnifier as if the indemnifier has no rights but only liability towards the indemnified.

In the logical state of things if we read Section 141 which deals with the rights of surety, we can easily conclude that the indemnifier's right would also be same as that of surety.

Where one person has agreed to indemnify the other, he will, on making good the indemnity, be entitled to succeed to all the ways and means by which the person indemnified might have protected himself against or reimbursed himself for the loss. [Simpson v Thomson]

Principle of Subrogation is applicable because it is an essential part of law of indemnity and is based on equity and the Contract Act contains no provision in contravention with [Maharaja Shri Jarvat Singhji v Secretary of State for India]

Contract of guarantee, surety, principal debtor and creditor:

A "contract of guarantee " is a contract to perform the promise, or discharge the liability, of a third person in case of his default. The person who gives the guarantee is called the " surety";

the person in respect of whose default the guarantee is given is called the " principal debtor ", and the person to whom the guarantee is given is called the " creditor ". A guarantee may be either oral or written.

Consideration for guarantee.-Anything done, or any promise made, for the benefit of the principal debtor, may be a sufficient consideration to the surety for giving the guarantee.

Illustrations

(a) B requests A to sell and deliver to him goods on credit. A agrees to do so, provided C will guarantee the payment of the price of the goods. C promises to guarantee the payment in consideration of as promise to deliver the goods. This is a sufficient consideration for Cs promise.

(b) A sells and delivers goods to B. C afterwards requests A to forbear to sue B for the debt for a year, and promises that, if he does so, C will pay for them in default of payment by B. A agrees to forbear as requested. This is a sufficient consideration for Cs promise.

(c) A sells and delivers goods to B. C afterwards, without consideration, agrees to pay for them in default of B. The agreement is void.

Suretys Liability

The liability of the surety is coextensive with that of the principal debtor, unless it is otherwise provided by the contract.

Illustration

A guarantees to B the payment of a bill of exchange by C, the acceptor. The bill is dishonoured by C. A is liable not only for the amount of the bill but also for any interest and charges which may have become due on it.

Continuing Guarantee

A guarantee which extends to a series of transactions is called a "continuing guarantee".

Revocation of Continuing Guarantee

A continuing guarantee may at any time be revoked by the surety, as to future transactions, by notice to the creditor.

Discharge of surety by variance in terms of contract

Any variance, made without the suretys consent, in the terms of the contract between the principal [debtor] and the creditor, discharges the surety as to transactions subsequent to the variance.

Discharge of surety by release or discharge of principal debtor

The surety is discharged by any contract between the creditor and the principal debtor, by which the principal debtor is released or by any act or omission of the creditor, the legal consequence of which is the discharge of the principal debtor.

Discharge of surety when creditor compounds with, gives time to, or agrees not to sue, principal debtor.

A contract between the creditor and the principal debtor, by which the creditors makes a composition with, or promises to give time to, or not to sue, the principal debtor, discharges the surety, unless the surety assents to such contract.

Surety not discharged when agreement made with third person to give time to principal debtor. Where a contract to give time to the principal debtor is made by the creditor with a third person, and not with the principal debtor, the surety is not discharged.

Release of one co-surety does not discharge others

Where there are co-sureties, a release by the creditor of one of them does not discharge the others; neither does it free the surety so released from his responsibility to the other sureties. Discharge of surety by creditors act or omission impairing suretys eventual remedy.

Guarantee obtained by misrepresentation invalid.

Any guarantee which has been obtained by means of misrepresentation made by the creditor, or with his knowledge and assent, concerning a material part of the transaction, is invalid.

Guarantee on contract that creditor shall not act on it until co-surety joins

Where a person gives a guarantee upon a contract that the creditor shall not act upon it until another person has joined in it as co-surety, the guarantee is not valid if that other person does not join.

Co-sureties liable to contribute equally

Where two or more persons are CO-sureties for the same debt or duty, either jointly or severally, and whether under the same or different contracts, and whether with or without the knowledge of each other, the co-sureties, in the absence of any contract to the contrary, are liable, as between themselves, to pay each an equal share of the whole debt, or of that part of it which remains unpaid by the principal debtor.

Liability of co-sureties bound in different sums

Co-sureties who are bound in different sums are liable to pay equally as far as the limits of their respective obligations permit.

Difference between Indemnity and Guarantee

In a contract of indemnity there are two parties i.e. indemnifier and indemnified. A contract of guarantee involves three parties i.e. creditor, principal debtor and surety.

An indemnity is for reimbursement of a loss, while a guarantee is for security of the creditor.

In a contract of indemnity, the liability of the indemnifier is primary and arises when the contingent event occurs. In case of contract of guarantee the liability of surety is secondary and arises when the principal debtor defaults.

The indemnifier after performing his part of the promise has no rights against the third party and he can sue the third party only if there is an assignment in his favour. Whereas, in a contract of guarantee, the surety steps into the shoes of the creditor on discharge of his liability, and may sue the principal debtor.

CONTRACTS OF BAILMENT AND PLEDGE

A bailment is a special contract defined under section 148 of the Indian Contract Act, 1872. It is derived from a French word i.e., "bailer" which means "to deliver". The etymological meaning of bailment is "handing over" or "change of possession of goods". By bailment, we mean delivery of goods from one person to another for a special purpose on the contract that they shall reimburse the goods on the fulfilment of the purpose or dispose of them as per the direction of the bailor. The person who delivers the goods is known as bailor. And the person to whom the goods are given is known as Bailee. And the property bailed is known as bailed property.

Essentials of Bailment

- There shall be a contract between the parties for the delivery of goods,
- The goods shall be delivered for a special purpose only,
- Bailment can only be done for movable goods and not for immovable goods or money,
- There shall be a transfer of possession of goods,
- Ownership is not transferred to Bailee, therefore Bailor remains the owner,
- Bailee is duty bound to deliver the same goods back and not any other goods.

Exception. The money deposited in the bank shall not account to bailment as the money returned by the bank would not be the same identical notes. And it is one of the essentials of the bailment that same goods are to be delivered back.

Duties of a Bailor

Section 150 of the Indian Contract Act, 1872 bound the bailor with certain duties to disclose the latent facts specifically pertaining to defect in goods. Bailor's duty of disclosure are:

- **Gratuitous Bailment.** It is the duty of the bailor to disclose all the defects in the goods that he is aware of to the Bailee that can interfere with the use of goods or can expose him to extraordinary risks. And failure to do the same will make bailor liable for damages.
- **Non Gratuitous Bailment (Bailment for Reward).** This duty particularly deals with the goods given on hire. As per this provision, when the goods are bailed for hire, then in such a situation even if the bailor is aware of the defect in the goods or not will be held liable for the injury that has been caused due to the existence of such defect.

In *Hyman v Nye & Sons*, the plaintiff took a carriage on hire from the defendant but the carriage was not fit for the journey and subsequently, the plaintiff suffered injuries. The court held that even though the defendant was aware of such defect or not he shall be liable.

Duties of Bailee

Bailee has to fulfil several obligations as per Indian Contract Act, 1872. That is:

- Duty to take reasonable care: It is the duty of the Bailee to take care of goods as his own goods. He shall ensure all safety measures that are necessary to protect the goods. The standard of care should be such as taken care by a prudent man. The goods shall be taken care of equally whether they are gratuitous or non-gratuitous. The Bailee shall be held liable for payment of compensation if he fails to take due care. But if the Bailee has taken due care and instead of that the goods are damaged then in such a situation Bailee will not be liable to pay compensation. The Bailee is not liable for the loss of goods due to destruction by fire. (Section 151-152)
- Bailee is duty bound to use the goods for a specific purpose only and not otherwise. If he uses the goods for any other purpose than what is agreed for then the bailor has the right to terminate such bailment or is entitled with compensation for damage caused due to unauthorized use. (Section 153-154)
- Duty not to mix bailor's goods with his own goods: It is the duty of the Bailee not to mix bailor's goods with his own. But if he wants to do the same then he shall seek consent from the bailor for mixing of goods. If the bailor agrees for the mixing of the goods then the interest in the mixed goods shall be shared in proportion. In case, Bailee without the consent of bailor mixes the goods with his own then two situations arise: goods can be separated and goods can't be separated. In the former case the Bailee has to bear the cost of separation and in the latter case since there is the loss of the goods, therefore, bailor shall be entitled with damages of such loss. (Section 155-157)
- Duty to return the goods on the fulfilment of purpose. Bailee is duty bound to return the goods once the purpose is achieved or on the expiry of the time period for which the goods were bailed. But if the Bailee makes default in returning the goods on proper time then he will be responsible with the loss, destruction or deterioration of the goods if any. (Section 160-161)
  In the case of *Bank of India v. Grains & Gunny Agencies* the court held that if the goods are lost or destroyed due to the negligence of servant of Bailee, then in such case as well Bailee shall be liable.
- Duty to deliver to the bailor increase or profit if any on the goods bailed. The Bailee has a duty to return the goods along with increase or profit subject to contract to the contrary. Accretion that has accrued from the bailed goods is the part of the bailed goods and therefore bailor has the right over such accretions if any. And such accretions shall be handed over to the bailor along with the goods bailed. For instance, A leaves a cow in the custody of B and cow gives birth to the calf. Then B is duty bound to hand over the bailed goods along with accretion to the bailor. (Section 163)

Rights of a Bailor

As such Indian Contract Act, 1872 does not provide for Rights of a Bailor. But Rights of a Bailor is same as Duties of the Bailee i.e. Rights of Bailor = Duties of Bailee. So the rights of bailor are:

- Enforcement of Bailee's Duty. Since Right of the bailor is same as the right of the Bailee, therefore on the fulfilment of all duties of Bailee the bailor's right is accomplished. For example, it is the duty of the Bailee to give the accretions and it is the right of bailor to demand the same.
- Right to claim damages: If the Bailee fails to take care of the goods, the bailor has the right to claim damages for such loss. (Section 151)
- Right to Termination the Contract: If the Bailee does not comply with the terms of the contract and acts in a negligent manner in such case the bailor has the right to rescind the contract. (Section 153)
- Right to claim compensation: If the Bailee uses the goods for an unauthorized purpose or mixes the goods which cause loss of goods in such case bailor has the right to claim compensation.
- Right to demand the return of goods: It is the duty of the bailee to return the goods and the bailor has the right to demand the same.

Rights of a Bailee

- Right to recover expenses. In the contract of bailment, the bailee incurs expenses to ensure the safety of goods. The Bailee has the right to recover such expenses from the bailor. (Section 158)
- Right to remuneration: When the goods are bailed to the bailee, he is entitled to receive certain remuneration for services that he has rendered. But in case of gratuitous bailment, the bailee is not awarded any remuneration.
- Right to recover compensation. At times a situation arises wherein bailor did not have the capacity to contract for bailment. Such a contract causing loss to the Bailee, therefore the Bailee has the right to recover such compensation from the bailor. (Section 168)
- Right to Lien. Bailee has the right over Lien. By this, we mean that if the bailor fails to make payment of remuneration or does not pay the amount due, the Bailee has the right to keep the goods bailed in his possession till the time debtor dues are cleared. Lien is of two types: particular lien and general lien. (Section 170-171)

  In the case of Surya Investment Co. v. S.T.C, the court held that expenses incurred by Bailee during preservation of goods under lien shall be borne by bailor.
- Right to suit against a wrongdoer. After the goods have been bailed and any third party deprives the Bailee of use of such goods, then the Bailee or bailor can bring an action against the third party. (Section 180)

Pledge

Pledge is a kind of bailment. Pledge is also known as Pawn. It is defined under section 172 of the Indian Contract Act, 1892. By pledge, we mean bailment of goods as a security for the repayment of debt or loan advanced or performance of an obligation or promise. The person who pledges the goods as security is known as Pledger or Pawnor and the person in whose favour the goods are pledged is known as Pledgee or Pawnee.

Essentials of Pledge

Since Pledge is a special kind of bailment, therefore all the essentials of bailment are also the essentials of the pledge. Apart from that, the other essentials of the pledge are:

- There shall be a bailment for security against payment or performance of the promise,
- The subject matter of pledge is goods,
- Goods pledged for shall be in existence,
- There shall be the delivery of goods from pledger to pledgee,
- There is no transfer of ownership in case of the pledge.

Exception. In exception circumstances pledgee has the right to sell the movable goods or property that are been pledged.

Rights of Pawnor

As per Section 177 of the Indian Contract Act, 1872 the Pawnor has the Right to Redeem. By this, we mean that on the repayment of the debt or the performance of the promise, the Pawnor can redeem the goods or property pledged from the Pawnee before the Pawnee makes the actual sale. The right of redemption is extinguished once the actual sale is done by the Pawnee as per his right under section 176 of the Indian Contract Act, 1872.

Rights of a Pawnee

The rights of the Pawnee as per Indian Contract Act, 1872 are:

- **Right to retain the goods.** If the Pawnor fails to make the payment of a debt or does not perform as per the promise made, the Pawnee has the right to retain the goods pledged as security. Moreover, Pawnee can also retain goods for non-payment of interest on debt or non-payment of expenses incurred. But Pawnee cannot retain goods for any other debt or promise other than that agreed for in the contract. (Section 173-174)
- **Right to recover extraordinary expenses.** The expenses incurred by Pawnee on the preservation of goods pledged can be recovered from Pawnor. (Section 175)
- **The right of suit to procure debt and sale of pledged goods.** On the failure to make repayment to Pawnee of the debt, the Pawnee has two right: either to initiate suit proceedings against him or sell the goods. In the former case, the Pawnee retains the goods with himself as collateral security and initiate the court proceedings. He need not provide any notice of such proceedings to the Pawnor. And in the latter case, the Pawnee can sell the goods after giving due notice of sale to the Pawnor. If the amount received from the sale of goods is less than the amount due then the rest amount can be recovered from Pawnor. And if the Pawnee gets more amount than the due amount then such surplus is to be given back to Pawnor. (Section 176)

Difference between Bailment and Pledge

Basis	Bailment	Pledge
Meaning	Transfer of goods from one person to another for a specific purpose is known as the bailment.	Transfer of goods from one person to another as security for repayment of debt is known as the pledge.
Defined In	It is defined under section 148 of the Indian Contract Act, 1872.	It is defined under section 172 of the Indian Contract Act, 1872.
Parties	The person who delivers the bailed goods is known as Bailor and the person receiving such goods is known as Bailee.	The person who delivers the pledged goods is known as Pledger or Pawnor and the person receiving such goods is known as Pledgee or Pawnee.
Consideration	The consideration may or may not be present.	Consideration is always there.

Basis	Bailment	Pledge
Right to Sell	Bailee has no right to sell the goods bailed.	Pledgee or Pawnee has the right to sell the goods.
Use of Goods	Bailee can use the goods only for a specific purpose only and not otherwise.	Pledgee or Pawnee cannot use the goods pledged.
Purpose	The purpose of bailed goods is for safekeeping or repairs etc.	The purpose of pledged goods is to act as security for repayment of debt or performance of the promise.

CONTRACTS OF AGENCY

When a person employs another person to do any act for himself or to represent him in dealing with third persons, it is called a *'Contract of Agency'*. The person who is so represented is called the 'principal' and the representative so employed is called the 'agent (Sec. 182). The duty of the agent is to enter into legal relations on behalf of the principal with third parties. But, by doing so he himself does not become a party to the contract to the contract not does he incur any liability under that contract. Principal shall be responsible for all the acts of his agent provided they are not outside the scope of his authority.

Competence of the Parties to Enter into a Contract of Agency

The person employing the agent must himself have the legal capacity or be competent to do the act for which he has employed the agent. A minor or a person with unsound mind cannot appoint an agent so as to be legally represented by him (Sec. 183). But an agent so appointed need not necessarily be competent to contact (Sec: 184) and hence minor or an insane can be appointed as an agent he can bring about legal relations between the principal and the third party but such an incompetent agent cannot personally be held liable to the principal.

Consideration not required. Contract of agency requires no consideration. It comes under the category of those contracts which law has declared to be valid without consideration (Sec. 185).

Creation of Agency. Agency may be created by any of the following ways:

1. **Expressly (Sec. 187).** When an agent is appointed by words spoken or written, his authority is said to be express.
2. **Impliedly (Sec. 187).** When agency arises from the conduct of the parties or inferred from the circumstances of the case, it is called implied agency.

   Example. A of Calcutta has a shop in Delhi. B, the manager of the shop, has been ordering and purchasing goods from C for the purpose of the shop. The goods purchased were being regularly paid for but of the funds provided by A. B shall be considered to be an agent of A by his conduct.

   Partners, servants and wives are usually regarded as agents by implications because of their relationship.

   Wife as an implied agent to her husband

   (a) Where the husband and wife are living together in a domestic establishment of their own, the wife shall have an implied authority to pledge the credit of her husband for necessaries. The implied authority can be challenged by the husband only in the following circumstances.

   (1) The husband has expressly forbidden the wife from borrowing money or buying goods on credit.

(2) The articles purchased did not constitute necessities.

(3) Husband had given sufficient funds to the wife for purchasing the articles she needed to the knowledge of the seller.

(4) The creditor had been expressly told not to give credit to the wife.

(b) Where the wife lives apart from husband without any of her fault, she shall have an implied authority to bind the husband for necessaries, if he does not provide for her maintenance.

3. **Agency by necessity.** Under certain circumstances, a person may be compelled to act as an agent to the other, e.g. master of the ship can borrow money at a port where the owner of the ship has not agent, to carry out necessary repairs to the ship in order to complete the voyage. In such a case of necessity, person acting as an agent need not necessarily have the authority of the principal. However, the agent must act under pressing conditions and for the benefit of the principal.

Example. The master of the ship on finding that the cargo is rapidly perishing is entitled to dispose it of at the best price available so as to bind the consignor as an agent by necessity.

4. **Agency by estoppel (Sec. 237).** When an agent has without authority, done acts or incurred obligations to third persons on behalf of his principal, the principal is bound by such acts and obligations if he has by his words or conduct induced such third person to believe that such acts and obligations were within the scope of the agent's authority.

5. **Agency by ratification (Sec. 196 to 200).** Ratification means subsequent acceptance and adoption of an act by the principal originally done by the agent without authority. According to section 196. "Where acts are done by one person on behalf of another but without his knowledge or authority, he may check to ratify or to disown such act. If he ratifies them, the same effects will follow as if they had been performed by his previous authority."

Example. The manager of a company per porting to act as an agent on the company's behalf but without its authority, accepted an offer by L, the defendant L subsequently withdrew the offer, but the company ratified the manager's acceptance. L was held to be bound by the acceptance. His revocation of the offer was held to be invalid. Ratification relates back to the due when the agent had first acted and, therefore, subsequent revocation shall have no effect

In order that ratification may be legal and valid, it must satisfy the following essentials.

(1) The act must be done in the name of the principal.

(2) Principal must have been in existence and competent to contract at the time when agent acted on his behalf as well as on the date of ratification.

(3) The act must be legal which the principal must be competent to do.

(4) Ratification must be with full knowledge of all the material facts (Sec. 198).

(5) Ratification must relate to the whole act and not to a part of it. Ratification of a part of the act will not be valid (Sec. 199).

(6) There can be no valid ratification of an act which is to the prejudice of a third person (Sec. 200). ***Example:*** A holds a lease from B, terminable on three months notice, C, an unauthorised person gives notice to termination to A. The notice cannot be ratified by B, so as to be binding on A.

(7) Ratification of an act must be made, either within the time fixed for this purpose or within a reasonable time after the contract was entered into by the agent.

SALE OF GOODS ACT, 1930

Sale of commodities constitutes one of the important types of contracts under the law in India. India is one of the largest economies and also a great country where and thus has adequate checks and measures to ensure the safety and prosperity of its business and commerce community. Here we shall explain The Sale of Goods Act, 1930 which defines and states terms related to the sale of goods and exchange of commodities.

Sale of Goods Act, 1930 – Important Terms

The Sale of Goods Act, 1930 herein referred to as the Act, is the law that governs the sale of goods in all parts of India. It doesn't apply to the state of Jammu & Kashmir. The Act defines various terms which are contained in the act itself. Let us see below:

I. Buyer And Seller

As per the sec 2(1) of the Act, a buyer is someone who buys or has agreed to buy goods. Since, a sale constitutes a contract between two parties, a buyer is one of the parties to the contract.

The Act defines seller in sec 2(13). A seller is someone who sells or has agreed to sell goods. For a sales contract to come into existence, both the buyer and seller must be defined by the Act. These two terms represent the two parties of a sales contract.

A faint difference between the definition of buyer and seller established by the act and the colloquial meaning of buyer and seller is that as per the act, even the person who agrees to buy or sell is qualified as a buyer or a seller. The actual transfer of goods doesn't have to take place for the identification of the two parties of a sales contract.

II. Goods

One of the most crucial terms to define is the goods that are to be included in the contract for sale. The Act defines the term "Goods" in its sec 2(7) as all types of movable property. The sec 2(7) of the Act goes as follows:

"Every kind of movable property other than actionable claims and money; and includes stock and shares, growing crops, grass, and things attached to or forming part of the land which are agreed to be severed before sale or under the contract of sale will be considered goods"

As you can see, shares and stocks are also defined as goods by the Act. The term actionable claims mean those claims which are eligible to be enforced or initiated by a suit or legal action. This means that those claims where an action such as recovery by auction, suit, refunds etc. could be initiated to recover or realize the claim.

1. Existing Goods

The goods that are referred to in the contract of sale are termed as existing goods if they are present (in existence) at the time of the contract. In sec 6 of the Act, the existing goods are those goods which are in the legal possession or are owned by the seller at the time of the formulation of the contract of sale. The existing goods are further of the following types:

(A) **Specific Goods.** According to the sec 2(14) of the Act, these are those goods that are "identified and agreed upon" when the contract of sale is formed. For example, you want to sell your mobile phone online. You put u an add with its picture and information. A buyer agrees to the sale and a contract is formed. The mobile, in this case, is specific good.

(B) **Ascertained Goods.** This is a type not defined by the law but by the judicial interpretation. This term is used for specific goods which have been selected from a larger set of goods. For example, you have 500 apples. Out of these 500 apples, you decide to sell 200 apples. To sell these 200 apples, you will need to separate them from the 500 (larger set). Thus you specify 200 apples from a larger group of unspecified apples. These 200 apples are now the ascertained goods.

(C) **Unascertained Goods.** These are the goods that have not been specifically identified but have rather been left to be selected from a larger group. For example, from your 500 apples, you decide to sell 200 apples but you don't specify which ones you want to sell. A seller will have the liberty to choose any 200 apples from the lot. These are thus, the unascertained goods.

2. Future Goods

In sec 2(6) of the Act, future goods have been defined as the goods that will either be manufactured or produced or acquired by the seller at the time the contract of sale is made. The contract for the sale of future goods will never have the actual sale in it, it will always be an agreement to sell.

For example, you have an apple orchard with apples in it. You agree to sell 1000 apples to a buyer after the apples ripe. This is a sale that has to occur in the future but the goods have been identified already and the agreement made. Such goods are known as future goods.

3. Contingent Goods

Contingent goods are actually a subtype of future goods in the sense that in contingent goods the actual sale is to be done in the future. These goods are part of a sale contract that has some contingency clause in it. For example, if you sell your apples from your orchard when the trees are yet to produce apples, the apples are a contingent good. This sale is dependent on the condition that the trees are able to produce apples, which may not happen.

III. Delivery

The delivery of goods signifies the voluntary transfer of possession from one person to another. The objective or the end result of any such process which results in the goods coming into the possession of the buyer is a delivery process. The delivery could occur even when the goods are transferred to a person other than the buyer but who is authorized to hold the goods on behalf of the buyer.

There are various forms of delivery as follows:

- *Actual Delivery*. If the goods are physically given into the possession of the buyer, the delivery is an actual delivery.
- *Constructive delivery*. The transfer of goods can be done even when the transfer is effected without a change in the possession or custody of the goods. For example, a case of the delivery by attornment or acknowledgment will be a constructive delivery. If you pick up a parcel on behalf of your friend and agree to hold on to it for him, it is a constructive delivery.
- *Symbolic delivery*. This kind of delivery involves the delivery of a thing in token of a transfer of some other thing. For example, the key of the godowns with the goods in it, when handed over to the buyer will constitute a symbolic delivery.

IV. The Document of Title to Goods

From the Sec 2(4) of the act, we can say that this "includes the bill of lading, dock-warrant, warehouse keeper's certificate, railway receipt, multimodal transport document, warrant or order for the delivery of goods and any other document used in the ordinary course of business as proof of the possession or control of goods or authorizing or purporting to authorize, either by endorsement or by delivery, the possessor of the document to transfer or receive goods thereby represented."

V. Mercantile Agent [Section 2(9)]

Mercantile agent is someone who has authority in the customary course of business, either to sell or consign goods under the contract on behalf of the one or both of the parties. Examples include auctioneers, brokers, factors etc.

VI. Property [Section 2(11)]

In the Act, property means 'ownership' or the general property i.e. all ownership right of the goods. A sale constitutes the transfer of ownership of goods by the seller to the buyer or an agreement of the same.

VII. Insolvent [Section 2(8)]

The Act defines an insolvent person as someone who ceases to pay his debts in the ordinary course of business or cannot pay his debts as they become due, whether he has committed an act of insolvency or not.

VIII. Price [Section 2(10)]

In the Act, the price is defined as the money consideration for a sale of goods.

IX. Quality of Goods

In Sec 2(12) of the Act, the quality of goods is referred to as their state or condition.

A contract is a formal or verbal agreement that is enforceable by law. Every contract must have an agreement but every agreement is not a contract. The section 4(1) of the Sale of Goods Act, 1930 states that – 'A contract of sale of goods is a contract whereby the seller either transfers or agrees to transfer the property in goods to the buyer for a decided price.'

In Section 4(4) of the Act, it is maintained that for an agreement of sale to become a sale, the time has to elapse or the conditions have to be fulfilled subject to which the property in the goods is to be is to be transferred.

Sale

Here the property in goods is transferred at once to the buyer from the seller. The Section 4(3) of the Act says that "where under a contract of sale the property in the goods is transferred from the seller to the buyer, the contract is then known as a sale." A sale is carried out on deliverable goods. Goods are said to be in a deliverable state when they are in such a condition that the buyer would, under the contract, be bound to take delivery of them [Section 2(3)].

The transfer of goods may be affected directly, after the fulfillment of a contingency or to a party authorized by the seller.

SALE AND AGREEMENT TO SELL

We saw that in a sale the property in the goods is transferred from the seller to the buyer. However, in an agreement to sell, the ownership of the property in goods is not transferred immediately. The objective of the agreement is to transfer the goods at a future date, once some contingent clauses in the agreement or certain conditions are satisfied.

The Act in Section 4(3), defines what an agreement to sell is. The section 4(3) of the sale of Goods Act defines it as, "where the transfer of the property in the goods is to take place at a future time or subject to some condition thereafter to be fulfilled, the contract is called an agreement to sell."

Thus we see that a contract for the sale of goods may be either sale or agreement to sell. This depends on the condition whether it postulates an immediate transfer of property from the seller to the buyer or whether it postulates the transfer to take place at some future date.

Now the question is that how does this transition from agreement to sell to sale occur? The agreement to sell will become a sale if and only when the time elapses or the conditions are fulfilled subject to which the contract of sale is to be fulfilled.

Elements of a Contract of Sale

From the Sale of Goods Act, 1930, we see that certain elements must co-exist for a contract of sale to be constituted. They are as follows:

1. The presence of two parties is a must. As is the case with a contract, there must be at least two parties in the contract of sale. One shall become the seller and the other a buyer.
2. The clauses therein present in the contract of sale must limit their scope to only the movable property. This "movable property" may constitute existing goods, goods in the possession or the ownership of the seller or future goods.
3. One of the important elements is the consideration of price. A price in value (currency and not in kind) has to be paid or promised. The price consideration or the actual payment could be partly in kind and partly in money but never in kind alone.
4. The ownership of the property of goods must change from the seller to the buyer. In the contract of sale, like we saw in the elements of a contract, an offer has to be made and then accepted. The offer is made by a seller and then accepted by the buyer.

DOCTRINE OF CAVEAT EMPTOR

The doctrine of Caveat Emptor is an integral part of the Sale of Goods Act. It translates to "let the buyer beware". This means it lays the responsibility of their choice on the buyer themselves. It is specifically defined in Section 16 of the act "there is no implied warranty or condition as to the quality or the fitness for any particular purpose of goods supplied under such a contract of sale"

A seller makes his goods available in the open market. The buyer previews all his options and then accordingly makes his choice. Now, let's assume that the product turns out to be defective or of inferior quality. This doctrine says that the seller will not be responsible for this. The buyer himself is responsible for the choice he made.

So the doctrine attempts to make the buyer more conscious of his choices. It is the duty of the buyer to check the quality and the usefulness of the product he is purchasing. If the product turns out to be defective or does not live up to its potential the seller will not be responsible for this.

Let us see an example. A bought a horse from B. A wanted to enter the horse in a race. Turns out the horse was not capable of running a race on account of being lame. But A did not inform B of his intentions. So B will not be responsible for the defects of the horse. The Doctrine of Caveat Emptor will apply.

However, the buyer can shift the responsibility to the seller if the three following conditions are fulfilled.

- if the buyer shares with the seller his purpose for the purchase
- the buyer relies on the knowledge and/or technical expertise of the seller
- and the seller sells such goods

The doctrine of caveat emptor has certain specific exceptions. Let us take a brief look at these exceptions.

1. **Fitness of Product for the Buyer's Purpose.** When the buyer informs the seller of his purpose of buying the goods, it is implied that he is relying on the seller's judgment. It is the duty of the seller then to ensure the goods match their desired usage.

Say for example A goes to B to buy a bicycle. He informs B he wants to use the cycle for mountain trekking. If B sells him an ordinary bicycle that is incapable of fulfilling A's purpose the seller will be responsible. Another example is the case study of Priest v. Last.

2. **Goods Purchased under Brand Name.** When the buyer buys a product under a trade name or a branded product the seller cannot be held responsible for the usefulness or quality of the product. So, there is no implied condition that the goods will be fit for the purpose the buyer intended.
3. **Goods sold by Description.** When the buyer buys the goods based only on the description there will be an exception. If the goods do not match the description then in such a case the seller will be responsible for the goods.
4. **Goods of Merchantable Quality.** The section 16 (2) deals with the exception of merchantable quality. The sections state that the seller who is selling goods by description has a duty of providing goods of merchantable quality, i.e. capable of passing the market standards.

   So if the goods are not of marketable quality then the buyer will not be the one who is responsible. It will be the seller's responsibility. However if the buyer has had reasonable chance to examine the product, then this exception will not apply.
5. **Sale by Sample.** If the buyer buys his goods after examining a sample then the rule of Doctrine of Caveat Emptor will not apply. If the rest of the goods do not resemble the sample, the buyer cannot be held responsible. In this case, the seller will be the one responsible. For example, A places an order for 50 toy cars with B. He checks one sample where the car is red. The rest of the cars turn out orange. Here, the doctrine will not apply and B will be responsible.
6. **Sale by Description and Sample.** If the sale is done via sample as well as a description of the product, the buyer will not be responsible if the goods do not resemble the sample and/or the description. Then the responsibility will fall squarely on the seller.
7. **Usage of Trade.** There is an implied condition or warranty about the quality or the fitness of goods/products. But if a seller deviated from this then the rules of caveat emptor cease to apply. For example, A bought goods from B in an auction of the contents of a ship. But B did not inform A the contents were sea damaged, and so the rules of the doctrine will not apply here.
8. **Fraud or Misrepresentation by the Seller.** This is another important exception. If the seller obtains the consent of the buyer by fraud then caveat emptor will not apply. Also if the seller conceals any material defects of the goods which are later discovered on closer examination then again the buyer will not be responsible. In both cases, the seller will be the guilty party.

Concept of Condition and Warranty

In a contract of sale, parties may make certain statements about the stipulation or the course of trade. These stipulations in the contract of sale are made with reference to the subject matter of the sale. These stipulations may either be a condition or in the form of a warranty. The provisions of the conditions and warranty are provided in the sections 11 to 17 of the Act. The stipulations are the essence of the contract of sale and a breach of these stipulations provides a remedy to the grieved party.

Stipulations As To Time – Sec 11

To understand the concept of warranty and conditions, we need to learn about the stipulation as to time. The stipulation as to time may be with regards to the delivery of goods or it may be with regards to the payment of the price. However, it may be noted that stipulations as to the time of delivery of the goods are usually the essence of the contract. In Section 11 of the Act, the topic of the stipulation as to time has been discussed. The Sec 11 states the follows:

Stipulations as to time: Unless a different intention can be ascertained from the contract, stipulations as to the time of payment are not considered to be of the essence of a contract of sale. Whether any other stipulation as to time is of the essence of the contract or not will ultimately depend on the terms of the contract.

This means that whether the stipulations as to the time of payment of the price is of the essence of the contract or not depends on the terms of the contract. Unless the terms of the contract specify something different than this.

Conditions

A condition is a stipulation is essential to the main purpose of the contract, the breach of which gives the right to repudiate the contract and to claim damages. (Sec 12 (2)). We can understand this with the help of the following example:

Say 'X' wants to purchase a car from 'Y', which can have a mileage of 20 km/lt. 'Y' pointing at a particular vehicle says "This car will suit you." Later 'X' buys the car but finds out later on that this car only has a top mileage of 15 km/ liter. This amounts to a breach of condition because the seller made the stipulation which forms the essence of the contract. In this case, the mileage was a stipulation that was essential to the main purpose of the contract and hence its breach is a breach of condition.

Warranty

A warranty is a stipulation collateral to the main purpose of the said contract. The breach of warranty which gives rise to a claim for damages. However, it does give a right to reject the goods or treat the contract as repudiated. (Sec 12(3)). Let us understand this with the help of an example below.

A man buys a particular car, which is warranted to be quite to drive and very comfortable. It turns out that after some days the car starts to make a very unpleasant noise everytime it is operated. Also sitting inside it is also not very comfortable. Thus the buyer's only remedy is to claim damages. This is not a breach of condition but rather a breach of warranty, because the stipulation made by the seller was only a collateral one.

Identification of a Stipulation as a Condition or Warranty

Whether a stipulation is a condition or a warranty is a very important aspect to have the knowledge about. A stipulation in a contract of sale is either a condition or is a warranty depending in either case on the construction of the contract. A stipulation may be a condition, though called a warranty in the contract.

RIGHTS OF UNPAID SELLER AGAINST GOODS

Rights of Lien

Seller's Lien (Section 47)

According to subsection (1) of Section 47 of the Sale of Goods Act, 1930, an unpaid seller, who is in possession of the goods can retain their possession until payment. This is possible in the following cases:

1. He sells the goods without any stipulation for credit
2. The goods are sold on credit but the credit term has expired.
3. The buyer becomes insolvent.

Subsection (2) specifies that the unpaid seller can exercise his right of lien notwithstanding that he is in possession of the goods acting as an agent or bailee for the buyer.

Part-delivery (Section 48)

Further, Section 48 states that if an unpaid seller makes part-delivery of the goods, then he may exercise his right of lien on the remainder. This is valid unless there is an agreement between the buyer and the seller for waiving the lien under part-delivery.

Termination of Lien (Section 49)

According to subsection (1) of Section 49 of the Sale of Goods Act, 1930, an unpaid seller loses his lien:

- If he delivers the goods to a carrier or other bailee for transmission to the buyer without reserving the right of disposal of the goods.
- When the buyer or his agent obtain possession of the goods lawfully.
- By waiver.

Further, subsection (2) states that an unpaid seller, who has a lien, does not lose his lien by reason only that he has obtained a decree for the price of the goods.

Right of Stoppage in Transit

This right is an extension to the right of lien. The right of stoppage in transit means that an unpaid seller has the right to stop the goods while they are in transit, regain possession, and retain them till he receives the full price. If an unpaid seller has parted with the possession of the goods and the buyer becomes insolvent, then the seller can ask the carrier to return the goods back. This is subject to the provisions of the Act.

Duration of Transit (Section 51)

Goods are in the course of transit from the time the seller delivers them to a carrier or a bailee for transmission to the buyer until the buyer or his agent takes delivery of the said goods.

Some scenarios of the transit ending:

- The buyer or his agent obtain delivery before the goods reach the destination. In such cases, the transit ends once the delivery is obtained.
- Once the goods reach the destination and the carrier of bailee informs the buyer or his agent that he holds the goods, then the transit ends.
- If the buyer refuses the goods and even the seller refuses to take them back the transit is not at an end.
- In some cases, goods are delivered to a ship chartered by the buyer. Depending on the case, it is determined that if the master is functioning as an agent or carrier of the goods.
- If a part-delivery of the goods has been made and the unpaid seller stops the remaining goods in transit, then the transit ends for those goods. This is provided that there is no agreement to give up the possession of all the goods.

How Stoppage is Affected (Section 52)

There are two ways of stopping the transit of goods:

1. The seller takes actual possession of the goods
2. If the goods are in the possession of a carrier or other bailee, then the seller gives a notice of stoppage to him. On receiving the notice, the carrier or bailee must re-deliver the goods to the seller. The seller bears the expenses of the re-delivery.

Effect of Stoppage

Even if the unpaid seller exercises his right of stoppage in transit, the contract stays valid. The buyer can ask for delivery of the goods after making the payment.

Pledge by the Buyer (Section 53)

Unless the seller agrees, the right of lien or stoppage is unaffected by the buyer selling or pledging the goods. The principle is simple: the second buyer cannot be in a better position that the seller (first buyer). However, if the buyer transfers the document of title or pledges the goods to a sub-buyer in good faith and for consideration, then the right of stoppage is defeated.

There are two exceptions to make note of:

a. The seller agrees to resale, mortgage or other disposition of the goods
   If the seller agrees to the buyer selling, pledging or disposing of the goods in any other way, then he loses his right to lien.
b. Transfer of the document of title of goods by the buyer
   When the seller transfers the document of title of goods to the buyer and the buyer further transfers it to another buyer who purchases the goods in good faith and for a price, then:
   - If the last mentioned transfer is by way of sale, the original seller's right of lien and stoppage is defeated.
   - If the last mentioned transfer is by way of a pledge, the original seller's right of lien or stoppage can be executed subject to the rights of the pledgee.

Rights of Resale (Section 54)

The right of resale is an important right for an unpaid seller. If he does not have this right, then the right of lien and stoppage won't make sense. An unpaid seller can exercise his right of resale under the following conditions:

- **Goods are perishable in nature.** In such cases, the seller does not have to inform the buyer of his intention of resale.
- **Seller gives a notice to the buyer of his intention of resale.** The buyer needs to pay the price of the goods and ask for delivery within the time mentioned in the notice. If he fails to do so, then the seller can resell the goods. He can also recover the difference between the contract price and resale price if the latter is lower. However, if the resale price is higher, then the seller keeps the profits.
- **Unpaid seller resells the goods post exercising his right of lien or stoppage.** The subsequent buyer acquires a good title to the goods even if the seller has not given a notice of resale to the original buyer.
- **Property in the goods has not passed to the buyer.** The unpaid seller can exercise his right of withholding delivery of goods. This is similar to the right of lien and is called quasi-lien.

Rights of Unpaid Seller against Buyer

When the buyer of goods does not pay his dues to the seller, the seller becomes an unpaid seller. And now the seller has certain rights against the buyer. Such rights are the seller remedies against the breach of contract by the buyer. Such rights of the unpaid seller are additional to the rights against the goods he sold.

1. **Suit for Price.** Under the contract of sale if the property of the goods is already passed but he refuses to pay for the goods the seller becomes an unpaid seller. In such a case. The seller can sue the buyer for wrongfully refusing to pay him his due.
   But say the sales contract says that the price will be paid at a later date irrespective of the delivery of goods and on such a day the if the buyer refuses to pay, the unpaid seller may sue for the price of these goods. The actual delivery of the goods is not of importance according to the law.

2. **Suit for Damages for Non-Acceptance.** If the buyer wrongfully refuses or neglects to accept and pay the unpaid seller, the seller can sue the buyer for damages caused due to his non-acceptance of goods. Since the buyer refused to buy the goods without any just cause, the seller may face certain damages.

   The measure of such damages is decided by the Section 73 of the Indian Contract Act 1872, which deals with damages and penalties. Take an for example the case of seller A. He agrees to sell to B 100 liters of milk for a decided price. On the day, B refuses to accept the goods for no justifiable reason. A is not able to find another buyer and the milk goes bad. In such a case, A can sue B for damages.

3. **Repudiation of Contract before Due Date.** If the buyer repudiates the contract before the delivery date of the goods the seller can still sue for damages. Such a contract is considered as a rescinded contract, and so the seller can sue for breach of contract. This is covered in the Indian Contract Act and is known as Anticipatory Breach of Contract

4. **Suit for Interest.** If there is a specific agreement between the parties the seller can sue for the interest amount due to him from the buyer. This is when both parties have specifically agreed on the interest rate to be paid to seller from the date on which the payment becomes due.

But if the parties do not have such specific terms, still the court may award the seller with the interest amount due to him at a rate which it sees fit.

Remedies of Buyer Against the Seller

Just as the seller can rescind the contract, then so can the seller. When the seller breaches the contract the buyer also has certain remedies against the seller. Let us take a look at some remedies that the Sales Act prescribes for the buyer.

1. **Damages of Non-Delivery.** If the seller wrongfully or neglectfully refuses to deliver the goods to the buyer, then the buyer can sue for non-delivery of the goods. According to Section 57 of the Sale of Goods Act, if the buyer faces losses due to the wrongful actions of the seller (non-delivery) he can sue for damages caused due to this.

   Let's take for example A whose agrees to sell to B 10 pair of shoes for 1000/- each. B was going to sell the same shoes to C for 1100/- a pair. A neglects to deliver the goods to B. Now, B can sue A for non-delivery. He can sue for the amount of 100/- per pair, i.e. 1000/- (the difference between B's cost price and sale price)

2. **Suit for Specific Performance.** If the seller commits a breach of contract, the buyer can approach the court to ask the seller for specific performance. The court after deliberation can command the seller for specific performance. One important point to keep in mind is that this remedy is only available if the goods are ascertained or specific.

   Example. There was a contract between A and B, that A will sell to B a very expensive painting on a specific date. On the said day A refuses to sell. B can approach the court, who orders A to sell the painting to B at the ascertained price.

3. **Suit for Breach of Warranty.** When the seller breaches the warranty of the goods, the buyer cannot simply reject the goods on such basis. The buyer has two options in such a case,

   - set up against the buyer the said breach of warranty in the extinction of the price
   - or sue the seller for breach of warranty

4. **Repudiation of Contract.** If the seller repudiates the contract, the buyer does not have to wait until the date of the contract. He can treat the contract as rescinded and sue for damages immediately. This will be an anticipatory breach of contract.

5. **Sue for Interest.** The Act specifically states that nothing in the act will affect the right of the seller or the buyer to recover interest or special damages due to him by the contract. And if there is no specific clause in the contract, the court can come to the rescue of the affected party.

Rights and Duties of the Buyer

RIGHTS

1. To have delivery of the goods as per contract. (Sec. 31 & 32)
2. To reject the goods when they are not of the description, quality or quantity as specified in the contract (Sec 37).
3. To repudiate the contract when goods are delivered in installments without any agreement to that effects [Sec. 38 (1)]
4. To be informed by the seller, when the goods are to be sent by sea route, so that he may arrange for their insurance [Sec 39 (30)]
5. To have a reasonable opportunity to examine the goods for ascertaining whether they are in conformity with the contract. (Sec. 41)
6. To sue the seller for damages if the seller wrongfully neglects or refuses to deliver the goods to the buyer (Sec 57)
7. To sue the seller for specific performance
8. To sue the seller for damages for breach of a warranty or for breach of a condition treated as breach of a warranty (Sec 59)
9. To sue the seller the damages for anticipatory breach of contract (Sec 60)
10. To sue the seller for interest where there is a breach of contract on the part of the seller and price has to be refunded to the buyer (Sec 61)

DUTIES

1. To accept the delivery of goods, when the seller is willing to make the delivery as per the contract (Sec. 31)
2. To pay the price in exchange for possession of the goods
3. To apply for delivery of the goods. (Sec. 35)
4. To demand delivery of the goods at a reasonable hour [Sec 36 (4)]
5. To accept delivery of the goods in installments and pay for them, in accordance with the contract. [(Sec. 38 (2)]
6. To bear the risk of deterioration in the course of transit, when the goods are to be delivered at a place other than where they are sold (Sec 40)
7. To inform the seller in case the buyer refuses to accept or rejects the goods (Sec 43)
8. To take the delivery of the goods within a reasonable time after the seller tenders the delivery (Sec. 44)
9. To pay the price, where the property in the goods are passed to the buyer, in accordance with the terms of the contract (Sec 55)
10. To pay damages for non-acceptance of goods (Sec 56)

NEGOTIABLE INSTRUMENT ACT, 1881

Negotiable instruments, it is seen have a great significance over the modern business world. It has to be noted that these instruments have gained significant prominence as the principle instruments for paying and discharging business obligation.

So what essentially is a negotiable instrument? A negotiable instrument is any transferable document which satisfies certain conditions. These instruments pass freely from hand to hand and thus form an integral form part this modern businesses instruments.

It also has to be noted that in our country, the law relating to negotiable instruments, is governed by the Negotiable Instruments Act 1881.

This Negotiable Instruments Act, does not in specific define what a negotiable instrument is, it merely states that a negotiable instrument means "a promissory note, bill of exchange or cheque payable either to the bearer."

Section 13 of the Act, does not indicate the characteristics of a negotiable instrument but only states that three instruments-cheque, bill of exchange and a promissory note, are negotiable instruments.

Thus these three instruments are therefore negotiable instruments as per the statute. But it has to be noted that S.13, does not prohibit any other instrument which satisfies the essential features of negotiability, to be treated as a negotiable instrument.

Thomas, defines the negotiable instrument as an instrument is negotiable which it is, by a legally recognized custom of trade or law, transferable by delivery or by endorsement and delivery, without notice to the party liable, in such a way that a holder of it may for the time being may sue upon it in his own name. The property in it passes on to a bonafide transferee for value free from any defect in the title of the person from whom he obtained it.

Very simply putting it, a negotiable instrument is a transferable document either by the application of the law or by the custom of the trade concerned.

Thus it has to be noted that a negotiable instrument, firstly is easily transferable from person to person and the ownership of the property may be passed on by mere delivery. Secondly, a negotiable instrument confers absolute faith and good title on a transferee, provided that he takes it in good faith for value and without notice of the fact that the transferor had defective title thereto.

It is seen that negotiable instruments can be essentially classified in to two major types:

Negotiable instruments by statute. The three instruments, cheque, bill of exchange and promissory notes are negotiable instruments by statute

Negotiable instruments by custom or usage. Some instruments, have acquired the character of negotiability by custom or usage of trade. Section 137 of the Transfer of Property Act, 1882, also recognized that an instrument may be negotiable by law or custom. Therefore we have case of promissory notes, delivery order and hundis being held as negotiable instruments.

THE COMPANIES ACT, 2013

There are many definitions of a Company by various legal experts. However, Section 2(20) of the Companies Act, 2013, defines the term 'Company' as follows: "Company means a company incorporated under this Act or under any previous company law."

Hence, in order to understand the meaning of a company, it is important to look at the distinctive features that explain the realm of a company.

Features of a Company

One of the most distinctive features of a company, as compared to other organizations, is that it acquires a unique character of being a separate legal entity. Hence, when you register a company, you give it a legal personality with similar rights and powers as a human being.

The existence of a company is distinct and separate from that of its members. It can own property, bank accounts, raise loans, incur liabilities and enter into contracts. According to Law, it is altogether different from the subscribers to the Memorandum of Association.

Also, it has a distinct personality which is different from those who compose it. Member can also contract with the company and acquire a right against it or incur a liability to it. However, for any debts, the creditors can sue the company but the members cannot.

A company can own, enjoy, and dispose of a property in its own name. While the shareholders contribute to the capital and assets, the company is the rightful owner of such assets and capital. Further, the shareholders are not private or joint holders of the company's property.

Perpetual Succession

Another important feature of company is that it continues to carry on its business notwithstanding the death of change of its members until it is wound up on the grounds specified by the Act. Further, the shares of the company change hands infinitely, but that does not affect the existence of the company.

In simple words, the company is an artificial person which is brought into existence by the law. Hence, it can be ended by law alone and is unaffected by the death or insolvency of its members.

Limited Liability

One of the important features of a company is the limited liability of its members. The liability of a member depends on the type of company.

- In the case of a limited liability company, the debts of the company in totality do not become the debts of its shareholders. In such case, the liability of its members is limited to the extent of the nominal value of shares held by them. The shareholders cannot be asked to pay more than the unpaid value of their shares.
- In the case of a company limited by guarantee, members are liable only to the extent of the amount guaranteed by them. Further, this liability arises only when the company goes into liquidation.
- Finally, if it is an unlimited company, then the liability of its members is unlimited too. But such instances are very rare.

Artificial Legal Person

Another one of the features of a company is that it is known as an Artificial Legal Person.

- Artificial – because its creation is by a process other than natural birth.
- Legal – because its creation is by law, and
- Person – because it has similar rights to a human being.

Further, a company can own property, bank accounts, and do everything that a natural person can do except go to jail, marry, take an oath, or practice a learned profession. Hence, it is a legal person in its own sense.

Since a company is an artificial person, it needs humans to function. These humans are Directors who can authenticate the company's formal acts either on their own or through the common seal of the company.

Common Seal

While a company is an artificial person and works through the agency of human beings, it has an official signature. This is affixed by the officers and employees of the company on all its documents. This official signature is the Common Seal.

However, the Companies (Amendment) Act, 2015 has made the Common Seal optional. Section 9 of the Act does not have the phrase 'and a common seal' in it. This provides an alternative mode of authorization for companies who do not wish to have a common seal.

According to this amendment, if a company does not have a common seal, then the authorization shall be done by:

- Two Directors or
- One Director and the Company Secretary (if the company has appointed a Company Secretary).

Corporate Veil Theory

The Corporate Veil Theory is a legal concept which separates the identity of the company from its members. Hence, the members are shielded from the liabilities arising out of the company's actions.

Therefore, if the company incurs debts or contravenes any laws, then the members are not liable for those errors and enjoy corporate insulation. In simpler words, the shareholders are protected from the acts of the company.

This brings us to some important questions:

1. If lifting or piercing the corporate veil possible?
2. If yes, then what are the scenarios and the rules that govern piercing the corporate veil?

Piercing the Corporate Veil means looking beyond the company as a legal person. Or, disregarding the corporate identity and paying regard to the humans instead. In certain cases, the courts ignore the company and concern themselves directly with the members or managers of the company. This is called piercing the corporate veil. Usually, courts choose this option when the case involves a question of control rather than ownership.

Piercing the Corporate Veil

Scenarios under which the Courts consider piercing or lifting the corporate veil are as below,

1. **To Determine the Character of the Company.** There are cases where the courts need to understand if the company is an enemy or friend. In such cases, the courts adopt the test of control. The courts usually avoid piercing the corporate veil, unless the public interest is in jeopardy. However, to ascertain if a company is an enemy company, the court might choose to do so.

   So, how can a company be an enemy? It does not have a mind or consciousness and cannot be a friend or foe, right? However, if the affairs of a company are under the control of people from an enemy country, then the company might be an enemy too. In such cases, the court may examine the character of the humans who are at the helm of affairs of the company.

2. **To Protect Revenue or Tax.** In matters concerning evasion or circumvention of taxes, duties, etc., the Court might disregard the corporate entity.

   Imagine a company that is used to evade tax. In such cases, piercing the corporate veil allows the Court to understand the real owner of the income of the company and make the said person liable for legitimate taxes.

3. **If trying to avoid a Legal Obligation.** Sometimes the members of a company can create another company/subsidiary company to avoid certain legal obligations. In such cases, piercing the corporate veil allows the Courts to understand the real transactions.

   Imagine a company is liable to share 20 percent of its profits with its employees as a bonus. This is a legal obligation. To avoid this, the company opens a wholly owned subsidiary company and transfers its investment holdings to it. The new company formed has no assets of its own and no business income either. It is completely dependent on the principal company. By doing so, the principal company reduced the amount of bonus liable to be paid to its employees. The Courts, by piercing the corporate veil, can understand the real intention of the principal company and ensure that it fulfills its legal obligations.

4. **Forming Subsidiaries to act as Agents.** Sometimes, the basis of the formation of a company is to act as an agent or trustee of its members or of another company. In such cases, the company loses its individuality in favor of its principal. Also, the principal is liable for the acts of such a company.

5. **A company formed for fraud or improper conduct or to defeat the law.** In cases where a company is formed for some illegal or improper purposes like defeating the law, the courts might decide to lift or pierce the corporate veil.

One Person Company

The Companies Act, 2013 completely revolutionized corporate laws in India by introducing several new concepts that did not exist previously. On such game-changer was the introduction of One Person Company concept. This led to the recognition of a completely new way of starting businesses that accorded flexibility which a company form of entity can offer, while also providing the protection of limited liability which sole proprietorship or partnerships lacked.

Several other countries had already recognized the ability of individuals forming a company before the enactment of the new Companies Act in 2013. These included the likes of China, Singapore, UK, Australia, and the USA.

Definition of One Person Company

Section 2(62) of Companies Act defines a one person company as a company that has only one person as its member. Furthermore, members of a company are nothing but subscribers to its memorandum of association, or its shareholders. So, an OPC is effectively a company that has only one shareholder as its member.

Such companies are generally created when there is only one founder/promoter for the business. Entrepreneurs whose businesses lie in early stages prefer to create OPCs instead of sole proprietorship business because of the several advantages that OPCs offer.

Difference between OPCs and Sole Proprietorships

A sole proprietorship form of business might seem very similar to one person companies because they both involve a single person owning the business, but there actually exist some differences between them.

The main difference between the two is the nature of liabilities they carry. Since an OPC is a separate legal entity distinguished from its promoter, it has its own assets and liabilities. The promoter is not personally liable to repay the debts of the company.

On the other hand, sole proprietorships and their proprietors are the same persons. So, the law allows attachment and sale of promoter's own assets in case of non-fulfillment of the business' liabilities.

Features of a One Person Company

Here are some general features of a one-person company:

a. **Private company.** Section 3(1)(c) of the Companies Act says that a single person can form a company for any lawful purpose. It further describes OPCs as private companies.
b. **Single member.** OPCs can have only one member or shareholder, unlike other private companies.
c. **Nominee.** A unique feature of OPCs that separates it from other kinds of companies is that the sole member of the company has to mention a nominee while registering the company.
d. **No perpetual succession.** Since there is only one member in an OPC, his death will result in the nominee choosing or rejecting to become its sole member. This does not happen in other companies as they follow the concept of perpetual succession.
e. **Minimum one director.** OPCs need to have minimum one person (the member) as director. They can have a maximum of 15 directors.

f. **No minimum paid-up share capital.** Companies Act, 2013 has not prescribed any amount as minimum paid-up capital for OPCs.

g. **Special privileges.** OPCs enjoy several privileges and exemptions under the Companies Act that other kinds of companies do not possess.

Formation of One Person Companies

A single person can form an OPC by subscribing his name to the memorandum of association and fulfilling other requirements prescribed by the Companies Act, 2013. Such memorandum must state details of a nominee who shall become the company's sole member in case the original member dies or becomes incapable of entering into contractual relations.

This memorandum and the nominee's consent to his nomination should be filed to the Registrar of Companies along with an application of registration. Such nominee can withdraw his name at any point of time by submission of requisite applications to the Registrar. His nomination can also later be cancelled by the member.

Membership in One Person Companies

Only natural persons who are Indian citizens and residents are eligible to form a one person company in India. The same condition applies to nominees of OPCs. Further, such a natural person cannot be a member or nominee of more than one OPC at any point of time.

It is important to note that only natural persons can become members of OPCs. This does not happen in case of companies wherein companies themselves can own shares and be members. Further, the law prohibits minors from being members or nominees of OPCs.

Conversion of OPCs into other Companies

Rules regulating the formation of one person companies expressly restrict conversion of OPCs into Section 8 companies, i.e., companies that have charitable objectives. OPCs also cannot voluntarily convert into other kinds of companies until the expiry of two years from the date of their incorporation.

Privileges of One Person Companies

OPCs enjoy the following privileges and exemptions under the Companies Act:

- They do not have to hold annual general meetings.
- Their financial statements need not include cash flow statements.
- A company secretary is not required to sign annual returns; directors can also do so.
- Provisions relating to independent directors do not apply to them.
- Their articles can provide for additional grounds for vacation of a director's office.
- Several provisions relating to meetings and quorum do not apply to them.
- They can pay more remuneration to directors than compared to other companies.

Private Companies

Section 2(68) of Companies Act, 2013 defines private companies. According to that, private companies are those companies whose articles of association restrict the transferability of shares and prevent the public at large from subscribing to them. This is the basic criterion that differentiates private companies from public companies.

The Section further says private companies can have a maximum of 200 members (except for One Person Companies). This number does not include present and former employees who are also members. Moreover, more than two persons who own shares jointly are treated as a single member.

This definition had previously prescribed a minimum paid-up share capital of Rs. 1 lakh for private companies, but an amendment in 2005 removed this requirement. Private companies can now have a minimum paid-up capital of any amount.

Features of Private Companies

These are some features that distinguish private companies from other types of companies:

i. **No minimum capital required.** There was a minimum paid-up share capital requirement of Rs. 1 lakh previously, but that is omitted now.
ii. **Minimum 2 and maximum 200 members.** A private company can have a minimum of just two members (but just one is enough if it a One Person Company), and maximum of upto 200 members.
iii. **Transferability of shares restricted.** Private companies cannot freely transfer their shares to the public like public companies. This is why stock exchanges never list private companies.
iv. **"Private Limited".** All private companies must include the words "Private Limited" or "Pvt. Ltd." in their names.
v. **Privileges and exemptions.** Since private companies do not freely transfer their shares and involve limited interest by members, the law has granted them several exemptions that public companies do not enjoy.

Types of Private Companies

Private companies are of three types depending on their members' liabilities:

a. **Limited by shares.** Liability of the members is limited to the amount unpaid to the company with respect to the shares held by them.
b. **Limited by guarantee.** Here the members' liabilities are limited to the amount of money they guarantee to pay in case the company is wound-up.
c. **Unlimited liability.** Liability of members is unlimited in this type of private companies. Personal assets of members can be attached and sold when the company is being wound-up.

In terms of the number of members, a private company can also be a One Person Company. These types of companies have just one member/shareholder as their promoter. The new Companies Act of 2013 introduced such types of companies.

Further, even small companies that have limited paid-up share capitals and turnover amounts, as defined under Section 2(85), are treated as private companies under Indian company law.

Formation of Private Companies

Minimum 2 and maximum 200 members can come together to form a private company by submitting an application to that effect to the Registrar of Companies along with a subscribed copy of their Memorandum of Association and other required documents after payment of prescribed fees.

The Memorandum must state the name of the company (which should include the words "Private Limited"), the address of its registered office, its objects and purposes, and extent of liability of its members. It must also mention details of subscribers to the Memorandum.

Apart from this, the Companies Act has also prescribed certain other compliances, such as requirements relating to names of private companies, their Articles of Association, details of members, transferability of shares, etc.

Privileges of Private Companies

The Companies Act has provided certain privileges and exemptions to private companies that public companies do not possess. These privileges accord them greater freedom in conducting their affairs. Here are some examples of them:

- No need to prepare a report for annual general meetings.
- Only 2 minimum directors required.
- No need to appoint independent directors.
- They can adopt additional grounds for disqualification of directors and vacation of their office.
- They can pay greater remuneration to their directors than compared to some other types of companies.

Limitations of Private Companies

Despite all the advantages they offer, private companies also have the following limitations:

- Private companies cannot freely transfer shares to the public.
- They find it more difficult than public companies to access external financial support.
- Shareholders have greater risks and liabilities.

Section 8 Company

The Companies Act defines a Section 8 company as one whose objectives is to promote fields of arts, commerce, science, research, education, sports, charity, social welfare, religion, environment protection, or other similar objectives. These companies also apply their profits towards the furtherance of their cause and do not pay any dividend to their members.

These companies were previously defined under Section 25 of Companies Act, 1956 with more or less the same provisions. The new Act has, however, prescribed more objectives that Section 8 companies can have.

Famous examples of Section 8 companies include Federation of Indian Chambers of Commerce and Industry (FICCI) and Confederation of Indian Industries (CII). The objective of these companies is facilitating the growth of trade and commerce and India.

Features of a Section 8 Company

A Section 8 company comprises of the following distinct features that most other kinds of companies do not have:

i. **Charitable objectives.** Section 8 companies do not aim to make profits. Their objectives are purely charitable in nature. They aim to further causes like science, culture, research, sports, religion, etc.
ii. **No minimum share capital.** Section 8 companies, unlike all other companies, do not require a prescribed minimum paid-up share capital.
iii. **Limited liability.** Members of these companies can only have limited liability. Their liabilities cannot be unlimited in any case.
iv. **Government license:** Such companies can function only if they have the Central Government's license. The Government can revoke this license as well.
v. **Privileges:** Since these companies possess charitable objectives, the Companies Act has accorded several benefits and exemptions to them.
vi. **Firms as members:** Apart from individuals and associations of persons, Section 8 also allows firms to be members of these companies.

Formation of Section 8 Company

A person or an association of persons can make an application to the Registrar of Companies using requisite forms to form a company with charitable objectives under Section 8 of Companies Act. The Central Government, if satisfied, can accept such an application upon any terms and conditions imposed under the license granted by it. Once accepted, the Registrar of Companies will register the company after the applicants pay all requisite fees.

It is important to note that such companies can only be limited companies. All privileges and obligations of limited companies apply in this case. Further, these companies also do not need to include the words "Limited" or "Private Limited" in their names, as all other companies have to.

Since the existence of such companies is based on the license granted to them, they cannot even alter their memorandum or articles of association without the Central Government's permission. They also cannot do anything that the license disallows.

Cancellation of License

Section 8 companies require a grant of a license by the Central Government. All such licenses are revocable as well on the following grounds:

- the company contravenes provisions of Section 8;
- terms of the license are violated;
- when its conduct is fraudulent, or it violates its own objectives and public policy.

The Government can even order the company to be wound-up or amalgamated with another similar company under certain circumstances. The Government has to hear the company before passing cancellation order.

Winding Up

Section 8 companies can wind-up or dissolve themselves either voluntarily or under orders given by the Central Government. If any assets remain after satisfaction of debts and liabilities upon such winding-up, the National Company Law Tribunal can order the transfer of these assets to a similar company. It can also order that they must be sold and the proceeds of this sale should be credited to the Insolvency and Bankruptcy Fund.

Punishment for Contravention

Any company that contravenes provisions of Section 8 is punishable with a fine ranging from Rs. 10 lakhs to Rs. 1 crore. Further, directors and officers of the company are liable to punishment with imprisonment up to 3 years and a fine between Rs. 25,000 to Rs. 25 lakhs. Such officers can also face prosecution under stringent provisions of Section 447 (dealing with fraud) if they conduct any affairs with fraudulent motives.

Advantages/Privileges

People generally prefer to conduct charitable activities by forming Section 8 companies instead of regular NGOs and associations. This is because they have limited liability, so their personal assets will not be used in paying debts of the company. Here are some advantages that these companies enjoy:

- Members have limited liability.
- No minimum capital requirements.
- They get several tax exemptions.
- Stamp duties and high fees are not payable for registration.
- They have perpetual existence and separate legal status.
- Exemptions from carrying out several procedural compliances.
- More credibility than compared to NGOs, societies, and trusts because they are recognized by the Central Government's license.

Disadvantages

Despite numerous merits, these companies also have the following drawbacks:

- Members of the company cannot get any dividend.
- Officers and directors do not get benefits and allowances.
- Can only use the profits for furthering charitable aims and objectives.
- Amendment of memorandum and articles requires Central Government's permission.
- The license is revocable on several grounds.

Registration and Incorporation of a Company

Promoters

Section 2(69) of the Companies Act, 2013, defines promoters as an individual who:-

- Is named as a promoter in the prospectus or in the annual returns of the company.
- Controls the affairs of a company, directly or indirectly.
- Advises, directs, or instructs the Board of Directors.

Hence, we can say that promoters are people who originally come up with the idea of the company, form it and register it. However, solicitors, accountants, etc. who act in their professional capacity are NOT promoters of the company.

Formation of a Company

Section 3 of the Companies Act, 2013, details the basic requirements of forming a company as follows:

- Formation of a public company involves 7 or more people who subscribe their names to the memorandum and register the company for any lawful purpose.
- Similarly, 2 or more people can form a private company.
- One person can form a One-person company.

Registration or Incorporation of a Company

Section 7 of the Companies Act, 2013, details the procedure for incorporation of a company. Here is the procedure:

Filing of company registration papers with the registrar

To incorporate a company, the subscriber has to file the following company registration papers with the registrar within whose jurisdiction the location of the registered office of the proposed company falls.

1. The Memorandum and Articles of the company. All subscribers have to sign on the memorandum.
2. The person who is engaged in the formation of the company has to give a declaration regarding compliance of all the requirements and rules of the Act. A person named in the Articles also has to sign the declaration.
3. Each subscriber to the Memorandum and individuals named as first directors in the Articles should submit an affidavit with the following details:
   i. Declaration regarding non-conviction of any offense with respect to the formation, promotion, or management of any company.
   ii. He has not been found guilty of fraud or any breach of duty to any company in the last five years.
   iii. The documents filed with the registrar are complete and true to the best of his knowledge.

4. Address for correspondence until the registered office is set-up.
5. If the subscriber to the Memorandum is an individual, then he needs to provide his full name, residential address, and nationality along with a proof of identity. If the subscriber is a body corporate, then prescribed documents need to be provided.
6. Individuals mentioned as subscribers to the Memorandum in the Articles need to provide the details specified in the point above along with the Director Identification Number.

Issuing the of Certificate of Incorporation

Once the Registrar receives the information and company registration papers, he registers all information and documents and issues a Certificate of Incorporation in the prescribed form.

Corporate Identity Number (CIN)

The Registrar also allocates a Corporate Identity Number (CIN) to the company which is a distinct identity for the company. The allotment of CIN is on and from the company's incorporation date. The certificate carries this date.

Maintaining copies of Company registration papers

The company must maintain copies of all information and documents until dissolution.

Furnishing false information at the time of incorporation

During the formation of a company, an individual can:

- Furnish incorrect or false information
- Suppress any material information in the documents provided to the Registrar for the incorporation, on purpose

In such cases, the individual is liable for action for fraud under section 447.

The company is already incorporated based on false information

If a company is already incorporated but it is found at a later date that the information or documents submitted were false or incorrect, then the promoters, first directors, and persons making a declaration is liable for action for fraud under section 447.

Order of the National Company Law Tribunal (NCLT)

If a company is incorporated by furnishing false or incorrect information or representation or suppressing material facts or information in the documents furnished, the Tribunal can pass the following orders (if an application is made and the Tribunal is satisfied with it):

- Pass an order to regulate the management of the company. It can include changes in its Memorandum and Articles if required. This order is either in public interest or in the interest of the company and its members and creditors.
- Order removal of the name of the company from the Registrar of Companies
- Order the company to wind-up
- Pass any other order as it deems fit

Before passing an order, the Tribunal has to give the company a reasonable opportunity state its case. Also, the Tribunal should consider the transactions of the company including obligations contracted or payment of any liability.

Effects of Registration of a Company

According to Section 9 of the Companies Act, 2013, these are the effects of registration of a company:

- From the date of incorporation, the subscribers to the Memorandum and all subsequent members of the company are a body corporate.
- A registered company can exercise all functions of a company incorporated under the Act. Also, the company has perpetual succession with power to acquire, hold, and dispose of property of all forms. Also, it can contract, sue and be sued by the said name.
- Further, the company becomes a legal person separate from the incorporators from the date of incorporation. Also, a binding contract comes into existence between the company and its members as mentioned in the Memorandum and Articles of Association. Until the company dissolves or the Registrar removes it from the register, it has perpetual existence.

Classification of Capital

In simple words, the total contributions made by people to the common stock of the company is the capital of the company. Further, a share is the proportion of the capital to which each member has entitlement. Remember, a share is not an amount of money. It is an interest including different rights in the contract.

In this article, we will look at five ways in which the term capital is used in Company Law: nominal capital, issued capital, subscribed capital, called up capital and paid up capital.

Nominal or Authorized or Registered Capital

Section 2(8) of the Companies Act, 2013, defines Nominal Capital as the amount of capital that the Memorandum of the company authorizes as the share capital of the company. Hence, it is the registered amount authorized that can be raised by issuing shares. The company also pays stamp duty in this amount. Typically, you can calculate nominal capital by taking into consideration the working and reserve capital needs of the company.

Issued Capital

Issued capital is a part of the Authorized capital, offered by the company for the subscription. This includes the allotment of shares. Section 2(50) of the Companies Act, 2013, offers this definition. Further, it is mandatory for companies to disclose its issued capital in the balance sheet (Schedule III of the Act).

Subscribed Capital

Section 2(86) of the Companies Act, 2013, defines Subscribed capital as the part of the capital being subscribed by the members of the company. It is the number of shares that the public takes.

Further, if the company states Authorized Capital in any communication like notice, advertisement, official/business letter, etc., then it has to also specify subscribed and paid up capital in equally conspicuous characters. Also, Section 60 of the Act specifies that defaulters in this regard, the company and all officers who default, will be fined around Rs. 10,000 and Rs. 5,000 respectively.

Called Up Capital

According to Section 2(15) of the Companies Act, 2013, called up capital is the part of the capital which the company calls for payment. This is the total amount that the company calls-up on the issued shares.

Paid Up Capital

Paid up capital is the part of called up capital actually paid or credited by shareholders on the issued shares. Mathematically, Paid up capital = called up capital – calls in arrears. Paid up capital represents the money that the company has not borrowed. Also, it is the total amount of money that the company receives from shareholders in exchange for shares of stock.

Memorandum Of Association

Object of registering a Memorandum of Association or MOA

- The MOA of a company contains the object for which the company is formed. It identifies the scope of its operations and determines the boundaries it cannot cross.
- It is a public document according to Section 399 of the Companies Act, 2013. Hence, any person who enters into a contract with the company is expected to have knowledge of the MOA.
- It contains details about the powers and rights of the company.

Under no circumstance can the company depart from the provisions specified in the memorandum. If it does so, then it would be ultra vires the company and void.

Format of Memorandum of Association (MOA)

According to Section 4 of the Companies Act, 2013, companies must draw the MOA in the form given in Tables A-E in Schedule I of the Act. Here are the details of the forms:

- Table A: Form for the memorandum of association of a company limited by shares.
- Table B: Form for the memorandum of association of a company limited by guarantee and not having a share capital.
- Table C: Form for the memorandum of association of a company limited by guarantee and having a share capital.
- Table D: Form for the memorandum of association of an unlimited company.
- Table E: Form for the memorandum of association of an unlimited company and having share capital.

Content of the MOA

The following information is mandatory in an MOA:

Name Clause

1. For a public limited company, the name of the company must have the word 'Limited' as the last word
2. For the private limited company, the name of the company must have the words 'Private Limited' as the last words.

This is not applicable to companies formed under Section 8 of the Act who must include one of the following words, as applicable:

- Foundation
- Association
- Chambers
- Council
- Forum
- Federation
- Confederation
- Electoral Trust, etc.

Registered Office Clause

It must specify the State in which the registered office of the company will be situated.

Object Clause

It must specify the objects for which the company is being incorporated. Further, if a company changes its activities which are not reflected in its name, then it can change its name within six months of changing its activities. The company must comply with all name-change provisions.

Liability Clause

It should specify the liability of the members of the company, whether limited or unlimited. Also,

1. For a company limited by shares – it should specify if the liability of its members is limited to any unpaid amount on the shares that they hold.
2. For a company limited by guarantee – it should specify the amount undertaken by each member to contribute to:
   i. The assets of the company when it winds-up. This is provided that he is a member of the company when it winds-up or the winding-up happens within one year of him ceasing to be a member. In the latter case, the debts and liabilities considered would be those contracted before he ceases to be a member.
   ii. The costs, charges, and expenses of winding up and the adjustment of the rights of the contributors among themselves.

Capital Clause

This is valid only for companies having share capital. These companies must specify the amount of Authorized capital divided into shares of fixed amounts. Further, it must state the names of each member and the number of shares against their names.

Association Clause

The MOA must clearly specify the desire of the subscriber to form a company. This is the last clause.

Doctrine of Ultra Vires

The Doctrine of Ultra Vires is a fundamental rule of the Company Law. It states that the objects of a company, as specified in its Memorandum of Association, can be departed from only to the extent permitted by the Act. Hence, if the company does an act, or enters into a contract beyond the powers of the directors and/or the company itself, then the said act/contract is void and not legally binding on the company.

The term Ultra Vires means 'Beyond Powers'. In legal terms, it is applicable only to the acts done in excess of the legal powers of the doers. This works on an assumption that the powers are limited in nature. Since the Doctrine of Ultra Vires limits the company to the objects specified in the memorandum, the company can be:

- Restrained from using its funds for purposes other than those specified in the Memorandum
- Restrained from carrying on trade different from the one authorized.

The company cannot sue on an ultra vires transaction. Further, it cannot be sued too. If a company supplies goods or offers service or lends money on an ultra vires contract, then it cannot obtain payment or recover the loan.

However, if a lender loans money to a company which has not been expended yet, then he can stop the company from parting with it via an injunction. The lender has this right because the company does not become the owner of the money as it is ultra vires to the company and the lender remains the owner.

Further, if the company borrows money in an ultra vires transaction to repay a legal loan, then the lender is entitled to recover his loan from the company.

Sometimes an act which is ultra vires can be regularized by the shareholders of the company. For example,

- If an act is ultra vires the power of directors, then the shareholders can ratify it.
- If an act is ultra vires the Articles of the company, then the company can alter the Articles.

Remember, you cannot bind a company through an ultra vires contract. Estoppel, acquiescence, lapse of time, delay, or ratification cannot make it 'Intravires'.

Summing up the Doctrine of Ultra Vires

1. An act, legal in itself, but not authorized by the object clause of the Memorandum of Association of a company or statute, is Ultra Vires the company. Hence, it is null and void.
2. An act ultra vires the company cannot be ratified even by the unanimous consent of all shareholders.
3. If an act is ultra vires the directors of a company, but intra vires the company itself, then the members of the company can pass a resolution to ratify it.
4. If an act is Ultra Vires the Articles of Association of a company, then the same can be ratified by a special resolution at a general meeting.

The Flip-side

While the main advantage of the Doctrine of Ultra Vires is the protection of shareholders and creditors, it has disadvantages too. This doctrine prevents the company from changing its activities in a direction agreed by all members. Further, a special resolution can alter the object clause of the Memorandum. This defeats the core purpose of the doctrine.

Winding up of a joint company

In case of voluntary winding up of company, the company must call for a meeting of creditors on the day or the day next following the day, on which there is to be conducted the general meeting of the company at which the resolution for voluntary winding up is to be proposed. The notice for meeting of creditors is to be sent by post to the creditors at the same time with the sending of the notices related to the general meeting of the company for voluntary winding up.

In addition to sending of the notice for meeting of creditors by post, the company must also cause to be advertised one time at least in the official gazette and one time at least in two newspapers circulating in the district where the registered office or principal place of business of the company is situated.

At the meeting of creditors, the Board of directors of the company must present a statement of the position of the company affairs jointly with a list of the creditors of the company and the projected amount of their claims. It is the duty of the appointed director to be in charge of at the meeting of creditors to attend the meeting and preside at the same.

Based on the decision of the two-thirds in value of creditors of the company, the next course of action on winding up of the company would be decided as follows:

- If it is in the interest of all parties so as to the company be wound up on a voluntary basis, then the company will be wound up voluntarily; or
- If the company may not be able to pay for its debts in full from the assets proceeds sold in voluntary winding up, then a resolution can be passed for winding up of the company by a Tribunal.

The notice of any resolution that is passed at a meeting of creditors must be filed with the Registrar within a period of 10 days of passing. If a company contravenes to the provisions related to this section, the company will be punishable with fine which will not be less than fifty thousand rupees but which may perhaps extend to Rs. two lakh and the director of the company who is in default will be punishable with imprisonment for a term which could extend to six months or with fine which will not be lesser than Rs. 50,000 but which may perhaps extend to Rs. 2 lakh, or with both.

LIMITED LIABILITY PARTNERSHIP (LLP)

Limited Liability Partnership is a new corporate structure that combines the flexibility of a partnership and the advantages of limited liability of a company at a low compliance cost. In other words, it is an alternative corporate business vehicle that provides the benefits of limited liability of a company, but allows its members the flexibility of organising their internal management on the basis of a mutually arrived agreement, as is the case in a partnership firm.

Owing to flexibility in its structure and operation, it would be useful for small and medium enterprises, in general, and for the enterprises in services sector, in particular. Internationally, LLPs are the preferred vehicle of business, particularly for service industry or for activities involving professionals.

LLP is governed by the provisions of the Limited Liability Partnership Act 2008, the salient features of which are as follows:

a. The LLP shall be a body corporate and a legal entity separate from its partners. Any two or more persons, associated for carrying on a lawful business with a view to profit, may by subscribing their names to an incorporation document and filing the same with the Registrar, form a Limited Liability Partnership. The LLP will have perpetual succession.

b. The mutual rights and duties of partners of an LLP inter se and those of the LLP and its partners shall be governed by an agreement between partners or between the LLP and the partners subject to the provisions of the LLP Act 2008 . The act provides flexibility to devise the agreement as per their choice.

c. The LLP will be a separate legal entity, liable to the full extent of its assets, with the liability of the partners being limited to their agreed contribution in the LLP which may be of tangible or intangible nature or both tangible and intangible in nature. No partner would be liable on account of the independent or un-authorized actions of other partners or their misconduct. The liabilities of the LLP and partners who are found to have acted with intent to defraud creditors or for any fraudulent purpose shall be unlimited for all or any of the debts or other liabilities of the LLP.

c. Every LLP shall have at least two partners and shall also have at least two individuals as Designated Partners, of whom at least one shall be resident in India. The duties and obligations of Designated Partners shall be as provided in the law.

d. The LLP shall be under an obligation to maintain annual accounts reflecting true and fair view of its state of affairs. A statement of accounts and solvency shall be filed by every LLP with the Registrar every year. The accounts of LLPs shall also be audited, subject to any class of LLPs being exempted from this requirement by the Central Government.

e. The Central Government has powers to investigate the affairs of an LLP, if required, by appointment of competent Inspector for the purpose.

f. The compromise or arrangement including merger and amalgamation of LLPs shall be in accordance with the provisions of the LLP Act 2008.

g. A firm, private company or an unlisted public company is allowed to be converted into LLP in accordance with the provisions of the Act. Upon such conversion, on and from the date of certificate of registration issued by the Registrar in this regard, the effects of the conversion shall be such as are specified in the LLP Act. On and from the date of registration specified in the certificate of registration, all tangible (moveable or immoveable) and intangible property vested in the firm or the company, all assets, interests, rights, privileges, liabilities, obligations relating to the firm or the company, and the whole of the undertaking of the firm or the company, shall be transferred to and shall vest in the LLP without further assurance, act or deed and the firm or the company, shall be deemed to be dissolved and removed from the records of the Registrar of Firms or Registrar of Companies, as the case may be.

h. The winding up of the LLP may be either voluntary or by the Tribunal to be established under the Companies Act, 1956. Till the Tribunal is established, the power in this regard has been given to the High Court.

i. The LLP Act 2008 confers powers on the Central Government to apply provisions of the Companies Act, 1956 as appropriate, by notification with such changes or modifications as deemed necessary. However, such notifications shall be laid in draft before each House of Parliament for a total period of 30 days and shall be subject to any modification as may be approved by both Houses.

j. The Indian Partnership Act, 1932 shall not be applicable to Limited Liability Partnerships.

FORMATION OF LLP IN INDIA

A. Starting a LLP

To register a Indian LLP, you need to first apply for a Designated Partner Identification Number (DPIN), which can be done by filing eForm for acquiring the DIN or DPIN. You would then need to acquire your Digital Signature Certificate and register the same on the portal. Thereafter, you need to get the LLP name approved by the Ministry. Once the LLP name is approved, you can register the LLP by filing the incorporation form.

Step 1 : Application for DIN or DPIN

All designated partners of the proposed LLP shall obtain "Designated Partner Identification Number (DPIN)". You need to file eForm DIR-3 in order to obtain DIN or DPIN. In case you already have a DIN (Director Identification Number), the same can be used as a DPIN.

Step 2 : Acquire/ Register DSC

The Information Technology Act, 2000 provides for use of Digital Signatures on the documents submitted in electronic form in order to ensure the security and authenticity of the documents filed electronically. This is the only secure and authentic way that a document can be submitted electronically. As such, all filings done by the LLP(s) are required to be filed with the use of Digital Signatures by the person authorised to sign the documents.

Acquire DSC -A licensed Certifying Authority (CA) issues the digital signature. Certifying Authority (CA) means a person who has been granted a license to issue a digital signature certificate under Section 24 of the Indian IT-Act 2000.

Register DSC - Role check can be performed only after the signatories have registered their Digital signature certificates (DSC) with LLP application. To know about it click Register a DSC

Step 3 : New User Registration

To file an eForm or to avail any paid service on LLP portal; you are first required to register yourself as a user in the relevant user category, such as registered and business user. To register now click New User Registration

Step 4 : Incorporate a LLP

Apply for the name of the LLP to be registered by filing Form 1 (Application for reservation or change of name) for the same. After that depending upon the proposed LLP, file required incorporation Form 2 (Incorporation document and Subscriber's statement)

Once the form has been approved by the concerned official of the Ministry, you will receive an email regarding the same and the status of the form will get changed to Approved. To know more about e-Filing process click "All About e-Filing"

Step 5 : File LLP Agreement

After incorporation of LLP, an initial LLP agreement is to be filed within 30 days of incorporation of LLP. The user has to file the information in Form 3 (Information with regard to Limited Liability Partnership Agreement and changes, if any, made therein).

Convert existing partnership into LLP

Any existing partnership firm that is willing to get converted into LLP will need to apply through Form 17 (Application and statement for the conversion of a firm into LLP. Form 17 needs to be filed along with Form 2 (Incorporation document and Subscriber's statement).

THE COMPETITION ACT, 2002

On December 16, 2002, the Lok Sabha passed a Bill to replace the MRTP (Monopolies and Restrictive Trade Practices) Act, 1969 which was enacted to curb the tendency to create monopoly in commerce, trade and industry. The Act is known as Competition Act, 2002 or Antitrust Law.

In 1999, Government of India appointed a committee on "Competition Policy and Law" under the Chairmanship of Sri S.V.S. Raghvan. In the year 2000, this committee submitted its report. Accordingly, the competition Act, 2002 was framed and passed on the basis of recommendation of this committee.

This Act was enforced on 13th January 2003. Later on, the government made some amendments through passing of competition (Amendment) Bill, 2007. This Act covers whole of India except Jammu and Kashmir. This Act smoothly replaced the MRTP Act.

Under the new laws, hardly 100 of the 6,000 big industries would come under the purview of the Act. An industry having assets of Rs 1,000 crore Or more or having a annual turnover of Rs 3,000 crore or more would attract the provisions of the new law, i.e., Competition Law or Antitrust Law.

The Act provides for the constitution of Competition Commission of India (CCI) which is a corporate body with quasi-judicial powers. The order of this Commission can be challenged only in the Supreme Court. The Commission shall be headed by a Chairman and there would not be more than 10 members of the Commission to be appointed by the Government of India. After its formation, the CCI has taken over MRTP commission (MRTPC). Accordingly MRTPC was dissolved and all pending cases of MRTPC were either disposed within a year or shifted to CCI. The pending unfair Trade Practice (UTPs) cases have been shifted to concerned consumer courts formed under consumer protection Act. 1986.

The competition Act 2002 was formulated with following objectives:

1. To promote healthy competition in the market.
2. To prevent those practices which are having adverse effect on competition.
3. To protect the interests of concerns in a suitable manner.
4. To ensure freedom of trade in Indian markets.
5. To prevent abuses of dominant position in the market actively.
6. Regulating the operation and activities of combinations (acquisitions, mergers and amalgamation).
7. Creating awareness and imparting training about the competition Act.

Following are some important features of the competition Act:

1. Competition Act is a very compact and smaller legislation which includes only 66 sections.
2. Competition commission of India (CCI) is constituted under the Act.
3. This Act restricts agreements having adverse effect on competition in India.

4. This Act suitably regulates acquisitions, mergers and amalgamation of enterprises.
5. Under the purview of this Act, the central Government appointed director General for conducting detail investigation of anti-competition agreements for arresting CCI.
6. This Act is flexible enough to change its provisions as per needs.
7. Civil courts do not have any jurisdiction to entertain any suit which is within the purview of this Act.
8. This Act possesses penalty provision.
9. Competition Act has replaced MRTP Act.
10. Under this Act, "Competition Fund" has been created.

Competition Act is not applicable in the following cases:

1. Public Financial Institutions.
2. Foreign Institutional Investors (FIIs).
3. Banks.
4. Venture capital Funds (VCFs).
5. Agreements related to intellectual property rights (IPRs) such as trademarks, patents, copyrights etc.
6. Central Government has the authority to exempt any class of enterprises from the provisions of Act in the common interest of national security or public interest.

It can now be concluded that the competition Act, 2002 is landmark legislation. The main aim of this Act is to promote competition and curb all anti-competitive agreements. This Act restricts the abuses of dominant enterprises. It can also regulate any kind of combinations beyond a particular size. Thus this Act does not curb monopolies rather it curbs abuses of monopolies.

Thus, the competition Act is expected to play a responsible role in changing the control mechanism related to monopoly and restrictive trade practices and is also expected to protect the interest of the small and medium industries in the country besides giving consumers more powers to redress their grievances.

THE INFORMATION TECHNOLOGY ACT, 2000

The **Information Technology Act, 2000** is an Act of the Indian Parliament (No 21 of 2000) notified on 17 October 2000. It is the primary law in India dealing with cybercrime and electronic commerce. It is based on the *United Nations Model Law on Electronic Commerce 1996* (UNCITRAL Model) recommended by the General Assembly of United Nations by a resolution dated 30 January 1997.

The bill was passed in the budget session of 2000 and signed by President K. R. Narayanan on 9 May 2000. The bill was finalised by group of officials headed by then Minister of Information Technology Pramod Mahajan.

The original Act contained 94 sections, divided in 13 chapters and 4 schedules. The laws apply to the whole of India. Persons of other nationalities can also be indicted under the law, if the crime involves a computer or network located in India.

The Act provides legal framework for electronic governance by giving recognition to electronic records and digital signatures. The formations of Controller of Certifying Authorities was directed by the Act, to regulate issuing of digital signatures. It also defines cyber crimes and prescribed penalties for them. It also established a Cyber Appellate Tribunal to resolve disputes rising from this new law. The Act also amended various sections of Indian Penal Code, 1860, Indian Evidence Act, 1872, Banker's Book Evidence Act, 1891, and Reserve Bank of India Act, 1934 to make them compliant with new technologies.

A major amendment was made in 2008. It introduced the Section 66A which penalized sending of "offensive messages". It also introduced the Section 69, which gave authorities the power of "interception or monitoring or decryption of any information through any computer resource". It also introduced for child porn, cyber terrorism and voyeurism. It was passed on 22 December 2008 without any debate in Lok Sabha. The next day it was passed by the Rajya Sabha. It was signed into law by President Pratibha Patil, on 5 February 2009.

List of offences and the corresponding penalties

Section	Offence	Punishment	Bailability and Congizability
65	Tampering with Computer Source Code	Imprisonment up to 3 years or fine up to Rs 2 lakhs	Offence is Bailable, Cognizable and triable by Court of JMFC.
66	Computer Related Offences	Imprisonment up to 3 years or fine up to Rs 5 lakhs	Offence is Bailable, Cognizable
66-A	Sending offensive messages through Communication service, etc...	Imprisonment up to 3 years and fine	Offence is Bailable, Cognizable and triable by Court of JMFC
66-B	Dishonestly receiving stolen computer resource or communication device	Imprisonment up to 3 years and/or fine up to Rs. 1 lakh	Offence is Bailable, Cognizable and triable by Court of JMFC
66-C	Identity Theft	Imprisonment of either description up to 3 years and/or fine up to Rs. 1 lakh	Offence is Bailable, Cognizable and triable by Court of JMFC
66-D	Cheating by Personation by using computer resource	Imprisonment of either description up to 3 years and /or fine up to Rs. 1 lakh	Offence is Bailable, Cognizable and triable by Court of JMFC
66-E	Violation of Privacy	Imprisonment up to 3 years and /or fine up to Rs. 2 lakh	Offence is Bailable, Cognizable and triable by Court of JMFC
66-F	Cyber Terrorism	Imprisonment extend to imprisonment for Life	Offence is Non-Bailable, Cognizable and triable by Court of Sessions
67	Publishing or transmitting obscene material in electronic form	On first Conviction, imprisonment up to 3 years and/or fine up to Rs. 5 lakh On Subsequent Conviction imprisonment up to 5 years and/or fine up to Rs. 10 lakh	Offence is Bailable, Cognizable and triable by Court of JMFC
67-A	Publishing or transmitting of material containing sexually explicit act, etc... in electronic form	On first Conviction imprisonment up to 5 years and/or fine up to Rs. 10 lakh On Subsequent Conviction imprisonment up to 7 years and/or fine up to Rs. 10 lakh	Offence is Non-Bailable, Cognizable and triable by Court of JMFC
67-B	Publishing or transmitting of material depicting children in sexually explicit act etc., in electronic form	On first Conviction imprisonment of either description up to 5 years and/or fine up to Rs. 10 lakh On Subsequent Conviction imprisonment of either description up to 7 years and/or fine up to Rs. 10 lakh	Offence is Non Bailable, Cognizable and triable by Court of JMFC
67-C	Intermediary intentionally or knowingly contravening the directions about Preservation and retention of information	Imprisonment up to 3 years and fine	Offence is Bailable, Cognizable.

Section	Offence	Punishment	Bailability and Congizability
68	Failure to comply with the directions given by Controller	Imprisonment up to 2 years and/or fine up to Rs. 1 lakh	Offence is Bailable, Non-Cognizable.
69	Failure to assist the agency referred to in sub section (3) in regard interception or monitoring or decryption of any information through any computer resource	Imprisonment up to 7 years and fine	Offence is Non-Bailable, Cognizable.
69-A	Failure of the intermediary to comply with the direction issued for blocking for public access of any information through any computer resource	Imprisonment up to 7 years and fine	Offence is Non-Bailable, Cognizable.
69-B	Intermediary who intentionally or knowingly contravenes the provisions of sub-section (2) in regard monitor and collect traffic data or information through any computer resource for cybersecurity	Imprisonment up to 3 years and fine	Offence is Bailable, Cognizable.
70	Any person who secures access or attempts to secure access to the protected system in contravention of provision of Sec. 70	Imprisonment of either description up to 10 years and fine	Offence is Non-Bailable, Cognizable.
70-B	Indian Computer Emergency Response Team to serve as national agency for incident response. Any service provider, intermediaries, data centres, etc., who fails to prove the information called for or comply with the direction issued by the ICERT.	Imprisonment up to 1 year and/or fine up to Rs. 1 lakh	Offence is Bailable, Non-Cognizable
71	Misrepresentation to the Controller to the Certifying Authority	Imprisonment up to 2 years and/or fine up to Rs. 1 lakh.	Offence is Bailable, Non-Cognizable.
72	Breach of Confidentiality and privacy	Imprisonment up to 2 years and/or fine up to Rs. 1 lakh.	Offence is Bailable, Non-Cognizable.
72-A	Disclosure of information in breach of lawful contract	Imprisonment up to 3 years and/or fine up to Rs. 5 lakh.	Offence is Cognizable, Bailable
73	Publishing electronic Signature Certificate false in certain particulars	Imprisonment up to 2 years and/or fine up to Rs. 1 lakh	Offence is Bailable, Non-Cognizable.
74	Publication for fraudulent purpose	Imprisonment up to 2 years and/or fine up to Rs. 1 lakh	Offence is Bailable, Non-Cognizable.

RIGHT TO INFORMATION ACT, 2005

The Right to Information Act, simply known as RTI, is a revolutionary Act that aims to promote transparency in government institutions in India. The Act came into existence in 2005, after sustained efforts of anti-corruption activists.

It is termed revolutionary because it opens government organisations up for scrutiny. Equipped with knowledge about RTI, a common man can demand any government agency to furnish information. The organisation is bound to provide the information, that too within 30 days, failing which the officer concerned is slapped with a monetary fine.

RTI Act has been made by legislation of Parliament of India on 15 June 2005. The Act came into effect on 12 October 2005 and has been implemented ever since to provide information to crores of Indian citizens. All the constitutional authorities come under this Act, making it one of the most powerful laws of the country.

1. HOW TO FILE RTI?

Every Indian should know about RTI filing. The procedure to File RTI is simple and hassle-free.

a. Write the application (or get it typed, your choice) on a paper in English/Hindi/the official language of the state. Some states have prescribed format for RTI applications. Address it to the PIO (Public Information Officer) of the department concerned.

b. Ask specific questions. See to it that they are clear and complete, and not confusing whatsoever.

c. Write your full name, contact details and address, where you want the information/response to your RTI be sent.

d. Take a photocopy of the application for your record. If you're sending the application by post, it's advisable to send it via registered post, as then you will have an acknowledgement of your request's delivery. If you're submitting the application to the PIO in person, remember to take an acknowledgement from him/her.

Some important points:

a. The Act is so people-friendly that if an illiterate person approaches a PIO and wants some info under the RTI, he/she can tell his requirement to the PIO and the officer is obliged to write it down for them and read it to them before processing it.

b. One need not write the application on a clean sheet of paper. Even a crumpled, old, torn piece of paper will do, so long as your written content on it is legible.

c. Until the RTI Act empowered the common man to demand information from government, only the members of Parliament had the privilege of seeking this information.

d. If you are hesitant about sending your RTI application by post and can't take a day off work to catch hold of the PIO concerned, you can go to your post office and submit your application to the assistant PIO. The postal department has appointed many APIOs across its many offices. Their job is to receive RTI applications and forward them to the PIO or appellate authority concerned.

2. HOW TO FILE ONLINE RTI?

Currently, Central and a few State government departments have facility for filing Online RTI. However, there are multiple independent websites that let you file your application online. They charge you a nominal amount, for which they draft your application and send it to the relevant department. This is as good as sending an RTI application without having to worry about the particulars.

3. WHICH GOVERNMENT ORGANISATIONS ARE REQUIRED TO GIVE RTI INFORMATION UNDER RTI ACT?

All government agencies, whether they are under a state government or the Centre, come under the purview of the Act. For example, Municipal Corporations, PSUs (Public Sector Units), Government departments, Ministries at the State as well as Central level, Judiciary, Government owned Companies, Government Universities, Government Schools, Works Departments, Road Authorities, Provident Fund department etc. The list is quite an exhaustive one.

You can ask a government how much money is being spent on renovation of its ministers' bungalows, what their telephone bill or fuel expenditure is. Or you can ask what amount was spent on MLAs'/MPs' foreign trips.

You can ask how much of allocated money your elected representatives have utilised on improving their constituency; you are entitled to ask for even a break-up of the amount spent, project-wise. This RTI information is available because it is the taxpayers' money that is being spent here. Few ministries and departments make online rti replies available to the public. You can see them on the respective websites.

Not only governments and their departments, but also smaller units such as your city corporation or gram panchayat fall under the ambit of RTI. Be it police, passport office, your electricity/water supply company or even the IRCTC, all are required to furnish RTI information.

4. WHICH GOVERNMENT DEPARTMENTS ARE EXEMPTED FROM THE ACT?

Twenty-odd organisations are exempted from RTI. But all these entities are related to the country's defence and intelligence, such as RAW, BSF, CRPF, CISF, Intelligence Burearu, National Security Guard etc.

Further, there are some specific instances whereby RTI information cannot be furnished. These instances relate to matters which:

a. Would affect national security, sovereignty, strategic, economic and/or scientific interest.
b. Have been disallowed by the court to be released.
c. Have been disallowed by the court to be released.
d. Relates to trade secrets or intellectual property, information which might affect/harm the competitive position of a third party.
e. Relates to information under fiduciary relationship.
f. Relates to foreign government information.
g. Would affect the life/physical safety of any person.
h. Would affect the process of an investigation.
i. Relates to cabinet papers.
j. Relates to personal information without any public interest.
k. However, RTI law says that any information which cannot be denied to a Members of Parliament or state legislature cannot be denied to any citizen.

5. HOW TO SOLVE PROBLEMS USING RTI?

Which Personal Problems can be solved using RTI

a. Pending Income Tax return
b. Delayed PF withdrawal
c. Delayed PF Transfer
d. Delayed Passport
e. Delayed Aadhar card
f. Delayed IRCTC Refund
g. Copies of answer sheets
h. Property Documents like Occupancy Certificate/Completion Certificate
i. Status of FIR
j. Status of a complaint
m. Status of EPF
l. Delay in Scholarship

Which Social Problems can be solved using RTI

a. Fix roads with pot holes
b. Conduct social audit of government projects
c. Know how your MP/MLA spent the fund allocated to him
d. Know how a particular government project or scheme was implemented

6. IIOW MANY DAYS DOES IT TAKE TO GET RTI RESPONSE?

As per law, the RTI information should be provided in 30 days. However, sometimes government records are misplaced or missing. Or the agency you've written to needs to co- ordinate with another department to provide you the information you want. In such situations, the information may take more than 30 days to arrive. In such case, the PIO concerned needs to send you a written intimation about the possible delay and the reason. If he/she fails to do so and you don't receive the info within 30 days, penalty can be levied on the PIO if the matter taken up with appellate authorities.

7. WHAT IS THE FEE FOR SEEKING INFORMATION UNDER THE RTI?

For central government departments one needs to pay Rs. 10 with every RTI application. Mode of payment may vary from government to government. While submitting application in person, some organisations accept cash while some do not. Some ask for Court Fee Stamp, some ask for Indian postal order (IPO). When sending an RTI application by post, we can use IPO/ court fee stamp of Rs. 10.

Those below poverty line (BPL) do not have to pay Rs. 10 as fee for filing an RTI.

If you've asked the government office to furnish copies of some records, you will need to pay Rs. 2 per page. Once the office receives your request and ascertains the amount you will need to pay towards making copies, you will get intimation via post. You can make the payment by sending postal order/ court fee stamp/demand draft of the said amount.

INTELLECTUAL PROPERTY RIGHTS (IPRs)

a. The first legislation in India relating to patents was the Act VI of 1856. The objective of this legislation was to encourage inventions of new and useful manufactures and to induce inventors to disclose secret of their inventions. The Act was subsequently repealed by Act IX of 1857 since it had been enacted without the approval of the British Crown . Fresh legislation for granting 'exclusive privileges' was introduced in 1 859 as Act XV of 1859. This legislation contained certain modifications of the earlier legislation, namely, grant of exclusive privileges to useful inventions only and extension of priority period from 6 months to 12 months. This Act excluded importers from the definition of inventor. This Act was based on the United Kingdom Act of 1852 with certain departures which include allowing assignees to make application in India and also taking prior public use or publication in India or United Kingdom for the purpose of ascertaining novelty.

b. In 1872, the Act of 1859 was consolidated to provide protection relating to designs. It was renamed as "The Patterns and Designs Protection Act" under Act XIII of 1872. The Act of 1872 was further amended in 1883 (XVI of 1883) to introduce a provision to protect novelty of the invention, which prior to making application for their protection were disclosed in the Exhibition of India. A grace period of 6 months was provided for filing such applications after the date of the opening of such Exhibition.

c. This Act remained in force for about 30 years without any change but in the year 1883, certain modifications in the patent law were made in United Kingdom and it was considered that those modifications should also be incorporated in the Indian law. In 1888, an Act was introduced to consolidate and amend the law relating to invention and designs in conformity with the amendments made in the U.K. law.

d. The Indian Patents and Designs Act, 1911, (Act II of 1911) replaced all the previous Acts. This Act brought patent administration under the management of Controller of Patents for the first time. This Act was further amended in 1920 to enter into reciprocal arrangements with UK and other countries for securing priority. In 1930, further amendments were made to incorporate, inter-alia, provisions relating to grant of secret patents, patent of addition, use of invention by Government, powers of the Controller to rectify register of patent and increase of term of the patent from 14 years to 16 years. In 1945, an amendment was made to provide for filing of provisional specification and submission of complete specification within nine months.

e. After Independence, it was felt that the Indian Patents & Designs Act, 1911 was not fulfilling its objective. It was found desirable to enact comprehensive patent law owing to substantial changes in political and economic conditions in the country. Accordingly, the Government of India constituted a committee under the Chairmanship of Justice (Dr.) Bakshi Tek Chand, a retired Judge of Lahore High Court, in 1949 t o review the patent law in India in order to ensure that the patent system is conducive to the national interest. The terms of reference included:
   - To survey and report on the working of the patent system in India;
   - To examine the existing patent legislation in India and to make recommendations for improving it, particularly with reference to the provisions concerned with the prevention of abuse of patent rights;
   - To consider whether any special restrictions should be imposed on patent regarding food and medicine;
   - To suggest steps for ensuring effective publicity to the patent system and to patent literature, particularly as regards patents obtained by Indian inventors;
   - To consider the necessity and feasibility of setting up a National Patents Trust;
   - To consider the desirability or otherwise of regulating the profession of patent agents
   - To examine the working of the Patent Office and the services rendered by it to the public and make suitable recommendations for improvement; and
   - To report generally on any improvement that the Committee thinks fit to recommend for enabling the Indian Patent System to be more conducive to national interest by encouraging invention and the commercial development and use of inventions.

f. The committee submitted its interim report on 4th August, 1949 with recommendations for prevention of misuse or abuse of patent right in India and suggested amendments to sections 22, 23 & 23A of the Patents & Designs Act, 1911 on the lines of the United Kingdom Acts 1919 and 1949. The committee also observed that the Patents Act should contain clear indication to ensure that food and medicine and surgical and curative devices are made available to the public at the cheapest price commensurate with giving reasonable compensation to the patentee.

g. Based on the above recommendation of the Committee, the 1911 Act was amended in 1950(Act XXXII of 1950) in relation to working of inventions and compulsory licence/revocation. Other provisions were related to endorsement of the patent with the words 'licence of right' on an application by the Government so that the Controller could grant licences. In 1952 (Act LXX of 1952) an amendment was made to provide compulsory licence in relation to patents in respect of food and medicines, insecticide, germicide or fungicide and a process for producing substance or any invention relating to surgical or curative devices. The compulsory licence was also available on notification by the Central Government. Based on the recommendations of the Committee, a bill was introduced in the Parliament in 1953 (Bill No.59 of 1953). However, the Government did not press for the consideration of the bill and it was allowed to lapse.

h. In 1957, the Government of India appointed Justice N. Rajagopala Ayyangar Committee to examine the question of revision of the Patent Law and advise government accordingly. The report of the Committee, which comprised of two parts, was submitted in September, 1959. The first part dealt with general aspects of the Patent Law and the second part gave detailed note on the several clauses of the lapsed bills 1953. The first part also dealt with evils of the patent system and solution with recommendations in regards to the law. The committee recommended retention of the Patent System, despite its shortcomings. This report recommended major changes in the law which formed the basis of the introduction of the Patents Bill, 1965. This bill was introduced in the Lok Sabha on 21st September, 1965, which however lapsed. In 1967, again an amended bill was introduced which was referred to a Joint Parliamentary Committee and on the final recommendation of the Committee, the Patents Act, 1970 was passed. This Act repealed and replaced the 1911 Act so far as the patents law was concerned. However, the 1911 Act continued to be applicable to designs. Most of the provisions of the 1970 Act were brought into force on 20 th April 1972 with publication of the Patent Rules, 1972.

i. This Act remained in force for about 24 years without any change till December 1994. An ordinance effecting certain changes in the Act was issued on 31 st December 1994, which ceased to operate after six months. Subsequently, another ordinance was issued in 1999. This ordinance was subsequently replaced by t he Patents (Amendment) Act, 1999 that was brought into force retrospectively from 1 st January, 1995. The amended Act provided for filing of applications for product patents in the areas of drugs, pharmaceuticals and agro chemicals though such patents were not allowed. However, such applications were to be examined only after 31-12-2004. Meanwhile, the applicants could be allowed Exclusive Marketing Rights (EMR) to sell or distribute these products in India, subject to fulfilment of certain conditions.

j. The second amendment to the 1970 Act was made through the Patents (Amendment) Act, 2002 (Act 38 0f 2002). This Act came into force on 20 th May 2003 with the introduction of the new Patent Rules, 2003 by replacing the earlier Patents Rules, 1972

k. The third amendment to the Patents Act 1970 was introduced through the Patents (Amendment) Ordinance, 2004 w.e.f. 1 st January, 2005. This Ordinance was later replaced by the Patents (Amendment) Act 2005 (Act 15 Of 2005) on 4 th April, 2005 which was brought into force from 1-1-2005.

PATENTS RULES

Under the provisions of section 159 of the Patents Act, 1970 the Central Government is empowered to make rules for implementing the Act and regulating patent administration. Accordingly, the Patents Rules, 1972 were notified and brought into force w.e.f. 20.4.1972. These Rules were amended from time to time till 20 May 2003 when new Patents Rules, 2003 were brought into force by replacing the 1972 rules. These rules were further amended by the Patents (Amendment) Rules, 2005 and the Patents (Amendment) Rules, 2006. The last amendments are made effective from 5 th May 2006.

COPYRIGHT & RELATED RIGHTS

The subject-matter of copyright is the literary, dramatic and musical or artistic work, a cinematograph film and a sound recording. Literary work includes computer programmes, tables and compilations including computer databases.

The object of this right is not the material thing produced, but the form impressed upon it by the maker. The picture, in the abstract sense of the artistic form made by visible by that paint and canvas, belongs to him who made it.

TRADE MARK

Trademark is anything which identifies the origin of the goods or services. It can be a name, symbol, logo, colour, sound etc. Trademark symbolizes the value or goodwill associated with the goods and its specific source. It distinguishes one firm from others. Benefits of trademarks are several-fold:

It helps consumers to identify products with desirable attributes quickly. It encourages firms to improve quality of their product. In absence of any identification mark, it would be difficult to distinguish the duplicates from high quality products. This will lower the incentive of the firm to make high quality products as the returns would be same as that of inferior products. Trademark protection gives a "monopoly power" over the distinctive trademark in the sense that others are debarred from using the same or a confusingly similar trademark. However this kind of monopoly power does not involve any welfare loss as its aim is not to prevent similar products but only to prevent use of similar or deceptive marks with the aim of confusing the consumer. As a result, trademarks have mostly a positive incentive effect. It may seem that overall the economics of trademark protection and the intellectual property law of those marks are non-conflicting. There are, however, some grey areas:

Issue of umbrella branding (brand extension) whereby a company uses a trademark made famous by sale of one product to enter into another market. For example Reliance entering retail marketing, entertainment industry, restaurants etc. Such brand extension strategies raise legitimate competition policy issues as a firm is essentially using an advantage acquired in other market to sell its products. Consumers are likely to try the products associated with a well-known brand name rather than an unknown brand with same quality making it difficult for a new company to enter the market.

Compulsory licensing of trademarks - Competition policies forcing companies to license their trademark may result in shoddy work at premium price associated with the brand. This will also ruin the reputation associated with the brand. This would affect the firm 's incentive to provide consumers with high quality goods.

PATENTS

The subject-matter of a patent-right is an invention. He whose skill or labour produces the idea of a new process, instrument or manufacture has that idea as his own in law. He alone is entitled to use it and to draw from it the profit inherent in it.

Geographical Indications

A geographical indication is a name or sign used on certain products which corresponds to a specific geographical location or origin (e.g. a town, region, or country). India, as a member of the World Trade Organization (WTO), enacted the Geographical Indications of Goods (Registration and Protection) Act, 1999 has come into force with effect from 15 September 2003. GIs have been defined under Article 22(1) of the WTO Agreement on Trade-Related Aspects of Intellectual Property Rights(TRIPS) Agreement as: "Indications which identify a good as originating in the territory of a member, or a region or a locality in that territory, where a given quality, reputation or characteristic of the good is essentially attributable to its geographic origin."

Industrial Design

Industrial design means only the features of shape, configuration, pattern, ornament or composition of lines or colours applied to any article whether in two dimensional or three dimensional or both forms, by any industrial process or means whether manual, mechanical or chemical, separate or combined, which in the finished article appeal to and are judged solely by the eye; but does not include any mode or principle of construction and does not include any trademark.

Lay-Out Designs of Integrated Circuits

In the case of layout designs of integrated circuits the property consists in the exclusive right to apply the layout design registered under statute in relation to the class of goods for which it is registered for a prescribed period. The right can also be licensed for use by third party or assign to any person.

Protection of Undisclosed Information:

Confidential information and know-how can be protected only so long as the owner is able to keep them secret and takes action against unlawful use of such information by others by an action for breach of confidence or contract.

The law relating to property and intellectual property has similarities regarding the nature the mode of acquisition, the nature of rights conferred, the commercial exploitation of those rights, the enforcement of those rights and the remedies available against infringement of those rights. Property rights include not all a person's right but only his corporeal property rights consisting of material things. But intellectual property is in the nature of intangible incorporeal property. The rights of intellectual property are created by statute. The invention may relate to a new product or an improvement of an existing product or a new process of manufacturing an existing or a new product. The acquisition of the monopoly of intellectual property, the conditions to be satisfied for acquisition, its duration, the licensing of this monopoly rights or their assignment to others are strictly governed by the statutes. The commercial exploitation of intellectual property may be assigned his rights or license them to industrialists for a lump sum payment or on a royalty basis the right of material property is transferred for sufficient consideration. As per the TRIPS Agreement, member countries of WTO may provide for criminal procedures and penalties to be applied in other cases of infringement of IPRs, in particular where they are committed willfully on a commercial scale. In respect of trademark, the civil remedied available against infringement are an injunction, either damages or an account of profits and the delivery-up of the infringing articles for destruction. Civil and criminal remedies are available against infringement of intellectual property.

Recent Trends in IPS

Invention in Softwares

While identifying what kind of protection is to be granted to an IP, one needs to identify on what is the "intellectual" in that property, is it an invention or a literary work? Software i.e. computer programme has found its mode of protection in the Indian Copyright Act, 1957. S. 2(ffc) defines computer programme as "a set of instructions expressed in words, codes, schemes or in any other form, including a machine readable medium, capable of causing a computer to perform a particular task or achieve a particular result". These are as such included in "literary work" defined in S.2 (o) of the Act, "literary work includes computer programmes, tables, and compilations including computer literary databases."

On the other hand, the Indian Patents Act, 1970 expressly excludes computer programmes from the ambit of patentable subject- matter, visavis including it in Section 3 what are not inventions, S. 3 (k) a mathematical or business method or a computer programs per se or algorithms; and S.3 (m) a mere scheme or rule or method of performing mental act or method of playing game; expressly excludes computer programs from patentable subject matter.

However, the Patent Office prescribes guidelines to outline various regulations and explanations regarding patentability of computer related inventions (CRIs), last updated on 30 June, 2017.

The legislative intent to attach the suffix per se to computer programme is evident by the following view expressed by Joint Parliamentary Committee while introducing Patents (Amendment) Act, 2002:

"In the new proposed clause (k) the words "per se" have been inserted. This change has been proposed because sometimes the computer programme may include certain other things, ancillary thereto or development thereon. The intention here in not to reject them for grant of patent if they are inventions. However, the computer programmes as such are not intended to be granted patent. This amendment has been proposed to clarify the purpose".

Example

1. In Accenture Global Service GMBH Vs. The Assistant Controller Of Patents & Designs, relates to Indian patent application number 1398/DELNP/2003, which is now a granted patent as patent number 256171, whose present legal status at the patent office database is, "Enforce with Due date of next renewal as 21/02/2017". This patent application was initially refused for patent registration by patent office under the provisions of Section 3(k) of the Indian patents act.
   However, the patent applicant appealed before the IPAB and as per the controller's decision, it was held that the instant invention as claimed is not software per se but, a system is claimed which is having the improvement in web services and software. Accordingly, it was held that the invention since not falling in the category of section 3(k), viz software per se, corresponding objection was waived and the patent was granted.
2. Nissan Motor filed a series of patent applications in 2017 with respect to the computer softwares inter alia a travel control device and method for vehicle comprising: a target acquisition means for acquiring target information which includes the location of an avoidance target that exists near a vehicle, a vehicle information acquisition function for acquiring information which includes the location of a vehicle, and drive assist device which is a driving assistance device for assisting driving when a host vehicle is changing lanes wherein the device is provided with; a position measurement means for measuring the position of the host vehicle; a detection means provided to the host vehicle the detection means detecting the conditions around the host vehicle; a database for recording map information.
   The aforementioned claims of Nissan Motor are claims concerning Computer Related Inventions (CRIs) which mean to perform the function as mentioned above and hence, are termed as means + functions defined in the Guidelines for Examination of Computer Related Inventions.
   In light of the guidelines published by the Indian patent office for examination of software patents / computer related inventions (CRIs), software patents can be applied in India by way of combination of hardware and software features, which are novel, inventive and possess industrial applications. It may be categorized as hardware based inventions: apparatus/ system/ device, Method/process based, Computer program product/computer readable medium. Unless the software is a computer program per se, it may be granted a patent in India, and hence Nissan stands a fair chance to be granted the aforementioned patents. However, in the case of any conflict between The Indian patents Act and the said guidelines, the Act is to prevail and for such instances, it is essential to have rules with the effect of laws incorporating CRIs in patentable subject matter.
   On the same lines European Patent Convention expressly excludes computer programs, per se, from the purview of patentable subject matter.

Whereas in USA, there is no specific exclusion of software or business methods from patentable subject matter. The law states that the subject matter, to be patentable, must be a useful process, machine, manufacture or composition of matter. According to the US Supreme Court, the Congress intended the statutory patentable subject matter to include "anything under the sun made by man," but the laws of nature, natural phenomena and abstract ideas are three specific areas which are not patentable.

Emerging New IPS

Seps and Frand Licensing

A patent that protects technology essential to a standard is called a standard-essential patent. A standardis a document that sets out requirements for a specific item, material, component, system or service, or describes in detail a particular method or procedure. For example, a modern laptop computer implements around 251 interoperability standards.

The concept of SEPs evolved in India when Ericson in 2011 objected to the importation of handsets by Kingtech Electronics (India), claiming that the handsets infringed several of their SEPs in AMR Codec (Adaptive Multi-Rate) technology. The Indian Patents Act, 1970 does not contain any special provision for SEPs. Although, the same have been recognized by the jurisprudence, SEP is defined as "...for a technology that forms a part of a standard, the patent is regarded as an essential patent for such standard. An essential patent can be said to be a patent that corresponds to an industry standard. The same standard is mutually agreed by various service providers, equipment manufacturers etc to be mandatorily implemented for a particular technology (such standards are recognized and implemented by the concerned government authority as well). It is meant to ensure that complete compatibility is achieved. It is impossible to claim compatibility with a technology (as defined by the concerned standards) without actually infringing the specific patent (and hence the requirement to obtain a license).

Following Cases in India

1. Ericsson and Micromax case,
2. Ericsson and Intex case
3. Ericsson and Best It World (India)
4. Ericsson and Xiaomi Technology
5. Ericsson and Lava International Private Limited
6. Telefonaktiebolaget lm Ericsson (publ) v.Competition Commission of India and another,

have established clearly that the necessary steps to be taken by any company / legal entity, intending to incorporate any technology in its product that is standardized by any SSO (Standard Setting Organisation). It has to,

1. Incorporate the patent which is essential to obtain that standard.
2. To enable themselves of the use of aforesaid patent, without infringing it, they require obtaining a license from the holder of the aforesaid patent.

However, such a situation can have an obvious monopolistic outcome in the hands of the patent holder, and to curb such a situation before-hand, the patent holder has its commitments as a member of the SSOs, these commitments are known as FRAND commitments. Whereas the question remains as to what are the clear boundaries of fair, reasonable and non-discriminatory license terms, is to be determined by the consensus reached by the parties, and if the parties are unable to reach such consensus, they may appoint a mediator for the purpose, and yet if the party seeking the license considers the license terms to be abusive of the dominant powers of the patentee, the CCI holds proper jurisdiction to inquire and investigate into the same.

GOODS AND SERVICES TAX (GST)

GST is an Indirect Tax which has replaced many Indirect Taxes in India. The Goods and Service Tax Act was passed in the Parliament on 29th March 2017. The Act came into effect on 1st July 2017; Goods & Services Tax Law in India is a comprehensive, multi-stage, destination-based tax that is levied on every value addition.

In simple words, Goods and Service Tax (GST) is an indirect tax levied on the supply of goods and services. This law has replaced many indirect tax laws that previously existed in India.GST is one indirect tax for the entire country.

Under the GST regime, the tax is levied at every point of sale. In the case of intra-state sales, Central GST and State GST are charged. Inter-state sales are chargeable to Integrated GST.

Now let us try to understand the definition of Goods and Service Tax - "GST is a comprehensive, multi-stage, destination-based tax that is levied on every value addition."

The manufacturer who makes biscuits buys flour, sugar and other material. The value of the inputs increases when the sugar and flour are mixed and baked into biscuits.

The manufacturer then sells the biscuits to the warehousing agent who packs large quantities of biscuits and labels it. That is another addition of value after which the warehouse sells it to the retailer.

The retailer packages the biscuits in smaller quantities and invests in the marketing of the biscuits thus increasing its value.

GST is levied on these value additions i.e. the monetary value added at each stage to achieve the final sale to the end customer.

Consider goods manufactured in Maharashtra and are sold to the final consumer in Karnataka. Since Goods & Service Tax is levied at the point of consumption. So, the entire tax revenue will go to Karnataka and not Maharashtra.

The GST journey began in the year 2000 when a committee was set up to draft law. It took 17 years from then for the Law to evolve. In 2017 the GST Bill was passed in the Lok Sabha and Rajya Sabha. On 1st July 2017 the GST Law came into force.

In the earlier indirect tax regime, there were many indirect taxes levied by both state and centre. States mainly collected taxes in the form of Value Added Tax (VAT). Every state had a different set of rules and regulations.

Interstate sale of goods was taxed by the Centre. CST (Central State Tax) was applicable in case of interstate sale of goods. Other than above there were many indirect taxes like entertainment tax, octroi and local tax that was levied by state and centre.

This led to a lot of overlapping of taxes levied by both state and centre.

For example, when goods were manufactured and sold, excise duty was charged by the centre. Over and above Excise Duty, VAT was also charged by the State. This lead to a tax on tax also known as the cascading effect of taxes.

The following is the list of indirect taxes in the pre-GST regime:

- Central Excise Duty
- Additional Duties of Excise
- Special Additional Duty of Customs
- State VAT
- Purchase Tax
- Entertainment Tax
- Taxes on advertisements
- Duties of Excise
- Additional Duties of Customs
- Cess
- Central Sales Tax
- Luxury Tax
- Entry Tax
- Taxes on lotteries, betting, and gambling

CGST, SGST, and IGST has replaced all the above taxes.

However, the chargeability of CST for Inter-state purchase at a concessional rate of 2%, by issue and utilisation of c-Form is still prevalent for certain Non-GST goods such as:

(i) Petroleum crude; (ii) High-speed diesel;
(iii) Motor spirit (commonly known as petrol); (iv) Natural gas;
(v) Aviation turbine fuel; and (vi) Alcoholic liquor for human consumption.

In respect of following transactions only:

- Resale
- Use in manufacturing or processing
- Use in the telecommunication network or in mining or in the generation or distribution of electricity or any other power

A single common "Goods and Services Tax (GST)" was proposed and given a go-ahead in 1999 during a meeting between the Prime Minister Atal Bihari Vajpayee and his economic advisory panel. Mr Vajpayee set up a committee headed by the then finance minister of West Bengal, Asim Dasgupta to design a GST model. Later, Finance Minister P Chidambaram in February 2006 continued work on the same. It finally was implemented on July 1st, 2017 to be a comprehensive, destination-based indirect tax that has replaced various indirect taxes that were implemented by the State and Centre such as VAT, excise duty, and others. The government of India also formed a GST Council to govern the rules the Goods and Services Tax.

The GST council is the key decision-making body that will take all important decisions regarding the GST. The GST Council dictates tax rate, tax exemption, the due date of forms, tax laws, and tax deadlines, keeping in mind special rates and provisions for some states. The predominant responsibility of the GST Council is to ensure to have one uniform tax rate for goods and services across the nation.

The Goods and Services Tax (GST) is governed by the GST Council. Article 279 (1) of the amended Indian Constitution states that the GST Council has to be constituted by the President within 60 days of the commencement of the Article 279A.

According to the article, GST Council will be a joint forum for the Centre and the States. It consists of the following members:

- The Union Finance Minister, Arun Jaitley will be the Chairperson
- As a member, the Union Minister of State will be in charge of Revenue of Finance
- The Minister in charge of finance or taxation or any other Minister nominated by each State government, as members.

Article 279A (4) specifies that the Council will make recommendations to the Union and the States on the important issues related to GST, such as, the goods and services will be subject or exempted from the Goods and Services Tax.

They lay down GST laws, principles that govern the following:

- Place of Supply
- Threshold limits
- GST rates on goods and services
- Special rates for raising additional resources during a natural calamity or disaster
- Special GST rates for certain States

The GST Council meets to discuss and lay GST laws that will benefit dealers across the nation. The outcome of the previous latest GST Council meet was that the Council decided to implement GST provisions on e-way bills that requires goods of more than Rs.50,000 in value to be registered online before they can be moved. They have also extended the deadline to file GSTR-1.

The Council will also set up anti-profiteering screening committees that will make the National Anti-Profiteering Authority stronger under the GST law.

Other than laying GST laws, the GST Council have taken decisions as such:

- The threshold limit for exemption of GST would be set at Rs.20 lakh per year for all States (except for special category states)
- The threshold for special States is set at Rs 10 lakh per year
- For composition scheme is set at Rs. 75 lakh for all States (except for the North East States and Himachal Pradesh - Set at Rs 50 lakh per year)
- Ice cream, tobacco, pan masala, and other edible ice manufacturers shall not be eligible for composition levy (except for restaurant services)

GST Council also looks into drafting GST rules on registration, payment, valuation, input tax credit, composition, return, refund and invoice, and transitional provisions, among other things.

BENEFITS OF GST

Logistics. In a vast country like India, the logistics sector forms the backbone of the economy. We can fairly assume that a well organized and mature logistics industry has the potential to leapfrog the "Make In India" initiative of the government of India to its desired position.

E-commerce. The e-commerce sector in India has been growing by leaps and bounds. In many ways, GST will help the e-com sector's continued growth but the long-term effects will be particularly interesting because the GST law specifically proposes a Tax Collection at Source (TCS) mechanism, which e-commerce companies are not too happy with. The current rate of TCS is at 1%.

Pharma. On the whole, GST is benefiting the pharma and healthcare industries. It will create a level playing field for generic drug makers, boost medical tourism and simplify the tax structure. If there is any concern whatsoever, then it relates to the pricing structure (as per latest news). The pharma sector is hoping for a tax respite as it will make affordable healthcare easier to access by all.

Telecommunications. In the telecom sector, prices will come down after GST. Manufacturers will save on costs through efficient management of inventory and by consolidating their warehouses. Handset manufacturers will find it easier to sell their equipment as GST has negated the need to set up state-specific entities, and transfer stocks. The will also save up on logistics costs.

Textile. The Indian textile industry provides employment to a large number of skilled and unskilled workers in the country. It contributes about 10% of the total annual export, and this value is likely to increase under GST. GST would affect the cotton value chain of the textile industry which is chosen by most small medium enterprises as it previously attracted zero central excise duty (under optional route).

Real Estate. The real estate sector is one of the most pivotal sectors of the Indian economy, playing an important role in employment generation in India. The impact of GST on the real estate sector cannot be fully assessed as it largely depends on the tax rates. However, the sector will see substantial benefits from GST implementation, as it has brought to the industry much-required transparency and accountability.

Agriculture. The agricultural sector is the largest contributing sector the overall Indian GDP. It covers around 16% of Indian GDP. One of the major issues faced by the agricultural sector is the transportation of agri-products across state lines all over India. GST will resolve the issue of transportation.

FMCG. The FMCG sector is experiencing significant savings in logistics and distribution costs as the GST has eliminated the need for multiple sales depots.

Freelancers. Freelancing in India is still a nascent industry and the rules and regulations for this chaotic industry are still up in the air. But with GST, it will become much easier for freelancers to file their taxes as they can easily do it online. They are taxed as service providers, and the new tax structure has brought about coherence and accountability in this sector.

Automobiles. The automobile industry in India is a vast business producing a large number of cars annually, fueled mostly by the huge population of the country. Under the previous tax system, there were several taxes applicable to this sector like excise, VAT, sales tax, road tax, motor vehicle tax, registration duty which will be subsumed by GST.

Startups. With increased limits for registration, a DIY compliance model, tax credit on purchases, and a free flow of goods and services, the GST regime truly augurs well for the Indian startup scene. Previously, many Indian states had different VAT laws which were confusing for companies that have a pan-India presence, especially the e-com sector. All of this has changed under GST.

GST WORKING

The idea of moving towards the GST was first mooted by the then Union Finance Minister in his Budget for 2006-07. The talks of ushering in GST took concrete shape with the introduction of Constitution (122nd Amendment) Bill, 2014. The Bill was passed by the Parliament on 8 August 2016. This was followed by the ratification of the Bill by more than 15 states. On 12 April 2017, the Central Government enacted four GST bills:

- Central GST (CGST) Bill
- Integrated GST (IGST) Bill
- Union Territory GST (UTGST) Bill
- The GST (Compensation to States) Bill

In a short span of time, all the states approved their State GST (SGST) laws. Union territories with legislatures, i.e., Delhi and Puducherry, have adopted the SGST Act and the other 5 union territories without legislatures have adopted the UTGST Act.

The GST Council, a recommendatory body consisting of representatives of Central as well as state governments, has met on several occasions and taken important decisions relating to tax rate structure, exemptions, rules, composition scheme etc. Over the period, the Council has recommended a reduction in the tax rates of various goods and services. It is also considering the various issues faced by trade and industry and endeavoring to simplify the new tax regime and ease compliance.

On the compliance front, all registered persons have to file monthly returns in Form GSTR-3B (containing a summary of outward and inward supplies) by the 20th of the succeeding month. Additionally, an invoice-wise return of outward supplies needs to be submitted in Form GSTR-1 by the 10th of the succeeding month. Taxpayers with turnover upto INR 1.5 crores can file Form GSTR-1 on quarterly basis. The Government has suspended the requirement of filing Form GSTR-2 (containing details of inward supplies) and GSTR-3 (a consolidated statement of inward and outward supplies).

The GST Council has approved a simplified GST return format wherein the taxpayers will be required to file only one monthly return. Input tax credit will be available based on invoice details of outward supplies uploaded by the supplier. Taxpayers having turnover below INR 5 crores will have an option to file return on quarterly basis.

Under GST, there is a provision for the person in charge of a conveyance to carry electronic way bill (e-way bill) if the consignment value exceeds INR50,000. E-way bill can be generated through various modes such as web (online), Android app, SMS using Bulk Upload Tool and API-based site-to-site integration. The e-way bill system has become effective for inter-state as well as intra-state movement of goods.

GST has been a major transition in the Indian tax framework. It has evolved significantly from the time of its inception. It is expected that Government's pro-active measures and industry's active participation, will make it a truly "Good and Simple Tax" in the times to come.

DUAL GST

Many countries in the world have a single unified GST system i.e. a single tax applicable throughout the country. However, in federal countries like Brazil and Canada, a dual GST system is prevalent whereby GST is levied by both the federal and state or provincial governments. In India, a dual GST is proposed whereby a Central Goods and Services Tax (CGST) and a State Goods and Services Tax (SGST) will be levied on the taxable value of every transaction of supply of goods and services.

Impact on Prices of Goods and Services:-The GST is expected to foster increased efficiencies in the economic system thereby lowering the cost of supply of goods and services. Further, in the Indian context, there is an expectation that the aggregate incidence of the dual GST will be lower than the present incidence of the multiple indirect taxes in force. Consequently, the implementation of the GST is expected to bring about, if not in the near term but in the medium to long term, a reduction in the prices of goods and services. The expectation is that the dealers would start passing on the benefit of the reduced tax incidence to the customers by way of reduced prices. As regards services, it could be that their short term prices would go up given the expectation of an increase in the tax rate from the present 10% to approximately 14% to 16%.

Benefits of Dual GST

The Dual GST is expected to be a simple and transparent tax with one or two CGST and SGST rates. The dual GST is expected to result in:-

- reduction in the number of taxes at the Central and State level
- decrease in effective tax rate for many goods
- removal of the current cascading effect of taxes
- reduction of transaction costs of the taxpayers through simplified tax compliance
- increased tax collections due to wider tax base and better compliance

Certainty of implementation. The Finance Minister has made a categorical statement in Parliament that GST will be implemented on April 1, 2013. In his subsequent media interactions, he has further indicated that he is keen to implement the GST even if some of the States are not ready or willing to implement GST by this date. Accordingly, based on the present indications, as also on the basis of our subsequent interactions with senior Government Officials, we believe that the April 1, 2013 timeline for introduction of the dual GST will be met.

Who would be impacted. All businesses, whether engaged in sales / supply of goods or supply of services, would be impacted by GST. The impact would be on supply chains, ERP, product pricing, dealer margins etc.

Applicability to service providers. Unlike the transition from the sales tax regime to the VAT, where only businesses dealing in goods were affected, in the case of GST, as the name suggests, both goods and service providers will be impacted. Thus, even pure service providers need to plan for the transition to the GST.

Time to Plan for GST. The draft laws will clarify finer aspects of GST such as rates, classification and compliances. However, based on the material in the public domain, one can begin with spreading awareness among various stakeholders within the organization and identifying broad areas of action before the draft laws are published. Experience of VAT implementation suggests that there may not be enough lead-time available between the date of announcement of GST implementation and the actual date of GST implementation.

Taxable event. The "Taxable event" will be the "supply of goods? and the "supply of services?. Hence, the current taxable events such as 'manufacture of goods', 'sale of goods?' and ' rendition of services' will not be relevant under the GST regime.

Applicability of both CGST and the SGST on all transactions. A transaction of 'supply of goods' will attract both the CGST & SGST as applicable on goods. Similarly, a 'supply of service' will attract both the CGST & SGST as applicable on services.

GST collection model. GST is collected on the value added at each stage of sale or purchase in the supply chain. The tax on value addition is ensured through a tax credit mechanism throughout the supply chain. GST paid on the procurement of goods and services is available for set-off against the GST payable on the supply of goods or services. The idea is that the final consumer will bear the GST charged to him by the last person in the supply chain. It is thus a consumption based indirect tax.

Applicability of taxes on imports of goods. It must be understood that customs duties will remain outside the GST regime. Thus, the applicable basic customs duty will continue to be leviable on import of goods. In addition, both the CGST and the SGST are expected to be levied on imports of goods. Thus, the additional duty of customs in lieu of excise (CVD) and the additional duty of customs in lieu of sales tax / VAT will both be subsumed in the import GST.

Tax on import of services and person liabile to pay. Importation of services will be taxed and both the CGST & the SGST will apply on such imports. The tax will be payable on a reverse charge mechanism and the importer of services will hence need to self declare and pay the tax. As to which State will have authority to collect the relevant SGST, this will be determined based on the place of supply rules that the government is expected to notify for this purpose.

Separate enactments for the Central and State GST. There will be separate enactments. The CGST will be a common code throughout India. Further, each State will legislate its own enactment to levy and collect the SGST. However, it is understood that a white paper will be released by the Federal Government/Empowered Committee of State Finance Ministers based on which each State will legislate. The expectation is therefore is that a majority of the provisions will be uniform across the States.

Expected aggregate rate of GST. The aggregate rate of GST, across the Central and State GST, is expected to be approximately 16%. This is currently the subject matter of discussion within the Empowered Committee.

Different rates for goods and for services. It is expected that there will be one single rate of GST on services at the Central and State level and the understanding is that there would be not one but a few rates of Central and State GST for goods.

Carry forward of Input Tax Credits (ITC) and CENVAT Credit (CC) balances. Going by the precedence at the time of VAT implementation, it is believed that the accumulated ITC and CC will both be allowed to be carried forward under the GST regime, albeit upon fulfilment of prescribed conditions, if any.

Refund of un-utilised CC on inputs and input services. It is envisaged that under the proposed Dual GST model there would be refund of unutilized accumulated CCs at the end of each fiscal year and that refunds would not be restricted only to those relating to exports.

Cross utilization of credits between goods and services. Under the GST regime, the incidence of tax will be on supplies, be it supplies of goods or services. The taxes will be levied in parallel by the Centre and the States who will levy the CGST and SGST respectively on each supply of goods/ services. Accordingly, the cross utilization of credits for goods and services would be allowed subject to the fact that cross utilization of credits between the CGST and SGST would not be permissible.

Threshold limits for e-levy of GST. No threshold limits have been prescribed as yet. However, it has been indicated that the thresholds will be uniform and will be based on the cumulative turnover of goods and services. Dealers with turnover below these thresholds will not be covered under the ambit of the GST.

Uniformity under the various indirect tax legislations. The Dual GST model envisages uniform threshold limits under both the Central and the State GST.

Exemptions from GST, lists of exempted goods and exempted services. Under the GST, exemptions are expected to be minimal. Further, a common list of exemptions for both the Central and State GST with little flexibility for States to deviate therefrom is envisaged.

Benefits availed presently by EOUs (exemption from excise duty and Central Sales Tax (CST) on domestic procurement of goods). CST will be phased out and will have no place in the GST regime. It is expected that the benefits presently availed by the EOUs by way of exemptions would continue to be available in the GST regime as well.

Status of Software Technology Parks/ 100% Export Oriented Units/Special Economic Zone units. Typically, in view of the common list of exemptions, the exemption would extend to both the CGST and the State GST. With regard to the position on the Software Technology Parks/ 100% Export Oriented Units/Special Economic Zone units, it is envisaged that the status quo will remain.

Continuation of exemption currently available :-In view of the fact that under the GST scheme, exemptions would be minimal, it may not be correct to proceed on the assumption that the present exemptions would continue under the GST dispensation.

Position with regard to investors who enjoy area-based exemptions or who have entered into a Memorandum of Understanding with the Governments in respect of exemption, subsidy etc.:-All exemption schemes are proposed to be converted to post-tax cash refund schemes. However, it is advised that companies approach the Government to negotiate their MOUs so that their interests are not jeopardized and that the incentives granted under the present tax regime are protected.

Taxation of Inter-State sale transactions: Presently, inter-State sales are subject to Central Sales Tax (CST), which is origin based. However, the GST regime would work under a destination / consumption based concept and hence the tax on inter- State sale transactions will accrue to the destination State. As a corollary, it will be zero rated in the Origin State.

Treatment of stock transfers. The taxable event will be the supply of goods and therefore the stock transfers could be taxed. However, certainty will only emerge once the GST law is finalized.

Taxation of inter State supply of services. Detailed place of supply rules will be framed for such transactions. Taxation of such supplies will however continue to pose a challenge. Practices currently being followed in the European Union, Canada and Brazil are being studied. Policymakers are also looking at different options of taxing inter State supplies of services based on whether they are Business to Business (B2B) or Business to Customer (B2C)

Fresh registrations and registration of existing VAT and Service tax dealers :-The position in this regard is not clear at present. However, the rules are expected to be assessee- friendly in this regard with appropriate soft-landing provisions for the transition phase.

Single return or multiple returns. It is expected that a single return will be required to be prepared by the assessee and copies filed with the Central GST and State GST authorities. The draft GST laws / Rules will provide further details.

Process of assessment under the dual GST. The dual GST is expected to be a self assessed tax. The Tax administration would have powers to audit and re-assess the taxpayers on a selective basis.

Relevancy of concepts / principles surrounding "manufacture?, "MRP based valuation?, "works contracts? etc. under the GST. As GST is on all economic value addition involving all supplies of goods and services, the above concepts/principles could lose relevance under the GST.

Refunds on exports. In view of the Government policy that no taxes should be exported, refund of GST paid on inputs should be available in case of exports of goods and services, which will both be zero rated.

Uniformity in classification of goods, procedures, forms etc. across the States:-Based on the current discussions in the Empowered Committee, it is expected that there should be uniformity in classification of goods, procedures and forms across States.

MULTIPLE CHOICE QUESTIONS

1. Which of the following is not an essential element of a valid contract?
(1) Offer (2) Acceptance
(3) Consideration (4) Cancellation

2. Which of the following is not a type of contract under the Indian Contract Act, 1872?
(1) Oral contract
(2) Written contract
(3) Implied contract
(4) Virtual contract

3. What is the legal age of majority for the purpose of entering into a contract in India?
(1) 18 years (2) 19 years
(3) 20 years (4) 21 years

4. What is the legal term used to describe a contract that is created by the conduct of the parties rather than through a written or spoken agreement?
(1) Implied contract (2) Unilateral contract
(3) Express contract (4) Void contract

5. Which of the following is not a type of free consent?
(1) Coercion
(2) Undue influence
(3) Misrepresentation
(4) Fraud

6. Which of the following is not a mode of discharge of a contract?
(1) Performance (2) Breach
(3) Frustration (4) Ratification

7. Which of the following is a right available to an aggrieved party in case of a breach of contract?
(1) Specific performance
(2) Monetary damages
(3) Restitution
(4) All of the above

8. Which of the following is not a quasi-contract under the Indian Contract Act, 1872?
(1) Quantum meruit (2) Quantum valebant
(3) Quantum sufficit (4) Unjust enrichment

9. Which of the following is an example of a void contract?
(1) A contract to sell an illegal substance
(2) A contract to sell a car with a clear title
(3) A contract to buy a piece of land from a government agency
(4) A contract to buy a TV from a retail store

10. Which of the following is not a requirement for a valid offer under the Indian Contract Act, 1872?
(1) The offer must be communicated to the offeree
(2) The offer must be made with a view to obtaining the acceptance of the offeree
(3) The offer must be made in writing
(4) The terms of the offer must be certain or capable of being made certain

11. Which of the following is not a type of consideration under the Indian Contract Act, 1872?
(1) Payment of money
(2) Performance of a legal duty
(3) Love and affection
(4) Promise to perform an act in the future

12. Which of the following is not a requirement for a valid acceptance under the Indian Contract Act, 1872?
(1) The acceptance must be communicated to the offeror
(2) The acceptance must be made with a view to accepting the offer
(3) The acceptance must be in writing
(4) The acceptance must be absolute and unqualified

13. Which of the following is not a type of free consent under the Indian Contract Act, 1872?
(1) Coercion
(2) Undue influence
(3) Misrepresentation
(4) Duress

14. Which of the following is not a consequence of coercion?
(1) The contract is voidable at the option of the party subjected to coercion

(2) The contract is voidable at the option of the party using coercion

(3) The party using coercion may be held criminally liable

(4) The party subjected to coercion may be entitled to damages

15. Which of the following is not a type of undue influence under the Indian Contract Act, 1872?

(1) Actual undue influence

(2) Constructive undue influence

(3) Presumptive undue influence

(4) Fraudulent undue influence

16. Which of the following is not a cause of frustration of a contract?

(1) Impossibility of performance

(2) Change of circumstances

(3) Failure of consideration

(4) Illegality

17. Which of the following is not a type of breach of contract?

(1) Actual breach

(2) Anticipatory breach

(3) Material breach

(4) Breach of friendship

18. Which of the following is not a remedy available to an aggrieved party in case of a breach of contract?

(1) Specific performance

(2) Rescission of the contract

(3) Monetary damages

(4) Spiritual intervention

19. Which of the following is an example of a quasi-contract?

(1) X agrees to sell his car to Y for Rs. 50,000 and Y agrees to buy the car for that amount

(2) X repairs Y's house and Y agrees to pay X for the repairs

(3) X promises to mow Y's lawn every week in exchange for free use of Y's swimming pool

(4) X promises to lend Rs. 10,000 to Y but later changes her mind

20. Which of the following is an example of a voidable contract?

(1) A contract entered into by a minor

(2) A contract entered into through fraud

(3) A contract entered into for an illegal purpose

(4) A contract entered into for a charitable purpose

21. Which of the following is an example of an express contract?

(1) A written contract signed by both parties

(2) A contract created by the conduct of the parties

(3) A contract created by law

(4) A contract created by a court of law

22. Which of the following is not a factor to consider when determining the capacity of a party to enter into a contract?

(1) Age (2) Mental soundness

(3) Gender (4) Legal status

23. Which of the following is a requirement for free consent under the Indian Contract Act, 1872?

(1) The consent must be obtained through fraud

(2) The consent must be obtained through undue influence

(3) The parties to the contract must be of equal social status

(4) None of the above

24. Which of the following is an example of a quasi-contract?

(1) X agrees to sell his car to Y for Rs. 50,000 and Y agrees to buy the car for that amount

(2) X repairs Y's house and Y agrees to pay X for the repairs

(3) X promises to mow Y's lawn every week in exchange for free use of Y's swimming pool

(4) X promises to lend Rs. 10,000 to Y but later changes her mind

25. Which of the following is an example of a condition precedent in a contract?

(1) X agrees to sell his car to Y if Y agrees to pay Rs. 50,000

(2) X agrees to perform a dance at Y's wedding party

(3) X agrees to lend Rs. 10,000 to Y if Y agrees to pay interest at the rate of 10%

(4) X agrees to mow Y's lawn every week in exchange for free use of Y's swimming pool

26. Which of the following is not a requirement for a contract to be discharged by performance?

(1) Performance must be exact

(2) Performance must be substantial

(3) Time of performance must be specified in the contract
(4) Performance must be completed within a reasonable time

27. Which of the following is not a consequence of fraud under the Indian Contract Act, 1872?
(1) The contract is voidable at the option of the party defrauded
(2) The party defrauded may be entitled to damages
(3) The party defrauded may be entitled to rescission of the contract
(4) The party using fraud may be held criminally liable

28. Which of the following is an example of a implied-in-fact contract?
(1) X agrees to sell his car to Y for Rs. 50,000 and Y agrees to buy the car for that amount
(2) X repairs Y's house and Y agrees to pay X for the repairs
(3) X promises to mow Y's lawn every week in exchange for free use of Y's swimming pool
(4) X promises to lend Rs. 10,000 to Y but later changes her mind

29. Which of the following is not a consequence of undue influence?
(1) The contract may be voidable at the option of the party subjected to undue influence
(2) The party using undue influence may be held criminally liable
(3) The contract may be voidable at the option of the party using undue influence
(4) The party subjected to undue influence may be entitled to damages

30. Which of the following is not a remedy available to an aggrieved party in case of anticipatory breach of contract?
(1) Rescission of the contract
(2) Monetary damages
(3) Specific performance
(4) Injunction

31. Which of the following is an example of a quasi-contract?
(1) X agrees to sell his car to Y for Rs. 50,000 and Y agrees to buy the car for that amount
(2) X repairs Y's house and Y agrees to pay X for the repairs
(3) X promises to mow Y's lawn every week in exchange for free use of Y's swimming pool
(4) X promises to lend Rs. 10,000 to Y but later changes her mind

32. Which of the following is not a factor to consider when determining the capacity of a party to enter into a contract?
(1) Age (2) Mental soundness
(3) Nationality (4) Legal status

33. Which of the following is not a requirement for a valid consideration under the Indian Contract Act, 1872?
(1) The consideration must move from the promisee
(2) The consideration must be in cash or money's worth
(3) The consideration must be adequate
(4) The consideration must have been given or promised at the desire of the promisor

34. Which of the following is an example of a void contract?
(1) A contract to sell an illegal substance
(2) A contract to deliver a legal substance
(3) A contract to buy a piece of land from a government agency
(4) A contract to lend money to a friend

35. Which of the following is an example of a collateral contract?
(1) X agrees to sell his car to Y for Rs. 50,000 and Y agrees to buy the car for that amount
(2) X repairs Y's house and Y agrees to pay X for the repairs
(3) X promises to mow Y's lawn every week in exchange for free use of Y's swimming pool
(4) X promises to pay for Y's medical bills if Y promises to take care of X's pet

36. Which of the following is not a remedy available to an aggrieved party in case of breach of contract?
(1) Specific performance
(2) Rescission of the contract
(3) Punitive damages
(4) Monetary damages

37. Which of the following is not a cause of frustration of a contract?
(1) Impossibility of performance
(2) Change of circumstances

(3) Failure of consideration
(4) Illegality

38. Which of the following is not a type of free consent?
(1) Coercion
(2) Undue influence
(3) Misrepresentation
(4) Duress

39. Which of the following is not a requirement for a valid offer under the Indian Contract Act, 1872?
(1) The terms of the offer must be certain
(2) The offer must be communicated to the offeree
(3) The offer must be accepted within 30 days
(4) The offer must be made with a view to obtaining the acceptance of the offeree

40. Which of the following is not a requirement for a valid acceptance under the Indian Contract Act, 1872?
(1) The acceptance must be communicated to the offeror
(2) The acceptance must be absolute and unqualified
(3) The acceptance must be in writing
(4) The acceptance must be made with a view to accepting the offer

Directions: Each of the following items consists of two statements, one labelled as Assertion (A) and other labelled as Reason (R). You are to examine these two statements carefully and decide if the (A) and the (R) are individually true and if so, whether (R) is the correct explanation of (A). Select your answers to these items using the codes given below:
(1) Both (A) and (R) are true and the (R) is a correct explanation of the (A).
(2) Both (A) and (R) are true, but the (R) is not a correct explanation of the (A).
(3) The (A) is true, but the (R) is false.
(4) The (A) is false, but the (R) is true.

41. **Assertion (A):** A contract is an agreement enforceable by law.
Reason: An agreement is enforceable by law only if it satisfies the essential elements of a valid contract.

42. **Assertion (A):** A void contract is a contract that is not enforceable by law.
Reason: A void contract is a contract that does not satisfy the essential elements of a valid contract.

43. Which of the following is not a type of special contract?
(1) Contract of indemnity
(2) Contract of guarantee
(3) Contract of sale
(4) Contract of bailment

44. Which of the following is not a party to a contract of indemnity?
(1) Indemnifier (2) Indemnitee
(3) Beneficiary (4) None of these

45. What is the primary purpose of a contract of indemnity?
(1) To pool risk between two parties
(2) To transfer risk from one party to another
(3) To compensate for loss or damage suffered by one party
(4) To create a partnership between two parties

46. What is the difference between a contract of indemnity and a contract of guarantee?
(1) A contract of indemnity involves two parties, while a contract of guarantee involves three parties.
(2) A contract of indemnity compensates the indemnified party for loss suffered, while a contract of guarantee involves a promise to pay if another party fails to perform.
(3) A contract of indemnity is enforceable even without the occurrence of loss, while a contract of guarantee requires proof of loss before it becomes enforceable.
(4) A contract of indemnity is a form of insurance, while a contract of guarantee is a form of security.

47. What is the primary purpose of a contract of guarantee?
(1) To pool risk between two parties
(2) To transfer risk from one party to another
(3) To compensate for loss or damage suffered by one party
(4) To ensure the performance of a third party's obligations

48. What is the difference between a contract of bailment and a contract of pledge?
(1) A contract of bailment involves transfer of ownership, while a contract of pledge involves transfer of possession.
(2) A contract of bailment involves transfer of possession, while a contract of pledge involves transfer of ownership.

(3) A contract of bailment does not involve transfer of possession, while a contract of pledge involves transfer of possession.
(4) A contract of bailment and a contract of pledge are the same thing.

49. Which of the following is not an essential element of a contract of bailment?
(1) Delivery of goods
(2) Acceptance of goods
(3) Consideration
(4) Return of goods

50. What is the difference between a contract of bailment and a contract of sale?
(1) A contract of bailment involves transfer of ownership, while a contract of sale involves transfer of possession.
(2) A contract of bailment involves transfer of possession, while a contract of sale involves transfer of ownership.
(3) A contract of bailment does not involve exchange of something of value, while a contract of sale does.
(4) A contract of bailment and a contract of sale are the same thing.

51. What is the primary purpose of a contract of agency?
(1) To create a partnership between two parties
(2) To transfer ownership of one party's assets to another party
(3) To create an obligation on one party to perform a specific task for another party
(4) To give one party the power to act on behalf of another party

52. What is the difference between an express agency and an implied agency?
(1) An express agency is created by the conduct of the parties, while an implied agency is created through a written agreement.
(2) An express agency is created through a written agreement, while an implied agency is created by the conduct of the parties.
(3) An express agency and an implied agency are the same thing.
(4) An express agency is created by a third party, while an implied agency is created by the principal.

53. What is the difference between a general agency and a special agency?
(1) A general agency involves a broad scope of authority, while a special agency involves a limited scope of authority.
(2) A general agency involves a principal and several agents, while a special agency involves a principal and a single agent.
(3) A general agency involves a long-term relationship between the principal and the agent, while a special agency involves a short-term relationship.
(4) A general agency and a special agency are the same thing.

54. What is the primary purpose of a contract of guarantee?
(1) To pool risk between two parties
(2) To transfer risk from one party to another
(3) To compensate for loss or damage suffered by one party
(4) To ensure the performance of a third party's obligations

55. Which of the following is not an example of a bailment?
(1) A customer leaves her car at a valet parking service.
(2) A person buys a new house and takes possession of the keys.
(3) A company rents a forklift from a leasing company.
(4) A person lends a lawnmower to a neighbor.

56. Which of the following is not a duty of the bailee in a contract of bailment?
(1) To take reasonable care of the goods
(2) To return the goods to the bailor on demand
(3) To compensate the bailor for any loss or damage suffered
(4) To sell the goods to a third party

57. Which of the following is not a requirement for a valid agency relationship?
(1) The principal must have contractual capacity
(2) The agent must have contractual capacity
(3) There must be a mutual agreement between the principal and the agent
(4) There must be consideration exchanged between the principal and the agent

58. Which of the following is not an example of a pledge?

(1) A person takes out a loan and pledges his car as collateral.
(2) A person leaves his watch with a pawnbroker in exchange for a loan.
(3) A person rents a car from a rental agency.
(4) A person buys a used car and takes possession of the keys.

59. Which of the following is not a duty of the pledgee in a contract of pledge?
(1) To take reasonable care of the pledged goods
(2) To return the pledged goods to the pledgor on demand
(3) To compensate the pledgor for any loss or damage suffered
(4) To sell the pledged goods to a third party

60. What is the primary purpose of a contract of guarantee?
(1) To pool risk between two parties
(2) To transfer risk from one party to another
(3) To compensate for loss or damage suffered by one party
(4) To ensure the performance of a third party's obligations

61. Which of the following is not a type of guarantee?
(1) Specific guarantee
(2) Continuing guarantee
(3) Absolute guarantee
(4) Conditional guarantee

62. Which of the following is not an example of a contract of agency?
(1) A company hires a sales agent to sell its products.
(2) A patient hires a doctor to treat her illness.
(3) A writer hires an agent to negotiate deals with publishers.
(4) An athlete hires an agent to negotiate contracts with sports teams.

63. Which of the following is not an essential element of a contract of guarantee?
(1) Consent of the surety
(2) Consideration
(3) Writing
(4) Competent parties

64. Which of the following is not a requirement for a valid pledge?
(1) Delivery of possession
(2) Existence of a debt or obligation
(3) Movable property as the subject matter of the pledge
(4) Consent of the pledgor

65. What is the difference between a pledge and a mortgage?
(1) A pledge involves transfer of possession, while a mortgage involves transfer of ownership.
(2) A pledge and a mortgage are the same thing.
(3) A pledge is used to secure a personal debt, while a mortgage is used to secure a real estate debt.
(4) A pledge involves transfer of ownership, while a mortgage involves transfer of possession.

66. What is the difference between an actual authority and an apparent authority in a contract of agency?
(1) Actual authority is the authority that is granted explicitly, while apparent authority is the authority that is assumed by the agent.
(2) Actual authority is the authority that is assumed by the agent, while apparent authority is the authority that is granted explicitly.
(3) Actual authority and apparent authority are the same thing.
(4) Actual authority is the authority to act on behalf of another, while apparent authority is the authority to act on behalf of oneself.

67. Which of the following is not a type of agency relationship?
(1) Gratuitous agency
(2) Agency by estoppel
(3) Agency by ratification
(4) Agency by inheritance

68. What is the primary purpose of a contract of indemnity?
(1) To pool risk between two parties
(2) To transfer risk from one party to another
(3) To compensate for loss or damage suffered by one party
(4) To create a partnership between two parties

69. Which of the following is not an essential element of a contract of guarantee?

(1) Consent of the surety
(2) Consideration
(3) Writing
(4) Competent parties

70. What is the difference between a guarantee and a letter of credit?

(1) A guarantee involves a direct promise to pay, while a letter of credit involves a promise to pay upon the satisfaction of certain conditions.
(2) A guarantee and a letter of credit are the same thing.
(3) A guarantee involves transfer of legal ownership, while a letter of credit involves transfer of physical ownership.
(4) A guarantee involves transfer of physical possession, while a letter of credit involves transfer of legal possession.

71. Which of the following is not a type of contract of bailment?

(1) Gratuitous bailment
(2) Deposit bailment
(3) Commission bailment
(4) Rental bailment

72. Which of the following is not an essential element of a contract of agency?

(1) Mutual agreement between principal and agent
(2) Consideration
(3) Consent of principal and agent
(4) Capacity to contract

73. Which of the following is not a requirement for a valid guarantee?

(1) The guarantee must be in writing
(2) The guarantee must be supported by consideration
(3) The guarantor must have the capacity to contract
(4) The guarantor must have possession of the property being guaranteed

74. Which of the following is not a duty of the bailee in a contract of bailment?

(1) To take reasonable care of the goods
(2) To return the goods to the bailor on demand
(3) To compensate the bailor for any loss or damage suffered
(4) To sell the goods to a third party

75. An agreement to sell becomes a sale when

(1) Payment has been made
(2) Delivery has been made
(3) The goods conform to the contract
(4) Both parties have performed their obligations

76. In an agreement to sell, the transfer of property occurs at the time of

(1) Payment (2) Delivery
(3) Agreement (4) Custom

77. A contract for the sale of goods is

(1) Void (2) Voidable
(3) Valid (4) Unenforceable

78. Which of the following is not a condition of a contract of sale?

(1) The goods must be as described
(2) The goods must be of satisfactory quality
(3) The goods must be fit for a particular purpose
(4) The goods must be shipped in a timely manner

79. Which of the following is not a warranty of a contract of sale?

(1) The goods must be as described
(2) The goods must be of satisfactory quality
(3) The goods must be fit for a particular purpose
(4) The goods must be shipped in a timely manner

80. Which of the following is true about the Doctrine of Caveat Emptor?

(1) The seller has no obligation to disclose defects in the goods
(2) The buyer has no obligation to inspect the goods before purchase
(3) The buyer has the burden of proving defects in the goods
(4) The seller has the burden of proving the goods are defect-free

81. The Sale of Goods Act, 1930 applies to

(1) The sale of movable goods
(2) The sale of immovable goods
(3) The sale of all kinds of goods
(4) The sale of services

82. The price of goods is determined by

(1) The buyer and seller together
(2) The buyer

(3) The seller
(4) Customs and usage of trade

83. The duties of a seller under a contract of sale include
(1) Delivering the goods
(2) Passing the property in the goods
(3) Warranting the goods are as described
(4) Payment of price

84. If goods are delivered to a buyer and they are not as described, the buyer can
(1) Refuse to accept the goods
(2) Accept the goods and claim damages from the seller
(3) Claim the goods and refuse to pay
(4) None of the above

85. The buyer has the right to inspect the goods before purchase under the Doctrine of
(1) Caveat Emptor
(2) Implied Warranty
(3) Express Warranty
(4) Unconditional Warranty

86. The risk of loss or damage to the goods passes from the seller to the buyer
(1) When the goods are shipped
(2) When the goods are loaded onto the carrier's vehicle
(3) When the goods are delivered to the buyer
(4) When the buyer accepts the goods

87. Which of the following is not a right of an unpaid seller?
(1) The right to resell the goods
(2) The right to withhold delivery
(3) The right to claim damages
(4) The right to demand price at any time

88. When can an unpaid seller of goods exercise the right of lien on the goods?
(1) At any time after the delivery of the goods
(2) Only before the delivery of the goods
(3) Only after the buyer has accepted the goods
(4) Only after the buyer has paid for the goods

89. The right of stoppage in transit is available to
(1) The buyer (2) The carrier
(3) The seller (4) The insurer

90. The right to resale of goods is available to
(1) The buyer (2) The seller
(3) The carrier (4) The insurer

91. The right to claim damages for breach of contract is available to
(1) The buyer (2) The seller
(3) The carrier (4) The insurer

92. The right to payment of the price is available to
(1) The buyer (2) The seller
(3) The carrier (4) The insurer

93. A contract of sale is void if
(1) The goods are damaged
(2) The price is not agreed upon
(3) The goods are not in conformity with the contract
(4) The consideration is illegal

94. When can a buyer reject the goods under a contract of sale?
(1) When the goods do not conform to the contract
(2) When the price is too high
(3) When the buyer changes his mind
(4) None of the above

95. When can the buyer claim damages under a contract of sale?
(1) When the buyer accepts the goods and later discovers defects
(2) When the buyer rejects the goods based on defects
(3) When the buyer decides not to go through with the purchase
(4) None of the above

96. Which of the following is not a document of title?
(1) Bill of lading (2) Warehouse receipt
(3) Invoice (4) Delivery order

97. Who is a buyer in possession of goods under a contract of sale?
(1) A buyer who has received delivery of the goods but has not paid for them
(2) A buyer who has paid for the goods but has not received delivery of them
(3) A buyer who has paid for the goods and has received delivery of them
(4) None of the above

98. Who is a seller in possession of goods under a contract of sale?
(1) A seller who has received payment for the goods but has not delivered them
(2) A seller who has delivered the goods but has not received payment for them

(3) A seller who has delivered the goods and has received payment for them
(4) None of the above

99. A seller's lien applies to
(1) Only movable goods
(2) Movable and immovable goods
(3) Only immovable goods
(4) None of the above

100. An unpaid seller can stop the goods in transit if
(1) The buyer has received delivery of the goods
(2) The carrier has delivered the goods to the buyer
(3) The buyer has failed to pay the price of the goods
(4) The carrier has not delivered the goods to the buyer

101. When can an unpaid seller exercise the right of withholding delivery of the goods?
(1) When the goods are in transit
(2) When the seller is in possession of the goods
(3) When the buyer has already paid for the goods
(4) When the buyer has already taken delivery of the goods

102. When can an unpaid seller sue for the price of the goods?
(1) When the goods are in transit
(2) When the seller is in possession of the goods
(3) When the buyer has already paid for the goods
(4) When the buyer has already taken delivery of the goods

103. In a sale of unascertained goods, property in the goods passes to the buyer
(1) At the time of the contract
(2) At the time of delivery
(3) At the time of payment
(4) None of the above

104. In a sale of goods where the goods are to be delivered to a carrier, property in the goods passes to the buyer
(1) At the time of the contract
(2) At the time of delivery to the carrier
(3) At the time of acceptance by the carrier
(4) At the time of payment

105. A buyer can reject the goods under a contract of sale if
(1) The goods are damaged
(2) The goods do not conform to the contract
(3) The price is too high
(4) The buyer changes his mind

106. In a sale of goods by sample, the goods must
(1) Conform to the description given by the seller
(2) Conform to the sample provided by the seller
(3) Be of the same quality as the goods provided by the seller on a previous occasion
(4) None of the above

107. A buyer has a duty to
(1) Accept delivery of the goods
(2) Inspect the goods before accepting them
(3) Pay the full price of the goods before delivery
(4) None of the above

108. In a sale of goods by description, the goods must
(1) Conform to the sample provided by the seller
(2) Be of the same quality as the goods provided by the seller on a previous occasion
(3) Conform to the description given by the seller
(4) None of the above

109. In a sale of goods by sample as well as by description, the goods must
(1) Conform to the sample provided by the seller
(2) Conform to the description given by the seller
(3) Conform to both the sample and description provided by the seller
(4) None of the above

110. In a contract of sale, delivery means
(1) The physical transfer of goods
(2) The transfer of title to goods
(3) The payment of the full price of goods
(4) None of the above

111. In a sale of goods, the term 'FOB' means
(1) Free on Board
(2) Freight on Board
(3) Forward on Board
(4) None of the above

112. In a sale of goods, the term 'CIF' means
(1) Cost, Insurance, and Freight

(2) Credit, Interest, and Freight
(3) Cash, Insurance, and Freight
(4) None of the above

113. The right of resale of goods by an unpaid seller is subject to the rules of
(1) Caveat Emptor
(2) Sales of Goods Act, 1930
(3) Unconditional Warranty
(4) None of the above

114. The right of stoppage in transit by an unpaid seller is subject to the rules of
(1) Caveat Emptor
(2) Sales of Goods Act, 1930
(3) Unconditional Warranty
(4) None of the above

Directions: Each of the following items consists of two statements, one labelled as Assertion (A) and other labelled as Reason (R). You are to examine these two statements carefully and decide if the (A) and the (R) are individually true and if so, whether (R) is the correct explanation of (A). Select your answers to these items using the codes given below:
(1) Both (A) and (R) are true and the (R) is a correct explanation of the (A).
(2) Both (A) and (R) are true, but the (R) is not a correct explanation of the (A).
(3) The (A) is true, but the (R) is false.
(4) The (A) is false, but the (R) is true.

115. Assertion (A): An agreement to sell is a bilateral contract between a buyer and a seller.
Reason: In an agreement to sell, the transfer of ownership occurs when the contract is agreed upon.

116. Assertion (A): The Doctrine of Caveat Emptor places a duty on the seller to disclose all defects in the goods.
Reason: The buyer has the obligation to inspect the goods before purchase.

117. Assertion (A): An unpaid seller has the right of lien on goods as long as they remain in his possession.
Reason: The right of lien on goods can only be exercised by an unpaid seller before the goods are delivered to the buyer.

118. Assertion (A): The right to stoppage in transit is available to an unpaid seller and a carrier.
Reason: The right to stoppage in transit is exercised by the person who has the legal right to possession of the goods at the time they are in transit.

119. Assertion (A): The right to resale of goods is available only to an unpaid seller.
Reason: The right to resale of goods allows the seller to recover the price of the goods from the defaulting buyer.

120. The Negotiable Instruments Act, 1881 applies to
(1) Promissory notes (2) Bills of exchange
(3) Cheques (4) All of these

121. A promissory note is
(1) A promise to pay a sum of money to a specific person
(2) A written order to pay a sum of money to a specific person
(3) A written order to pay a sum of money to the bearer of the note
(4) None of the above

122. A bill of exchange is
(1) A promise to pay a sum of money to a specific person
(2) A written order to pay a sum of money to a specific person
(3) A written order to pay a sum of money to the bearer of the note
(4) None of the above

123. A cheque is
(1) A promise to pay a sum of money to a specific person
(2) A written order to pay a sum of money to a specific person
(3) A written order to pay a sum of money to the bearer of the note
(4) None of the above

124. Which of the following is true about a negotiable instrument?
(1) It can be transferred by endorsement and delivery
(2) It can be transferred by delivery alone
(3) It can be transferred by endorsement alone
(4) It cannot be transferred

125. Which of the following is true about an endorsement of a negotiable instrument?
(1) It must be in writing
(2) It must be signed by the endorser
(3) It must be on the instrument itself or on a slip of paper attached to it
(4) All of the above

126. Which of the following is true about a blank endorsement of a negotiable instrument?
(1) It can only be done by the original payee
(2) It can be done by anyone
(3) It transfers the instrument to the bearer
(4) It is not allowed under the law

127. Which of the following is true about a restrictive endorsement of a negotiable instrument?
(1) It specifies the person to whom the instrument is to be paid
(2) It transfers the instrument to the endorsee and all subsequent holders
(3) It transfers the instrument to the endorsee only
(4) It is not allowed under the law

128. Which of the following is not a type of endorsement of a negotiable instrument?
(1) Blank endorsement
(2) Restrictive endorsement
(3) Conditional endorsement
(4) Special endorsement

129. A promissory note can be transferred by
(1) Delivery alone
(2) Endorsement and delivery
(3) Endorsement alone
(4) None of the above

130. A bill of exchange can be transferred by
(1) Delivery alone
(2) Endorsement and delivery
(3) Endorsement alone
(4) None of the above

131. A cheque can be transferred by
(1) Delivery alone
(2) Endorsement and delivery
(3) Endorsement alone
(4) None of the above

132. Which of the following is true about a negotiable instrument that is overdue?
(1) It cannot be negotiated
(2) It can be negotiated, but the holder takes it subject to any defects of title
(3) It can be negotiated, and the holder takes it free from any defects of title
(4) None of the above

133. What is the period of limitation for filing a suit on a promissory note?
(1) One year from the date of maturity
(2) Three years from the date of maturity
(3) Ten years from the date of maturity
(4) There is no limitation period for a promissory note

134. What is the period of limitation for filing a suit on a bill of exchange or cheque?
(1) One year from the date of issuance
(2) Three years from the date of issuance
(3) Six years from the date of issuance
(4) There is no limitation period for a bill of exchange or cheque

135. A negotiable instrument that is not payable on demand is called a
(1) Promissory note
(2) Bill of exchange
(3) Cheque
(4) None of the above

136. Which of the following is not a type of crossing of a cheque?
(1) General crossing
(2) Special crossing
(3) Open crossing
(4) Restrictive crossing

137. Which of the following is true about an open cheque?
(1) It can only be paid to the payee whose name is written on the cheque
(2) It can be paid to any person who presents it for payment
(3) It can only be paid to the bank where the cheque is drawn
(4) None of the above

138. Which of the following is true about a crossed cheque?
(1) It can only be paid to the payee whose name is written on the cheque
(2) It can be paid to any person who presents it for payment
(3) It can only be paid to the bank where the cheque is drawn
(4) None of the above

139. Which of the following is true about a dishonoured cheque?
(1) It is an instrument that is not payable on demand
(2) It is an instrument that is not honoured by the bank due to lack of funds
(3) It is an instrument that is not properly endorsed
(4) It is an instrument that is past its due date

140. Which of the following is true about a promissory note?
(1) It can be payable on demand or at a future date
(2) It is always payable on demand
(3) It is always payable at a future date
(4) None of the above

141. Which of the following is true about a bill of exchange?
(1) It can be payable on demand or at a future date
(2) It is always payable on demand
(3) It is always payable at a future date
(4) None of the above

142. A cheque is always
(1) Payable on demand
(2) Payable at a future date
(3) Payable to the bearer
(4) None of the above

143. Which of the following is true about a promissory note payable to order?
(1) It is a negotiable instrument
(2) It is non-negotiable
(3) It can only be endorsed and delivered to the payee
(4) None of the above

144. Which of the following is true about a promissory note payable to bearer?
(1) It is a negotiable instrument
(2) It is non-negotiable
(3) It can only be endorsed and delivered to the payee
(4) None of the above

145. A promissory note cannot be crossed because
(1) It is non-transferable
(2) It is not payable on demand
(3) It is payable to a specific person
(4) None of the above

146. A bill of exchange can be endorsed
(1) Only once
(2) As many times as necessary
(3) Only by the holder of the instrument
(4) None of the above

147. Which of the following is true about an order cheque?
(1) It can only be paid to the payee whose name is written on the cheque
(2) It can be paid to any person who presents it for payment
(3) It can only be paid to the bank where the cheque is drawn
(4) None of the above

148. Which of the following is true about a bearer cheque?
(1) It can only be paid to the payee whose name is written on the cheque
(2) It can be paid to any person who presents it for payment
(3) It can only be paid to the bank where the cheque is drawn
(4) None of the above

149. The period of limitation for filing a suit on a dishonoured cheque is
(1) One year from the date of dishonour
(2) Three years from the date of dishonour
(3) Six years from the date of dishonour
(4) There is no limitation period for a dishonoured cheque

150. Which of the following is not a party to a bill of exchange?
(1) Drawer (2) Payee
(3) Acceptor (4) Endorsee

151. Which of the following is not a party to a promissory note?
(1) Maker (2) Payee
(3) Acceptor (4) Endorsee

152. Which of the following is not a party to a cheque?
(1) Drawer (2) Payee
(3) Drawee (4) Endorsee

153. Which of the following is a type of endorsement of a negotiable instrument?
(1) Blank (2) Conditional
(3) Special (4) All of these

154. The legal transferee of a promissory note gets
(1) Better title than the transferor
(2) Same title as the transferor
(3) Inferior title than the transferor
(4) None of the above

155. The legal transferee of a cheque gets
(1) Better title than the transferor
(2) Same title as the transferor
(3) Inferior title than the transferor
(4) None of the above

156. A crossed cheque is
(1) One that has been marked with two parallel lines
(2) One that has been marked with the words 'Not Negotiable'
(3) One that has been marked with the words 'Account Payee Only'
(4) All of the above

157. A cancelled cheque is one that
(1) Has been torn or defaced to prevent its further use
(2) Has been paid by the bank
(3) Has been returned by the bank unpaid
(4) All of the above

158. A promissory note can be made by
(1) A company
(2) An individual
(3) A partnership firm
(4) All of the above

159. The notification of dishonour of a negotiable instrument should be given by
(1) The drawee
(2) The holder of the instrument
(3) The legal representative of the holder
(4) All of the above

160. **Assertion (A):** A cheque is a type of bill of exchange.
Reason: A cheque is payable on demand and is drawn on a bank.
(1) Both assertion and reason are true and the reason is a correct explanation of the assertion.
(2) Both assertion and reason are true, but the reason is not a correct explanation of the assertion.
(3) The assertion is true, but the reason is false.
(4) The assertion is false, but the reason is true.

161. What is the minimum number of members required to form a private limited company?
(1) 1 (2) 2
(3) 3 (4) 7

162. What is the minimum number of members required to form a public limited company?
(1) 1 (2) 2
(3) 3 (4) 7

163. Which of the following is the most common type of company in India?
(1) Private limited company
(2) Public limited company
(3) One person company
(4) Unlimited company

164. What is the maximum number of members allowed in a private limited company?
(1) 50 (2) 100
(3) 200
(4) There is no maximum limit

165. Which of the following is true about a public limited company?
(1) Its shares can be freely traded on the stock exchange
(2) It can have no more than 50 members
(3) It cannot issue debentures
(4) It is not required to file an annual report with the Registrar of Companies

166. Which of the following is true about a private limited company?
(1) Its shares cannot be freely traded on the stock exchange
(2) It can have more than 50 members
(3) It can issue debentures
(4) It is not required to file an annual report with the Registrar of Companies

167. Which of the following is true about a one person company?
(1) It can have only one member
(2) It can have up to 5 members
(3) It can issue debentures
(4) Its shares can be freely traded on the stock exchange

168. Which of the following is not a type of joint stock company?
(1) Private limited company
(2) Public limited company
(3) One person company
(4) Unlimited company

169. Which of the following is true about a not-for-profit company?
(1) It is formed for the purpose of making a profit
(2) It is exempt from paying taxes
(3) Its profits are distributed to its members
(4) It is not allowed to issue shares

170. Which of the following is true about a Section 8 company?
(1) It is formed for the purpose of making a profit

(2) It is exempt from paying taxes
(3) Its profits are distributed to its members
(4) It is not allowed to issue dividends

171. Which of the following statements is true about the memorandum of association of a company?
(1) It defines the powers of the directors
(2) It defines the rights of the shareholders
(3) It defines the objects of the company and the powers incidental to those objects
(4) It defines the duties of the auditor

172. Which of the following statements is true about the articles of association of a company?
(1) It defines the powers of the directors
(2) It defines the rights of the shareholders
(3) It defines the objects of the company and the powers incidental to those objects
(4) It defines the duties of the auditor

173. Which of the following statements is true about the directors of a company?
(1) They are appointed by the shareholders
(2) They are employees of the company
(3) They are responsible for managing the affairs of the company
(4) They are not allowed to hold shares in the company

174. Which of the following is true about the requirement for a company to have a registered office?
(1) It must be located in the same city as the company's head office
(2) It must be registered with the Registrar of Companies within 30 days of incorporation
(3) It must be open to the public during business hours
(4) It can be changed at any time without notifying the Registrar of Companies

175. Which of the following statements is true about the annual general meeting of a company?
(1) It is held every 3 years
(2) It is a meeting of the directors only
(3) It must be held within 6 months of the end of the financial year
(4) It cannot be held via video conference

176. Which of the following is not a power of the Registrar of Companies?
(1) To approve the name of a company
(2) To register the memorandum and articles of association of a company
(3) To issue shares on behalf of a company
(4) To strike off the name of a defunct company from the register

177. Which of the following is true about the power of the Tribunal to remove a director of a company?
(1) It can only be done with the approval of the shareholders
(2) It can be done on the application of any member of the company
(3) It can be done only if the director is convicted of a criminal offence
(4) It cannot be done under any circumstance

178. Which of the following is not a ground for the winding up of a company by the Tribunal?
(1) The company is unable to pay its debts
(2) The company has violated the provisions of the Companies Act
(3) The company has committed fraud or mismanagement
(4) The shareholders wish to liquidate the company voluntarily

179. Which of the following is not a type of resolution passed by a company?
(1) Ordinary resolution
(2) Special resolution
(3) Democratic resolution
(4) Written resolution

180. Which of the following is true about an extraordinary general meeting of a company?
(1) It is held every 3 years
(2) It is a meeting of the directors only
(3) It can be called by the directors or by the shareholders
(4) It must be held in person at the registered office of the company

181. Which of the following is true about a dormant company?
(1) It is not allowed to enter into any business activity
(2) It must file an annual return and financial statements with the Registrar of Companies
(3) It is required to have a minimum of 2 members
(4) Its shares can be freely traded on the stock exchange

182. Which of the following is not a requirement for the incorporation of a company?
(1) A registered office address

(2) A minimum paid-up capital
(3) A unique name
(4) A memorandum of association

183. Which of the following is true about the duties of a company secretary?
(1) Keeping the minutes of meetings
(2) Advising the directors on legal and regulatory compliance
(3) Signing off on financial statements
(4) All of the above

184. Which of the following is true about the quorum for a board meeting?
(1) It must be at least 1/3rd of the total number of directors
(2) It must be at least 1/4th of the total number of directors
(3) It must be at least 2/3rds of the total number of directors
(4) It can be any number of directors present at the meeting

185. Which of the following is true about the quorum for a general meeting?
(1) It must be at least 1/3rd of the total number of members
(2) It must be at least 1/4th of the total number of members
(3) It must be at least 2/3rds of the total number of members
(4) It can be any number of members present at the meeting

186. Which of the following is not a power of a company to borrow money?
(1) Loans from directors
(2) Public deposits
(3) Issuance of debentures
(4) A loan from a foreign bank

187. Which of the following is true about the liability of members of a company?
(1) It is limited to the amount of their investment in the company
(2) It is unlimited
(3) It is limited to a fixed amount mentioned in the memorandum of association
(4) It is limited to a fixed amount mentioned in the articles of association

188. Which of the following is not an example of a resolution that requires a special resolution to be passed?
(1) Changing the name of the company
(2) Increasing the authorised share capital
(3) Appointing a director
(4) Altering the articles of association

189. Which of the following is true about the requirement for a prospectus for public issue of shares?
(1) It is not required by law
(2) It must be filed with the Registrar of Companies
(3) It must be signed by every director of the company
(4) It is required only for private limited companies

190. Which of the following is not a type of director of a company?
(1) Managing director
(2) Whole-time director
(3) Independent director
(4) Honorary director

191. Which of the following is the correct order of steps for the incorporation of a company?
(1) Obtain a name approval, draft the memorandum and articles of association, file the incorporation documents, obtain the certificate of incorporation
(2) Draft the memorandum and articles of association, obtain a name approval, file the incorporation documents, obtain the certificate of incorporation
(3) Obtain a name approval, file the incorporation documents, draft the memorandum and articles of association, obtain the certificate of incorporation
(4) File the incorporation documents, obtain a name approval, draft the memorandum and articles of association, obtain the certificate of incorporation

192. Which of the following is not a requirement for the registration of a company?
(1) The company must have at least one registered office
(2) The company must have a minimum of one member
(3) The company must have a minimum of two directors
(4) The company must have a unique name

193. Which of the following is true about the appointment of a director of a company?
(1) It must be done by the shareholders at a general meeting

(2) It can be done by the directors at a board meeting
(3) It can be done by the company secretary
(4) It cannot be done without the approval of the Registrar of Companies

194. A public limited company must have a minimum paid-up capital of
(1) Rs. 1 lakh (2) Rs. 5 lakhs
(3) Rs. 10 lakhs (4) Rs. 50 lakhs

195. A private limited company can issue shares only to
(1) Its members
(2) The general public
(3) Its employees
(4) The government

196. A company can only change its memorandum of association by
(1) Passing an ordinary resolution
(2) Passing a special resolution
(3) Obtaining the approval of the Tribunal
(4) Obtaining the approval of the Registrar of Companies

197. A company can pass a written resolution
(1) Only if it is a private limited company
(2) Only if it is a public limited company
(3) Only in certain circumstances as specified in the Companies Act
(4) If all the members entitled to vote on the resolution sign it

198. Which of the following is not a ground for the removal of a director of a company by the Tribunal?
(1) The director has been convicted of a criminal offence
(2) The director has absconded
(3) The director has breached the provisions of the Companies Act
(4) The director is not a resident of India

199. Which of the following is true about the winding up of a company voluntarily?
(1) It can only be done with the approval of the Tribunal
(2) It can be done without the approval of the Tribunal
(3) It can be done only if there are no creditors of the company
(4) It can be done only if all the members of the company agree to it unanimously

200. Which of the following is not a requirement for the appointment of an auditor of a company?
(1) The approval of the members at a general meeting
(2) The approval of the Registrar of Companies
(3) The agreement of the auditor to act as auditor
(4) The filing of a notice of appointment with the Registrar of Companies

201. **Assertion (A):** The articles of association of a company define the rights and duties of the directors.
Reason: The articles of association also define the powers and duties of the shareholders.
(1) Both assertion and reason are true and the reason is a correct explanation of the assertion.
(2) Both assertion and reason are true, but the reason is not a correct explanation of the assertion.
(3) The assertion is true, but the reason is false.
(4) The assertion is false, but the reason is true.

202. What is the minimum number of designated partners required to form an LLP?
(1) 1 (2) 2
(3) 3 (4) 4

203. Which of the following is not a requirement for the name of an LLP?
(1) It must be unique
(2) It must not be offensive
(3) It must not be identical or too similar to an already registered name
(4) It must contain the words "Limited Liability Partnership" or "LLP"

204. Which of the following is the maximum number of partners allowed in an LLP?
(1) 10 (2) 30
(3) 50
(4) There is no maximum limit

205. Which of the following statements is true about the partners of an LLP?
(1) They are personally liable for the debts of the LLP
(2) They must be natural persons
(3) They must be Indian citizens
(4) They must be shareholders of the LLP

206. Which of the following is true about the liability of partners in an LLP?

(1) They are personally liable for the debts of the LLP
(2) They are liable only to the extent of their contribution to the LLP
(3) They are liable only if the LLP is unable to pay its debts
(4) They are not liable under any circumstances

207. Which of the following is true about the requirement for a registered office for an LLP?
(1) It must be located in the same city as the LLP's head office
(2) It must be open to the public during business hours
(3) It must be registered with the Registrar of LLP within 30 days of incorporation
(4) It can be changed at any time without notifying the Registrar of LLP

208. Which of the following statements is true about the incorporation document of an LLP?
(1) It must be signed by all the designated partners
(2) It must be filed with the Registrar of Companies
(3) It must be notarized
(4) It must be certified by a practicing professional

209. Which of the following is not a requirement for the incorporation of an LLP?
(1) A minimum paid-up capital
(2) A designated partner
(3) An LLP agreement
(4) A unique name

210. Which of the following is true about the LLP agreement?
(1) It is optional for an LLP
(2) It must be filed with the Registrar of LLP
(3) It must be signed by all the partners
(4) It must contain the amount of capital contribution by each partner

211. Which of the following is not a power of the Registrar of LLP?
(1) To approve the name of an LLP
(2) To register the incorporation document of an LLP
(3) To issue tax registrations for an LLP
(4) To strike off the name of a defunct LLP from the register

212. Which of the following is true about the obligation to maintain books of account for an LLP?
(1) It is not required by law
(2) It must be maintained at the registered office of the LLP
(3) It must be audited annually by a chartered accountant
(4) It must be maintained for a period of 7 years from the end of the financial year

213. Which of the following statements is true about a partner's right to transfer their share in an LLP?
(1) It is restricted by the LLP agreement
(2) It can be freely transferred to any person
(3) It can be transferred only with the approval of all the other partners
(4) It can be transferred only to a family member

214. Which of the following is true about an LLP's right to sue or be sued?
(1) It does not have the right to sue or be sued
(2) It can only be sued if all the partners are named as parties
(3) It can sue or be sued in its own name
(4) It can only sue or be sued if the LLP agreement permits it

215. Which of the following is true about the obligation to file an annual return and financial statements for an LLP?
(1) It is required only for LLPs with a turnover of more than Rs. 40 lakhs
(2) It must be filed with the Registrar of LLP within 60 days of the end of the financial year
(3) It is not required for LLPs with no activity during the financial year
(4) It must be certified by a practicing chartered accountant

216. Which of the following is true about the obligation to maintain statutory registers for an LLP?
(1) It is not required by law
(2) It must be maintained at the registered office of the LLP
(3) It must be audited annually by a practicing chartered accountant
(4) It must be maintained for a period of 10 years from the end of the financial year

217. Which of the following is true about the quorum for a meeting of the partners of an LLP?
(1) It must be at least 1/3rd of the total number of partners

(2) It must be at least 1/4th of the total number of partners

(3) It must be at least 2/3rds of the total number of partners

(4) It can be any number of partners present at the meeting

218. Which of the following is not a type of resolution passed by an LLP?

(1) Ordinary resolution

(2) Special resolution

(3) Consensus resolution

(4) Written resolution

219. Which of the following is true about the obligation to obtain a tax registration for an LLP?

(1) It is optional

(2) It must be done within 30 days of incorporation

(3) It is required only for LLPs with a turnover of more than Rs. 40 lakhs

(4) It can be done only through a chartered accountant

220. Which of the following is true about the obligation to obtain a GST registration for an LLP?

(1) It is optional

(2) It must be done within 30 days of the threshold limit being crossed

(3) It is required only for LLPs with a turnover of more than Rs. 20 lakhs

(4) It can be done only through a chartered accountant

221. Which of the following is true about the obligation to obtain a TAN registration for an LLP?

(1) It is optional

(2) It must be done within 30 days of incorporation

(3) It is required only for LLPs with employees

(4) It can be done only through a chartered accountant

222. Which of the following is true about the power of a partner to bind the LLP?

(1) It can be done only with the approval of all the other partners

(2) It can be done only if the LLP agreement permits it

(3) It can be done without the approval of the other partners

(4) It cannot be done under any circumstance

223. Which of the following is not a requirement for the registration of an LLP?

(1) The designated partner must have a Designated Partner Identification Number

(2) The designated partner must have a Digital Signature Certificate

(3) The designated partner must be a resident of India

(4) The designated partner must not be disqualified under the Companies Act

224. Which of the following is not a type of designated partner?

(1) Managing partner

(2) Whole-time partner

(3) Nominee partner

(4) Executive partner

225. Which of the following statements is true about the obligation to file income tax returns for an LLP?

(1) It is not required by law

(2) It must be filed annually with the Income Tax Department

(3) It must be filed within 6 months of the end of the financial year

(4) It must be certified by a practicing chartered accountant

226. Which of the following is not a ground for the dissolution of an LLP?

(1) The expiry of the term of the LLP

(2) The inability of the LLP to pay its debts

(3) The decision of the partners to dissolve the LLP

(4) The disqualification of a designated partner

227. Which of the following is true about the obligation to file a statement of account and solvency for an LLP?

(1) It is required only for LLPs with a turnover of more than Rs. 5 crores

(2) It must be filed with the Registrar of LLP within 30 days of the end of 6 months of the financial year

(3) It must be certified by a practicing chartered accountant

(4) It is not required for LLPs that have not carried on business during the financial year

228. Which of the following is not a advantage of forming an LLP over a traditional partnership?

(1) Limited liability protection for partners

(2) Greater tax flexibility
(3) Greater operational flexibility
(4) Easier access to funding

229. Which of the following statements is true about the obligation to maintain a seal for an LLP?
(1) It is not required by law
(2) It must be maintained at the registered office of the LLP
(3) It must be used on every document executed by the LLP
(4) It must be certified by the Registrar of LLP

230. Which of the following is true about the obligation to file GST returns for an LLP?
(1) It is required only for LLPs with a turnover of more than Rs. 20 lakhs
(2) It must be filed annually with the GST Department
(3) It must be certified by a practicing chartered accountant
(4) It must be filed within 3 months of the end of the financial year

231. Which of the following is true about the requirement for a Designated Partner Identification Number (DPIN) for an LLP?
(1) It is mandatory for all partners of the LLP
(2) It is optional for the partners of the LLP
(3) It is required only for the designated partners of the LLP
(4) It is required only for the partners who are Indian citizens

Directions: Each of the following items consists of two statements, one labelled as Assertion (A) and other labelled as Reason (R). You are to examine these two statements carefully and decide if the (A) and the (R) are individually true and if so, whether (R) is the correct explanation of (A). Select your answers to these items using the codes given below:
(1) Both (A) and (R) are true and the (R) is a correct explanation of the (A).
(2) Both (A) and (R) are true, but the (R) is not a correct explanation of the (A).
(3) The (A) is true, but the (R) is false.
(4) The (A) is false, but the (R) is true.

232. **Assertion (A):** An LLP agreement is mandatory for the formation of an LLP.
Reason: An LLP agreement defines the rights and duties of the partners and the manner in which the LLP is to be managed.

233. **Assertion (A):** The liability of partners in an LLP is limited to their contribution to the LLP.
Reason: The requirement for limited liability protection is the primary reason for forming an LLP.

234. The Competition Act, 2002 was enacted to
(1) Regulate unfair trade practices
(2) Promote competition and protect consumers
(3) Control the monopoly of large corporations
(4) None of the above

235. Which body is responsible for enforcing the Competition Act, 2002?
(1) Central Board of Direct Taxes
(2) Competition Commission of India
(3) Passport Office
(4) Customs Department

236. Which of the following is not an objective of the Competition Act, 2002?
(1) To prohibit anti-competitive agreements
(2) To regulate mergers and acquisitions
(3) To restrict foreign investments
(4) To prevent abuse of dominance

237. Which section of the Competition Act, 2002 provides for the establishment of the Competition Commission of India?
(1) Section 6 (2) Section 8
(3) Section 16 (4) Section 21

238. The Competition Commission of India consists of
(1) A chairperson and two members
(2) A chairperson and four members
(3) A chairperson and six members
(4) A chairperson and eight members

239. The main function of the Competition Commission of India is to
(1) Regulate foreign investments
(2) Enforce anti-competitive laws
(3) Promote monopoly in the market
(4) None of the above

240. The Competition Act, 2002 prohibits
(1) Abuse of dominance
(2) Monopoly
(3) Cartels
(4) Both (1) and (3)

241. Which of the following is an example of an anti-competitive agreement?
(1) An agreement to form a joint venture
(2) An agreement between competitors to fix prices
(3) An agreement to share technology
(4) An agreement to collaborate on research and development

242. Which of the following is not a type of anti-competitive agreement?
(1) Cartels
(2) Price discrimination
(3) Bid rigging
(4) Collusive bidding

243. Which section of the Competition Act, 2002 provides for the regulation of combinations (mergers and acquisitions)?
(1) Section 6 (2) Section 20
(3) Section 24 (4) Section 29

244. Which of the following is not a ground for the Competition Commission of India to approve a combination?
(1) The combination would lead to substantial lessening of competition
(2) The combination would result in the creation of a monopoly
(3) The combination would benefit consumers
(4) The combination would result in unfair trade practices

245. Which of the following is not a factor taken into consideration by the Competition Commission of India when approving a combination?
(1) The size of the parties to the combination
(2) The market share of the parties to the combination
(3) The entry barriers to the market
(4) The political affiliation of the parties to the combination

246. The Competition Commission of India has the power to
(1) Impose fines on parties to anti-competitive agreements
(2) Order divestiture of assets to restore competition
(3) Both (1) and (2)
(4) None of the above

247. Which section of the Competition Act, 2002 provides for the regulation of abuse of dominance?
(1) Section 4 (2) Section 8
(3) Section 16 (4) Section 21

248. Which of the following is not considered abuse of dominance under the Competition Act, 2002?
(1) Charging discriminatory prices
(2) Refusing to deal with a customer
(3) Offering low prices to attract customers
(4) Predatory pricing

249. The Competition Commission of India has the power to inquire into any alleged contravention of the Competition Act, 2002
(1) On its own
(2) On receipt of a complaint
(3) Both (1) and (2)
(4) None of the above

250. The Competition Commission of India can direct an investigation by the Director General
(1) Only in cases of alleged anti-competitive agreements
(2) Only in cases of alleged abuse of dominance
(3) In all cases of alleged contravention of the Competition Act, 2002
(4) None of the above

251. Which of the following is not a power of the Director General under the Competition Act, 2002?
(1) The power to search and seize documents
(2) The power to impose fines
(3) The power to summon witnesses and take evidence
(4) The power to conduct investigations

252. The Chairman and members of the Competition Commission of India
(1) Hold office for a term of 4 years
(2) Hold office for a term of 5 years
(3) Hold office for a term of 6 years
(4) Hold office for a term of 7 years

253. The principal officer of the Competition Commission of India is
(1) The Chairperson
(2) The Secretary
(3) The Director General
(4) The Registrar

254. The Competition Commission of India can impose a penalty of up to ________ for a contravention of the Competition Act, 2002.
(1) Five lakh rupees
(2) Ten lakh rupees

(3) One crore rupees
(4) One hundred crore rupees

255. The Competition Act, 2002 provides for the constitution of the Competition Appellate Tribunal to hear appeals against
(1) Orders of the Competition Commission of India
(2) Orders of the High Court
(3) Orders of the Supreme Court
(4) None of the above

256. The Competition Appellate Tribunal consists of
(1) A chairperson and two members
(2) A chairperson and four members
(3) A chairperson and six members
(4) A chairperson and eight members

257. The term of office of the chairperson and members of the Competition Appellate Tribunal is
(1) 4 years (2) 5 years
(3) 6 years (4) 7 years

258. The Competition Appellate Tribunal can
(1) Set aside, modify or confirm the orders of the Competition Commission of India
(2) Impose fines on parties to anti-competitive agreements
(3) Order divestiture of assets to restore competition
(4) None of the above

259. The Competition Act, 2002 applies to
(1) All sectors of the economy
(2) Only the manufacturing sector
(3) Only the service sector
(4) Only the agricultural sector

260. The Competition Act, 2002 provides for the establishment of the
(1) Competition Tribunal
(2) Competition Appellate Authority
(3) National Company Tribunal
(4) None of the above

261. The Competition Act, 2002 is applicable to enterprises
(1) Registered in India
(2) Registered in any part of the world
(3) Registered in India and having a substantial presence outside India
(4) Registered outside India and having a substantial presence in India

262. Which of the following is not a form of abuse of dominance?
(1) Bundling of products
(2) Refusal to deal
(3) Tying and leveraging
(4) Income tax evasion

263. Which of the following is not an objective of the Competition Appellate Tribunal?
(1) To promote competition in the market
(2) To ensure consumer protection
(3) To provide an effective and expeditious appellate forum
(4) To encourage foreign investments

264. Which of the following is not a power of the Competition Commission of India?
(1) The power to order an investigation into an alleged contravention of the Competition Act, 2002
(2) The power to impose fines on parties to anti-competitive agreements
(3) The power to regulate foreign investments
(4) The power to approve or disapprove combinations

265. The Competition Act, 2002 came into force on
(1) 1st June, 2004
(2) 1st September, 2010
(3) 1st September, 2009
(4) 1st June, 2011

266. The jurisdiction of the Competition Commission of India extends to
(1) The whole of India
(2) Only in urban areas
(3) Only in rural areas
(4) Only in the Northeastern states

267. The term "enterprise" under the Competition Act, 2002 includes
(1) A company registered under the Companies Act, 2013
(2) A firm registered under the Partnership Act, 1932
(3) An association of individuals
(4) All of the above

268. The term "group" under the Competition Act, 2002 includes
(1) Two or more companies where one holds more than 50% of the voting rights in the other
(2) Two or more entities where one has control over the other

(3) Two or more individuals carrying on business in partnership

(4) All of the above

269. The penalties under the Competition Act, 2002 can be imposed on

(1) Any individual

(2) Any firm

(3) Any association of individuals

(4) All of the above

270. The Competition Act, 2002 provides for the establishment of the

(1) National Company Law Appellate Tribunal

(2) National Company Law Tribunal

(3) National Trade Tribunal

(4) None of the above

271. The Competition Act, 2002 provides for the power of the Commission to

(1) Supervise the activities of businesses

(2) Regulate foreign investments

(3) Compel businesses to merge

(4) None of the above

272. The Competition Appellate Tribunal can

(1) Pass interim orders

(2) Impose fines on parties to anti-competitive agreements

(3) Issue directions to the Competition Commission of India

(4) None of the above

273. The Competition Commission of India can initiate a suo motu inquiry

(1) Only in cases where a complaint has been received

(2) Only in cases where the Director General has recommended an inquiry

(3) On its own, even without receiving a complaint or recommendation from the Director General

(4) None of the above

Directions: Each of the following items consists of two statements, one labelled as Assertion (A) and other labelled as Reason (R). You are to examine these two statements carefully and decide if the (A) and the (R) are individually true and if so, whether (R) is the correct explanation of (A). Select your answers to these items using the codes given below:

(1) Both (A) and (R) are true and the (R) is a correct explanation of the (A).

(2) Both (A) and (R) are true, but the (R) is not a correct explanation of the (A).

(3) The (A) is true, but the (R) is false.

(4) The (A) is false, but the (R) is true.

274. Assertion (A): The Competition Act, 2002 prohibits anti-competitive agreements.

Reason: Anti-competitive agreements restrict competition and harm consumers.

275. Assertion (A): The Competition Act, 2002 aims to promote competition and protect consumers.

Reason: Competition helps to ensure lower prices and better quality products for consumers.

276. Assertion (A): The Competition Act, 2002 provides for the regulation of combinations (mergers and acquisitions) that have an adverse impact on competition in the market.

Reason: Mergers and acquisitions can lead to increased market power and harm competition if they result in the creation of a monopoly or a substantial lessening of competition.

277. Assertion (A): The Competition Act, 2002 provides for the regulation of abuse of dominance in the market.

Reason: Abuse of dominance can harm competition and harm consumers by restricting output, increasing prices, and limiting consumer choice.

278. The Information Technology Act, 2000 was enacted to

(1) Regulate the use of computers and the internet

(2) Protect privacy and personal information

(3) Promote e-governance and e-commerce

(4) All of the above

279. The Information Technology Act, 2000 applies to

(1) All sectors of the economy

(2) Only the information technology sector

(3) Only the manufacturing sector

(4) Only the service sector

280. The Information Technology Act, 2000 provides for the establishment of

(1) Cybercrime Cell

(2) Indian Computer Emergency Response Team

(3) Both (1) and (2)

(4) None of the above

281. Which section of the Information Technology Act, 2000 provides for the punishment for hacking?
(1) Section 65 (2) Section 66
(3) Section 67 (4) Section 69

282. Which section of the Information Technology Act, 2000 provides for the punishment for publishing or transmitting obscene content in electronic form?
(1) Section 65 (2) Section 66
(3) Section 67 (4) Section 69

283. Which section of the Information Technology Act, 2000 provides for the punishment for cyber terrorism?
(1) Section 66F (2) Section 67C
(3) Section 69A (4) Section 70A

284. Which section of the Information Technology Act, 2000 provides for the punishment for identity theft?
(1) Section 66 (2) Section 66C
(3) Section 66D (4) Section 67

285. The term "cyber crime" refers to
(1) Crimes committed using the internet or electronic devices
(2) Crimes committed in cyberspace
(3) Crimes committed by technology companies
(4) Crimes committed by hackers

286. Which of the following is not a type of cyber crime?
(1) Hacking (2) Identity theft
(3) Robbery (4) Cyberstalking

287. Which section of the Information Technology Act, 2000 provides for the punishment for cyber stalking?
(1) Section 66A (2) Section 66B
(3) Section 66C (4) Section 67B

288. Which section of the Information Technology Act, 2000 provides for the punishment for publishing or transmitting false information?
(1) Section 66D (2) Section 67A
(3) Section 69B (4) Section 70B

289. Which of the following is not a provision of the Information Technology Act, 2000?
(1) Digital signatures
(2) Data protection
(3) Cyber squatting
(4) Encryption

290. The Information Technology Act, 2000 provides for the appointment of a Controller of
(1) Digital Signatures
(2) Data Protection
(3) Internet Services
(4) None of the above

291. Which section of the Information Technology Act, 2000 provides for the punishment for publishing or transmitting information that is false and causes harm?
(1) Section 66D (2) Section 67A
(3) Section 69B (4) Section 70B

292. The term "cyber terrorism" refers to
(1) The use of computers to carry out terrorist acts
(2) The use of the internet to spread terrorism propaganda
(3) The use of social media to incite violence
(4) None of the above

293. The term "computer virus" refers to
(1) A software program that can copy itself and spread from one computer to another
(2) A software program that provides protection against cyber crimes
(3) A hardware device that can be used to store and transfer data
(4) None of the above

294. Which section of the Information Technology Act, 2000 provides for the punishment for phishing?
(1) Section 66C (2) Section 66D
(3) Section 66E (4) Section 67C

295. Which of the following is not a type of cyber security threat?
(1) Viruses (2) Phishing
(3) Hacking (4) Physical attacks

296. Which section of the Information Technology Act, 2000 provides for the punishment for tampering with computer source code?
(1) Section 66 (2) Section 66A
(3) Section 66B (4) Section 66E

297. Which section of the Information Technology Act, 2000 provides for the punishment for electronic fraud?
(1) Section 65 (2) Section 66
(3) Section 67 (4) Section 69

298. Which section of the Information Technology Act, 2000 provides for the punishment for cyber bullying?

(1) Section 66A (2) Section 66B
(3) Section 66D (4) Section 67B

299. Which section of the Information Technology Act, 2000 provides for the punishment for child pornography?
(1) Section 65 (2) Section 66C
(3) Section 67B (4) Section 69D

300. Which of the following is not a provision of the Information Technology Act, 2000 related to e-commerce?
(1) Validity of electronic contracts
(2) Digital signatures
(3) Data protection
(4) Electronic payment systems

301. The Information Technology Act, 2000 provides for the establishment of
(1) Electronic Authentication Authority
(2) Electronic Payment Systems Authority
(3) Electronic Trading Authority
(4) None of the above

302. Which of the following is a legal aspect of e-commerce under the Information Technology Act, 2000?
(1) Digital signatures
(2) Data encryption
(3) Data protection
(4) None of the above

303. Which section of the Information Technology Act, 2000 provides for the punishment for destruction of electronic evidence?
(1) Section 65 (2) Section 66A
(3) Section 67B (4) Section 69A

304. Which of the following is not a provision of the Information Technology Act, 2000 related to data protection?
(1) Right to privacy
(2) Protection of personal information
(3) Right to access information
(4) Data security standards

305. Which section of the Information Technology Act, 2000 provides for the punishment for breach of confidentiality and privacy?
(1) Section 66A (2) Section 66B
(3) Section 66C (4) Section 72

306. The term "cyber forensic" refers to
(1) The use of technology to investigate cyber crimes
(2) The use of legal expertise to investigate cyber crimes
(3) The use of physical evidence to investigate cyber crimes
(4) None of the above

307. Which section of the Information Technology Act, 2000 provides for the punishment for stealing a computer resource?
(1) Section 66 (2) Section 66B
(3) Section 66D (4) Section 66E

308. Which of the following is not a type of cyber security defense mechanism?
(1) Firewalls (2) Antivirus software
(3) Encryption (4) Physical barriers

309. The term "spam" refers to
(1) Unsolicited commercial messages sent via email, text or social media
(2) Malware that infects computers and steals information
(3) A type of phishing attack
(4) None of the above

310. Which section of the Information Technology Act, 2000 provides for the punishment for publishing or transmitting material containing sexually explicit acts?
(1) Section 65 (2) Section 66
(3) Section 67 (4) Section 67A

311. Which section of the Information Technology Act, 2000 provides for the punishment for unauthorised access to a computer system or hacking?
(1) Section 65 (2) Section 66
(3) Section 67 (4) Section 69

312. The term "hacker" refers to
(1) A person who gains unauthorised access to computer systems with malicious intent
(2) A person who tests computer systems for vulnerabilities
(3) A person who develops cybersecurity software
(4) None of the above

313. Which section of the Information Technology Act, 2000 provides for the punishment for violation of privacy?
(1) Section 65 (2) Section 66C
(3) Section 66D (4) Section 67

314. The term "phishing" refers to
(1) A type of cyber attack where a person is tricked into giving away sensitive information

(2) A type of virus that infects computers
(3) A type of spam email
(4) None of the above

315. Which section of the Information Technology Act, 2000 provides for the punishment for dishonestly receiving stolen computer resources?
(1) Section 66A (2) Section 66B
(3) Section 66D (4) Section 66E

316. The term "data hacking" refers to
(1) The unauthorised access to or modification of electronic data
(2) The sending of unsolicited commercial messages
(3) The use of viruses to disrupt computer systems
(4) None of the above

317. Which section of the Information Technology Act, 2000 provides for the punishment for tampering with computer systems?
(1) Section 66 (2) Section 66A
(3) Section 66B (4) Section 66E

Directions: Each of the following items consists of two statements, one labelled as Assertion (A) and other labelled as Reason (R). You are to examine these two statements carefully and decide if the (A) and the (R) are individually true and if so, whether (R) is the correct explanation of (A). Select your answers to these items using the codes given below:
(1) Both (A) and (R) are true and the (R) is a correct explanation of the (A).
(2) Both (A) and (R) are true, but the (R) is not a correct explanation of the (A).
(3) The (A) is true, but the (R) is false.
(4) The (A) is false, but the (R) is true.

318. **Assertion (A):** The Information Technology Act, 2000 protects individuals from the unauthorised use of their personal data.
Reason: Personal data is often used for criminal purposes such as identity theft and cyberstalking.

319. **Assertion (A):** The Information Technology Act, 2000 provides for the punishment of cyber crimes such as hacking, phishing and identity theft.
Reason: Cyber crimes can cause significant harm to individuals, businesses and society as a whole.

320. **Assertion (A):** The Information Technology Act, 2000 provides for the regulation of e-commerce activities.
Reason: E-commerce transactions are vulnerable to cyber crimes such as hacking and fraud, and require legal protection.

321. The RTI Act, 2005 provides for the right to information to
(1) All citizens of India
(2) All permanent residents of India
(3) All permanent residents and citizens of India
(4) None of the above

322. The RTI Act, 2005 applies to
(1) All levels of government
(2) Only the central government
(3) Only the state governments
(4) Only the local governments

323. The RTI Act, 2005 provides for the establishment of
(1) Central Information Commission
(2) State Information Commissions
(3) Both (1) and (2)
(4) None of the above

324. Which section of the RTI Act, 2005 provides for the appointment of a Chief Information Commissioner by the central government?
(1) Section 12 (2) Section 13
(3) Section 14 (4) Section 15

325. Which section of the RTI Act, 2005 provides for the appointment of State Information Commissioners by the state governments?
(1) Section 12 (2) Section 13
(3) Section 14 (4) Section 15

326. Which section of the RTI Act, 2005 provides for the punishment for destroying, tampering or concealing information?
(1) Section 18 (2) Section 19
(3) Section 20 (4) Section 21

327. The term "information" under the RTI Act, 2005 includes
(1) Any material in any form
(2) Any data in any form
(3) Any opinion in any form
(4) All of the above

328. The term "public authority" under the RTI Act, 2005 includes
(1) Any government office
(2) Any non-government organisation that receives government funding

(3) Any private organisation that performs a public function
(4) All of the above

329. Which section of the RTI Act, 2005 provides for the time limit for providing information to an applicant?
(1) Section 7 (2) Section 8
(3) Section 9 (4) Section 10

330. Which section of the RTI Act, 2005 provides for the time limit for filing an appeal against a decision of the public authority?
(1) Section 19 (2) Section 20
(3) Section 21 (4) Section 22

331. Which section of the RTI Act, 2005 provides for the punishment for obstructing furnishing of information?
(1) Section 17 (2) Section 18
(3) Section 19 (4) Section 20

332. Which section of the RTI Act, 2005 provides for the punishment for refusing to receive a request for information?
(1) Section 7 (2) Section 8
(3) Section 9 (4) Section 10

333. Which section of the RTI Act, 2005 provides for the appointment of Information Officers by public authorities?
(1) Section 4 (2) Section 5
(3) Section 6 (4) Section 7

334. Which section of the RTI Act, 2005 provides for the punishment for providing false information to an applicant?
(1) Section 18 (2) Section 19
(3) Section 20 (4) Section 21

335. Which section of the RTI Act, 2005 provides for the establishment of appropriate commissions for appeals and complaints?
(1) Section 12 (2) Section 13
(3) Section 14 (4) Section 15

336. Which section of the RTI Act, 2005 provides for the punishment for destroying records?
(1) Section 20 (2) Section 21
(3) Section 22 (4) Section 23

337. Which of the following is not a provision of the RTI Act, 2005 related to fees and costs?
(1) Application fees
(2) Processing fees
(3) Fee for obtaining copies of documents
(4) Fees for submitting an appeal

338. Which section of the RTI Act, 2005 provides for the punishment for unauthorised removal of records?
(1) Section 20 (2) Section 21
(3) Section 22 (4) Section 23

339. The term "applicant" under the RTI Act, 2005 refers to
(1) Any citizen of India who files a request for information
(2) Any person who files a request for information
(3) Any legal entity that files a request for information
(4) None of the above

340. Which section of the RTI Act, 2005 provides for the punishment for causing obstruction, damage or destruction of records?
(1) Section 20 (2) Section 21
(3) Section 22 (4) Section 23

341. Which section of the RTI Act, 2005 provides for the exemption from disclosure of information that may cause harm to national security?
(1) Section 8(1) (2) Section 9(1)
(3) Section 10(1) (4) Section 11(1)

342. Which of the following is not a provision of the RTI Act, 2005 related to exemptions from disclosure?
(1) Information that may harm national security
(2) Information that may infringe on personal privacy
(3) Information that may reveal trade secrets
(4) Information that may be embarrassing to the government

343. Which section of the RTI Act, 2005 provides for the exemption from disclosure of information that may infringe on personal privacy?
(1) Section 8(1) (2) Section 9(1)
(3) Section 10(1) (4) Section 11(1)

344. Which section of the RTI Act, 2005 provides for the exemption from disclosure of information that may be confidential or make an impact on India's foreign relations?
(1) Section 8(1) (2) Section 9(1)
(3) Section 10(1) (4) Section 11(1)

345. Which of the following is a provision of the RTI Act, 2005 related to proactive disclosure?
(1) Public authorities are required to publish certain types of information proactively

(2) The public can demand proactive disclosure of any information
(3) Proactive disclosure is optional for public authorities
(4) None of the above

346. Which section of the RTI Act, 2005 provides for the exemption from disclosure of information that may reveal trade secrets?
(1) Section 8(1) (2) Section 9(1)
(3) Section 10(1) (4) Section 11(1)

347. Which of the following is a provision of the RTI Act, 2005 related to transparency?
(1) The right to information is a fundamental right
(2) Public authorities are required to maintain information in an electronic form
(3) Appeals against decisions of the public authority must be heard in a public forum
(4) All of the above

348. Which section of the RTI Act, 2005 provides for the exemption from disclosure of information that may affect the integrity of the judiciary?
(1) Section 8(1) (2) Section 9(1)
(3) Section 10(1) (4) Section 11(1)

349. Which of the following is not a duty of public authorities under the RTI Act, 2005?
(1) To maintain records in a manner that facilitates easy access
(2) To provide information in a timely and accurate manner
(3) To maintain the confidentiality of all information received
(4) To publish certain types of information proactively

350. Which section of the RTI Act, 2005 provides for the exemption from disclosure of information that may affect commercial interests?
(1) Section 8(1) (2) Section 9(1)
(3) Section 10(1) (4) Section 11(1)

351. Which of the following is not a provision of the RTI Act, 2005 related to appeals?
(1) The time limit for filing an appeal is 30 days
(2) Appeals are heard by the Central Information Commission or State Information Commission
(3) The decision of the Commission is binding
(4) The appellant must bear the cost of the appeal

352. Which section of the RTI Act, 2005 provides for the exemption from disclosure of information that may be prejudicial to the conduct of an inquiry?
(1) Section 8(1) (2) Section 9(1)
(3) Section 10(1) (4) Section 11(1)

353. Which of the following is a provision of the RTI Act, 2005 related to accountability?
(1) Public authorities are required to maintain records in a manner that facilitates easy access
(2) Public authorities are required to provide reasons for their decisions
(3) Appeals against decisions of the public authority must be heard in a public forum
(4) All of the above

354. Which section of the RTI Act, 2005 provides for the exemption from disclosure of information that may be prejudicial to the prevention or detection of a crime?
(1) Section 8(1) (2) Section 9(1)
(3) Section 10(1) (4) Section 11(1)

355. The term "third party" under the RTI Act, 2005 refers to
(1) Any person other than the applicant and the public authority
(2) Any person who provided the information to the public authority
(3) Any person who is mentioned in the information requested
(4) None of the above

356. Which section of the RTI Act, 2005 provides for the exemption from disclosure of information that may affect the security of the country?
(1) Section 8(1) (2) Section 9(1)
(3) Section 10(1) (4) Section 11(1)

357. The term "record" under the RTI Act, 2005 includes
(1) Any document in any form
(2) Any data in any form
(3) Any opinion in any form
(4) All of the above

358. Which section of the RTI Act, 2005 provides for the exemption from disclosure of information that may affect intellectual property?
(1) Section 8(1) (2) Section 9(1)
(3) Section 10(1) (4) Section 11(1)

359. Which of the following is not a provision of the RTI Act, 2005 related to the role of the Information Commissioners?
(1) To provide an independent and impartial adjudication process
(2) To ensure a fair and speedy resolution to appeals and complaints
(3) To represent the interests of the public
(4) To promote a culture of transparency and accountability

360. Which section of the RTI Act, 2005 provides for the exemption from disclosure of information that may affect the strategic interests of the country?
(1) Section 8(1) (2) Section 9(1)
(3) Section 10(1) (4) Section 11(1)

Directions: Each of the following items consists of two statements, one labelled as Assertion (A) and other labelled as Reason (R). You are to examine these two statements carefully and decide if the (A) and the (R) are individually true and if so, whether (R) is the correct explanation of (A). Select your answers to these items using the codes given below:
(1) Both (A) and (R) are true and the (R) is a correct explanation of the (A).
(2) Both (A) and (R) are true, but the (R) is not a correct explanation of the (A).
(3) The (A) is true, but the (R) is false.
(4) The (A) is false, but the (R) is true.

361. **Assertion (A):** The RTI Act, 2005 aims to promote transparency and accountability in government.
Reason: The right to information is a fundamental right enshrined in the Indian Constitution.

362. **Assertion (A):** The RTI Act, 2005 provides for exemptions from disclosure of certain types of information.
Reason: The disclosure of certain types of information may harm national security, personal privacy, trade secrets and other interests.

363. What is a patent?
(1) A form of protection for creative works
(2) A form of protection for inventions
(3) A form of protection for names and symbols
(4) None of the above

364. What is a trademark?
(1) A form of protection for creative works
(2) A form of protection for inventions
(3) A form of protection for names and symbols
(4) None of the above

365. What is a copyright?
(1) A form of protection for creative works
(2) A form of protection for inventions
(3) A form of protection for names and symbols
(4) None of the above

366. Which of the following is not a type of patent?
(1) Utility patent
(2) Design patent
(3) Plant patent
(4) Algorithm patent

367. Which of the following is the correct term for a registered trademark?
(1) TM (2) R
(3) C
(4) None of the above

368. Which of the following is the correct term for an unregistered trademark?
(1) TM (2) SM
(3) R (4) None of the above

369. Which of the following is not protected by copyright?
(1) Literary works
(2) Musical compositions
(3) Ideas and concepts
(4) Artistic works

370. Which of the following is a requirement for obtaining a patent?
(1) The invention must be new
(2) The invention must be useful
(3) The invention must not be obvious to someone skilled in the field
(4) All of the above

371. Which of the following is the correct term for a symbol used to indicate that a trademark is currently being used?
(1) TM (2) R
(3) C (4) SM

372. Which of the following is not a requirement for obtaining a trademark?
(1) The name or symbol must be unique
(2) The name or symbol must be used in commerce

(3) The name or symbol must be registered with a government office
(4) The name or symbol must not be offensive or misleading

373. Which of the following is not protected by trademark law?
(1) Logos (2) Colors
(3) Slogans (4) Ideas

374. Which of the following is not a requirement for obtaining copyright protection?
(1) The work must be fixed in a tangible form
(2) The work must be original
(3) The work must be registered with a government office
(4) The work must have some level of creativity

375. Which of the following is a benefit of obtaining a patent?
(1) Exclusive right to use the invention for a set period of time
(2) Monetary compensation for infringement of the patent
(3) Increased visibility for the invention
(4) All of the above

376. Which of the following is a benefit of obtaining trademark protection?
(1) Exclusive right to use the name or symbol for a set period of time
(2) Monetary compensation for infringement of the trademark
(3) Increased sales and brand recognition
(4) All of the above

377. Which of the following is a benefit of obtaining copyright protection?
(1) Exclusive right to reproduce, distribute, and display the work for a set period of time
(2) Monetary compensation for infringement of the copyright
(3) Increased visibility for the work
(4) All of the above

378. Which of the following is not a type of trademark?
(1) Service mark
(2) Trade dress
(3) Copyright mark
(4) Certification mark

379. Which of the following is not a requirement for registering a trademark?
(1) The name or symbol must be unique
(2) The name or symbol must be used in commerce
(3) The name or symbol must not be offensive or misleading
(4) The name or symbol must be registered with a government office

380. Which of the following is not an example of intellectual property?
(1) Patents (2) Company assets
(3) Copyrights (4) Trademarks

381. Which of the following is a challenge associated with protecting intellectual property rights internationally?
(1) Different laws and regulations in different countries
(2) Lack of enforcement mechanisms in some countries
(3) Uneven economic policies across countries
(4) All of the above

382. Which of the following is not a benefit of protecting intellectual property rights?
(1) Encourages innovation and creativity
(2) Allows for fair competition
(3) Provides a way to monetize intellectual property
(4) Limits access to knowledge and ideas

383. Which of the following is a concern related to patent trolls?
(1) They do not actually use or produce any products
(2) They prevent innovation by hoarding patents
(3) They often use litigation to obtain financial settlements from companies
(4) All of the above

384. Which of the following is a concern related to patent thickets?
(1) They make it difficult for companies to use new technology without infringing on patents
(2) They make it more difficult for companies to obtain patents
(3) They limit competition in a given field
(4) None of the above

385. Which of the following is a concern related to copyright term extensions?
(1) They limit access to creative works

(2) They limit the ability of artists to control their work

(3) They increase corporate control over creative works

(4) All of the above

386. Which of the following is a benefit of open access policies for intellectual property?

(1) Increases access to knowledge and ideas

(2) Promotes collaboration and sharing of information

(3) Encourages innovation and creativity

(4) All of the above

387. Which of the following is a benefit of open source software?

(1) Increased security due to more eyes on the code

(2) Greater flexibility in customization and use

(3) Cost savings for both users and creators

(4) All of the above

388. Which of the following is a concern related to patent pools?

(1) They limit access to technologies and increase costs for companies

(2) They limit competition in a given field

(3) They increase the risk of patent infringement for companies

(4) None of the above

389. Which of the following is a benefit of licensing intellectual property?

(1) Provides a way to monetize intellectual property

(2) Promotes innovation and sharing of ideas

(3) Encourages development of new technologies

(4) All of the above

390. Which of the following is a concern related to patent portflio acquisitions?

(1) They limit competition in a given field

(2) They increase costs for companies

(3) They make it more difficult for small companies and startups to innovate

(4) All of the above

391. Which of the following is a concern related to copyright and fair use?

(1) It is difficult to determine what constitutes fair use

(2) It can limit creativity and expression

(3) It can restrict access to knowledge and ideas

(4) All of the above

392. What is a patent infringement?

(1) Using or producing an invention that is covered by a patent without permission from the patent owner

(2) Using a product that has a registered trademark without permission from the trademark owner

(3) Reproducing a work that is covered by copyright without permission from the copyright owner

(4) None of the above

393. What is a trademark infringement?

(1) Using or producing a product that has a registered trademark without permission from the trademark owner

(2) Using an invention that is covered by a patent without permission from the patent owner

(3) Reproducing a work that is covered by copyright without permission from the copyright owner

(4) None of the above

394. What is a copyright infringement?

(1) Reproducing a work that is covered by copyright without permission from the copyright owner

(2) Using or producing an invention that is covered by a patent without permission from the patent owner

(3) Using a product that has a registered trademark without permission from the trademark owner

(4) None of the above

395. Which organisation is responsible for enforcing intellectual property rights in the United States?

(1) U.S Patent and Trademark Office

(2) U.S. Copyright Office

(3) Federal Trade Commission

(4) None of the above

396. Which organisation is responsible for enforcing international intellectual property rights?

(1) World Intellectual Property Organization

(2) United Nations Human Rights Council

(3) International Trade Commission

(4) None of the above

397. Which of the following is not a type of copyright license?

(1) Attribution license

(2) Commercial license

(3) Share-alike license
(4) Non-disclosure license

398. Which of the following is not a benefit of open access journals?
(1) Increases access to knowledge and ideas
(2) Promotes collaboration and sharing of information
(3) Reduces the quality of academic research
(4) None of the above

399. What is the purpose of a non-disclosure agreement?
(1) To protect intellectual property from disclosure to competitors
(2) To protect the reputation of a company or individual
(3) To protect against patent trolls
(4) All of the above

400. Which of the following is a benefit of open access policies for government-funded research?
(1) Increases access to knowledge and ideas
(2) Promotes collaboration and sharing of information
(3) Ensures that the public receives a return on their investment in research
(4) All of the above

401. Which of the following is not a concern related to copyright enforcement on the internet?
(1) It can be difficult to identify the copyright owner
(2) It can be difficult to distinguish between fair use and infringement
(3) It can result in over-enforcement and limiting access to information
(4) None of the above

Directions: Each of the following items consists of two statements, one labelled as Assertion (A) and other labelled as Reason (R). You are to examine these two statements carefully and decide if the (A) and the (R) are individually true and if so, whether (R) is the correct explanation of (A). Select your answers to these items using the codes given below:
(1) Both (A) and (R) are true and the (R) is a correct explanation of the (A).
(2) Both (A) and (R) are true, but the (R) is not a correct explanation of the (A).
(3) The (A) is true, but the (R) is false.
(4) The (A) is false, but the (R) is true.

402. Assertion (A): Patents provide the exclusive right to use an invention for 20 years.
Reason: Patents prevent others from producing or selling an invention without permission.

403. Assertion (A): Copyright law protects material that is expressed in a tangible form.
Reason: Copyright law protects the specific expression of an idea, but not the underlying idea itself.

404. When was GST introduced in India?
(1) 2016 (2) 2017
(3) 2018 (4) 2019

405. What is the objective of implementing GST in India?
(1) To simplify the tax structure
(2) To increase revenue collection for the government
(3) To reduce tax evasion
(4) All of the above

406. What is the full form of GST?
(1) General Sales Tax
(2) Goods and Services Tax
(3) Government Service Tax
(4) Gross Sales Tax

407. How many types of GST are there in India?
(1) One (2) Two
(3) Three (4) Four

408. What is the name of the authority responsible for implementing and monitoring GST in India?
(1) Central Board of Direct Taxes
(2) Securities and Exchange Board of India
(3) Central Board of Indirect Taxes and Customs
(4) Reserve Bank of India

409. Which of the following types of taxes are subsumed under GST in India?
(1) Service Tax
(2) Central Excise Duty
(3) Value Added Tax (VAT)
(4) All of the above

410. Which of the following is not a benefit of GST?
(1) Increased tax compliance
(2) Elimination of cascading effect of taxes
(3) Reduction in tax rates
(4) Higher tax burden on consumers

411. What is the threshold limit for GST registration for businesses in India?
(1) Rs. 10 lakhs (2) Rs. 20 lakhs
(3) Rs. 50 lakhs (4) Rs. 1 crore

412. Which rate slab is applicable to items like milk, vegetables, and bread under GST in India?
(1) 0% (2) 5%
(3) 12% (4) 18%

413. Which rate slab is applicable to items like luxury cars and aerated drinks under GST in India?
(1) 5% (2) 12%
(3) 18% (4) 28%

414. Which of the following is a disadvantage of GST?
(1) Increased tax compliance
(2) Higher tax revenue for the government
(3) Increased administrative burden for businesses
(4) Elimination of the cascading effect of taxes

415. What is the concept of input tax credit under GST?
(1) Refund of excess tax paid by the taxpayer
(2) Tax credit for tax paid on inputs used in the production of goods or services
(3) Exemption from tax for small businesses
(4) None of the above

416. Which of the following sectors come under the purview of GST in India?
(1) Agriculture (2) Healthcare
(3) Education (4) All of the above

417. Which of the following is a benefit of GST for the common man?
(1) Reduction in overall tax burden
(2) Increased prices of essential items
(3) Difficulty in understanding tax structure
(4) All of the above

418. Which of the following is not a provision of GST?
(1) Reverse charge mechanism
(2) Composition scheme for small businesses
(3) Input tax credit only for services used in the same state
(4) GST refund system

419. Which of the following types of taxes are not subsumed under GST in India?
(1) Income Tax
(2) Excise Duty on petroleum products
(3) Stamp Duty
(4) Customs Duty

420. Which of the following is the correct method of calculating GST?
(1) GST = (Taxable amount / (100 + GST rate)) × GST rate
(2) GST = Taxable amount × GST rate
(3) GST = Taxable amount + GST rate
(4) GST = Taxable amount – GST rate

421. Which of the following is the correct rate of GST for exports in India?
(1) 0% (2) 5%
(3) 12% (4) 18%

422. What is the composition scheme under GST?
(1) A voluntary scheme for small businesses to pay a fixed percentage of their turnover as tax
(2) A mandatory scheme for all businesses to pay a fixed percentage of their turnover as tax
(3) A scheme for refunding excess tax paid by businesses
(4) None of the above

423. What is the full form of IGST?
(1) Integrated Goods and Service Tax
(2) Integrated General Sales Tax
(3) Inter-State Goods and Service Tax
(4) Inter-State General Sales Tax

424. Which of the following is the correct method of claiming input tax credit under GST?
(1) File GST returns for the month in which the input was received
(2) File GST returns for the month in which the input was used
(3) File GST returns for the month in which the input was purchased
(4) None of the above

425. Which of the following is a benefit of GST for small businesses?
(1) Increased tax burden
(2) Simplified tax structure
(3) Higher tax rates
(4) None of the above

426. What is the due date for filing GST returns in India?
(1) 10th of the month following the tax period
(2) 15th of the month following the tax period
(3) 20th of the month following the tax period
(4) 25th of the month following the tax period

427. Which of the following services is exempted from GST in India?
(1) Healthcare services
(2) Educational services
(3) Financial services
(4) All of the above

428. Which of the following types of taxpayers are required to register under GST?
(1) Businesses with turnover above the threshold limit
(2) Casual taxable persons
(3) Non-resident taxable persons
(4) All of the above

429. Which of the following is a disadvantage of multiple tax rates under GST?
(1) Complexity in tax structure
(2) Increased tax compliance
(3) Higher tax rates
(4) None of the above

430. What is the concept of Place of Supply under GST?
(1) The location where goods or services are delivered
(2) The location where goods or services are produced
(3) The location of the taxpayer's business
(4) None of the above

431. Which of the following is the correct method of calculating GST on discounts?
(1) GST on the original price of the product
(2) GST on the discounted price of the product
(3) No GST on discounts
(4) GST on the net price after discount

432. Which of the following types of GST is applicable to intra-state transactions?
(1) CGST (2) SGST
(3) IGST (4) None of the above

433. Which of the following types of GST is applicable to inter-state transactions?
(1) CGST (2) SGST
(3) IGST (4) None of the above

434. Which of the following is the correct method of filing GST returns for small businesses under the Composition Scheme?
(1) Quarterly (2) Monthly
(3) Half-yearly (4) Yearly

435. Which of the following is a benefit of GST for businesses?
(1) Input tax credit
(2) Simplified tax structure
(3) Reduced paperwork
(4) All of the above

436. Which of the following is the correct method of calculating GST on a reverse charge basis?
(1) GST on the original price of the product
(2) GST on the discounted price of the product
(3) No GST on discounts
(4) GST on the net price after discount

437. What is the due date for payment of GST in India?
(1) 5th of the month following the tax period
(2) 10th of the month following the tax period
(3) 15th of the month following the tax period
(4) 20th of the month following the tax period

438. Which of the following is the correct method of calculating GST on a transaction involving multiple tax rates?
(1) Calculate GST separately for each tax rate
(2) Apply highest tax rate across all items
(3) Apply weighted average tax rate across all items
(4) None of the above

439. Which of the following is a benefit of GST for the government?
(1) Increased tax revenue
(2) Simplified tax structure
(3) Lower tax rates
(4) None of the above

440. Which of the following is the correct method of calculating IGST on an inter-state transaction?
(1) Calculate CGST and SGST separately
(2) Calculate IGST at the applicable rate
(3) No IGST is applicable on inter-state transactions
(4) None of the above

441. Which of the following is a disadvantage of GST for businesses?
(1) Increased tax compliance
(2) Higher tax rates
(3) Inability to claim input tax credit
(4) None of the above

442. Which of the following is a benefit of GST for consumers?
(1) Reduced prices of goods and services
(2) Increased prices of goods and services
(3) Complexity in tax structure
(4) None of the above

443. What is the correct format for GST registration number in India?
(1) 15 digits (2) 16 digits
(3) 17 digits (4) 18 digits

ANSWERS

1. (4)	2. (4)	3. (1)	4. (1)	5. (4)	6. (4)	7. (4)	8. (3)	9. (1)	10. (3)
11. (3)	12. (3)	13. (4)	14. (2)	15. (4)	16. (3)	17. (4)	18. (4)	19. (2)	20. (2)
21. (1)	22. (3)	23. (4)	24. (1)	25. (1)	26. (3)	27. (3)	28. (2)	29. (3)	30. (4)
31. (2)	32. (3)	33. (3)	34. (1)	35. (4)	36. (3)	37. (3)	38. (4)	39. (3)	40. (3)
41. (1)	42. (1)	43. (3)	44. (3)	45. (3)	46. (1)	47. (4)	48. (1)	49. (3)	50. (2)
51. (4)	52. (2)	53. (1)	54. (4)	55. (2)	56. (4)	57. (4)	58. (4)	59. (4)	60. (4)
61. (3)	62. (2)	63. (3)	64. (1)	65. (1)	66. (1)	67. (4)	68. (3)	69. (3)	70. (1)
71. (3)	72. (2)	73. (4)	74. (4)	75. (4)	76. (1)	77. (3)	78. (4)	79. (1)	80. (1)
81. (1)	82. (1)	83. (1)	84. (1)	85. (1)	86. (4)	87. (4)	88. (2)	89. (3)	90. (2)
91. (1,2)	92. (2)	93. (4)	94. (1)	95. (1)	96. (3)	97. (1)	98. (1)	99. (1)	100. (4)
101. (2)	102. (4)	103. (4)	104. (2)	105. (2)	106. (2)	107. (2)	108. (3)	109. (3)	110. (1)
111. (1)	112. (1)	113. (2)	114. (2)	115. (3)	116. (4)	117. (1)	118. (4)	119. (2)	120. (4)
121. (1)	122. (2)	123. (2)	124. (1)	125. (4)	126. (3)	127. (3)	128. (4)	129. (2)	130. (2)
131. (2)	132. (2)	133. (2)	134. (2)	135. (4)	136. (4)	137. (2)	138. (3)	139. (2)	140. (1)
141. (1)	142. (1)	143. (1)	144. (1)	145. (4)	146. (2)	147. (1)	148. (2)	149. (2)	150. (4)
151. (3)	152. (4)	153. (4)	154. (2)	155. (2)	156. (4)	157. (1)	158. (4)	159. (4)	160. (1)
161. (2)	162. (4)	163. (1)	164. (3)	165. (1)	166. (1)	167. (1)	168. (4)	169. (4)	170. (4)
171. (3)	172. (1)	173. (3)	174. (2)	175. (3)	176. (3)	177. (2)	178. (4)	179. (3)	180. (3)
181. (2)	182. (2)	183. (4)	184. (1)	185. (4)	186. (4)	187. (1)	188. (3)	189. (2)	190. (4)
191. (1)	192. (3)	193. (1)	194. (1)	195. (1)	196. (2)	197. (4)	198. (4)	199. (2)	200. (2)
201. (2)	202. (2)	203. (2)	204. (4)	205. (2)	206. (2)	207. (3)	208. (1)	209. (1)	210. (3)
211. (3)	212. (2)	213. (1)	214. (3)	215. (2)	216. (2)	217. (4)	218. (3)	219. (2)	220. (3)
221. (2)	222. (2)	223. (3)	224. (4)	225. (2)	226. (4)	227. (2)	228. (4)	229. (1)	230. (1)
231. (3)	232. (2)	233. (1)	234. (2)	235. (2)	236. (3)	237. (2)	238. (3)	239. (2)	240. (4)
241. (2)	242. (2)	243. (1)	244. (4)	245. (4)	246. (3)	247. (1)	248. (3)	249. (3)	250. (3)
251. (2)	252. (2)	253. (1)	254. (4)	255. (1)	256. (1)	257. (2)	258. (1)	259. (1)	260. (4)
261. (4)	262. (4)	263. (4)	264. (3)	265. (1)	266. (1)	267. (4)	268. (2)	269. (4)	270. (4)
271. (1)	272. (1)	273. (3)	274. (1)	275. (1)	276. (1)	277. (1)	278. (4)	279. (1)	280. (3)
281. (2)	282. (3)	283. (1)	284. (2)	285. (1)	286. (3)	287. (4)	288. (1)	289. (3)	290. (1)
291. (1)	292. (1)	293. (1)	294. (2)	295. (4)	296. (1)	297. (2)	298. (4)	299. (3)	300. (3)
301. (4)	302. (1)	303. (1)	304. (3)	305. (4)	306. (1)	307. (2)	308. (4)	309. (1)	310. (3)
311. (2)	312. (1)	313. (2)	314. (1)	315. (2)	316. (1)	317. (1)	318. (2)	319. (1)	320. (2)
321. (1)	322. (1)	323. (3)	324. (1)	325. (4)	326. (3)	327. (4)	328. (4)	329. (1)	330. (1)
331. (4)	332. (4)	333. (2)	334. (3)	335. (1)	336. (1)	337. (4)	338. (1)	339. (1)	340. (1)
341. (1)	342. (4)	343. (1)	344. (1)	345. (1)	346. (1)	347. (2)	348. (1)	349. (3)	350. (1)
351. (4)	352. (1)	353. (4)	354. (1)	355. (1)	356. (1)	357. (4)	358. (1)	359. (3)	360. (1)
361. (1)	362. (1)	363. (2)	364. (3)	365. (1)	366. (4)	367. (2)	368. (1)	369. (3)	370. (4)
371. (1)	372. (3)	373. (4)	374. (3)	375. (4)	376. (4)	377. (4)	378. (3)	379. (4)	380. (2)
381. (4)	382. (4)	383. (4)	384. (1)	385. (1)	386. (4)	387. (4)	388. (4)	389. (4)	390. (4)
391. (4)	392. (1)	393. (1)	394. (1)	395. (4)	396. (4)	397. (4)	398. (3)	399. (1)	400. (4)
401. (4)	402. (1)	403. (1)	404. (2)	405. (4)	406. (2)	407. (4)	408. (3)	409. (4)	410. (4)
411. (2)	412. (1)	413. (4)	414. (3)	415. (2)	416. (4)	417. (1)	418. (3)	419. (1)	420. (2)
421. (1)	422. (1)	423. (1)	424. (1)	425. (2)	426. (3)	427. (1)	428. (4)	429. (1)	430. (1)
431. (4)	432. (1)	433. (3)	434. (1)	435. (4)	436. (4)	437. (4)	438. (1)	439. (1)	440. (2)
441. (1)	442. (1)	443. (2)							

UNIT 10

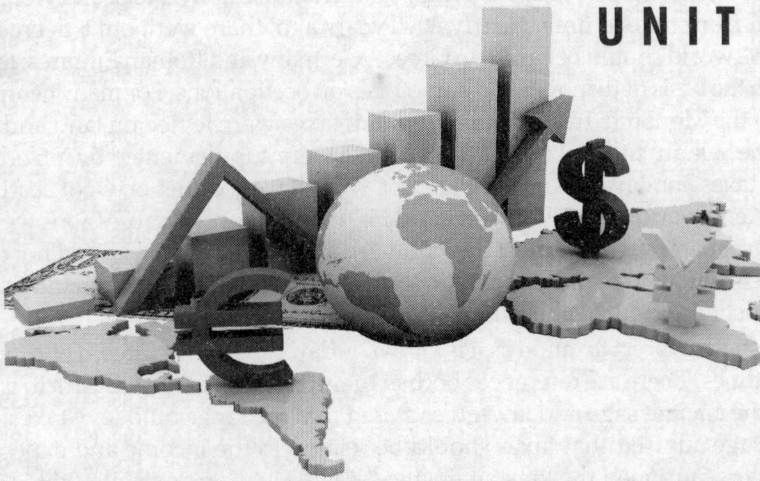

INCOME-TAX AND CORPORATE TAX PLANNING

SYLLABUS

- Income-tax: Basic concepts; Residential status and tax incidence; Exempted incomes; Agricultural income; Computation of taxable income under various heads; Deductions from Gross total income; Assessment of Individuals; Clubbing of incomes
- International Taxation: Double taxation and its avoidance mechanism; Transfer pricing
- Corporate Tax Planning: Concepts and significance of corporate tax planning; Tax avoidance versus tax evasion; Techniques of corporate tax planning; Tax considerations in specific business situations: Make or buy decisions; Own or lease an asset; Retain; Renewal or replacement of asset; Shut down or continue operations
- Deduction and collection of tax at source; Advance payment of tax; E-filing of income-tax returns

INCOME TAX

It is a matter of general belief that taxes on income and wealth are of recent origin but there is enough evidence to show that taxes on income in some form or the other were levied even in primitive and ancient communities. The origin of the word "Tax" is from "Taxation" which means an estimate. These were levied either on the sale and purchase of merchandise or livestock and were collected in a haphazard manner from time to time. Nearly 2000 years ago, there went out a decree from Ceaser Augustus that all the world should be taxed. In Greece, Germany and Roman Empires, taxes were also levied sometime on the basis of turnover and sometimes on occupations. For many centuries, revenue from taxes went to the Monarch. In Northern England, taxes were levied on land and on moveable property such as the Saladin title in 1188. Later on, these were supplemented by introduction of poll taxes, and indirect taxes known as "Ancient Customs" which were duties on wool, leather and hides. These levies and taxes in various forms and on various commodities and professions were imposed to meet the needs of the governments to meet their military and civil expenditure and not only to ensure safety to the subjects but also to meet the common needs of the citizens like maintenance of roads, administration of justice and such other functions of the State.

In India, the system of direct taxation as it is known today, has been in force in one form or another even from ancient times. There are references both in Manu Smriti and Arthasastra to a variety of tax measures. Manu, the ancient sage and law-giver stated that the king could levy taxes, according to Sastras. The wise sage advised that taxes should be related to the income and expenditure of the subject. He, however, cautioned the king against excessive taxation and stated that both extremes should be avoided namely either complete absence of taxes or exorbitant taxation. According to him, the king should arrange the collection of taxes in such a manner that the subjects did not feel the pinch of paying taxes. He laid down that traders and artisans should pay 1/5th of their profits in silver and gold, while the agriculturists were to pay 1/6th, 1/8th and 1/10th of their produce depending upon their circumstances. The detailed analysis given by Manu on the subject clearly shows the existence of a well-planned taxation system, even in ancient times. Not only this, taxes were also levied on various classes of people like actors, dancers, singers and even dancing girls. Taxes were paid in the shape of gold-coins, cattle, grains, raw-materials and also by rendering personal service.

The learned author K.B. Sarkar commends the system of taxation in ancient India in his book "Public Finance in Ancient India", (1978 Edition) as follows:-

"Most of the taxes of Ancient India were highly productive. The admixture of direct taxes with indirect Taxes secured elasticity in the tax system, although more emphasis was laid on direct tax. The tax-structure was a broad based one and covered most people within its fold. The taxes were varied and the large variety of taxes reflected the life of a large and composite population".

In our present day economy structure Income Tax plays a vital role as a source of Revenue and a measure of removal economic disparity. Our Taxation structure provides for Two types of Taxes: DIRECT and INDIRECT; Income Tax , Wealth Tax and Gift Tax are Direct Taxes whereas Sales Tax and Excise Duties are Indirect Taxes.

On the recommendation of Law Commission & Direct Taxes Enquiry Committee and in consultation with Law Ministry a Bill was framed. This Bill was referred to a select committee and finally passed in Sept. 1961. This Act came into force from 1st.April 1962 in whole of the country. Income Tax Act, 1961 is a comprehensive Act and consists of 298 Sections. Sub-Sections running into thousands Schedules, Rules, Sub-Rules, etc. and is supported by other Acts and Rules. This Act has been amended by several amending Acts since 1961. The Annual Finance Bills presented to Parliament along with Budget make far-reaching amendments in this Act every year.

TAX MANAGEMENT

Tax Management is now an integral part of business management. It involves not only due compliance of law in timely and regular manner, but also arranging the affairs in such a manner that it reduces the tax liability burden. Specifics are :

- Filling of Return.
- Maintenance of Accounts.
- Getting the Accounts Audited.
- Complying with the notices of Income Tax Department.
- Payment of Advance Tax.
- Timely deduction of Tax at Source and its payment.

Person

The word "Person" is a very wide term and embraces in itself the following :

- **Individual.** It refers to a natural human being whether Male or Female, Minor or Major.
- **Hindu Undivided Family (HUF).** It is a relationship created due to operation of Hindu Law. The Manager of HUF is called " Karta" and its member are called 'Coparceners'.
- **Company.** It is an artificial person registered under Indian Companies Act 1956 or any other Law.
- **Firm.** It is an entity which comes into existence as a result of partnership agreement. The Income Tax accepts only these entities as firms which are accessed as firms under Section 184 of the Act.
- **Association of Persons (AOP) or Body of Individuals (BOI).** Co-operative societies, MARKFED, NAFED, etc. are the example of such persons. When persons combine together to carry on a joint enterprise and they do not constitute partnership under the ambit of law, they are assessable as an Association of Persons. An A.O.P. can have firms, companies, associations and individuals as its members. A Body of Individual (B.O.I.) cannot have non-individuals as its members. Only natural human being can be members of a Body of Individuals.
- **Local Authority.** Municipality, Panchayat, Cantonment Board, Port Trust etc. are called Local Authority.
- **Artificial Judicial Person.** Statutory Corporations like Life Insurance Corporation, University etc. are called Artificial Judicial Persons.

These are seven categories of person chargeable to tax under the Act. The aforesaid definition is inclusive and not exhaustive . Therefore, any person, not falling in the above-mentioned seven categories, may still fall in the four corners of the term "Person" and accordingly may be liable to tax under Sec. 4.

ASSESSEE

Assessee means a person by whom any tax or any other sum of money is payable under this Act and includes the following:

(i) Every person in respect of whom any proceeding under the Income-tax Act has been taken:

a. for the assessment of his income or the income of any other person in respect of which he is assessable; or

b. to determine the loss sustained by him or by such other person; or

c. to determine the amount of refund due to him or to such other person.

(ii) A person who is deemed to be an assessee under any provisions of this Act i.e. a person who is treated as an assessee. This would include the legal representative of a deceased person or the legal guardian of minor if minor is taxable separately.

(iii) Every person who is deemed to be an assessee in default under any provisions of this Act. A person is said to be an assessee in default if he fails to comply with the duties imposed upon him under the Income-tax Act. For example: a person, paying interest to another person, is responsible for deducting tax at source on this amount and to deposit the tax with the Government. If he fails in either of these duties i.e., if he does not deduct the tax, or deducts the tax but does not deposit it with the government, he shall be deemed to be an assessee in default.

INCOME

The Definition given u/s 2 (24) is inclusive and not exhaustive. According to English dictionary, the term "Income" means periodical monetary return coming in regularly from definite sources like one's business, Land, Work, Investments etc.".

It's nowhere mentioned that "Income" refers to only monetary return. It includes value of Benefits and Perquisites.

The term "Income" includes not only what is received by using the property but also the amount saved by using it himself. Any thing which is convertible into income can be regarded as source of accrual of income.

" Income includes ":

- **Profit and Gains.** For instance, Profit generated by a businessman is taxable as "Income".
- **Dividend.** For instance, "Dividend" declared/paid by a company to a shareholders is taxable as " income" in the hands of shareholders.
- **Voluntary contribution received by a Trust.** In the hands of a Trust, income includes voluntary contributions received by it. This rule is applicable in the following cases..
  - Such contribution is received by a trust created wholly or partly for charitable or religious purpose ; or
  - Such contribution is received by a scientific research association ; or
  - Such contribution is received by any fund or institution established for charitable purposes ; or
  - Such contribution is received by any university or other educational institutions or hospital.

Features of Income

The following features of income can help a person to understand the concept of income.

1. **Definite Source.** Income has been compared with a fruit of a tree or a crop from the field. Fruit comes from a tree and crop from fields. Thus the source of income is definite in both cases. The existence of a source for income is somewhat essential to bring a receipt under the charge of tax.
2. **Income must come from Outside.** No one can earn income from himself. There can be no income from transaction between head office and branch office. Contributions made by members for the mutual benefit and found surplus cannot be termed as income of such group.
3. **Tainted Income.** Income earned legally or illegally remains income and it will be taxed according to the provisions of the Act. Assessment of illegal income of a person does not grant him immunity from the applicability of the provisions of other Act. Any expenditure incurred to earn such illegal income is allowed to be deducted out of such income only.

4. **Temporary or Permanent.** Whether the income is permanent or temporary, it is immaterial from the tax point of view.
5. **Voluntary Receipt.** The receipts which do not arise from the exercise of a profession or business or do not amount to remuneration and are made for reasons purely of personal nature are not included in the scope of total income.
6. **Dispute regarding the Title.** In case a person is receiving some income but his title to such receipts is disputed, it will not free him from tax liability. The receipt of such income has to pay tax.
7. **Income in Money or Money's worth.** The income may be in cash or in kind. It is taxable in both cases.

Tax Treatment of Income

For the purposes of treatment of income for tax purposes it can be divided into three categories :

A. **Taxable Income.** These incomes form part of total income and are fully taxable. These are treated u/s 14 to 69 of the Act. These are Salaries, Rent, Business Profits, Professional Gain, Capital Gain, Interest, Dividend, Winning from Lotteries, Races etc.

B. **Exempted Incomes.** These incomes do not from part of total income either fully or partially. Hence, No Tax is payable on such incomes. These incomes are given u/s 10(1) to 10(32) of the Act.

C. **Rebateable (Tax Free) Incomes.** These incomes form part of total income and are fully taxable. Tax is calculated on total income out of which a rebate of tax at average rate is allowed . The Rebateable incomes given u/s 86 of the Act are :

- Share of income received by a member of an association of persons provided the total income of such AOP is assessed to tax at the rates applicable to an individual.
- Share of income received by a partner of a firm assessed as an association of persons (PFAOP) provided the total income of such PFAOP is assessed to tax at the rates applicable to an individual.

GTI

U/s 14 the term "Gross Total Income" [GTI] means aggregate of incomes computed under the following Five heads :

- Income under the head "Salaries"
- Income under the head " House Property"
- Income under the head "Profit and Gains of Business or Profession".
- Income under the head "Capital Gain".
- Income under the head " Other Sources".

After aggregating income under various heads, losses are adjusted and the resultant figure is called " Gross Total Income" [GTI]

From Gross Total Income , Deductions u/s 80 are allowed. The resultant figure is called "Total Income " on which Rates of Taxes are applied

Assessment Year

"Assessment Year" means the period of 12 months commencing on the 1st day of April every year.

In India, the Govt. maintains its accounts for a period of 12 months i.e. 1st April to 31st March every year. As such it is known as Financial Year. The Income Tax department has also selected same year for its Assessment procedure.

The Assessment Year is the Financial Year of the Govt. of India during which income a person relating to the relevant previous year is assessed to tax. Every person who is liable to pay tax under this Act, files Return of Income by prescribed dates. These returns are processed by the Income Tax Department Officials and Officers. This processing is called Assessment. Under this income returned by the assessee is checked and verified.

Tax is calculated and compared with the amount paid and assessment order is issued. The year in which whole of this process is under taken is called Assessment Year.

At present the Assessment Year 2008-2009 (1-4-2018 to 31-3-2019) is going on.

Previous Year

As the word 'Previous' means 'coming before' , hence it can be simply said that the Previous Year is the Financial Year preceding the Assessment Year e.g. for Assessment Year 2008-2009 the Previous Year should be the Financial Year ending 31st March 2008.

- **Previous Year in case of a continuing Business.** It is the Financial Year preceding the Assessment Year. As such for the assessment year 2008-2009, the Previous Year for continuing business is 2007-2008 i.e. 1-4-2007 to 31-3-2008.
- **Previous Year in case of newly set up Business.** The Previous Year in case of newly started business shall be the period between commencement of business and 31st March next following . e.g. in case of a newly started business commencing its operations on Diwali 2007, the Previous Year in relation to Assessment Year 2008-2009. shall be the period between Diwali 2007 to 31 March 2008.
- **Previous Year in case of newly created source of income.** In such case the Previous Year shall be the period between the day on which such source comes existence and 31st March next following.

Sl. No.	Income	Section	Previous Year
1	Cash Credit	[68]	Financial Year in which found to be entered.
2	Unexplained Investment	[69]	Financial Year preceding the Assessment Year
3	Unexplained Bullion, Cash, Jewelley	[69A]	Financial Year in which found in the possession of the assessee.
4	Partly explained Investment	[69B]	Financial Year in which Investment was made.
5	Unexplained Expenditure	[69C]	Financial Year in which expenditure was incurred.
6	Payment of Hundi, Money in Cash	[69D]	Financial Year in which such payment was made.

Heads of Income

There are 5 different Income heads. The Income under each head will be charged to Income Tax. Thus the tax will be computed on the basis of total income.

1. Salaries including Allowances, value of Perquisites, Profits in lieu of salary and Pensions.
2. Income from House Property whether residential, commercial or let out.
3. Profits & Gains of Business / Profession.
4. Capital Gains - Short & Long Term.
5. Income from other Sources including Bank Interest, Interest on Securities, Lotteries, Cross word Puzzles, Races, Games, Gift received on or after 1-9-2004 in excess of Rs. 50,000 in cash etc. from unrelated persons.

Who need to pay Income Tax?

a. Individual including Non-resident, Hindu Undivided Families (HUF), Bodies of Individuals (BOI), Association of Persons (AOP) & Artificial Juridical Persons (such as Deities of Temples) having taxable income exceeding Rs. 1.5 lakh (Rs. 1,80,000 for Resident Women assesses below 65 Years and Rs. 2,25,000 for Resident Senior Citizens.)
b. Societies & Charitable / Religious Trusts having taxable income exceeding Rs.1.5 lakh.
c. All Partnership Firms irrespective of their Income.
d. Co-Op. Societies irrespective of their Income.
e. All Companies irrespective of Income.
f. Local Authorities like, Panchayats, Municipal Corporation etc.

How is income tax charged?

Income Tax is charged on 5 different heads. Aggregate of taxable income under each head of income is known as Gross Total Income and so

Taxable Income = Gross Total Income - Allowance Deductions.

Deduction of Expenditures

In computing income under various heads, deduction is allowed towards expenditure incurred in relation to earning the income. However, no deduction shall be allowed in respect of expenditure incurred in relation to incomes exempt from tax.

Computation of Gross Total Income

It is the aggregate of incomes under various heads of income calculated after set-off of unabsorbed depreciation/loss, carried forward from earlier years.

Set-off and Carry Forward

Set-off means adjustment of certain losses against the income under other sources / heads. Carry forward implies carrying forward of certain losses for set-off in subsequent years.

Total / Taxable Income

Total / Taxable Income is computed after deducting permissible deductions under section 80A to 80U, from the Gross Total Income.

Where the Gross Total Income of the Assesses includes Short-Term Capital Gains from transfer of equity shares / units of an equity oriented mutual fund subject to Securities Transaction Tax or any Long-Term Capital Gains, then no deduction shall be allowed against such Capital Gains.

On this Taxable Income, Tax will be calculated as per the applicable rates.

AGRICULTURAL INCOME

Sec.10(1) exempts Agricultural Income from Income-Tax. By virtue of Sec.2(1)a the expression "Agricultural Income" means :

- Any Rent or Revenue derived from Land which is situated in India and is used for agricultural purposes. [Sec. 2(1A)(a)]
- Any income derived from such land :
  - Use for Agricultural purposes ; or
  - Used for agricultural operations means- irrigating and harvesting , sowing, weeding, digging, cutting etc. It involves employment of some human skill, labour and energy to get some income from land. ; or

According to Sec. 2(1)(a) , if the following 3 conditions are satisfied, income derived from land can be termed as "Agricultural Income".

Condition-1 : Income derived from Land

It is essential that for any income to be termed as agricultural Land must be effective and immediate source of Income and not indirect and secondary.

As a result, interest on arrears of land revenue, dividend paid by a company out of its profits which included agricultural income also and salary paid to a manager for managing agricultural farms are not agricultural incomes because in all these cases land is not the effective and immediate source of income.

Condition-2 : Land is used for Agricultural Purposes

To term any income as agricultural income, it is necessary that income must be the result of agricultural operations performed on agricultural land. Agriculture means performance of some basic operations— irrigating and harvesting , sowing, weeding, digging, cutting etc. it involves employment of some human skill, labour and energy to get some income form land.

Condition-3 : Land is situated in India

To qualify the exemption u/s 10(1) of the Act, it is necessary that agricultural income must be derived from land situated in India. In case income is derived from agricultural land situated outside India or is from any non-agricultural land, it will not be exempted u/s 10(1). It is taxable income under the head "Income from other Sources".

What is the Tax Treatment of Income which is partially Agricultural and partially from Business [Rules 7, 7A, 7B and 8]

For disintegrating a composite business income which is partly agriculture and partly non-agricultural, the following rules are applicable:

Type of Income	Business Income	Agricultural Income
❍ Tea Business	40%	60%
❍ Coffee Business	40%	60%
❍ Rubber Business	40%	65%

DEDUCTIONS TO BE MADE IN COMPUTING TOTAL INCOME

[Sections 80A to 80U (Chapter VIA)]

The aggregate of income computed under each head, after giving effect to the provisions for clubbing of income and set off of losses, is known as "Gross Total Income". In computing the total income of an assessee, certain deductions are permissible under sections 80C to 80U from Gross Total Income.

These deductions are however not allowed from the following incomes although these incomes are part of Gross Total Income:

a. Long-term capital gains.

b. Short-term capital gain on transfer of equity shares and units of equity oriented fund through a recognised stock exchange i.e. short-term capital gain covered under section 111A.

c. Winnings of lotteries, races, etc.

d. Incomes referred to in sections 115A, 115AB, 115AC, 115ACA, 115AD and 115D.

These deductions are of two types:

1. Ddeductions on account of certain payments and investments covered under sections 80C to 80GGC.

2. Deductions on account of certain incomes which are already included under Gross Total Income covered under sections 80-IA to 80U.

The income arrived at, after claiming the above deductions from Gross Total Income, is known as Total Income. It may also be called Taxable Income. The Total Income, thus calculated, should be rounded off to the nearest Rs. 10.

Basic Rules of Deductions [Sections 80A/80AB/80AC]

1. **Deductions cannot exceed Gross Total Income [Section 80A(2)].** The aggregate amount of deductions under sections 80C to 80U. i.e., under Chapter VI-A shall not, in any case, exceed the "Gross Total Income" (exclusive of long-term capital gains, short-term capital gain covered under section 111A, winnings of lotteries, crossword, puzzles, etc. and income referred to in sections 115A to 115AD and 115D) of the assessee. Therefore, the total income after deductions will either be positive or nil. It cannot be negative due to deductions. If the "Gross total income" is negative or nil, no deduction can be permitted under this Chapter.
2. **Deduction not allowed to members if allowed to AOP/BOI [Section 80A(3)].** If a deduction is allowed under the above sections to the AOP or BOI then deductions for the same payment/ income will not be allowed to the members of the AOP/BOI. [Section 80A(3)].
3. **Double deduction not allowed and deduction cannot exceed the profit of the particular undertaking or unit or enterprise, etc. [Section 80A(4)].** Notwithstanding anything to the contrary contained in section 10AA or in any provisions of this Chapter under the heading "C.-Deductions in respect of certain incomes" (i.e. deductions under sections 80-IA to 80RRB), where, in the case of an assessee, any amount of profits and gains of an undertaking or unit or enterprise or eligible business is claimed and allowed as a deduction under any of those provisions for any assessment year, deduction in respect of, and to the extent of, such profits and gains shall not be allowed under any other provisions of this Act for such assessment year and shall in no case exceed the profits and gains of such undertaking or unit or enterprise or eligible business, as the case may be.
4. **Deduction allowed only when it is claimed by the assessee [Section 80A(5)].** Where the assessee fails to make a claim in his return of income for any deduction under section 10AA or under any provision of this Chapter under the heading "C.-Deductions in respect of certain incomes" (i.e. sections 80-IA to 80RRB), no deduction shall be allowed to him thereunder.
5. **Profit or gain to be recomputed if inter unit or inter business transfer is not at market value [Section 80A(6)]**
6. **Assessee's duty to place relevant material.** If an assessee approaches a statutory authority for obtaining a concession under the taxing statute, he should in fairness place all the material before the said authority and be also in a position to satisfy the said authority that he was entitled to obtain the concession.
7. **Deduction to be allowed in respect of net income included in Gross Total Income [Section 80-AB].** Where any deduction is required to be made or allowed under any section in respect of any income then for the purpose of computing the deduction under that section, the net income computed in accordance with the provisions of the Income-tax Act (before making any deduction under this chapter i.e. Chapter VIA) shall alone be regarded as the income received by the assessee and which is included in his Gross Total Income. [Section 80AB].
8. **Benefits of certain deductions not to be allowed in cases where return is not filed within the specified time limit [Section 80AC].** Where in computing the total income of an assessee, any deduction is admissible under section 80-IA or section 80-IAB or section 80-IB or section 80-IC or section 80-ID or section 80-IE, no such deduction shall be allowed to him unless he

furnishes a return of his income for such assessment year on or before the due date specified under section 139(1).

Deduction under Chapter VI-A

[Sec.- 80C, 80CCC, 80CCD, 80CCF, 80CCG, 80D, 80DD, 80DDB, 80E, 80EE, 80G, 80GG, 80GGA, 80GGB, 80GGC, 80 IA, 80IB, 80IC, 80ID, 80IE, 80JJA, 80JJAA, 80LA, 80P, 80QQB, 80RRB, 80TTA, 80U]

DEDUCTION UNDER CHAPTER VI-A IN RESPECT OF 'PAYMENTS'

Section	Nature of Payment	Who can Claim
80C	Life Insurance Premia, Provident Fund Contribution [Maximum: Rs. 1,50,000]	Individuals
80CCC	Pension Fund [Maximum: Rs. 1,50,000]	Individuals
80CCD(1)	Deduction available in respect of Employee's/Assessee's Contribution to National Pension Scheme (NPS) [Section 80CCD(1)]	Individuals
80CCD(1B)	Additional Deduction of Rs. 50,000 is available in respect of Employee's/Assessee's Contribution to National Pension Scheme (NPS) [Section 80CCD(1B)]	Individuals
80CCD(2)	Deduction available in respect of Eemployer's Contribution to National Pension Scheme (NPS) [Section 80CCD(2)]	Employees
80D	Deduction in respect of Health or Medical Insurance Premium	Individual/HUF
80DD	Deduction in respect of Maintenance Including Medical Treatment of a Dependent who is a Person with Disability	Resident Individual/ Resident HUF
80DDB	Deduction in respect of Medical Treatment , etc.	Resident Individual/ Resident HUF
80E	Payment of interest of Loan taken for higher studies	Individual
80EE	Deduction in respect of Interest on Loan taken for Residential House Property	Individual
80G	Deduction in respect of Donations to certain Funds, Charitable Institutions , etc. [Section 80G]	All Assessee
80GG	Deduction in respect of Rents Paid [Section 80GG]	Individual
80GGA	Deduction in respect of certain Donations for Scientific Research or Rural Development [Section 80GGA]	All assesses not having any income chargeable under the head 'Profits and gains of business or profession'
80GGB/GGC	Contribution to Political Parties	

DEDUCTION UNDER CHAPTER VI-A IN RESPECT OF 'CERTAIN INCOMES'

Section	Nature of Income	Who can Claim
80-IA	Deduction in respect of Profit and Gains from Industrial Undertaking or Enterprises engaged in infrastructure Development [Section 80IA]	All Assessee
80-IAB	Deduction in respect of profits and gains by an undertaking or an enterprise engaged in development of Special Economic Zone (SEZ)	Developers
80-IAC	Special Provision in respect of Eligible Business of Eligible Start Up [Section 80-IAC] [W.e.f. A.Y. 2017-18]	Companies / LLPs
80-IB	Deduction in respect of Profit & Gain from certain Industrial Undertaking other than Infrastructure Development Undertaking [Section 80-IB]	All Assessee
80-IBA	Deduction in respect of Profits and Gains from Housing Projects [Section 80-IBA]	All Assessee

80-IC	Deduction in respect of Profits and Gains of CertainUndertaking or Enterprises in certain Special Category States. [Section 80-IC]	All Assessee
80-ID	Deduction in respect of Profits and Gains from Business of Hotels and Convention center in NCR	All Assessee
80-IE	Deduction in respect of certain undertaking in North-Eastern States	All Assessee
80-JJA	Deduction In Respect Of Profit And Gains From Business Of Collecting And Processing Of Bio-Degradable Waste	All Assessee
80-JJAA	Deduction In Respect Of Employment Of New Employees [Section 80-JJAA] w.e.f. A.Y. 2017-18	All Assessee
80LA	Deduction in respect of certain incomes of Offshore Banking Units and International Financial Services Centre	Scheduled Banks
80P	Deduction in respect of income of Co-operative Societies	Co-operatives Societies
80PA	Deduction in respect of income of Farm Producer Companies [W.e.f. A.Y. 2019-20]	Producers Companies
80QQB	Deduction in respect of royalty income, etc., of authors of certain books other than text books [Maximum Rs. 3,00,000]	Resident Individuals
80RRB	Deduction in respect of royalty on patents [Maximum Rs. 3,00,000]	Resident Individuals
80TTA	Deduction in respect of interest on deposits in savings accounts to the maximum extent of Rs. 10,000	Individuals / HUF
80TTB	Senior citizen to be allowed a deduction of Rs. 50,000 on account of interest on deposits with Banks/co-operative bank/post office. [W.e.f. A.Y. 2019-20]	Senior Citizens
80U	Deduction in case of a person with disability [Maximum : Rs.1,25,000]	Resident Individuals

ASSESSMENT OF INDIVIDUAL

Section 140A – Self Assessment

All persons having taxable income are required to file income tax return each year. While filing a tax return, the assess computes the income earned and pays tax as per the return filed by him/her. This process of self-calculation of income and payment of tax is called self-assessment. Section 140A of the Income Tax Act deals with self-assessment of income tax. Section 140A is reproduced below for reference:

Self-assessment

"140A. (1) Where a return has been furnished under section 139 and the tax payable on the basis of that return as reduced by any tax already paid under any provision of this Act exceeds five hundred rupees, the assessee shall pay the tax so payable within thirty days of furnishing the return.

(2) After a provisional assessment under section 141 or a regular assessment under section 143 or section 144 has been made, any amount paid under sub-section (1) shall be deemed to have been paid towards the provisional assessment or regular assessment, as the case may be.

(3) If any assessee fails to pay the tax or any part thereof in accordance with the provisions of sub-section (1), he shall, unless a provisional assessment under section 141 or a regular assessment under section 143 or section 144 has been made before the expiry of thirty days referred to in that sub-section, be liable, by way of penalty, to pay such amount as the Income-tax Officer may direct, so however, that the amount of penalty does not exceed fifty per cent, of the amount of such tax or part, as the case may be:

Provided that before levying any such penalty, the assessee shall be given a reasonable opportunity of being heard.".

Section 143(3) – Scrutiny Assessment

After filing an income tax return, a tax officer may be assigned by the Income Tax department randomly based on certain criteria to undertake an examination. If a taxpayer is selected for scrutiny assessment, the Assessment Officer would issue an income tax notice to the taxpayer under Section 143(2) informing that the taxpayer has been selected for scrutiny assessment. Further, the tax officer would request certain information, documents and book of accounts for undertaking the scrutiny assessment. On producing the information and documents requested, the income tax officer would complete an assessment and compute the amount of income and tax payable by the taxpayer. If there is any mismatch in the amount of taxable income or taxes to be paid, the taxpayer could agree with the order passed by the Officer and pay the demand or accept any amount of refund, or loss as determined by the tax officer.

The taxpayer can also apply for rectification of income tax return under Section 154 if any clerical error persists. Else, he/she can also make a revision application to the Commissioner of Income Tax under Section 263 or Section 264. Finally, if the orders passed in a scrutiny assessment is not acceptable, the taxpayer can move an appeal to the CIT (A), after that to ITAT, thereafter to the High Court and then the Supreme Court, if required.

Section 144 – Best Judgement Assessment

Best judgement assessment means the computation of income and tax payable is based on the best judgement of the income tax officer undertaking an examination of the taxpayer. Best judgement assessments are performed when the assessee does not cooperate with the Income Tax officer's request for information or does not file a tax return or does not maintain the book of accounts. Hence, the best judgement assessment is made by an Income Tax officer for the following cases:

- The taxpayer does not file income tax return.
- The taxpayer does not comply with an income tax notice issued for filing income tax return or conduct of audit of accounts.
- The taxpayer does not comply with the requests for information and documents during a scrutiny assessment.
- The tax officer is not sastisfied with the information or documents presented by the assessee.

Before completing and passing order, the Income Tax Offer must provide an opportunity to the taxpayer for being heard.

Section 147 – Income Escaping Assessment

The Income Tax department has powers to open an assessment upto 6 years. Hence, if a tax officer believes that the income of an assessment has escaped assessment, he/she can reopen the assessment and complete it as per the newly available information and documents. To begin an income escaping assessment, the tax officer must issue a notice under Section 148 to the taxpayer.

CLUBBING OF INCOMES

Under the Income Tax Act a person has to pay taxes on his income. While computing the gross total income, if the income of any other person in a family is included, then its called Clubbing of Income. Section 64 of the Income Tax Act, 1961 deals with clubbing of income. Clubbing of income ensures that taxpayers do not circumvent their tax liability by transferring their incomes and assets within the family. In this article, we look at provisions relating to clubbing of income in detail.

As per Income Tax Act, every person has to pay taxes on his income. No person is allowed to divert his income to any the relatives to reduce tax liability. Clubbing of income means income of other person is included in the taxpayer's total income while computing income tax payable.

Many taxpayers in India have attempted to reduce their income tax liability by transferring their incomes and assets to their family members, in such a way that most of the income falls under the taxable amount. The clubbing of incomes regulations ensure that such practices are curbed.

Clubbing of incomes is needed under following circumstance:

- Investing money in the form of fixed deposit in children name.
- Earning assets in the name of relatives (wife or child).
- Creating saving bank accounts for dependants.
- Mutual funds for child.
- Shares in the name of spouse / child.
- Post office savings for family members.

Also, if you decided to transfer the ownership of an asset and the income from the asset to a dependant, it will continued to be added to your income under the clubbing of income provisions. Here is an example for better understanding:

If a person purchasing a flat in the name of one of his family member and that person let out this flat, the rental income earned by the person in name of his family member is taxable. As per section 64 of Income Tax, the income would be clubbed with person purchasing the flat.

Clubbing of income relates to income from investments made on behalf of a spouse, minor child, spouse or daughter-in-law. These incomes are integrated together and taxed on the overall income. The following are some of the major rules relating to clubbing of income:

When a person retaining the ownership of an asset but transfers the income from the asset to any of his relatives by an agreement or any other way. – As per Section 64 of Income Tax Act, such income will be taxable in the hands of the transferor.

Let have a look at this example of income transfer.

Assume that person "A" owns 10000, 50% debentures of XYZ private limited of Rs. 500 each. But he is transferring the interest income to his family member "B" without transferring the ownership of Debentures. In this case, although interest will be received by a family member, it is taxable in the hands of "A".

If an asset is transferred under a revocable transfer, income from such asset is taxable in the hands of the transferor.

For example, if a person "M" transfers his house to one of his friend N. And, M has right to revoke the transfer during the lifetime of N, then the income arising from the house property will be taxable in the hands of M.

Clubbing of spouse income is the most common under Section 64 of the Income Tax Act. The following are some of the major aspects of clubbing of spouse income:

Remuneration to Spouse

A person's income is to be clubbed with spouse's income if any payment is received from the spouse through the following methods:

- Salary or remuneration paid to spouse directly.
- Wage or remuneration or commission paid to spouse from a concern in which the assessee has a substantial interest.

For example, if Mithun has a substantial interest in a Company and his wife Anila is working in the company and she is not in any technical or professional qualification. – In this case, the salary income of Anila will be taxable in the hands of her husband Mithun.

The key criteria is the technical or professional qualification of the spouse. Hence, clubbing of income would not be applicable, if the spouse possesses technical or professional qualification and income of the spouse is related with such technical or professional knowledge.

Income from assets transferred to spouse

If an asset is transferred by a Person to his spouse directly or indirectly, any income from such asset will be considered as income of the transferor. However, the transfer must not be in connection with an agreement of divorce settlement or with adequate consideration.

For example, if a flat is transferred by Arun to his wife Divya. Rental income on the flat will be considered as income of Arun. However, clubbing of income provisions will not be applicable if the transfer of the asset is made through an agreement of divorce or settlement or to live apart.

Any income of the minor child is to be clubbed with the parent whose income is higher.

The parent with whom the income is clubbed will be allowed an income tax deduction of Rs.1500 per minor child. Under section 80U of Income Tax Act, clubbing is not to be done when income arises from manual work or application of his skill or specialized knowledge and experience of the minor child suffering from any disability.

Know more about clubbing income of minor.

Finally, clubbing of income is applicable if a person transferred an asset without adequate consideration to son's wife or daughter-in-law. Any income from such an asset would be considered as income of the transferor.

INTERNATIONAL TAXATION

Every state may tax their subject. However an issue is raised when there is an incidence of tax levied by two countries on the same property or person. The OECD committee on fiscal affairs stated the problem as "imposition of comparable taxes in two or more states on the taxpayer in respect of the same subject matter and for identical periods:"

Generally, a country will tax its citizens on their worldwide income and also the income and gains at source. The source principle envisages that a country will tax their citizens and also non-resident person's incomes and gains in the country. The issue of jurisdiction arising from residence and source is one of the main issues on international taxation. Many Corporations select destinations to save taxes and the International tax policy would be to control such activities.

The incidence of double taxation is of the following two types :

- **Juridical Double Taxation.** This occurs where two countries impose tax on the same property or person in a way that there is a heavier tax burden on the subject as compared to the burden he would have if he were within the jurisdiction of one country.
- **Economic double taxation.** This occurs when two persons are taxed for the same income

In order to remedy double taxation countries are entering into treaties. The Organisation for Economic Co-Operation and Development is an international body of which set out a model on avoidance double taxation. In substance India follows the UN model which is adapted from the OECD model. Generally such treaties have a tie breaker clause and the treaty decides which country will have the right to tax the individual or corporation involved.

With globalization the focus has shifted from double taxation to double non taxation. Nowadays developed nations are trying to find a way to curb MNE's from avoiding double taxation. In order to do this the following measures have been put in place :

- Controlled Foreign Companies Regime

- Transfer Pricing; and
- Thin Capitalization

The above measures have been recognized by the OECD and have been incorporated in the model law. According to the OECD these measures do not contravene any principles of International Tax.

In India, the Government has been given the authority under Section 90 of Indian Income Tax Act to join in Double Tax Avoidance Treaties (DTAA).

DOUBLE TAXATION AND ITS AVOIDANCE MECHANISM

Double taxation is a taxation principle referring to income taxes paid twice on the same source of earned income. It can occur when income is taxed at both the corporate level and personal level. Double taxation also occurs in international trade when the same income is taxed in two different countries.

Double taxation is often an unintended consequence of tax legislation.

Double taxation often occurs because corporations are considered separate legal entities from their shareholders. As such, corporations pay taxes on their annual earnings, just like individuals. When corporations pay out dividends to shareholders, those dividend payments incur income-tax liabilities for the shareholders who receive them, even though the earnings that provided the cash to pay the dividends were already taxed at the corporate level.

The concept of double taxation on dividends paid to shareholders has prompted significant debate. While some argue that taxing dividends received by shareholders is an unfair double taxation of income because it was already taxed at the corporate level, others contend this tax structure is fair.

Proponents of keeping the "double taxation" on dividends point out that without taxes on dividends, wealthy individuals could enjoy a good living off the dividends they received from owning large amounts of common stock, yet pay essentially zero taxes on their personal income. As well, supporters of dividend taxation point out that dividend payments are voluntary actions by companies and, as such, companies are not required to have their income "double taxed" unless they choose to make dividend payments to shareholders.

Most tax systems attempt, through the use of varying tax rates and tax credits, to have an integrated system where income earned by a corporation and paid out as dividends and income earned directly by an individual is, in the end, taxed at the same rate.

International Double Taxation

International businesses are often faced with issues of double taxation. Income may be taxed in the country where it is earned, and then taxed again when it is repatriated in the business' home country. In some cases, the total tax rate is so high, it makes international business too expensive to pursue.

To avoid these issues, countries around the world have signed hundreds of treaties for the avoidance of double taxation, often based on models provided by the Organization for Economic Cooperation and Development (OECD). In these treaties, signatory nations agree to limit their taxation of international business in an effort to augment trade between the two countries and avoid double taxation.

Avoiding Double Taxation

India, at present, has entered into DTAAs with various countries. Relief of double taxation is generally available under two methods:

A. **Exemption method.** Under this method, either of the state has an exclusive right to tax the income arising in the source state.

B. **Tax credit method.** Under this method, foreign tax credit is given in the resident state in respect of tax paid in the source state on the doubly taxed income.

In India, taxability depends on the residential status and the source of income. In India while a Non- Resident ('NR')/Not Ordinarily Resident ('NOR') is taxed on the Indian sourced income, a Resident and Ordinarily Resident (ROR') is taxed on worldwide income. In the example given below, we look at two scenarios of double taxation and how the same can be avoided.

A UK employee working in India qualifying to be a ROR during FY 2014-2015 returns to his home country on July 31, 2014

In the present case, since the employee qualifies to be an ROR in India, his worldwide income would be subject to tax in India. Hence, the salary income earned by him in the UK during the period August 1, 2014 to March 31, 2015 would be subject to tax in India. Further, under the UK laws, assuming he also qualifies to be a resident of the UK from August 1, 2014, UK would also tax his salary income from August 1, 2014.

However, a DTAA exists between India and the UK and the employee can avail of the benefits of the DTAA to the extent it is more beneficial to him. Typically, under the DTAA, where an individual is a resident of both countries, the tie-breaker test would have to be applied to ascertain the country of residence according to DTAA. Under the tie-breaker clause, conditions such as existence of permanent home, closeness of economic and social ties and the like are factors in determining the residency and the same has to be examined. In the present case, the individual is deputed from the UK. Assuming his residency tie- breaks to the UK, under the India-UK DTAA, he will be exempt from tax in India on salary earned during the period August 1, 2014 to March 31, 2015 under Article 16 of the India UK DTAA. However, according to the provisions of the Indian tax law, a Tax Residency Certificate (TRC) would be required to be obtained from the UK authorities to claim the exemption along with Form 10F under the Income-tax Act, 1961 (Act).

In this scenario, double tax is avoided by an exemption method.

An Indian employee deputed outside India and providing services outside India qualifying to be an ROR in India in the year of deputation (assuming he is deputed to the UK with effect from January 1, 2015).

Where an employee is deputed to the UK and qualifies to be an ROR in the year of deputation (i.e. FY2014-2015), he would be taxable on global income in India including salary for the period January 1, 2015 to March 31, 2015. Assuming he qualifies as resident of the UK with effect from January 1, 2015, he would also be taxable in UK on salary income earned in the UK for the period January 1, 2015 to March 31, 2015. Now assuming his residency tie-breaks to India, then under the India-UK DTAA he would be eligible to claim credit in India of taxes paid in the UK on such doubly taxed income in accordance with the India-UK DTAA.

In this case, double tax is avoided by the credit method.

As it is evident from above, where your income is derived in one state and you are resident of another state, double tax can be avoided by applying the DTAA. However, where double tax is avoided by exemption method, it is relevant to obtain TRC from the resident country. Where double tax is avoided by claiming foreign tax credit, it is imperative that the proof of taxes paid (such as tax return, tax receipts, tax certificates) in the other country is maintained as evidence. Further, one should be mindful to examine each Article of the respective country DTAA to claim an exemption or take credit.

It would be relevant to note that even in the absence of a DTAA entered with that country, a resident of India can claim foreign tax credit under the domestic tax laws in accordance with section 91 of the Act subject to evidence being maintained.

Transfer Pricing

Transfer price is the price at which divisions of a company transact with each other, such as the trade of supplies or labor between departments. Transfer prices are used when individual entities of a larger multi-entity firm are treated and measured as separately run entities. A transfer price can also be known as a transfer cost.

A transfer price arises for accounting purposes when different divisions of a multi-entity company are in charge of their own profits. When divisions are required to transact with each other, a transfer price is used to determine costs. Transfer prices generally do not differ much from the market price. If the price does differ, then one of the entities is at a disadvantage and would ultimately start buying from the market to get a better price.

Transfer pricing is closely monitored within a company's financial reporting and requires strict documentation that is included in financial reporting documents for auditors and regulators. This documentation is closely scrutinized. If inappropriately documented, it can lead to added expenses for the company in the form of added taxation or restatement fees. These prices are closely checked for accuracy to ensure that profits are booked appropriately within arm's length pricing methods and associated taxes are paid accordingly.

Transfer prices are most often used when companies sell goods to divisions in other international jurisdictions. This type of transfer pricing is common, and a large part of intentional commerce is actually done within companies as opposed to between unrelated companies.

Transfer pricing can also refer to regulations that governments and tax authorities use for regulating intercompany transfers. Intercompany transfers done internationally have tax advantages, which has led regulatory authorities to frown upon using transfer pricing for tax avoidance. When transfer pricing occurs, companies can book profits of goods and services in a different country that may have a lower tax rate. In some cases, the transfer of goods and services from one country to another within an interrelated company transaction can allow a company to avoid tariffs on goods and services exchanged internationally. The international tax laws are regulated by the Organisation for Economic Cooperation and Development (OECD), and auditing firms within each international location audit financial statements accordingly.

Adjustments required for differences in;

1. **Quantity discount.** In case similar discount is offered by C Ltd., the price that was charged by C Ltd. would have been lower by INR 500/MT.
2. **Freight & Insurance (FOB Vs CIF).** In case the purchase from C Ltd. was also on FOB, then price charged by C Ltd. would have been lesser. Hence, the cost of freight & insurance must be reduced from purchase price.
3. **Credit period.** In case the similar credit was offered by C Ltd., then price charged by them would have been more after factoring such cost. Hence, 1.25% pm must be added to the purchase price.

Resale Price Method or Resale Minus Method

In this method, it takes the prices at which the associated enterprise sells its product to the third party. This price is referred to as the resale price. The gross margin which is determined by comparing the gross margins in a comparable uncontrolled transaction is then reduced from this resale price. After this, costs which are associated with the purchase of such product such as the customs duty are deducted. What remains is considered as arm's length price for a controlled transaction between the associated enterprises.

Cost Plus Method

With Cost Plus Method, you emphasize on costs of the supplier of goods or services in the controlled transaction. Once you're aware of the costs, you need to add a markup. This markup must reflect the profit for the associated enterprise on basis of risks and functions performed. The result is the arm's' length price. Generally, the markup in the cost plus method would be calculated after the direct and indirect cost related to production or supply is considered. But, operating expenses of an enterprise (like overhead expenses) aren't part of this markup.

Problems associated with Transfer Pricing

There are quite a few problems associated with the transfer prices. Some of these issues include:

- There could be differences in opinions among organizational divisional managers with respect to how transfer price needs to be set.
- Additional time, costs and manpower would be required for executing the transfer prices and designing the accounting system to match the requirements of transfer pricing rules.
- Arm's length prices might cause dysfunctional behavior among the managers of organizational units.
- For some of the divisions or departments, for instance, a service department, arm's length prices don't work equally well as such departments don't offer measurable benefits.
- The transfer pricing issue in a multinational setup is very complicated.

Domestic Transfer Pricing

Till March 2013, the transfer pricing provisions were limited to international transactions alone. From April 2013 Transfer Pricing provisions have been extended to SDTs (Specified Domestic Transactions) and are applicable from the assessment year 2013-14.

Transactions which are covered under the Specified Domestic Transactions include:

- Expenditures in which payment has been made or would be made to:
  a. A director
  b. A relative of the director
  c. An entity where a director or the company has the voting interest exceeding 20%
- Transactions which relates to transfer of goods or services provided in Section 80-IA (8) & (10) (i.e. deductions which are related to profits and gains from enterprises engaged in infrastructure development or industrial undertakings, producers and distributors of power or Telecommunication Service Providers). SDT is also applicable to the transactions between the entity located in a tax holiday area, and the one which is situated in a non-tax holiday area in case both are under same management structure.

The above transactions would be treated as Specified Domestic Transactions only if the aggregate value of such transactions exceeds INR 5 crore.

CORPORATE TAX PLANNING

Corporate tax planning provides strategies that are significant in minimizing taxes. Some valuable ways to save include sponsoring a retirement plan, writing off company assets, claiming depreciation expense, taking deductions on business automobiles, office expenses, self employment health insurance, employer sponsored child care resources, and using a home office for the company. Business tax planning involves understanding what it means to be self-employed. A company owner needs to be aware of anything that might impact taxes paid. Self-employment tax, company expenses and deductions, business assets, charitable contributions, shifting income, and retirement planning are important considerations.

Self-employment tax is due from those who are receiving income as an independent contractor, sole proprietor, or anyone who is conducting business through selling services or products. Corporate tax planning provides some ways that a business owner can save on income taxes both short-term and long-term. Income received must be reported but deductions can reduce the amount that is actually owed. The deductions can vary depending upon the type of industry and what are considered legitimate deductions.

Some company owners shift income to a family member as a tax advantage. In order to do this a family member must be providing some benefit to the business and the amount should be in line with the type of compensation. Shifting income legitimately can lower a company into a lower tax bracket. Of course the shifting of income to a family member could raise their income bracket and this should be considered. This is a business tax planning venture that should benefit both parties and should be done ethically and reasonably. To shift a large amount of income to a family member just to avoid paying taxes would be unethical unless there were a legitimate reason such as payment for services.

A retirement plan is a tax advantage to a person who is self-employed. This can be done with or without employees. However, it would affect the type of plan that is embraced. A self-employed person can place pre-tax dollars into a retirement account. Having employees mean providing for them the capability of doing the same. A company owner can also choose other employee benefit plans to attract employees. Corporate tax planning involves looking out for employees by offering retirement, cafeteria and medical benefit plans. Cafeteria plans allow employees to use a portion of pre-tax income for medical or child care expenses. Corporations do not have to pay payroll taxes or workers company premiums on the dollars that are paid into a cafeteria plan or medical benefits plan.

There are many deductions that a company can take advantage of including start-up costs, business trip expenses, home office use, the use of automobiles, and other assets. The costs of health care expenses are often deductible especially for the owner and dependents. In addition, any contributions made to a health savings account are also deductible expenses. Business tax planning includes knowing what plans provide the greatest benefits and implementing those plans to not only provide benefits to the company but benefits to employees as well.

There is a degree of burden that is felt from tax legislation by any and every owner. However, there are positive ways that a corporation can comply with obligations and find ways to develop a strong company otherwise. Business tax planning includes taking advantage of opportunities to provide relief when possible. A corporate planning attorney can provide some good advice on how to structure a company to be optimally successful while remaining compliant with considerations such as paying taxes. Information can be found on the Internet that can help prepare a new business owner with how to be compliant in every area when it comes to reporting income and deducting expenses.

Charitable contributions are a great way for a company to save on taxes and help those in the community. Many non profit organizations are set up to help those who are less fortunate within the community that they reside and some offer services to anyone who they can help no matter where they are located. There are limits on how much of a contribution that can be counted and the organization has to fit the guidelines used by the IRS to be considered a legitimate charitable organization. Some of the ones who usually do qualify are churches, educational companies, scientific or medical research institutions, those that provide true charitable services and organizations who help animals. There is more information on the Internet about organizations that truly qualify as charitable.

Long-range tax financial planning involves strategically placing liquid assets where monies can earn the greatest return. Investing in mutual funds, stocks and bonds, purchasing real estate, and saving for retirement or college are all smart moves for consumers who want to minimize tax obligations over the long haul. Most individuals spend a lifetime earning as much money as possible, but few are aware of the legal means of protecting assets and keeping the government from dipping into savings. There are three major ways to minimize taxes: reduce net taxable income, investigate and take advantage of all allowable credits, and increase deductions by itemizing every allowable expense.

Thousands of taxpayers fail to take more than standard deductions simply because of a lack of knowledge about federal and state credits. A prime example is the Earned Income Tax Credit (EITC) which helps taxpayers without children reduce taxable income. Military personnel and ministers also qualify for EITC. The Child Tax Credit makes parenting just a little more appealing and provides a credit of up to $1,000 for qualifying child. Grandparents under the age of 65, foster parents, siblings raising younger brothers and sisters, and biological Moms and Dads can all reduce taxable income by taking advantage of the Child Tax Credit. While "rendering unto Caesar the things that are Caesar's" is commendable, protecting personal finances through tax financial planning is not only legal, but also wise and prudent. "For wisdom is better than rubies; and all the things that may be desired are not to be compared to it. I wisdom dwell with prudence, and find out knowledge of witty inventions".

Short-term tax financial planning includes increasing the number of dependents on 9-to-5 employment so that more money is taken out during the year. At the end of the year, individuals who increase dependents allowed by law will usually wind up getting a refund or owing much less to the government than those who claim fewer dependents. Of course, the Internal Revenue Service may take a closer look at a single man claiming an excessive number of dependents that are not in residence at least six months out of the year.

While most taxpayers dread pulling out records and receipts to prepare returns, there is a benefit to itemizing as many deductions as possible. The more deductions claimed, the less net taxable income to report. Self-employed individuals and those with home businesses frequently neglect to take deductions for gasoline, travel and meals. Deductions for a home office, no matter how small, can also reduce net taxable income. Simply measure the in-home office, figure the percentage of the home's total square footage, and take a deduction equal to that percentage of all utilities, mortgage, and other household expenses.

Big spenders who want to shield liquid assets from Uncle Sam should look into offshore tax planning. Taxpayers usually pay revenue on capital assets owned in the country in which they reside; but the rich and famous have discovered a way to minimize and eliminate paying revenue by investing money into offshore properties. Exotic islands may be the playground for the wealthy, but they are also prime low tax jurisdictions. The islands of Barbados, the Turks, and Caicos; Switzerland; Canada; and China all offer investors seeking to minimize or reduce taxes a place to dispose of wealth which would normally be heavily assessed in the U.S. The savings are so substantial that corporations routinely move operations offshore to shield assets.

Individuals and entrepreneurs seeking to keep as much annual earnings as possible should seek the advice of financial planning professionals who can suggest a myriad of ways to protect assets. It is never too early to begin long-range planning; and the sooner individuals begin securing a financial future, the sooner the benefits of sound fiscal management can be enjoyed. Businesses desiring to avoid paying excessive revenue should include offshore tax planning as part of a sound fiscal strategy. A small percentage of assets placed in a low tax jurisdiction can net excellent returns without incurring liability.

TAX AVOIDING VS TAX EVASION

Every assessee wants to escape from paying taxes, which encourages them to use various means to avoid such payment. And when it's about savings if taxes, the two most common practices that can be seen all around the world are tax avoidance and tax evasion. **Tax avoidance** is an exercise in which the assessee legally tries to defeat the basic intention of the law, by taking advantage of the shortcomings in the legislature.

On the contrary, **tax evasion** is a practice of reducing tax liability through illegal means, i.e. by suppressing income or inflating expenses or by showing lower income. In other words, Tax Avoidance is completely lawful because only those means are employed which are legal, while Tax Evasion is considered as a crime in the whole world, as it resorts to various kinds of deliberate manipulations.

Basis for Comparison	Tax Avoidance	Tax Evasion
Meaning	Minimization of tax liability, by taking such means which do not violate the tax rules, is Tax Avoidance.	Reducing tax liability by using illegal ways is known as Tax Evasion.
What is it?	Hedging of tax	Concealment of tax
Attributes	Immoral in nature, which involves bending the law without breaking it.	Illegal and objectionable, both in script and moral.
Concept	Taking unfair advantage of the shortcomings in the tax laws.	Deliberate manipulations in accounts resulting in fraud.
Legal implication	Use of Justified means	Use of such means that are forbidden by law
Happened when	Before the occurrence of tax liability.	After tax liability arises.
Type of act	Legal	Criminal
Consequences	Deferment of tax liability	Penalty or imprisonment
Objective	To reduce tax liability by applying the script of law.	To reduce tax liability by exercising unfair means.

An arrangement made to beat the intent of the law by taking unfair advantage of the shortcomings in the tax rules is known as Tax Avoidance. It refers to finding out new methods or tools to avoid the payment of taxes which are within the limits of the law.

This can be done by adjusting the accounts in a manner that it will not violate any tax rules as well as the tax incurrence will also be minimised. Formerly tax avoidance is considered as lawful, but now it comes to the category of crime in some special cases.

The only purpose of tax avoidance is to postpone or shift or eliminate the tax liability. This can be done investing in government schemes and offers like the tax credit, tax privileges, deductions, exemptions, etc., which will result in the reduction in the tax liability without making any offence or breach of law.

An illegal act, made to escape from paying taxes is known as Tax Evasion. Such illegal practices can be deliberate concealment of income, manipulation in accounts, disclosure of unreal expenses for deductions, showing personal expenditure as business expenses, overstatement of tax credit or exemptions suppression of profits and capital gains, etc. This will result in the disclosure of income which is not the actual income earned by the entity.

Tax Evasion is a criminal activity for which the assessee is subject to punishment under the law. It involves acts like:

- Deliberate misrepresentation of material facts.
- Hiding relevant documents.
- Not maintaining complete records of all the transactions.
- Making false statements.

The following are the major differences between Tax Avoidance and Tax Evasion:

1. A planning made to reduce the tax burden without infringement of the legislature is known as Tax Avoidance. An unlawful act, done to avoid tax payment is known as Tax Evasion.

2. Tax avoidance refers to hedging of tax, but tax evasion implies the suppression of tax.
3. Tax avoidance is immoral that tends to bend the law without causing any damage to it. Unlike tax evasion, which is illegal and objectionable both according to law and morality.
4. Tax avoidance aims at minimising the tax burden by applying the script of law. However, tax evasion minimises the tax liability by exercising unfair means.
5. Tax Avoidance involves taking benefit of the loopholes in the law. Conversely, Tax Evasion includes the deliberate concealment of material facts.
6. The arrangement for tax avoidance is made prior to the occurrence of tax liability. Unlike Tax Evasion, where the arrangements for it, are made after the occurrence of the tax liability.
7. Tax avoidance is completely legal however Tax Evasion is a criminal activity.
8. The result of tax avoidance is the postponement of tax, whereas the consequence of tax evasion if the assessee is found guilty of doing so, is either imprisonment or penalty or both.

Tax Avoidance and Tax Evasion both are meant to reduce the tax liability ultimately but what makes the difference is that the former is justified in the eyes of the law as it does not make any offence or breaks any law. However, it is biased as the honest tax payers are not fools, but they can also make arrangements for postponing unnecessary tax. If we talk about the latter, it is completely unjustified because it is a fraudulent activity, because it involves the acts which are forbidden by the law and hence it is punishable.

TECHNIQUES OF CORPORATE TAX PLANNING

The avid goal of every taxpayer is to minimize his Tax Liability. To achieve this objective taxpayer may resort to following three methods :

1. Tax Planning
2. Tax Avoidance
3. Tax Evasion

MEANING OF TAX PLANNING

Tax Planning involves planning in order to avail all exemptions, deductions and rebates provided in Act. The Income Tax law itself provides for various methods for Tax Planning, Generally it is provided under exemptions u/s 10, deductions u/s 80C to 80U and rebates and relief's. Some of the provisions are enumerated below :

- Investment in securities provided u/s 10(15) . Interest on such securities is fully exempt from tax.
- Exemptions u/s 10A, 10B, and 10BA
- Residential Status of the person
- Choice of accounting system
- Choice of organization.

For availing benefits, one should resort to bonafide means by complying with the provisions of law in letter and in spirit.

Where a person buys a machinery instead of hiring it, he is availing the benefit of depreciation. If it's his exclusive right either to buy or lease it . In the same manner to choice the form of organization, capital structure, buy or make products are the assesse's exclusive right. One may look for various tax incentives in the above said transactions provided in this Act, for reduction of tax liability. All this transaction involves tax planning.

Why Every Person Needs Tax Planning ?

Tax Planning is resorted to maximize the cash inflow and minimize the cash outflow. Since, Tax is kind of cast, the reduction of cost shall increase the profitability. Every prudence person, to maximize the return, shall increase the profits by resorting to a tool known as a tax planning.

How is Tool of Tax Planning Exercised ?

Tax Planning should be done by keeping in mine following factors :

- The Planning should be done before the accrual of income. Any planning done after the accrual income is known as Application of Income an it may lead to a conclusion of that there is a fraud.
- Tax Planning should be resorted at the source of income.
- The choice of location of business , undertaking, or division also play a very important role.
- Residential Status of a person. Therefore, a person should arranged his stay in India such a way that he is treated as NR in India.
- Choice to Buy or Lease the Assets. Where the assets are bought, depreciation is allowed and when asset is leased, lease rental is allowed as deduction.
- Capital Structure decision also plays a major role. Mixture of debt and equity fund should be balanced, to maximize the return on capital and minimize the tax liability. Interest on debt is allowed as deduction whereas dividend on equity fund is not allowed as deduction

Methods of Tax Planning

Various methods of Tax Planning may be classified as follows :

1. **Short Term Tax Planning.** Short range Tax Planning means the planning thought of and executed at the end of the income year to reduce taxable income in a legal way.

   Example. Suppose , at the end of the income year, an assessee finds his taxes have been too high in comparison with last year and he intends to reduce it. Now, he may do that, to a great extent by making proper arrangements to get the maximum tax rebate u/s 88. Such plan does not involve any long term commitment, yet it results in substantial savings in tax.
2. **Long Term Tax Planning.** Long range tax planning means a plan called out at the beginning or the income year to be followed around the year. This type of planning does not help immediately as in the case of short range planning but is likely to help in the long run; e.g. If an assessee transferred shares held by him to his minor son or spouse, though the income from such transferred shares will be clubbed with his income u/s 64, yet is the income is invested by the son or spouse, then the income from such investment will be treated as income of the son or spouse. Moreover, if the company issue any bonus shareds for the shares transferred , that will also be treated as income in the hands of the son or spouse.
3. **Permissive Tax Planning.** Permissive Tax Planning means making plans which are permissible under different provisions of the law, such as planning of earning income covered by Sec.10, specially by Sec. 10(1) , Planning of taking advantage of different incentives and deductions, planning for availing different tax concessions etc.
4. **Purposive Tax Planning.** It means making plans with specific purpose to ensure the availability of maximum benefits to the assessee through correct selection of investment, making suitable programme for replacement of assets, varying the residential status and diversifying business activities and income etc.

TAX CONSIDERATIONS IN SPECIFIC BUSINESS SITUATIONS

Make or Buy Decisions

The make-or-buy decision is vital process in management field. It is basically action of making a tactical choice between producing an item internally (in-house) or purchasing it externally (from an outside supplier). The buy side of the decision also is called outsourcing. Make-or-buy decisions generally develop when company that has produced a product or part or considerably changed a product or part is having concern with current dealers, or has weakening capacity or varying demand. The make-or-buy issue is complicated which represents a major dilemma faced by several companies. In aggressive competitive business environment, all the manufacturing and services companies must have to reassess their existing processes, technologies, products and services in order to get an opportunity to positively impact the bottom line by making strategically-drawn out make-or-buy decisions.

Make-or-buy analysis is done at the strategic and operational level. Clearly, the strategic level is the more long-range of the two. Variables considered at the strategic level comprise of analysis of the future, as well as the current environment. There are numerous issues that affect make or buy decisions that include government regulation, competing firms, and market trends. Companies should make items that emphasise or are in-line with their core capabilities. In current business situation, people are more aware of make-or-buy decision therefore organizations have difficulty when deciding between keeping technologies/processes in-house and purchasing them from an outside dealer. The highly vibrant nature of the market demand-supply environment forces firms to consider, and reassess, make-or-buy decisions that are based on not just the basic cost-related factors, but also on a multitude of other reasons. Additionally, the make or buy decision are visualized as an operational or tactical level as well as at strategic level. There are longer-term strategic considerations entwined with the make-or-buy decision that has great significance.

Companies that adopt the process of lean manufacturing has prompted an increase in outsourcing. Manufacturers are tending to purchase subassemblies instead of piece parts, and are outsourcing activities that range from logistics to administrative services. In their 2003 book World Class Supply Management, David Burt, Donald Dobler, and Stephen Starling gave a rule of thumb for out-sourcing. It recommended that company outsource all items that do not fit one of the following three categories: (1) the item is critical to the success of the product, including customer perception of important product attributes; (2) the item requires specialized design and manufacturing skills or equipment, and the number of capable and reliable suppliers are extremely limited; and (3) the item fits well within the firm's core competencies, or within those the firm must develop to fulfil forthcoming plans. Items that are suitable under one of these three categories are considered strategic in nature and should be produced internally if possible.

Make-or-buy decisions also happen at the operational level. Analysis in separate texts by Burt, Dobler, and Starling, as well as Joel Wisner, G. Keong Leong, and Keah-Choon Tan, propose these considerations that favour making a part in-house:

- Cost considerations (less expensive to make the part)
- Desire to integrate plant operations
- Productive use of excess plant capacity to help absorb fixed overhead (using existing idle capacity)
- Need to exert direct control over production and/or quality
- Better quality control
- Design secrecy is required to protect proprietary technology
- Unreliable suppliers

- No competent suppliers
- Desire to maintain a stable workforce (in periods of declining sales)
- Quantity too small to interest a supplier
- Control of lead time, transportation, and warehousing costs
- Greater assurance of continual supply
- Provision of a second source
- Political, social or environmental reasons (union pressure)
- Emotion (e.g., pride)

Various factors that may influence company to buy a part externally are as follows:

1. Lack of expertise
2. Suppliers' research and specialized know-how exceeds that of the buyer cost considerations (less expensive to buy the item)
3. Small-volume requirements
4. Limited production facilities or insufficient capacity
5. Desire to maintain a multiple-source policy
6. Indirect managerial control considerations
7. Procurement and inventory considerations
8. Brand preference
9. Item not essential to the firm's strategy

The two vital factors that must be considered in a make-or-buy decision are cost and the availability of production capacity. Burt, Dobler, and Starling advised that "no other factor is subject to more varied interpretation and to greater misunderstanding" Cost considerations comprises of all relevant costs and be long-term in nature. Apparently, the buying firm will compare production and purchase costs. Burt, Dobler, and Starling provide the major elements included in this comparison. Elements of the "make" analysis include:

1. Incremental inventory-carrying costs
2. Direct labour costs
3. Incremental factory overhead costs
4. Delivered purchased material costs
5. Incremental managerial costs
6. Any follow-on costs stemming from quality and related problems
7. Incremental purchasing costs
8. Incremental capital costs

Cost considerations for the "buy" analysis include:

1. Purchase price of the part
2. Transportation costs
3. Receiving and inspection costs
4. Incremental purchasing costs
5. Any follow-on costs related to quality or service

It is to be noted that six of the costs to consider are incremental. Incremental costs would not be incurred if the parts were purchased from an outside source. If a firm does not have the capacity to make the part, incremental costs will include variable costs plus the full portion of fixed overhead allocable to the part's manufacture. If the firm has more capacity that can be used to produce the part in question, only the variable overhead caused by production of the parts are considered incremental.

Senior management normally face issues of make and buy decision who want to reveal and exploit capability within the links of the supply chain. Make or buy is a decision not to be made on the basis of monetary considerations, since procurement or loss of core competencies may also be involved. Companies must determine how that decision will affect the end product quality and the company's technology when making best make-or-buy decision. There are four stages for successful make-or-buy decision:

1. Building incentive for outsourcing,
2. Exploring strategic implications,
3. Analysing costs/performance,
4. Selecting providers.

Advantage of make or buy decision. Make or buy decisions are imperative when manufacturers consider the benefits and shortcomings of buying materials and parts from retailers as opposed to making these items internally. A make or buy decision contributes company's development but it may not be the correct decision for the long term. Make or buy decisions relate to autonomy, and these decisions helps in choosing among more than one option instead of simply accepting the available option. Make or buy decision can save business money if company can lower its materials costs by making items in house. Making these items will possibly increase labour costs, however, company need to balance the savings on materials against the added payroll cost to see whether making items in house or buying them from an outside retailer makes the most financial sense.

There is a flexibility in make or buy decisions to weigh and evaluate a range of considerations, from employee morale to production deadlines. When orders are down and company is unwilling to lay off employees, deciding to produce materials in house can keep workers employed, encouraged and available for any requirement. These benefits may compensate a financial consideration such as a short-term elevated expense for production labour. If deadlines are tight, the option to produce materials in house allows company to continue manufacturing if parts are slow to arrive. Make or buy decisions beneficial to company by control over the materials that go into the products to customers. If company is displeased with the quality of the materials that vendors provide, it can make them itself, in accordance with according to company's specifications. This way, company can offer high quality product.

To summarize, the make-or-buy procedure is critical strategic decisions within logistics outsourcing and should be taken in a structured and reliable way. The steps of the make-or-buy decision should be altered according to the specific organization and outsourcing situation. Major steps for make and buy decisions include evaluate whether outsourcing is right for company, determine exactly what functions to outsource and the performance expectations, use a well-defined professional selection process to evaluate and select which provider(s) are right for the job. These decisions are always individual decisions, which have to be taken into consideration as the specific characteristics of each company.

OWN OR LEASE AN ASSET

There are many factors to consider when you're acquiring equipment, buildings or automobiles. And one of the primary ones is, should you lease or should you buy? Both options have advantages and disadvantages based on your particular business situation.

To help you make the best decision in any given situation, you'll want to ask yourself the following questions:

How long do you plan to keep the asset? If you're only planning to keep it for the short term, you may find that leasing is a better alternative than buying it and trying to resell it when you no longer need it. You'll want to find out if there's a buyout option at the end of the lease if you decide you want to keep the asset after the original lease is over.

Is new or used equipment the best fit for your needs? Do you need new equipment, or can you utilize used equipment? Used equipment is often available at a lower cost, and while you'll save money on the purchase price, you may not have the option to lease it. New equipment, on the other hand, is often available for either buying or leasing.

One important task you'll want to undertake is to analyze the cost/benefit of new vs. used equipment, especially if you're just starting out. Investing in a lot of new equipment when you're just getting started can place an undue burden on your cash flow and finances. It might be better to start small and increase your capital acquisitions as you increase your profits and can support the growth.

How frequently does technology change with this asset? For assets that become outdated rapidly, it may be wiser to take on a short leases so you can always have the most recent technology, especially if technology is critical to your business. If your company isn't reliant on the latest technology, you'll often find it more cost effective to update you technology products a little less frequently, such as every three years.

What are my financing options for purchasing vs. leasing? Purchasing tends to require a higher monetary outlay initially in addition to having to finance your purchase through a lender. Depending on your situation, this may not be a viable option if you don't have a large enough cash reserve. Leasing generally requires less cash down, and the monthly payments are often smaller.

What are the tax benefits of buying vs. leasing? It's critical that you consider all related tax ramifications for both options as they relate to your particular business situation. There's usually a tax benefit associated with leasing where you get to deduct the full lease payment immediately. You should be sure to consult with your tax professional because each type of lease has a different accounting for tax purposes as to how much you get to deduct as an expense on your profit/loss statement.

When it comes to purchasing and financing the asset, you only get to deduct the interest portion as an expense. The principal amount that you're paying on the loan isn't considered a taxable deduction on your profit/loss Statement-it's considered a reduction of your loan liability.

Leasing and buying both offer advantages to companies. The key to making the right decision is understanding exactly what your company's needs are and the purpose of the asset. Answering the questions above will help ensure that you're making the best choice for your situation.

TAXATION

The main tax consideration which one has to keep in mind is whether expenditure on repair, replacement or renewal is deductible as revenue expenditure u/s 30,31, or 37(1). It the expenditure is deductible as revenue expenditure under these sections, then cost of financing such expenditure is reduced to the extent of tax save.

On the other hand if such expenditure is not allowed as deduction u/s 30,31 or 37(1) then it may be capitalized and on the amount so capitalized depreciation is available if certain conditions are satisfied.

"Repair" implies the existence of a thing has malfunctioned and can be set right by effecting repairs which may involve replacement of some parts, thereby making the thing as efficient as it was before or close to it as possible. After repair the thing to which the repair was carried out continues to be available for use. Replacement is different from repair.

"Replacement" implies the removal or discarding of the things that was in use, by a different or new thing capable of performing the same function with the same or greater efficiency. The replacement of a section in a series of machines which are interconnected , in a segment of the production process which together form an integrated whole may in some circumstances , be regarded as amounting to repair when without such replacement that unit in that segment will not function. That logic cannot be extended to the entire manufacturing facility from the stage of Raw Material to the delivery of the final finished product.

Difference Between Revenue and Capital Expenditure

Capital Expenditure	Revenue Expenditure
Cost of acquisition and installment charges of a fixed asset is a capital expenditure.	Purchase price of a current asset for resale or manufacture is a revenue expenditure.
Expenditure incurred to free oneself from a capital liability is a capital expenditure.	Expenditure incurred to free oneself from a revenue liability is a revenue expenditure.
Expenditure incurred towards acquisition of a source of income is a capital expenditure.	Expenditure incurred towards an income is a revenue expenditure.
Expenditure incurred to increase the operating capacity of fixed assets is capital expenditure.	Expenditure incurred to maintain the fixed assets is a revenue expenditure
Expenditure incurred for obtaining capital by issue of shares is a capital expenditure	Expenditure incurred towards raising loans or issue of debentures is a revenue expenditure.

"Current Repair" implies the expenditure must have been incurred to 'preserve and maintain' an already existing asset and the object of the expenditure must not be to bring a new asset into existence of for obtaining a new advantage.

Shifting of Administrative Office. Expenditure incurred for shifting the administrative office from one city to another city as a result of amalgamation of three companies having a number of activities in various centers is allowable as Revenue Expenditure.

Shifting of Head Office from one place to another is Capital Expenditure. Where the assessee-company shifted its head office from one place to another place after it Board of Directors resolved that it would be commercially prudent to centralized the Registered Office of the company in one place, in connection with the shifting , it incurred huge expenses including a certain payment made to the lawyers, the expenses incurred on this account could not be on revenue account.

Expenditure of shifting of employees is Revenue Expenditure. Expenditure incurred by assessee on shifting of employees to another place consequent on shifting of factory to another site due to labour unrest was allowable as Revenue Expenditure.

Decoration of reception / dining halls in Hotels is revenue expenditure. Expenses incurred in putting up decorative mirrors in the wall, plaster molded roof, plywood panels, etc. in reception-cum dinning halls of a Hotel, in order to deep the place fir and attract customers, is deductible as revenue expenditure.

Expenditure on renovation an modernization of Hotel Premises is Revenue Expenditure. Expenditure incurred solely for repairs and modernizing the Hotel and replacing the existing components of the building, furniture, and fittings, with a view to create a conductive and beautiful atmosphere for the purpose of running of a business of a Hotel , will fall under the category of Revenue Expenditure only, and is hence deductible.

Expenditure on Wall to Wall Carpet for office is capital expenditure. Expenditure on purchase of wall-to-wall carpet, for being used in the office, has nothing to do with the augmenting, preserving or protecting the turnover or profits of the business and hence it is in the nature of capital expenditure.

Repairs to building can be capital or revenue, depending on nature of change brought about. So long as the repair does not bring into existence an additional advantages or benefit of an enduring nature or change the nature, character or the identity of the building itself, the expenditure must be regarded as a revenue expenditure. On the other hand, if it does, it will be in the nature of a Capital Expenditure.

Replacement of Assets as a whole is not 'Repair'. Where substantial repairs are carried out in order to put to use an existing asset, the same could be termed as Revenue Expenditure. But where there is replacement 'As a Whole', it amounts to reconstruction and not repairs. It is pertinent that the asset in its old form must continue to exist to say that the expenditure involved in improving the assets is Revenue Expenditure. Where effacement takes place and a new asset comes into being, then expenditure involved would become a Capital Expenditure.

Repairs for converting Godown into Administrative Office. Where the assessee incurred expenditure on repairs to a godown used for business purpose so as to convert it into an Administrative Office, the expenditure was allowable as revenue expenditure, since the business asset has retained its character and only its use had changed, and the use at both points of time, i.e. before and after the expenditure was incurred, related to the business of the assessee without there being any addition to or expansion of the profit-making apparatus of the assessee.

Remodeling of furniture in retail outlet is revenue expenditure. The expenditure incurred by the assessee company towards the remodeling of furniture in its various retails depots which was necessitated by changes in design, was deductible as revenue expenditure.

Repair and replacement of false ceiling in cinema building is revenue expenditure. Expenditure on repair and replacement of false ceiling in cinema building owned by the assessee was allowable as revenue expenditure, since it was incurred for keeping the business running.

Replacement of electric wiring in cinema building is revenue expenditure, since it was incurred for keeping the business running.

Expenditure in repairs to car damaged during riots are deductible. Expenditure to repair damage to car in which director of assessee-company was traveling to the business premises, was allowable as business expenditure.

SHUT DOWN OR CONTINUE OPERATIONS

A shutdown point is a level of operations at which a company experiences no benefit for continuing operations, and therefore decides to shut down temporarily (or in some cases permanently). It results from the combination of output and price where the company earns just enough revenue to cover its total variable costs. The shutdown point denotes the exact moment when a company's (marginal) revenue is equal to its variable (marginal) costs - in other words, it occurs when the marginal profit becomes negative.

At this point, there is no economic benefit to continuing production. If an additional loss occurs, either through a rise in variable costs or a fall in revenue, the cost of operating will outweigh the revenue. At that point, shutting down operation is more practical than continuing, even if the company continues to experience losses in other areas, such as fixed costs. If the reverse occurs, continuing production is more practical.

If a company can produce revenues greater or equal to its total variable costs, it can use the additional revenues to pay down its fixed costs, assuming fixed costs, such as lease contracts or other lengthy obligations, will still be incurred when the firm shuts down. When a company can earn a positive contribution margin, it should remain in operations despite an overall marginal loss.

The shutdown point does not include an analysis of fixed costs in its determination. It is based entirely on determining at what point the marginal costs associated with operation exceed the revenue being generated by those operations.

A shutdown point can apply to all of the operations a business participates in, or just a portion of its operations. Certain seasonal businesses, such as Christmas tree farmers, may shut down almost entirely during the off-season. While fixed costs remain during the shutdown, variable costs can be eliminated.

Other businesses may experience fluctuations or produce some goods year-round, while others are only produced seasonally. For example, Cadbury chocolate bars are produced year-round, while Cadbury Cream Eggs are considered a seasonal product. The main operations, focused on the chocolate bars, may remain operational year-round while the cream egg operations may go through periods of shutdown during the off-season.

The length of a shutdown may be temporary or permanent, depending on the nature of the economic conditions leading to the shutdown. For non-seasonal goods, an economic recession may reduce demand from consumers, forcing a temporary shutdown (in full or in part) until the economy recovers. Other times, demand dries up completely due to changing consumer preferences or technological change. For instance, nobody produces cathode-ray tube (CRT) televisions or computer monitors any longer, and it would be a losing prospect to open a factory these days to produce them.

Fixed costs are the costs that remain regardless of what operations are taking place. This can include payments to maintain the rights to the facility, such as rent or mortgage payments, along with any minimum utilities that must be maintained. Minimum staffing costs are considered fixed if a certain number of employees must be maintained even when operations cease.

Variable costs are more closely tied to actual operations. This can include, but is not limited to, employee wages for those whose positions are tied directly to production, certain utility costs or the cost of the materials required for production.

DEDUCTION AND COLLECTION OF TAX AT SOURCE

TDS

TDS or Tax Deducted at Source is income tax reduced from the money paid at the time of making specified payments such as rent, commission, professional fees, salary, interest etc. by the persons making such payments. Usually, the person receiving income is liable to pay income tax. But the government with the help of Tax Deducted at Source provisions makes sure that income tax is deducted in advance from the payments being made by you. Any person making specified payments mentioned under the Income Tax Act are required to deduct TDS at the time of making such specified payment. But no TDS has to deducted if the person making the payment is an individual or HUF whose books are not required to be audited.

However, in case of rent payments made by individuals and HUF exceeding Rs 50,000 per month, are required to deduct TDS @ 5% even if the individual or HUF is not liable for a tax audit. Also, such Individuals and HUF liable to deduct TDS @ 5% need not apply for TAN. The Tax Deducted at Source must be deposited to the government by 7th of the subsequent month. Tax Deducted at Source has to be deposited using Challan ITNS-281 on the government portal. Filing Tax Deducted at Source returns is mandatory for all the persons who have deducted TDS. TDS return is to be submitted quarterly and various details need to be furnished like TAN, amount of TDS deducted, type of payment, PAN of deductee, etc. Also, different forms are prescribed for filing returns depending upon the purpose of the deduction of TDS. Form 16, Form 16A, Form 16 B and Form 16 C are all TDS certificates. TDS certificates have to be issued by a person deducting TDS to the assessee from whose income TDS was deducted while making payment. For instance, banks issue Form 16A to the depositor when TDS is deducted on interest from fixed deposits. Form 16 is issued by the employer to the employee.

ADVANCE PAYMENT OF TAX

As the name suggests, it refers to paying a part of your yearly taxes in advance. Advance tax is the income tax payable if your tax liability exceeds Rs 10,000 in a financial year. Advance tax should be paid in the year in which the income is received. Hence, it is also known as the 'pay-as-you-earn' scheme.

Advance tax is applicable when an individual has sources of income other than his/her salary. For instance, if one is earning through capital gains, interest on investments, lottery, house property or business, the concept becomes relevant.

Any rebate due fetches you an interest of 0.5 per cent every month, or, six per cent annually, as in the case of an income tax refund. However, if you don't pay the advance tax on time, you'll be charged one per cent every month, or, 12 per cent a year.

Who should file it?

If you are salaried, you need not pay advance tax as your employer deducts tax at source (TDS). However, you still need to file it if you have other sources of income, increasing your liability to more than Rs 10,000. Professionals (self-employed) and businessmen will have to pay taxes in advance as, given their business income, the liability can be huge. The same goes for companies and corporates.

When to file advance tax?

Advance tax or self-assessment taxes have to be paid on the 15th of September, December and March, in instalments of 30 per cent, 30 per cent and 40 per cent, respectively, for non-corporates. Corporates need to pay it on the 15th of June, September, December and March.

While employers deduct TDS on salaries, advance tax is paid on income that has not been subjected to TDS.

How to file it?

You can pay advance tax using the tax payment challan at the bank branches empanelled with the Income Tax (I-T) department. It can be deposited with the Reserve Bank of India, State Bank of India, ICICI Bank, HDFC Bank, Indian Overseas Bank, Indian Bank, and other authorised banks. There are 926 branches in India that can accept advance tax payments. You could also pay it online through the I-T department or the National Securities Depository site.

E-Filing if ITRs

E-filing or electronic filing is submitting your income tax returns online. There are two ways to file your income tax returns. The traditional way is the offline way, where you go the Income Tax Department's office to physically file your returns. The other way is when you e-file through the internet. Over the past few years, e filing has become popular because it is easier, doesn't require prints of documents, and can be done for free!

Am I Required to File Income Tax Returns?

It is mandatory to file income tax returns in India if any of the below conditions are applicable to you (as per the Income Tax Act):

Earn gross annual income more than:

	Amount
For individuals below 60 years	Rs 2.5 Lakhs
For individuals above 80 years	Rs 5.0 Lakhs

- Earn income other than salary like house property, etc
- Want to claim income tax refund from the department

- Earn from or have invested in foreign assets
- Wish to apply for visa or loan applications
- Company or a firm, irrespective of profit or loss

Difference Between AY and FY

Financial Year is the period between 1st April to 31st March. Assessment Year is the next year in which the income is liable to tax.

For example, if your financial year is from 1 April, 2015 to 31 March 2016, then it is known as FY 2015-16. The assessment year for income earned during this period would begin after the financial year ends–that is on 1 April 2016 until 31 March 2017.

After successfully submitting your income tax return, you get an acknowledgement from the IT department called the ITR-V or Income Tax Return-Verification. You receive a mail on your registered e-mail Id from the Income Tax Department containing the ITR-V.

MULTIPLE CHOICE QUESTIONS

1. What is the name of the tax levied on income in India?
   (1) Excise tax (2) Income tax
   (3) Sales tax (4) Service tax
2. Which of the following is not an objective of income tax in India?
   (1) To raise revenue for the government
   (2) To reduce income inequality
   (3) To promote economic growth
   (4) To control inflation
3. Which agency is responsible for administering income tax in India?
   (1) Reserve Bank of India
   (2) Central Board of Direct Taxes
   (3) Securities and Exchange Board of India
   (4) Ministry of Finance
4. What is the residential status of an individual who stays in India for more than 182 days during a financial year?
   (1) Non-resident
   (2) Resident
   (3) Resident but not ordinarily resident
   (4) Non-resident but deemed resident
5. Which of the following is not an exempted income under income tax in India?
   (1) Agricultural income
   (2) Dividend income
   (3) Interest income from savings bank account
   (4) All of the above are exempted income
6. What is the tax rate for agricultural income in India?
   (1) 0% (2) 10%
   (3) 20% (4) 30%
7. Which of the following is not a head of income for computation of taxable income under income tax in India?
   (1) Salary income
   (2) Business income
   (3) House property income
   (4) Gifts received from friends
8. Which of the following is a deduction available under section 80C of income tax?
   (1) Education loan interest paid
   (2) Medical insurance premium paid
   (3) Donation to charitable institutions
   (4) All of the above
9. What is the maximum amount of deduction available under section 80C of income tax?
   (1) Rs. 50,000 (2) Rs. 1,00,000
   (3) Rs. 1,50,000 (4) Rs. 2,00,000
10. What is the due date for filing income tax returns in India for the financial year 2020-21?
    (1) 31st July 2020
    (2) 31st August 2020
    (3) 31st December 2020
    (4) 31st March 2021
11. What is the penalty for late filing of income tax returns in India?
    (1) Rs. 5,000 (2) Rs. 10,000
    (3) Rs. 15,000 (4) Rs. 20,000
12. What is the tax rate for long-term capital gains on sale of equity shares in India?
    (1) 10% (2) 15%
    (3) 20% (4) 25%
13. Which of the following is not included in the calculation of gross total income under income tax in India?
    (1) Salary income
    (2) Rental income from house property
    (3) Dividend income
    (4) Municipal tax paid on house property
14. Which of the following is not a type of tax return form for filing income tax returns in India?
    (1) ITR 1 (2) ITR 2
    (3) ITR 3 (4) ITR 4
15. Which of the following is not a type of taxable income under income tax in India?
    (1) Salary income
    (2) Business income
    (3) Gifts received from family members
    (4) Capital gains

16. What is the tax rate applicable to income earned by non-residents and foreign companies in India?
(1) 10% (2) 20%
(3) 30% (4) 40%
17. Which of the following is an example of income from other sources under income tax in India?
(1) Salary income
(2) Rental income from house property
(3) Dividend income
(4) Gifts received from friends
18. Which of the following is a deduction available under section 80D of income tax?
(1) Medical insurance premium paid for parents
(2) Education loan interest paid
(3) Donation to charitable institutions
(4) All of the above
19. Which of the following is a benefit of filing income tax returns in India?
(1) Claiming tax refunds
(2) Avoiding penalties for non-filing
(3) Establishing proof of income
(4) All of the above
20. Which of the following taxes is not levied on income in India?
(1) Income tax
(2) Value Added Tax (VAT)
(3) Wealth tax
(4) None of the above
21. Which of the following is a benefit of tax planning?
(1) Minimising tax liability
(2) Maximising tax refunds
(3) Avoiding penalties for non-payment of taxes
(4) All of the above
22. Which of the following is not a source of income under income tax in India?
(1) Salary income
(2) Interest income from savings bank account
(3) Gifts received from relatives
(4) Rental income from commercial property
23. Which of the following is a benefit of e-filing income tax returns in India?
(1) Faster processing of returns
(2) Avoiding mistakes in returns
(3) Accessing tax return documents online
(4) All of the above
24. What is the tax rate for short-term capital gains on sale of equity shares in India?
(1) 10% (2) 15%
(3) 20% (4) 25%
25. Which of the following is not a required document for filing income tax returns in India?
(1) Form 16 (2) Aadhaar card
(3) PAN card
(4) All of the above are required documents
26. Which of the following is a deduction available under section 80G of income tax?
(1) Medical insurance premium paid for self and family
(2) Donations to certain charitable institutions
(3) Interest paid on education loan
(4) All of the above
27. Which of the following types of taxpayers are not eligible to use ITR 1 form for filing income tax returns in India?
(1) Individuals with income from salary/pension
(2) Individuals with income from house property
(3) Individuals with income from capital gains
(4) All of the above are eligible to use ITR 1
28. What is the tax rate for short-term capital gains on sale of debt mutual funds in India?
(1) 10%
(2) 20%
(3) Depends on the individual's income tax bracket
(4) No tax on short-term capital gains on sale of debt mutual funds
29. Which of the following is a benefit of claiming deductions under income tax in India?
(1) Reducing the taxable income
(2) Avoiding tax liability
(3) Maximising tax refunds
(4) All of the above
30. Which of the following is not a taxable income for minors in India?
(1) Income from salary
(2) Income from house property
(3) Income from gifts received from non-relatives
(4) Income from investments

31. Which of the following is a deduction available under section 80GG of income tax?
(1) Rent paid for residential accommodation
(2) Medical insurance premium paid for parents
(3) Education loan interest paid
(4) None of the above

32. Which of the following is not a head of income for computation of income from business and profession?
(1) Salary income
(2) Rental income
(3) Profit from sale of goods
(4) Income from freelance work

33. What is the tax rate for long-term capital gains on sale of debt mutual funds in India?
(1) 10%
(2) 20%
(3) Depends on the individual's income tax bracket
(4) No tax on long-term capital gains on sale of debt mutual funds

34. Which of the following is a benefit of maintaining proper records for income tax purposes?
(1) Easy calculation of taxable income
(2) Avoiding mistakes in returns
(3) Responding to tax notices effectively
(4) All of the above

35. Which of the following types of taxpayers are required to conduct tax audits under income tax in India?
(1) Individuals with income above a certain threshold
(2) Companies and firms
(3) Trusts and institutions
(4) All of the above

36. Which of the following is an example of indirect tax in India?
(1) Income tax
(2) Goods and Services Tax (GST)
(3) Wealth tax
(4) None of the above

37. Which of the following is not included in the calculation of net income under income tax in India?
(1) Deductions under section 80C to 80U
(2) Taxes paid on income
(3) Interest income from savings bank account
(4) None of the above

38. Which of the following is the date from which income tax returns are processed by the Income Tax Department in India?
(1) 1st April (2) 1st July
(3) 1st October (4) 1st January

39. Which of the following is a benefit of filing income tax returns even if no tax is due?
(1) Establishing financial credibility
(2) Accessing bank loans and credit cards easily
(3) Proof of income for visa applications
(4) All of the above

40. Which of the following is a required document for verification after e-filing income tax returns in India?
(1) Form 16
(2) PAN card
(3) Aadhaar card
(4) None-verification is done online

41. What is the tax rate for long-term capital gains on sale of property in India?
(1) 10%
(2) 20%
(3) Depends on the individual's income tax bracket
(4) No tax on long-term capital gains on sale of property

42. Which of the following is a benefit of tax audit under income tax in India?
(1) Avoiding penalties for non-compliance
(2) Recording transactions accurately
(3) Minimising tax liability
(4) All of the above

43. What is the mode of payment for income tax in India?
(1) Cash only
(2) Cheque only
(3) Demand draft only
(4) Online payment allowed

44. Which of the following is a head of income for computation of income from house property?
(1) Salary income
(2) Profit from sale of goods
(3) Rental income
(4) None of the above

45. Which of the following is a deduction available under section 80E of income tax?
(1) Education loan interest paid for self and family
(2) Donations to certain charitable institutions
(3) Medical insurance premium paid for self and family
(4) None of the above

46. Which of the following is a prerequisite for e-filing of income-tax return?
(1) Possession of a computer
(2) Possession of a digital signature
(3) Possession of a smartphone
(4) None of the above

47. Which of the following types of taxpayers are required to prepare and maintain books of accounts under income tax in India?
(1) Individuals with income above a certain threshold
(2) Businesses and professions
(3) Trusts and institutions
(4) All of the above

48. Which of the following is not a head of income for computation of income from other sources?
(1) Interest income from savings bank account
(2) Rental income from house property
(3) Dividend income
(4) Income from freelance work

49. Which of the following types of taxpayers are required to file income tax returns in India?
(1) Individuals with income above a certain threshold
(2) Companies and firms
(3) Trusts and institutions
(4) All of the above

50. What is the tax rate for short-term capital gains on sale of property in India?
(1) 10%
(2) 20%
(3) Depends on the individual's income tax bracket
(4) No tax on short

51. What is double taxation?
(1) When a person is taxed twice on their income in two different countries
(2) When a person is taxed twice on their income in the same country
(3) When a person is taxed once on their income in two different countries
(4) When a person is not taxed on their income in any country

52. What is the purpose of the double taxation avoidance agreement (DTAA)?
(1) To prevent taxpayers from avoiding tax
(2) To prevent double taxation of income
(3) To encourage taxpayers to invest in foreign countries
(4) To increase tax revenue for host countries

53. Which of the following is not a mechanism for avoiding double taxation?
(1) Tax credits
(2) Tax treaties
(3) Transfer pricing
(4) Exemption

54. What is transfer pricing?
(1) When a company transfers its assets to another country to avoid tax
(2) When a company prices its goods or services for transfer between two entities within the same company group
(3) When a company transfers its profits to a tax haven
(4) When a company transfers its liabilities to another country to avoid tax

55. Which of the following is not a method for determining arm's length price in transfer pricing?
(1) Comparable uncontrolled price method
(2) Resale price method
(3) Market capitalization method
(4) Profit split method

56. What is the purpose of thin capitalization rules?
(1) To prevent companies from incurring too much debt
(2) To prevent companies from avoiding tax through excessive interest expenses
(3) To prevent companies from investing in foreign countries
(4) To increase tax revenue for host countries

57. Which of the following is not a factor that determines tax residency of an individual?
(1) Days present in a country
(2) Nationality
(3) Employment status
(4) Place of permanent residence

58. What is base erosion and profit shifting (BEPS)?
(1) A global tax reform initiative to address tax avoidance
(2) A strategy used by companies to evade tax
(3) A tax planning technique to Minimise tax liability
(4) None of the above

59. What is Controlled Foreign Corporation (CFC) rules?
(1) Rules that prevent multinational companies from shifting profits to tax havens
(2) Rules that prevent companies from operating in foreign countries
(3) Rules that prevent companies from involving in cross-border transactions
(4) Rules that prevent companies from investing in foreign countries

60. Which of the following is not a challenge in enforcing transfer pricing rules?
(1) Difficulty in determining arm's length price
(2) Complexity of inter-company transactions
(3) Influence of customs and traditions on pricing
(4) Difficulty in obtaining information from multinational companies

61. Which of the following is an example of a tax treaty between two countries?
(1) India-US Double Taxation Avoidance Agreement
(2) US-Mexico Free Trade Agreement
(3) China-India Bilateral Investment Treaty
(4) All of the above

62. Which of the following is not a mechanism for resolving transfer pricing disputes?
(1) Advance pricing agreement
(2) Independent arbitration
(3) Mutual agreement procedure
(4) Legal action in international court

63. Which of the following is an example of a fixed place of business for tax purposes?
(1) Home office
(2) Shared office space
(3) Warehouse for storing goods
(4) All of the above

64. What is the purpose of the general anti-avoidance rule (GAAR)?
(1) To prevent taxpayers from avoiding tax
(2) To prevent double taxation of income
(3) To encourage taxpayers to invest in foreign countries
(4) To increase tax revenue for host countries

65. Which of the following is not a type of permanent establishment for tax purposes?
(1) Fixed place of business
(2) Construction site
(3) Dependent agent
(4) Temporary stay

66. Which of the following is not a method for resolving tax disputes between two countries?
(1) Advance pricing agreement
(2) Independent arbitration
(3) Mutual agreement procedure
(4) Legal action in national court

67. Which of the following is not an example of transfer pricing methods under OECD guidelines?
(1) Cost plus method
(2) Transactional net margin method
(3) Comparable uncontrolled price method
(4) Random pricing method

68. Which of the following is an example of a tax haven?
(1) Luxembourg (2) Switzerland
(3) Indonesia (4) South Africa

69. Which of the following is not a purpose of transfer pricing regulations?
(1) To prevent tax avoidance
(2) To ensure fair allocation of taxable income
(3) To encourage foreign investment
(4) To promote transparency of inter-company transactions

70. Which of the following is not a type of tax credit?
(1) Foreign tax credit
(2) Income tax credit
(3) Property tax credit
(4) Sales tax credit

71. What is the meaning of the term 'permanent establishment'?
(1) A physical place of business in a foreign country
(2) A place of business that is not permanent in a foreign country
(3) A company resident in a foreign country
(4) A subsidiary of a company in a foreign country

72. What is the meaning of the term 'tax treaty'?
(1) A treaty signed between two countries for the purpose of avoiding double taxation
(2) A treaty signed between two countries for the purpose of increasing tax revenue
(3) A treaty signed between two countries for the purpose of promoting foreign investment
(4) A treaty signed between two countries for the purpose of avoiding tax havens

73. Which of the following is an example of a tax credit?
(1) Exemption from tax
(2) Reduction in tax rate
(3) Reduction in tax liability
(4) Deduction from taxable income

74. Which of the following is not a reason for transfer pricing disputes?
(1) Difficulty in determining arm's length price
(2) Different accounting standards in different countries
(3) Stricter transfer pricing regulations in some countries compared to others
(4) Complexity of inter-company transactions

75. What is the meaning of the term 'thin capitalization'?
(1) A situation where a company has excess capital
(2) A situation where a company has inadequate capital
(3) A situation where a company has no capital
(4) None of the above

76. Which of the following is not a type of transfer pricing adjustment?
(1) Primary adjustment
(2) Secondary adjustment
(3) Tertiary adjustment
(4) None of the above

77. What is the purpose of the Mutual Agreement Procedure (MAP)?
(1) To resolve disputes between two countries on tax matters
(2) To increase tax revenue for host countries
(3) To prevent tax avoidance by multinational companies
(4) None of the above

78. What is the meaning of the term 'tax haven'?
(1) A country or region with a low tax rate
(2) A country or region with strict tax regulations
(3) A country or region with high tax rate
(4) None of the above

79. Which of the following is not a type of tax treaty?
(1) Bilateral tax treaty
(2) Multilateral tax treaty
(3) Regional tax treaty
(4) Global tax treaty

80. Which of the following is not a transfer pricing method used by tax authorities?
(1) Secret comparables method
(2) Resale price method
(3) Transactional net margin method
(4) Comparable uncontrolled price method

81. What is the meaning of the term 'tax residency'?
(1) The country where a person is born
(2) The country where a person is living
(3) The country where a person pays taxes
(4) The country where a person works

82. Which of the following is an example of a tax treaty organisation?
(1) OECD (2) UN
(3) World Bank (4) IMF

83. What is the meaning of the term 'Foreign Account Tax Compliance Act (FATCA)'?
(1) A US law aimed at preventing tax evasion by US taxpayers holding foreign financial assets
(2) A tax treaty between US and foreign countries to avoid double taxation
(3) A US law aimed at preventing tax evasion by foreign taxpayers holding US financial assets
(4) A foreign law aimed at preventing tax evasion by US taxpayers

84. What is the meaning of the term 'transfer pricing adjustment'?
(1) Adjustment made by a company to its transfer pricing policies
(2) Adjustment made by tax authorities to a company's transfer pricing policies
(3) Adjustment made by a company to its accounting policies
(4) Adjustment made by tax authorities to a company's accounting policies

85. Which of the following is an example of a treaty anti-abuse provision?

(1) Limitation of benefits clause
(2) General anti-avoidance rule
(3) Thin capitalization rule
(4) None of the above

86. What is the meaning of the term 'advance pricing agreement (APA)'?
(1) Agreement between a taxpayer and tax authorities on transfer pricing methodology
(2) Agreement between two countries on tax treaty issues
(3) Agreement between a taxpayer and tax authorities on tax liability
(4) None of the above

87. Which of the following is an example of a principal place of business for tax purposes?
(1) Head office
(2) Branch office
(3) Factory
(4) All of the above

88. What is the meaning of the term 'permanent accounting period'?
(1) A tax period that lasts for multiple years
(2) A tax period that begins and ends on the same date each year
(3) A tax period that can be changed by the taxpayer
(4) None of the above

89. Which of the following is not a mechanism for avoiding double taxation of income?
(1) Exemption (2) Tax treaty
(3) Tax credit (4) Tax evasion

90. Which of the following is not a transfer pricing method used by companies?
(1) Cost plus method
(2) Market capitalization method
(3) Comparable uncontrolled price method
(4) Resale price method

91. Which of the following is an example of a tax credit carryforward?
(1) Foreign tax credit carryforward
(2) Income tax credit carryforward
(3) Property tax credit carryforward
(4) Sales tax credit carryforward

92. What is the meaning of the term 'underlying tax'?
(1) The tax on the income of a company in the country where it resides
(2) The tax on the income of a company in the country where it operates
(3) The tax on the income of a company's subsidiaries in foreign countries
(4) None of the above

93. Which of the following is not a mechanism for avoiding transfer pricing disputes?
(1) Advance pricing agreement
(2) Independent arbitration
(3) Mutual agreement procedure
(4) Legal action in national court

94. What is the purpose of the Country-by-Country Reporting (CbCR) framework?
(1) To increase transparency in inter-company transactions
(2) To prevent tax avoidance by multinational companies
(3) To increase tax revenue for host countries
(4) All of the above

95. Which of the following is an example of a transfer pricing adjustment made by tax authorities?
(1) Increase in the selling price of goods
(2) Decrease in the buying price of goods
(3) Increase in the royalty fees paid to a related party
(4) Decrease in the management fees paid to a related party

96. What is the meaning of the term 'bifurcation of income'?
(1) Separation of income into two categories for tax purposes
(2) Separation of income into taxable and non-taxable categories
(3) Separation of income into domestic and foreign categories
(4) None of the above

97. What is the main purpose of corporate tax planning?
(1) To reduce tax liabilities legally
(2) To evade taxes
(3) To avoid tax laws
(4) To reduce tax liabilities illegally

98. What is the difference between tax avoidance and tax evasion?
(1) Tax avoidance is legal while tax evasion is illegal
(2) Tax avoidance is illegal while tax evasion is legal

(3) Tax avoidance and tax evasion are both legal
(4) Tax avoidance and tax evasion are both illegal

99. Which of the following is not a technique of corporate tax planning?
(1) Income shifting
(2) Expense shifting
(3) Tax evasion
(4) Timing of income and expenses

100. What is the meaning of the term 'income shifting' in corporate tax planning?
(1) Transfer of income from a high-tax entity to a low-tax entity
(2) Transfer of income from a low-tax entity to a high-tax entity
(3) Transfer of losses from a high-tax entity to a low-tax entity
(4) Transfer of losses from a low-tax entity to a high-tax entity

101. What is the meaning of the term 'expense shifting' in corporate tax planning?
(1) Transfer of expenses from a high-tax entity to a low-tax entity
(2) Transfer of expenses from a low-tax entity to a high-tax entity
(3) Transfer of profits from a high-tax entity to a low-tax entity
(4) Transfer of profits from a low-tax entity to a high-tax entity

102. Which of the following is not a tax consideration in make or buy decisions?
(1) Tax deductibility of expenses
(2) Tax credits for investments
(3) Indirect taxes
(4) Depreciation benefits

103. What is the meaning of the term 'leaseback' in corporate tax planning?
(1) Leasing of an asset without an agreement to purchase it later
(2) Leasing of an asset with an agreement to purchase it later
(3) Selling an asset and then leasing it back from the buyer
(4) None of the above

104. Which of the following is not a tax consideration in own or lease an asset decision?
(1) Availability of depreciation benefits
(2) Indirect taxes
(3) Cost of financing
(4) Maintenance expenses

105. What is the meaning of the term 'depreciation recapture' in tax planning?
(1) A tax on the gain realized upon the disposal of a depreciated asset
(2) A tax on the depreciation of an asset
(3) A tax on the purchase of a new asset
(4) None of the above

106. Which of the following is not a tax consideration in retain or renewal/replacement of asset decision?
(1) Availability of depreciation benefits
(2) Indirect taxes
(3) Maintenance expenses
(4) Corporate social responsibility

107. What is the meaning of the term 'tax credit'?
(1) A deduction from taxable income
(2) A reduction in the tax rate
(3) A reduction in the tax liability
(4) None of the above

108. Which of the following is not a tax consideration in shut down or continue operations decision?
(1) Availability of depreciation benefits
(2) Indirect taxes
(3) Cost of terminating employees
(4) Corporate social responsibility

109. Which of the following is an example of a tax haven?
(1) UK (2) USA
(3) Switzerland (4) China

110. What is the meaning of the term 'transfer pricing' in corporate tax planning?
(1) Transfer of profits from one entity to another within the same corporate group
(2) Transfer of assets from one country to another to avoid taxes
(3) Transfer of liabilities from one entity to another within the same corporate group
(4) None of the above

111. Which of the following is an example of a timing technique of corporate tax planning?
(1) Electing accelerated depreciation methods
(2) Income shifting
(3) Expense shifting
(4) None of the above

112. What is the meaning of the term 'tax liability'?
(1) The amount of taxes owed to the government
(2) The amount of taxes paid to the government
(3) The amount of taxes deducted from income
(4) None of the above

113. Which of the following is a tax exemption available to a company?
(1) Interest expense deduction
(2) Depreciation deduction
(3) Capital gains tax exemption
(4) Property tax deduction

114. What is the meaning of the term 'tax audit'?
(1) Examination of a company's financial statements by the government to ensure compliance with tax laws
(2) Examination of a company's marketing strategies by the government to ensure fair competition
(3) Examination of a company's human resources policies by the government to ensure compliance with labour laws
(4) None of the above

115. Which of the following is not a tax credit available to a company?
(1) Research and development tax credit
(2) Foreign tax credit
(3) Social security tax credit
(4) Charity tax credit

116. What is the meaning of the term 'tax shield'?
(1) Reduction in the taxable income due to tax deductions
(2) Reduction in the tax liability due to tax exemptions
(3) Reduction in the tax rate due to tax credits
(4) None of the above

117. What is the meaning of the term 'offshore tax planning'?
(1) Tax planning in a country that is not the domicile of the company
(2) Tax planning in the country of the domicile of the company
(3) Tax planning in a tax haven
(4) None of the above

118. Which of the following is not a tax consideration in shut down or continue operations decision?
(1) Availability of depreciation benefits
(2) Indirect taxes
(3) Cost of terminating employees
(4) Corporate social responsibility

119. What is the meaning of the term 'debt-equity ratio'?
(1) Ratio of debt to equity in a company's capital structure
(2) Ratio of debt to profit in a company's financial statements
(3) Ratio of borrowing to lending in a company's financial operations
(4) None of the above

120. Which of the following is not a technique of income shifting in corporate tax planning?
(1) Transfer pricing
(2) Licensing intellectual property
(3) Payment of royalties
(4) None of the above

121. What is the meaning of the term 'low-tax jurisdiction' in corporate tax planning?
(1) A country with a high corporate tax rate
(2) A country with a low corporate tax rate
(3) A country with strict tax laws
(4) None of the above

122. Which of the following is not a technique of expense shifting in corporate tax planning?
(1) Thin capitalization
(2) Transfer pricing
(3) Double deduction
(4) None of the above

123. What is the meaning of the term 'tax holiday' in corporate tax planning?
(1) A period of time when a company is exempt from paying taxes
(2) A period of time when a company pays a reduced tax rate
(3) A period of time when a company is audited by the government
(4) None of the above

124. Which of the following is not a tax consideration in own or lease an asset decision?
(1) Availability of depreciation benefits
(2) Indirect taxes
(3) Cost of financing
(4) Maintenance expenses

125. What is the meaning of the term 'expensing' in corporate tax planning?

(1) Deducting the cost of an asset in the year it was purchased
(2) Deducting a portion of the cost of an asset each year
(3) Deducting the cost of a liability in the year it was incurred
(4) None of the above

126. Which of the following is an example of a tax exemption available to individuals?
(1) Retirement savings contribution credit
(2) Home mortgage interest deduction
(3) Earned income tax credit
(4) None of the above

127. What is the meaning of the term 'amortization' in corporate tax planning?
(1) Deducting the cost of an asset in the year it was purchased
(2) Deducting a portion of the cost of an asset each year
(3) Deducting the cost of a liability in the year it was incurred
(4) None of the above

128. Which of the following is not a technique of timing in corporate tax planning?
(1) Electing accelerated depreciation methods
(2) Income shifting
(3) Expense shifting
(4) None of the above

129. What is the meaning of the term 'capital expenditure' in corporate tax planning?
(1) An expenditure that is deductible in the year it was incurred
(2) An expenditure that is added to the cost of an asset and deducted over time
(3) An expenditure that is capitalized and not deducted
(4) None of the above

130. Which of the following is a tax consideration in make or buy decisions?
(1) Tax deductibility of expenses
(2) Tax credits for investments
(3) Indirect taxes
(4) Depreciation benefits

131. What is the meaning of the term 'pass-through entity' in tax planning?
(1) An entity that distributes its profits to shareholders
(2) An entity that distributes its profits to a charity
(3) An entity that does not pay taxes
(4) None of the above

132. Which of the following is not a tax credit available to a company?
(1) Research and development tax credit
(2) Foreign tax credit
(3) Social security tax credit
(4) Charity tax credit

133. What is the meaning of the term 'inversion' in corporate tax planning?
(1) A corporate strategy to change the domicile of the company to a low-tax jurisdiction
(2) A corporate strategy to change the corporate structure of the company
(3) A corporate strategy to increase the profitability of the company
(4) None of the above

134. Which of the following is a tax exemption available to a company?
(1) Interest expense deduction
(2) Depreciation deduction
(3) Capital gains tax exemption
(4) Property tax deduction

135. What is the meaning of the term 'tax treaty' in international tax planning?
(1) An agreement signed between two countries to avoid double taxation
(2) An agreement signed between two countries to increase tax revenue
(3) An agreement signed between a company and the government to avoid taxes
(4) None of the above

136. Which of the following is not a tax consideration in retain or renewal/replacement of asset decision?
(1) Availability of depreciation benefits
(2) Indirect taxes
(3) Maintenance expenses
(4) Corporate social responsibility

137. What is the meaning of the term 'tax deductible expenses'?
(1) Expenses that are deductible to reduce the taxable income
(2) Expenses that cannot be deducted for tax purposes

(3) Expenses that have to be paid in order to reduce taxes
(4) None of the above

138. Which of the following is an example of a tax efficiency strategy?
(1) Reducing the number of employees to reduce payroll taxes
(2) Reducing the wages of employees to reduce payroll taxes
(3) Increasing investment in research and development to claim tax credits
(4) None of the above

139. What is the meaning of the term 'bonus depreciation' in corporate tax planning?
(1) A method of depreciating an asset over a shorter period of time
(2) A method of depreciating an asset over a longer period of time
(3) A method of depreciating a portion of an asset in the year of purchase
(4) None of the above

140. What is the threshold limit for TDS deduction on salary?
(1) Rs. 1,80,000
(2) Rs. 2,50,000
(3) Rs. 5,00,000
(4) Rs. 10,00,000

141. What is the rate of TDS on interest income?
(1) 10% (2) 20%
(3) 30% (4) 40%

142. What is the threshold limit for TDS deduction on non-salary payments?
(1) Rs. 10,000
(2) Rs. 15,000
(3) Rs. 20,000
(4) Rs. 30,000

143. What is the rate of TDS on rent paid?
(1) 2% (2) 5%
(3) 10% (4) 15%

144. What is the rate of TDS on commission paid to agents?
(1) 5% (2) 10%
(3) 15% (4) 20%

145. What is the rate of TDS on professional fees paid?
(1) 5% (2) 10%
(3) 15% (4) 20%

146. What is the meaning of the term 'Form 16'?
(1) A certificate of TDS deduction on salary
(2) A certificate of TDS deduction on non-salary payments
(3) A certificate of advance tax payment
(4) A certificate of e-filing of income-tax return

147. Who is responsible for deducting and depositing TDS?
(1) The payer of income
(2) The receiver of income
(3) The government
(4) None of the above

148. What is the meaning of the term 'challan' in TDS?
(1) A form used for depositing TDS with the government
(2) A form used for claiming TDS refund
(3) A form used for e-filing of income-tax return
(4) A form used for applying for PAN card

149. What is the threshold limit for TDS deduction on sale of immovable property?
(1) Rs. 30 lakhs
(2) Rs. 50 lakhs
(3) Rs. 75 lakhs
(4) Rs. 1 crore

150. What is the meaning of the term 'Form 16A'?
(1) A certificate of TDS deduction on salary
(2) A certificate of TDS deduction on non-salary payments
(3) A certificate of advance tax payment
(4) A certificate of e-filing of income-tax return

151. What is the rate of TDS on payments made to non-residents?
(1) 20% (2) 25%
(3) 30% (4) 35%

152. Which of the following payments is exempt from TDS deduction?
(1) Dividend income
(2) Interest income from savings bank account
(3) Interest income from fixed deposits
(4) Rent paid for accommodation

153. What is the rate of TDS on lottery winnings?
(1) 10% (2) 20%
(3) 30% (4) 40%

154. Whose TAN is to be used for TDS deduction if the payer does not have a TAN?

(1) The TAN of the government
(2) The TAN of the receiver of income
(3) The TAN of the payer of income
(4) None of the above

155. What is the threshold limit for TDS deduction on rent paid?
(1) Rs. 1,80,000 (2) Rs. 2,40,000
(3) Rs. 3,60,000 (4) Rs. 5,00,000

156. What is the threshold limit for TDS deduction on payment to contractors?
(1) Rs. 10,000 (2) Rs. 15,000
(3) Rs. 20,000 (4) Rs. 30,000

157. Which of the following is not a penalty for non-compliance related to TDS?
(1) Penalty for non-deduction or short deduction of TDS
(2) Penalty for non-filing of TDS return
(3) Penalty for incorrect information in TDS return
(4) Penalty for e-filing of income-tax return

158. What is the threshold limit for TDS deduction on payment to professionals and consultants?
(1) Rs. 10,000 (2) Rs. 15,000
(3) Rs. 20,000 (4) Rs. 30,000

159. What is the rate of TDS on payments made to transporters?
(1) 1% (2) 2%
(3) 5% (4) 10%

160. What is the meaning of the term 'Form 26AS'?
(1) A statement of TDS deducted and deposited
(2) A certificate of TDS deduction on salary
(3) A certificate of TDS deduction on non-salary payments
(4) A certificate of advance tax payment

161. What is the rate of advance tax for senior citizens?
(1) 15% (2) 20%
(3) 30% (4) 40%

162. What is the due date for payment of first installment of advance tax for non-corporate taxpayers?
(1) 15th June (2) 15th September
(3) 15th December (4) 15th March

163. What is the meaning of the term 'advance tax'?
(1) Payment of tax in installments during the financial year
(2) Payment of tax at the end of the financial year
(3) Payment of tax before the financial year begins
(4) None of the above

164. What is the rate of interest charged on late payment of advance tax?
(1) 1% (2) 2%
(3) 3% (4) 4%

165. Which of the following payments is not eligible for payment of advance tax?
(1) Interest income from savings bank account
(2) Interest income from fixed deposits
(3) Short-term capital gains from sale of equity shares
(4) Long-term capital gains from sale of property

166. What is the due date for payment of second installment of advance tax for non-corporate taxpayers?
(1) 15th June (2) 15th September
(3) 15th December (4) 15th March

167. What is the rate of interest paid on refund of excess advance tax?
(1) 2% (2) 4%
(3) 6% (4) 8%

168. What is the due date for payment of third installment of advance tax for non-corporate taxpayers?
(1) 15th June
(2) 15th September
(3) 15th December
(4) 15th March

169. What is the due date for payment of fourth installment of advance tax for non-corporate taxpayers?
(1) 15th June
(2) 15th September
(3) 15th December
(4) 15th March

170. What is the meaning of the term 'Form 15CA'?
(1) A declaration of payments made to non-residents
(2) A declaration of TDS deduction on salary
(3) A certificate of TDS deduction on non-salary payments
(4) A certificate of advance tax payment

171. What is the meaning of the term 'Form 15CB'?
(1) A certificate of a chartered accountant verifying the amount of payment made to non-residents
(2) A certificate of TDS deduction on salary
(3) A certificate of TDS deduction on non-salary payments
(4) A certificate of advance tax payment

172. What is the due date for submission of Form 15CA and Form 15CB?
(1) Before the payment is made
(2) Within 7 days of the payment
(3) Within 15 days of the payment
(4) Within 30 days of the payment

173. What is the meaning of the term 'e-filing'?
(1) Online filing of income-tax return
(2) Filing of income-tax return through post
(3) Filing of income-tax return through a tax consultant
(4) None of the above

174. What is the last date for e-filing of income-tax return for non-audit cases?
(1) 31st July (2) 31st August
(3) 30th September (4) 31st October

175. What is the last date for e-filing of income-tax return for audit cases?
(1) 30th November (2) 31st December
(3) 31st January (4) 28th February

176. What is the threshold limit for e-filing of income-tax return?
(1) Rs. 5 lakhs (2) Rs. 8 lakhs
(3) Rs. 10 lakhs (4) Rs. 12 lakhs

177. Which of the following taxpayers is required to e-file their income-tax return mandatorily?
(1) All taxpayers
(2) Individuals with income over Rs. 5 lakhs
(3) Individuals with income over Rs. 8 lakhs
(4) Corporates

178. What is the meaning of the term 'Form 26AS' in e-filing of income-tax return?
(1) A statement of TDS deducted and deposited
(2) A certificate of TDS deduction on salary
(3) A certificate of TDS deduction on non-salary payments
(4) A certificate of advance tax payment

179. What is the meaning of the term 'Form 16' in e-filing of income-tax return?
(1) A certificate of TDS deduction on salary
(2) A certificate of TDS deduction on non-salary payments
(3) A certificate of advance tax payment
(4) A certificate of e-filing of income-tax return

180. What is the due date for submission of income-tax return for individuals and HUFs who do not have any business income?
(1) 31st July
(2) 31st August
(3) 30th September
(4) 31st October

181. What is the meaning of the term 'Form 16A' in e-filing of income-tax return?
(1) A certificate of TDS deduction on salary
(2) A certificate of TDS deduction on non-salary payments
(3) A certificate of advance tax payment
(4) A certificate of e-filing of income-tax return

182. What is the meaning of the term 'PAN' in e-filing of income-tax return?
(1) Permanent Account Number
(2) Personal Account Number
(3) Public Account Number
(4) None of the above

183. Which of the following is not a benefit of e-filing of income-tax return?
(1) Faster processing of returns
(2) Lower possibility of mistakes
(3) Higher chance of scrutiny
(4) Availability of past records

184. What is the meaning of the term 'XML' in e-filing of income-tax return?
(1) Extensible Markup Language
(2) Extraordinary Mining Language
(3) External Management Language
(4) None of the above

ANSWERS

1. (2)	**2.** (4)	**3.** (2)	**4.** (2)	**5.** (2)	**6.** (1)	**7.** (4)	**8.** (4)	**9.** (3)	**10.** (1)
11. (1)	**12.** (1)	**13.** (4)	**14.** (4)	**15.** (3)	**16.** (4)	**17.** (3)	**18.** (1)	**19.** (4)	**20.** (2)
21. (4)	**22.** (3)	**23.** (4)	**24.** (2)	**25.** (4)	**26.** (2)	**27.** (3)	**28.** (3)	**29.** (1)	**30.** (4)
31. (1)	**32.** (1)	**33.** (2)	**34.** (4)	**35.** (4)	**36.** (2)	**37.** (2)	**38.** (1)	**39.** (4)	**40.** (4)
41. (2)	**42.** (4)	**43.** (4)	**44.** (3)	**45.** (1)	**46.** (4)	**47.** (4)	**48.** (2)	**49.** (4)	**50.** (3)
51. (1)	**52.** (2)	**53.** (3)	**54.** (2)	**55.** (3)	**56.** (2)	**57.** (3)	**58.** (1)	**59.** (1)	**60.** (3)
61. (1)	**62.** (4)	**63.** (4)	**64.** (1)	**65.** (4)	**66.** (4)	**67.** (4)	**68.** (1)	**69.** (3)	**70.** (4)
71. (1)	**72.** (1)	**73.** (3)	**74.** (2)	**75.** (2)	**76.** (3)	**77.** (1)	**78.** (1)	**79.** (4)	**80.** (1)
81. (3)	**82.** (1)	**83.** (1)	**84.** (2)	**85.** (1)	**86.** (1)	**87.** (4)	**88.** (2)	**89.** (4)	**90.** (2)
91. (1)	**92.** (1)	**93.** (4)	**94.** (4)	**95.** (3)	**96.** (1)	**97.** (1)	**98.** (1)	**99.** (3)	**100.** (1)
101. (2)	**102.** (4)	**103.** (3)	**104.** (4)	**105.** (1)	**106.** (4)	**107.** (3)	**108.** (4)	**109.** (3)	**110.** (1)
111. (1)	**112.** (1)	**113.** (3)	**114.** (1)	**115.** (3)	**116.** (1)	**117.** (1)	**118.** (4)	**119.** (1)	**120.** (4)
121. (2)	**122.** (3)	**123.** (1)	**124.** (4)	**125.** (1)	**126.** (4)	**127.** (2)	**128.** (4)	**129.** (2)	**130.** (4)
131. (1)	**132.** (3)	**133.** (1)	**134.** (3)	**135.** (1)	**136.** (4)	**137.** (1)	**138.** (3)	**139.** (3)	**140.** (2)
141. (1)	**142.** (1)	**143.** (2)	**144.** (1)	**145.** (2)	**146.** (1)	**147.** (1)	**148.** (1)	**149.** (2)	**150.** (2)
151. (3)	**152.** (2)	**153.** (3)	**154.** (4)	**155.** (2)	**156.** (4)	**157.** (4)	**158.** (4)	**159.** (2)	**160.** (1)
161. (1)	**162.** (1)	**163.** (1)	**164.** (1)	**165.** (1)	**166.** (2)	**167.** (3)	**168.** (3)	**169.** (4)	**170.** (1)
171. (1)	**172.** (1)	**173.** (1)	**174.** (1)	**175.** (3)	**176.** (1)	**177.** (1)	**178.** (1)	**179.** (1)	**180.** (1)
181. (2)	**182.** (1)	**183.** (3)	**184.** (1)						

ADDITIONAL MULTIPLE CHOICE QUESTIONS

1. Which one of the following statements is correct?

(1) The purpose of issuing different types of rules and regulations by SEBI is to bring monetary gains to investors.
(2) SEBI has been constituted under the Securities (Contract and Regulation) Act, 1956.
(3) One of the objectives of setting up SEBI is to protect the interests of investors.
(4) SEBI is constituted from amongst the directors of various stock exchanges.

2. Match the items of List I with the items of List II and choose the correct answer from the code given below.

LIST I	LIST II
(a) Rival Firms	(i) External Environments
(b) Technology	(ii) Social and Cultural Environment
(c) Improving Quality	(iii) Internal Environment
(d) Ethics in Business	(iv) Global Environment

Code :

(1) (a)–(ii), (b)–(iii), (c)–(iv), (d)–(i)
(2) (a)–(iv), (b)–(i), (c)–(ii), (d)–(iii)
(3) (a)–(i), (b)–(ii), (c)–(iii), (d)–(iv)
(4) (a)–(iii), (b)–(i), (c)–(iv), (d)–(ii)

3. Combined leverage can be used to measure the relationship between

(1) Sales and EPS
(2) PAT and EPS
(3) EBIT and EPS
(4) Sales and EBIT

4. Which among the following is not an internal factor of pricing decision ?

(1) Price elasticity as per sales of product
(2) Consumers expectation from company by past pricing
(3) Consumer behaviour for given product
(4) Position of product in product cycle

5. Match the items of List I with the items of List II and choose the correct answer from the code given below.

LIST I

(a) Compensation received by an employee from his employer on termination of job
(b) Pension received by the widow of an employee
(c) Foreign allowance for rendering services abroad
(d) Children hostel allowance

LIST II

(i) Exemption up to specified limit
(ii) Profits in lieu of salary
(iii) Income from other sources
(iv) Fully exempt from tax

Code :

(1) (a)–(ii), (b)–(iv), (c)–(iii), (d)–(i)
(2) (a)–(ii), (b)–(iii), (c)–(iv), (d)–(i)
(3) (a)–(iv), (b)–(iii), (c)–(i), (d)–(ii)
(4) (a)–(iii), (b)–(iv), (c)–(ii), (d)–(i)

6. The companies having business in a large number of countries around the world at present are called

(1) Multinational Enterprises (MNEs)
(2) Global Corporations (GCs)
(3) Transnational Corporations (TNCs)
(4) Multinational Corporations (MNCs)

7. Banking Ombudsman Scheme was introduced by RBI with effect from

(1) 2005 (2) 1998
(3) 2001 (4) 1995

8. If a perpendicular on X-axis from the point of intersection of both 'less than' and 'more than' frequency curves is drawn, it gives the value of
(1) Median
(2) Mode
(3) Third quartile
(4) Arithmetic mean

9. Choose the correct code for the following statements being correct or incorrect

Statement I : An identifiable group of people contributing their efforts towards attainment of goals is called organization.

Statement II : In its broadest sense, organization refers to the relationship between the various factors present in a given endeavour.

Code :
(1) Both the statements I and II are incorrect.
(2) Both the statements I and II are correct.
(3) Statement II is correct, but I is incorrect.
(4) Statement I is correct, but II is incorrect.

10. Match the items of List I with the items of List II and choose the correct answers from the code given below.

LIST I	LIST II
(a) Job context	(i) Procedures used
(b) Job-related tangibles and intangibles	(ii) Work schedule
(c) Work activities	(iii) Work standards
(d) Work performance	(iv) Services rendered

Code:
(1) (a)–(ii), (b)–(iv), (c)–(i), (d)–(iii)
(2) (a)–(iv), (b)–(iii), (c)–(i), (d)–(ii)
(3) (a)–(iii), (b)–(iv), (c)–(ii), (d)–(i)
(4) (a)–(i), (b)–(iv), (c)–(ii), (d)–(iii)

11. Given below are two statements, one labelled as Assertion (A) and the other labelled as Reason (R). Read the statements and choose the correct answer using the code given below.

Assertion (A) : There exists excess capacity of the production for the firms if these incur losses

Reason (R) : Their production level has to remain below their economic capacity level.

Code :
(1) (A) is incorrect but (R) is correct.
(2) Both (A) and (R) are correct but (R) is not the right explanation of (A).
(3) (A) is correct but (R) is incorrect.
(4) Both (A) and (R) are correct and (R) is the right explanation of (A).

12. Second generation reforms in our country do not comprise of which one of the following?
(1) Exploiting the knowledge based global economy
(2) Population control measures
(3) Growing Indian transnational corporations
(4) Clean environment

13. Match the items of List I with the items of List II and choose the correct answer from the code given below.

LIST I	LIST II
(a) Claims	(i) Company car, club membership, paid holidays, furnished house
(b) Fringe benefits	(ii) Telephone/mobile allowance, internet allowance, medical allowance
(c) Perquisites	(iii) Canteen, uniform, accident relief

Code :
(1) (a)–(iii), (b)–(ii), (c)–(i)
(2) (a)–(ii), (b)–(iii), (c)–(i)
(3) (a)–(ii), (b)–(i), (c)–(iii)
(4) (a)–(i), (b)–(ii), (c)–(iii)

14. The monopoly involves a social cost mainly due to its emphasis on which one of the following?
(1) Earning net profit in all possible situations.
(2) Charging different prices from different categories of buyers of the same product.
(3) Attempting to stall entry of other firms in the market.
(4) Lower output at a higher cost in a normal profit situation.

15. Arrange the following stages of staffing in correct sequence and indicate the code of correct sequence.
(i) Performance appraisal
(ii) Recruitment
(iii) Transfers
(iv) Selection
(v) Induction and orientation

Choose the correct answer from the code given below.

Code :

(1) (iv), (ii), (v), (iii), (i)

(2) (i), (ii), (iv), (v), (iii)

(3) (ii), (iv), (v), (i), (iii)

(4) (ii), (i), (iv), (v), (iii)

16. Which one of the following demands states consumers are adequately buying all the products put into the marketplace ?

(1) Latent demand

(2) Irregular demand

(3) Full demand

(4) Overfull demand

17. Choose the correct code for the following statements being correct or incorrect.

Statement I : Thousands of employees die every day in factories due to accidents.

Statement II : To make an accident-free plant adds to cost and decreases productivity.

Code :

(1) Both the statements I and II are correct.

(2) Both the statements I and II are incorrect.

(3) Statement I is correct, but II is incorrect.

(4) Statement II is correct, but I is incorrect.

18. Who among the following is not an observer country of the SAARC?

(1) Iran (2) China

(3) Canada (4) USA

19. Which one of the following is not true for introducing multiple brands in a category?

(1) Increasing shelf presence and retailer dependence in the store

(2) Yielding economies of scale in advertising, sales, merchandising and physical distribution

(3) Decreasing internal competition within the firm

(4) Attracting consumers seeking variety who may otherwise have switched to another brand

20. Given below are two statements, one labelled as Assertion (A) and the other labelled as Reason (R). Read the statements and choose the correct answer using the code given below.

Assertion (A) : Databases assist in market segmentation, especially behavioural segmentation such as developing loyalty segments.

Reason (R) : Customer Relationship Management (CRM) databases have become an asset for the analysis of customer behaviour.

Code :

(1) Both (A) and (R) are correct and (R) is the right explanation of (A).

(2) (A) is correct but (R) is not correct.

(3) Both (A) and (R) are correct but (R) is not the right explanation of (A).

(4) Both (A) and (R) are incorrect.

21. "Skimming" in e-banking is a method of

(1) stealing credit card information.

(2) transferring cash from one account to another account.

(3) converting Debit Card into Credit Card.

(4) intimating the customer about his heavy withdrawals

22. Everyone benefits when the focus is on common interest and promotion of harmony "is the underlying assumption of which one of the approaches to industrial relations

(1) Pluralistic approach

(2) Human relation approach

(3) Unitary approach

(4) Marxist approach

23. Sales of a firm are Rs 40 Lakh ;variable costs Rs 10 lakh; fixed costs Rs 15 lakh ; Interest Rs 5 lakh. Combined leverage of the firm will be

(1) 2 (2) 2.5

(3) 3 (4) 8

24. Under Sec. 194 IB of the Income Tax Act, 1961 an individual or HUF (who is not required to get his accounts audited u/s 44 AB) who is responsible for paying to a resident any rent, shall deduct income tax, for the use of any land and building or both, if the rent exceeds

(1) 50,000 per month

(2) 15,000 per month

(3) 25,000 per month

(4) 40,000 per month

25. Which one of the following is not an advantage of external recruitment?

(1) Scope for resentment, jealousies and heartburn are avoided

(2) Benefits of new skills, new talents and new experiences to organisations are available

(3) Compliance with reservation policy becomes easy

(4) Good performance is rewarded

26. When RBI reduces CRR, it results into
(1) Increase in deposits
(2) Increase in lendable resources
(3) Decrease in lendable resources
(4) Decrease in deposits

27. The Industrial Policy, 1956 has been prompted by which combination of the following developments?
(i) Adoption of the Constitution of India.
(ii) Implementation of Economic Planning.
(iii) Acceleration of Economic Growth and Industrialisation.
(iv) Availability of Sufficient Funds for Investment in Public Sector.

Choose the correct answer from the code given below :

Code:
(1) Only (i) and (ii)
(2) Only (ii), (iii) and (iv)
(3) Only (ii) and (iv)
(4) Only (i), (ii) and (iv)

28. Match the items of List I with the items of List II and choose the correct answer from the code given below.

LIST I	LIST II
(a) Balance of trade	(i) Imports and exports of goods and services and unilateral transfer of goods and services
(b) Current account	(ii) Transactions leading to changes in the financial assets and liabilities of a country
(c) Balance of payments	(iii) All economic transactions between a countries residents and residents of other countries
(d) Capital account	(iv) Value of exports and imports of a country

Code :
(1) (a)–(iii), (b)–(ii), (c)–(iv), (d)–(i)
(2) (a)–(i), (b)–(ii), (c)–(iii), (d)–(iv)
(3) (a)–(iv), (b)–(iii), (c)–(ii), (d)–(i)
(4) (a)–(iv), (b)–(i), (c)–(iii), (d)–(ii)

29. Choose the correct code for the following statements being correct or incorrect.

Statement I : Punctuality and team spirit among employees of an organisation has great contribution in enhancing profits of the business but they do not appear as an asset in the balance sheet.

Statement II : Financial statements do not reflect the correct financial position of a business.

Code :
(1) Both the statements I and II are incorrect.
(2) Both the statements I and II are correct.
(3) Statement I is correct, but II is incorrect.
(4) Statement I is incorrect, but II is correct.

30. Choose the correct code for the following statements being correct or incorrect.

Statement I : Intellectual Property (IP) is a category of property that includes intangible creations of the human intellect.

Statement II : IPR does not include trade secrets and moral rights.

(1) Both the statements I and II are incorrect.
(2) Statement II is correct, but I is incorrect.
(3) Both the statements I and II are correct.
(4) Statement I is correct, but II is incorrect.

31. Choose the correct code for the following statements being correct or incorrect.

Statement I: If the value of β_2, i.e., μ_4/σ_4, of a distribution gives the value more than 3, its curve is platykurtic.

Statement II: In a moderately asymmetrical distribution, the standard deviation is 1.25 times of mean deviation.

Code :
(1) Both the statements I and II are incorrect.
(2) Both the statements I and II are correct.
(3) Statement I is correct, but II is incorrect.
(4) Statement II is correct, but I is incorrect.

32. Which one of the following statements is not true?
(1) Cost of sales is a better numerator than sales while calculating stock turnover.
(2) Conversion of debentures into preference shares will decrease debt-equity ratio.
(3) Higher operating ratio indicates higher profits.
(4) Long-term liabilities due for payment within a year should be treated as current liabilities.

33. Which of the following sources of finance has an implicit cost of capital?
(1) Equity share capital
(2) Preference share capital
(3) Debentures
(4) Retained earnings

34. Given below are two statements, one labelled as Assertion (A) and the other labelled as Reason (R). Read the statements and choose the correct answer using the code given below.
Assertion (A) : Technological change and skill requirements have been made a subject of investigation in an organization.
Reason (R) : The neo-classical economic theory stated that technological changes require a broader variety of skills and higher average skills from the workers.
Code :
(1) Both (A) and (R) are correct but (R) is not the right explanation of (A).
(2) (A) is correct but (R) is incorrect.
(3) Both (A) and (R) are correct and (R) is the right explanation of (A).
(4) Both (A) and (R) are incorrect.

35. Choose the correct code for the following statements being correct or incorrect.
Statement I : An option which gives its holder the privilege of selling to other party a fixed amount of some stock at a stated price on or before a predetermined date is known as call option.
Statement II : In an option, the holder has the privilege of purchasing from other party a fixed amount of some stock at a stated price on or before a predetermined date is known as put option.
Code :
(1) Both the statements I and II are correct.
(2) Statement II is correct, but I is incorrect.
(3) Statement I is correct, but II is incorrect.
(4) Both the statements I and II are incorrect.

36. Which one of the following is agricultural income under Income Tax Act?
(1) Income from the sale of replanted trees where denuded parts of the forest are replanted and subsequent operations in forestry are carried out.
(2) Income from dairy farm, poultry farm, etc.
(3) Dividend from a company engaged in agriculture.
(4) Income from the land used for storing agricultural produce.

37. The inverse relationship between the variation in the price and the variation in the quantity demanded is not due to
(1) Price effect
(2) Gossen's laws of consumption
(3) Entry and exit of buyers
(4) Law of substitution

38. Which one of the following is not the fund based business of commercial banks?
(1) RTGS/NEFT transactions
(2) Issuance of Letters of Credit
(3) Overdraft facility
(4) Acceptance of deposits

39. For performance assessment of employees, "helping to meet legal requirements" is the application of which one of the following?
(1) Administrative purpose
(2) Organisational maintenance purpose
(3) Documentation purpose
(4) Developmental purpose

40. Which one of the following items is not a part of job specification?
(1) Judgement (2) Initiative
(3) Location
(4) Emotional characteristics

41. In which one of the following modes of entry into foreign market are risk and profit potential the highest?
(1) Indirect exporting
(2) Direct investment
(3) Direct exporting
(4) Joint ventures

42. Cost plus pricing is considered appropriate for which combination of the following?
(i) Product Tailoring
(ii) Public Utility Pricing
(iii) Refusal Pricing
(iv) Monopoly Pricing
Choose the correct answer from the code given below:
Code :
(1) Only (i) and (ii)
(2) Only (ii), (iii) and (iv)
(3) Only (iii) and (iv)
(4) Only (i), (ii) and (iii)

43. Which one of the following is not the function of the Reserve Bank of India ?

(1) Custodian of Cash Reserves of Commercial Banks
(2) Controller of credit
(3) Accepting deposits and advancing loans to public
(4) Issue of Bank notes

44. Choose the correct code for the following statements being correct or incorrect.

Statement I : The geometric mean of the two regression coefficients of X and Y variables gives the value of the coefficient of correlation.

Statement II : If the population distribution is not normal and a sampling distribution of mean is prepared by taking small sized samples, the sampling distribution of mean is not normal.

Code :

(1) Statement I is correct, but II is incorrect.
(2) Statement II is correct, but I is incorrect.
(3) Both the statements I and II are correct.
(4) Both the statements I and II are incorrect.

45. Given below are two statements, one labelled as Assertion (A) and the other labelled as Reason (R). Read the statements and choose the correct answer using the code given below.

Assertion (A) : The multilateral trading system is an attempt by governments to make the business environment stable and predictable.

Reason (R) : Promising not to raise trade barriers can be as important as lowering one, because the promise gives businesses a clearer view of their future market opportunities.

Code :

(1) (A) is correct but (R) is incorrect.
(2) Both (A) and (R) are correct and (R) is the right explanation of (A).
(3) Both (A) and (R) are correct but (R) is not the right explanation of (A).
(4) Both (A) and (R) are incorrect.

46. Which among the following is not included in seven Ps of marketing and Bitner?

(1) Politics
(2) Process
(3) People
(4) Physical Evidence

47. Match the items of List I with the items of List II and choose the correct code given below.

LIST I

(a) The economy was characterised by marketing small regional suppliers who sold goods on a local basis
(b) Standardised, branded goods were sold at national level
(c) Era of market differentiation based on demographic, socio-economic and life style factors
(d) Technological advancements, especially in the area of digital communication, allow marketers to communicate with individual consumers or very small groups

LIST II

(i) Mass marketing
(ii) Hyper-segmentation
(iii) Segmentation
(iv) Fragmentation

Code :

(1) (a)–(iv), (b)–(i), (c)–(iii), (d)–(ii)
(2) (a)–(iv), (b)–(i), (c)–(ii), (d)–(iii)
(3) (a)–(i), (b)–(ii), (c)–(iii), (d)–(iv)
(4) (a)–(i), (b)–(iv), (c)–(ii), (d)–(iii)

48. Which one among the following is the oldest form of organization?

(1) Project Organization
(2) Functional Organization
(3) Committee Organization
(4) Line Organization

49. Merger of two companies under the Board for Industrial and Financial Reconstruction (BIFR) supervision is known as

(1) Offer for sale
(2) Negotiated merger
(3) Reverse merger
(4) Arranged merger

50. According to Donald Kirkpatrick, training programmes can be evaluated at four levels. Indicate the code of correct sequence from the following:

(i) Result (ii) Reaction
(iii) Learning (iv) Behaviour

Choose the correct answer from the code given below:

Code :

(1) (iv), (iii), (ii), (i) (2) (i), (ii), (iii), (iv)
(3) (ii), (iii), (iv), (i) (4) (iii), (iv), (i), (ii)

51. Which of the following statements relating to the sampling theory are correct?

(i) The values of the statistical measures based on the sampled units are called values of statistic.
(ii) In the simple random sampling technique, the element of the population and the unit of the sample are different.
(iii) Snow-ball sampling technique is a probability-based sampling technique.
(iv) The 'law of statistical regularity' and the 'law of inertia of large are the main bases of the sample to become representative of the population.

Choose the correct answer from the code given below

Code :

(1) (i) and (iv) (2) (ii) and (iii)
(3) (ii), (iii) and (iv) (4) (i), (ii) and (iii)

52. Which one of the following statements is not true?

(1) Profits earned from non-operating activities is added to net profit while calculating profits from operations.
(2) Major source of working capital in the long run, is profits from operations.
(3) Depreciation is a source of funds.
(4) Any transaction that increases working capital is a source of funds.

53. Which one of the following is not the advantage of database management system?

(1) Improved data integrity
(2) Centralized control
(3) High acquisition costs
(4) Shared data

54. The probable error of the coefficient of correlation (r) is calculated by which one of the following formulae?

(1) $0.6745\sqrt{\frac{1-r^2}{n}}$ (2) $0.6745\frac{(1-r^2)}{\sqrt{n}}$

(3) $0.6745\frac{1+r^2}{\sqrt{n}}$ (4) $0.6745\frac{(1+r^2)}{n}$

55. To examine whether the company is pursuing its best opportunities with respect to markets, products, and channels is the purpose of which one of the following types of marketing control ?

(1) Strategic control
(2) Annual-plan control
(3) Efficiency control
(4) Profitability control

56. Choose the correct code for the following statements being correct or incorrect.

Statement I : A well-chosen marketing channel must be aligned to company's marketing strategy with respect to segmentation, targeting and positioning.

Statement II : Marketing channels are set of interdependent organizations participating in the process of making the product available for the use of consumption.

Code :

(1) Statement II is correct, but I is incorrect.
(2) Both the statements I and II are incorrect.
(3) Both the statements I and II are correct.
(4) Statement I is correct, but II is incorrect.

57. Foreign investment can be made through which of the following routes ?

(i) Foreign Direct Investment (FDI)
(ii) Foreign Portfolio Investment (FPI)
(iii) Private Equity Investment (PEI)
(iv) Foreign Venture Capital Investors (FVCI)

Choose the correct answer from the code given below :

Code :

(1) (i), (iii) and (iv) (2) (i), (ii), (iii) and (iv)
(3) (i), (ii) and (iv) (4) (i) and (iv)

58. Given below are two statements, one labelled as Assertion (A) and the other labelled as Reason (R). Read the statements and choose the correct answer using the code given below.

Assertion (A): Training aids in encouraging and achieving self-development and self-confidence.

Reason (R): It helps a person handle stress, tension, frustration and conflict.

Code :

(1) Both (A) and (R) are correct but (R) is not the right explanation of (A).
(2) Both (A) and (R) are incorrect.
(3) (A) is correct but (R) is not correct.
(4) Both (A) and (R) are correct and (R) is the right explanation of (A).

59. Match the items of List I with the items of List II and choose the correct answer from the code given below.

LIST I	LIST II
(a) AS-1	(i) Accounting for fixed assets
(b) AS-3	(ii) Disclosure of accounting policies

(c) AS – 10 (iii) Leases and its accounting
(d) AS – 19 (iv) Cash flow statements
(1) (a)–(iii), (b)–(i), (c)–(iv), (d)–(ii)
(2) (a)–(iii), (b)–(iv), (c)–(ii), (d)–(i)
(3) (a)–(i), (b)–(ii), (c)–(iii), (d)–(iv)
(4) (a)-(ii), (b)-(iv), (c)-(i), (d)-(iii)

60. Which of the following are included in the international liquidity ? Indicate the correct code.
(i) Foreign exchange reserve
(ii) Borrowing capacity of the various countries
(iii) Gold reserves

Choose the correct answer from the code given below :

Code :
(1) (ii) and (iii) (2) (i) and (ii)
(3) (i) and (iii) (4) (i), (ii) and (iii)

61. X Ltd. forfeited 40 shares of 10 each and on which 4 per share were paid. If the forfeited shares are reissued as 8 per share paid up, what is the minimum price the company must charge?
(1) 2 per share (2) 4 per share
(3) 10 per share (4) 8 per share

62. Which one of the following initiatives is not the strategy for managing shortage of employees in an organisation ?
(1) Attempt to reduce turnover
(2) Employee training
(3) Hire temporary employees
(4) Offer incentives to postpone retirement

63. A firm has inventory turnover of 3 and cost of goods sold is Rs. 2,70,000/- with better inventory management, the inventory turnover is increased to 5. This would result in
(1) Decrease in inventory by 90,000
(2) Increase in cost of goods sold by 20,000
(3) Decrease in inventory by 36,000
(4) Increase in inventory by 54,000

64. Which of the following variables is not known in Internal Rate of Return method of capital budgeting?
(1) Life of the project
(2) Discount rate
(3) Amount of cash outflows
(4) Amount of cash inflows

65. Match the items of List I with the items of List II and choose the correct answer from the code given below.

LIST I (Propounder of Theory)	LIST II (Theory of Motivation)
(a) Dr. William Ouchi	(i) X theory
(b) Douglas McGregor	(ii) Need Hierarchy Theory
(c) Frederick McGregor	(iii) Z Theory
(d) A.H. Maslow	(iv) Hygiene Theory

Code :
(1) (a)–(iii), (b)–(i), (c)–(iv), (d)–(ii)
(2) (a)–(iv), (b)–(i), (c)–(iii), (d)–(ii)
(3) (a)–(ii), (b)–(iii), (c)–(iv), (d)–(i)
(4) (a)–(ii), (b)–(i) ,(c)–(iii), (d)–(iv)

66. Which one of the following is not the correct property of normal distribution?
(1) Equality of central values (Mean, Mode and Median)
(2) Uni-modal distribution
(3) Standard deviation is the sole parameter of the distribution
(4) Continuous distribution

67. Production function is based on which combination of the main characteristics of the inputs from the following:
(i) Substitutability (ii) Complementarily
(iii) Flexibility (iv) Specificity

Choose the correct answer from the code given below :

Code :
(1) Only (iii) and (iv)
(2) Only (i), (ii) and (iv)
(3) Only (i) and (ii)
(4) Only (ii), (iii) and (iv)

68. Indicate the most popular route of privatisation adopted by the Government of India in recent decades.
(1) Spontaneous Privatisation
(2) Cross Holdings
(3) Management-Employee Buyout
(4) Strategic sale

69. Which of the following is not a method of preparation of cash budget?
(1) Adjusted Net Income method
(2) Proforma Balance Sheet method
(3) Cash Cycle method
(4) Receipts and Payments method

70. Corporations are controlled and directed by which one of the following?

(1) Corporate codes
(2) Corporate governance
(3) Corporate ethics
(4) Corporate mechanism

71. Choose the correct code for the following statements being correct or incorrect.

Statement I : FX Spot is an agreement between two parties to buy one currency against selling another currency at an agreed price for settlement on the spot date.

Statement II : The date of maturity of a forward contract is more than two business days in future.

Code :

(1) Both the statements I and II are correct.
(2) Statement II is correct, but I is incorrect.
(3) Statement I is correct, but II is incorrect.
(4) Both the statements I and II are incorrect.

72. Which of the following statements is/are true?

(i) Tax-shield on depreciation and interest is an important variable both for the lessor and the lessee.
(ii) Lease transactions in India are governed by the Lease Act.
(iii) A lessee should evaluate the lease options against the buying option.
(iv) As per AS – 19, financial lease is shown in the balance sheet of the lessee as an asset.

Choose the correct answer from the code given below :

Code :

(1) (i), (iii) and (iv) (2) Only (ii)
(3) (ii), (iii) and (iv) (4) (i) and (iv)

73. A company proposes to introduce a new product in the market. The company wants to maintain P/V ratio at 25%. If variable cost of the product is 300, what will be the selling price?

(1) Rs. 400 (2) Rs. 100
(3) Rs. 200 (4) Rs. 300

74. The correct code for the following statements being correct or incorrect.

Statement I: When the two securities returns are perfectly positively correlated, the risk of their portfolio is just a weighted average of the individual risks of the securities. In such case, diversification does not provide risk reduction but only risk averaging.

Statement II : Total risk of a portfolio of two risk securities can be completely eliminated when their returns are perfectly negatively correlated and their proportionate holdings in the portfolio are inversely related to the relative individual risks of the securities.

Code :

(1) Both the statements I and II are incorrect.
(2) Both the statements I and II are correct.
(3) Statement I is correct, but II is incorrect.
(4) Statement II is correct, but I is incorrect.

75. Match the items of List I with the items of List II and choose the correct answer from the code given below.

LIST I (Type of Interview)	LIST II (Usual Application)
(a) Structured	(i) A realistic approach that yields comparable answers plus in-depth insights
(b) Unstructured	(ii) Useful to understand applicants reasoning and analytical abilities under modest stress
(c) Mixed	(iii) Useful for valid results, especially when dealing with large number of applicants
(d) Behavioural	(iv) Useful when the interviewer tries to probe personal details of the candidate to analyse why they are not fit for the job

Code :

(1) (a)–(iii), (b)–(i), (c)–(ii), (d)–(iv)
(2) (a)–(i), (b)–(iv), (c)–(ii), (d)–(iii)
(3) (a)–(iii), (b)–(iv), (c)–(i), (d)–(ii)
(4) (a)–(iv), (b)–(ii) ,(c)–(i), (d)–(iii)

76. Given below are two statements, one labelled as Assertion (A) and the other labelled as Reason (R). Read the statements and choose the correct answer using the code given below.

Assertion (A) : Consumers need to be given legal protection against certain trade practices and business methods.

Reason (R) : Protection as per market forces and 'Caveat Emptor' is not enough as perfectly competitive market is an economics dream and consumer sovereignty is a myth.

Code :
(1) Both (A) and (R) are correct but (R) is not the right explanation of (A).
(2) (A) is correct but (R) is incorrect.
(3) (A) is incorrect but (R) is correct.
(4) Both (A) and (R) are correct and (R) is the right explanation of (A).

77. Banks are required to classify Non-Performing Assets into
(1) Doubtful assets, bad debts and loss assets
(2) Standard assets, and sub-standard assets
(3) Sub-standard assets, doubtful assets, and loss assets
(4) Doubtful assets, and bad debts

78. Cardinal utility analysis of consumer's behaviour is based on which combination of the following assumptions:
(i) Utility is measurable in terms of cardinal numbers.
(ii) Constancy of the marginal utility of money.
(iii) Utilities of different goods are interdependent.
(iv) Gossen's first law of consumption.
Choose the correct answer from the code given below :
Code :
(1) Only (iii) and (iv)
(2) Only (i), (ii) and (iv)
(3) Only (ii), (iii) and (iv)
(4) Only (i) and (ii)

79. Which one of the following is the main government agency responsible for development and monitoring international trade in India?
(1) Export Promotion Council
(2) Department of Commerce
(3) Indian Institute of Foreign Trade
(4) Federation of Indian Export Organisations

80. Which of the following statements Ware false?
(i) Capital profits can never be distributed as dividends to the shareholders.
(ii) Dividends are paid out of profits and, therefore, do not affect the liquidity position of the firm.
(iii) Every company should follow the policy of low dividend payment.
(iv) Walter's model suggests that dividend payment does not affect the market price of the share.
Choose the correct answer from the code given below :
Code :
(1) (iii) and (iv)
(2) (ii), (iii) and (iv)
(3) (i), (ii), (iii) and (iv)
(4) (i), (ii) and (iii)

81. A and B are partners in a firm sharing profits in the ratio of 3 : 2. They admit X as a partner for 1/3 share in profits of the firm. The new profit sharing ratio of A, B and X is
(1) 3:2:2 (2) 3:2:1
(3) 6:4:5 (4) 3:2:3

82. Advertising method in which a commercial is broadcast simultaneously on several radio stations and/or television channels is known as
(1) Road block (2) Road side
(3) Exclusive drive
(4) Intensified campaign

83. Which one of the following is not the basic function of WTO?
(1) To facilitate the expansion and balanced growth of international trade
(2) To facilitate the implementation, administration and operation of trade agreements
(3) To settle differences and disputes among its member countries
(4) To carry out periodic reviews of the trade policies of its member countries

84. Bretton Woods Conference resulted into the establishment of which of the following?
(1) IBRD and IFC (2) IMF and IDA
(3) IDA and ADB (4) IMF and IBRD

85. Which one of the following modes is not an example of Direct and Database marketing communication?
(1) Mailings
(2) Social media marketing
(3) Catalogues
(4) Telemarketing

86. Given below are two statements, one labelled as Assertion (A) and the other labelled as Reason (R). Read the statements and choose the correct answer using the code given below.
Assertion (A) : A low debt-equity ratio is generally recommended for a newly started business.
Reason (R) : During the initial years of the business, debt servicing will prove to be less burdensome.

Code :

(1) (A) is not correct but (R) is correct.
(2) Both (A) and (R) are correct and (R) is the correct explanation of (A).
(3) (A) is correct but (R) is not correct.
(4) Both (A) and (R) are correct but (R) is not the correct explanation of (A).

87. Match the items of List I with the items of List II and choose the correct answer from the code given below.

LIST I

(a) Direct investment overseas aimed at manufacturing products not manufactured by the firm in the home country.
(b) Direct investment in a foreign country aimed to sell the output of the firm's domestic production.
(c) Direct investment overseas aimed at providing inputs for the firms production process in the home country.
(d) Foreign firms investing overseas and taking control over foreign assets

LIST II

(i) Inward FDI
(ii) Backward Vertical FDI
(iii) Conglomerate FDI
(iv) Forward Vertical FDI

(1) (a)–(iv), (b)–(iii), (c)–(ii), (d)–(i)
(2) (a)–(iii), (b)–(iv), (c)–(ii), (d)–(i)
(3) (a)–(i), (b)–(iv), (c)–(ii), (d)–(iii)
(4) (a)–(iii), (b)–(ii) ,(c)–(i), (d)–(iv)

88. Given below are two statements, one labelled as Assertion (A) and the other labelled as Reason (R). Read the statements and choose the correct answer using the code given below.

Assertion (A): Among all methods of charging depreciation on fixed assets, diminishing balance method is the best method.

Reason (R): Diminishing balance method of charging depreciation has been permitted under the Income Tax Act, 1961 for claiming deduction for depreciation.

Code :

(1) (A) is correct but (R) is not correct.
(2) Both (A) and (R) are correct but (R) is not the correct explanation of (A).
(3) Both (A) and (R) are correct and (R) is the correct explanation of (A).
(4) (A) is incorrect but (R) is correct.

89. The theory suggesting that the patterns of international trade are determined by factor endowment rather than productivity was propounded by which one of the following?

(1) Adam Smith
(2) Michael Porter
(3) David Ricardo
(4) Heckscher and Bertil Ohlin

90. Match the items of List I with the items of List II and choose the correct answer from the code given below.

List I	List II
(a) Behaviour referent	(i) Wide ranging cultural, structural and personnel strategies
(b) Focus of attention for interventions	(ii) Manage climate and culture
(c) Conflict handling	(iii) Few
(d) Job categories and grades	(iv) Values/mission

(1) (a)–(i), (b)–(ii), (c)–(iv), (d)–(iii)
(2) (a)–(iii), (b)–(i), (c)–(ii), (d)–(iv)
(3) (a)–(iv), (b)–(i), (c)–(ii), (d)–(iii)
(4) (a)–(iv), (b)–(ii), (c)–(i), (d)–(iii)

91. Critical path indicates which one of the following?

(1) Average time of completing a task
(2) Shortest route of completing a task
(3) Longest route of completing a task
(3) Recorded time of completing a task

92. Given is the information related to a house

Municipal Value (M. V.)	Rs. 1,50,000/-
Fair Rent	Rs. 1,80,000/-
Standard Rent	Rs. 1,60,000/-
Actual Rent	Rs. 20000/-pm

Municipal tax paid by owner is 20% of M.V. Unrealised rent 40,000 (conditions of rule 4 satisfied). What is the annual value of the house?

(1) Rs. 1,60,000/- (2) Rs. 1,50,000/-
(3) Rs. 2,10,000/- (4) Rs. 1,70,000/-

93. Match the items of List I with the items of List II and choose the correct answer from the code given below.

List I

(a) Income elasticity less than unity
(b) Cross elasticity less than unity

(c) Cross elasticity less than zero
(d) Income elasticity less than zero

List II

(i) Competitive goods
(ii) Inferior goods
(iii) Superior goods
(iv) Complementary goods

Code :

(1) (a)–(i), (b)–(ii), (c)–(iii), (d)–(iv)
(2) (a)–(iv), (b)–(i), (c)–(ii), (d)–(iii)
(3) (a)–(iii), (b)–(i), (c)–(iv), (d)–(ii)
(4) (a)–(iv), (b)–(iii), (c)–(i), (d)–(ii)

94. Match the items of List I with the items of List 11 and choose the correct answer from the code given below.

List I	**List II**
(a) Mobile Defense	(i) Occupying the most desirable position in consumers' minds, making the brand almost impregnable.
(b) Contraction Defense	(ii) The leader stretches its domain over new territories through market broadening and market diversification.
(c) Position Defense	(iii) Large companies give up weaker markets and reassign resources to stronger ones.

Code :

(1) (a)–(ii), (b)–(iii), (c)–(i)
(2) (a)–(i), (b)–(ii), (c)–(iii)
(3) (a)–(i), (b)–(iii), (c)–(ii)
(4) (a)–(ii), (b)–(i), (c)–(iii)

95. For the following two statements regarding infrastructural services in the country, choose the correct code for the statements being correct or incorrect.

Statement I : Most infrastructure services are provided by public monopolies which generally suffer with severe problems like lack of accountability, low productivity, poor financial performance and over-employment.

Statement II : There is a need now to induce more private sector investment and participation in provision of social overheads as it may encourage better risk sharing, accountability, monitoring and management of infrastructure sector.

(1) Both I and II are correct.
(2) I is incorrect, but II is correct.
(3) Both I and II are incorrect.
(4) I is correct, but II is incorrect.

96. In which one of the following forms of workers participation in management is the role of the workers council not just advisory but the management is under a moral obligation to acknowledge, accept and implement the unanimous decision of the council?

(1) Associative Participation
(2) Administrative Participation
(3) Consultative Participation
(4) Decisive Participation

97. Match the items of List I with the items of List II and choose the correct answer from the code given below.

List I	**List II**
(a) NPA	(i) The percentage of deposits to be kept with RBI in the form of cash.
(b) SLR	(ii) the rate at which RBI lends money to commercial banks.
(c) Repo Rate	(iii) Loans and advances not paid for more than 90 days.
(d) CRR	(iv) The percentage of net demand and time liabilities to be kept in the form of liquid assets.

Code :

(1) (a)–(iii), (b)–(ii), (c)–(iv), (d)–(i)
(2) (a)–(iii), (b)–(iv), (c)–(ii), (d)–(i)
(3) (a)–(iii), (b)–(iv), (c)–(i), (d)–(ii)
(4) (a)–(ii), (b)–(iii), (c)–(iv), (d)–(i)

98. Given below are two statements, one labelled as Assertion (A) and the other labelled as Reason (R). Read the statements and choose the correct answer using the code given below.

Assertion (A) : Purchase decisions are not based on how customers perceive prices but, on the marketers, stated price.

Reason (R) : Customers may have a lower price threshold, below which prices signal inferior or unacceptable quality, and an upper price threshold where the product appears not worth the money.

Code :

(1) Both (A) and (R) are correct but (R) is not the right explanation of (A).
(2) Both (A) and (R) are incorrect.
(3) Both (A) and (R) are correct and (R) is the right explanation of (A).
(4) (A) is incorrect but (R) is correct.

99. 'Finance for exporting companies' as part of major programmes of the Exim Bank of India does not include?

(1) Post-shipment credit
(2) Overseas investment finance
(3) Term loans
(4) Working capital

100. On fulfilling certain conditions, for an undertaking set up in special economic zones, deduction under section 10 AA of the Income Tax Act is allowed for?

(1) 10 years (2) Unlimited period
(3) 5 years (4) 15 years

101. The central bank can significantly influence the savings, investments and consumer spending in the economy through which of the following policy ?

(1) Fiscal Policy
(2) Monetary Policy
(3) Industrial Policy
(4) Foreign Exchange Policy

102. Which one of the following is not the characteristic of capitalism ?

(1) Individuals and associations behave with economic motive of maximising their profit with least sacrifice or cost.
(2) The country's major means of production are either owned by the Government or their use is controlled by the Government.
(3) Producers, consumers and employees compete among themselves, as the resources and opportunities are limited.
(4) Price, the invisible hand, plays a predominant role in the flow of the factors of production and consumption.

103. Which of the following is not the salient feature of the industrial policy developments since 1991?

(1) The scope of the private sector has been enormously expanded.
(2) Public sector has been withdrawing partially or fully from several of the enterprises by divestment.
(3) The Indian industry is increasingly exposed to foreign competition.
(4) Monopoly or dominant position for the public sector in most of the industries and control of the commanding heights of the economy by the public sector.

104. Which of the following does not form the part of the important information to be incorporated in the Memorandum of Association as specified in the Companies Act, 2013 ?

(1) The name of the company and the state in which it is situated.
(2) The objects for which the company is proposed to be incorporated.
(3) The rules, regulations and bye-laws for the internal management of the company.
(4) The liability of the members of the company, whether limited or unlimited.

105. Assertion (A) : The volume of imports tends to be very high when there is a conjecture of high rate of economic growth and a sharp fall in the relative price of imports and vice versa.

Reason (R) : High rate of growth, ceteris paribus, is associated with rise in imports and increase in the imports, ceteris paribus, is associated with a fall in the relative price of imports.

Code :

(1) Both (A) and (R) are correct and (R) is the right explanation of (A).
(2) Both (A) and (R) are correct but (R) is not the right explanation of (A).
(3) (A) is correct but (R) is not correct.
(4) (R) is correct but (A) is not correct.

106. Which of the following statements is not correct relating to consumerism ?

(1) Consumerism is a manifestation of the failure of the business to guarantee and ensure consumer legitimate rights.
(2) The government does not have any role in consumer protection as it is the part of business organisations alone.
(3) The consumers should accept consumerism as a means of asserting and enjoying their rights.
(4) Consumerism evolution is not a set-back for marketing but rather points to the next stage in the evolution of enlightened marketing.

107. Which one of the following is not covered in the approach adopted by "Niti Aayog" ?

(1) Five year planning approach
(2) Three year action agenda
(3) Seven year strategy
(4) Fifteen year vision

108. Assertion (A) : Personal transactions of the owners of the business are not recorded in the books.

Reasoning (R) : According to the business entity concept, each business enterprise is considered as an accounting unit separate from owners.

Code :

(1) Both (A) and (R) are correct and (R) is the correct explanation of (A).
(2) Both (A) and (R) are correct but (R) is not the correct explanation of (A).
(3) (A) is correct but (R) is not correct.
(4) (A) is wrong but (R) is correct.

109. Which one of the following is not an example of 'financing activities' with reference to cash flow statement ?

(1) Repayment of bank loan
(2) Interest on debentures/Dividend paid
(3) Cash proceeds from public deposits
(4) Sale of fixed assets

110. Which one of the following statements is true about estimated costs and standard costs ?

(1) Standard costs are based on scientific analysis and engineering studies while estimated costs are based on historical basis.
(2) Standard cost emphasis is on "what cost will be" while estimated cost emphasis is on "what cost should be".
(3) Standard costs are more frequently revised compared to estimated cost.
(4) Estimated costs are more stable than standard costs.

111. Which one of the following statements is not true ?

(1) An expenditure intended to benefit current year is revenue expenditure.
(2) Amount paid for acquiring goodwill is capital expenditure.
(3) Wages paid for installation of a new machine is usually debited to wages account.
(4) Revenue expenditure is not intended to benefit future period.

112. X Ltd. forfeited 20 shares of ' 10 each, ' 8 called up, on which John had paid application and allotment money of ' 5 per share, of these, 15 shares were reissued to Parker as fully paid up for ' 6 per share. What is the balance in the share Forfeiture Account after the relevant amount has been transferred to Capital Reserve Account ?

(1) NIL (2) Rs. 5
(3) Rs. 25 (4) Rs. 100

113. X and Y sharing profits in the ratio of 7 : 3, admit Z for 3/7 share in the new firm in which he takes 2/7 from X and 1/7 from Y. The new ratio of X, Y and Z will be :

(1) 7 : 3 : 3 (2) 4 : 2 : 3
(3) 14 : 6 : 15 (4) 29 : 11 : 30

114. Assertion (A) : A high operating ratio indicates a favourable position.

Reasoning (R) : A high operating ratio leaves a high margin to meet non operating expenses.

Code :

(1) (A) and (R) both are correct and (R) correctly explains (A).
(2) Both (A) and (R) are correct but (R) does not explain (A).
(3) Both (A) and (R) are incorrect.
(4) (A) is correct but (R) is incorrect.

115. The following are the two statements regarding concept of profit. Indicate the correct code of the statements being correct or incorrect.

Statement (I) : Accounting profit is a surplus of total revenue over and above all paid-out costs, including both manufacturing and overhead expenses.

Statement (II) : Economic or pure profit is a residual left after all contractual costs have been met, including the transfer costs of management, insurable risks, depreciation and payments to shareholders sufficient to maintain investment at its current level.

Code :

(1) Both the statements are correct.
(2) Both the statements are incorrect.
(3) Statement (I) is correct while Statement (II) is incorrect.
(4) Statement (I) is incorrect while Statement (II) is correct.

116. Which one of the following sets is incorrect to show the inter-relationships among price elasticity coefficient, change in price and change in total revenue ?

Price elasticity coefficient	Change in price	Change in Total Revenue
(1) Zero	Increase	Increase
	Decrease	Decrease
(2) Less than 1	Increase	Decrease
	Decrease	Increase
(3) Equal to 1	Increase	No change
	Decrease	No change
(4) More than 1	Increase	Decrease
	Decrease	Increase

117. Which one of the following is not the basic property of indifference curves ?

(1) Indifference curves have a negative slope.
(2) Indifference curves of imperfect substitutes are concave to the origin.
(3) Indifference curves do not intersect nor are they tangent to one another.
(4) Upper indifference curves indicate higher level of satisfaction.

118. When labour is plotted on X-axis and capital is plotted on Y-axis and an iso-quant is prepared, then which of the following statements is/are false ?

(a) Marginal rate of technical substitution of labour for capital is equal to the slope of the iso-quant.
(b) Marginal rate of technical substitution of labour for capital is equal to change in the units of capital divided by the change in the units of labour.
(c) Marginal rate of technical substitution of labour for capital is the ratio of marginal productivity of capital to marginal productivity of labour.

Code :

(1) (a) and (b) statements
(2) Only (c) statement
(3) Only (a) statement
(4) Only (b) statement

119. Match the items of List - II with the items of List - I and indicate the code of correct matching. The items relate to economies of scale/scope.

List - I	List - II
(a) Economies of scale	(i) arise with lower average costs of manufacturing a product when two complementary products are produced by a single firm
(b) Internal economies	(ii) Mean lowering of costs of production by producing in bulk
(c) External economies	(iii) Arise when cost per unit depends on size of the firm
(d) Economies of scope	(iv) Arise when cost per unit depends on the size of the industry, not the firm

Codes :

	(a)	(b)	(c)	(d)
(1)	(ii)	(iv)	(i)	(iii)
(2)	(i)	(ii)	(iii)	(iv)
(3)	(ii)	(iii)	(iv)	(i)
(4)	(iv)	(iii)	(ii)	(i)

120. A firm that produces highly substitute goods can adopt which one of the following pricing strategies ?

(1) Transfer pricing
(2) Going Rate pricing
(3) Product bundling
(4) Full cost pricing

121. In a perfectly competitive market, a firm in the long run operates at the level of output where

(1) AC = MC when MC is lowest
(2) MC = AR = MR when MC is lowest
(3) MR = MC
(4) AR = MR =AC = MC

122. Assignment of numerals to the objects to represent their attributes is known as :

(1) Nominal data (2) Ordinal data
(3) Interval data (4) Ratio data

123. A graph of a cumulative frequency distribution is called :

(1) Frequency polygon
(2) Frequency curve
(3) Ogive
(4) Pie diagram

124. In the case of classification of data, the class having its upper limit is treated as the lower limit of its next class is called :

(1) Open ended class
(2) Close ended class
(3) Exclusive class
(4) Inclusive class

125. For a standard normal probability distribution, the mean (μ) and the standard deviation (s) are

(1) $\mu = 0, \sigma = 1$ (2) $\mu = 16, \sigma = 4$

(3) $\mu = 25, \sigma = 5$ (4) $\mu = 100, \sigma = 10$

126. Match the items of List - II with the items of List - I and select the code of correct matching.

List - I	List - II
(a) Standard error of mean	(i) Ha : $\mu_1 \neq \mu_2$
(b) Base of point estimate of the mean of the population	(ii) Values based on all the observations of the population
(c) Non-specific hypothesis	(iii) Mean of the sampling distribution of mean
(d) Parameter value of descriptive statistics	(iv) Standard deviation of the sampling distribution of mean

Codes :

	(a)	(b)	(c)	(d)
(1)	(iv)	(iii)	(i)	(ii)
(2)	(i)	(ii)	(iii)	(iv)
(3)	(iv)	(iii)	(ii)	(i)
(4)	(iii)	(iv)	(i)	(ii)

127. There is a very high inverse relationship between measures of 'Overweight' and 'life expectancy'. Which one of the following value of the coefficient of correlation is consistent with the statement ?

(1) 0.80 (2) 0.20

(3) –0.20 (4) –0.80

128. Match the items of List - II with the items of List-I & select the code of correct matching.

List - I	List - II
(a) Chi-square Test	(i) Testing the significance of the differences of the mean values among more than two sample groups.
(b) ANOVA (F-test)	(ii) Testing the goodness of fit of a distribution
(c) Z - test	(iii) Testing the significance of the difference of the mean values between two large sized samples
(d) *t* - test	(iv) Testing the significance of the difference of the mean values between two small sized samples when population standard deviation is not available

Codes :

	(a)	(b)	(c)	(d)
(1)	(i)	(ii)	(iii)	(iv)
(2)	(iv)	(iii)	(ii)	(i)
(3)	(i)	(ii)	(iv)	(iii)
(4)	(ii)	(i)	(iii)	(iv)

129. Match the items of List - II with List - I and choose the correct code :

List - I	List - II
(a) Sales Executive	(i) Top- middle Management
(b) Branch Manager	(ii) Middle Management
(c) Foreman	(iii) Lower Management
(d) Production Manager	(iv) Operating Force

Codes :

	(a)	(b)	(c)	(d)
(1)	(iv)	(ii)	(iii)	(i)
(2)	(ii)	(iii)	(iv)	(i)
(3)	(iii)	(iv)	(ii)	(i)
(4)	(i)	(ii)	(iii)	(iv)

130. Select the correct code of the statements being correct or incorrect.

Statement (I) : It is a significant feature of human that he plans.

Statement (II) : A plan is a trap to capture the future.

Code :

(1) Statement (I) is correct but (II) is incorrect.

(2) Statement (II) is correct but (I) is incorrect.

(3) Both the statements (I) and (II) are correct.

(4) Both the statements (I) and (II) are incorrect.

131. Assertion (A) : Management is a set of principles relating to its functions.

Reasoning (R) : Management is essential to run all types of organizations.

Code :

(1) (A) and (R) both are correct ; and (R) is the right explanation of (A).

(2) (A) and (R) both are correct ; but (R) is not the right explanation (A).

(3) Both (A) and (R) are incorrect.
(4) (A) is correct ; but (R) is incorrect.

132. Match the items of List - II with List - I ; and choose the correct code :

List - I (Critical Control Standards)	List - II (Critical Points)
(a) Physical standards	(i) Material cost per unit
(b) Cost standards	(ii) Labour hours per unit of output
(c) Revenue standards	(iii) Timing of production
(d) Program standards	(iv) Average sales per customer

Codes :

	(a)	(b)	(c)	(d)
(1)	(ii)	(i)	(iv)	(iii)
(2)	(ii)	(i)	(iii)	(iv)
(3)	(i)	(ii)	(iv)	(iii)
(4)	(iv)	(i)	(iii)	(ii)

133. Which among the following is not a correct statement with regard to Corporate Governance in India ?
(1) Every company must appoint an individual or firm as auditor.
(2) The independent directors must attend at least three meetings a year.
(3) One or more women directors are recommended for certain classes of companies.
(4) The maximum number of permissible directors cannot exceed 15 in a public limited company.

134. The popular statement, "if all you have is a hammer, everything looks like a nail", is given by :
(1) A.H. Maslow (Hierarchy of Needs)
(2) Henry Fayol (Industrial and General Administration)
(3) F.W. Taylor (Scientific Management)
(4) Fredrick Herzberg (Hygiene Theory)

135. Functional Leadership Theory is associated with
(1) Hackman and Walton and McGrath
(2) Bernard and Ordway Tead
(3) Koontz and O'Donnell
(4) Alford and Beatty

136. When two separate companies or two divisions within the same company agree to place both of their respective brands on a particular product or enterprise, this arrangement is termed as :
(1) Differential Branding
(2) Cobranding
(3) Dual Branding
(4) Both Cobranding and Dual Branding

137. The tangible goods for which a consumer wants to compare quality, price and perhaps style in several stores before making a purchase are called :
(1) Convenience Goods
(2) Shopping Goods
(3) Speciality Goods
(4) Unsought Goods

138. When a company treats each single customer as a separate segment, this is called :
(1) Niche Marketing
(2) Nano Marketing
(3) Single Marketing
(4) Micro Marketing

139. Under which of the following conditions, the level of consumer's involvement will not be high ?
(1) The consumer considers the amount of money involved to be large.
(2) The product is seen as having low potential for providing significant benefits.
(3) The consumer lacks information about alternatives for satisfying the need.
(4) The product has considerable social importance.

140. **Statement (I) :** The mindset which is commonly associated with a long - ago era when the demand for goods generally exceeded the supply, and the primary focus in business was to effectively produce medium quantities of products ; finding the customers was viewed as a relatively major function.

Statement (II) : The firms with product orientation typically focus on the quality and quantity of offerings while assuming that customers will seek out and buy reasonably priced, well made products.

From the above statements indicate the correct code of being statements correct or incorrect The statements relate to concepts of marketing.
(1) Both the statements (I) and (II) are not correct.
(2) Both the statements (I) and (II) are correct.
(3) Statement (I) is correct but statement (II) is not correct.

(4) Statement (I) is not correct but statement (II) is correct.

141. Match the items of List - II with List - I to identify the correct code which are related to legal forces affecting international marketers.

List - I	List - II
(a) Tariff	(i) A regulation specifying the proportion of a finished product's components and labour that must be provided by importing country.
(b) Import Quota	(ii) Tax imposed on product entering a country and used to protect domestic producers and/or raise revenue.
(c) Local-content Law	(iii) A requirement that a product contain or exclude certain ingredients or that it be tested and certified as meeting certain restrictive standards.
(d) Local-operating Law	(iv) Limiting amount of a particular product that can be brought into a country, to protect domestic industry or broadening access to its markets.
(e) Standards and Certification	(v) A refusal to buy products from a particular company or country.
(f) Boycott	(vi) A constraint on how, when or where retailing can be conducted.

Codes :

	(a)	(b)	(c)	(d)	(e)	(f)
(1)	(iii)	(iv)	(ii)	(i)	(vi)	(v)
(2)	(vi)	(ii)	(i)	(iv)	(iii)	(v)
(3)	(ii)	(iv)	(i)	(vi)	(iii)	(v)
(4)	(iv)	(vi)	(i)	(ii)	(iii)	(v)

142. Match the items of List - II with List - I which are related to personal selling process and identify the correct code :

List - I	List - II
(a) Prospecting	(i) Attention, Interest, Desire, Action
(b) Preapproach	(ii) Identifying Profiles, leads, Records and Qualifying capability and willingness
(c) Presentation	(iii) Reduce Dissonance, Build goodwill
(d) Post sales services	(iv) Information, habits, preferences

Codes :

	(a)	(b)	(c)	(d)
(1)	(i)	(iii)	(iv)	(ii)
(2)	(iii)	(iv)	(ii)	(i)
(3)	(ii)	(iv)	(i)	(iii)
(4)	(iv)	(iii)	(ii)	(i)

143. Which of the following is not an approach to the Capital Structure ?

(1) Gross Profit Approach

(2) Net Operating Income Approach

(3) Net Income Approach

(4) Modigliani and Miller Approach

144. Which one of the following methods of Capital Budgeting assumes that cash-inflows are reinvested at the project's rate of return ?

(1) Net Present Value

(2) Accounting Rate of Return

(3) Internal Rate of Return

(4) Discounted Pay Back Period

145. Cost of Equity Share Capital is more than cost of Debt because :

(1) Equity shares are not easily saleable.

(2) Equity shares do not provide the fixed dividend rate.

(3) Generally the face value of equity shares is less than the face value of debentures.

(4) Equity shares have high risk than debts.

146. Negative Net Working Capital implies that :

(1) Long-term funds have been used for fixed assets.

(2) Short-term funds have been used for fixed assets.

(3) Long-term funds have been used for current assets.

(4) Short-term funds have been used for current assets.

147. Which of the following is an implicit cost of increasing proportion of debt of a company ?

(1) P.E. Ratio of the company would increase.

(2) Rate of return of the company would decrease.

(3) Tax-shield would not be available on new debts.

(4) Equity shareholders would demand higher return.

148. Profitability Index of a Project is the ratio of present value of cash inflows to :

(1) Total cash inflows

(2) Total cash outflows

(3) Present value of cash outflows

(4) Initial cost minus Depreciation

149. Which one of the following statements is false ?

(1) Effective dividend policy is an important tool to achieve the goal of wealth maximisation.

(2) According to Walter, the optimal payout ratio for a growth firm is 100%.

(3) MM model asserts that the value of the firm is not affected whether the firm pays dividend or not.

(4) 'Bird-in-the-hand theory' in reference to dividend decision has been developed by Myron Gordon.

150. Which one of the following statements defines the correct meaning of the term "boundary spanning" ?

(1) It refers to an obligation of an individual, firm or institution to account for its activities and accept responsibility for them.

(2) It refers to the process that helps the organization and its employees to link with their external environment through specific activities/functions.

(3) It refers to the science of morals, principles and rules of conduct.

(4) It refers to multiculturism management.

151. The VRIO framework, used in HR function in today's era, refers to four criteria. Identify the correct code which stands as correct explanation to VRIO as proposed by Barney.

(1) Valence - Recruiting - Industrial relations - Opportunities

(2) Vision - Rewards - Improvements - Options

(3) Value-Rarity-Imitability - Organization

(4) Versatile - Resource - Information - Outsourcing

152. Assertion (A) : Induction is an informal information sharing session on miscellaneous issues in an organization.

Reasoning (R) : The rationale of induction is to ensure effective integration of staff into or across the organization for their mutual benefit.

Code :

(1) Assertion (A) and Reasoning (R) both are correct and (R) is correct explanation of (A).

(2) Assertion (A) and Reasoning (R) both are correct but (R) is not the correct explanation of (A).

(3) Assertion (A) is correct statement but Reasoning (R) is an incorrect statement.

(4) Assertion (A) is an incorrect statement but Reasoning (R) is a correct statement.

153. Match the items of List - II with the items of List - I pertaining to the ranking methods used in performance management systems ; and select the code of correct matching.

List - I (Ranking methods)	List - II (Methodology)
(a) Simple ranking	(i) Based on overall performance.
(b) Alternation ranking	(ii) Ends up with predetermined number of people in each group.
(c) Paired comparison	(iii) Based on particular trait only for quantity/quality of work
(d) Forced distribution	(iv) Based on a trait or a set of trait and avoids central tendency.

Codes :

	(a)	(b)	(c)	(d)
(1)	(ii)	(iii)	(iv)	(i)
(2)	(i)	(iv)	(iii)	(ii)
(3)	(iv)	(ii)	(i)	(iii)
(4)	(iii)	(i)	(ii)	(iv)

154. Assertion (A) : Compensation has two vital domains economic concept and psychological concept.

Reasoning (R) : Compensation basically represents an employment contract.

Code :

(1) (A) is correct and (R) is right explanation of (A).

(2) (A) is correct but (R) is not the right explanation of (A).

(3) (A) is correct but (R) is incorrect.

(4) (A) is incorrect but (R) is correct.

155. Which of the following is not the primary objective of industrial relations and labour laws ?

(1) Maintaining social equity
(2) Providing credit facilities to industries
(3) International uniformity
(4) Promoting economic growth

156. **Assertion (A) :** In real terms, workers' participation in management has failed in India.

Reasoning (R) : There is lack of attitudinal change, multiplicity of unions and absence of a procedure to determine a sole bargaining agent in an organization.

Code :

(1) (A) is correct and (R) is correct explanation of (A).
(2) (A) is correct but (R) is not the correct explanation of (A).
(3) (A) is correct but (R) is incorrect.
(4) (A) is incorrect but (R) is correct.

157. Which one of the following is not the function of NABARD ?

(1) To provide refinance assistance by way of short term credit to state cooperative banks and sectoral rural banks, etc., approved by the RBI for some specific purposes.
(2) To undertake inspection of cooperative societies other than primary cooperative societies and RRBs.
(3) To promote research in various aspects of the problems of urban development.
(4) To subscribe to share capital or invest in securities of any institution concerned with agricultural and rural development.

158. Which one of the following financial institutions co-ordinates the functions and operations of all the financial institutions into a single integrated financial structure so that each may contribute to the growth of the economy ?

(1) IFCI (2) UTI
(3) IDBI (4) SIDBI

159. **Assertion (A) :** The Reserve Bank of India is entrusted with the management of the public debt and issue of new loans and treasury bills on behalf of the central and state Governments.

Reasoning (R) : The Governor and the Deputy Governors of Reserve Bank of India are appointed by the Central Government.

Code :

(1) (A) is correct but (R) is not correct.
(2) (A) and (R) both are correct but (R) is not the right explanation of (A).
(3) (A) and (R) both are correct and (R) is the right explanation of (A).
(4) (A) and (R) both are not correct.

160. __________ refers to the process of removing or stripping the legal status of a currency.

(1) Digitisation (2) Financial Inclusion
(3) Demonetisation (4) Micro finance

161. Which one of the following is not the objective of UTI ?

(1) To mobilise savings of the community by offering savers the triple benefits of safety, liquidity and profitability of Investments.
(2) To channelise the pooled savings into productive outlets.
(3) To provide finance under hire purchase finance and housing finance to its members.
(4) To give every one a chance to indirectly own shares and securities in a large number of select companies.

162. Which one of the following is the main objective of IFCI ?

(1) To offer both small and large investors the means of acquiring shares in the widening prosperity resulting from the steady industrial growth of the country.
(2) To upgrade technology, modernization and to promote marketing of products of small scale sector.
(3) To serve as the apex institution for term finance for industry with coordination, regulation and supervision of the working of other financial institution.
(4) To provide medium and long term financial assistance to industrial undertakings, particularly in those circumstances in which banking accommodation is in appropriate or resource to capital market is impracticable.

163. Match the items of List - II with the items of List - I and indicate the correct code :

List - I	List - II
(a) Term finance	(i) Providing finance to new or existing industrial units for encouraging commercial application of technology/expansion.
(b) Refinance	(ii) Delivering of banking services at affordable

	cost to the vast sections of disadvantaged and low income groups.
(c) Financial inclusion	(iii) Providing replenishment finance to eligible institutions for their loans to industrial concerns.
(d) Venture capital	(iv) Providing finance to the borrowers for expansion and modernization of plant and equipment.

Codes :

	(a)	(b)	(c)	(d)
(1)	(i)	(ii)	(iii)	(iv)
(2)	(i)	(ii)	(iv)	(iii)
(3)	(iv)	(iii)	(ii)	(i)
(4)	(iv)	(iii)	(i)	(ii)

164. Assertion (A) : An export processing zone is different from free trade zone as it promotes units primarily devoted to exports.

Reasoning (R) : Goods imported to a free trade zone may be re-exported without any processing, in the same form. But, goods exported by units in an EPZ are expected to have undergone some value addition by manufacturing/processing.

Code :

(1) (A) is correct and (R) is correct explanation of (A).

(2) (A) is correct but (R) is not the correct explanation of (A).

(3) (A) is correct but (R) is incorrect.

(4) (A) is incorrect but (R) is correct.

165. Match the items of List - II with the items of List - I relating to liberalisation of agricultural trade.

List - I	List - II
(a) Tariffication	(i) They have demonstrably adverse effects on other member countries.
(b) Prohibited subsidies	(ii) They act on goods which are contingent upon export performance.
(c) Actionable subsidies	(iii) Replacement of existing non-tariff restrictions.
(d) Non-actionable subsidies	(iv) For industrial research in disadvantaged regions.

Codes :

	(a)	(b)	(c)	(d)
(1)	(ii)	(iii)	(i)	(iv)
(2)	(iv)	(i)	(ii)	(iii)
(3)	(iii)	(ii)	(i)	(iv)
(4)	(ii)	(iv)	(iii)	(i)

166. Match the items of List - II and with the items of List - I relating to WTO impact :

List - I	List - II
(a) NAMA	(i) Liberalisation of international investments.
(b) GATTS	(ii) Includes industrial goods, textile, jewellery, fish and fisheries product manufacturing industries.
(c) TRIMs	(iii) Liberalisation of trade in goods and services.
(d) TRIPs	(iv) Provides monopoly power to owners of intellectual property.

Codes :

	(a)	(b)	(c)	(d)
(1)	(ii)	(i)	(iv)	(iii)
(2)	(iv)	(ii)	(iii)	(i)
(3)	(ii)	(iii)	(i)	(iv)
(4)	(iii)	(ii)	(iv)	(i)

167. Indicate the correct code of the following statements being correct or incorrect. The statements relate to the type of transactions recorded in the current/capital accounts of the Balance of Payments.

Statement (I) : The capital account consists of long-term capital transactions only.

Statement (II) : The current account includes all transactions which give rise to or use up national income.

Code :

(1) Both the statements are correct.

(2) Both the statements are incorrect.

(3) Statement (I) is correct while Statement (II) is incorrect.

(4) Statement (I) is incorrect while Statement (II) is correct.

168. Select the correct code of the following statements being correct or incorrect.

Statement (I) : International liquidity encompasses the international reserves only.

Statement (II) : International liquidity covers only official holdings of gold, foreign exchange, SDRs and reserve position in the IMF available for the settlement of the international transactions.

Code :

(1) Both the statements are correct.
(2) Both the statements are incorrect.
(3) Statement (I) is correct while Statement (II) is incorrect.
(4) Statement (I) is incorrect while Statement (II) is correct.

169. Match the items of List - II with the items of List - I and select the code of correct matching. The items relate to International Trade Theories.

List - I	List - II
(a) Comparative Cost Theory	(i) Adam Smith
(b) Opportunity Cost Theory	(ii) Gottfried Haberler
(c) Factor Endowment Theory	(iii) David Ricardo
(d) Absolute Cost Theory	(iv) Eli Heckscher and Bertil Ohlin

Codes :

	(a)	(b)	(c)	(d)
(1)	(i)	(ii)	(iii)	(iv)
(2)	(iii)	(ii)	(iv)	(i)
(3)	(iv)	(iii)	(ii)	(i)
(4)	(i)	(iv)	(iii)	(ii)

170. Which one of the following is not the guiding principle of the World Bank regarding it's lending operations ?

(1) Proper assessment of the repayment prospects of loans.
(2) Lending should be only for specific projects which are economically and technically sound and of a high priority nature.
(3) The lending should be to enable a country to meet foreign exchange content ot the project cost.
(4) The bank does expect the borrowing country to spend the loan in a particular country.

171. Total return on a security is equal to the following :

(1) $\frac{\text{Periodic cash receipts + Capital gains}}{\text{Purchase Price of the security}}$

(2) $\frac{\text{Periodic cash receipts + Capital gains}}{\text{Current Market Price of the security}}$

(3) $\frac{\text{Periodic cash receipts}}{\text{Current Market Price of the security}}$

(4) $\frac{\text{Periodic cash receipts – Capital gains}}{\text{Purchase Price of the security}}$

172. Risk of a portfolio can be minimised by which one of the following ?

(1) Combining two securities having perfect positive correlation in their expected returns.
(2) Combining two securities having perfect negative correlation in their expected returns.
(3) Combining two securities having partially positive correlation in their expected returns.
(4) Combining two securities having partially negative correlation in their expected returns.

173. The certificate which evidences an unsecured corporate debt of short-term maturity, is known as :

(1) Certificate of Deposit
(2) Short-term loan certificate
(3) Treasury Bill
(4) Commercial paper

174. Which of the following statements are false? Indicate the correct code.

(a) Grey market is a market for dealing in listed securities.
(b) OTCEI is mainly intended for big investors.
(c) Insider Trading is legally permitted in the capital market.
(d) The device adopted to make profit out of the differences in prices of a security in two different markets is called 'arbitrage'.

Code :

(1) (a), (b), (c) (2) (a), (b), (d)
(3) (a), (b), (c), (d) (4) (b), (c), (d)

175. Which of the following statements are false ? Indicate the correct code.

(a) Share capital issued by a company for the first time is known as venture capital.
(b) All Venture Capital Funds in India are promoted by the Government.

(c) In addition to capital, venture capitalists provide managerial and technical support also to the assisted firms.

(d) Benefits from venture capital financing can be realised in long run only.

Code :

(1) (a), (b) and (d) (2) (a) and (b)

(3) (b), (c) and (d) (4) (c) and (d)

176. Match the items of List - II with the items of List - I and select the correct code :

List - I	List - II
(a) Liquidity Risk	(i) Risk related to purchasing power of Income.
(b) Business Risk	(ii) Risk related to Firm's capital structure.
(c) Financial Risk	(iii) Risk related to inability to pay its dues on time.
(d) Inflation Risk	(iv) Risk related to fluctuation in profits.

Codes :

	(a)	(b)	(c)	(d)
(1)	(ii)	(iii)	(iv)	(i)
(2)	(i)	(iv)	(iii)	(ii)
(3)	(iii)	(ii)	(iv)	(i)
(4)	(iii)	(iv)	(ii)	(i)

177. Statement (I) : Designing a distribution system for a service (for-profit or non-business context) involves to select the parties only through which ownership will pass.

Statement (II) : The ownership channel for most of the services is long and quite complex because of inseparability characteristic.

Statement (III) : Short channels usually mean more control on the part of the seller. Identify the correct code of being the statements correct or incorrect. These statements relate to channel strategies of products/services.

(1) Statements (I) and (II) are correct but (III) is not correct.

(2) Statements (I) and (III) are correct but (II) is not correct.

(3) Statements (I) and (II) are not correct but (III) is correct.

(4) Statements (I), (II) and (III) all are not correct.

178. An enormous collection of data on various topics from a variety of internal and external sources, compiled by a firm for its own use or for use by its clients, is called :

(1) Data-base (2) Data warehouse

(3) Data mining (4) M.I.S.

179. Statement (I) : A form of non-store retailing that uses advertising to contact consumers who, in turn, purchase products without visiting a retail store is called Direct selling.

Statement (II) : A form of non-store retailing in which personal contact between a sales person and a consumer occurs away from a retail store is called Direct Marketing.

In the light of above statements, identify the correct code of statements being correct or incorrect.

(1) Statement (I) is correct but Statement (II) is not correct.

(2) Statement (I) is not correct but Statement (II) is correct.

(3) Both the statements are correct.

(4) Both the statements are not correct.

180. 34% of the customers who fall in one of the categories of diffusion process who are deliberate customers to accept an innovation just before the average adopter in a social system. Such customers who are above average in social and economic measures, rely quite a bit on advertisements and salesmen are known as :

(1) Early Adopters (2) Early Majority

(3) Late Majority (4) Late Adopters

181. The G. E. Business Model is explained on which one of the following parameters ?

(1) Market Attractiveness and Business Position.

(2) Business Attractiveness and Market Position.

(3) Industry Growth rate and Company's Market share.

(4) Company's Growth rate and Industry's Position.

182. A reduction from the list price that is offered by a seller to buyers in payment for marketing functions the buyers will perform is known as :

(1) Trade Discount

(2) Functional Discount

(3) Cash Discount

(4) Both Trade and Functional Discount

183. Match the items of List-II with the items of List-I relating to Personnel Management (PM) and Human Resource Management (HRM) & select the code of correct matching.

List - I	List - II
(a) Focus of PM	(i) Development attitude by making people contribute their best.
(b) Focus of HRM	(ii) Exercising it as a functional area of management.
(c) Philosophy of PM	(iii) Exercising it as humane management.
(d) Philosophy of HRM	(iv) Profit maximization by controlling people.

Codes :

	(a)	(b)	(c)	(d)
(1)	(ii)	(iii)	(iv)	(i)
(2)	(iii)	(ii)	(i)	(iv)
(3)	(iv)	(i)	(ii)	(iii)
(4)	(i)	(iii)	(iv)	(ii)

184. Select the correct code of the following statements being correct or incorrect.

I Strategic HRM focuses on specific organizational intentions about what needs to be done while HR strategies focus on long-term issues only.

II Strategic HRM focuses on macro concerns such as structure and culture while HR strategy focuses on specific issues assigned.

III Human Resource strategy decisions are derived from strategic HRM.

Code :

(1) Statements I and II are correct while III is incorrect.
(2) Statements II and III are correct while I is incorrect.
(3) Statements I and III are correct while II is incorrect.
(4) All the statements are correct.

185. Which of the following code represents the full form of the term "BARS" in performance management systems ?

(1) Business Appraisal & Rating Systems.
(2) Balanced Assessment Reviewing Scorecard.
(3) Behaviourally Anchored Rating Scale.
(4) Benchmarking Appraisal Reviewing Strategy.

186. Match the items of List - II with the items of List - I relating to training, and select the code of correct matching.

List - I	List - II
(a) Andragogy	(i) Strategies or styles of instructions
(b) Pedagogy	(ii) Ultimate knowledge level with which trainee leaves the training sessions
(c) Terminal behaviour	(iii) Lack of commitment of management and scarcity of resources in training
(d) Training impediments	(iv) Art and Science of training the adults

Codes :

	(a)	(b)	(c)	(d)
(1)	(i)	(iv)	(iii)	(ii)
(2)	(ii)	(iii)	(i)	(iv)
(3)	(iv)	(i)	(ii)	(iii)
(4)	(iii)	(ii)	(iv)	(i)

187. Which of the following statements does not stand as a principle of compensation administration ?

(1) An enterprise should have a clear -cut plan to determine differential pay level in terms of divergent job requirements.
(2) People and jobs should never be mingled.
(3) The compensation system should be designed with subjectivity with respect to individual skill sets exercised from time to time.
(4) There should be established wage grievance handling procedures.

188. Match the items of List - II with the items of List - I relating to industrial relations and select the code of correct matching.

List - I	List - II
(a) Healthy labour–management relations	(i) Industrial Disputes Act
(b) Industrial Peace Law	(ii) Guiding principles for a grievance procedure
(c) Industrial Democracy	(iii) Workers' participation in management
(d) National Commission on Labour, 1969	(iv) Voluntary arbitration and responsible trade union

Codes :

	(a)	(b)	(c)	(d)
(1)	(iv)	(i)	(iii)	(ii)
(2)	(ii)	(iii)	(iv)	(i)
(3)	(iii)	(i)	(iv)	(ii)
(4)	(ii)	(iv)	(i)	(iii)

189. In recent years which among the following countries has been the largest source of foreign investment in India ?

(1) Australia (2) Japan
(3) China (4) Mauritius

190. Assertion (A) : The Government of India has been opening up domestic market to foreign players in baby steps.

Reasoning (R) : Allowing foreign firms free play in India's retail sector has always been a political hot potato.

Code :

(1) (A) and (R) both are correct ; and (R) is the right explanation of (A).
(2) (A) and (R) both are correct ; but (R) is not the right explanation of (A).
(3) (A) and (R) both are incorrect.
(4) (A) is correct ; but (R) is incorrect.

191. Select the correct code of the following statements being correct or incorrect.

Statement (I) : A Global Depositary Receipt (GDR) is a bank certificate issued in more than one country for shares in a foreign company.

Statement (II) : A GDR is very similar to American Depositary Receipt (ADR)

Statement (III) : GDRs are called EDRs when private markets are attempting to obtain Euros.

Code :

(1) Statements (I), (II) and (III) are correct.
(2) Statements (I) and (II) are correct but (III) is incorrect.
(3) Statements (I) and (III) are correct but (II) is incorrect.
(4) Statements (II) and (III) are correct but (I) is incorrect.

192. Capital budgeting means

(1) Planning for Capital Assets
(2) Planning for Profit
(3) Planning for Cash
(4) Planning for Sales

193. Select the correct code of the following statements being correct or incorrect.

Statement (I) : The 'law of one price' states that in competitive markets free of transportation costs and barriers to trade, identical products sold in different countries must sell for the same price when their price is expressed in terms of the same currency.

Statement (II) : An 'Efficient market' has no impediments to the free flow of goods and services, such as trade barriers.

Code :

(1) Statement (I) is correct but (II) is incorrect.
(2) Statement (II) is correct but (I) is incorrect.
(3) Both statements (I) and (II) are correct.
(4) Both statements (I) and (II) are incorrect.

194. Which among the following is not a correct statement regarding patent ?

(1) A patent is a legal protection granted for an invention that is new, non-obvious and useful.
(2) The patent grants the patent holder the exclusive right to make use or sell the patented products or process.
(3) The exclusive purpose of the patent system is to benefit the patent holder.
(4) The Indian Patent Act, 1970, was amended and made effective from January 1, 2005.

195. Which one of the following is agricultural income under the Income Tax Act, 1961 ?

(1) Interest on arrears of rent in respect of agricultural land.
(2) Interest received by a money-lender in the form of agricultural produce.
(3) Income from sale of trees of forest which are of spontaneous growth and in relation to which forestry operations alone are performed.
(4) Interest on capital received by a partner from the firm engaged in agricultural operations.

196. Under the Income Tax Act, 1961 "block of assets" for the purpose of charging depreciation means :

(1) Value of all the assets after depreciation
(2) Value of all tangible assets after charging depreciation
(3) Value of all those assets to which one rate of depreciation is applicable
(4) Gross value of machinery and plant less accumulated depreciation

197. The maximum amount of exemption of compensation received at the time of voluntary retirement U/S 10(10C) of the Income Tax Act, 1961, is :

(1) ₹ 1,00,000 (2) ₹ 2,50,000
(3) ₹ 5,00,000 (4) ₹ 10,00,000

198. Which one of the following statements is not correct with reference to the assessment of firms ?

(1) All partnership firms formed under the Indian Partnership Act, 1932, are assessed as firms under the Income Tax Act, 1961.
(2) Income of a firm is taxable at a flat rate of 30% without any exemption.
(3) Partners' share in the income of a firm is not chargeable to tax in the hands of partners.
(4) Remuneration paid to partners of a firm (assessed as such) is allowed as deduction subject to statutory limit.

199. The due date of first instalment of advance tax by assessees other than companies is

(1) 15th April (2) 15th June
(3) 15th September (4) 15th December

200. Which one of the following items is not allowed as deduction while computing income from business and profession ?

(1) Fees paid to the lawyer for drafting partnership deed
(2) Loss due to embezzlement by an employee
(3) Legal expenses paid to protect the building of the business
(4) Cost of installing a new telephone

201. **Assertion (A) :** Buyers, for several industries, are potential competitors-they may integrate backwards.

Reasoning (R) : They have different degrees of bargaining power.

Code :

(1) (A) and (R) are correct and (R) is the correct reasoning of (A).
(2) (A) and (R) are correct but (R) is not the correct reasoning of (A).
(3) (A) is incorrect while (R) is a correct statement.
(4) Both (A) and (R) are incorrect.

202. Which one of the following is the governing factor in deciding the type of redressal agency which will deal with the dispute of a consumer?

(1) Area of sale of goods and services
(2) Type of goods and services sold
(3) The choice of the consumer
(4) The value of goods and services sold

203. Match List - I with List - II relating to the roles played by government in an economy and indicate the correct code of their matching.

List - I (Roles)	List - II (Examples)
(a) Regulatory role	(i) Deciding timing and usage of resources
(b) Promotional role	(ii) Capital intensive projects of public sector
(c) Enterpreneurial role	(iii) Imposing of high import duty
(d) Planning role	(iv) Measures to control and cover risk in priority sectors

Codes :

	(a)	(b)	(c)	(d)
(1)	(iv)	(ii)	(i)	(iii)
(2)	(iii)	(i)	(iv)	(ii)
(3)	(iii)	(iv)	(ii)	(i)
(4)	(i)	(iii)	(iv)	(ii)

204. Which one of the following statement is not correct relating to Competition Policy and Law?

(1) Collusion and dominance have potential for unfair competition.
(2) The appeal against decisions of Competition Commission of India can be made to the Competition Appellate Tribunal.
(3) State monopolies, government's business policies and functioning of Regulatory Authorities cannot be scrutinized under this law.
(4) Abuse of dominance rather than dominance should be the key for Competition Policy/Law.

205. Which one of the following is not correct with reference to standard costing ?

(1) Standard costing is a system where pre determined costs are used for control of entire organisation
(2) Standard may be expressed in quantitative and monetary measures
(3) Only adverse variances are investigated intensively
(4) Standard is determined for each element of cost

206. Which one of the following is not correct ?

(1) Margin of Safety $\frac{\text{Profit}}{\text{P/V Ratio}}$

(2) P/V Ratio = $\frac{\text{Change in Contribution}}{\text{Change in sales}} \times 100$

(3) Break-even point in units = $\frac{\text{Fixed cost}}{\text{Contribution per unit}}$

(4) Required sales to earn desired profits = $\frac{\text{Desired profit}}{\text{P/V ratio}}$

207. Schedule III Part II of the Companies Act, 2013 deals with which one of the following ?

(1) Format of Balance Sheet
(2) Format of Profit and Loss Account
(3) Format of Trading Account
(4) Format of Cash Flow

208. Which one of the following statements is not true ?

(1) When there is one liquidation and one formation it is known as external construction
(2) Goodwill or Capital reserve arises only when the amalgamation is in the nature of merger
(3) Under the pooling of interest method, the transferee company incorporates the assets and liabilities of the transferor company at book value
(4) The vendor company transfers preliminary expenses (at the time of absorption) to equity shareholders' account

209. **Statement - I :** The least - cost or optimal input combination of labour and capital requires that the marginal revenue productivity ratio of the two inputs should be equal to their price ratio.

Statement-II : In a hypothetical production function of the following form

$Q = -L^3 + 15L^2 + 10L$

Where, Q = Quantity of the product and L=No. of variable input (labour), the marginal physical productivity of labour is $-L^2 + 15L + 10$.

Code :

(1) Both the statements are true.
(2) Both the statements are false.
(3) Statement - I is true while statement - II is false.
(4) Statement - I is false while statement - II is true.

210. Match the items of List - I with the items of List - II and indicate the code of correct matching.

List - I	List - II
(a) Technological advantages	(i) Managerial economies
(b) Large scale purchase of material	(ii) Economies in transport and storage inputs
(c) Specialized departments under Specialized personnel	(iii) Economies in marketing
(d) Oil companies having their own fleet of tankers	(iv) Economies in production

Codes :

	(a)	**(b)**	**(c)**	**(d)**
(1)	(iv)	(iii)	(i)	(ii)
(2)	(iii)	(iv)	(ii)	(i)
(3)	(iii)	(i)	(ii)	(iv)
(4)	(iv)	(ii)	(iii)	(i)

211. Manufacturing of T.V. sets and refrigerators and their pricing in India belong to which one of the following market structures ?

(1) Monopolistic competition
(2) Perfect competition
(3) Monopoly
(4) Oligopoly

212. **Statement - I :** Pricing at par with the market price of the existing brands is considered to be the most reasonable pricing strategy for a product which is being sold in a strongly competitive market.

Statement - II : Pricing below the market price has been found to be more successful when a seller intends to achieve a prestigious position among the sellers in the locality for selling prestigious goods of much superior quality.

Code :

(1) Both the statements are correct
(2) Both the statements are incorrect
(3) Statement - I is correct while Statement - II is incorrect
(4) Statement - I is incorrect while Statement - II is correct

213. Which of the following statements are true ? Select the correct code.

(a) The coefficient of rank correlation has the same limits as the Karl Pearson's coefficient of correlation.
(b) The coefficient of correlation is independent of the change of origin but not of scale.

(c) The covariance between X and Y is defined as $\frac{\Sigma xy}{n}$ where $x=(X-\bar{X})$, $y=(Y-\bar{Y})$ and n = no. of paired observations.

(d) b_{xy} is called regression coefficient of X variable on Y variable.

(e) If b_{xy} is 0.4 and b_{yx} is 1.6, coefficient of determination would be 0.8.

Code :

(1) (a), (b) and (c) (2) (a), (c) and (d)
(3) (c), (d) and (e) (4) (b), (c) and (e)

214. The application of χ^2-test as parametric test will be in which one of the following situations ?

(1) Test of independence of attributes
(2) Test of goodness of fit of a specific type of distribution
(3) Test for population variance on the basis of small sized sample variance
(4) Test of homogeneity of several populations with respect to some characteristic of interest

215. In which one of the following situations is the application of t-test is most appropriate ?

(1) Testing the significance of coefficient of correlation between paired observations of small sized sample
(2) Testing the significance of coefficient of correlation between paired observations of large sized sample
(3) Comparing variances of two small sized samples
(4) Testing the significance of the difference among mean values of more than two samples groups

216. Which of the following is not a logical data structure ?

(1) Chain (2) Stack
(3) List (4) Tree

217. Match the items of List - I with those of List - II; and choose the correct code of combination :

List - I	**List - II**
(a) A committee consist of a group of people specifically designated to perform some administrative work	(i) C.I. Barnard
(b) Staff service in organisation means the service or advice or council, as distinguished from the function of authority or command	(ii) W.H. Newman
(c) Organisation is informal when the aggregate interpersonal relationships are without conscious joint purpose	(iii) McFarland
(d) An identifiable group of people contributing their efforts towards the attainment of goals is called organisation	(iv) James D. Mooney

Codes :

	(a)	(b)	(c)	(d)
(1)	(ii)	(iv)	(i)	(iii)
(2)	(iv)	(ii)	(iii)	(i)
(3)	(iv)	(iii)	(i)	(ii)
(4)	(i)	(ii)	(iv)	(iii)

218. Which among the following is not a physical barrier of communication ?

(1) Poor vocabulary
(2) Noise
(3) Improper time
(4) Overload information

219. Statement - I : Management control seeks to compel events to conform to plans.

Statement - II : Controlling is determining what is motivational to the employees of the organization.

Code :

(1) Statement - I is correct but II is incorrect
(2) Statement - II is correct but I is incorrect
(3) Both the statements I and II are correct
(4) Both the statements I and II are incorrect

220. Assertion (A) : Sound planning is one of the essential elements for the success of corporate entities.

Reasoning (R) : Planning is deciding in advance what is to be done. It involves the selection of objectives, policies, procedures and programmes from among alternatives.

Code :

(1) Both (A) and (R) are correct and (R) is the right explanation of (A).
(2) Both (A) and (R) are correct but (R) is not the right explanation of (A).
(3) Both the statements (A) and (R) are incorrect.
(4) (A) is correct but (R) is incorrect.

221. Match the items of List - I with List - II and denote the code of correct matching :

List - I	**List - II**
(a) Acceptability	(i) Convenience Aspect

(b) Affordability (ii) Functional and Psychological Aspects

(c) Accessibility (iii) Information and knowledge Aspects

(d) Awareness (iv) Economic and Psychological Aspects

Codes :

	(a)	(b)	(c)	(d)
(1)	(i)	(iii)	(ii)	(iv)
(2)	(iii)	(ii)	(i)	(iv)
(3)	(ii)	(iv)	(i)	(iii)
(4)	(iv)	(ii)	(i)	(iii)

222. Match the items of List - I with the items of List - II which are related to dimensions of brand personality. Denote the code of correct matching.

List - I	List - II
(a) Sincerity	(i) Upper class, Charming
(b) Excitement	(ii) Reliable, Intelligent, Successful
(c) Competence	(iii) Down to earth, Cheerful, Wholesome
(d) Sophistication	(iv) Outdoors, Tough
(e) Ruggedness	(v) Spirited, Imaginative, Up-to-date

Codes :

	(a)	(b)	(c)	(d)	(e)
(1)	(v)	(ii)	(i)	(iii)	(iv)
(2)	(i)	(iv)	(iii)	(ii)	(v)
(3)	(iii)	(v)	(ii)	(i)	(iv)
(4)	(ii)	(i)	(iii)	(v)	(iv)

223. One of the techniques of stimulating creativity for developing new product where you start with an idea then thinking of the next idea and link, then think of the next association and do this with all association that come up with each new idea, is known as :

(1) Attribute Listing
(2) Forced Relationship
(3) New Contexts (4) Mind Mapping

224. Statement - I : We are motivated to re-evaluate our beliefs, attitudes, opinions or values occurred at two different time.

Statement - II : The difference due to some intervention occurred at either point of time motivates us to search a newer option and thus satisfies our mind/ anxiety.

Code :

(1) Statement - I is correct, Statement - II is not correct.
(2) Statement - II is correct, Statement - I is not correct.
(3) Both statements are correct.
(4) Both statements are incorrect.

225. Operating Leverage and Financial Leverage of a firm are 3 and 2, respectively. If sales increase by 6%, then earnings before tax will rise by :

(1) 18% (2) 12%
(3) 36% (4) 30%

226. Match the items of List - I with those of List - II and indicate the correct code :

List - I	List - II
(a) Net Income Approach	(i) Working Capital Management
(b) Profitability Index	(ii) Over- capitalisation
(c) Concentration Banking	(iii) Capital Structure Planning
(d) Lower Rate of Return	(iv) Capital Budgeting Decision

Codes :

	(a)	(b)	(c)	(d)
(1)	(iii)	(iv)	(i)	(ii)
(2)	(iii)	(iv)	(ii)	(i)
(3)	(iv)	(ii)	(iii)	(i)
(4)	(ii)	(iii)	(i)	(iv)

227. Statement - I : In payback period method, the risk of the project is adjusted by lessening the target payback period.

Statement - II : Sensitivity Analysis helps in calculation of net present value of the proposal.

Code :

(1) Statement - I is correct, but statement - II is wrong
(2) Statement - I is wrong, but statement - II is correct
(3) Statement - I and statement - II, both are correct
(4) Statement - I and statement - II, both are wrong

228. Dividend irrelevance argument of MM Model is based on :

(1) Hedging (2) Issue of Debentures
(3) Liquidity (4) Arbitrage

229. Match the items of List - I with List - II and indicate the correct code of their matching relating to human resource management philosophy :

List - I	List - II
(a) Rational System Approach	(i) F.W. Taylor

(b)	The Ahmedabad Experiments to improve productivity	(ii)	Max Weber's theory of bureaucracy
(c)	Social System Approach	(iii)	A.K. Rice
(d)	Functional organisation concept	(iv)	Hawthorne studies

Codes :

	(a)	(b)	(c)	(d)
(1)	(ii)	(iv)	(iii)	(i)
(2)	(iii)	(ii)	(iv)	(i)
(3)	(iv)	(iii)	(i)	(ii)
(4)	(iii)	(i)	(ii)	(iv)

230. Which one of the following is not a method of deciding acceptable level of reliability or consistency of measurement in selection methods?

(1) Regiocentric approach
(2) Split half method
(3) Test related method
(4) Expectancy diagrams

231. Put the following steps of discrete selection process in correct sequence and select the correct code :

(a) Preliminary interview
(b) Completion of application blank
(c) Background investigation
(d) Physical examination
(e) Employment tests
(f) Comprehensive interview
(g) Final employment decision

Code :

(1) (b), (a), (c), (d), (e), (f), (g)
(2) (b), (a), (e), (f), (c), (d), (g)
(3) (a), (b), (e), (f), (c), (d), (g)
(4) (a), (b), (d), (c), (e), (f), (g)

232. Match List - I with List - II relating to wage theories and its propounders and indicate the code representing correct matching :

List - I (Theory)	List - II (Propounder)
(a) Subsistence Theory	(i) Karl Marx
(b) Surplus Value Theory	(ii) Francis Walker
(c) Wage Fund Theory	(iii) David Richardo
(d) Residual Claimant Theory	(iv) Adam Smith

Codes :

	(a)	(b)	(c)	(d)
(1)	(ii)	(iv)	(i)	(iii)
(2)	(iv)	(i)	(ii)	(iii)
(3)	(iii)	(i)	(iv)	(ii)
(4)	(iv)	(ii)	(iii)	(i)

233. A perfectly competitive firm attains equilibrium when

(A) AC = AR (B) MR = MC
(C) MC = AC (D) TC = TR

234. 'RWA' with regard to capital adequacy stands for which one of the following ?

(1) Risk Withdrawal Adjustments
(2) Risk Withdrawal Arrangements
(3) Risk Weighted Assets
(4) Risk-free Weighted Assets

235. Match the items of List - I with List - II and denote the code of correct matching :

List - I	List - II
(a) Future	(i) Consists of purchase or sale of commodities in two different markets with the expectations that a future change in price in one market will be off set by an opposite change in the other market
(b) Swap	(ii) A contract in which a seller agrees to deliver an asset to a buyer at a predetermined price at some future date as privately negotiated
(c) Hedging	(iii) A contractual agreement for exchanging a steam of payments with opposite and matching needs, to reap the benefit arising due to market discrepancies
(d) Forward	(iv) A contract covering the purchase and sale of physical commodities or financial instruments for future delivery on a future exchange floor

Codes :

	(a)	(b)	(c)	(d)
(1)	(iv)	(iii)	(ii)	(i)
(2)	(i)	(ii)	(iii)	(iv)
(3)	(ii)	(i)	(iii)	(iv)
(4)	(iv)	(iii)	(i)	(ii)

236. Which of the following are the forms of e - banking ? Select the correct code.
(a) Internet Banking
(b) Telephone Banking
(c) Electronic Cheque Conversion
(d) Electronic Bill Payment
(e) Direct Fund Transfer Through RTGS
Code :
(1) (a), (c) and (d)
(2) (a), (b), (c) and (d)
(3) (b), (c) and (d)
(4) (a), (b), (c), (d) and (e)

237. Which one among the following has the largest share of exports from India ?
(1) Agriculture and Allied Commodity
(2) Gems and Jewellery
(3) Handicrafts
(4) Electronic Goods

238. Which one among the following is not a part of TRIPS agreement ?
(1) Industrial Design
(2) Geographical Indications
(3) Interior Design
(4) Layout Designs of Integrated Circuits

239. Which one among the following is not correct ?
(1) IMF's headquarters is in Washington, D.C.
(2) IMF has 198 countries as its members.
(3) IMF is an outcome of the Bretton Woods Conference.
(4) IMF was found on July 7, 1944.

240. **Statement - I :** Served From India Scheme (SFIS) has been replaced with Service Exports from India Scheme (SEIS).

Statement - II : The rate of reward under SEIS would be based on net foreign exchange earned.
Code :
(1) Statement - I is correct but statement - II is incorrect.
(2) Statement - II is correct but statement - I is incorrect.
(3) Both the statements - I and II are incorrect.
(4) Both the statements - I and II are correct.

241. Match the items of List - I with those of List - II and indicate the correct code :

List - I (Accounting standard)	List - II (Relationship)
(a) AS - 6	(i) Accounting for Consolidated Financial Statements
(b) AS - 3	(ii) Accounting For Fixed Assets
(c) AS - 10	(iii) Depreciation Accounting
(d) AS - 21	(iv) Accounting For Cash Flow Statement

Codes :

	(a)	(b)	(c)	(d)
(1)	(ii)	(iv)	(iii)	(i)
(2)	(iii)	(iv)	(ii)	(i)
(3)	(iv)	(iii)	(i)	(ii)
(4)	(i)	(ii)	(iii)	(iv)

242. Which of the following statements are False ? Indicate the correct code.
(a) RBI has prescribed guidelines for the operations of credit rating agencies in India.
(b) All venture capital funds in India have been promoted by Government.
(c) A mutual fund can operate as venture capital fund.
(d) Credit rating is an authoritative guarantee regarding the credit position of a person.
Code :
(1) (a), (b), (c) and (d) (2) (a), (b) and (d)
(3) (a), (b) and (c) (4) (a) and (c)

243. Which of the following are the examples of systematic risk ? Indicate the correct code.
(a) Elimination of Government Subsidy
(b) Increase in Bank Rate
(c) Labour Problem
(d) High Levered Fund
Code :
(1) (a), (b) and (c) (2) (a), (b) and (d)
(3) (a) and (b) (4) (a) and (d)

244. Which of the following are the benefits of responsibility accounting ?
(a) It facilitates the centralisation of decision taking.
(b) It provides a system of closer control.
(c) It measures the performance of individuals in an objective manner.
(d) It develops a sense of cost consciousness among managers and their subordinates.
Code :
(1) (a), (b) and (c) (2) (b), (c) and (d)
(3) (a), (b) and (d) (4) (a), (c) and (d)

245. Which of the following statements are True? Indicate the correct code.
(a) Tax-shield on depreciation and interest is an important variable both for lessor and lessee.
(b) A lessee may evaluate the lease options as against the buying option.

(c) Sale and Lease-back, and leveraged lease are types of financial lease.

(d) Lease financing is a type of capital budgeting decision from the point of view of the lessee.

Code :

(1) (a), (b) and (d) (2) (b), (c) and (d)

(3) (a), (c) and (d) (4) (a), (b) and (c)

246. Which one of the following methods of Inflation Accounting has been proposed by Sandilands Committee of U.K ?

(1) General Price Level Method

(2) Specific Price Level Method

(3) Current Cost Accounting Method

(4) Generally Accepted Accounting Principles

247. Which of the following are the motives of mergers ? Indicate the correct code.

(a) To gain the economies of scale.

(b) To utilise under - utilised resources.

(c) To break the monopoly.

(d) To reduce the tax liability.

Code :

(1) (a), (c) and (d) (2) (a), (b) and (d)

(3) (b), (c) and (d) (4) (a), (b) and (c)

248. A research technique used particularly in retailing (online and offline), in which consumers are recruited by researchers to act as anonymous buyers in order to evaluate customer satisfaction, service quality and customer's own evaluation of their experiences, is known as :

(1) Consumer Jury

(2) Projective Technique

(3) Mystery Shopping

(4) Semiotic Research

249. Match the items of List - I with items of List - II and select the correct code of matching :

List - I	List - II
(a) Market Leader	(i) Avoid hostile attacks on rivals
(b) Market Challenger	(ii) Attack the market leader
(c) Market Follower	(iii) Provide high level of specialisation
(d) Market Nicher	(iv) Attack the market

Codes :

	(a)	(b)	(c)	(d)
(1)	(iv)	(ii)	(i)	(iii)
(2)	(ii)	(iv)	(iii)	(i)
(3)	(iii)	(i)	(iv)	(ii)
(4)	(i)	(iii)	(iv)	(ii)

250. Which of the statements are correct ? Select correct code.

Statement (I) : Opinions can be described as the slow responses we might give to opinion poll questions about any issue.

Statement (II) : Attitudes are held with a greater degree of conviction, over longer duration and more likely to influence behaviour.

Statement (III) : Values are held more strongly than attitudes and underpin our attitudinal behaviour.

Code :

(1) (I) and (II) (2) (II) and (III)

(3) (I) and (III) (4) (I), (II) and (III)

251. Which of the following is not a major aspect of digital marketing ?

(1) Jurisdiction (2) Ownership

(3) Security (4) Entertainment

252. Which of the following statements are correct ? Select the correct code.

Statement (I) : Horizontal conflict between channel members is caused due to channel members impinge on the market territory of other intermediaries at different level.

Statement (II) : Vertical conflict is caused due to intense price competition, disagreement about promotional activities, attempts to bypass intermediary and distribute direct, differing expectations as to channel or intermediary performance.

Statement (III) : Hybrid channel conflict arises due to grey marketing.

Code :

(1) (I) and (III) (2) (I) and (II)

(3) (II) and (III) (4) (I), (II) and (III)

253. Which of the following statements are incorrect ? Indicate the correct code.

Statement (I) : As consumer's income increases, the percentage of income spent for food items decreases, for rent, fuel and light remains the same, for clothing remains the same and for sundries increases.

Statement (II) : Societal marketing period was from 1960 onwards.

Statement (III) : Our debt to social anthropology decreases more and more as we use qualitative market research approaches.

Statement (IV) : The economic concepts of perfect competition and matching of supply and demand underlie the marketing concept, particularly in relation to the concepts of the price at which goods are sold and quantity distributed.

Code :

(1) (I) and (II) (2) (II) and (III)
(3) (II) and (IV) (4) (I) and (IV)

254. Which of the following statements are correct ? Indicate the correct code.

Statement (I) : Virtue ethics is a form of ethical approach associated with Aristotle which stresses the importance of developing virtuous principles, 'right' character and the pursuit of a virtuous life.

Statement (II) : Utilitarianism is an ethical approach where an action is right if, and only if, it conforms to the principle of utility, whereby utility is minimised and pain and unhappiness minimised more than any alternative.

Statement (III) : 'Deontological Ethics' is an ethical approach where rightness or wrongness of an action or decision is not judged to be based exclusively on the consequences of that action or decision.

Code :

(1) (I), (II) and (III) (2) (I) and (II)
(3) (I) and (III) (4) (II) and (III)

255. Assertion (A) : The matter of succession planning is often deferred.

Reasoning (R) : The succession charts need utmost confidentiality.

Code :

(1) (A) is correct and (R) is right reasoning of it.
(2) (A) is correct but (R) is not the correct reasoning of it.
(3) (A) is correct but (R) is not correct statement.
(4) (A) is not correct while (R) is a correct statement.

256. Bethel Maine of USA was the pioneer of which one of the following Laboratory training methods of employee training ?

(1) Transactional Analysis
(2) Business Games
(3) Critical Incident Technique
(4) T-group

257. Which of the following statements relating to appraisal methods are not correct ? Indicate the correct code.

Statement (I) : The MBO program is built on the assumption that individuals always need not be responsible and self - directed and thus need to be motivated to work towards objectives.

Statement (II) : Forced distribution method was developed by Karl Marx.

Statement (III) : Peer evaluation and self - appraisal need to be done on well - defined parameters in check-list method.

Statement (IV) : Forced choice method consists of seven main factors on three point rating scale.

Code :

(1) Statements (I) and (II)
(2) Statements (III) and (IV)
(3) Statements (I), (II) and (III)
(4) Statements (I), (II), (III) and (IV)

258. Match the main concerns of HRD sub-systems given in List - I with List - II and choose the correct code of matching :

List - I (HRD sub-systems)	List - II (Main concerns)
(a) Individual's career	(i) Competence
(b) Development of teams	(ii) Power
(c) Socialisation of organisation	(iii) Commitment & integration
(d) Management of organization	(iv) Values

Codes :

	(a)	(b)	(c)	(d)
(1)	(ii)	(iv)	(i)	(iii)
(2)	(iv)	(ii)	(iii)	(i)
(3)	(iii)	(i)	(iv)	(ii)
(4)	(ii)	(iii)	(i)	(iv)

259. Match the items of List - I with List - II and indicate the correct code of matching :

List - I (Wage Theory)	List - II (Basis of determining wage)
(a) Subsistence theory	(i) Capitalists first set aside predetermined surplus income and then decide the wages
(b) Surplus value theory of wages	(ii) Growth of the population brings down to level of subsistence
(c) Wage Fund theory	(iii) Balance claimed upon the output of industry
(d) Residual Claimant theory	(iv) Natural price for labour

Codes :

	(a)	(b)	(c)	(d)
(1)	(iv)	(ii)	(i)	(iii)
(2)	(ii)	(iv)	(i)	(iii)
(3)	(iii)	(i)	(ii)	(iv)
(4)	(i)	(iii)	(iv)	(ii)

260. **Statement (I) :** Selection of wrong criteria during performance appraisal can result in serious dysfunctional consequences.

Statement (II) : Generally the evaluator becomes more critical about performance evaluation technique rather than which criteria need to be evaluated.

Code :

(1) Both the statements are correct.
(2) Both the statements are incorrect.
(3) Statement - I is correct while statement - II is incorrect.
(4) Statement - I is incorrect while statement - II is correct.

261. Which of the statements are not correct ? Indicate the correct code.

Statement (I) : Social assistance is financed by tripartite or bipartite contributions.

Statement (II) : Social insurance ignores the income and means of liable relation.

Statement (III) : Social assistance makes the beneficiary a first charge on the liable relations.

Statement (IV) : Social assistance aims at to provide maximum subsistence to those who can not make it on their own.

Code :

(1) (I) and (II) (2) (II) and (III)
(3) (I) and (IV) (4) (III) and (IV)

262. According to which one of the following theories, differences in nominal interest rates will be eliminated in the exchange rate ?

(1) Leontief Paradox Trade Theory
(2) Fisher Effect Economic Theory
(3) Purchasing Power Parity Theory
(4) Combined Equilibrium Theory

263. According to the Purchasing Power Parity Theory, the level of foreign exchange rate is determined by which of the following ?

(1) Domestic Price level (P) divided by foreign price level (P*)
(2) P*–P
(3) P–P*
(4) P*/P

264. Match the items of List - I with List - II and choose the correct code of combination :

List - I	List - II
(a) It abolishes all restrictions on trade among the members	(i) Common Market
(b) It not only eliminates all restrictions on trade among members but also adopts a uniform commercial policy against the non-members	(ii) Economic Union
(c) It allows free movement of labour and capital within the common market	(iii) Free Trade Area
(d) It achieves some degree of harmonization of national economic policies, through a common central bank, unified monetary and fiscal policy, etc.	(iv) Customs Union

Codes :

	(a)	(b)	(c)	(d)
(1)	(iv)	(ii)	(i)	(iii)
(2)	(iv)	(iii)	(i)	(ii)
(3)	(iii)	(iv)	(i)	(ii)
(4)	(ii)	(i)	(iv)	(iii)

265. **Assertion (A) :** Indian companies have established subsidiaries and joint ventures in a number of countries in different manufacturing industries and service sectors.

Reasoning (R) : By restricting the areas of operations and growth, the government policy seriously constrained the potential of Indian companies to make a foray into the foreign countries.

Code :

(1) Both (A) and (R) are correct and (R) is the right explanation of (A).
(2) Both (A) and (R) are correct but (R) is not the right explanation of (A).
(3) Both (A) and (R) are incorrect.
(4) (A) is correct but (R) is incorrect.

266. **Statement (I) :** Automatic variations in the exchange rates, in accordance with the variations in the balance of payments position, tend to automatically restore the balance of payments equilibrium.

Statement (II) : A deficiency in the balance of payments increases the exchange rate.

Code :

(1) Statement (I) is correct but (II) is incorrect.
(2) Statement (II) is correct but (I) is incorrect.
(3) Both the statements (I) and (II) are incorrect.
(4) Both the statements (I) and (II) are correct.

267. Which among the following is not a correct statement ?

(1) Designated bank refers to any bank in India, which has been authorised by the RBI to act as banker to FII.

(2) Domestic custodian includes any person carrying on the activities of providing custodial services in respect of securities.

(3) Sub-account includes those institutions, established or incorporated in India, whether incorporated or not, on whose behalf investments are proposed to be made in India by FIIs.

(4) A domestic portfolio manager or domestic asset management company shall also be eligible to be registered as FII to manage the funds of sub-accounts.

268. Identify the incorrect statement from the following :

(1) Broken-date contract is a full - month forward contract.

(2) Currency arbitrage refers to making profit by buying a currency cheap in one market and selling it dear in the other market at a particular point of time.

(3) Currency Futures Market refers to organised foreign exchange market where a fixed amount of a currency is exchanged on a fixed maturity date in the pit.

(4) Currency Options Market refers to market for the exchange of currency where the option buyer enjoys the privilege of not exercising the option if the rate is not favourable.

269. Dividends declared by Unit Trust of India or by mutual fund is :

(1) Fully exempt in the hands of unit holders

(2) Fully taxable in the hands of unit holders

(3) Fully exempt in the hands of individual unit holders and fully taxable in the hands of institutional unit holders

(4) Included in the gross total income but a deduction is allowed under section 80 L

270. Match the items of List - I with the items of List - II and choose the correct answer from the code given below :

List - I (Types of Income)	**List - II (Heads of Income)**
(a) Salary, bonus, commission, etc. received by a working partner from the firm	(i) Income from other Sources
(b) Pension received by the widow of a government employee	(ii) Income from (short term) Capital Gains
(c) profits on the sale of machinery used in business	(iii) Income from Capital Gains
(d) Compensation received from the government on compulsory acquisition of land and profit earned	(iv) Income from Business and Profession
	(v) Income from Salaries

Codes :

	(a)	(b)	(c)	(d)
(1)	(v)	(ii)	(i)	(iii)
(2)	(iv)	(ii)	(iii)	(v)
(3)	(v)	(iv)	(iii)	(ii)
(4)	(iv)	(i)	(ii)	(iii)

271. Which of the following will be considered as tax planning effort ?

(a) Mr. A purchased a house for self residence of Rs. 80 lacs by taking a loan of Rs. 60 lacs from SBI at 10% interest, instead of using his own funds.

(b) Mr. A made investment in purchasing 12% redeemable debentures of TISCO worth Rs. 1.50 lac

(c) Mr. A purchased 100 gram gold biscuits of Rs. 2.5 Lac from SBI on the occasion of Diwali.

(d) Mr. A invested Rs. 1 crore in purchasing 5 acres of agricultural land in his native village in Gaya.

Code :

(1) (a) and (b) (2) (b) and (c)

(3) (a) and (d) (4) (c) and (d)

272. Assertion (A) : If the interest is payable outside India, tax must be deducted at source.

Reason (R) : If tax has not been deducted at source, the amount paid as interest will not be allowed as a deduction in computing business income.

Select the correct answer from the code given below :

(1) Both (A) and (R) are correct and (R) is the correct explanation of (A).

(2) (A) and (R) both are correct but (R) is not the correct explanation of (A).

(3) (A) is correct but (R) is wrong.
(4) (A) is wrong but (R) is correct.

273. Under the Income Tax Act, 1961 the education cess of (2% + 1%) is calculated on the amount of
(1) Income Tax
(2) Income Tax Plus surcharge (if any)
(3) Gross total Income
(4) Taxable Income

274. Exemption, under Sec.54 F of the Income Tax Act, 1961, shall not be allowed if the assessee, on the date of transfer owns :
(1) Any residential house
(2) A residential house which is let out
(3) A house which is self occupied
(4) More than one residential house

275. The income from the sale of a machinery used in business is treated as :
(1) Income from business and profession
(2) Short-term capital gain
(3) Long-term capital gain
(4) Income from other sources

276. When Walt Disney World's Magic kingdom lets customers visit a fairy kingdom, a pirate ship, or a haunted house, then what is marketed in this example ?
(1) Services (2) Events
(3) Experiences (4) Ideas

277. Which one of the following statements is true according to VALS framework of psychographic segmentation ?
(1) The consumers who are primarily motivated by ideals are guided by knowledge and principles.
(2) The consumers who are motivated by achievement look for knowledge and principles.
(3) The consumers who are motivated by self expression don't desire social or physical activity, variety, and risk.
(4) The consumers who are motivated by achievement desire social or physical activity, variety, and risk.

278. From the following two statements of Assertion (A) and Reason (R), indicate the correct code :

Assertion (A) : A transformational appeal of communication elaborates on a non-product related benefit or image.

Reasoning (R) : Transformational appeals often do not attempt to stir up emotions that will motivate purchase.

Code :
(1) (A) and (R) both are correct.
(2) (A) is correct (R) is not correct.
(3) (A) is not correct (R) is correct.
(4) (A) and (R) both are incorrect.

279. Select the correct sequence for Hierarchy-of-effects model related to marketing communication :
(1) Awareness → Knowledge → Liking → Preference → Conviction → Purchase
(2) Knowledge → Awareness → Liking → Conviction → Preference → Purchase
(3) Awareness → Liking → Knowledge → Conviction → Preference → Purchase
(4) Liking → Awareness → Knowledge → Preference → Conviction → Purchase

280. Match the items of List - I with the items of List - II and denote the code of correct matching :

List - I	List - II
(a) Basic Product	(i) Set of attributes and conditions buyers normally expect
(b) Expected Product	(ii) Possible augmentation and transformation the product might undergo in future
(c) Augmented Product	(iii) Exceed customer expectations
(d) Potential Product	(iv) Converting core benefits into product

Codes :

	(a)	(b)	(c)	(d)
(1)	(iii)	(iv)	(i)	(ii)
(2)	(i)	(iii)	(iv)	(ii)
(3)	(i)	(iv)	(iii)	(ii)
(4)	(iv)	(i)	(iii)	(ii)

281. Which of the following statements is false ?
(1) The opportunity cost of an input is considered in capital budgeting
(2) Capital budgeting decisions are reversible in nature
(3) Cash flows and accounting profits are different
(4) An expansion decision is a capital budgeting decision

282. Match the items of List - I with those of List - II and indicate the correct code :

List - I	List - II
(a) ABC Analysis	(i) Dividend Decision

(b) Walter Model		(ii) Capital Budgeting Decision	
(c) Capital Rationing		(iii) Capital Structure Decision	
(d) Net Operating Income		(iv) Working Capital Management Decision Approach	

Codes :

	(a)	(b)	(c)	(d)
(1)	(i)	(iii)	(ii)	(iv)
(2)	(ii)	(i)	(iii)	(iv)
(3)	(iv)	(i)	(ii)	(iii)
(4)	(iii)	(i)	(ii)	(iv)

283. Main objective of employing Financial Leverage is to :

(1) Reduce the risk associated with profits

(2) Maintain the stability in profits

(3) Decrease the cost of debt capital

(4) Magnify the return on equity share capital

284. Which one of the following is not a method of calculating cost of equity capital ?

(1) Dividend yield method

(2) Dividend yield plus growth method

(3) Yield to maturity method

(4) Earnings yield method

285. Which one of the following equates the present value of cash out flows and the present value of expected cash inflows from a project ?

(1) Net Present Value

(2) Internal Rate of Return

(3) Pay back Period

(4) Accounting Rate of Return

286. Which one of the following is not true ?

(1) Material resources are subject to laws of mechanics and they cannot have an output greater than the input.

(2) Human resources are capable of exponential growth and development.

(3) Human resources cannot yield an output that may be far greater than what the value of their input warrants.

(4) In current scenario, gradually, the emphasis has shifted from muscle power to use of mind power.

287. The pluralistic approach of industrial conflict is based on which one of the following basic assumption / premise ?

(1) That conflict occurs when the tendency of industrial society is to treat worker as an isolated individual and deprive him of all control over his environment

(2) That an enterprise contain people with coalition of different interests

(3) That industrial conflict is a part of the broader social conflict between classes

(4) That no consensus is possible, in case of conflicts, because people are with different socio - cultural backgrounds.

288. The Job Description Index (JDI) Technique is used for measuring which one of the following ?

(1) Job attitudes

(2) Job descriptions / definitions

(3) Job analysis records

(4) Job skill requirements

289. From the following two statements of Assertion (A) and Reasoning (R) indicate the correct code :

Assertion (A) : Development in HRM is a short-term educational process with temporary intervention.

Reasoning (R) : It is a educational process utilizing a systematic and organized procedure for development of operative employees performance in current jobs.

Code :

(1) (A) is correct and (R) is correct explanation of (A).

(2) (A) is correct, but (R) is not correct explanation of (A).

(3) (A) is not correct, but (R) is correct.

(4) (A) and (R) both are not correct.

290. Match items of List - I with List - II relating to methods of performance appraisal and indicate the correct code of matching.

List - I	List - II
(a) Paired comparison method	(i) Reviewing employee records and holding interview on definite test questions.
(b) Forced choice description method	(ii) Set of pair phrases or descriptive statements
(c) Critical Incidents method	(iii) Differentiating between effective and non - effective performance on basis of achievements

(d) Field review method		(iv) Relative ranking method	

Codes :

	(a)	(b)	(c)	(d)
(1)	(iv)	(ii)	(iii)	(i)
(2)	(ii)	(iii)	(iv)	(i)
(3)	(iii)	(i)	(iv)	(ii)
(4)	(ii)	(iv)	(i)	(iii)

291. Match the following items of List - I with the items of List - II and indicate the code of correct matching :

List - I (Name of organisation)	List - II (Year of establishment)
(a) IDBI	(i) 1956
(b) ICICI	(ii) 1955
(c) LIC of India	(iii) 1990
(d) SIDBI	(iv) 1964

Codes :

	(a)	(b)	(c)	(d)
(1)	(iii)	(i)	(ii)	(iv)
(2)	(iii)	(i)	(iv)	(ii)
(3)	(iv)	(ii)	(i)	(iii)
(4)	(i)	(ii)	(iii)	(iv)

292. Statement (I) : Capital adequacy norms help banks in strengthening their capital base.

Statement (II) : Capital adequacy norms help banks in sanctioning more loans.

Code :

(1) Both the Statements (I) and (II) are correct.
(2) Both the Statements (I) and (II) are incorrect.
(3) Statement (I) is correct but (II) is incorrect.
(4) Statement (I) is incorrect but (II) is correct.

293. What is Hawala ?

(1) Tax evasion
(2) Illegal trading in stock exchanges
(3) Bank robbery
(4) Illegal transactions of foreign exchange

294. The best definition of 'capital employed' in calculating the rate of return on investment is

(1) Current assets + gross fixed assets
(2) Current assets + net fixed assets
(3) Working capital + gross fixed assets
(4) Working capital + net fixed assets

295. Assertion (A) : The future will see mostly the electronic money clearance through satellite networking.

Reasoning (R) : RBI is encouraging e-banking.

Code :

(1) (A) is true but (R) is false.
(2) (A) is false but (R) is true.
(3) Both (A) and (R) are true and (R) is the correct explanation of (A).
(4) Both (A) and (R) are true but (R) does not support (A).

296. Statement (I) : Developing countries can borrow more than their quota under Extended Fund Facility (EFF) of IMF.

Statement (II) : The Extended Fund Facility (EFF) was created in 1984 to help the developing countries over longer period upto 3 years.

Code :

(1) Statement (I) is correct but (II) is not correct.
(2) Statement (II) is correct but (I) is not correct.
(3) Both the statements (I) and (II) are correct.
(4) Both the statements (I) and (II) are not correct.

297. Match the items of List - I with those of List - II; and choose the correct code of combination :

List - I	List - II
(a) Poverty Reduction and Growth Facility(PRGF)	(i) 1997
(b) Supplemental Reserve Facility (SRF)	(ii) 1974
(c) Extended Fund Facility(EFF)	(iii) 1999

Codes :

	(a)	(b)	(c)
(1)	(iii)	(i)	(ii)
(2)	(iii)	(ii)	(i)
(3)	(ii)	(i)	(iii)
(4)	(i)	(iii)	(ii)

298. Who among the following has given Absolute Advantage Model of international trade ?

(1) Adam Smith
(2) David Recardo
(3) Hackscher Ohlin
(4) William Petty

299. Which among the following is not an international economic institution ?

(1) IMF (2) IBRD
(3) ADB (4) IFRS

300. Assertion (A) : The fall in aggregate expenditure or aggregate demand in the economy works to reduce imports and help in solving the balance of payment problems.

Reasoning (R) : The important way to reduce imports and thereby reduce deficit in balance of payments is to adopt monetary and fiscal policies that aims at reducing aggregate expenditure in the economy.

Code :

(1) (A) and (R) both are correct and (R) supports (A).
(2) (A) and (R) both are correct but (R) does not support (A).
(3) (A) is correct but (R) is incorrect.
(4) (R) is correct but (A) is incorrect.

301. As per Section 80G maximum deduction allowed for any cash donation is upto

(1) Rs. 1.000 (2) Rs. 2.000
(3) Rs. 5.000 (4) Rs. 10.000

302. In Leontief production function, L is considered as

(1) Structural constraint in the production process
(2) Degree of Homogeneity
(3) Binding constraint in the production process
(4) Optimisation constraint in the production process

303. EPRG framework in International Business refers to

(1) Ethno, Poly, Regio, Geo Transformations
(2) Ethnocentric, Polycentric, Regiocentric and Geocentric Orientations
(3) Ethics, Policies, Regulations, Guidelines Orientations
(4) Every Person Refers Global Framework

304. Which one of the following is not a major direct selling company in India?

(1) Eureka Forbes
(2) Amway India Enterprises
(3) Modicare
(4) Hindustan Unilever Ltd.

305. Which one of the following statements is 'True' in partnership?

(1) In the absence of any provision in the partnership deed, only a working partner is entitled to remuneration.
(2) Any firm which earns normal profit has no goodwill.
(3) The business of the firm must be carried on by all the partners.
(4) Interest on loan given by a partner to the firm shall be paid if there are profits.

306. Which of the following relationships is true in a model distribution?

(1) Mean — Mode = 3 (Mean — Median)
(2) Mode = 3 Median — 2 Mean
(3) 3 Median = 2 Mean + Mode
(4) 2 Median — 3 Quartile Deviation = 2 Mean

307. In continuous compounding, the time it takes to double the sum grossly follow 'Rule of 69'. If it is changed to discrete compounding, the relevant rule of thumb is ________.

(1) Rule of 69.3 (2) Rule of 72
(3) Rule of 84 (4) Rule of 64

308. The 'going concern concept' is the underlying basis for

(1) Disclosing the market value of securities
(2) Consolidating the accounts of subsidiary companies with those of parent company
(3) Depreciating fixed assets over their useful lives
(4) Disclosing the sales and other operating information in the income statement

309. 'Constraint Optimisation' is closer to which of the following objectives of business firm?

(1) Sales maximisation
(2) Profit maximisation
(3) Satisfying behaviour
(4) Rent seeking

310. In a rising consumer income scenario, the preferred decision choice of business firms for low income elastic products will be ________.

(1) Product promotion (2) Cost control
(3) Product repositioning
(4) Product improvement

311. If an estimated Cobb-Douglas production function is $Q = 10K^{06}L^{08}$. What type of returns to scale does this production function indicate?

(1) Increasing returns
(2) Decreasing returns
(3) Constant returns
(4) Negative returns

312. Pricing strategy of setting a high price when a product is introduced and gradually lowering its price is known as

(1) Skimming (2) Penetration pricing
(3) Peak load pricing (4) Dumping

313. Which one of the following is not true for Mass Marketing?
(1) Provides very little scope for customisation
(2) Deals with customers directly
(3) Normally followed in case of FMCG and SMCG Goods
(4) Relies heavily on advertising

314. A manufacturing enterprise monthly consumes 1.350 units of raw material at the cost of Rs 20 per unit. Determine its economic order quantity given the ordering cost of Rs 2400 and carrying cost of inventory being 30 percent of the price paid.
(1) 3.600 units (2) 2.400 units
(3) 4.800 units (4) 2,700 units

315. The portfolio theory articulates diversification to reduce which of the following risks?
(1) Market risk (2) Financial risk
(3) Unsystematic risk
(4) Business risk

316. When foreign currency assets and liabilities match in terms of amount of exposure and timing of maturities, it is described as :
(1) Financial hedge (2) Natural hedge
(3) Perfect hedge (4) Netting

317. What is the probability that a randomly chosen card from a deck of cards will either be a King or a Spade?
(1) 0.3077 (2) 0.3209
(3) 0.0384 (4) 0.3160

318. The standard deviation of the binomial distribution is :
(1) np (2) $\sqrt{np}$
(3) npq (4) $\sqrt{npq}$

319. When sampling is done without replacement then standard error of mean is :
(1) $SE_{\bar{X}} = \frac{\sigma}{\sqrt{n}}$ (2) $SE_{\bar{X}} = \frac{\sigma}{\sqrt{n}}\sqrt{\frac{N-n}{N-1}}$
(3) $SE_{\bar{X}} = \frac{\sigma}{\sqrt{n}}\sqrt{\frac{N-1}{N-n}}$
(4) $SE_{\bar{X}} = \frac{\sigma}{\sqrt{n}}\sqrt{1-\frac{n}{N}}$

320. Which of the following is not an example of compressed data?
(1) Data array
(2) Frequency distribution
(3) Histogram
(4) Ogive

321. The Human Relations Approach rejected the 'rabble hypothesis' by giving which of the following argument?
(1) The worker does not work for money only.
(2) A worker operates in a techno-economic system with no room for emotions.
(3) Authoritarian style of leadership is more productive.
(4) Individual pays attention to self-achievement irrespective of informal group norms.

322. Which of the following is not correct with respect to matrix organisation?
(1) It is a combination of functional and product organisation
(2) Functional departments are not permanent fixtures of a matrix organisation
(3) Product departments are created as the need for them arises
(4) Team members have functional home when they are not needed on a project

323. As per Carroll Model, the four levels of Corporate Social Responsibility are :
(1) Physical, economic, social and legal
(2) Physical, economic, legal and ethical
(3) Philanthropic, economic, legal and ethical
(4) Philanthropic, economic, social and ethical

324. Who coined the term 'Collective Bargaining'?
(1) Reed Richardson (2) Kurt Lewin
(3) W.E. Deming
(4) Sydney Webb and Beatrice Webb

325. The headquarters of the ASEAN is located in which of the following country?
(1) Indonesia (2) Vietnam
(3) Thailand (4) Singapore

326. What is the rate of tax deduction at source from insurance commission in case of 'Person' :
(1) 2 percent (2) 5 percent
(3) 10 percent (4) 4 percent

327. Which of the following is a long term source of finance?
(1) Commercial Paper (CP)
(2) External Commercial Borrowings (ECB)
(3) Factoring
(4) Line of Credit (LOC)

328. What is a 'Repo Rate'?
(1) Is the rate at which RBI lends to State Government

(2) Is the rate at which International aid agencies lends to RBI
(3) Is the rate at which the RBI lends to Banks in case of short maturity
(4) Is the rate at which RBI borrows funds from the Commercial Banks in the country

329. In Marketing. DSA stands for
(1) Delivery Staff Agency
(2) Direct Supplier Agent
(3) Direct Selling Agent
(4) Distribution and Supply Agency

330. In which of the following stages of product life cycle a company reduces sales promotion to take advantage of heavy consumer demand?
(1) Introduction (2) Growth
(3) Maturity (4) Decline

331. In which of the following price adjustment strategies, a company reduces prices to reward customer responses such as volume purchases, paying early or promoting the product?
(1) Discount and allowance pricing
(2) Psychological pricing
(3) Promotional pricing
(4) Dynamic pricing

332. Some doctors charge patients for missed appointments because the service value existed only at that point and disappeared when the patient did not show up, is an example of which one of the following four service characteristics?
(1) Inseparability (2) Intangibility
(3) Variability (4) Perishability

333. Which one is False as per the relevant provisions of the Indian Contract Act, 1872?
(1) A void agreement is one that is not enforceable by law
(2) Assignment is the obvious mode of discharge of a contract
(3) Where a party waives its rights under the contract, the other party is released of its obligations under the contract
(4) Where the subject matter of a contract is destroyed for no fault of the promisor, the contract does not become void by impossibility of performance

334. Which of the following is not an implied condition in a contract of sale?
(1) Condition as to quality or fitness
(2) Condition as to merchantable quality
(3) Condition as to wholesomeness
(4) Condition as to free from encumbrances

335. Which of the following does not come under the definition of "Information" under RTI Act, 2005?
(1) Log Books (2) Circulars
(3) File Notings in the process
(4) Data material held in any electronic form

336. Under which section of Information Technology Act of 2000, updated in 2008, stealing any digital asset or information is considered as cyber crime?
(1) 65 (2) 65-D
(3) 67 (4) 70

337. Which one of the following statements is true for the set off and carry forward of loss under the head "house property" in India?
(1) Can be carried forward for 8 years
(2) Can not be carried forward
(3) Can be carried forward for 4 years
(4) Can be carried forward infinitely

338. Surcharge of 10% (percent) is payable by an Individual where the total income exceeds
(1) Rs. 7,50,000/- (2) Rs. 8,50,000/-
(3) Rs. 50,00,000/- (4) Rs. 20,00,000/-

339. Mohan, has rendered his services in India and retired in 2015. He then shifted and settled in Singapore. The pension received by him for such services would be _____?
(1) Deemed to accure or arise outside India
(2) Deemed to accure or arise in India only when it is received in India
(3) Deemed to accure or arise in India only when it is received outside India
(4) Deemed to accure or arise in India

340. Sugam is also known as :
(1) ITR-1 (2) ITR-2
(3) ITR-4 (4) ITR-6

341. Mercosur, a South American Trade block is a :
(1) Free Trade Area
(2) Common Market
(3) Custom Union
(4) Economic Cooperation

342. Which of the following are possible negative impacts of FDI on domestic firms in host countries?
(A) Market monopoly
(B) Technology dependence

(C) Increased competition
(D) Profit outflow

Choose the correct answer from the options given below :

(1) (A), (B) only (2) (B), (C) only
(3) (A), (B), (D) only (4) (B), (C), (D) only

343. Charging different prices for the same product in different markets until the MR of last unit sold equals the MC of the product sold in each market is described by ______.

(A) Price discrimination of first degree
(B) Price discrimination of second degree
(C) Price discrimination of third degree
(D) Equilibrium price
(E) Price discrimination

Choose the correct answer from the options given below :

(1) (A) and (B) only (2) (A) and (C) only
(3) (C) and (E) only (4) (A) and (D) only

344. Arrange the following steps in logical sequence of operation of the Arbitrage Pricing Theory (APT).

(A) Estimate the Factor Sensitivities
(B) Estimate the Risk Premium for Factor(s)
(C) Identify the Macroeconomic Factors

Choose the correct answer from the options given below :

(1) (A), (B), (C) (2) (B), (A), (C)
(3) (C), (B), (A) (4) (C), (A), (B)

345. Cost audit for Materials covers :

(A) Goods inward procedure.
(B) Methods of calculating standard cost variance.
(C) Classification of overhead.
(D) Accounting for scrap, wastage, materials transfers
(E) Accounting treatment of under or over absorption

Choose the most appropriate answer from the options given below :

(1) (A), (D) only (2) (A), (E) only
(3) (A), (B) only (4) (E), (C) only

346. Which of the following explains the declining slope of indifference curves?

(A) Diminishing marginal utility
(B) Diminishing Marginal Rate of substitutions between the commodities
(C) Diminishing Marginal Rate of technical substitution
(D) Ordinal measurement of utilities
(E) Diminishing Marginal utility of money

Choose the most appropriate answer from the options given below :

(1) (A) and (D) only (2) (B) and (D) only
(3) (C) and (D) only (4) (A) and (E) only

347. Which of the following is/are condition(s) for price discrimination of product?

(A) Firm must have some monopoly power.
(B) Price elasticities of demand for the product in different market must differ
(C) Market must be separable or able to be segmented
(D) Free entry and exit of firms

Choose the correct answer from the options given below :

(1) (A) and (D) only
(2) (B), (C) and (D) only
(3) (A), (C) and (D) only
(4) (A), (B) and (C) only

348. Consumer rationality in business economics is collective manifestation of which of the following assumptions?

(A) Non-Satiation
(B) Clarity of preferences
(C) Divisibility of goods and services
(D) Economic selfish motive
(E) Possession of information

Choose the most appropriate answer from the options given below :

(1) (A), (B) and (D) only
(2) (A), (C) and (E) only
(3) (A), (B), (C) and (D) only
(4) (A), (B), (D) and (E) only

349. Net Present Value (NPV) and Internal Rate of Return (IRR) methods yield conflicting outcomes due to _____.

(A) Unconventional cash flows
(B) Investment size disparity
(C) Investment life disparity
(D) Cash flow pattern disparity

Choose the most appropriate answer from the options given below :

(1) (A) and (B) only (2) (A) and (C) only
(3) (A), (B) and (C) only
(4) (B), (C) and (D) only

350. In which of the following situations, the payback period method is advised for evaluation of investment opportunities?

(A) Overleveraged businesses
(B) Cash rich businesses
(C) Uncertain market conditions
(D) Stable market conditions
Choose the most appropriate answer from the options given below:
(1) (A) and (B) only (2) (A) and (C) only
(3) (B) and (C) only (4) (C) and (D) only

351. The Regression Coefficient is independent of the change of
(A) Scale only (B) Origin only
(C) Both Scale and Origin
(D) Neither Scale nor Origin
Choose the most appropriate answer from the options given below :
(1) (A) only (2) (B) only
(3) (C) only (4) (D) only

352. Which of the following are positional averages?
(A) Arithmetic Mean (B) Median
(C) Mode (D) Geometric Mean
(E) Harmonic Mean
Choose the most appropriate answer from the options given below :
(1) (B), (C) only (2) (B), (C), (D) only
(3) (B), (C), (A) only
(4) (A), (B), (C), (D) only

353. Which of following is not correct about properties of correlation coefficient?
(A) Depends on the origin.
(B) Depends on the scale.
(C) Depends on both origin and scale.
(D) Is independent with respect to origin.
(E) Is independent with respect to unit of scale.
Choose the correct answer from the options given below :
(1) (A), (D), (E) only (2) (A), (B), (D) only
(3) (A), (B), (C) only (4) (D), (E), (B) only

354. What type of defense mechanism is used by a person when he gets angry at his child or spouse because he had a bad day at work?
(A) Denial (B) Repression
(C) Projection (D) Displacement
(E) Regression
Choose the most appropriate answer from the options given below :
(1) (A) and (B) only (2) (B) only
(3) (D) only (4) (E) only

355. Out of the following statements which of them explains the difference between enculturation and acculturation as a part of Cross-Cultural Training?
(A) Enculturation refer to the process of learning and adopting host cultural norms, and acculturation is the process of learning our own native culture.
(B) Enculturation is a anthropological term used for socialisation like acculturation.
(C) Both terms refer to the process of Learning through social interaction.
(D) Enculturation refers to the process of learning our own culture, and acculturation refers to the process of learning host cultural norms.
Choose the most appropriate answer from the options given below :
(1) (A), (B), (C) only (2) (B), (D) only
(3) (B), (C), (D) only
(4) (A), (B), (C) and (D) only

356. Which of the following financial institution(s) got merged with their subsidiary?
(A) UTI (B) IFCI
(C) ICICI (D) IDBI
(E) Global Trust Bank
Choose the correct answer from the options given below :
(1) (A), (B) only (2) (B), (C) only
(3) (C), (D) only (4) (C), (E) only

357. Objectives of IMPS (Immediate Payment Service) are :
(A) To enable bank customers to use mobile instruments as a channel for accessing their banks accounts and remit funds 24 × 7.
(B) Making payments simpler just with the mobile number of the beneficiary.
(C) To build the foundation for a full range of mobile based banking services
(D) To create competition with NEFT and RTGS
Choose the most appropriate answer from the options given below :
(1) (A), (B), (C) only (2) (B), (C), (D) only
(3) (A), (B), (D) only (4) (B), (D) only

358. Which among the followings are correct statements with regard to NBFC in India?
(A) All NBFCs should be registered with RBI.
(B) NBFCs cannot accept demand deposits.

(C) NBFCs do not form part of the payment and settlement system and cannot issue cheques drawn on itself.

(D) Deposit insurance facility of Deposit Insurance and Credit Guarantee Corporation is not available to depositors of NBFCs.

Choose the correct answer from the options given below :

(1) (A), (B), (C) only
(2) (A), (B), (C), (D) only
(3) (A), (B), (D) only (4) (A), (D) only

359. Which of the following are true about delivering customer value?

(A) A company can go alone in creating customer value

(B) Company must work within a broader network of partners to accomplish customer value.

(C) Individual companies and brands compete: their entire value delivery networks don't.

(D) Individual companies and brands don't compete: their entire value delivery networks do.

(E) Value = Contribution/cost (offer higher contribution through product or service to clients and lowers the cost).

Choose the most appropriate answer from the options given below :

(1) (A) and (E) only
(2) (A), (B) and (E) only
(3) (B), (C) and (E) only
(4) (B), (D) and (E) only

360. Market for automobiles needs to be segmented on the basis of :

(A) Buying behaviour
(B) Psychographics
(C) Geographies
(D) Demographics

Choose the most appropriate answer from the options given below :

(1) (A), (D) only (2) (C), (D) only
(3) (A), (B), (D) only (4) (A), (B), (C), (D)

361. The strategies of flanking defense preemptive defense mobile defense contractor defense and counter offensive defense is used by which market player?

(A) Market challenger (B) Market leader
(C) Market follower (D) Market Nicher
(E) Start up Marketer

Choose the most appropriate answer from the options given below

(1) (A) only (2) (B) only
(3) (C) only (4) (B), (E) only

362. Out of the following statements, which is not correct about the RTI Act, 2005?

(A) The RTI Act come into force from October 13, 2005.

(B) Any citizen may request information from a Public Authority (Both Govt. and Private)

(C) Reply for information asked can be given within 30 days.

(D) There is a nominal application fee that are needs to pay to get information under the RTI application.

(E) For getting information, applicant has to pay Rs. 10/- per page of information for Central Govt. Departments.

Choose the correct answer from the options given below :

(1) (A), (B), (E) only (2) (B), (E) only
(3) (C), (E) only (4) (B), (C), (D), (E) only

363. Out of the following, which are not the features of GST 2017 in India.

(A) GST is applicable on 'supply' of Goods and Services.

(B) GST is based on the principle of origin based taxation rather than principle of destination based consumption.

(C) Import of Goods is treated as Inter-State supplies and would be subject to IGST in addition to applicable Custom Duties.

(D) It is a dual taxation with Centre and State simultaneously levying it on a common base.

(E) GST is applicable to all Goods and Services without any exemptions.

Choose the correct answer from the options given below :

(1) (A), (B), (E) only (2) (B), (C), (E) only
(3) (B), (E) only (4) (C), (D), (E) only

364. Which of the followings is correct about deduction available in respect of contribution to various provident funds in case of salaried employees?

(A) Employers contribution to recognised provident fund is exempted upto 12% of salary.

(B) Employers contribution to unrecognised provident fund is exempted from tax.

(C) Employer does not contribute to Public Provident Fund.

(D) Deduction under Section 80 C is available for employer's contribution in unrecognized provident fund.

Choose the correct answer from the options given below :

(1) (A), (B), (C) only (2) (A), (B), (D) only
(3) (B), (C), (D) only (4) (A), (C), (D) only

365. Which of the following expenses debited to Profit and Loss a/c but disallowed while computing income from Business?

(A) General Expenses
(B) Personal Expenses
(C) Expenses of Income which is taxable under the other heads of income
(D) Charities and donations

Choose the correct answer from the options given below :

(1) (A), (B), (C) only (2) (B), (C), (D) only
(3) (C), (D) only (4) (A), (B), (C), (D) only

366. Match List I with List II

List I Authors of Trade Theory	List II Name of Theory
(A) Steffan Linder	(I) Product Life Cycle Theory
(B) Raymond Vernon	(II) Country Similarity Theory
(C) Hecksher-Ohlin	(III) Absolute Advantage Theory
(D) Adam Smith	(IV) Factor Proportion Theory

Choose the correct answer from the options given below :

(1) (A)-(IV), (B)-(III), (C)-(II), (D)-(I)
(2) (A)-(II), (B)-(I), (C)-(IV). (D)-(III)
(3) (A)-(I), (B)-(III), (C)-(IV), (D)-(II)
(4) (A)-(III), (B)-(II), (C)-(I), (D)-(IV)

367. Match List I with List II

List I	List II
(A) Standard Costing	(I) Financial forecasting and planning
(B) Margin of Safety	(II) Sales minus break-even sales
(C) Ratio Analysis	(III) Control of inventory
(D) JIT System	(IV) Management by exception

Choose the correct answer from the options given below :

(1) (A)-(IV), (B)-(II), (C)-(I), (D)-(III)
(2) (A)-(III), (B)-(I), (C)-(II), (D)-(IV)
(3) (A)-(II), (B)-(III), (C)-(I), (D)-(IV)
(4) (A)-(I), (B)-(II), (C)-(IV), (D)-(III)

368. Match the market forms in the List I and the role of the selling costs in the List II

List I Market Forms	List II Role of selling costs
(A) Perfect Competition	(I) Sustained survival of firm
(B) Monopoly	(II) Influencing buying behaviour
(C) Monopolistic Competition	(III) Increasing market size
(D) Oligopoly	(IV) Intimation of product or service

Choose the correct answer from the options given below :

(1) (A)-(I), (B)-(III), (C)-(IV)- (D)-(II)
(2) (A)-(IV), (B)-(II), (C)-(I), (D)-(III)
(3) (A)-(III), (B)-(IV), (C)-(II), (D)-(I)
(4) (A)-(II), (B)-(I), (C)-(III), (D)-(IV)

369. Match List I with List II

List I	List II
(A) Mezzanine Capital	(I) It is the speedy source of finance less regulated by the regulatory environment of debt and capital markets.
(B) Private Equity	(II) It is long term capital embraced by the high networth and high risk appetite investors.
(C) Global Depository Receipts	(III) It is an equity instrument issued in overseas markets and is listed and traded on bourses on an OTC basis.
(D) Venture Capital	(IV) It refers to subordinated debt or preferred equity that allows firms to borrow additional capital beyond the levels lenders are willing to finance through the bank loans.

Choose the correct answer from the options given below :

(1) (A)-(II), (B)-(IV), (C)-(I), (D)-(III)
(2) (A)-(I), (B)-(III), (C)-(IV), (D)-(II)

(3) (A)-(IV), (B)-(I), (C)-(III), (D)-(II)
(4) (A)-(III), (B)-(II), (C)-(I), (D)-(IV)

370. Match List I with List II

List I

(A) Bayes' Theorem
(B) Conditional Probability
(C) Theorem of complementary events
(D) Theorem of addition

List II

(I) $P(\bar{E}) = 1 - P(E)$
(II) $P(E_1 \cup E_2) = P(E_1) + P(E_2)$
(III) $P(E_2 / E_2) = \frac{P(E_1 \cap E_2)}{P(E_1)}$
(IV) $P(H_1 / E) = \frac{P(H_1 \cap E)}{P(E)}$

Choose the correct answer from the options given below :

(1) (A)-(I), (B)-(IV), (C)-(III), (D)-(II)
(2) (A)-(III), (B)-(IV), (C)-(II), (D)-(I)
(3) (A)-(III), (B)-(IV), (C)-(I), (D)-(II)
(4) (A)-(IV), (B)-(III), (C)-(I), (D)-(II)

371. Match List I with List II

List I	List II
(A) I am Not OK, you are Not OK	(I) Dependent
(B) I am OK, you are Not OK	(II) Confronting
(C) I am OK, you are OK	(III) Withdrawn
(D) I am Not OK, you are OK	(IV) Task obsessive

Choose the correct answer from the options given below :

(1) (A)-(III), (B)-(IV), (C)-(II), (D)-(I)
(2) (A)-(III), (B)-(II), (C)-(IV), (D)-(I)
(3) (A)-(I), (B)-(II), (C)-(III), (D)-(IV)
(4) (A)-(II), (B)-(I), (C)-(II), (D)-(IV)

372. Match List I with List II

List I Capital Structure Preposition(s)

(A) Target Capital Structure
(B) Optimum Capital Structure
(C) Cost of financial distress
(D) MM preposition-II

List II Description(s)

(I) Expected yield on the equity capital is equal to the pure equity return plus a premium for financial risk.
(II) It refers to the perceived costs due to increased ratio of debt in the firm.
(III) It is the debt ratio the firm strives to achieve.
(IV) It is the debt-equity ratio that maximises the value of the firm.

Choose the correct answer from the options given below :

(1) (A)-(II), (B)-(III), (C)-(I), (D)-(IV)
(2) (A)-(III), (B)-(IV), (C)-(II), (D)-(I)
(3) (A)-(IV), (B)-(II), (C)-(III), (D)-(I)
(4) (A)-(I), (B)-(III), (C)-(II), (D)-(IV)

373. Match List I with List II

List I (Authors)	List II (Ideas)
(A) Bill Bishop	(I) Managing in the Market Space
(B) D. Bird	(II) Commonsense Direct Marketing
(C) Daniel S. Jonal	(III) Strategic Marketing for the Digital Age
(D) Jeffery F. Rayport	(IV) On-line Marketing

Choose the correct answer from the options given below :

(1) (A)-(III), (B)-(II), (C)-(IV), (D)-(I)
(2) (A)-(I), (B)-(II), (C)-(III), (D)-(IV)
(3) (A)-(II), (B)-(I), (C)-(IV), (D)-(III)
(4) (A)-(IV), (B)-(III), (C)-(II), (D)-(I)

374. Match List I with List II

List I

(A) Limited Liability Partnership
(B) Particular Partnership
(C) Partnership
(D) Mutual Agency

List II

(I) It can be formed with a minimum of two individuals or body corporate through their nominees.
(II) It is formed for a specific venture or for a particular period.
(III) It is an association of two or more individuals.
(IV) A partner is both an agent and a principal in a partnership firm.

Choose the correct answer from the options given below :

(1) (A)-(I), (B)-(II), (C)-(III), (D)-(IV)
(2) (A)-(II), (B)-(III), (C)-(I), (D)-(IV)

(3) (A)-(II), (B)-(I), (C)-(III), (D)-(IV)
(4) (A)-(IV), (B)-(II), (C)-(I), (D)-(III)

375. Match List I with List II

List I	List II
(A) 80 GG	(I) Deduction in respect of contribution given by companies to political parties.
(B) 80 GGA	(II) Deduction in respect of contribution given by any person to political parties.
(C) 80 GGB	(III) Deduction in respect of scientific research.
(D) 80 GGC	(IV) Deduction in respect of rent paid.

Choose the correct answer from the options given below :
(1) (A)-(IV), (B)-(III), (C)-(I), (D)-(II)
(2) (A)-(III), (B)-(IV), (C)-(II)- (D)-(I)
(3) (A)-(IV), (B)-(III), (C)-(II), (D)-(I)
(4) (A)-(IV), (B)-(II), (C)-(I), (D)-(III)

376. Arrange the following legal enactments m India in the chronological sequence from the first to the last.
(A) The Mines Act
(B) The Minimum Wages Act
(C) The Payment of Gratuity Act
(D) The Child Labour (Prolnbition and Regulation) Act
(E) The Apprentices Act
Choose the correct answer from the options given below
(1) (B), (D), (C), (A), (E)
(2) (B), (A), (E), (C), (D)
(3) (A), (E), (B), (C), (D)
(4) (E), (B), (A), (C), (D)

377. Arrange in the sequence of decisions in manufacturing enterprises
(A) Making of forecasts
(B) Determination of key factors
(C) Consideration of alternative combination of forecasts
(D) Preparation of budgets
(E) Combination of factors
Choose the correct answer from the options given below :
(1) (A), (B), (C), (E), (D)
(2) (C), (A), (E), (B), (D)
(3) (B), (A), (C), (E), (D)
(4) (A), (C), (B), (E), (D)

378. Arrange the following products in the increasing order of price elasticities
(A) Homogeneous products
(B) Differentiated products
(C) Necessities (D) Durable goods
Choose the correct answer from the options given below :
(1) (C), (B), (D) and (A)
(2) (A), (B), (C) and (D)
(3) (A), (C), (B) and (D)
(4) (C), (A), (B) and (D)

379. Arrange the following financing choices in order of preference suggested by the pecking order theory
(A) Reinvestment of earnings
(B) New issue of equity
(C) Issue of debt
Choose the correct answer from the options given below :
(1) (A), (B), (C) (2) (A), (C), (B)
(3) (B), (C), (A) (4) (B), (A), (C)

380. Arrange the following stages of research in a proper sequence
(A) Report Writing (B) Budgeting
(C) Data Collection (D) Field Work
(E) Research outcomes
Choose the correct answer from the options given below
(1) (B), (D), (C), (E), (A)
(2) (D), (A), (B), (C), (E)
(3) (D), (C), (B), (E), (A)
(4) (B), (E), (D), (C), (A)

381. Arrange the following steps of creating a market competitive pay plan in a sequence from the first to the last
(A) Choose benchmark jobs and select compensable factors
(B) Define each compensable factor and determine its degree in each job
(C) Establish rate changes
(D) Develop pay grades
(E) Compare and adjust current and market wage rates for jobs
Choose the correct answer from the options given below :
(1) (B), (A), (E), (D), (C)
(2) (A), (C), (B), (D), (E)
(3) (A), (B), (E), (D), (C)
(4) (A), (B), (C), (E), (D)

382. Arrange the following initiatives taken by the Government of India to tackle the Non-performing assets in their ascending order of chronology :

(A) Corporate Debt Restructuring
(B) Compromise Settlement
(C) The Debt Recovery Tribunals (DRTs)
(D) Credit Information Bureau
(E) SARFAESI Act

Choose the correct answer from the options given below :

(1) (C), (D), (A), (B), (E)
(2) (A), (B), (E), (C), (D)
(3) (C), (D), (B), (E), (A)
(4) (D), (C), (B), (E), (A)

383. Arrange the following steps of marketing process in proper sequence

(A) Construct an integrated marketing programme that delivers superior value
(B) Capture value from customers to create profits and customer equity
(C) Understand the market place and customer needs and wants
(D) Engage customers, build profitable relationships, and create customer delight
(E) Design a customer value-driven marketing strategy

Choose the correct answer from the options given below :

(1) (C), (A), (E), (D), (B)
(2) (B), (E), (A), (C), (D)
(3) (D), (A), (B), (C), (E)
(4) (C), (E), (A), (D), (B)

384. Which one is the correct sequence implied in the Indian Contract Act 1872?

(A) Offer of proposal (B) Contract
(C) Promise (D) Agreement
(E) Acceptance

Choose the correct answer from the options given below :

(1) (C), (E), (A), (D), (B)
(2) (D), (B), (C), (A), (E)
(3) (B), (D), (C), (E), (A)
(4) (A), (E), (C), (D), (B)

385. Arrange the following procedure of Income Tax return e-Filling in India

(A) Login (B) Register
(C) Verification
(D) Downloading utility and preparing return
(E) e-filing Income Tax Return

Choose the correct answer from the options given below

(1) (A), (B), (C), (D), (E)
(2) (A), (C), (B), (E), (D)
(3) (B), (A), (E), (D), (C)
(4) (B), (A), (D), (E), (C)

386. Given below are two statements.

Statement (I): Monetary policy causes a deliberate change in government revenue and expenditure with a view to influencing the price level and the quantum of national output.

Statement (II): Fiscal Policy regulates the money supply and the cost and availability of credit.

In the light of the above statements, choose the most appropriate answer from the options given below :

(1) Both Statement (I) and Statement (II) are correct
(2) Both Statement (I) and Statement (II) are incorrect
(3) Statement (I) is correct but Statement (II) is incorrect
(4) Statement (I) is incorrect but Statement (II) is correct

387. Given below are two statements : One is labelled as Assertion (A) and the other is labelled as Reason (R).

Assertion (A): Firms opt for buying an asset if the equivalent annual cost of ownership and operation is less than the best lease rate it can get.

Reason (R): Operating leases are attractive to equipment users if the lease payment is less than the user's equivalent annual cost of buying the equipment.

In the light of the above statements, choose the most appropriate answer from the options given below :

(1) Both (A) and (R) are correct and (R) is the correct explanation of (A)
(2) Both (A) and (R) are correct but (R) is NOT the correct explanation of (A)
(3) (A) is correct but (R) is not correct
(4) (A) is not correct but (R) is correct

388. Given below are two statements : One is labelled as Assertion (A) and the other is labelled as Reason (R).

Assertion (A): According to Herzberg, preventing or reducing dissatisfaction at work is not the same as providing satisfaction.

Reason (R): Under the 'two factor theory', job satisfaction and dissatisfaction are the two different aspects of work motivation.

In the light of the above statements, choose the correct answer from the options given below :

(1) Both (A) and (R) are true and (R) is the correct explanation of (A)

(2) Both (A) and (R) are true but (R) is NOT the correct explanation of (A)

(3) (A) is true but (R) is false

(4) (A) is false but (R) is true

389. Given below are two statements : One is labelled as Assertion (A) and the other is labelled as Reason (R).

Assertion (A): Trade mark registration gives exclusive proprietary rights to the trademark owner.

Reason (R): A trademark is a recognizable sign, design or expression which identifies products or services of a particular source from those of others and are used to claim exclusive proprietary rights of products or services.

In the light of the above statements, choose the correct answer from the options given below :

(1) Both (A) and (R) are true and (R) is the correct explanation of (A)

(2) Both (A) and (R) are true but (R) is NOT the correct explanation of (A)

(3) (A) is true but (R) is false

(4) (A) is false but (R) is true

390. Given below are two statements.

Statement (I): Gratuity received by Government employee is exempted from tax under Section 10(10)(i) of the Indian Income Tax Act. 1961.

Statement (II): Gratuity received by local authority employee is exempted from tax.

In the light of the above statements, choose the correct answer from the options given below :

(1) Both Statement (I) and Statement (II) are true

(2) Both Statement (I) and Statement (II) are false

(3) Statement (I) is correct but Statement (II) is false

(4) Statement (I) is incorrect but Statement (II) is true

Answer Question No. 391 to 395 on the basis of the following passage :

Burnout is a psychological syndrome emerging as a prolonged response to chronic interpersonal stressors on the job. The three key dimensions of this response are an overwhelming exhaustion, feelings of cynicism and detachment from the job, and a sense of ineffectiveness and lack of accomplishment. The significance of this three-dimensional model is that it clearly places the individual stress experience within a social context and involves the person's conception of both self and others.

The exhaustion dimension was also described as wearing out, loss of energy, depletion, debilitation, and fatigue. The cynicism dimension was originally called depersonalization (given the nature of human services occupations), but was also described as negative or inappropriate attitudes towards clients, irritability, loss of idealism, and withdrawal. The inefficacy dimension was originally called reduced personal accomplishment, and was also described as reduced productivity or capability, low morale, and an inability to cope.

There have been various conceptual models about the development of burnout and its subsequent impact. At first, the focus was on the relationship between the three dimensions of burnout, which was often described in sequential stages. Exhaustion was assumed to develop first, in response to high demands and overload, and then this would precipitate detachment and negative reactions to people and the job (depersonalization or cynicism). If this continued, then the next stage would be feelings of inadequacy and failure (reduced personal accomplishment or professional inefficacy).

More recently, burnout models have been based on theories about job stress, and the notion of imbalances leading to strain. Its three stages are: (a) Job stressors, (b) individual strain, and (c) defensive coping. Subsequently, two developmental models of the demands-resources imbalance have emerged : the Job Demands-Resources (JD-R) model and the conservation of Resources (COR) model. The JD-R model focuses on the notion that burnout arises when individuals experience incessant job demands and have inadequate resources available to address and to reduce those demands. The COR model follows a basic motivational theory assuming that burnout arises as a result of persistent threats to available resources. A different variation of an imbalance model of burnout is the Areas of Worklife (AW) model, which frames job stressors ill terms of person-job imbalances, or mismatches, but identifies six key areas in which these imbalances take place : workload, control, reward, community, fairness and values. Mismatches in these areas affect an individuals level of experienced burnout, which in turn determines various outcomes, such as job performance, social behaviors, and personal wellbeing.

391. Which of the following has the correct sequence of the stages of burnout?

(1) Fatigue due to excessive work, dislike for work, failure to achieve targets
(2) Negative feelings about work, dislike for work, effort to quit work
(3) Initial good interpersonal relations, depersonalization, loss of idealism
(4) Cynicism, inadequacy, inefficiency

392. Given below are two statements.

Statement (I): Cynicism stage of Burnout is often experienced by employees, engaged in production activity, due to excessive work pressure.

Statement (II): In Cynicism stage of burnout, person withdraws from others and shows lack of interest towards them.

In the light of the above statements, choose the correct answer from the options given below :

(1) Both Statement (I) and Statement (II) are true
(2) Both Statement (I) and Statement (II) are false
(3) Statement (I) is correct but Statement (II) is false
(4) Statement (I) is incorrect but Statement (II) is true

393. Match List I with List II

List I	**List II**
(A) Exhaustion	(I) Not able to complete work
(B) Cynicism	(II) No energy for work
(C) Inefficiency	(III) No interest in customer

Choose the correct answer from the options given below :

(1) (A)-(I), (B)-(II), (C)-(III)
(2) (A)-(III), (B)-(II), (C)-(I)
(3) (A)-(II), (B)-(III), (C)-(I)
(4) (A)-(II), (B)-(I), (C)-(III)

394. Which of the following is not a resource-imbalance model of Burnout'?

(1) Job Demands-Resources Model
(2) Conservation of Resources Model
(3) Three Dimensional Model
(4) Areas of Worklife Model

395. Which of the following are caused by Burnout?

(A) Concern for clients
(B) Negative Social Behaviour
(C) Physical and Mental Strain

Choose the most appropriate answer from the options given below :

(1) (A) only (2) (A) and (B) only
(3) (B) and (C) only (4) (A) and (C) only

Answer Question No. 396 to 400 on the basis of the following passage :

It is desirable for consumers to be aware of their rights, and to exercise those rights responsibly and intelligently. In these days of audio-video publicity on the public and private media, it is indeed very difficult, if not impossible, to verify the exaggerated or false claims made by producers, manufacturers, distributors and dealers of various goods and services. The all-pervasive, exaggerated and often false claims, made for services and goods, emphasize the imperative need for Consumer Protection Legislation and creation of awareness about it among the general public.

In this connection, there are a number of enactments, in India such as the prevention of Food Adulteration Act, 1954, the Essential Commodities Act, 1955, the Hire Purchases Act, 1972, the Standards Weight and Measure Act, 1976 etc. However, the remedies prescribed there under are time-consuming, inadequate and expensive. As in other areas of Judicial Processes, the offenders are hardly caught, proceeded against and rarely, if ever, got convicted. When violators go scot-free, the victims have no remedy and gets frustrated.

396. Which among the following is a correct statement based on the passage?

(1) Consumers laws are not explained well in India
(2) Indian Judiciary System needs a drastic reform to facilitate consumers' welfare
(3) Indian manufacturers are clever
(4) The Indian Consumers have no remedy and get frustated

397. Which among the following is a correct statement based on the passage?

(1) Consumers in India are aware of their rights

(2) Consumers in India exercise their rights responsibly
(3) Consumers in India are unaware of their rights and hence, they do not exercise them
(4) None of the above could be ascertained on the basis of paragraph given here above

398. Which among the following is a correct statement based on the passage?
(1) The Government of India has enacted sufficient number of laws for protection of consumer interests
(2) The paragraph does not give comprehensive list of laws in favour of consumers
(3) Legal environment for consumers in India is not conducive
(4) Legal environment for consumers in India is conducive

399. Who among the followings could be considered at the center point in the passage?
(1) Consumers
(2) Judicial Process
(3) Manufacturers
(4) Government

400. Which among the following is a correct statement based on the passage?
(1) Producers and manufacturers are sensitive about consumers' rights.
(2) Producers and manufacturers are insensitive about consumers' rights.
(3) Producers and manufacturers are neutral about consumers' rights.
(4) Producers and manufacturers are basically governed by ethics and values.

ANSWERS

1. (3) 2. (3) 3. (1) 4. (3) 5. (2) 6. (4) 7. (4) 8. (1) 9. (2) 10. (1)
11. (4) 12. (2) 13. (1) 14. (4) 15. (3) 16. (3) 17. (2) 18. (3) 19. (2) 20. (1)
21. (1) 22. (3) 23. (3) 24. (1) 25. (4) 26. (2) 27. (2) 28. (4) 29. (2) 30. (4)
31. (1) 32. (3) 33. (4) 34. (3) 35. (4) 36. (1) 37. (2) 38. (2) 39. (3) 40. (3)
41. (2) 42. (1) 43. (3) 44. (3) 45. (2) 46. (1) 47. (1) 48. (4) 49. (3) 50. (3)
51. (1) 52. (1) 53. (3) 54. (2) 55. (1) 56. (3) 57. (2) 58. (4) 59. (4) 60. (4)
61. (2) 62. (2) 63. (3) 64. (2) 65. (1) 66. (3) 67. (3) 68. (4) 69. (2) 70. (2)
71. (1) 72. (1) 73. (1) 74. (2) 75. (3) 76. (4) 77. (3) 78. (2) 79. (2) 80. (3)
81. (3) 82. (1) 83. (1) 84. (4) 85. (2) 86. (2) 87. (2) 88. (4) 89. (4) 90. (3)
91. (3) 92. (1) 93. (3) 94. (1) 95. (1) 96. (4) 97. (2) 98. (4) 99. (1) 100. (4)
101. (2) 102. (2) 103. (4) 104. (3) 105. (1) 106. (2) 107. (1) 108. (1) 109. (4) 110. (1)
111. (3) 112. (3) 113. (2) 114. (3) 115. (1) 116. (2) 117. (2) 118. (4) 119. (3) 120. (3)
121. (4) 122. (1) 123. (3) 124. (3) 125. (1) 126. (1) 127. (4) 128. (4) 129. (1) 130. (3)
131. (2) 132. (1) 133. (4) 134. (1) 135. (1) 136. (2) 137. (2) 138. (4) 139. (2) 140. (2)
141. (3) 142. (3) 143. (1) 144. (3) 145. (4) 146. (2) 147. (4) 148. (3) 149. (2) 150. (2)
151. (3) 152. (4) 153. (2) 154. (2) 155. (2) 156. (1) 157. (3) 158. (3) 159. (2) 160. (3)
161. (3) 162. (4) 163. (3) 164. (1) 165. (3) 166. (3) 167. (4) 168. (4) 169. (2) 170. (4)
171. (1) 172. (2) 173. (4) 174. (1) 175. (2) 176. (4) 177. (3) 178. (2) 179. (4) 180. (2)
181. (1) 182. (2) 183. (3) 184. (2) 185. (3) 186. (3) 187. (3) 188. (1) 189. (4) 190. (1)
191. (2) 192. (1) 193. (3) 194. (3) 195. (3) 196. (3) 197. (3) 198. (1) 199. (3) 200. (1)
201. (2) 202. (4) 203. (3) 204. (3) 205. (3) 206. (4) 207. (2) 208. (2) 209. (1) 210. (1)
211. (4) 212. (3) 213. (1) 214. (3) 215. (1) 216. (2) 217. (1) 218. (1) 219. (1) 220. (1)
221. (3) 222. (3) 223. (4) 224. (3) 225. (3) 226. (1) 227. (1) 228. (4) 229. (1) 230. (1)
231. (3) 232. (3) 233. (2) 234. (3) 235. (4) 236. (4) 237. (2) 238. (3) 239. (2) 240. (4)
241. (2) 242. (1) 243. (3) 244. (2) 245. (2) 246. (3) 247. (2) 248. (3) 249. (1) 250. (4)
251. (1) 252. (3) 253. (2) 254. (3) 255. (2) 256. (4) 257. (4) 258. (3) 259. (4) 260. (3)
261. (1) 262. (2) 263. (1) 264. (3) 265. (4) 266. (1) 267. (3) 268. (1) 269. (2) 270. (4)
271. (1) 272. (1) 273. (2) 274. (4) 275. (1) 276. (3) 277. (1) 278. (2) 279. (1) 280. (4)
281. (2) 282. (3) 283. (4) 284. (3) 285. (2) 286. (3) 287. (2) 288. (1) 289. (4) 290. (1)
291. (3) 292. (3) 293. (4) 294. (4) 295. (3) 296. (1) 297. (1) 298. (1) 299. (4) 300. (1)
301. (2) 302. (3) 303. (2) 304. (4) 305. (4) 306. (3) 307. (2) 308. (3) 309. (3) 310. (2)
311. (1) 312. (1) 313. (2) 314. (4) 315. (3) 316. (2) 317. (1) 318. (4) 319. (2) 320. (1)
321. (1) 322. (2) 323. (3) 324. (4) 325. (1) 326. (2) 327. (2) 328. (3) 329. (3) 330. (2)
331. (1) 332. (4) 333. (4) 334. (4) 335. (3) 336. (1) 337. (3) 338. (3) 339. (4) 340. (3)
341. (3) 342. (4) 343. (3) 344. (4) 345. (1) 346. (2) 347. (4) 348. (4) 349. (4) 350. (2)
351. (2) 352. (1) 353. (3) 354. (3) 355. (3) 356. (3) 357. (1) 358. (2) 359. (4) 360. (4)
361. (2) 362. (2) 363. (3) 364. (1) 365. (4) 366. (2) 367. (1) 368. (1) 369. (3) 370. (4)
371. (2) 372. (2) 373. (1) 374. (1) 375. (1) 376. (2) 377. (1) 378. (4) 379. (2) 380. (1)
381. (3) 382. (1) 383. (4) 384. (4) 385. (4) 386. (2) 387. (1) 388. (1) 389. (1) 390. (1)
391. (1) 392. (4) 393. (3) 394. (3) 395. (3) 396. (4) 397. (4) 398. (3) 399. (1) 400. (2)

MODEL PAPERS (Revised Pattern)

SET–1

Note : This paper contains **hundred** (100) Objective type questions, each question carrying **two** (2) marks. Attempt all of them.

1. The arithmetic mean of 10 items is 50. If each item is increased by 5, then new arithmetic mean would be:

(1) 50 (2) 55
(3) 60 (4) 45

2. Which of the following are NOT sources of secondary data?

(a) Interview (b) Questionnaire
(c) Observation (d) Unpublished thesis
(e) Annual report

Choose the correct option from the following:

(1) (a), (d) and (e) (2) (b), (c) and (d)
(3) (c), (d) and (e) (4) (a), (b) and (c)

3. The attitude based on beliefs, opinion, knowledge or information about the particular event which the employees possesses is:

(1) Behavioral attitude
(2) Positive attitude
(3) Cognitive attitude
(4) Affective attitude

4. **Assertion (A):** Brainstorming technique demands generation of a number of alternatives to a problem.

Reason (R): Participants generate as many alternatives as possible without evaluating them in brainstorming sessions.

In the context of the above two statements, which one of the of the following codes is correct?

(1) Statement (A) is correct and (R) is the correct explanation of (A)
(2) Both (A) and (R) are correct but (R) is not the right explanation of (A)
(3) Statement (A) is correct but (R) is incorrect
(4) Both (A) and (R) are correct

5. Which of the following is the predecessor of the IRDA Act, 1999?

(1) The Insurance Act, 1938
(2) The Life Insurance Corporation Act, 1956
(3) The Marine Insurance Act, 1963
(4) The Pubic Liability Insurance Act, 1991

6. A 'sale and lease back' arrangement is more suitable for a lessee having:

(1) Liquidity crisis (2) Surplus fund
(3) High profit (4) No-profit no-loss

7. **Statement (I):** The arithmetic mean is an all-purpose average.

Statement (II): Median and mode are called positional averages. In the context of the above two statements, which one of the following codes is correct?

(1) Both the statements (I) and (II) are correct
(2) Both the statements (I) and (II) are incorrect
(3) Statement (I) is correct but (II) is incorrect
(4) Statement (II) is correct but (I) is incorrect

8. Match List-I with List-II:

List-I	List-II
(a) Net income approach	(i) Inventory Management
(b) Gordan model	(ii) Capital Budgeting

(c) Internal rate of Return (iii) Capital structure theory

(d) Reorder level (iv) Dividend theory

Choose the correct option from those given below:

(1) (a)-(ii); (b)-(iii); (c)-(iv); (d)-(i)
(2) (a)-(iii); (b)-(iv); (c)-(ii); (d)-(i)
(3) (a)-(iii); (b)-(iv); (c)-(i); (d)-(ii)
(4) (a)-(ii); (b)-(i); (c)-(iv); (d)-(iii)

9. Which of the following types of goodwill is considered to be the best?

(1) Dog goodwill (2) Cat goodwill
(3) Rat goodwill (4) Cow goodwill

10. Which of the following are included in digital payment system?

(a) RTGS (b) Demand draft
(c) NEFT (d) Cheque

Choose the correct option from the following:

(1) (a), (c) and (d) (2) (b) and (d) only
(3) (a) and (c) only (4) (b), (c) and (d)

11. **Assertion (A):** At times, a business may face the situation where it has to shut down its operations.

Reason (R): If the revenue is less than its variable cost, the operation should be closed down.

In the context of the above two statements, which one of the following codes is correct?

(1) (A) is correct but (R) is not correct
(2) (A) and (R) both are correct and (R) is the right explanation of (A)
(3) (A) and (R) both are correct and (R) is not the right explanation of (A)
(4) Both (A) and (R) is incorrect

12. One belt, one road initiative (BRI) is not intended to:

(1) Trade protectionism
(2) Strengthening logistic and supply chain
(3) Improve cost competitiveness
(4) Rebalance trade dominance

13. Following are the events of an organizational culture:

(a) Customer orientation and employee policies
(b) Quality orientation, directing and motivating stylesv
(c) Decision-making, products and services and responsibilities to society
(d) Reaction to competitors and gratitude towards nation
(e) Role ambiguities, trade union and policies

Select the correct sequence for the above events:

(1) (a), (b), (d) and (e)
(2) (a), (c), (d) and (e)
(3) (b), (c), (d) and (e)
(4) (a), (b), (c) and (d)

14. The social environment of the job affects people and is also affected by them and not by management alone, is the main proposition of:

(1) Contingency theory of organization
(2) System theory of organization
(3) Classical theory of organization
(4) Neo-classical theory of organization

15. The channel alternative is NOT to be assessed on the basis of:

(1) Economic criteria
(2) Control criteria
(3) Adaptive criteria
(4) Accumulation criteria

16. 'Motivation-force or level of efforts is not equal to satisfaction and performance' is propounded by

(1) Porter-Lawler model
(2) Vroom's expectancy theory
(3) X and Y theory
(4) Adam's equity theory

17. As per Section 52 of the companies Act, 2013, the balance in the Security Premium Account cannot be utilized for:

(1) Payment of dividend
(2) Writing off discount on issue of shares
(3) Issue of fully paid-up bonus share
(4) Capital losses

18. Match List-I with List-II:

List-I	List-II
(a) Cyber Crime	(i) Intellectual Property Right Act
(b) Doctrine of Caveat Emptor	(ii) Negotiable Instrument Act
(c) Dishonour of Bill	(iii) Sale of Goods Act
(d) Patent and Copyrights	(iv) The Information Technology Act

Choose the correct option from those given below:

(1) (a)-(iii); (b)-(iv); (c)-(i); (d)-(ii)
(2) (a)-(iii); (b)-(ii); (c)-(iv); (d)-(i)
(3) (a)-(iv); (b)-(iii); (c)-(ii); (d)-(i)
(4) (a)-(ii); (b)-(iv); (c)-(iii); (d)-(i)

19. Chalapathi Rao Committee was constituted for restructuring of:
(1) State Financial Corporation in India
(2) Commercial Banks in India
(3) Co-operative Banks in India
(4) Regional Rural Banks in India

20. Product A requires 10 kg of material at the rate of Rs. 5 per kg. The actual consumption of material for the manufacturing of product A comes to 12 kg of material at the rate of Rs. 6 per kg. Direct material cost variance is:
(1) Rs. 22 (favourable)
(2) Rs. 22 (unfavourable)
(3) Rs. 12 (favourable)
(4) Rs. 12 (unfavourable)

21. Which among the following is NOT included in negotiable instrument?
(1) Cheque (2) Demand Draft
(3) Promissory Note (4) Mutual Fund

22. Building long-term mutually satisfying relations with key customers, suppliers, distributors in order to earn and retain their long-term preference and business is known as
(1) Relationship marketing
(2) Social marketing
(3) Niche marketing
(4) Service marketing

23. Credit worthiness score in India ranges between:
(1) 300 to 600 (2) 300 to 900
(3) 500 to 1000 (4) 900 to 1600

24. If two regression coefficients are –0.8 and –0.2, then the value of coefficient of correlation is:
(1) –0.16 (2) –0.50
(3) +0.40 (4) –0.40

25. Excess capacity is NOT noticed in which of the following market conditions?
(1) Monopoly
(2) Monopolistic competition
(3) Oligopoly
(4) Perfect competition

26. New reform in Indian banking system include:
(a) Digitization of bank operations
(b) Banking consolidation
(c) Borrowing from Government
(d) Agency work

Choose the correct option from the following:
(1) (a) and (b) (2) (c) and (d)
(3) (b), (d) and (c) (4) (a), (c) and (d)

27. Match List-I with List-II:

List-I	List-II
(a) 80 TTA	(i) Deduction in respect of payment of interest on loan taken for higher education
(b) 80 CCD	(ii) Deduction in respect of interest on loan taken for residential house property
(c) 80 E	(iii) Deduction in respect of interest on deposits in savings account
(d) 80 EE	(iv) Deduction in respect of contribution to national pension system

Choose the correct option from those given below:
(1) (a)-(iii); (b)-(iv); (c)-(i); (d)-(ii)
(2) (a)-(iii); (b)-(iv); (c)-(ii); (d)-(i)
(3) (a)-(iii); (b)-(i); (c)-(ii); (d)-(iv)
(4) (a)-(i); (b)-(ii); (c)-(iii); (d)-(iv)

28. List out from the given statements the important ethical principles that a business should follow:
(a) To take the necessary action for the development of the concerned industry or business.
(b) Pay taxes and discharge other obligations promptly.
(c) To ensure the best utilization of the human resources.
(d) Refrain from secret kickbacks or pay-offs to customers, suppliers, administrators, etc.
(e) Ensure payment of fair wages and fair treatment of employees.

Choose the correct answer from the options given below:
(1) (c), (d) and (e) (2) (b), (d) and (e)
(3) (a), (b) and (c) (4) (a), (c) and (e)

29. A company issues 10% irredeemable preference shares. The face value per share is Rs. 100, but the issue price is Rs. 95. What is the cost of preference share?

(1) 10.63% (2) 10.73%
(3) 10.83% (4) 10.53%

30. Under which of the following situations, the decision outcome on evaluate of investment opportunities vary under NPV and IRR methods per se?

(a) Time disparity (b) Cost disparity
(c) Life disparity (d) Volume disparity

Choose the correct combination of situations:

(1) (a) and (d) only
(2) (b) and (d) only
(3) (a), (b) and (c) only
(4) (b), (c) and (d) only

31. Which of the following does NOT fall in the ambit of the objectives of Competition Act, 2002?

(1) Encourage Competition
(2) Prevent abuse of dominant position
(3) Prevent monopolistic rights arising out of intellectual property
(4) Regulate mergers and acquisitions

32. Match List-I with List-II:

List-I	List-II
(a) Sec 6 (i)	(i) Agriculture Income
(b) Sec 10AA	(ii) Leave Travel Concession
(c) Sec 10 (i)	(iii) Resident
(d) Sec 10 (5)	(iv) Leave Salary

Choose the correct option from those given below:

(1) (a)-(i); (b)-(iv); (c)-(iii); (d)-(ii)
(2) (a)-(iii); (b)-(iv); (c)-(ii); (d)-(i)
(3) (a)-(iii); (b)-(ii); (c)-(iv); (d)-(i)
(4) (a)-(iii); (b)-(iv); (c)-(i); (d)-(ii)

33. Find the marginal revenue of a firm that sells a product at a price of Rs. 10 and the price elasticity of demand for the product is (–) 2.

(1) Rs. 5 (2) Rs. 10
(3) Rs. 30 (4) Rs. 15

34. When a company distributes its products through a channel structure that includes one or more resellers, it is known as

(1) Direct marketing
(2) Indirect marketing
(3) Integrated marketing
(4) Multi-level marketing

35. After US dollar, which of the following currencies has largest weightage in determining the value of SDR?

(1) Japanese Yen
(2) Chinese Yuan (Renminbi)
(3) Euro
(4) British Pound

36. Organization structure that shows a unique combination of strategy, structure and management process is known as:

(1) Free-form organization
(2) Virtual organization
(3) Network organization
(4) Horizontal organization

37. Redeemable preference shares of Rs. 2,00,000 are to be redeemed at par for which fresh equity shares of Rs. 80,000 are issued at a discount of 10%. What amount should be transferred to Capital Redemption Reserve Account?

(1) Rs. 2,00,000 (2) Rs. 1,20,000
(3) Rs. 1,28,000 (4) Rs. 72,000

38. Match List-I with List-II:

List-I	List-II
(a) Ind AS-16	(i) Income tax
(b) Ind AS-38	(ii) Leasing
(c) Ind AS-17	(iii) Intangible assets
(d) Ind AS-12	(iv) Property, plant and equipment's

Choose the correct option from those given below:

(1) (a)-(iv); (b)-(iii); (c)-(i); (d)-(ii)
(2) (a)-(iv); (b)-(iii); (c)-(ii); (d)-(i)
(3) (a)-(iii); (b)-(ii); (c)-(iv); (d)-(i)
(4) (a)-(iv); (b)-(ii); (c)-(i); (d)-(iii)

39. Deduction u/s 37 (1) is allowed under tax laws for those expenditures which are:

(1) Revenue
(2) Capital
(3) Both revenue and capital
(4) Deferred revenue expenses

40. The current market price of a company's share is Rs. 90 and the expected dividend per share next year is Rs. 4.5. If the dividend is expected to grow at a constant rate of 8%, the shareholder's required rate of return will be:

(1) 8% (2) 5%
(3) 20% (4) 13%

41. Which of the following is NOT a main stage in a customer relationship life cycle?
(1) Customer acquisition
(2) Customer development
(3) Customer satisfaction
(4) Customer annoyance

42. Capital structure and leverage decisions come in the ambit of:
(1) Investment decisions
(2) Distribution decisions
(3) Financing decisions
(4) Dividend decisions

43. Quantitative import restrictions that limit the quantity of a product being imported is called:
(1) Embargo (2) Quota
(3) Trade restraint (4) Import tariff

44. Miller-Orr model is used in the management of:
(1) Inventory (2) Leverage
(3) Receivables (4) Cash

45. SUGAM is also known as:
(1) ITR-1 (2) ITR-2
(3) ITR-3 (4) ITR-4

46. **Statement (I):** t-test and f-test are based on the identical assumptions.
Statement (II): t-test is used for comparison between two groups whereas f-test is used for comparison between more than two groups.
In the context of the above two statements, which one of the following codes is correct?
(1) Both the Statements (I) and (II) are correct
(2) Both the Statements (I) and (II) are incorrect
(3) Statement (I) is correct but (II) is incorrect
(4) Statement (II) is correct but (I) is incorrect

47. Promoting team spirit, harmony and unity within the organization is the principle of
(1) Order (2) Scalar chain
(3) Spirit de corps (4) Equity

48. Match List-I with List-II:

List-I (Objectives of business Firms)	**List-II (Hypothesis)**
(a) Maximization of firms' growth rate	(i) Baumol's hypothesis
(b) Managerial Utility function	(ii) Marris hypothesis
(c) Satisfying behavior	(iii) Williamson hypothesis
(d) Sales Maximization	(iv) Cyert-March hypothesis

Choose the correct option from those given below:
(1) (a)-(ii); (b)-(iii); (c)-(iv); (d)-(i)
(2) (a)-(iii); (b)-(iv); (c)-(i); (d)-(ii)
(3) (a)-(iv); (b)-(i); (c)-(ii); (d)-(iii)
(4) (a)-(i); (b)-(i); (c)-(iii); (d)-(iv)

49. Following are the steps in the activity-based cost allocation:
(a) Identification of the main activities
(b) Collection of cost pool
(c) Determination of the activity cost drivers
(d) Calculation of activity driver rate
(e) Charging the cost of activities to products
Select the correct sequence of the above steps:
(1) (a), (b), (c), (e), (d)
(2) (a), (b), (e), (d), (c)
(3) (a), (b), (c), (d), (e)
(4) (a), (d), (c), (b), (e)

50. Which one of the following analysis is suitable for risk-return analysis in financial decisions?
(1) CAPM analysis (2) SWOT analysis
(3) Capital gearing (4) EVA analysis

51. **Statement (I):** Agreement without consideration is always valid.
Statement (II): All contracts are agreements but all agreements are not contracts.
In the context of the above two statements, which one of the following codes is correct?
(1) Statements (I) and (II) both are correct
(2) Both Statement (I) and (II) re incorrect
(3) Statement (I) is incorrect and Statement (II) is correct
(4) Statement (I) is correct and Statement (II) is incorrect

52. Which of the following is an instance of non-conventional dumping?
(1) Sporadic dumping
(2) Predatory dumping
(3) Reverse dumping
(4) Persistent dumping

53. Shopping goods have which of the following features?

(a) These products are generally durable in nature
(b) Consumers generally compare the goods of various sellers and then buy such goods
(c) Per unit price of these gods is generally high
(d) These goods are regularly and continuously in demand
(e) These goods are sold as a result of aggressive promotional efforts.

Choose the right answer from the options given below:

(1) (c), (d) and (e) (2) (a), (b) and (c)
(3) (b), (c) and (d) (4) (a), (c) and (e)

54. Which among the following is NOT a correct statement?

(1) Hedge funds are not mutual funds.
(2) Hedge funds can be sold to public.
(3) Investors in mutual funds must pay various fees and expenses.
(4) Mutual funds provide economies of scale to investment decisions.

55. In tax laws, donation to approved and notified association for scientific research is allowed as:

(1) 125% of the donation
(2) 100% of the donation
(3) 175% of the donation
(4) 150% of the donation

56. Consumer behavior does NOT consist which of the following activities?

(1) Obtaining (2) Consuming
(3) Disposition (4) Producing

57. Which among the following institutions is NOT a part of World Bank group?

(1) International Development Association (IDA)
(2) International Monetary Fund (IMF)
(3) International Finance Corporation (IFC)
(4) Multilateral Investment Guarantee Agency (MIGA)

58. Currency swap is a method of:

(1) Hedging against foreign exchange risk
(2) speculating in foreign exchange
(3) leverage instrument used by cooperative banks
(4) mode of payment in international trade

59. Study the following information:

Covariance between X and Y series = –17.8
Standard deviation of X series = 6.6
Standard deviation of Y series = 4.2
No. of pairs of observation = 20

The coefficient of correlation is:

(1) –0.642 (2) 0.642
(3) 0.253 (4) –0.253

60. Which of the following are considered non-parametric tests?

(a) Mann-Whitney U test
(b) Kruskal-Wallis test
(c) F-test
(d) T-test
(e) Chi-square test

Choose the correct option from the following:

(1) (a), (b) and (e)
(2) (a), (b) and (c)
(3) (a), (b), (c) and (d)
(4) (a), (b), (c), (d) and (e)

61. SIDBI was set up as a subsidiary of IDBI to:

(1) Takeover the functions of small business financing of IDBI
(2) Takeover the venture capital operation of IDBI
(3) Reconstruct and rehabilitate the sick and closed industrial units financed by IDBI
(4) Facilitate, finance and promote India's foreign trade

62. Which one of the following is NOT the prerequisite of price discrimination?

(1) Firm must have monopoly power
(2) Product have multiple close substitutes and different uses
(3) Markets and separated and segmented
(4) Price elasticity of product must differ in different markets

63. Which one of the following is used for international money transfer?

(1) RTGS (2) NEFT
(3) SWIFT (4) DD

64. In which of the following pricing policies, a firm charges higher initial price for the product and reduces it over time as the demand at higher price is satisfied?

(1) Peak load pricing
(2) Incremental pricing
(3) Skimming
(4) Penetration pricing

65. X is an individual of 55 years of age having gross total income Rs. 3,50,000. What is the tax liability for assessment year 2018-19?

(1) Rs. 5,000 (2) Rs. 2,500

(3) Rs. 2,580 (4) Rs. 3,000

66. Match List-I with List-II:

List-I	List-II
(a) Interbank call market	(i) Money Market
(b) Commercial bills	(ii) Promissory note
(c) Commercial papers	(iii) Short-term Maturity
(d) Treasury bills	(iv) Government Papers

Choose the correct option from those given below:

(1) (a)-(i); (b)-(ii); (c)-(iv); (d)-(iii)

(2) (a)-(iii); (b)-(i); (c)-(ii); (d)-(iv)

(3) (a)-(i); (b)-(iii); (c)-(iv); (d)-(ii)

(4) (a)-(iv); (b)-(iii); (c)-(ii); (d)-(i)

67. Which one is NOT true regarding the Market Stabilization Scheme (MSS)?

(1) It absorbs surplus liquidity of enduring nature arising out of large capital flows.

(2) It absorbs surplus liquidity through sale of short-dated government securities and treasury bills

(3) Mobilized surplus liquidity is held in the MSS account with the Reserve Bank of India

(4) MSS account liquidity can be used for normal government expenditure of capital nature

68. Which of the following committees is related to the investor protection?

(1) Bhagwati Committee

(2) N.K. Mitra Committee

(3) J.R. Verma Committee

(4) L.C. Gupta Committee

69. Which of the most appropriate mode of entry in international business to an enterprise with little experience of international markets?

(1) Acquisition (2) Strategic Alliance

(3) Joint Venture (4) Exporting

70. Amount unutilized in capital gain account scheme for which exemption claimed u/s 54 shall be treated as long-term capital gain, if:

(1) 2 years have expired from the date of transfer

(?) 2 years have expired from the date of deposit

(3) 3 years have expired from the date of transfer

(4) 3 years have expired from the date of deposit

71. Which of the following does NOT come under the definition of 'information' as per the Right to Information Act (RTI Act), 2005?

(1) Logbooks

(2) Data material held in electronic from

(3) File noting

(4) Circular

72. A statement of change in financial position typically would NOT disclose the effect of:

(1) Share capital issued to acquire productive facilities

(2) Dividends on share declared

(3) Cash dividend declared but not yet paid

(4) Purchase and retirement of treasury stock

73. The retail supply chain does NOT include:

(1) Manufactures (2) Retailers

(3) Wholesalers (4) Regulators

74. Peter F. Drucker noted the relationship between selling and marketing in which of the following terms?

(1) Marketing is a subsidiary component of selling

(2) The aim of marketing is to make selling superfluous

(3) The aim of selling is to make marketing superfluous

(4) Selling and marketing are essentially the same thing

75. A firm consumes 90000 units of a certain item of raw material in its production process annually. It costs Rs. 3 per unit, the cost per purchase order is Rs. 300 and the inventory carrying cost is 20% per year. What is the EOQ?

(1) 9470 units (2) 9487 units

(3) 9480 units (4) 9840 units

76. Match List-I with List-II:

List-I

(a) $j = \frac{\bar{X} - M}{\sigma}$ (b) $j = \frac{Q_3 - Q_1 - 2M_e}{Q_3 - Q_1}$

(c) $j = \frac{P_{90} - P_{10} - 2P_{50}}{Q_{90} - Q_{10}}$

List-II

(i) Kelly's coefficient of skewness
(ii) Bowley's measure of Skewness
(iii) Karl Pearson's coefficient of skewness

Choose the correct option from those given below:

(1) (a)-(iii); (b)-(ii); (c)-(i)
(2) (a)-(iii); (b)-(i); (c)-(ii)
(3) (a)-(i); (b)-(ii); (c)-(iii)
(4) (a)-(ii); (b)-(i); (c)-(iii)

77. 'Doctrine of Caveat Emptor' means:

(1) Buyer should make payment well in time
(2) Buyer should be beware of all aspects of buying
(3) Buyer will be responsible for the whole payment
(4) Buyer will not be responsible at any cost

78. For a very large population the ratio between SE $\overline{X}$ and σ is 8:40. The Sample size n will be:

(1) 5 (2) 25
(3) 32 (4) 48

79. Return of income is submitted under which Section of Income-tax Act?

(1) Section 138 (1) (2) Section 142 (1)
(3) Section 139 (1) (4) Section 129 (1)

80. The essence of the law of diminishing returns is:

(1) Inelastic production
(2) Negative marginal production
(3) Declining total production
(4) Declining average production

81. Which among the following is NOT true about BASEL?

(1) Initially it was named as Committee of Banking Regulations and Supervisory Practices (CBRS)
(2) BASEL was established by the Central Bank Governors of fifteen countries
(3) It was established by the end of 1974
(4) Disturbances in international currency and banking markets were responsible for its establishment

82. Following are the information for a house property:

Municipal value	Rs. 4,50,000
Fair rental value	Rs. 5,00,000
Standard rant	Rs. 4,80,000
Actual rent	Rs. 4,20,000

What is the gross annual value of the house property?

(1) Rs. 4,80,000 (2) Rs. 5,00,000
(3) Rs. 4,20,000 (4) Rs. 4,50,000

83. Statement (I): Though closely related, job evaluation and performance appraisal are not the same.

Statement (II): The purpose of job evaluation is to fix the remuneration and other relevant benefits.

In the context of the above two statements, which one of the following codes is correct?

(1) Both the Statements (I) and (II) are correct
(2) Both the Statements (I) and (II) are incorrect
(3) Statement (I) is correct, while Statement (II) is incorrect
(4) Statement (I) is incorrect, while Statement (II) is correct

84. Under which of the following situations, economies of scale exist to the potential and persists?

(1) When firm is too small and too specialized.
(2) When firms' decision to hire inputs do not result in an increase in the input costs.
(3) When firm is too large and overdiversified.
(4) When long-run cost of producing a unit falls as the output increases.

85. Redressal mechanism for consumer disputes under Section 9 of the Consumer Protection Act envisages a:

(1) Single-tier system
(2) Two-tier system
(3) Three-tier system
(4) Open system independent of hierarchy

86. In which of the following commodities, when a consumer spends so much that negative income effect overwhelms the positive substitution effect so as the underlying demand curve is positively sloped?

(1) Inferior goods (2) Superior goods
(3) Giffen goods (4) Normal goods

87. Statement (I): If the tax liability as been reduced within the legal frame work, it is tax planning.

Statement (II): If tax liability has been reduced to get benefit of deduction available under the income tax, it is called tax evasion.

In the context of the above two statements, which one of the following codes is correct?

(1) Both the Statements (I) and (II) are correct
(2) Statement (I) is correct but (II) is incorrect
(3) Both Statements (I) and (II) are incorrect
(4) Statement (II) is correct but (I) is incorrect

88. Which of the following characteristics are related to relationship marketing?
(a) Product feature orientation
(b) Product benefit orientation
(c) Frequent consumer contact
(d) High concern for quality
Choose the correct option from the following:
(1) (b), (c) and (d)
(2) (a), (b) and (c)
(3) (a), (c) and (d)
(4) (a), (b) and (d)

89. Arrange the following in order of their manifestations:
(a) Offer (b) Acceptance
(c) Breach of contract
(d) Contract
Choose the correct option from the following:
(1) (a), (b), (c) and (d)
(2) (a), (b), (d) and (c)
(3) (b), (c), (a) and (d)
(4) (a), (d), (c) and (b)

90. What is the probability that sum of outcomes on pair of dice is equal to 8?
(1) 6/36 (2) 5/36
(3) 4/36 (4) 3/36

91. Match List-I with List-II:
List-I
(a) Fiscal, monetary and industrial policies
(b) Social obligations towards several stakeholders
(c) Consumers, shareholders, suppliers, creditors etc.
(d) Moral principles that defines the right or wrong
List-II
(i) Social responsibilities
(ii) Stakeholders/interest group
(iii) Business ethics
(iv) Economic policies
Choose the correct option from those given below:
(1) (a)-(iii); (b)-(i); (c)-(iv); (d)-(ii)
(2) (a)-(i); (b)-(ii); (c)-(iv); (d)-(iii)
(3) (a)-(ii); (b)-(iv); (c)-(iii); (d)-(i)
(4) (a)-(iv); (b)-(i); (c)-(ii); (d)-(iii)

92. Which of the following commodities is kept outside the purview of GST?
(1) Tobacco products
(2) Petroleum products
(3) Edible oils
(4) Insurance products

93. Which of the following reflects the sum of perceived tangible and intangible benefits and costs to a customer?
(1) Customer satisfaction
(2) Customer delight
(3) Customer value
(4) Customer expectation

94. Which of the following are the rights of a Statutory Auditor?
(a) To receive remuneration
(b) To attend Board of Doctors' Meeting
(c) To attend the General Meeting
(d) To visit the branch office
Choose the correct answer from the following:
(1) (a) and (b)
(2) (a), (b) and (d)
(3) (a), (c) and (d)
(4) (a), (b), (c) and (d)

95. Match List-I with List-II:

List-I (Trade and Finance Institution)	List-II (Headquarters)
(a) WTO	(i) Brussels
(b) IMF	(ii) Geneva
(c) FAO	(iii) Washington
(d) EU	(iv) Rome

Choose the correct option from those given below:
(1) (a)-(ii); (b)-(iii); (c)-(iv); (d)-(i)
(2) (a)-(i); (b)-(ii); (c)-(iii); (d)-(iv)
(3) (a)-(iii); (b)-(ii); (c)-(i); (d)-(iv)
(4) (a)-(i); (b)-(iii); (c)-(ii); (d)-(iv)

96. Which of the following is true about India Policy (Export-Import), 2015-2019?
(a) Doubling the exports (both merchandise and services)
(b) Achieve 3.5% share in global exports
(c) Introduced two new schemes (MEIS and SEIS)
(d) Introduced simplified Aayat-Niryat Form

Choose the correct answer from the following:
(1) (a) and (b) only
(2) (a) and (c) only
(3) (a), (b) and (c) only
(4) All are correct

97. Match List-I with List-II:

List-I (Theories of Profit)	**List-II (Economists)**
(a) Risk theory of profit	(i) Schumpeter
(b) Innovation theory of Profit	(ii) Walker
(c) Rent theory of profit	(iii) Hawley
(d) Dynamic theory of Profit	(iv) Clark

Choose the correct option from those given below:
(1) (a)-(iii); (b)-(iv); (c)-(ii); (d)-(i)
(2) (a)-(iv); (b)-(ii); (c)-(iii); (d)-(i)
(3) (a)-(iii); (b)-(i); (c)-(ii); (d)-(iv)
(4) (a)-(iv); (b)-(i); (c)-(ii); (d)-(iii)

98. Assertion (A): Reserve Bank of India is an important regulatory and administrative authority to execute FEMA provisions.
Reason (R): Being monetary authority and custodian of foreign exchange, Reserve bank of India enjoys requisite expertise of FEMA administration.
In the context of the above two statements, which one of the following options is correct?
(1) Both (A) and (R) are correct and (R) is the right explanation of (A)
(2) Both (A) and (R) are correct but (R) is not the right explanation of (A)
(3) Both (A) and (R) are incorrect
(4) (A) is correct and (R) is not correct

99. Assertion (A): U-shaped long-run average cost curve is based on the assumption that economies of scale prevail at small levels of production and diseconomies of scale prevails at larger level of production.
Reason (R): Decreasing returns to scale arises primarily because as the scale of operation increases, it becomes even more difficult to manage the firm effectively.
In the context of the above two statements, which one of the following codes is correct?
(1) Both (A) and (R) are correct and (R) is the right explanation of (A)
(2) Both (A) and (R) are correct but (R) is not the right explanation of (A)
(3) (A) is correct and (R) is not correct
(4) Both (A) and (R) are incorrect

100. Assertion (A): According to Net Income (NI) approach, capital structure decision is relevant in the valuation of firm.
Reason (R): A firm can change its total value and its overall cost of capital by change in the degree of leverage in its capital structure.
In the context of the above two statements, which one of the following options is correct?
(1) Both (A) and (R) are correct and (R) is the right explanation of (A)
(2) Both (A) and (R) are correct but (R) is not the right explanation of (A)
(3) Both (A) and (R) are incorrect
(4) (A) is correct and (R) is not correct

ANSWERS

1. (2)	**2.** (4)	**3.** (3)	**4.** (1)	**5.** (1)	**6.** (1)	**7.** (4)	**8.** (2)	**9.** (4)	**10.** (3)
11. (2)	**12.** (1)	**13.** (4)	**14.** (4)	**15.** (4)	**16.** (1)	**17.** (1)	**18.** (3)	**19.** (4)	**20.** (2)
21. (4)	**22.** (1)	**23.** (2)	**24.** (3)	**25.** (1)	**26.** (1)	**27.** (1)	**28.** (2)	**29.** (4)	**30.** (3)
31. (3)	**32.** (4)	**33.** (1)	**34.** (2)	**35.** (3)	**36.** (1)	**37.** (3)	**38.** (2)	**39.** (1)	**40.** (4)
41. (4)	**42.** (3)	**43.** (2)	**44.** (4)	**45.** (4)	**46.** (1)	**47.** (3)	**48.** (1)	**49.** (3)	**50.** (1)
51. (3)	**52.** (3)	**53.** (2)	**54.** (2)	**55.** (2)	**56.** (4)	**57.** (2)	**58.** (1)	**59.** (1)	**60.** (1)
61. (1)	**62.** (2)	**63.** (3)	**64.** (3)	**65.** (2)	**66.** (2)	**67.** (4)	**68.** (3)	**69.** (4)	**70.** (3)
71. (3)	**72.** (3)	**73.** (4)	**74.** (2)	**75.** (1)	**76.** (2)	**77.** (2)	**78.** (2)	**79.** (3)	**80.** (4)
81. (2)	**82.** (1)	**83.** (1)	**84.** (4)	**85.** (3)	**86.** (3)	**87.** (2)	**88.** (1)	**89.** (2)	**90.** (2)
91. (4)	**92.** (2)	**93.** (3)	**94.** (3)	**95.** (1)	**96.** (4)	**97.** (3)	**98.** (1)	**99.** (1)	**100.** (1)

SET–2

Note : This paper contains **hundred** (100) Objective type questions, each question carrying **two** (2) marks. Attempt all of them.

1. Which one of the following is NOT correct according Consumer Protection Act?
   (1) District Forum shall consist of a lady social worker
   (2) State Commission shall consist of person who is or has been a Judge of a High Court
   (3) District Forum shall consist of four members
   (4) National Consumer Disputes Redressal Commission shall consist of a person who is or has been a Judge of the Supreme Court

2. According to FEMA, foreign exchange does NOT include
   (1) Deposits payable in any foreign currency
   (2) Bills of exchange drawn in Indian currency but payable in any foreign currency
   (3) Travellers cheques drawn by institutions outside India but payable in Indian currency
   (4) Drafts drawn by banks outside India and payable in foreign currency

3. Which of the following laws affect business organizations?
   (1) Incorporation and Bankruptcy laws
   (2) Environmental Protection Laws
   (3) Occupational Health and Safety Laws
   (4) Competition Laws

4. Which one is odd?
   (1) Economic Policies
   (2) Economic Planning
   (3) Socio - cultural factors
   (4) Macro - economic scenario

5. Which of the following is NOT a method for calculating or ascertaining the amount of purchase consideration?
   (1) Net Payment Method
   (2) Net Assets Method
   (3) Gross Receipts Method
   (4) Share Exchange Method

6. Which of the following sections of Companies Act, 2013 facilitates amalgamation, absorption and reconstruction of companies?
   (1) 319 (2) 320
   (3) 410 (4) 502

7. Which of the following is NOT part of the process of management audit?
   (1) Identification of responsibility center
   (2) Review of performance of each responsibility center
   (3) Review of organizational structure
   (4) Investigating the depreciation method and its application on fixed assets in the company

8. Which of the following statements is NOT correct regarding the duties of an auditor?
   (1) Physical verification of fixed assets is primarily the responsibility of the auditor
   (2) Ownership of fixed assets should be verified by examining the title deed by the auditor
   (3) Auditor should ascertain that the assets are in the possession of the client
   (4) The auditor should satisfy himself that the assets have been valued in the financial statements according to the accounting principles

9. 'Maximization of firm's growth rate subject to managerial and financial constraints' as one of the important alternative objectives of especially large business corporation was pleaded by:
   (1) Milton Friedman (2) Robin Marris
   (3) Cyert and March (4) H.A. Simon

10. On which of the following assumptions, the theory of consumer behaviour on cardinal utility approach is NOT based?
   (1) Consumer is rational
   (2) Limited money income of the consumer
   (3) Maximization of total satisfaction
   (4) Diminishing marginal utility of money

11. The following are the two statements regarding elasticity of demand and its measurement
   Statement I : On every point on the straight line demand curve, the point elasticities are all equal.

Statement II : On every point on the rectangular hyperbola shaped demand curve, the point elasticities are not equal.

Select the correct option for those below:

(1) Both the statements are correct
(2) Both the statements are not correct
(3) Statement I is correct while Statement ll is incorrect
(4) Statement I is incorrect while Statement ll is correct

12. A production function expressed as

$$Q = A[\alpha K^{-\beta} + (1-\alpha)L^{-\beta}]^{\frac{-1}{\beta}}$$

or

$$Q = A[\alpha L^{-\beta} + (1-\alpha)K^{-\beta}]^{\frac{-1}{\beta}}$$

When $A > 0, 0 < \alpha < 1$ and $\beta -1$

Where L = labour, K = Capital and A, α and β are three parameters is called

(1) Constant elasticity substitution function
(2) Variable elasticity substitution function
(3) Leontief - type function
(4) Cobb - Douglas function

13. Under which of the following approaches, the cost of equity is assumed to increase linearly with leverage, i.e., the average cost of capital remains constant with increased use of leverage?

(1) Net Operating Income Approach
(2) Net Income Approach
(3) Traditional Approach
(4) Walter Approach

14. If the risk - free return (Rt) is 6%, Beta value (β) is 1.5 and market rate of return (Km) is 10%, the expected rate of return would be

(1) 15% (2) 12%
(3) 17.5% (4) 16%

15. A company raises Rs. 1,00,000 by issue of 1000, 10% debentures of Rs. 100 each at a discount of 2% redeemable after 10 years. If the corporate tax rate is 40%, what would be the cost of capital?

(1) 6.82% (2) 5.98%
(3) 6.18% (4) 5.5%

16. In which of the following years, the Bretton Woods Agreement was signed by the delegates from 44 nations which led to the establishment of the IMF?

(1) 1940 (2) 1952
(3) 1944 (4) 1957

17. The sum total of the values of two variables 'X' and 'Y' is equal for all the observations. The value of the coefficient of correlation between 'X' and 'Y' is:

(1) + 1 (perfectly positive)
(2) - 1 (perfectly negative)
(3) Zero (No correlation)
(4) > 0 < 1 (Imperfect correlation)

18. Which of the following statements is false?

(1) When value of correlation coefficient is one, the two regression lines coincide
(2) The regression coefficients are independent of the change of origin and of scale
(3) The sign of the regression coefficients are always the same
(4) The square of the coefficient of correlation is called coefficient of determination

19. Which of the following is the non-random method of selecting samples from a given population?

(1) Stratified Sampling
(2) Systematic Sampling
(3) Quota Sampling
(4) Multi - stage Sampling

20. Which of the following is an incomplete experimental research design?

(1) Before and after with control group design
(2) Factorial design
(3) One group before-after design
(4) Latin Square design

21. Which of the following is NOT a factor contributing to MBO program failure?

(1) Altering goals to meet changes in circumstances
(2) Easy goals
(3) Lack of management support
(4) Setting of unrealistically difficult goals

22. Which of the following terms means the tendency of a supervisor to rate a subordinate lower than his performance?

(1) Horns Effect
(2) Halo Effect
(3) Central Tendency
(4) Pointing Tendency

23. The informal group's communication system is called

(1) Group Dynamics (2) Grapevine

(3) Exchange (4) Interaction

24. Quality circle is a type of

(1) Problem- solving team
(2) Cross-functional team
(3) Self-directed team
(4) Project team

25. Choose incorrect statement from the following:

(1) 28 Days T - bills were introduced in 1998
(2) 364 Days T - bills were introduced in 1992
(3) 182 Days T - bills were introduced in 1986
(4) 273 Days T - bills were introduced in 2006

26. 14 Days intermediate T - bills were brought into effect from 1996 - 97 after the abolition of which of the following?

(1) 91 Days T - bills (2) 182 Days T - bills
(3) 273 Days T - bills (4) 364 Days T - bills

27. Which among the following is NOT a correct statement?

(1) The Reserve Bank of India worked as Central Bank of Burma till April 1947
(2) The Reserve Bank of India worked as Central Bank of Pakistan till June 1948
(3) The Reserve Bank of India worked as Central Bank of Bangladesh from January 'I972 to December 1975
(4) The Reserve Bank of India commenced its operations on April 1, 1935

28. National Housing Bank was established in 'I987 as wholly owned subsidiary of which of the following?

(1) State Bank of India
(2) Life Insurance Corporation of India
(3) Reserve Bank of India
(4) Industrial Finance Corporation of India

29. In e-commerce, one of the key design elements of an effective website - community refers to

(1) Its layout and design
(2) The way site enables user to user communication
(3) Site's ability to tailor itself to different users or to allow users to personalize the site
(4) Degree that the site is linked to the other sites

30. Which of the following is NOT true about web marketers?

(1) Web marketers usually try to attract prospects to their site through email, advertisements in newspapers
(2) Use attractions like discounts, gifts and contests
(3) Ask customers to give their personal data mandatorily
(4) Give a lot of publicity to the discount schemes

31. Companies that are becoming skilled in Customer Relationship Management (CRM) focus on:

(1) Understanding the perceived performance and buyer's expectations
(2) Giving benefits to the customers by reducing cost
(3) Developing programs to attract and retain the right customers and meeting the individual needs of valued customers
(4) Giving the quality in features and characteristics of a product or service that bear on its ability to satisfy stated or implied needs

32. In the recent years - the major gain in logistical efficiency have come from which one of the following?

(1) Advances in Information Technology
(2) Reduction in petroleum prices
(3) Fast order processing
(4) Increase in production of commercial vehicles

33. Which of the following is NOT a presumption about a negotiable instrument?

(1) Date (2) Consideration
(3) Stamp
(4) Absolute and good title to the transferee

34. Which one of the following relates to warranty?

(1) It is of vital importance for completion of contract
(2) If there is breach, the aggrieved party can repudiate the contract
(3) It is essential to the main purpose of the contract
(4) In case of breach, the aggrieved party can claim only damages

35. Which of the following is the odd one out?

(1) Specific goods
(2) Un-ascertained goods
(3) Future goods
(4) Ascertained goods

36. The indemnity holder is NOT entitled to

(1) All damages which he may be compelled to pay in any suit in respect of any matter

to which the promise applies
(2) All costs that he may be compelled to bear in defending any such suit
(3) All sums that he may have paid under the terms of any compromise of such suit
(4) Damages for liability incurred which is not absolute

37. ADEN Rules, 1953 is related to which of the following?
(1) Tax exemption
(2) Residential status
(3) Double taxation relief
(4) Assessment of corporate entity

38. What percentage of income from compensation on disaster is exempted from tax liability?
(1) 100% (2) 75%
(3) 50% (4) 25%

39. Which among the following is a correct statement about residential status of a company?
(1) A company can be classified as "not ordinarily resident"
(2) A company can never be classified as "not ordinarily resident"
(3) A company can be classified as "not ordinarily resident" with the permission from Ministry of Finance
(4) A company can be classified as "not ordinarily resident" with the permission from Ministry of Commerce

40. Under which of the following categories, a partner of partnership firm will be assessed?
(1) An individual
(2) HUF
(3) Firm
(4) Body of an individual

41. What are the drivers of globalization?
(a) Population mobility especially of labour
(b) Financial flows
(c) Exporting
(d) Assembly operations
Choose the correct answer from the following
(1) (a) and (d) (2) (b) and (d)
(3) (a) and (b) (4) (c) and (d)

42. Which of the following are part of Corporate Social Responsibility (CSR) to consumers?
(a) Reasonable chances and proper system for accomplishment and promotion
(b) To supply goods at reasonable prices even when there is seller's market
(c) Improving the efficiency of the business operation
(d) To provide an opportunity for being heard and redress genuine grievances
Choose the correct answer from the options given below
(1) (a) and (b) (2) (b) and d)
(3) (b) and (c) (4) (a) and (c)

43. Which among the following are NOT qualified to be appointed as auditor of a company?
(a) An individual who is a Chartered Accountant and holds a Certificate of Practice as per CA Act, 1949
(b) A limited liability partnership firm, which has all partners as Chartered Accountants
(c) Officer or employee of a company who is qualified Chartered Accountant degree holder too
(d) Any Chartered Accountant whose appointment will result in the person being the auditor of more than 10 companies
Choose the most appropriate option:
(1) (a) and (b)
(2) (b), (c) and (d)
(3) (c) and (d)
(4) (a), (b) and (d)

44. Which of the following are the methods of determining cost behaviour?
(a) High and low point method
(b) Least square regression method
(c) Accounting or analytical approach
(d) Non-parametric method
Choose the correct answer from the options given below
(1) (a), (b) and d) (2) (a), (c) and (d)
(3) (b), (c) and (d) (4) (a), (b) and (c)

45. Which two of the following statements are correct?
(a) In the short - run, Δ TFC = 0, therefore Δ TC = Δ WC
(b) if decrease in AFC < increase in AVC, then AC decreases
(c) If decrease in AFC = increase in AVC, AC remains constant
(d) if decrease in AFC > increase in AVC, then AC increases
Choose the correct answer from the options given below
(1) (a) and (c) (2) (b) and (c)
(3) (b) and d) (4) (a) and (d)

46. Which two of the following statements are true?
(a) A simple monopoly firm always earns super normal profit
(b) Sweezy's kinked demand curve model is the best known model explaining relatively more satisfactory behaviour of oligopoly firm for price rigidity
(c) A perfectly competitive firm is price - taker
(d) Firms under monopolistic competition earn only normal profits
Choose the correct option from those below
(1) (a) and (d) (2) (b) and d)
(3) (b) and (c) (4) (a) and (c)

47. Which of the following statements are correct?
(a) Dividend payout ratio refers to that portion of total earnings which is distributed among equity shareholders of the company
(b) ' Bird in hand' argument is given by Gordon's model
(c) MM model suggest that dividend payment is very relevant for value of the firm
(d) Walter's Model suggests that dividend payment does not affect the market price of the share
(1) (a) and (b) (2) (a) and (c)
(3) (b) and (c) (4) (c) and (d)

48. Which of the following statements are true?
(a) Pay - back period method considers all cash flows of a PYOJGCI
(b) Pay - back period method concerns more with the recovery of cost than profitability
(c) Net Present Value represents net addition to the wealth of shareholders
(d) Accounting Rate of Return method incorporates risk as well as time value of money
Choose the
(1) (a) and (b) (2) (a) and (d)
(3) (b) and (c) (4) (b) and d)

49. Which of the following statements are true?
(a) Transaction exposure is inherent in all foreign currencies denominated contractual transactions
(b) Translation exposure relates to the change in accounting income and balance sheet statements caused by change in exchange rate
(c) Economic exposure has an impact on the valuation of a firm
(d) Operating exposure does not have any impact on the firm's future operatlng revenues or future operating costs
Choose the correct option from those below:
(1) (a) and (b) only (2) (b) and (c) only
(3) (b) and d) only (4) (a), (b) and (c) only

50. Which two of the following measures of central tendency are NOT capable of algebraic treatment?
(a) Geometric Mean (b) Median
(c) Arithmetic Mean (d) Mode
(e) Harmonic Mean
Choose the correct answer from the options given below:
(1) (a) and (b) (2) (d) and (e)
(3) (b) and (d) (4) (c) and (e)

51. Which two of the following statements are true?
(a) The sum of the deviations from mean (ignoring algebraic signs) is greater than the sum of the deviations from median (ignoring algebraic signs)
(b) Standard deviation is independent of change of origin and change of scale
(c) In a symmetrical distribution, mean deviation equals 4/5 of standard deviation
(d) In a symmetrical and bell shaped distribution, quartile deviation is 1/3 of standard deviation
Choose the correct answer from the options given below
(1) (b) and d) (2) (a) and (c)
(3) (c) and (d (4) (a) and (b)

52. Which two of the following statements are true?
(a) Skewness studies the flatness or peakedness of the distribution
(b) A positively skewed distribution curve is stretched more to the right than to the left
(c) On the basis of empirical relationship between mean, mode and median for moderately asymmetrical distribution, Karl Pearson's coefficient of skewness can be measured by 3 (Mean - Median) divided by Standard Deviation
(d) If mean < mode, the distribution is positively skewed
Choose the correct option from those below:
(1) (a) and (b) (2) (b) and (c)
(3) (c) and (d) (4) (b) and d)

53. Which of the following types of authorities are found in most organizations?
(a) Division Authority

(b) Line Authority
(c) Staff Authority
(d) Functional Authority

Choose the correct option from those given bellow:
(1) (a) and (b) only
(2) (b) and (c) only
(3) (a), (b) and (c) only
(4) (b), (c) and (d) only

54. The theories that explain the formation of Informal Groups are to include which of the following?
(a) Propinquity Theory
(b) Similarity (or) Balance Theory
(c) Displacement Theory
(d) Need for achievement Theory

Choose the correct option from those given below:
(1) (a) and (d) only
(2) (a) and (b) only
(3) (a), (b) and (c) only
(4) (a), (b), (c) and (d)

55. Functions of a first-level or front line supervisors are to include which of the following?
(a) To determine individual job assignment
(b) To attend to grievances and resolve conflicts
(c) To provide technical knowledge and guidance to workers
(d) To supply strategic information relating to production to management

Choose the correct answer from the options given below
(1) (a) and (b) only (2) (a) and (c) only
(3) (a), (b) and (c) only
(4) All of them - (a), (b), (c), and (d)

56. Non-Banking Financial Companies can be classified as:
(a) Asset Finance Company (AFC)
(b) Investment Company (IC)
(c) Loan Company (LC)
(d) Foreign Trade Company (FTC)

Choose the correct answer from the options given below:
(1) (a), (b) and (c) only
(2) (b), (c) and (d) only
(3) (a), (c) and (d) only
(4) (a), (b) and (d) only

57. Which three of the following types of cyber attacks may occur in the process of mobile banking?
(a) Backdoor attack
(b) Front door attack
(c) Denial of service attack
(d) Direct access attack

Choose the correct option from those given below:
(1) (a), (b) and (c) (2) (b), (c) and (d)
(3) (a),(b) and d) (4) (a), (c) and (d)

58. Michael Porter proposed generic strategies that provide good starting points for strategic thinking. Identify them from the below mentioned strategies
(a) Overall cost leadership
(b) Innovation
(c) Focus
(d) Differentiation

Choose the correct answer from the options given below:
(1) (a) and (b) only
(2) (a),(c) and (d) only
(3) (a), (b) and d) only

59. Given below are two statements, one labelled as Assertion (A) and the other labelled as Reason (R).

Assertion (A): Auto companies and other consumer goods companies offer cash rebates to encourage purchase of the manufacturer's products within a specified period

Reason (R): The same product is priced differently at different times

In the context of the two statements above related to pricing strategy, which one of the following options is correct?
(1) Both (A) and (R) are correct
(2) Both (A) and (R) are not correct
(3) (A) is correct, but (R) is not correct
(4) (A) is not correct, but (R) is correct

60. According to Sale of Goods Act, which two of the following are defined as 'goods :
(a) Moveable property
(b) Growing crops
(c) Actionable claims
(d) Book debt

Choose the
(1) (a) and (d) (2) (b) and (c)
(3) (a) and (b) (4) (d) and (b)

61. Which of the following are true about conditions according to the Sale of Goods Act?
(a) Title (b) Description
(c) Quite possession (d) Encumbrances
Choose the correct answer from the following options
(1) (a) and (d) only
(2) (b) and (c) only
(3) (a), (c) and (d) only
(4) (a) and (b) only

62. Who are the parties to a cheque?
(a) Drawer (b) Payee
(c) Acceptor (d) Holder
Choose the correct answer from the following options:
(1) (a) and (b) only
(2) (a), (b) and d) only
(3) (a) and (c) only
(4) All of these - (a), (b), (c) and (d)

63. Which two of the following are correct about TDS Certificates?
(a) TDS on non-salary payment - Form 16
(b) TDS on salary payment - Form 16 A
(c) TDS on sale of property - Form 16 B
(d) TDS on rent - Form 16 C
Choose the correct option from those given below:
(1) (a) and (b) (2) (c) and (d)
(3) (a) and (d) (4) (b) and (c)

64. Which two of the following are correct in terms of rate of tax deduction at source (TDS)?
(a) Income by way of winning from horse race: @ 30%
(b) Insurance Commission: @ 10%
(c) Rent of Plant & Machinery: @ 5%
(d) Rent of furniture: @ 5%
Choose the correct option from the following:
(1) (a) and (b) (2) (a) and (c)
(3) (a) and (d) (4) (b) and (c)

65. Which two of the following are correct about the due date of issue of the TDS certificate?
(a) Form No 16 - Annual
(b) Form No 16 A - Quarterly
(c) Form No 16 B - Half Yearly
(d) Form No 16 C - Monthly
Choose the correct option from those below:
(1) (a) and (d) (2) (a) and (c)
(3) (a) and (b) (4) (c) and (d)

66. Match List I with List II

List I	List II
(a) Size of the market	(i) Globalization of business
(b) Demographic environment	(ii) Foreign trade policy
(c) Export - oriented units	(iii) Macro-environment
(d) Multinational corporations	(iv) Non-economic environment

Choose the correct option from those given below
(1) (a)–(iv); (b)–(ii); (c)–(iii); (d)–(i)
(2) (a)–(ii); (b)–(iii); (c)–(i); (d)–(iv)
(3) (a)–(iii); (b)–(ii); (c)–(i); (d)–(iv)
(4) (a)–(iii); (b)–(iv); (c)–(ii); (d)–(i)

67. Match List I with List II

List I	List II
(a) Qualified Report	(i) Auditor Duty
(b) Examine Valuation and Disclosure	(ii) Auditor Liabilities
(c) Access to records of Company and its subsidiaries	(iii) Auditor Report
(d) Mis-statement in prospectus in company issue of capital	(iv) Auditor Right

Choose the correct option from those given below:
(1) (a)–(ii); (b)–(i); (c)–(iv); (d)–(iii)
(2) (a)–(iii); (b)–(i); (c)–(iv); (d)–(ii)
(3) (a)–(iii); (b)–(i); (c)–(ii); (d)–(iv)
(4) (a)–(iv); (b)–(ii); (c)–(iii); (d)–(i)

68. Match the following theories of profit with their propounders

Theory	Propounder
(a) Profit as Rent of Ability	(i) F. B. Hawley
(b) Dynamic Theory of Profit	(ii) Joseph A Schumpeter
(c) Risk Theory of Profit	(iii) J. B. Clark
(d) Innovation Theory of Profit	(iv) F. A. Walker

Choose the correct option from those given below:
(1) (a)–(iv); (b)–(ii); (c)–(iii); (d)–(i)

(2) (a)–(i); (b)–(ii); (c)–(iii); (d)–(iv)
(3) (a)–(iv); (b)–(iii); (c)–(i); (d)–(ii)
(4) (a)–(iii); (b)–(i); (c)–(ii); (d)–(iv)

69. Match the following methods of capital budgeting with their respective formula:

Method	**Formula**
(a) ARR method	(i) Present Value of Cash Inflows - Present Value of Cash Outflows
(b) pay back period Method	(ii) Present Value of Case Inflows ÷ Present Value of Cash Outflows
(c) NPV Method	(iii) Average Income + Average Investment
(d) Probability Index	(iv) Investment + Annual Cash Inflows

Choose the correct option from those given below:
(1) (a)–(iii); (b)–(i); (c)–(iv); (d)–(ii)
(2) (a)–(iii); (b)–(iv); (c)–(i); (d)–(ii)
(3) (a)–(i); (b)–(ii); (c)–(iii); (d)–(iv)
(4) (a)–(i); (b)–(iv); (c)–(ii); (d)–(iii)

70. Match the tests with suitable situations of their application for hypothesis-testing:

Test	**Situation**
(a) z-test	(i) Comparing the differences in the mean values of more than two sample groups (Parametric data)
(b) ANOVA	(ii) Testing the significance of the difference between averages of two large sized sample groups (Parametric data)
(c) Chi-Square Test	(iii) Comparing the differences in the mean values of more than two sample groups (Non-parametric data)
(d) Kruskal – Wallis Test	(iv) Testing the significance of the association between two attributes

Choose the correct option from those given below
(1) (a)–(i); (b)–(ii); (c)–(iii); (d)–(iv)
(2) (a)–(ii); (b)–(i); (c)–(iv); (d)–(iii)
(3) (a)–(ii); (b)–(iii); (c)–(i); (d)–(iv)
(4) (a)–(i); (b)–(iv); (c)–(ii); (d)–(iii)

71. Match the 'Category of Compensation' with 'Compensation Plan'

(Category of Compensation)	**(Compensation Plan)**
(a) Pay for time not worked	(i) Savings Plan
(b) Services and Perquisites	(ii) Stock Option
(c) Protection Programme	(iii) Pension
(d) Incentive Pay	(iv) Sick Leave
(e) Deferred Pay	(v) Low Cost Meals

Choose the correct option from those given below
(1) (a)–(iii); (b)–(iv); (c)–(ii); (d)–(i); (e)–(v)
(2) (a)–(iv); (b)–(v); (c)–(iii), (d)–(ii); (e)–(i)
(3) (a)–(iv); (b)–(v); (c)–(i); (d)–(ii); (e)–(iii)
(4) (a)–(iii); (b)–(v); (c)–(i); (d)–(iv); (e)–(ii)

72. Match the following Banking Sector reform committees with their respective purposes:

Committee	**Purpose**
(a) Y.V. Reddy Committee	(i) Revised method of lending in place of cash credit system
(b) Rashid Jilani Committee	(ii) Rationalization of interest rate on small savings
(c) SM Kelkar Committee	(iii) Working capital lending norms
(d) I. T Vaz Committee	(iv) Regional Rural Banks

Choose the correct option from those given below
(1) (a)–(i), (b)–(ii), (c)–(iii); (d)–(iv)
(2) (a)–(ii); (b)–(i); (c)–(iv); (d)–(iii)
(3) (a)–(iv); (b)–(iii); (c)–(ii); (d)–(i)
(4) (a)–(ii); (b)–(iii); (c)–(iv); (d)–(i)

73. Match the modes of communication in marketing and their communication platforms

(Mode of Communication)	**(Communication Platform)**
(a) Advertising	(i) Blogs
(b) Sales Promotion	(ii) Brochures & Booklets
(c) Word of mouth marketing	(iii) Sales meetings

(d) Personal selling (iv) Contests

Choose the correct option

(1) (a)–(ii); (b)–(iii); (c)–(iv); (d)–(i)

(2) (a)–(ii); (b)–(iv); (c)–(i); (d)–(iii)

(3) (a)–(iv); (b)–(iii); (c)–(ii); (d)–(i)

(4) (a)–(iv); (b)–(iii); (c)–(i); (d)–(ii)

74. Match List I with List II

List I	List II
(a) Transfer of ownership	(i) Negotiable Instrument
(b) Sale of goodwill after dissolution	(ii) Contract of sale of goods
(c) Buy - back of securities firm	(iii) Dissolution of partnership
(d) Promissory Note	(iv) Share capital of company

Choose the correct option from those given below

(1) (a)–(ii); (b)–(iii); (c)–(iv); (d)–(i)

(2) (a)–(iii); (b)–(iv); (c)–(ii); (d)–(i)

(3) (a)–(iv); (b)–(ii); (c)–(i); (d)–(iii)

(4) (a)–(i); (b)–(ii); (c)–(iii); (d)–(iv)

75. Match the following countries with the types of Double Taxation Avoidance Agreement signed by India with them:

Country	Type of Agreement
(a) Austria	(i) Limited Agreement
(b) Bahamas	(ii) Comprehensive Agreements
(c) Lebanon	(iii) Comprehensive Agreements/ Limited Multilateral Agreement
(d) Sri Lanka	(iv) Tax Information Exchange Agreement

Choose the correct option from those given below:

(1) (a)–(iv), (b)–(ii); (c)–(i); (d)–(iii)

(2) (a)–(ii); (b)–(iv); (c)–(i); (d)–(iii)

(3) (a)–(ii); (b)–(iv); (c)–(iii); (d)–(i)

(4) (a)–(i); (b)–(ii); (c)–(iii); (d)–(iv)

76. Which two of the following are the function of WTO

(a) To facilitate the implementation, administration and operation of trade agreement

(b) To carry out periodic reviews of the trade policies of its member countries

(c) To assist in the establishment of a multilateral system of payments

(d) To promote international monetary cooperation

Choose the correct option from the following:

(1) (a) and (d) (2) (b) and (c)

(3) (c) and (d) (4) (a) and (b)

77. Following are the events which generally happen in the life of a public limited company

(a) Public issue of shares (IPO)

(b) Firm Incorporation

(c) Preliminary expenditures

(d) Issue of equity shares to promoters of the company

Choose the correct sequence (chronological order) of the events from the options given below:

(1) (a) → (b) → (c) → (d)

(2) (b) → (c) → (d) → (a)

(3) (c) → (b) → (a) → (d)

(4) (c) → (b) → (d) → (a)

78. In the case consumers equilibrium to be explained through an ordinal approach, when there are two commodities with their prices given and with limited income of the consumer, the following information is required

(a) Price line/budget line

(b) Indifference map

(c) Point of tangency between IC and budget line

(d) Equality of the slopes of IC and budget line

Arrange the information required in the correct sequence and choose the right option from those below

(1) (b) → (d) → (a) → (c)

(2) (b) → (a) → (d) → (c)

(3) (a) → (d) → (b) → (c)

(4) (a) → (b) → (c) → (d)

79. Which one of the following is the correct sequence of various stages of operating cycle of a manufacturing company?

(1) Raw material conversion period, work-in-progress conversion period, Finished goods conversion period, Receivables conversion period

(2) Raw material conversion period, work-in-progress conversion period, Creditors payment period, Receivables conversion period

(3) Creditors payment period, Raw material conversion period, Receivables conversion period, work-in- progress conversion period

(4) Raw material conversion period, Finished goods conversion period, work-in-progress conversion period, Receivables conversion period

80. Which measure assesses the volatility of an investment compared to the overall market?

(1) Beta (2) Alpha

(3) Standard Deviation (4) Sharpe Ratio

81. What is the typical sequence in which the following selection devices are used by the company?

(a) Reference checks

(b) Physical examination

(c) Application Blank

(d) Hire

(e) Conditional Offers

(f) More interviews

(g) Screening interviews

(h) Tests

Choose the correct answer from the options given below

(1) (c) → (g) → (h) → (f) → (a) → (e) → (b) → (d)

(2) (d) → (g) → (f) → (h) → (a) → (e) → (b) → (c)

(3) (c) → (h) → (g) → (a) → (f) → (e) → (b) → (d)

(4) (d) → (g) → (h) → (f) → (a) → (e) → (b) → (d)

82. Arrange the following financial institutions in ascending order of their year of establishment:

(a) National Housing Bank

(b) Export - Import Bank of India

(c) NABARD

(d) Unit Trust of India

Choose the correct option from those below

(1) (b) → (d) → (c) → (a)

(2) (d) → (b) → (a) → (c)

(3) (d) → (b) → (c) → (a)

(4) (d) → (c) → (b) → (a)

83. Market logistic planning has the following four steps. Arrange the steps in correct sequence

(a) Develop operational excellence in sales forecasting, warehouse management, transportation and material management

(b) Select the best channel design and network strategy for reaching the customers

(c) Implement the solution with the best information systems, equipment, policies and procedures

(d) Decide on company's value proposition to its customers

Select the correct option from those below

(1) (a) → (b) → (c) → (d)

(2) (d) → (b) → (a) → (c)

(3) (d) → (b) → (c) → (a)

(4) (d) → (c) → (b) → (a)

84. Which one of the following is a void contract?

(1) Unilateral contract

(2) A contract which ceases to be enforceable by law

(3) Implied contract

(4) Express contract

85. Arrange the steps to e-filing of Income Tax Return in correct sequence:

(a) Register yourself

(b) Verify ITR V

(c) Select the requisite form

(d) Fill form and upload

Choose the correct option from those below:

(1) (a) → (c) → (d) → (b)

(2) (a) → (b) → (c) → (d)

(3) (a) → (b) → (d) → (c)

(4) (c) → (a) → (d) → (b)

86. Which of the following is a macroeconomic indicator?

(1) Consumer price index (CPI)

(2) Price elasticity of demand

(3) Marginal utility

(4) Production cost

87. What is a common motive for FDI known as the "efficiency-seeking" motive?

(1) Access to a large consumer base

(2) Cost differences in production

(3) Political stability

(4) Technology transfer

88. Which regulatory body oversees the functioning of cooperative banks in India?

(1) Reserve Bank of India (RBI)

(2) National Bank for Agriculture and Rural Development (NABARD)

(3) Securities and Exchange Board of India (SEBI)

(4) Ministry of Finance

88. What is the Weighted Average Cost of Capital (WACC)?
   (1) The average cost of all sources of capital, weighted by their proportion in the capital structure
   (2) The cost of capital for debt financing only
   (3) The cost of equity financing only
   (4) The average cost of retained earnings

90. Which of the following is not a requirement for a valid offer under the Indian Contract Act, 1872?
   (1) The offer must be communicated to the offeree
   (2) The offer must be made with a view to obtaining the acceptance of the offeree
   (3) The offer must be made in writing
   (4) The terms of the offer must be certain or capable of being made certain

Read the passage carefully and answer the questions that follow:

Life Insurance in its modern form came to India from England in the year 1818. The Oriental Life Insurance Company started by Europeans in Calcutta was the first life insurance company on Indian soil. All the insurance companies established during that period were brought up with the purpose of looking after the needs of the European community and Indian natives were not being insured by these companies. However, later with the efforts of eminent people like Babu Muttylal Seal, foreign insurance companies started insuring Indian lives too. But Indian lives were being treated as sub standard lives and heavy extra premium were being charged upon them. The Bombay Mutual Life Assurance Society heralded the birth of the first Indian life insurance company in the year 1870 and covered Indian lives at normal rates. Starting as an Indian enterprise with highly patriotic motives, insurance companies came into existence to carry the message of insurance and social security through insurance to various sectors of society. In 1907, the Hindustan Co-operative Insurance Company took birth in one of the rooms of 'The Jorsanko', house of the great poet Rabindranath Tagore in Calcutta. The Indian Mercantile, General Assurance and Swadeshi Life (later Bombay Life) were some of the companies established during the same period. Prior to 1912, India had no legislation to regulate the insurance business. In the year 1912, Life Insurance Companies Act and Provident Fund Act were passed. The Life Insurance Companies Act, 1912 made it necessary that the premium rate tables and periodical valuations of companies should be certified by an actuary. But the Act discriminated between foreign and Indian Companies on many accounts, putting Indian Companies at a disadvantage.

Sub questions

91. The paragraph is about which of the following?
   (1) Genesis of insurance in India
   (2) Struggle of insurance business
   (3) Conflict of insurance business
   (4) Complications of insurance business

92. Identify the correct statement from the following
   (1) Initially, insurance companies used to discriminate Indian and European clients
   (2) There was no discrimination in Indian and European clients by the insurance companies initially
   (3) Indian clients were charged lower premium by the insurance companies in the beginning
   (4) Indian insurance companies charged higher premium to Europeans at a later stage

93. Which one among the following grew along with insurance business in India?
   (1) Pension Fund (2) Provident Fund
   (3) Gratuity (4) Arbitrage

94. The insurance business in India was started first by which one of the following?
   (1) Americans (2) Indian merchants
   (3) European (4) Afro-Indians

95. Which among the following was later renamed as Bombay Life?
   (1) The Indian Mercantile General Assurance
   (2) The Oriental Life Insurance Company
   (3) National Insurance
   (4) Swadeshi Life

Question Numbers : (96 to 100).

Question Label : Comprehension

Read the given passage carefully and answer the questions that follow:

Companies often define themselves in terms of products: They are in the "auto business" or the "clothing business". 'Market definitions of a business, however, describe the business as a customer - satisfying process. Products are transient, basic needs and customer groups endure forever. Transportation is a need: the horse and carriage, automobile, railroad, airline, ship and truck are products that meet the need. Viewing business in terms of customers can suggest additional growth opportunities. There exists a difference between a target market definition and a strategic market definition. To define its mission, a company should address Peter Drucker's classic question: What is our business?

Sub questions

96. Pepsi could define its 'target market' as:
(1) Everyone who drinks carbonated soft drinks and are competitors
(2) Anyone who drinks liquid
(3) Everyone who drinks non-milk drinks
(4) Anyone who drinks competitor's drinks

97. Which of the following is the correct market definition of 'BPCL'?
(1) We distribute oil products
(2) We are the largest oil supply company in India
(3) We supply energy
(4) Bharat's own oil distribution company

98. Which of the following is the correct product definition of 'Blue Star'?
(1) We provide climate control in homes and offices
(2) We supply air conditioners
(3) We make air cooling systems
(4) We make air conditioners

99. Which of the following is NOT a major characteristic of a good mission statement?
(1) They have very limited words
(2) They focus on a limited number of goals
(3) They stress the company's major competitive spheres in which company will operate
(4) They have a long term view

100. Which of the following is the correct combination Product Definition and Market Definition of Xerox Company?
(1) Product Definition - We sell photocopies Market Definition - We help improve office efficiency
(2) Product Definition - We make photo machines Market Definition - We improve copy speeds
(3) Product Definition - We sell copying equipment Market Definition - We make office more efficient
(4) Product Dentition - We make copying equipment Market Definition - We help improve office productivity

ANSWERS

1. (3)	**2.** (3)	**3.** (1)	**4.** (3)	**5.** (3)	**6.** (4)	**7.** (4)	**8.** (1)	**9.** (2)	**10.** (4)
11. (4)	**12.** (1)	**13.** (1)	**14.** (2)	**15.** (1)	**16.** (3)	**17.** (2)	**18.** (2)	**19.** (3)	**20.** (3)
21. (1)	**22.** (1)	**23.** (2)	**24.** (1)	**25.** (4)	**26.** (1)	**27.** (3)	**28.** (3)	**29.** (2)	**30.** (3)
31. (3)	**32.** (1)	**33.** (3)	**34.** (4)	**35.** (1)	**36.** (4)	**37.** (3)	**38.** (1)	**39.** (2)	**40.** (1)
41. (3)	**42.** (2)	**43.** (3)	**44.** (4)	**45.** (1)	**46.** (3)	**47.** (1)	**48.** (3)	**49.** (4)	**50.** (3)
51. (3)	**52.** (2)	**53.** (4)	**54.** (3)	**55.** (3)	**56.** (1)	**57.** (4)	**58.** (2)	**59.** (1)	**60.** (3)
61. (4)	**62.** (2)	**63.** (2)	**64.** (1)	**65.** (3)	**66.** (4)	**67.** (2)	**68.** (3)	**69.** (2)	**70.** (2)
71. (2)	**72.** (4)	**73.** (2)	**74.** (1)	**75.** (2)	**76.** (4)	**77.** (4)	**78.** (4)	**79.** (1)	**80.** (1)
81. (1)	**82.** (4)	**83.** (2)	**84.** (2)	**85.** (1)	**86.** (1)	**87.** (2)	**88.** (1)	**89.** (1)	**90.** (3)
91. (1)	**92.** (1)	**93.** (2)	**94.** (3)	**95.** (4)	**96.** (1)	**97.** (3)	**98.** (2)	**99.** (1)	**100.** (4)

PREVIOUS YEARS' PAPERS

NOVEMBER, 2021

COMMERCE

Paper-II

Note : This paper contains **hundred (100)** objective type questions of **two (2)** marks each. **All** questions are **compulsory**.

1. Bretton Woods resolutions led to the formation of

(1) WTO (2) GATT
(3) UNCTAD (4) IMF

2. The mode of joint venturing in international business that allows a company to conduct business in another country whose laws discourage foreign ownership is known as

(1) International Franchising
(2) Licensing
(3) Contract manufacturing
(4) Joint ownership

3. Fill in the blanks

The collapse of Eastern Europe in ______ and USSR in ______ lead to emergence of the transitory economies.

(1) 1989, 1991 (2) 1988, 1995
(3) 1997, 1991 (4) 1980, 1987

4. The resource seeking FDI moves to a country where

(1) Per capita income and size of the market are large
(2) Technologies are available to improve productivity
(3) Raw materials and manpower are in abundance
(4) Financial resources help MNCs improve their efficiency

5. 'A', 'B' and 'C' are partners sharing profits in the ratio of 3:2:1. 'D' is admitted for $1/6^{th}$ share and 'C' should retain his original share.

The sacrificing ratio of A and (B) will be:

(1) 1 : 2/1 : 2 (2) 2 : 3/2 : 3
(3) 3 : 2/3 : 2 (4) 2 : 1/2 : 1

6. From the following information about a firm, what will be the contribution to sales (c/s) ratio and the profit?

Sales = ₹ 100,000
Fixed Cost = ₹ 20,000
Break-even Point = ₹ 40,000

(1) C/S = 25% and Profit = ₹ 60,000
(2) C/S = 50% and Profit = ₹ 60,000
(3) C/S = 50% and Profit = ₹ 30,000
(4) C/S = 60% and Profit = ₹ 30,000

7. Which one of the following is a structured review of the systems and procedures of an organisation in order to evaluate whether they are being conducted efficiently and effectively?

(1) Financial audit (2) Safety audit
(3) Management audit (4) Cost audit

8. Fill in the blanks

For a holding company, all pre-acquisition profits/losses of the subsidiary company are ____________, while all postacquisition profits/losses of the subsidiary company are ________.

(1) revenue profits/losses, capital profits/losses
(2) capital profits, capital losses
(3) revenue profits, revenue losses
(4) capital profits/losses, revenue profit/losses

9. When the sum of exponents exceeds one (a + b > 1) in the Cobb - Douglas production function, it causes which one of the following?

(1) Constant returns to scale
(2) Increasing returns to scale
(3) Decreasing returns to scale
(4) Variable returns to scale

10. A price ceiling below the equilibrium price often leads to a shortage of the commodity and possibly

(1) Commodity glut
(2) Black marketing
(3) Price manipulations
(4) Increased consumption

11. The cross-price elasticity of demand for complementary commodities is
(1) Positive (2) Zero
(3) Greater than one (4) Negative

12. Which market form leads to more technological change and product improvements than alternative forms of market structure?
(1) Perfect competition
(2) Monopoly
(3) Monopolistic competition
(4) Oligopoly

13. The practice of delaying receipts from the foreign currency designated receivables whose currencies are likely to appreciate and delaying foreign currency designated payables whose currencies are likely to depreciate is known as
(1) Leading (2) Netting
(3) Lagging (4) Risk hedging

14. Companies strive to stockpile internally generated cash. Such a cash reserve is called
(1) Margin of safety
(2) Financial float
(3) Reserve float
(4) Financial slack

15. What is the sustainable growth rate of the company that enjoys return on equity = 30 percent and a dividend payout ratio of 40 percent?
(1) 12 per cent (2) 18 per cent
(3) 30 per cent (4) 40 per cent

16. Which one of the following is considered a necessary precondition by Richard Roll for markets to become efficient?
(1) Traders who make a living by 'beating the market' through trading
(2) Free access to and flow of information
(3) Costless trading
(4) Prices approximate a random walk

17. An economy grows at 5%, 12%, and 7% over the last three years. The average annual increase over this period would be
(1) Equal to 8% (2) At least 8%
(3) Less than 8% (4) 8% or less

18. Which one of the following is CORRECT?
(1) $PE = \frac{.6475(1-r^2)}{\sqrt{n}}$
(2) $PE = \frac{.6745(1-r^2)}{\sqrt{n}}$
(3) $PE = \frac{.6475\sqrt{n}}{(1-r^2)}$
(4) $PE = \frac{.6475(1-r^2)}{n}$

19. If each value in a given set is increased by K, it will
(1) Increase the Pearson's coefficient of skewness value
(2) No change in Pearson's coefficient of skewness value
(3) No change in Bowley's coefficient of skewness value
(4) Reduce the value of Pearson's coefficient of skewness

20. A certain bivariate data b_{yx} and b_{xy} have been calculated which is equal to 2.4 and 0.4, respectively. If the value of the x series are all multiplied by 5 and all values of y series are divided by 2, how would it affect the value of the two coefficients?
(1) Both the coefficients remains unchanged
(2) Both the coefficients get multiplied so b_{yx} = 6.0 and b_{xy} = 4.0
(3) The coefficients are revised by b_{yx} = 0.24 and b_{xy} = 4.0
(4) The coefficients are revised by b_{yx} = 24 and b_{xy} = 0.04

21. Which one of the following training methods is most suitable for developing problem-solving skills?
(1) Lecture (2) Case study
(3) Role playing (4) Sensitivity training

22. Which one of the following is the most suitable coping mechanism if 'fear of overload' is the source of resistance to change?
(1) Participation and involvement
(2) Support of resources
(3) Role redefinition and re-orientation
(4) Role clarity and definition

23. Which one of the following is NOT true for the functional organization?
(1) It is based on the principle of unity of command
(2) The discipline tends to become loose
(3) It is useful for large-scale business
(4) Functional managers are specialists in their respective areas

24. According to Plutchik, which one of the following is NOT a secondary emotion?

(1) Hostility (2) Insecurity
(3) Distrust (4) Fear

25. In Banking Technologies, Star Topology involves:

(1) Each node is joined to the central node by a separate medium
(2) Devices are connected in a close loop
(3) Information is passed from one node to another in series
(4) Devices on the network are connected to a single continuous cable

26. Which one of the following statement is FALSE regarding transactions of Internet Banking?

(1) Statement of account is for a specific period
(2) Withdrawal of cash anywhere in India
(3) Balance inquiry
(4) Transfer of funds from one account to another account

27. Which of the following is NOT the feature of the Indian capital market?

(1) Government rules and regulations
(2) Utilises intermediaries
(3) Link between savers and investment opportunities
(4) Co-promotes state-level venture funds

28. Which one of the following statements are the advantages of the Decision Support System (DSS)?

(1) Unaware of Assumptions
(2) Generates new evidence in support of a decision
(3) Difficulty in quantifying all the data
(4) System design failure

29. Which one of the following generations is more pragmatic and individualistic?

(1) Silent generation (2) Baby Boomers
(3) Gen X (4) Gen Y

30. Which one of the following vehicles is used when traffic building is the consumer promotion objective?

(1) Discount sales (2) Special events
(3) Coupons (4) Catalogue offers

31. In which one of the following services price sensitivity is high?

(1) Airlines (2) Car rentals
(3) Sea Transport (4) Retailing

32. With reference to product hierarchy, life insurance is an example of:

(1) Product family (2) Product class
(3) Product line (4) Product type

33. In which of the following cases, the Doctrine of Supervening impossibility will apply?

(1) Difficulty in performance
(2) Commercial Impossibility
(3) Impossibility known to the parties at the time of making of the contract
(4) Strikes, Locks-outs, and civil disturbances

34. Which one of the following State Taxes have NOT been replaced by GST?

(1) Taxes on lotteries, betting, and gambling
(2) Special additional duty of customs
(3) Purchase Tax
(4) Luxury Tax

35. Which one of the following statements are TRUE about the contract of Bailment?

(1) Hiring of bank locker is a contract of Bailment
(2) Bailee has a right of the general lien
(3) Money deposited in fixed deposit with a bank is a contract of Bailment
(4) A contract of Bailment does not result when a person leaves some goods with his friend for being looked after

36. Which one of the following is NOT true regarding input tax credit to avoid cascading effect?

(1) Input Tax credits of SGST can be utilised for payment of SGST first and balance for payment of IGST on outward supply
(2) Input Tax credit of UTGST can be utilised for payment of UTGST first and balance for payment of IGST on outward supply
(3) Input Tax credit of SGST/UTGST can be utilised for payment of CGST
(4) Input Tax credit of CGST can be utilised for payment of CGST first and balance for payment of IGST on outward supply

37. Tax Audit is compulsory in case a person is carrying on a business whose gross turn over/receipts exceeds:

(1) Rs. 40 lakh (2) Rs. 50 lakh
(3) Rs. 1 crore (4) Rs. 60 lakh

38. The due date of the first instalment of advance tax paid by an assessee other than the company is:
(1) 15th April (2) 15th June
(3) 15th September (4) 15th December

39. Section 80GGC of Income tax is:
(1) Deduction in respect of contribution given by any person to political parties
(2) Deduction in respect of contribution given by any company to political parties
(3) Deduction in respect of certain donation for scientific research
(4) Deduction in respect of rent paid

40. The partial integration of agricultural with non-agricultural income is done in case of:
(1) Firm (2) Company
(3) Co-operative society
(4) AOP/BOI

41. Buoyancy is a basic principle of taxation which means:
(A) The system should be such that cost of collection is least
(B) Tax obligation of the payers should be well determined
(C) The system should be such that the tax revenue has the inherent tendency to increase as the economy grows
(D) Tax base should be fairly diversified so that the tax burden is widely spread

Choose the correct answer from the options given below :
(1) (A) only (2) (A) and (B) only
(3) (C) only (4) (D) only

42. The term current account transaction is defined as a transaction other than a capital account transaction and without prejudice to the generality of the foregoing, such transaction includes:
(A) Overseas direct investment, (ODIs) from India
(B) Payment due as interest on loans and as net income from investments
(C) Remittances for living expenses of parents, spouse, and children residing abroad
(D) Borrowing or lending in foreign exchange and in Indian rupees

Choose the correct answer from the options given below :
(1) (A) and (D) only (2) (A) and (B) only
(3) (B) and (C) only (4) (D) only

43. The technique of marginal costing is based upon which of the following assumptions:
(A) Fixed cost will tend to remain constant or unchanged for the entire volume of production
(B) Variable cost remains constant per unit of output irrespective of the level of output
(C) There will not be any change in pricing policy due to change in volume, competition, etc.
(D) Operating efficiency of the firm may increase or decrease

Choose the correct answer from the options given below :
(1) (A) and (B) only
(2) (A), (B) and (D) only
(3) (A), (B), (C) and (D)
(4) (A), (B), and (C) only

44. The sources of the Indian GAAP (IGAAP) include:
(A) Indian Companies Act, 2013
(B) Notifications issued by Ministry of Finance
(C) Accounting standards
(D) ICAI's pronouncements

Choose the correct answer from the options given below :
(1) (A) and (C) only
(2) (B), (C), and (D) only
(3) (A), (B), and (C) only
(4) (A), (C), and (D) only

45. Which among the following are generally accepted methods of accounting for price level changes?
(A) Replacement Cost Method
(B) Current Purchasing Power Method
(C) Opportunity Cost Method
(D) Current Cost Accounting Method
(E) Standard Cost Method

Choose the correct answer from the options given below :
(1) (A) and (C) only (2) (A), (B) and (C) only
(3) (B) and (D) only (4) (C), (D) and (E) only

46. Identify three conditions that a firm must meet to practice price discrimination:
(A) The firm must have some control over the price and the product
(B) The firm must operate in the growth phase of its product life cycle

(C) The markets in which products are sold must be separable
(D) Price elasticity of demand for the product must differ
(E) The firm operates its plant at full capacity

Choose the correct answer from the options given below :
(1) (A), (B) and (C) only
(2) (A), (C) and (D) only
(3) (B), (D) and (E) only
(4) (B), (C) and (D) only

47. A U-shaped long-run average cost curve is based on the assumptions that
(A) Economies of scale prevails at small levels of output
(B) Diseconomies of scale prevails at larger levels of output
(C) Benefits of the division of labour and specialisation accrue more at the lower scale of production
(D) Managerial inefficiencies are prone to a higher scale of operations

Choose the correct answer from the options given below :
(1) (A), (B) and (C) only
(2) (B), (C) and (D) only
(3) (A), (C), and (D) only
(4) (A), (B), (C) and (D)

48. Cash flows are presumably reinvested in capital budgeting decisions at
(A) Discount rate (B) Market rate
(C) Cost of capital (D) Riskless rate
(E) Internal rate of return

Choose the correct answer from the options given below :
(1) (A), (C) and (E) only
(2) (B), (C) and (D) only
(3) (C), (D) and (E) only
(4) (A), (C) and (D) only

49. The basic premise of the MM-approach is based on which of the following assumptions?
(A) Asymmetrical information
(B) Efficient capital markets
(C) Investor rationality
(D) Diverse business risk profile
(E) 100% dividend payout ratio

Choose the correct answer from the options given below :
(1) (A), (B) and (C) only
(2) (C), (D), and (E) only
(3) (A), (C) and (E) only
(4) (B), (C) and (E) only

50. Identify the components of the credit policy of a business firm from the following:
(A) Collection policy (B) Factoring
(C) Credit rating (D) Credit analysis
(E) Terms of sale

Choose the correct answer from the options given below :
(1) (B), (C) and (D) only
(2) (A), (D) and (E) only
(3) (C), (D) and (E) only
(4) (A), (C) and (D) only

51. The values in one of the series in a bivariate data set are multiplied by a constant K, which of the following would change as a result of this?
(A) Karl Pearson's coefficient of correlation
(B) Standard deviation
(C) Covariance between the variables
(D) Rank correlation coefficient

Choose the correct answer from the options given below :
(1) (A), (B) and (C) only
(2) (B) and (C) only
(3) (A), and (D) only
(4) (A), (B), and (D) only

52. Which of the following statements are CORRECT?
(A) The critical value of Z for two tailed test with $\alpha = 0.5$ is 1.96
(B) The critical value of Z for a two tailed test with $\alpha = 0.01$ is 2.575
(C) The critical value of Z for one tailed test with $\alpha = 0.05$ is 1.96
(D) The critical value of Z for a left-tailed test with $\alpha = 0.01$ is -2.33

Choose the correct answer from the options given below :
(1) (A), (B) and (C) only
(2) (B), (C) and (D) only
(3) (A), (B) and (D) only
(4) (A) and (B) only

53. Incentives schemes where earnings differ at different levels of output are:

(A) Gantt Task System (B) Halsey Plan
(C) Rowan Plan (D) Bedaux Plan
(E) Emerson's Efficiency Plan
Choose the correct answer from the options given below :
(1) (B) and (E) only
(2) (A), (C) and (E) only
(3) (A), (C) and (D) only
(4) (A) and (E) only

54. The functions of lower management are:
(A) Executing plans in accordance with the policies and directives of the top management
(B) Maintaining discipline among the workers
(C) Selecting suitable operative and supervisory personnel
(D) Providing training to the workers
(E) Maintaining good human relations
Choose the correct answer from the options given below :
(1) (A) and (B) only
(2) (C) and (D) only
(3) (B), (D) and (E) only
(4) (A), (B) and (C) only

55. Which of the following are the limitations in the creation of credit of commercial banks?
(A) The amount of cash that commercial banks possess
(B) Supply of collateral security
(C) Monetary policy of the central bank
(D) Allied deposits scheme
(E) Deposits linked with special benefits
Choose the correct answer from the options given below :
(1) (A), (D) and (E) only
(2) (A), (C) and (E) only
(3) (C) and (D) only
(4) (D) and (E) only

56. Which of the following is INCORRECT about ways, the RBI can affect the structure of interest rates?
(A) By changing the treasury bill rate
(B) Blending of leading and trading activities
(C) By changing the Bank rate
(D) Fixing the maximum interest on time deposits with the bank
(E) Ineffective tapping and mobilization of savings
Choose the correct answer from the options given below :
(1) (A) and (D) only
(2) (D) and (E) only
(3) (B) and (E) only
(4) (A), (C), (D) and (E) only

57. Constituents of Integrated marketing are:
(A) Customers
(B) Price
(C) Communications
(D) Products and services
(E) Channels
Choose the correct answer from the options given below :
(1) (A), (B) and (C) only
(2) (C), (D) and (E) only
(3) (B), (C), (D) and (E) only
(4) (A), (B), (D) and (E) only

58. Factors that reduce price sensitivity are:
(A) Buyers cannot store the product
(B) The expenditure is a larger part of the buyer's total income
(C) Buyer are aware of substitutes
(D) The product is used in conjunction with assets previously bought
(E) Part of the cost is borne by another party
Choose the correct answer from the options given below :
(1) (A) and (B) only
(2) (A), (D) and (E) only
(3) (C), (D) and (E) only
(4) (B), (D) and (E) only

59. The characteristics of online and social media marketing are:
(A) Personal (B) Rich
(C) Timely (D) Interactive
(E) Up to date
Choose the correct answer from the options given below :
(1) (A), (D) and (E) only
(2) (B) and (E) only
(3) (B), (D) and (E) only
(4) (A), (C) and (D) only

60. A contract is said to be discharged by rescission:
(A) When terms of a contract are altered
(B) When a party makes novation of a contract

(C) When an aggrieved party exercises his option to avoid the contract
(D) When a party to a contract waives his rights under the contract
(E) Where none of the parties has performed its part for a long time and no other party has objected against it

Choose the correct answer from the options given below :
(1) (A), (D) and (E) only
(2) (B), (C) and (E) only
(3) (C) and (E) only
(4) (B) and (D) only

61. Which of the following are objectives of the Competition Act, 2002?
(A) To prevent practices having an adverse effect on competition
(B) To impede and torment competition in the market
(C) To protect the interests of sellers
(D) To ensure freedom of trade carried on by other participants in markets

Choose the correct answer from the options given below :
(1) (A), (B) and (C) only
(2) (B), (C) and (D) only
(3) (A), (B) and (D) only
(4) (A) and (D) only

62. Which of the following statements are TRUE in a contractual capacity?
(A) Law presumes that every person is competent to contract unless otherwise proved
(B) That a minor can make a contract for necessities of life
(C) That a person of unsound mind can enter into the family contracts
(D) A convict cannot enter into a valid contract nor can sue
(E) That a wife can always make valid business contracts and bind her husband

Choose the correct answer from the options given below :
(1) (B), (D) and (E) only
(2) (A), (C) and (E) only
(3) (A) and (E) only
(4) (B) and (D) only

63. Which of the following are required to be studied for a deep understanding of Income Tax procedures?
(A) The Income Tax Act, 1961
(B) The Income Tax Rules, 1962
(C) Notifications, circulars and classification issued from time to time by the CBDT.
(D) Judicial decisions
(E) Companies Act, 2013

Choose the correct answer from the options given below :
(1) (A), (C), (D) and (E) only
(2) (A), (B), (C) and (D) only
(3) (B), (C), (D) and (E) only
(4) (A), (B) and (E) only

64. Which of the following losses are NOT deductible from business Income?
(A) Loss incurred in closing down the business
(B) Loss incurred due to damage destruction etc. of capital assets
(C) Loss of stock-in-trade due to enemy action
(D) Loss sustained before the business is commenced
(E) Loss of raw material finished good-in-transit

Choose the correct answer from the options given below :
(1) (A), (B), (C) only (2) (A), (B), (D) only
(3) (C), (D), (E) only (4) (A), (D), (E) only

65. An ITR-1 can be used by an individual having an income from
(A) One house property
(B) Pension
(C) Interest on Fixed Deposits in Banks
(D) Winnings from lottery

Choose the correct answer from the options given below :
(1) (A), (B) and (C) only
(2) (B), (C) and (D) only
(3) (A), (C) and (D) only
(4) (A), (B) and (D) only

66. Match List I with List II

List I Events	List II Year
(A) Bretton Woods Conference	(I) 1948
(B) GATT established	(II) 1974
(C) Multi-fibre Agreement	(III) 1944
(D) WTO replaced GATT	(IV) 1995

Choose the correct answer from the options given below :

(1) (A)-(II), (B)-(I), (C)-(IV)- (D)-(III)
(2) (A)-(IV), (B)-(II), (C)-(I), (D)-(III)
(3) (A)-(III), (B)-(I), (C)-(II), (D)-(IV)
(4) (A)-(IV), (B)-(III), (C)-(I), (D)-(II)

67. Match List I with List II

List I	List II
(A) Ind- AS: 1	(I) Provisions, Contingent Liabilities and Contingent Assets
(B) Ind-AS: 29	(II) Consolidated Financial Statements
(C) Ind-AS: 37	(III) Presentation of Financial Statements
(D) Ind-AS: 110 110	(IV) Financial reporting in Hyperinflationary Economies

Choose the correct answer from the options given below :
(1) (A)-(IV), (B)-(III), (C)-(II), (D)-(I)
(2) (A)-(III), (B)-(IV), (C)-(I), (D)-(II)
(3) (A)-(III), (B)-(I), (C)-(II), (D)-(IV)
(4) (A)-(IV), (B)-(III), (C)-(I), (D)-(II)

68. Match the market forms in the List I and the role of the selling costs in the List II

List I Nature of commodities	List II Income Elasticities of Demand
(A) Normal goods	(I) Greater than one
(B) Inferior goods	(II) Between zero and one
(C) Luxurious commodities	(III) Greater than zero (positive)
(D) Necessities	(IV) Less than zero (negative)

Choose the correct answer from the options given below :
(1) (A)-(III), (B)-(I), (C)-(IV)- (D)-(II)
(2) (A)-(II), (B)-(IV), (C)-(I), (D)-(III)
(3) (A)-(III), (B)-(IV), (C)-(I), (D)-(II)
(4) (A)-(II), (B)-(IV), (C)-(III), (D)-(I)

69. Match List I with List II

List I Hedging Concepts	List II Description
(A) European option	(I) Option contract exercised on any date up to maturity
(B) Option premium	(II) When the immediate exercise of an option yields positive value to its holder
(C) In-money option	(III) Option contract exercised only on the maturity date
(D) American option	(IV) It is paid by the buyer of the options upfront to the option seller

Choose the correct answer from the options given below :
(1) (A)-(I), (B)-(II), (C)-(IV), (D)-(III)
(2) (A)-(III), (B)-(IV), (C)-(II), (D)-(I)
(3) (A)-(I), (B)-(II), (C)-(III), (D)-(IV)
(4) (A)-(I), (B)-(IV), (C)-(II), (D)-(III)

70. Match List I with List II

List I	List II
(A) Dispersion	(I) Involving relationship between the median and quartile
(B) Karl Pearson's measures of skewness	(II) Based on the relationship between the averages
(C) Bowley's measures of skewness	(III) Using percentile
(D) Kelly's measure of skewness	(IV) Amount of variation in given data

Choose the correct answer from the options given below :
(1) (A)-(IV), (B)-(II), (C)-(I), (D)-(III)
(2) (A)-(IV), (B)-(I), (C)-(II), (D)-(III)
(3) (A)-(IV), (B)-(III), (C)-(II), (D)-(I)
(4) (A)-(I), (B)-(II), (C)-(III), (D)-(IV)

71. Match List I with List II

List I Ego Defence Mechanism	List II Description
(A) Projection	(I) Returning to a previous stage of development
(B) Regression	(II) Acting out unacceptable impulses in a socially acceptable way

(C) Repression (III) Placing unacceptable impulses in yourself onto someone else

(D) Sublimation (IV) Pulling into the unconscious

Choose the correct answer from the options given below :

(1) (A)-(III), (B)-(I), (C)-(IV), (D)-(II)
(2) (A)-(III), (B)-(IV), (C)-(I), (D)-(II)
(3) (A)-(I), (B)-(III), (C)-(II), (D)-(IV)
(4) (A)-(II), (B)-(I), (C)-(IV), (D)-(III)

72. Match List I with List II

List I	List II
(A) Role of Commercial Bank	(I) Help to consumers
(B) NBFC service	(II) Mutual saving bank
(C) Non-depository Institution	(III) Hire purchase
(D) Depository Institution	(IV) Mutual fund

Choose the correct answer from the options given below :

(1) (A)-(II), (B)-(I), (C)-(III), (D)-(IV)
(2) (A)-(I), (B)-(III), (C)-(IV), (D)-(II)
(3) (A)-(IV), (B)-(II), (C)-(I), (D)-(III)
(4) (A)-(III), (B)-(IV), (C)-(II), (D)-(I)

73. Match List I with List II

List I (Authors)	List II (Ideas)
(A) Value added by Channel Members-Low; Market Growth Rate-Low	(I) Introductory stage
(B) Value added by Channel Members-High; Market Growth Rate-Low	(II) Growth stage
(C) Value added by Channel Members-Low; Market Growth Rate-High	(III) Mature stage
(D) Value added by Channel Members-High; Market Growth Rate-High	(IV) Decline stage

Choose the correct answer from the options given below :

(1) (A)-(I), (B)-(IV), (C)-(III), (D)-(II)
(2) (A)-(II), (B)-(I), (C)-(III), (D)-(IV)
(3) (A)-(IV), (B)-(I), (C)-(III), (D)-(II)
(4) (A)-(III), (B)-(I), (C)-(IV), (D)-(II)

74. Match List I with List II

List I	List II
(A) Actionable claim	(I) Goods to be manufactured after the making of the contract
(B) Appropriation of goods	(II) Goods owned by the seller at the time of the making of the contract of sale
(C) Existing goods	(III) Separating the goods sold from other goods so as to determine and identify the actual goods to be delivered
(D) Future goods	(IV) Recovered only by means of a suit or an action in a court of law

Choose the correct answer from the options given below :

(1) (A)-(III), (B)-(I), (C)-(IV), (D)-(II)
(2) (A)-(I), (B)-(II), (C)-(III), (D)-(IV)
(3) (A)-(II), (B)-(IV), (C)-(I), (D)-(III)
(4) (A)-(IV), (B)-(III), (C)-(II), (D)-(I)

75. Match List I with List II

List I	List II
(A) Section 10 (1)	(I) Amount received involuntary retirement
(B) Section 10 (10 C)	(II) Agricultural Income
(C) Section 10 (13 A)	(III) Leave Encashment
(D) Section 10 (10 AA)	(IV) House Rent Allowance

Choose the correct answer from the options given below :

(1) (A)-(II), (B)-(I), (C)-(IV), (D)-(III)
(2) (A)-(II), (B)-(I), (C)-(III)- (D)-(IV)

(3) (A)-(IV), (B)-(III), (C)-(I), (D)-(II)
(4) (A)-(IV), (B)-(III), (C)-(II), (D)-(I)

76. Arrange the following levels of economic integration, from least integrated to the most integrated:
(A) Customs Union
(B) Free Trade Area
(C) Economic Union
(D) Common Market
(E) Political Union
Choose the correct answer from the options given below
(1) (E), (D), (C), (A), (B)
(2) (B), (A), (D), (C), (E)
(3) (D), (C), (A), (B), (E)
(4) (A), (B), (C), (D), (E)

77. Which of the following order is followed in the issue of shares under the "Fixed Price Offer Method"?
(A) Issue of a prospectus
(B) Receipt by the company of application for share
(C) Selection of merchant banker
(D) Issue of share certificates
(E) Allotment of shares to the applicant
Choose the correct answer from the options given below :
(1) (A), (D), (E), (C), (B)
(2) (C), (B), (A), (D), (E)
(3) (C), (A), (B), (E), (D)
(4) (E), (B), (A), (C), (D)

78. Logically sequence the following steps in the managerial decision-making process
(A) Determining the objective
(B) Selecting the best solution
(C) Implementing the decision
(D) Defining the problem
(E) Identifing possible solutions
Choose the correct answer from the options given below :
(1) (D), (A), (C), (E), (B)
(2) (D), (A), (E), (B), (C)
(3) (A), (E), (D), (B), (C)
(4) (A), (E), (B), (C), (D)

79. Arrange the following economic regions in increasing order of FDI inflows, as per the UNCTAD Report, 2020?
(A) Developing economies
(B) Transition economies
(C) North America
(D) Developed economies
(E) Europe
Choose the correct answer from the options given below :
(1) (B), (A), (C), (E), (D)
(2) (E), (B), (D), (C), (A)
(3) (B), (A), (D), (E), (C)
(4) (A), (B), (C), (E), (D)

80. Arrange the following steps in the process of hypothesis testing in proper sequence:
(A) Select the level of significance
(B) Setup null and alternative hypothesis
(C) Establish the decision rule
(D) Performance computations
(E) Select test statistics
(F) Draw conclusion
Choose the correct answer from the options given below
(1) (A), (B), (C), (D), (E), (F)
(2) (A), (B), (E), (D), (C), (F)
(3) (B), (A), (C), (D), (E), (F)
(4) (B), (A), (E), (C), (D), (F)

81. The characteristics of different levels of leaders are given below. Arrange these in an increasing order of levels
(A) He contributes to the achievement of group objectives and works effectively with others in a group
(B) He builds enduring greatness through a paradoxical combination of professional will and personal humanity
(C) He makes a productive contribution through talent, knowledge, skills, and good work habits
(D) He catalyses commitment to and vigorous pursuit of a clear and compelling vision and stimulates the group to high-performance standards
(E) He organises people and resources towards the effective and efficient pursuit of predetermined objectives

Choose the correct answer from the options given below :
(1) (C), (E), (D), (A), (B)
(2) (A), (E), (D), (B), (C)
(3) (A), (C), (E), (B), (D)
(4) (C), (A), (E), (D), (B)

82. Arrange the following steps in a logical sequence of the claim settlement procedure in the Insurance

(A) Scrutinisation
(B) Investigation of an assessment
(C) Claim form
(D) Notice of loss
(E) Settlement and Arbitration

Choose the correct answer from the options given below :

(1) (A), (B), (C), (D), (E)
(2) (C), (A), (D), (B), (E)
(3) (C), (B), (A), (E), (D)
(4) (D), (C), (A), (B), (E)

83. Arrange the steps of market segmentation process in the proper sequence

(A) Segment "Acid Test"
(B) Segment Attractiveness
(C) Need Based Segmentation
(D) Segment Profitability and Segment Positioning
(E) Segment Identification

Choose the correct answer from the options given below :

(1) (C), (E), (B), (D), (A)
(2) (E), (C), (D), (B), (A)
(3) (A), (E), (C), (D), (B)
(4) (A), (B), (C), (E), (D)

84. Arrange in the sequence, steps in the procedure for calling a statutory meeting of the company

(A) Contents of the statutory report
(B) A list of members must be produced at the commencement
(C) Twenty-one days notice
(D) Certification of the statutory report by not less than two directors, one of whom must be the managing director
(E) A certified copy of the statutory report must be delivered to the Registrar

Choose the correct answer from the options given below :

(1) (B), (E), (C), (A), (D)
(2) (A), (D), (E), (B), (C)
(3) (D), (C), (B), (A), (E)
(4) (C), (A), (D), (E), (B)

85. Arrange in sequence the steps in the procedure of e-filing of an Income Tax Return

(A) Login
(B) Register
(C) Verification
(D) e-filing
(E) Downloading utility and preparing the return

Choose the correct answer from the options given below

(1) (B), (A), (E), (D), (C)
(2) (A), (B), (C), (D), (E)
(3) (A), (B), (E), (C), (D)
(4) (A), (B), (C), (E), (D)

86. Given below are two statements.

Assertion A: Quick ratio is a more penetrating test of liquidity than the current ratio, yet a high quick ratio does not necessarily imply sound liquidity.

Reason R: A company with a high value of quick ratio can suffer from a shortage of funds if it has slow-paying, doubtful and long duration outstanding debtors

In light of the above statements, choose the most appropriate answer from the options given below:

(1) Both (A) and (R) are correct and (R) is the correct explanation of (A)
(2) Both (A) and (R) are correct but (R) is NOT the correct explanation of (A)
(3) (A) is correct but (R) is not correct
(4) (A) is not correct but (R) is correct

87. Given below are two statements : One is labelled as Assertion (A) and the other is labelled as Reason (R).

Assertion (A): Two companies with the same general earning power and same general position in an industry, the one paying larger dividend will almost always sell at a higher price

Reason (R): The discounted value of near dividends is higher than the present worth of distant dividends

In the light of the above statements, choose the most appropriate answer from the options given below :

(1) Both (A) and (R) are correct and (R) is the correct explanation of (A)
(2) Both (A) and (R) are correct but (R) is NOT the correct explanation of (A)
(3) (A) is correct but (R) is not correct
(4) (A) is not correct but (R) is correct

88. Given below are two statements.

Statement (I): The aim of marketing is to make selling superfluous

Statement (II): Marketing should result in a customer who is ready to buy

(1) Both Statement (I) and Statement (II) are true
(2) Both Statement (I) and Statement (II) are false
(3) Statement (I) is correct but Statement (II) is false
(4) Statement (I) is incorrect but Statement (II) is true

89. Given below are two statements.

Statement (I): patents are defined as monopoly rights which one granted by the government, for full disclosure of invention for a limited period of time, that is for 20 years

Statement (II): The purpose of granting patents is to encourage inventions by promoting their protection and utilization so as to contribute to the development of Industries

(1) Both Statement (I) and Statement (II) are true
(2) Both Statement (I) and Statement (II) are false
(3) Statement (I) is correct but Statement (II) is false
(4) Statement (I) is incorrect but Statement (II) is true

90. Given below are two statements.

Statement (I): Assessee is always a person but a person may or may not be an assessee

Statement (II): The term 'person' includes an individual, a HUF, a company, a firm, an association of persons, local authority and every artificial juridical person

(1) Both Statement (I) and Statement (II) are true
(2) Both Statement (I) and Statement (II) are false
(3) Statement (I) is correct but Statement (II) is false
(4) Statement (I) is incorrect but Statement (II) is true

Answer Question No. 91 to 95 on the basis of the following passage :

For a developing economic nation, its industrial policy requires regular updation to meet the growing demands of the industry as well as to increase the share of manufacturing in overall GDP. As India's GDP has been dominated by services rather than agriculture or manufacturing, there are structural modifications always required so that manufacturing activity be increased substantially to meet the global market requirements. This requires legal amendments, with the new laws

aimed to facilitate better manufacturing and exports. Actually, India faces two challenges, rather opportunities that the bullishness on the Indian economy is to be export-oriented as well as to feed its ever-growing domestic consumption. Also, no economy can only be consumption oriented as its people should also save and invest actively. This brings to an important direction of banking system which plays a critically important role in achieving the above two objectives. The public sector banks require to build on to the

capabilities and expertise on the due diligence methods for the credit appraisal for the loan requirements. Worth mentioning here is the data that the non-performing assets valuing Rs. 7.7 lakh crore (as on December 2017) as per the latest figures of the Finance Ministry. Nevertheless, given their large structure and geographic percolation, the public sector banks must be recognized in India's development and that there is "no country in the world where banks have not

had a problem."

91. What problem is highlighted in the above passage?

(1) Low growth in GDP
(2) Balance of payments issue
(3) High fiscal deficit
(4) Role of banking sector

92. Which of the following is not a feature of the consumption economy?

(1) Increasing population with increasing consumption
(2) More contribution to indirect taxes
(3) It also prompts more exports than imports
(4) The unsold goods create problems

93. Which of the following set defines Sustainable Consumption and Production (SCP)?

(A) The use of services and related products which respond to basic needs and bring a better quality of life.
(B) Minimizing the use of natural resources and toxic materials as well as the emission of waste as pollutants.

(C) Pertinent use of service or product so as not to jeopardise the needs of future generations.

(D) Planned cities with a lower cost of production minimizing the retail inflation.

Choose the correct answer from the options given below :

(1) (A), (B) and (D) only
(2) (B), (C) and (D) only
(3) (A), (B) and (C) only
(4) (A), (B), (C) and (D)

94. The credit appraisal process by a bank does NOT involve evaluation if the borrower on:

(1) Technical feasibility
(2) Economic viability
(3) Bank ability or credit worthiness
(4) Loan offtakes and paying ability of related companies in the geographical area

95. The Indian banking sector requires that it:

(1) build more manpower and ICT resources
(2) be more technology dependent
(3) evaluate loan disbursals
(4) increase the frequency of change of the bank rates

Question Numbers : (96 to 100). Question Label: Comprehension

Answer Question No. 96 to 100 on the basis of the following passage :

The Economic Survey cautions against extended forbearance of credit default, drawing the lessons that extended forbearance in the wake of the 2007-08 global financial crisis led to the build-up of bad loans and dragged down investment rates and economic growth.

If followed through, this would mean a major squeeze on company finances, as they scramble for resources to service loans

to avoid bankruptcy, and a big demand on the government to recapitalize the banks it owns, after they recognize and provide for a mass of bad loans

Regulatory forbearance must be an emergency medicine, not a staple diet, is sound advice. A moratorium by banks on debt service by borrowers has been a part of the COVID cushioning to corporates. Many of these firms would face acute liquidity problems when the moratorium ends

Fast growth that embraces all businesses would avert a crisis. Such Goldilocks perfection rarely materializes in real life.

Many companies that could survive with access to liquidity could go under when banks think it is time to do their asset quality reviews. The solution is to provide such companies with capital that does not need to be serviced when they do not make a profit on equity

Companies would need a whole lot of capital, to service existing loans and to invest in new production, to cater to the demand thrown up by economic revival. The government had promised a fund to funds that would mobilize large volumes of capital to invest in micro, small and medium enterprises.

This is the time to walk the talk. The equity stakes can be sold later, hopefully at a profit. Special situation funds, private equity, and allocations from retirement savings can be tapped for the needed capital. Managing the investment is the challenge.

96. Which could be a suitable title for the above paragraph?

(1) Forbearance and Corporate Funding in Crisis Times
(2) Funding during crisis
(3) Bad loans and Indian corporates
(4) Funding crisis and COVID-19

97. What is the theme of the paragraph narrated above?

(1) Crisis of corporate funding during crisis times
(2) Forbearance of credit default
(3) Liquidity and survival of companies
(4) Moratorium by banks on debt service

98. Given below are two statements, one is labelled as Assertion (A) and the other is labelled as Reason (R)

Assertion (A): The government had promised a fund of funds that would mobilize large volumes of capital to invest in micro, small and medium enterprises

Reason (R): Companies would need a whole lot of capital, to service existing loans and to invest in new production, to cater to the demand thrown up by economic revival.

In light of the above statements, choose the most appropriate answer from the options given below:

(1) Both (A) and (R) are correct and (R) is the correct explanation of (A)
(2) Both (A) and (R) are correct but (R) is NOT the correct explanation of (A)

(3) (A) is correct but (R) is not correct
(4) (A) is not correct but (R) is correct

99. Given below are two statements:

Statement I: For bearance of credit default is a common phenomenon in Indian banking system

Statement II: Global financial crisis influences the quantum of bad loans in India

In light of the above statements, choose the correct answer from the options given below

(1) Both Statement (I) and Statement (II) are true
(2) Both Statement (I) and Statement (II) are false
(3) Statement (I) is correct but Statement (II) is false
(4) Statement (I) is incorrect but Statement (II) is true

100. Given below are two statements, one is labelled as Assertion A and the other is labelled as Reason R

Assertion A: A moratorium by banks on debt service by borrowers has been a part of the COVID cushioning to corporates

Reason R: Regulatory forbearance must be an emergency medicine but not a staple diet

In light of the above statements, choose the most appropriate answer from the options given below

(1) Both (A) and (R) are correct and (R) is the correct explanation of (A)
(2) Both (A) and (R) are correct but (R) is NOT the correct explanation of (A)
(3) (A) is correct but (R) is not correct
(4) (A) is not correct but (R) is correct

ANSWERS

1. (4)	**2.** (2)	**3.** (1)	**4.** (3)	**5.** (3)	**6.** (3)	**7.** (3)	**8.** (4)	**9.** (2)	**10.** (2)
11. (4)	**12.** (4)	**13.** (3)	**14.** (4)	**15.** (2)	**16.** (1)	**17.** (3)	**18.** (2)	**19.** (2)	**20.** (3)
21. (2)	**22.** (4)	**23.** (1)	**24.** (4)	**25.** (1)	**26.** (2)	**27.** (4)	**28.** (2)	**29.** (3)	**30.** (2)
31. (1)	**32.** (3)	**33.** (3)	**34.** (2)	**35.** (1)	**36.** (3)	**37.** (3)	**38.** (2)	**39.** (1)	**40.** (4)
41. (3)	**42.** (3)	**43.** (4)	**44.** (4)	**45.** (3)	**46.** (2)	**47.** (4)	**48.** (1)	**49.** (4)	**50.** (2)
51. (2)	**52.** (3)	**53.** (4)	**54.** (1)	**55.** (4)	**56.** (3)	**57.** (3)	**58.** (2)	**59.** (3)	**60.** (3)
61. (4)	**62.** (4)	**63.** (2)	**64.** (2)	**65.** (1)	**66.** (3)	**67.** (2)	**68.** (3)	**69.** (2)	**70.** (1)
71. (1)	**72.** (2)	**73.** (3)	**74.** (4)	**75.** (1)	**76.** (2)	**77.** (3)	**78.** (2)	**79.** (2)	**80.** (4)
81. (4)	**82.** (4)	**83.** (1)	**84.** (4)	**85.** (1)	**86.** (1)	**87.** (1)	**88.** (1)	**89.** (1)	**90.** (1)
91. (3)	**92.** (3)	**93.** (1)	**94.** (1)	**95.** (1)	**96.** (1)	**97.** (1)	**98.** (1)	**99.** (1)	**100.** (1)

SEPTEMBER, 2022

COMMERCE

Paper-II

Note : This paper contains **hundred (100)** objective type questions of **two (2)** marks each. **All** questions are **compulsory.**

1. Pricing of housing loan by a commercial bank may follow the following step in a logical sequence

(A) Competitive price determination
(B) Specification of spread
(C) Application of MCLR
(D) Conduct of Credit Assessment
(E) Quoting to prospective borrower

Choose the correct answer from the options given below:

(1) (C), (B), (A), (D), (E)
(2) (A), (B), (D), (E), (C)
(3) (B), (A), (D), (E), (C)
(4) (D), (C), (B), (A), (E)

2. Presumptive taxation involves which one of the following?

(1) The use of indirect methods to calculate tax liability, which differ from the usual sales based on the tax payers accounts.
(2) Transfer of tax liability from State to the Centre.
(3) Calculation of short term capital gain
(4) Calculation of rebate U/S 89.

3. Sequentially arrange the following themes related to globalization of Indian businesses since independence:

(A) FDI in various sectors opened along with slashing of custom duties.
(B) Partial opening of economy to external trade and de-licensing of some key sectors.
(C) Govt. - led investments in large public sector units in steel, chemicals and power.
(D) Indian businesses became competitive and started to reap rewards of various phases of development learning.
(E) Increased government involvement in industry with sustained focus on import substitution.

Choose the correct answer from the options given below :

(1) (C), (E), (B), (D), (A)
(2) (E), (C), (B), (A), (D)
(3) (C), (E), (B), (A), (D)
(4) (A), (C), (E), (B), (D)

4. Which one of the following is a myth about rural markets?

(1) All villages are not equally populated.
(2) Rural buyers are a heterogeneous lot.
(3) Rural buyers are able to discriminate between products and brands.
(4) Only low priced products sell in rural markets.

5. The pricing practice to extract all of the consumer surplus from consumers to maximize the total revenue and profits from the sale of a particular quantity of product is called:

(1) First degree price discrimination
(2) Second-degree price discrimination
(3) Third degree price discrimination
(4) Penetration pricing

6. As per the Agency Theory of Corporate Governance, which of the following statements are relevant?

(A) Governance approach is materialistic.
(B) Managers are motivated by the principal's objectives.
(C) Interests of the managers and principals converge.
(D) Behaviour pattern is opportunistic.
(E) Owner's attitude is to avoid risks.

Choose the most appropriate answer from the options given below :

(1) (A), (C), (E) only (2) (B), (C), (D) only
(3) (B), (D), (E) only (4) (A), (D), (E) only

7. A company should undergo a step-Wise process before selecting a final price. Accordingly, arrange the following steps of pricing policy process to help 'KYZ' company to decide the final price of its product.

(A) Selecting the pricing method.

(B) Examining competitor's costs, prices and offers.

(C) Estimating the demand curve and the probable quantities company will sell at each possible price.

(D) Selecting the pricing objective of the company.

(E) Estimating costs for different levels of output, for different levels of accumulated production experience, and for differentiated marketing offers.

Choose the correct answer from the options given below :

(1) (D), (B), (E), (C), (A)

(2) (D), (C), (E), (B), (A)

(3) (A), (B), (C), (E), (D)

(4) (A), (D), (E), (C), (B)

8. Match List I with List II

List – I	List – II
(A) Consensus ad idem	(I) Something in return
(B) Quid pro quo	(II) As much as earned
(C) Quantum meruit	(III) Buyer beware
(D) Cave-ate emptor	(IV) Meeting of minds

Choose the correct answer from the options given below:

(1) (A)-(I), (B)-(III), (C)-(IV), (D)-(II)

(2) (A)-(IV), (B)-(I), (C)-(II), (D)-(III)

(3) (A)-(II), (B)-(I), (C)-(III), (D)-(IV)

(4) (A)-(I), (B)-(IV), (C)-(II), (D)-(III)

9. Arrange the following stages of delegation in correct sequence:

(A) Establish proper controls.

(B) Select the person in light of the job to be done.

(C) Reward effective delegation and successful assumption of authority.

(D) Define assignments and delegate authority in light of results expected.

(E) Maintain open lines of communication.

Choose the correct answer from the options given below :

(1) (A), (B), (C), (E), (D)

(2) (B), (D), (E), (A), (C)

(3) (D), (B), (E), (A), (C)

(4) (C), (D), (B), (E), (A)

10. Rates of Income Tax under new regime applicable for financial year 2021-22 in India are:

(A) 5% (B) 10%

(C) 12% (D) 15%

(E) 20%

Choose the correct answer from the options given below :

(1) (A), (B), (C) only

(2) (A), (B), (D) only

(3) (A), (B), (D), (E) only

(4) (B), (C), (D), (E) only

11. If the subject matter of insurance is the ship, the marine insurance is called:

(1) Cargo insurance

(2) Hull insurance

(3) Freight insurance

(4) Voyage insurance

12. As per Section 68 of the Indian Companies Act a company may purchase its own share out of which of the following?

(A) Free reserves

(B) Securities premium account

(C) General reserve

(D) Proceeds of any other shares

(E) Proceeds of same kind of shares

Choose the correct answer from the options given below :

(1) (A), (B), (C) and (E) only

(2) (A), (B), (C) and (D) only

(3) (B), (C), (D) and (E) only

(4) (A), (C), (D) and (E) only

13. Match List I with List II

List I - Type of Exposure	List II - Description
(A) Economic Exposure	(I) Potential changes in all future cash flows of a firm that result from unanticipated changes in exchange rates.
(B) Translation Exposure	(II) It arises when items of financial statements that are stated in foreign currencies are restated in the home currency of an MNC.

(C) Transaction Exposure	(III) It arises when a firms contract obligations are exposed to unanticipated changes in exchange rate.
(D) Operating Exposure	(IV) When a firms real assets are exposed to unanticipated changes in exchange rates.

Choose the correct answer from the options given below:

(1) (A)-(III), (B)-(IV), (C)-(II), (D)-(I)
(2) (A)-(I), (B)-(II), (C)-(III), (D)-(IV)
(3) (A)-(IV), (B)-(III), (C)-(II), (D)-(I)
(4) (A)-(I), (B)-(IV), (C)-(III), (D)-(II)

13. Match List I with List II

List I - Statistical Distribution	List II - Characteristical Expression
(A) Negatively Skewed Distribution	(I) Mean = Mode, $P(x \leq \mu) = 0.50$
(B) Positively Skewed Distribution	(II) $\bar{x}$ > Median > Mode; P > 0.5
(C) Binomial Distribution	(III) $\bar{x}$ > Median > Mode
(D) Normal Distribution	(IV) Y > Median > Mode

Choose the correct answer from the options given below:

(1) (A)-(III), (B)-(I), (C)-(II), (D)-(IV)
(2) (A)-(I), (B)-(II), (C)-(III), (D)-(IV)
(3) (A)-(II), (B)-(III), (C)-(IV), (D)-(I)
(4) (A)-(III), (B)-(IV), (C)-(II), (D)-(I)

15. Which of the following are key assumptions of Gordon's Dividend Model?

(A) Ke > br
(B) *r* and Ke are changing
(C) The firm is not all-equity firm
(D) The firm has perpetual life
(E) The retention ratio, once decided is constant

Choose the correct answer from the options given below :

(1) (A), (D), (E) only (2) (B), (C), (E) only
(3) (A), (B), (D) only (4) (C), (D), (E) only

16. Given below are two statements :

Statement I: Display of goods by a shopkeeper with prices marked on them is not an offer but an invitation to the public to make an offer to buy the goods.

Statement II: Price quotations, catalogues and advertisements in newspaper for sale of an article do constitute a valid offer.

In the light of the above statements, choose the most appropriate answer from the options given below :

(1) Both Statement I and Statement II are correct
(2) Both Statement I and Statement II are incorrect
(3) Statement I is correct but Statement II is incorrect
(4) Statement I is incorrect but Statement II is correct

17. Which of the following are key features of prudent accounting concepts and conventions?

(A) It includes revenues and profits in the accounts when they are realised.
(B) It prevents profits from being overstated.
(C) It prevents a trader from more withdrawing from the business than is wise.
(D) Managerial efficiency and expertise.
(E) Good customer relations.

Choose the most appropriate answer from the options given below :

(1) (C), (D), (E) only (2) (A), (D), (E) only
(3) (B), (C), (D) only (4) (A), (B), (C) only

18. Match List I with List II

List – I Description	List – II Conceptualisation
(A) Net Stable Funding Ratio	(I) Asset Liability Management
(B) Innovative Perpetual Debt Instrument	(II) Tier - I capital
(C) Time Maturity Gap	(III) Tier - II capital
(D) Risk Weighted Assets	(IV) Basel - III norms

Choose the correct answer from the options given below:

(1) (A)-(IV), (B)-(II), (C)-(I), (D)-(III)
(2) (A)-(I), (B)-(IV), (C)-(III), (D)-(II)
(3) (A)-(II), (B)-(III), (C)-(IV), (D)-(I)
(4) (A)-(IV), (B)-(III), (C)-(II), (D)-(I)

19. Economists' adjustment to reality limited by individual consumers preferences, intelligence and environmental factors is called :
(1) Rationality
(2) Homo economics
(3) Bounded rationality
(4) Consumer sovereignity

20. A contract is discharged by supervening impossibility under which of the following situations?
(A) Destruction of subject matter
(B) Death or disablement of parties
(C) Rescission
(D) Remission
(E) Accord and satisfaction
Choose the most appropriate answer from the options given below :
(1) (A), (C) and (D) only
(2) (A) and (B) only
(3) (A), (B), and (E) only
(4) (C) and (D) only

21. Which of the following statements are correct?
(A) Internal reliability is described as the consistency of a measure taken at two different points of time.
(B) A distribution is random walk if it has a mean of 0 and variance of 1.
(C) Increase and decrease in scores measured overtime that produce a variance of less than 50% is reliable.
(D) Normal distribution cannot be applied to real life situations.
(E) Factor Analysis supersedes multiple discriminate analysis.
Choose the most appropriate answer from the options given below :
(1) (A), (B), (E) only (2) (C), (D), (E) only
(3) (B), (C), (D) only (4) (B), (D), (E) only

22. Total revenue of a business firm increases as long as :
(1) $|Ep| > 1$ (2) $|Ep| = 1$
(3) $|Ep| < 1$ (4) $|Ep| < 0$

23. Which of the following are thinly veiled disguises that essentially restrict imports?
(A) Voluntary import restrictions
(B) Labeling requirements showing origin and contents
(C) Import tariffs and quotas
(D) Safety regulations for automobile and electrical equipments
(E) Health regulations for hygiene production and packaging of imported food production
Choose the most appropriate answer from the options given below :
(1) (A), (B) and (C) only
(2) (B), (C) and (D) only
(3) (C), (D) and (E) only
(4) (B), (D) and (E) only

24. According to Herzberg's Two Factor Theory, which one of the following is not a maintenance factor?
(1) Affiliation or Acceptance
(2) Esteem or Status
(3) Security or Safety
(4) Physiological Needs

25. Steps involved in computation of Book Profit under MAT regime are as follows:
(A) Arrive NP as per statement of P/L A/C of the company.
(B) Specific adjustments in case of merger.
(C) Make adjustments pertaining to OCI items.
(D) Adjust the book profit with stipulated exclusion and inclusion.
(E) Net amount of Book Profit for application of MAT rate.
Choose the correct sequence from the options given below :
(1) (A), (D), (B), (C), (E)
(2) (A), (B), (D), (C), (E)
(3) (A), (C), (B), (D), (E)
(4) (A), (B), (C), (D), (E)

26. Given below are two statements :
Statement I: Policies are guides to action, rather than to thinking.
Statement II: Policies define an area within which a decision is to be made.
In the light of the above statements, choose the most appropriate answer from the options given below :
(1) Both Statement I and Statement II are correct
(2) Both Statement I and Statement II are incorrect
(3) Statement I is correct but Statement II is incorrect
(4) Statement I is incorrect but Statement II is correct

27. Given below are two statements : One is labelled as Assertion (A) and the other is labelled as Reason (R) :

Assertion (A): Capital structure is determined within debt capacity of a company and it should not be exceeded.

Reason (R): Debt capacity of a company depends on its ability to generate cash flows. It should generate cash enough to pay lenders' fixed charges and principal sum.

In the light of the above Statements, choose the most appropriate answer from the options given below :

(1) Both (A) and (R) are correct and (R) is the correct explanation of (A)
(2) Both (A) and (R) are correct but (R) is NOT the correct explanation of (A)
(3) (A) is correct but (R) is not correct
(4) (A) is not correct but (R) is correct

28. Michael Porter has identified five forces that determine the intrinsic long-term attractiveness of a market. According to the model, which of the following are true?

(A) A segment is unattractive if it already contains numerous aggressive competitors.
(B) A segment is unattractive if it is stable or declining.
(C) A segment is unattractive if it has high entry barriers and low exit barriers.
(D) A segment is unattractive if the company's suppliers are able to raise prices.
(E) A segment is unattractive when there are actual or potent substitutes for the product.

Choose the most appropriate answer from the options given below :

(1) (A) and (B) only
(2) (B) and (C) only
(3) (A), (C) and (D) only
(4) (A), (B), (C) and (E) only

29. Dimensions of VALS^{TM} framework to include which one of the following:

(1) Consumer motivation and consumer resources
(2) Consumer personality and consumer resources
(3) Consumer motivation and consumer preferences
(4) Consumer needs and consumer resources

30. Under Indian Income Tax Act, allowances which are non-taxable for the individual assesses are:

(A) Sumptuary allowances.
(B) Compensatory allowance paid to judges.
(C) Overtime allowance.
(D) Allowances paid to Govt. employees posted abroad.
(E) Non-practicing allowance.

Choose the most appropriate answer from the options given below:

(1) (A), (B), (D), (E) only
(2) (A), (C), (D), (E) only
(3) (A), (B), (D) only
(4) (A), (B), (C), (D), (E)

31. A prudent financial policy suggested by Marris Hypothesis to maximize balanced growth of the firm is based on which of following financial ratios?

(A) Return on investment ratio
(B) Debt equity ratio
(C) Return on capital employed ratio
(D) Liquidity ratio
(E) Retention ratio

Choose the most appropriate answer from the options given below :

(1) (A), (B), (C) only
(2) (B), (C), (D) only
(3) (A), (C), (D) only
(4) (B), (D), (E) only

32. Preference share in India is issued by a company for a maximum period of:

(1) 10 years (2) 13 years
(3) 20 years (4) Unliminted period

33. Which one of the following theories describes FDI flows in ecosystems?

(1) Product Life Cycle Theory
(2) Factor Endowment Theory
(3) Waterfall Theory
(4) New Trade Theory

34. Break-even point is not affected with the changes in which one of the following?

(1) Sale price per unit
(2) Variable cost per unit
(3) Number of units sold fair it
(4) Total fixed costs

35. Match List I with List II

List-I International Trade Theories	List-II Expounders
(A) Absolute Advantage	(I) David Ricardo

(B) Factor Endowments	(II) Minhas. Leontief et. al.
(C) Factor - Intensity Reversal	(III) Adam Smith
(D) Comparative Advantage	(IV) Heckscher - Ohlin

Choose the correct answer from the options given below:

(1) (A)-(III), (B)-(II), (C)-(IV), (D)-(I)
(2) (A)-(III), (B)-(IV), (C)-(II), (D)-(I)
(3) (A)-(I), (B)-(IV), (C)-(II), (D)-(III)
(4) (A)-(III), (B)-(I), (C)-(II), (D)-(IV)

36. The qualified characteristics determining (constituting) consumer 'rationality' includes which of the following?

(A) Economic selfish motives
(B) Risk-return optimiser
(C) Clarity of preferences
(D) Possession of information
(E) Non-satiation of needs

Choose the most appropriate answer from the options given below :

(1) (A), (B) and (C) only
(2) (C), (D) and (E) only
(3) (A), (B), (C) and (D) only
(4) (A), (C), (D) and (E) only

37. The current market price per share of New Age Limited is Rs. 80. The dividend expected a year from now is Rs. 4 and it is expected to grow at a constant rate of 10 percent. The floatation (issue! cost for the new issue will be 8 percent. What is the cost of new equity?

(1) 15.43 percent (2) 15.00 percent
(3) 5.00 percent (4) 5.43 percent

38. From the following, select the right option with reference to the working capital:

(1) Higher net working capital leads to higher liquidity and higher profitability.
(2) According to hedging approach, current assets should be financed from long-term sources.
(3) There is an inverse relationship between the length of operating cycle of a firm and its working capital requirements.
(4) Trade-off plan, in general, is considered an appropriate financing strategy for working capital.

39. Arrange the following steps in the process of GDR Issues:

(A) Registration with prescribed authority
(B) Appointment and vesting of shares with the custodian
(C) Approval of the regulatory authorities
(D) Listing of GDR
(E) GDR allotment

Choose the correct answer from the options given below :

(1) (C), (A), (B), (E), (D)
(2) (A), (B), (C), (D), (E)
(3) (A), (C), (B), (E), (D)
(4) (B), (A), (C), (D), (E)

40. Arrange the following negotiation rounds of WTO (World Trade Organisation) in reverse chronological order:

(A) Uruguay Round (B) Geneva Round
(C) Kennedy Round (D) Doha Round
(E) Tokyo Round

Choose the correct answer from the options given below :

(1) (A), (C), (D), (B), (E)
(2) (D), (A), (E), (C), (B)
(3) (B), (A), (C), (E), (D)
(4) (D), (E), (A), (C), (B)

41. In case of a warranty, the buyer can :

(1) Repudiate the contract
(2) Claim damages only
(3) Return the goods
(4) Refuse to pay the price

42. Written plan containing the details regarding the conduct of a particular audit is called:

(1) Audit Memorandum
(2) Audit Planning Procedure
(3) Audit Notebook
(4) Audit Programme

43. A price ceiling below the equilibrium price possibly leads to which of the following?

(A) Black marketing
(B) Commodity glut
(C) Shortage of commodity
(D) Commodity export
(E) Price decline

Choose the correct answer from the options given below :

(1) (A) and (B) only
(2) (D) and (E) only
(3) (A) and (C) only
(4) (A), (B), and (C) only

44. Which one of the following is an example of Secondary Reserves?
(1) Cash in hand and balances with other banks in current account
(2) Balances with RBI for CRR
(3) Investment in Commercial Paper
(4) Investment in Government Securities for SLR

45. When a monopolist switches from charging a single price to perfect price discrimination. It reduces:
(1) The quantity produced
(2) The firm's profit
(3) Consumer surplus
(4) Total surplus

46. Choose the correct options regarding banking:
(A) Chain banking indicates the form of bank cartel that occurs when a small group of people control atleast three banks that are independently chartered.
(B) PAN number is required for deposits in a commercial bank for Rs. 50.000 and above.
(C) Upon detection of counterfeit notes at the counter, the bank can impound the note and issue receipt.
(D) The interest rates on bank's contribution to Rural Infrastructure Development Fund is fixed by NABARD.
(E) RBI Act, 1934 prohibits the making or issuing of a promissory note expressed to be payable to the bearers thereof.
Choose the most appropriate answer from the options given below :
(1) (B), (D), (E) only (2) (B), (C) only
(3) (A), (D), (E) only (4) (A), (B), (C) only

47. Under the Vivad se Vishwas Act, 2020 the amount payable by the declarant U/S 3 on or after January 1, 2021 is:
(1) Amount of disputed tax
(2) The aggregate of the amount of disputed tax and 10% of disputed tax
(3) Amount of penalty and amount computed by CBDT
(4) Average of tax arrears for last three assessment years

48. In a statistical experiment, an effect size is described as:
(1) Effective testing of hypothesis
(2) Probable success of an experimental manipulation
(3) Quantitative measurement of the magnitude of the experimental effect
(4) Standardised measure of the magnitude of the effect observed in an experiment

49. Sequence the following in copyright ecosystem for literary creation under the Indian Copyright Act. 1957 :
(A) Public communication
(B) Copyright assignment
(C) Content development
(D) Relinquish copyright
(E) Copyright transmission
Choose the correct answer from the options given below :
(1) (A) → (E) → (B) → (D) → (C)
(2) (C) → (A) → (B) → (E) → (D)
(3) (E) → (C) → (B) → (D) → (A)
(4) (B) → (C) → (E) → (A) → (D)

50. The standard error is a statistical measure of :
(1) The normal distribution of scores around the sample mean.
(2) The extent to which a sample mean is likely to differ from the population mean.
(3) The clustering of scores at each end of a survey scale.
(4) The degree to which the sample has been accurately stratified.

51. Logically sequence the following economic entities/identities in understanding the theory of consumer choice:
(A) Budget line
(B) Utility analysis
(C) Demand curve analysis
(D) Indifference curve analysis
(E) Consumer equilibrium
Choose the correct answer from the options given below :
(1) (D) → (E) → (A) → (B) → (C)
(2) (B) → (D) → (A) → (E) → (C)
(3) (B) → (C) → (D) → (A) → (E)
(4) (B) → (D) → (A) → (C) → (E)

52. "If you know the enemy and know yourself, you need not fear the result of a hundred battles."
Above statement of Sun Tzu corresponds to which one of the following components of Porter's Five Forces Model?
(1) Threat of substitutes
(2) Threat of Competitor

(3) Bargain Power of Supplier
(4) Threat of New Entrants

53. Which one of the following is false with respect to interest rate structure in the Indian money market?
(1) A very tight liquidity position will increase the call rates while excess liquidity will give fairly low and stable rates.
(2) If the liquidity crunch of the banks is passed on to the system, it may lead to high volatility in the call rates.
(3) Call rates under normal liquidity conditions are the cap rate for the term money market.
(4) In a volatile call market situation, lending will yield high return and by selling Interbank participation, the bank will have more money to play in the call market.

54. A co-efficient of correlation having a value of +0.81 implies that :
(1) Co-efficient of correlation is strong and positive.
(2) Co-efficient of determination is extremely weak.
(3) The relationship between two variables is weak, but positive.
(4) The relationship between two variables is strong.

55. In Fund Flow Statement, which one of the following is not a valid statement?
(1) It is prepared to know the total sources and their uses in a year.
(2) Dividend received is a source of funds.
(3) Its preparation is at the discretion of the management.
(4) It is useful for external financial management.

56. Which of the following statements are correct?
(A) The difference between sample variance and population variance computation is μ replaced by $\overline{x}$.
(B) Cronbach alpha value less than 0.30 indicates reliability of research instrument.
(C) The value of $R^2 = 1$ may imply that regression is spurious.
(D) The identical observation of sample and population parameters shows that every sample can be substituted as population.
(E) Randomise control trial is a qualitative approach to research.

Choose the correct answer from the options given below :
(1) (C), (D), (E) only
(2) (A), (B), (C), (D) only
(3) (A), (C), (D), (E) only
(4) (B), (C), (D) only

57. The banks wherein a majority of depositors are non-residents are called
(1) Cross Payment Banks
(2) Currency Banks
(3) Foreign Banks (4) Offshore Banks

58. Given below are two statements :
Statement I: Marketing managers must calculate customer lifetime values of their customer base to understand their profit implications.
Statement II: Activity – based costing, an accounting technique, is very useful for conducting customer profitability analysis.
In the light of the above Statements, choose the most appropriate answer from the options given below :
(1) Both Statement I and Statement II are correct
(2) Both Statement I and Statement II are incorrect
(3) Statement I is correct but Statement II is incorrect
(4) Statement I is incorrect but Statement II is correct

59. Which one of the following motives characterizes dominant organizational climate of university teaching departments/scientific organizations?
(1) Affiliation (2) Extension
(3) Expert power (4) Achievement

60. Which of the following decision choices are valid in relation to marginal costing?
(A) Costing 'special' or 'one off' opportunities.
(B) Deciding whether to make or buy a product.
(C) Most appropriate technique because of application of more automation in the industry.
(D) Choosing between competing alternative actions.
(E) Employing a penetration or destroyer pricing strategy.

Choose the correct answer from the options given below :
(1) (A), (B), (D) and (E) only

(2) (A), (B), (C) and (E) only
(3) (B), (C), (D) and (E) only
(4) (A), (D) and (E) only

61. "Hospital administration may think that patients want better food, but patients may be more concerned with nurse responsiveness" Above statement pertains to which one of the following service gaps?
(1) Gap between consumer expectation and management perception.
(2) Gap between management perception and service-quality specification.
(3) Gap between service delivery and external communication.
(4) Gap between service-quality specifications and service delivery.

62. Which of the following constructs hold true for research analysis and design?
(A) Research design is a framework for every stage of the collection and analysis of data.
(B) The choice between qualitative and quantitative methods in a research experiment depends upon Cronbach alpha.
(C) Experiments as source of data is not appropriate for a qualitative study.
(D) Plagarism is the failure of researcher to acknowledge the borrowed material in his! Her publication.
(E) Content Analysis is a method commonly used in qualitative research to aid data collection.
Choose the most appropriate answer from the options given below:
(1) (A), (B), (E) only (2) (B), (C), (D) only
(3) (A), (C), (D), (E) only
(4) (B), (E) only

63. Answer the correct material usage variance from the information given below :
Standard material cost for manufacturing 1000 units of an output is 400 kgs of material at Rs. 2.50 per kg. When 2000 units are produced, it is found that actual consumption was of 825 kgs material at a price of Rs. 2.70 per kg. :
(1) Rs. 67.50 Favourable
(2) Rs. 67.50 Adverse
(3) Rs. 62.50 Favourable
(4) Rs. 62.50 Adverse

64. A spot sale of a currency combined with a forward repurchase of the same currency is called which one of the following?
(1) Forex swap (2) Swap rate
(3) Forward rate (4) Spot rate

65. Under which one of the following the Basel framework places restrictions on participation by banks in system-wide credit booms with the aim of reducing their losses in credit bust?
(1) Catastrophic Reserve Capital
(2) Counter cyclical Capital Buffer
(3) Deferred Capital
(4) Conservative Preference Capital

66. Which one of the following is not an advantage of organization structure by territory?
(1) Makes control easy for top management
(2) Places responsibility at a lower level
(3) Improves coordination in a region
(4) Takes advantage of economies of local operations

67. From which of the following, employees derive authority?
(A) Position (B) Experience
(C) Moral worth (D) Past service
(E) Intelligence
Choose the most appropriate answer from the options given below :
(1) (A), (B) only (2) (A), (E) only
(3) (B), (C), (E) only (4) (A), (B), (C), (D), (E)

68. Arm's length price computation method under 92 (C) of the Income Tax Act. 1961 does not include which one of the following?
(1) Comparable uncontrolled price
(2) Transaction net margin
(3) Resale price
(4) Slum sale price method

69. Match List I with List II

List I – Inds AS	List II – Topic
(A) Inds AS 1	(I) Income Taxes
(B) Inds AS 12	(II) Related Party Disclosures
(C) Inds AS 24	(III) Intangible Assets
(D) Inds AS 38	(IV) Presentation of Financial Statements

Choose the correct answer from the options given below :
(1) (A)-(I), (B)-(II), (C)-(III), (D)-(IV)
(2) (A)-(IV), (B)-(I), (C)-(II), (D)-(III)
(3) (A)-(IV), (B)-(III), (C)-(II), (D)-(I)
(4) (A)-(II), (B)-(IV), (C)-(I), (D)-(III)

70. Match List I with List II

List I Promotional Campaign	List II Company
(A) # StayStrong Moms	(I) Pepsico India
(B) # JeetKiOre	(II) Hindustan Uniliver (HUL)
(C) # Lets unstereotypelndia	(III) Indian Tobacco Company (ITC)
(D) # Freedomtolove	(IV) Brooke Bond India

Choose the correct answer from the options given below:
(1) (A)-(III), (B)-(I), (C)-(IV), (D)-(II)
(2) (A)-(II), (B)-(IV), (C)-(I), (D)-(III)
(3) (A)-(II), (B)-(I), (C)-(III), (D)-(IV)
(4) (A)-(I), (B)-(III), (C)-(IV), (D)-(II)

71. Which one of the following is a Trade related entry mode in international markets?
(1) Management Contract
(2) International Licensing
(3) International Leasing
(4) Portfolio Investments

72. Which of the following are essentially anti-competetive agreements as per the Competition Act. 2002 in India?
(A) Exclusive distribution agreement
(B) Resale price maintenance
(C) Exclusive supply agreement
(D) Non-compete agreement
(E) Tie-in agreement
Choose the correct answer from the options given below :
(1) (A), (B) and (C) only
(2) (C), (D) and (E) only
(3) (A), (B), (C) and (D) only
(4) (A), (B), (C) and (E) only

73. Match List I with List II

List I – Personality Factor	List II – Bipolar Dimension
(A) Warmth	(I) Imaginative vs practical
(B) Abstractedness	(II) Controlled vs casual
(C) Openness to change	(III) Outgoing vs reserved
(D) Perfectionism	(IV) Experimental vs conservative

Choose the correct answer from the options given below:
(1) (A)-(II), (B)-(II), (C)-(IV), (D)-(III)
(2) (A)-(III), (B)-(I), (C)-(IV), (D)-(II)
(3) (A)-(I), (B)-(IV), (C)-(III), (D)-(II)
(4) (A)-(III), (B)-(II), (C)-(IV), (D)-(I)

74. Which one of the following is not valid as per the Limited Liability Partnership Act, 2008?
(1) LLP shall maintain its books of accounts on double entry system and on cash or accrual basis.
(2) LLP shall prepare a Statement of Account and Solvency for each financial year.
(3) Every LLP shall file an annual return with the Registrar of Companies.
(4) Every LLP is a separate legal entity independent of its partners.

75. Which are the major factors that lead to capital rationing?
(A) Imperfection of capital market.
(B) Reluctance to broaden the equity share-base for the fear of losing control.
(C) Inability to manage.
(D) Deficiencies in market information which might affect the availability of capital.
(E) Efficiency of Capital Market.
Choose the correct answer from the options given below :
(1) (A), (B), (D) only
(2) (C), (D), (E) only
(3) (A), (B), (C), (E) only
(4) (A), (B), (C), (D) only

76. Match List I with List II

List I Income Tax Disposition	List II Particular/Section
(A) Donation to National Defence Fund	(I) Section 1-10 (A)
(B) Hedging of Tax	(II) Tax Management
(C) Compliance with Legal Formalities	(III) Tax Avoidance
(D) Permanent Account Number (PAN)	(IV) 100% Deduction

Choose the correct answer from the options given below:
(1) (A)-(III), (B)-(II), (C)-(I), (D)-(IV)
(2) (A)-(IV), (B)-(III), (C)-(II), (D)-(I)

(3) (A)-(II), (B)-(I), (C)-(III), (D)-(IV)
(4) (A)-(I), (B)-(IV), (C)-(II), (D)-(III)

77. Why do Central banks intervene to affect exchange rates?
(A) To influence domestic production
(B) To influence trade flows
(C) To influence domestic interest rates
(D) To inject liquidity in domestic markets
(E) To smoothen fluctuations in exchange rates
Choose the correct answer from the options given below :
(1) (A), (B) and (C) only
(2) (C), (D) and (E) only
(3) (B), (C) and (D) only
(4) (A), (B) and (E) only

78. If the information sought has been supplied by third party or is treated as confidential by that third party, the third party must give a representation before the PIO in reply to the notice issued to it within how many days from the date of receipt of such notice?
(1) 5 days (2) 15 days
(3) 10 days (4) 7 days

79. Which of the following factors favour product standardization in the international markets?
(A) High cost of adaptation.
(B) Variations in conditions of use.
(C) Country of origin effect.
(D) Economies in R & D.
(E) Differences in technical standards.
Choose the most appropriate answer from the options given below :
(1) (A) and (E) only
(2) (A), (C) and (D) only
(3) (A), (B), (C) and (D) only
(4) (C) and (D) only

80. Banker sale of a mortgage portfolio by setting up a mortgage pass-through securities is an example of :
(1) Credit enhancement
(2) Unbundling
(3) Derivatives
(4) Securitisation

81. Match List I with List II

List – I Nature of goods	**List – II** Income Elasticity (E_i) of demand
(A) Normal goods	(I) E_i is greater than one
(B) Inferior goods	(II) E^i is greater than zero
(C) Luxury goods	(III) E_i is between zero and one
(D) Necessities	(IV) E_i is less than zero

Choose the correct answer from the options given below:
(1) (A)-(II), (B)-(IV), (C)-(I), (D)-(III)
(2) (A)-(III), (B)-(I), (C)-(IV), (D)-(II)
(3) (A)-(II), (B)-(I), (C)-(III), (D)-(IV)
(4) (A)-(I), (B)-(III), (C)-(II), (D)-(IV)

82. Which one of the following is not an assumption of simple linear regression model?
(1) The set of expected values of the dependent variable y for given values of independent variable x. are normally distributed.
(2) The standard deviation and variance of expected values of the dependent Variable about the regression line are constant for all values of the independent variable x for the set of observations in a sample.
(3) The dependent variable y is a continuous random variable.
(4) The holiday in the value of y are identical in successive observations.

83. Tax holiday under the Income Tax Act 1961 has been used in the context of which one of the following?
(1) Section 80 IA (2) Section 80 D
(3) Section 80 CCC (4) Section 10(5)

84. Given below are two statements : One is labelled as Assertion (A) and the other is labelled as Reason (R) :
Assertion (A): Substitution effect is usually much larger than the income effect.
Reason (R): Consumer usually spends only a small portion of her/his income on any one commodity.
In the light of the above Statements, choose the correct answer from the options given below :
(1) Both (A) and (R) are true and (R) is the correct explanation of (A)
(2) Both (A) and (R) are true but (R) is NOT the correct explanation of (A)
(3) (A) is true but (R) is false
(4) (A) is false but (R) is true

85. Which one of the following tools is not used for forecasting personnel needs (Labour Demand) by an organization?

(1) Trend Analysis (2) Markov Analysis
(3) Ratio Analysis (4) Scatter Plot

86. Who among the following are indentified as the Key managerial personnel in the Indian Companies Act, 2013?

(A) Chief Executive Officer
(B) Whole Time Director
(C) Company Secretary
(D) Chief Risk Officer
(E) Manager

Choose the most appropriate answer from the options given below :

(1) (A), (B) and (D) only
(2) (A) and (B) only
(3) (A), (B), (C) and (D) only
(4) (A), (B), (C) and (E) only

87. In order to maintain its market share, a market follower can employ :

(1) Counterfeiting strategy
(2) Specialization strategy
(3) Counter offensive strategy
(4) Preemptive strategy

88. Under Indian Income Tax Act, in order to claim deduction of interest on home loan for house property, which of the following things need to be taken care of ?

(A) The home loan must be used for the purchase construction of the house property.
(B) The loan must be taken on or after 1st April, 2019.
(C) The amount of loan must be used within 10 days from the date of loan taken.
(D) The purchase or construction must be completed within 5 years from the end of Financial Year in which the loan was taken.
(E) The rate of interest on loan cannot exceed 22%.

Choose the most appropriate answer from the options given below :

(1) (A), (B), (D) only
(2) (A), (C), (D), (E) only
(3) (B), (C), (D), (E) only
(4) (A) and (D) only

89. What will be the sequence of steps involved in 'Net Benefit Model' of Human Resource Accounting'?

(A) The gross value of services to be rendered in future by the employee in their individual as well as their collective capacity is determined.
(B) The excess of the value of future human resources over the value of future payments is ascertained.
(C) The present value of the net benefit is determined by applying a pre-determined discount rate.
(D) The value of future payments to the employees is determined.
(E) The amount calculated under 'C' will be the value of human resources to the organisation.

Choose the correct sequence from the options given below :

(1) (A), (D), (B), (C), (E)
(2) (A), (B), (C), (D), (E)
(3) (A), (C), (D), (B), (E)
(4) (B), (A), (C), (D), (E)

90. Which of the following are the main platforms for social media?

(A) Search Engines
(B) Online communities and forums
(C) Blogs
(D) Social Networks
(E) Web 1.0

Choose the correct answer from the options given below :

(1) (B), (C) and (D) only
(2) (B) and (D) only
(3) (B), (C), (D) and (E) only
(4) (A), (B), (C) and (E) only

Read the following passage and answer the question.

GOI has reaffirmed its intent in amendments to the Finance Bill to use tax as a deterrent to speculation in virtual digital assets. The amendments disallow losses on the sale of one crypto asset to be set off against gains on another. No deduction is permitted for any expenditure other than the cost of acquisition for computation of income from sale of cryptos and non-fungible tokens (NFTs). Every transfer of crypto assets will be taxed, at the proposed 30% rate, irrespective of whether they are a capital asset or not. Only the proposed 1% rate of tax deducted at source will apply to transactions in digital assets. Penalties have been imposed for taxpayers who have claimed a deduction of surcharge and cess from their taxable income, but have not, on their own accord, paid the tax and interest on the deduction they have claimed. The inability to set off losses will skew the risk-reward profile of digital assets, and crypto exchanges fear it could push trading activity beyond Indian jurisdiction to decentralized exchanges and foreign platforms accessed through virtual private networks. The industry feels not allowing tax deduction on the costs of mining cryptos will eventually force blockchain companies and the talent they hire to operate outside the country. To the extent that the proposed tax regime drives users from exchanges compliant with know-your-customer (KYC) rules towards underground peer-to-peer platforms, deterrence would be diluted.

Nirmala Sitharaman, in her statement while moving the amendments, has clarified the tax on private digital assets does not indicate GOI's stance on their legitimacy. The regulatory position could become clearer once the Reserve Bank of India (RBI) is ready with its digital currency. Fiat digital currencies, which make transactions and monetary transmission more efficient, are inevitable as the use of cash plateaus in several countries. Speculation, and a reflex to curb it, must not draw attention away from the inherent superiority of digital currencies. This is the future of money.

91. Which one of the following is done by the Digital Currency Regulatory Framework?
(1) Eventually force blockchain companies to operate from outside.
(2) Attract users towards exchanges which are compliant with know-your-customer rules.
(3) Motivate the operators to operate outside the country.
(4) Promote underground Peer to peer crypto platforms.

92. Digital currency regulations will result into which one of the following?
(1) Scare digital currencies away.
(2) Permit deduction of any expenditure other than the cost of acquisition for computation of income.
(3) Impose penalties for tax payers who have claimed a deduction of surcharge and cess from their taxable income.
(4) Attract 30% tax on every transfer of crypto asset.

93. Given below are two statements :
Statement I: Non-fungible tokens cannot be splitted.
Statement II: Non-fungible tokens can be replicated at convenience.
In the light of the above Statements, choose the most appropriate answer from the options given below :
(1) Both Statement I and Statement II are correct
(2) Both Statement I and Statement II are incorrect
(3) Statement I is correct but Statement II is incorrect
(4) Statement I is incorrect but Statement II is correct

94. Government of India's intent towards virtual digital assets is which one of the following?
(1) To promote speculation
(2) To be silent on speculation
(3) To discourage speculation
(4) To stop speculation

95. Given below are two statements : One is labelled as Assertion (A) and the other is labelled as Reason (R) :
Assertion (A): Crypto exchanges fear that the new amendments could push trading activity beyond Indian jurisdiction to decentralized exchanges.
Reason (R): The new amendments disallow losses on the sale of new crypto asset to be set off against gains on another.
In the light of the above Statements, choose the most appropriate answer from the options given below :
(1) Both (A) and (R) are correct and (R) is the correct explanation of (A)
(2) Both (A) and (R) are correct but (R) is NOT the correct explanation of (A)
(3) (A) is correct but (R) is not correct
(4) (A) is not correct but (R) is correct

Read the given passage and answer the question.

Naik, AGM Materials, is fuming and fretting. He bumped into Kamath. GM (Materials), threw the resignation letter on his table, shouted and walked out of the room swiftly.

Naik has reason for his sudden outburst. He has been driven to the wall. Perhaps, details of the story will tell the reasons for Naiks bile and why he put in his papers, barely four months after he took up his present assignment.

The year was 2021 when Naik quit the prestigious SAIL plant at Vishakapatnam. As a manager materials, Nail; enjoyed powers – he could even place an order for materials worth Rs. 25 lakh. He needed nobody's prior approval.

Nails joined a pulp-making plant located at Harihar in Karnataka, as AGM Materials. The plant is a part of the multiproduct and multiplant-conglomerate owned by a prestigious business house in India.

Obviously, perks, designation and reputation of the conglomerate lured Naik away from the public sector steel monolith.

When he joined the eucalyptus pulp making company, little did Nail realise that he needed prior approval to place an order for materials worth Rs. 12 lakh. He had presumed that he had the authority to place an order by himself worth half the amount of what he used to do at the mega steel maker. He placed the order, materials arrived, were received, accepted and used up in the plant.

Trouble started when the bill for Rs. 12 lakh came from the vendor. The accounts department Withheld payment for the reason that the bill was not endorsed by Kamath, Kamath refused to sign on the bill as his approval was not taken by Naik before placing the order.

Naik felt fumigated and cheated. A brief encounter with Kamath only aggravated the problem. Naik was curtly told that he should have known company rules before venturing, Naik decided to quit.

96. What is the most ineffective in the organisation?
(1) Recruitment policy (2) Selection policy
(3) Induction programme
(4) Promotion policy

97. The job of AGM materials is to
(1) Place order (2) Receive material
(3) Inspect material (4) Issue material

98. Given below are two statements :
Statement I: Naik's presumption that he could place an order for materials Worth Rs.2-5 lakh was right.
Statement II: Perks and reputation of the conglomerate were the reasons for Mr. Nail joining the eucalyptus pulp making company.
In the light of the above Statements, choose the most appropriate answer from the options given below :
(1) Both Statement I and Statement II are correct
(2) Both Statement I and Statement II are incorrect
(3) Statement I is correct but Statement II is incorrect
(4) Statement I is incorrect but Statement II is correct

99. As per the passage, who is at fault?
(1) Mr. Naik (2) Mr. Kamath
(3) Both Mr. Naik and Mr. Kamath
(4) Human Resource Department

100. Given below are two statements : One is labelled as Assertion (A) and the other is labelled as Reason (R):
Assertion (A): It was right on the part of accounts department to withheld payment.
Reason (R): Mr. Naik had the authority to place the order for materials worth Rs. 25 lakh.
In the light of the above Statements, choose the correct answer from the options given below :
(1) Both (A) and (R) are true and (R) is the correct explanation of (A)
(2) Both (A) and (R) are true but (R) is NOT the correct explanation of (A)
(3) (A) is true but (R) is false
(4) (A) is false but (R) is true

ANSWERS

1. (4)	**2.** (1)	**3.** (3)	**4.** (4)	**5.** (4)	**6.** (4)	**7.** (2)	**8.** (2)	**9.** (3)	**10.** (3)
11. (2)	**12.** (2)	**13.** (2)	**14.** (4)	**15.** (1)	**16.** (3)	**17.** (4)	**18.** (1)	**19.** (3)	**20.** (2)
21. (1)	**22.** (1)	**23.** (4)	**24.** (2)	**25.** (1)	**26.** (4)	**27.** (2)	**28.** (4)	**29.** (1)	**30.** (3)
31. (4)	**32.** (3)	**33.** (1)	**34.** (3)	**35.** (2)	**36.** (4)	**37.** (1)	**38.** (4)	**39.** (3)	**40.** (2)
41. (2)	**42.** (4)	**43.** (3)	**44.** (3)	**45.** (3)	**46.** (2)	**47.** (2)	**48.** (3)	**49.** (2)	**50.** (2)
51. (2)	**52.** (2)	**53.** (3)	**54.** (1)	**55.** (4)	**56.** (3)	**57.** (4)	**58.** (1)	**59.** (3)	**60.** (1)
61. (1)	**62.** (3)	**63.** (4)	**64.** (1)	**65.** (2)	**66.** (1)	**67.** (4)	**68.** (4)	**69.** (2)	**70.** (1)
71. (1)	**72.** (4)	**73.** (2)	**74.** (4)	**75.** (4)	**76.** (2)	**77.** (4)	**78.** (3)	**79.** (2)	**80.** (4)
81. (1)	**82.** (4)	**83.** (1)	**84.** (1)	**85.** (2)	**86.** (4)	**87.** (1)	**88.** (4)	**89.** (1)	**90.** (1)
91. (2)	**92.** (4)	**93.** (3)	**94.** (3)	**95.** (1)	**96.** (3)	**97.** (1)	**98.** (4)	**99.** (4)	**100.** (3)

MARCH, 2023
COMMERCE
Paper-II

Note : This paper contains **hundred (100)** objective type questions of **two (2)** marks each. **All** questions are **compulsory**.

1. Which one of the following non-tariff barriers is to be adequately addressed by India while signing FTA with any country that has potential to import fruits, vegetables and other plant-based products from India?
(1) Phytosanitary Regulations
(2) Sanitary Regulations
(3) Complex Registrations
(4) Restrictive customs procedure

2. According to the Heckscher-Ohlin theory, which one of the following statements is correct?
(1) Trade should take place among countries that have greater differences in their factor endowments.
(2) A country with a relatively cheaper cost of labour would export labour-intensive products.
(3) Country benefits from international trade even if it is less efficient than other nations.
(4) Countries with the proximity of geographical locations would have greater trade compared to the distant ones.

3. Which one of the following FTA was signed in February 2022 and came into force in May 2022?
(1) AI-ECTA Australia - India Economic Cooperation and Trade Agreement
(2) India-UAE Comprehensive Economic Partnership Agreement (CEPA)
(3) India-Nepal Treaty of Trade
(4) India-Singapore Comprehensive Economic Cooperation Agreement (CECA)

4. The Government of India on 27-9-22 extended the existing Foreign Trade Policy (2015-20) up to which one of the following on account of volatile global economic and geo-political situation and currency fluctuations?
(1) December 2022 (2) March 2023
(3) September 2023 (4) December 2023

5. Which one of the following Ind AS is related to "The Effects of Changes in Foreign Exchange Rates"?
(1) Ind AS 19 (2) Ind AS 115
(3) Ind AS 103 (4) Ind AS 21

6. Policy of 'Playing Safe' followed by the accountant is based on which one of the following concepts?
(1) Dual Aspect Concept
(2) Conservation Conventions
(3) Money Measurement Concept
(4) Realization Concept

7. X and Y are partners in a firm sharing profits in the ratio 4:5. X surrenders 1/4 of his share and Y surrenders 1/5 of his share in favour of Z, the new partner. What will be the new profit-sharing ratio of the firm's partners?
(1) 3:4:2 (2) 55:44:81
(3) 4:5:2 (4) 44:55:81

8. Net profit after taxes of a firm is Rs.1,00,000 and its fixed interest charges on long term debt are Rs. 20,000. What is the interest coverage ratio if the rate of income tax is 60%?
(1) 13 times (2) 13.5 times
(3) 12.5 times (4) 5 times

9. The study of unemployment is the subject matter of which one of the following Economics?
(1) Descriptive Economics
(2) Normative Economics
(3) Micro Economics
(4) Macro Economics

10. Which one of the following commodities has the most inelastic demand?
(1) Cigarette (2) Soap
(3) Ice-cream (4) Salt

11. 'Sales Revenue Maximization' as an alternate objective of business firms was postulated by whom of the following?

(1) O.E. Williamson (2) Cyert and March
(3) W.J. Baumol (4) K.W. Rothschild

12. Which one of the following statements is correct regarding the slope and the point elasticity on all the points on a rectangular hyperbola shaped demand curve of a product?
(1) Slope remains the same while point elasticity goes on changing.
(2) Slope goes on changing while point elasticity remains the same.
(3) Both slope and point elasticity remain the same.
(4) Both slope and point elasticity go on changing.

13. The current market price of a company's share is Rs. 90 and the expected dividend per share next year is Rs. 4.50. If the dividends are expected to grow at a constant rate of 8%, the shareholders required rate of return is
(1) 5% (2) 8%
(3) 13% (4) 20%

14. The Kinked-shaped revenue curve of a firm relates to which one type of the market structure?
(1) Perfect Competition
(2) Oligopoly
(3) Monopoly
(4) Monopolistic Competition

15. 'Value-additivity principle' implies in which one of the following methods of capital budgeting?
(1) Payback period method
(2) NPV method
(3) IRR method (4) ARR method

16. The risk-free rate is 6 per cent, the market risk premium is 9 per cent and the beta of share is 1.54, then what is cost of equity?
(1) 23% (2) 19%
(3) 13% (4) 20%

17. While averaging rates and ratios where time factor is variable and the act being performed is constant, which one of the following measures of Central Tendency is appropriate?
(1) Arithmetic average
(2) Mode
(3) Harmonic mean
(4) Geometric mean

18. If two regression coefficients are 0.8 and 1.2, which one of the following is the value of coefficient of correlation?
(1) 0.97 (2) 0.96
(3) 1.00 (4) 0.80

19. Which one of the following statements is true?
(1) For a symmetrical distribution $\beta_1 = 0$.
(2) Kurtosis means 'lack of symmetry'.
(3) β_2 can be negative.
(4) Skewness studies the flatness or peakedness of the distribution.

20. Which one of the following statements is incorrect?
(1) Algebraic sum of deviations taken from Arithmetic Mean is zero.
(2) The sum of absolute deviations taken from Median is the largest.
(3) Standard deviation is always less than range.
(4) The sum of the squares of deviations of a given set of observations is minimum, when taken about the arithmetic mean.

21. Which one of the following is referent source of power?
(1) Perception or belief that the manager has some special knowledge.
(2) Manager's desire to identify with or imitate the subordinate.
(3) Ability of the manager to reward the subordinate for obeying orders.
(4) Ability of the manager to punish the subordinate for not obeying orders.

22. Which one of the following is NOT an advantage of the line organization?
(1) It ensures excellent discipline.
(2) It fixes responsibility for the performance of tasks.
(3) It is suitable for big organizations.
(4) It is not expensive.

23. A scale that measures a fair sample of the tasks and skills actually needed for the job in question is known as
(1) Test validity (2) Criterion validity
(3) Content validity (4) Construct validity

24. Training technique which teaches the importance of resolving matters is known as:
(1) Built-in-Tension (2) Shadowing
(3) Tag Teams (4) Mirroring

25. When Central Bank conducts a sale of securities, the cash reserve of commercial banks shall
(1) Increase at slow rate
(2) Decrease

(3) Remain constant
(4) Increase at fast rate

26. 'Average clause' in insurance is applicable for which one of the following cases?
(1) Double Insurance
(2) Re-insurance
(3) Over insurance
(4) Under insurance

27. ABC Ventures is private equity investor considering investing Rs. 1,000 million in the equity of XYZ ltd. ABC Ventures requires a return of 30% on investment with planned holding period of 5 years. The likely debt of XYZ ltd. will be Rs. 1000 million and cash balance of Rs. 300 million with a projected EBITDA of Rs. 1500 million for the year 5. The desired ownership share of ABC Ventures in XYZ ltd., given FVF0.30,5= 3.713, will be
(1) 37.13% (2) 30.00%
(3) 37.90% (4) 7.13%

28. One of the assumptions in Black-Scholes Option Pricing Model is that underlying asset prices are
(1) Equi-distributed
(2) Marginally distributed
(3) Log-normally distributed
(4) Normally distributed

29. In which one of the following service products, price sensitivity of the customers is low?
(1) Car rentals (2) Transport
(3) Medical services (4) Retailing

30. Which one of the following is correct while segmenting consumer markets on demographic basis?
(1) Low predictability of consumer choice behaviour and high cost of measurement.
(2) Low predictability of consumer choice behaviour and low cost of measurement.
(3) High predictability of consumer choice behaviour and low cost of measurement.
(4) High predictability of consumer choice behaviour and high cost of measurement.

31. Which one of the following is NOT a market-oriented definition of a business?
(1) We run a railroad.
(2) We help improve office productivity.
(3) We supply energy.
(4) We distribute information.

32. In which one of the following concepts, a buyer is passively involved in an exchange transaction, and he accepts whatever is offered to him by a marketer?
(1) Production concept
(2) Product concept
(3) Selling concept
(4) Marketing concept

33. If invoice discounting is not confidential in nature, the customers of the client are advised to make payment directly to the factor. This facility, when offered with a non-recourse, is known as:
(1) Agency Factoring
(2) Protected invoice discounting
(3) Full factoring
(4) Odd line factoring

34. The practice of forging a return address on an e-mail so that the recipient is fooled into revealing private information is termed as:
(1) Hacking (2) Cracking
(3) Dumpster diving (4) Spoofing

35. If anyone fraudulently or dishonestly makes use of the electronic signature, password or any other unique identification feature of any other person then under which section of IT Act 2000, punishment shall be given?
(1) Section 63 (2) Section 66B
(3) Section 66C (4) Section 67B

36. From Dec. 1, 2022 which body handles all complaints related to Profiteering under Goods and Services Tax (GST)?
(1) National Anti-Profiteering Authority (NAA)
(2) NITI Aayog
(3) Competition Commission of India (CCI)
(4) GST Council

37. Section 80 GGC of Income Tax Act is related with which one of the following?
(1) Deduction in respect of contribution given by any company to political parties.
(2) Deduction in respect of contribution given by any person to political parties.
(3) Deduction in respect of rent paid.
(4) Deduction in respect of certain donation for scientific research.

38. Which one of the following is NOT correct for Tonnage Tax System?
(1) It is a scheme of presumptive taxation.

(2) It is applicable for the taxation of income derived from shipping activities.
(3) It is applicable for both Indian as well as foreign companies.
(4) Computation of tonnage income is covered U/S 115 VG.

39. Tax on declared dividend is paid by whom?
(1) Shareholders/ Receiver of the dividend
(2) Manager
(3) Distributor of the dividend
(4) Company

40. Which one of the following is NOT related to Income Tax in India?
(1) Taxpayer Identification Number (TIN)
(2) Dearness Allowance (DA)
(3) Leave Travel Allowance (LTA)
(4) Tax Deduction and Collection Account Number (TAN)

41. After COVID-19, which of the following are the upskilling enablers for women in India?
A. Introduction of electric vehicles.
B. Flexible work opportunities.
C. Work from home.
D. Need to stay relevant, especially in technology.
E. Willingness to return to work.
Choose the most appropriate answer from the options given below:
(1) A and B only (2) C and D only
(3) C, D and E only (4) B, C, D and E only

42. E-commerce and large retailers in India bet big on mega consumption events on which of the following days?
A. Republic Day
B. Independence Day
C. Black Friday
D. Cyber Monday
E. Akshya Tritiya
Choose the most appropriate answer from the options given below:
(1) A and B only (2) C and D only
(3) A, B and E only (4) A, B, C, D and E

43. Which of the following are NOT assumptions of Marginal Costing?
A. The total cost can be segregated into fixed and variable components.
B. Fixed costs per unit of production remains constant.
C. Variable cost remains constant per unit of output.
D. The selling price per unit remains unchanged.
E. Variable cost is variable per unit.
Choose the correct answer from the options given below:
(1) A and B only (2) B and E only
(3) C and D only (4) B and C only

44. Which of the following transactions are related to Financing Activities?
a. Share issued for cash.
b. Dividend distributed to shareholders.
c. Sale of machinery.
d. Redemption of debentures.
e. Provision for depreciation.
Choose the correct answer from the options given below:
(1) a and e only (2) a and c only
(3) a, b and d only (4) a, b, c and d only

45. Which of the following statements are correct?
A. A monopolist can charge any price to maximize profits.
B. The slope of monopoly's MR curve is twice that of AR curve.
C. A necessary condition for monopoly's long-run equilibrium is AC = AR = MC = MR.
D. A monopolist is in equilibrium where MC = MR.
E. Equilibrium price of a monopolist is always higher than that of a competitive firm.
Choose the correct answer from the options given below:
(1) A, B and C only (2) B, C and D only
(3) B, D and E only (4) C, D and E only

46. Which of the following factors hinder the formation and sustainability of Cartels?
a. Less number of firms in the industry.
b. Presence of differentiated products.
c. Different cost structures.
d. Low frequency sales coupled with huge amounts of output.
e. Absence of monopolies and restrictive trade practices.
Choose the most appropriate answer from the options given below:
(1) b, c and d only (2) a, d and e only
(3) c, d and e only (4) b, c and e only

47. Which of the following factors determine the requirements of working capital of a firm?
 a. Nature of Business
 b. Technology and Manufacturing Policy
 c. Management Skills
 d. Credit Policy
 e. Market and Demand Conditions

 Choose the correct answer from the options given below:
 (1) a, b, c and d only (2) a, b, d, and e only
 (3) c, d and e only (4) a, b and e only

48. Which of the following are related to primary capital market?
 a. IPO b. Long Term Loans
 c. Venture Capital d. Letters of Credit
 e. Participation Certificates

 Choose the most appropriate answer from the options given below:
 (1) a, b and e only (2) c, d and e only
 (3) a, b and c only (4) a, d and e only

49. Which among the following are the measures of Central Tendency or Measures of Location?
 A. Mean B. Range
 C. Mode D. Median
 E. Variance

 Choose the most appropriate answer from the options given below:
 (1) A, B, C and E only
 (2) C, D and E only
 (3) A, C and D only
 (4) B, C and D only

50. In which of the following practical situations, Poisson Distribution can be used?
 A. Number of customers arriving at the super markets per hour.
 B. Number of typographical errors per page in a typed material.
 C. Number of accidents taking place per day on a busy road.
 D. Dice throwing problems.
 E. Number of defective material say, blades, etc. in a packing manufactured by a good concern.

 Choose the most appropriate answer from the options given below:
 (1) B, D and E only
 (2) A, B, C and E only
 (3) A, C, D and E only
 (4) A, B, C and D only

51. Which of the following attributes are true in systems approach to performance appraisal?
 A. Low degree of formality.
 B. Occasional appraisal frequency.
 C. Individual-oriented reward practices.
 D. Facilitative leadership practices.
 E. Problem solving as primary goal.

 Choose the most appropriate answer from the options given below:
 (1) A, D and E only (2) A, B and D only
 (3) B, C and E only (4) A, C, D and E only

52. Which of the following are the distinct features of the Principles of Management?
 A. Flexibility
 B. Universal application.
 C. Principles are absolute, not relative.
 D. Based on situation.
 E. Derived out of experience.

 Choose the correct answer from the options given below:
 (1) A, C and E only (2) A, B and D only
 (3) B, C, D and E only
 (4) A, B, D and E only

53. According to Henri Fayol, which of the following are the Principles of Management?
 A. Discipline
 B. Decentralization
 C. Unity of Command
 D. Equity
 E. Instability of Tenure

 Choose the correct answer from the options given below:
 (1) A, C, D only (2) A, B, C, E only
 (3) A, B, D only (4) B, C, E only

54. Which of the following are the functions of Reserve Bank of India?
 A. Issue of Currency
 B. Accepting Deposits
 C. Banker of Government
 D. Bankers Bank E. Credit Control

 Choose the correct answer from the options given below:
 (1) B and C only (2) A and D only
 (3) A, B, C and D only
 (4) A, C, D, and E only

55. For ongoing maintenance of regulatory capital, which of the following risks were covered by Pillar-1 Minimum Capital Requirement?

A. Credit Risk B. Financial risk
C. Operation Risk D. Market Risk
E. Reputational Risk

Choose the correct answer from the options given below:

(1) A, B and C only (2) A, B and D only
(3) B, C and D only (4) A, C and D only

56. Which of the following are the advantages of Mobile Banking?

A. Insecure B. Fraud reduction
C. Time saving
D. Separate internet required
E. Increased efficiency

Choose the most appropriate answer from the options given below:

(1) B, C and E only (2) A, B and D only
(3) C, D and E only (4) B, D and E only

57. Which of the following are to be determined to estimate current market demand?

A. Total Market potential
B. Area Market potential
C. Analyse past sales
D. Sales force's input
E. Market share

Choose the most appropriate answer from the options given below:

(1) A, C and E only (2) B, D and E only
(3) A, C and D only (4) A, B and E only

58. Which of the following are social factors influencing consumer's behaviour?

A. Culture B. Social class
C. Groups D. Family
E. Roles and status

Choose the most appropriate answer from the options given below:

(1) A, D and E only (2) B, C, D and E only
(3) C, D and E only (4) B and C only

59. Which of the following are true when an organization uses intensive distribution of its products?

A. Customers are moderate in number.
B. Widespread market coverage
C. Customers are brand-conscious
D. Mass advertising
E. Pleasant shopping conditions

Choose the most appropriate answer from the options given below:

(1) B, D and E only (2) A, B and C only
(3) B and D only (4) B, C and D only

60. As per RTI Act, 2005, which of the following are exempted from disclosure [U/S 8(1)]?

a. Information, the disclosure of which cause a breach of privilege of Parliament or the State Legislature.
b. The monthly remuneration received by employee.
c. Information received in confidence from foreign government.
d. Information which relates to personal information the disclosure of which has no relationship to any public activity or interest.
e. A statement of the categories of documents that are held by public authority or under its control.

Choose the correct answer from the options given below:

(1) a, b and e only (2) a, c and d only
(3) c, d and e only (4) b, c and d only

61. An instrument is to be called 'Negotiable' as per Negotiable Instruments Act, 1881, if it possesses which of the following characteristics?

a. Can be transferred infinitum.
b. Having minimum lock-in period.
c. Freely transferable.
d. The holder cannot sue in his own name.
e. Holder's title free from defects.

Choose the correct answer from the options given below:

(1) a, c and e only (2) a, b and e only
(3) b, d and e only (4) a, b, c and e only

62. Intellectual Capital of an enterprise includes its:

A. Processes
B. Designs
C. Relationships developed with its customers and suppliers.
D. Internet domain names.
E. Copyrights

Choose the correct answer from the options given below:

(1) A, B, C and D only
(2) B, C and E only
(3) C, D and E only
(4) A, B, C, D and E

63. Income received and accrued or arisen outside India from a business controlled in or a profession set up in India, is taxed in the hands of which of the following?

a. Every citizen of India
b. Domicile of India
c. Ordinary Resident
d. Non-Ordinarily Resident
e. Non-Resident

Choose the correct answer from the options given below:

(1) a and c only (2) a and b only
(3) c and d only (4) c, d and e only

64. Which of the following are related to tax-evasion?

a. Claiming bogus expenses and losses.
b. Hiding capital nature of profits.
c. Showing sales transactions.
d. Showing excess transactions.
e. Showing real income and expenses.

Choose the correct answer from the options given below:

(1) a and b only (2) a, b and d only
(3) a, b and c only (4) c and e only

65. Which of the following conditions should be fulfilled by an Assessee to avail deduction u/s. 91 of Income Tax Act. 1961?

a. The Assessee is a tax resident in India during the relevant previous year.
b. The income accrues or arises to him/her outside India.
c. There is an agreement for relief from double taxation between India and the other country when the income has accrued or arisen.
d. The Assessee has paid tax on his/her foreign income in the foreign country.
e. India does not have any agreement for relief from double taxation with the country.

Choose the most appropriate answer from the options given below:

(1) a and e only (2) b and c only
(3) a, b, d and e only (4) a, b and e only

66. Match List I with List II:

List I (COP 27)	List II (COP 27 Action Plan)
A. Mitigation	I. Promote climate know-how solutions.
B. Capitalize	II. Empowering all stakeholders to engage in climate action.
C. Technology	III. Phase down unabated coal power.
D. Capacity Building	IV. Creation of "gloss and damage fund"

Choose the correct answer from the options given below:

(1) A- II, B- III, C- IV, D- I
(2) A- IV, B- III, C- II, D- I
(3) A- III, B- IV, C- I, D- II
(4) A- IV, B- III, C- I, D- II

67. Match List I with List II:

List I (Issue)	List II (Description)
A. Cut-off	I. Assets, Liabilities and Equity balances exist at the end of the period.
B. Classification	II. Transactions and events have been recorded in proper accounts.
C. Occurrence	III. Whether all assets and liabilities are reported in the appropriate period.
D. Existence	IV. Transactions recognized in the financial statements have occurred and relate to the entity.

Choose the correct answer from the options given below:

(1) A- II, B- I, C- III, D- IV
(2) A- IV, B- III, C- II, D- I
(3) A- I, B- III, C- II, D- IV
(4) A- III, B- II, C- IV, D- I

68. Match List I with List II:

List I	List II
A. Margin of Safety	I. Profit ~ sales/PV Ratio
B. Break Even Point	II. Difference between total revenue and total variable costs
C. P V Ratio	III. Total Sales-Total Variable Cost/ Total Sales
D. Contribution	IV. Equality between contribution and total fixed costs.

Choose the correct answer from the options given below:

(1) A- I, B- II, C- III, D- IV
(2) A- I, B- IV, C- III, D- II

(3) A III, B I, C II, D IV
(4) A- IV, B- I, C- II, D- III

69. Match List I with List II:

List I	List II
A. Finance Lease	I. The lessee and the owner of the equipment are two different entities.
B. Operating Lease	II. Lessee sells an asset for cash to a prospective lessor and then leases back the same assets.
C. Sale and Lease back	III. The lessor does not transfer all the risk and rewards incidental to the ownership of the assets.
D. Direct lease	IV. The lessor transfers substantially all the risks and rewards incidental to the ownership of the assets to the lessee.

Choose the correct answer from the options given below:
(1) A- IV, B- III, C- II, D- I
(2) A- IV, B- III, C- I, D- II
(3) A- I, B- II, C- III, D-IV
(4) A- I, B- II, C- IV, D- III

70. Match List I with List II:

List I (Type of Test)	List II (Subject matter of the problem)
A. Kruskal-Wallis test	I. Parametric test to compare means of more than two population groups.
B. Z-test	II. Non-parametric test to compare means of more than two population groups.
C. ANOVA test	III. Non-parametric test to test the goodness of fit.
D. Chi-square test	IV. Testing the difference between means of two sample groups.

Choose the correct answer from the options given below:
(1) A- II, B- IV, C- I, D- III
(2) A- II, B- III, C- IV, D- I
(3) A- III, B- I, C- II, D- IV
(4) A- I, B- II, C- III, D-IV

71. Match List I with List II:

List I (Characteristic)	List II (Leadership Mode)
A. Source of power	I. Power extension
B. Concept of power	II. Empowerment
C. Dominant need	III. Building culture
D. Managing style	IV. Multiplying

Choose the correct answer from the options given below:
(1) A- II, B- IV, C- I, D- III
(2) A- IV, B- II, C- I, D- III
(3) A- II, B- IV, C- III, D-I
(4) A- II, B- III, C- I, D- IV

72. Match List I with List II:

List I (Application narratives)

A. Time interval between successive arrival of customers in a queue.
B. Distribution of income, property and certain human abilities in a capitalistic society.
C. Movement of stock prices and distributing of income in a socialistic society.
D. Distribution of rare events i.e. the probability of occurrence is very small but the number of trials are very large.

List II (Statistical distributions)

I. Pareto distribution
II. Poisson distribution
III. Exponential distribution
IV. Lognormal distribution

Choose the correct answer from the options given below:
(1) A- II, B- IV, C- III, D- I
(2) A- III, B- I, C- IV, D- II
(3) A- I, B- IV, C- II, D- III
(4) A- I, B- II, C- III, D- IV

73. Match List I with List II:

List I (Sales Promotion Method)	List II (Goal)
A. Stock allowances	I. To incentivize customers to try a new product.
B. Premiums	II. To incentivize stores to try a new product.

C. Sampling — III. To incentivize stores to keep selling a product.

D. Advertising — IV. To incentivize customers to increase their consumption.

Choose the correct answer from the options given below:

(1) A- II, B- IV, C- I, D- III
(2) A- IV, B- II, C- I, D- III
(3) A- II, B- IV, C- III, D- I
(4) A- III, B- IV, C- I, D- II

74. Match List I with List II:

List I	List II
A. Sale by Auction	I. 15
B. Breach of Warranty	II. 27
C. Sale by Description	III. 13
D. Transfer of Title	IV. 64

Choose the correct answer from the options given below:

(1) A- IV, B- III, C- I, D- II
(2) A- IV, B- I, C- III, D- II
(3) A- III, B- IV, C- II, D- I
(4) A- III, B- I, C- II, D- IV

75. Match List I with List II:

List I (Income Tax Return)	List II (Relationship with)
A. ITR-2	I. For a company other than a company claiming exemption under section 11.
B. ITR-6	II. For presumptive business income covered u/s 44 AD and 44 AE.
C. ITR-7	III. For a person (including a company who are required to furnish return u/s 139 (4A) or 139 (4B) or 139 (4C) or 139 (4D).
D. ITR-4 (Sugam)	IV. For individual and HUF not having income for business and profession.

Choose the correct answer from the options given below:

(1) A- IV, B- I, C- II, D- III
(2) A- IV, B- I, C- III, D- II
(3) A- III, B- II, C- IV, D- I
(4) A- II, B- I, C- IV, D- III

76. Sequence the following different settlement stages of the WTO dispute settlement System.

A. Retaliation
B. Implementation
C. Panel Review
D. Appellate
E. Consultations

Choose the correct answer from the options given below:

(1) D, E, A, C, B
(2) E, D, C, A, B
(3) E, C, D, B, A
(4) D, E, C, A, B

77. Arrange in proper sequence the following benefits available to Information System Auditor who uses CATT:

A. Check susceptibility to threat. Much of the accounting is done through cloud accounts or other online system.
B. Evaluating the system
C. Data security
D. Bolsters controls
E. Develop IT Governance

Choose the correct answer from the options given below:

(1) E, D, C, B, A
(2) C, B, A, D, E
(3) A, B, C, D, E
(4) B, A, E, C, D

78. Arrange the following steps in a proper sequence to forecast the demand for a product systematically and scientifically.

A. Making choice of method for demand forecasting.
B. Estimation and interpretation of results.
C. Specifying the objectives.
D. Determining the time perspective.
E. Collection of data and data adjustment.

Choose the correct answer from the options given below:

(1) C, A, E, D, B
(2) C, D, A, E, B
(3) A, C, D, B, E
(4) E, D, C, A, B

79. Arrange the following steps involved in the budgeting in a proper sequence:

A. Screening the proposal.
B. Evaluation of various proposals.
C. Identification of Investment proposal.
D. Performance review.
E. Implementing the proposal.

Choose the correct answer from the options given below:

(1) A, C, B, D, E (2) C, A, D, B, E
(3) C, A, B, E, D (4) A, B, C, D, E

80. Arrange the following steps involved in a research process to carry out orderly and systematic research:

A. Formulating hypothesis.
B. Collection and analysis of data.
C. Defining research problem.
D. Prepare research design.
E. Interpretation and report writing.

Choose the correct answer from the options given below:

(1) D, A, C, E, B (2) C, A, D, B, E
(3) A, B, C, D, E (4) C, B, A, E, D

81. Arrange the following examples of human needs in the hierarchy of their increasing importance.

a. Insurance for accidents.
b. Recognition and respect from others.
c. Food and shelter provisions.
d. Accomplishing distinction in chosen area by maximising potential.
e. Developing meaningful relations with others.

Choose the correct answer from the options given below:

(1) a, c, e, b, d (2) c, a, b, e, d
(3) a, c, e, d, b (4) c, a, e, b, d

82. Arrange the following industry verticals in the ascending order of their weightages in the index of core industries in India.

A. Coal B. Cement
C. Refinery Products D. Electricity
E. Steel

Choose the correct answer from the options given below:

(1) A, C, D, B, E (2) E, B, D, A, C
(3) B, A, E, D, C (4) B, E, D, C, A

83. Arrange the following stages of buying decision process in the logical sequence.

A. Comprehension
B. Adoption
C. Need recognition
D. Legitimization
E. Attitude forming

Choose the correct answer from the options given below:

(1) A, C, D, E, B (2) C, A, B, D, E
(3) C, A, E, D, B (4) C, E, D, A, B

84. Arrange the Intellectual Capital Management Process Flow Stages in a proper sequential order:

A. Index B. Capture
C. Replicate D. Identify
E. Store

Choose the correct answer from the options given below:

(1) B, D, A, E, C (2) B, D, A, C, E
(3) D, B, A, E, C (4) D, A, B, E, C

85. Computation of income from house property for let-out house, the following items are deducted. Arrange them in a proper sequence:

a. Local taxes/Municipal Taxes.
b. Standard deductions.
c. Unrealized Rent.
d. Interest on loan for the period the prior to previous year in which the house is completed (in five equal annual instalments).
e. Interest on loan taken for purchase, construction or repair of the house, relating to the previous year.

Choose the correct answer from the options given below:

(1) a, b, e, d, c (2) c, a, b, e, d
(3) a, c, b, e, d (4) d, a, b, e, c

86. Given below are two statements:

Statement I: Monetary policy on its own cannot influence economic growth but can only support it by creating congenial factors.

Statement II: Monetary policy rates change get transmitted across the markets and eventually get reflected in lending rates, mortgage rates and yields. Hence, monetary policy can address the current inflation.

In the light of the above statements, choose the most appropriate answer from the options given below:

(1) Both Statement I and Statement II are true.
(2) Both Statement I and Statement II are false.
(3) Statement I is true but Statement II is false.
(4) Statement I is false but Statement II is true

87. Given below are two statements:

One is labelled as Assertion A and the other is labelled as Reason R.

Assertion 'A': When holding company holds more than 50% (but not whole) shares of a company, then the holders of the rest of shares will be known as "Minority".

Reason 'R': Minority interest is calculated by considering proportionate shares and reserves of Holding Company.

In the light of the above statements, choose the most appropriate answer from the options given below:

(1) Both A and R are true and R is the correct explanation of A.

(2) Both A and R are true but R is not the correct explanation of A.

(3) A is true but R is false.

(4) A is false but R is true.

88. Given below are two statements:

One is labelled as Assertion A and the other is labelled as Reason R.

Assertion 'A': The theories of price determination under oligopoly are found to be inapplicable to real life market conditions.

Reason 'R': Real life oligopoly market situation is characterized by small number of sellers, interdependence of decision making, barriers to entry, indeterminate price and output; all leading to wide variety of situations.

In the light of the above statements, choose the most appropriate answer from the options given below:

(1) Both A and R are correct and R is the correct explanation of A.

(2) Both A and R are correct but R is not the correct explanation of A.

(3) A is correct but R is not correct.

(4) A is not correct but R is correct.

89. Given below are two statements:

Statement I: Translation exposure refers to the exchange gain or loss occurring from the difference in the exchange rate at the beginning and the end of the accounting period.

Statement II: Transaction exposure refers to the change in the value of the firm caused by the unexpected changes in the exchange rate.

In the light of the above statements, choose the most appropriate answer from the options given below:

(1) Both Statement I and Statement II are correct.

(2) Both Statement I and Statement II are incorrect.

(3) Statement I is correct but Statement II is incorrect.

(4) Statement I is incorrect but Statement II is correct.

90. Given below are two statements:

Statement I: If a population from which a sample is to be drawn does not constitute a homogenous group, stratified sampling technique is generally applied in order to obtain a representative sample.

Statement II: In the case of small samples, z-test is applied even if the population standard deviation is not available (given).

In the light of the above statements, choose the most appropriate answer from the options given below:

(1) Both Statement I and Statement II are correct.

(2) Both Statement I and Statement II are incorrect.

(3) Statement I is correct but Statement II is incorrect.

(4) Statement I is incorrect but Statement II is correct.

Read the Comprehension below and answer the following question:

The economy of India is a mixed, middle-income, developing social market economy. It is the world's fifth-largest economy by nominal GDP and the third-largest by Purchasing Power Parity (PPP). According to the International Monetary Fund (IMF), on a per capita income basis, India ranked 142nd by GDP (nominal) and 125th by GDP (PPP). From Independence in 1947 until 1991, successive governments promoted protectionist economic policies, with extensive state intervention and economic regulation. This is characterized as dirigisme, in the form of the Licence Raj. The end of the Cold war and an acute balance of payments crisis in 1991 led to the adoption of a broad economic liberalization in India. Since the start of the 21st century, annual average GDP growth has been 6% to 7%, and from 2013 to 2018, India was the world's fastest growing major economy, surpassing China. Economy of the Indian subcontinent was the largest in the world for most of the recorded history until the onset of colonialism in early 19th century. Share of Indian economy is 7.5% of world economy by PPP terms. The long-term growth perspective of the Indian economy remains positive due to its young population and corresponding low dependency ratio, healthy savings, and investment rates, increasing globalization in India and integration into the global economy. Nearly 70% of India's GDP is driven by domestic private consumption. The country remains the world's sixth-largest consumer market. Apart from private consumption, India's GDP is also fuelled by government spending, investments, and exports. India has been a member of the World Trade Organization since 1 January 1995. It ranks 37th on the Ease of Doing Business Index and 37th on the Global Competitiveness Report. Due to extreme rupee/dollar rate fluctuations, India's nominal GDP too fluctuates significantly. With 50 crore (500 million) workers, the Indian labour force is the world's second-largest. India has one of the world's highest number of billionaires and extreme income inequality. Because of several exemptions, barely 2% of Indians pay income taxes.

91. Given below are two statements:

Statement I: India has one of the world's highest number of billionaires and extreme income inequality. Because of several exemptions, barely 5% of Indians pay income taxes.

Statement II: With 50 crore (500 million) workers, the Indian labour force is the world's second largest.

In the light of the above statements, choose the most appropriate answer from the options given below:

(1) Both Statement I and Statement II are correct.
(2) Both Statement I and Statement II are incorrect.
(3) Statement I is correct but Statement II is incorrect.
(4) Statement I is incorrect but Statement II is correct.

92. Which of the following is NOT a correct statement?

(1) The economy of India is a mixed, middle-income, developing social market economy.
(2) India's GDP is also fuelled by government spending, investments, and exports.
(3) India has been a member of the World Trade Organization since 1 January 1996.
(4) Economy of the Indian subcontinent was the largest in the world for most of the recorded history until the onset of colonialism in early 19th century.

93. Which one of the following is NOT a supportive factor to the Indian economy's long-term growth perspective?

(1) Young population and corresponding low dependency ratio.
(2) Healthy savings and investment rates.
(3) Increasing globalization in India and integration into the global economy.
(4) Continuous increasing defence expenditure.

94. Given below are two statements:

Statement I: Since the start of the 21st century, annual average GDP growth rate of India has been 6% to 7%.

Statement II: From 2013 to 2018, India was the world's fastest growing major economy, surpassing China.

In the light of the above statements, choose the most appropriate answer from the options given below:

(1) Both Statement I and Statement II are correct.
(2) Both Statement I and Statement II are incorrect.
(3) Statement I is correct but Statement II is incorrect.
(4) Statement I is incorrect but Statement II is correct.

95. Given below are two statements:

One is labelled as Assertion A and the other is labelled as Reason R.

Assertion 'A': Nearly 70% of India's GDP is driven by domestic private consumption.

Reason 'R': The country (India) remains the world's sixth-largest consumer market.

In the light of the above statements, choose the most appropriate answer from the options given below:

(1) Both A and R are correct and R is the correct explanation of A.
(2) Both A and R are correct but R is not the correct explanation of A.
(3) A is correct but R is not correct.
(4) A is not correct but R is correct.

Read the Comprehension below and answer the following question:

India began laying the foundation for a more digital economy more than a decade ago with the launch of a national identification program called Aadhaar. The system creates biometric IDs to establish proof of residence and has been instrumental in digitizing financial transactions, among other benefits. This initiative is now part of India Stack, a decentralized public utility offering a low-cost comprehensive digital identity, payment and data management system. "IndiaStack is likely to lead to a massive change in how India spends, borrows and accesses healthcare", says an expert. IndiaStack has broad applications including a network for lowering credit costs, making loans more accessible and affordable for both consumers and businesses. Credit availability is an important component of economic growth, and "India is currently one of the most under leveraged countries in the world", says the expert, whose team thinks the ratio of credit to GDP could increase from 57% to 100% over the next decade. Indian consumers are also likely to have more disposable income. India's income distribution could flip over the next decade, and consequently overall consumption in the country could be more than double from $2 trillion in 2022 to $4.9 trillion by the end of the decade - with the greatest gains going to non-grocery retail, including apparel and accessories, leisure and recreation, and household goods and services, among other categories.

96. Which one of the following explains Aadhaar?
(1) National Identification program
(2) National Citizenship program
(3) Unified Identification program
(4) Unified census program

97. Which one of the following describes India Stack better?
A. A decentralized public utility offering a low-cost comprehensive digital identity.
B. Payment and data-management system.
C. A network for lowering credit costs.
D. A trading platform.
Choose the correct answer from the options given below:
(1) A, B and C only (2) B, C and D only
(3) A, B and D only (4) A, C and D only

98. Given below are two statements:
Statement I: Credit availability is an important component of economic growth.
Statement II: India is currently one of the most under leveraged countries in the world.
In the light of the above statements, choose the most appropriate answer from the options given below:
(1) Both Statement I and Statement II are true.
(2) Both Statement I and Statement II are false.
(3) Statement I is true but Statement II is false.
(4) Statement I is false but Statement II is true.

99. "The system creates biometric IDs to establish proof of residence and has been instrumental in digitizing financial transactions, among other benefits." The above statement talks about which one of the following?
(1) PAN (2) DIN
(3) Aadhaar (4) GST

100. Given below are two statements:
One is labelled as Assertion A and the other is labelled as Reason R.
Assertion 'A': India's income distribution could flip over the next decade.
Reason 'R': Overall consumption in the country could be more than double from $2 trillion in 2022 to $4.9 trillion by the end of the decade.
In the light of the above statements, choose the most appropriate answer from the options given below:
(1) Both A and R are true and R is the correct explanation of A.
(2) Both A and R are true but R is not the correct explanation of A.
(3) A is true but R is false.
(4) A is false but R is true.

ANSWERS

1. (1)	**2.** (1)	**3.** (2)	**4.** (2)	**5.** (4)	**6.** (2)	**7.** (1)	**8.** (2)	**9.** (4)	**10.** (4)
11. (3)	**12.** (2)	**13.** (3)	**14.** (2)	**15.** (2)	**16.** (4)	**17.** (3)	**18.** (1)	**19.** (1)	**20.** (2)
21. (2)	**22.** (3)	**23.** (3)	**24.** (1)	**25.** (2)	**26.** (4)	**27.** (3)	**28.** (3)	**29.** (3)	**30.** (2)
31. (1)	**32.** (1)	**33.** (1)	**34.** (4)	**35.** (3)	**36.** (3)	**37.** (2)	**38.** (3)	**39.** (1)	**40.** (1)
41. (4)	**42.** (4)	**43.** (2)	**44.** (3)	**45.** (3)	**46.** (1)	**47.** (2)	**48.** (3)	**49.** (3)	**50.** (2)
51. (1)	**52.** (4)	**53.** (1)	**54.** (4)	**55.** (4)	**56.** (1)	**57.** (4)	**58.** (3)	**59.** (3)	**60.** (2)
61. (1)	**62.** (4)	**63.** (3)	**64.** (2)	**65.** (3)	**66.** (3)	**67.** (4)	**68.** (2)	**69.** (1)	**70.** (1)
71. (1)	**72.** (2)	**73.** (1)	**74.** (1)	**75.** (2)	**76.** (3)	**77.** (3)	**78.** (2)	**79.** (3)	**80.** (2)
81. (4)	**82.** (3)	**83.** (3)	**84.** (3)	**85.** (2)	**86.** (3)	**87.** (3)	**88.** (1)	**89.** (3)	**90.** (3)
91. (4)	**92.** (3)	**93.** (4)	**94.** (1)	**95.** (2)	**96.** (1)	**97.** (1)	**98.** (1)	**99.** (3)	**100.** (1)

DECEMBER, 2023

COMMERCE

Paper-II

Note : This paper contains **hundred (100)** objective type questions of **two (2)** marks each. **All** questions are **compulsory**.

1. _______ as defined under the Foreign Trade Policy (FTP), implemented by Director General of Foreign Trade has the main aim to "mentor new and potential exporters on the intricacies of foreign trade through counselling, training and outreach programmes" so that they can get into international trade.

(1) Niryat Bharat Scheme
(2) Niryat Sandhu Scheme
(3) Niryat Benefit Scheme
(4) Niryat Border Scheme

2. ______ is a marketing term for any design to prompt an immediate response or encourage an immediate sale.

(1) Call for Promotion
(2) Call for Activity
(3) Call to Action
(4) Call to Aspiration

3. The exporting firm is termed 'rider' where the other firm with an established distribution channel in the target country is termed as 'Carrier'. This phenomenon is known as:

(1) Counter Trade (2) Barter
(3) Piggy Backing (4) Switch Trading

4. In International Commercial Terms (INCOTERMES), identify the one, under which the delivery of goods to the named place of destination (discharge) takes place at the seller's expense. Buyers assumes the cargo insurance, import custom clearance, payment of custom duties, taxes and other costs and risk.

(1) Carriage and Insurance Paid To (CIP)
(2) Cost, Insurance and Freight (GIF)
(3) Carriage Paid To (CPT)
(4) Cost and Freight (CFR)

5. In which ratio, will the remaining partners compensate the retiring partner for a share of goodwill?

(1) Profit-sharing ratio
(2) Sacrificing ratio
(3) Gaining ratio
(4) Capital ratio

6. Which one of the following accounting concepts and conventions consider it reasonable to use the historical cost to record long-lived assets?

(1) The entity concept
(2) Going concern convention
(3) Materiality convention
(4) The periodicity convention

7. Luxmi industries issued shares of Rs. 1000 at a premium of Rs. 10 per share, payable Rs. 20 on application, Rs. 35 on allotment (including premium) and the balance on the first and final call. Mr. X who held 200 shares has paid only the application money and these shares were subsequently forfeited by the company. In this regard, by which amount share forfeiture account will be credited?

(1) Rs. 4000 (2) Rs. 2000
(3) Rs. 3000 (4) Rs. 200

8. Which of the following frameworks is considered as the Open International Standard for Digital Business Reporting?

(1) CSR reporting (2) TBL reporting
(3) XBRL reporting (4) PPP reporting

9. Which one of the following statements is the most relevant to the substitution effect?

(1) In the real world, substitution effect is much larger than the income effect
(2) Most of the goods are not reasonable substitutes
(3) In reality, the income effect represents its predominance over the substitution effect
(4) Substitution and income effects cannot be separated easily

10. Identify the source of oligopoly which is also applicable to monopoly firms:

(1) Economies of scale may operate over a small range of outputs

(2) Huge capital investments and specialized inputs are required to enter the market
(3) Large firms may own a patent for the exclusive right to produce a commodity
(4) New firms have chances to win customer loyalty

11. Which one of the following statements does not support the concept of third degree price discrimination?
(1) The firm must have monopoly power
(2) This type of price discrimination is most likely to occur in the manufacturing industries
(3) The firm must be able to keep the two markets separate
(4) The price elasticity and demand for the commodity must be different in the two markets

12. Which one of the following concepts measures the amount of capital that the firm can give up by using one additional unit of labour and still remain on the same isoquant?
(1) Diminishing Marginal Rate of Substitution
(2) Economic Trade-off Region
(3) Diminishing Marginal Rate of Technical Substitution
(4) Diminishing Marginal Utility

13. Which of the following theories of capital structure articulates that a firm borrows up to the point where the tax benefit from extra debt is exactly equal to the cost that comes from the increased probability of financial distress?
(1) The static theory
(2) Net income approach
(3) Modigliani-Miller theory
(4) Net operating income approach

14. When a target company makes a counter bid for the stock of the bidder the defensive strategy in reference is called?
(1) Greenmail (2) Poison pill
(3) Pacman defense (4) Golden parachute

15. The earning per share for Avanti corporation is Rs. 4.0. The rate of return on investments is 16 per cent and the return required by its shareholders is 12 percent. What will be the price per share as per the Walter model if the payout ratio is 40 per cent?
(1) Rs. 24 (2) Rs. 36
(3) Rs. 40 (4) Rs. 12

16. Which one of the following instruments is often used to protect the value of a foreign currency denominated transaction?
(1) Forward contract
(2) Forward swap
(3) Forward hedge
(4) Forward premium

17. A discrete probability distribution ______.
(1) is a listing of all possible values of the random variable
(2) assigns a probability to each possible value of the random variable
(3) can assume the value between –1 and +1
(4) is independent of the parameters of the distribution

18. The price earnings ratio for firms in a certain industry follows the normal distribution. A firm's price-earnings ratio has a standardized value (Z)= 1.0 and it is included in the highest ______ of firms in the industry.
(1) 99.73% (2) 68.27%
(3) 15.87% (4) 34.13%

19. In one-factor ANOVA, the computed F-value will be negative
(1) when there is no difference in the treatment of means
(2) when there is no difference within treatments
(3) when SST (total variance) is larger than SSE (error variance)
(4) under no circumstances

20. In a certain population, 22% of people are smokers, 57% of people are males and 12% males are smokers. If a person is chosen at random from the population, what is that probability that selected person is either a male or a smoker?
(1) 0.79 (2) 0.22
(3) 0.45 (4) 0.67

21. Effective mentoring requires trust and the level of trust reflects the mentor's:
(1) Competence, consistency, communication abilities and control sharing readiness
(2) Concerned, cooperativeness, communication abilities and coordination skills
(3) Competence, consistency, complexity and communication abilities
(4) Communication abilities, competence, concerned behaviour control sharing readiness

22. Which one of the following consists of physical

working conditions, work schedule, incentives and the number of people with whom the employee would normally interact?

(1) Job profile (2) Job content
(3) Job context (4) Job specification

23. Which one of the following beliefs and behaviors does not characterise 'collectivism'?
(1) Relations are moral not contractual
(2) Relations take precedence over tasks
(3) Individual opinions are independent of collective opinions
(4) Maintaining harmony is highly valued

24. Honeywell Inc's move from a hierarchical management structure to a much flatter and team-based structure is a good description of which one of the following?
(1) Centralisation (2) Decentralisation
(3) Span of control
(4) Work specialization

25. Companies use _______ when they lack financial resources to carry out direct marketing and when they can earn more by doing so.
(1) Intermediaries
(2) Internationalisation
(3) Influencers (4) Innovation

26. Which one of the following committees has suggested the establishment of NBFCs' regulatory framework?
(1) Raj Study Group (1975)
(2) Chakkravarty Committee (1985)
(3) Vaghul Committee (1987)
(4) Shah Committee (1992)

27. The sequential stages of moral development in business organisations are characterised by
(1) Conceptualised disposition, consistency and harmony, principled oriented
(2) Consistency and harmony, conceptualized disposition, principled oriented
(3) Principled oriented, conventional and preconventional
(4) Preconventional, conventional, principled oriented

28. Which one of the fallowing are disposed to promote financial inclusion?
(1) Poor quality of services rendered
(2) High transaction costs
(3) Universal access to financial services
(4) Lack of trust in the system

29. Which one of the following digital payment systems is developed and managed by the National Payments Corporation of India?
(1) Paytm (2) BharatPe
(3) Mastercard (4) RuPay

30. Which amongst the following methods is not a method of generating sales leads in personal selling?
(1) Referrals (2) Networking
(3) Coupons (4) Cold calls

31. _______ takes into account a host of inputs, such as buyers image of the product performance, the channel deliverables, the warranty quality, customer support and softer attributes such as the suppliers reputation, trust worthiness and esteem.
(1) Target rate-of-return pricing
(2) Auction-type pricing
(3) Economic-value-to-customer pricing
(4) Competitive pricing

32. The present value of future profits, the individual or segment will generate over a lifetime relationship with a brand or firm, is known as
(1) Lifelong Value (2) Lifetime Value
(3) Longlife Value (4) Longterm value

33. A charitable trust Registered under section 12 AB of the Income Tax Act) is registered under GST in New Delhi. It provided yoga training to middle-aged people, coaching for Basket-ball to teenagers and skill development services to persons over the age of 65 years residing in New Delhi in the month of July This trust is liable to pay GST on:
(1) Yoga training
(2) Skill-development services
(3) Coaching for basket-ball
(4) Coaching for basket-ball and Yoga training

34. Which one of the following is invalid for the relationship among the agent the sub-agent and the principal?
(1) Sub-agent works under the control and on the directions of the agent
(2) Sub-agent is responsible to the agent only
(3) Privity of contract exists between the principle and the sub-agent
(4) Agent is responsible to the principle for the acts of the sub-agent

35. In case of anti-competitive activities by a firm, the Competition Commission of India can impose a penalty which shall be not more than

(1) Five percent of the average turnover/income of the firm of the three preceding financial years.
(2) Ten percent of the average turnover/income of firm of the three preceding financial years
(3) Fifteen percent of the average turnover/income of firm of the three preceding financial years
(4) Five percent of the average turnover/income of firm of the five preceding financial years

36. Which one of the following is an exception to the doctrine of Constructive Notice

(1) Doctrine of Subrogation
(2) Doctrine of Ultra Vires
(3) Corporate Veil
(4) Turquand Rule

37. As per the sub-section (8A) of Section 130 of the Income Tax Act, a person may furnish an updated return of his income for the previous year relevant to such assessment year within from the end of assessment year?

(1) 6 months (2) 12 months
(3) 24 months (4) 36 months

38. Mr. X is holding equity shares of ABC Ltd with voting power of 26 per cent. Mrs. X is working in ABC Ltd at a salary of Rs. 20,000 pm. The other income of Mr. X and Mrs. X are Rs. 6,00,000 and Rs. 3,00,000, respectively. The grass total income of Mr. X and Mrs. X are respectively for the Assessment Year 2023-24.

(1) Rs. 6.00.000 and Rs. 5.40,000
(2) Rs. 7,90.000 and Rs. 3.00,000
(3) Rs. 6.00,000 and Rs. 4.90.000
(4) Rs. 8.40.000 and Rs. 3.00.000

39. Every seller who receives an amount exceeding as consideration for sale of a motor vehicle, shall collect tax @ 1% of the sale consideration from the buyer at the time of receipt of such an amount.

(1) Rs. 25 lakhs (2) Rs. 15 lakhs
(3) Rs. 10 lakhs (4) Rs. 50 lakhs

40. Which one of the following is the allowable deduction as per the Income Tax Act, 1961 in respect of entertainment allowance paid to a government employee?

(1) Lower of one-fourth of basic salary or Rs. 5000 or entertainment allowance received.
(2) Lower of one-fifth of basic salary or Rs. 5000 or entertainment allowance received
(3) Lower of one-fifth of salary or Rs. 5000 or entertainment allowance received.
(4) Lower of one-fourth of salary or Rs. 5000 or entertainment allowance received.

41. For Forigen Direct Investment, it is argued that a location in question attracts FDI because it combines the unique advantage of which of the following conditions?

A. Internalisation Advantage
B. First Mover Advantage
C. Knowledge Advantage
D. Ownership Advantage
E. Location Advantage

Choose the correct answer from the options given below

(1) E, A and C Only (2) E, A and D Only
(3) C B and D Only (4) C, E and D Only

42. Channel power is the ability to alter channel members' behaviour so that they take actions they would not have taken otherwise. From the following channel powers, list the ones which are subjective in nature:

A. Legal Power B. Coercive Power
C. Expert Power D. Referent Power
E. Reward Power

Choose the correct answer from the options given below:

(1) D, A and C Only
(2) D, A and B Only
(3) A, B and E Only
(4) A, C and E Only

43. SAFTA (South Asian Free Trade Agreement) categorises member nations as Non-Least Developed Contracting States (NLDCS) and Least Developed Contracting States (LDCS). Identify the NLDSC stales from the following

A. Bangladesh B. Pakistan
C. Bhutan D. India
E. Sri Lanka

Choose the correct answer from the options given below:

(1) A, B and D Only (2) A, C and E Only
(3) E, A and B Only (4) E, D and B Only

44. Which of the following ratios are critically significant for an investor
A. Debt-Equity ratio B. Price-Earning ratio
C. Dividend yield D. Asset turnover ratio
E. Debtor turnover ratio
Choose the correct answer from the options given below:
(1) A, B and C Only (2) D and E Only
(3) B, C and D Only (4) A, D and E Only

45. By reducing the sales price from Rs. 80 per unit to Rs. 78 per unit, the sales manager has succeeded in selling 1000 units more of a product. Which of the following decisive conclusions can be drawn from this?
A. Sales price variance is unfavourable
B. Sales volume variance is favourable
C. Total sales variance is unfavourable
D. Sales activity variance is Rs. 80000 (favourable)
E. Sales price variance is Rs. 2000 (unfavourable)
Choose the correct answer from the options given below:
(1) A, B and C Only (2) C, D and E Only
(3) A, B and D Only (4) B, D and E Only

46. Which of the following are considered as the limitations of Cost-Volume-Profit analysis?
A. Constant selling price regardless of sales volume
B. Firm efficiency and productivity are constant and the costs are linear
C. Margin of safety is constant at varied levels of sales
D. Sales mix and the inventory levels are constant
E. Profit is constant at varied levels of sales price
Choose the correct answer from the options given below:
(1) A, B and C only (2) B, C and D only
(3) C, D and E only (4) A, B and D only

47. Which of the following are relevant in technological innovations?
A. Most innovations are incremental
B. Most innovations involve the commercial utilization of ideas
C. Innovations cannot be explained with isoquants
D. Introduction of innovations is not stimulated by strong domestic rivalry and geographic concentrations
E. The risk in introducing innovations is usually high
Choose the correct answer from the options given below:
(1) B, D and E only (2) A, C and E only
(3) A, B and E only (4) A, B and C only

48. Which of the following are relevant in deciding among different courses of action, the manager needs to consider the differential revenue and costs of alternatives?
A. Opportunity costs and economic profits
B. Fixed and Sunk Costs
C. Marginal Revenue and Marginal Cost
D. Incremental and marginal costs
E. Economies and dis-economies of scale
Choose the correct answer from the options given below:
(1) A and D Only (2) B and C Only
(3) D and E Only (4) A and B Only

49. Which of the following are the reasons for substitution between domestic and MNC goods?
A. Increased knowledge of foreign products due to international information revolution
B. No need to conduct advertising campaigns
C. Transportation costs having fallen to very low levels for most products
D. Restricted international travel
E. Tastes are consistent at the global level
Choose the correct answer from the options given below:
1 A and C Only 2 D and E Only
3 C and D Only 4 A and B Only

50. Which of the following are constituents of the trilemma of international finance?
A. Fixed exchange rate
B. Independent monetary policy
C. Free mobility of capital
D. Global recessionary tendency
E. Rising inflationary conditions
Choose the correct answer from the options given below:
(1) A, B and C Only (2) C, D and E Only
(3) B, C and E Only (4) A, C and D Only

51 Which of the following factors are attributed to the weakening of Indian rupee?

A. Rupee payment for international trade
B. Rising cost of imports
C. Widening trade deficit
D. Opening of Rupee vostro accounts
E. Rupee UPI payments for overseas transactions

Choose the most appropriate answer from the options given below:

(1) A, B and C Only (2) C, D and E Only
(3) A, D and E Only (4) B, C and D Only

52. When a country's currency is accepted as a reserve currency, the potential conflict may arise between which of following policy objectives?

A. Domestic monetary policy
B. Domestic fiscal policy
C. External currency policy
D. Foreign trade policy
E. Inland trade policy

Choose the correct answer from the options given below:

(1) A, B, and C Only (2) A, C and D Only
(3) B, D and E Only (4) C, D and E Only

53. In order to conduct exploratory data analysis, which of following are used by a researcher in the five number summary?

A. Median B. First quartile
C. Mean D. Third quartile
E. Smallest and largest values

Choose the correct answer from the options given below:

(1) A, C, D and E Only
(2) A, B, D and E Only
(3) B, C, D and E Only
(4) A, B, C and E Only

54. Which of the following are considered while avoiding conflict?

A. Conflict based on interpersonal relationships
B. All conflicts are not bad and can be taken positively
C. Conflict over content and goals of the work
D. Conflicts do not support a group's goal and improve its performance
E. Conflict over how work gets done

Choose the correct answer from the options given below:

(1) A, B and C Only (2) A, B and E Only
(3) A, C and E Only (4) B, C and D Only

55. Which of following are pre-experimental designs?

A. One-group pretest-post test
B. Pre-test post-test control group
C. Quasi-experiments
D. Static group comparison
E. After-only study

Choose the correct answer from the options given below:

(1) D, B, C Only (2) A, D, E Only
(3) A, C, E Only (4) E, B, D Only

56. Which of the following managerial actions are followed to reduce resistance to change?

A. Education and communication are strong tools for resistance to change
B. Allows participation to those who oppose a change to participate in decision making
C. Negotiation may become vital when resistance comes from a powerful source
D. Employee counseling does not serve the purpose
E. Coercion can be used to get support easily

Choose the correct answer from the options given below:

(1) A, B and C Only (2) B, C and D Only
(3) B, C and E Only (4) A, C and D Only

57. Which of the following are objectives of Immediate Payment Service (IMPS)?

A. To enable bank clients to use mobile instruments as a channel for accessing their bank accounts and remit funds
B. To build the foundation for a full range of mobile based banking services.
C. To sub-serve the goal of Reserve Bank of India (RBI) in digital payments.
D. To make payments simpler with the mobile number of the beneficiary
E. To restrain a nation-wide payment system facilitating one-to-one funds transfer

Choose the most appropriate answer from the option given below:

(1) A, C, D and E Only
(2) A, B, C and D Only
(3) B, C, D and E Only
(4) B, A, E and D Only

58. Which of the following are functions of the Reserve Bank of India?

A. Bank of issue
B. Banker's bank and lender of the last resort
C. Regulator of fiscal policy
D. Controller of credit
E. Custodian of foreign exchange reserves

Choose the most appropriate answer from the option given below:
(1) A, B, C and D Only
(2) A, B, D and E Only
(3) B, C, D and E Only
(4) A, B and D Only

59. The concept of product life cycle is based on which of the following key assumptions?
A. Profits remain stable at different stages of product life cycle
B. Products have an unlimited life
C. Product sales pass through distinct stages, each posing different challenges, opportunities and problems to the seller
D. Products require different marketing, financial manufacturing, purchasing and human resource strategies in each of the life cycle stages
E. Products have a limited life

Choose the most appropriate answer from the option given below:
(1) B, C and D Only (2) A, B and C Only
(3) A, C and D Only (4) C, D and E Only

60. Emotional appeal is one of the types of advertising appeals, based on three ideas, namely
A. Rational appeals generally go unnoticed
B. Consumers watch all ads
C. It can capture attention and foster an attachment
D. Consumers ignore most ads
E. Rational appeal generally gets noticed

Choose the correct answer from the options given below
(1) C, E, and D Only (2) C, E and B Only
(3) C, A and D Only (4) C, A and B Only

61. Which are the states where every supplier of goods and/or services is required to obtain registration if his aggregate turnover exceeds the threshold limit of Rs. 20 lakh for supply of goods and/or services?
A. Arunachal Pradesh B. Meghalaya
C. Manipur D. Mizoram
E. Sikkim

Choose the most appropriate answer from the option given below:
(1) B, C and A Only (2) C, D and E Only
(3) E, B and A Only (4) A, B and D Only

62. Which of the following can become the member of an LLP?
A. Resident Indians
B. Limited Liability Partnership
C. Corporation Sole
D. Co-operative society
E. Companies (including foreign companies)

Choose the most appropriate answer from the option given below:
(1) A, B and C Only (2) A, C and D Only
(3) A, B and D Only (4) A, E and B Only

63. The trademarks can be broadly classified into which of the following categories?
A. Descriptive B. Normative
C. Generic D. Explanatory
E. Invented

Choose the most appropriate answer from the option given below:
(1) A, B and D Only (2) D, E and C Only
(3) B, C and E Only (4) C, A and E Only

64. Which of the following are deemed to be dividend for the purpose of computing income chargeable under the head, Income from other sources, as per the Income Tax Act, 1961?
A. Payment on buy-back of shares
B. Payment to shareholders on reduction of capital
C. Distribution of debentures to shareholders
D. Loan granted to shareholders in the ordinary course of business
E. Loan granted to shareholders by a closely held company

Choose the correct answer from the options given below
(1) B and C Only (2) B, C and E Only
(3) A, B and C Only (4) A and C Only

65. Which of the following will be clubbed into the income of Mr. Q whose Income from Profession is Rs. 85,000?
A. Income from Mrs. Q's profession, Rs. 45,000
B. Mrs. Q's salary as a clerk, Rs. 66.000
C. Minor son's earned interest on deposits of money gifted to him by his uncle, Rs. 15,000

D. Minor daughter's earnings from sports, Rs. 85,000

E. Minor son's winnings from lottery, Rs. 1,05,000

Choose the correct answer from the options given below:

(1) A, C, D and E Only
(2) C, D and E Only
(3) C and D Only (4) C and E Only

66. Match List I with List II

List I Nature of Business Activity	List II FDI Permitted under Automatic Route
A. Trading in Transferable Development Rights (TDK)	I. 49%
B. Multi-Brand Retail Trading	II. Prohibited
C. Satellite (Establishment and Operations)	III. 51%
D. Petroleum Refining (by PS Us)	IV. 100%

Choose the correct answer from the option given below

(1) A- IV, B-II, C-III, D-I
(2) A-II, B-III, C-IV, D-I
(3) A-I, B-III, C-II, D-IV
(4) A-IV, B-II, C-I, D-III

67. Match List I with List II

List I Activity Based Cost Centers	List II Costs incurred and accounted for
A. Unit-level activity center	I. Patent, trademark and copyright fees
B. Batch level activity center	II. Direct material and labour costs
C. Product level activity center	III. Plant depreciation and maintenance expenses
D. Facility level activity center	IV. Material handling costs

Choose the correct answer from the option given below:

(1) A-II, B- IV, C- I, D-III
(2) A-II, B- IV, C-III, D-I
(3) A-I, B-III, C-II, D-IV
(4) A-III, B-I, C-IV, D-II

68. Match List I with List II

List I types of Effect	List II Description
A. Veblen effect	I. Conspicuous consumption
B. Snob effect	II. Reduction in relative price of commodity
C. Bandwagon effect	III. Negative network externality
D. Substitution effect	IV. Positive network externality

Choose the correct answer from the option given below

(1) A-I, B-II, C-III, D-IV
(2) A-IV, B-III, C-II, D-I
(3) A-II, B-III, C-IV, D-I
(4) A-I, B-III, C-IV, D-II

69. Match List I with List II

List I Bond rates and risk	List II Description
A. Coupon rate	I. The interest rate required in the market on a bond
B. Yield to maturity	II. It is obtained by dividing annual coupon (stated interest payment) by the bond price
C. Interest rate risk	III. It germinates and originates from fluctuating interest rates
D. Current (bond) yield	IV. The annual coupon (stated interest payment) divided by the face value of a bond

Choose the correct answer from the option given below

(1) A-IV, B-I, C-III, D-II
(2) A-II, B-III, C-I, D-IV
(3) A-III, B-II, C-IV, D-I
(4) A-I, B-III, C-II, D-IV

70. Match List I with List II

List I Description identifiers	List II Research design
A. The time dimension	I. Exploratory study
B. The purpose of the study	II. Statistical study

C.	The topical scope of the study	III.	Descriptive study
D.	The degree to which the research question has been crystallized	IV.	Cross-section study

Choose the correct answer from the option given below:

(1) A-I, B- II, C- III, D- IV
(2) A-III, B-I, C- IV D- II
(3) A-IV, B-III, C- II, D-I
(4) A-II, B-IV, C-I, D-III

71. Match List I with List II

List I Management Thinkers		**List II Approach Dimensions**	
A.	Kurt Lewin	I.	Position power, Task structure, Leader member relations
B.	Fred E Fiedler	II.	Authority and Responsibility, Unity of command, Scalar chain
C.	Henri Fayol	III.	Power, Affiliation, Achievement
D.	David C. McClelland	IV.	Unfreezing, Moving, Refreezing

Choose the correct answer from the option given below

(1) A-I, B-II, C-III, D-IV
(2) A-IV, B-I, C-II, D-III
(3) A-IV, B-III, C-I, D-II
(4) A-II, B-IV, C-III, D-I

72. Match List I with List II

List I Asset classes		**List II Type of Investments**	
A.	Asset Class A	I.	Equity shares of companies traded in futures and options segments
B.	Asset Class C	II.	Government securities and state development loans
C.	Asset Class E	III.	Alternate Assets
D.	Asset Class G	IV.	Corporate bonds/ debentures which are listed and rated not below A

Choose the correct answer from the option given below:

(1) A-I, B-IV, C-II, D-III
(2) A-III, B-II, C- IV, D-I
(3) A-III, B-IV, C-I, D-II
(4) A-I, B-III, C-II, D-IV

73. Match List I with List II

List I Concepts (Targeting)		**List II Definition**	
A.	Target Compatibility	I.	Reflects the ability of a market segment to create superior value for the company
B.	Tactical Targeting	II.	A reflection of the company's ability, to create superior customer value
C.	Target Attractiveness	III.	Focuses on customising company's offerings according to the customers' needs
D.	Strategic Targeting	IV.	Ways in which the company can reach strategically important customers

Choose the correct answer from the option given below

(1) A-I, B-II, C-III, D-IV
(2) A-II, B- IV, C-I, D-III
(3) A-II, B-III, C-I, D-IV
(4) A-IV, B-III, C-II, D-I

74. Match List I with List II

List I Features		**List II Remedies for breach of contract**	
A.	Breach of promise to many	I.	Suit for injunction
B.	Part performance (as much as earned)	II.	Rescission of contract
C.	Absolvation from all obligations	III.	Sue for quantum meruit
D.	Mode of securing the specific performance of negative terms of contract	IV.	Vindictive damage

Choose the correct answer from the option given below

(1) A-IV, B-III, C-II, D-I
(2) A-I, B-II, C-III, D-IV
(3) A-III, B-IV, C-I, D-II
(4) A-II, B-I, C-IV, D-III

75. Match List I with List II

List I Assets Transferred	List II Exemptions of capital gains Sections 54-54 EC Income Tax Act
A. Agricultural Land	I. Section 54 B
B. Residential House	II. Section 54 EC
C. Land or Building or Both	III. Section 54 D
D. Land and Building forming part of an Industrial undertaking	IV. Section 54

Choose the correct answer from the option given below
(1) A-III, B-II, C-I, D-IV
(2) A-I, B- IV, C-II, D-III
(3) A-IV, B- III, C-I, D-II
(4) A-III, B-I, C- IV D-II

76. Arrange the following rounds for multilateral trade negotiations under GATT/WTO in a chronological order.
A. Kennedy B. Doha
C. Annecy D. Torquay
E. Tokyo
Choose the correct answer from the option given below:
(1) C, D, A, E, B (2) D, C, E, A, B
(3) B, A, E, C, D (4) B, E, A, D, C

77. Arrange the steps in the book building process for public issue of shares in India
A. Determine issue price, market clearing price and price discovery
B. Book runner and syndicate members generate awareness, create demand and run the order book
C. Appointment of the merchant banker and syndicate members (SEBI registered intermediaries) as underwriters
D. Preparation and filing of red herring prospectus with the SEBI for approval
E. Allotment and listing of shares on stock exchange(s)
Choose the correct answer from the option given below:
(1) C, D, B, A, E (2) D, C, A, B, E
(3) A, B, C, D, E (4) B, C, D, E, A

78. Arrange the following in a sequence with regard to price leadership sustainability:
A. Small firms in the industry are allowed to sell all they want at that price
B. Dominant firm acts as the residual supplier of the commodity
C. The dominant firm sets the price for the commodity that maximizes its profits
D. Small firms in the industry behave as price takers
E. Dominant firm then comes into fill the market
Choose the correct answer from the option given below:
(1) A, B, C, D, E (2) E, D, C, B, A
(3) A, C, B, D, E (4) C, A, E, B, D

79. Sequentially arrange the following impacts of the evolving global monetary system on the economies.
A. Protectionism and nationalism
B. Capital flows driving economic development
C. Increased world trade with limited capital flows
D. Expanded open economies
E. Industrial economies increasingly open and emerging nations open slowly
Choose the correct answer from the option given below:
(1) B, D, A, C, E (2) C, A, D, E, B
(3) C, E, D, A, B (4) E, B, D, A, C

80. Arrange the following steps of a well planned experiment in the sequential order.
A. Specify the treatment levels
B. Assign subject to groups and conduct pilot test
C. Choose an experimental design suited to the hypotheses
D. Control the environmental and extraneous factors
E. Select relevant variables for testing
Choose the correct answer from the option given below:
(1) C, D, E, A, B (2) A, C, D, E, B
(3) E, A, D, C, B (4) D, C, B, A, E

81. Arrange the following group member's behavior outcomes in a sequence as per the successive stages of group building process.
A. Eager, Anxious, Gather data about similarities and differences among members and keep things simple
B. Upset and Depressed
C. Less dissatisfied and a feeling of belongings to the group

D. Confront the differences, feel angry or frustrated, lot of competition and hostilities
E. Inter dependence in personal relations, tendency to get involved in and problem solving

Choose the correct answer from the option given below:

(1) A, D, C, E, B (2) A, B, C, D, E
(3) E, C, D, B, A (4) B, C, E, A, D

82. Arrange the following SBI-sponsored RRBs in an increasing order of their existence since formation.

A. Rajasthan Marudhara Gramin Bank
B. Telangana Gramin Bank
C. Sausashtra Gramin Bank
D. Madhyanchal Gramin Bank
E. Arunachal Pradesh Rural Bank

Choose the correct answer from the option given below:

(1) A, D, B, E, C (2) C, E, D, A, B
(3) B, A, C, E, D (4) D, E, A, B, C

83. Place the following service differentiators in a logical sequence:

A. Speed and timing of delivery
B. Maintenance and repair
C. Returns
D. Installation, training and consulting
E. Ease of ordering

Choose the correct answer from the option given below:

(1) E, D, B, C, A (2) E, A, D, B, C
(3) E, D, A, C, B (4) E, C, A, B, D

84. Arrange the following steps in the investigation process of combinations by the Competition Commission of India in the correct order

A. Call for a report from the Director General
B. Invite any person, affected parties to file written objections
C. Direct the parties of combination to publish details of the combination
D. Call for additional information from the parties of the combination
E. Issue a notice for show-cause to the parties of the combination

Choose the correct answer from the option given below:

(1) A, B, C, D, E (2) E, A, C, B, D
(3) B, A, C, D, E (4) C, A, D, E, B

85. Arrange the following in the ascending order of applicable TDS (Tax deducted at source) rates for the Financial Year. 2023-24.

A. Payment of Rs. 6,55,000 rent by an individual in a year
B. Payment of Rs. 20,000 on winnings from horse races
C. Payment of Rs. 8.000 as dividend by cheque
D. Payment of Rs. 35,000 to an individual contractor for repair by a university
E. Payment of Rs. 38,000 as fees for professional and technical services by a call center

Choose the correct answer from the option given below:

(1) A, B, C, D, E (2) D, E, A, C, B
(3) E, D, C, B, A (4) A, E, C, D, B

86. Given below are two statements: one is labelled as Assertion A and the other is labelled as Reason R

Assertion A: A promoter, invariably is the one who has been associated with formation of the company

Reason R: A promoter is the one who undertakes to form a company with reference to a given object and who takes the necessary steps to accomplish that purpose

In the light of the above statements, choose the most appropriate answer from the options given below:

(1) Both A and R are correct and R is the correct explanation of A.
(2) Both A and R are correct but R is NOT the correct explanation of A.
(3) A is correct but R is not correct.
(4) A is not correct but R is correct

87. Given below are two statements: one is labelled as Assertion A and the other is labelled as Reason R

Assertion A: Persons with high self-esteem are less susceptible to influence, more confident of achieving goals and more effective in social networking

Reason R: Self-esteem manifests in several behaviours. Persons with high self-esteem tend to report fewer negative emotions than persons with low self-esteem

In the light of the above statements, choose the most appropriate answer from the options given below:

(1) Both A and R are true and R is the correct explanation of A.
(2) Both A and R are true but R is NOT the correct explanation of A.
(3) A is true but R is false.
(4) A is false but R is true

88. Given below are two statements:

Statement I: The ordinary treasury bills that are marketable and have a secondary market are issued to the public and financial institutions.

Statement II: Ad hoc treasury bills are issued only in favour of the Reserve Bank of India which is authorized to issue currency notes against them.

In the light of the above statements, choose the most appropriate answer from the options given below:
(1) Both Statement I and Statement II are true
(2) Both Statement I and Statement II are false
(3) Statement I is true but Statement II is false
(4) Statement I is false but Statement II is true

89. Given below are Two statements: one is labelled as Assertion A and the other is labelled as Reason R

Assertion A: Consumes may prefer to choose the channels based on their own shopping goals as well as price, product assortment and convenience.

Reason R: Some consumers are unwilling to "trade-up" to retailers offering higher-end goods, and "trade down" to discount retailers for private-label.

In the light of the above statements, choose the most appropriate answer from the options given below:
(1) Both A and R are correct and R is the correct explanation of A.
(2) Both A and R are correct but R is NOT the correct explanation of A.
(3) A is correct but R is not correct.
(4) A is not correct but R is correct

90. Given below are two statements:

Statement I: For a given sample size and level of significance (a), the critical value of Student's t always exceeds that of z.

Statement II: For a given level of significance (a), the critical value of Student's t increases as n increases.

In the light of the above statements, choose the correct answer from the options given below:
(1) Both Statement I and Statement II are true
(2) Both Statement I and Statement II are false
(3) Statement I is true but Statement II is false
(4) Statement I is false but Statement II is true

Read the given passage and answer the questions that follow:

For most of its existence as a modern field of study since the 18th century, economics has fared reasonably well at explaining consumer and producer behavior. It explained why buyers choose the products they do, how firms produce them to maximize profit, and how markets discover the most efficient prices. This changed with the Great Depression, when aggregate variables came into play that needed a better understanding than an assumption that markets return to equilibrium after shocks. Thus came into existence macroeconomics, the most dismal aspect of the dismal science. Economics has since diversified into quite a few other branches, such as those employing statistics and psychology, but most of its disrepute originates from its failure to predict financial crises.

'Macro' by its very nature - dealing with GDP employment, inflation and other important but soporific matters and parameters - is headline-grabbing stuff. Governments come into play here, as do international relations. Yet, macro eludes the scientific method of testing hypotheses with repeated experiments: one can't conceivably wreck an economy to establish the effects of a shock. Instead, macroeconomists can only back-test their models against data that may be of questionable provenance. This makes prediction of the next stock market crash forever embarrassingly less exact than the return of Halley's Comet.

Microeconomics, the reputable part of the endeavor, suffers from fewer limitations to controlled parameter experiments and delivers less equivocal insights. The explosion of commerce in the modem world owes itself in no small measure to predicting actions by the smallest economic agents: humans. Here, too, heroic assumptions are made, the foremost being that human beings are rational and information is free.

The crisis in economic modelling arises from aggregating billions of micro truths into one macro truth. Models are improving, so are quantitative capabilities, and the qualitative judgements that drive macro policy will become more refined.

91. Which one of the following is the reason, as per the given passage, for crises in economic modelling?
(1) Aggregating billions of micro truths into one macro truth
(2) Only equalization factors are considered in economic models
(3) Economic activities are not sufficient to study the macro environment
(4) Human beings behave irrationally

92. Match List I with List II

List-I Phenomenon	List-II Reasons
A. Economics defines	I. Better understanding of aggregate variables
B. Learning of Great Depression	II. GDP Employment, and Inflation
C. Macro-economic variables	III. Human beings are rational and information is free
D. Pitfalls of Micro economics	IV. How markets discover the most efficient prices

Choose the correct answer from the options given below:
(1) A-I, B-II, C-III, D-IV
(2) A-II, B-III, C-I, D - IV
(3) A-III, B-IV, C-II, D-I
(4) A-IV, B-I, C-II, D-III

93. Which of the following, as per the passage are the major contribution of economics?
A. Buyers behavior towards the products
B. Firm's behaviors for maximising profit
C. Retailers behavior to maximize sale
D. Market behavior to the most efficient prices
E. Stakeholder's behaviors to maximise wealth

Choose the correct answer from the options given below:
(1) A, B and D Only (2) A, B and C Only
(3) B, D and E Only (4) A, B and E Only

94. **Statement I:** Macroeconomists can only back-test their models against data that may be of questionable provenance.
Statement II: Macroeconomic variables elude the scientific method of testing hypotheses with repeated experiments.
In the light of the above statements, choose the most appropriate answer from the options given below:
(1) Both Statement I and Statement II are true
(2) Both Statement I and Statement II are false
(3) Statement I is true but Statement II is false
(4) Statement I is false but Statement II is true

95. Which of the following is the reason, as per the passage, for driving more effective macro policies?
(1) Assumption that markets return to equilibrium after shocks
(2) Improved economic models are capable to understand qualitative and quantitative factors
(3) Economics has fared reasonably well during financial crises
(4) Every small measure is not capable to predict economic outcomes

Read the given passage and answer the questions that follow:

Over $350 billion of private capital has been deployed over the last decade, which has propelled more than 5,000 enterprises. These new businesses are anchored in innovative business models combining the full potential of technology, facilitating every Indian to fulfil their aspirations.

The big shift in the last decade is the reimagination of India as an addressable market of 300 million households, a massive shift from only 20 million households in tier-1 cities earlier. This has been propelled by the strong partnership between entrepreneurs and the PE/VC ecosystem. The share of FDI funnelled into PE/VC has surged to 50-60%, up from 20-30% two decades back.

Besides the tremendous focus on value creation, the PE/VC industry has brought about multidimensional progress in the economy. The principles of responsible investing that this industry is committed to have enabled the building of a more equitable, inclusive economy, and one that has earned the trust of large global investors as an attractive investment destination.

The PE/VC ecosystem sparked a renaissance, empowering young minds to take a bold leap. This led to a change in mindset where entrepreneurship is now an accepted livelihood and, indeed, a proud way of life. Today, startups and new businesses are celebrated, and many are giving up established careers to follow their heart, with families standing as stalwart supporters of entrepreneurship. The proportionality of risk and reward has been embraced, forging a harmonious relationship between uncertainty and achievement.

Stories at home and those that went global are a testament to the power of partnerships between the capital provider and entrepreneurs, transforming a large democracy to be self-reliant, and elevating over a billion people to a new world of greater aspirations and confidence.

This revolution has been largely possible because of GoI's thrust towards attracting capital. The frameworks of alternative investment funds (AIFs), GIFT City IFSC, Startup India programme and budget allocations, coupled with progressive amendments such as GST and India Stack, have made India an attractive destination for investment.

96. In the recent years, the focus of private equity and venture capital in India, has been on
(1) Self-reliance (2) Job creation
(3) Inclusive growth (4) Value creation

97. The principles of responsible investing to which private equity and venture capital industry is committed have resulted in which of the following outcomes for the Indian economy?
A. Democratic decentralization
B. Balanced regional growth
C. Inclusive and equitable economy
D. Larger export orientation
E. Earned the trust of global investors
Choose the correct answer form the options given below
(1) B and C Only (2) A and D Only
(3) C and E Only (4) B, C and D Only

98. Which of following according to the passage, have made India an attractive destination for investments?
A. Startup India program
B. Make in India program
C. Goods and Services Tax facilitation
D. Alternative Investment funds
E. Standup India program
Choose the most appropriate answer from the options given below:
(1) A, B and C Only (2) A, C and D Only
(3) A, D and E Only (4) C, D and E Only

99. According to the passage, which of the following is now being accepted as a way of life and livelihood?
(1) PE/VC ecosystem
(2) Risk and uncertainty
(3) Innovation and achievement
(4) Entrepreneurship

100. Given below are Two statements: one is labelled as Assertion A and the other is labelled as Reason R
Assertion A: The private equity and venture capital ecosystem has sparked a renaissance, empowering young minds to take a bold leap.
Reason R: Today, startups and new business are celebrated and many are given up their established careers to follow their heart, with families standing as stalwart supporters.
In the light of the above statements, choose the correct answer from the options given below:
(1) Both A and R are true and R is the correct explanation of A
(2) Both A and R are true but R is NOT the correct explanation of A
(3) Ais true but R is false.
(4) A is false but R is true.

ANSWERS

1. (2)	**2.** (3)	**3.** (3)	**4.** (3)	**5.** (3)	**6.** (2)	**7.** (1)	**8.** (3)	**9.** (1)	**10.** (2)
11. (2)	**12.** (3)	**13.** (1)	**14.** (3)	**15.** (3)	**16.** (3)	**17.** (2)	**18.** (3)	**19.** (4)	**20.** (4)
21. (1)	**22.** (3)	**23.** (3)	**24.** (2)	**25.** (1)	**26.** (4)	**27.** (4)	**28.** (3)	**29.** (4)	**30.** (3)
31. (3)	**32.** (2)	**33.** (2)	**34.** (3)	**35.** (2)	**36.** (4)	**37.** (3)	**38.** (2)	**39.** (3)	**40.** (2)
41. (2)	**42.** (1)	**43.** (4)	**44.** (1)	**45.** (3)	**46.** (4)	**47.** (3)	**48.** (1)	**49.** (1)	**50.** (1)
51. (4)	**52.** (2)	**53.** (2)	**54.** (3)	**55.** (2)	**56.** (3)	**57.** (2)	**58.** (2)	**59.** (4)	**60.** (3)
61. (*)	**62.** (4)	**63.** (4)	**64.** (2)	**65.** (4)	**66.** (2)	**67.** (1)	**68.** (4)	**69.** (1)	**70.** (3)
71. (2)	**72.** (3)	**73.** (2)	**74.** (1)	**75.** (2)	**76.** (1)	**77.** (1)	**78.** (4)	**79.** (2)	**80.** (3)
81. (1)	**82.** (2)	**83.** (2)	**84.** (2)	**85.** (2)	**86.** (4)	**87.** (1)	**88.** (1)	**89.** (1)	**90.** (3)
91. (1)	**92.** (4)	**93.** (1)	**94.** (1)	**95.** (2)	**96.** (4)	**97.** (3)	**98.** (2)	**99.** (4)	**100.** (1)

OOO

SEPTEMBER, 2024

COMMERCE

Paper-II

Note : This paper contains **hundred (100)** objective type questions of **two (2)** marks each. **All** questions are **compulsory**.

1. Which of the following is the apex decision - making body of WTO?
(1) General Council
(2) Executive Council
(3) Ministerial Conference
(4) TRIMS

2. The authentication to be affected by use of asymmetric crypto system and hash function is known as:
(1) E-commerce
(2) Virtual signature
(3) Digital signature
(4) E-verification

3. Revenue from sale of products, ordinarily is reported as part of the earning in the period when
(1) The sale is made
(2) The cash is collected
(3) The products are manufactured
(4) The profit is computed

4. Arrange the following new product planning process in proper sequence.
A Idea screening
B. Idea generation
C. Concept Development and testing
D. Market strategy development
E. Business Analysis

Choose the *correct* answer from the options given below:
(1) A, B, C, D, E (2) B, A, C, D, E
(3) A, B, C, E, D (4) E, D, B, A, C

5. Which of the following are the participants in T-Bills Market?
A. Reserve Bank of India
B. Commercial Banks
C. Foreign Banks
D. Provident Funds
E. Corporates

Choose the *correct* answer from the options given below:
(1) B, C, D & E Only
(2) A, B, C & E Only
(3) A, B, D & E Only
(4) A, B, C, D & E

6. Compute the tax liability under default tax regime of Mr. X (35 year), having total income of ₹ 51,75,000 for the assessment year 2024-25. Assume that his total income comprises salary, income from house property and interest on fixed deposit:
(1) 13.75,000 (2) 13,77,750
(3) 14.30,000 (4) 14,75,000

7. Match the List-I with List-II

LIST I (Section)	LIST II (Ceiling limit)
A. 80-C	I. 50,000
B. 80- CCD (1)	II. 10% of salary or 20% of gross total income as per case
C. 80-CCD (1B)	III. 14% of salary
D. 80- CCD (2)	IV. 1,50.000

Choose the *correct* answer from the options given below:
(1) A-I, B-II, C-III, D-IV
(2) A-IV, B-II, C-I, D-III
(3) A-IV, B-III, C-II, D-I
(4) A-III, B-IV, C-I, D-II

8. What is the time limit within which an information is to be provided regarding the life and liberty of a person under RTI Act, 2005?
(1) 30 days (2) 60 days
(3) 24 hours (4) 48 hours

9. Match the List I with List II

LIST I	LIST II
A. Right to Safety	I. Consumers have a right against the marketing of goods, products or services

			which are hazardous to life & property:
B.	Right to be assured	II.	Consumers have a right to know about the quality; quantity; potency; purity; standard and price of goods or services.
C.	Right to be informed	III.	Consumers have a right to be assured that their interest will receive due consideration at appropriate commission
D.	Right to be heard	IV.	Consumer has the opportunity to choose from a wide range of products at reasonable rates.

Choose the *correct* answer from the options given below:

(1) A-I, B-IV, C-II, D-III
(2) A-II, B-III, C-I, D-IV
(3) A-III, B-II, C-I, D-IV
(4) A-IV, B-III, C-II, D-I

10. Which of the following are the benefits of globalisation?

A. Increase in competition would make companies more cost & quality conscious and innovative.
B. An open economy spurs innovation with fresh ideas from abroad.
C. Liberalisation & global competition enhances consumer choice and consumer surplus.
D. Developing countries could be very vulnerable to the harmful effects of globalisation.
E. Globalisation opens up enormous domestic and global opportunities for firms in developing countries.

Choose the *correct* answer from the options given below:

(1) A, B, C & D Only
(2) C, D & E Only
(3) B, C, D & E Only
(4) A, B, C & E Only

11. Match the List I with List II

	LIST I Instruments		LIST II Market
A.	Forwards	I	Primary Market
B.	Certificate of Deposits	II.	Money Market
C	FPO	III.	Derivative Market
D.	IPO	IV.	Stock Market

Choose the *correct* answer from the options given below:

(1) A-I, B-III, C-II, D-IV
(2) A-II, B IV, C-I, D-III
(3) A-IV, B-II, C-III, D-I
(4) A-III, B-II, C-IV, D-I

12. Arrange the online registration process of a new private limited company in proper sequence.

A. Select and Reserve Company Name
B. Acquire DIN & DSC of promoters
C. Draft Memorandum and Articles of Association
D. Get Company Registration Certificate
E. File SPICE+Applicaiton

Choose the *correct* answer from the options given below:

(1) A, B, C, E, D
(2) A, B, E, D, C
(3) B, A, C, E, D
(4) B, A, C, D, E

13. Match the List I with List II

	LIST I		LIST II
A.	Transfer of ownership	I	Negotiable Instrument
B.	Sale of goodwill after dissolution	II.	Contract of Sale of Goods
C	Buy back of shares	III.	Dissolution of Partnership Finn
D.	Promissory Note	IV.	Share Capital of Company

Choose the *correct* answer from the options given below:

(1) A-II. B-III. C-IV, D-I
(2) A-I. B-II. C-III. D-IV
(3) A-II, B-III. C-I. D-IV
(4) A-I, B-III, C-II. D-IV

14. When the number of trials (n) is large but the probability of success (p) is small. Bionomial probability distribution can be approximated using:

(1) Normal Distribution
(2) Hypergeometric Distribution
(3) Poisson Distribution
(4) Bernoulli Distribution

15. Match the offences and their corresponding penalties as per I.T. Act-2000.

LIST I	LIST II
A. Tampering with computer source documents (Sec.65)	I. Imprisonment upto 2 years and, or fine upto ₹ 1 lakh
B. Penalty' for mis-representation (Sec. 71)	II. Imprisonment upto 3 years, or fine of ₹ 2 lakh or both
C. Penalty for Breach of confidentiality and privacy (Sec.72)	III. Imprisonment upto 2 years or fine which may extend to one lakh rupees or with both.
D. Punishment for cyber terrorism (Sec.66F)	IV. Imprisonment extends to imprisonment for life.

Choose the *correct* answer from the options given below:

(1) A-I, B-II, C-III, D-IV
(2) A II, B-I, C-IV, D-III
(3) A-II, B-III, C-I, D-IV
(4) A-III, B-IV C-I, D-II

16. Arrange the following strategic decisions in international business in proper sequence.

A. Market Selection Decision
B. International Business Decision
C. Entry and Operating Decision
D. International organisation & HR Decisions
E. Marketing Mix Decision

Choose the *correct* answer from the options given below:

(1) A, B, C, D, E
(2) A, B, C, E, D
(3) B, A, C, E, D
(4) B, C, A, E, D

17. "Fiduciary relationship" is a relationship based on

(1) Legal obligations
(2) Absolute trust and reliance
(3) Trade relation
(4) Monetary benefits

18. Match the List I with List II

LIST I	LIST II
A. Capital Asset Pricing Model	I. $\frac{E}{V}\gamma_E+\frac{D}{V}\gamma_D(1-T_C)$
B. Gordon Model	II. $R_E = R_F + P_E(R_M - R_f)$
C. Weighted Average Cost of Capital	III. $P = m\left(D+\frac{E}{3}\right)$
D. Traditional Model	IV. $P_0 = \frac{E_1(1-b)}{k-br}$

Choose the *correct* answer from the options given below:

(1) A-IV, B-I, C-II, D-III
(2) A-II, B-III, C-I, D-IV
(3) A-I, B-II, C-III, D-IV
(4) A-II, B-IV, C-I, D-III

19. From the following identify the measures of dispersion

A. Mean Deviation
B. Range
C. Standard Deviation
D. Coefficient of Variation
E. Coefficient of Correlation

Choose the *correct* answer from the options given below:

(1) B, C, D & E Only
(2) A, B, D & E Only
(3) A, C, D & E Only
(4) A, B, C & D Only

20. Determine the correct sequence of the steps involved in the process of hypothesis testing

A. Setting the null and alternative hypothesis
B. Setting the level of significance
C. Determining the appropriate statistical test
D. Setting the decision rule
E. Analysing the collected data

Choose the *correct* answer from the options given below:

(1) B, A, C, D, E
(2) B, C, A, D, E
(3) A, C, B, D, E
(4) A, C, B, E, D

21. The tax planning strategies used by multinational enterprises that exploit gaps and mismatches in tax rules to avoid paying tax is known as:

(1) AEPS (2) BEPS
(3) EBPS (4) CEPS

22. Which environment shapes the attitudes of human beings, though there may be great diversity in its impact ?

(1) The Political Environment
(2) International Environment
(3) The Socio-Cultural Environment
(4) The Economic Environment

23. The liquidator after realizing the assets of the company should distribute the proceeds among below mentioned claimants in which order?

A. Liquidator's remuneration and cost of expenses of winding up.
B. Legal charges
C. Claims of secured creditors
D. Preferential creditors and creditors secured by floating charges
E. Unsecured creditors

Choose the *correct* answer from the options given below:

(1) A, B, C, D, E (2) B, A, C, D, E
(3) B, C, A, D, E (4) A, C, B, E, D

24. Match the List I with List II

LIST I	LIST II
A. Buyer's Mind	I. Members of Social-club
B. Personal Factor	II. Motivation
C. Psychological Factor	III. Life Style
D. Reference Group	IV. Black Box

Choose the *correct* answer from the options given below:

(1) A-I, B-II, C-III, D-IV
(2) A-II, B-III, C-IV, D-I
(3) A III, B-IV, C-I, D-II
(4) A-IV, B-III, C-II, D-I

25. The profit volume ratio of a company is 50% and the margin of safety is 40%. Calculate net profit if the sales volume is ₹ 1,00.000.

(1) 10.000 (2) 15.000
(3) 20.000 (4) 25,000

26. The supply function is given as $q = -100+10p$. Find the elasticity of supply (Es) using point method, when price is ₹ 15.

(1) Es = 2 (2) Es = 3
(3) Es = 3.5 (4) Es = 4

27. Arrange the following phases of International Monetary System in chronological order (old to new).

A. Gold Bullion Standard
B. Gold Specie Standard
C. Floating Exchange Rate
D. Gold Exchange Standard
E. Bretton Woods System

Choose the *correct* answer from the options given below:

(1) A, B, E, D, C (2) A, D, E, C, B
(3) B, A, D, E, C (4) B, D, A, C, E

28. Matrix organisation violates which of the following management principles?

(1) Span of Management
(2) Scalar Chain
(3) Unity of Direction
(4) Unity of Command

29. The effect of exchange rate fluctuations on a firm's future cost and revenues is termed as:-

(1) Transaction Exposure
(2) Translation Exposure
(3) Accounting Exposure
(4) Operating Exposure

30. The Bretton Woods monetary system was based on the fixed rate monetary system. It lasted between the years:

(1) 1946 To 1974 (2) 1944 To 1974
(3) 1940 To 1974 (4) 1944 To 1971

31. Which of the following is not a feature of capitalist economy?

(1) Right of private property
(2) Freedom of choice to consumers
(3) Government Interference
(4) High level of competition

32. Which of the following is correct to compute Labour Mix Variance (LMV)?

(1) LMV = Actual rate (Revised Std. time-Actual tune)
(2) LMV = Actual time (Std. Rate-Actual rate)
(3) LMV = Std. Rate (Revised Std. time - Actual time)
(4) LMV = Std. time (Actual rate - Std. Rate)

33. Which of the following is the most frequently held meeting of a company?

(1) Statutory Meeting
(2) Annual General Meeting
(3) Class Meeting
(4) Director's Meeting

34. Arrange the following steps of sampling design process in correct order.

A. Sampling frame must be determined
B. Target population should be defined according to objective

C. Sampling process must be effectively executed
D. Selecting a sampling technique
E. Number of elements to be included in the study must be carefully determined

Choose the *correct* answer from the options given below:

(1) B, D, E, C, A (2) A, B, D, E, C
(3) A, C, B, D, E (4) B, A, D, E, C

35. Arrange the steps of research process in the correct logical order.

A. Formulate a research question
B. Literature review
C. Collect data
D. Develop a research plan
E. Interpret the result

Choose the *correct* answer from the options given below:

(1) B, A, D, C, E (2) A, B, D, C, E
(3) A, C, D, B, E (4) B, A, C, D, E

36. Providing a total package of related goods and services to solve a customer's needs is called

(1) Complete Selling
(2) Conglomerate Selling
(3) Wholesale Selling
(4) Systems Selling

37. The distribution of data which has a long left tail is known as

(1) Positively skewed distribution
(2) Negatively skewed distribution
(3) Symmetrical distribution
(4) Mesokurtic distribution

38. Nicosia Model of consumer behaviour is divided into four major fields, which of the following is the third field under this model?

(1) Feedback
(2) Act of purchase
(3) Firm's and consumer's attributes
(4) Search and evaluation

39. Match the List I with List II

LIST I	LIST II
A. Personal selling	I. Commercially significant news
B. Advertising	II. Advertising within buses, railway compartments
C. Transit advertising	III. Non-personal communication
D. Publicity	IV Two way communication

Choose the *correct* answer from the options given below:

(1) A-I, B-II, C-III, D-IV
(2) A-II, B-III, C-IV, D-I
(3) A-I, B-III, C-II, D-IV
(4) A-IV, B-III, C-II, D-I

40. Match the List I with List II

LIST I Act/ Institution	LIST II Year
A. Consumer Protection Act	I. 1964
B. FEMA	II. 1945
C. IMF	III. 1999
D. UNCTAD	IV. 2019

Choose the *correct* answer from the options given below:

(1) A-IV, B-III, C-II, D-I
(2) A-II, B-III, C-I, D-IV
(3) A-III, B-IV, C-II, D-I
(4) A-I, B-II, C-III, D-IV

41. Match the List I with List II

LIST I Technique	LIST II Description
A. Gordon Technique	I. Teaching the importance of resolving matters
B. Morphological Analysis	II. Insight into a given interaction
C. Built-in- Tension	III. Listing of alternative solution to problems
D. Manodrama	IV Steering a discussion to cry stallise solutions

Choose the *correct* answer from the options given below:

(1) A-I, B-II, C-III, D-IV
(2) A-II, B-III, C-I, D-IV
(3) A-III, B-IV, C-II, D-I
(4) A-IV, B-III, C-I, D-II

42. Transmission of shares is effected by which of the following?

A. Sale B. Death
C. Insolvency D. Maturity

Choose the *correct* answer from the options given below:

(1) A & B Only (2) A & C Only
(3) B & D Only (4) B & C Only

43. Arrange the following forms in correct sequence of first appeal to final appeal by an assesse under Income Tax Act-1961

A. Supreme Court B. High Court
C. Appellate Tribunal
D. Joint Commissioner

Choose the *correct* answer from the options given below:

(1) A, B, C, D (2) D, C, B, A
(3) B, D, A, C (4) C, A, D, B

44. What will be the dividend per share of Rohtas Industries for the year 2024 given the following information about the company ?

EPS for 2024 = ₹ 3
DPS for 2023 = ₹ 1.2
Target Payout Ratio = 4 0.6
Adjustment Rate = ₹ 0.7

(1) ₹ 1.8 (2) ₹ 1.62
(3) ₹ 1.52 (4) ₹ 1.72

45. Arrange the following steps involved in the process of IPO issue in correct order.

A. Verification by SEBI
B. Hiring an under writer
C. Registration for IPO
D. Pricing of IPO
E. Allotment of shares

Choose the *correct* answer from the options given below:

(1) A, C, D, B, E (2) A, D, C, B, E
(3) B, C, D, A, E (4) B, C, A, D, E

46. Which of the following is the pre-condition for applying Chi-square test?

(1) Data should not be presented in percentage or ratio form.
(2) The sample should consists of at least 100 observations.
(3) The sample should not be drawn randomly.
(4) All the individual observations in a sample should not be independent.

47. Which of the following is/are included in salary as per section- 17 of Income Tax Act 1961?

A. Wages B. Perquisite
C. Profits in lieu of salary
D. Compensation on termination of employment

Choose the *correct* answer from the options given below:

(1) A & B Only (2) B & C Only
(3) A, B & C Only (4) A, B, C & D

48. Which of the following are the assumption underlying MM Theory of capital structure?

A. Perfect capital Market
B. Heterogeneous Expectations
C. Absence of Taxes
D. 100% Dividend Payout
E. Equivalent Risk Class

Choose the *correct* answer from the options given below:

(1) A, C, & E Only (2) B, C & E Only
(3) A, B, C & D Only (4) B, C, D & E Only

49. According to Proposition II of Modigliani-Miller theory of capital structure, which of the following statement is true?

(1) Financial Leverage has no effect on the wealth of shareholders.
(2) Financial Leverage increases with wealth of shareholders.
(3) Rate of return expected by shareholders increases with the increase in equity financing.
(4) Rate of return expected by shareholders increases with financial leverage.

50. Which organisational structure promotes control and co-ordination within a department because of similarity in the tasks being performed?

(1) Divisional Structure
(2) Functional Structure
(3) Formal Structure
(4) Matrix Structure

51. Which of the following means management should promote a team-spirit of unity and harmony among employees?

(1) Unity of Command
(2) Unity of Direction
(3) Scalar chain
(4) Espirit De Corps

52. Which of the following are the rights of the equity shareholders?

A. Right to Income
B. Right to claim Dividend
C. Right to Control
D. Right to Liquidation
E. Pre-emptive Rights

Choose the *correct* answer from the options given below:

(1) A, B, C, D & E (2) B, C & E Only
(3) A, B, C & D Only (4) A, C, D & E Only

53. Tax treaties are generally based on which of the following convention?

A. OECD Model Tax Convention
B. UN Model Tax Convention
C. WTO Model Tax Convention
D. IMF Model Tax Convention

Choose the *correct* answer from the options given below:

(1) A & B only (2) A & C only
(3) B & D only (4) A, B & C only

54. An appeal that elaborate on a non-product related benefit or linage and attempts to induce emotional responses from consumers is called:

(1) Physiological Appeals
(2) Informational Appeal
(3) Sociological Appeal
(4) Transformational Appeal

55. Calculate Debt Service coverage ratio from the following data

Net profit before interest and Tax ₹ 50,000

10% Debenture (payable in 10 years in equal instalments) ₹ 1.00,000

Tax rate is 50%

(1) 1.27 (2) 1.67
(3) 2.27 (4) 2.67

56. Which of the following are included in Foreign Direct Investment?

A. Wholly owned subsidiary
B. Joint venture
C. Investment in GDR
D. Acquisition
E. Investment by FIIs

Choose the *correct* answer from the options given below:

(1) A & B Only (2) B, C & D Only
(3) C, D & E Only (4) A, B & D Only

57. The price of one kg of tea is < 30. At this price ₹ 5 kg of tea is demanded. If the price of coffee rises from ₹ 25 to ₹ 35 per kg. the quantity demanded of tea rises from 5 kg to 8 kg. Find the cross price elasticity of tea.

(1) (+)0.5 (2) (+) 1.0
(3) (+)1.5 (4) (-) 1.8

58. According to Dividend Growth Model, the cost of Equity is *equal* to

(1) Retained Earning + Dividend yield
(2) Dividend yield + Expected Growth in Dividend
(3) Retained Earning + Expected Growth in Dividend
(4) Dividend yield + Intrinsic value

59. What is the valuation formula based on the Walter's model if

P: Price per equity share
D: Dividend per share
E: Earnings per share
r: Rate of return on investment
k: Cost of equity

(1) $P = \frac{D + (E - k)/r}{r}$

(2) $P = \frac{E + (D - E)r/k}{k}$

(3) $P = \frac{D + (E - D)r/k}{k}$

(4) $P = \frac{E + (E - D)r/k}{k}$

60. In the context of an organisation, the process of making subordinates to act in a desired manner to achieve certain organisational goals is known as:

(1) Employee participation
(2) Co-partnership
(3) Affiliation
(4) Motivation

61. Which of the following are true about chi-square test and chi-square distribution?

A. Chi-square test is a non-parametric test.
B. Chi-square test was developed by spearman.
C. Chi-square distribution can never be negative.
D. Chi-square distribution is a discrete distribution.
E. Chi-square distribution is a function of its degree of freedom.

Choose the *correct* answer from the options given below:

(1) B, C & D Only (2) A, C & E Only
(3) A, B & D Only (4) B, D & E Only

62. The general consideration applicable to tax planning in the field of business deduction revolve around which of the following?

A. Allowability
B. Year of allowability
C. Extent of allowability
D. Carry forward to future years

Choose the *correct* answer from the options given below:

(1) A & B Only (2) A & C Only

(3) A, B & C Only (4) A, B, C & D

63. Match the List I with List II

LIST I	LIST II
A. Unit of Command	I. Maintaining high morale among employees is imperative
B. Unit of Direction	II. Hierarchical, formalised communication channel
C. Scalar Chain	III. Functions have only one plan and one boss
D. Espirit de Corps	IV. Sub-ordinates reports to only one boss

Choose the *correct* answer from the options given below:

(1) A-I, B-II, C-III, D-IV

(2) A-I, B-IV, C-III, D-II

(3) A-IV, B-III, C-II, D-I

(4) A-II, B-III, C-IV, D-I

64. Arrange the following process of incorporation of a new LLP in proper sequence

A. Reserve LLP name

B. Procure Digital Signature Certificate

C. Prepare documents for incorporation of LLP

D. LLP incorporation and DIN Application

E. Drafting and Filling LLP Agreement

F. Apply for PAN and TAN

Choose the *correct* answer from the options given below:

(1) A, B, C, D, F, E (2) B, A, D, C, E, F

(3) B, A, C, D, F, E (4) A, B, C, D, E, F

65. Arrange the steps of Capital Budgeting Process in correct sequence

A. Preparation of Capital Budget and Appropriation

B. Performance Review

C. Assembling of Investment proposals

D. Identification of Investment opportunities

E. Decision Making

Choose the *correct* answer from the options given below:

(1) D, C, E, A, B (2) A, C, D, B, E

(3) A, D, C, B, E (4) B, D, C, E, A

66. Match the List I with List II

LIST I	LIST II
A. Organisational Structure	I. Refers to the delegation of authority throughout the organisation.
B. Span of Management	II. Groups activities on the basis of products.
C. Divisional Structure	III. Refers to the number of subordinates under a supervisor.
D. Dec entralisation	IV. The framework within which managerai and operating tasks are operated.

Choose the *correct* answer from the options given below:

(1) A-I, B-II, C-III, D-IV

(2) A-III, B-II, C-I, D IV

(3) A-II, B-III, C-IV, D-I

(4) A-IV, B-III, C-II, D-I

67. Which of the following sections of the Income-Tax ACT- 1961. provide for double taxation relief in India?

A. Section- 89 B. Section- 90

C. Section- 91 D. Section- 92

E. Section- 93

Choose the *correct* answer from the options given below:

(1) A & B Only (2) B & C Only

(3) C & D Only (4) A, B & E Only

68. In case of performance appraisal, an assessment should focus on

A. Technology to intervene between appraiser and appraisee.

B. Individual traits

C. Behaviours exhibited by the assesses

D. Knowledge/ skills possessed

E. Results achieved

Choose the *correct* answer from the options given below:

(1) A, B, C & D Only (2) A, B, & C Only

(3) B, C & D Only (4) B, C, D & E Only

69. Arrange the following stages of investigation in proper sequence.
A. Plan work to be done and timing.
B. Obtain instructions from the client and prepare terms of reference
C. Make necessary calculation to eliminate inconsistencies.
D. Collect necessary information and documents.
E. Formulate conclusions/ analysis of findings.
Choose the *correct* answer from the options given below:
(1) A, B, C, D, E (2) A, C, B, D, E
(3) B,A, D, C,E (4) A, B, D, C, E

70. Which of the following are included under EPRG framework of internationalisation?
A. Eco centrism B. Ethno centrism
C. Poly centrism D. Regio centrism
E. Geo centrism
Choose the *correct* answer from the options given below:
(1) B, C, D & E Only
(2) A, B, C & E Only
(3) A, C, D & E Only
(4) A, B, D & E Only

71. A firm wants to launch a new brand of television and refrigerator. The firm conducted a survey and found that 60% of the households have television. 65% have a refrigerator and 35%, both a television and a refrigerator. If a household is randomly selected, what is the probability that the household has either a television or refrigerator?
(1) 0.70 (2) 0.90
(3) 0.80 (4) 0.60

72. Which of the following capital budgeting Techniques follows the discounting criteria?
A. Net Present Value
B. Benefit- cost Ratio
C. Accounting Rate of Return
D. Internal Rate of Return
E. Payback Period
Choose the *correct* answer from the options given below:
(1) A, B, C, D Only (2) B, C, D Only
(3) A, B, D Only (4) A, C, D Only

73. Which of the following is NOT a part of micro environment?
(1) Suppliers
(2) Customers
(3) Competitors
(4) Technology

74. Which of the following are different types of dumping?
A. Persistent dumping
B. Predatory dumping
C. Sporadic dumping
D. Nomadic dumping
Choose the *correct* answer from the options given below:
(1) A & B Only
(2) A, B & C Only
(3) B & C Only
(4) C & D Only

75. What is the privilege of a holder in due course?
(1) The right to cancel the instrument at any time
(2) Instrument cleansing of all defects.
(3) Exemption from legal obligations.
(4) Unrestricted transfer of the instrument.

76. Match the List I with List II

LIST I	LIST II
A. Joint occurrence of Events	I. Collective Exhaustive Events
B. Outcome of an experiment consisting of all possible events	II. Equally likely Events
C. One of the events can not be expected to occur in preference over the other	III. Compound Event
D. The occurance of one event implies that the other can not occur	IV. Mutually Exclusive Events

Choose the *correct* answer from the options given below:
(1) A-III, B-I, C-II, D-IV
(2) A-IV, B-II, C-I, D-III
(3) A-III, B-II, C-I, D-IV
(4) A-I, B-II, C-III, D-IV

77. Which of the following can file a petition for winding up of a company?
A. Shareholders

B. The creditor or prospective creditors
C. The legal heirs
D. The person authorised by the central government

Choose the *correct* answer from the options given below:
(1) A, B & C Only (2) B, C & D Only
(3) A, C & D Only (4) A, B & D Only

78. Arrange the following anti-dumping process in proper sequence.
A. Initiation
B. Preliminary screening
C. Rejection under deminimis, unsubstantiated information etc.
D. Exporting country allowed to modify practice.
E. Preliminar findings followed by final finding and measures

Choose the *correct* answer from the options given below:
(1) B, C, A, D, E (2) A, B, C, D, E
(3) B, A, C, D, E (4) B, C, A, E, D

79. A company has Return on Assets (ROA) of 10% and profit margin of 2%. Compute the total assets turnover.
(1) 2.5% (2) 5%
(3) 7.5% (4) 10%

80. Match the List I with List II

LIST I	LIST II
A. Informal organisation	I. Grouping of jobs of similar nature
B. Formal organisation	II. Interaction among people at work gives rise to a network of social-relationship among employees
C. Divisional structure	III. The organisation structure comprises separate business units
D. Functional structure	IV. Specifies clearly the boundaries of authority' and responsibility

Choose the *correct* answer from the options given below:
(1) A-II, B-III, C-IV, D-I
(2) A-II, B-III, C-I, D-IV
(3) A-II, B-IV, C-III, D-I
(4) A-II, B-IV, C-I, D-III

81. A company prices one litre bottle of its mineral water at ₹ 20/- but 100 ml of the same water in a moisturizer spray for ₹ 50/-. This is an example of which one of the following pricing practices?
(1) Customer-Segment Pricing
(2) Image Pricing
(3) Product-form Pricing
(4) Mark-up Pricing

82. Which of the following are the schemes promoted by NABARD?
A. Kisan Credit Card (KCC)
B. Capital Investment Subsidy Scheme
C. Special Economic Zone Scheme
D. Rural Innovation Fund
E. Tribal Development Fund

Choose the *correct* answer from the options given below:
(1) A, B, C & D Only
(2) B, C, D & E Only
(3) A, B, D & E Only
(4) A, C, D & E Only

83. Which of the following are the principal functions of UNCTAD?
A. To promote International trade with a view to accelerating economic development.
B. To assist economic development of developing countries by promoting private enterprises.
C. To negotiate multinational trade agreements.
D. To make proposals for putting its principles and policies into effect.

Choose the *correct* answer from the options given below:
(1) A, B & C Only (2) B, C & D Only
(3) A, B & D Only (4) A, C & D Only

84. Arrange the following steps of securitisation in a correct sequence
A. Forming SPV
B. Transfer to SPV
C. Credit Enhancement
D. Seasoning
E. Issuance of securities

Choose the *correct* answer from the options given below:

(1) A, B, C, D, E (2) B, C, A, D, E
(3) D, C, A, B, E (4) D, C, B, A, E

85. Assessment made not only from inside the company bin from groups outside the organisation is known as:
(1) 360 - Degree Feedback
(2) 720 - Degree Feedback
(3) Performance Appraisal
(4) MBOM

86. Match the List I with List II

LIST I Trader	LIST II Function/Activity
A. Hedger	I. Buying and selling shares quickly
B. Speculator	II. Reducing investment Risk
C. Arbitrageur	III. Taking increased Risk willingly
D. Scalper	IV. Taking advantage of the mismatch of the prices in two marktes

Choose the *correct* answer from the options given below:
(1) A-I, B-II, C-III, D-IV
(2) A-II, B-I, C-III, D-IV
(3) A-II, B-III, C-IV, D-I
(4) A-III, B-IV, C-II, D-I

87. The management of Vibgyor Fabrics subscribes to the NOI approach and believes that its cost of debt and overall cost of capital will remain at 9% and 12% respectively. If the debt-equity ratio is 0.8, what is the cost of equity?
(1) 16.4% (2) 12.4%
(3) 14.4% (4) 8.12%

88. Which of the following section of Companies Act, 2013 deals with amalgamation, absorption and reconstruction?
(1) Section 139 (2) Section 219
(3) Section 319 (4) Section 391

89. Who among the following has given this definition of CSR? "Wealth created from society has to be ploughed back into society."
(1) Milton (2) Henry Ford
(3) Mahatma Gandhi (4) Kay and Silberston

90. Which of the following are the price-adaption strategies?
A. Price discounts and allowances
B. Target return pricing
C. Geographical pricing
D. Differentiated pricing
E. Going rate pricing

Choose the *correct* answer from the options given below:
(1) A, C & E Only (2) B, C & D Only
(3) A, C & D Only (4) A, B & D Only

Solar Tech Ltd., a global solar panel manufacturer, sought to expand into emerging markets to counteract stagnation in its domestic market. After analyzing global opportunities, the company targeted India due to its favourable renewable energy policies and growing demand for sustainable energy solution.

Solar Tech Ltd. established a joint venture with a local firm to leverage their market knowledge arid distribution network. They also customized their products to meet local regulatory standards and climatic conditions. Despite initial challenges, such as navigating regulatory complexities and cultural differences, solar tech achieved a 25% market share within two years.

The success of the company was attributed to strategic partnerships, product customization and effective market entry tactics. However it faced ongoing issues with supply chain- disruption and the need for continuous innovation to stay competitive.

91. What was a key factor in Solar Tech, ability to achieve a 25% market share in India?
(1) Price reduction
(2) Aggressive advertising campaigns
(3) Strategic partnership and product customisation
(4) Government subsidies

92. How did Solar Tech Ltd. initially approached the market entry into India?
(1) By setting up a wholly owned subsidiary
(2) Through a joint venture with a local firm
(3) By acquiring a local competition
(4) By exporting products directly

93. Despite its success, what ongoing issue did Solar Tech Ltd. encounter?
(1) Decreasing customer base
(2) Increased competition from local brands
(3) Supply chain disruption
(4) Difficulties in securing financing

94. What was the primary reason for Solar Tech, to expand its business to Indian market?
(1) Declining domestic demand

(2) Favourable policies and growing demand in India

(3) Lower production cost in India

(4) Saturated international market

95. What were some of the challenges Solar Tech. Ltd. faced in Indian Market?

(1) Labour shortage and high tariffs

(2) High inflation rate

(3) Political instability and poor infrastructure

(4) Regulatory complexities and cultural differences

The finance manager of ABC: Ltd., a company based in Bangalore has gone on vacation to an island with his family. The island has very poor connectivity and hence he is unable to make or receive calls. The CEO of the company send him a SMS to provide certain information related to financial statement as he was unable to connect due to network problems and C EO has a meeting with the chairman next day.

The finance manager has no documents with him and he was also not able to take the help of internet to send the desired information due to lack of internet facility on the island. On the basis of his memory, he was able to send the following information to the CEO through SMS, which was delivered after 2 hours.

a) Current Debt to Total Debt Ratio : 0.40
b) Total Debt to owner's equity : 0.60
c) Fixed Assets to owner's equity : 0.60
d) Total Assets turnover : 2 Times
e) Inventory turnover : 8 Times
f) Owner's equity : ₹ 1,00,000

The CEO is puzzled to get the SMS, as he was unable to find the required information. You are required to help the CEO in finding relevant information from the SMS as indicated hi the following questions:

96. What would be the value of sales as per the data given in case

(1) ₹ 1,60.000 (2) ₹ 2,20.000
(3) ₹ 3.00.000 (4) ₹ 3,20,000

97. What would be the value of fixed assets as per the ratio given in the case?

(1) ₹ 50.000 (2) ₹ 60.000
(3) ₹ 70.000 (4) ₹ 75.000

98. Compute the value of inventory' horn the data given hi case

(1) ₹ 40,000 (2) ₹ 45,000
(3) ₹ 50.000 (4) ₹ 60,000

99. Find out the value of total assets from the given information

(1) ₹ 80,000 (2) ₹ 1,20,000
(3) ₹ 1,45,000 (4) ₹ 1,60.000

100. Identify the value of long term debt from the given data

(1) ₹ 32.000 (2) ₹ 35.000
(3) ₹ 36.000 (4) ₹ 39.500

ANSWERS

1. (4)	2. (4)	3. (2)	4. (1)	5. (4)	6. (1)	7. (2)	8. (4)	9. (2)	10. (3)
11. (4)	12. (1)	13. (4)	14. (3)	15. (4)	16. (2)	17. (2)	18. (2)	19. (3)	20. (1)
21. (1)	22. (3)	23. (4)	24. (2)	25. (4)	26. (1)	27. (2)	28. (4)	29. (1)	30. (4)
31. (2)	32. (4)	33. (4)	34. (2)	35. (3)	36. (1)	37. (2)	38. (4)	39. (1)	40. (1)
41. (4)	42. (3)	43. (3)	44. (2)	45. (2)	46. (4)	47. (1)	48. (1)	49. (1)	50. (2)
51. (1)	52. (2)	53. (3)	54. (1)	55. (2)	56. (1)	57. (2)	58. (3)	59. (4)	60. (3)
61. (4)	62. (1)	63. (4)	64. (3)	65. (4)	66. (3)	67. (3)	68. (4)	69. (3)	70. (4)
71. (4)	72. (3)	73. (3)	74. (4)	75. (3)	76. (2)	77. (3)	78. (1)	79. (1)	80. (2)
81. (4)	82. (1)	83. (3)	84. (4)	85. (3)	86. (4)	87. (3)	88. (4)	89. (4)	90. (4)
91. (3)	92. (1)	93. (4)	94. (3)	95. (2)	96. (3)	97. (4)	98. (3)	99. (2)	100. (4)

OOO

DECEMBER, 2024

COMMERCE

Paper-II

Note : This paper contains **hundred (100)** objective type questions of **two (2)** marks each. **All** questions are **compulsory.**

1. Which of the following is not the characteristics of theory of comparative cost advantage?

A. There is full employment of the factors of production

B. There are two countries, two commodities and two factors of production

C. There are two countries, two commodities and one factor of production

D. There is absence of transportation cost

E. The countries are capital intensive only.

Choose the *correct* answer from the options given below:

(1) A, B, C Only (2) B, C, D Only

(3) A, C, D Only (4) A, B, E Only

2. Which one of the following is the developmental role of RBI?

(1) Formulates, implements and monitors the monitary policy

(2) Prescribes broad parameters of banking operations

(3) Issues, exchanges end destroys currency notes

(4) Performs a wide range of promotional functions to support national objectives

3. Arrange the following Securities Exchange Board of India (SEBI) regulations in the ascending year of of their enactment.

A. ICDR regulations

B. Intermediaries regulations

C. Real estate investment Trusts regulations

D. Buy - Back of Securities by listed companies regulations

E. Listing Obligations and Disclosures Requirements Regulations

Choose the *correct* answer from the options given below:

(1) D, B, A, C, E (2) D, A, E, C, B

(3) A, C, D, E, B (4) B, A, E, D, C

4. The Consumer Protection Act came into force first on

(1) 14 June, 1986

(2) 20 January, 1987

(3) 24 December, 1986

(4) 14 July, 1987

5. Match the **LIST-I** with **LIST-II**

LIST-I (Concept)	**LIST-II (Meaning)**
A. Exchange Rate	I. It refers to the price of one unit of foreign currency in terms of some units of home currency
B. Forward market	II. It is the process of making risk less profits by exploiting price differences of assets in different market.
C. Arbitrage	III. Where transactions are entered into for settlement on a future date
D. Direct Quotation	IV. It is a price of one unit of a currency in terms of some units of another currency

Choose the **correct** answer from the options given below:

(1) A-IV, B-III, C-II, D-I

(2) A-III, B-IV, C-II, D-I

(3) A-I, B-II, C-III, D-IV

(4) A-I, B-III, C-II, D-IV

6. Which of the following are the characteristics of a high customer centric Organization?

A. Market driven B. Process Oriented

C. Value Driven D. Price Driven

E. Making competitor irrelevant

Choose the **correct** answer from the options given below:

(1) A, B, E Only (2) A, C, E Only
(3) B, C, D Only (4) C, D, E Only

7. Beta Company Ltd issued 10% perpetual debt of ₹ 1,00,000. The company's tax rate is 50%. Determine the cost of capital (before tax as well as after tax) assuming the debt is issued at 10 percent premium.

(1) Before tax cost = 9.09% and after tax cost = 4.54%
(2) Before tax cost = 4.54% and after tax cost = 9%
(3) Before tax cost = 9.90% and after tax cost = 4.45%
(4) Before tax cost = 10.09% and after tax cost = 5.54%

8. Match the **LIST-I** with **LIST-II**

LIST-I Personality Type	**LIST-II** Congruent Occupation
A. Social	I. Mechanic
B. Conventional	II. Mathematician
C. Investigative	III. Corporate Manager
D. Realistic	IV. Teacher

Choose the **correct** answer from the options given below:

(1) A-IV, B-III, C-II, D-I
(2) A-III, B-IV, C-II, D-I
(3) A-IV, B-II, C-III, D-I
(4) A-II, B-IV, C-I, D-III

9. _____ is the result of the Bretton Wood Conference of nations held in 1944.

(1) WTO (2) IMF
(3) IBRD (4) ADB

10. Arrange the following stages of conflict process in the proper sequence.

A. Outcomes
B. Potential opposition or incompatibility
C. Behaviour
D. Cognition and personalization
E. Intentions

Choose the *correct* answer from the options given below:

(1) D, B, E, C, A (2) B, D, E, C, A
(3) A, B, E, D, C (4) D, C, B, E, A

11. Match the **LIST-I** with **LIST-II**

LIST-I Financial Inclusion Yojana	**LIST-II** Year
A. PM Jan Dhan	I. 2016
B. PM Mudra	II. 2014
C. Stand Up India	III. 2017
D. Vaya Vandana	IV. 2015

Choose the **correct** answer from the options given below:

(1) A-II, B-IV, C-I, D-III
(2) A-II, B-I, C-IV, D-III
(3) A-IV, B-I, C-III, D-II
(4) A-II, B-III, C-I, D-IV

12. In which one of the following the effectiveness of brainstorming as group decision making technique is high?

(1) Social Pressure
(2) Task Orientation
(3) Potential for interpersonal conflict
(4) Money Costs

13. Which of the following are the disadvantages of Graphics rating scale as an appraisal tool?

A. Standards may be unclear
B. Halo Effect
C. Time consuming
D. Difficult to develop
E. Leniency

Choose the *correct* answer from the options given below:

(1) A, B, E Only (2) A, B, C Only
(3) B, C, E Only (4) A, C, D, E Only

14. Which one of the following is not a behavioral symptom of stress?

(1) Lower Job Satisfaction
(2) Lower Job Performance
(3) Higher Absenteeism
(4) Higher Labour Turnover

15. Which of the following tool is used for projecting supply of personnel?

(1) Trend Analysis (2) Ratio Analysis
(3) Markov Analysis
(4) Managerial Judgement

16. Match the **LIST-I** with **LIST-II**

LIST-I Concept	**LIST-II** Explanation
A. Higher Indifference Curve	I. Higher Satisfaction

B.	Converse Indifference Curve	II.	Diminishing Marginal Rate of Substitution
C.	Price Line	III.	Same satisfaction on the curve
D.	Indifference Curve	IV.	Constant Price Ratio

Choose the *correct* answer from the options given below:

(1) A-I, B-II, C-III, D-IV
(2) A-I, B-II, C-IV, D-III
(3) A-I, B-III, C-IV, D-II
(4) A-IV, B-II, C-III, D-I

17. Which of the following curves cannot be U-shaped?

(1) A.V.C Curve (2) A.F.C Curve
(3) A.C. Curve (4) M.C. Curve

18. Arrange the following steps in logical sequence regarding how to compute Net Present Value (NPV).

A. Calculate Net Present Value (NPV) i.e. Present Value of all cash inflows - present value of all cash outflows
B. Calculate all the cash outflows associated with the project
C. Calculate all the cash inflows associated with the project
D. Calculate the present value of all cash inflows associated with the project
E. Calculate the present value of all cash outflows associated with the project

Choose the *correct* answer from the options given below:

(1) A, B, C, E, D (2) B, C, E, D, A
(3) A, C, B, E, D (4) A, C, B, D, E

19. Which of the following are taxes (GST) applicable in the case of supply of goods

I. From West Bengal to Chandigarh
II. From Puducherry to Chennai

Note: **CGST:** Central Goods and Services Tax
IGST: Integrated Goods and Services Tax
UTGST: Union territory Goods and Services Tax
SGST: State Goods and Services Tax

(1) I. CGST II. IGST
(2) I. IGST II. IGST
(3) I. UTGST II. UTGST
(4) I. SGST II. UTGST

20. Match the **LIST-I** with **LIST-II**

LIST-I (Sections)	LIST-II (TDS)
A. Section 194 of the Income Tax Act, 1961	I. Payment on account of repurchase of units by mutual fund
B. Section 194C of the Income Tax Act, 1961	II. Payment to the non-resident sportsman
C. Section 194E of the Income Tax Act, 1961	III. Payment to contractor and sub-contractor
D. Section 194F of the Income Tax Act, 1961	IV. Dividend

Choose the **correct** answer from the options given below:

(1) A-IV, B-III, C-II, D-I
(2) A-I, B-II, C-III, D-IV
(3) A-I, B-III, C-II, D-IV
(4) A-III, B-IV, C-I, D-II

21. What is the value of Standard Deviation of first seven natural numbers?

(1) $\sqrt{48}$ (2) 2
(3) $\sqrt{8}$ (4) 4

22. Identify which of the following statements are True

A. Assessment Year means the period of 12 months commencing on the first day of April every year
B. Rounding off of total income is defined under section 288B of the Income Tax Act, 1961
C. Rounding off of tax is defined under section 288 A of the Income Tax Act, 1961
D. Assessee is always a person but a person may or may not be an assessed
E. A person may not have assessable income but may still be an assessed

Choose the *correct* answer from the options given below:

(1) B and C only (2) A, D, E Only
(3) A, B, C Only (4) B, C, D Only

23. Arrange the following channels in the increasing order of value-addition of sales.

A. Retail Store B. Sales force
C. Internet

D. Value-added partners
E. Distributors

Choose the *correct* answer from the options given below:

(1) A, E, C, D, B (2) C, A, E, B, D
(3) C, A, E, D, B (4) B, C, A, E, D

24. Match the **LIST-I** with **LIST-II**

LIST-I Statistical Test	**LIST-II** Explanation
A. Z-Test	I. Tests the significance of the association between two attributes
B. Chi - Square	II. Compares the difference in the mean values of two independent sample groups (non-parametric data)
C. ANOVA	III. Tests the significance of the different between average of two large sized sample groups (Parametric data)
D. Mann-Whitney Test (U-test)	IV. Compares the difference in the mean values of more than two sample groups (Parametric data)

Choose the **correct** answer from the options given below:

(1) A-I, B-II, C-III, D-IV
(2) A-III, B-I, C-IV, D-II
(3) A-II, B-III, C-I, D-IV
(4) A-IV, B-I, C-III, D-II

25. Which of the following is a situation of adverse balance of trade?

(1) Import more than exports
(2) Exports more than imports
(3) Exports equal to imports
(4) Export Surplus

26. Which of the following points are considered as essential characteristics of a Promissory Note?

A. It must be in writing
B. It must not contain an undertaking or promise to pay
C. The promise to pay must be conditional
D. A promissory note must be signed by the maker.
E. Promise to pay money only

Choose the *correct* answer from the options given below:

(1) A, D and E Only (2) A, B and E Only
(3) B, C and D Only (4) B and D Only

27. Match the **LIST-I** with **LIST-II**

LIST-I Thoery	**LIST-II** Author(s)
A. Theory of Comparative Cost Advantage	I. Heckseher & Ohlin
B. Theory of Opportunity Cost	II. David Ricardo
C. Endowment Theory of Factor	III. Haberler
D. Theory of Absolute Advantage	IV. Adam Smith

Choose the **correct** answer from the options given below:

(1) A-II, B-III, C-I, D-IV
(2) A-II, B-III, C-IV, D-I
(3) A-III, B-II, C-I, D-IV
(4) A-IV, B-III, C-II, D-I

28. Which of the following is a non-probability method of selecting sample from a population?

(1) Simple Random Sampling
(2) Multi Stage Sampling
(3) Cluster Sampling
(4) Snow Ball Sampling

29. Which of the following points are considered as salient features of Limited Liability Partnership (LLP)?

A. LLP is a body corporate
B. LLP is a legal entity separate from its partners
C. LLP does not enjoy a perpetual succession
D. Partners of LLP have unlimited liability
E. LLP is an artificial legal person

Choose the *correct* answer from the options given below:

(1) A, B and E Only (2) B, C and D Only
(3) C, D and E Only (4) C and D Only

30. Total production is maximum when

(1) Average production is maximum
(2) Marginal production is maximum

(3) Marginal production is zero
(4) Average production is zero

31. Which one of the following consists of comparing entries in the books of account with documentary evidence in support thereof.

(1) Internal check (2) Internal control
(3) Vouching (4) Verification

32. Match the **LIST-I** with **LIST-II**

LIST-I (Key definition Under IT Act 2000)	**LIST-II (Sections)**
A. Addressee	I. Section 2(1)(f) of the Information Technology Act 2000
B. Adjudicating Officer	II. Section 2(1)(d) of the Information Technology Act 2000
C. Affixing Electronic Signature	III. Section 2(1)(c) of the Information Technology Act 2000
D. Asymmetric Crypto System	IV. Section 2(1)(b) of the Information Technology Act 2000

Choose the **correct** answer from the options given below:

(1) A-IV, B-III, C-II, D-I
(2) A-III, B-IV, C-I, D-II
(3) A-II, B-I, C-III, D-IV
(4) A-I, B-II, C-III, D-IV

33. Current assets are Rs 4,00,000
Inventories are Rs 2,00,000
Working capital is Rs 2,40,000
Calculate Current Ratio.

(1) 2:1 (2) 2.5: 1
(3) 1.5:1 (4) 1:2

34. Which of the following are True for a random variable?

A. A random variable is a certain quantity, whose value depends on chance.
B. A continuous random variable can assume at most two countable number of values.
C. A discrete random variable can assume at most a countable number of values.
D. A random variables is a function of the simple space.
E. A random variables is a uncertain quantity, whose value depends on chance.

Choose the *correct* answer from the options given below:

(1) A, B, D Only (2) A, B, C Only
(3) B, C, D Only (4) C, D, E Only

35. Match the **LIST-I** with **LIST-II**

LIST-I INSTITUTION	**LIST-II YEAR OF ESTABLISHMENT**
A. UNCTAD	I. 1967
B. WTO	II. 1994
C. NAFTA	III. 1964
D. ASEAN	IV. 1995

Choose the **correct** answer from the options given below:

(1) A-I, B-II, C-III, D-IV
(2) A-III, B-IV, C-II, D-I
(3) A-I, B-III, C-IV, D-II
(4) A-I, B-II, C-IV, D-III

36. Match the **LIST-I** with **LIST-II**

LIST-I ECONOMISTS	**LIST-II CONTRIBUTION**
A. Adam Smith	I. Principles of Economics
B. A. Marshall	II. Value and Capital
C. J.R. Hicks	III. The Wealth of Nations
D. Wassily Leontief	IV. Input Output Economics

Choose the **correct** answer from the options given below:

(1) A-I, B-III, C-II, D-IV
(2) A-I, B-II, C-IV, D-III
(3) A-III, B-I, C-II, D-IV
(4) A-III, B-II, C-I, D-IV

37. Arrange the following management research questions in the ascending order.

A. Management Question
B. Measurement Question
C. Management dilemma
D. Research Question
E. Investigative Question

Choose the *correct* answer from the options given below:

(1) C, A, B, D, E (2) C, A, D, E, B
(3) A, C, D, E, B (4) B, C, A, D, E

38. Which of the following statements are true regarding admission of a new partner?

A. According to section 25 of the Indian Partnership Act, 1932, a person can be admitted as partner.

B. New Profit - sharing ratio is the ratio in which all partners, including new partners, will share future profits and loses of the firm.

C. New Profit Share = Profit Share Sacrificed - Old Profit Share

D. Sacrificing Ratio = Old Profit Share New Profit Share

E. The Profit or loss which arises from Revaluation Account will be transferred to partner's capital account

Choose the *correct* answer from the options given below:

(1) B, D and E Only (2) A, B and C Only
(3) B, C and D Only (4) C, D and E Only

39. Which of the following are the features of Treasury Bills?

A. Negotiable Securities

B. Issued at par and are repaid at premium on maturity.

C. High liquidity on account of short tenure

D. Assured Yield

E. High transaction cost

Choose the *correct* answer from the options given below:

(1) A, B, E Only (2) A, C, D Only
(3) B, C, D Only (4) A, C, D, E Only

40. A proposal requires a cash outflow of ₹ 18,500 and is expected to generate cash inflows of ₹ 8,000, ₹ 6,000, ₹ 4,000, ₹ 2,000 and ₹ 2,000 over next 5 years respectively. The payback period is

(1) 4 Years (2) 3.25 Years
(3) 3.50 Years (4) 4.25 Years

41. Match the **LIST-I** with **LIST-II**

LIST-I Product Life Cycle (PLC) Stage	**LIST-II Distribution Strategy**
A. Introduction	I. Phase out unprofitable outlets
B. Growth	II. Build Selective distribution
C. Maturity	II. Build intensive distribution
D. Decline	IV. Build more intensive distribution

Choose the **correct** answer from the options given below:

(1) A-III, B-II, C-IV, D-I
(2) A-III, B-II, C-I, D-IV
(3) A-II, B-III, C-IV, D-I
(4) A-IV, B-III, C-I, D-II

42. Which of the following are the assumptions of the oligopoly?

A. One seller and large number of buyers

B. A few sellers and large number of buyers

C. Large number of sellers and large number of buyer

D. Entry of new seller is restricted

E. Firms Interdependence

Choose the *correct* answer from the options given below:

(1) C, D, E Only
(2) A, B, C Only
(3) B, D, C Only
(4) B, D, E Only

43. Arrange the following point (Section wise from Section 14 to 18) of the Indian Contract Act

A. Definition of free consent

B. Misrepresentation

C. Fraud

D. Undue influence

E. Coercion

Choose the *correct* answer from the options given below:

(1) E, D, C, B, A (2) D, E, C, A, B
(3) B, D, E, A, C (4) A, E, D, C, A

44. Arrange the prefatory information of report writing in a logical sequence.

A. Executive Summary

B. Authorization Statement

C. Title Page

D. Letter of transmittal

E. Table of Contents

Choose the *correct* answer from the options given below:

(1) A, B, C, D, E (2) C, D, E, B, A
(3) D, C, B, A, E (4) D, B, C, E, A

45. Quasi contracts are based on the doctrine of

(1) Unjust enrichment
(2) Just enrichment

(3) Unjust Richment
(4) Misrepresentation

46. Identify correct statements from the following regarding Time Value of money.

A. The interest which may be earned/saved on the money held at present underlines the concept of time value of money.

B. The money which is receivable at present has less value than the money receivable in future.

C. The relationship that exists between the value of money receivable at present and the value of money receivable in future is referred as time value of the money.

D. Value of money receivable at present = value of money receivable in future - Time value of money.

E. Future value of money is the value of money held presently at some given future time at a given rate of Interest.

Choose the *correct* answer from the options given below:

(1) B and D Only (2) A, C and E Only
(3) B, C and D Only (4) C, D and E Only

47. Match the **LIST-I** with **LIST-II**

LIST-I Conflict Handling intentions	LIST-II Description
A. Competing	I. A situation in which each party in a conflict desires to satisfy fully the concerns of all parties.
B. Collaborating	II. The willingness of one party in a conflict to place the negotiating partners interest above their own.
C. Accommodating	III. A situation in which each party to a conflict is willing to give up something to resolve the conflict.
D. Compromising	IV. A desire to satisfy one's interests regardless of the impact on the other party to the conflict.

Choose the **correct** answer from the options given below:

(1) A-I, B-IV, C-II, D-III
(2) A-IV, B-I, C-II, D-III
(3) A-IV, B-I, C-III, D-II
(4) A-IV, B-II, C-I, D-III

48. Which one of the following refers to the firms investment in the current assets?

(1) Gross Working Capital
(2) Net Working Capital
(3) Gross Current liabilities
(4) Operating cycle

49. Arrange the following points in their section-wise order (Section 23 to 27) as per the Income Tax Act, 1961

A. Deemed ownership

B. Provision for arrears of rent and unrealized rent received subsequently

C. Determination of annual value

D. Treatment of income from co-owned property

E. Deduction from (Annual Value) Income from house property

Choose the *correct* answer from the options given below:

(1) A, C, B, D, E (2) C, E, B, D, A
(3) A, B, C, D, E (4) B, C, D, E, A

50. Match the **LIST-I** with **LIST-II**

LIST-I Act	LIST-II Year
A. Indian Contract Act	I. 2013
B. Sales of Goods Act	II. 1872
C. Negotiable Instruments Act	III. 1930
D. Companies Act	IV. 1881

Choose the **correct** answer from the options given below:

(1) A-II, B-III, C-IV, D-I
(2) A-I, B-II, C-III, D-IV
(3) A-IV, B-III, C-II, D-I
(4) A-III, B-IV, C-I, D-II

51. Match the **LIST-I** with **LIST-II**

LIST-I (Accounting Concept & Convention)	LIST-II (Meaning)
A. Conservatism	I. Use of same accounting policies by a firm from period to period
B. Dual aspect	II. Enterprise is treated as separate

			from owner and other persons associated with it
C.	Separate Business entity	III.	Every transaction has a twofold effect
D.	Consistency	IV.	Anticipate no profit, but provide for all possible losses

Choose the **correct** answer from the options given below:

(1) A-IV, B-III, C-II, D-I
(2) A-I, B-II, C-III, D-IV
(3) A-II, B-III, C-I, D-IV
(4) A-III, B-IV, C-I, D-II

52. Which of the following points are considered as factors determinating the working capital of a firm?

A. Basic nature of Business
B. Business cycle fluctuations
C. Credit Policy of the firm
D. Long term source of finance
E. Employee Skills

Choose the *correct* answer from the options given below:

(1) A, B and D Only (2) B, C and D Only
(3) A, B and C Only (4) D and E Only

53. Arrange the following steps in the proper sequence to develop effective marketing communication.

A. Design the communication
B. Select the communication channel
C. Identify the target audience
D. Choose the communication mix
E. Choose the communication objectives

Choose the *correct* answer from the options given below:

(1) E, A, C, B, D (2) C, A, B, D, E
(3) E, B, C, A, D (4) C, E, A, B, D

54. Standard Deviation of Sampling Distribution is called

(1) Sampling Error (2) Probable Error
(3) Standard Error (4) Measurable Error

55. If new contract is substituted in place of an existing contract, it is called

(1) Waiver (2) Remission
(3) Novation (4) Alteration

56. The Capital Adequacy Ratio (CAR) for Indian Public Sector banks set by RBI is:

(1) 9% (2) 10%
(3) 11% (4) 12%

57. Arrange the following Institutions in ascending order of their year of establishment.

A. SEBI
B. Reserve Bank of India
C. State Bank of India
D. SIDBI
E. NABARD

Choose the *correct* answer from the options given below:

(1) C, B, E, A, D (2) B, C, E, D, A
(3) B, C, A, E, D (4) E, B, C, D, A

58. Which of the following are true for Skewness

A. It is a measure of symmetry of a frequency distribution.
B. For the right-skewed distribution, the mean is to be to the right of median.
C. For the right-skewed distribution, the mean is to be to the right of mode.
D. For the right-skewed distribution, the mean is to be to the left of median.
E. For the right-skewed distribution, the mean is to be to the left of mode.

Choose the *correct* answer from the options given below:

(1) A, B, C Only (2) A, C, D Only
(3) A, D, E Only (4) A, B, D Only

59. Arrange the organizational aspect of employees need hierarchy in the increasing order.

A. Cohesive and supportive co-workers
B. Work place conditions
C. Work safety
D. Responsibilities
E. Job Challenge

Choose the *correct* answer from the options given below:

(1) C, B, D, A, E (2) B, C, A, D, E
(3) A, C, B, E, D (4) B, A, C, D, E

60. "To what degree will there be rules and regulations to direct employees and managers" is defined as

(1) Departmentalization
(2) Centralization and decentralization
(3) Formalization
(4) Boundary Spanning

61. Identify, which of the following statements are True.

A. Commuted pension received by a government employee is fully exempted from Income Tax
B. Section 30 of the Income Tax Act 1961 discusses deduction in respect of rent, rates, taxes, repairs and insurance of building used by the assessee for the purpose of business
C. Section 33 of the Income Tax Act 1961, defines provision regarding depreciation of tangible assets
D. Capital gain arises from transfer of any assets
E. Short term Capital assets is defined under section 2(42 A) of the Income Tax Act 1961

Choose the *correct* answer from the loptions given below:

(1) A, B, and E Only (2) C, D and E only
(3) A and B only (4) C and D only

62. Which of the following is correct?

(1) A firm under perfect competition is in equilibrium where AR = MR
(2) A firm under monopoly is in equilibrium where TR = MR
(3) A firm under monopolistic competition is in equilibrium where AC = MC
(4) A firm under oligopoly is in equilibrium where MR = MC

63. According to Job characteristics model, the psychological state of an experienced meaningfulness of the work is due to the following core job dimensions -

A. Autonomy B. Skill Variety
C. Task Identity D. Feedback
E. Task Significance

Choose the *correct* answer from the options given below:

(1) A, B, D Only (2) B, C, E Only
(3) A, C, E Only (4) A, B, D, E Only

64. When all the factors of production are changed in same proportion, it is called as;

A. Long run production function
B. Law of equal proportion
C. Law of return to scale
D. Law of return to a factor
E. Law of Variable proportion

Choose the *correct* answer from the options given below:

(1) A, B, C Only (2) B, C, D Only
(3) C, D, E Only (4) A, C, E Only

65. Bret Lee, an Australian cricket player visits India for 100 days in every financial year. This has been his practice for the past 10 financial Years. Find out his residential status for the assessment Year 2023-24.

(1) Resident in India
(2) Resident and ordinarily resident in India
(3) Resident but not ordinarily resident in India
(4) Non-resident in India

66. Which one of the following sections of the Income Tax Act, 1961 defines method for computing Arm Length Price?

(1) 90 C (2) 91 C
(3) 92 C (4) 93 C

67. Which of the following statements are correct:

A. Call-in-advance is the amount paid by the shareholders in excess of amount due from them.
B. When the number of shares applied is more than the number of shares offered to the public for subscription, the issue is termed as under subscription.
C. Section 49 of the Companies Act prohibits the issue of shares other than sweat equity shares at discount.
D. Unless or until the fortified shares are reissued, the balance on the shares fortified account will be deducted from the paid up capital.
E. The securities premium is an amount in excess of nominal value of face value of the securities.

Choose the *correct* answer from the options given below:

(1) A and E Only (2) B, C and D Only
(3) A, B and C Only (4) A, D and E Only

68. When price of a good X rises, the demand for substitute good Y will;

(1) Rise (2) Fall
(3) Remain unchanged
(4) Falls initially and then rises

69. Determine the P/V ratio from the following particulars.

Total Fixed Cost Rs 12,000
Actual Sales Rs 48,000
Margin of Safety Rs 8,000

(1) 20% (2) 25%
(3) 30% (4) 40%

70. Which of the following are the features of F.E.M.A?

A. Central government can regulate payments to and from a person situated outside country.
B. Holding of immovable property outside India is restricted.
C. R.B.I can restrict the transaction from capital account even if it is done by authorized person.
D. All foreign financial transactions are to be done through F.E.M.A authorized person.
E. F.E.M.A applies to Indian citizens living abroad.

Choose the *correct* answer from the options given below:

(1) A, B, C Only (2) B, D, E Only
(3) A, B, E Only (4) A, C, D Only

71. Which of the following statements are true regarding the buying dynamics of individual consumers?

A. To successfully compete in the market and create customer value, managers must fully understand the reality rather than theory of consumer behavior.
B. In marketing, perceptions are more important than reality because they affect consumers actual behavior.
C. People emerge with same perceptions of the same object.
D. Consumers are constructive decision makers and are subject to many contextual influences.
E. A consumer's buying behavior is influenced by cultural, social and personal tactics. Of theses personal factors exert the broadest and deepest influence on people's perception and desires.

Choose the *correct* answer from the options given below:

(1) B, D Only (2) A, B, D Only
(3) A, C, E Only (4) B, C, D, E Only

72. Which of the following research designs is the most precise one?

(1) Experimental (2) Exploratory
(3) Diagnostic (4) Descriptive

73. Which one the following is not the behavioral factor of the customer profile involved in tactical targeting?

(1) Purchase Frequency
(2) Income
(3) Purchase Quantity
(4) Price Sensitivity

74. Which one of the following refers to the composition of long term funds such as debentures, long term borrowing, preference shares, equity shares in the capitalization of a company?

(1) Cost of capital
(2) Capital budgeting
(3) Working Capital
(4) Capital structure

75. Which of the following is not a monetary measure for correcting disequilibrium in Balance of Payment?

(1) Monetary Contraction
(2) Devaluation
(3) Exchange Control
(4) Abolution of Export Duties

76. A contract of Indemnity is a :

(1) Wagering Agreement
(2) Quasi Contract
(3) Void Contract
(4) Contingent Contract

77. Which one of the following structure of the marketing department will be most suitable for the companies that produce many products for many markets?

(1) Geographic Organization
(2) Product or Brand Organization
(3) Functional Organization
(4) Matrix Organization

78. Which one of the following conditions is not true in case of marketing skimming as the pricing objective?

(1) The market is highly price sensitive
(2) A sufficient number of buyers signal a high demand
(3) The high initial price does not attract more competitors to the market
(4) The high price communicates the image of a superior product

79. Arrange the following points step by step regarding computation of Gross Total Income

A. Computation of Gross Total Income
B. Set off and carry forward of Losses
C. Clubbing of Income of spouse, minor child etc.
D. Computation of Income under each head of Income
E. Determination of Residential Status

Choose the correct answer from the options given below:
(1) E, D, C, B, A (2) A, B, C, D, E
(3) C, D, E, A, B (4) B, C, D, E, A

80. Match the **LIST-I** with **LIST-II**

LIST-I (Direct Material Variance)	**LIST-II (Formula)**
A. Direct material cost variance	I. Standard price × (Revised standard quantity – Actual Quantity)
B. Direct material price variance	II. Standard price × (Standard Quantity for actual output quantity – Actual Quantity)
C. Direct material usage variance	III. Actual Quantity × (Standard price – actual price)
D. Direct material mix variance	IV. Standard cost for actual output actual cost

Choose the **correct** answer from the options given below:
(1) A-I, B-II, C-III, D-IV
(2) A-IV, B-III, C-I, D-II
(3) A-IV, B-III, C-II, D-I
(4) A-III, B-IV, C-II, D-I

81. Which section of the Income Tax Act 1961 mentions unilateral relief?
(1) 90 (2) 89
(3) 91 (4) 92

82. Which one of the following is value added service of EXIM Bank?
(1) Export Facilitation
(2) Export product Development
(3) Workshops and Seminars
(4) Export Marketing

83. Arrange the following levels of economic integration in increasing order.

A. Political Union B. Free Trade Area
C. Customs Union D. Common Market
E. Economic Union

Choose the *correct* answer from the options given below:
(1) B, C, D, E, A (2) B, A, C, D, E
(3) B, A, D, C, E (4) E, D, B, A, C

84. Which one of the following is not a social network of social media platform?
(1) Facebook (2) Blogs
(3) Twitter (4) YouTube

85. Arrange the practical steps involved in the preparation of process account where there is work in progress.
A. Prepare process account
B. Prepare statement of Evaluation
C. Prepare statement of cost per equivalent unit
D. Prepare statement of equivalent production
E. Determine and analyze the number of physical units in the form of inputs (transferred from previous process) and output

Choose the *correct* answer from the options given below:
(1) A, B, C, D, E (2) E, D, C, B, A
(3) C, D, E, A, B (4) B, C, D, A, E

86. Which one of the following conditions is not true as per IRDA Act, 1999, for entry of private players into the insurance market?
(1) The company's sole purpose is to carry on life insurance business or general insurance business or reinsurance business.
(2) The minimum paid up equity capital for life insurance or general insurance business is ₹ 100 crore.
(3) The minimum paid up capital for carrying reinsurance business is ₹ 300 crore.
(4) Insurance companies are required to invest not less than 15 percent of their funds in infrastructure and social sectors.

87. The Securities Exchange Board of India (SEBI) regulates and supervises the securities through
A. Regulations B. Rules
C. Guidelines D. Scheme
E. Orders

Choose the *correct* answer from the options given below:

(1) A, B, E Only (2) B, C, D Only
(3) A, B, C, D, E (4) A, C, D, E Only

88. Arrange the following actions of a manager in the increasing degree of control.

A. Manager defines limits and asks for group decisions
B. Manager offers tentative decisions to change
C. Manager sells decisions
D. Manager lets subordinates function within limits defined by him
E. Manager presents problems, invites suggestions and makes decisions

Choose the *correct* answer from the options given below:

(1) A, D, B, E, C (2) C, B, E, A, D
(3) D, A, E, B, C (4) D, A, B, E, C

89. Prepaid Insurance is which type of account?

(1) Real Account
(2) Personal Account
(3) Nominal Account
(4) Real and Nominal Both

90. Which of the following refers to an attempt to avoid payment of taxes by using illegal means?

(1) Tax Management (2) Tax Planing
(3) Tax Avoidance (4) Tax Evasion

The first phase of modern banking in India began after independence in 1947, when the government nationalized the major banks and introduced various reforms to promote financial inclusion and social welfare. The second phase started in the 1990s, when the liberalization of the economy and the advent of technology enabled the emergence of new private and foreign banks, offering competitive and innovative products and services to the customers. In the 2000s, the third phase commenced when the Internet and mobile penetration increased, leading to the rise of online and mobile banking, as well as the entry of Non-Banking Financial Companies (NBFCs) and fintech startups, offering digital solutions to cater to the unbanked and underbanked segments of the population. The fourth and current phase of banking in India is characterized by the emergence of neo banks, which are digital-only banks that operate without physical branches and offer a range of banking and financial services through mobile apps and web platforms. Neo banks often function by partnering with licensed banks to provide their services to customer. While the digital banking landscape in India is evolving rapidly, there are still many challenges and gaps that need to be addressed. One of the major challenges is the lack of standardization and interoperability among the various players, platforms, and systems in the ecosystem. For instance, there are multiple payment methods, such as UPI, IMPS, NEFT, RTGS, cards, wallets and QR codes, each with its own features, limitations and charges. This creates confusion and inconvenience for customers, who have to switch between different apps and interfaces to make payments and access their accounts.

Artificial Intelligence (AI) is a potent technology that can help digital banks to overcome the challenges and gaps mentioned above, and add value to their customers and stakeholders. AI can enable digital banks to leverage data and analytics, machine learning, natural language processing, computer vision, and other advance techniques to automate and enhance various banking processes, such as customer identification and verification, customer service and support, product recommendation and cross-selling, fraud detection and risk management, credit scoring and underwriting, and regulatory compliance and reporting.

91. What is one-of the major challenges in the digital banking landscape in India?

(1) Lack of internet penetration
(2) Overabundance of physical branches
(3) Lack of standardization and interoperability
(4) Over regulation by the government

92. What marked the beginning of the second phase of modern banking in India?

(1) Nationalization of major banks
(2) Liberalization of the economy
(3) Emergence of fintech startup
(4) Introduction of Internet banking

93. How can artificial intelligence (AI) help digital banks to overcome challenges?

(1) By reducing Internet penetration
(2) By increasing physical branches
(3) By providing advanced analytics
(4) By reducing customer base

94. What is the primary focus of neo banks in India?

(1) Offering physical branch services
(2) Catering to the unbanked and underbanked segments
(3) Providing traditional banking services
(4) Emphasizing paper - based transaction

95. What is consequence of the lack of standardization and interoperability in the digital banking ecosystem?

(1) Convenience for customers
(2) Increased trust in digital banking
(3) Confusing and inconvenience for costumers
(4) Reduction in transaction costs

The major source for the revenue for the government is indirect tax. The Central Board of Indirect Taxes and Customs (CBIC) (erstwhile Central Board of Excise and Customs) is the apex regulatory body that supervises the levy and administration of Indirect Taxes in India. CBIC is a part of the Department of Revenue under the Ministry of Finance, Government of India. It deals with the tasks of formulation of policy concerning levy and collection of customs, Central Excise duties, Central Goods & Services Tax and IGST, prevention of smuggling and administration of matter relating to customs, Central Excise, Central Goods & Services Tax (CGST), IGST and narcotics to the extent under CBIC's purview. The board is the administrative authority for its subordinate organizations, including Custom Houses, Central Excise and Central GST Commissionerate's and the Central Revenue Control Laboratory. In recent years, the Indian government has undertaken significant reforms under the indirect taxation system. This includes the implementation of Goods and Services Tax (GST). Goods and Services Tax (GST) is an indirect tax has replaced many indirect taxes in India. The Goods and Services Tax Act was passed in the Parliament on March 29, 2017. This Act came into effect on July 01, 2017. GST is a destination based tax on consumption with credit of taxes paid at previous stages available as set-off. In nutshell. Only value addition will be taxed and the burden of tax is to be borne by the final consumer.

Destination based tax on consumption means the tax would accrue to the taxing authority which has jurisdiction over the place of consumption which is also termed as place of supply. GST has removed the cascading effect of taxes. This cascading effect implies charging tax on tax. In other words, at the time of levy of tax, the total value is considered which is inclusive of all taxes paid up to the points. In this manner, if the tax is always charged on the selling price of the products, the burden of tax keeps on increasing at each point of sales. In this process, the effect of taxation magnifies as at each level tax is calculated on value, which includes taxes already levied and paid. The charging of tax on tax is called the 'Cascading Effect of Tax'.

96. What is the significance of the term "destination - based tax" in the context of GST?

(1) Tax is based on the destination of goods only
(2) Tax is levied based on the origin of goods
(3) Tax is collected at the point of sale.
(4) Tax accrues to the taxing authority at the place of consumption.

97. What does the term "cascading effect of taxes" refer to?

(1) Tax evasion (2) Tax avoiding
(3) Charging tax on tax
(4) Tax exemption

98. How does GST eliminate the cascading effect of taxes?

(1) By increasing tax rates
(2) By reducing the number of tax types
(3) By allowing tax credit on previous stages
(4) By exempting certain product from tax

99. Who bears the burden of tax in the GST system?

(1) Manufacturers (2) Retailers
(3) Final Consumer (4) Government

100. Which department oversees the administration of matters related to custom, central excise, Central Goods & Services Tax (CGST), (IGST), and narcotics under the Indian government?

(1) Ministry of Finance
(2) Central Board of Direct Taxes
(3) Central Board of Indirect Taxes and Customs (CBIC)
(4) Department of Revenue

ANSWERS

1. (4)	**2.** (4)	**3.** (1)	**4.** (3)	**5.** (1)	**6.** (2)	**7.** (1)	**8.** (1)	**9.** (2,3)	**10.** (2)
11. (1)	**12.** (2)	**13.** (1)	**14.** (1)	**15.** (3)	**16.** (2)	**17.** (2)	**18.** (2)	**19.** (2)	**20.** (1)
21. (2)	**22.** (2)	**23.** (3)	**24.** (2)	**25.** (1)	**26.** (1)	**27.** (1)	**28.** (4)	**29.** (1)	**30.** (3)
31. (3)	**32.** (1)	**33.** (2)	**34.** (4)	**35.** (2)	**36.** (3)	**37.** (2)	**38.** (1)	**39.** (2)	**40.** (2)
41. (3)	**42.** (4)	**43.** (4)	**44.** (3)	**45.** (1)	**46.** (2)	**47.** (3)	**48.** (1)	**49.** (2)	**50.** (1)
51. (1)	**52.** (3)	**53.** (4)	**54.** (3)	**55.** (3)	**56.** (4)	**57.** (2)	**58.** (1)	**59.** (2)	**60.** (3)
61. (1)	**62.** (4)	**63.** (2)	**64.** (1)	**65.** (3)	**66.** (3)	**67.** (1)	**68.** (1)	**69.** (3)	**70.** (4)
71. (1)	**72.** (1)	**73.** (2)	**74.** (4)	**75.** (4)	**76.** (4)	**77.** (4)	**78.** (1)	**79.** (1)	**80.** (3)
81. (3)	**82.** (3)	**83.** (1)	**84.** (3)	**85.** (2)	**86.** (3)	**87.** (3)	**88.** (3)	**89.** (2)	**90.** (4)
91. (3)	**92.** (2)	**93.** (3)	**94.** (2)	**95.** (3)	**96.** (4)	**97.** (3)	**98.** (3)	**99.** (3)	**100.** (4)

JUNE, 2025

COMMERCE

Paper-II

Note : This paper contains **hundred (100)** objective type questions of **two (2)** marks each. **All** questions are **compulsory.**

1. Match the **LIST-I** with **LIST-II**

LIST-I Concept	LIST-II Formula
A. Present Value	I. Cash flow x $(1+r)^t$
B. Future Value	II. Cash flow/ $(1+r)^t$
C. Future Value of Annuity	III. R (PVIFi,n)
D. Present Value of Annuity	IV. R (FVIFAi,n)

Choose the *correct* answer from the options given below:
(1) A-II, B-I, C-IV, D-III
(2) A-I, B-II, C-IV, D-III
(3) A-III, B-IV, C-I, D-II
(4) A-I, B-III, C-II, D-IV

2. Match the **LIST-I** with **LIST-II**

LIST-I TRADE TARIFF	LIST-II Explanation
A. Specific Tariff	I. Fixed percentage of the value of the commodity
B. Ad valorem tariff	II. Fixed amount of money per unit
C. Compound Tariff	III. Duty fixed to bring the price of imported commodity to the level of domestic support price
D. Variable Tariff	IV. Combination of Ad valorem and Specific Tariff

Choose the *correct* answer from the options given below:
(1) A-I, B-II, C-III, D-IV
(2) A-II, B-I, C-IV, D-III
(3) A-III, B-IV, C-II, D-I
(4) A-IV, B-III, C-II, D-I

3. Which of the following is NOT the feature of business environment?
(1) Complex (2) Dynamic
(3) Multi faceted (4) Static

4. Identify the correct sequence of Research Design Process
A. Measurement technique selection
B. Research approach selection
C. Data collection technique selection
D. Sample design selection
E. Data analysis method selection
Choose the correct answer from the options given below:
(1) A, B, C, D, E
(2) B, A, D, C, E
(3) D, C, E, A, B
(4) C, E, D, B, A

5. A Ltd. makes plastic buckets. Selling price per bucket is ₹ 210 and variable cost per bucket is 60. Fixed cost of making buckets is ₹ 1,50,000 for the year. The number of buckets to be sold to get a profit of ₹ 90000 is:
(1) 714 buckets
(2) 428 buckets
(3) 1000 buckets
(4) 1600 buckets

6. Identify the correct sequence of sampling design process
A. Determine the Sample size
B. Select a sampling technique
C. Selection of sampling frame
D. Defining target population
Choose the correct answer from the options given below:
(1) A, B, C, D (2) B, A, D, C
(3) A, B, D, C (4) D, C, B, A

7. The ongoing process of systematically identify-

ing, assessing, and developing organizational leadership to enhance job performance is known as which of the following?
(1) Strategy and Workforce Planning
(2) Predictive workforce monitoring
(3) Succession Planning
(4) Managerial Decision

8. Arrange the following examples of business cycles in chronological order. (Old to New)
A. Dot Com bubble burst
B. Great Depression
C. Covid Pandemic
D. Global Financial Crisis
Choose the correct answer from the options given below:
(1) A, B, C, D (2) B, A, D, C
(3) D, B, A, C (4) C, D, A, B

9. Arrange the following Development Financial Instituition in chronological order of their eastablishment (Old to New)
A. IFCI B. IDBI
C. NABARD D. SIDBI
Choose the correct answer from the options given below:
(1) A, B, C, D (2) B, A, C, D
(3) C, D, A, B (4) D, C, B, A

10. Which of the following is a horizontal agreement?
(1) Tie in arrangement
(2) Resale Price maintenance
(3) Cartel
(4) Exclusive Distribution

11. Match the **LIST-I** with **LIST-II**

LIST-I Concept	**LIST-II** Formula
A. Deduction of Tax at source on fees for professional and technical services	I. Section 194 B
B. Deduction of Tax at source from income by way of rent	II. Section 193
C. Deduction of Tax at source from winnings from lotteries or crossword puzzles, etc.	III. Section 194-1
D. Deduction of Tax at source from interest on securities	IV. Section 194J

Choose the *correct* answer from the options given below:
(1) A-I, B-II, C-III, D-IV
(2) A-IV, B-III, C-II, D-I
(3) A-IV, B-III, C-I, D-II
(4) A-II, B-I, C-IV, D-III

12. Which of the following statements are correct with regard to mathematical properties of standard deviation?
A. Standard deviation is independent of change of origin and change of scale.
B. Standard deviation is independent of change of origin but not of scale.
C. The standard deviation of first n natural numbers is $\sqrt{\frac{n^2-1}{12}}$
D. The standard deviation of first n natural numbers is $\sqrt{\frac{n^2-1}{6}}$
E. For moderately skewed distributions standard deviation is 0.8 of mean deviation.
Choose the correct answer from the options given below:
(1) B and C Only
(2) B, C, and E Only
(3) A and C Only
(4) B, D and E Only

13. Arrange the following steps of incorporation of a new Limited Liability Partnership in proper sequence.
A. Reserve LLP Name
B. Preparation of Documents for Incorporation of LLP
C. Procure Digital Signature Certificate
D. LLP incorporation and DIN Application and apply for PAN and TAN
E. Drafting and filling LLP Agreement
Choose the correct answer from the options given below:
(1) B, A, C, D, E
(2) A, B, C, E, D
(3) C, A, B, D, E
(4) D, E, B, A, C

14. A company has 10%, 20 lakh debentures. The EBIT of the company is ₹ 5,00,000 and the equity capitalisation rate is 16%. Calculate overall cost of capital.

(1) 9.5% (2) 10.8%
(3) 12.9% (4) 14.5%

15. Symbols, Icons, Rituals and values are the manifestations of:
(1) Social class (2) Culture
(3) Sub-culture (4) Social Factors

16. What does 'L' denote in the PESTLE framework?
(1) Labor (2) Legal
(3) Land (4) Latest

17. Match the **LIST-I** with **LIST-II**

LIST-I Relative measures of Skewness	LIST-II Formula
A. Karl Pearson's coefficient of skewness	I. $\frac{(\mu_3)^2}{(\mu_2)^3}$
B. Bowley's coefficient of skewness	II. $(P_{90} + P_{10}$-2 Median)/ $(P_{90}-P_{10})$
C. Kelly's coefficient of skewness	III. $(Q_3 + Q_{10}$-2 Median)/(Q_3-Q_1)
D. Moment coefficient of skewness	IV. (Mean-Mode)/ Standard Deviation

Choose the *correct* answer from the options given below:
(1) A-I, B-II, C-III, D-IV
(2) A-IV, B-III, C-II, D-I
(3) A-II, B-III, C-IV, D-I
(4) A-III, B-IV, C-I, D-II

18. Match the **LIST-I** with **LIST-II**

LIST-I (Stages of Product Life Cycle)	LIST-II (Types of Customers)
A. Presentation	I. Laggard
B. Development	II. Early Adopters
C. Maturity	III. Middle majority
D. Obsolescence	IV. Innovator

Choose the *correct* answer from the options given below:
(1) A-I, B-II, C-III, D-IV
(2) A-II, B-III, C-I, D-IV
(3) A-IV, B-II, C-III, D-I
(4) A-III, B-II, C-IV, D-I

19. Geographical Price differentials include which of the following?
A. F.O.B Factory Pricing
B. Zone Pricing
C. Loss Leader Pricing
D. Postage Stamp Pricing
E. Basing Point Pricing

Choose the correct answer from the options given below:
(1) A, B, C and D Only
(2) B, C, D and E Only
(3) A, B, D and E Only
(4) B, D and E Only

20. Match the **LIST-I** with **LIST-II**

LIST-I Components commonly present in reports	LIST-II Contents
A. Prefatory Information	I. Executive Summary
B. Introductory Information	II. Glossary
C. Main Research Body	III. Problem Definition
D. Supplementary Information	IV. Research Design

Choose the *correct* answer from the options given below:
(1) A-I, B-II, C-III, D-IV
(2) A-II, B-I, C-IV, D-III
(3) A-I, B-III, C-II, D-IV
(4) A-I, B-III, C-IV, D-II

21. Any assessee (except an eligible assessee in respect of an eligible business referred to in section 44 AD or 44 ADA) must pay upto 75 percent of advance tax payable:
(1) on or before June 15 of the previous year
(2) on or before September 15 of the previous year
(3) on or before December 15 of the previous year
(4) on or before March 15 of the previous year

22. Arrange the following human needs as per Maslow's Hierarchy of needs.
A. Social Needs B. Safety Needs
C. Esteem Needs
D. Physiological Needs
E. Self-actualisation Needs

Choose the correct answer from the options given below:
(1) D, B, A, C, E (2) A, B, C, D, E
(3) B, D, C, E, A (4) D, A, B, C, E

23. Match the **LIST-I** with **LIST-II**

LIST-I Concept	LIST-II Formula
A. Total Utility	I. $MU_1 + MU_2 + \ldots MU_n$
B. Marginal Utility	II. $TU_n - TU_n - 1$
C. Average Fixed Cost	III. $\Delta TC / \Delta Q$
D. Marginal Cost	IV. TFC/Q

Choose the ***correct*** answer from the options given below:

(1) A-IV, B-III, C-II, D-I
(2) A-II, B-I, C-III, D-IV
(3) A-I, B-II, C-IV, D-III
(4) A-III, B-II, C-I, D-IV

24. Match the **LIST-I** with **LIST-II**

LIST-I Concept	LIST-II Formula
A. Section 2 (85)	I. Associate Company
B. Section 455	II. Producer Company
C. Section 378A	III. Dormant Company
D. Section 2 (6)	IV. Small Company

Choose the ***correct*** answer from the options given below:

(1) A-I, B-II, C-III, D-IV
(2) A-I, B-III, C-II, D-IV
(3) A-II, B-III, C-I, D-IV
(4) A-IV, B-III, C-II, D-I

25. What rights does an unpaid seller have against the goods?

A. Right of lien
B. Right to sue for specific performance
C. Right of resale
D. Right of stoppage of goods in transit
E. Right to reorganise possession of goods

Choose the correct answer from the options given below:

(1) A, B and C Only
(2) B, C and D Only
(3) C, D and E Only
(4) A, C, D Only

26. What is the amount of net cash from operating activities of A Ltd. if it has net profit before tax ₹ 5,90,000: Depriciation on Property, Plant and Equipment ₹ 4,30,000: Decrease in current Assets ₹ 30,000: Decrease in Current Liabilities ₹ 85000: and Tax Paid ₹ 80000

(1) ₹ 9,65,000 (2) ₹ 8,85,000
(3) ₹ 10,75,000 (4) ₹ 9,95,000

27. Match the **LIST-I** with **LIST-II**

LIST-I	LIST-II
A. Ind AS 2	I. Property, Plant and Equipment
B. Ind AS 16	II. Fair Value Measurement
C. Ind AS 103	III. Inventories
D. Ind AS 113	IV. Business Combinations

Choose the ***correct*** answer from the options given below:

(1) A-I, B-II, C-III, D-IV
(2) A-IV, B-III, C-II, D-I
(3) A-III, B-I, C-IV, D-II
(4) A-III, B-I, C-II, D-IV

28. Which of the following statements are incorrect for amalgamation in the nature of merger?

A. All the assets and liabilities of the transferor company are taken over by transferee company.
B. Shareholders holding not less than 95% of the face value of the equity shares of the transferor company become equity shareholders of the transferee company.
C. Payment of purchase consideration may be made in cash per share.
D. Journal entries for recording the merger are passed by pooling of interest method.
E. The business of the transferor company is not intended to be carried on by the transferee company.

Choose the correct answer from the options given below:

(1) A, B, and C Only
(2) B, C and D Only
(3) A and D Only
(4) B, C and E Only

29. The term 'marketing myopia' was coined by:

(1) Philip Kotler
(2) Gary Armstrong
(3) Peter Drucker
(4) Theodore Levitt

30. In case the income of an individual includes the income of ₹ 25,000 of his minor child in terms of section 64(IA), such individual shall be entitled to an exemption under section 10 (32) of:

(1) ₹ 25,000 (2) ₹ 1,500
(3) ₹ 2,500 (4) ₹ 15,000

31. The cross price elasticity between two goods 'A' and 'B' is (-) 0.8. If the price of good 'B' rise by 20%, how will the demand for 'A' change?

(1) (-) 16% (2) 2.6%
(3) (-) 8% (4) (-) 12%

32. ABC ltd. issued 2,000, 10% preference shares of 100 each at 95. Calculate the cost of preference shares.

(1) 8.50% (2) 10.53%
(3) 12.35% (4) 15.25%

33. Match the **LIST-I** with **LIST-II**

LIST-I Item	**LIST-II** Section
A. Deduction in respect of medical insurance premium	I. Section 80CCH
B. Deduction in case of a person with disability	II. Section 80D
C. Deduction in respect of interest on loan taken for higher education	III. Section 80U
D. Deduction in respect of contribution to Agnipath Scheme	IV. Section 80E

Choose the ***correct*** answer from the options given below:

(1) A-IV, B-I, C-II, D-III
(2) A-III, B-IV, C-I, D-II
(3) A-II, B-III, C-IV, D-I
(4) A-I, B-II, C-III, D-IV

34. Arm's length price as per section 92F is the price applied or proposed to be applied when:

(1) two unrelated persons enter into a transaction in uncontrolled conditions
(2) two related persons enter into a transaction in uncontrolled conditions
(3) two unrelated persons enter into a transaction in controlled conditions
(4) two related persons enter into a transaction in controlled conditions

35. Which of the following are the applications of the conservatism principle of accounting?

A. Valuation of stock in trade at the lower of cost or market value
B. Debiting drawings account and crediting purchases account when goods are withdrawn by the proprietor
C. Making provision for bad and doubtful debts
D. Making provision for discount on creditors
E. Creation of investment fluctuation fund

Choose the correct answer from the options given below:

(1) A and C Only (2) A, B and D Only
(3) B, C and E Only (4) A, C and E Only

36. Which of the following methods belong to the category of demand/market-based pricing?

A. Surge pricing
B. Premium pricing
C. 'What the traffic can bear' pricing
D. Discount pricing
E. Parity pricing

Choose the correct answer from the options given below:

(1) A, B, C and D Only
(2) B, C and D Only
(3) A, B and C Only
(4) C, D and E Only

37. A term loan becomes Non Performing Asset (NPA) if its interest and/or instalment of principal remains overdue for a period of more than:

(1) 30 days (2) 60 days
(3) 75 days (4) 90 days

38. The scheme of partial integration of tax or non-agricultural income with income derived from agricultural is applicable if an individual has:

(1) Non-Agricultural income of more than the exemption limit or agricultural income exceeding ₹ 5000
(2) Non-Agricultural income of more than the exemption limit or agricultural income exceeding ₹ 2500
(3) Non-Agricultural income of more than the exemption limit and agricultural income exceeding ₹ 2500
(4) Non-Agricultural income of more than the exemption limit and agricultural income exceeding ₹ 5000

39. Which of the following are the key objectives of WTO?

A. To set rules for international trade
B. To resolve trade disputes
C. To resolve border disputes
D. To provide a forum for negotiating trade liberalisation

Choose the correct answer from the options given below:

(1) A, B, D Only
(2) A, C Only
(3) B, C, D Only
(4) A, B, C and D

40. In India, the term of every utility patent granted shall be of years.

(1) 10 (2) 20
(3) 30 (4) 50

41. The working of current Purchasing Power Accounting requires classification of balance sheet items into Monetary Items and Non-Monetary Items. Which of the following is a Non-Monetary Item as per current Purchasing Power Accounting?

(1) Cash
(2) Debertures
(3) Debtors
(4) Inventories

42. Arrange the following steps of Multinational Capital Budgeting in correct order

A. Estimate net cash flow from the project
B. Determine net investment outlay
C. Apply appropriate evaluation technique
D. Identify appropriate discount rate

Choose the correct answer from the options given below:

(1) A, B, C, D
(2) C, A, B, D
(3) D, C, B, A
(4) B, A, D, C

43. Which of the following Ind AS specifically deals with consolidated financial statements?

(1) Ind AS 29
(2) Ind AS 101
(4) Ind AS 41
(3) Ind AS 110

44. Which of the following types of FDI includes creation of new assets and production facilities in the country?

(1) Brownfield investment
(2) Merger and Acquisition
(3) Strategic alliances
(4) Greenfield investment

45. What is the Harmonic Mean of two numbers whose Arithmetic Mean and Geometric Mean are 30 and 24 respectively?

(1) 4.8 (2) 9.6
(3) 19.2 (4) 76.8

46. What is the primary liability of the drawer of a bill of exchange or cheque?

(1) Liability to compensate the holder incase of dishonour.
(2) Liability to pay the amount at maturity.
(3) Liability to provide sufficient funds to the drawee.
(4) Liability to pay the holder without any condition.

47. In case of transmission of shares, which of the following is correct?

A. No instrument of transfer is required.
B. Transmission of securities is generally made without any consideration.
C. Shares continue to be subject to the original liabilities.
D. Transmission takes place on death or insolvency of a holder of securities.
E. Stamp duty is payable on transmission of securities.

Choose the correct answer from the options given below:

(1) A, B, C and D Only
(2) B, C and D Only
(3) C, D and E Only
(4) A, B, C Only

48. Which of the following statements are correct with regard to tax avoidance?

A. Tax avoidance is legitimate arrangement of affairs in such a way so as to minimize tax liability.
B. There is an element of malafide motive involved in tax avoidance.
C. Tax avoidance takes into account the loopholes of law.
D. Tax avoidance is intentional attempt to avoid payment of tax after the liability to tax has arisen.
E. Tax avoidance is same as tax omission.

Choose the correct answer from the options given below:

(1) A and C Only
(2) A, B and C Only
(3) B, D and E Only
(4) A, C and E Only

49. Arrange the following steps of New Product Development in sequential order:
A. Product Development
B. Feasibility Analysis
C. Concept Development and Testing
D. Identifying Prospective customers
E. Idea Generation
Choose the correct answer from the options given below:
(1) A, B, C, E, D
(2) D, E, B, C, A
(3) E, D, C, B, A
(4) E, B, C, A, D

50. Which of the following are properties of regression coefficient?
A. The coefficient of correlation and the two regression coefficients have the same signs.
B. The coefficient of correlation is the harmonic mean between the regression coefficients.
C. If one of the regression coefficient is greater than unity, the other must also be greater than unity.
D. If one of the regression coefficient is greater than unity, the other must be less than unity.
E. The regression coefficient are independent of change of origin but not of scale.
Choose the correct answer from the options given below:
(1) A and D Only
(2) B, C and E Only
(3) A, B and C Only
(4) A, D and E Only

51. Arrange the following stages of Adoption process in correct order:
A. Interest
B. Awareness
C. Trial
D. Evaluation
E. Adoption
Choose the correct answer from the options given below:
(1) A, D, C, B, E
(2) A, B, C, D, E
(3) B, C, A, E, D
(4) B, A, D, C, E

52. Arrange the following in chronological order of their establishment (Old to New)
A. NAFTA B. European Union
C. SAARC D. ASEAN
Choose the correct answer from the options given below:
(1) A, B, C, D (2) B, A, D, C
(3) D, C, B, A (4) C, D, A, B

53. Match the **LIST-I** with **LIST-II**

LIST-I Concept	**LIST-II Formula**
A. Production Function	I. K (K, L)
B. Average Product	II. TPn - TPn - 1
C. Marginal Product	III. Total Product/No. of units of variable factor
D. Constant Return to scale	IV. Qf (a, b, c, ...n)

Choose the *correct* answer from the options given below:
(1) A-I, B-II, C-III, D-IV
(2) A-II, B-I, C-IV, D-III
(3) A-I, B-II, C-IV, D-III
(4) A-IV, B-III, C-II, D-I

54. Which of the following are the discounted cash flow techniques of capital budgeting?
A. Payback Period
B. Accounting rate of return (ARR)
C. Net Percent Value (NPV)
D. Internal Rate of Return (IRR)
E. Profitability Index
Choose the correct answer from the options given below:
(1) A, C, D Only
(2) B, C, E Only
(3) C and D Only
(4) C, D and E Only

55. If a random variable X follows a Poisson distribution such that : P(X=1) 4P (X=2)
The variance of X is
(1) 1/2 (2) 1
(3) 2 (4) 1/4

56. A type of validity which demonstrates statistically a relationship between scores on a selection procedure and job performance is called:
(1) Test validity
(2) Criterion validity

(3) Content validity
(4) Construct validity

57. Which of the following is NOT an element of Micro environment?
(1) Customers
(2) Suppliers
(3) Technology
(4) Competitors

58. "Active concealment of fact" is associated with which one of the following?
(1) Misrepresentation
(2) Undue influence
(3) Fraud
(4) Mistake

59. A company hold raw material for 60 days. It gets credit from suppliers for 15 days, production process take 15 days, finished goods are held for 30 days and 30 days credit is given to debtors. Calculate the total working capital cycle.
(1) 150 days (2) 120 days
(3) 100 days (4) 90 days

60. Match the **LIST-I** with **LIST-II**

LIST-I	LIST-II
A. Job enlargement	I. A list of jobs 'human requirements', i.e the requisite education, skills, personality etc.
B. Job descriptions	II. A list of jobs duties, responsibilities, reporting relatonships, working conditions and supervisory responsibilities.
C. Job specifications	III. Assigning workers additional same level activities.
D. Job enrichment	IV. Redesigning jobs in a way that increases the opportunities for the workers to experience feelings of responsibility, achievement, growth and recognition.

Choose the *correct* answer from the options given below:
(1) A-III, B-II, C-I, D-IV
(2) A-IV, B-II, C-I, D-III
(3) A-III, B-I, C-II, D-IV
(4) A-IV, B-II, C-III, D-I

61. Which of the following requirements have to be satisfied in order that an assessee is entitled to claim deduction under section 91 for doubly taxed income?
A. The assessee must have been non- resident in India in the relevant previous year.
B. The assessee must have been resident in India in the relevant previous year.
C. Income must have been accrued or arisen to him during that previous year in India.
D. Income must have been accrued or arisen to him during that previous year outside India.
E. In respect of that income which accrued or arouse outside India, he must have paid by deduction or otherwise tax under the law in force in the country in question.

Choose the correct answer from the options given below:
(1) A and C Only
(2) B and D Only
(3) B, D and E Only
(4) A, C and E Only

62. The price of a product decreases from ₹ 100 to ₹ 60 per unit. If the price elasticity of demand in 1.5 and the original quantity demanded in 30 units, What will be the new quantity demanded?
(1) 38 (2) 48
(3) 56 (4) 62

63. Which of the following statement is incorrect for Management Audit?
(1) Management audit is a statutory requirement.
(2) Management audit is a comprehensive and critical review of all aspects of management process.
(3) Management audit covers wide area of management activities and may be for more than one financial year.
(4) The shareholders or board of directors may appoint the management auditor.

64. The questions that are actually asked from the respondent are known as:
(1) Management Questions
(2) Research Questions

(3) Investigative Questions
(4) Measurement Questions

65. State Bank of India came into existence in which of the following years?
(1) 1947 (2) 1950
(3) 1955 (4) 1969

66. Identify the areas of macro economics:
A. National Income
B. Balance of Payments
C. Level of savings and investment
D. Location of industry
E. Behaviour of firms
Choose the correct answer from the options given below:
(1) A, B and C Only
(2) B, C and E Only
(3) B, C and D Only
(4) A, B, C, D and E

67. In which of the following year Investor Protection and Education Fund Regulations was issued by the Securities and Exchange Board of India?
(1) 1992 (2) 1999
(3) 2003 (4) 2009

68. According to Levitt and Drucker, the essence of marketing is:
(1) Profit Orientation
(2) Product Orientation
(3) Market Orientation
(4) Customer Orientation

69. Arrange the following in chronological order of the Milestone achieved by the National Stock Exchange of India
A. Commencement of Trading in Index options
B. Launch of securities Lending and Borrowing Scheme
C. Commencement of Derivatives Trading in Index Futures
D. Launch of Mutual Fund Service System
E. Launch of S & P CNX Nifty
Choose the correct answer from the options given below:
(1) B, D, E, A, C
(2) A, C, E, B, D
(3) E, A, C, D, B
(4) E, C, A, B, D

70. Which of the following types of audit report are termed together as modified reports as per standards on Auditing (SA) 705?
A. Qualified Report
B. Audit Report with an 'Emphasis of Matter' paragraph
C. Disclaimer of opinion Report
D. Adverse Report
Choose the correct answer from the options given below:
(1) A and B Only
(2) A, B and C Only
(3) B and C Only
(4) A, C and D Only

71. Which of the following formula correctly show the relationship Average Revenue (AR), Margianl Revenue (MR) and Price elasticity of demand?
(1) MRAR + e – 1
(2) AR – MR × e – 1/e
(3) MR=AR × (e – 1)/e
(4) MRAR + e – 1/e + 1

72. Arrange the following exchange rate arrangements of international monetary system in chronological order (Old to New)
A. Gold Standard
B. Commodity Specie Standard
C. Fixed parity System
D. Floating exchange Rate
Choose the correct answer from the options given below:
(1) A, B, C, D (2) B, A, C, D
(3) C, B, D, A (4) B, C, A, D

73. Who can file petition to the Tribunal for the Winding up of a Limited Liability Partnership?
A. Secured Creditors
B. LLP or any of its Partners
C. Registrar of Companies
D. Any person authorised by the central Government
E. Any Voluntary Association
Choose the correct answer from the options given below:
(1) A, B, C Only
(2) A and B Only
(3) A, B, C and D Only
(4) B, C and E Only

74. If the employee pays tax within the parameters of alternative tax regime under section 115 BAC then from assessment year 2025-26, standard deduction from salary income is:
(1) NIL
(2) ₹ 50,000 or gross salary, whichever is lower
(3) 75,000 or gross salary, whichever is lower
(4) 40,000 or gross salary, whichever is lower

75. Which of the following are part of micro economics?
A. Product pricing
B. Consumer behaviour
C. Interest rate
D. Factor pricing
Choose the correct answer from the options given below:
(1) A, B and C Only
(2) A, B and D Only
(3) A and D Only
(4) A, B, C and D

76. An unsecured short term promissory note, negotiable and transferable by endorsement and delivery with a fixed maturity period, issued at a discount by creditworthy corporates, primary dealers and all-India financial institutions is known as:
(1) Treasury Bill
(2) Commercial Paper
(3) Certificates of Deposit
(4) Repo

77. The type of market where few sellers are selling competing products to many buyers is known as:
(1) Monopoly
(2) Monopolistic Competition
(3) Oligopoly
(4) Perfect Competition

78. A company produces and sells 10,000 toys. The selling price per toy is ₹ 500, variable cost is 200 per unit and fixed operating cost is ₹ 25,00,000. Calculate operating Leverage.
(1) 4 times (2) 5 times
(3) 6 times (4) 8 times

79. Which of the following statements is correct?
A. If a company is an Indian company then it will automatically be considered a domestic company.
B. Foreign company means a company which is not a domestic company.
C. The resident status of an Indian company can be non-resident in India.
D. The resident status of a foreign company can never be resident in India.
E. Foreign income of a resident company is taxable in India.
Choose the correct answer from the options given below:
(1) Only A, B and C
(2) Only B, C and D
(3) Only A, C and E
(4) Only A, B and E

80. Identify the correct order in which the assets of the firm shall be applied in case of dissolution of a partnership firm
A. Paying to each partner rateably what is due to him from the firm for advances as distinguished from capital.
B. Paying the residues if any to partners in the proportion in which they were entitled to share profit.
C. Paying the debts of the firm to third parties.
D. Paying to each partner rateably what is due to him on account of capital.
Choose the correct answer from the options given below:
(1) A, C, D, B
(2) C, A, B, D
(3) C, A, D, B
(4) A, B, C, D

81. Identify the factors that determine the demand.
A. Price of the Commodity
B. Income of the Consumer
C. Taste and Preferences of Consumer
D. Size of Population
Choose the correct answer from the options given below:
(1) A and B Only
(2) A, B and C Only
(3) B, C and D Only
(4) A, B, C and D

82. Arrange the following steps involved in the process of Voluntary Liquidation of a Limited Liability Partnership in correct order.
A. Declaration of Solvency

B. Designated Partners' Meeting
C. Partners' Meeting
D. Identification of an Insolvency Professional as liquidator
E. Filling of resolutions with registrar of Companies and Insolvency and Bankruptcy Board of India (IBBI)

Choose the correct answer from the options given below:
(1) A, B, C, D, E
(2) C, B, D, A, E
(3) A, D, B, C, E
(4) E, D, C, B, A

83. Matrix Structure can be made more effective by following which of the guidelines given below?

A. Collective learning, coordination and integration of skills for obtaining the streams of technology.
B. Define the objectives of the project or task.
C. Clarify the roles, authority and responsibilities of managers and team members.
D. Ensure that influence is based on knowledge, information, rather than on rank.
E. Balance the power of functional and project managers.

Choose the correct answer from the options given below:
(1) A, B, C, D Only
(2) A, B, D and E Only
(3) B, C, D, and E Only
(4) A, B, C, E Only

84. Match the **LIST-I** with **LIST-II**

LIST-I Concept	LIST-II Formula
A. Perception	I. A descriptive thought that a person holds about something.
B. Learning	II. A person's consistently favourable or unfavourable evaluations, feelings and tendencies toward an object or idea.
C. Belief	III. Changes in an individual's behaviour arising from experience.
D. Attitude	IV. The process by which people select, organise and interpret information to form a meaningful picture of the world.

Choose the *correct* answer from the options given below:
(1) A-I, B-II, C-III, D-IV
(2) A-III, B-IV, C-II, D-I
(3) A-IV, B-III, C-I, D-II
(4) A-II, B-III, C-I, D-IV

85. Match the **LIST-I** with **LIST-II**

LIST-I BOP	LIST-II Concept
A. Balance of payment-current A/C	I. Inflow and outflow of capital
B. Balance of payment-capital A/C	II. International Transactions of goods and services
C. Balance of Trade	III. Import and export of goods only
D. Balancing item	IV. Entry for net errors and omissions

Choose the *correct* answer from the options given below:
(1) A-I, B-II, C-III, D-IV
(2) A-III, B-II, C-IV, D-I
(3) A-IV, B-III, C-I, D-II
(4) A-II, B-I, C-III, D-IV

86. Which of the following countries were part of NAFTA?

A. United States
B. Canada
C. Mexico
D. Brazil

Choose the correct answer from the options given below:
(1) A, B Only
(2) A, B, C Only
(3) B, C, D Only
(4) B, C Only

87. Arrange the following theories of international trade in chronological order (old to new)

A. Mercantilism Theory
B. Comparative Advantage Theory
C. Product Life Cycle Theory
D. Hecksher-Ohlin Theory

Choose the correct answer from the options given below:

(1) A, B, C, D (2) A, B, D, C
(3) C, B, A, D (4) B, A, C, D

88. Keeping a record of uncommonly good or undesirable examples of an employee's work-related behaviour and reviewing it with the employee at pre-determined times is known as:
(1) Behaviorally Anchored Rating Scale
(2) Critical Incident Method
(3) Paired Comparison Method
(4) Mixed Standard Scales

89. The parametric test that can be used for hypothesis testing of paired samples is:
(1) t test:
(2) z test
(3) Chi-Square test
(4) Mann-whitney test

90. Match the **LIST-I** with **LIST-II**

LIST-I Term	**LIST-II Explanation**
A. Nostro Account	I. Account held by a foreign bank with a local bank
B. Vostro Account	II. An Indian Bank's Swiss Franc A/C with a bank in Switzerland.
C. Bid	III. Price at which the dealer is willing to buy another currency.
D. Offer	IV. Price at which the dealer is willing to sell another currency.

Choose the ***correct*** answer from the options given below:
(1) A-I, B-II, C-III, D-IV
(2) A-II, B-I, C-III, D-IV
(3) A-III, B-II, C-IV, D-I
(4) A-IV, B-III, C-I, D-II

Read the following passage and answer the questions:

A mid-sized IT firm in India is facing multiple HR challenges as it expands. The company recently hired 200 employees but is struggling with high attrition, lack of structured training program and a weak performance appraisal system. Employees often feel over worked and underappreciated, leading to low engagement and motivation. The HR manager Priya wants to improve HR practices by implementing a structured performance appraisal system launching employee wellness program and using HR technology for recruitment. However she face resistance from senior management, who think those initiative will increase cost without direct financial benefits. Additionally, employee feedback indicates dissatisfaction with work life balance and unclear career progression. Some employees also feel that promotions are biased and that the company lack a proper succession plan.

Priya is considering introducing flexible work arrangements, setting up leadership development program and adopting AI- driven HR analytics to improve decision making. However, she needs to convince top management of the long term benefits of these changes.

91. Which strategy would be most effective in retaining employees and reducing attrition rate?
(1) Making the resignation process more difficult
(2) Increasing workload
(3) Offering voluntary retirement
(4) Offering increments and career growth opportunities

92. Priya needs to address employee dissatisfaction with career progression. What should be her first step?
(1) Encouraging empoyee to find new jobs
(2) Reducing training budgets
(3) Conducting skill gap analysis and creating career development plan
(4) Promoting only senior employee

93. To convince senior management about HR investments, Priya should highlight:
(1) The number of training program conducted
(2) The positive feed back of customers
(3) The financial impact of HR initiatives on business growth
(4) The employees performance appraisal methods

94. If Priya wants to use HR analytics to predict labour turn over, Which data should she analyse?
(1) Employees social media engagements
(2) Attrition trends and exit interview feedback
(3) The number of training program
(4) The number of leaves taken by employees

95. Which HR strategy will help develop future leaders in the organization?
    (1) Implement an intensive employee development program
    (2) Hiring only external candidates for leadership roles
    (3) Implementation of performance linked bonuses
    (4) Promoting employees on the basis of seniority

Read the following passage and answer the questions:

A large real estate company in India is facing challenges in raising funds for expansion. Despite solid track record the company is struggling to attract investors due to increasing concern about liquidity in the financial market. The company has earlier relied on bank loans and debt instruments for financing but now looking for other funding option.

The CFO of the company is evaluating different option such as corporate bonds, Private equity, public deposit and securitization to raise capital. He is also looking at the evolving role of financial institution such as investment banks, development banks and insurance companies in providing finance. However, he is concerned about the volatility of the stock market and the risk of inflation affecting company's future cashflow.

To address these challenges, the company plan to consult with financial advisors and explore new avenues of funding, including green bonds and venture capital. The CFO must navigate the complex world of financial markets to ensure that the company secures the right funding at the right cost.

96. In a volatile stock market, how the company can reduce financing risk when raising funds through equity?
    (1) Issue share only when market is at peak
    (2) Raise funds through long term bonds only
    (3) Reduce dividend payout to increase internal funds
    (4) Diversify source of funds by combining debt and equity financing

97. Which of the following is a primary function of financial markets in the economy?
    (1) Facilitating buying and selling of financial instruments
    (2) Offering financial advice to individual investors
    (3) Providing loan without collateral
    (4) Increasing revenues for the Government

98. What would be the main concern for the company if it has to issue green bonds for financing?
    (1) High interest rate
    (2) Less repayment period
    (3) Limited investor demand due to niche market
    (4) Government restriction

99. What is the main advantage of raising capital through venture capital?
    (1) To avoid giving up ownership or control
    (2) To access expertise and guidance from investors
    (3) To get the fund for a very long term
    (4) To get a low cost funding

100. The company is considering corporate bonds as a funding option. Which factor is most likely to affect the interest rate of bond?
    (1) The number of projects completed by the company
    (2) The interest rate on Government securities
    (3) The credit rating of the bond
    (4) The level of Foreign Direct Investment

ANSWERS

1. (1)	**2.** (2)	**3.** (4)	**4.** (2)	**5.** (4)	**6.** (4)	**7.** (3)	**8.** (2)	**9.** (1)	**10.** (3)
11. (3)	**12.** (1)	**13.** (3)	**14.** (3)	**15.** (2)	**16.** (2)	**17.** (2)	**18.** (3)	**19.** (3)	**20.** (4)
21. (3)	**22.** (1)	**23.** (3)	**24.** (4)	**25.** (4)	**26.** (2)	**27.** (3)	**28.** (4)	**29.** (4)	**30.** (2)
31. (1)	**32.** (2)	**33.** (3)	**34.** (1)	**35.** (4)	**36.** (3)	**37.** (4)	**38.** (4)	**39.** (1)	**40.** (2)
41. (4)	**42.** (4)	**43.** (3)	**44.** (4)	**45.** (3)	**46.** (1)	**47.** (1)	**48.** (1)	**49.** (3)	**50.** (4)
51. (4)	**52.** (3)	**53.** (1)	**54.** (4)	**55.** (1)	**56.** (2)	**57.** (3)	**58.** (3)	**59.** (2)	**60.** (1)
61. (3)	**62.** (2)	**63.** (4)	**64.** (1)	**65.** (3)	**66.** (1)	**67.** (4)	**68.** (4)	**69.** (4)	**70.** (4)
71. (3)	**72.** (2)	**73.** (3)	**74.** (3)	**75.** (2)	**76.** (2)	**77.** (3)	**78.** (3)	**79.** (4)	**80.** (3)
81. (4)	**82.** (3)	**83.** (3)	**84.** (3)	**85.** (4)	**86.** (2)	**87.** (2)	**88.** (2)	**89.** (1)	**90.** (2)
91. (4)	**92.** (3)	**93.** (3)	**94.** (2)	**95.** (1)	**96.** (4)	**97.** (1)	**98.** (3)	**99.** (2)	**100.** (3)

JANUARY, 2026

COMMERCE

Paper-II

Note : This paper contains **hundred (100)** objective type questions of **two (2)** marks each. **All** questions are **compulsory.**

1. Which of the following statements are correct for tax Evasion ?

A. All methods by which tax liability is illegally avoided is termed as tax evasion

B. Tax evasion takes into account loopholes of Law

C. Tax evasion is tax godging within framework of Law

E. Tax evasion is intentional attempt to avoid payment of tax after the liability to tax has arisen

D. Tax evasion has legal sanction

Choose the correct answer from the options given below:

(1) B and D Only (2) B, C and D Only
(3) A, E and C Only (4) A and E Only

2. Select the correct option from the followings. The Balance of payment (BoP):

(1) Includes only exports and imports of goods and services.

(2) Is always balanced because every credit entry has a corresponding debit entry.

(3) Excludes unilateral transfers like remittance.

(4) Shows only the financial account of transactions.

3. What are the GST rates applicable after 22nd September 2025 ?

A. 5% B. 12%
C. 18% D. 28%
E. 40%

Choose the correct answer from the options given below :

(1) A, B, C and D Only
(2) B, C, D and E Only
(3) A, C and E Only
(4) B, C and E Only

4. Arrange the followings on the basis of Sections of Indian Contract Act, 1872 in ascending order:

A. Agreement in restraint of Marriage

C. Agreement with unlawful objects or consideration

B. Agreement made without consideration

D. Agreement in restraint of Trade

E. Agreement by way of wager

Choose the **correct** answer from the options given below:

(1) C, B, A, D, E (2) C, A, D, B, E
(3) A, B, C, E, D (4) D, B, A, C, E

5. Which of the followings are the properties of Indifference Curve ?

A. Indifference curve slopes downward to right

B. Indifference curve is concave to origin

D. Indifference Indi curves cannot intersect each other but can be tangent to each other

C. Indifference curve is convex to origin

E. Higher indifference curve represents higher level of satisfaction

Choose the correct answer from the options given below:

(1) A, B, D and E Only
(2) A, C, D and E Only
(3) A, C and E Only
(4) A, B, C and D Only

6. For assessment year 2025-26, 'Health and Education Cess' shall be levied at the rate of:

(1) 1% on Income Tax (2) 2% on Income Tax
(3) 3% on Income Tax (4) 4% on Income Tax

7. Where a company incurs any expenditure (not being expenditure in the nature of cost of any land or building) on any notified skill development project, then such company can claim as deduction under section 35CCD:

(1) Only 25% of such expenditure
(2) Only 50% of such expenditure
(3) Only 75% of such expenditure
(4) 100% of such expenditure

8. Which one of the followings are not the Objectives of HRM ?

(1) Societal Objectives
(2) Organizational Objectives
(3) Functional Objectives
(4) Group Objectives

9. Charge collected from the investors by a Mutual Fund Scheme when it sells its units to investors is called:

(1) Exit Load (2) Entry Load
(3) Switch (4) Sale Price

10. Given below are two statements one is labelled as Assertion (A) and the other is labelled as Reason (R).

Assertion (A): The minimum level of service the customer expects represents the threshold level of expectations.

Reason (R): The gap between the desired and adequate service has been called as the zone of intolerance.

In the light of the above statements, choose the most appropriate answer from the options given below:

(1) Both (A) and (R) are correct and (R) is the correct explanation of (A)
(2) Both (A) and (R) are correct but (R) is not the correct explanation of (A)
(3) (A) is correct but (R) is not correct
(4) (A) is not correct but (R) is correct

11. Which of the followings are the techniques of Monetary Control adopted by RBI ?

A. Loans and Advances to the Industries
B. Cash Reserve Ratio
C. Open Market Operations
D. Statutory Liquidity Ratio
E. Repo Rates

Choose the correct answer from the options given below:

(1) A, B, C, D Only (2) A, B, D, E Only
(3) B, C, D, E Only (4) A, C, D, E Only

12. Arrange the following steps of Personal Selling in sequence :

A. Pre approach
B. Presentation and Demonstration
C. Approach
D. Prospecting and Qualifying
E. Handling Objections

Choose the correct answer from the options given below :

(1) A, D, C, E, B (2) A, C, D, E, B
(3) C, A, D, B, E (4) D, A, C, B, E

13. Which one of the followings is not a category under Balance of Payments?

(1) Current Account (2) Capital Account
(3) Drawings Account
(4) Official Reserve Account

14. Arrange the following steps of Capital Budgeting Process in correct order :

A. Preliminary Screening Process
B. Project Generation
C. Detailed Project Evaluation
D. Control of Capital Expenditure
E. Project Selection and its implementation

Choose the correct answer from the options given below :

(1) A, B, C, D, E (2) B, A, C, E, D
(3) A, B, C, E, D (4) B, A, C, D, E

15. Given below are two statements one is labelled as Assertion (A) and the other is labelled as Reason (R).

Assertion (A): Heckscher and Ohlin developed a theory to explain the reasons for differences in relative commodity prices and competitive advantages between two nations. According to this theory, a nation will export the commodity whose production requires intensive use of nation's relatively abundant and cheap factors and import the commodity whose production requires intensive use of the nation's scarce and expensive factors.

Reason (R): Thus, a country with an abundance of cheap labour would import labour intensive products and export capital intensive goods and vice-versa.

In the light of the above statements, choose the most appropriate answer from the options given below:

(1) Both (A) and (R) are correct and (R) is the correct explanation of (A)
(2) Both (A) and (R) are correct but (R) is not the correct explanation of (A)
(3) (A) is correct but (R) is not correct
(4) (A) is not correct but (R) is correct

16. Which one of the followings is not a type of conflict?

(1) Task Conflict (2) Relationship Conflict
(3) Process Conflict (4) Product Conflict

17. Which statement best captures the difference between FDI and FPI ?

(1) FDI is investment with lasting interest and managerial control; FPI is passive investment without control.
(2) FDI involves only equity investment; FPI involves both equity and debt security.
(3) FDI is recorded in current account; FPI is recorded in capital account.
(4) Both FDI and FPI give investors voting rights in the host country.

18. An empirical test was carried out in 1951 on Heckscher Ohlin model to find out whether or not the US, which has abundant capital resources, exports capital intensive goods and imports labour intensive goods. But, it was found that the US exported more labour -intensive commodities and imported more capital intensive products, which was contrary to the result of Heckscher - Ohlin model. Who has conducted the test?

(1) Staffan B. Linder (2) David Ricardo
(3) J. B. Say (4) Wassily Leontief

18. Given below are two statements one is labelled as Assertion (A) and the other is labelled as Reason (R).

Assertion (A): Section 91 provides for grant of unilateral relief in the case of resident taxpayers on income which has been taxed in India as well as in the country with which there is no Double Taxation Avoidance Agreement.

Reason (R): The relief under section 91 is granted by allowing to the tax payer a deduction from tax liability of an amount equal to the tax calculated at the average Indian rate of tax or the amount of tax calculated at the rate of tax of that other country on the doubly taxed income, whichever is higher.

In the light of the above statements, choose the most appropriate answer from the options given below:

(1) Both (A) and (R) are correct and (R) is the correct explanation of (A)
(3) (A) is correct but (R) is not correct
(2) Both (A) and (R) are correct but (R) is not the correct explanation of (A)
(4) (A) is not correct but (R) is correct

19. Given below are two statements one is labelled as Assertion (A) and the other is labelled as Reason (R).

Assertion (A): The skimming price policy is adopted where close substitute of a new product are not available.

Reason (R): This policy requires fixing a lower initial price designed to penetrate the market as quickly as possible and is intended to maximize the profit in the long run.

In the light of the above statements, choose the most appropriate answer from the options given below:

(1) Both (A) and (R) are correct and (R) is the correct explanation of (A)
(2) Both (A) and (R) are correct but (R) is not the correct explanation of (A)
(3) (A) is correct but (R) is not correct
(4) (A) is not correct but (R) is correct

20. Arrange the following in ascending order of sections of Income Tax Act related to permissible deduction from Gross Total Income:

A. Deduction in respect of Medical Insurance Premia
B. Deduction in respect of Royalty Income of Author
C. Deduction in respect of Payment of Interest on Loan taken for Higher Education
D. Deduction in respect of Interest on Deposits in Saving Accounts
E. Deduction in respect of Donations to Certain Funds, charitable Institutions, etc.

Choose the correct answer from the options given below:

(1) A, B, C, D, E (2) E, D, C, B, A
(3) A, C, E, D, B (4) A, C, E, B, D

22. Match List - I with List - II.

List - I (Tax Deducted at Source)	**List - II (Sections of Income Tax Act)**
A. Deduction of Tax at Source on Fees for Professional or Technical Services	I. Section 194 A
B. Deduction of Tax at Source from Payment of life Insurance Policy	II. Section 194B
C. Deduction of Tax at Source from Winnings from Lotteries or Crossword Puzzles	III. Section 194DA
D. Deduction of Tax at Source from Interest other than Interest on Securities	IV. Section 194J

Choose the correct answer from the options given below:

(1) A-I, B-II, C-III, D-IV
(2) A-IV, B-III, C-II, D-I
(3) A-I, B-II, C-IV, D-III
(4) A-II, B-I, C-III, D-IV

23. The Break Even point expressed in amount of sales in rupees of X Ltd having selling Price of ₹ 20 per unit, variable cost of ₹ 14 per unit and fixed cost of ₹ 7,92,000 is:

(1) ₹ 11,28,571 (2) ₹ 1,32,000
(3) ₹ 39,600 (4) ₹ 26,40,000

24. The right of the insurer to stand in the place of insured after the settlement of a claim and it gives the insurer right to recover from an alternative source, the principle involved in this case is called :

(1) Principle of Insurable Interest
(2) Principle of Subrogation

(3) Principle of Causa Proxima
(4) Principle of Contribution

25. Which of the followings are the myths about Rural Market?
A. All Villages are equally populated
B. Rural Consumers are a hetrogeneous lot
C. Being illiterate, rural consumer is not able to discriminate between products and brands
D. Only low priced products will sell in rural India
E. Rural markets are the consumer durable markets

Choose the correct answer from the options given below:
(1) A, B, C and D Only (2) A, C and D Only
(3) C, D and E Only (4) B, C, D and E Only

26. Given below are two statements one is labelled as Assertion (A) and the other is labelled as Reason (R).
Assertion (A): New Issue of Capital is costlier than Retained Earnings.
Reason (R): The cost of Retained Earnings is the return foregone by the shareholders on the dividend income.
In the light of the above statements, choose the most appropriate answer from the options given below:
(1) Both (A) and (R) are correct and (R) is the correct explanation of (A)
(2) Both (A) and (R) are correct but (R) is not the correct explanation of (A)
(3) (A) is correct but (R) is not correct
(4) (A) is not correct but (R) is correct

27. Match **List - I** with **List - II.**

List - I	List - II
A. Operating Leverage	I. Contribution/EBT
B. Combined Leverage	II. Contribution/EBIT
C. Earning Per Share	III. EBIT/EBT
IV. EAT/No. of Equity Shares	D. Financial Leverage

Choose the correct answer from the options given below :
(1) A-I, B-II, C-IV, D-III
(2) A-II, B-I, C-IV, D-III
(3) A-II, B-I, C-III, D-IV
(4) A-I, B-II, C-III, D-IV

28. Which one of the followings is not a type of organizational culture ?
(1) Non-Entrepreneurial Culture
(2) Power Culture
(3) Role Culture (4) Task Culture

29. Which one of the followings is not a component of formal (organized) financial system ?
(1) Financial Markets
(2) Financial Instruments
(3) Chit-fund Companies
(4) Financial Services

30. Match **List - I** with **List - II.**

List - I	List - II
A. Probable Error of Correlation Coefficient	I. $\frac{\text{Explained Variation}}{\text{Total Variation}}$
B. Standard Error of Correlation Coefficient	II. $\frac{\text{Unexplained Variation}}{\text{Total Variation}}$
C. Coefficient of Determination	III. $\frac{1-r^2}{\sqrt{n}}$
D. Coefficient of Alienation	IV. $0.6745\left[\frac{1-r^2}{\sqrt{n}}\right]$

Choose the correct answer from the options given below:
(1) A-I, B-II, C-III, D-IV
(2) A-IV, B-III, C-II, D-I
(3) A-III, B-IV, C-I, D-II
(4) A-IV, B-III, C-I, D-II

31. Match **List - I** with **List - II.**

List - I	List - II
A. Ind AS 7	I. Impairment of Assets
B. Ind AS 24	II. Related Party Disclosures
C. Ind AS 36	III. Consolidated Financial Statement
D. Ind AS 110	IV. Statement of Cash Flows

Choose the correct answer from the options given below :
(1) A-I, B-II, C-III, D-IV
(2) A-IV, B-II, C-I, D-III
(3) A-III, B-IV, C-I, D-II
(4) A-IV, B-III, C-II, D-I

32. Arrange the following in descending order on the basis of number of sellers in the Market.
A. Duopoly B. Oligopoly
C. Monopolistic Competition
D. Perfect Competition

Choose the correct answer from the options given below:
(1) D, C, B, A (2) B, A, C, D
(3) A, B, C, D (4) B, D, A, C

33. Which of the followings is/are the part of external environment (macro) of Business ?

A. Customers B. Economic factors
C. Natural factors
D. Marketing Intermediaries
E. Competitors

Choose the correct answer from the options given below:
(1) B and D Only (2) B and C Only
(3) A, B, C and D Only
(4) B, C, D and E Only

34. Arrange the followings in the correct sequence in which they are computed for determining Net Cash from operating activities as per AS-3 (Revised):
A. Operating profit before Working Capital Changes
B. Cash flow before extra ordinary items
C. Cash generated from operations
D. Net Profit before taxation and extra ordinary items

Choose the correct answer from the options given below :
(1) A, B, C, D (2) D, B, A, C
(3) C, D, B, A (4) D, A, C, A

35. Suppose a production function is given as
$Q = -L^3 + 5L^2 + 10L$
Which law of production is revealed by this production function:
(1) Law of diminishing return
(2) Law of increasing return
(3) Law of constant return
(4) Law of return to scale

36. Arrange the following steps of process of consumer buying in proper sequence:
A. Evaluation of Alternatives
B. Search for Alternatives
C. Need Recognitions
D. Decision
E. Development of Decision Criteria

Choose the correct answer from the options given below:
(1) C, B, A, E, D (2) C, A, B, E, D
(3) C, E, B, A, D (4) B, A, C, E, D

37. An infinite series of equal cash flow occurring at regular time interval is known as:
(1) An Annuity (2) An Annuity Due
(3) Perpetuity (4) Future Value

38. Match **List - I** with **List - II**.

List - I	**List - II**
A. Occurs when a true null hypothesis is rejected	I. Type II Error
B. Occurs when false null hypothesis does not get rejected	II. Type I Error
C. Used for data from interval or ratio scales	III. Nonparametric Tests
D. Used to test hypotheses with nominal and ordinal data	IV. Parametric Tests

Choose the correct answer from the options given below :
(1) A-I, B-II, C-III, D-IV
(2) A-I, B-II, C-IV, D-III
(3) A-II, B-I, C-IV, D-III
(4) A-II, B-I, C-III, D-IV

39. Which one of the followings is not a method of New Issues?
(1) Public Issue through Prospectus
(2) Right Issue
(3) Bonus Issue (4) Book Building

40. If demand equation is given by
$D = 10{,}000 - P$
and the supply equation is given by
$S = 1000 + 4P$, the equilibrium price would be
(1) 1600 (2) 1800
(3) 1700 (4) 2000

41. Which of the following statements is incorrect for Amalgamation in the nature of merger ?
(1) All assets and liabilities of the transferor company taken over by the transferee company
(2) Shareholders of the transferor company need not become equity shareholders of the transferee company
(3) Payment of purchase consideration is made in cash only for fractional shares, if any.
(4) The business of Transferor Company is intended to be carried on, after amalgamation, by the transferee company

42. Process of ensuring access to appropriate financial products and services needed by all sections of the society in general and vulnerable group such as weaker sections and low-income groups in particular at an affordable cost in a fair and transparent manner by mainstream institutional players is referred to as:
(1) Financial Integration
(2) Financial Instability
(3) Financial Inclusion
(4) Monetary Instability

43. Mr. A, a resident in India, aged 60 years, earned agricultural income of ₹ 5,00,000 and non-agricultural income of ₹ 3,80,000 for assessment year 2025-26. The tax liability of Mr. A assuming that he does not opt to be taxed under the old tax regime is :

(1) ₹ 38,000 (2) ₹ 3,640
(3) ₹ 8,000 (4) Nil

44. What will be the value of AR, if elasticity of demand is unit elastic and the value of MR is 5?

(1) 2.5 (2) 5
(3) 1 (4) 10

45. Arrange the following steps of Sampling Design Process in correct order :

A. Determine the sample size
B. Select a sampling technique
C. Selection of sampling frame
D. Target Population definitions

Choose the correct answer from the options given below :

(1) A, B, C, D (2) D, C, B, A
(3) C, D, B, A (4) B, D, C, A

46. Arrange the following steps of Selection Process in correct order :

A. Selection Tests
B. Reference and Background Analysis
C. Preliminary Interview
D. Employment Interview
E. Job Offer

Choose the correct answer from the options given below :

(1) A, B, C, D, E (2) C, A, B, D, E
(3) C, A, D, B, E (4) A, C, B, D, E

47. Which of the followings are the types of decentralisation in an organisation ?

A. Profit Centres B. Service Centres
C. Cost Centres D. Investment Centres

Choose the correct answer from the options given below:

(1) A, B and C Only (2) A, C and D Only
(3) A, B and D Only (4) B, C and D Only

48. Arrange the following committees as per their year of formation in ascending order:

A. Narasimham Committee - I
B. Padmanabhan Committee
C. Verma Committee
D. Saraf Committee
E. Rashid Jilani Committee

Choose the correct answer from the options given below:

(1) A, B, C, D, E (2) A, E, D, B, C
(3) A, E, B, D, C (4) A, D, E, B, C

49. Arrange the following institutions as per their year of establishment in ascending order:

A. NAFTA B. EU
C. ASEAN D. UNCTAD

Choose the correct answer from the options given below :

(1) A, B, C, D (2) D, A, C, A
(3) B, D, C, A (4) B, C, A, D

50. Match **List - I** with **List - II**.

List - I	List - II
A. Standard Deduction under Section 16(ia)	I. Income under the head Capital Gains
B. Standard Deduction under Section 24	II. Income under the head Profits and Gains of Business or Profession
C. Depreciation Allowance under Section 32	III. Income Under the Head Income from House Property
D. Exemption Under Section 54 for Profit on transfer of house property used for residence	IV. Income Under the Head Salaries

Choose the correct answer from the options given below:

(1) A-I, B-II, C-III, D-IV
(2) A-IV, B-III, C-II, D-I
(3) A-III, B-IV, C-II, D-I
(4) A-III, B-IV, C-I, D-II

51. India's participation in SAARC and ASEAN trade pacts primarily reflects which level of Regional Economic Integration ?

(1) Customs Union (2) Free Trade Area
(3) Economic Union (4) Common Market

52. Which of the followings is not a core function of WTO ?

(1) Providing a forum for trade negotiation
(2) Administering agreement such as GATS, TRIPS and TRIMS
(3) Monitoring trade policies
(4) Providing Concessional loans and financial aid to developing countries

53. Non-receipt of dividend by Investors is categorised in which type of complaints received by the SEBI ?

(1) Type I (2) Type II
(3) Type III (4) Type IV

54. Which of the following statements are incorrect?

A. Management audit is not compulsory under any law.
C. Section 148 of the Companies Act, 2013 has made Cost Audit mandatory for some limited companies

B. Vouching is concerned only with items of balance sheet.

D. The object of vouching is to satisfy the auditor as to existence, ownership, possession, completeness, valuation and disclosure of items mentioned in the Balance Sheet.

E. Independent financial audit has been made compulsory for many entities established under respective Acts.

Choose the correct answer from the options given below:

(1) B, C and E Only (2) A, B and C Only
(3) B and D Only (4) A, C and E Only

55. Match **List - I** with **List - II.**

List - I (Human Resource Valulation Approaches)	List - II (Propounders)
A. Historical Cost Approach	I. Brummet, Flamholtz and Plye
B. Opportunity Cost approach	II. Hekimian and Jones
C. Standard Cost Approach	III. David Watson
D. Present Value of Future Earning Model	IV. Lav and Schwartz

Choose the correct answer from the options given below:

(1) A-I, B-II, C-III, D-IV
(2) A-II, B-I, C-IV, D-III
(4) A-IV, B-III, C-I, D-II
(3) A-III, B-IV, C-I, D-II

56. Match **List - I** with **List - II.**

List - I	List - II
A. Greenfield Investment	I. Direct Investment overseas aimed to sell the output of a firm's domestic production process
B. Foreign Portfolio Investment	II. Overseas investment to acquire existing facilities
C. Forward Vertical FDI	III. Overseas investment to create new facilities from the ground up
D. Brownfield Investment	IV. Investment in foreign financial instruments such as foreign stock, government bonds etc.

Choose the correct answer from the options given below:

(1) A-III, B-IV, C-II, D-I
(2) A-I, B-II, C-III, D-IV
(3) A-IV, B-III, C-I, D-II
(4) A-III, B-IV, C-I, D-II

57. Which of the following sections of research reports contains Executive Summary?

(1) Prefatory Information
(2) Introductory Information
(3) Main Research Body
(4) Supplementary Information

58. Which one of the followings is not a type of Organisation charts ?

(1) Vertical Chart (2) Circular Chart
(3) Diagonal Chart (4) Horizontal Chart

59. Match **List - I** with **List - II.**

List - I	List - II
A. Making provision for bad and doubtful debts and for discount on debtors	I. Cost Concept
B. Expenses should be recognised in the period in which associated revenue is recognized	II. Going Concern
C. Assets are not shown at their current realisable value	III. Matching Concept
D. Internally generated goodwill is not recorded in the books of account	IV. Conservatism

Choose the correct answer from the options given below:

(1) A-I, B-II, C-III, D-IV
(2) A-IV, B-III, C-II, D-I
(3) A-IV, B-II, C-III, D-I
(4) A-II, B-I, C-IV, D-III

60. Arrange the following Acts in ascending order as per their year of enactment:

A. RTI (Rights to Information Act)
B. Competitions Act
C. Information Technology Act
D. Negotiable Instrument Act
E. Indian Contract Act

Choose the correct answer from the options given below :

(1) E, D, C, B, A (2) A, B, C, D, E
(3) A, B, E, D, C (4) E, D, C, A, B

61. Karl Pearson's Coefficient of Skewness for a distribution having mean of 6.82, median of 6.8 and standard Deviation of 1.4 is:
(1) 0.014 (2) 0.028
(3) 0.043 (4) 0.056

62. Match **List - I** with **List - II.**

List - I	List - II
A. Doctrine of Caveat Emptor	I. Special Contract
B. Bailment and Pledge	II. Limited Liability Partnership
C. Holder in due Course	III. Sales of Goods Act
D. DPIN	IV. Negotiable Instrument

Choose the correct answer from the options given below :
(1) A-IV, B-I, C-II, D-III
(2) A-I, B-II, C-IV, D-III
(3) A-II, B-I, C-III, D-IV
(4) A-III, B-I, C-IV, D-II

63. Given below are two statements one is labelled as Assertion (A) and the other is labelled as Reason (R).
Assertion (A): An effective appraisal system can contribute to competitive advantage by improving employee job performance.
Reason (R): One serious challenge facing the performance appraisal relates to assessment of self-managed teams.
In the light of the above statements, choose the most appropriate answer from the options given below:
(1) Both (A) and (R) are correct and (R) is the correct explanation of (A)
(3) (A) is correct but (R) is not correct
(2) Both (A) and (R) are correct but (R) is not the correct explanation of (A)
(4) (A) is not correct but (R) is correct

64. A, B and C were partners in a firm sharing profits and losses in the ratio of 4 : 3 : 2. A died on September 15, 2025. At that time, the capitals of B and C after all the adjustments were ₹ 3,56,000 and ₹ 2,44,000 respectively. B and C decided to adjust their capitals according to their new profit sharing ratio by opening current accounts. The new capital of B is:
(1) ₹ 1,33,333 (2) ₹ 2,00,000
(3) ₹ 2,40,000 (4) ₹ 3,60,000

65. If the first quartile is 48 and quartile deviation is 6, the value of median assuming the distribution to be symmetrical is:
(1) 50 (2) 52
(3) 54 (4) 56

66. Match **List - I** with **List - II.**

List - I	List - II
A. Highest Reach	I. Publicity
B. Most Persuasive	II. Advertising
C. Immediate Effect on Sales	III. Personal Selling
D. No Cost Involved	IV. Sales Promotion

Choose the correct answer from the options given below :
(1) A-I, B-II, C-III, D-IV
(2) A-II, B-I, C-III, D-IV
(3) A-II, B-III, C-IV, D-I
(4) A-IV, B-I, C-II, D-III

67. Arrange the following steps of Control Process in the correct order :
A. Measurement of Actual Performance
B. Establishment of Standards
C. Corrective action where required
D. Comparison of actual performance with the standards
Choose the correct answer from the options given below:
(1) B, A, C, D (2) B, A, D, C
(3) A, B, C, D (4) A, B, D, C

68. An assessee who declares his business/professional income in accordance with the provisions of Section 44 AD(1) or Section 44 ADA(1), must pay up to 100 percent of advance tax payable on or before:
(1) December 15 of the previous year
(2) January 15 of the previous year
(3) February 15 of the previous year
(4) March 15 of the previous year

69. Given below are two statements one is labelled as Assertion (A) and the other is labelled as Reason (R). Assertion (A)
Assertion (A): Filter questions in questionnaire measure the familiarity of the respondents with the topic of research.
Reason (R): Questions that try to capture multiple information at once are referred to as leading questions.
In the light of the above statements, choose the most appropriate answer from the options given below:
(1) Both (A) and (R) are correct and (R) is the correct explanation of (A)
(2) Both (A) and (R) are correct but (R) is not the correct explanation of (A)
(3) (A) is correct but (R) is not correct
(4) (A) is not correct but (R) is correct

70. According to Walter's Model of Dividend, market value of the share of a declining firm (having $r < k_e$) will be maximum at:
(1) 0% Dividend Payout
(2) 100% Dividend Payout
(3) 50% Dividend Payout
(4) 75% Dividend Payout

71. Which one of the followings is not an external technique of Foreign Exchange Risk Management?
(1) Forward Contracts
(2) Currency Futures
(3) Netting (4) Swaps

72. Under which of the following, a firm well publicized changes in price and price changes are generally followed by the rival firms. This kind of price leadership may not necessarily come from the largest firm of the industry.
(1) Biometric Price Leadership
(2) Barometric Price Leadership
(3) Price Leadership by low cost firm
(4) Price Leadership by dominant firm

73. Arrange the following types of motivating needs as identified by Maslow in ascending order:
A. Physiological Needs
B. Social Needs
C. Self-actualization Needs
D. Safety Needs
E. Esteem Needs
Choose the correct answer from the options given below:
(1) A, D, B, C, E (2) A, D, B, E, C
(3) A, B, D, E, C (4) A, B, C, D, E

74. Arrange the following steps of research process in correct order:
A. Developing an approach to the problem
B. Problem definition
C. Data Collection, Preparation and analysis
D. Research design formulation
E. Report writing and presentation
Choose the correct answer from the options given below:
(1) A, B, C, D, E (2) B, A, D, C, E
(3) D, B, A, E, C (4) A, B, D, E, C

75. Given below are two statements one is labelled as Assertion (A) and the other is labelled as Reason (R).
Assertion (A): RTGS system is a funds transfer mechanism where transfer of money takes place from one bank to another on a real time and on gross basis.
Reason (R): There is no minimum ceiling for the RTGS transactions.
In the light of the above statements, choose the most appropriate answer from the options given below:
(1) Both (A) and (R) are correct and (R) is the correct explanation of (A)
(2) Both (A) and (R) are correct but (R) is not the correct explanation of (A)
(3) (A) is correct but (R) is not correct
(4) (A) is not correct but (R) is correct

76. Which of the following is a measure of relative risk and is calculated by dividing the standard deviation by its expected value ?
(1) Variance
(2) Coefficient of Variance
(3) Co-Variance
(4) Geometric Mean

77. Which of the followings are properties of Normal Distribution ?
A. The normal curve approaches the x-axis asymptotically as we proceed in either direction away from the mean.
B. The normal curve has its points of inflection at $\overline{X} \pm 2\sigma$
C. Irrespective of the shape, the total area under the normal curve and above the horizontal axis is always equal to 1
D. About 68.27% of the total area under the normal curve is covered from $\mu - 2\sigma$ to $\mu + 2\sigma$.
E. The normal distribution is unimodal.
Choose the correct answer from the options given below:
(1) A, B and E Only (2) B, C and D Only
(3) C, D and E Only (4) A, C and E Only

78. Match **List - I** with **List - II**.

List - I	List - II
A. Managerial Grid	I. Charles Bird
B. Hawthorne Experiments	II. Alderfer
C. Trait Theory	III. Blake and Mouton
D. ERG Theory	IV. Elton Mayo

Choose the correct answer from the options given below :
(1) A-I, B-II, C-III, D-IV
(2) A-III, B-IV, C-I, D-II
(3) A-I, B-III, C-II, D-IV
(4) A-III, B-IV, C-II, D-I

79. A possible cost of FDI to the host country is:
(1) Employment opportunities may increase in the short run but long run competitiveness will be reduced.

(2) Technology transfer always leads to dependency and no local innovation gets encouraged.
(3) Repatriation of profits may lead to capital outflows.
(4) FDI inflows always worsen the host country's BoP position.

80. The probability that a leap year selected at random contains either 53 Sundays or 53 Mondays is:

(1) $\frac{1}{7}$ (2) $\frac{2}{7}$
(3) $\frac{3}{7}$ (4) $\frac{4}{7}$

81. Given below are two statements one is labelled as Assertion (A) and the other is labelled as Reason (R).

Assertion (A): A gentlemen died leaving a young widow. The relatives of the deceased threatened the widow to adopt a boy otherwise they would not allow her to remove the dead body of her husband for cremation. The widow adopted the boy.

Reason (R): The widow subsequently cancelled the adoption. The court held her consent was not free due to coercion.

In the light of the above statements, choose the most appropriate answer from the options given below:
(1) Both (A) and (R) are correct and (R) is the correct explanation of (A)
(2) Both (A) and (R) are correct but (R) is not the correct explanation of (A)
(3) (A) is correct but (R) is not correct
(4) (A) is not correct but (R) is correct

82. Match **List - I** with **List - II.**

List - I (Theories of Profit)	**List - II (Propounders)**
A. Risk theory of Profit	I. Joseph A Schumpeter
B. Dynamic theory of Profit	II. F.A. Waker
C. Innovation theory of Profit	III. F.B. Hawley
D. Profit as rent of ability	IV. J.B. Clark

Choose the correct answer from the options given below:
(1) A-III, B-II, C-I, D-IV
(2) A-III, B-IV, C-I, D-II
(3) A-II, B-III, C-I, D-IV
(4) A-IV, B-II, C-I, D-III

83. Which of the followings are the approaches of determining the financing mix for working capital:
A. Matching Approach
B. Conservative Approach
C. Operating Cycle Approach
D. Aggressive Approach

Choose the correct answer from the options given below:
(1) B, C and D Only
(2) A, B and D Only
(3) A, C and D Only
(4) A, B and C Only

84. Given below are two statements: one is labelled as Assertion (A) and the other is labelled as Reason (R).

Assertion (A): Minority interest is that part of the net assets of a subsidiary attributable to interest which is held by outsiders.

Reason (R): Minority interest should be presented in the consolidated balance sheet as a part of equity of the parent's shareholders.

In the light of the above statements, choose the most appropriate answer from the options given below:
(1) Both (A) and (R) are correct and (R) is the correct explanation of (A)
(2) Both (A) and (R) are correct but (R) is not the correct explanation of (A)
(3) (A) is correct but (R) is not correct
(4) (A) is not correct but (R) is correct

85. Which of the following types of audit report is issued when the auditor concludes that the financial statements are prepared, in all material respects, in accordance with the applicable financial reporting framework?
(1) Audit report with an 'emphasis of matter paragraph
(2) Qualified report
(3) Disclaimer of opinion report
(4) Unmodified opinion report

86. Match **List - I** with **List - II.**

List - I	**List - II**
A. NPV	I. Which equates the aggregate present value of the net cash Inflows with the aggregate present value of cash outflows.
B. IRR	II. Dividing the average annual profit after tax by average investment over the life of the project.

C. ARR — III. Summation of the present values of cash proceeds in each year minus the summation of the present values of the net cash outflow in each year.

D. PI — IV. Dividing the present value of future cash inflow by the present value of cash outflow.

Choose the correct answer from the options given below:

(1) A-I, B-III, C-II, D-IV
(2) A-III, B-II, C-IV, D-I
(3) A-III, B-I, C-II, D-IV
(4) A-I, B-II, C-III, D-IV

87. Which of the followings is not valid for ordinal school of consumer preferences ?

(1) Consumer preferences can be plotted on an indifference curve
(2) Ranking of Utility is important
(3) Magnitude of Utility is important
(4) Utility is not additive

88. Arm's length price as per section 92 F of the Income Tax Act is the price applied or proposed to be applied when:

(1) two related persons enter into a transaction in uncontrolled conditions.
(2) two unrelated persons enter into a transaction in controlled conditions.
(3) two related persons enter into a transaction in controlled conditions.
(4) two unrelated persons enter into a transaction in uncontrolled conditions.

89. Match **List - I** with **List - II**.

List - I	**List - II**
A. EXIM Bank	I. Advancing Credit for agriculture and other economic activities in rural area
B. NHB	II. Financing Exports and Imports
C. IDBI	III. Promoting Housing Finance Institution
D. NABARD	IV. Financing, Promoting and Developing industries

Choose the correct answer from the options given below:

(1) A-I, B-II, C-III, D-IV
(2) A-II, B-I, C-IV, D-III
(3) A-II, B-III, C-IV, D-I
(4) A-II, B-III, C-I, D-IV

90. Identify the correct equation of Cobb-Douglas production function:

(1) $Q = A + L^{\alpha}K^{\beta}$ (2) $Q = A \times L^{\alpha}K^{\beta}$
(3) $Q = A \div L^{\alpha}K^{\beta}$ (4) $Q = A - L^{\alpha}K^{\beta}$

Read the following passage and answer the questions :

An application was sent to registrar of companies to obtain the certificate of incorporation on 30 June 2024. One of the promotors, Raj, made the allotment of shares of the company on 28 June 2024. He also made a contract to buy a certain machinery from Pooja by representing himself as an agent of the company on 20 June 2024.

Raj also signed the Memorandum of Association (MOA) of the company on behalf of all seven members to obtain the certificate of incorporation.

Inspite of all these, the certificate of incorporation was issued in respect of ABC company but wrongly dated as 25 June 2024.

After sometimes, it is also found that two of the members out of seven members named in MOA were minors.

He also entered into a contract after the incorporation of company to buy a building from Prakash for Rs. 1,00,00,000 but before obtaining the certificate of commencement of business.

91. The certificate of incorporation of ABC is :

(1) Void as it is obtained by forged document
(2) Void as it is obtained by including minor promotors
(3) Valid, even if irregular, cannot be cancelled
(4) Valid, but from 30th June 2024 and not from 25th June

92. Which of the followings is correct?

(1) Pooja can claim payment of machinery from the company as Raj acted on behalf of the company.
(2) Pooja can claim the payment from Raj, who will be personally liable as she is considering that it is a provisional contract.
(3) Raj will be personally liable as for all pre-incorporation contracts, promotors are personally liable
(4) Raj will not be liable as the machinery was used by the company not by Raj for his personal benefits.

93. The allotment of shares was challenged as it was done before sending the application to the Registrar of Companies. Choose the correct answer:

(1) The allotment of shares is void as the certificate of incorporation is not valid
(2) The allotment of shares is valid as it is made after obtaining the certificate of incorporation

(3) The allotment of shares is void as application to obtain certificate was sent on 30th June

(4) The allotment of shares is void as the certificate was obtained by forged document

94. The contract to buy a building from Prakash for ₹ 1,00,00,000 will be called:
(1) Pre-incorporation Contract
(2) Provisional Contract
(3) Preliminary Contract
(4) Void Contract

95. The contract made with Pooja on 20 June 2024 will be called:
(1) Pre-incorporation Contract
(2) Provisional Contract
(3) Preliminary Contract
(4) Standard Contract

Read the following passage and answer the questions :

Ecofresh Pvt. Ltd, a startup in India, produces eco-friendly home cleaning products such as liquid detergents, floor cleaners and dishwashing liquids. The company follows a green marketing approach and highlights its products as biodegradable, safe and affordable.

To reach its customers, Ecofresh sells through online Platforms, retail stores and direct sales agents. The firm has designed its marketing mix carefully. Pricing is slightly above competitors due to its ecofriendly positioning but promotions include digital campaigns, social media advertising and discounts on bulk purchases.

Recently Ecofresh launched a new product; a herbal air freshener. During its product life cycle's introduction stage, the firm invested heavily in promotion and awareness building activities. The company also engages in customer relationship management by offering loyalty points and personalised recommendation to repeat buyers.

96. By selling through online platforms, retail stores and direct sales agents, Ecofresh is focusing on:
(1) Pricing Strategies
(2) Promotional Mix
(3) Service Marketing
(4) Multi Channel distribution

97. Ecofresh use of digital campaigns, social media and discounts reflects decisions related to:
(1) Distribution Mix (2) Promotion Mix
(3) Product Mix (4) Pricing Policy

98. The launch of herbal air freshener during its introduction stage of the product life cycle primarily requires heavy investment in promotion and awareness building activity. It will lead to (in short run):
(1) High Profit
(2) Low/Negative Profit
(3) High Revenue, low cost
(4) High Revenue, High cost

99. The use of loyalty points is an example of :
(1) Advertising (2) Sales Promotion
(3) Personal Selling (4) Sponsorship

100. Ecofresh's emphasis on biodegradable safe product reflects which marketing approach ?
(1) Production approach
(2) Selling approach
(3) Societal marketing approach
(4) Product approach

ANSWERS

1. (4)	2. (2)	3. (3)	4. (1)	5. (3)	6. (4)	7. (4)	8. (4)	9. (2)	10. (3)
11. (3)	12. (4)	13. (3)	14. (2)	15. (3)	16. (4)	17. (1)	18. (4)	19. (3)	20. (3)
21. (4)	22. (2)	23. (4)	24. (2)	25. (2)	26. (2)	27. (2)	28. (1)	29. (3)	30. (4)
31. (2)	32. (1)	33. (2)	34. (4)	35. (1)	36. (3)	37. (3)	38. (3)	39. (3)	40. (2)
41. (2)	42. (3)	43. (4)	44. (1)	45. (2)	46. (3)	47. (2)	48. (2)	49. (3)	50. (2)
51. (2)	52. (4)	53. (2)	54. (3)	55. (1)	56. (4)	57. (1)	58. (3)	59. (2)	60. (1)
61. (3)	62. (4)	63. (2)	64. (4)	65. (3)	66. (3)	67. (2)	68. (4)	69. (3)	70. (2)
71. (3)	72. (2)	73. (2)	74. (2)	75. (3)	76. (2)	77. (4)	78. (2)	79. (3)	80. (3)
81. (1)	82. (2)	83. (2)	84. (3)	85. (4)	86. (3)	87. (3)	88. (4)	89. (3)	90. (2)
91. (3)	92. (3)	93. (2)	94. (2)	95. (1)	96. (4)	97. (2)	98. (2)	99. (2)	100. (3)